HALSBURY'S
Laws of England

ANNUAL ABRIDGMENT
1980

EDITOR

KENNETH MUGFORD
of Lincoln's Inn, Barrister

ASSISTANT EDITOR

GILLIAN MATHER LLB

BUTTERWORTHS

LONDON

ENGLAND   Butterworth & Co (Publishers) Ltd
88 Kingsway, London WC2B 6AB

AUSTRALIA   Butterworth Pty Ltd
586 Pacific Highway, Chatswood, Sydney,
NSW 2067
Also at Melbourne, Brisbane, Adelaide and Perth

CANADA   Butterworth & Co (Canada) Ltd
2265 Midland Avenue, Scarborough,
Toronto M1P 4S1

NEW ZEALAND   Butterworths of New Zealand Ltd
33–35 Cumberland Place, Wellington

SOUTH AFRICA   Butterworth & Co (South Africa) (Pty) Ltd
152–154 Gale Street, Durban

USA   Butterworth & Co (Publishers) Inc
10 Tower Office Park, Woburn, Boston,
Mass 01801

EDITORIAL STAFF: JANE RUDDICK LLB of Gray's Inn, Barrister
GOURI PREECE BA of Gray's Inn, Barrister
SHEILA SELLARS BA
WENDY SPILLING BA
ANNE RADFORD BA
MADELEINE JONES LLB Solicitor
CELIA TRENTON BA
CAROLINE HOLMES-KAUSHESH BA

INDEXER: ELISABETH INGHAM ALA

ADMINISTRATION: PHYLLIS BUCK (Manager)
CLARE HORNSBY BA

ISBN 0 406 03367 6

Typeset by CCC in Great Britain by William Clowes (Beccles) Limited, Beccles and
London

PUBLISHERS' NOTE

This is the seventh Annual Abridgment and covers the year 1980. The Abridgment constitutes year by year a comprehensive survey of English case law, statute law and subordinate legislation. European Community law and decisions of Commonwealth courts are given attention commensurate with their importance. Further, the Abridgment chronicles and tabulates topics which may be of interest to lawyers. Such topics are derived from government papers, reports of committees, the EEC official journal, legal periodicals and the daily press.

Each Annual Abridgment is complete without any recourse to any other publication.

The alphabetical arrangement, the comprehensive tables and index and the inclusion of destination and derivation tables of consolidation legislation make the work an ideal aid in research. At the same time, the typography and presentation have been so designed that the Abridgment is suitable for independent study. A section entitled "In Brief", which immediately follows the table of contents, shows at a glance the year's main developments.

When referring to this volume reference should be made to both the year and the relevant paragraph number: e.g. "1980 Halsbury's Abridgment para. 2039".

This volume covers the law made in 1980 and is compiled from sources available in London on 31st December 1980.

BUTTERWORTH LAW PUBLISHERS LTD

TABLE OF CONTENTS

IN BRIEF

A summary of the year's main developments

Administrative law

A taxpayer may have sufficient interest, where another taxpayer has been relieved from paying tax, to bring an action to compel the Revenue to collect the tax: *R v Inland Revenue Comrs, ex parte National Federation of Self Employed and Small Businesses Ltd*, para. 8.

The House of Lords has held that at a public inquiry into the proposed construction of a motorway, there was no breach of natural justice when objectors were refused permission to cross-examine Government witnesses: *Bushell v Secretary of State for the Environment*, para. 24.

Agriculture

A notice to quit an agricultural holding is valid, notwithstanding that the notice is shorter than that statutorily required, where both parties agree that it is to be treated as if it were a notice of the statutory length: *Elsden v Pick*, para. 52.

Banking

A bank's confidential relationship with its clients does not extend to concealing a client's fraud; further a court may order discovery in support of a Mareva injunction, even though the client has not been served with a writ in respect of the main action: *Bankers Trust Co v Shapira*, para. 891.

Charities

A trust set up for the encouragement of football and other sports in schools and universities, with a view to promoting the physical education and development of pupils, has been held to be a charitable trust: *Inland Revenue Comrs v McMullen*, para. 319.

Companies

The Companies Act 1980 makes various amendments to the law relating to companies, including the making of insider dealing in company securities unlawful: para. 363.

Consumer protection

The Competition Act 1980 abolishes the Price Commission and provides for the investigation and control of practices which restrict competition or abuse a monopoly position: para. 2890.

Contempt of court

Disclosure of the secrets of the jury room is not per se a contempt of court: *Attorney General v Statesman and Nation Publishing Co Ltd*, para. 467.

Contempt of court cannot be committed in respect of a local valuation court, as it is not a court of law: *A-G v British Broadcasting Corporation*, para. 465.

Contract

There is no rule of law by which exclusion clauses are eliminated where there has been a fundamental breach of contract: *Photo Production Ltd v Securicor Transport Ltd*, para. 480.

Where a party mistakenly believes he is entitled to rescind under the terms of a contract, his attempt to rescind does not amount to repudiation: *Woodar Investment Development Ltd v Wimpey Construction UK Ltd*, para. 495.

Coroners

An inquest should be held with a jury, where the circumstances of the death were such that similar fatalities might possibly recur and it is reasonable to expect action to be taken to prevent a recurrence: *Re Peach (Dec'd); Peach v Burton*, para. 520.

Courts

Contempt of court cannot be committed in respect of a local valuation court, as it is not a court of law: *A-G v British Broadcasting Corporation*, para. 465.

Criminal law

Although one person can be convicted of conspiracy, a jury may be directed either to convict or to acquit all the defendants if there would otherwise be a serious risk of inconsistent verdicts: *R v Holmes*, para. 573.

A provision in an Act which empowers the court to make a forfeiture order for an offence under that Act, does not cover conspiracy to contravene the Act: *R v Cuthbertson, Todd and McCoy*, para. 584.

Where an accused receives a cheque believing it to represent stolen goods his belief does not entitle a jury to infer that it did represent stolen goods: *Attorney General's Reference (No. 4 of 1979)*, para. 598.

It has been held that a police officer who, acting upon her chief constable's standing instruction, removed clothing from an arrested person, was not acting in the execution of her duty: *Lindley v Rutter*, para. 566.

In deciding whether a person is guilty of wilfully neglecting a child, the subjective test must be applied: *R v Sheppard*, para. 582.

Criminal procedure

Jury vetting is permissible where it is necessary in order to exclude disqualified jurors: *R v Mason*, para. 1681.

Discovery

A defendant can claim privilege from discovery of documents in a copyright action, on the grounds that by doing so he would incriminate himself, even though this might effectively deny the copyright owner a remedy: *Rank Film Distributors Ltd v Video Information Centre*, para. 2181.

The High Court has the power to make an order for discovery in support of a Mareva injunction, where it is necessary to do so in order to ensure the proper and effective exercise of the Mareva jurisdiction: *A v C*, para. 890.

A bank's confidential relationship with its clients does not extend to concealing a client's fraud; further a court may order discovery in support of a Mareva injunction, even thought the client has not been served with a writ in respect of the main action: *Bankers Trust Co v Shapira*, para. 891.

Case records of children in the local authority's care should not be disclosed, even when the child himself seeks discovery when bringing an action in negligence against the authority: *Gaskin v Liverpool City Council*, para. 899.

Press and television companies are not entitled to refuse to disclose their sources of information on the grounds of public interest: *British Steel Corpn v Granada Televison Ltd*, para. 896.

A person to whom the court grants an order for discovery of documents, impliedly undertakes that the documents will not be used except for the purposes of the action in which they have been disclosed: *Home Office v Harman*, para. 889.

Employment
The House of Lords has laid down a test as to whether an employer, who has sold part of his business to another, is liable for redundancy payments to his former employees: *Melon v Hector Powe Ltd*, para. 1069.

Estoppel
Issue estoppel is not an absolute bar to the bringing of an action where a decision has already been made on the issue in dispute: *McIlkenny v Chief Constable of West Midlands and the Home Office*, para. 1102.

European Communities
If appeal to the House of Lords is unobtainable, then the Court of Appeal is the final court of appeal for the purpose of referring a question of interpretation of the EEC Treaty to the European Court: *Reinold Hagen v Fratelli D & G Moretti SNC and Molnar Machinery Ltd*, para. 541.

The European Court of Justice has held that where an EEC national is granted permission to enter the United Kingdom and stay for a limited time only, this is a restriction on the free movement of persons: *R v Pieck*, para. 1177.

Execution
A charging order may be made, under the Charging Orders Act 1979, in respect of a beneficial interest under a trust for sale: *National Westminster Bank v Stockman*, para. 1238.

Foreign relations law
A Convention has been signed providing for the return of children improperly removed from the custody of a parent and taken to another Convention country: para. 1329.

The House of Lords has considered the circumstances in which "travaux préparatoires" may be used in an English court: *Fothergill v Monarch Airlines*, para. 197.

Housing

A local authority's duty to provide "assistance in kind" to avoid a child being taken into care includes the provision of accommodation, even if the child's parents are intentionally homeless: *Attorney-General, on the relation of Tilley v Wandsworth LBC*, para. 1431.

Where a family is intentionally homeless a local authority must give the family a reasonable time to find another home: *Lally v Kensington and Chelsea Royal Borough*, para. 1432.

The Housing Act 1980 provides, inter alia, for the giving to the tenants of local authorities, security of tenure and the right to buy their homes: para. 1436.

A number of orders and regulations have been made concerning the operation of the "right to buy" provisions under the Housing Act 1980: paras. 1449–1458.

Husband and wife

A wife in actual occupation of the matrimonial home has an overriding interest in the property: *Williams and Glyn's Bank Ltd v Boland*; *Williams and Glyn's Bank Ltd v Brown*, para. 2012.

A husband cannot exclude his wife from premises of which he is the tenant, by surrendering the tenancy and asking the landlord to relet the premises to another tenant: *Hoggett v Hoggett*, para. 1491.

Immigration

A person is guilty of harbouring an illegal immigrant in his home, even if the immigrant is the person's spouse and has a right to live in the matrimonial home: *R v Mistry*; *R v Asare*, para. 1529.

Guidelines have been given to assist a court in considering whether to make a recommendation for deportation of an immigrant who has been convicted of a criminal offence: *R v Nazari*, para. 1506.

The Commission for Racial Equality has power to make an investigation into the control of immigration in carrying out its duties to promote equality of opportunity and good relations between persons of different racial groups: *Home Office v Commission for Racial Equality*, para. 1502.

The European Court of Justice has held that where an EEC national is granted permission to enter the United Kingdom and stay for a limited time only, this is a restriction on the free movement of persons: *R v Pieck*, para. 1177.

Income taxation

A taxpayer may have sufficient interest, where another taxpayer has been relieved from paying tax, to bring an action to compel the Revenue to collect the tax: *R v Inland Revenue Comrs, ex parte National Federation of Self Employed and Small Businesses Ltd*, para. 8.

Injunctions

The High Court has the power to make an order for discovery in support of a Mareva injunction, where it is necessary to do so in order to ensure the proper and effective exercise of the Mareva jurisdiction: *A v C*, para. 890.

A bank's confidential relationship with its clients does not extend to concealing a client's fraud; further a court may order discovery in support of a Mareva injunction, even though the client has not been served with a writ in respect of the main action: *Bankers Trust Co v Shapira*, para. 891.

A Mareva injunction can be granted against a defendant who is not a foreigner or foreign based: *Barclay-Johnson v Yuill*, para. 1625; *Bin Turki v Abu-Taha*, para. 1626.

A Mareva injunction is available in a personal injuries action to a legally aided plaintiff, notwithstanding his inability to pay damages if the action should fail: *Allen v Jambo Holdings Ltd*, para. 1629.

Judgments and orders

Where the costs of proceedings are increased by the bringing of a counterclaim, the counterclaim should bear only the amount of that increase: *Millican v Tucker*, para. 1772.

Where, due to the nature of a writ, a plaintiff may not enter judgment in default of appearance, the court may nevertheless grant leave to enter judgment to prevent an abuse of the court's process: *The Venus Destiny, Stewart Chartering Ltd v C & O Managements SA*, para. 1673.

The doctrine of merger applies only to contract and covenant and cannot override a provision of a statute: *Ealing London Borough Council v El Isaacs*, para. 1445.

Juries

Jury vetting is permissible where it is necessary in order to exclude disqualified jurors: *R v Mason*, para. 1681.

Land charges

An unregistered option to purchase land is void as against a purchaser of the legal estate for money or money's worth, irrespective of the purchaser's bona fides or the adequacy of the consideration: *Midland Bank Trust Co Ltd v Green*, para. 1685.

Land registration

A wife in actual occupation of the matrimonial home has an overriding interest in the property: *Williams and Glyn's Bank Ltd v Boland*; *Williams and Glyn's Bank Ltd v Brown*, para. 2012.

Landlord and tenant

The Court of Appeal has reviewed the rights of a tenant where a notice to quit is served during a "disregarded period": *Landau v Sloane*; *Midgalski v Corvin*, para. 1722.

A husband cannot exclude his wife from premises of which he is the tenant, by surrendering the tenancy, and asking the landlord to relet the premises to another tenant: *Hoggett v Hoggett*, para. 1491.

The doctrine of frustration can apply to a lease of land so as to bring it to an end: *National Carriers Ltd v Panalpina (Northern) Ltd*, para. 1710.

Legal aid

Regulations have been made providing the means to obtain assistance by way of representation, introduced by the Legal Aid Act 1979: para. 1781.

Where a charge in favour of the legal aid fund is registered on a house, the Law Society has a discretion to accept a substitute charge on another house: *Hanlon v Law Society*, 1790.

The payment of a plaintiff's debts by the defendant, instead of the payment of damages, will not avoid a legal aid fund statutory charge: *Manley v The Law Society*, para. 1787.

Limitation of actions

The Court of Appeal has considered the basis of the rule of practice whereby a party may not be joined as a defendant to an action where the claim against him is statute-barred: *Liff v Peasley*, para. 1799.

Local government

A local authority's duty to provide "assistance in kind" to avoid a child being taken into care includes the provision of accommodation, even if the child's parents are intentionally homeless: *Attorney-General, on the relation of Tilley's v Wandsworth LBC*, para. 1431.

Where a family is intentionally homeless a local authority must give the family a reasonable time to find another home: *Lally v Kensington and Chelsea Royal Borough*, para. 1432.

Minors

A Convention has been signed providing for the return of children improperly removed from the custody of a parent and taken to another Convention country: para. 1329.

Case records of children in the local authority's care should not be disclosed, even when the child himself seeks discovery when bringing an action in negligence against the authority: *Gaskin v Liverpool City Council*, para. 899.

In certain circumstances a court can abrogate a parent's rights as a tenant, for the temporary protection of the children: *B v B*, para. 1972.

Negligence

Where negligence is alleged against a professional person, an error of judgment might or might not amount to negligence: *Whitehouse v Jordan*, para. 2063.

Practice and procedure

A plaintiff can discontinue an action in England and pursue it in a foreign court if by doing so he is likely to obtain greater damages: *Castanho v Brown and Root (UK) Ltd*, para. 2206.

A civil court cannot make a declaration with regard to the legality of an act, when criminal proceedings on the issue are pending: *Imperial Tobacco Ltd v Attorney General*, para. 258.

The House of Lords has considered the circumstances in which "travaux préparatoires" may be used in an English court: *Fothergill v Monarch Airlines*, para. 197.

Race relations

An employer did not discriminate against an employee, even though the employee was demoted for disclosing information about the employer's discriminatory practices: *Kirby v Manpower Services Commission*, para. 2278.

The Commission for Racial Equality has power to make an investigation into the control of immigration in carrying out its duties to promote equality of opportunity and good relations between persons of different racial groups: *Home Office v Commission for Racial Equality*, para. 1502.

Sex discrimination

Dismissal on the grounds of pregnancy is not unlawful discrimination, as a pregnant woman cannot be compared to a man: *Turley v Allders Department Stores Ltd*, para. 2577.

The principle that a man and a woman should receive equal pay for equal work applies even though their periods of employment were not contemporaneous: *Macarthys Ltd v Smith*, paras. 1196, 2580.

Once a job evaluation scheme has been carried out in which it is concluded that a woman's job is of equal value to a man's, the woman's contract is to be treated as containing the same terms as the man's, irrespective of whether the pay structure has been adjusted: *O'Brien v Sim-Chem Ltd*, para. 2581.

Shipping

The Hague Rules should be used only as a defence to an action, not as a means of attack: *Mogul Line Ltd v Commerce International Incorp*, para. 2602.

Tort

It is no defence to an action for conversion that the person withholding the goods from their rightful owner fears industrial action by his employees should he release those goods: *Howard E Perry & Co v British Railways Board*, para. 2854.

Trade and industry

The Competition Act 1980 abolishes the Price Commission and provides for the investigation and control of practices which restrict competition or abuse a monopoly position: para. 2890.

Trade unions

Where ACAS is asked to decide whether to recommend recognition of a trade union for collective bargaining purposes, the courts can only interfere with its recommendation if no reasonable person would have made such a recommendation: *United Kingdom Association of Professional Engineers v Advisory Conciliation and Arbitration Service*, para. 2956.

The House of Lords has held that where trade union officers put pressure on the Government, believing that it would assist in bringing a strike to a successful conclusion, their acts were in furtherance of a trade dispute: *Duport Steels Ltd v Sirs*, para. 2933.

It is not an abdication of its statutory functions for ACAS to defer its inquiry or report on a recognition issue, if it is of the opinion that this would improve industrial relations: *Engineers' and Managers' Association v Advisory, Conciliation and Arbitration Service*, para. 2939.

Where, by its rules, a union is affiliated to the Labour Party, this does not prevent one of its branches from making a contribution to the Conservative Party: *Parkin v Association of Scientific, Technical and Managerial Staffs*, para. 2959.

The Employment Act 1980 makes a number of important amendments relating to the law of industrial relations: para. 2949.

Unfair dismissal

Failure to comply with the Industrial Relations Code of Practice does not per se make the dismissal of an employee unfair: *Rasool v Hepworth Pipe Co Ltd (No. 2)*, para. 3036.

REFERENCES AND ABBREVIATIONS

ACTR	Australian Capital Territory Reports
All ER	All England Law Reports
ALJ	Australian Law Journal
ALJR	Australian Law Journal Reports
ALR	Australian Law Reports
ATC	Annotated Tax Cases
BJAL	British Journal of Administrative Law
BLR	Business Law Review
Brit J Criminol	British Journal of Criminology
BTR	British Tax Review
CCC	Canadian Criminal Cases
CLJ	Cambridge Law Journal
CLR	Commonwealth Law Reports (Australia)
CMLR	Common Market Law Reports
CML Review	Common Market Law Review
Conv	Conveyancer
Conv (NS)	Conveyancer and Property Lawyer
Cr App Rep	Criminal Appeal Reports
Crim LR	Criminal Law Review
Decisions and Reports	Decisions and Reports of European Commission on Human Rights
DLR	Dominion Law Reports (Canada)
EA	East Africa Law Reports
ECR	European Court Reports
EHRR	European Human Rights Reports
Fam Law	Family Law
FR	Federal Court Reports (Canada)
FSR	Fleet Street Reports
ICLQ	International and Comparative Law Quarterly
ICR	Industrial Cases Reports
IJR	Irish Jurist Reports
ILJ	Industrial Law Journal
ILT	Irish Law Times
ILTR	Irish Law Times Reports
Imm AR	Immigration Appeals
IR	Irish Reports
IRLR	Industrial Relations Law Reports
JBL	Journal of Business Law
JCL	Journal of Criminal Law
JP	Justice of the Peace Reports
JP Jo	Justice of the Peace Journal
JPL	Journal of Planning and Environmental Law
JR	Juridical Review
JSPTL	Journal of the Society of Public Teachers of Law
KIR	Knight's Industrial Reports
LE	Legal Executive
LG	Law Guardian
LGC	Local Government Chronicle
LGR	Local Government Reports
Lloyd's Rep	Lloyd's Reports

LMCLQ	Lloyd's Maritime and Commercial Law Quarterly
LQR	Law Quarterly Review
LS Gaz	Law Society Gazette
LS Gaz R	Law Society Gazette Reports
L(TC)	Income Tax Leaflets
Med Sci & Law	Medicine Science & The Law
MLR	Modern Law Review
NI	Northern Ireland Reports
NILQ	Northern Ireland Law Quarterly
NLJ	New Law Journal
NSWLR	New South Wales Law Reports
NZLR	New Zealand Law Reports
OJC	Official Journal of the European Communities— communications and information series
OJL	Official Journal of the European Communities— legislation series
OR	Ontario Reports
PL	Public Law
P & CR	Property and Compensation Reports
RA	Rating Appeals
RPC	Reports of Patent Etc. Cases
RRC	Ryde's Rating Cases
RTR	Road Traffic Reports
RVR	Rating and Valuation Reporter
SASR	South Australian State Reports
SC	Session Cases
SCR	Supreme Court Reports (Canada)
SLG	Scottish Law Gazette
SLT	Scots Law Times
Sol Jo	Solicitors' Journal
STC	Simon's Tax Cases
TC	Tax Cases
TR	Taxation Reports
Traff Cas	Traffic Cases
VATTR	Value Added Tax Tribunal Reports
VR	Victorian Reports
WAR	Western Australian Reports
WIR	West Indian Reports
WLR	Weekly Law Reports
WWR	Western Weekly Reports (Canada)

TABLE OF STATUTES

TABLE OF STATUTORY INSTRUMENTS

TABLE OF SECONDARY LEGISLATION OF THE EUROPEAN COMMUNITIES

TABLE OF CASES

Decisions of the European Court of Justice are listed both alphabetically and numerically. The numerical table follows the alphabetical.

Annual Abridgment 1980

ADMINISTRATIVE LAW

Halsbury's Laws of England (4th edn.) Vol. 1, paras 1–300

1   **Article**

Judicial Review: Locus Standi, Henry E. Markson: 124 Sol Jo 386.

2   **Certiorari—application to High Court—jurisdiction—whether matter relating to trial on indictment**

See *R v Sheffield Crown Court, ex parte Brownlow*, para. 718.

3   **—— availability—disciplinary tribunal—failure to meet procedural requirements**

Canada

The applicant was found guilty of professional misconduct by the hearing committee of the Law Society of British Columbia. She applied for the verdict to be quashed on the grounds that the committee had been inquorate, that there had been a breach of natural justice and likelihood of bias. *Held*, (i) the legislation which provided for the committee's quorum had been enacted for the benefit of the public interest and could not be waived in any event. (ii) The committee had failed to observe the rules of the Law Society by not inviting submissions from the applicant which was a breach of the rules of natural justice. (iii) A remark prior to the hearing by a committee member that he had considered from the beginning that there was a clear cut case for disbarment constituted bias and was sufficient to disqualify him. Although the applicant had a right of appeal against the decision, the discretionary remedy of certiorari would be more effective. Accordingly the application would be granted.

CONNOR v LAW SOCIETY OF BRITISH COLUMBIA [1980] 4 WWR 638 (Supreme Court of British Columbia).

4   **—— —— jurisdiction of court ousted by statute**

See *South East Asia Fire Bricks Sdn Bhd v Non-Metallic Mineral Products Manufacturing Employees Union*, para. 558.

5   **Declaration—writ issued in Chancery Division—circumvention of procedure for application for judicial review**

Following prison riots, the plaintiff, a prisoner, was disciplined by the prison board of visitors. He issued a writ in the Chancery Division for a declaration that the adjudication of the board of visitors was null and void. The board contended that the plaintiff should have applied for judicial review to the Divisional Court of the Queen's Bench Division under RSC Ord 53, and applied for all further proceedings in the action to be stayed. *Held*, it was technically open to plaintiff to apply for a declaration, either by bringing an action in the Chancery Division or by applying for judicial review in the Divisional Court of the Queen's Bench Division. In the present case, since the plaintiff was seeking a review of a quasi-judicial determination, it was more appropriate for proceedings to be brought under RSC Ord 53 since (i) the Queen's Bench Division had more experience in dealing with questions concerning administrative or quasi-judicial proceedings and could deal expeditiously with them and (ii) since the plaintiff was indirectly seeking judicial review of a determination he should not be permitted to circumvent the requirement to obtain leave under RSC Ord 53. Accordingly the board's application would be allowed.

HEYWOOD v HULL PRISON BOARD OF VISITORS [1980] 3 All ER 594 (Chancery Division: GOULDING J).

6   Declaratory judgment—jurisdiction—declaration as to legality of act—criminal proceedings pending

See *Imperial Tobacco Ltd v A-G*, para. 258.

7   Judicial control—exercise of discretion conferred by statute—abuse

See *A-G v Ryan*, para. 18.

8   Judicial review—application by body of taxpayers—whether sufficient interest to claim declaration

The Board of Inland Revenue granted a tax amnesty to a large number of casual workers in the newspaper industry who had evaded income tax. It was suggested that the amnesty had been granted under the threat of industrial action and in order to lay the foundations for the successful working of the new scheme. A body of taxpayers, represented by the federation, sought a declaration that the Board had acted unlawfully in granting the amnesty, and an order of mandamus directing the Board to assess and collect income tax from the casual workers. It fell to be determined whether, under RSC Ord. 53, r. 3 (5), the federation had sufficient interest in the matter to bring such an action. *Held*, LAWTON LJ dissenting, the federation had sufficient interest in the matter and were entitled to have the merits of the dispute decided.

LORD DENNING MR held that it may have been that the Board had no power to make the amnesty as an agreement not to prosecute an offender was an unlawful agreement. However, the court would proceed by allowing the federation to bring a complaint on the grounds that public authorities should be required to perform their duties as a matter of public interest and because the federation had a genuine grievance.

ACKNER LJ held that he could see no distinction between a ratepayer who could reasonably assert that he had a genuine grievance based on the difference between his assessment and that of others in the same rating area, and the position of a taxpayer whose sense of justice was offended by the unlawful act of the Revenue in allowing fellow taxpayers not to pay their tax.

R v INLAND REVENUE COMRS, EX PARTE NATIONAL FEDERATION OF SELF-EMPLOYED AND SMALL BUSINESSES LTD [1980] 2 All ER 378 (Court of Appeal: LORD DENNING MR, LAWTON and ACKNER LJJ). Dictum of Lord Wilberforce in *Arsenal Football Club Ltd v Ende* [1979] AC 1, HL, 1977 Halsbury's Abridgment para. 2231, *R v Hereford Corporation, ex parte Harrower* [1970] 3 All ER 640, DC, and *R v Greater London Council, ex parte Blackburn* [1976] 3 All ER 184, CA, 1976 Halsbury's Abridgment para. 2503 applied. *R v Lewisham Union Guardians* [1897] 1 QB 498, DC, overruled.

For a discussion of this case, see The public interest in 'Mickey Mouse', Justinian: Financial Times, 3rd March 1980.

9   —— coroner's inquest

See *Re Evans and Milton*, para. 521.

10   —— decision of justices—likelihood of bias

The Divisional Court quashed a decision of justices dismissing an information by a council house tenant against the council alleging a statutory nuisance in respect of the premises, on the ground that the husband of one of the adjudicating justices had previously been a member of the council and the chairman of the housing committee concerned with the property complained of.

R v SMETHWICK JJ, EX PARTE HANDS (1980) Times, 4th December (Queen's Bench Division: DONALDSON LJ and KILNER BROWN J).

11   —— duty to act reasonably—transfer of health authority's functions to other persons

An area health authority grossly exceeded its authorised expenditure and was required to make economies. It failed to do so and the Minister made a direction under the National Health Service Act 1977, s. 86, that in consideration of the failure to control the expenditure he had declared an emergency and the authority's functions were to be performed by other persons until further notice. On an ex parte application for judicial review of his decision *held*, the minister, on the evidence, could have reasonably concluded that the authority had created an absolute ban on reducing staff, services and patient activities, and thus there was material upon which he could have decided to exercise his discretion under s. 86. However, he had failed to give proper consideration to the possibility of making a s. 17 direction, under which he could have given the authority directions with regard to the exercise of its functions. In default he could then have replaced its members in accordance with s. 85. Further, a s. 86 order was to be made only in times of crisis and was not to be used to take over the authority's functions for an unlimited period in order to control the financial affairs of the area. The direction was accordingly invalid.

R v SECRETARY OF STATE FOR SOCIAL SERVICES, EX PARTE LEWISHAM, LAMBETH AND SOUTHWARK LONDON BOROUGH COUNCILS (1980) Times, 26th February (Queen's Bench Division: WOOLF J).

In the light of this decision, the Secretary of State decided not to appeal, but instead to arrange for the members of the authority to resume their functions from 1st April 1980: see Times, 4th March 1980. Legislation has been passed to give legal effect to decisions and actions taken under the invalid direction; see National Health Service (Invalid Direction) Act 1980, para. 2030.

12   —— order for transfer of housing from GLC to London boroughs

See *Brent London Borough Council v GLC*, para. 1835.

13   Mandamus—availability—application by taxpayer to amend case stated—availability of remedy

See *R v Inland Revenue Comrs, ex parte Emery*, para. 1575.

14   —— ——application to compel highway authority to perform its duty to remove obstruction on footpath

See *R v Surrey County Council, ex parte Send Parish Council*, para. 1404.

15   —— committee member's right to see report—report containing defamatory material

See *R v Clerk to Lancashire Police Committee, ex parte Hook*, para. 1818.

16   —— law against obscene publications—application to compel enforcement of law

See *R v Metropolitan Police Comr, ex parte Blackburn*, para. 2155.

17 — refusal by Crown Court of application for leave to appeal out of time against decision of justices

A magistrates' court made a finding in the applicant's absence that he was the father of the respondent's child and made an order of £5 per week against him. That order was not served on the applicant until 20 days had elapsed after the period of 21 days within which he could have appealed against the justices' decision. As soon as he received the order he applied to the Crown Court for leave to appeal and for an extension of time for appealing, giving a explanation as to why he had failed to attend at the magistrates' court. The Crown Court judge refused leave without giving his reasons despite several requests for a reconsideration. The applicant then applied to the Divisional Court for a judicial review in respect of the matter which was also refused without reasons. On appeal, *held*, the refusals to grant leave were manifestly wrong. The court would accordingly grant an order of mandamus directed to the Crown Court directing it to exercise its powers under the Crown Court Rules in relation to the extension of time for appealing, so as to enable the applicant to appeal against the order of the justices.

RE WORTH'S APPLICATION (1979) 10 Fam Law 54 (Court of Appeal: ORR, ORMROD and GEOFFREY LANE LJJ).

18 Natural justice—duty to act judicially or fairly—application for citizenship

The Bahamas

In June 1974 a resident of the Bahamas who possessed Bahamian status applied for registration as a citizen of the Bahamas under the Constitution of the Bahamas, art. 5, which provided that a person possessing Bahamian status and who was ordinarily resident in the Bahamas was entitled, on making an application before July 1974, to be registered as a citizen, subject to exceptions prescribed in the interests of national security or public policy. These exceptions were provided for under the Bahamas Nationality Act 1973 which empowered the minister concerned to refuse an application for specified reasons or any other sufficient reason of public policy. The decision did not have to be reasoned and was not subject to review by the courts. The resident's application for citizenship was refused by the minister and he issued a summons against the Attorney General for a declaration that under the Constitution he was entitled to be registered as a citizen. *Held*, (i) by virtue of the 1973 Act, the Minister had legal authority to determine questions concerning the rights of individuals. He was therefore bound to observe the principles of natural justice when exercising that authority; his failure to inform the applicant of the reasons for the refusal of the application constituted a breach of natural justice and accordingly the decision to refuse the application was void. (ii) The provisions of the Constitution which empowered Parliament to impose limitations on entrenched rights given by the Constitution were not to be construed so as to enable Parliament to pass legislation depriving the individual of the substance of his constitutional rights. Any provision such as those under the 1973 Act purporting to confer on a Minister the power of a sole judge of what constituted "any other sufficient reason of public policy" was ultra vires the Constitution and void. (iii) Clauses preventing ministerial actions becoming subject to judicial review extended only to prohibiting the court from re-examining the decision of an inferior tribunal, including executive authorities exercising quasi-judicial powers, if the decision was one which the tribunal had jurisdiction to make. A decision affecting legal rights of individuals arrived at by a procedure which offended natural justice was outside the jurisdiction of the decision-making authority. Thus the Minister's decision was made without jurisdiction and the court was not prevented from inquiring into its validity. The application would be remitted to the Minister to be determined according to law.

A-G v RYAN [1980] AC 718 (Privy Council: LORD DIPLOCK, VISCOUNT DILHORNE, LORD RUSSELL OF KILLOWEN, LORD KEITH OF KINKEL and SIR CLIFFORD RICHMOND). Dictum of Lord Selborne in *Spackman v Plumstead District Board of Works* (1885) 10 App Cas 299 at 240, HL and *Anisminic Ltd v Foreign Compensation Commission* [1969] 2 AC 147, HL applied.

19   **—— opportunity to be heard**

After failing to supply certain requested information the taxpayer appealed against his estimated assessment to capital gains tax. He caused the hearing to be adjourned several times before it finally went ahead in his absence. He alleged that he had telephoned the clerk to inform the court that he would be unable to attend, and applied for judicial review on the ground that there had been a breach of the rules of natural justice, although he failed to state a case within the time limit prescribed by the Taxes Management Act 1970, s. 56. *Held*, in the light of the delays, the opportunities given to the taxpayer to put his case, and his failure to challenge the decision or raise the natural justice issue earlier, the court would not grant judicial review of the decision.

PAGE v DAVENTRY GENERAL COMRS [1980] STC 698 (Court of Appeal: STEPHENSON, OLIVER LJJ, and SIR JOHN WILLIS).

20   A motorist entered a plea of not guilty to a charge of driving without due care and attention, and wrote to the magistrates requesting an adjournment. The magistrate directed that the summons be heard in the motorist's absence and he applied for judicial review. *Held*, although the motorist had notified the court of his inability to attend, the reasons given by the magistrate for his decision were impeccable and he had directed himself properly, therefore the application would fail.

R v OLD STREET JJ, EX PARTE RUTMAN [1980] RTR 403 (Queen's Bench Division: LORD WIDGERY CJ and PARK J).

21   **—— —— banning of minicab drivers by airport authority**

See *Cinnamond v British Airports Authority*, para. 186.

22   **—— —— disciplinary hearing**

See *Connor v Law Society of British Columbia*, para. 3.

23   **—— —— investigation by Commission for Racial Equality—right of cross-examination**

See *R v Commission for Racial Equality, ex parte Cottrell & Rothon*, para. 2272.

24   **—— —— public inquiry—right of cross-examination**

A public inquiry was held into two motorway schemes. At the inquiry the inspector refused to allow the cross-examination of Department of Environment witnesses on their evidence concerning traffic forecasts. The inspector recommended that both schemes proceed. The objectors to the schemes requested that the inquiry be re-opened in the light of new evidence relating to traffic forecasts but the minister refused on the ground that he was satisfied that the evidence did not affect the inspector's decision. The objectors unsuccessfully applied for an order to quash the minister's decision, but the Court of Appeal, by a majority decision, allowed the appeal on the ground that the inquiry had not been conducted with due regard to the rules of natural justice. On appeal by the minister, *held*, LORD EDMUND-DAVIES dissenting, the decision to determine priorities in the construction of future stretches of the national network of motorways by reference to their respective traffic needs in years ahead, could properly be described as government policy. The merits of the methods adopted to determine those needs were an essential element of that policy and were not appropriate for investigation at different local inquiries. Cross-examination of witnesses as to their views on the comparative merits of different methods of forecasting would not therefore have served any useful purpose. The objectors had been allowed to voice their own criticisms of the methods used and to call expert witness and accordingly there had been no denial of natural justice or unfairness and the appeal would therefore be allowed.

BUSHELL v SECRETARY OF STATE FOR THE ENVIRONMENT [1980] 2 All ER 608 (House of Lords: LORD DIPLOCK, VISCOUNT DILHORNE, LORD EDMUND-DAVIES, LORD FRASER OF TULLYBELTON and LORD LANE). Decision of Court of Appeal (1979) 123 Sol Jo 605, 1979 Halsbury's Abridgment para. 15 reversed.

25   Parliamentary Commissioner—complaint against Department of Health and Social Security—removal of property without consent

See para. 2778.

26   —— complaint against Driver and Vehicle Licensing Centre

See para. 2380.

27   —— investigation into procedure on application for hill livestock compensatory allowance

A person dissatisfied with the decision of the Minister of Agriculture, Fisheries and Food on an application for a hill livestock compensatory allowance is given the opportunity of making oral representations to a regional panel. The panel deliberates in private and makes recommendations to the minister who makes the final decision on the application. According to general practice the divisional executive officer who made the initial decision helps to arrange the membership of the panel for the hearing, presents the case for the minister at the hearing and, after the hearing, is responsible for conveying the minister's final decision to the applicant.

After oral representations had been made at the hearing in question, the applicant was asked to leave the room whilst the officer remained behind to discuss the case with the panel. The panel concluded its deliberations on the case and then, accompanied by the officer, went to lunch. Following a complaint to the Parliamentary Commissioner for Administration and on investigation, the minister has agreed to discontinue the practice of such officials conferring in private with members of the panel following the oral representations and before the panel's recommendations have been formulated. The ministry has also agreed to review the practice of the officers lunching with members of the panel since it is recognised that this practice is open to misinterpretation. The ministry informed the Parliamentary Commissioner, however, that the regional panel procedure was not a quasi-judicial appeal procedure but rather a non-statutory procedure introduced "in the interests of visibly more informed administration".

Case C494/79, Parliamentary Commissioner for Administration Selected Cases, 1980, Vol. 3, p. 6.

28   —— investigation of complaints

In January 1978 a group of about 40 gipsy families illegally entered and occupied land belonging to the Ministry of Defence which was in the hands of the Property Services Agency of the Department of the Environment for disposal as surplus to need. They were joined a few days later by several families of Irish travellers. Serious damage occurred to empty buildings. The lack of sanitary facilities and the behaviour of many of the gipsies (the term being used in reference to all occupying the land illegally) created a serious health hazard for local residents, particularly for a farmer whose land adjoined the area occupied. It was not until nearly Christmas 1978 that the various public authorities concerned were able to agree and execute a scheme to limit the number of gipsies and the area occupied and so reduce, to some extent, the adverse effects on the amenities and property of the local residents. The farmer complained to the Parliamentary Commissioner, inter alia, of actions of the government departments so far as they had administrative responsibility for permitting gipsies to occupy government land, for removing them and for preventing or mitigating any nuisance caused by occupation of the land. The farmer complained of a fall in net profit from farming attributable to the gipsies' behaviour and also strain, distress and illness suffered by his family. In accepting jurisdiction the Commissioner had to consider whether the farmer had a remedy for the material damage which he suffered in the courts. The Commissioner said that it would be unreasonable to expect him to sue persons whose identities would be difficult to establish and whose whereabouts and resources were ephemeral. See, Investigation of a complaint about the occupation by gipsies of surplus government land, HC 249 (session 1979–80).

29   **Prohibition—coroner's inquest—reasonable apprehension of bias**

See *Re Evans and Milton*, para. 521.

30   **Tribunals—Council on Tribunals—annual report and report on functions**

The Council on Tribunals has published its annual report for 1978–79 (HC 359). In the report it comments that, whilst not favouring an inflexible rule on the matter, it considers that it should be the normal practice of all chairmen of tribunals to disclose their names and those of their members to persons appearing before them. It also registers concern that, in some instances, inspectors of taxes are issuing notices of hearing before the general commissioners of income tax and notifying appellants of their decisions. The Council on Tribunals adds that the principle that the clerks of these tribunals should alone be responsible for such documents has been accepted by the Inland Revenue and the Lord Chancellor's department but not yet implemented. The report includes a list of tribunals under the general supervision of the Council as at 31st July 1979.

The Council has produced a special report on its functions (Cmnd 7805). It proposes that it should have clear power to act over the whole area of administrative adjudication and the organisation of tribunals and the clear right to be consulted in relation to legislation and procedural rules. It recommends that differences in the wording of its responsibilities in relation to different tribunals be removed and that it be given statutory power to investigate certain matters of principle in relation to tribunals and inquiries and that members of the Council should have the power to visit private hearings of tribunals under the Council's supervision.

31   —— **rent assessment committee—duty to give reasoned decisions**

See *Guppy's Properties Ltd v Knott*, para. 1735.

ADMIRALTY

Halsbury's Laws of England (4th edn.), Vol. 1, paras. 301–600

32   **Action in rem—arrest of vessel—clause conferring exclusive jurisdiction on English courts—arrest abroad—injunction to restrain proceedings**

See *Mike Trading and Transport Ltd v Pagnan*, para. 427.

33   —— —— **failure of owners to secure release of vessel—liability of owners**

See *Richmond Shipping Ltd v Vestland*, para. 2609.

34   —— **renewal of writ—change in ownership of defendant vessel**

The plaintiffs, a Canadian company, issued a writ in an action in rem against three ships owned by the defendants, a Cypriot company. During the subsequent year none of the ships came within the jurisdiction, therefore the writ was allowed to lapse. However, a few weeks later one of the ships docked in London and the Admiralty registrar agreed to renewal of the writ. But between the date of the lapsing of the writ and its renewal the defendants had transferred ownership of the ship to another company within the same group of companies. The new owners moved to set aside the renewal of the writ and to release unconditionally the ship, which was under arrest. *Held*, the cause of action was not statute-barred, and as the plaintiffs had gone to considerable lengths to try to serve the writ promptly, there was no objection to renewal on that ground. Although the ship was no longer owned by the company liable in personam the writ could be renewed, and indeed ought to be to prevent the defendants from secretly depriving the plaintiffs from their right to proceed with the action. The change of ownership in the present case had taken place between two companies within the same group, and thus it was probable that the new owners were aware of the action in rem before purchasing the ship. In any event any purchasers would not be prejudiced by the renewal of a writ in these circumstances as it was possible for them to protect themselves against a claim by taking an indemnity from the seller.

THE HELENE ROTH [1980] 1 All ER 1078 (Queen's Bench Division: SHEEN J). Dictum of Brandon J in *The Monica S* [1967] 3 All ER 740, at 769 applied.

35   Maritime lien—ship-repairers' lien—whether class to be extended

See *Bankers Trust International Ltd v Todd Shipyard Corpn*, para. 2627.

AFFILIATION AND LEGITIMATION

Halsbury's Laws of England (4th edn.), Vol. 1, paras. 601–700

36   Article

The Reform of Illegitimacy Law, Ruth Deech: 10 Fam Law 101.

37   Affiliation order—application by Supplementary Benefits Commission—mother in receipt of supplementary benefit and child benefit—whether supplementary benefit paid to meet child's requirements

The mother of an illegitimate child received supplementary benefit and child benefit. The Supplementary Benefits Commission applied for an affiliation order against the putative father. The justices refused to make an order on the grounds that the child's requirements were being met by the mother's entitlement to child benefit; hence supplementary benefit was not being paid to meet the child's requirements and the Commission was not entitled to apply for an affiliation order under the Supplementary Benefits Act 1976, s. 19. On appeal by way of case stated, *held*, under the 1976 Act, Sch. 1, para. 3 (2) payment was made to one representative of the family unit, the requirements and resources of which were aggregated. Section 19 (1) provided that benefit would be paid to meet requirements which included those of an illegitimate child. It therefore came into operation as soon as the requirements, as a result of which a sum was paid by way of supplementary benefit, included a requirement related to an illegitimate child. The justices had adopted the wrong approach in refusing to make an affiliation order and the case would be remitted to them.

ROBINSON v LOWTHER (1980) Times, 8th April (Family Division: LATEY and PURCHAS JJ).

The Supplementary Benefits Commission has now been abolished; see Social Security Act 1980, s. 6, para. 2761.

38   —— paternity—blood tests

The Blood Tests (Evidence of Paternity) (Amendment) Regulations 1980, S.I. 1980 No. 887 (in force on 25th July 1980), increase the fees payable under the Blood Tests (Evidence of Paternity) Regulations 1971 in respect of blood tests carried out for the purpose of determining paternity in civil proceedings.

39   Domestic Proceedings and Magistrates' Courts Act 1978—commencement

See para. 1976.

AGENCY

Halsbury's Laws of England (4th edn.), Vol. 1, paras. 701–1000

40   **Agent—authority—apparent authority—reliance by third party upon representation by principal**

Canada

An employee had his employers' actual authority to negotiate for, and effect, the sale of sulphur. During negotiations with a prospective purchaser, his authority was qualified in that approval had to be obtained for the sale. The question arose whether the employers were bound by a contract entered into by the employee for which approval had not been obtained, the purchaser having no knowledge of the restriction on the employee's authority. *Held*, the employee had negotiated with the purchaser with the employers' actual authority. His authority was subsequently curtailed without notice to the purchaser. This amounted to a representation by the employers of the employee's authority, on which the purchaser relied. Accordingly, the employers were bound by the contract.

Rockland Industries Inc v Amerada Minerals Corpn of Canada Ltd (1980) 108 DLR (3d) 513 (Supreme Court of Canada). Decision of Supreme Court of Alberta (1978) 95 DLR (3d) 64, 1979 Halsbury's Abridgment para. 34 reversed.

41   **—— —— ostensible authority—estoppel**

Canada

Between 1962 and 1969 a company bought large quantities of platinum from a supplier. The platinum was ordered by an employee of the company and during that period he fraudulently took possession of quantities of the metal and resold it to the supplier as scrap in the name of a fictitious customer of the company wishing to deal directly with the supplier. In 1966 the supplier made inquiries about the transactions and was referred by a purchasing agent of the company to the employee. In 1968 the supplier made further inquiries resulting in an action by the company against the supplier for damages for conversion. *Held*, in the absence of any act by a responsible member of staff of the company, the company was not estopped from denying the employee's authority to sell the platinum. In the circumstances the conduct of the company's purchasing agent in 1966 amounted to a holding out of the employee as having authority to act on the company's behalf in relation to the transactions. The company was therefore only entitled to damages in respect of the transactions until 1966.

Canadian Laboratory Supplies Ltd v Engelhard Industries of Canada (1979) 97 DLR (3d) 1 (Supreme Court of Canada).

42   **—— duty to principal—agent accepting fee from third party— whether full disclosure made**

Canada

A mortgage broker who had been authorised to find a lender intended to accept a fee from the lender. He included in the document which was signed by his client an acknowledgment that he might receive a fee. *Held*, this did not amount to the full disclosure which was necessary, and the failure to make such disclosure deprived the broker of any right to the agreed commission.

Advanced Realty Funding Corpn v Bannink (1979) 27 OR (2d) 193 (Court of Appeal of Ontario).

43   **—— —— —— whether in breach of fiduciary duty**

Canada

The Supreme Court of British Columbia has held that an agent's fiduciary duty to his principal is broken only when the agent's activities are inconsistent with his undertaking as an agent. Thus, a mortgage broker authorised to find a lender was not in breach of his fiduciary duty to the borrower by agreeing to accept a fee from a potential lender.

TURNER V LAURENTIDE FINANCIAL REALTY CORPN (WESTERN) LTD (1979) 97 DLR (3d) 429 (Supreme Court of British Columbia).

44　　　　—— estate agent—commission—agreement—construction

A flat owner instructed a firm of estate agents to assist him in the sale of his flat. He agreed that if the estate agents effected an introduction of a person ready, able and willing to purchase the flat they might look to him for their commission. The estate agents introduced a ready, able and willing purchaser to the owner. Prior to the introduction, the owner's solicitors had exchanged contracts for the sale of the flat with another purchaser. The estate agents claimed their commission. *Held*, there was an implied term in the contract that a commission was not payable if the property had already been sold before the ready, able and willing purchaser was introduced. The commission was not payable.

A A DICKSON & CO V O'LEARY [1980] LS Gaz R 39 (Court of Appeal: LORD DENNING MR, BRIDGE LJ and SIR DAVID CAIRNS). Dicta of Bucknill LJ in *E P Nelson & Co v Rolfe* [1949] 2 All ER 584, at 586–7 applied.

45　　　　—— remuneration—breach of contract by principal—agent's entitlement to remuneration

The plaintiffs introduced the defendants to a third party, and the defendants and the third party then entered into a contract for the sale of cement. An agency agreement between the plaintiffs and the defendants provided that the defendants would cover the plaintiffs by way of commission for the profit the plaintiffs would have made if the plaintiffs had made the contract with the third party. The defendants failed to perform the contract with the third party. The plaintiffs sued the defendants in damages for a sum in respect of the commission. *Held*, the defendants had failed to perform their contract with the third party and had broken their contract of agency with the plaintiffs, who were accordingly entitled to damages equal to the amount of commission they would have received had the defendants performed the contract.

ALPHA TRADING LTD V DUNNSHAW-PATTEN LTD [1980] 2 Lloyd's Rep 284 (Queen's Bench Division: MOCATTA J).

This decision has been affirmed by the Court of Appeal; see [1981] 1 All ER 482.

46　　　　Existence of agency relationship—test to be applied by court

A language teacher organised educational courses for overseas students which were booked through overseas organisations. A value added tax tribunal held that, in acting as the alter ego of the organisations in relation to the foreign students, the teacher was an agent for them, and her services were taxable at a zero-rate pursuant to the Finance Act 1972, Sch. 4, Group 9, item 1. On appeal by the commissioners, *held*, the true test of agency for the purposes of Sch. 4, Group 9, item 1 was whether a relationship existed between two persons one of whom consented, expressly or by implication, that the other should act on his behalf, and the other of whom consented so to act, and was not dependent on effecting legal relationships with third parties. The appeal would be allowed.

CUSTOMS AND EXCISE COMRS V JOHNSON [1980] STC 624 (Queen's Bench Division: WOOLF J). *Kidd & Zigrino Ltd v Customs and Excise Comrs* [1974] VATTR 173, disapproved.

Finance Act 1972, Sch. 4, Group 9, item 1 now amended: S.I. 1978 No. 1064; 1979 No. 244.

47　　　　Forwarding agents—carriage by air—loss of goods—duty to claim against carriers

See *Marbrook Freight Ltd v KMI (London) Ltd*, para. 198.

AGRICULTURE

Halsbury's Laws of England (4th edn.), Vol 1, paras. 1001–1853

48   **Agricultural holding—application for succession to holding of deceased tenant—eligibility—occupier of commercial unit**

An agricultural land tribunal held that an applicant for succession to a deceased tenant's holding under the Agriculture (Miscellaneous Provisions) Act 1976 was ineligible as he was the occupier of a commercial unit of agricultural land. A commercial unit is defined by reference to the Agriculture Act 1967 as a unit which in the opinion of the appropriate minister is capable of providing full-time employment as there stated. In coming to its decision the tribunal did not apply its mind to the question whether the land was a commercial unit in the opinion of the minister but based the decision on its own opinion. *Held*, the tribunal had erred and its decision would be quashed.

R v AGRICULTURAL LAND TRIBUNAL (WALES), EX PARTE HUGHES (1980) 255 Estates Gazette 703 (Queen's Bench Division: DONALDSON LJ and BRISTOW J).

49   **—— —— suitability—onus of proof**

In proceedings under the Agriculture (Miscellaneous Provisions) Act 1976, s. 20, a widow's application for a tribunal's direction entitling her to succession to a tenancy was dismissed on the basis that she was not suitable to farm the holding satisfactorily and profitably. On appeal, *held*, (i) the tribunal members were entitled to consider whether the widow could farm the holding profitably in the light of their own experience. (ii) The tribunal were not obliged, in considering certain factors determining profitability, first to give the parties the opportunity of making submissions on them. (iii) The onus of proof was correctly placed on the widow to prove her own suitability.

DAGG v LOVETT (1980) 256 Estates Gazette 491 (Court of Appeal: LORD DENNING MR, CUMMING-BRUCE and ACKNER LJJ).

50   **—— cessation of agricultural activity—determination of tenancy**

In a case where it was alleged that under an agricultural tenancy agreement, the tenant changed the agricultural user and accordingly the tenancy ceased to be an agricultural tenancy within the Agricultural Holdings Act 1948, questions arose as to (i) whether a court had jurisdiction to deal with such an issue, and (ii) when an agricultural tenancy ceased to be an agricultural tenancy. *Held*, (i) it was for the court and not the Agricultural Land Tribunal to determine whether a tenancy had ceased altogether to be an agricultural tenancy under the 1948 Act. (ii) A tenancy ceased to be an agricultural tenancy if the agricultural activity was abandoned during the course of the tenancy. This applied whether or not the landlord consented to the agricultural activity being stopped; strong evidence, however, was needed to show that agricultural user had been abandoned.

WETHERALL v SMITH [1980] 2 All ER 530 (Court of Appeal: STEPHENSON and ACKNER LJJ and SIR DAVID CAIRNS). Dicta of Jenkins LJ in *Hawkins v Jardine* [1951] 1 All ER 320 at 329 and of Somerville LJ in *Blackmore v Butler* [1954] 2 All ER 403 at 406 applied.

51   **—— compensation to outgoing tenant—calculation**

The Agriculture (Calculation of Value for Compensation) (Amendment) Regulations 1980, S.I. 1980 No. 751 (in force on 1st July 1980), amend the 1978 Regulations, 1978 Halsbury's Abridgment para 37, substituting new tables for calculating the compensation payable to the outgoing tenant of an agricultural holding arising under the provisions of the Agricultural Holdings Act 1948 in the case of tenancies which terminate on or after 1st July 1980.

52   —— notice to quit—length of notice required

The Agricultural Holdings Act 1948, s. 23 provides that a notice to quit an agricultural holding is invalid if it purports to terminate the tenancy before the expiration of twelve months from the end of the then current year of the tenancy.

A landlords' agent agreed to accept as valid a notice by a tenant of his intention to quit a farm. The length of the notice was a day short of the twelve months required by s. 23. Subsequently the tenant contended that the notice was ineffective because it contravened the section. The landlords sought a declaration that they were entitled to possession of the farm occupied by the tenant. *Held*, s. 23 provided that a short notice to quit was invalid as against the recipient. It did not, however, preclude the determination of an agricultural tenancy by shorter notice than that required by the Act if both parties agreed that the notice was to be treated in all respects as if it were a notice of the statutory length. The agent's agreement to accept the notice to quit as a valid notice effectually determining the tenancy on a specific date had the effect of a binding waiver of any defect in the notice and of a binding agreement that the tenancy should accordingly end on that date. Such a waiver and agreement were not contrary to s. 23 and the landlords would be entitled to the declaration sought.

ELSDEN v PICK [1980] 3 All ER 235 (Court of Appeal: BUCKLEY, SHAW and BRIGHTMAN LJJ).

Agricultural Holdings Act 1948, s. 23 now Agricultural Holdings (Notices to Quit) Act 1977, s. 1.

53   Agricultural land—meaning for purposes of protected tenancy

See *Bradshaw v Smith*, para. 1721.

54   Agricultural levy—reliefs

The Agricultural Levy Reliefs (Frozen Beef and Veal) Order 1980, S.I. 1980 No. 211 (in force on 28th February 1980), requires the Minister of Agriculture, Fisheries and Food to allocate the UK's share of a quota for the levy-free import of frozen beef and veal under the provisions of Council Regulation (EEC) 2956/79. Entitlement to relief is determined by the issue of licences.

55   Agricultural Wages Committees—nomination of representatives

The Agricultural Wages Committees (Amendment) Regulations 1980, S.I. 1980 No. 1005 (in force on 1st September 1980), amend the 1949 Regulations by enabling the Council of the Farmers' Union of Wales to participate in the nomination of representatives of employers to Agricultural Wages Committees established under the Agricultural Wages Act 1948, s. 2 for counties in Wales. Such members are to be nominated by the Council and the Council of the Farmers' Union in such proportions as may be agreed between them.

56   Agriculture and horticulture—grant scheme

The Agriculture and Horticulture Grant Scheme 1980, S.I. 1980 No. 1072 (in force on 1st October 1980) supersedes and largely consolidates the provisions of the Farm Capital Grant Scheme 1973 (as varied) and the Horticultural Capital Grant Scheme 1973 (as varied). Applications for grants under these two schemes will not be acceptable after 30th September 1980.

57   Apple and pear development

See para. 2895.

58   Artificial insemination—cattle

The Artificial Insemination of Cattle (England and Wales) Regulations 1980, S.I. 1980 No. 448 (in force on 1st May 1980), supersede the 1977 Regulations, 1977 Halsbury's Abridgment para. 42. These regulations continue, with certain changes, the system for the control and practice of artificial insemination of cattle in England and Wales.

59   **Butter—subsidy**

The Butter Subsidy (Protection of Community Arrangements) Regulations 1980, S.I. 1980 No. 1990 (in force on 21st January 1981), consolidate, with amendments, provisions previously made, enabling a subsidy paid on butter under certain EC Council Regulations to be recovered where the butter has been exported from the United Kingdom, or has, without the authority of the Intervention Board for Agricultural Produce, been used for manufacture. The Regulations further prohibit the use of subsidised butter for manufacture unless the Board has authorised such use and requires records to be kept and information to be furnished about exports of subsidised butter.

The Butter Subsidy (Protection of Community Arrangements) Regulations 1979, as amended, 1979 Halsbury's Abridgment paras. 59 and 60, are revoked.

60   **Central Council for Agricultural and Horticultural Co-operation— grants**

The Agricultural and Horticultural Co-operation (Variation) Scheme 1980, S.I. 1980 No. 1382 (in force on 1st October 1980), varies the 1971 Scheme in so far as the amount of grant given in relation to capital expenditure and the 1977 Scheme, 1977 Halsbury's Abridgment para. 46 ceases to apply to proposals submitted to the Council after 1st October 1980.

61   **—— extension of period**

The Agricultural and Horticultural Co-operation Grants (Extension of Period) Order 1980, S.I. 1980 No. 636 (in force on 15th May 1980), extends the period during which applications for grants can be made until 14th May 1983.

62   **Common agricultural policy—common organisation of market— compensation for damage arising from legislative measures**

See Cases 116 and 124/77: *GR Amylun NV and Tunnel Refineries Ltd v EC Council and EC Commission*; Case 143/77: *Koninklijke Scholten Honig NV v EC Council and EC Commission*, para. 1186.

63   **—— effect of national price freezing measures**

In the course of national proceedings a French court referred to the European Court certain questions, inter alia, as to whether member states were prohibited from applying price freezing rules to products subject to a common organisation of the market. *Held*, in sectors governed by a common organisation of the market, in particular where that organisation was based on a common price system, member states were no longer free to apply unilateral measures, such as a price freeze, which jeopardised the aims and functioning of the market in question. However, the question whether and to what extent the relevant national measure was compatible with the Community legislation governing the market in question was for the national court to decide, taking into account the particular nature of that market organisation. Further, although price freezing measures which were equally applicable to both domestic and imported products did not in themselves constitute a measure of equivalent effect to a quantitative restriction as prohibited by EEC Treaty, art. 30, they could have that effect and thus be so prohibited in so far as they fixed prices at a level which made the sale of imported products either impossible or more difficult than that of domestic products. This again was a question for the national court to decide.

The Court pointed out that a national rule imposing a price freeze did not constitute an agreement between undertakings or a concerted practice within art. 85.

Case 5/79: PROCUREUR GENERAL v BUYS [1979] ECR 3203, [1980] 2 CMLR 493 (European Court of Justice).

64   A reference was made to the European Court for a preliminary ruling under EEC Treaty, art. 177, concerning the interpretation of art. 30 which provides that quantitative restrictions on imports and all measures having equivalent effect are prohibited between member states. The question arose in the course of criminal proceedings by a national government ministry against traders in animal feed stuffs accused of increasing prices without notifying the minister concerned in accordance with certain conditions laid down by national law. The conditions, in effect, were rules imposing a price freeze and the traders contended that this amounted to a measure having equivalent effect to a quantitative restriction and was therefore prohibited under art. 30. *Held,* a national system of price control constituted a measure having equivalent effect to a quantitative restriction on imports prohibited by art. 30 to the extent to which it made the marketing of products imported from other member states either impossible or more difficult than that of similar national products, or had the effect of favouring the markets of the national products to the detriment of imported products. Further, such national rules were incompatible with the common organisation of the market established for cereals under Council Regulation (EEC) 120/67 in so far as they jeopardised the objectives and functioning of that market organisation.

Cases 16–20/79: OPENBAAR MINISTERIE v JOSEPH DANIS [1979] ECR 3327 (European Court of Justice).

65   See also Joined Cases 95 and 96/79: *Procureur du Roi v Charles Kefer and Louis Delmelle,* para. 1158.

66   —— **currency revaluation—compensation**

On a previous reference by a German court the European Court had held that the distinction between agricultural livestock producers and industrial livestock producers, for the purposes of receiving compensation as a result of currency re-valuation, was valid. The national court referred a further question to the European Court arising out of the same proceedings, on the validity of excluding industrial calf fatteners from receiving compensation if agricultural calf fatteners used the same industrially produced feeding stuffs as industrial calf fatteners. *Held,* although the same feeding-stuffs might be used, fatteners in the agricultural sector were nevertheless subject to the risks inherent in farming land. Accordingly, such a distinction was justified since agricultural producers were more likely to suffer a loss of income as a result of re-valuation, and since the distinction was not arbitrary it could not be regarded as discrimination between producers.

Case 36/79: DENKAVIT FUTTERMITTEL GmbH v FINANZAMT WARENDORF [1979] ECR 3439 (European Court of Justice). For earlier proceedings see [1978] ECR 1675, 1979 Halsbury's Abridgment para. 57.

67   —— **expiration of transitional period—products not subject to common organisation of market—retention of national restriction on imports—validity of restriction**

The Commission instituted proceedings before the European Court seeking a declaration under EEC Treaty, art. 169 that France, by continuing to apply its restrictive national system to the importation of lamb from the United Kingdom, had failed to fulfil its obligations under EEC Treaty, arts. 12 and 30 concerning the free movement of goods between member states. France claimed that it was entitled to maintain the import restrictions until the products were covered by a common organisation of the markets. *Held,* the national organisation was incompatible with the Treaty provisions since it included the fixing of a threshold price protected by a system of import bans and the levying of a duty on imports of lamb coming from another member state. A member state was not entitled unilaterally to adopt measures to protect trade. If it was still considered necessary to take special measures they should be adopted within the Community system which was designed to guarantee that the general public interest of the Community was protected. Since the transitional period for implementing the provisions had expired France had failed to fulfil its obligations under arts. 12 and 30.

The Commission sought to amend its conclusions with reference to Case 231/78: *Re Import of Potatoes: EC Commission v United Kingdom* [1979] 2 CMLR 427, ECJ,

1979 Halsbury's Abridgment para. 72, in order to back-date the period of alleged unlawful action. The amended conclusions were held to be inadmissible since they would invoke a new set of legal rules.

Case 232/78: Re RESTRICTION ON IMPORTS OF LAMB: EC COMMISSION v FRANCE [1979] ECR 2729, [1980] 1 CMLR 418 (European Court of Justice).

68 —— export refunds—rules for granting of refunds

Council Regulation (EEC) 3035/80 (OJ No. L 323, 29.11.80) lays down general rules for granting export refunds on certain agricultural products exported in the form of goods not covered by EEC Treaty, Annex II, and the criteria for fixing the amount of such refunds.

69 —— farm improvement grants

See Case 1652/79: *Lee v Minister for Agriculture*, para. 1131.

70 —— fisheries—agreement between member states and third countries

Council Regulation (EEC) 3062/80 (OJ No. L 322, 28.11.80) details the conclusion of the agreement on fisheries between the member states of the Community and Spain which establishes the principles and rules governing the fishing activities of the vessels of either party within the fishing zones falling under the jurisdiction of the other party. (See also OJ No. C263, 10.10.80.)

71 —— —— —— effect of Community law

See Case 812/79: *A-G v Burgoa*, para. 1220.

72 —— —— conservation

Council Regulation (EEC) 2527/80 (OJ No. L 258, 1.10.80) lays down technical measures for the conservation of fishery resources, specifying, inter alia, the mesh size, by-catch rates and fish sizes permitted.

73

Council Regulation (EEC) 3458/80 (OJ No. L 360, 31.12.80), lays down technical measures for the conservation of fishing resources, extending until 31st January 1981 the provisions of Council Regulation (EEC) 2527/80, para. 72.

74 —— —— national law—validity

The skipper of a French fishing vessel, whilst fishing off the Welsh coast, was arrested and was subsequently charged with carrying on board a fishing vessel, within British fishery limits, a net which failed to comply with the provisions of the Fishing Net (North-East Atlantic) Order 1977, as amended. Questions arose as to the validity of the regulations and their compatability with Council Regulation (EEC) 101/76 relating to a common structural policy for the fishing industry. *Held*, national fishery conservation regulations setting mesh limits for nets which were duly notified to the Commission and member states, but which were introduced without their approval, did not infringe Regulation 101/76.

R v TYMEN [1980] 3 CMLR 101 (Crown Court at Cardiff: WATKINS J). Case 61/77: *Re Sea Fishery Restrictions: EC Commission v Ireland* [1978] 2 CMLR 466, 1978 Halsbury's Abridgment para. 1334 and Case 141/78: *Re Fishing Net Mesh Sizes; France v UK* [1980] 1 CMLR 6, para. 1130 distinguished.

75 —— —— power of member states to act unilaterally

See Case 141/78: *Re Fishing Net Mesh Sizes*, para. 1130.

76 —— green pound—conversion rate

See Case 49/79: *Pool v EC Council*, para. 1188.

77　　　—— horticulture—national law incompatible with Community provisions

A Dutch trader was prosecuted by the relevant national authority after having sold certain ornamental plants in the Netherlands without having been a member of the relevant statutory trade association. Questions arose as to the interpretation and application of EEC Treaty, arts. 30 and 34 and Council Regulation (EEC) 234/68 on the establishment of a common organisation of the market in ornamental plants. *Held*, in so far as intra-Community trade was concerned, the common organisation of the ornamental plants market introduced by Regulation 234/68 was based on commercial transactions and was opposed to any national rule which hindered, directly or indirectly, actually or potentially, intra-Community trade. Any national provisions or practices which modified the patterns of imports or exports by not allowing producers to market those products freely were incompatible with that market organisation. This applied to rules forbidding traders to market, nationally or transnationally, plant propagation material unless they were members of specific organisations; such a restriction violated the regulation which laid down the principle of an open market.

Case 94/79: Re Pieter Vriend [1980] ECR 327, [1980] 3 CMLR 473 (European Court of Justice).

78　　　—— impact of European Monetary System

Council Regulation (EEC) 1523/80 (OJ No. L152, 20.6.80) amends Council Regulation (EEC) 652/79, 1979 Halsbury's Abridgment para. 64, on the impact of the European Monetary System on the common agricultural policy.

79　　　—— licences—import and export licences

Commission Regulation (EEC) 3183/80 (OJ No. L338, 13.12.80) lays down common detailed rules for the application of the system of import and export licences and advance fixing certificates for agricultural products.

80　　　—— milk—payment of premium—disposal of dairy herd and farm—effect

On a reference to the European Court for an interpretation of certain provisions of Council Regulation (EEC) 1975/69 relating to the payment of premiums to farmers for the non-marketing of milk and disposal of their dairy herd, the Court stated that an undertaking entered into by the recipient of a premium bound the recipient personally and did not attach to the property. If the property, or the right to the use of the property, was disposed of, the recipient lost his entitlement to the premium and was obliged to return any amount received if the marketing of milk had not ceased at the property in question.

Case 77/79: Damas v Fonds D'orientation et de Regularisation des Marches Agricoles [1980] 3 CMLR 387 (European Court of Justice).

81　　　—— notice of invitation to tender—decision—whether of direct and individual concern to tenderers

See Case 92/78: *Simmenthal SpA v EC Commission*, para. 1126.

82　　　—— poultrymeat—limitation of production

The owner of a slaughterhouse for poultry infringed national provisions limiting the number of fowl to be slaughtered for the purpose of poultrymeat. The provisions were introduced in order to counter the fall in the price of poultrymeat which resulted from surplus production. Questions concerning the validity of the provisions arose, in particular whether the provisions were compatible with Community law, namely Council Regulation (EEC) 123/67 on the common organisation of the market in poultrymeat and EEC Treaty, arts. 30–37 concerning the elimination of quantitative restrictions between member states. *Held*, once the

Community had, pursuant to art. 40, legislated for the establishment of the common organisation of the market in a given agricultural sector, member states were under an obligation to refrain from taking any measures which undermined or created exceptions to it. Council Regulation (EEC) 123/67 omitted any provision for the withdrawal of products from the poultrymeat market as a deliberate choice of economic policy. The organisation of the market was based upon freedom of commercial transactions under conditions of genuine competition and therefore national measures designed to limit the number of poultry slaughtered as a means of market regulation infringed that regulation. Furthermore, voluntary trade measures taken with Community encouragement to reduce the number of poultry on the market were equally a violation of the regulation.

Case 111/76: OFFICIER VAN JUSTITIE V BEERT VAN DEN HAZEL [1980] 3 CMLR 12 (European Court of Justice).

83   —— **production refunds—compensation for loss arising from abolition of refunds—liability of Community**

See Case 238/78: *Ireks-Arkady GmbH v EC Council and EC Commission*, para. 1187.

84   —— **sheepmeat**

Council Regulation (EEC) 1837/80 (OJ No. L183, 16.7.80) establishes a common organisation of the market in sheepmeat and goatmeat, comprising a price system and a trading system.

85   Commission Regulation (EEC) 2755/80 (OJ No. L284, 29.10.80) having regard to Council Regulation (EEC) 1837/80, para. 84, on the common organisation of the market in sheepmeat and goatmeat, provides for the conditions for implementing and suspending intervention buying in that market.

86   —— —— **protection of Community arrangements**

The Common Agricultural Policy (Agricultural Produce) (Protection of Community Arrangements) (Amendment) Order 1980, S.I. 1980 No. 1562 (in force on 20th October 1980), amends the Common Agricultural Policy (Agricultural Produce) (Protection of Community Arrangements) (No. 2) Order 1973 by extending the powers provided for in that order, in respect of keeping records and entering premises for the protection of the Community support system to cover the common regime for sheepmeat and goatmeat.

87   The Common Agricultural Policy (Protection of Community Arrangements) (Amendment) Regulations 1980, S.I. 1980 No. 1565 (in force on 20th October 1980), amend the Common Agricultural Policy (Protection of Community Arrangements) Regulations 1973 by extending the powers provided for in those regulations, such as the requirement to keep records and the power to enter premises, for the protection of the Community support system to cover the common regime for sheepmeat and goatmeat.

88   —— —— **variable slaughter premium**

Commission Regulation (EEC) 2956/80 (OJ No. L306, 15.11.80) fixes for the United Kingdom the level of the variable slaughter premium for sheep and the amounts to be charged on products leaving that member state.

89   —— **sugar—restructuring of market organisation**

The common organisation of the market in sugar is governed by Council Regulation (EEC) 3330/74 while Council Regulation (EEC) 3331/74 concerns the allocation and alteration of the basic quotas for sugar and provides for derogations from Regulation 3330/74. Article 2 (2) of Regulation 3331/74 provides that Italy may alter quotas in so far as it is necessary for the implementation of restructuring plans for beet and sugar sectors. Two sugar manufacturers challenged the validity of a decree which reduced the basic quotas allotted to them and increased the basic quota allotted to a third manufacturer. On a reference to the European Court concerning the validity and interpretation of Regulation 3331/74, art. 2 (2), *held*, although the power in art. 2 (2) was not subject to specific quantitative limits its exercise was subject to the existence of restructuring plans and should not exceed what was necessary for the implementation of those plans. Accordingly art. 2 (2) came within the objective laid down in the basic regulation. Restructuring plans formed part of the common organisation of the market in sugar and were accordingly an element of the common agricultural policy as a whole. The concept of restructuring plans within art. 2 (2) was to be defined both by its objectives, which were to redress the unbalance between different agricultural regions and to adapt the sugar and beet sectors in Italy to the requirements of the common organisation of the market, and also by its effects which was to allow the competent authorities to redistribute the basic quotas between several undertakings.

Case 230/78: SpA Eridania-Zuccherifici Nazionali v Minister of Agriculture and Forestry [1979] ECR 2749 (European Court of Justice).

90   —— trade arrangements

Council Regulation (EEC) 3033/80 (OJ No. L323, 29.11.80) lays down the trade arrangements applicable to certain goods resulting from the processing of agricultural products.

91   —— wine

Commission Regulation (EEC) 2313/80 (OJ No. L 233 4.9.80) lays down detailed rules and conditions for granting temporary abandonment premiums and premiums for the renunciation of replanting in the wine sector.

92   —— —— restrictions on new planting of vines—validity

See Case 44/79: *Hauer v Land Rheinland-Pfalz*, para. 1136.

93   Eggs—levy

The Eggs Authority (Rates of Levy) Order 1980, S.I. 1980 No. 325 (in force on 1st April 1980), specifies the rate of levy to be raised in respect of the accounting period beginning 1st April 1980 and ending 31st March 1981 to meet the aggregate of the amounts determined for financing the functions of the Eggs Authority.

94   Farm and horticulture improvements—grant

The Agriculture and Horticulture Development Regulations 1980, S.I. 1980 No. 1298 (in force on 1st October 1980), supersede and consolidate the 1978 Regulations, 1978 Halsbury's Abridgment para. 97, as amended. The regulations provide for aid for agricultural and horticultural businesses in relation to development plans.

95

The Farm and Horticulture Development (Amendment) Regulations 1980, S.I. 1980 No. 97 (in force on 1st February 1980), amend the Farm and Horticulture Development Regulations 1978, 1978 Halsbury's Abridgment, para. 97, in order to change the level of grant payable to those applying for assistance on or after 1st February 1980. They also restrict the total amount of expenditure which may be approved for grants in respect of such applications, taking into account similar approved expenditure during the preceding six years.

In addition the amendments:
(a) introduce the European Currency Unit (ECU) to replace the unit of account;
(b) increase the lower and upper limits relating to approved expenditure in connection with the breeding and keeping of pigs;
(c) increase the limits for expenditure per labour unit that may be approved for grant on a development plan;
(d) increase the amount of grant payable for keeping accounts.

These regulations have been replaced; see para. 94.

96   The Farm and Horticulture Development (Amendment) (No. 2) Regulations 1980,
            S.I. 1980 No. 419 (in force on 1st April 1980), are made under the European
            Communities Act 1972. They further amend the 1978 Regulations, 1978
            Halsbury's Abridgment para. 97, in order to withdraw from applications for
            guarantees received by a guarantor on or after 1st April 1980 the facility previously
            granted under reg. 4 for defrayment of guarantee fees by the Minister.
                The definitions of "eligible agricultural business" and "eligible persons" are now
            contained in the interpretation regulation, reg. 2.
                These regulations have been replaced; see para. 94.

97   The Farm and Horticulture Development (Amendment) (No. 3) Regulations 1980,
            S.I. 1980 No. 928 (in force on 1st October 1980), further amend the 1978
            Regulations, 1978 Halsbury's Abridgment para. 97. The amendment brings
            forward the final date by which applications for assistance under the 1978
            Regulations must be received by the appropriate Minister from 18th April 1982 to
            30th September 1980.
                These regulations have been replaced; see para. 94.

98   The Farm Capital Grant (Variation) Scheme 1980, S.I. 1980 No. 103 (in force on 1st
            February 1980), varies the Farm Capital Grant Scheme 1973, as varied. The
            principal changes are that in respect of applications received on or after 1st February
            1980:—
                (a) some of the rates of grant payable under the scheme have been changed;
                (b) the total amount of expenditure within any six year period incurred on or
            after 1st February 1980 which may qualify for grant under this scheme is restricted,
            taking into account grant-aided expenditure under the Horticulture Capital Grant
            Scheme and the Farm and Horticulture Development Regulations for which
            applications for approval are received on or after 1st February 1980;
                (c) no expenditure can be approved under this scheme if the applicant has a
            development plan approved under the Farm and Horticulture Development
            Regulations 1978 which has not been completed.
                In addition, this scheme introduces the European Currency Unit (ECU) to replace
            the unit of account, increases the limit on eligible expenditure per labour unit and
            increases both the lower and upper limits relating to expenditure which may be
            approved in connection with the breeding and keeping of pigs.

99   The Farm Capital Grant (Variation) (No. 2) Scheme 1980, S.I. 1980 No. 930 (in
            force on 1st October 1980), varies the 1973 Scheme. The Scheme brings forward
            the final date before which applications for approval of expenditure under the 1973
            Scheme must be received by the appropriate Minister from 1st January 1981 to 1st
            October 1980, except for applications for works certified under the Farm
            Amalgamation and Boundary Adjustment Schemes which remain at 1st January
            1981. Further, the scheme provides that claims for a grant must be received before
            1st January 1984 and for the replacement of para 8 (3) of the 1973 Scheme
            concerning claims made under that Scheme.

100   The Horticulture Capital Grant (Variation) Scheme 1980, S.I. 1980 No. 104 (in
            force on 1st February 1980), amends the Horticulture Capital Grants Scheme
            1973. The principal changes are that in respect of applications received on or after
            1st February 1980:—
                (a) the amount of grant payable under the scheme towards approved expenditure
            on land improvements, buildings and the provision of services is reduced;
                (b) the total of expenditure which may qualify for grant under this scheme
            within any six year period is restricted, taking into account grant-aided expenditure
            under the Farm Capital Grant Scheme and the Farm and Horticulture Development
            Regulations for which applications for approval are received on or after 1st February
            1980;
                (c) no expenditure can be approved under this scheme if the applicant has a
            development plan approved under the Farm and Horticulture Development
            Regulations 1978 which has not been completed.
                In addition, this scheme introduces the European Currency Unit (ECU) to replace
            the unit of account and increases the limit on eligible expenditure per labour unit.

101   The Horticulture Capital Grant (Variation) (No. 2) Scheme 1980, S.I. 1980 No. 929 (in force on 1st October 1980), varies the 1973 Scheme. The changes are (i) the bringing forward of the final date before which applications for approval of expenditure under the 1973 Scheme must be received by the appropriate Minister from 1st January 1981 to 1st October 1980; (ii) the provision that claims for grants must be received before 1st January and (iii) the replacement of para. 10 of the 1973 Scheme concerning claims made under that Scheme.

102   ## Fertilisers—sampling and analysis

The Fertilisers (Sampling and Analysis) (Amendment) Regulations 1980, S.I. 1980 No. 1130 (in force on 1st November 1980), amend the 1978 Regulations, 1978 Halsbury's Abridgment para. 94, in order to prescribe additional methods of analysis, to extend the application of the 1978 Regulations to fertilisers marked in accordance with the Fertilisers and Feeding Stuffs Regulations 1973 and to revoke the 1973 Regulations, as amended, in so far as they apply to the sampling and analysis of fertilisers.

103   ## Hill livestock—compensatory allowances

The Hill Livestock (Compensatory Allowances) (Amendment) Regulations 1980, S.I. 1980 No. 2028 (in force on 1st January 1981), amend the 1979 Regulations, 1979 Halsbury's Abridgment, para. 85. The regulations increase the compensatory allowance payable for cattle and sheep and increase the overall limit on payments for each hectare of eligible land in accordance with Council Directive (EEC) 80/666.

104   ## —— —— procedure on application for allowance

See para. 27.

105   ## Home-Grown Cereals Authority—levy scheme

The Home-Grown Cereals Authority (Rate of Levy) Order 1980, S.I. 1980, No. 862 (in force on 1st August 1980), specifies in respect of home-grown wheat, barley and oats the rate of levy to be raised for the year beginning 1st August 1980 to meet the amounts apportioned by the Ministers to these kinds of home-grown cereals to finance the Home-Grown Cereals Authority in the performance of their non-trading functions under the Cereals Marketing Act 1965. The order also includes provisions as to the quantity of such cereals in respect of which a levy is to be imposed. The levy will be recovered in accordance with the provisions of a scheme under the 1965 Act, s. 16.

106   ## Intervention Board for Agricultural Produce—monetary compensatory amounts

The Customs and Excise (Positive Monetary Compensatory Amounts) Regulations 1980, S.I. 1980 No. 927 (in force on 1st August 1980), require the Commissioners of Customs and Excise to pay to the Intervention Board for Agricultural Produce sums equivalent to the monetary compensatory amounts charged on imports into the United Kingdom from other member states of the European Economic Community.

107   ## Plant breeders' rights

The Plant Breeders' Rights (Amendment) Regulations 1980, S.I. 1980 No. 316 (in force on 4th April 1980), amend the Plant Breeders' Rights Regulations 1978, Sch. 3, 1978 Halsbury's Abridgment para. 103. Composite schemes having been made to enable Plant Breeders' Rights to be granted in respect of cereals, oil and fibre plants, vegetables and soft fruit, the regulations specify the reproductive and other plant material to be delivered when an application is made for a grant of Plant Breeders' Rights in respect of plant varieties of those kinds and also in respect of other plant varieties for which there are existing schemes not replaced by the aforesaid composite schemes.

108   —— **fees**

The Plant Breeders' Rights (Fees) Regulations 1980, S.I. 1980 No. 351 (in force on 4th April 1980), revoke the 1978 Regulations, 1978 Halsbury's Abridgment para. 105. They prescribe the fees payable to the Controller of Plant Variety Rights in regard to matters arising out of the application for granting plant breeders' rights.

109   —— **schemes—cereals**

The Plant Breeders' Rights (Cereals) Scheme 1980, S.I. 1980 No. 321 (in force on 4th April 1980), replaces previous schemes in respect of barley, oats, wheat and maize and adds rye as plant varieties of cereals for which plant breeders' rights may now be granted.

110   —— —— **oil and fibre plants**

The Plant Breeders' Rights (Oil and Fibre Plants) Scheme 1980, S.I. 1980 No. 318 (in force on 4th April 1980), prescribes the varieties of oil and fibre plants in respect of which grants of plant breeders' rights may be exercised.

111   —— —— **soft fruits**

The Plant Breeders' Rights (Soft Fruits) Scheme 1980, S.I. 1980 No. 331 (in force on 4th April 1980), replaces previous schemes in respect of strawberries, raspberries and blackcurrants and adds gooseberries to those soft fruits for which plant breeders' rights may be granted.

112   —— —— **vegetables**

The Plant Breeders' Rights (Vegetables) (including Field Beans and Field Peas) Scheme 1980, S.I. 1980 No. 319 (in force on 4th April 1980), replaces previous schemes and adds beetroot and cauliflower to those vegetables for which plant breeders' rights may be granted.

113   **Plant health—import and export—chrysanthemums**

The Chrysanthemum (Temporary Prohibition on Landing) (Great Britain) Order 1980, S.I. 1980 No. 1942 (in force on 17th December 1980), prohibits for three months the landing in Great Britain of chrysanthemums grown in the Netherlands. The order is to take effect as though contained in the Import and Export (Plant Health) (Great Britain) Order 1980, para. 114.

114   —— —— **plants**

The Import and Export (Plant Health) (Great Britain) Order 1980, S.I. 1980 No. 420 (in force on 1st May 1980), revokes the Importation of Plants, Plant Produce and Potatoes (Health) (Great Britain) Order 1971, and implements Council Directive (EEC) 77/93, which prohibits the import into member states of the EEC of certain pests harmful to plants and prescribes controls on the movement of plants, plant products and soil. In addition, the Order prescribes controls in respect of the import of genetically manipulated material, in respect of direct trade in plants, plant products and soil with countries outside the EEC and in respect of restrictions on the planting of potatoes in Great Britain.

115   —— —— **trees, wood and bark**

See para. 1352.

116   —— **plant pests**

The Plant Pests (Great Britain) Order 1980, S.I. 1980 No. 499 (in force on 1st May 1980), applies to Great Britain and revokes the Sale of Diseased Plants Order 1927 and the Destructive Pests and Diseases of Plants Order 1965. The order relates to the control of non-indigenous plant pests.

117   Potatoes—seed potatoes—fees

The Seed Potatoes (Fees) Regulations 1980, S.I. 1980 No. 480 (in force on 5th May 1980), revoke the 1979 Regulations, 1979 Halsbury's Abridgment para. 95. The Regulations prescribe the fees payable in respect of certain matters arising under the Seed Potatoes Regulations 1978, 1978 Halsbury's Abridgment para. 110.

118   Seeds—cereal

The Cereal Seeds Regulations 1980, S.I. 1980 No. 900 (in force on 1st August 1980), revoke and replace the 1976 Regulations, 1976 Halsbury's Abridgment para. 93. The regulations regulate the marketing in Great Britain of cereal seeds but exclude cereals used for research, experiment or selection processes, uncleaned seeds marketed with a view to processing or other treatment and seeds marketed under prescribed multiplication contracts.

119   —— fees

The Seeds (Fees) Regulations 1980, S.I. 1980 No. 901 (in force on 1st August 1980) revoke the 1979 Regulations, 1979 Halsbury's Abridgment para. 98, and prescribe the new fees payable under the Vegetable Seeds Regulations 1979, 1979 Halsbury's Abridgment para. 101, the Cereal Seeds Regulations 1980, para. 118, supra, the Fodder Plant Seeds Regulations 1980, para. 121, infra, the Beet Seeds Regulations 1976, 1976 Halsbury's Abridgment para. 93, the Oil and Fibre Plant Seeds Regulations 1979, 1979 Halsbury's Abridgment para. 99 and the Seeds (Regulation and Licensing) Regulations 1974, 1974 Halsbury's Abridgment para. 106.

120

The Seeds (National Lists of Varieties) (Fees) Regulations 1980, S.I. 1980 No. 330 (in force on 4th April 1980), replace the 1978 Regulations, 1978 Halsbury's Abridgment para. 112. They prescribe fees in respect of matters arising under the Seeds (National Lists of Varieties) Regulations 1979, 1979 Halsbury's Abridgment para. 100. Provision is made for the mitigation of fees for tests of a plant variety where that variety is the subject of the application for a grant of plant breeders' rights and fees for tests are being charged in respect of it in accordance with the Plant Breeders' Rights (Fees) Regulations 1980, para. 108.

121   —— fodder plants

The Fodder Plant Seeds Regulations 1980, S.I. 1980 No. 899 (Sch. 2, Pt. I para. 7 (b), (c) in force on 1st January 1981, the remainder in force on 1st August 1980), revoke the Fodder Plant Seeds Regulations 1976, 1976 Halsbury's Abridgment para. 95. The Regulations regulate the marketing in Great Britain of seeds of fodder plants but exclude seeds used for research, experiment or selection processes, uncleaned seeds marked with a view to processing or other treatment and seeds marketed under prescribed multiplication contracts. They further give effect to Council Directive (EEC) 66/401, as amended.

122   —— national lists of varieties

The Seeds (National List of Varieties) (Amendment) Regulations 1980, S.I. 1980 No. 898 (in force on 1st August 1980), make amendments to certain of the botanical names given to kinds of plants subject to the Seeds (National List of Varieties) Regulations 1979, 1979 Halsbury's Abridgment para. 100 which are included in National Lists published in accordance with these regulations.

123   Sheep—annual premium

The Sheep Annual Premium Regulations 1980, S.I. 1980 No. 1577 (in force on 10th November 1980), make provision for those matters left to member states under Council Regulations (EEC) 2643/80, 2660/80 and 1837/80, para. 84 which introduced a common organisation of the market for sheepmeat and goatmeat. The present regulations appoint the "competent authority" responsible for administering the scheme in the United Kingdom, specify the circumstances for payment of the premium, and provide for powers of entry on to land by authorised officers acting on behalf of the competent authority for the purposes of inspecting and counting ewes and examining relevant documents. Furthermore, the regulations create a number of offences which are punishable on summary conviction by a fine.

124 —— guaranteed payments—termination

The Common Agricultural Policy (Termination of Guarantee Arrangements) (Fat Sheep) Order 1980, S.I. 1980 No. 1564 (in force on 20th October 1980), provides that the United Kingdom arrangements for guarantee payments to producers of fat sheep cease to have effect as from 20th October 1980.

125 —— variable premium—protection of payments

The Sheep Variable Premium (Protection of Payments) Order 1980, S.I. 1980 No. 1563 (in force on 20th October 1980), makes provision for the protection of payments to be made under arrangements of the European Economic Community for the regulation of the market in sheepmeat introduced by Council Regulation (EEC) 1837/80, para. 84. The order requires the marking of any animal or carcase qualifying for a premium payment before certification of such payment, and contains other provisions designed to prevent the payment of more than one premium in respect of the same animal or carcase. The order further provides for the keeping and production of records relating to the purchase, sale or slaughter of certified animals or carcases and that any contravention of the order is an offence under the Agriculture Act 1957, s. 7.

126 The Sheep Variable Premiums (Protection of Payments) (No. 2) Order 1980, S.I. 1980 No. 1811 (in force on 29th November 1980), replaces the 1980 Order, para. 125. The order makes provision for the protection of payments to be made under arrangements of the European Economic Community for the regulation of the market in sheepmeat introduced by Council Regulation (EEC) 1837/80, para. 84. The general supervision of the protection provisions will be undertaken by the Intervention Board for Agricultural Produce. The order requires the marking of any animal or carcase qualifying for a premium payment before certification of such payment, and contains other provisions designed to prevent payment of more than one premium in respect of the same animal or carcase.

127 —— —— recovery powers

The Sheep Variable Premium (Recovery Powers) Regulations 1980, S.I. 1980 No. 1578 (in force on 21st October 1980), enable the Intervention Board for Agricultural Produce to recover a sheep variable premium payment made under Community arrangements if contrary to the provisions of the Sheep Variable Premiums (Protection of Payments) Order 1980, para. 125, the animal in respect of which it was paid has been used for breeding.

128 Suckler cow—premiums

The Suckler Cow Premium Regulations 1980, S.I. 1980 No. 1239 (in force on 19th August 1980), make provision for the proper implementation of the payments of premiums for maintaining the suckler cows scheme introduced by Council Regulation (EEC) 1357/80.

129 The Suckler Cow Premium (Amendment) Regulations 1980, S.I. 1980 No. 1770 (in force on 21st November 1980), amend the 1980 Regulations, para 128, so as to include a reference to Commission Regulation (EEC) 2879/80 concerning the closing date for the receipt of applications for premiums for 1980, and further modifies the powers of entry on land by authorised officers for the purposes of inspecting and counting cattle and of examining relevant documents.

130　　The Suckler Cow Premium (Amendment) (No. 2) Regulations 1980, S.I. 1980 No. 1979 (in force on 19th December 1980), further amend the 1980 Regulations, para. 128. The definition of "the Regulation of the Commission" is amended so as to include a reference to Commission Regulation (EEC) 3154/80 which extends the closing date for the receipt of applications for premiums for 1980 for maintaining suckler cows to 20th December 1980.

131　　**Sugar beet—research and education**

The Sugar Beet (Research and Education) Order 1980, S.I. 1980 No. 257 (in force on 1st April 1980), provides for the assessment and collection of contributions towards the programme of research and education for the year beginning 1st April 1980 from the British Sugar Corporation Ltd and growers of home grown beet.

132　　**Tractor cabs—safety**

The Agriculture (Tractor Cabs) (Amendment) Regulations 1980, S.I. 1980 No. 1036 (in force on 29th August 1980), amend the 1974 Regulations, 1974 Halsbury's Abridgment para. 109, so as to conform with Council Directives (EEC) 77/311 and 77/536 regarding the safety of tractor cabs.

133　　**Tree pests—control**

See para. 1353.

134　　**Wool—marketing—Welsh region**

The British Wool Marketing Scheme (Amendment) Order 1980, S.I. 1980 No. 1238 (in force on 8th August 1980), further amends the 1950 Scheme, increasing the number of regional members of the British Wool Marketing Board from ten to eleven by dividing the Welsh region into two regions, Welsh Southern and Welsh Northern.

ANIMALS

Halsbury's Laws of England (4th edn.), Vol. 2, paras. 201–500

135　　**Animal pathogens—importation restrictions**

The Importation of Animal Pathogens Order 1980, S.I. 1980 No. 1212 (in force on 1st October 1980), prohibits the importation of animal pathogens or carriers of such pathogens without a licence issued by the appropriate minister and in accordance with any conditions of that licence. Further, the order contains powers for the seizure of any animal pathogen or carrier imported in contravention to the order, or in breach of any licence conditions and makes the intentional contravention of certain provisions of the order an indictable offence. The order has no application to any animal pathogen or carrier contained in a medicinal product the importation of which is permitted under the Medicines Act 1968.

136　　**Bees—importation restrictions**

The Importation of Bees Order 1980, S.I. 1980 No. 792 (in force on 1st July 1980), is made under the Bees Act 1980, s. 1, para. 137 and prohibits the importation of bees into Great Britain except under the authority of a licence issued by the Minister of Agriculture, Fisheries and Food, the Secretary of State for Scotland or the Secretary of State for Wales. Licences may be general or limited to specific consignments of bees and may be issued unconditionally or subject to specified conditions.

The Importation of Bees Order 1978, 1978 Halsbury's Abridgment para. 118 and the Importation of Bees (Prohibition) Orders 1979, 1979 Halsbury's Abridgment paras. 106, 107 are revoked.

137 Bees Act 1980

The Bees Act 1980 extends the power of the Minister of Agriculture, Fisheries and Food and the Secretaries of State for Scotland and Wales to take action to prevent the introduction of pests and diseases of bees into Great Britain. It replaces in an extended form the Agriculture (Miscellaneous Provisions) Act 1954, s. 10 on imports of bees and re-enacts and extends to Scotland provisions in the Agriculture (Miscellaneous Provisions) Act 1941 for preventing the spreading of bee pests and diseases within the country. The Act received the royal assent on 20th March 1980 and came into force on 10th June 1980: S.I. 1980 No. 791.

Section 1 empowers the Ministers to prohibit or regulate, by order, the importation into or movement within Great Britain of bees and their associated natural products and containers, for the purpose of preventing the introduction or spreading of bee diseases. It enables authorised persons to examine and take samples of bees and other things controlled by an order and to destroy, without compensation, any such bees or other things if they are infected or have been exposed to infection, or if they have been illegally imported. Other matters for which provision may be made by order are indicated in the Schedule.

Section 2 confers on authorised persons a power of entry for the purpose of exercising powers arising under the Act.

Section 3 gives definitions.

Section 4 provides for corresponding provision to be made for Northern Ireland by Order in Council subject to the negative resolution procedure, and s. 5 deals with short title, commencement, repeals, transitional provision and extent.

138 Carriage of animals—carriage by air—liability of carrier—offence committed in foreign territory

The House of Lords were faced with the question as to whether there was a punishable offence in England under the Diseases of Animals Act 1950 and the Transit of Animals (General) Order 1973, which prohibits the carriage of animals in conditions likely to cause injury to the animals, where an Indian airline carried a cargo of birds from Bombay to London in conditions which constituted a breach of the statutory provisions. The birds however died before the aircraft entered British airspace. *Held*, in construing Acts of Parliament there was an established principle that in the absence of words to the contrary an "offence-making" section was not intended to make conduct outside the territorial jurisdiction of the Crown an offence triable in the English courts. It was apparent that the statutory provisions in the present case were confined to the ambit of animals carried in aircraft actually landing and taking off in England and where the offences occurred within British airspace. Further the offence under the 1973 Order was a continuing offence so long as the birds were carried on the aircraft in such a way as to cause suffering to them. The commission of the offence ceased at the moment when suffering ended. As the death of the birds happened outside British airspace no offence was committed.

AIR INDIA v WIGGINS [1980] 2 All ER 593 (House of Lords: LORD DIPLOCK, LORD EDMUND-DAVIES, LORD KEITH OF KINKEL, LORD SCARMAN and LORD ROSKILL). *Cox v Army Council* [1963] AC 48 and *R v Jameson* [1896] 2 QB 425 applied. Decision of Queen's Bench Divisional Court [1980] 1 All ER 192, 1979 Halsbury's Abridgment para. 108 reversed.

139 Dangerous wild animal—licence—whether enclosure in street constitutes circus

The proprietor of a zoological garden was charged with keeping a lioness without a licence contrary to the Dangerous Wild Animals Act 1976, s. 1, after removing the animal from the zoo and allowing it to perform tricks in an enclosure in a crowded street. At first instance he successfully argued that the tricks and manoeuvres performed by the lioness brought the enclosure within the definition of "circus" in s. 7 (4), and consequently exempted the proprietor from the provisions of the Act pursuant to s. 5. On appeal, *held*, the definition section defined a circus as that word was commonly understood and could not be extended to cover such an enclosure in a high street. The removal of the lioness from the zoological gardens, albeit temporary, was a breach of the provisions of the Act.

HEMMING V GRAHAM-JONES (1980) Times, 23rd October (Queen's Bench Division: DONALDSON LJ and McNEILL J).

140 Deer—welfare

The Welfare of Livestock (Deer) Order 1980, S.I. 1980 No. 593 (in force on 20th May 1980), provides that "livestock" in the Agriculture (Miscellaneous Provisions) Act 1968, Part I is to include deer kept for the production of antlers in velvet.

141 The Removal of Antlers in Velvet (Anaesthetics) Order 1980, S.I. 1980 No. 685 (in force on 11th June 1980), prohibits the performance without anaesthetic of the operation of removing any part of the antlers of a deer while those antlers are in velvet except where authorised under the Cruelty to Animals Act 1876 or in an emergency for the purpose of saving life or relieving pain.

142 The Welfare of Livestock (Deer) Regulations 1980, S.I. 1980 No. 1004 (in force on 17th July 1980), prohibit the removal of any part of the antlers while in velvet of a deer which is livestock for the time being situated on agricultural land. They do not apply to any act lawfully done under the Cruelty to Animals Act 1876, nor do they affect the rendering of first aid to save life or relieve pain, or the performance by a veterinary surgeon of an operation which he considers necessary as treatment for disease or injury.

143 Deer Act 1980

The Deer Act 1980 makes provision to prevent the poaching of deer, to control the sale and purchase of venison and to amend the Deer Act 1963. It received the royal assent on 8th August 1980 and came into force on 8th November 1980, except ss. 2, 3, which came into force on 1st November 1980.

Section 1 makes provision for the prevention of poaching. Any person guilty of an offence under s. 1 is liable on summary conviction to a fine not exceeding £500 or imprisonment for a term not exceeding three months or both: s. 1 (5). Section 2 makes it an offence to sell and purchase venison in certain prescribed circumstances and prescribes penalties for offences under s. 2. Licensed game keepers are required to keep records of all purchases and receipts of venison: s. 3, Sch. 1.

Powers of search, seizure and arrest of persons suspected of committing or having committed an offence under the Act are provided for in s. 4. Upon conviction of any offence the court may order forfeiture of any deer or venison, or vehicle or other thing used to commit the offence, may disqualify that person from holding a game licence and may also cancel any firearm or shotgun certificate held by him: s. 5. Where offences are shown to have been committed by a body corporate, a director, manager secretary or other person may also be guilty of the offences and punished accordingly: s. 6.

Section 7 and Sch. 2 amend the Deer Act 1963, ss. 5–8. Section 8 relates to interpretation and s. 9 to short title, repeals, extent and commencement.

144 Diseases of animals—administration—provision of quarantine station at airport—use of station by airline

A local authority sought a declaration against an airline that on the true construction of the Diseases of Animals Act 1950, s. 61, the airline was liable to pay the charges prescribed by the byelaws relating to the authority's animal quarantine station at an airport, made pursuant to s. 61, for the use of the quarantine station to keep animals imported by air. *Held*, an airline which was licensed as a carrying agent for animals and which, as the person in charge of an animal at the time of landing, was under a duty under the Rabies (Importation of Dogs, Cats and other Mammals) Order 1974, art. 7 (1) (b), to remove the animal to an approved temporary quarantine station provided by the local authority at an airport, made use of the station within s. 61 (4) of the 1950 Act on discharging that duty, and hence was liable to pay the local authority's charges for use of the station. The airline, as the person in charge of the animal at the time of landing, could not be regarded in this context as the mere agent of the owner and although the airline might be able to recover the cost from the owner by virtue of some personal nexus in contract or quasi contract, the owner was not the person who directly incurred the toll.

Where the authorised carrying agent and the person in charge of the animal at the time of landing were different persons it was the latter who was personally liable for the toll, although the former might have to hand over the money where the person providing the quarantine accommodation could and did insist upon advance payment.

CITY OF LONDON CORPN v BRITISH CALEDONIAN AIRWAYS LTD [1980] 2 All ER 297 (Chancery Division: GOULDING J).

145   —— African swine fever

The African Swine Fever Order 1980, S.I. 1980 No. 145 (in force on 4th March 1980), extends the definition of disease in the Diseases of Animals Act 1950, s. 84 to include African swine fever for all the purposes of the Act and enables animals affected or suspected of being affected with that disease, or exposed to infection, to be slaughtered. It also applies certain provisions relating to foot-and-mouth diseases for African swine fever.

146   The African Swine Fever (Compensation) Order 1980, S.I. 1980 No. 146 (in force on 4th March 1980), prescribes the scale of compensation payable to animals slaughtered under the Diseases of Animals Act 1950, s. 17 because they were affected or suspected of being affected with African swine fever or had been exposed to the infection of that disease. The Diseases of Animals (Ascertainment of Compensation) Order 1959 applies in respect of such slaughtered animals.

147   —— cattle—brucellosis

The Brucellosis (England and Wales) (Amendment) Order 1980, S.I. 1980 No. 890 (in force on 18th July 1980), further amends the Brucellosis (England and Wales) Order 1978, 1978 Halsbury's Abridgment para. 119. Where an officer of the Ministry of Agriculture, Fisheries and Food considers it necessary for the purpose of eradicating brucellosis he may serve a notice on the owner or person in charge of the bovine animals kept within an eradication area requiring him to remove them to a place specified in the notice. During the time the notice is in force the animals must not be moved from the specified place except under the authority of a licence issued by the appropriate officer. Schedules 1 and 2 of the 1979 Order, 1979 Halsbury's Abridgment para. 113 are replaced.

148   The Brucellosis (England and Wales) (Amendment) (No. 2) Order 1980, S.I. 1980 No. 1689 (in force on 1st December 1980), further amends the 1978 Order, 1978 Halsbury's Abridgment para. 119, by making certain deletions and amending certain definitions.

149   —— —— enzootic bovine leukosis

The Enzootic Bovine Leukosis Order 1980, S.I. 1980 No. 79 (in force on 21st February 1980), applies the Diseases of Animals Act 1950, which relates to the slaughter of diseased animals, to all forms of bovine leukosis, especially epizootic bovine leukosis. The order prescribes the methods of detecting and dealing with the disease and the duties of occupiers of premises and any other person involved with animals. The 1977 Order, 1977 Halsbury's Abridgment para. 140 and the 1978 Order, 1978 Halsbury's Abridgment para. 124 are revoked.

150   The Enzootic Bovine Leukosis (Compensation) Order 1980, S.I. 1980 No. 80 (in force on 21st February 1980), provides that the amount of compensation which has to be paid under the Diseases of Animals Act 1950, s. 17 (3), in respect of a bovine animal slaughtered on account of bovine leukosis, is an amount equal to its market value or the sum of £567 whichever is the less. The 1978 Order, 1978 Halsbury's Abridgment para. 125 is revoked.

151　　—— disinfectants

The Diseases of Animals (Approved Disinfectants) (Amendment) Order 1980, S.I. 1980 No. 25 (in force 31st January 1980), amends the Diseases of Animals (Approved Disinfectants) Order 1978, 1978 Halsbury's Abridgment para. 126, by adding to the list of approved disinfectants, newly approved disinfectants and by deleting other disinfectants.

152

The Diseases of Animals (Approved Disinfectants) (Amendment) (No. 2) Order 1980, S.I. 1980 No. 955 (in force on 29th July 1980), further amends the Diseases of Animals (Approved Disinfectants) Order 1978, 1978 Halsbury's Abridgment para. 126 by substituting new lists of approved disinfectants and of disinfectants removed from the list but were to be used as approved disinfectants until 31st December 1980.

153

The Diseases of Animals (Fees for the Testing of Disinfectants) Order 1980, S.I. 1980 No. 1383 (in force on 10th October 1980), revokes the 1979 Order, 1979 Halsbury's Abridgment para. 118. The Order prescribes revised fees payable for the testing of disinfectants for the purpose of determining their suitability for listing as approved disinfectants in the Diseases of Animals (Approved Disinfectants) Order 1978, 1978 Halsbury's Abridgment para. 126.

154　　—— importation of animals—poultry

The Importation of Animal Products and Poultry Products Order 1980, S.I. 1980 No. 14 (in force on 1st March 1980), prohibits the landing in Great Britain of any animal product or poultry product from outside a place in Great Britain unless under the authority of a licence. The landing of animal carcases or poultry carcases or any part thereof is similarly prohibited. Exemptions are provided in the Schedule.

The order contains provisions relating to contravention of the order and deliberate contravention is an indictable offence.

The importation into Great Britain of embryos, ova or semen is subject to the provisions of the Importation of Embryos, Ova and Semen Order 1980, para. 156.

155

The Importation of Animal Products and Poultry Products (Amendment) Order 1980, S.I. 1980 No. 1934 (in force on 1st January 1981), amends the Importation of Animal Products and Poultry Products Order 1980, Sch., para. 154, by omitting cooked meat and cooked poultry meat. A licence is therefore required to land these products in Great Britain and they must be landed in accordance with the conditions of that licence.

156　　—— importation of embryos, ova and semen

The Importation of Embryos, Ova and Semen Order 1980, S.I. 1980 No. 12 (in force on 1st March 1980), prohibits the landing in Great Britain of the embryos, ova or semen of certain animals from a place outside Great Britain except under the authority of a licence. However, the prohibition does not apply to semen which is landed in Great Britain in accordance with the Agriculture (Miscellaneous Provisions) Act 1943, s. 17 (3). Veterinary inspectors are given power by the order to take action in case of contravention. This is without prejudice to any court proceedings for an offence arising out of the contravention. Deliberate contravention is an indictable offence.

157　　Horses—breeding

The Horse Breeding (Amendment) Rules 1980, S.I. 1980 No. 592 (in force on 23rd May 1980), increase the fees payable under the Horse Breeding Rules 1948 and amend the forms prescribed by the principal rules relating to an application for a licence or a permit and application for a referee's inspection.

158   **Wild birds—conservation of migratory species**

Under a Convention on the Conservation of Migratory Species of Wild Animals signed at Bonn, 23rd June 1979, the contracting parties have undertaken individually or in co-operation with each other to take the steps necessary to conserve migratory species and their habitat. The convention calls for immediate protection for species specified in App. I and for the parties to endeavour to conclude agreements covering the conservation and management of species included in App. II. The convention lays down measures which the parties should adopt for the protection of species listed in App. I and sets out guidelines for agreements relating to species listed in App. II. The convention requires fifteen parties to ratify, accept, approve or accede to it before it enters into force. It has not been ratified by the United Kingdom. For the text of the convention, see Cmnd. 7888.

159   —— **protection—offence—defence**

See *Robinson v Whittle*, para. 1841.

ARBITRATION

Halsbury's Laws of England (4th edn.), Vol. 2, paras. 501–700

160   **Arbitration clause—reference to arbitration—injunction restraining proceedings**

A salvage agreement made between a shipping company and a salvage company provided that the amount of the salvors' remuneration for services rendered during the relevant period was to be determined by an arbitrator. By a notice of motion the shipping company applied for an injunction restraining the salvors from taking any steps in arbitration proceedings. *Held*, the shipping company had agreed that the salvors' reward would be determined by arbitration and it was an implied term of such an agreement that both parties would co-operate in bringing the matter before the arbitrator within a reasonable period of time. An injunction would only be granted if one party to the agreement had, by his conduct, shown that he repudiated the contract and that the other party had accepted that "repudiation" so that the contract was rescinded. There had been no such repudiation of the contract and the application would be dismissed.

THE ANNA MARIA [1980] 1 Lloyd's Rep 192 (Queen's Bench Division: SHEEN J).

161   —— **service of notice of writ out of jurisdiction—availability**

See *The Vikfrost, W. & R Fletcher (New Zealand) Ltd v Sigurd Haavik Aksjeselskap*, para. 2614.

162   —— **time limit for claim—court's power to extend time**

Shipowners failed to claim arbitration over salvage remuneration, within the time limit provided by the salvage agreement. They applied for an extension of the time limit under the Arbitration Act 1950, s. 27, but the judge held that he had no jurisdiction to grant an extension, because s. 27 applied to causes of action only. The shipowners appealed. *Held*, "claims" in s. 27 was not confined to causes of action and applied to a claim to fix the amount of salvage award in arbitration. The appeal would therefore be allowed.

SIOUX INC v CHINA SALVAGE CO, KWANGCHOW BRANCH [1980] 3 All ER 154 (Court of Appeal: LORD DENNING MR, BRIDGE LJ and SIR DAVID CAIRNS).

163   **Arbitrator—appointment—time for appointment—discretion of court to extend time**

A contract dated 25th June 1973 provided for the sale of 1,500 tonnes of soya bean meal, shipment to be in 250 tonne lots from April to September 1973. The sellers made no shipment in June. They subsequently tendered part of the June shipment, leaving an unfulfilled balance by September, when the buyers became insolvent. The buyers claimed in arbitration proceedings that they were entitled to damages under the default clause of the contract. The sellers contended that the operative clause was the one relating to insolvency and that under that clause, which overrode the default clause, there was a sum due to them. They also contended that the buyers' claim was time-barred, since the contract provided for the appointment of an arbitrator by September 1973 and this had not been done until October 1974. The Board of Appeal of GAFTA held that the sellers were liable to the buyers, but that the latter's claim was time-barred. They stated their award in the form of a special case. *Held*, the insolvency clause dealt with a situation where there was an existing entitlement to deliver and it was to the unfulfilled deliveries which the seller was entitled to make that that clause was directed. The sellers had no right whatever to deliver and insist on acceptance of any further amount. They were liable to pay damages under the default clause.

As to whether the buyers' claim was time-barred, the contract provided that in the event of non-compliance with the rules as to arbitration, claims should be deemed to be waived and barred unless the Board of Appeal should in their absolute discretion otherwise determine. This relieving power was general and hence the Board had power to waive the non-compliance with the provision concerning the appointment of an arbitrator. This was a complete discretion and the Board had declined to exercise it, with the result that the claim was time-barred. The buyers had applied for an extension of time under the Arbitration Act 1950, s. 27, but this was not a case to which s. 27 applied since there was not here a bar for failure to comply but a deemed waiver unless the Board should in their absolute discretion otherwise determine. Even if s. 27 applied, this was not a case where the court ought to exercise its discretion. The application for an extension of time would be refused and the buyers' claim would fail.

TIMMERMAN'S GRAAN-EN MAALHANDEL EN MAALDERIJ BV v SACHS [1980] 1 Lloyd's Rep 194 (Queen's Bench Division: PARKER J). *Bunge SA v Kruse* [1979] 1 Lloyd's Rep 279 not followed. *Ets Soules & Cie v International Trade Development Co Ltd* [1979] 2 Lloyd's Rep 122, 1979 Halsbury's Abridgment para. 483 and *Edm J M Mertens & Co PVBA v Veevoeder Import Export Vimex BV* [1979] 2 Lloyd's Rep 372, para. 165 applied.

164   —— ——validity of appointment—jurisdiction of court to intervene

A firm of builders agreed to construct two ships, the *Hull 1704* and the *Hull 1705*, for separate shipowners; disputes arose concerning both ships and were referred to arbitration in accordance with clauses in the respective contracts. Two arbitrators were appointed for the *1704* hearing. The builders and owners then varied the arbitration clause relating to the *1704* by executing a written submission to arbitration in which they appointed an umpire themselves instead of leaving his appointment to the arbitrators. The *1704* hearing was adjourned in August 1978; by October 1978 the builders and owners of the *1705* believed, as a result of letters between them, that the tribunal constituted for the *1704* arbitration would hear the *1705* dispute; however, there was no written submission in respect of the *1705*. By autumn 1979 the owners decided that it would be better to replace the *1704* tribunal in order to expedite the hearing of the *1705* dispute. The builders did not agree. The owners claimed that (i) the umpire had not been validly appointed for the *1705* arbitration since there had been no written submission and (ii) the court should replace the *1704* arbitrators and umpire for the *1705* dispute. *Held*, (i) the umpire's appointment was not conditional on the execution of a written submission in the same terms as the *1704* arbitration. An arbitration could be conducted perfectly well under the ordinary procedural rules and therefore the umpire had been validly appointed; (ii) the court had no jurisdiction to interfere in the appointment of the tribunal members under the Arbitration Act 1950, s. 13 (3) since the arbitrators were not responsible for the delay in hearing the *1705* dispute: they had not taken any action because they had not been asked to do so. The court would not interfere under s. 10 since it applied only when an arbitrator refused to act or was incapable of acting. Furthermore, the court would only interfere with an established tribunal under s. 1 if convinced that it was the only right thing to do. However, the arbitrators and umpire for the *1705* dispute had been agreed on by letters between the builders and owners and had been retained in office for over a year. In the circumstances, there were no grounds for intervention by the court.

SUCCULA LTD AND POMONA SHIPPING CO LTD v HARLAND AND WOLFF LTD [1980] 2 Lloyd's Rep 381 (Queen's Bench Division: MUSTILL J).

165   — — — **whether time-barred**

The sellers sold a quantity of soya bean meal c.i.f. Rotterdam for shipment monthly. The contract incorporated the provisions of the Arbitration Rules of the Grain and Feed Trade Association (GAFTA), Nos. 100 and 125 concerning the appointment of an arbitrator in the case of a dispute. As a result of flooding the US government restricted the export of soya bean meal and the sellers were unable to deliver one instalment. The sellers later appropriated under a bill of lading a quantity of soya bean meal and the buyers accepted the tender in part performance of the sellers' obligations whilst reserving all their contractual rights. A month later the buyers sent a telex demanding compensation for non-performance of the contract and appointing an arbitrator. The sellers contended that the buyers' claim was time-barred since they did not appoint an arbitrator within the time limit set out in GAFTA 125 and, in so far as the Board of Appeal purported to extend the buyers' time for appointing their arbitrator, they had no jurisdiction to do so. They also claimed that the buyers had waived their rights to hold the sellers in default. The dispute was referred to arbitration and the Board of Appeal decided in favour of the buyers but stated their award in the form of a special case for the decision of the court. *Held*, it was clear from the facts and the construction of GAFTA 100 and 125 that the arbitrator had been appointed within the time limit and the buyers' claim was not time-barred; and the Board was entitled to extend the time for the buyers to appoint their arbitrator. There appeared no sufficient finding of any representation by the buyers and no reliance by the sellers for a waiver to operate.

EDM J M MERTENS & CO PVBA v VEEVOEDER IMPORT EXPORT VIMEX BV [1979] 2 Lloyd's Rep 372 (Queen's Bench Division: LLOYD J). *Ets Soules & Cie v International Trade Developments Co Ltd* [1979] 2 Lloyd's Rep 122, 1979 Halsbury's Abridgment para. 483, and *Bremer Handelsgesellschaft mbH v Vanden Avenne-Izegem PVBA* [1978] 2 Lloyd's Rep 109, 1978 Halsbury's Abridgment para. 499 applied.

166   — **duty to conduct fair hearing—final award set aside—effect on interim award**

The applicants complained of defects in common parts of the buildings in which they had purchased several flats. They claimed £130,000 damages, which included the cost of strengthening the roof in order that a roof garden could be made for the flat-dwellers, or, in the event of that part of the claim being disallowed, £93,000. The arbitrator made an interim award disallowing the part of the claim relating to the roof garden. He later made a final award of £12,471, without giving any reasons. The applicants sought the removal of the arbitrator and an order to set aside the award on the ground that he had failed to conduct a fair hearing within the principles of natural justice. *Held*, where such a large part of a claim had been dismissed the arbitrator was bound to give a reasoned decision. The aggrieved party had no remedy if he could not establish whether the deficiency he found was one of fact or of law. The award would therefore be set aside and a new arbitrator appointed. The interim award would stand as there had been no application to the court relating to it.

FISHER v P. G. WELLFAIR LTD (1980) 124 Sol Jo 15 (Queen's Bench Division: ACKNER J).

167   — **grounds for removal—misconduct**

In arbitration proceedings, the arbitrator made an interim award involving a point of law without hearing or inviting submissions from the plaintiff. On appeal by the plaintiff, *held*, the Arbitration Act 1950, s. 23 (1), provided that where an arbitrator had misconducted himself or the proceedings, the High Court might remove him. In the present case the arbitrator had decided a case against a party without hearing him. It was clearly a breach of natural justice and the arbitrator had misconducted the proceedings within s. 23 of the Act. Further, the arbitrator had given no explanation or assurance that such an occurrence would not happen again. It was right that the parties to arbitration proceedings had confidence in an arbitrator's ability to come to a correct conclusion. Accordingly the award would be quashed and the arbitrator would be removed and another appointed in his place.

MODERN ENGINEERING (BRISTOL) LTD v MISKIN & SON LTD (1980) Times, 12th July (Court of Appeal: LORD DENNING MR and DUNN LJ).

168   —— jurisdiction—power to impose conditions on interim award

A dispute between the owners and the charterers of a ship, concerning a claim and a cross-claim, was referred to arbitration. The arbitrators issued an interim award to the charterers on condition that the charterers put up security for the return of it in case the owners were successful in their claim. The charterers applied for a declaration that the arbitrators were acting in excess of their jurisdiction in imposing such a condition. The High Court held that it had the power to grant such a declaration and did grant it on the ground that the arbitrators had no power to impose such a condition. On appeal, *held*, the High Court had an inherent jurisdiction to supervise the conduct of arbitrators and it was within its power to grant the declaration in question. However by the Arbitration Act 1950, s. 14 the arbitrators could impose any proper condition they thought fit when making an interim award and the condition which they had imposed was not unreasonable in view of the fact that the claim and cross-claim were so closely connected.

JAPAN LINE LTD v AGGELIKI CHARIS COMPANIA MARITIMA SA AND DAVIES AND POTTER, THE ANGELIC GRACE [1980] 1 Lloyd's Rep 288 (Court of Appeal: LORD DENNING MR and WALLER LJ).

169   Award—appeal—grant of leave to appeal—guidelines

See *Pioneer Shipping Ltd v BTP Tioxide Ltd*, para. 483.

170   —— grounds for setting aside—misconduct of arbitrator or umpire

A dispute between the owners of a vessel and its charterers for the outstanding hire charge was referred to arbitration. The arbitrators found in favour of the owners and the charterers applied for the award to be set aside on the ground that the arbitrators had misconducted themselves in making their award after considering documents and written submissions which had not been disclosed to them. *Held*, the arbitrators were not under an obligation to provide the charterers with the submissions and full supporting documents of the owners. It was only necessary that a party was not taken by surprise by either the evidence or the arguments advanced by the other party. In the present case, the charterers' arbitrator had requested further information from them in order to meet the case advanced by the owners, and both parties were aware of the nature of the dispute and of the issues involved. There was nothing in the owners' submissions which had taken the charterers by surprise even though the precise details of the submissions had not been seen by the charterers. Accordingly the application would be refused.

THE DUSAN, ALPINE SHIPPING CO v VINBEE (MANCHESTER) LTD [1980] 1 Lloyd's Rep 400 (Queen's Bench Division: ROBERT GOFF J). *The Myron* [1969] 1 Lloyd's Rep 411 applied.

171   —— second arbitration—res judicata

A dispute arose between buyers and sellers about the construction of a force majeure clause in a contract. The buyers referred the dispute to arbitration in terms limiting the reference to the issue of liability for non-delivery. The arbitrators found in favour of the buyers, who then submitted a debit note to the sellers in the amount of the damages which they claimed. The sellers refused payment and the buyers referred the claim for damages to arbitration. The sellers contended that having chosen to limit the first arbitration to the issue of liability, the buyers could not now pursue a claim for damages in a second arbitration. The arbitrators' decision in favour of the buyers was upheld and the sellers further appealed. *Held*, the rule that there could not be serial claims for damages based upon the same cause of action did not apply to this case as there had not been two claims for damages. If the matter had arisen in litigation, regard would have to be had to the principle that no one should be twice vexed by the same cause; however, in this case, there were two causes, the first being an alleged breach of an obligation to deliver and the second being concerned with remedies for that breach. Regard should also be had to the principle that there should be an end to litigation and to whether the right to claim damages had become merged in the declaration of liability. In any event, the buyers would succeed because an award of damages could not have been made in the first arbitration; its jurisdiction was consensual and depended on a reference of the dispute to it, and the only dispute at that time was as to the application of the force majeure clause. Therefore the buyers were not estopped from claiming damages by reason of the previous proceedings and the appeal would be dismissed.

COMPAGNIE GRANIERE SA v FRITZ KOPP AG [1980] 1 Lloyd's Rep 463 (Court of Appeal: LORD DENNING MR, LAWTON and GEOFFREY LANE LJJ). Decision of Donaldson J [1978] 1 Lloyd's Rep 511, 1978 Halsbury's Abridgment para. 153 affirmed.

172   —— special case—mode of stating case—insufficient facts

In a case where a vessel was detained in the Middle East an arbitrator was asked to settle a dispute between the owners and charterers of the vessel on the basis of very unsatisfactory evidence. The question arose whether the arbitrator had provided all the materials needed for the purposes of arguing a special case for the opinion of the court. *Held*, it was possible that while the arbitrator was unable to reach conclusions on some of the mixed questions of fact and law he might be able to give the court the benefit of further background facts from which the court might be able to draw inferences as a matter of law. In the circumstances the award would be remitted to the arbitrator for further consideration but neither party would have the right to address him further.

THE BETIS, TRANSAMERICAN SHIPPING CORPN v TRADAX EXPORT SA [1980] 1 Lloyd's Rep 107 (Queen's Bench Division: DONALDSON J).

The procedure for making an award in the form of a special case has ceased to have effect: Arbitration Act 1979, s. 1 (1). There is now a right of appeal to the High Court on any question of law arising out of an award made under an arbitration agreement: 1979 Act, s. 1 (2).

173   Costs of arbitration—costs apportioned between parties—departure from ordinary rule—umpire's discretion

The owners succeeded on a reference to arbitration in respect of a substantial sum of money owed to them by charterers. In his award the umpire ordered the parties to pay their own costs. The owners applied for the award to be remitted for reconsideration on the ground that the umpire should have shown good reason for departing from the ordinary rule, that the award of costs should follow the event, and accordingly be made in favour of the owners. *Held*, an umpire was not obliged to give reasons for an award but was required to exercise his discretion judicially. In the present case the umpire should have disclosed good reason for departing from the ordinary rule. Since the court could not substitute its own discretion for that of the umpire the award would be remitted for reconsideration on the matter of costs with a direction that in the event of departure from the ordinary rule, justification was to be given in any fresh order.

PATROCLOS SHIPPING CO v SOCIÉTÉ SECOPA [1980] 1 Lloyd's Rep 405 (Queen's Bench Division: PARKER J). *Tramountana Armadora SA v Atlantic Shipping Co SA* [1978] 1 Lloyd's Rep 391, 1978 Halsbury's Abridgment para. 155 applied.

174 — — **whether a justifiable departure from general rule that successful party should obtain costs**

Arbitrators made an award in favour of a charterer for damages for deterioration of his cargo whilst on the owner's ship. Two-thirds of the damage had been due to improper stowage and one-third to inherent vice. The arbitrators stated a special case and the court of first instance upheld the award. An appeal was allowed by the Court of Appeal and the award was remitted to the arbitrators, who held that the charterer's claim for damages failed in its entirety and apportioned costs between the charterer and the owner, making a separate award as to costs in respect of the improper stowage issue. The owner applied to the court to set aside the award or remit it on grounds of technical misconduct. He contended that, although arbitrators had a discretion as to costs, the normal position was that the successful party obtained costs, and if the arbitrators departed from that rule reasons had to be given which justified such a departure. *Held*, there was no obligation on the arbitrators to give reasons for an order as to costs, although it was considered desirable to do so when an unusual order was made. The arbitrators had thought it correct in the exercise of their discretion to make a special order of costs on one issue of the case and it was open to them to make a special order requiring a successful party to pay the costs of a particular issue. It would therefore be wrong to interfere with the exercise of their discretion and the application would be dismissed.

THE CIECHOCINEK (No. 2), ISMAIL v POLISH OCEAN LINES [1980] 1 Lloyd's Rep 97 (Queen's Bench Division: ROBERT GOFF J).

For substantive proceedings in the Court of Appeal, see [1976] 1 All ER 902, 1976 Halsbury's Abridgment para. 2351.

175 **County court—proceedings referred to arbitration—jurisdiction of judge to appoint himself as arbitrator—power to set aside award without parties' consent**

The defendant applied to set aside an award made by the registrar in favour of the plaintiff in arbitration proceedings. The county court judge set aside the award, then ordered another reference to be made in which he appointed himself as arbitrator, acting under the provisions of the County Courts Act 1959, s. 92 and CCR Ord. 19, r. 1. He then made an award in favour of the plaintiff, which was for the same amount as that awarded by the registrar. On appeal the defendant contended that he was not given an opportunity to expound his application to set aside as being an appeal on its merits. *Held*, there could only be an appeal if it was shown that the judge had no jurisdiction, that there was some error of law on the face of the award or that there was some misconduct by the judge. By virtue of the proviso to s. 92 (3) of the Act, a county court judge may with the consent of the parties, revoke the reference or order another reference to be made. The consent of the parties was only necessary to revoke a reference and accordingly the judge had jurisdiction to order another reference to be made and under CCR Ord. 19, r. 1 to appoint himself as arbitrator and make an award in place of the one set aside. The appeal would be dismissed.

LEUNG v GARBETT [1980] 2 All ER 436 (Court of Appeal: MEGAW and TEMPLEMAN LJJ and SIR PATRICK BROWNE).

176 **Notice of arbitration—notice served outside time limit—whether claim time-barred**

A contract for the sale of goods provided that notice of the intention to proceed with arbitration had to be given within three months of the expiry of the shipment period and, in the event of non-compliance, claims for quality were deemed to be waived and absolutely barred unless the Board of Appeal, in their discretion, determined otherwise. The buyers under the contract brought a claim for non-delivery of goods. The shipment period expired on 31st August 1973 and the buyers gave notice on 3rd December, 1973. The sellers contended that the claim was time-barred. *Held*, claims should not be time-barred except by clear words. Thus the provision in question would not be construed as one which barred all claims, with the proviso that quality claims might be allowed at the discretion of the Board; instead it was to be construed as one which only applied to quality claims and not to other claims. As the claim in the instant case did not relate to the quality of the goods it was not time-barred.

BUNGE SA v DEUTSCHE CONTI-HANDELSGESELLSCHAFT mbH (No. 2) [1980] 1 Lloyd's Rep 352 (Queen's Bench Division: DONALDSON J).

177   Stay of court proceedings—application for removal of stay— whether arbitration agreement incapable of being performed

An order was made staying proceedings on a contract containing an arbitration clause. The plaintiff applied for the removal of the stay under the Arbitration Act 1975, s. 1, on the ground that the arbitration agreement was incapable of being performed because his financial position was such that he could not find the deposit required by the rules of the International Chamber of Commerce to initiate proceedings, and the defendant company was not prepared to do so itself. *Held*, where an agreement stated that disputes were to be settled by arbitration and only one party wanted so to settle it, but could not do so, and the other party would not, it was a matter of common sense that the matter was incapable of being performed. The stay would be removed.

PACZY v HAENDLER AND NATERMANN GmbH [1980] LS Gaz R 793 (Chancery Division: WHITFORD J).

AVIATION

Halsbury's Laws of England (4th edn.), Vol. 2, paras. 801–1500

178   Aerodromes—customs and excise airports

The list of aerodromes designated as places for the landing or departure of aircraft for the purposes of customs and excise legislation has been revised. With effect from 20th October 1980 (see the Civil Aviation (Customs and Excise Airports) Order 1980, not in the S.I. series) the designated airports are: Aberdeen (Dyce), Belfast (Aldergrove), Biggin Hill, Birmingham, Blackpool, Bournemouth (Hurn), Bristol (Lulsgate), Cambridge, Cardiff, Coventry, East Midlands, Edinburgh, Exeter, Gatwick, Glasgow, Heathrow, Humberside, Kirkwall, Leeds and Bradford, Liverpool, Luton, Lydd, Manchester International, Manston, Newcastle (Woolsington), Norwich, Plymouth (Roborough), Prestwick, Southampton, Southend, Stansted, Staverton, Sumburgh, Tees-side, and Valley.

179   Air navigation

The Air Navigation Order 1980, S.I. 1980 No. 1965 (in force on 9th February 1981), consolidates the Air Navigation Order 1976, as amended, 1976 Halsbury's Abridgment para. 158. Helicopters and gyroplanes engaged on certain flights are no longer required to take off from and land at a Government aerodrome, an aerodrome owned or managed by the Civil Aviation Authority or a licensed aerodrome. The order also re-classifies the criminal offences created by the order to make only the more serious offences triable on indictment and to increase the penalties.

180   —— services—joint financing

The Civil Aviation (Joint Financing) (Third Amendment) Regulations 1980, S.I. 1980 No. 1892 (in force on 1st January 1981), further amend the Civil Aviation (Joint Financing) Regulations 1978, 1978 Halsbury's Abridgment para. 172 by altering the charge payable by aircraft operators to the Civil Aviation Authority in respect of crossings between Europe and North America. The charges altered are those attributable to the Danish and Icelandic air navigation services and are payable in pursuance of the 1956 Agreements on the Joint Financing of Certain Air Navigation Services.

181   Airports—shops—hours

The Cardiff-Wales Airports Shops Order 1980, S.I. 1980 No. 774 (in force on 1st July 1980), designates Cardiff-Wales Airport as an airport having a substantial amount of international passenger traffic, by virtue of which designation, traders at the airport are exempt from the provisions of Part I of the Shops Act 1950, which relates to hours of closing.

182   Aviation security fund—contributions to fund—prescribed aerodromes

The Aviation Security Fund (Second Amendment) Regulations 1980, S.I. 1980 No. 88 (in force on 1st February 1980), further amend the Aviation Security Fund Regulations 1978, 1978 Halsbury's Abridgment para. 177. As from 1st February 1980, the sum which, multiplied by the number of passengers over 2,000 who arrive by air each month at an aerodrome, is equal to the contribution payable in respect of the aerodrome for that month, is increased from 85p to £1.60. Passengers carried by helicopters are excluded from the calculation. The regulations update the definition of "aerodrome" and add Humberside and Stornoway to the list of aerodromes in respect of which contributions are required to be made. They also allow each aerodrome authority until the end of August, rather than June, to give the Secretary of State certified particulars of the number of passengers who arrived by air during the previous year.

183   British Aerospace—borrowing powers

The British Aerospace Borrowing Powers (Increase of Limit) Order 1980, S.I. 1980 No. 1208 (in force on 8th August 1980), increases the borrowing limit of British Aerospace and its wholly owned subsidiaries to £250 million.

184   British Aerospace Act 1980

The British Aerospace Act 1980 provides for the dissolution of British Aerospace and the vesting of its property, rights, liabilities and obligations in a company to be nominated by the Secretary of State (see para. 185), the shares of which will initially be held on behalf of the Crown. The Act received the royal assent on 1st May 1980 and came into force on that date.

Section 1, Sch. 1 and S.I. 1980 No. 1988 provide for the vesting of the property, rights, liabilities and obligations in the company on 1st January 1981. By s. 2 British Aerospace's liability in respect of its commencing and public dividend capital is to be extinguished immediately before that day and s. 3 provides for shares in the company to be allotted to the Secretary of State and requires the consent of the Treasury for their disposal. The opening accounts of the company are to be the closing accounts of British Aerospace, with the company's share capital substituted for the capital of British Aerospace. Any excess of the amount of former Government investment in British Aerospace over the nominal amount of the company's initial share capital is to be carried to a special reserve for fully paying up bonus shares: s. 4. The Secretary of State may, with the consent of the Treasury, acquire ordinary voting shares in the company and securities of the company or of any of its subsidiaries: s. 5. By s. 6 he may also appoint nominees to receive shares under s. 3, to acquire shares and securities under s. 5 and to hold and deal with such shares. A target limit is to be set on the proportion of issued voting shares held by the Secretary of State or his nominees: s. 7. The company is to be liable for judgment debts of companies which become its wholly-owned subsidiaries on 1st January 1981, where the cause of action arises before that day: s. 8. Those outstanding liabilities of British Aerospace which become the company's liabilities are to be discharged by the Secretary of State in the event of the company being wound up: s. 9. Section 10 provides for the dissolution of British Aerospace and makes certain transitional provisions. Sections 11 to 13 and Sch. 3 contain supplementary provisions and ss. 14 and 15 contain provisions relating to interpretation, citation, repeals and extent.

185 ── **nominated company**

The British Aerospace (Nominated Company) Order 1980, S.I. 1980 No. 1989 (in force on 16th December 1980), provides that the company nominated for the purposes of the British Aerospace Act 1980, para. 184, is British Aerospace Limited.

186 **British Airports Authority—statutory powers—power to ban mini cabs—validity of banning notice**

The Airports Authority invoked a byelaw and notified a minicab driver who had numerous convictions for loitering and touting at an airport that he was prohibited from entering the airport for any purpose other than as a bona fide passenger until further notice. The driver unsuccessfully claimed declarations that the authority had no power to ban him from the airport and that the banning notice was invalid and in breach of the rules of natural justice. The driver appealed. *Held*, the Airports Authority was not in the same position as a private landowner who could prohibit anyone from entering his premises, but it had the implicit power to prohibit entry to the airport where it would be fair and reasonable to do so, under the Airports Authority Act 1975, s. 2 (1), (3), which empowers it to do anything calculated to facilitate the discharge of its duties. A minicab driver could take a passenger to the airport, but if he abused that lawful authority by touting whilst at the airport, he became a trespasser from the beginning. The byelaw invoked was necessary and desirable for regulating the operation of the airport and it should be interpreted so as to make it valid; the byelaw gave sanction to the power in s. 2 (3) of the Act. Further, the contention that there had been a breach of the rules of natural justice because there had been no opportunity of making representations before the ban was imposed failed as the drivers could not have expected a hearing in view of their conduct.

CINNAMOND v BRITISH AIRPORTS AUTHORITY [1980] 2 All ER 368 (Court of Appeal: LORD DENNING MR, SHAW and BRANDON LJJ). Decision of Forbes J [1979] RTR 331, 1979 Halsbury's Abridgment para. 2177 affirmed.

187 **British Airways Board—borrowing powers**

The British Airways Board (Borrowing Powers) Order 1980, S.I. 1980 No. 500 (in force on 8th April 1980), specifies £850m as the maximum permissible limit of the aggregate of the amount outstanding in respect of the principal of the moneys borrowed by the British Airways Board and the payments made to the Board by way of public dividend capital, under the British Airways Board Act 1977, s. 9 (1).

188 **Carriage by air—limitation of liability—conversion rate**

The Carriage by Air (Sterling Equivalents) Order 1980, S.I. 1980 No. 281 (in force on 21st March 1980), supersedes the Carriage by Air (Sterling Equivalents) Order 1979, 1979 Halsbury's Abridgment para. 174. The Order specifies new sterling equivalents of amounts, expressed in gold francs, as the limit of the air carrier's liability both under the amended Warsaw Convention of 1929 and under corresponding provisions applying to carriage by air to which that Convention does not apply.

This order has been superseded: see para. 189.

189 The Carriage by Air (Sterling Equivalents) (No. 2) Order 1980, S.I. 1980 No. 1873 (in force on 1st January 1981), supersedes the Carriage by Air (Sterling Equivalents) Order 1980, para. 188. The order specifies the new sterling equivalent of amounts, expressed in gold francs, as the limit of the air carrier's liability both under the amended Warsaw Convention of 1929 and under corresponding provisions applying to carriage by air to which the amended Convention does not apply.

190 **Civil Aviation Act 1971—Isle of Man**

The Civil Aviation Act 1971 (Isle of Man) (Amendment) Order 1980, S.I. 1980 No. 188 (in force on 13th March 1980), amends the 1972 Order, which extends the Civil

Aviation Act 1971 to the Isle of Man subject to the modifications specified in the Schedule to that Order.

191   Civil Aviation Act 1980

The Civil Aviation Act 1980 provides for the reduction of public dividend capital of the British Airways Board (the Board), for an increase of the Board's financial limits and for the vesting of its property etc. in a company nominated by the Secretary of State. It also makes amendments of the law relating to civil aviation which concern the Secretary of State's emergency powers, amendments of the Civil Aviation Act 1971 and the Protection of Aircraft Act 1973, charges for air navigation services, sound proofing grants, aircraft accident investigations, the extension of the powers of the British Airports Authority and byelaws relating to lost property. The Act received the royal assent on 13th November 1980 and came into force on that date.

Part I. The British Airways Board
Section 1 reduces the Board's public dividend capital by £160 million and s. 2 increases its financial limits. On a day to be appointed, all the property, rights, liabilities and obligations of the Board are to be vested in a company (known as the successor company) nominated by the Secretary of State: s. 3 and Sch. 1. Shares in the successor company are initially to be held on behalf of the Crown and the Secretary of State may give directions for their disposal: s. 4. Section 5 deals with the financial structure of the company and its subsidiaries and s. 6 with government investment in the company's shares and securities. Section 7 provides a target investment limit for government shareholdings under ss. 4, 6. Section 8 and Sch. 3 repeal the British Airways Board Act 1977 thus dissolving the Board but make transitional arrangements in Sch. 2 for it to remain in existence after the day appointed under s. 3. The application of the Trustee Investments Act 1961 in relation to investment in the successor company is provided for by s. 9 and s. 10 concerns interpretation of Part I.

Part II. Miscellaneous amendments of the law relating to Civil Aviation
Section II gives the Secretary of State powers over British air transport businesses in case of emergency. Sections 12 to 18 are concerned with amendments of the Civil Aviation Act 1971. The general objectives of the Civil Aviation Authority are covered by s. 12. Section 13 requires the Authority to make periodical publications of policies concerning its air transport licensing function and s. 14 deals with its borrowing powers. Section 15 is concerned with the Authority's duties in relation to certain air transport services and ss. 16, 17 with designated aerodromes and disclosure of information. Section 18 abolishes certain government controls over the Authority. Under s. 19, charges for air navigation services are payable to the Authority and under s. 20 sound proofing grants are to be taken into account in determining compensation for depreciation. Section 21 relates to aircraft accident investigations. Sections 22, 23 amend the Protection of Aircraft Act 1973 in relation to the Secretary of State's powers to give directions to aerodrome managers regarding searches and with respect to directions under the 1973 Act, ss. 9, 11. The British Airports Authority's powers in relation to aerodromes and the acquisition of land are dealt with in ss. 24, 25 respectively. Section 26 enables byelaws to be made relating to lost property. Interpretation of Pt. II and repeals consequent on that Part are contained in ss. 27, 28 and Sch. 3.

Part III. Supplementary provisions
Section 29 provides for administrative expenses, s. 30 for application of the Act to overseas territories and s. 31 for citation and extent.

192   Civil Aviation Authority—charges payable to Authority—navigation services

The Civil Aviation (Navigation Services Charges) (Fourth Amendment) Regulations 1980, S.I. 1980 No. 317 (in force on 1st April 1980), further amend the Civil

Aviation (Navigation Services Charges) Regulations 1977, 1977 Halsbury's Abridgment para. 200. The Regulations increase charges payable to the Civil Aviation Authority for navigation services at certain aerodromes, for services provided within the Shanwick Oceanic Control Area and for a helicopter flight from the United Kingdom to an offshore installation in a specified area.

193   The Civil Aviation (Navigation Services Charges) (Fifth Amendment) Regulations 1980, S.I. 1980 No. 1349 (in force on 1st October 1980), further amend the 1977 Regulations by increasing the charges payable to the Civil Aviation Authority for navigation services provided in connection with the use of specified aerodromes, and by increasing the charge payable by the operator of an aircraft which flies within the Shanwick Oceanic Control Area and in respect of which a flight plan is communicated to the appropriate air traffic control unit.

194   —— —— —— route charges

The Civil Aviation (Route Charges for Navigation Services) Regulations 1980, S.I. 1980 No. 356 (in force on 1st April 1980), revoke and replace the Civil Aviation (Route Charges for Navigation Services) Regulations 1978 as amended, see 1978 Halsbury's Abridgment paras. 185, 186 and 1979 Halsbury's Abridgment para. 181. The regulations extend Eurocontrol's power to recover charges for navigation services to ten other states and introduce increased charges for navigation services.

195   International carriage—loss of and damage to goods—jurisdiction

English suppliers of goods agreed with a Saudi Arabian airline that it would carry the goods from Amsterdam to Jeddah. Some of them were lost or damaged in transit. The suppliers served a writ on the carriers at their branch office in London. On an application to set the writ aside the question arose as to the interpretation of "ordinarily resident" in art. 28 (1) of the Warsaw Convention, which enables an action to be brought in the place where the carrier is ordinarily resident. The suppliers appealed against an order that there was no jurisdiction in England. *Held*, as an international convention the Warsaw Convention should be construed without reference to the technical rules of English law. On the true construction of art. 28 (1) a foreign corporation was not "ordinarily resident" in England if it only had a branch office there. Accordingly the appeal would be dismissed and the writ set aside.

ROTHMANS OF PALL MALL (OVERSEAS) LTD v SAUDI ARABIAN AIRLINES CORPORATION [1980] 3 All ER 359 (Court of Appeal: ROSKILL and ORMROD LJJ). Dicta of Lord Wilberforce and Lord Salmon in *Buchanan & Co Ltd v Babco Forwarding and Shipping (UK) Ltd* [1977] 3 All ER 1048, HL, 1977 Halsbury's Abridgment para. 316 applied.

196   —— loss of baggage—liability of airline—method of calculating loss

An airline passenger lost one of her six pieces of luggage in transit. She successfully claimed £304 against her insurance company for the value of the lost suitcase and its contents. The insurance company sought to recover that sum from the airline. Under the Carriage by Air Act 1961, Sch. 1, art. 22 (2) (b) compensation for registered baggage is paid according to the number of kilogrammes lost. The total weight of the passenger's baggage was 75 kilograms but the individual pieces had not been weighed separately. The airline therefore recreated another suitcase similar to the lost one and containing similar items, and asked the passenger whether this corresponded in weight to the lost suitcase. The suitcase weighed 13 kilogrammes and the appropriate value under art. 22 (2) (b) was therefore £145. The insurance company maintained that the airline had not proved the weight precisely and that when they realised that one suitcase had been lost they ought to have weighed the remaining five and deducted their weight from the total of 75 kilogrammes so as to obtain the exact weight of the missing case. *Held*, it was open to the airline to prove the weight by any evidence available to it for the purpose, and the method adopted was as good as any could be. Accordingly, the insurance company could recover only £145 from the airline.

BLAND v BRITISH AIRWAYS BOARD (1980) Times, 24th June (Court of Appeal: LORD DENNING MR, WALLER and DUNN LJJ).

197　　—— loss of baggage contents—time limit for complaint

A passenger, after an international flight, discovered that his suitcase was damaged and subsequently that some items from the case were missing. In an action for damages against the airline questions arose as to the interpretation of the Warsaw Convention, art. 26 (2), as set out in the Carriage by Air Act 1961, Sch. 1. If art. 26 (2) applied the loss of contents should have been reported to the airline within seven days of the flight. *Held*, the purpose of art. 26 (2) was to enable an airline to check the nature of the "damage", make inquiries as to how and when the "damage" occurred and to assess its possible liability. The text was ambiguous as the English and French translations differed in their interpretation of the word "damage". "Damage" was not confined to physical injury and included partial loss of contents. The action therefore would be time-barred if a complaint was not made to the airline within seven days of the flight.

The majority of the court considered whether "travaux préparatoires" could be used in interpreting international conventions in English courts. In the interests of uniformity of application of such conventions a court ought to have regard to the general practice applied in the courts of other contracting states. There might be cases where travaux préparatoires could be profitably used but certain conditions had to be fulfilled before such use. The conditions were (i) that the material involved was public and accessible, and (ii) that the travaux préparatoires clearly and indisputably pointed to a definite legislative intention. Although international conventions owed their enforceability in the United Kingdom to embodiment in an authorisation by an Act of Parliament, they nevertheless owed their origin and wording to prior law-preparing processes in which Parliament did not participate. The language of international conventions was addressed to a wider and more varied judicial audience than an Act of Parliament dealing with purely domestic law and they should be interpreted unconstrained by technical rules of English law, or by English precedent, but on broad principles of general acceptance.

FOTHERGILL v MONARCH AIRLINES [1980] 2 All ER 696 (House of Lords: LORD WILBERFORCE, LORD DIPLOCK, LORD FRASER OF TULLYBELTON, LORD SCARMAN and LORD ROSKILL). *Day v Transworld Airlines Inc* (1975) 523 F 2d 31 and *James Buchanan & Co Ltd v Babco Forwarding and Shipping (UK) Ltd* [1977] 3 All ER 1048, 1977 Halsbury's Abridgment para. 316 followed. Decision of the Court of Appeal [1979] 3 All ER 445, 1979 Halsbury's Abridgment para. 184 reversed.

198　　—— loss of goods—duty of freight forwarders to claim against carriers

Freight forwarders arranged for a consignment of clothing belonging to exporters to be flown from London to Lagos. The goods were transported by a carrier in accordance with agreed conditions of carriage which provided that there could be an action for damages on the loss of goods only where written notice of the loss had been presented to the carrier within thirty days from the date of issue of the air waybill. A week later the exporters were informed by the consignees that part of the consignment was missing and immediately informed the forwarders of the loss. Three weeks later the forwarders informed the carriers that they held the carriers responsible for the loss but their claim was later rejected for being out of time. The exporters then claimed the value of the lost goods from the forwarders. *Held*, there was in the contractual arrangement between the parties an implied obligation on the part of the forwarders to submit the claim to the carriers. Further the facts of the case showed that that implied term was accepted and acted upon by the parties. Accordingly, in failing to make the claim against the carriers within the specified time period the forwarders were responsible for the loss.

MARBROOK FREIGHT LTD v KMI (LONDON) LTD [1979] 2 Lloyd's Rep 341 (Court of Appeal: MEGAW, BRIDGE and TEMPLEMAN LJJ).

199   Noise insulation grants

The Gatwick Airport–London Noise Insulation Grants Scheme 1980, S.I. 1980 No. 154 (in force on 1st April 1980), requires the British Airports Authority to pay grants towards the cost of domestic sound insulation of dwellings whose construction was completed before 1st April 1980 and which are situated in a specified area.   The closing date for applications is 31st March 1983 and the insulation work must be completed before 1st April 1985.   The amount of grant payable in respect of an eligible dwelling is 100 per cent of the actual cost of the insulation works reasonably incurred, subject to the provisions set out in the scheme.   There is no uniform ceiling applying in all cases and minimum specifications for ventilation work have been modified.   The Gatwick Airport–London Noise Insulation Grants Scheme 1975, 1975 Halsbury's Abridgment para. 191, as amended, is revoked.

200   The Heathrow Airport–London Noise Insulation Grants Scheme 1980, S.I. 1980 No. 153 (in force on 1st April 1980), requires the British Airports Authority to pay grants towards the cost of domestic sound insulation of dwellings whose construction was completed before 1st April 1980 and which are situated in a specified area.   The closing date for applications is 31st March 1983 and the insulation work must be completed before 1st April 1985.   The amount of grant payable in respect of an eligible dwelling is 100 per cent of the actual cost of the insulation works reasonably incurred, subject to the provisions set out in the scheme.   There is no uniform ceiling applying in all cases and minimum specifications for ventilation work have been modified.   The Heathrow Airport–London Noise Insulation Grants Scheme 1975, 1975 Halsbury's Abridgment para. 192, as amended, is revoked.

201   Restriction of flying

The Air Navigation (Restriction of Flying) (Exhibition of Flying) Regulations 1980, S.I. 1980 No. 631 (in force on 29th May 1980), restrict the holding of flying exhibitions by the Red Arrows display team to not below 5,500 feet above ground level over certain areas on specified days.

BAILMENT

Halsbury's Laws of England (4th edn.), Vol. 2, paras. 1501–1589

202   Bailee—recovery from bailor of expenses incurred in storing goods—salvage agreement

See *China-Pacific SA v The Food Corpn of India*, para. 2692.

203   —— standard of care—duty of garage in relation to customer's vehicle

A motor car dealer had, over a period of months, taken cars to a garage proprietor for repairs.   On one occasion a car which the dealer had left with the garage proprietor was stolen from the proprietor's forecourt.   It was later recovered but had been seriously damaged by the removal of mechanical parts.   The garage proprietor was held liable in negligence on the grounds that it was foreseeable that someone would enter the forecourt to steal components from the car.   On appeal, *held*, there was no absolute duty on bailees of motor cars to keep them behind locked doors.   In the present case, the car could not be driven away under its own power as the cylinder head had been removed.   Further the practical difficulties of locking the car up were known to the car dealer and outweighed the foreseeability of the risk of components being stolen.   Accordingly, the proprietor was not liable in negligence and the appeal would be allowed.

IDNANI v ELISHA (trading as GRAFTON SERVICE STATION) [1979] RTR 488 (Court of Appeal: MEGAW, ORMROD and TEMPLEMAN LJJ).   *Cowan v Blackwill Motor Caravan Conversions Ltd* [1978] RTR 421, CA, 1978 Halsbury's Abridgment para. 203, applied.

BANKING

Halsbury's Laws of England (4th edn.), Vol. 2, paras. 1–200

204   Articles

Mistaken Payment of Countermanded Cheques, A. M. Tettenborn: 130 NLJ 273.
Money Paid Under Mistake of Fact, P. Matthews (in the light of *Barclays Bank Ltd v W. J. Simms Son and Cooke (Southern) Ltd* [1979] 3 All ER 522, 1979 Halsbury's Abridgment para. 1888): 130 NLJ 587.
Recent developments in money transfer methods, Ann Arora: LMCLQ 416.

205   Bank—duty of care—bank as trustee of settlement

See *Bartlett v Barclays Bank Trust Co Ltd*, para. 2993.

206   —— relationship with customer—confidentiality—disclosure to assist person to trace and recover property of which he is fraudulently deprived

See *Bankers Trust Co v Shapira*, para. 891.

207   Bank account—application for order to inspect bank account— whether notice required

See *R v Marlborough St. Metropolitan Stipendiary Magistrate, ex parte Simpson*, para. 681.

208   Bank notes—fiduciary note issue—amount of issue

The Fiduciary Note Issue (Extension of Period) Order 1980, S.I. 1980 No. 192 (in force on 14th March 1980), extends for a further two years, from 14th March 1980, the period during which the Fiduciary Note Issue may stand at amounts continuously exceeding £1,575 million.

209   Bankers' books—copies of entries as evidence in legal proceedings—husband's bank account

A wife was charged with the theft of a sum of money which she alleged had been paid into her husband's bank account. An application was made under the Bankers' Books Evidence Act 1879, s. 7 which provides that on an application of any party to a legal proceeding a court may order that the party may inspect any entries in a banker's book for any of the purposes of such proceedings. An order was granted. On an application for judicial review, it was contended that the order should not have been made since it went behind the principle that a spouse was a competent although not compellable witness. *Held*, the purpose of the Act was to enable any evidence which was relevant to proceedings to be obtained . In the present case it was necessary to have the evidence in order to confirm or refute the wife's contention. The order was necessary since the husband was not a compellable witness.

R v ANDOVER JJ, EX PARTE RHODES (1980) Times, 14th June (Queen's Bench Division: DONALDSON LJ and WOOLF J).

210   —— —— whether "microfilm" a book

A Divisional Court of the Queen's Bench Division has held that microfilms used by banks to keep records are included in the definition of bankers' books for the purpose of the Bankers' Books Evidence Act 1879, notwithstanding that they are not normally called books. Section 4 of the Act provides that copies of entries of books are not admissible as evidence in legal proceedings unless the book is one of the ordinary books of the bank and the entry is made in the usual course of business of the bank. Books are defined as including ledgers, day books, cash books, account books and all other books used in the ordinary course of business.

BARKER v WILSON [1980] 1 All ER 81 (Queen's Bench Division: BRIDGE LJ and CAULFIELD J).

211   Banking Act 1979—excepted persons

The Banking Act 1979 (Excepted Persons) Order 1980, S.I. 1980 No. 347 (in force on 1st April 1980), adds certain Scottish savings banks and the Crown Agents for Overseas Governments and Administrations to the list of persons set out in the Banking Act 1979, Sch. 1, to whom the prohibition in s. 1 (1) of the Act on the acceptance of a deposit does not apply.

212   —— exempt transactions

The Banking Act 1979 (Exempt Transactions) (Amendment) Regulations 1980, S.I. 1980 No. 345 (in force on 1st April 1980), amend and make additions to the Banking Act 1979 (Exempt Transactions) Regulations 1979, 1979 Halsbury's Abridgment para. 193. The circumstances under which deposit-taking by charities will be an exempt transaction for the purposes of the Banking Act 1979, s. 1, 1979 Halsbury's Abridgment para. 192, are altered. Two further exempt transactions are provided for; deposit-taking from their members by certain agricultural, forestry and fisheries associations and deposit-taking by certain co-operative societies.

213

The Banking Act 1979 (Exempt Transactions) (Amendment) (No. 2) Regulations 1980, S.I. 1980 No. 346 (in force on 1st April 1980), make further additions to the Banking Act 1979 (Exempt Transactions) Regulations 1979, 1979 Halsbury's Abridgment para. 193, by prescribing an additional transaction, the acceptance by certain public undertakings of deposits made by other such undertakings, which is exempt for the purposes of the Banking Act 1979, s. 1, 1979 Halsbury's Abridgment para. 192.

214   —— recognition and licences

Under the Banking Act 1979, s. 3, the Bank of England is empowered to recognise an institution as a bank for the purposes of the Act or to license it to carry on a deposit-taking business. The Bank of England has published a list of the institutions to which recognition and licences have been granted. The list also contains the names of 350 institutions which were carrying on deposit-taking business on 1st October 1979 in respect of which applications to the Bank of England under s. 3 of the Act were being considered. The names of the recognised and licensed institutions were published in The Times, 3rd April 1980.

215   —— —— refusal to grant or revoke—appeals

The Banking Act 1979 (Appeals) Regulations 1980, S.I. 1980 No. 353 (in force on 2nd April 1980), make provision with respect to appeals under the Banking Act 1979, s. 11 against Bank of England decisions to refuse to grant or revoke recognition, or a licence or to give a direction under s. 8 of the Act. Provision is made, inter alia, as to the period and manner in which appeals are to be brought, procedure and evidence at the hearing and the payment of costs of appeals.

216   Community legislation—list of credit institutions

The Commission has issued a list of credit institutions in accordance with Council Directive (EEC) 77/780, 1979 Halsbury's Abridgment para. 195 concerning the coordination of laws, regulations and administrative provisions relating to the taking up and pursuit of the business of credit institutions. The Directive has been implemented in the United Kingdom by virtue of the Banking Act 1979, 1979 Halsbury's Abridgment para. 192.

The list reflects the situation as at 31.12.79 excepting those sections of the list concerning United Kingdom credit institutions which contain only those establishments authorised as at 30.4.80. A revised list will be published annually in the form of a special communication.

Further, the list has no legal significance and confers no right in law on the institutions named. (See OJ No. C 229 8.9.80.)

217   Company's account—winding up—disposition of assets after commencement of winding up—validity

See *Re Gray's Inn Construction Co Ltd*, para. 391.

218   Credit card—false representation by holder—relevance of bank's contractual arrangements with shop

See *R v Lambie*, para. 619.

219   Duty of care—mortgagee—exercise of power of sale—duty of mortgagee

See *Bank of Cyprus (London) Ltd v Gill*, para. 2049.

220   Guarantee—guarantee delivered in escrow—effect

See *Barclays Bank Ltd v Thomas*, para. 1377.

221   Letter of credit—illegality—letter of credit in breach of Peruvian exchange control regulations—enforceability

A British company entered into an agreement with a Peruvian company for the supply of a glass fibre forming plant. Payment was to be made by letter of credit issued by the defendants. The Peruvian company asked for the price of the quotation to be doubled and that they be allowed to pay the surplus in United States dollars to a company with an office in Miami. The glass fibre forming plant was shipped and the documents presented for payment. The defendants refused to pay out on the letter of credit contending that the agreement between the British company and the Peruvian company was illegal and unenforceable as contrary to public policy, having been entered into to secure the transfer of funds out of Peru contrary to the country's exchange control regulations. They further contended that it was also in breach of the Bretton Woods Agreement (which was incorporated into the law of both countries) prohibiting exchange control contrary to the regulations of any member state. On the question of whether the letter of credit was enforceable, *held*, after hearing evidence on Peruvian law, the contract between the British and Peruvian companies could be described as constituting an exchange contract by being a monetary transaction in disguise contrary to the exchange control regulations of Peru and in breach of the Bretton Woods Agreement. Any payment under the confirmed letter of credit would be to give effect to the illegal contract. The court could not enable the Bretton Woods Agreement to be avoided and it would not therefore enforce the letter of credit.

UNITED CITY MERCHANTS (INVESTMENTS) LTD v ROYAL BANK OF CANADA (No. 2) [1979] 2 Lloyd's Rep 498 (Queen's Bench Division: MOCATTA J).

On the question of costs see [1980] 1 Lloyd's Rep 251.

For earlier proceedings relating to the enforcement of the contract between the English and Peruvian companies see [1979] 1 Lloyd's Rep 267, 1979 Halsbury's Abridgment para. 1904.

222   National Savings Bank—ordinary deposits—withdrawal limits

The National Savings Bank (Amendment) Regulations 1980, S.I. 1980 No. 619 (in force on 2nd June 1980), increase the limits of the amount of ordinary deposits which may be withdrawn in certain cases. In particular, the limit for withdrawals from any savings bank office without previous notice is increased to £100.

223　Securities—forged transfers—damage to third party—liability

See *Yeung v Hong Kong and Shanghai Banking Corpn*, para. 1378.

224　Trustee savings banks—accounts and deposits

The Trustee Savings Banks (Amendment) Regulations 1980, S.I. 1980 No. 1061 (in force on 25th July 1980), amend the Trustee Savings Banks Regulations 1972, as amended, and dispense with some of the regulations affecting management, payment and transfer of accounts by trustee savings banks. The provisions which relate to the extent to which trusts affecting accounts may be acknowledged by a trustee savings bank are revoked together with the requirements relating to withdrawals by or for minors and on behalf of mentally disordered persons and bankrupts. The provisions in respect of transfers from one account to another with the same trustee savings bank and in respect of the addition of names to an account are also deleted. The Regulations also revoke the provisions relating to the proof of death of a depositor or a nominee, and the rules applicable on the death of a depositor and to payment without a grant of representation. The procedural requirements for the transfer of an account are also abolished.

225　—— interest-bearing receipts

The Trustee Savings Banks (Interest-bearing Receipts) Order 1980, S.I. 1980 No. 584 (in force on 21st May 1980), increases the rate of interest allowed to trustee savings banks on sums standing to their credit in the Fund for the Banks for Savings to 7.50 per cent per annum.

The Trustee Savings Banks (Interest-bearing Receipts) Order 1978, 1978 Halsbury's Abridgment para. 213 is revoked.

226　—— settlement of disputes—power of Chief Registrar of Friendly Societies

On a dispute concerning the beneficial ownership of a joint account at a trustee savings bank, the Chief Registrar of Friendly Societies (by analogy with the powers of the High Court; see *Nielson-Jones v Fedden* [1974] 3 All ER 38, at 50, per Walton J, 1974 Halsbury's Abridgment para. 2788) regards himself as having the power to sever the joint interest in the account and to award to the applicant such share of the deposits as the registrar finds him entitled to.

Re Samuel William Little, Peter Albert Little and the Trustee Savings Bank—South East. Report of the Chief Registrar of Friendly Societies for 1978, Part 1, p. 39.

BANKRUPTCY AND INSOLVENCY

Halsbury's Laws of England (4th edn.), Vol. 3, paras. 201–1100

227　Adjudication order—application for annulment—no prior public examination

A creditor filed a bankruptcy petition against a debtor. A receiving order was made and a date fixed for the debtor's public examination. The debtor failed to attend. An adjudication order was therefore made and the public examination adjourned sine die. When the debtor continued to fail to attend he was committed to prison for contempt of court, but was released on giving an undertaking to attend the public examination. Subsequently he applied for an annulment of the adjudication order under the Bankruptcy Act 1914, s. 29 (1) on the grounds that the debt in question had been paid in full. He filed an affidavit in support of his application and the registrar granted an annulment. The creditor appealed, claiming that the registrar's order should be set aside since the proceedings before him had been defective in that he had refused to allow the creditor's counsel to cross-examine the debtor on the contents of his affidavit and, further, that a public examination had not been held as required by s. 15 (1) of the Act. *Held*, (i) although the debtor's affidavit had not only been filed, but also used in the proceedings, the judge still had a discretion whether to order cross-examination; only in exceptional circumstances should he refuse. In the present case, however, since the creditor had not defined clear issues of fact to which cross-examination could be directed, such questioning would have been oppressive. (ii) Section 29 displaced s. 15 and conferred an unfettered discretion on the court to annul an adjudication order even though a public examination had not taken place. That discretion was to be exercised in the light of all the circumstances of the case. In the present case, the debtor had paid all his debts owed to the petitioning creditor. Furthermore, since the Official Receiver had advised that a public examination would serve no useful purpose, the judge was right to give due weight to his advice; he had not exercised his discretion unjustly and the appeal would be dismissed.

The court pointed out that it was proper to take into account a petitioning creditor's motive for contesting the annulment of an adjudication order. In the present case, it was relevant that the creditor had no direct financial interest, but was motivated by other reasons to ensure that the debtor remained bankrupt.

RE A DEBTOR (No. 37 OF 1976) (LIVERPOOL), EX PARTE TAYLOR V THE DEBTOR [1980] 1 All ER 129 (Chancery Division: FOX and BROWNE-WILKINSON JJ). *Comet Products UK Ltd v Hawkex Plastics Ltd* [1971] 1 All ER 1141, CA applied.

228   ———— **statement of practice by Chief Registrar**

In the course of his judgment in *Re a Debtor (No 37 of 1976)* [1980] 1 All ER 129, para. 227, FOX J quoted the following extract from a statement of practice from the Chief Registrar in relation to applications for annulment:

Unless the public examination has been dispensed with under the Bankruptcy Act 1914, s. 15 (10) (or the Insolvency Act 1976, s. 6) it is the practice of the High Court not to entertain, except in exceptional circumstances, an application for annulment under s. 29 of the 1914 Act, on the ground of payment in full, until the bankrupt has undergone a public examination and that examination has been concluded.

229   **Bankruptcy procedures—proposed changes**

The Insolvency Law Review Committee have produced an interim report (Cmnd. 7968) on bankruptcy procedures. They recommend an improved procedure known as a "debts arrangement order" system to be administered by the county courts along the lines of the existing administration order procedure. This would be complemented by a procedure for voluntary arrangements under which the trustee would have many of the powers of a trustee in bankruptcy and a creditor would not be able to insist on a full bankruptcy. These procedures would be supplemented by both a compulsory procedure short of the full bankruptcy procedure and the full bankruptcy procedure.

The government has published a consultative document (Cmnd. 7967) in which it indicates that it would prefer a simpler, more straightforward bankruptcy procedure and to withdraw the official receiver from his administrative responsibilities in bankruptcy. The new procedure would be administered by private receivers whose initial costs and remuneration would be underwritten by the petitioner. The receiver would be appointed by the court when the receiving order was made and empowered to apply to the court for a vesting order where there was need to realise assets and distribute the proceeds among the creditors. The consultative document sets out the proposed new procedure commencing with the petition.

230   **Bankruptcy Rules—amendment**

The Bankruptcy (Amendment) Rules 1980, S.I. 1980 No. 2044 (in force on 2nd February 1981), increase the deposit payable on setting down an appeal; amend the forms to be sent to the Chief Land Registrar on the filing of a petition and making of a receiving order and prescribe a new form giving notice to him of any amendment to the title of the proceedings. The order also deletes the reference to a prescribed fee for examination of the list of proofs by the chief clerk in a county court.

231 Deed of arrangement—fees

The Deeds of Arrangement Fees Order 1980, S.I. 1980 No. 509 (in force on 17th April 1980), abolishes the use of adhesive stamps and increases the registration fees payable to the Registrar of Deeds of Arrangement and the Department of Trade in connection with various proceedings concerning deeds of arrangements. The Deeds of Arrangement Fees Order 1973 is revoked.

232 Fees

The Bankruptcy Fees (Amendment) Order 1980, S.I. 1980 No. 683 (in force on 8th June 1980), amends the Bankruptcy Fees Order 1975, 1975 Halsbury's Abridgment para. 222. It increases court fees payable in bankruptcy proceedings and amalgamates or abolishes a number of fees.

This order has been revoked; see para. 234.

233

The Bankruptcy Fees (Amendment No. 2) Order 1980, S.I. 1980 No. 1186 (in force on 18th August 1980), further amends the Bankruptcy Fees Order 1975, 1975 Halsbury's Abridgment para. 222. The order abolishes the combined stationery and Gazette fee, and provides that, in cases where the receiving order is made on or after 18th August 1980, separate fees will be charged for stationery, etc. and for each insertion of a notice in the London Gazette.

This order has been revoked; see para. 234.

234

The Bankruptcy Fees Order 1980, S.I. 1980 No. 2007 (in force on 1st January 1981), revokes and replaces the Bankruptcy Fees Order 1975 as amended, 1975 Halsbury's Abridgment, para. 222. Table A of the order was replaced by the Bankruptcy Fees (Amendment) Order 1980 supra, and is now replaced without further change. Table B is updated with certain increases in the fees taken by the Department of Trade.

235 Offence—undischarged bankrupt obtaining credit—obtaining credit for a third party—whether an offence

The defendant was charged with obtaining credit whilst being an undischarged bankrupt contrary to the Bankruptcy Act 1914, s. 155 (2). At the close of the prosecution case the trial judge ruled that an offence under s. 155 (a) was committed if an undischarged bankrupt procured the granting of credit to a third party. The defendant subsequently changed his plea to guilty and on conviction applied for leave to appeal on the ground that the ruling by the judge was wrong in law. *Held*, the trial judge had erred in his interpretation of s. 155 (a). If the facts disclosed that credit was not obtained for the undischarged bankrupt but for another person there was then no offence. Where there was an issue of fact as to whether the credit was extended to the bankrupt personally or was given to a business, it became a question for a jury to decide. The question was whether, on evidence, the bankrupt held himself out as the person for whom credit was sought or whether it was for a genuine and separate business. In the circumstances there was overwhelming evidence that the defendant himself had obtained the credit and on the facts a jury would have convicted the defendant had he disputed the facts. The application would accordingly be refused.

R v GODWIN (1980) 71 Cr App Rep 97 (Court of Appeal: CUMMING-BRUCE LJ, KILNER BROWN and HOLLINGS JJ).

236 Property available for distribution—estate taken by trustee in bankruptcy—whether subject to third party's irrevocable licence to stay in property

The debtor purchased a property, two-thirds of the purchase price being loaned to him by his aunt. In return for the loan the aunt was to live with the debtor and his wife in the property. Three years later a receiving order was made against the debtor and his trustee in bankruptcy contracted to sell the property with vacant possession. He had received no replies to letters addressed to the aunt, inquiring as to her interest in the property, but at the date of the contract she made a claim to the property as having either a beneficial interest under a resulting trust by virtue of the loan, or a right under an irrevocable licence to stay in the property until repayment of the loan. The trustee in bankruptcy claimed possession. *Held*, where moneys were advanced by way of a loan, the lender was not entitled to the property under a resulting trust because, if she were to have such an interest she would be repaid twice, both on repayment of the loan and on taking her share of the proceeds of sale. However, where the parties proceeded on a common assumption that one of them was to enjoy a right to reside in the property and, on that assumption, expended money, the court would imply an irrevocable licence or trust to give effect to the arrangement. The aunt had therefore acquired an interest in the property before the bankruptcy. Her failure to reply to the trustee's inquiries did not preclude her from enforcing that interest. The trustees took the property subject to her interest therefore and she was entitled to remain in the property until the loan had been repaid.

RE SHARPE, A BANKRUPT, EX PARTE THE TRUSTEE OF THE BANKRUPT v SHARPE [1980] 1 All ER 198 (Chancery Division: BROWNE-WILKINSON J). *Errington v Errington* [1952] 1 All ER 149, *Tanner v Tanner* [1975] 3 All ER 776 CA, 1975 Halsbury's Abridgment para. 2031, *Hardwick v Johnson* [1978] 2 All ER 935 CA, 1977 Halsbury's Abridgment para. 1281 and *DHN Food Distributors Ltd v Tower Hamlets London Borough Council* [1976] 3 All ER 462 CA, 1976 Halsbury's Abridgment para. 388, applied.

237　　—— matrimonial home—husband and wife joint owners—husband adjudicated bankrupt

A husband and wife owned the matrimonial home jointly. On their divorce the wife applied for a property adjustment order. The husband was adjudicated bankrupt and the trustee in bankruptcy sought an order for possession and sale under the Law of Property Act 1925, s. 30. The wife claimed that the bankruptcy petition was merely a device to prevent her from being granted a property transfer order. *Held*, the husband was, in fact, unable to pay his debts, and his motive alone was not enough to amount to an abuse of the court's process. In exercising its discretion under s. 30 the court had to consider whose claim prevailed in equity, without reference to the powers of property transfer, which were not available against the trustee in bankruptcy. Even though the children were not direct beneficiaries under the trust for sale their needs had to be considered as part of the wife's obligation to provide a home for them, and so the house should not be sold without her consent until the two eldest children had reached the age of seventeen.

RE HOLLIDAY (A BANKRUPT), EX PARTE THE TRUSTEE OF THE BANKRUPT v THE BANKRUPT [1980] 3 All ER 385 (Court of Appeal: BUCKLEY and GOFF LJJ and SIR DAVID CAIRNS). Dictum of Buckley LJ in *Burke v Burke* [1974] 2 All ER at 947–948 followed; *Buchanan-Wollaston's Conveyance, Curtis v Buchanan-Wollaston* [1939] 2 All ER 302, *Jones v Challenger* [1960] 1 All ER 785 and *Re Turner* [1975] 1 All ER 5 applied.

238　　—— transfer by trustee to bankrupt—validity

The registered proprietor of property which was subject to a legal charge was adjudicated bankrupt, and an inhibition registered in respect of his property. In order to give him locus standi to pursue a cause of action the proprietor asked the trustee in bankruptcy to transfer the beneficial interest in the property to him. The trustee did so, but failed to register the transfer. The bank, which was the chief unsecured creditor, contended that the transfer was invalid. The bankrupt claimed that he was purchaser for value of an equitable interest without notice. *Held*, the transfer was not a sale authorised by the Bankruptcy Act 1914, s. 55 (1) because it lacked the requisite consideration; nor was the necessary consent obtained for the purposes of a transaction pursuant to s. 56 (8). The trustee therefore had no power to carry out the transaction, and the transfer was rendered voidable. The bankrupt was the purchaser of an equitable interest, but the court would not order the trustee to do anything further in breach of trust. The bankrupt would therefore be unable to perfect his title so would not be able to establish that he was a purchaser for value without notice. Accordingly, the prior rights of the creditors on bankruptcy prevailed and the transfer would be set aside.

MICHAELIDES v BANK OF CYPRUS (LONDON) LTD (1980) Times, 11th December (Chancery Division: BROWNE-WILKINSON J).

239   Receiving order—order made by High Court—transfer of proceedings to county court—jurisdiction of county court to rescind order

A receiving order was made in the High Court against a debtor. The High Court ordered the proceedings to be transferred to a county court under the Bankruptcy Act 1914, s. 100 (2). The debtor made provision for payment of his debts in full and applied to the county court for the receiving order to be rescinded. The official receiver of the county court applied to the High Court to have the proceedings transferred back so that the order could be rescinded by the High Court. The debtor objected to the application; he contended that the prevailing practice in the county court of rescinding High Court receiving orders when the proceedings had been transferred to the county court should be followed. *Held*, when proceedings were transferred under the 1914 Act, s. 100 (2) from one court to another having parallel bankruptcy jurisdiction, the first court was replaced by the second for all purposes of the 1914 Act. Therefore, the second court could exercise the first court's jurisdiction without the first court being involved. It was not necessary to transfer the proceedings back to the High Court and the receiving order could be rescinded by the county court.

RE A DEBTOR (No 2A of 1980, COLCHESTER) [1980] 3 All ER 641 (Chancery Division: GOULDING J).

240   Reciprocal enforcement of orders—orders in aid—British court with jurisdiction in bankruptcy—désastre proceedings in Jersey against insolvent debtor

The Bankruptcy Act 1914, s. 122 provides that the High Court, the county courts, the courts having jurisdiction in bankruptcy in Scotland and Ireland, and every British court elsewhere having jurisdiction in bankruptcy or insolvency are bound to act in aid of and be auxiliary to each other in bankruptcy matters; and an order of court seeking aid with a request to the court whose aid is sought, enables the latter court to exercise, in regard to matters directed by the order, such jurisdiction as either of the two courts could exercise in regard to similar matters within their respective jurisdiction.

A solicitor practised in both England and Jersey. In 1975 he sold his practices in England and subsequently went to live and practise his profession in Jersey. In 1976 he found himself in financial difficulties and an order of the Royal Court of Jersey initiated a process of sequestration of his movable property known under local law as en désastre. Désastre was a declaration of bankruptcy, the effect of which was to deprive an insolvent debtor of the possession of his movable estate and invest that possession in the Viscount of the Royal Court of Jersey whose duty it was to liquidate that estate for the benefit of the creditors who proved their claims. Before the order was made the solicitor returned to England and established a profitable practice in London. The Royal Court of Jersey set in motion the procedure provided for in Bankruptcy Act 1914, s. 122 and the Viscount was proposed as receiver of all the solicitor's movable property in England with power to realise and sell it and with authority to do all that was necessary for those purposes. The solicitor contended that the application did not fall within s. 122. On the construction of s. 122 in the light of the facts of the case, *held*, (i) there was no doubt that the Royal Court of Jersey was a British court within s. 122 and it was also apparent that the procedure termed désastre, although only defined at common law, was similar to the English statutory rules on bankruptcy. It followed therefore, that if two British courts were to conduct their insolvency business according to practically similar rules, in the one jurisdiction reduced to a statutory code, and in the other established as unwritten customary law, both courts were entitled to invoke s. 122. (ii) "Bankruptcy" was left undefined by the Act and dependent on its definition was whether or not the procedure of désastre was "a matter of bankruptcy" within s. 122. "Bankruptcy" could mean (a) the condition of a person unable to pay his creditors in England a person was not declared a bankrupt until adjudicated as such under the Act, or, (b) a class of judicial or administrative process which was for the protection of creditors from one another and dishonest debtors and for the protection of debtors from the extreme enforcement of the legal rights of creditors. "Bankruptcy" in s. 122 was to be construed in a wide sense, including both definitions put forward by the court, for the section was designed to produce co-operation between courts acting under different systems of law. It appeared that désastre was "a matter of bankruptcy" within the section and the Viscount's powers were exercisable over the solicitor's movables wherever they might be located. It required strong evidence to show that, in the present circumstances, a British court overseas had fundamentally mistaken the territorial extent of its own process under its own law and accordingly the Viscount would be entitled to the solicitor's after-acquired property and the application would succeed.

RE A DEBTOR, VISCOUNT OF THE ROYAL COURT OF JERSEY v THE DEBTOR [1980] 3 All ER 665 (Chancery Division: GOULDING J). Dicta of Farwell J in *Re Osborn* [1931–32] B & CR at 194 and of Lowry LCJ in *Re Jackson* [1973] NI at 71, 72 applied.

BARRISTERS

Halsbury's Laws of England (4th edn.), Vol. 3, paras. 1101–1221

241　　Barristers in employment—revised rules

The following rules for employed barristers were approved at the annual general meeting of the Bar on 15th July 1980 (see the *Law Society's Gazette*, 23rd July 1980, p. 759). The rules do not apply to barristers employed in the government legal service, nor to barristers employed by (i) a law centre (or similar), (ii) (in respect of certain matters) by a trade association, or (iii) (in respect of certain matters) by an insurance company. Subject to certain conditions, a barrister with appropriate qualification (or exemption) and experience may undertake any form of conveyancing work (rr. 5, 6). The conditions relate to insurance cover (except in the case of a local government employee) and the relevant payments being made to the barrister's employer (r. 7). Failure to honour any undertaking given is prima facie professional misconduct (r. 9). A barrister so acting may not act for a fellow employee (r. 8). An employed barrister may instruct a practising barrister without the intervention of a solicitor except in relation to instructions: (a) to appear as counsel where civil or criminal proceedings or arbitration have already been commenced in the United Kingdom; or (b) to draft documents for litigation or arbitration in the United Kingdom (r. 10). Notwithstanding r. 10, a barrister employed by a prosecuting authority may instruct a practising barrister without the intervention of a solicitor in a prosecution by that authority; and any existing practice whereby barristers employed by public authorities instruct practising barristers direct may continue; an employed barrister (other than one employed by a local government or other public body) who instructs a practising barrister is responsible for paying his fees (rr. 11, 12). Any employed barrister exercising rights under these rules must first be registered in respect of those rights by the Senate (r. 4). See *Annual Statement* 1979–80, p. 52 et seq.

242　　Conduct of case—voluntary absence of accused—counsel's discretion to continue to take part in case

See *R v Shaw*, para. 725.

243   Defending counsel—cross-examination of co-defendant—duty to test veracity of witnesses' evidence

See *R v Fenlon*, para. 686.

244   Disciplinary tribunal—composition and procedure

The Senate has effected changes in the composition and procedure of disciplinary tribunals. The membership of a tribunal is limited to five, including a chairman and a lay representative. The chairman will be a judge and a member of the Senate. Spare members will be nominated to fill vacancies among the barrister members before the start of the hearing. The President is empowered to nominate members who are not members of the Senate and also to appoint a judge who is a member of the Senate to hold a summons for directions. The documents to be laid before a tribunal are specified. The finding and any sentence must be recorded in writing and signed by all members of the tribunal. The procedure for determining the effective date of a sentence is specified and arrangements for publication of the finding and any sentence have been clarified. See *Annual Statement*, 1979–80, p. 37.

245   Fees—quantum

The Law Society and the Bar Council have agreed that the fee for each piece of work (whether interlocutory or on the brief) should be "fair and reasonable" and based on the "weight of the work" and the time and attention involved. The fee for interlocutory work should not therefore embody any element of discount based on counsel's expectation of a brief fee. Similarly, a brief fee should not reflect any element of compensation in respect of interlocutory work. See Joint Statement by the Bar Council and the Law Society: LS Gaz, 20th September 1980, p. 918.

246   Interviewing witnesses—prosecution counsel—Bar Council statement

The Bar Council has amplified its guidance to counsel concerning the attendance of witnesses at conferences, to cover conferences with counsel for the prosecution. It is pointed out those considerations apply to prosecution counsel which are different to that applicable to counsel in other instances. As counsel for the prosecution is in overall conduct of the case, he should not regard himself as appearing for a party. He may see, and confer with, investigator witnesses in the case; but he may do so only if they have discharged some supervisory responsibility in the investigation. Counsel for the prosecution ought not, however, to confer with investigators or receive factual instructions directly from them on particular aspects of evidence to be given by them about which there is known, or may reasonably be anticipated, to be dispute. See LS Gaz, 30th January 1980, p. 98.

247   Qualifications—recognition of qualifications of Community nationals

The European Communities (Service of Lawyers) (Amendment) Order 1980, S.I. 1980 No. 1964 (in force on 1st February 1981), amends the 1978 Order, 1978 Halsbury's Abridgment para. 1225, to include lawyers qualified in the Hellenic Republic among the EEC lawyers whom that order enables, under certain conditions, to provide services in the United Kingdom which could otherwise be provided only by advocates, barristers or solicitors.

248   Queen's Counsel—brief to appear without junior

In the particular circumstances in which a solicitor intends to instruct a Queen's Counsel to appear without a junior at the hearing of any matter but either proposes to instruct, or has already instructed, a junior to do the drafting or other interlocutory work in the same proceedings, he should give notice of such intention at the earliest possible date to the junior so instructed. See the Joint Statement of the Bar Council and the Law Society: LS Gaz, 24th September 1980, p. 918.

249   Retainers—abolition of retainer rules

The Bar Council has announced the abolition of the Retainer Rules with effect from 4th August 1980. Retainer Rules 20 (appeals), and 21 (embarrassment) are to be embodied in the Bar's Code of Conduct.

The abolition does not affect the "retainers" recognised in relation to the appointment of Treasury counsel. See LS Gaz, 24th September 1980, p. 918.

250   Right of audience—Crown Court—private criminal prosecution— right of prosecutor to appear in person

See *R v George Maxwell (Developments) Ltd*, para. 722.

BETTING, GAMING AND LOTTERIES

Halsbury's Laws of England (4th edn.), Vol. 4, paras. 1–300

251   Amusements—monetary limits

The Amusements with Prizes (Variation of Monetary Limits) Order 1980, S.I. 1980 No. 29 (in force on 3rd March 1980), increases the maximum amounts to be paid or offered in amusements provided at certain fairs as prizes under the Lotteries and Amusements Act 1976, s. 16 (3).

252   Betting, Gaming and Lotteries (Amendment) Act 1980

The Betting, Gaming and Lotteries (Amendment) Act 1980 amends the Betting, Gaming and Lotteries Acts 1963–1971 in relation to the number of races on which betting may take place on dog racecourses on any day and in relation to the number of special betting days. The Act implements recommendations made in the Final Report of the Royal Commission on Gambling 1978. It received the royal assent on 31st March 1980 and came into force on that date.

Section 1 amends s. 7 of the 1963 Act so as to increase the number of races on which betting may take place on any day on dog racecourses, from eight to ten and on any special betting day from sixteen to twenty. Section 2 amends s. 2 of the 1971 Act so as to increase the number of special betting days for any particular track from four to six. The Secretary of State may by order, subject to annulment by Parliament, substitute any other number of days in relation to special betting days as he thinks fit.

253   Bingo—value added tax—exempt supply—consideration for entry fee

See *Tynewydd Labour Working Men's Club and Institute Ltd v Customs and Excise Comrs*, para. 3061.

254   Dog racecourse totalisator—percentage

The Dog Racecourse Totalisator (Percentage) Order 1980, S.I. 1980 No. 1771 (in force on 22nd December 1980), has the effect of increasing from 15 per cent to 17½ per cent the percentage which the operator of a totalisator on a dog racecourse is permitted to deduct from the amounts staked. The Dog Racecouse Totalisator (Percentage) Order 1975, 1975 Halsbury's Abridgment para. 247 is revoked.

255   Gaming—charges

The Gaming (Small Charges) (Amendment) Order 1980, S.I. 1980 No. 1127 (in force on 1st December 1980), increases from £3 to £6 the maximum daily charge which may be made in clubs and miners' welfare institutes in respect of a person taking part in gaming when the only games played are bridge and whist.

256   Gaming Board for Great Britain—report

See para. 328.

257   Gaming licence duty

See para. 330.

258   Lottery—legality of sales promotion scheme—declaration as to legality of scheme subject of criminal proceedings

Cigarette manufacturers adopted a sales promotion scheme whereby each packet of cigarettes contained a ticket, some of which entitled the holder to a prize. The Director of Public Prosecutions commenced criminal proceedings against the manufacturers, alleging that they were holding unlawful lotteries and competitions. The manufacturers sought a declaration in the civil courts that the scheme was lawful. This was granted by the Court of Appeal, and on appeal the questions for the House of Lords were (i) whether the scheme was in fact lawful and (ii) whether a declaration in respect of legality should have been made when criminal proceedings were pending. *Held*, (i) in order to establish the existence of an unlawful lottery within the Lotteries and Amusements Act 1976, s. 1 it was necessary that there was a distribution of prizes by lot or chance and that the chance should be secured by some payment, contribution or consideration by those persons taking part. Where a person purchased two things for one price it was impossible to say that he paid only for one of them. There was therefore payment for chance when, in return for money paid, the customer secured a chance in addition to a packet of cigarettes, and the scheme was an unlawful lottery. However, the scheme was not an unlawful competition within s. 14 as it could not be said to be a competition at all; a competition involved the exercise of some degree of skill. (ii) Where criminal proceedings had been commenced it was not open to a civil court to grant a declaration that the facts to be alleged by the prosecution did not constitute the unlawful acts charged. The administration of justice would become chaotic if after the start of a prosecution declarations of innocence could be obtained from a civil court. Accordingly the appeal would be allowed.

IMPERIAL TOBACCO LTD v A-G [1980] 1 All ER 866 (House of Lords: VISCOUNT DILHORNE, LORD EDMUND-DAVIES, LORD FRASER OF TULLYBELTON, LORD SCARMAN and LORD LANE). Decision of Court of Appeal [1979] 2 All ER 592, 1979 Halsbury's Abridgment para. 242, reversed. *Taylor v Smetten* (1883) 11 QBD 207 applied, *Willis v Young and Stembridge* [1907] 1 KB 448 disapproved and *Whitbread & Co Ltd v Bell* [1970] 2 All ER 64 overruled.

259   Pool Competitions Act 1971—continuation

The Pool Competitions Act 1971 (Continuance) Order 1980, S.I. 1980 No. 876 (in force on 26th July 1980), continues in force the Pool Competitions Act 1971 until and including 26th July 1981.

BILLS OF EXCHANGE AND OTHER NEGOTIABLE INSTRUMENTS

Halsbury's Laws of England (4th edn.), Vol. 4, paras. 301–600

260   Bill of exchange—dishonoured bill—estoppel

The plaintiffs, suppliers of foreign-built hydrofoils, advertised in trade journals for sales agents for their vessels. The defendants saw the advertisement and as a result of negotiations entered into an agency agreement. By a schedule annexed to the agreement it was provided that the defendants were to buy two vessels, which the plaintiffs considered to be necessary for the proper carrying on of the agency. The defendants, as required, paid the full amount for one of the vessels immediately and ten per cent of the total price of the other vessel. The defendants gave the plaintiffs three bills of exchange which were for the balance of the purchase price. The bills of exchange were for the wrong amount of money and the plaintiffs returned the drafts to the defendants on the understanding that they would receive new drafts for the correct sum. Shortly afterwards, the defendants were informed that production of the vessels had stopped and that the plaintiffs would not be able to supply them. They accepted the repudiation of the agreement but failed to send to the plaintiffs the drafts for the correct sum. The plaintiffs claimed the balance of the purchase price of the goods sold, or, alternatively for breach of the undertaking by the defendants to forward the cheques. The defendants contended they had a counterclaim and set-off against the plaintiffs in that they had been induced by oral representations, to the effect that the plaintiffs had access to and sufficient supply of the vessels, and had guaranteed their profits for the first year, to enter into the agreement. *Held*, although the plaintiffs might have been induced to part with the bill of exchange by the promise of a cheque they were not to be treated as someone who had in their possession a dishonoured cheque. Estoppel did not operate to turn a person not suing on a cheque into a person who was. The counterclaim and set-off put forward by the defendants was substantial and on the evidence submitted the defendants had been induced to enter into the agreement by the assurances made and unconditional leave to defend would be granted to the defendants.

AQUAFLITE LTD v JAYMAR INTERNATIONAL FREIGHT CONSULTANTS LTD [1980] 1 Lloyd's Rep 36 (Court of Appeal: STEPHENSON AND LANE LJJ and DUNN J). *Morgan & Son Ltd v S. Martin Johnson & Co Ltd* [1949] 1 KB 107 applied.

261   —— foreign bill—bill issued by Canadian bank drawn on foreign agency—residence of bank—proper law to be applied

Canada

A life assurance company had its head office in Canada and also conducted business in the United States. It held a "head office account" with a branch of a Canadian bank situated in New York known as the Agency. In response to a request from its New York representative, the company issued a number of cheques in Canada payable to named insurance policy holders resident in the United States. The cheques were cashed in New York by means of forged indorsements and passed to the Agency where they were debited to the company's account. The company brought proceedings in Canada against the bank for the restoration of the money to its account. The liability of the bank depended on whether the law of Canada or the law of New York was to be applied in determining the legal effect of the forged indorsements; this depended on the interpretation of certain provisions of the Canadian Bills of Exchange Act 1970. *Held*, s. 161 provided that the interpretation of the indorsement of a foreign bill was subject to the law of the place where the contract was made; however the indorsement of inland bills in a foreign country was subject to the law of Canada as regards the payer. Section 25 defined an inland bill as one drawn and payable within Canada or drawn within Canada upon someone resident there. A bank was capable of having more than one residence in which its business might be conducted and in which for those purposes it was resident. Accordingly the bank was resident in a foreign country for the purposes of the cheques drawn on its foreign agency. Since the cheques were directed to the Agency it was not sufficient that the bank had its head office in Canada. Accordingly a bill of exchange drawn on a foreign agency of a Canadian bank was a foreign bill. It followed that whether or not s. 161 extended to the legal effect of an indorsement, New York law was applicable, since the cheques were payable there, indorsed, negotiated and paid there. Under New York law, the bank was entitled to rely on the indorsements as a good defence to the action.

CANADA LIFE ASSURANCE CO v CANADIAN IMPERIAL BANK OF COMMERCE (1979) 98 DLR (3d) 670 (Supreme Court of Canada).

For the corresponding English legislation see the Bills of Exchange Act, 1882, ss. 4, 72.

262 **Cheques—cheque drawn on partnership bank account—printed name of partnership and one partner's signature—whether payee entitled to recover money from other partner**

H and W were partners who had a bank account in the name of the partnership. It was agreed that the bank would pass any cheque signed by one partner. H wrote and signed a crossed cheque for £500, on behalf of the firm, in favour of the plaintiff. H then disappeared without trace and W instructed the bank not to honour any cheques signed by him. When the plaintiff sought payment of the cheque at the bank, he was told of its orders not to pay but that he could present it through his own bank. The court ordered W to pay the money to the plaintiff. He appealed, contending that although it might be banking practice for one partner's signature on a cheque with the partnership name printed on it to bind the other partner, that was not the true position in law. He claimed that under the Bills of Exchange Act 1882, s. 23 (2), the other partner was only liable if the firm "signed" the cheque through some link between the signature and the printed name, such as "pp" before the printed words. He alternatively argued that the cheque had not been "presented" as required by s. 45 of the Act, as a crossed cheque could only be presented by passing it through a bank account. *Held*, it was a necessary inference that a partner who signed his name under the printed name was making a cheque on the firm and all its partners. In the present case there was certainly sufficient "signature" on the cheque for the purposes of s. 23 (2). No other physical link was required. Further, the cheque had been "presented" within the meaning of s. 45 even though no attempt had been made to have it paid through a bank account. The appeal would be dismissed.

RINGHAM v HACKETT (1980) 124 Sol Jo 201 (Court of Appeal: MEGAW, LAWTON and ORMROD LJJ).

263 **Holder in due course—defective title—whether bill obtained by fraud**

A company drew a bill of exchange on the defendants. The defendants accepted it and it was subsequently indorsed by the company to the plaintiff (the defendants' bank). When the bill was presented for payment it was dishonoured. The plaintiff brought an action against the defendants claiming the full amount on the ground that the plaintiff was a holder in due course within the Bills of Exchange Act 1882, s. 29 (1). On an application by the plaintiff for summary judgment, the defendants applied for unconditional leave to defend contending that the plaintiff's title to the bill was defective and that it could not therefore claim the rights of a holder in due course, because at the time the bill was drawn the plaintiff had known that the company was insolvent and indorsement of the bill therefore constituted a fraudulent preference amounting to a fraud within ss. 29 (2), 30 (2) of the 1882 Act. The judge gave summary judgment in favour of the plaintiff and the defendant appealed. *Held*, in ss. 29 (2), 30 (2) "fraud" meant common law fraud and a fraudulent preference was not, per se, a common law fraud. On the evidence there was no allegation of common law fraud to which the bank was a party and, accordingly the appeal would be dismissed.

ÖSTERREICHISCHE LÄNDERBANK v S'ELITE LTD [1980] 2 All ER 651 (Court of Appeal: ROSKILL and BRIGHTMAN LJJ and SIR DAVID CAIRNS).

BILLS OF SALE

Halsbury's Laws of England (4th edn.), Vol. 4, paras 601–830

264 **Charges created by overseas company—charges not registered— application of Bills of Sale Acts**

See *NV Slavenburg's Bank v Intercontinental Natural Resources Ltd*, para. 382.

BRITISH NATIONALITY AND ALIENAGE

Halsbury's Laws of England (4th edn.), Vol. 4, paras. 901–1100

265   British   nationality—categories   of   citizenship—proposed alterations

The Home Office has issued a white paper *British Nationality Law* (Cmnd. 7987) outlining the government's proposals for changes in the law in the light of comments received on the similarly entitled green paper issued in 1977 (Cmnd. 6795). The government proposes three categories of citizenship: British citizenship, citizenship of the British dependent territories and British overseas citizenship. The first category would comprise persons who are at present citizens of the United Kingdom and colonies who have a close personal connection with the United Kingdom; in general terms, people who or whose parents or grandparents were born, adopted, naturalised or registered in the United Kingdom; also those citizens of the United Kingdom and colonies from overseas who have been settled here for some time. Citizenship of the British dependent territories would be acquired by those citizens of the United Kingdom and colonies who have that citizenship by reason of their own, or their parents' or grandparents' birth, naturalisation or registration in an existing dependency or associated state. Citizens of the United Kingdom and colonies who do not fall within the preceding two categories would become British overseas citizens. The white paper elaborates on the acquisition etc. of the categories of citizenship and sets out the proposed transitional provisions.

266   Citizenship

The British Nationality (Amendment) Regulations 1980, S.I. 1980 No. 197 (in force on Zimbabwe Independence Day, 18th April 1980), amend the British Nationality Regulations 1975, 1975 Halsbury's Abridgment para. 260, in consequence of the transitional provisions as to applications for registration as a citizen of the United Kingdom and Colonies contained in the Zimbabwe Act 1979, Sch. 1, 1979 Halsbury's Abridgment para. 342.

267   —— application for registration—licence to marry obtained by deception—public policy

A German national married a citizen of the United Kingdom and Colonies using a false name. Her application for registration as a British citizen under the British Nationality Act 1948, s. 6 (2), as amended, made under her real name, was refused. She then applied for a declaration of the validity of her marriage, which was refused although it was accepted that the marriage was valid. On her reapplication for registration as a British citizen, *held*, although the disqualifying provisions in the Act did not specifically apply in the applicant's case, Parliament must be deemed to have been aware of the public policy that a court ought not to assist a criminal to benefit from his crime. Since citizenship was not only a matter of private right but also of public status and concern, it could not have been intended that a woman should be entitled to claim citizenship by relying on a marriage celebrated on the basis of perjury and fraud. The application would be dismissed.

R v SECRETARY OF STATE FOR THE HOME DEPARTMENT, EX PARTE PUTTICK [1981] 1 All ER 776 (Queen's Bench Division: DONALDSON LJ and FORBES J).

For proceedings relating to validity of the marriage, see *Puttick v A-G and Puttick* [1979] 3 All ER 463, 1979 Halsbury's Abridgment para. 1473.

268   —— citizen by registration—registration by fraudulent means— validity of registration—power of Secretary of State to detain

See *R v Secretary of State for the Home Department, ex parte Akhtar*, para. 1508.

269   —— fees

The British Nationality (Amendment) (No. 2) Regulations 1980, S.I. 1980 No. 358 (in force on 1st April 1980), amend the British Nationality Regulations 1975, 1975 Halsbury's Abridgment para. 260, as amended, by increasing the fees payable in respect of the conferment on adults of citizenship of the UK and Colonies or British subject status. They also provide for the payment of a fee in respect of the conferment on minors of citizenship of the UK and Colonies.

270   Immigration

See IMMIGRATION.

271   Race relations

See RACE RELATIONS.

BUILDING CONTRACTS, ARCHITECTS AND ENGINEERS

Halsbury's Laws of England (4th edn.), Vol. 4, paras. 1101–1500

272   Article

NHBC Scheme 1979 Revision, J. E. Adams: 130 NLJ 171.

273   Builder—duty of care—express warranty

See *Fraser-Reid v Droumtsekas*, para. 2462.

274   Engineer—duty of care—soil test

See *Surrey (District) v Carroll-Hatch & Associates Ltd*, para. 2043.

275   Fixed price contract—adjustments

Australia
A contract for the erection of a high rise building contained a clause which provided that the amount payable to the builder for the part of the building remaining to be completed would rise or fall with alterations in the conditions of the employment of the workmen. Certain increases in expenditure occurred, namely, increases in amounts payable for fares, sick leave and long service leave, increases in the cost of holiday pay, and increases in the cost of workers' compensation insurance. The question arose as to whether those items of expenditure fell within the clause. *Held*, although normally the costs of compensation insurance would not be included within the "conditions of employment", the adjustment clause expressly covered all alterations in pay loadings, and evidence had been adduced to show that "pay loadings" commonly included workers' compensation insurance; therefore insurance costs were covered by the clause. Amounts payable for fares, sick leave and long service leave, which were independent of wage increases, were conditions of employment and therefore fell within the clause, but the increases in respect of holiday pay occurred consequentially upon wage increases and therefore they would not be separately covered by the adjustments clause.

MAX COOPER & SONS PTY LTD v SYDNEY CITY COUNCIL (1980) 29 ALR 77 (Privy Council: LORD DIPLOCK, LORD SIMON OF GLAISDALE, LORD SALMON, LORD RUSSELL OF KILLOWEN and LORD KEITH OF KINKEL).

276   Implied terms—warranty of fitness—television mast

See *Independent Broadcasting Authority v BICC Construction Ltd*, para. 485.

277   Quasi-judicial functions—certification of progress—duty of fairness

New Zealand

A drainage board accepted a tender for the laying of sewer pipes and incidental work. The contract provided for progress payments to be made on the certificate of the board's engineer. Following disagreement over the need for an adjustment the engineer delayed certification, whereupon the contractor suspended work. The engineer informed the contractor that sufficient progress had not been made to ensure completion within the time specified in the contract (which had already passed) and arranged for completion by other contractors in reliance on the forfeiture clause in the contract. On a claim by the board for extra expenses incurred, *held*, under the terms of the contract the contractor had not been entitled to suspend work. In certifying progress and acting under the forfeiture clause the engineer was bound to act fairly and impartially. By not certifying progress and by calling for completion within a time which had already passed he had not acted fairly. The board had been wrong in purporting to act under the forfeiture clause by taking the work out of the contractor's hands.

CANTERBURY PIPE LINES LTD v CHRISTCHURCH DRAINAGE BOARD [1979] 2 NZLR 347 (Court of Appeal).

278   Structural engineer—duty of care—duty to consider effect of weather conditions on design of television mast

See *Independent Broadcasting Authority v BICC Construction Ltd*, para. 485.

BUILDING SOCIETIES

Halsbury's Laws of England (4th edn.), Vol. 4, paras. 1501–1723

279   Accounts and annual return

The Building Societies (Accounts and Annual Return) (Amendment) Regulations 1980, S.I. 1980 No. 1472 (in force on 6th December 1980), amend the 1976 Regulations, 1976 Halsbury's Abridgment para. 267 so as to reflect the increase in the special advances limit from £20,000 to £25,000 prescribed by the Building Societies (Special Advances) Order 1979, 1979 Halsbury's Abridgment para. 267 for the purposes of the Building Societies Act 1962. The regulations also change the levels by reference to which directors' and employees' emoluments are to be disclosed, so as to correspond with the equivalent disclosure requirements for companies prescribed by the Companies (Accounts) Regulations 1979, 1979 Halsbury's Abridgment para. 346.

280   Fees

The Building Societies (Fees) Regulations 1980, S.I. 1980 No. 1741 (in force on 1st January 1981), supersede the Building Societies (Fees) Regulations 1979, 1979 Halsbury's Abridgment para. 265 and increase the fees payable in connection with the exercise by the Central Office and the Chief Registrar of their functions under the Building Societies Act 1962.

281   Special advances

The Building Societies (Special Advances) Order 1980, S.I. 1980 No. 2003 (in force on 1st January 1981), increases to £37,500 the limit beyond which an advance made by a building society to an individual is to be treated as a special advance for the purposes of the Building Societies Act 1962.

The 1979 Order, 1979 Halsbury's Abridgment para. 267, is revoked.

CAPITAL GAINS TAXATION

Halsbury's Laws of England (4th edn.), Vol. 5, paras 1–300

282   Article

CTT and CGT: Treatment of Reversionary Interests, Barry McCutcheon: 130 NLJ 355.

283   Assessment—appeal in absence of taxpayer—judicial review

See *Page v Daventry General Comrs*, para. 19.

284   Deductions—allowable   expenditure—cost   of   acquisition— conditional contract—valuation of shares given as consideration

The taxpayer company negotiated a conditional contract with an insurance company for the purchase of securities. The contract price was to be satisfied by the allotment by the taxpayer company to the insurance company of certain shares in the taxpayer company. The issue price of each share for the purpose of satisfying the consideration was stated in the contract as £1.60. A few weeks later, the conditions of the contract were satisfied and the consideration shares were alloted to the insurance company. The middle market price then obtainable for those shares was £1.25 each. The taxpayer company subsequently sold some of the securities, thereby realising gains. The taxpayer company successfully contended that the contractual price of the shares (£1.60 each) was deductible under the Finance Act 1965, Sch. 6, para. 4 (1) (a) in respect of chargeable gains on its assessment to corporation tax. The Crown appealed, contending that the value of the shares should be determined by reference to their market price at the time when the contract came into effect (£1.25). *Held*, the consideration given for the assets should not be ascertained by reference to any contractual price agreed by the parties, but by reference to the value of the consideration at the date when the contract became unconditional and took effect. The appeal would be allowed.

STANTON (INSPECTOR OF TAXES) V DRAYTON COMMERCIAL INVESTMENT CO LTD [1980] STC 386 (Chancery Division: VINELOTT J).

Finance Act 1965, Sch. 6, para. 4 now Capital Gains Tax Act 1979, s. 32 (1)–(3).

285   —— —— —— reorganisation of share capital of wholly-owned subsidiary

Scotland

The taxpayer company entered into a tax avoidance scheme involving the reorganisation of the share capital of its wholly-owned subsidiary. A rights issue was made to existing members at a predetermined price per share. The subsidiary was then voluntarily wound up and its only asset, a sum of money, was distributed to the taxpayer company. The Crown claimed that in computing the chargeable gains or allowable loss arising to the taxpayer company on the disposal of its shares in the subsidiary (i.e. on the liquidation) the taxpayer company was not entitled to deduct the sum which it had paid for the new shares. The taxpayer company contended that the transactions constituted a reorganisation of the subsidiary's share capital within the Finance Act 1965, Sch. 7, para. 4 (1) and it should therefore by virtue of para. 4 (2), (3) be deemed that there had been no disposition or acquisition of the shares, so that the cash paid by the taxpayer company for the shares fell to be treated as having been given in consideration for the original shares and was deductible in computing the allowable loss on the disposal of the taxpayer company's entire shareholding in the subsidiary. The Crown contended that at the date of the reorganisation the taxpayer company and its subsidiary were not transacting at arm's length, so that s. 22 (4) came into play and the relevant consideration which was deductible was not the cash paid but the market value of the rights issue shares at the time of reorganisation. *Held*, the word "acquisition" in s. 22 (4) referred only to an acquisition for capital gains tax purposes. Under para. 4 (2) reorganisation of a company's share capital did not involve any such acquisition as respects the company's new holding within para. 4 (1), and para. 4 (3) was concerned only with the treatment of consideration given for something which under para. 4 (2) was not to be treated as an acquisition for capital gains tax purposes. Accordingly, in computing the chargeable gains or allowable loss accruing to the taxpayer company on the disposal of its new holding in the subsidiary, there was nothing in para. 4 which entitled one to apply market value under s. 22 (4) to the rights issue shares in ascertaining the deductible consideration. The taxpayer company's claim would be upheld.

INLAND REVENUE COMRS v BURMAH OIL CO LTD [1980] STC 731 (Inner House). Finance Act 1965, s. 22 (4), Sch. 7, para. 4 (1), (2), (3) now Capital Gains Tax Act 1979, ss. 19 (3), 77 (1), (2), 78, 79 (1).

286   —— **expenditure incurred on asset—whether value of taxpayer's labour included**

The taxpayer bought a derelict uninhabited house and renovated it himself. At no time was it his main residence. He sold it at a considerable profit. On a question of assessment of the amount of capital gains tax payable on disposal, he contended that the sum of £1,700, representing the estimated value of his work in man-hours, fell to be deducted from the total gain. The Finance Act 1965, Sch. 6, para. 4 (1) (b) allowed relief on any expenditure incurred for the purpose of enhancing the asset. *Held*, "expenditure" contemplated expenditure in the sense of a reduction of his stock of anything by a precisely ascertainable amount and included money and goods. The taxpayer's own labour was not capable of being quantified in this way. Nor was there any machinery in the Act that provided for the conversion of labour costs into money terms. Further, had the Revenue deducted the sum for notional expenditure, it would have then been open to it to charge him to income tax in respect of his notional receipt of £1,700 as money earned as a builder. The sum was not therefore allowable as a deduction from the total gain.

ORAM (INSPECTOR OF TAXES) v JOHNSON [1980] 2 All ER 1 (Chancery Division: WALTON J).

Finance Act 1965, Sch. 6, para. 4 now Capital Gains Tax Act 1979, s. 32 (1)–(3).

287   **Disposal of assets—deemed disposals—capital sum derived from assets—deferred consideration for shares**

In 1970 the taxpayer agreed to sell shares in a private company, the consideration for which was partly a fixed sum per share to be paid immediately and partly a deferred payment to be calculated in accordance with the agreement. The relevant date for calculating the amount of the deferred consideration was 5th December 1972. The question for the court was whether, on that date, capital gains tax was chargeable on the deferred sum on the basis of the Finance Act 1965, s. 22 (3), which provides that there is a disposal of assets by their owner where any capital sum is derived from assets notwithstanding that no asset is acquired by the person paying the capital sum. The taxpayer contended, (i) that s. 22 (3) did not apply because an asset, the shares, was acquired by the person paying the capital sum and, (ii) if s. 22 (3) was applicable he was exempted by Sch. 7, para. 11 (1) which provides that where a person incurs a debt to another no chargeable gain accrues to that creditor on a disposal of the debt except in the case of a debt on a security. *Held*, (i) there was an asset in the form of the obligation to pay the deferred consideration and, when paid in 1972, the deferred consideration was a capital sum derived from that asset. The application of s. 22 (3) was not limited to situations where no asset was acquired but was to be interpreted as meaning that it would apply whether or not an asset was acquired and accordingly ss. 22 (3) applied to the case. (ii) Further, Sch. 7, para. 11 (1) did not operate to exempt the taxpayer. A possible liability to pay an unascertained sum on an unknown date was not a debt. There was accordingly, a deemed disposal in 1972 and chargeable gains arose.

MARREN (INSPECTOR OF TAXES) v INGLES [1980] 3 All ER 95 (House of Lords: LORD WILBERFORCE, VISCOUNT DILHORNE, LORD SALMON, LORD FRASER OF TULLYBELTON and LORD RUSSELL OF KILLOWEN). Decision of Court of Appeal

[1979] STC 637, 1979 Halsbury's Abridgment para 272 affirmed.　Dicta of Walton J in *Inland Revenue Comrs v Montgomery* [1975] STC 189 disapproved.

Finance Act 1965, s. 22, Sch. 7, para. 11 now Capital Gains Tax Act 1979, ss. 20, 134.

288　　　——　—— disposal of interest in settled property

A taxpayer paid a Jersey company to arrange a tax avoidance scheme whereby he could reduce his liability to capital gains tax in respect of a sale of shares by incurring an allowable loss which he could then deduct for the purposes of ascertaining his liability to tax.　First, a settlement was created in Jersey with the taxpayer as beneficiary of the reversionary interest.　Secondly, he borrowed money from the company to purchase the reversionary interest in a Gibraltar settlement.　The trustees of the latter then exercised their special powers of appointment to make an appointment out of the trust fund to the trustees of the Jersey settlement.　The taxpayer then sold both his reversionary interests, the interest in the Gibraltar settlement at a loss, and used the combined proceeds of sale in both settlements to repay the loan from the company.　He contended that he had incurred an allowable loss, being the difference between the price he had paid for the reversionary interest in the Gibraltar scheme and the selling price he had received for the interest in the remaining sum left unappointed in the Gibraltar settlement.　He further maintained that no chargeable gain had accrued on the sale of the reversionary interest in the Jersey settlement, as he was not a person who had acquired or derived his title from one who acquired that interest for a consideration in money or money's worth within the Finance Act 1965, Sch. 7, para. 13 (1).　*Held*, the taxpayer's contentions would be rejected.　The sum transferred to the Jersey settlement remained, from and after the date of the appointment, settled on trusts having their genesis in the Gibraltar settlement and the taxpayer's reversionary interest in the Gibraltar settlement continued to extend to that sum.　Thus, the sale by the taxpayer of his reversionary interest in the appointed fund under the Jersey settlement, was the sale of part of his reversionary interest in the Gibraltar settlement.　The proceeds resulting therefrom were not exempt from tax under Sch. 7, para. 13 (1) but fell to be taken into account, together with the proceeds of sale from the remainder of his reversionary interest in the Gibraltar settlement, in computing the allowable loss accruing to him from transactions involving the acquisition and sale of his reversionary interest in the Gibraltar settlement.

EILBECK (INSPECTOR OF TAXES) v RAWLING [1980] 2 All ER 12 (Court of Appeal: BUCKLEY, TEMPLEMAN and DONALDSON LJJ).　Decision of Slade J [1979] STC 16, 1979 Halsbury's Abridgment para. 271 affirmed on different grounds.

Finance Act 1965, Sch. 7, para. 13 (1) now Capital Gains Tax Act 1979, s. 58.

289　　　—— transfer to trustees—total or partial disposal

In 1972 the taxpayer executed a deed of settlement whereby he transferred shares and stock to a Guernsey company as trustees for his benefit for life.　By the same settlement he sold the reversionary interest in the trust fund to a Jersey company for £14,500, its full market value.　In the following tax year he assigned his life interest in the income to a Bahamian company for £130,753.　He was assessed to capital gains tax on the basis that he had made a total disposal of the shares and stock to trustees in the year 1971–72.　His appeal was allowed and the assessment reduced on the ground that the disposal of his reversionary interest to the Jersey company was a part disposal within the Finance Act 1965, s. 22 (2).　The Crown appealed, contending firstly that the transfer to the trustees was a gift in settlement within s. 22 (2) and so was a disposal of the entire property by virtue of that subsection.　The Crown contended secondly that the transfer to the trustees was not the result of an arm's length bargain and hence was deemed by s. 22 (4) (a) to be for a consideration equal to the market value of the stock and shares.　*Held*, BUCKLEY LJ dissenting, the Crown's first contention would be rejected.　The transfer to the trustees did not amount to a gift and the Crown's construction would be giving the word a meaning it did not normally bear.　The second contention also failed because the disposal was a part disposal within s. 22 (2) (b), the life interest remaining undisposed of. The appeal would be dismissed.

BERRY v WARNETT (INSPECTOR OF TAXES) [1980] 3 All ER 798 (Court of Appeal: BUCKLEY, ACKNER and OLIVER LJJ). Decision of Goulding J [1978] 1 WLR 957, 1978 Halsbury's Abridgment para. 282 affirmed.

Finance Act 1965, ss. 22 (2), (4), 25 (2), now Capital Gains Tax Act 1979, ss. 19 (2), (3), 53.

290　　—— whether right to payment constitutes separate and chargeable asset

On 31st March 1965 the taxpayer sold land to a development company for £47,000. Under the terms of the agreement the company was bound to enter into a supplemental agreement on the following terms: the company was to pay the taxpayer £7,500 per acre for each acre of land it was permitted to develop, and if the land was compulsorily acquired from the company it should pay the taxpayer half the compensation money it received. In January 1976, after being granted planning permission for the development of the land, the company came to an agreement with the taxpayer whereby the taxpayer would relinquish his rights under the supplemental agreement in exchange for £348,250. The taxpayer was assessed to capital gains tax on this sum, on the ground that the rights under the supplemental agreement constituted a separate and chargeable asset within the Finance Act 1965, s. 22 (1) and that on receipt of the sum of £348,250 there was a disposal of the asset within the meaning of s. 22 (3). Under the Finance Act 1965, Sch. 6, para. 14 (5) the consideration for a disposal is brought into the computation of the gain without any discount for postponement of the right to receive any part of it. The taxpayer contended that if the Act had been in force in March 1965 not only the payment of £47,000 but also the payments of £7,500 per acre under the supplemental agreement would have been taxable at their full value, and no further charge would have arisen in respect of the payments in 1976. He argued in the alternative that Sch. 7, para. 11 applied, whereby no chargeable gain accrues on the disposal of a debt and that the payment of £348,250 was received in satisfaction of a debt. *Held*, consideration for the disposal of an asset fell to be taken into account in computing a chargeable gain under Sch. 6, para. 14 (5) only when it was contingent and ascertainable in amount. On 31st March 1965 the amount of additional consideration which the company might have to pay was unascertainable since compulsory acquisition of the land prior to the granting of planning permission would deprive the taxpayer of his right to receive the £7,500 per acre, and entitle him to only half the compensation money, which was itself unascertainable. Furthermore a contingent liability which might never ripen into a present debt was not a "debt" within Sch. 7, para. 11 (1). The rights under the supplemental agreement were, in fact, a separate chargeable asset and the payment of £348,250 was a disposal of that asset arising in 1976, despite the fact that at that time no asset was acquired by the company in exchange for the payment; for under s. 22 (3) of the 1965 Act there was a disposal of an asset where any capital sum was derived from the asset notwithstanding that no asset was acquired by the person paying the capital sum. The taxpayer was therefore liable to capital gains tax on the payment.

MARSON (INSPECTOR OF TAXES) v MARRIAGE [1980] STC 177 (Chancery Division: FOX J). *Marren (Inspector of Taxes) v Ingles* [1979] STC 673, 1979 Halsbury's Abridgment para. 272 applied.

Finance Act 1965, s. 22 (1), (3) now Capital Gains Tax Act 1979, ss. 19 (1), 20 (1); 1965 Act, Sch. 6, para. 14 (5) and Sch. 7, para. 11 now 1979 Act ss. 40 (2) and 134.

291　Exemptions and reliefs—charities—donations by one charity to another—donations accumulated by recipient charity

See *Inland Revenue Comrs v Helen Slater Charitable Trust Ltd*, para. 1567.

292　　—— disposal of only or main residence—meaning of "residence"

In 1959 a taxpayer built a house for himself and his family on land which he owned in the country. From 1961 onwards they all lived in London during the week in

a flat purchased by his employer. He bought the flat himself in 1966. At the same time he decided to employ a caretaker for his country house and built a bungalow on his land next to the house. The bungalow had its own access road and was separately rated. In 1967 the taxpayer elected to treat the house as his main residence and from 1974 he lived there all the time. He then sold the bungalow and was assessed to capital gains tax. He claimed that the gain was exempt under Finance Act 1965, s. 29. *Held*, under 1965 Act, s. 29 (1), (2) a gain was exempt if it was attributable to the disposal of a dwelling house or part of a dwelling house which was a person's only or main residence. For the purposes of s. 29, a residence included not only a main dwelling house but also any appurtenant building, which could be another separate dwelling house. The bungalow, which was appurtenant to the taxpayer's dwelling house, was occupied for the benefit of his house and therefore was occupied by him through his caretaker. As the bungalow formed part of the taxpayer's residence, the gain on disposal was exempt under s. 29.
BATEY (INSPECTOR OF TAXES) v WAKEFIELD [1980] STC 572 (Chancery Division: BROWNE-WILKINSON J).
Finance Act 1965, s. 29 (1), (2) now Capital Gains Tax Act 1979, ss. 101 (1), (2), 102 (1).

293 —— —— **owner occupiers who let hiring accommodation in their homes**

The Inland Revenue have, by a statement of practice no. SP 14/80, given an indication to owner occupiers who are, or are contemplating, letting the whole or part of their homes, as to whether they will be liable to capital gains tax when they dispose of their homes.

294 —— **gain accruing to charity—distribution by trustees to charity as residuary beneficiary—whether gain accruing to charity**

A testatrix left her residuary estate on trust for sale in favour of a number of charities, subject to the payment of certain annuities. As the annuities did not exhaust the estate income, the trustees sold certain trust property and paid the proceeds to the charities. The taxpayer, a trustee, was assessed to capital gains tax in respect of the gain on sale. He contended that the gain accrued to the charities, not himself, and was therefore exempt under Finance Act 1965, s. 35 (1). *Held*, the gain accrued to the trustees, not the charities; it could only be regarded as accruing to the charities if they were absolutely entitled as against the trustees within Finance Act 1965, s. 22 (5). However, the charities could not direct how the trust property was to be dealt with before sale, nor could they object if the trustees, before the actual distribution, decided to retain a larger amount as cover for the annuities. Therefore, as the gain accrued to the trustees, not the charities, the taxpayer was liable to capital gains tax.
PREST (INSPECTOR OF TAXES) v BETTINSON [1980] STC 607 (Chancery Division: DILLON J).
Finance Act 1965, ss. 22 (5), 35 now Capital Gains Tax Act 1979, ss. 46 (1), 145 respectively.

295 —— **gilt-edged securities**

The Capital Gains Tax (Gilt-edged Securities) (No. 1) Order 1980, S.I. 1980 No. 507 (made on 27th March 1980), adds 13¾ per cent Treasury Stock 2000–2003 'A', 15 per cent Treasury Stock 1985, 14 per cent Treasury Stock 1998–2001, 14 per cent Exchequer Stock 1984, 13½ per cent Exchequer Stock 1983 and 12½ per cent Treasury Stock 2003–2005 'A' to the category of stock and bonds which are exempt from tax on capital gains if held for more than twelve months.

296 The Capital Gains Tax (Gilt-edged Securities) (No. 2), Order 1980, S.I. 1980 No. 922 (made on 2nd July 1980), adds 14 per cent Treasury Stock 1996, 9 per cent Conversion Stock 2000, 13½ per cent Treasury Stock 2004–2008, 13½ per cent Exchequer Stock 1992, 3 per cent Treasury Stock 1985 and 13½ per cent Exchequer Stock 1994 to the category of stocks and bonds which are exempt from tax on capital gains if held for more than twelve months.

297 The Capital Gains Tax (Gilt-edged Securities) (No. 3) Order 1980, S.I. 1980 No. 1910, adds 12½ per cent Exchequer Stock 1985 "A", 13 per cent Treasury Stock 2000, 12 per cent Treasury Stock 1987, 3 per cent Exchequer Stock 1983 "A", 11¾ per cent Treasury Stock 1991 "A", 12 per cent Exchequer Stock 1998 "A", 11¾ per cent Exchequer Stock 1986 to the category of stocks and bonds which are exempt from tax on capital gains if held for more than twelve months.

298 —— **replacement of business assets—occupation for purposes of trade**

A taxpayer sold nine plots of land on his farm land, thus acquiring a capital gain, and used a further two to build houses for his sons who were partners with him. He appealed against his assessment to capital gains tax on the ground that as the two houses were used and occupied by the partnership for trading purposes, he was entitled to "roll-over relief" in respect of the gain on the sale of the land, under the Finance Act 1965, s. 33. *Held*, although the houses were "used" for the purposes of the trade they were not "occupied" for the purposes of the trade unless the occupation was essential to the performance of the duties of the person who lived there, or unless by living there that person could better perform his duties and there was an express contractual term that he should live there. The appeal would be dismissed.

ANDERTON (INSPECTOR OF TAXES) v LAMB [1981] STC 43 (Chancery Division: GOULDING J). *Commissioner of Valuation for Northern Ireland v Fermanagh Protestant Board of Education* [1969] 3 All ER 352, HL, applied.

1965 Act, s. 33, now Capital Gains Tax Act 1979, s. 115.

299 —— **transfer of shares—beneficial interest**

The taxpayer and other shareholders transferred their shares to trustees to be held by them subject to the terms of an agreement. The taxpayer successfully appealed against an assessment to capital gains tax which had been made on the basis that the transfer gave rise to a chargeable gain. On appeal by the Crown, *held*, the Finance Act 1965, s. 22 (5) provided that where assets were held by a person as trustee for two or more other persons jointly absolutely entitled as against the trustee, they were to be regarded as if they were vested in those persons. In the present case, on the creation of the trust the settlors were concurrently and absolutely entitled to the shares as against the trustees and were entitled to terminate the settlement. Since the shares were pooled in a trust fund, the beneficial interest remained unaffected and there was no transfer. Accordingly there was no chargeable gain and the appeal would be dismissed.

BOOTH v ELLARD (INSPECTOR OF TAXES) [1980] 3 All ER 569 (Court of Appeal: BUCKLEY, ACKNER and OLIVER LJJ). Decision of Goulding J [1978] STC 487, 1978 Halsbury's Abridgment para. 289 affirmed. *Stephenson v Barclays Bank Trust Co Ltd* [1975] 1 All ER 625, 1975 Halsbury's Abridgment para. 324, and *Kidson v MacDonald* [1974] Ch 339, 1974 Halsbury's Abridgment para. 269 applied.

Finance Act 1965, s. 22 (5), now Capital Gains Tax Act 1979, s. 46 (1).

300 **Finance Act 1980**

See para. 2328.

301 **Gain—computation—assets held on 6th April 1965—lease of business premises**

In 1960 the taxpayer was granted a tenancy of business premises. In 1974, following proceedings under the Landlord and Tenant Act 1954, Pt. II, he was granted a new lease. He was assessed to capital gains tax on the gain arising from the disposal of the lease in 1976 on the basis that the 1974 lease was a new asset for tax purposes, acquired for the first time when it was granted. He successfully appealed, contending that the 1974 lease was a continuation of the original lease and accordingly, in computing the chargeable gains arising on its disposal, the time apportionment provisions of the Finance Act 1965, Sch. 6, para. 24 (2), relating to assets held on 6th

April 1965, applied so as to enable the gain to be spread over the whole period from the commencement of the 1960 lease. On appeal by the Crown, *held*, a tenancy granted under the 1954 Act, Pt. II, was a new tenancy, as it might have different terms, subject-matter or rent. Hence the asset disposed of in 1976 was the lease granted in 1974, which was a new asset granted for the first time on that occasion. The provisions of the 1965 Act, Sch. 6, para. 24 (9), to the effect that in certain circumstances the period of ownership of one asset could include the period of ownership of another asset, did not apply to the two leases, since the value of the new lease was not derived from the original lease within Sch. 6, para. 8. The appeal would be allowed.

BAYLEY (INSPECTOR OF TAXES) v ROGERS [1980] STC 544 (Chancery Division: BROWNE-WILKINSON J).

Finance Act 1965, Sch. 6, para. 24, now Capital Gains Tax Act 1979, Sch. 5, para. 11.

302   —— ——**consideration for disposal—reallocation of consideration**

A new company was incorporated with a share capital consisting of two £1 shares. The taxpayer company transferred its assets to the new company in exchange for those two shares plus £61,680, to be left outstanding in the new company's loan account with the taxpayer company. The taxpayer company subsequently agreed to sell the shares in the new company to a third party for £35,000. In addition, under the agreement the taxpayer company was entitled to withdraw a certain sum from the loan account in full and final settlement of the new company's liability under that account. At the date of the agreement, the new company's balance on the loan account was £55,839 and the amount withdrawn by the taxpayer company in pursuance of the agreement was £20,969. The taxpayer company was assessed to corporation tax in respect of the chargeable gains arising on the sale of the shares on the basis that the consideration for the sale was £35,000. The company contended that the consideration was £130, since of the £55,969 received under the agreement (ie £35,000 plus £20,969), £55,839 was referable to the satisfaction of the debt. *Held*, where parties to a composite transaction had, as a result of negotiation between themselves, provided that part of the consideration was to be paid for one part of the transaction and part for another, they could not subsequently seek to reallocate the consideration for tax purposes. The agreement between the taxpayer company and the third party expressly provided that £35,000 was to be the total consideration for the shares and that part repayment of the loan account by the new company to the taxpayer company was to be in full and final settlement of any balance due on the loan account. Therefore, for tax purposes, the shares ought to be treated as having been disposed of for £35,000.

E. V. BOOTH (HOLDINGS) LTD v BUCKWELL (INSPECTOR OF TAXES) [1980] STC 578 (Chancery Division: BROWNE-WILKINSON J).

303   —— ——**election for valuation on 6th April 1965—whether lease and goodwill indivisible asset**

The tenant of shop premises commenced business on 6th April 1965, and sold it in June 1970; by that time there was a valuable goodwill but a decrease in the value of the lease. The taxpayer submitted a notice under the Finance Act 1965, Sch. 6, Part II, para. 25 (1) electing for the gains to be computed with reference to the market value on 6th April 1965. The Revenue contended that the lease and the goodwill should be treated as separate assets so that there could be no valid election in respect of the goodwill, which did not exist before 6th April 1965, and so that, owing to the decrease in value of the lease before its disposal, it would be treated as neither a loss nor a gain, under para. 25 (2). *Held*, on the facts, the goodwill and the lease were to be treated as separate assets, therefore para. 25 (1) did not apply to either and the assessment would have to be determined in varying amounts rather than with reference to the market value on 6th April 1965.

BUTLER v EVANS (INSPECTOR OF TAXES) [1980] STC 613 (Chancery Division: DILLON J).

Finance Act 1965, Sch. 6, para. 25 (1) now Capital Gains Tax Act 1979, Sch. 5, para. 12 (1)

304   Settled property—disposal of interest arising under settlement—tenant in common of proceeds of sale of property—liability to tax

Property was conveyed on trust for sale by executors to a taxpayer, his brother and sister who were beneficiaries under a will. On the death of the taxpayer's brother the property was vested in the taxpayer and his sister as trustees for sale for themselves as tenants in common in equal shares. They personally managed the property, letting it to tenants. The property was later sold and the proceeds of sale divided equally between them. The taxpayer was assessed to capital gains tax in respect of his half share in the proceeds of sale. The taxpayer contended firstly that no chargeable gain accrued on the sale of the property because he sold as a beneficiary and not as a trustee, the sale was a disposal of an interest created by or arising under a settlement and he was a person for whose benefit the settlement was created within the Finance Act 1965, Sch. 7, para. 13. Secondly he contended that the management of the property by himself and his sister constituted a family business and he had fulfilled the conditions providing for relief on the disposal of a family business within the 1965 Act, s. 34. *Held*, (i) the case fell within s. 22 (5), which provided that assets held by a trustee for another person absolutely entitled as against the trustee were to be regarded as if they were vested in that other person; thus as the taxpayer and his sister were absolutely entitled to the proceeds of sale, the sale should be seen as one by the taxpayer and his sister as co-owners and it followed therefore that there was no disposal of an interest within Sch. 7, para. 13 and accordingly the taxpayer was properly chargeable in respect of his share of the gains accruing. (ii) For the taxpayer to claim relief under s. 34 he had to show that what had been disposed of was a business. The taxpayer and his sister held the property as landowners receiving rent, and this did not amount to a business. The taxpayer would be liable for capital gains tax on the half share of the proceeds of sale.

HARTHAN v MASON (INSPECTOR OF TAXES) [1980] STC 94 (Chancery Division: Fox J). *Kidson (Inspector of Taxes) v Macdonald* [1974] STC 54, 1974 Halsbury's Abridgment, para. 269 followed.

Finance Act 1965, ss. 22 (5), 34 and Sch. 7, para. 13 now Capital Gains Tax Act 1979, ss. 46 (1), 124 and 58 respectively.

305   —— resident beneficiaries of non-resident trusts—apportionment of gains between persons with interests in settled property—nature of interests

Property was settled on non-resident trustees to hold capital and income on trust for such of the settlor's grandchildren born within the perpetuity period as the trustees should appoint but subject to a discretionary power either to apply income to any of them or to accumulate it. Funds undistributed at the close of the perpetuity period were to go to such grandchildren then living, with remainders over. No relevant distribution was made by the trustees and the only potential beneficiaries were five grandchildren. Capital gains accrued to the trustees in respect of the settled property and the Crown sought to apportion, under the Finance Act 1965, s. 42 (2), to the five grandchildren the capital gains tax which would have been recoverable from the trustees had they been United Kingdom residents. *Held*, the final words of s. 42 (2) required that in the case of a defeasible interest, the possibility of any defeasance should be ignored. The Crown's contention, that "defeasible interest" should be given a wide meaning to include all contingent interests and that the holders of such interests should be treated as holders of absolute vested interests, was unacceptable. There was no basis for extending the meaning of the phrase beyond its ordinary significance. The provision resulted in any interest in default of appointment being considered without regard to the possibility of it being defeated by a future exercise by the trustees of their power of appointment.

Section 42 (2) provided for apportionment in such manner as was just and reasonable between persons having interests in the settled property as near as may be according to the respective values of those interests. The question was what the relevant interests of the beneficiaries were. The rights of a mere object of a discretionary trust of income or of a power of appointment could not have a value and thus could not amount to an interest for the purposes of s. 42 (2). Hence the only relevant interests of the beneficiaries were their contingent interests in the capital. The market value of those interests was negligible. Section 42 required the whole of the gain to be apportioned between those having interests and therefore the gains accruing to the trustees had to be apportioned equally between the five beneficiaries, notwithstanding that their interests were so small. The prospects of the beneficiaries receiving benefits were to be taken into account in considering whether it was just and reasonable to apportion between the five grandchildren having interests under the settlement. Although those prospects were not marketable and did not themselves amount to interests in the settled property, there was no reason for disregarding them in considering the justice and reason of applying the section to the interests that they had. Accordingly, the beneficiaries were liable to tax under s. 42 (2).

LEEDALE (INSPECTOR OF TAXES) v LEWIS; PEARSON (INSPECTOR OF TAXES) v PAGE [1980] STC 679 (Chancery Division: DILLON J). *Gartside v Inland Revenue Comrs* [1968] 1 All ER 121 applied.

Finance Act 1965, s. 42, now Capital Gains Tax Act 1979, s. 17.

306 ——— **residuary gift subject to payment of annuity—whether residuary beneficiary absolutely entitled as against trustees**

See *Prest (Inspector of Taxes) v Bettinson*, para. 294.

CARRIERS

Halsbury's Laws of England (4th edn.), Vol. 5, paras. 301–500

307 **British Airports Authority—statutory powers—power to ban minicabs—validity of banning notice**

See *Cinnamond v British Airports Authority*, para. 186.

308 **Carriage by air**

See AVIATION.

309 **Carriage by Air and Road Act 1979—commencement**

The Carriage by Air and Road Act 1979 (Commencement No. 1) Order 1980, S.I. 1980 No. 1966, brought into force on 28th December 1980, ss. 3 (3), 4 (2), (4) (part), 5 (part), 6 (1) (b) of the Act, as a consequence of the entry into force of a Protocol to the Convention on the Contract for the International Carriage of Goods by Road. The Protocol introduces a new unit of account for the purposes of the Convention.

310 **Carriage by sea**

See SHIPPING AND NAVIGATION.

311 **Carriage of goods—carriage by road—liability of carrier for loss of container**

A carrier contracted to transport a container from Harwich docks to London where it was to be unloaded, and from there to transport the empty container to Leighton Buzzard. The container was duly unloaded but it never reached its final destination. The contract of carriage incorporated the conditions of carriage of the Road Haulage Association Ltd 1967 whereby a carrier incurs no liability for loss or non-delivery of the "whole of the consignment or of any separate package forming part of the consignment" unless he is advised of the loss or non-delivery within twenty-eight days. In an action for damages the question arose whether the carrier escaped liability by virtue of that clause. *Held*, in construing the conditions of carriage as a whole an empty container was equivalent to a whole consignment of goods and the carrier therefore would not be liable for its loss or non-delivery.

ACME TRANSPORT LTD v BETTS (1980) Times, 10th October (Court of Appeal: CUMMING-BRUCE, GRIFFITHS and O'CONNOR LJJ).

312   —— cash-on-delivery service—liability to value added tax

See Case 126/78: *NV Nederlandse Spoorwegen v Secretary of State for Finance*, para. 1212.

313   —— international carriage of goods—carriage by road—convention—parties to convention

The Carriage of Goods by Road (Parties to Convention) (Amendment) Order 1980, S.I. 1980 No. 697 (in force on 1st June 1980), amends the Carriage of Goods by Road (Parties to Convention) Order 1967 by specifying additional countries as parties to the 1956 Convention on the Contract for the International Carriage of Goods by Road. The Carriage of Goods by Road (Parties to Convention) (Amendment) Order 1969 and the Carriage of Goods by Road (Parties to Convention) Order 1973 are revoked.

314   —— —— —— liability of carrier for damage to goods

The defendants hired a trailer to a third party and arranged for a load of yarn to be carried on it. The yarn was damaged by rain in transit, due to the defective condition of the trailer's cover, and was rejected by the plaintiffs, the consignees. Their claim against the defendants was settled by consent and the defendants then sought in third party proceedings to recover the sum paid by them to the plaintiffs under the convention scheduled to the Carriage of Goods by Road Act 1965 ("CMR"), art. 37 (a), which provides that a carrier who has paid compensation is entitled to recover it from the other carriers who have taken part in the carriage, subject to the provision that the carrier responsible for the loss or damage is solely liable for the compensation, whether paid by himself or by another carrier. The third party relied on art. 17 (2), which provides that the carrier is to be relieved of liability if the damage was caused through circumstances which the carrier could not avoid and the consequences of which he is unable to prevent. The defendants in turn relied on art. 17 (3), which provides that the carrier is not to be relieved of liability by reason of the defective condition of the vehicle used by him to perform the carriage. *Held*, art. 17 (2) clearly applied to matters other than the defective condition of the vehicle, such as an accident for which it could not possibly be contended that the carrier bore any responsibility. There was therefore no justification for not applying art. 17 (3). Hence the defendants were entitled to recover against the third parties under art. 37 (a).

WALEK & CO v CHAPMAN AND BALL (INTERNATIONAL) LTD [1980] 2 Lloyd's Rep 279 (Queen's Bench Division: MOCATTA J).

CHARITIES

Halsbury's Laws of England (4th edn.), Vol. 5, paras. 501–984

315   Appointment of receiver and manager—extent of powers

See *A-G v Schonfeld*, para. 2317.

316   Charitable corporation—winding up—distribution of assets—whether company trustee of assets

The memorandum of association of a charitable company provided that upon the winding up of the company any surplus assets should be transferred to a charitable institution with similar objects. Upon an application for directions as to the manner of distribution the Attorney General argued that the corporation was trustee of its assets and that the Companies Act 1948, ss. 265 and 302, which together provide that surplus assets should be distributed among members subject to their interest in the company, would not apply. *Held*, although the company was in a position analogous to that of a trustee it was not a trustee in the strict sense because it was capable of incurring liabilities in its own name, and consequently must hold the assets beneficially. The surplus assets were the property of the company to be dealt with according to s. 265 and distributed among those entitled, but the benefits of s. 302 to the members were ousted by the express direction in the memorandum of association that the assets be transferred to other designated persons. Accordingly the court would exercise its jurisdiction to order an appropriate cy-pres scheme.

LIVERPOOL AND DISTRICT HOSPITAL FOR DISEASES OF THE HEART v A-G (1980) Times, 4th November (Chancery Division: SLADE J).

317   Charitable gift—donations by one charity to another—donations accumulated by recipient charity—liability to tax of donor charity

See *Inland Revenue Comrs v Helen Slater Charitable Trust Ltd*, para. 1567.

318   Charitable trust—charitable purposes—religion—society for the study of ethical principles

A religious and ethical society's objects were for "the study and dissemination of ethical principles and the cultivation of a rational religious sentiment". The society's trustees sought a declaration as to whether its objects were for the advancement of religion or otherwise charitable. *Held*, a requirement of a charity was that there should be some element of public benefit and it should not be a club devoted to the self improvement of its own members. It was established that a trust could be a valid charitable trust for the advancement of religion, even though the religion sought to be advanced was not a Christian religion, but the meaning of "religion" did not warrant extension to incorporate all other beliefs and philosophies. "Religion" was concerned with man's relation to God. "Ethics" was concerned with man's relation to man. The two were not the same and it was impossible to say that the society's objects were for the advancement of religion, but they were charitable for the advancement of education or for other purposes beneficial to the community.

BARRALET v ATTORNEY-GENERAL [1980] 3 All ER 918 (Chancery Division: DILLON J). Dicta of Lord Parker of Waddington in *Bowman v Secular Society Ltd* [1917] AC at 445 applied.

319   —— —— trust for promotion of sport

The Football Association established a trust the objects of which were to encourage the sport of association football and other sports in schools and universities with a view to promoting the physical education and development of pupils. The trust was registered as a charity by the Charity Commissioners but the Inland Revenue successfully appealed against their decision. The Court of Appeal upheld the court's decision and the trustees appealed to the House of Lords. The question for their Lordships was whether a valid charitable trust for the advancement of education had been established. *Held*, the mere playing of games for enjoyment or competition was not per se charitable or educational. However, the Education Act 1944 did not limit education to the development of mental, practical or vocational skills and there was express recognition of the contribution that extra-curricular activities and voluntary societies could play. The meaning of education was sufficiently wide to cover all the activities envisaged by the trust. Further, the limitation as to the pupils of schools and universities was a sufficient association with the provision of formal education to prevent any danger of vagueness in the objects of the trust or capriciousness in application by the trustees. The appeal would accordingly be allowed.

INLAND REVENUE COMRS v MCMULLEN [1980] 1 All ER 884 (House of Lords: LORD HAILSHAM OF ST. MARYLEBONE, LORD DIPLOCK, LORD SALMON, LORD RUSSELL OF KILLOWEN and LORD KEITH OF KINKEL). Decision of Court of Appeal [1979] 1 All ER 588, 1979 Halsbury's Abridgment para. 305 reversed.

320   Charity Commissioners—annual report

The Report of the Charity Commissioners for England and Wales 1979 has been published as HC 608. During 1979 3,299 charities were registered; of these 1,736 were new charities founded during the year. The commissioners removed 208 charities from the register. The number of charities at present on the register is 132,303. During the year the commissioners established 914 schemes and made a further 3,812 orders relating to charities. The report includes, as an appendix, a set of notes for the guidance of charity trustees which can be used as a checklist when preparing their accounts.

321   Inquiries—procedure

In *Rule v Charity Commissioners for England and Wales* (1979) (referred to in the Report of the Charity Commissioners for England and Wales 1979, HC 608, at p. 12) Fox J had to consider a claim, inter alia, that the conduct of an inquiry had been unfair and contrary to the rules of natural justice. After reviewing the authorities, he differentiated between inquiries involving a charge or accusation or subjection to pains and penalties from purely fact-finding inquiries and concluded that the inquiry was an administrative one concerned only with obtaining information. He added that the investigator was the master of his own procedure and was entitled to obtain information in any way he thought fit. He must, however, give those affected a fair opportunity to comment on or contradict relevant statements which were prejudicial to them; but no higher duty was imposed on the investigator. In particular, he was not required to put to the persons affected the conclusions which he had reached upon the matter.

CHOSES IN ACTION

Halsbury's Laws of England (4th edn.), Vol. 6, paras. 1–200

322   Assignment of chose in action—whether champertous

The plaintiff company successfully claimed damages against a bank which had defaulted by refusing to honour its letter of credit. An appeal to the House of Lords was pending however. The plaintiff company had been financed throughout the action by the defendant company to whom it owed a large sum of money. The defendant threatened to bankrupt the plaintiff unless it assigned the benefit of its chose in action against the bank to the defendant. A purported agreement to that effect was signed in Geneva, the agreement to be governed by Swiss law. The defendant then assigned the right of action to an undisclosed third party for $1 million. The defendant then negotiated with the bank who agreed to pay $8 million damages. This sum was then paid over to the third party. The plaintiff brought an action in England, inter alia, to set aside the Geneva agreement. The questions for the court were (i) whether the agreement was valid or invalid. If the latter, the exclusive jurisdiction clause fell with it. (ii) If the agreement was valid, whether the proceedings should continue in England because there was no process compelling discovery of documents in Switzerland. *Held,* (i) the crime and the tort of maintenance and champerty had been abolished by the Criminal Law Act 1967, although by s. 14 (2) the abolition did not affect any rule of law as to cases in which a contract was to be treated as contrary to public policy or otherwise illegal. It was therefore now legal to assign an impersonal right to litigate provided that the circumstances reasonably warranted it. The defendant had a genuine pre-existing financial interest in maintaining the plaintiff's solvency, as it had financed the transaction which had given rise to the cause of action and was a creditor for large sums arising out of the transaction. The assignment was therefore valid. (ii) The exclusive jurisdiction clause had to be given effect unless it was unreasonable and unjust. Both the plaintiff and defendant were Swiss corporations and all the transactions had taken place in Switzerland. Further, there was no reason to suppose that justice could not be done in Switzerland notwithstanding that there was no process compelling discovery of documents there. Accordingly the action to set aside the agreement would be stayed.

TRENDTEX TRADING CORPN v CREDIT SUISSE [1980] 3 WLR 367 (Court of Appeal: LORD DENNING, MR, BRIDGE and OLIVER LJJ). *Guy v Churchill* (1888) 40 Ch D 481, *Glegg v Bromley* [1912] 3 KB 474, CA, *Martell v Consett Iron Co Ltd* [1955] Ch 363, CA, and *McShannon v Rockware Glass Ltd* [1978] AC 795, HL, 1978 Halsbury's Abridgment para. 422, applied.

For earlier proceedings by the plaintiff against the bank, see *Trendtex Trading Corpn v Central Bank of Nigeria* [1977] 1 All ER 881, CA, 1977 Halsbury's Abridgment para. 1356.

CLUBS

Halsbury's Laws of England (4th edn.), Vol. 6, paras. 201–500

323   Article

The Dissolution of Unincorporated Non-Profit Associations, B. Green: 43 MLR 626.

324   Bingo duty—exemptions

The Bingo Duty (Exemptions) Order 1980, S.I. 1980 No. 19 (in force on 3rd March 1980), increases the maximum amounts permitted:
  (a) to be paid for a card in any one game of bingo, from 10p to 20p;
  (b) to be taken as total payment for any one game, from £5.00 to £10.00;
  (c) to be offered as a money prize, from 10p to 20p;
under the exemptions from bingo duty in respect of bingo played at small scale amusements provided commercially.

325   Gaming—monetary limits

The Gaming Act (Variation of Monetary Limits) Order 1980, S.I. 1980 No. 28 (in force on 3rd March 1980), increases the maximum amounts to be paid or offered in respect of gaming for prizes at licensed club premises under the Gaming Act 1968, s. 21.

The Gaming Act (Variation of Monetary Limits and Fees) Order 1975, 1975 Halsbury's Abridgment para. 251 is revoked.

326   —— —— bingo

The Gaming Act (Variation of Monetary Limits) (No. 2) Order 1980, S.I. 1980 No. 1429 (in force on 1st December 1980), amends the Gaming Act 1968 s. 20 (3) by increasing the maximum aggregate sum permitted to be paid to players as winnings in respect of all "linked" games of bingo played in any one week in a group of licensed bingo clubs.

327   Gaming (Amendment) Act 1980

The Gaming (Amendment) Act 1980 amends the Gaming Act 1968, s. 20 (3) which provides that the maximum permitted aggregate amount of winnings in respect of bingo played in one week on different premises is to be £1,000. The Act received the royal assent on 20th March 1980 and came into force on that date.

Section 1 of the Act provides that at the end of the 1968 Act, s. 20 (3), there should be added a provision allowing the Secretary of State to amend the limit of £1,000. The Act will then take effect with the amended limit. Section 2 deals with the short title.

328   Gaming Board for Great Britain—report

The Report of the Gaming Board for Great Britain 1979 (HC561) discloses that at the end of 1979 there were 128 clubs licensed for gaming other than bingo, bridge or whist (casino gaming; with a total drop (i.e. money changed for chips) in 1978–79 of £919 million (£727 million in 1977–78). At the end of 1979 there were 1,510 clubs licensed for bingo (1,530 in 1978) (excluding Scotland). At the end of June 1979 there were 916 clubs registered under Part II of the Gaming Act 1968 and 17,238 registered under Part III. Seventeen licensees continued to operate pools competitions under the Pool Competitions Act 1971. By the end of 1979 356 local authorities and 972 societies had registered lottery schemes.

In relation to jackpot machines, the board states that it does not expect its inspectors to take action under the Gaming Act 1968, s. 31 (4) if a player is paid a prize otherwise than by means of coins delivered by the machine when the machine first becomes defective. The agreement between the board and the trade associations that jackpot machines should have a basic payout of not less than 75 per cent of the money inserted by players has been modified (in the light of the introduction of value added tax and the increase of that duty to 15 per cent) to give effect to a minimum payout of 71 per cent. The board also state that it should not be assumed that all video games are exempt from control; in particular, video pin-tables can only be supplied in accordance with s. 28 of the 1968 Act. The board particularly deplores three activities in relation to casino gaming: (i) the introduction by persons acting on behalf of the licence holder of guests who participate in the gaming; (ii) the payment of a commission based on a guest's gaming losses to a club member who introduces the guest, and (iii) the allowing to a person who introduces a guest of a percentage discount from the gaming losses of the introducer. The board regard these activities as infringing s. 12 of the Act and the last, in particular, may also contravene s. 16.

329   Gaming clubs—charges

The Gaming Clubs (Hours and Charges) (Amendment) Regulations 1980, S.I. 1980 No. 27 (in force on 3rd March 1980), increase the maximum charges which may be made for admission to gaming on bingo club premises in England and Wales.

The Gaming Clubs (Hours and Charges) (Amendment) Regulations 1978, 1978 Halsbury's Abridgment para. 318 are revoked.

330   Gaming licence duty

The Gaming Licence Duty Regulations 1980, S.I. 1980 No. 1147 (in force on 1st September 1980, except reg. 7 which comes into force on 1st October 1981), provide for the administration of the new system of gaming licence duty introduced by the Finance Act 1980, s. 6, para. 2328, by (i) prescribing the form of application for a gaming licence and the form of licence; (ii) providing for regular returns of financial information and for the inspection of accounts and other records and (iii) providing for duty to be paid in accordance with a certified statement of gross gaming yield. The 1980 Regulations apply to licences for periods beginning after 30th September 1980 subject to transitional provisions in the case of periods beginning before 1st October 1981. The Gaming (Licence Duty) Regulations 1970 are revoked as from 1st October 1981.

COMMONS

Halsbury's Laws of England (4th edn.), Vol. 6, paras. 501–800

331   Registration—search of register—fees

The Commons Registration (General) (Amendment) Regulations 1980, S.I. 1980 No. 1195 (in force on 5th September 1980), provide for the increase of fees prescribed in the Commons Registration (General) Regulations 1966 for searches of the Registers of Common Land and Town and Village Greens and for providing certified copies of entries in the registers. They also prescribe a new form on which searches of the registers are to be made, which provides for a compulsory search of both registers. The Commons Registration (General) (Amendment) Regulations 1970 are revoked.

332   Right of common—common of pasture by reason of vicinage— whether a right of common or merely a defence to trespass

The New Forest Act 1949, s. 9 empowers the verderers of the forest to make byelaws for regulating the animals that may be depastured in the forest by virtue of a right of common. The byelaws in force are set out in the Schedule to the New Forest (Confirmation of Byelaws) Order 1962. Byelaw 4A provides that "no commoner or other person" who has a right of common of pasture shall allow a bovine animal to be depastured in the forest unless it is marked by an agister and the appropriate payment is made.

The appellant allowed three cows to depasture in the forest when they had not been marked and the fee had not been paid. By reason of his rights of pasture over the wastes of a neighbouring manor he enjoyed a right of common of pasture pur vicinage over the forest land. He was convicted of an offence under byelaw 4A and appealed, contending that the verderers had been incorrect in holding that vicinage was a right of common within byelaw 4A. *Held*, it was established that common of pasture pur vicinage was a right of common, and not merely an excuse for trespass, although its extent was limited. It was not a separate right, but a means by which a commoner obtained rights of pasture over another piece of land. The appellant was a "commoner or other person" exercising a right of common of pasture and was therefore subject to the byelaws. The appeal would be dismissed.

NEWMAN v BENNETT [1980] 3 All ER 449 (Queen's Bench Division: WALLER LJ and PARK J). Dictum of Archibald J in *Cape v Scott* (1874) 4 LR 9 QB at 277 applied.

COMMONWEALTH AND DEPENDENCIES

Halsbury's Laws of England (4th edn.), Vol. 6, paras. 801–1206

333   African Development Fund—further payments to capital stock

The African Development Fund (Further Payments to Capital Stock) Order 1980, S.I. 1980 No. 781 (in force on 4th June 1980), provides for a further payment in accordance with arrangements made with the African Development Fund of a sum not exceeding £18,499,854 to the capital stock of that Fund in respect of its second operating period and for the redemption of non-interest bearing and non-negotiable notes issued by the Minister of Overseas Development in respect of the payment.

334   Anguilla Act 1980

The Anguilla Act 1980 makes provision for the separation of Anguilla from the associated state of St. Christopher, Nevis and Anguilla. The Act received the royal assent on 16th December 1980 and came into force on that date. Section 1 provides for the future status and administration of Anguilla. On 19th December 1980, Anguilla ceased to form part of the territory of the above mentioned associated state: S.I. 1980 No. 1953. Provision is made for the government of Anguilla, its independence and other connected matters. The section also provides for the repeal of the Anguilla Act 1971 which it supersedes. Section 2 deals with citation and provides that the Act is to extend to the associated state of St. Christopher, Nevis and Anguilla notwithstanding the provisions of the West Indies Act 1967.

335   Bahamas—constitution—application for citizenship

See *A-G v Ryan*, para. 18.

336 **Channel Islands—Guernsey and Jersey—extension of certain provisions of Merchant Shipping Act 1979**

See para. 2675.

337 **Crown Agents—authorised agency activities**

The Crown Agents (Additional Powers) Order 1980, S.I. 1980 No. 689 (in force on 17th June 1980) adds the activity of arranging insurance to those which the Crown Agents are empowered to carry out as agents under the Crown Agents Act 1979, 1979 Halsbury's Abridgment para. 318.

338 **Hong Kong—appeal to Privy Council**

See para. 553.

339 **Isle of Man—transfer of functions**

The Isle of Man (Transfer of Functions) Order 1980, S.I. 1980 No. 399 (in force on 1st April 1980), modifies certain specified enactments and orders. The effect of these modifications is to transfer, in respect of the Isle of Man, the functions conferred by those provisions on the Customs and Excise Commissioners (or officers of those Commissioners) or the Governor of the Isle of Man to the authorities or persons specified in the Schedule to the order.

340 **Jamaica—constitution—rights entrenched in constitution—trial by jury**

Jamaica

The appellant was tried and convicted in respect of serious firearms offences by a Jamaican Supreme Court judge sitting without a jury as prescribed by the Gun Court Act 1974. Before the Jamaican Constitution came into force in August 1962, such offences were triable by a Supreme Court judge sitting with a jury. The Constitution provided that the Supreme Court had such jurisdiction and powers as might be conferred on it by the Constitution or any other law and that the Supreme Court in existence immediately before August 1962 was the Supreme Court for the purpose of the Constitution. Provision was also made for any legislation affecting a constitutionally entrenched right to be passed in accordance with a special procedure. The appellant contended that the various constitutional provisions implied that the right to trial by jury existing before 1962 was entrenched in the Constitution; therefore, as the 1974 Act had not been passed under the special procedure, the trial was unconstitutional and void. *Held*, there were no grounds for implying an entrenched right to trial by jury. The expression "Supreme Court" in the Constitution described the judges who, sitting alone or with a jury, were entitled to exercise the jurisdiction exercised by the Court before 1962. However, whether a judge sat alone or with a jury was a matter of practice and procedure rather than jurisdiction: there was nothing in the Constitution regarding the power to regulate practice and procedure which entrenched the right to trial by jury. Even if the mode of trial could be regarded as a matter of jurisdiction or power, the appellant could not rely on the Constitution. It clearly authorised "any other law" such as the 1974 Act to extend the jurisdiction or powers of the Court existing before 1962 to cover trial without a jury in the case of serious offences.

STONE V R [1980] 1 WLR 880 (Privy Council: LORD DIPLOCK, LORD SALMON, LORD ELWYN-JONES, LORD RUSSELL OF KILLOWEN and LORD KEITH OF KINKEL). *Hinds v R* [1977] AC 195, PC, 1976 Halsbury's Abridgment para. 328 applied.

341 **Malaysia—availability of certiorari**

See *South East Asia Fire Bricks Sdn Bhd v Non-Metallic Mineral Products Manufacturing Employees Union*, para. 558.

342   **New Hebrides Act 1980**

The New Hebrides Act 1980 makes provision in connection with the attainment by the New Hebrides of independence within the Commonwealth. The Act received the royal assent on 20th March 1980 and came into force on that date, except for sections 1 (2), 2, Schs. 1, 2 which came into force on 30th July 1980: S.I. 1980 No. 1079.

Section 1 modifies the British Nationality Act 1948 so as to confer the status of British subject and Commonwealth citizen on citizens of the New Hebrides with effect from its independence. The date of independence is to be appointed by Order in Council. Section 2 provides for the modification of certain United Kingdom enactments with effect from the attainment by the New Hebrides of independence and provides for the repeal of certain measures relating to the New Hebrides in consequence of the change in its status. These provisions are specified in Schedules 1 and 2 respectively. Section 3 enables provision to be made by Order in Council regarding any appeals and petitions for leave to appeal from courts in the New Hebrides which may be pending before the Judicial Committee of the Privy Council on the date of the attainment of independence.

The New Hebrides is now known as Vanuatu.

343   **Overseas Development and Co-operation Act 1980**

The Overseas Development and Co-operation Act 1980 consolidates certain enactments relating to overseas development and co-operation, and repeals, as unnecessary, the West Indies Act 1967, s. 16 (1), (2). The Act received the royal assent on 13th November 1980 and came into force on 13th December 1980. Tables showing the destination of enactments consolidated and the derivation of the new Act are set out on pages 76–81 following.

DESTINATION TABLE

This table shows in column (1) the enactments repealed by the Overseas Development and Co-operation Act 1980 and in column (2) the provisions of that Act corresponding to the repealed provisions.

(1)	(2)	(1)	(2)
Bretton Woods Agreements Act 1945 (c 19)	Overseas Development and Co-operation Act 1980 (c 63)	Overseas Service Act 1958 (c 14)	Overseas Development and Co-operation Act 1980 (c 63)
s 1	Rep., 1968 c 13, s 24 (2), Sch 6, Pt I	s 1 (1)	s 10 (1)
2 (1) (a)	Rep., 1977 c 6, s 8 (3), Sch 2	(2)–(5)	(3)–(6)
(b)–(d)	Rep., 1979 c 29, s 6 (1), Sch, Pt I	(6)	(7), (8)
(e)	s 5 (1)	(7)	13 (3), (4)
(2)	(4) (a)	(8)	10 (9)
(3)	Rep., 1968 c 13, s 24 (2), Sch 6, Pt I	2	Rep., 1973 c 21, s 6 (2), Sch 2
(4)	s 5 (2), (3)	3 (1)	Rep., 1973 c 21, s 6 (2), Sch 2
3 (1)	9 (1), (2)	(2)	Rep., 1965 c 10, s 9 (5), Sch 4, Pt III
(2)	(3), (4)	(3)	Rep., 1973 c 21, s 6 (2), Sch 2
(3)	———	(4), (5)	Rep., 1965 c 83, ss 2 (1) (c), 8 (1) (b), Sch 3, Pt II
(4)	9 (1)	(6), (7)	Rep., 1973 c 21, s 6 (2), Sch 2
4	———	4	Rep., 1973 c 21, s 6 (2), Sch 2
Colonial Loans Act 1949 (c. 50)		5 (1)	s 11 (1)
s 1 (1)	8 (1), (2)	(2)	(2), (3)
(2), (3)	(4), (5)	(3)	Rep., 1976 c 35, s 13 (2), Sch 3
(4)–(7)	(7)–(10)	(4)	s 11 (4)
2	———	6	———
Colonial Loans Act 1952 (c 1)		7 (1)	10 (1), 13 (1)
s 1 (1)	8 (1), (4), (5)	(2)	10 (2)
(2)	(3)	(3)	13 (2)
(3)	(5) (d), (6)	(4)	———
(4)	(10)	8	———
2	———	International Bank and Monetary Fund Act 1959 (c 17)	
International Finance Corporation Act 1955 (c 5)		s 1	5 (1) (a)
s 1	See s 5 (4) (b)	2	———
2 (1), (2)	Rep., 1968 c 13, s 24 (2), Sch 6, Pt I	Commonwealth Scholarships Act 1959 (c 6)	
(3)	s 5 (4) (b)	s 1 (1)	15 (1), (2), 17
3 (1)	9 (1), (2)	(2)–(5)	15 (3)–(6)
(2)	(3), (4)	(6)	(7), (8)
(3)	———	(7)	(9), (10)
(4)	9 (5)	(8), (9)	(11), (12)
4	———	2	16
		3	———

(1)	(2)
International Development Association Act 1960 (c 35)	Overseas Development and Co-operation Act 1980 (c 63)
s 1	——
2 (1), (2)	Rep., 1968 c 13, s 24 (2), Sch 6, Pt I
(3)	——
(4)	Rep., 1968 c 57, s 1 (3)
3 (1)	s 9 (1), (2)
(2)	(3), (4)
(3)	——
(4)	9 (5)
4	
Commonwealth Teachers Act 1960 (c 40)	
s 1 (1)	14 (1), 17
(2)	14 (2)
(3), (4)	Rep., 1966 c 21, s 6 (1)
2	——
Colonial Loans Act 1962 (c 41)	
s 1 (1)	s 8 (2)
(2)	(1) (c), (4), (5)
	(d)
(3)	Rep., 1980 c 16, s 2 (2), Sch 2
2	——
Commonwealth Scholarships (Amendment) Act 1963 (c 6)	
s 1	s 17
2, 3	——
International Development Association Act 1964 (c 13)	
s 1	See s 6 (1)
2 (1)	s 6 (1) (a)
(2)	Rep., 1968 c 13, s 24 (2), Sch 6, Pt I
(3)	——
3	

(1)	(2)
Overseas Development and Service Act 1965 (c 38)	Overseas Development and Co-operation Act 1980 (c 63)
s 1	Rep., S.L.(R.)A. 1976
2 (1)–(5)	s 12 (1)–(5)
(6)	(6), (7)
(7)	(8), 13 (1), (2)
(8)	——
3 (1)	
(2)	Rep., S.L.(R.)A. 1976
(3)	Rep., S.L.(R.)A. 1974
Schedule	Rep., S.L.(R.)A. 1974
Overseas Aid Act 1966 (c 21)	
s 1 (1)	s 1 (1)–(4)
(2)	(5)
(3)–(5)	Rep., S.L.(R.)A. 1976
(6)–(9)	s 1 (6)–(9)
2 (1) (a), (b)	——
(c)	7 (1) (b)
(2)	Rep., 1968 c 13, s 24 (2), Sch 6, Pt I
(3)	s 7 (5) (a)
(4)	Rep., 1968 c 13, s 10
	(6)
3	Rep., S.L.(R.)A. 1977
4	Rep., 1978 c 2, s 18 (1), Sch 2
5	Rep., S.L.(R.)A. 1976
6 (1)	Rep., S.L.(R.)A. 1974
(2)	s 14 (1) (b)
7	Rep., 1973 c 21, s 6 (2), Sch 2
8	——
West Indies Act 1967 (c 4)	
s 16 (1), (2)	——
National Loans Act 1968 (c 13)	
s 2†	s 5 (3)
10 (1)	5 (1), 6 (1), (9)
(2)	5 (4)
(6)†	
Sch 2	(3)

† Repealed in part

(1)	(2)
Gas and Electricity Act 1968 (c 39)	Overseas Development and Co-operation Act 1980 (c 63)
s 5	s 2 (1)–(3), (6), Sch 1, Pt I
Overseas Aid Act 1968 (c 57)	
s 1 (1), (2)	6 (1)
(3), (4)	
(5)	6 (2)
(6)	
(7)	6 (3)
2 (1), (2)	4 (1), (2)
(3)	
(4)	(3)
3 (1)–(3)	7 (1)–(3)
(4)	(5) (b)
(5)	(1)
4	Rep., 1973 c 21, s 6 (2), Sch 2
5	
Post Office Act 1969 (c 48)	
s 8 (b)	s 2 (1) (a), (6), Sch 1, Pt I
Development of Tourism Act 1969 (c 51)	
s 5 (4)	2 (1)–(3), (6), Sch 1, Pt I
Coal Industry Act 1971 (c 16)	
s 5 (1)	2 (1)–(3), Sch 1, Pt III
(2)	2 (4)
(3)	(6)
Overseas Investment and Export Guarantees Act 1972 (c 40)	
s 1, 2	Rep., 1978 c 18, s 16 (2) Sch
3 (1)	s 3 (1), (2)
(2)	(3)
4	Rep., 1975 c 19, s 6 (8) Sch
5 (1)	

(1)	(2)
Overseas Investment and Export Guarantees Act 1972 (c 40)	Overseas Development and Co-operation Act 1980 (c 63)
s 5 (2)	s 3 (5)
(3)	(4)
Gas Act 1972 (c 60)	
s 6 (7)	2 (1)–(3), (6), Sch 1, Pt III
Development of Rural Wales Act 1976 (c 75)	
s 7	2 (1)–(3), (6) Sch 1, Pt III
Aircraft and Shipbuilding Industries Act 1977 (c 3)	
s 3 (6)	2 (1)–(3), (6), Sch 1, Pt III
International Finance, Trade and Aid Act 1977 (c 6)	•
s 1, 2	Rep., 1979 c 29, s 6 (1), Sch Pt I
3	Rep., 1979 c 30, s 5 (2), Sch
4	Rep., 1978 c 18, s 16 (2), Sch
5, 6	Rep., 1978 c 2, s 18 (1), Sch 2
7 (1)	
(2)	s 4 (1), (2)
(3)	
8	
Sch 1	Rep., 1978 c 18, s 16 (2), Sch
2	
Coal Industry Act 1977 (c 39)	
Sch 4, para 4	s 2 (4)
National Health Service Act 1977 (c 49)	
s 24	2 (1)–(3), (6), Sch 1, Pt II

TABLE OF DERIVATIONS

This table shows in the right hand column the legislative source from which the sections of the Overseas Development and Co-operation Act 1980 in the left hand column have been derived. In the table the following abbreviations are used:

1945	=	The Bretton Woods Agreements Act 1945 (9 & 10 Geo. 6. c. 19)
1949	=	The Colonial Loans Act 1949 (12 & 13 Geo. 6. c. 50)
1952	=	The Colonial Loans Act 1952 (1 Eliz. 2. c. 1)
1955	=	The International Finance Corporation Act 1955 (4 & 5 Eliz. 2. c. 5)
1958	=	The Overseas Service Act 1958 (6 & 7 Eliz. 2. c. 14)
1959 (a)	=	The International Bank and Monetary Fund Act 1959 (7 & 8 Eliz. 2. c. 17)
1959 (b)	=	The Commonwealth Scholarships Act 1959 (8 Eliz. 2. c. 6)
1960 (a)	=	The International Development Association Act 1960 (8 & 9 Eliz. 2. c. 35)
1960 (b)	=	The Commonwealth Teachers Act 1960 (8 & 9 Eliz. 2. c. 40)
1962	=	The Colonial Loans Act 1962 (10 & 11 Eliz. 2. c. 41)
1963	=	The Commonwealth Scholarship (Amendment) Act 1963 (1963 c. 6)
1964 (a)	=	The International Development Association Act 1964 (1964 c. 13)
1964 (b)	=	The Police Act 1964 (1964 c. 48)
1965	=	The Overseas Development and Service Act 1965 (1965 c. 38)
1966	=	The Overseas Aid Act 1966 (1966 c. 21)
1967	=	The Police (Scotland) Act 1967 (1967 c. 77)
1968 (a)	=	The National Loans Act 1968 (1968 c. 13)
1968 (b)	=	The Gas and Electricity Act 1968 (1968 c. 39)
1968 (c)	=	The Overseas Aid Act 1968 (1968 c. 57)
1969 (a)	=	The Post Office Act 1969 (1969 c. 48)
1969 (b)	=	The Development of Tourism Act 1969 (1969 c. 51)
1971	=	The Coal Industry Act 1971 (1971 c. 16)
1972 (a)	=	The Overseas Investment and Export Guarantees Act 1972 (1972 c. 40)
1972 (b)	=	The Gas Act 1972 (1972 c. 60)
1976	=	The Development of Rural Wales Act 1976 (1976 c. 75)
1977 (a)	=	The Aircraft and Shipbuilding Industries Act 1977 (1977 c. 3)
1977 (b)	=	The International Finance, Trade and Aid Act 1977 (1977 c. 6)
1977 (c)	=	The Coal Industry Act 1977 (1977 c. 39)
1977 (d)	=	The National Health Service Act 1977 (1977 c. 49)
1977 (e)	=	The Asian Development Bank (Extension of Limit on Guarantees) Order 1977 (S.I. 1977 No. 485)
1978	=	The National Health Service (Scotland) Act 1978 (1978 c. 29)
1979 (a)	=	The Electricity (Scotland) Act 1979 (1979 c. 11)
1979 (b)	=	The Ministry of Overseas Development (Dissolution) Order 1979 (S.I. 1979 No. 1451).

Section of Act	Derivation
1 (1)–(4)	1966 s. 1 (1).
(5)	1966 s. 1 (2).
(6)–(9)	1966 s. 1 (6)–(9).
2 (1)–(3)	See derivations of Schedule 1.
(4)	1971 s. 5 (2); 1977 (c) s. 15, Sch. 4 para. 4.
(6)	See 1979 (b) Art. 3 (1).
3 (1), (2)	1972 (a) s. 3 (1).
(3)	1972 (a) s. 3 (2).
(4), (5)	1972 (a) s. 5 (2), (3).
4 (1)	1968 (c) s. 2 (1); 1977 (b) s. 7 (2) (a), (b).
(2)	1968 (c) s. 2 (2); 1977 (b) s. 7 (2) (c).
(3)	1968 (c) s. 2 (4).

Section of Act	Derivation
5 (1) (a)	1945 s. 2 (1) (e); 1959 (a) s. 1 (b); 1968 (a) s. 10 (1).
(b)	1945 s. 2 (1) (e).
(2)	1945 s. 2 (4).
(3)	1945 s. 2 (4); 1968 (a) s. 2, Sch. 3.
(4)	1945 s. 2 (2); 1955 s. 2 (3); 1968 (a) s. 10 (2).
6 (1) (a)	1964 (a) s. 2 (1); 1968 (a) s. 10 (1); 1968 (c) s. 1 (2) (a), (b).
(b)	1968 (c) s. 1 (2) (c).
(2)	1968 (c) s. 1 (5).
(3)	1968 (c) s. 1 (7).
7 (1) (a)	1968 (c) s. 3 (1).
(b)	1966 s. 2 (1) (c).
(2), (3)	1968 (c) s. 3 (2), (3); 1977 (e).
(4)	1968 (c) s. 3.
(5)	1966 s. 2 (3); 1968 (c) s. 3 (4).
8 (1)	1949 s. 1 (1); 1952 s. 1 (1); 1962 s. 1 (2).
(2)	1949 s. 1 (1); 1962 s. 1 (1).
(3)	1952 s. 1 (2)
(4)	1949 s. 1 (2); 1952 s. 1 (1); 1962 s. 1 (2).
(5)	1949 s. 1 (3); 1952 s. 1 (1), (3); 1962 s. 1 (2).
(6)	1962 s. 1 (2).
(7)–(9)	1949 s. 1 (4)–(6).
(10)	1949 s. 1 (7); 1952 s. 1 (4).
9 (1), (2)	1945 s. 3 (1); 1955 s. 3 (1); 1960 (a) s. 3 (1).
(3), (4)	1945 s. 3 (2); 1955 s. 3 (2); 1960 (a) s. 3 (2).
(5)	1955 s. 3 (4); 1960 (a) s. 3 (4).
(6)	[Savings.]
10 (1)	1958 ss. 1 (1), 7 (1).
(2)	1958 s. 7 (2).
(3)–(7)	1958 s. 1 (2)–(6).
(8)	1958 s. 1 (6).
(9)	1958 s. 1 (8).
(10), (11)	See 1958 s. 1.
11 (1)	1958 s. 5 (1).
(2)	1958 s. 1 (2); 1964 (b) Sch. 4 para. 2; 1967 Sch. 4.
(3)	1958 s. 5 (2).
(4)	1958 s. 5 (4).
12 (1), (2)	1965 s. 2 (1), (2).
(3), (4)	1965 s. 2 (3), (4); Minister for the Civil Service Order 1968 (S.I. 1968 No. 1656) Art. 2 (2), Sch.
(5), (6)	1965 s. 2 (5), (6).
(7)	1965 s. 2 (6), proviso.
13 (1)	1958 s. 7 (1); 1965 s. 2 (7).
(2)	1958 s. 7 (2); 1965 s. 2 (7).
(3), (4)	1958 s. 1 (7).
14 (1)	1960 (b) s. 1 (1); 1966 s. 6 (2).
(2)	1960 (b) s. 1 (2).
15 (1), (2)	1959 (b) s. 1 (1).

Section of Act	Derivation
(3)–(7)	1959 (b) s. 1 (2)–(6).
(8), (9)	1959 (b) s. 1 (6)–(7).
(10)–(12)	1959 (b) s. 1 (7)–(9).
16	1959 (b) s. 2.
17	1959 (b) s. 1 (1); 1960 (b) s. 1 (2); 1963 s. 6 (2).
18	[Repeals, revocations and saving.]
19	[Short title, commencement and extent.]
Sch. 1	
Part I	1968 (b) s. 5 (Area Electricity Board and Central Electricity Generating Board and Electricity Council); 1969 (b) s. 5 (4) (British Tourist Authority, English Tourist Board, Scottish Tourist Board and Wales Tourist Board); 1979 s. 16 (North of Scotland Hydro-Electric Board and South of Scotland Electricity Board); 1969 (a) s. 8 (*b*) (Post Office).
Part II	1977 (d) s. 24.
Part III	1972 (b) s. 6 (7) (British Gas Corporation); 1977 (a) s. 3 (6) (British Shipbuilders); 1976 s. 7 (Development Board for Rural Wales); 1971 s. 5 (1), (3) (National Coal Board).
Part IV	1978 s. 17.
Sch. 2	Enactments repealed and orders revoked.

344   **Papua New Guinea, Western Samoa and Nauru (Miscellaneous Provisions) Act 1980**

The Papua New Guinea, Western Samoa and Nauru (Miscellaneous Provisions) Act 1980 makes provision in connection with Papua New Guinea's independence within, and Western Samoa and Nauru's membership of, the Commonwealth. The Act received the royal assent on 31st January 1980 and came into force on that date.

Section 1 modifies the British Nationality Act 1948 so as to confer the status of British subject and Commonwealth citizen on citizens of Papua New Guinea, Western Samoa and Nauru. Section 2 enables births and deaths which have occurred in Papua New Guinea since 16th September 1975, the date of its independence, to be entered in the register of the British High Commission there. Section 3 and the Schedule provide for the consequential amendment and repeal of certain United Kingdom enactments.

345   **Singapore—appeal to Privy Council—validity of death penalty**

Singapore

The defendants were convicted of trafficking in heroin and under national law, where the amount of heroin in a trafficking offence exceeded fifteen grammes, the death penalty was mandatory. Accordingly the defendants were sentenced to death. On appeal to the Privy Council the question arose whether the mandatory death penalty was unconstitutional in view of various provisions in the Constitution of Singapore. *Held*, the Privy Council, in its judicial capacity, was not concerned with the arguments against capital punishment or its efficacy as a deterrent to such offences. That was a matter for the legislature of Singapore. The primary object of the death penalty was that it should deter and there was nothing unusual in such a penalty being mandatory. All criminal law involved the classification of individuals for the purpose of punishment. Equality before the law and equal protection of the law required that like should be compared with like. The constitution, in assuring the individual of equal treatment with other individuals in like circumstances, did not forbid discrimination in punitive treatment between one class of individuals and another where there was a difference in the circumstances in which the offence had been committed. The discrimination complained of in the instant case was discrimination between two distinct classes, individuals trafficking in less than fifteen grammes of heroin and those in more. It was not unreasonable for the legislature to decide that a dealer trafficking in significant quantities of heroin required a stronger deterrent than a dealer on a smaller scale. Accordingly the provisions for a mandatory death penalty were not unconstitutional and the appeal would be dismissed.

ONG AH CHUAN v PUBLIC PROSECUTOR; KOH CHAI CHENG v PUBLIC PROSECUTOR [1980] 3 WLR 855 (Privy Council: LORD DIPLOCK, LORD KEITH OF KINKEL, LORD SCARMAN and LORD ROSKILL).

346   **Southern Rhodesia—constitution of Zimbabwe—elections and appointments**

The Southern Rhodesia (Constitution of Zimbabwe) (Elections and Appointments) (Amendment) Order 1980, S.I. 1980 No. 243 (in force on 26th February 1980), amends the Southern Rhodesia (Constitution of Zimbabwe) (Elections and Appointments Order) 1979, 1979 Halsbury's Abridgment para. 344 by deferring, until after Independence Day, the election of the presiding officer of the Senate and House of Assembly. The electoral college for the purpose of the election of the first President of Zimbabwe is to be convened and presided over by a person to be prescribed by regulations to be made by the Governor. The order also safeguards the Governor's powers to take steps necessary to ensure that the election to the House of Assembly is, as a whole free and fair.

This order has now been revoked, see para. 347.

347   —— —— **transitional, supplementary and consequential matters**

The Zimbabwe Constitution (Transitional, Supplementary and Consequential Provisions) Order 1980, S.I. 1980 No. 395 (in force on 17th April 1980), makes provision for certain transitional, supplementary and consequential matters connected with the Constitution set out in the Zimbabwe Constitution Order 1979, Sch., 1979 Halsbury's Abridgment para. 343 and revokes the Southern Rhodesia (Constitution) Orders in Council 1961, 1964, the Southern Rhodesia Constitution (Interim Provisions) Order 1979, 1979 Halsbury's Abridgment para. 330, the Southern Rhodesia (Constitution of Zimbabwe) (Elections and Appointments) Order 1979, 1979 Halsbury's Abridgment para. 344 and the Southern Rhodesia (Constitution of Zimbabwe) (Elections and Appointments) (Amendment) Order 1980, para. 346.

348   **—— date of independence as Zimbabwe**

The Zimbabwe Independence Order 1980, S.I. 1980 No. 394 (in force on 21st March 1980), appointed the 18th April 1980 as the day on which Southern Rhodesia became independent as the Republic of Zimbabwe.

349   **Vanuatu**

The New Hebrides attained independence under the name of Vanuatu on 30th July 1980. See further para. 342.

350   **Zimbabwe—grants of probate—resealing by English courts**

See para. 2221.

351   **—— independence and membership of the Commonwealth—consequential provisions**

The Zimbabwe (Independence and Membership of the Commonwealth) (Consequential Provisions) Order 1980, S.I. 1980 No. 701 (having effect from Independence Day, 18th April 1980), makes provision in the UK law consequent upon Zimbabwe becoming independent and a member of the Commonwealth. Article 2 adds Zimbabwe to the list of those Commonwealth countries having a separate citizenship with the consequence that citizens of Zimbabwe also have the status of British subjects or Commonwealth citizens. Articles 3, 4 repeal temporary provisions of the Zimbabwe Act 1979, 1979 Halsbury's Abridgment para. 342. Article 5 continues the applicability of the Colonial Stocks Acts to stock issued by the Southern Rhodesian Government or for which that Government assumed responsibility. Article 6 modifies the Southern Rhodesia (Legal Proceedings and Public Liabilities) Order 1979, 1979 Halsbury's Abridgment para. 333 so that, inter alia, references to the Crown in right of Southern Rhodesia may be read as including references to the Government of Zimbabwe. Article 7 and the Schedule modify a number of other enactments. Zimbabwe is accorded the status of a Commonwealth country in relation to the Commonwealth Institute, and to service and visiting forces law.

COMPANIES

Halsbury's Laws of England (4th edn.), Vol. 7, paras. 1–1868

352   **Articles**

Boundaries of "Fraudulent Trading", D. W. Fox: 124 Sol Jo 354.
Company Cases—Incorporation and Operation, Henry E. Markson: 124 Sol Jo 6.
Company Cases: Termination, Henry E. Markson: 124 Sol Jo 657.
Company Cheques—Personal Liability Again, Henry E. Markson: 124 Sol Jo 72.
The New Companies Act, Derrick Owles (the Companies Act 1980, para. 363): Accountant, 12th June 1980, p. 870.
Tax and Company Unveiling Again, Henry E. Markson: 130 NLJ 428.

353 Accounts—disclosure of information in accounts—oversea companies

The Oversea Companies (Accounts) (Exceptions) Order 1980, S.I. 1980 No. 1786 (in force on 22nd December 1980), supersedes the Oversea Companies (Accounts) (Exceptions) Order 1977, 1977 Halsbury's Abridgment, para. 382. An oversea company need not disclose in the accounts that it delivers to the registrar of companies certain information, relating to transactions with the company's directors and connected persons, in accordance with Companies Act 1980, ss. 54 and 56, para. 363.

354 —— —— unregistered companies

The Companies (Unregistered Companies) (Amendment) Regulations 1980, S.I. 1980 No. 1784 (in force on 22nd December 1980), amend the Companies (Unregistered Companies) Regulations 1975, 1975 Halsbury's Abridgment para. 387. The Companies Act 1980, ss. 54–58, 62–66, para. 363, which require the disclosure in a company's accounts and otherwise of certain information relating to transactions with the company's directors and connected persons, now apply to unregistered companies.

355 —— form and content

A new standard accounting practice (SSAP No. 16) has been published on current cost accounting (see *Accountancy*, April 1980, 97 et seq.). The standard applies to most listed companies and other large entities whose annual financial statements are intended to give a true and fair view of the financial position and profit or loss. Such financial statements are required to include current cost accounts prepared in accordance with the standard, in addition to historical cost accounts or historical cost information. The current cost accounts should contain a profit and loss account and balance sheet, together with explanatory notes. The information required to be disclosed is: the current cost profit and loss account; interest/income relating to the net borrowing on which the gearing adjustment has been based; the gearing adjustment; taxation; extraordinary items; and current cost profit or loss (after tax) attributable to shareholders. A reconciliation should be provided between the current cost operating profit and the profit or loss before charging interest and taxation calculated on the historic cost basis. The current cost balance sheet must show the assets and liabilities of the entity on the bases required by the standard. The notes attached to the current cost accounts are required to describe the bases and methods adopted in preparing the accounts particularly in relation to the value to the business of fixed assets and the depreciation thereon; the value to the business of stock and work in progress and the cost of sales adjustment; the monetary working capital adjustment; the gearing adjustment; the basis of translating foreign currencies and dealing with translation differences arising; other material adjustments to the historical cost information; and the corresponding amounts. An appendix to the standard provides an example of the presentation of current cost accounts.

356 Articles of association—alteration by agreement of shareholders acting together—validity

A company had an issued share capital of £30,000 of which half was vested in the defendants and half in trustees on trust for the plaintiff. The articles of association provided that the chairman should have a casting vote at meetings, but an agreement in 1967 purported to withdraw that right. On the determination of the trust the plaintiff became absolutely entitled to her share and, due to a disagreement between the plaintiff and the defendants, a deadlock occurred in the affairs of the company. The question arose as to whether the articles of association had been effectively altered by the 1967 agreement. The defendants contended that in the light of the Companies Act 1948, s. 10 and s. 141, the articles could only be altered by a special resolution passed at a meeting. *Held*, it was a fundamental principle that all the shareholders, acting together, could do anything which was intra vires the company. That principle was not undermined by s. 10, which merely laid down a procedure whereby some only of the shareholders could validly alter the articles. The 1967 agreement had therefore been effective to alter the articles of association and the chairman was not entitled to a casting vote.

CANE v JONES [1980] 1 WLR 1451 (Chancery Division: MICHAEL WHEELER QC). *Re Duomatic Ltd* [1969] 1 All ER 161, applied.

357   Auditors—negligence—client's contributory lack of care

See *Simonius Vischer & Co v Holt & Thompson*, para. 471.

358   Capital—reduction of capital—purchase of own shares

The Secretary of State for Trade has published a consultative document (Cmnd 7944) on the purchase by a company of its own shares. The bulk of the document is taken up by a statement on the present position, comparing it with that in other countries and considering alternative ways of amending the law, by Prof. L. C. B. Gower, research adviser on company law to the Department of Trade.

359   Charitable corporation—winding-up—distribution of assets

See *Liverpool and District Hospital for Diseases of the Heart v A-G*, para. 316.

360   Companies Act 1976—commencement

The Companies Act 1976 (Commencement No. 7) Order 1980, S.I. 1980 No. 1748 brought into force on 22nd December 1980, s. 37 (4) and part of s. 42 (2) and Sch. 3, which repeal provisions enabling the Secretary of State to prescribe fees to be paid to the registrar of companies in respect of certain of his functions. The Secretary of State's power to prescribe fees is now contained in s. 37 of the Act.

361   —— —— fees

The Companies (Fees) Regulations 1980, S.I. 1980 No. 1749 (in force on 22nd December 1980), prescribe those fees to be paid to the registrar of companies on the exercise of certain of his functions. Some fees are increased, and the regulations introduce new fees for the re-registration of a private company as a public company and vice versa, pursuant to Companies Act 1980, ss. 5, 10.

362

The Companies (Fees) (Amendment) Regulations 1980, S.I. 1980 No. 1980 (in force on 22nd December 1980), amend the Companies (Fees) Regulations 1980, supra, with respect to the fee payable for inspection of documents by the registrar.

363   Companies Act 1980

The Companies Act 1980 amends the law relating to companies. Its main objects are to implement the EEC Second Directive on Company Law, Council Directive (EEC) 77/91, 1977 Halsbury's Abridgment para. 1165; to make further provision in relation to directors' duties and transactions giving rise to conflicts of interest for directors; to make insider dealing in company securities unlawful; and to make further provision in relation to the interests of employees and members of companies. The Act also revises the penalties and modes of trial for offences under the Companies Acts 1948 to 1976. The Act received the royal assent on 1st May 1980. The following provisions of the Act came into force on 23rd June 1980: ss. 46, 68–73, 80, 81, 83, 84 (1) (c), (2), (3), 86 (part), 87 (1), (5)–(7), 88 (part), 89, 90, Schs. 2, 3 (part), 4 (part): S.I. 1980 No. 745. The remaining provisions came into force on 22nd December 1980, with the exception of ss. 65 (1) (b) (part), 82 (f), 88 (2) (part), Sch. 4 (part), which come into force on a day or days to be appointed: S.I. 1980 No. 1785.

Classification and registration of companies, etc.
Part I provides a fresh classification of companies and deals with the registration and re-registration of companies and related matters.

Classification of companies. Section 1 defines public and private companies and provides that no company may be formed as, or become, a company limited by guarantee with a share capital. Section 2, together with Sch. 1, sets out requirements as to the constitution of a public company in respect of its name, memorandum of association and minimum number of members.

Registration and re-registration of companies, etc. Section 3 makes provision for the registration of public and private companies. A public company registered as such on its original incorporation is prohibited from doing business or exercising any borrowing powers unless it meets requirements as to its issued share capital, and has obtained a certificate from the registrar of companies: s. 4. Section 5 provides for a private company to be re-registered as a public company if it passes a special resolution to be so re-registered, makes the necessary changes in its memorandum and articles and meets requirements as to its net assets and requirements imposed by s. 6 as to its issued share capital. The operation of s. 5 in the case of an unlimited company is modified by s. 7. Section 8 provides for the re-registration as public companies of old public companies. Section 9 makes it an offence for an old public company not to obtain a new classification under s. 8. A public company may re-register as a private company if it passes a special resolution to do so which is not cancelled by the court: s. 10. Section 11 sets out the procedure for an application to the court to cancel a resolution by an old public company not to be re-registered as public, or a resolution by a public company to be re-registered as private, and specifies the powers of the court on such an application. A public company is required to re-register as a private company where the court confirms a reduction of its issued share capital below the minimum level required for a public company: s. 12. Section 13 provides for the registration as a public company of a joint stock company formed otherwise than under the Companies Acts.

The capital of a company
Part II, which deals with the share capital of public and private companies, sets out requirements as to the issue of, and payment for, share capital, the maintenance of share capital, and the variation and registration of class rights.

The issue of share capital. Section 14 prohibits directors from exercising any powers of a public or private company to allot shares and certain other securities of the company without the required authority. Private limited companies with a share capital are prohibited from offering their shares or debentures to the public: s. 15. Where an increase in share capital of a public company is not fully subscribed for, no allotment may be made of any of the share capital unless the terms of the offer provides that there may be an allotment in that case: s. 16.

Pre-emption rights. Section 17 requires a company proposing to issue equity securities for cash, to offer them first to existing equity shareholders, or, if the articles of the company so provide in the case of equity securities of a particular class, first to equity shareholders of that class, and subsequently to equity shareholders generally. Companies may qualify or withdraw the statutory pre-emption rights: s. 18. Section 19 makes transitional provisions in relation to pre-emption rights.

Payment for share capital. Sections 20 to 31 lay down rules for the payment for shares allotted by public companies. Some of the provisions also extend to private companies. Section 20 provides that shares allotted by public and private companies may only be paid up in money or money's worth, which includes good will and know-how. It also provides that a public company may not accept an undertaking to do work or perform services as payment for shares. The allotment of shares by public and private companies at a discount is prohibited: s. 21. A public company may not allot a share unless at least one-quarter of the nominal value and the whole of any premium on that share has been paid to the company: s. 22. Section 23 provides that a public company may not allot shares in consideration of an undertaking to transfer a non-cash asset to the company at a future date except on terms that the asset is to be transferred within five years from the date of the allotment. The section also makes provision for where such a term is broken. A public company may not allot shares for a non-cash consideration, unless that consideration has been the subject of a report with respect to its value made by a person qualified to be an auditor of that company. He must value the asset himself, unless it appears to him reasonable to accept a valuation made by some other person: s. 24. Section 25 contains provisions supplementary to the requirement for experts' reports and valuations in s. 24. A public company, other than a company re-registered under s. 8, may not, within an initial period, agree to acquire an asset from the subscribers to its memorandum, or, in the case of a company re-registered as a public company, from its members at the time of re-registration if the consideration for the asset is equal in value to at least one-tenth of the company's issued capital, unless there has been a valuation and report on the asset and the acquisition has been approved by an ordinary resolution of the company: s. 26. Section 27 contains provisions supplementary to s. 26. A person who is liable under ss. 20, 23, 24 or 26 in relation to payment for any share or who is liable by virtue of any undertaking given in payment for such shares may apply to the court for relief. A person who is liable to make a contribution may also be relieved by the court from his liability to make that contribution: s. 28. In the case of a public company, shares taken by the subscribers to the memorandum are to be paid up in cash: s. 29. It is an offence to contravene any of the provisions of ss. 20 to 24, 26 and 29, and undertakings given in contravention of some of those provisions remain enforceable: s. 30. Section 31 applies ss. 20, 22 to 25 and 28 to 30 to companies which are in the process of becoming public companies.

Class rights. Section 32 deals with the conditions under which rights attached to special classes of shares may be varied. This section covers both public and private companies. Particulars of special rights attaching to any of a company's shares and particulars of variations of those rights must be delivered to the registrar of companies: s. 33.

Maintenance of capital. Sections 34 to 38 deal with the maintenance of capital of public companies. Some of the provisions also extend to private companies. Section 34 requires the directors of a public company, when they become aware that the net assets of the company are half or less of the amount of the company's called-up share capital, to convene an extraordinary general meeting of the company to consider what measures if any should be taken. A limited company is generally prohibited from acquiring its own shares: s. 35. Section 36 provides that where a person acquires shares in a limited company as nominee for that company and fails to pay sums due to the company on them, the subscribers or the directors are to be jointly and severally liable with him. Where shares in a public company other than an old public company are forfeited or surrendered to the company in respect of a failure to pay sums due on those shares, the company must dispose of them within three years or cancel them: s. 37. Section 38 prohibits, subject to exceptions, any charges by a public company over its own shares.

Restrictions on distribution of profits and assets
Part III lays down rules regulating distributions to members of the company.

Section 39 provides that a company must not make a distribution except out of profits available for the purpose, and defines those profits. A public company may make a distribution only when its net assets are not less than the aggregate of its called-up share capital and undistributable reserves and to the extent that the distribution does not reduce the amount of those assets to less than that aggregate: s. 40. Section 41 provides that investment companies may also make other distributions, and lays down other rules regulating distributions by those companies. Section 42 makes special provision in respect of the realised profits of insurance companies. The right of a company to make a distribution and the amount of any distribution is to be determined by reference to accounts complying with specified requirements: s. 43. Section 44 sets out the consequences for shareholders of unlawful distributions. Section 45 makes ancillary provisions relating to distributions.

Duties of directors and conflicts of interest
Part IV contains provisions relating to the general duties of directors and to transactions which may give rise to conflicts of interest. It also provides for the disclosure in the accounts of particulars of transactions involving directors and others.

Duty in relation to employees. Section 46 provides that directors are to have regard to the interests of the company's employees generally, as well as the interests of its members.

Particular transactions giving rise to a conflict of interest. A term in a director's contract of employment under which the period of his employment is to continue, or may be continued, otherwise than at the instance of the company, for a period exceeding five years is prohibited unless the term is first approved by a resolution of the company in general meeting: s. 47. A company may not without a prior resolution in general meeting to do so enter into specified substantial property transactions with directors or persons connected with them: s. 48. As a general rule, companies may not make loans to their directors or to directors of their holding companies, and companies are prohibited from entering into similar transactions involving guarantees or the provision of security: s. 49. Section 50 deals with exceptions from s. 49 and s. 51 defines the amounts relevant for determining whether a transaction falls within those exceptions. The civil and criminal consequences of a contravention of s. 49 are contained in ss. 52 and 53.

Disclosure of transactions involving directors and others. Section 54 provides for the disclosure in the company accounts of specified substantial contracts in which a director or a person connected with a director has a material interest. Section 55 lists the particulars which are required to be included in the accounts by s. 54. Section 56 contains particulars of amounts outstanding to be included in the accounts. Section 57 contains further provisions relating to recognised banks. Section 58 concerns transactions excluded from ss. 54 and 57 and s. 59 concerns the duty of the auditors of a company in breach of ss. 54 or 56. The provisions of the Companies Act 1948 relating to disclosure by a director of his interest in a contract with the company extend to any transaction or arrangement: s. 60. Section 61 extends the Companies Act 1967, s. 26, relating to disclosure of a director's service contract with a company.

Supplemental. Under s. 62, the Secretary of State is empowered to increase the financial limits under Part IV. Section 63 concerns shadow directors and s. 64 defines persons who are connected with a director. Sections 65 and 66 deal with interpretation and consequential repeals and savings and s. 67 applies ss. 54–58 and 62–66 to unregistered companies.

Insider dealing
Part V contains provisions which prohibit insider dealing by individuals in company securities on a stock exchange, provides for certain duties of disclosure in private deals and sets out the criminal and civil consequences of breach. It also confers power to appoint inspectors to investigate infringements.
Section 68 imposes a number of prohibitions on dealing on a recognised stock exchange in securities when in the possession of inside information. Section 69 contains similar prohibitions in relation to inside information obtained by servants of the Crown. Sections 68 and 69 also apply in relation to certain deals in advertised securities otherwise than on a recognised stock exchange: s. 70. Section 71 contains exceptions in relation to international bonds. A contravention of ss. 68 and 69 is a criminal offence: s. 72. Section 73 deals with interpretation.

Miscellaneous and general
Interests of employees and members. Section 74 empowers a company when closing down or transferring the whole or any part of its business to make provision for employees or former employees of the company or its subsidiaries. The court has power to intervene on the application of a member of the company or the Secretary

of State where the affairs of the company are being conducted in a manner unfairly prejudicial to the interests of some of the members or where any act or omission is or would be so prejudicial: s. 75.

Miscellaneous. Section 76 prohibits trading under a misleading name. A company with the Welsh equivalent of "public limited company" in its name is required to state in English that it is such a company: s. 77. Section 78 deals with alternatives and Welsh equivalents of statutory designations of companies. Section 79 imposes requirements for qualifications of company secretaries. Section 80, together with Sch. 2, revises the mode of trial and penalties for offences under the Companies Acts 1948 to 1976. Certain provisions of the Companies Act 1948 are amended and repealed: ss. 81, 82. Section 83 provides for the continued application of provisions of the Protection of Depositors Act 1963.

General. Section 84 sets out sections of the Companies Acts which are applicable to the enforcement of the 1980 Act. The authorised minimum in respect of the share capital of public companies is £50,000 or such sum as the Secretary of State may by order specify instead: s. 85. Section 86 deals with the application of the 1980 Act to certain companies not formed under the 1948 Act. Section 87 deals with interpretation. Section 88 and Schs. 3 and 4 contain minor and consequential amendments and repeals. Section 89 relates to Northern Ireland and s. 90 deals with short title, citation, commencement and extent.

364   Company forms

The Companies (Forms) Regulations 1980, S.I. 1980 No. 1826 (in force on 22nd December 1980), set out the forms required under the provisions of the Companies Act 1980 (see para. 363).

365   —— acquisition of shares of dissenting shareholders

The Companies (Forms) (Amendment) Regulations 1980, S.I. 1980 No. 2016 (in force on 22nd December 1980), provide for the statutory notice and manner of effecting a takeover of shares under the Companies Act 1948, s. 209 (1), (2) (a).

366   Debenture—appointment of receiver—action carried on by receiver after winding up of company—liability of receiver for costs of action

A debenture holder appointed a receiver of a company, who continued an action by the company against a sub-contractor. Subsequently another company was joined to the action as second defendants. The plaintiff company was compulsorily wound up and the receiver continued the action and provided security for the second defendants' costs. The action was then settled as against the sub-contractor. The Official Referee ordered the company to provide further security for the second defendants' costs, which it failed to do. Consequently the Official Referee dismissed the action against the second defendants and ordered the company to pay their costs. Because the second defendants ranked only as unsecured creditors in the company's liquidation in respect of the order for costs, it was sought to make the receiver personally liable for the costs. The second defendants obtained leave to join the receiver as third defendant and applied for an order that he should pay their costs from the date of the winding up order. *Held*, the receiver would be ordered to pay those costs, provided he had recourse for them against the debenture holders. The court had power under the Supreme Court of Judicature (Consolidation) Act 1925, s. 50 (1), to order a receiver appointed under a debenture to pay the costs of an action carried on by him after the company had been compulsorily wound up which had been incurred after the winding up order. It was just and equitable to make such an order because if the action had been continued by the liquidator and not by the receiver, the second defendants would have ranked as secured creditors in the liquidation for their costs. The slip rule could not be applied to amend the Official Referee's order to provide for payment of the costs by the receiver as well as the plaintiff company. However, the receiver had been properly joined as a defendant to the action because it remained sufficiently alive for that purpose despite the fact that it had been dismissed as against the second defendants. Accordingly, the second defendants were not required to bring a fresh action against the receiver to determine whether he should pay their costs.

BACAL CONTRACTING LTD v MODERN ENGINEERING (BRISTOL) LTD [1980] 2 All ER 655 (Queen's Bench Division: JUDGE FAY QC). *Samuels v Linzi Dresses Ltd* [1980] 1 All ER 803, para. 1668 applied.

367   Director—compensation for loss of office—prohibition—ex gratia payment—validity

Scotland

A company ceased trading and four days before it went into voluntary liquidation the directors resolved that an ex gratia payment be made to one of them as there was no provision for a pension. A shareholder presented a petition under the Companies Act 1948, s. 333 for an order that the sum be paid to the liquidator. He contended that the payment was unlawful in that it had not been approved by the company as required by s. 191 of the Act, which provided that such a payment to a director as compensation for loss of office was unlawful if the proposed payment had not been disclosed to and approved by the members of the company. The company claimed that the payment was "of the nature of a superannuation or similar payment" within s. 194 (3) which permitted such payments to directors on loss of office. *Held*, ss. 191–194 were not relevant where a company was being wound up. In the absence of any express power, those sections were subject to the overriding principle that the validity of an ex gratia payment to a director by way of pension in respect of past services depended upon proof that the payment was made to benefit the company as a whole. In this case, the directors had no express power to make such a payment. The payment was a gratuitous one, the result of which was to diminish the assets remaining for distribution among the members. Hence it was impossible to regard it as a payment made in the interests of the company as a whole. Thus as the payment was invalid, the order sought would be made.

GIBSON'S EXECUTOR v GIBSON 1980 SLT 2 (Outer House).

368   —— fiduciary duty—accountability for profits

Canada

The defendant was the director of two companies, one of which financed the building business of the other. Both companies ran into financial difficulties and a third company was formed by the director to acquire and lease equipment to the building company. The newly formed company made a profit but the building company became insolvent, and debts owing to the finance company remained outstanding. Creditors of the finance company sued the director for breach of trust arising out of a fiduciary relationship. *Held*, the director was clearly in a fiduciary relationship with the building company and a constructive trust would have arisen out of that relationship, but such a relationship was limited to the company itself and did not extend to the creditors of the company. The director could not therefore be compelled to account to the creditor company for the profits made from transactions with the building company even though he was also a director of the creditor company.

WESTERN FINANCE CO LTD v TASKER ENTERPRISES LTD (1979) 106 DLR (3d) 81 (Court of Appeal of Manitoba).

369   —— —— sale of company property—duty to account for profit

Canada

In a case concerning the profitable sale of company property by a director prior to the company becoming insolvent, it was held that there was no general rule for determining whether or not a director had committed a breach of fiduciary duty. Each case was to be considered on its own facts. The determining factor in this case was that the transaction occurred just before the company was declared insolvent.

If, as a result of the disposal of an asset by a company in such a position, a right was acquired by a director, the director had to account to the trustee in bankruptcy for any profit realised from the disposal of that right.

WEBER FEEDS LTD v WEBER (1979) 24 OR (2d) 754 (Court of Appeal of Ontario). *Canadian Aero Service Ltd v O'Malley* (1973) 40 DLR (3d) 371, 1974 Halsbury's Abridgment para. 340 followed.

370   Directors' report—disabled employees

The Companies (Directors' Report) (Employment of Disabled Persons) Regulations 1980, S.I. 1980 No. 1160 (in force on 1st Septerner 1980), require the directors' report to include a statement as to the policy the company has applied during the financial year as to the employment training, career development and promotion of disabled people. The Regulations do not apply where the average number of persons employed by a company per week during the relevant financial year does not exceed 250 and no account is to be taken of persons working wholly or mainly outside the United Kingdom. The regulations only apply to directors' reports prepared for financial years which begin on or after 1st September 1980.

371   —— particulars of political or charitable contributions

The Companies (Directors' Report) (Political and Charitable Contributions) Regulations 1980, S.I. 1980 No. 1055 (in force on 1st September 1980), change the requirements of the Companies Act 1967, s. 19 as to the particulars of contributions for political or charitable purposes to be contained in the directors' report of a company. A statement as to the amount of money given for political or charitable purposes or both, particulars of gifts for political purposes and particulars of gifts by way of donations or subscriptions to a political party need only be contained in the report where the amount in question exceeds £200. This figure was formerly £50.

372   Fees

The Companies (Department of Trade) Fees Order 1980, S.I. 1980 No. 2008 (in force on 1st January 1981), amends the Companies (Department of Trade) Fees Order 1975, 1975 Halsbury's Abridgment para. 397 by increasing fees taken by the Department of Trade in winding-up proceedings.

373   —— amendment

The Companies (Department of Trade) Fees (Amendment) Order 1980, S.I. 1980 No. 1187 (in force on 18th August 1980), further amends the Companies (Department of Trade) Fees Order 1975, 1975 Halsbury's Abridgment para. 397 by abolishing the combined stationery and Gazette fee and provides that, in cases where the winding-up is made on or after 18th August 1980 separate fees will be charged for stationery, etc, and for each insertion of a notice in the London Gazette.

374   —— fees payable to registrar

See paras 361 and 362.

375   Investigation of company's affairs—appointment of inspectors— duty of inspectors to conduct investigation fairly

The managing director of a company, registered under the Companies Act 1948, s. 408 as an overseas company carrying on business in Great Britain, was previously the chairman of a similar company which had been wound up as a result of investigations carried out by the Department of Trade and Industry. Some of the inspectors involved in the earlier investigation were authorised under the Companies Act 1967, s. 109 to investigate the new company. They served a notice on the director requiring him to produce all accounting and correspondence records of the new company. He applied for judicial review and sought a declaration that the inspection should be carried out fairly. *Held*, before the powers in s. 109 could be exercised the Secretary of State and officers of the Department had to suspect that there were matters to be investigated. The officers carrying out an investigation were potential prosecutors and their duty under s. 109 to act fairly was a duty not to exceed or abuse the discretion granted to them under the section nor to use that discretion for an ulterior motive. In the circumstances there was no evidence that the inspectors had acted unfairly and the application would be refused.

R v SECRETARY OF STATE FOR TRADE, EX PARTE PERESTRELLO [1980] 3 All ER 28 (Queen's Bench Division: WOOLF J). Dictum of Lord Parker CJ in *Re HK (An Infant)* [1967] 2 QB 617 at 630 applied. *Metropolitan Properties Co (FGC) Ltd v Lannon* [1969] 1 QB 577 distinguished.

376 —— —— evidence given to inspectors—admissibility in subsequent proceedings by company

A company, which was in liquidation, sued the defendants, a firm of accountants for negligence in auditing its accounts. Inspectors were appointed under the Companies Act 1948, s. 165 to investigate the company's affairs. The inspectors took evidence on oath from four of the defendants' partners and from an employee, giving them no express assurance of confidentiality. It was agreed that the inspectors' report was not admissible in the proceedings, but that passages from it might be put to a witness in cross-examination; if the witness agreed with the passages they became part of the evidence. The defendants, however, contended that if the witness did not agree, the evidence was not admissible as it was given in confidence and the plaintiffs had obtained it in breach of confidence. *Held*, it had to be shown not only that the communication was made in confidence, but that the confidence was of a kind which the public interest required to be protected. However, it was fundamentally important that the confidentiality of evidence given to inspectors was not complete, as a potential witness would know that his evidence and identity might be subsequently disclosed in some way. Evidence given to inspectors would be admissible both under the general law and under the Companies Act 1967, s. 50. Further, as such evidence was admissible in proceedings by the Department of Trade in the company's name, under s. 37 of the 1967 Act, the public interest in preserving confidentiality could not be preserved by drawing a distinction between such proceedings and proceedings by the company or the liquidators. The public interest in all relevant evidence being available to the court should prevail over the public interest in preserving confidentiality.

LONDON AND COUNTY SECURITIES LTD v NICHOLSON [1980] 3 All ER 861 (Chancery Division: BROWNE-WILKINSON J). *Re Rolls Razor Ltd* [1968] 3 All ER 698 and *D v National Society for the Prevention to Cruelty to Children* [1978] AC 171, HL, 1977 Halsbury's Abridgment para. 916 applied. *Re Pergamon Press Ltd* [1970] 3 All ER 535, CA, distinguished.

377 —— conduct of inquiries—duties of inspectors

The Secretary of State for Trade has announced in an answer to a parliamentary question that in future inspectors would be expected to report (or at least produce an interim report) within twelve months of appointment. The Department of Trade would also indicate to the inspectors the particular matters on which a report was required. It was intended to make use of the services of senior members of the Bar who had other heavy commitments on their time less frequently for these purposes. It is intended that the guidance notes provided to inspectors would be published. The Secretary of State stated that inspectors should be appointed only where the information necessary to take decisions with regard to prosecutions or petitions to wind up could not be obtained from an examination of the company's books and papers. Witnesses who made difficulties over appearing before the inspectors might make themselves liable to proceedings for contempt. See 985 H of C Official Report 19th May 1980, Written Answers.

378 Parent company—power over subsidiary company's documents

See *Lonrho Ltd v Shell Petroleum Co Ltd*, para. 902.

379 **Pre-incorporation undertaking to court—enforceability—British Steel Corporation**

A company was party to an agreement which in 1965 involved it in proceedings under the Restrictive Trade Practices Act 1956. As a result of the proceedings the company undertook not to enter into or make any other restrictive agreement without the leave of the court. In 1967 the British Steel Corporation was established by statute and by statutory instrument all property, rights, liabilities and obligations of the company were vested in the corporation. In 1974 the corporation entered a restrictive agreement without leave of the court. A motion was laid before the court for leave to issue a sequestration order for contempt of court against the corporation in respect of the 1974 agreement. *Held*, the burden of the undertaking, which was similar in its effect to an injunction, was transferred to the corporation by the statutory instrument. Accordingly, in entering into the 1974 agreement without leave, the corporation had committed a contempt of court. It would be fined appropriately.

RE AN AGREEMENT BETWEEN MEMBERS OF THE BRITISH CONCRETE PIPE ASSOCIATION (1980) Times, 18th December (Restrictive Practices Court: MOCATTA J presiding).

380 **Production of company's books—application for production by Director of Public Prosecutions—exercise of judge's jurisdiction to make order—availability of appeal**

The Director of Public Prosecutions made an application under the Companies Act 1948, s. 441 (1) for an order for the production and inspection of a company's books and records on the ground that he had reasonable cause to believe that a company officer had committed an offence in connection with the management of the company's affairs. The application was refused but later granted on appeal notwithstanding s. 441 (3) which provides that a decision made under s. 441 (1) was "not appealable". On the issues of availability of appeal under this provision and the ambit of the jurisdiction of the High Court and Court of Appeal in such cases, *held*, an order under s. 441 (1), if made on an ex parte application, authorised a step in a criminal investigation which would otherwise have been unlawful in the absence of the company's consent. It did not decide any issue other than the authority to inspect and the requirement to produce documents. "Not appealable" meant that there was no appeal from a decision taken under that section, and to allow an appeal process in a situation in which the section applied would be to endanger its object. The Court of Appeal had no jurisdiction to entertain such an appeal and the order it purported to make ordering production and inspection of the company's books and records would be set aside. It followed that the House of Lords, in turn, had no jurisdiction to enter on a consideration of whether or not the refusal of the application was right or wrong.

RE RACAL COMMUNICATIONS LTD [1980] 2 All ER 634 (House of Lords: LORD DIPLOCK, LORD SALMON, LORD EDMUND-DAVIES, LORD KEITH OF KINKEL, LORD SCARMAN). *Anisminic Ltd v Foreign Compensation Commission* [1969] 2 AC 147 considered and *Pearlman v Harrow School* [1979] 1 All ER 365, 1978 Halsbury's Abridgment para. 1766 disapproved. Decision of the Court of Appeal sub nom *Re A Company* [1980] 1 All ER 284, 1979 Halsbury's Abridgment para 372 reversed.

381 **Registration of charges—building agreement—lease—equitable charge affecting land**

An agreement between two companies, L and W, provided that L could enter onto W's land and erect certain buildings in accordance with plans approved by W's surveyors and that those plans could be varied only by mutual consent. On completion of each building W was to grant a ninety-nine year lease to L of the appropriate piece of land, the provisions of each lease to be taken from the building agreement. Until each lease was granted L's interest in the land was as a tenant at will. By a mortgage permitted under the terms of the agreement L assigned to the plaintiff as mortgagee all interests under the agreement as security for a sum to be advanced by the plaintiff to finance the development. The mortgage contained a covenant to execute a legal mortgage if any lease was granted under the agreement whilst money remained due under the mortgage. L registered the particulars of the mortgage under the Companies Act 1948, s. 95. W granted to L two leases, which L assigned for value to the defendants who remained in possession of the land contained in the leases. Money secured by the mortgage remained due from L to the plaintiff. In proceedings to enforce the mortgage, the question arose whether the defendants' interest was subject to the equitable charge created by the mortgage. The plaintiff contended that their interest was subject to the charge because they had acquired the leases with actual notice of the charge since the building agreement conferred an equitable interest in the land on L. The charge had been registered under s. 95 which constituted registration of a charge under the Land Charges Act 1972, s. 3 (7) and this, by virtue of the Law of Property Act 1925, s. 198, constituted actual notice of the charge to the defendants. The defendants contended either that (i) the building agreement could not confer any interest in the land on L and the mortgage was not an equitable charge affecting the land registrable under s. 95, or (ii) the mortgage contained two separate equitable charges, one on L's chose in action entitling it to require a grant of a lease by W, which had become spent on the grant of such leases by W, and the other on leases when granted, conferred by the covenant to execute a legal mortgage, which had not been lawfully registered, or (iii) registration under s. 95 did not effect registration under the 1972 Act because it was not registered in the name of the estate owner, W. *Held*, the defendants' interest was subject to an equitable charge created by a mortgage because (i) a contract gave an interest in land if it also gave power to require a grant of the land without further permission of the owner; (ii) the charge constituted by the mortgage was a single continuing charge and could not be split. Hence L had an equitable interest in the land at the date of the mortgage and the mortgage was an equitable charge affecting the land which was registrable under s. 95; (iii) the registration of an equitable charge under s. 95, although it could not be effected in the name of the owner of the underlying legal estate, nevertheless operated as an effective registration of the charge for the purposes of the Land Charges Act 1972.

PROPERTY DISCOUNT CORPN LTD v LYON GROUP LTD [1980] 1 All ER 334 (Chancery Division: GOULDING J). Dicta of Jessel MR and Sir James Hannen in *London and South Western Railway Co v Gomm* (1882) 20 Ch D 562 at 581, 586 applied.

This decision has been affirmed by the Court of Appeal; see [1981] 1 All ER 379.

382 ——**charges created by overseas company not registered in England—validity of unregistered charges against foreign liquidator**

The defendant company was incorporated in Bermuda and had an established place of business in England. It entered into agreements with a Dutch bank whereby the bank provided the company with credit facilities. The company created charges in favour of the bank which included the assignment of its entire business including its present and future trading stock. Subsequently the bank withdrew its credit facilities and the company ceased trading. The parties agreed that the company's property which was stored in England should be sold and the proceeds paid into a joint account in the names of the parties' solicitors. The rights of each in the proceeds were to be the same as their rights in the property before sale. A Bermudian court made a winding up order in respect of the company and appointed joint liquidators. Neither the company nor the particulars of the charges had been registered in England and it was argued that the charges were void against the liquidators for non-registration by virtue of the combined effect of the Companies Act 1948, ss. 95 and 106 or that the documents which created the charges were void against them as unregistered bills of sale. *Held*, (i) the charges were void against the liquidators by virtue of ss. 95 and 106. Section 95 was applied by s. 106 to a company "incorporated outside England" and therefore applied to an overseas company. The operation of s. 106 was not dependent on registration of the company under s. 407 since s. 95 did not require registration of a charge to render it valid but only the delivery of particulars of the charge. It was sufficient for the operation of s. 106 that the overseas company had an established place of business in

England. The bank could have preserved the validity of the charges by delivering particulars to the registrar even though the company was not registered under s. 407. (ii) Although the primary meaning of "liquidator" in s. 95 was a liquidator in an English winding up, for the purpose of s. 106 it could extend to a liquidator in a foreign winding up. (iii) Section 95 applied to floating charges and applied to future property as well as existing property in England. (iv) Under the agreement between the parties, the charges were not spent and accordingly s. 95 applied to the proceeds of sale.

If a company came within the registration provisions of the relevant Companies Act, the Bills of Sale Acts did not apply and it was irrelevant that a particular charge was not registrable. The Bills of Sale (1878) Amendment Act 1882, s. 17 exempted from registration any debentures "issued by any mortgage, loan or other incorporated company". Thus it applied only to individuals and not to corporations. Accordingly, if the charges had not been void under s. 95 they would have been enforceable against the liquidators.

N V SLAVENBURG'S BANK v INTERCONTINENTAL NATURAL RESOURCES LTD [1980] 1 All ER 955 (Queen's Bench Division: LLOYD J). *National Provincial and Union Bank of England v Charnley* [1924] 1 KB 431 applied; *Clark v Balm, Hill & Co.* [1908] 1 KB 667 followed.

383   **Shareholders—rights of minority shareholders—right to sue for compensation on behalf of the company**

The plaintiff company, a minority shareholder in the defendant company, brought a representative action claiming inter alia, compensation on behalf of the defendant company. Two directors of the defendant company had induced its shareholders, by a misleading and tricky circular, to pass a resolution at a general meeting authorising a transaction which was to the detriment of the defendant company and for the benefit of a third company in which the directors held shares through a nominee. The defendant company's board was similarly deceived. The question for the court, inter alia, was whether the action was barred by the rule in *Foss v Harbottle* (1843) 2 Hare 461, under which the proper plaintiff in an action for a wrong alleged to have been done to a company was, prima facie, the company itself. *Held*, where there was a fraud on a minority the rule in *Foss v Harbottle* was relaxed in favour of the minority. The exception to the rule was not confined to the case where the alleged wrongdoer had voting control but extended to the case where it could be shown that, unless the minority were allowed to sue on the company's behalf, the interests of justice would be defeated, in that an action which ought to have been pursued on behalf of the company could not be pursued. As the board had also been deceived there was no real possibility that it would have been able to present the facts to the shareholders in such a way as to enable them to exercise a proper judgment on whether or not it was in the company's interests to sue. Accordingly the interests of justice required that a minority action should be permitted.

The court stated that the exception to the rule in *Foss v Harbottle* is not limited to cases where conscious and deliberate wrongdoing, or fraud, is alleged.

PRUDENTIAL ASSURANCE CO LTD v NEWMAN INDUSTRIES LTD (No. 2) [1980] 2 All ER 841 (Chancery Division: VINELOTT J).

For proceedings relating to the representative action in tort for conspiracy by the two directors see 1979 Halsbury's Abridgment para. 2152.

384   **Shares—issue of shares at a premium—obligation to transfer sum equal to value of premium to share premium account**

It fell to be determined, for tax purposes, whether the taxpayer company was obliged in law, under the Companies Act 1948, s. 56, to create a share premium account, following its acquisition of two companies with assets worth far more than the normal value of the shares which the taxpayer company issued in exchange for the issued share capitals of the two companies. *Held*, the case was indistinguishable on the facts from *Henry Head & Co Ltd v Ropner Holdings Ltd*, where the transfer of the excess value of the shares to a share premium account was required. Section 56 was mandatory and did not make any distinction between cash premiums and non-cash premiums.

SHEARER (INSPECTOR OF TAXES) v BERCAIN LTD [1980] STC 359 (Chancery Division: WALTON J). *Henry Head & Co Ltd v Ropner Holdings Ltd* [1951] 2 All ER 994 followed.

385 —— **purchase of shares—agreement for company to give financial aid for purchase of its own shares**

An agreement was entered into between the first two defendants and the other defendants, shareholders in a finance company, that the plaintiff company, all the shares in which were owned by the first two defendants, would purchase all the shares in the finance company for £500,000. That sum was used by the other defendants to finance the purchase of all the shares in the plaintiff company for £489,000. Soon afterwards the plaintiff company went into liquidation and it was discovered that the real value of the shares in the finance company was £60,000. The receiver commenced an action for damages on behalf of the plaintiff company against the defendants contending (i) that the purchase price of £500,000 was arrived at to enable the defendants to purchase the plaintiff company with money provided by the plaintiff, contrary to the Companies Act 1948, s. 54. Section 54 provides that it is unlawful for a company to give financial assistance for, or in connection with, the purchase of its own shares; (ii) that the defendants had conspired to carry into effect the sale and purchase of the plaintiff company's share capital contrary to s. 54; and (iii) that the defendants were liable as constructive trustees as having received money which was held in trust for the plaintiff in such circumstances as to render them accountable for it and as having knowingly participated in a fraudulent design on the part of those holding money in trust for the plaintiff. *Held,* (i) a breach of s. 54 occurred when a company purchased something from a third party with the sole purpose of putting the third party in funds to acquire shares in the company. Even though the agreement for the purchase of the share capital of the finance company by the plaintiff was a satisfactory commercial transaction for the defendants it nevertheless contravened s. 54. The transaction was merely part of a scheme to enable the defendants to acquire the plaintiff company at no cash cost to themselves. (ii) To establish a claim of conspiracy in civil proceedings the plaintiff had to show that there was a "combination" of the defendants to effect an unlawful act resulting in damage to the plaintiff. The claim of conspiracy had been established because there was a common intention among the defendants to do an act contrary to s. 54 which resulted in damage to the plaintiff company. (iii) The second defendants were further liable as constructive trustees of the sum received for the sale of the share capital of the plaintiff company because that money had been misapplied by the directors of the plaintiff company by virtue of the breach of s. 54. The second defendants had known all the circumstances of the transaction and had accordingly received trust funds (i.e. funds belonging to the plaintiff company of which its directors were trustees) in such a way as to become accountable for them. Due to the second defendants' genuine belief that the share capital of the finance company was worth £500,000 they had not knowingly participated in a fraudulent design and were not liable as constructive trustees on that account. The plaintiff would be awarded damages accordingly.

BELMONT FINANCE CORPN v WILLIAMS FURNITURE LTD (No. 2) [1980] 1 All ER 393 (Court of Appeal: BUCKLEY, GOFF and WALLER LJJ). *Mulcahy v R* (1868) LR 2 HL 306; dictum of Lord Simon LC in *Crofter Hand Woven Harris Tweed Co Ltd v Veitch* [1942] 1 All ER 142 at 147 and dictum of Lord Selborne LC in *Barnes v Addey* (1874) LR 9 Ch App 244 at 251–252 applied.

For previous proceedings see *Belmont Finance Corpn Ltd v Williams Furniture Ltd* [1979] 1 All ER 118, 1978 Halsbury's Abridgment para. 351.

386 —— —— **repayment of debt in part consideration of purchase— whether "financial assistance"**

Company A was a subsidiary of company B, the shareholders of which were company C and two individuals who were directors of companies A and B.

Company B owed company C a sum of money. Company C agreed to sell its shares in company B at par to the two directors in return for payment by company A in discharge of the debt owed by company B. Consequently the directors became the sole shareholders of company B. On the subsequent liquidation of companies A and B the question arose whether the payment was capable of constituting financial assistance for the purchase of shares contrary to the Companies Act 1948, s. 54. *Held*, s. 54 was not limited to financial assistance given to a purchaser of shares, but was directed to such assistance to anyone, provided that it was for the purpose of, or in connection with, the purchase of shares. Company A must have known that if it had not made the payment to company C, the share transaction between the directors and company C would not have taken place. The payment was therefore capable of constituting financial assistance within s. 54 (1).

ARMOUR HICK NORTHERN LTD v ARMOUR TRUST LTD [1980] 3 All ER 833 (Chancery Division: JUDGE MERVYN DAVIES QC). *E. H. Dey Pty Ltd v Dey* [1966] VR 464 applied.

387   —— transfer of shares—restrictions imposed by articles

A member of a private company died leaving a will in which he bequeathed his shares in the company to another member of the company. During administration of the estate the deceased's personal representative, a bank, was registered as holder of the shares. Upon completion of administration of the estate the bank declared that it regarded itself as trustee for the beneficiary and that it would not transfer the shares to the beneficiary unless instructed to do so. Under article 7 of the company's articles, if a member desired to transfer his shares he was obliged first to offer them pro rata to the other members. Article 8 provided an exception to the rule where the proposed transferee was a close relative of the transferor. The plaintiff, wishing to acquire under article 7 a proportion of the deceased's shares, claimed that upon completion of the estate administration the bank was obliged to offer the shares pro rata to all the members. *Held*, (i) the article 8 exception did not apply as the beneficiary was not a close relative of the deceased. (ii) However, the bank was not obliged to offer the shares pro rata to the members because (a) the expression "transfer of a share" covered only dispositions of the legal title in a share and took no account of transfers of solely equitable or beneficial rights, and (b) it was the desire of the person registered as holder of the shares to transfer the same which was relevant under article 7, and accordingly the desire of the deceased to transfer the shares was irrelevant. As the bank had no desire to transfer the legal title in the shares the plaintiff's claim failed.

SAFEGUARD INDUSTRIAL INVESTMENTS LTD v NATIONAL WESTMINSTER BANK LTD [1980] 3 All ER 849 (Chancery Division: VINELOTT J).

388   Stamp duty—raising of capital—basis of assessment

See Case 161/78: *P. Conradsen A/S v Ministry for Fiscal Affairs*, para. 1138.

389   Stock Exchange (Completion of Bargains) Act 1976—extension to unregistered companies

The Companies (Unregistered Companies) (Completion of Stock Exchange Bargains) Regulations 1980, S.I. 1980 No. 926 (in force on 1st August 1980), extend the Stock Exchange (Completion of Bargains) Act 1976, ss. 1, 2 to specified unregistered companies thereby enabling a computerised settlement and stock transfer system to be applied to the securities of such companies.

390   Winding up—application of bankruptcy rules—proof of claims— claim in tort for unliquidated damages

An assurance company, PGA, sought leave to bring an action for negligent misrepresentation against B, a company in compulsory liquidation since 1975. The loss resulting from the alleged misrepresentation which it sought to recover would only be suffered by PGA if B succeeded in another action commenced by the

Secretary of State for Trade on B's behalf pursuant to the Companies Act 1967, s. 37. In that action the liquidators of B were questioning, inter alia, the validity of a debenture in favour of A company, which it was alleged, was made to assist another company in the purchase of B's shares in contravention of the Companies Act 1948, s. 54. PGA's action for negligent misrepresentation against B was based upon certain representations made to it, by B, concerning the debenture, when PGA took over A company's share capital. PGA maintained that it would not have purchased A company, had it not been represented that the debenture was valid.

B's liquidators opposed the application for leave to bring an action for damages for negligent misstatement on the basis of the 1948 Act, s. 317, which restricts debts provable in the winding up of an insolvent company to those provable under bankruptcy law. Thus only those who would be entitled to prove and to receive dividends out of a bankrupt's assets would be entitled to prove in a winding up, and a claim for damages in tort was not provable in bankruptcy unless liquidated by judgment before the date of the receiving order. The liquidators of B maintained s. 317 was similarly applicable to every company in liquidation unless and until its assets were shown to be sufficient to meet its liabilities and the costs of winding up. Once it was shown to be solvent, a claim for unliquidated damages became provable under s. 316.

Held, a receiving order was not to be equated with a winding up order. Once the former was made the bankrupt's assets would be distributed in accordance with a statutory scheme. However, a company would initially be treated as insolvent until its assets were shown to be equal to its liabilities. Once it was shown to be solvent, it might again have to be treated as insolvent if the surplus assets were insufficient to meet the costs and expenses of winding up.

A proof of damages could not be admissible and inadmissible according to the financial health of the company. Section 317 thus was not to be treated as operating to exclude a claim for damages in tort which had not become liquidated by judgment before the commencement of the winding up, but only to exclude a claim not so liquidated at the date when the claimant came in to prove. Thus, leave would be given to bring the action for damages against B which was being wound up and which might be insolvent. The liability PGA sought to enforce would be admissible to proof if, and only if, liquidated by judgment before the company's assets were distributed.

RE BERKELEY SECURITIES (PROPERTY) LTD [1980] 3 All ER 513 (Chancery Division: VINELOTT J). Dictum of Vaughan Williams LJ in *Re Whitaker* [1901] 1 Ch at 12 and *Re McMurdo* [1902] 2 Ch at 684 applied.

391   —— compulsory winding up—disposition of company's assets after commencement of winding up—validity

On 3rd August a creditor of a company presented a petition to wind up the company. The company was trading at a loss and had an unsecured overdraft on its bank account. The bank became aware of the winding up petition on the 15th August. On the 9th October the court made a compulsory winding up order in respect of the company. The bank, without obtaining a validating order from the court, allowed the company to continue operating the account for the period 3rd August to 9th October (the relevant period). In doing this the bank did not consider whether it was in the interests of the unsecured creditors nor ensured that pre-liquidation debts were not paid out of the account after commencement of the winding up. During the relevant period, money was paid into the account by outstanding debtors, and the company paid to creditors sums owed in respect of goods and services supplied before commencement of the winding up. Throughout the relevant period the account remained overdrawn. The liquidator applied by summons for (i) a declaration that the payments made into and out of the account during the relevant period constituted dispositions of the company's property which were void under the Companies Act 1948, s. 227, and (ii) an order for payment of those sums to be made by the bank to the liquidator. *Held*, (i) the payments into the account during the relevant period constituted dispositions of the company's property within s. 227. As the account was overdrawn the company was a debtor to the bank for the amount of the overdraft. When the bank credited the account with sums paid in by the company, the bank, on the company's behalf, made a disposition in its own favour by discharging the company's liability on the overdraft. All payments out also constituted dispositions within s. 227. Unless validated by the court under s. 227 all payments into and out of the account during the relevant period were invalid. (ii) In exercising its discretion under s. 227 to make a validating order the court had to ensure that the interests of the unsecured creditor were not prejudiced. The court would not validate transactions which resulted in a pre-liquidation creditor being paid in full at the expense of other creditors who only received a dividend, unless there were special circumstances which made validation desirable in the interest of the unsecured creditors as a whole. Where a bank decided to allow a compay in liquidation to have facilities on an existing account, without obtaining a validating order, then if this resulted in loss to the creditors, the court would not necessarily absolve the bank from liability.

In the light of the circumstances of the case certain of the transactions would be declared valid and others invalid. Repayment of sums to the liquidator in respect of the latter transactions would be ordered.

RE GRAY'S INN CONSTRUCTION CO LTD [1980] 1 All ER 814 (Court of Appeal: BUCKLEY and GOFF LJJ and SIR DAVID CAIRNS). Dictum of Oliver J in *Re Leslie Engineers Co Ltd* [1976] 2 All ER 85 at 95, 1976 Halsbury's Abridgment para. 356 applied.

392 —— ex gratia payment to director—validity

See *Gibson's Executor v Gibson*, para. 367.

393 —— injunction to restrain—condition attached to injunction— declaration of solvency by company

The defendant served on the plaintiff company a notice under the Companies Act 1948, s. 223 (a) requiring it to pay an alleged debt within twenty-one days. The company denied the debt claiming that the defendant was merely a contingent creditor of the company for the sum mentioned. The company issued a writ claiming an injunction restraining the defendant from presenting a petition to wind up the company based on the alleged debt and, by a notice of motion, sought an injunction to restrain him from doing so until the trial of the action or further order. An order was accordingly granted but on the condition that the directors filed a declaration of solvency. The company appealed. *Held*, there was no justification for the imposition of such a condition in granting the order. Since there was a bona fide dispute as to whether any money was due from the company to the defendant and there was evidence that the defendant nonetheless threatened to present a petition on the basis that it was due. The company was entitled to an injunction restraining the defendant from presenting a petition for winding up.

STONEGATE SECURITIES LTD V GREGORY [1980] 1 All ER 241 (Court of Appeal: BUCKLEY and GOFF LJJ and SIR DAVID CAIRNS). Dictum of Ungoed Thomas J in *Mann v Goldstein* [1968] 2 All ER 769 at 775 approved; dictum of Goulding J in *Holt Southey Ltd v Catnic Components Ltd* [1978] 2 All ER 276 at 280, 1978 Halsbury's Abridgment para. 377 disapproved.

394 —— petition by creditor—form of advertisement

A petition for the compulsory winding up of a company was presented by a creditor and supported by the Inland Revenue. The petition was advertised using an old form instead of the new form prescribed by the Companies (Winding-up) Rules 1949, as amended. The petitioner and the Inland Revenue contended that it would be unfair to order readvertisement of the petition. *Held*, under the Companies Act 1948, s. 319 preferential debts in a winding up were limited to those which had become payable or had been assessed within a specified period before the date of the winding up order. Therefore, any delay in making the order by requiring readvertisement of the petition was liable to prejudice preferential creditors by delaying the commencement of the specified period. The Inland Revenue, a preferential creditor, was not responsible for the form of advertisement used by the petitioner and it would be unjust to cause further delay by ordering readvertisement. Moreover, the old form of advertisement included all the relevant facts of the petition contained in the new form so creditors and contributories were not prejudiced by its use. Accordingly the defect in the advertisement would be waived and a compulsory winding up order granted.

RE ACCOUSTIC TRANSDUCER CO LTD (1980) Times, 12th November (Chancery Division: SLADE J).

395　　　—— —— —— petition in respect of unpaid bill of costs

See *Re Laceward Ltd*, para. 2808.

396　　　—— rules

The Companies (Winding-up) (Amendment) Rules 1980, S.I. 1980 No. 2031 (in force on 20th January 1981), amend certain rules in the Companies (Winding-up) Rules 1949, S.I. 1949 No. 330, by inserting references to Companies Act 1980, s. 75, para. 363 which provides for applications to the court to grant relief against a company where members are unfairly prejudiced.

397　　　—— two petitions—application for costs

The plaintiff company presented a petition to wind up a company. An earlier petition in respect of the same company had been advertised in the London Gazette, unknown to the plaintiffs, but the Companies Department had failed to carry out its usual practice of searching an unofficial register, and were unable to inform the plaintiff of the earlier petition. When the plaintiffs' petition was dismissed they applied for costs up to the time that they became aware of the earlier petition. *Held*, the advertisement in the Gazette did not in itself constitute notice to all the world, and the normal practice of the Companies Department entitled a prospective petitioner to assume that it was an adequate means of confirming that no earlier petition had been presented. The costs would accordingly be awarded in this case, but the judge added that for other purposes, such as the presenting of petitions in the county court, a petitioner who failed to search in the Gazette might be treated as doing so at his own risk as regards costs.

RE DRAMSTAR LTD (1980) 124 Sol Jo 807 (Chancery Division: SLADE J). *Re General Financial Bank* (1882) 20 Ch D 276 applied.

398　　　—— voluntary winding up—application by liquidators to distribute final dividend—whether subject to claims of late creditors

A company which manufactured aircraft engines went into voluntary liquidation in 1971. The liquidators were able to realise some of its assets, to pay off its debts and to make payments to its shareholders. There was a public announcement that final dividends were to be made to the shareholders. Before the payments were made writs were issued against the company for damages in respect of the deaths of aircraft passengers in a crash caused by a defective engine manufactured by the company. The company was insured for £53 million in respect of defective product liability, which the liquidators considered sufficient to settle the claims. They therefore applied to the court under the Companies Act 1948, s. 307 for, inter alia, liberty to distribute final dividends to members without regard to any claims arising out of the aircraft accident. *Held*, in deciding whether to make an order, under s. 307, notwithstanding a last-minute claim by persons who contended that they were creditors, the test was one of reasonableness. There was no rule that the claimants had to establish that they had not been guilty of either wilful default or lack of due diligence. Further, where the order was sought to facilitate a distribution amongst members, the court would be more reluctant to grant it than if the distribution was to be made to creditors. Whilst it was highly inconvenient to have the proposed distribution halted and postponed, justice required it as the rights of insurance could

not be regarded as providing any sufficient substitute.   The order would accordingly
be refused.
Re R-R Realisations Ltd (formerly called Rolls-Royce Ltd) [1980] 1 All
ER 1019 (Chancery Division: Sir Robert Megarry V-C).

COMPULSORY ACQUISITION OF LAND

Halsbury's Laws of England (4th edn.), Vol. 8, paras. 1–400

399   Articles

Agricultural Compensation: The Injustice of Market Value in Severance Cases.
Barry Denyer-Green: 80 JPL 505.
Resisting Compulsory Acquisition of Land, Dawn Oliver (resisting enforcement
of compulsory purchase order): [1980] JPL 236.

400   Compensation—assessment—betterment   reducing   compensation

Portsmouth Roman Catholic Diocesan Trustees Registered v Hampshire
County Council [1980] RVR 67: V. G. Wellings QC (a council compulsorily
purchased land under the Highways Act 1959 in order to construct a side road; the
owner retained an adjacent piece of land; he requested planning permission for a
residential development; the council refused to consider the application until after
the road was completed; questions arose as to the amount of compensation payable
for the land taken; the council contended that a reduction in the compensation
should be made for the betterment to the retained land due to the proposed
development; Tribunal held no reduction was necessary; the grant of any planning
permission for a residential development was not a benefit which the tribunal was
required to have regard to under the 1959 Act, s. 222 (6) (a); s. 222 (6) (a) related to
a benefit directly referable to the purpose for which the land was acquired; the grant
of planning permission was an indirect effect of that purpose).

401   —— —— community land

See para. 2864.

402   —— —— date of valuation

Hoveringham Gravels Ltd v Chiltern District Council (1980) 39 P & CR
414: Sir Douglas Frank QC and W. H. Rees FRICS (case remitted by Court of
Appeal for determination of compensation payable; claimant contended basis of
assessment should be current market value, not value at date of original hearing; date
of valuation should not be extended where there was an appeal or decision whether
or not to appeal might be affected; compensation assessed according to value at date
of original hearing).
As to previous proceedings, see (1977) 35 P & CR 295, CA, 1977 Halsbury's
Abridgment para. 422.

403   —— —— land devastated by fire—market value—loss of earnings

Singapore
Land in Singapore was subject to a head lease and two sub-leases both of which were
registered.   A fire destroyed buildings on the land occupied by the second sub-lessee,
a trading company.   Shortly thereafter a declaration that the land was required for
public purposes was made under the Land Acquisition Act and the government in
due course took possession.   Compensation was assessed and awarded to the three

lessees but a claim for loss of earnings by the trading company was disallowed. Answers to questions stated to the Court of Appeal in subsequent proceedings formed the basis of appeals by all parties to the Privy Council. Disallowing the lessees' appeal on one point, *held*, the declaration made set in motion the compulsory acquisition procedure and this constituted an acquisition of land within six months of the land's devastation by fire so as to bring the matter within s. 33 (1) of the Act. Allowing the lessees' appeal on their second point and the government's cross-appeal, *held*, (i) since the trading company whose unencumbered title appeared on the Register of Deeds was in a position to convey its interest in the land with vacant possession the land could not be said to be subject to encumbrances within s. 33 (1) whatever the position of the head-lessee. Consequently compensation should have been assessed at full and not one-third of full vacant possession value. (ii) In determining "actual earnings" which could be compensated under s. 33 (1) (d) account should only be taken of earnings which were being earned at the time of acquisition and whose loss was a result of the acquisition itself. Because the trading company was not operating at the time of acquisition it had lost no actual earnings and was not entitled to compensation.

ROBINSON AND CO LTD v COLLECTOR OF LAND REVENUE, SINGAPORE [1980] 1 WLR 1614 (Privy Council: LORD WILBERFORCE, LORD EDMUND-DAVIES, LORD RUSSELL OF KILLOWEN, LORD SCARMAN and LORD LANE).

404 ——— **Lands Tribunal decisions**

DAVIS v NOTTINGHAM CITY COUNCIL [1980] RVR 311: W. H. Rees FRICS (council compulsorily acquired freehold interest in premises comprising land enclosed by brick walls with no roof; claimant sought compensation of an amount referable to potential value after repairs, which she claimed had not been carried out because of threat of compulsory purchase; also claimed loss of rent for period prior to notice of entry and travelling expenses incurred in visiting premises; compensation payable was value of freehold interest before repairs, plus expenses; it was not an economical proposition to repair premises, the lack of repair was treated as the result of claimant's neglect, and nothing was payable for loss of rent prior to notice to treat).

405 FAWCETT v NEWCASTLE UPON TYNE METROPOLITAN DISTRICT COUNCIL [1980] RVR 300: Sir Douglas Frank QC (compulsory purchase of freehold interest, subject to protected tenancy; claimant valued house at £6,000 supported by sale with vacant possession of nearby houses; compensation payable was in fact the registered rent, less the amount due to furniture, less 22½ per cent for repairs, insurance and management; comparable houses with vacant possession of no assistance in assessment).

406 TOOTH v WOLVERHAMPTON BOROUGH COUNCIL [1980] RVR 60: W. H. Rees FRICS (compulsory acquisition of allotment land; claimant sought compensation on the basis of the value of all the allotments taken together; council's claim that lower figure should be paid upheld because planning permission for development of land as a single site would not be forthcoming and there was no direct access to it).

407 ——— **injury by authorised works—assessment—Lands Tribunal decision**

WEEKS v THAMES WATER AUTHORITY (1979) 39 P & CR 208: Sir Douglas Frank QC (applicant owned cottage in setting of exceptional charm; change in character of property due to improvement works to stream nearby; claim for compensation for injurious affection; compensation should represent difference in value of property before and after execution of works; date of assessment was date of execution; sum awarded; observation on inconsistency that Lands Tribunal did not have same powers as High Court to award interest on sum).

408   —— owner-occupiers' supplement

SAGHIR V BIRMINGHAM DISTRICT COUNCIL [1980] RVR 74: V. G. Wellings QC
(a house owner claimed payment of owner-occupiers' supplement under Housing
Act 1969, Sch 5, para. 1 (2) on the compulsory purchase of his house; prior to
purchasing the house the owner inquired as to the likelihood of compulsory
acquisition; the council stated the property would be surveyed within two years in
connection with compulsory acquisition for the purpose of slum clearance; the
council refused to pay the supplement; the Lands Tribunal had no jurisdiction to
inquire into the validity of the council's decision made under the 1969 Act, Sch 5,
para. 1 (2)).

409   —— —— full compulsory purchase value

A local housing authority acquired a dwelling house in a clearance area. At the date
of the declaration of the clearance area the claimant occupied the house with his
family. Before the local authority entered into possession of the house, the claimant
and his family moved but the claimant retained one room in the house, letting the
remainder to weekly tenants. The question arose whether, in assessing the "full
compulsory purchase value" for the purpose of calculating the owner-occupier
supplement as provided for under the Housing Act 1969, s. 68 and Sch. 5, account
was to be taken of the tenancies subsisting at the date when the local authority
entered into possession of the house or whether the premises were to be valued as
with vacant possession, the position at the date of declaration of the clearance area.
Held, Sch. 5 introduced the normal compulsory purchase code governing
compensation payable to an owner-occupier. There was nothing which stated that
compensation was to be assessed by reference to facts at the date of the declaration of
the clearance area, disregarding any subsequent event which might have affected the
value of the property in the open market at the date when the local authority took
possession. The supplement, therefore, would be calculated at the date of entry
subject to subsisting tenancies.

KHAN V BIRMINGHAM CITY COUNCIL (1980) 40 P & CR 412 (Court of Appeal:
MEGAW and SHAW LJJ and DAME ELIZABETH LANE). *Hunter v Manchester City
Council* [1975] 2 All ER 966, 1975 Halsbury's Abridgment para. 1703 distin-
guished. Decision of the Lands Tribunal [1978] RVR 231, 1979 Halsbury's
Abridgment para. 401 affirmed.

410   —— purchase notice—liability to development land tax—date of
disposal

See *Inland Revenue Comrs v Metrolands (Property Finance) Ltd*, para. 888.

411   Compulsory purchase order—application to quash order—
whether order made to deal with possible future need

A local authority resolved to acquire compulsorily a number of houses, including
that of the applicant, in a housing action area. However, they further resolved that
if satisfactory repairs were carried out subsequent to the confirmation of the
compulsory purchase order they would not take possession of the properties. At an
inquiry into objections to the order the inspector found that the applicant had a
deplorable record of maintenance and was unlikely to proceed expeditiously with
the necessary work. On the inspector's recommendation the Secretary of State
confirmed the compulsory purchase order. The applicant sought an order to quash
the decision on the ground that the Secretary of State's power of confirmation had
been exercised so as to deal with a possible future need. *Held*, the Secretary of State
had no power to authorise the acquisition of land in advance of the council's
requirements. However, the fact that the authority might not proceed with the
acquisition in the event of it becoming unnecessary did not invalidate the
authorisation. Nor had the authority disabled themselves from exercising

the compulsory powers of purchase by their undertaking, so that the Secretary of State could not confirm the order. The application would accordingly be refused.
VARSANI V SECRETARY OF STATE FOR THE ENVIRONMENT (1980) 40 P & CR 354 (Queen's Bench Division: SIR DOUGLAS FRANK QC).

412　　—— confirmation by confirming authority—consideration of alternative schemes—effect of failure to refer to minor scheme in decision

The plaintiffs objected to a compulsory purchase order being made in respect of their property. An inquiry was held and the plaintiffs put forward alternative schemes; a major scheme involving the whole site and a minor scheme affecting only three houses. The inspector's report noted both schemes and recommended confirmation of the order to the Secretary of State. The decision letter of the Secretary of State confirmed the order, stating that he accepted the finding of fact, conclusions and recommendation of the inspector, but made no reference to the minor scheme. The judge quashed the Secretary of State's decision on the ground that he had not had regard to a material consideration. On appeal, *held*, where the Secretary of State had not differed from the inspector on any relevant fact he was not wrong in mentioning in his decision letter some of the material considerations in the inspector's report and omitting others. The appeal would accordingly be allowed and the confirmation order of the compulsory purchase order restored.

LONDON WELSH ASSOCIATION LTD V SECRETARY OF STATE FOR THE ENVIRONMENT (1980) Times, 24th June (Court of Appeal: LAWTON, BRIDGE, SHAW LJJ). Decision of Forbes J (1979) 252 Estates Gazette, 1979 Halsbury's Abridgment para. 416 reversed.

413　　—— prescribed forms—land described by reference to map—accuracy of map denoting land

Fiji

A city council in Fiji successfully applied for authority to acquire compulsorily part of a plot of land. The council served notice of acquisition on the owner but failed to publish the notice in a local newspaper as required by Fijian legislation. The notice described the land as being twenty acres at the eastern end of a plot as shown on an attached sketch plan. The plan, which indicated an area of twenty acres, was not drawn to scale. Evidence showed that if the plan was treated as a scale plan, the area shown was more than twenty acres. The owner contested the validity of the acquisition. *Held*, (i) under Fijian legislation, a notice of compulsory acquisition was required to describe the relevant land "giving measurements and showing boundaries wherever practicable." This requirement was satisfied if the land was denoted by a sketch plan as long as its position and extent could be ascertained from the plan. As the description in the council's notice was sufficiently precise, it was irrelevant that the map was not to scale. (ii) The council had given sufficient notice of acquisition to the persons interested in the land. Accordingly, failure to comply with the provision requiring a notice to be advertised in a newspaper did not invalidate the acquisition.

MUKTA BEN V SUVA CITY COUNCIL [1980] 1 WLR 767 (Privy Council: LORD WILBERFORCE, LORD EDMUND-DAVIES, LORD RUSSELL OF KILLOWEN, LORD KEITH OF KINKEL and LORD LANE).

For similar legislation, see the Acquisition of Land (Authorisation Procedure) Act 1946, Sch. 1, Part 1.

414　　Disposal of surplus land—procedure

The Department of the Environment has issued a consultative paper on the procedure for disposal of surplus government land which had originally been acquired by or under threat of compulsion. The proposals include a general obligation to offer back to former owners surplus freehold land or property acquired by or under the threat of compulsion if it has not been materially changed in character since acquisition. (The term "material change" is defined in the document.) The obligation would include agricultural land acquired since 1st January 1935 (as at present) but would also extend to other land acquired within 25 years of the date of disposal. Consideration will be given to the claims of persons with other interests in land, particularly long leaseholders. The land would be disposed of at a price reflecting current market value. Certain specific categories are excluded from the obligation to offer the land back to the former owners: i.e. land needed by other public authorities, where such disposal would conflict with the original purpose of the acquisition, where such disposal might result in severance of the site and the resulting sale being at a substantially lower price, and where tenants of houses would have the first opportunity to purchase the freehold. Pending the formalisation of the new policy on disposals, the draft policy will be applied to any proposal for such disposal.

415   **Entry onto land—entry before completion—rate of interest after entry**

The Acquisition of Land (Rate of Interest after Entry) Regulations 1980, S.I. 1980 No. 1026 (in force on 18th August 1980), decrease from 17 per cent to 16 per cent the annual rate of interest payable, where entry is made before compensation, on land in England and Wales which is being acquired compulsorily. The Acquisition of Land (Rate of Interest after Entry) (No. 3) Regulations 1979, 1979 Halsbury's Abridgment para. 420 are revoked.

These regulations have been revoked; see para. 416.

416   The Acquisition of Land (Rate of Interest After Entry) (No. 2) Regulations 1980, S.I. 1980 No. 1944 (in force on 5th January 1981), decrease from 16 per cent to 14½ per cent the annual rate of interest payable where entry is made before payment of compensation on land in England and Wales which is being purchased compulsorily. The Acquisition of Land (Rate of Interest After Entry) Regulations 1980, para. 415, are revoked.

417   **Local Government, Planning and Land Act 1980**

See para. 1819.

418   **Notice to treat—notice bearing different date from that on which it was served—validity**

A local authority decided to clear a slum area and subsequently made a compulsory purchase order and accordingly gave notices to treat to the persons concerned, the owners of the property to be purchased. As a result of a number of private transactions concerning the property the local authority served two notices to treat in succession. Both were invalid on the ground that they were served on the wrong persons. The authority served a third notice to treat on the correct person but it bore a date different from that on which it was served. Furthermore, the authority was already in possession of the property prior to the serving of the third notice. Questions arose as to the validity of the notice and the effect of certain provisions of the Compulsory Purchase Act 1965 on the authority's actions. *Held*, the date which a notice to treat bore made no difference to its validity. The effect of a notice to treat was to establish a relationship analogous to that of vendor and purchaser and which bound the owner of the land to give up the land subject to his being paid compensation, and which bound the acquiring authority to take the land. The rights and obligations created by the service of a notice to treat were legal as distinct from equitable. There was nothing in the 1965 Act which prevented the local authority from serving a notice to treat after entering on the land. All that remained after the notice had been served was to agree the amount of compensation for the purpose of enabling the local authority to become the lawful owner. The authority was, furthermore, entitled to rectify matters and prevent any trespasses by serving the appropriate notices without having first to go out of possession.

COHEN V HARINGEY LONDON BOROUGH COUNCIL (1980) 125 Sol Jo 47 (Court of Appeal: LORD DENNING MR, ORMROD and O'CONNOR LJJ).

419   Planning blight—notice—Lands Tribunal decision

WYSE V NEWCASTLE UNDER LYME BOROUGH COUNCIL [1980] RVR 134: W H Rees FRICS (claimant served blight notice stating that hereditament was included in land falling within Town and Country Planning Act 1971, s. 192 (1); council served counter-notice; hereditament included in housing clearance programme but no resolution made to include it in clearance area; there was structure plan in force but no adverse plan affected hereditament; counter-notice valid; nothing to show hereditament blighted within s. 192 (1); housing programme not a structure plan within s. 192 (1) (a)).

CONFLICT OF LAWS

Halsbury's Laws of England (4th edn.), Vol. 8, paras. 401–800

420   Articles

A Different Approach to Choice of Law in Contract, A. Thomson: 43 MLR 650.
The Recognition of Foreign Nullity Decrees, Raymond Smith: 96 LQR 380.

421   Admiralty—maritime lien—priority over mortgage of ship on distribution of proceeds of sale—foreign claim

See Bankers Trust International Ltd v Todd Shipyard Corpn, para. 2627.

422   Bills of exchange—foreign bill—forged indorsement in foreign country—proper law to be applied

See Canada Life Assurance Co v Canadian Imperial Bank of Commerce, para. 261.

423   Consular Fees Act 1980

The Consular Fees Act 1980 re-enacts with amendments so much of the Consular Salaries and Fees Act 1891 as relates to consular fees together with certain enactments amending that Act. The Act received the royal assent on 1st May 1980 and came into force on that date.

Section 1 (1) enables Her Majesty by Order in Council to prescribe fees to be levied by persons authorised to exercise consular functions, or functions in the United Kingdom corresponding with consular functions. Section 1 (2) defines consular functions by reference to art. 5 of the Vienna Convention on Consular Relations, set out in the Consular Relations Act 1968, Sch. 1. Under s. 1 (3) the Secretary of State may make regulations governing the levying and handling of the fees. Section 1 (4) provides that tables of the fees, or extracts from them, are to be exhibited in any office where they are taken. Section 1 (5) repeals legislation which is replaced by this Act. Section 2 deals with short title.

424   Continental shelf—jurisdiction

The Continental Shelf (Jurisdiction) Order 1980, S.I. 1980 No. 184 (in force on 13th March 1980), revokes and re-enacts the provisions of the Continental Shelf (Jurisdiction) Order 1968, as amended. It also makes corresponding provision in respect of new areas designated as part of the Shelf by the Continental Shelf (Designation of Additional Areas) Order 1979, 1979 Halsbury's Abridgment para. 1842.

425   The Continental Shelf (Jurisdiction) (Amendment) Order 1980, S.I. 1980 No. 559 (in force on 20th May 1980), amends the Continental Shelf Jurisdiction Order 1980, *supra*, in respect of the definition of Scottish areas for the purposes of civil law and related matters.

426   ### Contract—foreign jurisdiction clause—application for stay of proceedings

The plaintiffs brought an action in the United Kingdom for damages for lost cargo shipped by the defendants, a Russian shipping company. The goods were shipped under a standard bill of lading which provided that any dispute was to be decided in the country where the carrier had its principal place of business. The defendants applied for the action to be stayed on the grounds that the dispute between the parties was one which the parties had agreed should be decided by the Russian court. *Held*, the court had a discretion whether or not to stay the proceedings. The general principle was to enforce such clauses as in the present case and it was for the plaintiffs to show strong grounds for not giving effect to the foreign jurisdiction clause. In the circumstances there were no such grounds and the application for stay of proceedings would be granted.

THE KISLOVODSK [1980] 1 Lloyd's Rep 183 (Queen's Bench Division: SHEEN J).

427   ### —— —— exclusive jurisdiction conferred on English courts—injunction to restrain proceedings in Italy

A ship bound for Italy broke down and was towed into a Tunisian port. The cargo-owners paid to have the ship towed to Italy in order to get the cargo to its destination and the shipowners refused to contribute towards the cost. The cargo-owners began legal proceedings in Italy and the ship was arrested there. The shipowners issued a writ in England claiming that the arrest of the ship in Italy was unlawful because of the exclusive jurisdiction clause in the bill of lading by which any and all legal proceedings against the carrier had to be brought in London. They applied for an interlocutory injunction for the release of the ship. *Held*, "any and all legal proceedings" should be construed as relating only to proceedings to establish liability and "carrier" did not include "ship". Hence the clause did not preclude proceedings in a foreign country for arrest of a ship. In any event, the English court would not grant an injunction to stop the arrest. When the arrest was made in good faith for the purpose of obtaining security for a just demand, English courts should not restrain it even though it might be said to be in breach of an exclusive jurisdiction clause. Justice required that the arrest should be upheld unless security for the ship's release was provided.

MIKE TRADING AND TRANSPORT LTD v PAGNAN (1980) Times, 2nd August (Court of Appeal: LORD DENNING MR, WALLER and DUNN LJJ).

428   ### —— —— when proceedings in England should be stayed

The plaintiffs brought an action in England for damages in respect of damaged cargo shipped by the defendants, an Egyptian company, to an English port. A clause of the bill of lading provided that any dispute was to be decided in the country where the carrier had its principal place of business. The defendants applied for the action to be stayed on the ground that the dispute between the parties was one which the parties had agreed should be decided by the Egyptian court. *Held*, the general principle was to enforce such clauses and it was for the plaintiffs to show strong grounds for not giving effect to a foreign jurisdiction clause. However, in the present case, the defendants contended that the deterioration of the cargo had occurred as a result of its unreasonably slow discharge in England, an event which had no direct connection with Egypt. Although there was a dispute as to when the cargo was damaged the most important evidence would be as to the condition of the cargo on its arrival, and that was in England. Further it was probable that the parties would obtain a more thorough investigation into the merits of the case in England and since the plaintiffs were entitled to invoke the Admiralty jurisdiction of the English courts, the defendants' application would be dismissed.

THE EL AMRIA, ARATRA POTATO CO LTD V EGYPTIAN NAVIGATION CO [1980] 1 Lloyd's Rep 390 (Queen's Bench Division: SHEEN J).

429   —— repudiation—overseas telex—breach committed outside jurisdiction

See *Brinkibon Ltd v Stahag Stahl und Stahlwarenhandelsgesellschaft MbH*, para. 490.

430   Divorce and nullity—jurisdiction of court to hear petition— domicile and habitual residence of respondent

A husband filed a petition for divorce and the question arose as to the wife's domicile and habitual residence, for the purposes of establishing the court's jurisdiction to hear the petition. The parties had moved to Canada in 1951 and had become Canadian citizens in 1956. They had returned to England in 1961 and had purchased a villa in Spain. In 1975 they had acquired the lease of a flat in Toronto and for fiscal reasons the husband had returned to Canada. The wife had purchased her own flat in London and had continued to live there except for visits to Canada and Spain. *Held*, both parties were domiciled in Canada. The wife's habitual residence was in England. She had been born and bred in England and had close relatives here. The Spanish villa was a holiday home only. The wife therefore was habitually resident in England over the relevant period.

OUNDIAN V OUNDIAN [1980] LS Gaz R 69 (Family Division: FRENCH J).

431   —— matrimonial orders—practice in magistrates' courts

See para. 1851.

432   —— recognition of foreign proceedings—nullity of marriage

Canada

A husband and wife were married in England. Both were resident in the United Kingdom but the husband was domiciled in Canada and the wife in America. The husband returned to Canada and the wife petitioned the High Court in England for a divorce. She was granted maintenance pending suit and after amending her petition she was granted a decree of nullity with further financial provision. Shortly afterwards the husband was granted a decree of nullity in Canada. The wife sought to have the order for further financial provision reciprocally enforced in Canada. The husband contended that the Canadian court did not have jurisdiction to enforce reciprocally the English order as the English court had not had jurisdiction to grant the nullity decree originally. *Held*, the English court had jurisdiction to annul a void marriage on the basis of one party's residence and the Canadian court had jurisdiction to annul a void marriage if the marriage was celebrated in Canada. Since both the domestic and foreign courts had jurisdiction the principle of reciprocity applied and the Canadian court had jurisdiction to hear an application to enforce reciprocally the financial provision order. Alternatively the English decree of nullity would be recognised on the basis of the "real and substantial connection" principle as the wife had lived continuously in England since prior to the marriage ceremony, and hence had a real and substantial connection with that country.

GWYN V MELLEN (1979) 101 DLR (3d) 608 (Court of Appeal of British Columbia). *Indyka v Indyka* [1969] 1 AC 33, HL applied.

433   Domestic Proceedings and Magistrates' Courts Act 1978— commencement

See para. 1976.

434   Domicile—acquisition of domicile of choice—relevant con- siderations

The testator, who had a domicile of origin in Rhode Island, moved to England at the age of four and spent fifty-eight of the remaining seventy-six years of his life there.

On the question as to where he was domiciled at the time of his death, the Crown argued that he had acquired a domicile of dependency in England, through his father, before he was twenty-one; or alternatively that he had acquired a domicile of choice in England. He had expressed his intention of returning to New York when he was no longer able to work actively on his English farm. *Held,* the testator's father had not acquired a domicile of choice in England at the relevant time and so the testator's most recent domicile of dependency was in Rhode Island. However, on the balance of probabilities the testator had acquired a domicile of choice in England, his expressed intention to return to the United States being based on a contingency which was indefinite, and the evidence being that he had made England his home with the intention of ending his days there.

Re FURSE, FURSE v IRC [1980] STC 596 (Chancery Division: Fox J).

435   Foreign judgments—reciprocal enforcement—Tonga

The Government has signed a convention with the Government of Tonga providing for the reciprocal enforcement and recognition of judgments in civil matters; see Cmnd. 7716. The convention applies to final and conclusive judgments of superior courts which make an order for the payment of money (other than taxes or sums in respect of a fine or other penalty) and are given after the date on which the convention enters into force. The judgment creditor may apply for the registration of the judgment within a period of six years; in England and Wales, the application is to be made to the High Court. The convention will enter into force three months after instruments of ratification have been exchanged.

436

The Reciprocal Enforcement of Foreign Judgments (Tonga) Order 1980, S.I. 1980 No. 1523 (in force on 18th December 1980), extends the Foreign Judgments (Reciprocal Enforcement) Act 1933, Pt. I to the judgments of the superior courts of Tonga and makes certain provisions regarding the registration and enforcement of such judgments.

437   Jurisdiction—action in rem—foreign proceedings—stay of English action

A judge in the Queen's Bench Division has held that the proper and natural forum for the resolution of a dispute concerning a collision six miles outside Stockholm was the Maritime Division of the Court in Stockholm.

The collision occurred in Swedish territorial waters between two vessels, one of which was being navigated by a Swedish pilot and the other led by a man who was qualified to act as a Swedish pilot. The two vessels had exchanged information in Swedish as to their movements by radio. Notwithstanding the fact that one of the parties' interests were being protected by an English insurance company, that party would not lose any legitimate personal or judicial advantage if the proceedings were heard in Stockholm and the English proceedings would accordingly be stayed.

THE WELLAMO, GULF OIL BELGIAN SA v FINLAND STEAMSHIP CO LTD [1980] 2 Lloyd's Rep 229 (Queen's Bench Division: SHEEN J).

438   —— restraint of proceedings in foreign court

See *Castanho v Brown & Root (UK) Ltd,* para. 2206.

439   Maintenance orders—reciprocal enforcement—Hague Convention countries—procedure

The Magistrates' Courts (Reciprocal Enforcement of Maintenance Orders) (Hague Convention Countries) Rules 1980, S.I. 1980 No. 108 (in force on 1st March 1980), make provision, in relation to magistrates' courts, for the various matters which are prescribed under the Maintenance Orders (Reciprocal Enforcement) Act 1972, Part I. The Reciprocal Enforcement of Maintenance Orders (Hague Convention Countries) Order 1979, Sch 3, 1979 Halsbury's Abridgment para. 438, sets out in full the provisions of the Act as they apply to the Hague Convention countries.

440   Procedure—limitation of actions—Law Commission recommendation

The Law Commission has provisionally recommended that all statutes of limitation (English and foreign) should be classified as substantive in this country for choice of law purposes. This recommendation is made subject to a recommendation that the effect given by English courts to the expiry of a period of limitation or prescription applicable under foreign law should be the same as would be given by a relevant foreign court and that there should be no change in the discretion of English courts in matters of public policy. The Law Commission further recommends that in applying a foreign statute of limitations English courts should have regard to the whole body of the domestic law of the lex causae, and in particular to any provisions which might operate to suspend the appropriate period; but where the period of limitation under the lex causae is suspended by reason of either party's absence from the jurisdiction, the English courts should apply the period of limitation without regard to such suspension. It is further suggested that, for the avoidance of doubt, it should be expressly stated by statute that a foreign judgment on a limitation point should be regarded by the English courts as giving rise to an estoppel per rem judicatam. See *Classification of Limitation in Private International Law* (Law Commission working paper 75) on which comments are invited by the Law Commission.

441   Property—movables—assignment—determination of title to goods

Works of art were stolen from the plaintiff in England and sold to the defendant in Italy. The defendant sent them to England for resale by a firm of auctioneers and the plaintiff brought an action in detinue and conversion. The question whether English or Italian domestic law was to be applied to determine title to the goods was directed to be heard as a preliminary issue on the assumption that the defendant had a good title to the goods under Italian law but not under English law. The plaintiff accepted the defendant's contention that the validity of a transfer of movable property was governed by the lex situs, but contended that because the case was largely connected with England, England should be regarded as the lex situs or an exception to the lex situs rule should be made on the ground of public policy in the case of stolen goods. *Held*, if personal property was disposed of in a way which was binding according to the lex situs, that disposition was binding everywhere. This rule applied to a transaction whereby a person acquired title under the lex situs and thus destroyed the proprietary rights of a former owner even if the former owner had never possessed the property in that country nor consented to its being taken there. Nor was there any exception to the rule in the case of stolen goods taken abroad and then returned to England. Italian law should be applied to determine title to the goods notwithstanding their connection with England, since to introduce a fictional English situs would lead to intolerable uncertainty.

WINKWORTH v CHRISTIE MANSON & WOODS LTD [1980] 1 All ER 1121 (Chancery Division: SLADE J). *Cammell v Sewell* (1860) 5 H & N 728, *Todd v Armsur* (1882) 9 R 901 and *Embiricos v Anglo-Austrian Bank* [1905] 1 KB 677, CA applied.

Detinue has been abolished: Torts (Interference with Goods) Act 1977, s. 2 (1).

442   Tort—location of tort—injury sustained in England caused by foreign machine—service of writ out of jurisdiction

RSC Ord. 11, r. 1 (h) provides that the service of a writ or notice of a writ out of the jurisdiction is permissible with the leave of the court if the action begun by the writ is founded on a tort committed within the jurisdiction.

An employee of an English company was injured by the malfunctioning of a German made machine bought in England. The English company contended that the manufacturers were joint tortfeasors in an action in tort brought by the employee. They subsequently obtained leave to issue and serve a third party notice on the manufacturers under RSC Ord. 11, r. 1 (h). The manufacturers appealed. *Held*, where a foreign company had a distribution network in England enabling

English companies to purchase their products, any tort committed in relation to those products was committed partly within and partly outside the jurisdiction, in that the product was distributed within but manufactured outside the jurisdiction. The court had to consider where the wrongful act from which the damage flowed was done and not where the damage was suffered. In the present case what gave the employee a cause of action was not the manufacture of the goods in Germany but the putting on to the English market of a defective product without any warning of the defect. The tort, therefore, if any, was committed within the jurisdiction and accordingly the appeal would be dismissed.

CASTREE v E. R. SQUIBB & SONS LTD [1980] 2 All ER 589 (Court of Appeal: BUCKLEY, ACKNER and OLIVER LJJ). *Distillers Co (Biochemicals) Ltd v Thompson* [1971] AC 458 and dicta of Lord Justice du Parcq in *George Munro Ltd v American Cyanamid and Chemical Corporation* [1944] 1 KB 432 at 440 applied.

CONSTITUTIONAL LAW

Halsbury's Laws of England (4th edn.), Vol. 8, paras. 801–1647

443   Civil Service—Pay Research Unit—withdrawal of services by Crown—breach of collective agreement

The Civil Service Pay Research Unit was set up to collate information about pay and conditions outside the Civil Service, for the purpose of comparability, on behalf of the Council of Civil Service Unions. An agreement in 1974 provided for six months' notice of a proposal for pay review and that the research unit should deliver a report for negotiations. Notice to terminate the 1974 agreement was given and the research unit refused to deliver the report for 1979–1980, claiming that its work had come to an end. The CCSU applied for an order that the report should be handed over. *Held*, the research unit was a Government body and the Crown therefore had the right to withdraw its services even if it involved a breach of the 1974 agreement. The machinery for negotiation of pay and conditions was based on extra legal sanctions and there was no right which could be asserted in a court action, proprietary or contractual, to require the pay research unit to deliver reports or continue its work.

KENDALL v MORGAN (1980) Times, 4th December (Chancery Division: VINELOTT J).

444   Coinage—Trial of the Pyx

The Trial of the Pyx (Amendment) Order 1980, S.I. 1980 No. 1967 (in force on 18th December 1980), amends the Trial of the Pyx Order 1975, 1975 Halsbury's Abridgment para. 461 by providing for the minimum numbers of coins to be set apart by the Deputy Master of the Mint for Trial.

445   Comptroller and Auditor General—functions and responsibilities

The government has published a Green Paper setting out its provisional views on the role and responsibilities of the Comptroller and Auditor General. This represents the first stage in a review of the Exchequer and Audit Departments Acts 1866 to 1957. It is suggested that the role of the comptroller should be: to provide a basic financial and regularity audit of departmental accounts; to undertake an examination of the economy and efficiency with which public funds are spent; and (in appropriate cases) to investigate the effectiveness of programmes and projects in meeting established policy goals. The effective working relationship between the comptroller and the Public Accounts Committee, it is suggested, should be preserved. In the case of non-departmental bodies, an important objective of the comptroller's examination should be to review the effectiveness of the arrangements under which ministers monitor and control the payment of public funds to the bodies. Decisions whether to provide for audit or inspection of such bodies by the comptroller should be taken case by case but the comptroller should not cover the nationalised industries. It is proposed that obsolete powers of direction under the Act should be repealed. It is also suggested that the independence of the Comptroller of both Parliament and of the executive should be maintained and that he should remain an office holder under the Crown. See *The Role of the Comptroller and Auditor General*, 1980, Cmnd 7845.

446　Criminal offence committed by Crown—Crown's immunity from prosecution—nomination of fictitious individual as defendant

See *Barnett v French*, para. 735.

447　Foreign Compensation Commission—financial provision

The Foreign Compensation (Financial Provisions) Order 1980, S.I. 1980 No. 186 (in force on 13th March 1980) directs the Foreign Compensation Commission to pay into the Exchequer, out of the funds paid to the Commission for the purpose of being distributed under the Foreign Compensation Acts 1950 and 1962, amounts in respect of the Commission's expenses during the period 1st October 1978 to 30th September 1979 in relation to the distribution of those funds.

448　Location of Offices Bureau—dissolution

The Location of Offices Bureau (Revocation) Order 1980, S.I. 1980 No. 560 (in force on 1st May 1980), dissolves the Bureau.

449　Ministers—salaries

The Ministerial and other Salaries and Pensions Order 1980 No. 1073 (in force on 28th July 1980), increases salaries payable to Ministers, salaried Members of the Opposition and the Speaker of the House of Commons under the Ministerial and other Salaries Act 1975, 1975 Halsbury's Abridgment para. 474. The salaries payable up to 12th June 1981 represent the second stage of the implementation of the recommended rates increased by certain percentages and those payable after that date represent the third and final stage of the implementation of those rates with increases. The order also provides that for pension purposes those salaries and those of certain other office holders should be regarded as being payable at the increased third stage rate. The Ministerial and other Salaries Order 1979, 1979 Halsbury's Abridgment para. 449 is revoked.

450　Northern Ireland

See NORTHERN IRELAND.

451　Public service pensions

See PENSIONS AND SUPERANNUATION.

452　Secretary of State—transfer of functions—legal aid in criminal proceedings and costs in criminal cases

See para. 1778.

453　Treasure trove—Crown's right—silver alloy coins

Roman coins, known as antoniniani and made mainly of base metal with a small percentage of silver, were found on land within the liberties of the Duchy of Lancaster and occupied by the defendants. The court was asked to determine whether the coins were the property of the duchy or of the defendants. *Held*, treasure trove had always been limited to coins that were gold or silver. On the facts, these coins were not silver, therefore they were not treasure trove and the Crown had no claim to them.

ATTORNEY-GENERAL OF THE DUCHY OF LANCASTER v G. E. OVERTON (FARMS) LTD

[1980] 3 All ER 503 (Chancery Division: DILLON J). *Case of Mines* (1568) 1 Plowd 310 and dictum of Lord Simon in *Palser v Grinling* [1948] AC 291, HL, applied.

CONSUMER PROTECTION AND FAIR TRADING

Halsbury's Laws of England (3rd edn.), Vol. 38, paras. 94–185

454   Article

Fair Trading at Home and Away, Gavin McFarlane: 124 Sol Jo 419.

455   Dangerous substances and preparations—safety

The Dangerous Substances and Preparations (Safety) Regulations 1980, S.I. 1980 No. 136 (in force, except for regulation 3, on 11th February 1980), implements Council Directive (EEC) 76/769, as amended by Council Directive (EEC) 79/663. Reg. 2 amends the Aerosol Dispensers (EEC Requirements) Regulations 1977, 1977 Halsbury's Abridgment para. 475, which prescribe technical specifications with which aerosol dispensers must comply. Reg. 4 lays down requirements regarding textile products intended to come into contact with the skin. Reg. 3 (which came into operation on 1st March 1980) prohibits the use of certain dangerous substances in certain types of ornamental objects.

456   Novelties—safety

The Novelties (Safety) Regulations 1980, S.I. 1980 No. 958 (in force on 15th July 1980, except reg. 2 (c) in force on 20th August 1980 and reg. 2 (a) in force on 9th October 1980), prohibit persons from supplying, offering or agreeing to supply, exposing for supply or possessing for supply any substance for making balloons which contains benzene either as part of a balloon-making kit or separately, any injurious tear-gas capsule, or any article containing more than 1·5 millilitres of sulphides of ammonia or any mixture or solution thereof which is designed or intended to afford amusement by means of the obnoxious properties of the sulphides.

457   Price marking—food

See FOOD, DAIRIES AND SLAUGHTERHOUSES.

458   —— petrol

The Price Marking (Petrol) Order 1980, S.I. 1980 No. 1121 (in force on 1st January 1981), prohibits the indication of the price of petrol by reference to the litre unless (i) the indication of the price of the petrol on the pump required to be given is followed by an adjacent indication of the equivalent price per gallon; (ii) the price of the petrol followed by the equivalent price per gallon are indicated in close proximity elsewhere on the pump or near the pump; or (iii) where the premises are price display premises, a price equivalent chart is displayed on the pump or near the pump. Where all or any of the pumps are being adapted to measure in litres there will be a transitional period of twenty-eight days to enable other pumps to be converted to metric sales. The Petrol Prices (Display) Order 1978, 1978 Halsbury's Abridgment para. 460 as amended is revoked.

459   Trade descriptions

See TRADE DESCRIPTIONS.

460   **Upholstered furniture—safety regulations**

The Upholstered Furniture (Safety) Regulations 1980, S.I. 1980 No. 725 (in force on 1st October 1980 except reg. 5 (1) which comes into force on 31st December 1982), apply to certain types of upholstered seating furniture, and prescribe tests to verify the resistance of the upholstery to ignition by smouldering cigarettes and by lighted matches (simulated in the tests by a butane flame). Furniture first supplied in the United Kingdom on or after 1st October 1980 and furniture supplied before that date but only to an own-brand dealer, must bear warning labels from that date if it does not satisfy those tests. Regulation 5 (1) will prohibit manufacturers and importers and own-brand dealers from supplying, offering to supply, agreeing to supply, exposing for supply or possessing for supply furniture which does not satisfy the smouldering cigarette test.

CONTEMPT OF COURT

Halsbury's Laws of England (4th edn.), Vol. 9, paras. 1–200

461   **Article**

Contempt of Court—the Leveller Case, A. Tettenborn (discussion of *A-G v Leveller Magazine* [1979] 1 All ER 745, HL, 1979 Halsbury's Abridgment para. 469): 124 Sol Jo 5.

462   **Breach of undertaking—pre-incorporation undertaking by predecessor company—whether contempt of court**

See *Re an agreement between members of the British Concrete Pipe Association*, para. 379.

463   —— **unintentional breach—whether contempt of court**

The Court of Appeal has held that a breach of an undertaking given to the court was a contempt of that court, notwithstanding that it may have been unintentional or accidental.

Pending the determination of an appeal to the House of Lords, the Inland Revenue returned certain documents, seized from the taxpayer, to him on his absolute undertaking given in court, that the documents would be redelivered to the Revenue if the House of Lords held that they had been lawfully seized pursuant to valid warrants granted under the Taxes Management Act 1970, s. 20C. The House of Lords found in favour of the Revenue, but the documents were not returned. The taxpayer maintained that they had been inadvertently discarded by his secretary and was fined £1,000 for contempt of court.

RE ROSSMINSTER LTD AND TUCKER (1980) Times, 23rd May (Court of Appeal: LORD DENNING MR, BRIGHTMAN LJ and SIR PATRICK BROWNE).

For substantive proceedings, see [1980] 1 All ER 80, HL, 1979 Halsbury's Abridgment para. 1532.

464   **Civil contempt—discovery of documents—abuse of process of discovery**

See *Home Office v Harman*, para. 889.

465   **Criminal contempt—contempt in connection with proceedings in an inferior court—local valuation court**

A religious sect sought to have its premises recognised as a place of public religious worship for the purpose of rate relief. The Attorney General and others sought injunctions restraining the BBC from televising a programme about the sect whilst the case before the local valuation court was still pending. By RSC Ord. 52, r. 1 (2) the Divisional Court had the power to make an order in respect of a contempt committed in connection with proceedings in an inferior court. The local valuation court was held to be an "inferior court" and the decision was upheld by the Court of Appeal. The BBC appealed. *Held*, a local valuation court was a court which discharged administrative functions and was not a court of law. It was therefore not within the class of "inferior courts of law" within RSC Ord. 52, r. 1 (2) to which the law of contempt applied. The appeal would therefore be allowed.

A-G v British Broadcasting Corpn [1980] 3 WLR 109 (House of Lords: Viscount Dilhorne, Lord Salmon, Lord Edmund-Davies, Lord Fraser of Tullybelton and Lord Scarman). Decision of the Court of Appeal [1979] 3 All ER 45, 1979 Halsbury's Abridgment para. 467 reversed.

466   —— contempt in face of court—intoxication

Canada

After attending court in the morning and finding that his case would not be called until the afternoon, the accused spent the interval drinking and consequently was unable to instruct his counsel or fully understand the proceedings. He was found guilty of contempt. On appeal, he contended that he had no intention to show disrespect to the court. *Held*, such an intention was not an essential ingredient of the offence. The appeal would be dismissed.

R v Perkins [1980] 4 WWR 763 (Court of Appeal of British Columbia).

467   —— publication of juror's account of jury room discussion—whether amounts to interference with administration of justice

The Attorney-General made an application for an order for contempt under RSC Ord. 52, r. 9 against the defendant publishers, with regard to an article in a publication, in which a juror in the trial of a well-known politician disclosed certain secrets from the jury room. The publication took place after the end of the trial. The defendants contended that once a trial was concluded, there was no interference with justice and therefore no contempt was committed in disclosing what had happened in the jury room. *Held*, there were powerful arguments against breaking the secrets of a jury room and serious consequences could arise from an approach to a juror, particularly after a trial which had attracted great publicity. However, disclosure of the secrets of the jury room was not a contempt of court per se. The test was whether in the light of the circumstances of the case, such disclosures tended to imperil the finality of jury verdicts or to affect adversely the attitude of future jurors and the quality of their deliberations. On the basis of the facts in, and circumstances of, the present case the publication of the article did not amount to a contempt of court and the application would be dismissed.

A-G v New Statesman and Nation Publishing Co Ltd [1980] 1 All ER 644 (Queen's Bench Division: Lord Widgery CJ and Park J). A-G v Leveller Magazine Ltd [1979] 1 All ER 745, HL, 1979 Halsbury's Abridgment para. 469 applied.

CONTRACT

Halsbury's Laws of England (4th edn.), Vol. 9, paras. 201–750

468   Articles

Breach of Contract and Exclusion Clauses, L W Melville: 130 NLJ 646.
The Nature of Fundamental Breach, L. W. Melville: 130 NLJ 307.
Ouster Clauses, Henry E. Markson: 124 Sol Jo 420.

469   Breach of contract—contractual licence—order for specific performance

An extremist political party contracted with a local council to hire a hall for a private conference. The party immediately paid the agreed hiring fee. Before the conference was held, a new local council was elected, and proceeded to rescind the agreement. The money was repaid to the party. The party was unable to find another venue for its conference and subsequently brought an action against the council claiming specific performance of the contract or, alternatively, damages for breach of contract. A summary judgment under RSC Ord. 14 was applied for. The council admitted repudiation of the contract without lawful excuse but contended that specific performance was inappropriate as it was likely that the party's use of the hall would provoke breaches of the peace. The case was dealt with under Ord. 14 and an order for specific performance was made. The council appealed. *Held*, the judge had not erred in dealing with the case under Ord. 14 because the issues were clear and the points of substance could be decided in such proceedings without ordering a trial. There was no reason why specific performance of a contractual licence of short duration could not be ordered by the court. It was the duty of the court to protect any interest in land, whether an estate or licence, by injunction or specific performance, if it was appropriate. In such an appropriate case the court could order specific performance where a licensee's licence was unlawfully repudiated before he entered into possession. Freedom of speech and assembly and the sanctity of contracts had to be considered in the present case before deciding whether to make an order for specific performance. The judge had not erred in the exercise of his discretion in making such an order and the appeal would be dismissed.

VERRALL v GREAT YARMOUTH BOROUGH COUNCIL [1980] 1 All ER 839 (Court of Appeal: LORD DENNING MR, ROSKILL and CUMMING-BRUCE LJJ). *Winter Garden Theatre (London) Ltd v Millenium Productions Ltd* [1947] 2 All ER 331 and dictum of Darling J in *Gilbey v Cossey* [1911–1913] All ER Rep 644 at 645 applied. *Glass v Woolgar and Roberts (No. 2)* (1897) 41 Sol Jo 573 and dictum of Lord Greene MR in *Booker v Palmer* [1942] 2 All ER 674 at 677 disapproved. *Thompson v Park* [1944] 2 All ER 477 not followed.

470   —— **fundamental breach—exclusion clause—effect of breach on validity of clause**

See *Photo Production Ltd v Securicor Transport Ltd*, para. 480.

471   —— **negligence—effect of plaintiff's lack of care**

Australia

The plaintiffs were a firm of wool brokers established in Switzerland and carrying on business in Australia. The defendants had acted as their auditors in Australia since 1936. A wool futures exchange was established in Sydney in 1960, whereupon the plaintiffs established a futures division and arranged for the audit contract to be extended accordingly. The plaintiffs traded both as brokers and on their own account. The Sydney office was given permission to trade in a limited way on the plaintiffs' account, but the office consistently exceeded its authority and members of the staff themselves traded on their own account, rendering the plaintiffs liable as principals. The plaintiffs suffered loss, caused primarily by unauthorised trading by the Sydney office and by trading by members of staff. They successfully sued the defendants for breach of contract, the court holding that they had not acted unreasonably in the conduct of their business and that the cause of the loss was the defendants' breach of duty. The defendants appealed, contending that certain terms, e.g. that the plaintiffs would inform them of known breaches of authority by staff, should be implied into the audit contract, and alleging contributory negligence. *Held*, it could not be said that the real or proximate cause of loss was the plaintiffs' lack of care rather than the defendants' breaches of their duties under the audit contract nor that the cause was any breach of terms implied by law into that contract. The appeal would be dismissed.

SIMONIUS VISCHER & CO v HOLT & THOMPSON [1979] 2 NSWLR 322 (Court of Appeal of New South Wales).

472   —— termination by innocent party—extent of liability of defaulting party

Canada
In 1966 shipowners agreed to carry cargoes to various European ports until a date in
1972. When they failed to provide ships in April and May 1970 the shippers
terminated the contract. In the ensuing action the shipowners contended that their
liability was confined to the failure to ship cargoes in 1970. *Held*, their liability
extended to their failure to ship during the remainder of the term of the contract.
    CELGAR LTD v STAR BULK SHIPPING CO (1979) 101 DLR (3d) 61 (Court of Appeal
of British Columbia).

473   —— waiver of breach—negotiations for extension of completion
date

See *Prosper Homes Ltd v Hambros Bank Executor and Trustee Co Ltd*, para. 2455.

474   Building contracts

See BUILDING CONTRACTS, ARCHITECTS AND ENGINEERS.

475   Capacity of parties—inter-office trading transactions—whether
genuine trading transactions

The Hamburg and Munich offices of a company often traded independently of each
other. The Hamburg office entered into a contract to sell a quantity of soya bean
meal to the buyers. Contracts for the buying and selling of soya bean meal were
made between the two offices. All the contracts were for shipment c.i.f. Rotterdam
and incorporated the terms of a standard form GAFTA contract which provided
that shippers had to give notice of appropriation to the first buyer within ten days
of the date of the bill of lading. Ten days after shipment was effected the Hamburg
office, as "shippers", gave notice of appropriation to the Munich office as first
buyers. The Munich office as "subsequent sellers" then gave notice of appropriation
to the buyer. The buyer contended that the notice was out of time and that the
Munich office could not be regarded as "subsequent sellers". *Held*, it was known in
the trade that the company's offices often traded as separate legal entities and the
buyer should have envisaged that there might be a chain of contracts. Once it was
established that there was a general trade practice regarding these inter-office
transactions as part of a chain it was possible to apply the words "buyer" and
"subsequent seller" to such transactions and it was in effect extending the words of the
GAFTA contract provision on notice of appropriation. The offices had therefore
entered into genuine transactions, the contracts were valid and notice of appropriation
was given in time.
    BREMER HANDELSGESELLSCHAFT mbH v TOEPFER [1980] 2 Lloyd's Rep 43 (Court
of Appeal: MEGAW, LAWTON and BROWNE LJJ). Decision of Donaldson J [1978] 1
Lloyd's Rep 643, 1978 Halsbury's Abridgment para. 484 affirmed.

476   Collateral contract—intention to create legal obligation—validity

See *Independent Broadcasting Authority v BICC Construction Ltd*, para. 485.

477   Construction—variation of contract—breach—waiver

A contract for the sale of American wheat made provision concerning the natural
weight of the wheat shipped, to be indicated by official inspection certificates at
loading. It was provided that a certificate would be acceptable even though issued
by a non-official laboratory or organisation, so long as it was independent, being a
certificate showing the natural weight of the goods in terms of kilograms per
hectolitre, showing the equivalent in those terms of the natural weight expressed in
the original American official certificates in terms of pounds per bushel.
Subsequently, the presentation of a certificate by an official laboratory in respect of
natural weight was required. Shortly after shipment, the sellers notified the buyers

of the natural weight which had been shipped, expressed in kilograms per hectolitre. At the same time they sent to the confirming bank official certificates of inspection, weight and analysis, together with an invoice based on the natural weight. The natural weight shown in the invoice was as stated in an unofficial laboratory certificate and was expressed in kilograms per hectolitre. The weight stated was not a mathematical conversion from the natural weight in pounds per bushel stated in the official certificate and was higher than the mathematical equivalent would be. The buyers did not see any of the documents presented to the bank. The buyers' claim for the amount overpaid against the invoice was rejected by the sellers. *Held*, the amendment of the contract to require a certificate issued by an official laboratory, did not alter the original contract in any other way than to make provision that it had to be issued by an official laboratory instead of being a certificate which could be provided by an independent laboratory or organisation. The certificates tendered by the sellers showed the natural weight in kilograms per hectolitre which was substantially greater than the correct equivalent of the pounds per bushel natural weight stated in the official certificate. It could not be said that merely by electing not to reject the documents the buyers had given up their right to claim damages in respect of damage caused to them by the breach of contract involved in the tendering of wrong documents. Nor were there any grounds for holding that the buyers were estopped from claiming damages, and therefore the buyers were entitled to the amount claimed.

ETS SOULES & CIE v INTERNATIONAL TRADE DEVELOPMENT CO LTD [1980] 1 Lloyd's Rep 129 (Court of Appeal: MEGAW, LAWTON and BROWNE LJJ). Decision of Robert Goff J [1979] 2 Lloyd's Rep 122, 1979 Halsbury's Abridgment para. 483 affirmed.

478　　Contractual term—innominate term—effect of breach of term

See *Bunge Corporation v Tradax Exports SA*, para. 2447.

479　　Exclusion clause—pre-shipment inspection clause excluding liability—provisions of clause not wholly complied with—effect on liability

See *Kollerich & Cie SA v State Trading Corpn of India*, para. 2439.

480　　—— scope of clause—fundamental breach—whether clause deprived of effect

An employee of the defendant security company deliberately lit a fire which set alight the plaintiffs' factory, while on night patrol duty. The factory and stock were destroyed. The defendants denied liability on the basis of exception clauses contained in their contract with the plaintiffs excluding liability for injurious acts or defaults by employees. The Court of Appeal held that the defendants could not rely on the exception clauses because they had committed a fundamental breach of contract. The defendants appealed. *Held*, there was no rule of law by which exception clauses were deprived of effect, regardless of their terms, where there was a fundamental breach of contract. In deciding whether an exception clause was to be applied, the question was one of construction of the contract as a whole. In the instant case, on their true construction the exception clauses were clear and unambiguous and covered deliberate acts of employees. The defendants' liability was therefore excluded and the appeal would, accordingly, be allowed.

PHOTO PRODUCTION LTD v SECURICOR TRANSPORT LTD [1980] 1 All ER 556 (House of Lords: LORD WILBERFORCE, LORD DIPLOCK, LORD SALMON, LORD KEITH OF KINKEL and LORD SCARMAN). Decision of the Court of Appeal [1978] 3 All ER 146, 1978 Halsbury's Abridgment para. 494 reversed. *Suisse Atlantique Société D'Armement Maritime SA v NV Rotterdemsche Kolen Centrale* [1966] 2 All ER 61, HL, explained and applied; *Charterhouse Credit Co Ltd v Tolly* [1963] 2 All ER 432, CA, *Harbutt's Plasticine Ltd v Wayne Tank and Pump Co Ltd* [1970] 1 All ER 225, CA, and *Wathes (Western) Ltd v Austins Menswear Ltd* [1976] 1 Lloyd's Rep 14, CA, 1975 Halsbury's Abridgment para. 522, overruled.

481   Foreign jurisdiction clause

See CONFLICT OF LAWS.

482   Frustration—application of doctrine to leases of land

See *National Carriers Ltd v Panalpina (Northern) Ltd*, para. 1710.

483   —— charterparty—effect   of   strike—whether   charterparty divisible

In November 1978 a vessel was chartered for seven consecutive voyages in 1979. After one voyage the vessel was unable to load the cargo due to a strike. The parties agreed to an addendum no. 2 to the charterparty by which the owners were permitted to take the vessel for one intermediate voyage, the charterparty was extended for a further seven voyages in 1980 and if the strike continued the situation was then to be discussed without obligation. The strike continued and by addendum no. 3 the charterers agreed to pay the owners compensation. An intermediate voyage took place and the charterers sought the return of the vessel in case the strike ended, but the owners fixed her for a further intermediate voyage. Arbitration took place on 26th September 1979 and the arbitrator held that the whole of the charterparty contract of November 1978 was frustrated, disregarding the addenda and considering only the seven voyages for 1979 and not those contemplated for 1980. The strike ended on 5th October. Leave to appeal was given and the Court of Appeal declined to interfere. On the hearing of the appeal, it was held that the charterparty and the addenda comprised one indivisible contract which was not frustrated. On further appeal by the owners, *held*, under the charterparty of November 1978 and the addendum no. 2 the contemplated voyages for 1979 and 1980 were distinct, separate and independent adventures and the arbitrator had rightly considered whether or not the charterparty for the 1979 season had been frustrated. Since the arbitrator had properly directed himself that, because of the strike, performance of the charterparty for 1979 must be radically different from what had been undertaken under the contract and his finding was reasonable, his conclusion that on 26th September 1979 the charterparty was frustrated in respect of the 1979 season should not have been interfered with. The appeal would be allowed.

The court laid down guidelines on the giving of leave to appeal under the Arbitration Act 1979. Under s. 1 (4), leave was not to be given unless the point of law could substantially affect the rights of one or both parties. Secondly, by reason of s. 1 (2), (3), (7), the decision of the arbitrator was final unless the judge gave leave. Having given leave, the judge's decision was final unless he certified that the question was of general importance or was one which for some reason should be considered by the Court of Appeal. In the case of a contractual clause which was not in a standard form, the interpretation of which was not likely to arise again, the judge should not give leave to appeal. In the case of a standard form clause, he should not give leave unless he considered it a really debatable point. Leave should be refused if the arbitrator had put upon the clause the meaning generally accepted in the trade. The decision of an arbitrator on frustration should normally be accepted.

PIONEER SHIPPING LTD v BTP TIOXIDE LTD [1980] 3 WLR 326 (Court of Appeal: LORD DENNING MR, TEMPLEMAN and WATKINS LJJ). *Larrinaga and Co Ltd v Société Franco-Americaine des Phosphates de Medulla, Paris* (1922) 28 Com Cas 1, CA (1923) 29 Com Cas 1, HL; *Jackson v Union Marine Insurance Co Ltd* (1874) LR 10 CP 125; *Davis Contractors Ltd v Fareham UDC* [1956] AC 696, HL applied.

484   Implied term—contract affected by intervening legislation—whether court can imply term to give efficacy to contract as result of legislation

See *Frobisher (Second Investments) Ltd v Kiloran Trust Co Ltd*, para. 1705.

485   —— contract for work and materials—liability of contractor

A television mast owned by a broadcasting company (IBA) was designed and constructed on behalf of a firm of contractors (EMI) by a company of structural engineers (BICC). The design of the mast was new and untested in the United Kingdom. It was common knowledge that the new design would be subjected to various stresses which were not fully understood and the IBA was concerned at the likelihood of the mast collapsing after a similar mast had swayed violently in adverse weather conditions. BICC, on the advice of an expert engineer in this field, wrote to the IBA guaranteeing the stability of the mast. The IBA interpreted this as a contractual warranty and took no further action. Three years after its installation the mast collapsed due to the accumulation of ice on the structure and low winds. The IBA brought an action against EMI as the principal contractors and BICC as sub-contractors claiming damages for breach of contract and negligence. *Held*, (1) the duty owed by BICC to the IBA was to use the care and skill to be expected of competent structural engineers. They had failed in that duty because they had omitted to take into account, in their design of the mast, the effect of stresses on the mast likely to be created in certain weather conditions. Although it had been found that the collapse was caused by two separate incidents at the same time, all that had to be shown was that a fault in BICC's design caused or materially contributed to the collapse. (ii) As the design was found to be negligent it followed that the statement made by BICC as to the mast's stability was negligent, but whether the statement amounted to a contractual warranty was a mixed question of law and fact. Collateral contracts had to be strictly proved and the existence of an animus contrahendi on the part of all parties had to be shown. In the present case the alleged warranty was not given at the time of making the main contract and so was not collateral to that contract. Further there was no evidence of any intention of creating such a contractual obligation. (iii) It was established that in a building contract for work and material there was an implied term that the main contractor accepted responsibility for materials provided by the nominated sub-contractor. In the present case therefore, EMI were liable for BICC and were in breach of their contract with the IBA.

INDEPENDENT BROADCASTING AUTHORITY v BICC CONSTRUCTION LTD (1980) 15th May (House of Lords: VISCOUNT DILHORNE, LORD SALMON, LORD EDMUND-DAVIES, LORD FRASER OF TULLYBELTON and LORD SCARMAN). *M'Gee v National Coal Board* 1973 SC (HL) 37, *Herbert Symons & Co v Buckleton* [1913] AC 30 and *Young & Marten Ltd v McManus Childs Ltd* [1969] 1 AC 454 applied. *Norta Wallpapers Ltd v John Sisk Ltd* [1978] IR 114 distinguished.

486   —— football contract—reasonable opportunity to perform

The plaintiff football club transferred a player to the defendant club. The agreement provided that an additional sum would be paid to the plaintiff when the player had scored twenty goals in first team competitive football. After a change in management the player was dropped by the defendant and subsequently transferred to another club. It was found that he had played eighteen games for the defendant. Although he had not scored the specified number of goals, the plaintiff claimed the additional fee. *Held*, BRIGHTMAN LJ dissenting, in order to give effect to the intention of the parties, it had to be implied that the player would be given a reasonable opportunity to play in a sufficient number of games so that he could have the chance of scoring twenty goals. By not affording that opportunity the defendant had prevented the plaintiff from earning the additional fee and was therefore in breach of contract.

BOURNEMOUTH AND BOSCOMBE ATHLETIC FOOTBALL CLUB CO LTD v MANCHESTER UNITED FOOTBALL CLUB LTD (1980) Times, 22nd May (Court of Appeal: LORD DENNING MR, DONALDSON and BRIGHTMAN LJJ). *Southern Foundries (1926) Ltd v Shirlaw* [1940] 2 All ER 445, HL applied.

487   —— indemnity—creation of rights of indemnity—enforceability

See *Yeung Kai Yung v Hong Kong and Shanghai Banking Corpn*, para. 1378.

488   —— loan agreement—securities acquired by English company with foreign bank loan—equitable charge

See *Swiss Bank Corpn v Lloyds Bank Ltd*, para. 1094.

489   Intention to create legal relations—retirement allowance stated to be at discretion of board of directors

Canada

The arrangements for the retirement of a company employee were stated to be at the pleasure of the board and subject to its sole discretion. It was held that the letter setting out the arrangements was not intended to create a legally binding contract and did not confer any legal rights on the recipient.

     Moir v J. P. Porter Co Ltd (1979) 103 DLR (3d) 22 (Supreme Court of Nova Scotia, Appeal Division).

490   Offer and acceptance—opening of letter of credit in accordance with offer—acceptance not communicated

The parties dealt in steel, the buyers in England acting for a Swiss company, the sellers in Austria where they were incorporated. The buyers, by a telex, offered to buy a quantity of steel. The sellers accepted the offer by telex subject to amendments and requested the buyers to open a letter of credit. The buyers issued instructions to a London bank to open the letter of credit required. Subsequently the sellers withdrew from the contract. The buyers were given leave to issue and serve notice of a writ out of the jurisdiction under RSC Ord. 11 alleging breach of contract. On appeal, *held*, the telex sent by the sellers was a counter-offer. The opening of a letter of credit within the jurisdiction in accordance with an offer did not constitute an acceptance since it only indicated that the buyers intended to accept the sellers' counter-offer. The general principle that an acceptance had to be communicated in order that a contract might be constitued applied in the present case. Furthermore the repudiation of a contract outside the jurisdiction communicated by telex did not constitute a breach of contract within the jurisdiction where the telex was received. Accordingly the appeal would be allowed.

     Brinkibon Ltd v Stahag Stahl und Stahlwarenhandelsgesellschaft mbH (1980) Times, 14th June (Court of Appeal: Stephenson and Templeman LJJ). *Entores Ltd v Miles Far East Corporation* [1955] 2 All ER 493, CA. *Atlantic Underwriting Agencies Ltd v Compagnia di Assicurazione di Miliano SpA* [1979] 2 Lloyd's Rep 240, 1979 Halsbury's Abridgement para. 427 applied.

491   Performance—implied   term—football   contract—reasonable opportunity to perform

See *Bournemouth and Boscombe Athletic Football Club Co Ltd v Manchester United Football Club Ltd*, para. 486.

492   Privity—clause conferring benefit on stranger to contract— reliance on clause by stranger

Canada

A marine carrier agreed under a contract with the owners, attested by a bill of lading, to carry a consignment of electronic calculators from Japan to Canada. On arrival in Canada one consignment was stored by a company of cargo-handlers in accordance with an agreement made with the carrier. Whilst being stored part of the consignment was stolen and the owners subsequently claimed damages for breach of contract. Both the carrier and cargo-handlers contended that, by virtue of the agreed provisions in the contract, bill of lading and agreement, they were exempt from liability. *Held*, in the absence of gross negligence on the carrier's part and since the loss was proved to have occurred after the goods were unloaded, the carrier was entitled to rely on a limitation of liability clause in the contract and that action against it would fail. When a bill of lading contained a "Himalaya" clause extending the benefit of a limitation of liability clause to a cargo-handler, he was entitled to the advantage of such an exemption even though he was not party to the bill of lading. The cargo-handlers relied primarily on their contract of services with the carrier in which it was provided that liability for the custody of the consignment was limited to the same extent as permitted by the original contract of carriage. The owners had accepted this term when they agreed the contract of carriage and the cargo-handlers were exempt to the same degree as the carrier. The action would be dismissed.

MARUBENI AMERICA CORPN v MITSUI OSK LINES LTD (1979) 96 DLR (3d) 518 (Federal Court of Canada, Trial Division).

493   Quasi-contract—money paid to the defendant's use—payment under compulsion

Canada

In order to obtain approval for subdivision of land into building lots a property developer paid money to a municipality under a byelaw which was ultra vires. He did not own the land and was not obliged to buy it. He had regarded the byelaw as ultra vires. On a claim for recovery of the money, *held*, it had been paid under a mistake of law. An exception to the general rule that money so paid was not recoverable applied where the payment was made under the compulsion of urgent and pressing necessity. The exception did not apply in the present case and the claim for recovery would fail.

G. GORDON FOSTER DEVELOPMENTS LTD. v TOWNSHIP OF LANGLEY (1979) 102 DLR (3d) 730 (Court of Appeal of British Columbia).

494   Repudiation—anticipatory repudiation—ability to perform contract

The plaintiffs agreed to sell a ship to the defendants. Under the contract a 10 per cent deposit was payable; the balance was due on delivery of the ship in February 1978. The defendants paid the deposit in November 1977. On 19th January 1978 they informed the plaintiffs by letter that they could not pay the balance of the purchase price but would "use every endeavour to secure alternative finance". The plaintiffs then suggested on 24th January that the defendants could resolve their financial difficulties by reselling the ship. The defendants replied on 26th January that they would try to do so. On 27th January the plaintiffs purported to accept an anticipatory repudiation of the contract by the defendants. *Held*, (BRANDON LJ dissenting), (i) the defendants' letter of 19th January did not give rise to and could not fairly have been treated as giving rise to a right to treat the contract as repudiated; (ii) there was nothing in the defendants' letter of 26th January to suggest that they had given up the idea of purchasing the ship or were unable to do so and (iii) the plaintiffs were not justified in assuming that the defendants would be unwilling or unable to pay any difference between the resale price of the ship and the balance due on completion. Therefore the defendants were not liable for anticipatory repudiation of the contract.

THE HAZELMOOR, ANCHOR LINE LTD v KEITH ROWELL LTD [1980] 2 Lloyd's Rep 351 (Court of Appeal: MEGAW, BRANDON and OLIVER LJJ).

495   —— implied repudiation—whether attempted rescission amounting to repudiation

The vendors agreed to sell certain property to the purchasers. The contract provided that the purchasers would be entitled to rescind the contract if prior to completion a statutory authority should have commenced to acquire the property compulsorily. At the date that the contract was signed, an authority had already commenced compulsory purchase proceedings. The purchasers purported to rescind the contract because of the authority's actions, but the vendors refused to accept. The vendors accordingly brought an action against the purchasers claiming a declaration that the purchasers were not entitled to rescind. The purchasers sought by their defence and counterclaim a declaration that they had validly rescinded the contract. The vendors then brought a second action against the purchasers claiming that the notice of rescission and the defence and counterclaim together amounted to a repudiation, which they accepted and which consequently entitled them to sue for damages. The Court of Appeal affirmed a decision in favour of the vendors, the purchasers having conceded that they were not entitled to rescind because the authority's actions had commenced before the date of the contract. The purchasers appealed on the issue of whether their attempted rescission amounted to repudiation. *Held*, LORD SALMON and LORD RUSSELL OF KILLOWEN dissenting, unjustified rescission of a contract did not always amount to repudiation; the circumstances and the purchasers' conduct as a whole had to be considered. In attempting to rescind, the purchasers were in fact relying on the contract rather than refusing to be bound by it, and because there was no evidence that they intended to abandon it or to refuse future performance, their erroneous and unsuccessful attempt at rescission did not amount to a repudiation. Further, LORD SALMON and LORD RUSSELL OF KILLOWEN concurring, the purchasers' defence and counterclaim had not carried their notice of rescission any further and their pleadings also, therefore, did not amount to repudiation. The appeal would be allowed.

WOODAR INVESTMENT DEVELOPMENT LTD v WIMPEY CONSTRUCTION UK LTD [1980] 1 All ER 571 (House of Lords: LORD WILBERFORCE, LORD SALMON, LORD RUSSELL OF KILLOWEN, LORD KEITH OF KINKEL and LORD SCARMAN). Dicta of Lord Cleridge in *Freeth v Burr* (1874) LR 9 CP 208 at 213, *James Shaffer Ltd v Findlay Durham and Brodie* [1953] 1 WLR 106, *Sweet & Maxwell Ltd v Universal News Services Ltd* [1964] 3 All ER 30 and *Spettabile Consorzio Veneziano di Armamento e Navigazione v Northumberland Shipping Co Ltd* [1918–19] All ER Rep 963 applied; *Federal Commerce and Navigation Ltd v Molena Alpha Inc* [1979] 1 All ER 307, CA, 1978 Halsbury's Abridgment para. 2609 distinguished.

496   —— necessity for acceptance—wrongful dismissal

See *Gunton v Richmond-upon-Thames LBC*, para. 1027.

497   Sale of goods

See SALE OF GOODS.

498   Sale of land

See SALE OF LAND.

499   Third party—bill of lading—exemptions and immunities

See *Port Jackson Stevedoring Pty Ltd v Salmond & Spraggon (Australia) Pty Ltd*, para. 2598.

COPYRIGHT

500   Article

Audio and Visual Recording—Piracy in the Home, Michael Flint: 130 NLJ 822.

501   Assignment of copyright—reversionary interest—collective work—song

By the Copyright Act 1911, s. 5 (2) proviso an assignment of a copyright did not vest any rights in the assignee beyond the expiration of 25 years from the author's death, and after that period the reversionary interest devolved upon the author's personal representatives for the benefit of his estate. However the assignment of copyright in a collective work was excepted.

In a complex case involving the ownership of a number of reversionary interests under the Copyright Acts 1911 and 1956, it fell to be determined, inter alia, whether a song, the words and music of which were written by different people, was a collective work and thus outside the protection of s. 5 (2) proviso.

Held, VISCOUNT DILHORNE dissenting on this point, copyright in a song existed only where the words and music were written by the same person, in which case that person would own the copyright of the song and he and his estate would have the protection of s. 5 (2) proviso. Where however, the words and music were written by two separate people, each had a separate copyright in relation to the words and music respectively. These copyrights could not be merged and thus the song itself had no copyright, and as a collective work had to have a copyright of its own, the exception to s. 5 (2) proviso did not apply. The exception related only to a collective work such as an encyclopaedia or dictionary, constituting work written in distinct parts by different authors or in which works or parts of works of different authors were incorporated, and in which copyright existed as a whole, in addition to, and apart from, any copyright which might have existed in its constituent parts. The song was accordingly afforded the protection of s. 5 (2) proviso.

CHAPPELL AND CO LTD V REDWOOD MUSIC LTD; REDWOOD MUSIC LTD V FRANCIS DAY AND HUNTER LTD [1980] 2 All ER 817 (House of Lords: VISCOUNT DILHORNE, LORD SALMON, LORD EDMUND-DAVIES, LORD RUSSELL OF KILLOWEN and LORD KEITH OF KINKEL). Decision of Court of Appeal [1980] RPC 385, 1979 Halsbury's Abridgment para. 540 affirmed.

502   Infringement—Anton Piller order—whether subject to privilege against self-incrimination

See *Rank Film Distributors Ltd v Video Information Centre*, para. 2181.

503   —— importation—effect of Community law

In an action for infringement of copyright the plaintiff was the exclusive licensee of the copyright in certain sound recordings. The alleged infringement consisted in, inter alia, the importation by the defendant into the United Kingdom of sound recordings lawfully manufactured in Portugal but in respect of which the plaintiff owned the United Kingdom copyright, contrary to the Copyright Act 1956, s. 16 (2). However, a trade agreement made in 1972 between the EEC and Portugal provides for the abolition of quantitive restrictions on imports and measures of equivalent effect (art. 14 (2)).

On the plaintiff's application for an interlocutory injunction the defendant sought an order under RSC Ord. 114 to stay the proceedings and to refer to the European Court certain questions on the interpretation and effect of the 1972 agreement, which the defendant claimed provided a defence to the action. The injunction was granted but an order to refer was refused on the ground that a ruling of the European Court was not necessary at the interlocutory stage. The defendant appealed. *Held*, the defendant's conduct came within s. 16 (2) of the 1956 Act and thus constituted an infringement of the plaintiff's copyright under English domestic law. However, it might be that s. 16 (2) was overridden by Community law on the point. A reference would therefore be made to the European Court for a ruling on the questions (i) whether art. 14 (2) of the 1972 agreement was directly enforceable in the Community, (ii) whether the enforcement of the plaintiff's copyright in the present circumstances constituted a measure of equivalent effect to a quantitive restriction and (iii) whether art. 14 (2) could afford a defence to an action such as the present. The English proceedings would be stayed accordingly.

POLYDOR LTD V HARLEQUIN RECORD SHOPS LTD [1980] 2 CMLR 413 (Court of Appeal: TEMPLEMAN AND ORMROD LJJ). Decision of Sir Robert Megarry V-C [1980] 1 CMLR 669 reversed in part.

For earlier interlocutory proceedings see [1979] 3 CMLR 432, 1979 Halsbury's Abridgment para. 529.

504   —— —— interlocutory injunction refused—difficult questions of law to be tried

The first and second plaintiffs were the worldwide owners of the copyright in certain sound recordings and the exclusive licensees of the right to manufacture and distribute those records in the United Kingdom respectively. Over a period of several years the defendant had established a business of importing into the United Kingdom for resale copies of those records lawfully manufactured in North America under parallel licences. The plaintiffs had been aware of the defendant's business for about three years before they issued a writ for infringement of copyright under the Copyright Act 1956, s. 16. On their application for an interlocutory injunction to restrain the defendant generally from selling or distributing in the United Kingdom any copies of sound recordings in respect of which the plaintiffs were the copyright owners or licensees, *held*, the injunction would be refused. First, there were clearly difficult questions of law to be decided at trial, in particular in relation to the construction and application of s. 16 and the effect of the provisions of the EEC Treaty regarding free movement of goods; the injunction sought would cause serious disturbance to the defendant's business which might ultimately prove to have been unjustified. Secondly, in the circumstances of the case it would be difficult to frame an injunction in terms that were fair to the defendant. Third, the plaintiffs' hesitation and delay in asserting the wide rights now claimed were important circumstances to be considered in relation to an interference with the defendant's trade.

WHO GROUP LTD v STAGE ONE (RECORDS) LTD [1980] 2 CMLR 429 (Chancery Division: GOULDING J).

505   —— **interlocutory   injunction—commercial   manufacture   of garments from knitting patterns book**

The plaintiff was a designer of original hand-knitted garments which she sold through her own retail outlet and to department stores. Pattern books containing instructions for knitting the garments were also for sale. The defendants reproduced the garments using the pattern books and sold them for a price considerably less than that which the plaintiff charged. The plaintiff applied for an interlocutory injunction restraining the defendants from infringing the copyright in her designs and from passing off. *Held*, the defendants' submission that, in the absence of express reservation, a purchaser of the pattern books was entitled to manufacture commercially from the patterns, would be rejected. The injunction would be granted as there was a prima facie infringement of copyright and a strong possibility that at the trial of the main action, a limitation on use of the patterns for commercial purposes would be imposed.

ROBERTS v CANDIWARE LTD [1980] FSR 352 (Chancery Division: VINELOTT J).

506   —— —— **likelihood of serious disturbance to defendant's business—injunction refused**

See *Who Group Ltd v Stage One (Records) Ltd*, para. 504.

507   —— **issue to public—Oscar statuette**

See *Oscar Trade Mark*, para. 513.

508   —— **reproduction of drawings—rights claimed not recognised in other EEC member states—effect of Community law**

In an action for infringement of copyright the plaintiff claimed to have the copyright in certain drawings relating to spare parts for cars. In exercise of that copyright they had granted or offered to grant licences to third parties to manufacture those parts. The terms of the licences were substantially similar and under each the plaintiffs undertook to take appropriate action against infringers. The alleged infringement by the defendant consisted in the unlicensed manufacture of those parts contrary to the Copyright Act 1956, ss. 3 (5), 48 (1).

In their defence the defendants claimed that the rights the plaintiffs sought to assert were not recognised under the laws of other EEC member states and that the plaintiffs' exercise of those rights, by the granting of licences and the prosecution of alleged infringers, was thus contrary to certain provisions of the EEC Treaty. The plaintiffs applied to have those parts of the defence relating to the Treaty struck out. *Held*, the application would be granted. First, the fact that the artistic copyright claimed by the plaintiffs was not recognised by the laws of other member states was irrelevant: EEC Treaty, art. 222, which expressly preserved national rules governing property ownership, clearly applied to industrial property. Secondly, the granting of licences on similar terms to third parties did not constitute a means of arbitrary discrimination or a disguised restriction on trade between member states so as to deprive the plaintiffs of the protection given to industrial property under art. 36. Thirdly, although the prosecution of the defendants for infringement might possibly constitute a concerted practice under art. 85, that action did not have the object or effect of distorting competition within the Common Market; rather, it was aimed at ensuring that all United Kingdom competitors were placed on an equal footing. The defences based on the EEC Treaty were therefore bad and would be struck out.

BRITISH LEYLAND MOTOR CORPN LTD v TI SILENCERS LTD [1980] 2 CMLR 332 (Chancery Division: WALTON J).

For earlier interlocutory proceedings see [1980] 1 CMLR 598, para. 2210.

509   —— —— whether discernible by layman

Hong Kong

The Supreme Court of Hong Kong has held that mere proof of reproduction of a three-dimensional reproduction of a drawing is insufficient to constitute an infringement, if the object would not appear to a layman to be a reproduction of the drawing within the Copyright Act 1956, s. 9 (8). The onus is on the prosecution to prove that s. 9 (8) does not afford relief to the defendant.

R v LEE [1980] FSR 314 (Supreme Court of Hong Kong).

510   —— reproduction of textile design—knowledge of infringement— whether sale amounted to publication

The plaintiffs were designers, manufacturers and retailers of printed textiles. At a meeting between the plaintiffs and the defendants, the defendants' buyer was shown one of the plaintiffs' designs. The buyer later went to Hong Kong where he was shown an identical design, although he did not recognise it as such, which he arranged to be made up into shirts and imported to and distributed in the UK. The plaintiffs became aware of the defendants' activities and wrote a letter requiring them to cease their activities. The defendants failed to comply and the plaintiffs sued for damages for infringement of copyright and conversion. The judge held that the importation into the UK constituted infringement, but that the plaintiffs could not recover in respect of the defendants' activities prior to the receipt of the plaintiffs' letter, as they had failed to prove knowledge of infringement as required by the Copyright Act 1956, ss. 5 (3), 18 until the receipt of that letter. The plaintiffs appealed against the limitation imposed on their remedy. *Held*, under s. 3 (5) (b) the copyright in an artistic work was infringed by publication and read together with s. 49 (2) (c), publication took place whenever reproductions had been issued. The defendants had infringed the copyright by issuing reproductions to the public and, as liability on the grounds of publication was not qualified by any requirement of knowledge, they were liable for such an infringement at any time. They were also liable in conversion under s. 18. They could not rely on ss. 17 (2), 18 (2) (a) (no reasonable grounds for suspecting that copyright existed in the design). It was incumbent on anyone who proposed to make use of any artistic work in a way which might infringe copyright, to make such inquiries and investigations as he could reasonably satisfy himself that the work was free of copyright.

INFABRICS LTD v JAYTEX LTD [1980] 2 WLR 822 (Court of Appeal: BUCKLEY and DONALDSON LJJ). Decision of Whitford J [1978] FSR 451, 1978 Halsbury's Abridgment para. 522 reversed in part.

511   —— right of action—exclusive licensee

The defendant purchased in the United States of America and imported into England for resale records made by an American company. The American company, as owner of the copyright in records made by it, had granted an exclusive licence in the United Kingdom of the copyright to an English subsidiary. The English subsidiary brought an action against the defendant for infringement of copyright, contending that the defendant had breached the Copyright Act 1956, s. 16 (2), (3), in that it had without the licence of the owner of the copyright imported an article into the United Kingdom and sold it when to the defendant's knowledge the making of that article would have constituted an infringement of copyright if the article had been made in the United Kingdom. *Held*, the defendant had not infringed the copyright at the suit of the English subsidiary. The latter could not claim to be treated as the owner of the copyright because the 1956 Act treated a licensee as having contractual, not proprietary, rights. The provisions of s. 49 (5), to the effect that persons who were entitled to the copyright, whether in consequence of a partial assignment or otherwise, were to be treated as the owner of the copyright, did not apply to exclusive licensees. An exclusive licensee was not a person who was entitled to the copyright and therefore was not the owner of the copyright within s. 49 (5).

Nor could the English subsidiary claim that for the purposes of s. 16 (2), (3) the hypothetical maker of the records if they had been made in the United Kingdom was the importer or any unauthorised person, since that hypothetical maker was assumed to be the person who actually made the article abroad. The manufacture of the records in the United Kingdom by the American company would not be an infringement since the 1956 Act, s. 1 (2), expressly excluded from the definition of infringement any acts done by the owner of the copyright. Hence neither the importation nor the resale of the records was caught by s. 16 (2), (3).

CBS United Kingdom Ltd v Charmdale Record Distributors Ltd [1980] 2 All ER 807 (Chancery Division: Browne-Wilkinson J).

512   —— sound recording—causing recording to be heard in public

New Zealand
The owner and operator of a hotel hired a disc jockey to play records in the lounge bar of the hotel. The disc jockey used his own records and equipment. There was no charge for admission to the bar, the prices of the drinks were not increased when music was provided, and people were not, in any case, obliged to purchase drinks. The plaintiff owned the copyright in one of the records which the disc jockey played. Neither the hotel owner nor the disc jockey had obtained a licence to play the record, although the plaintiff had asked the hotel owner to do so. The plaintiff claimed that the disc jockey had infringed the record's copyright by causing it to be played in public and receiving payment for so doing, and that the hotel owner had authorised that infringement. *Held*, the hotel owner, as the sole occupier controlling the premises, was the only person causing the record to be heard in public and the disc jockey had not, therefore, infringed the copyright. The hotel owner had received money for drinks, not for the music, and had not taken any action restricted by copyright.

Phonographic Performances (NZ) Ltd v Lion Breweries Ltd [1980] FSR 383 Court of Appeal.

513   —— unpublished work under United States law—copyright protection in United Kingdom

A company in the United Kingdom applied for registration of a trade mark consisting of the word "Oscar" and a silhouette of a statuette similar to that awarded by the Academy of Motion Picture Arts and Sciences. The Academy opposed the application and questions arose as to (i) whether the Academy had any copyright protection in the United Kingdom in the Oscar statuette and, (ii) whether, if the Academy had such protection, there was an infringement of copyright. *Held*, (i) the Oscar was an original artistic work of United States origin and was "unpublished" under United States law. English law defined publication as issue of copies to the public which meant an invitation to the public to acquire copies. The Academy only gave copies of the Oscar to named individuals and that was not an issue to the public under English law. The work was therefore unpublished but such works of United States origin enjoyed copyright protection in the United Kingdom under a series of statutory orders, so the Academy had United Kingdom copyright in the Oscar statuette. (ii) If the evidence given by the copyright owner showed a startling similarity between the work complained of and the copyright work, raising an inference of copying by the other party, infringement of copyright was proved unless evidence was adduced to the contrary. In the present case the similarity was so striking that such an inference was automatically raised, and in the absence of rebutting evidence the copyright owned by the Academy had been infringed.

OSCAR TRADE MARK [1980] FSR 429 (Queen's Bench Division: GRAHAM J). *British Northrop Ltd v Texteam Blackburn Ltd* [1974] RPC 57, *Francis Day & Hunter v Feldman & Co* [1914] 2 Ch 728 followed; *LB (Plastics) Ltd v Swish Products Ltd* [1979] RPC 551, HL 1979 Halsbury's Abridgment para. 531 applied.

514   International conventions

The Copyright (International Conventions) (Amendment) Order 1980, S.I. 1980 No. 1723 (in force on 10th December 1980), amends the 1979 order to take account of the accession of the Republic of Guinea to the Berne Copyright Convention. The order extends to dependent countries of the Commonwealth to which the 1979 order extends.

CORONERS

Halsbury's Laws of England (4th edn.), Vol. 9, paras. 1001–1200

515   Coroners Act 1980

The Coroners Act 1980 abolishes the legal obligation of coroners to view the bodies on which they hold inquests. The Act received the royal assent on 17th July 1980 and came into force on that date.

Section 1 provides for the abolition of the requirement for a coroner holding an inquest to view the body. Under s. 2, a coroner is empowered to hold inquests in areas other than that in which the body lies. On the assumption of jurisdiction to hold an inquest under s. 2, a coroner may assume all the powers and duties which would belong to him if the body were lying within his area, and the coroner within whose area the body is lying ceases to have any such powers and duties: s. 3. Section 4 empowers a coroner to order the exhumation of the body of a person buried within his jurisdiction for the purposes of an inquest or any criminal proceedings. Section 5 provides that the Act is to be construed as one with the other Coroners Acts and cited together with them as the Coroners Acts 1887 to 1980, the section also deals with extent. The repeal of the Coroners (Amendment) Act 1926, ss. 16, 17, certain other repeals and consequential amendments are contained in Schs. I and II.

516   Fees

The Coroner's Records (Fees for Copies) Rules 1980, S.I. 1980 No. 969 (in force on 1st September 1980), revoke and replace with appropriate modifications the 1975 Rules, 1975 Halsbury's Abridgment para. 570. They increase the fees payable to a coroner or other person for furnishing a copy of an inquisition, deposition or other document in his custody relating to an inquest.

517   Inquest—adjournment—amendment of rules

The Coroners (Amendment) Rules 1980, S.I. 1980 No. 557 (in force on 1st June 1980), substantially amend the 1953 Rules. The main changes relate to the requirement of notice of a post-mortem examination to be given to an inspector appointed under the Health and Safety at Work Act 1974 when that inspector is given notice of the accident or disease causing the death. The rules provide new forms for post-mortem examination reports and for notifying persons that an inquest is to be held. Further the verdict of justifiable or excusable homicide, as specified in the Form of Inquisition of the 1953 Rules, Sch. 3, Form 18, is replaced by a verdict that the killing was lawful.

518   The Coroners (Amendment) (Savings) Rules 1980, S.I. 1980 No. 668 (in force on 1st June 1980), exclude the application of the Coroners (Amendment) Rules 1980, para. 517, to an inquest begun, or to a post-mortem examination directed or requested by a coroner, before the coming into operation of those rules on 1st June 1980.

519   **—— examination of witnesses by interested person—availability of witnesses' statements to police**

See *R v HM Coroner, Hammersmith, ex parte Peach*, para. 520.

520   **—— inquest with jury—circumstances when jury required**

During a demonstration which had become a riot a man was struck on the head with a heavy instrument. It was alleged that the blow was struck by a policeman. The man subsequently died and the question arose as to whether the inquest was to be held with or without a jury. The Coroners (Amendment) Act 1926, s. 13 (2) (e) provides that if it appears to the coroner either before he proceeds to hold an inquest or in the course of an inquest which has begun without a jury, that there is reason to suspect that the death occurred in circumstances the continuance or possible recurrence of which is prejudicial to the health or safety of the public or any section of the public he shall proceed to summon a jury. The question was whether s. 13 (2) (e) applied to the present case. A Divisional Court of the Queen's Bench Division held that it did not.

The Court also held that statements taken from witnesses by the police which had been furnished to the coroner for the purpose of examination of the witnesses at the inquest were not available to be handed over to the applicant, the deceased's brother. Although the Coroners Rules 1953, r. 16, gave a right to any person who in the coroner's opinion was a properly interested person to examine a witness at the inquest, the word's "examine any witness" meant question a witness for the purpose of putting that person's allegations, and the denial of a sight of the statements was not a breach of the rules of natural justice.

On appeal against the Divisional Court's decision that s. 13 (2) (e) did not apply in the present case, *held*, s. 13 (2) (e) dealt with many circumstances in which anyone could realise that their "continuance or possible recurrence" might be "prejudicial to the health or safety of the public". A jury ought to be summoned where the circumstances were such that similar fatalities might possibly recur in the future and it was reasonable to expect some action to be taken to prevent such a recurrence, although a limitation had to be placed on the ambit of "circumstances" in s. 13 (2) (e); that provision did not apply solely to physical circumstances. In the present case, considered on a hypothetical basis as the allegations against the police had not been proved, the fatality occurred in circumstances in which a possible recurrence might be prevented, and therefore s. 13 (2) (e) required that there be an inquest with a jury. The appeal would be allowed.

R v HM CORONER, HAMMERSMITH, EX PARTE PEACH [1980] 2 All ER 7 (Court of Appeal: LORD DENNING MR, BRIDGE LJ and SIR DAVID CAIRNS). Decision of Divisional Court of the Queen's Bench Division [1980] 2 WLR 496 reversed.

521   **—— preliminary proceedings—whether subject to judicial review**

Canada

A man was killed by a bullet fired by a member of the Metropolitan Toronto Police Department. The death was investigated by a coroner, as a result of which the coroner issued a warrant for an inquest. A constable from the same police department was required to select the members of the jury, who were questioned by the coroner to determine whether they were likely to be biased. Prior to the opening of the inquest the coroner was given assistance by members of the same police department. All these preliminary stages were conducted in accordance with the relevant statutory provisions. The parents of the deceased, who had been granted the right to be represented at the inquest, as provided for by statute, applied for judicial review in respect of the preliminary proceedings, on the ground that there was a reasonable apprehension of bias. *Held*, proceedings concerning a coroner's inquest were not wholly immune from judicial review: the proceedings had the trappings of a trial and it was implicit that they were governed by the principles of natural justice. Prohibition would therefore lie where it was shown that the preliminary proceedings were such as to raise a reasonable apprehension of bias. In the present case, however, there was no reason to interfere with the holding of the inquest as convened: the relevant statutory provisions had been complied with precisely and the applicants had failed to show anything further from which a reasonable apprehension of bias could be inferred. The application would be dismissed.

RE EVANS AND MILTON (1979) 97 DLR (3d) 687 (Court of Appeal of Ontario).

COUNTY COURTS

Halsbury's Laws of England (4th edn.), Vol. 10, paras. 1–700

522   **Arbitration—county court judge—jurisdiction to appoint as arbitrator—power to set aside award without parties' consent**

See *Leung v Garbett*, para. 175.

523   **Costs—scale of costs—registrar's discretion to allow larger sums on taxation**

It has been held in the Court of Appeal that where a county court judge has refused to make a direction under CCR Ord. 47, r. 21 (2) that the registrar is not bound by the normal scale of costs on taxation, he is not prevented from exercising his discretion under Ord. 47 r. 21 (5) to allow larger sums on taxation than those allowed by the relevant scale unless the judge has also directed that r. 21 (5) is not to apply.

TRUSLER V TUDOR (1980) Times, 10th April (Court of Appeal: STEPHENSON and DUNN LJJ).

524   **County Court Rules—amendment**

The County Court (Amendment) Rules 1980, S.I. 1980 No. 329 (in force on 15th April 1980, except for the provisions regarding charging orders, which come into force on the day appointed for the coming into force of the Charging Orders Act 1979), amend the County Court Rules 1936 by (i) simplifying the procedure for serving proceedings abroad, (ii) increasing the time permitted for the acceptance of admissions and payments into court, (iii) expediting the enforcement of orders for oral examination, (iv) providing for the making of charging orders under the Charging Orders Act 1979, (v) increasing the registrar's powers regarding garnishee proceedings and the appointment of a receiver, (vi) removing provisions concerning exchange controls, (vii) providing for the enforcement of maintenance orders against persons resident in Hague Convention countries and (viii) amending the formal requirements regarding the status of the parties to an action.

525   The County Court (Amendment No. 2) Rules 1980, S.I. 1980 No. 628 (in force on 3rd June 1980), further amend the 1936 Rules relating to charging orders consequent on the entry into force of the Charging Orders Act 1979 and substitute revised forms of order for Forms 366 and 366A.

526   The County Court (Amendment No. 3) Rules 1980, S.I. 1980 No. 1807 (in force on 1st January 1981, except rr. 6, 7, 8, 14 and 18 which come into force on 21st April 1981 and r. 13 which comes into force on the day appointed for the coming into force of the Housing Act 1980, s. 142), amend the County Court Rules 1936 by (i) providing for the service of process on a state within the meaning of the State Immunity Act 1978, s. 14 and for the recovery and enforcement of a default judgment against such a state; (ii) enabling the joinder of a person as an alternative defendant to a counterclaim against the plaintiff; (iii) making further provision for the arbitration of disputes involving £500 or less; (iv) providing a procedure for enforcing a charging order by sale; (v) allowing proceedings under the Landlord and Tenant Act 1954, s. 38 (4) to be heard by a registrar; (vi) providing for proceedings under the Leasehold Reform Act 1967 which might previously have been transferred to the Lands Tribunal to be transferred to a leasehold valuation tribunal instead; (viii) reducing the ambit of certain provisions which restrict recovery of solicitors' costs; (ix) increasing the fixed costs recoverable in uncontested cases; (x) allowing the court more latitude in assessing costs and (xi) revising the forms of admission, defence and counterclaim.

527   The County Court (Amendment No. 4) Rules 1980, S.I. 1980 No. 1982 (in force on 1st January 1981), amend the County Court Rules 1936 by (i) providing that orders for the summary possession of land under Ord. 26 may be made by a judge, or, with leave of the judge, by a registrar and (ii) making it clear that a possession order under Ord. 26 may specify a date for possession, instead of taking effect forthwith, providing that the court could have specified a date for possession if the proceedings had been brought by action.

528   **Districts**

The County Court Districts (Frome) Order 1980, S.I. 1980 No. 694 (in force on 14th June 1980), closes the Frome County Court, divides its district between those of neighbouring courts and provides for sittings of the Trowbridge County Court to be held at Frome and Warminster as well as at Trowbridge and Devizes.

529   The County Court Districts (Romford) Order 1980, S.I. 1980 No. 1215 (in force on 6th October 1980), amends the County Court Districts Order 1970 by establishing a new county court at Romford.

530   **Divorce county courts**

See para. 921.

531   **Fees**

The County Court Fees (Amendment) Order 1980, S.I. 1980 No. 773 (in force on 7th July 1980), amends the County Court Fees Order 1978, 1978 Halsbury's Abridgment para. 539 by increasing the fees payable for (i) the commencement of all proceedings; (ii) bailiff service; (iii) warrants of delivery or execution and (iv) warrants of possession.

532   **Funds in court**

The County Court Funds (Amendment) Rules 1980, S.I. 1980 No. 1857 (in force on 1st January 1981), amend the County Court Funds Rules 1965, r. 24 (1) by lowering the rate of interest allowed on money in a short term investment account from 15 per cent to 12½ per cent per annum.

533   **Garnishee proceedings—undertaking to make periodical payments—whether "judgment or order"**

See *Gandolfo v Gandolfo*, para. 1241.

534   Judgment—application to set aside judgment—judgment in defendant's absence—material considerations

See *Rhodes Trust v Khan*, para. 1729.

535   Jurisdiction—proposed increase in limits

The Lord Chancellor's Office has published a consultation paper on the possible increase of the limits currently imposed on county court jurisdiction. The proposed limits would become: (i) general monetary limit, £5,000; (ii) limit in equity proceedings, £50 000; (iii) jurisdiction limit for registrars in both trials and arbitrations, £500; and (iv) consequential increases in the costs sanctions encouraging plaintiffs to commence proceedings in the county court rather than in the High Court. The consultation document has been published in the *Law Society's Gazette*, 27th August 1980, p. 805.

COURTS

Halsbury's Laws of England (4th edn.), Vol. 10, paras. 701–1000

536   Articles

Crown Court Productivity, I. R. Scott (discussion on number of cases heard by Crown Courts): [1980] Crim LR 293.

An End to House of Lords as Appeal Court?, Neville D. Vandyk: 124 Sol Jo 175.

537   Appeal—evidence—finding of fact by trial judge—inference from finding—substitution by appellate court of own inference

See *Whitehouse v Jordan*, para. 2063.

538   —— time for appeal—application for leave to appeal from Employment Appeal Tribunal to Court of Appeal—jurisdiction of appeal tribunal to extend time for application

See *Tether v Financial Times Ltd*, para. 1036.

539   Chancery Division—location of courts—location outside London

The Lord Chancellor, acting under the Courts Act 1971, s. 23 (1), has revised the arrangements for the disposal of High Court Chancery business outside London and the revised arrangements supersede those made on 2nd May 1973. With effect from 15th April 1980 Judge Blackett Ord V-C and Judge FitzHugh QC sit as deputy judges of the High Court for the hearing at such places as may be specified by the Lord Chancellor of all proceedings at any time assigned to the Chancery Division, including proceedings in the Companies Court, except: (a) proceedings directly concerning revenue; (b) bankruptcy proceedings; (c) proceedings before the Patent Court constituted as part of the Chancery Division under the Patents Act 1977, s. 96; (d) proceedings under the Mental Health Act 1959, Part VIII; (e) proceedings under the Defence Contracts Act 1958 or the Registered Designs Acts 1949 to 1961; (f) appeals to a Divisional Court of the Chancery Division; or (g) appeals, cases stated and questions referred for the opinion of the High Court which are mentioned in RSC Ord. 93, r. 10 (2), for the time being in force. See the Law Society Gazette, 28th May 1980, p. 545.

540   Court of Appeal—jurisdiction—error of law in construction of statute

See *Re Racal Communications Ltd*, para. 380.

541   **—— reference to European Court of Justice—whether Court of Appeal is court of final appeal**

The defendants sought to resist the grant of an injunction restraining the infringement of a patent. They contended that, in the light of the facts that the defendants hoped to establish at the trial and upon the true construction of the EEC Treaty, arts. 30 and 36 concerning the elimination of quantitative restrictions between member states, a patent which was valid in the United Kingdom but was invalid or was subject of prior user in one or more member states, was not enforceable by injunction although damages in lieu of an injunction might be awarded. The defendants sought leave to amend the defence so as to raise the point and introduce certain issues of fact which were relevant to that point but which would not otherwise be relevant in the trial of the action. *Held*, as there was no established body of case law on the question of the validity of the patent raised by the present case and since the question was essentially one of interpretation of the EEC Treaty, the question was one which ultimately would have to be referred to the European Court. If that was the prospect it was desirable that the pleadings were, from the outset, in a form enabling the defendants to lay the factual ground for the arguments which they would then wish to present. Further, if a United Kingdom court had to formulate questions for the European Court it was important that the court directing that reference knew what questions to ask the European Court and it would not know what were the correct questions to ask unless the relevant facts had been ascertained. Accordingly the defendants would be allowed to amend their defence.

The court further stated that the English Court of Appeal, if appeal to the House of Lords was unobtainable, was, for the purposes of a reference made to the European Court under art. 177, the final court of appeal and was therefore bound to refer any question regarding the interpretation of Community legislation to the European Court.

REINOLD HAGEN V FRATELLI D. & G. MORETTI SNC [1980] 3 CMLR 253 (Court of Appeal: BUCKLEY, TEMPLEMAN and BRIGHTMAN LJJ).

542   **—— right of appeal—exclusion of right of appeal**

See *Re Racal Communications Ltd*, para. 380.

543   **Court of original or appellate jurisdiction—definition**

See *Gayways Linings Ltd v Toczek*, para. 1774.

544   **Crown Court—joinder of informations—consent of defendant**

See *Sedwell v James*, para. 668.

545   **—— jurisdiction—appeal against conviction by magistrates— defendant previously sentenced by Crown Court**

The applicant was convicted of two offences by a juvenile court and was committed to the Crown Court for sentence. Sentence was passed on him on the understanding that he did not wish to appeal against conviction. Two months later, the applicant obtained leave to appeal out of time against the convictions. However, the Crown Court judge declined to hear the appeal on the ground that as the applicant had been sentenced there had been a final adjudication on conviction and sentence and the court was functus officio. The applicant applied by way of judicial review for an order of mandamus directing the Crown Court to hear his appeal. *Held*, in relation to a decision of justices, the Crown Court had two separate forms of jurisdiction; firstly, to hear and determine committals for sentence, and secondly, to hear appeals from decisions of the justices. A decision determining sentence under the jurisdiction on committal for sentence did not render the court functus officio in relation to the jurisdiction to hear an appeal against conviction. The order sought would be made.

R V CROYDON CROWN COURT, EX PARTE BERNARD [1980] 3 All ER 106 (Queen's Bench Division: LORD LANE CJ and WOOLF J).

546　—— —— appeal from justices on plea of guilty—power of court to inquire into proceedings before justices

In a case where a defendant pleaded guilty to a charge brought under the Vagrancy Act 1824 and was convicted, he appealed contending that in denying some of the prosecution's allegations his plea was equivocal. On the question as to whether the Crown Court had jurisdiction to remit the case for rehearing by the justices on the basis of a not guilty plea, *held*, the Crown Court could only remit to the justices for rehearing on a plea of not guilty a case in which the defendant originally pleaded guilty and then appealed against the conviction, when it had made proper inquiries into the circumstances surrounding the guilty plea and was satisfied that it had been equivocal.

R v MANCHESTER CROWN COURT, EX PARTE ANDERTON [1980] Crim LR 303 (Queen's Bench Division: LORD WIDGERY CJ and GRIFFITHS J). *R v Coventry Crown Court, ex parte Manson* (1978) 67 Cr App Rep 315, 1978 Halsbury's Abridgment para. 561 applied.

547　—— —— criminal bankruptcy order—variation

See *R v Saville*, para. 731.

548　—— plea of guilty before justices—committal for sentence—change of plea—case remitted to magistrates—jurisdiction

See *R v Inner London Crown Court, ex parte Sloper*, para. 734.

549　—— trial—private prosecution—right of prosecutor to appear in person

See *R v George Maxwell (Developments) Ltd*, para. 722.

550　District registries

The District Registries Order 1980, S.I. 1980 No. 1216 (in force on 1st October 1980 except in relation to Romford, which is established as a district registry with effect from 1st July 1981), consolidates the 1971 Order as amended. It also established new district registries at Croydon and Romford.

551　European Court of Justice

See EUROPEAN COMMUNITIES.

552　High Court—jurisdiction—application for certiorari to quash order of Crown Court—matter relating to trial on indictment

See *R v Sheffield Crown Court, ex parte Brownlow*, para. 718.

553　Judicial Committee of the Privy Council—appeal from Hong Kong—conditions of right of appeal

The Hong Kong (Appeal to Privy Council) (Amendment) Order 1980, S.I. 1980 No. 1078 (in force on 26th August 1980), further amends the 1909 Order by increasing the amount in dispute in respect of which there is a right of appeal to the Privy Council to $200,000. The maximum security that may be required from an appellant for due prosecution of an appeal and costs is increased to $100,000.

The order also gives the court a discretion to extend the period of fourteen days within which notice of appeal must be given.

554　—— fees

The Judicial Committee (Fees) Rules 1980, S.I. 1980 No. 714 (in force on 16th June 1980), substitute an increased scale of costs for that set out in the Judicial Committee Rules 1957, Sch. B, Pt. I, as amended.

555   —— jurisdiction—validity of death penalty

See *Ong Ah Chuan v Public Prosecutor; Koh Chai Cheng v Public Prosecutor*, para. 345.

556   Judicial review—availability of remedy—distinction between courts of law and administrative tribunals

See *Re Racal Communications Ltd*, para. 380.

557   Jurisdiction—declaration as to legality—subject matter already awaiting prosecution in criminal courts—jurisdiction to make declaration

See *Imperial Tobacco Ltd v A-G*, para. 258.

558   —— ouster of jurisdiction by statute

Malaysia
In a case concerning an industrial dispute, the question arose as to whether the High Court of Malaysia had jurisdiction to grant an order of certiorari quashing an award made by the appropriate national Industrial Court, notwithstanding that the legislation provided that "an award of the Court is to be final and conclusive, and no award is to be challenged, appealed against, reviewed, quashed or called into question by any Court of law." *Held*, the national legislation effectively excluded the power of the High Court to review the decision of the Industrial Court by certiorari. In determining whether certiorari was still available to correct an error on the face of the record notwithstanding the ouster, a distinction was to be drawn between an error of law which affected jurisdiction and one which did not. As the award was within the jurisdiction of the Industrial Court it followed that if it contained any errors of law on the face of the proceedings the legislation effectively ousted the jurisdiction of the High Court to quash the award by certiorari proceedings.

SOUTH EAST ASIA FIRE BRICKS SDN BHD V NON-METALLIC MINERAL PRODUCTS MANUFACTURING EMPLOYEES UNION [1980] 2 All ER 689 (Privy Council: LORD EDMUND-DAVIES, LORD FRASER OF TULLYBELTON, LORD RUSSELL OF KILLOWEN and LORD KEITH OF KINKEL). Dictum of Lane LJ in *Pearlman v Keepers and Governors of Harrow School* [1979] 1 All ER 365, 1978 Halsbury's Abridgment para. 1766 approved.

559   Right of audience—Crown Court—private criminal prosecution—right of prosecutor to appear in person

See *R v George Maxwell (Developments) Ltd*, para. 722.

CREMATION AND BURIAL

Halsbury's Laws of England (4th edn.), Vol. 10, paras. 1001–1243

560   Disused burial ground—faculty for enlargement of church—meaning of enlargement

See *Re St Thomas, Lymington*, para. 967.

CRIMINAL LAW

Halsbury's Laws of England (4th edn.), Vol. 11, paras. 1–1400

561   Articles

Aiding and Abetting: Criminal Intent, Alec Samuels: 130 NLJ 790.
Conditional intention to steal, L. Koffman (a discussion of recent cases which effectively abolish the "burglars' charter".): [1980] Crim LR 463.

Fraudulent Motorists and Shoppers. J. Kodwo Bentil: 124 Sol Jo 583.

Handling Stolen Goods—The Goods Must Be Proved To Be Stolen, Alec Samuels: 144 JP Jo 277.

Intention, Recklessness, and Probable Consequences, R. A. Duff: [1980] Crim LR 404.

Kidnapping: a Crime not so easily Determinable, J. Kodwo Bentil: 124 Sol Jo 177.

Murder by Instigating Suicide, D. J. Lanham: [1980] Crim LR 215.

Rebutting the Presumption of a Child's Criminal Incapacity, Jonathan Fischer: 130 NLJ 752.

Reckless Damage and the Unreasonable Man, M. D. Cohen: 130 NLJ 231.

Recklessness, R. A. Duff: [1980] Crim LR 282.

Taking the Joy out of Joy-Riding: The Mental Element of Taking a Conveyance Without Authority, S. White: [1980] Crim LR 609.

Three Rogues' Charters, Glanville Williams (law relating to attempted theft): [1980] Crim LR 263.

562 Abortion—defence of medical termination of pregnancy—termination by registered medical practitioner—participation by nurses—legality

See *Royal College of Nursing v Department of Health and Social Security*, para. 1875.

563 Assault—assault on constable in execution of duty—arrest—duty of constable to inform arrested person of grounds

On an appeal against a conviction of assaulting a constable in the execution of his duty the court held that it was important for a constable arresting or detaining a person to make it known to that person the fact that, and the grounds upon which, he was being arrested or detained. This was because a person could rely on the justification of self-defence if he assaulted an officer unlawfully arresting or detaining him, but not if the arrest or detention were lawful.

PEDRO V DISS (1980) Times, 16th December (Queen's Bench Division: LORD LANE CJ and WEBSTER J).

564 —— —— extent of constable's authority—defence of belief that constable not a police officer

A constable in plain clothes who believed the defendant to be about to perform actions which would lead to a breach of the peace drew him away from the scene. There was a brief struggle and the constable informed the defendant that he was a police officer and would arrest the defendant if he did not stop struggling. The defendant, who claimed that he did not believe the constable to be a police officer, then struck him several times. He was convicted of assault on a constable in the execution of his duty. On appeal, *held*, (i) a police officer, reasonably believing that a breach of the peace was about to take place, was entitled to take such steps as were necessary to prevent it, including the use of reasonable force and physical restraint. It was a question of fact and degree when a restraint had continued for so long that there must be a release or arrest, but on the facts that point had not been reached. The court indicated that when a breach of the peace was no longer threatened then restraint must end. (ii) In establishing his defence the defendant had to prove not only that he had used no more force than was reasonably necessary in the circumstances to protect himself and that he believed the constable not to be a police officer but also that his belief was based on reasonable grounds. On the evidence before the court the defendant failed to show reasonable grounds for his belief. His appeal would be dismissed.

ALBERT V LAVIN [1981] 1 All ER 628 (Queen's Bench Division: DONALDSON LJ and HODGSON J).

565   —— —— motorist detained for questioning—whether detention lawful

See *Daniel v Morrison*, para. 650.

566   —— —— removal by constable of accused's clothing—extent of constable's authority

In a case where the defendant was charged with assaulting a police constable in the execution of her duty when the defendant had been arrested and the constable was attempting to remove her brassiere for her own protection, the question arose as to the extent of a constable's authority to search and remove the clothing of a person in custody for his or her own safety. *Held*, it was the duty of a constable who lawfully had a prisoner in his charge to take all reasonable measures to ensure that he did not escape or assist others to do so, did not injure himself or others, did not destroy or dispose of evidence and did not commit further crime such as malicious damage to property. The adoption of any particular measures could never be justified without regard to all the circumstances of the particular case.

In this case, the conduct of the constable would require considerable justification. The constable was acting in accordance with the chief constable's standing orders and it was impossible to justify such a standing instruction or the constable's conduct based on it. Accordingly, the constable was not acting in the execution of her duty and the defendant was not guilty of the offence.

LINDLEY V RUTTER [1980] 3 WLR 660 (Queen's Bench Division: DONALDSON LJ and MUSTILL J).

567   —— defence of honest belief in right to use force—trespasser

The defendant was convicted of assault after using force to prevent bailiffs from taking possession of his house pursuant to a court order. He appealed on the ground that he honestly believed that the order had been obtained fraudulently and that he was therefore justified in using force to protect his property. He further claimed that he honestly believed the amount of force used by the bailiffs was unreasonable and he was acting in self defence. *Held*, the defence of honest mistake about legal rights did not extend to a refusal to accept an order of the court. Further, where excessive force was relied on by defendants to found the defence of self defence the test was objective and not subjective. The appeal would be dismissed.

R v BARRETT (1980) 124 Sol Jo 543 (Court of Appeal: CUMMING-BRUCE LJ, DRAKE and SMITH JJ).

568   Attempt—Law Commission recommendations—creation of statutory offence

The Law Commission has recommended that the offence of attempt at common law should be abolished and replaced by a statutory offence defined in terms of a draft Criminal Attempts Bill appended to their report. The statutory offence would continue to be distinct from the offences of incitement and conspiracy. The statutory offence would be committed by a person who did an act with intent to commit an offence which went so far towards the commission of the offence as to be more than an act of mere preparation. The question whether the act done was capable of being an attempt would be a question of law; whether it actually amounted to an attempt would be a question of fact. The mental element would be an intent to commit the offence attempted. The purpose, in very broad terms, would be to bring matters of practice and procedure in relation to attempts into line with the corresponding matters relating to the relevant substantive offence. See *Criminal Law: Attempt and Impossibility in relation to Attempt, Conspiracy and Incitement* (Law Commission No. 102; HC 646).

569   —— mens rea—perverting the course of justice—factors to be considered

See *R v Machin*, para. 625.

570   Automatism—evidence—necessity for medical evidence

See *Moses v Winder*, para. 687.

571   Commission of crime—joint participants—existence of duty of care

See *Ashton v Turner*, para. 2045.

572   Conspiracy—co-defendants—acquittal of one

On a charge of conspiracy it was held that since the Criminal Law Act 1977, ss. 5 (8) and (9) the trial judge is no longer obliged to give a direction that the jury must find both defendants guilty or both not guilty, even where the charge is one of conspiracy together but with no one else. The test is whether the evidence is such that a verdict of guilty in respect of one defendant and not guilty in respect of the other would be inexplicable and therefore inconsistent. If it would be, the judge should direct that the jury must reach the same verdict in respect of both defendants, adding that if they are unsure about the guilt of one, then both must be found not guilty. Where the evidence against each is markedly different the fairest result would be obtained by giving a separate verdict direction.

R v LONGMAN (1980) Times, 25th October (Court of Appeal: LORD LANE CJ, STOCKER and GLIDEWELL JJ). *R v Holmes* [1980] 1 WLR 1055, CA, para. 573 approved.

573   —— —— —— effect of statutory provisions

The Criminal Law Act 1977, s. 5 (8) provides that, the fact that a person or persons, who, so far as appears from the indictment on which any person has been convicted of conspiracy, were the only other parties to the agreement on which his conviction was based have been acquitted of conspiracy by reference to that agreement, shall not be a ground for quashing his conviction unless under all the circumstances of the case his conviction is inconsistent with the acquittal of the other person or persons in question.

Four defendants conspired to steal goods from unattended vehicles. During the course of the trial the question arose as to the effect of s. 5 (8). *Held*, the effect of s. 5 (8) was to complete the process begun by the House of Lords in *DPP v Shannon* [1974] 2 All ER 1009, 1974 Halsbury's Abridgment para. 598, of abandoning the common law doctrine of automatically quashing the conviction of one conspirator where the only other alleged conspirator had been acquitted. It followed that it was no longer necessary for trial judges to direct juries that they must either convict both, or acquit both. It did not however mean that such a direction might not be given in certain cases. If there was a serious risk of inconsistent verdicts the trial judge had a discretion to direct the jury, if he thought fit, to convict both or acquit both.

R v HOLMES [1980] 2 All ER 458 (Court of Appeal: ORMROD LJ, JUPP and COMYN JJ).

574   Corruption—bribery—police officers—accepting an advantage in capacity as public servants

Hong Kong

Two police officers were convicted of accepting a bribe contrary to Hong Kong law, in that being public servants they had accepted an advantage on account of their abstaining from performing an act in their capacity as public servants, namely taking police action in respect of an alleged dangerous drugs offence. The Hong Kong Court of Appeal allowed their appeal on the ground that the payment had not related to a previous offence, but had been made in respect of a possible future allegation of an offence, which would have been proved by planted evidence. Further, that they had not accepted the bribe in their capacity as public servants, the fabrication of evidence not being part of their duties as police officers. On appeal by the Attorney-General, *held*, "capacity" was not to be equated with "duty". However, the forbearing from planting evidence could have been perpetrated equally well by a stranger as by a member of the police force and the bribe would not therefore have been taken in the officers' capacity as public servants. The appeal would accordingly be dismissed.

A-G of Hong Kong v Ip Chiu [1980] 2 WLR 332 (Privy Council : Lord Wilberforce, Lord Edmund-Davies, Lord Russell of Killowen, Lord Keith of Kinkel and Lord Lane).

575   **Criminal damage—defence—lawful excuse—relevance of accused's drunkenness**

The defendant damaged a house which she believed was occupied by a man with whom she had a relationship such that she had his consent at any time to treat his property as if it were her own. In fact the house belonged to someone else. She was charged with damaging property contrary to the Criminal Damage Act 1971, s. 1 (1). She relied on s. 5 (2), which provides a defence if at the time of the act the accused believed that the person whom he believed to be entitled to consent to damage to the property would have consented to it if he had known of the damage and its circumstances. She was convicted, the justices holding that the defence was lost because she was drunk at the time of the act. On appeal, *held*, the defendant was not relying on her drunkenness to displace an inference of intent or recklessness but on her state of belief as called for by s. 5 (2). Section 5 (3) provided that for the purposes of s. 5 it was immaterial whether the accused's belief was justified if it was honestly held. A belief could be honestly held even if it was induced by intoxication. The justices were wrong in their holding and the appeal would be allowed.

Jaggard v Dickinson [1980] 3 All ER 716 (Queen's Bench Division: Donaldson LJ and Mustill J).

576   —— **mens rea—recklessness—appropriate test**

A fire occurred in the defendant's flat which was extinguished by the fire brigade. Shortly afterwards, as a result of the defendant lighting some matches, another fire occurred. The defendant was charged with arson, in that he deliberately or recklessly damaged the building contrary to the Criminal Damage Act 1971, s. 1 (1), (3). His defence was that either the second fire resulted from undetected smouldering left from the first fire, or, alternatively, that the lighting of a match had started the fire accidentally. He was convicted on the application of an objective test of recklessness. On appeal, *held*, the test of recklessness was subjective and knowledge of the risk of some damage must have entered the defendant's mind even though he might have suppressed it. Since the alternative defence was accident, the mental element was important and a jury which had been properly directed might not have arrived at the same conclusion. The conviction would be quashed.

R v Mullins [1980] Crim LR 37 (Court of Appeal: Lord Widgery CJ, Eveleigh LJ and Kilner Brown J). *R v Stephenson* [1979] 2 All ER 1198, CA, 1979 Halsbury's Abridgment para. 589, followed.

577   —— —— **specific or basic intent—effect of drunkenness**

The defendant was charged with arson, and arson with intent to endanger life or being reckless as to whether life would be endangered, contrary to the Criminal Damage Act 1971, ss. 1 (1) and 1 (2). Relying on the defence of drunkenness he pleaded not guilty to s. 1 (2) but guilty to s. 1 (1). The trial judge ruled that the offence under s. 1 (2) was one of basic intent and drunkenness was no defence. The defendant changed his plea to guilty and subsequently appealed against conviction on the ground that the judge's ruling was wrong in law. *Held*, an offence under s. 1 (2) was one of specific intent and evidence of drunkenness was relevant in determining whether the necessary mental element existed. The actus reus was the same in both ss. 1 (1) and 1 (2), but the mental element of intention or recklessness in s. 1 (2) was an aggravated circumstance which added to the actus reus. There was nothing inconsistent in treating an offence under s. 1 (1) as one of basic intent and under s. 1 (2) as one of specific intent. The appeal would be allowed.

R v Orpin [1980] 2 All ER 321 (Court of Appeal: Eveleigh LJ, Wien and Drake JJ).

578　　　—— possessing articles with intent to damage property

The defendant was seen carrying a bucket of white paint and a roller during a demonstration. He admitted that he had been painting over slogans on walls without permission to do so. He was charged with having the bucket of paint and the roller in his custody intending, without lawful excuse, to use it to damage property contrary to the Criminal Damage Act 1971, s. 3. On a submission of no case to answer the defence contended that there was insufficient evidence of intent to satisfy s. 3 and that the prosecution had failed to show that the activity intended would constitute damage if carried out. *Held*, there was no case to answer for in order to satisfy s. 3 specific intent had to be shown. The only evidence was of an intention to paint out slogans and although there might be an element of recklessness as to whether a wall would consequently be damaged, s. 3, unlike s. 1, did not include the concept of recklessness. There was no evidence to conclude that any wall would be damaged as it was difficult to see how the application of white paint on top of a slogan could damage a wall per se.

R v FANCY [1980] Crim LR 171 (Inner London Crown Court: JUDGE McNAIR).

579　　　—— whether series of offences of same or similar character

See *Re Prescott*, para. 729.

580　　　Criminal injuries—compensation—annual report of Criminal Injuries Compensation Board

The Fifteenth Report of the Criminal Injuries Compensation Board (Cmnd 7752) covers the twelve months ending on 31st March 1979. The number of applications to the board in 1978–79 was 21,960, an increase of 5·4 per cent over the previous year. The number of awards in the year totalled 16,357 and the board paid out a total of over £13 million in compensation. The highest award was £74,714, and during the year five awards in excess of £60,000 were made. In the board's report it comments on some of the applications considered by it. An award was refused in the case of an attack by an unaccompanied dog in the absence of evidence that someone had incited the dog (para. 18). An award was also refused where the victim was accidentally injured by a shot gun (para. 19), but where it was clear that an obstruction, which caused an accident, had been deliberately placed on an unlit road a full award was made (para. 22). The board comments (at para. 24) that it does not take future inflation into account in making awards in respect of future loss.

The Criminal Injuries Compensation Scheme is set out in App E to the report in the form in which it took effect from 21st May 1969. A statement by the board on the interpretation of that scheme is set out as App F. The scheme as further revised (applying to incidents occurring on or after 1st October 1979) is set out at App G and the corresponding statement by the board is set out at App H.

581　　　—— —— claim by spouse

The Criminal Injuries Compensation Board has refused to make any award to the wife of a man killed in a brawl at a public house. The man had a criminal record of 38 convictions and had been in jail on 16 occasions on sentences of up to 18 months. Since 1970 he had not held a job for more than three months. In refusing an award of compensation, the board said that his wife has suffered no financial loss by his death. See the *Daily Telegraph*, 2nd July 1980.

582　　　Cruelty to children—wilful neglect—meaning

Following the death of their sixteen month old son a young couple were charged with wilful neglect, contrary to the Children and Young Persons Act 1933, s. 1, by failing to provide him with adequate medical care during the days preceding his death. Their defence was that they genuinely failed to realise that the child needed any medical attention. The question arose whether a failure to provide medical care was deemed to be "wilful" neglect. *Held* (LORD FRASER OF TULLEYBELTON and LORD SCARMAN dissenting), the offence of wilfully neglecting a child contrary to s. 1 was not an offence of strict liability to be judged by the objective test of what a reasonable parent would have done in the circumstances, since the concept of negligence did not form part of the actus reus of the offence, nor was it part of the mens rea since that was encompassed in the word "wilfully". Although failure to provide adequate medical care was deemed by s. 1 (2) (a) to amount to "neglect" it was not deemed to amount to "wilful neglect". The prosecution was therefore required to prove that the parents had deliberately or recklessly failed to provide adequate medical care. It followed that a genuine failure to appreciate that the child needed medical attention was a good defence to the offence under s. 1.

Furthermore, the proper direction to be given to a jury on a charge of wilful neglect of a child under s. 1 by failing to provide adequate medical aid was that the jury had to be satisfied that the child required medical attention at the time of the parent's failure to provide it and that the parent was aware at that time that the child's health was at risk, or that the parent's unawareness of that fact was due to his not caring whether or not the child's health was at risk.

R v SHEPPARD [1980] 3 All ER 899 (House of Lords: LORD DIPLOCK, LORD EDMUND-DAVIES, LORD FRASER OF TULLEYBELTON, LORD KEITH OF KINKEL and LORD SCARMAN). R v Lowe [1973] 1 All ER 805 overruled. Decision of Court of Appeal (1980) 70 Cr App Rep 210 reversed.

583   Dangerous drug—cultivation—inference of cultivation of cannabis

Scotland

The respondent was charged with the offence of cultivating cannabis under the Misuse of Drugs Act 1971, s. 6. A number of plants were found growing in his flat which were identified as cannabis and cannabis seeds were also found. No inference of cultivation was found and he was acquitted. On appeal by the Crown, *held*, there was sufficient evidence to infer that the plants were being cultivated. The plants were healthy and had been positioned to enable them to receive sufficient light for growth. Further the presence of the seeds and the statements made by the defendant indicated that they were grown with a view to cropping them at the appropriate time. The appeal would be allowed.

TUDHOPE V ROBERTSON 1980 SLT 60 (High Court of Justiciary).

584   —— forfeiture order—conspiracy to produce controlled drug— validity of forfeiture order

The appellants, large scale drug traffickers, were convicted of conspiring to contravene the Misuse of Drugs Act 1971, s. 4 relating to the production and supply of a controlled drug. They had made vast profits from their crime and had transferred large sums abroad. The court made forfeiture orders in respect of the proceeds of their crime under s. 27 of the Act. The orders were upheld by the Court of Appeal. On appeal, *held*, s. 27 did not empower a court to make an order of forfeiture when the only offence of which a person had been convicted was one of conspiracy to contravene the 1971 Act. Conspiracy was not "an offence under this Act" within s. 27. In any event the power of forfeiture under s. 27 applied only to tangible things capable of being physically destroyed and not to choses in action or other intangibles. The orders would therefore be discharged.

LORD DIPLOCK noted that there was no jurisdiction to make orders purporting to transfer movable property situate abroad.

R v CUTHBERTSON, TODD AND MCCOY [1980] 2 All ER 401 (House of Lords: LORD DIPLOCK, LORD EDMUND-DAVIES, LORD KEITH OF KINKEL, LORD SCARMAN and LORD RUSSELL OF KILLOWEN). Decision of Court of Appeal [1979] Crim LR 665, 1979 Halsbury's Abridgment para. 586 reversed.

585   —— licence fees

The Misuse of Drugs (Licence Fees) (Amendment) Regulations 1980, S.I. 1980 No. 160 (in force on 1st April 1980), amend the Misuse of Drugs (Licence Fees) Regulations 1979, 1979 Halsbury's Abridgment, para. 594, by increasing the fees prescribed for licences under the Misuse of Drugs Act 1971.

586   —— possession—admissions by defendants—effect of admissions

See *R v Chatwood*, para. 688.

587   —— supply—distribution

B and G had decided to buy cannabis resin in bulk and had pooled their money for that purpose. B handed over their money to the supplier and received both his and G's share of the drug. He was found guilty and convicted of unlawfully supplying a controlled drug to G. On appeal he contended that when he received the drug it passed into the ownership and legal possession of G and there was thus no supply to G, G already being in possession. *Held*, pursuant to the Misuse of Drugs Act 1971, s. 37 (1) supplying included distributing and in dividing the drug between himself and G, B was distributing the drug. The appeal would be therefore dismissed.

R v BUCKLEY; R v LANE (1979) 69 Cr App Rep 371 (Court of Appeal: LANE LJ, SWANWICK and WATERHOUSE JJ).

588   Duress—objective and subjective tests

Australia

The Supreme Court of New South Wales has held that once the issue of duress has been raised the burden is on the prosecution to negative it. The defence has both subjective and objective elements. It is only available if the mind of the accused was in fact overborne, and where a reasonable man would have acted in the same way under the same duress.

R v LAWRENCE [1980] 1 NSWLR 123 (Supreme Court of New South Wales). *R v Steane* [1947] 1 All ER 813, CA, *Director of Public Prosecutions for Northern Ireland v Lynch* [1975] 1 All ER 913, HL, 1975 Halsbury's Abridgment para 680 and *R v Hudson and Taylor* [1971] 2 All ER 244, CA followed.

589   —— sufficiency of evidence a question of law—charge of rape

Canada

On a charge of rape the defence of duress was raised. The judge did not make a preliminary assessment of the evidence but left the question to the jury. The defendant was acquitted. On appeal, *held*, allowing the appeal, the question of sufficiency of evidence was a question of law for the judge. The defence was not open to the accused as he had several opportunities to leave the scene of the crime.

R v BERGSTROM [1980] 3 WWR 146 (Court of Appeal of Manitoba).

590   False accounting—whether documents made for accounting purpose—personal loan proposal forms

The Attorney-General referred to the Court of Appeal a question on the interpretation of the Theft Act 1968, s. 17 (1) (a). The accused tradesman had encouraged householders to give false particulars on personal loan proposal forms addressed to a finance company and the question was whether those proposal forms were documents made or required for an accounting purpose within the section. *Held*, the words "made or required" indicated that a distinction should be drawn between a document made specifically for accounting purposes and one made for some other purpose but also required for accounting purposes, so that, as in this case, a document would fall within the section if it was merely required for accounting purposes as a subsidiary consideration. The fact that the falsified information was contained in a different part of the document from that required for accounting purposes was irrelevant: the document must be examined as a whole. Accordingly, the question would be answered in the affirmative.

ATTORNEY-GENERAL'S REFERENCE (NO. 1 OF 1980) [1981] 1 WLR 34 (Court of Appeal: LORD LANE CJ, STOCKER and GLIDEWELL JJ).

591   False trade descriptions

See TRADE DESCRIPTIONS.

592   Firearms

See FIREARMS.

593   Forgery—forgery of witness statements—intention to deceive—meaning

The Court of Appeal has held that a police officer who forged two witnesses' statements had an intention to deceive and was therefore guilty, inter alia, of forgery under the Forgery Act 1913, s. 3 (3), notwithstanding that he had no "malus animus", that is, a hostile inclination against the accused, or an intention to frame him. Although the statements were in fact true in substance, and had the witnesses been called to give evidence, they would not have departed materially from the statements, there was sufficient mens rea if the intention to deceive had been proven. The conviction would accordingly be upheld and the police officer's appeal dismissed.

R v TURNER (1980) Times, 7th October (Court of Appeal: LORD LANE CJ, STOCKER and GLIDEWELL JJ).

594   —— —— whether "made evidence by law"

The Court of Appeal has given opinion on a point of law referred to it by the Attorney-General. The Court held, a police constable who forged, with intent to deceive, a written statement which was later tendered to a magistrates' court, committed an offence under the Forgery Act 1913, s. 3 (3) (g) of forging a document which was made evidence by law and an offence under s. 6 (1) of uttering a forged document which was made evidence by law.

The court rejected the argument that the document only became evidence when tendered to the court and that therefore at the time of the forgery had not achieved the status of a document tendered in evidence. "Document made evidence by law" was descriptive of a class of document, and not descriptive of the moment when its reception in evidence rendered it "evidence". Consequently a person committed an offence if he, with intention to deceive, forged any document which, if made and tendered in evidence in accordance with the terms and conditions of the relevant statute relating thereto, would become a document made evidence in law.

ATTORNEY-GENERAL'S REFERENCE (No. 2 OF 1980) [1981] 1 WLR 148 (Court of Appeal: LORD LANE CJ, STOCKER and GLIDEWELL JJ).

For proceedings relating to necessary mens rea required to constitute an "intention to deceive" see R v Turner (1980) Times, 7th October, CA, para. 593.

595   Handling stolen goods—goods marked for identification by owner—whether goods stolen

An employee stole four cartons of cigarettes from his employers and loaded them onto the back of a company lorry. The company security officer, knowing the cartons to be stolen, initialled them for future identification and notified the police. The defendant, a shopkeeper, was subsequently charged by the police with dishonestly handling stolen goods contrary to the Theft Act 1968, s. 22. On the question whether, on the facts, the stolen goods had been returned to the owners by virtue of the security officer's actions, held, by initialling the cartons and keeping them under observation the security officer did not take physical possession of the goods. Neither he nor the police were purporting to exercise any control over the goods but were merely waiting to see what happened to the goods after they left the premises. The cartons had not ceased to be stolen property when the defendant received them and accordingly he was guilty of contravening s. 22.

METROPOLITAN POLICE COMR v STREETER (1980) 71 Cr App Rep 113 (Queen's Bench Division: ACKNER LJ and MARS-JONES J).

596   —— knowledge or belief that goods stolen—deliberately shutting eyes to circumstances

The defendant was convicted of handling stolen goods. The jury were directed that in order to prove that, at the time the defendant received the stolen property dishonestly, he knew or believed it to be stolen property it was sufficient to show that he suspected that it was stolen and deliberately shut his eyes to the circumstances. On appeal, *held*, a direction that the offence was committed if the defendant, suspecting the goods to be stolen, deliberately shut his eyes to the circumstances, as an alternative to knowing or believing that they were stolen, was incorrect. It was however proper to direct the jury that, in common sense and in law, they might find that the defendant knew or believed the goods to be stolen because he deliberately shut his eyes to the circumstances. The appeal would be allowed.

R v LINCOLN [1980] LS Gaz R 794 (Court of Appeal: LORD LANE CJ, COMYN and MCNEILL JJ). *R v Griffiths* (1974) 60 Cr App Rep 14, CA, 1975 Halsbury's Abridgment para. 713 applied.

597　　　　—— —— evidential value of belief

The defendant was charged with dishonestly receiving goods, knowing or believing them to be stolen. There was no direct evidence that the goods were stolen but the prosecution submitted that the circumstances in which the defendant admitted having received the goods believing them to be stolen, were capable of proving that the goods were stolen. The defendant was convicted and appealed. *Held*, whether a belief had any evidential value depended on the facts of the case. It was the circumstances in which goods were received, not the admissions as to belief, which were capable of proving that the goods were stolen. The circumstances were such as to be capable of proving that the goods were stolen and the appeal would be dismissed.

R v MCDONALD [1980] Crim LR 242 (Court of Appeal: LAWTON LJ, CHAPMAN and WOOLF JJ).

598　　　　—— —— whether a cheque is "stolen goods"

The defendant was charged with dishonestly receiving stolen goods, namely a cheque for £288. A colleague of the defendant obtained cheques totalling £859 from their employer by deception and paid them into her bank account. After she handed the defendant the cheque her account stood at £641. On the question as to whether a jury was entitled to infer that the payment represented "stolen goods" within Theft Act 1968, s. 24 (2) (a) from the defendant's intention or belief that the money represented stolen goods, *held*, both a cheque and a bank account balance fell within the definition of "goods" under the 1968 Act and could, therefore, be goods which directly or indirectly represented stolen goods for the purposes of s. 24 (2) (a). In order to prove dishonest handling by receiving, it was necessary to prove that what was received was whole or part of the stolen goods. Proof was therefore required that (i) at the time of receipt, her colleague's bank balance comprised, in part, of that which represented the proceeds of stolen goods, and (ii) the defendant received such proceeds. An admission by the defendant as to her belief that the cheque was part of the stolen goods could not itself prove that her colleague's bank balance represented stolen goods within s. 24 (2) (a) or that part of such stolen goods had been received by the defendant. Her admission was admissible on the issue of her knowledge that the payment represented stolen goods and as to her honesty in receiving the money. On the issue as to whether the cheque she received represented stolen goods, the primary rule was that an accused could only make a valid and admissible admission of a statement of fact of which the accused could give admissible evidence. Unless the defendant knew the workings of her colleague's account, she could make no valid admission as to that. The jury therefore was not entitled to infer that the payment represented stolen goods from the defendant's belief that the money did so represent.

ATTORNEY-GENERAL'S REFERENCE (NO. 4 OF 1979) (1980) 71 Cr App Rep 341 (Court of Appeal: LORD LANE CJ, BOREHAM and GIBSON JJ). *Surujpaul v R* [1958] 1 WLR 1050 applied.

599　　　　—— similar fact evidence—evidence of possession of other stolen property within preceding year—admissibility

See *R v Bradley*, para. 700.

600   Harassment of residential occupier

See *R v Shepherd*, para. 1708.

601   Illegal immigration

See IMMIGRATION.

602   Jurisdiction—offence committed on high seas on foreign ship— British subject

Three British subjects were charged with offences of criminal damage aboard a Danish ship on the high seas. They demurred to the indictment on the ground that no British court had jurisdiction, but this was rejected because of the Merchant Shipping Act 1894, s. 686 (1), which provides that when a British subject is charged with having committed an offence on board a foreign ship to which he does not belong and he is within the jurisdiction of any court in Her Majesty's dominion, that court will have jurisdiction. The defendants appealed, contending that s. 686 (1) did not apply because the offence was not one triable by an English court if committed on a foreign ship on the high seas, and that anyway, as passengers, they did "belong" to the ship. *Held*, s. 686 gave the English courts extra-territorial jurisdiction to try such offences if committed by a British subject on the high seas. Further, those persons "belonged" to a vessel who had some reasonably permanent attachment to it, and this did not include passengers. The section did apply and the appeal would be dismissed.

R v KELLY [1981] 2 WLR 112 (Court of Appeal: LORD LANE CJ, STOCKER and GLIDEWELL JJ).

603   Juvenile offenders—proposed reform of law relating to juveniles

A White Paper entitled Young Offenders has been published as Cmnd. 8045. The Paper outlines proposals for strengthening the law relating to juvenile and young adult offenders.

The main proposals in relation to young adult offenders (aged 17–21) include (i) the repeal of the Criminal Justice Act 1961, s. 3 (power of courts to imprison young adult offenders); (ii) the replacement of sentences of borstal training and imprisonment by a single determinate sentence; (iii) a guarantee that offenders sentenced to between four and eighteen months will serve their sentences in designated training establishments; (iv) the retention of detention centres for male offenders sentenced to short terms of custody; (v) the supervision of offenders for up to one year following their release from custody.

In relation to juvenile offenders (aged under seventeen) the Paper proposes, inter alia, (i) the retention of detention centres for offenders aged fourteen to seventeen for short sentences; (ii) the power for the courts to impose sentences of four to eighteen months on offenders aged fifteen and sixteen; (iii) the establishment of a new order (on the recommendation of the supervising officer) specifying a programme of activities which the juvenile placed under supervision in the community agrees to undertake; (iv) the extension of the powers of probation and after-care committees; (v) the power for the courts to impose community service orders on offenders aged sixteen; (vi) the clarification and strengthening of the measures which enable parents to pay the fines of juveniles or to enter into recognisances.

604   Mens rea—attempt—perverting the course of justice

See *R v Machin*, para. 625.

605   —— criminal damage—defence of lawful excuse—relevance of accused's drunkenness

See *Jaggard v Dickinson*, para. 575.

606   —— handling stolen goods—knowledge or belief that goods stolen

See *R v Lincoln*, para. 596; *R v McDonald*, para. 597; *A-G's Reference (No. 4 of 1979)*, para. 598.

607 —— "malus animus"—intention to deceive

See *R v Turner*, para. 593.

608 —— recklessness—criminal damage

See *R v Mullins*, para. 576.

609 —— specific or basic intent—criminal damage

See *R v Orpin*, para. 577.

610 Murder — defence — diminished   responsibility — evidence   of mental imbalance

In a case where the defendant pleaded not guilty to murder but guilty to manslaughter on the grounds of diminished responsibility, it was held that such a plea, pursuant to the Homicide Act 1957, s. 2 (1), could only be accepted where there was clear evidence of mental imbalance.

R v VINAGRE (1979) 69 Cr App Rep 104 (Court of Appeal: LAWTON LJ, THOMPSON and HODGSON JJ).

611 —— —— drunkenness—intent to kill

In a case where the defendant raised the defence of drunkenness to a charge of murder it was held that the question for the jury was simply whether he had formed an intent to kill or do really serious bodily harm. The question was not whether he was capable or incapable of forming such an intent.

R v GARLICK (1980) Times, 3rd December (Court of Appeal: LORD LANE CJ, BOREHAM and WEBSTER JJ).

612 —— —— self-defence—objective and subjective tests

The defendant stabbed a man, M, with a pair of scissors. He was subsequently charged with murder and raised the defence of self-defence. At the trial there was conflicting evidence as to whether the defendant deliberately pulled the scissors out of his pocket or just picked them up off a nearby table. The trial judge directed the jury to consider whether the prosecution had satisfied them that the defendant had used more force than was reasonably necessary in the circumstances as that went solely to the question whether the defendant had lawfully killed M. The defendant was found guilty of manslaughter and appealed against the conviction on the ground of misdirection by the judge. *Held*, by directing the jury solely to consider whether the defendant had used unnecessary force in the circumstances, the judge might have precluded them from considering the real issue. What had to be considered was whether the stabbing was within the conception of necessary self-defence, as judged by the standards of common sense, bearing in mind the position of the defendant at the moment of stabbing. Further, the jury also had to consider whether the stabbing was purely angry retaliation or aggression. Such considerations bridged the gap between the "objective test" of what was reasonable judged from the viewpoint of an outsider, and the "subjective test" of what was reasonable from the defendant's viewpoint. It was necessary in cases of self-defence to draw a distinction between acts which were essentially defensive and those which were offensive, punitive or retaliatory in character. Such a distinction had not been made and the jury had failed to consider the defendant's state of mind at the time of the stabbing. The conviction was unsatisfactory and would be quashed.

R v SHANNON (1980) 71 Cr App Rep 192 (Court of Appeal: ORMROD LJ, CHAPMAN and JUPP JJ). Dictum of Lord Morris of Borth-y-Gest in *Palmer v R* [1971] AC 814 at 831 applied.

613 —— provocation—reasonable man test—nature of characteristics to be taken into account

The appellant, a chronic alcoholic, took a drug overdose when the woman with whom he had been living left him. A few days later, after drinking heavily, he killed a man who had allegedly made disparaging remarks about the woman. He raised the defence of provocation under the Homicide Act 1957, s. 3 but was convicted of murder. On appeal, he contended that the jury had been wrongly directed to consider the effect of the victim's remarks as if they had been made to a sober man. *Held*, it was necessary to consider the characteristics of the appellant. A characteristic had to have a sufficient degree of permanence to be regarded as part of an individual's character or personality. Further, there had to be a real connection between the nature of the provocation and the particular characteristics of the offender. In the present case the judge had been correct in not inviting the jury to take account of the appellant's chronic alcoholism, for it had no connection with the alleged words of provocation, and the effect of the drug overdose and the appellant's drunkenness at the time were of a transitory nature. Accordingly the appeal would be dismissed.

R v NEWELL (1980) 71 Cr App Rep 331 (Court of Appeal: LORD LANE CJ, PARK and ANTHONY LINCOLN JJ). *R v McGregor* [1962] NZLR 1069 applied.

614   Obscene articles—prohibition on import—exception based on public morality

See *R v Henn and Darby*, paras. 768, 1168.

615   Obscene publications—enforcement of law relating to pornography—application for mandamus against Metropolitan Police Commissioner

See *R v Metropolitan Police Comr, ex parte Blackburn*, para. 2155.

616   —— publishing an obscene article—video cassette used to show pornographic film—meaning of article

The Obscene Publications Act 1959, s. 2 created an offence of publishing an obscene article. The Attorney-General referred to the Court of Appeal the question whether a video cassette player containing pornographic video tape was an article within the 1959 Act. *Held*, under the 1959 Act, s. 1 (2) an article meant any description of article containing matter to be read or looked at, any sound record and any film or other record of a picture. The object of s. 1 (2) was to bring all articles which produced words, pictures or sounds within the 1959 Act, subject to two exceptions which were not relevant to the case. This was shown by s. 1 (2) itself and the terms of s. 1 (3) (b) which provided that a person published an article if he showed, played or projected an article containing matter to be looked at or a record. The words "showed, played or projected" were sufficiently wide to cover what happened when pictures were produced by using a video cassette. Therefore a video cassette was an article within the meaning of s. 1 (2).

ATTORNEY-GENERAL'S REFERENCE (No. 5 OF 1980) [1980] 3 All ER 816 (Court of Appeal: LAWTON LJ, CHAPMAN and BOREHAM JJ).

617   —— search warrant—whether warrant may be used twice

See *R v Adams*, para. 723.

618   Obstruction—police officer—refusal to comply with plain clothes policeman's request

The defendant picked up a prostitute and drove her to a secluded place. Plain clothes policemen followed him in order to arrest the prostitute. They opened the car door and asked the prostitute to get out. Since they had shown no identification, the defendant believed that they were intending to rob him and drove away and reported the incident. A private prosecution was instituted charging him with wilfully obstructing the police officers in the execution of their duty contrary to the Police Act 1964, s. 51 (3). The justices dismissed the information. On appeal by way of case stated, *held*, the justices had applied the law correctly in stating that a person could not obstruct a police constable if he did not reasonably believe him to be a police officer, especially where the act done would not be an offence if done in respect of anyone else. Further, a private prosecutor was under the same duty as a public prosecutor, which was not to obtain a conviction at any cost but to submit the full facts before the justices. Accordingly the appeal would be dismissed.

OSTLER V ELLIOTT [1980] Crim LR 584 (Queen's Bench Division: DONALDSON LJ and KILNER BROWN J).

619 **Obtaining a pecuniary advantage by deception—credit card transaction—false representation by card owner—inducement of seller**

The defendant used a credit card to obtain goods from a shop when she had already exceeded her credit limit. She was convicted of obtaining a pecuniary advantage by deception contrary to the Theft Act 1968, s. 16 (1), (2) (a), by dishonestly obtaining for herself the evasion of a debt for which she then made herself liable by a false representation that she was authorised to use the credit card to obtain the goods. On appeal, *held*, it was clear that the defendant had made a false representation to the shop assistant that she was authorised by the bank to use her credit card. The question was whether there was evidence upon which it could be found that the false representation induced the assistant to sell the goods to the defendant. The test for inducement was whether the assistant was induced by the false representation in the sense that she acted on the strength of its truth. By its contract with the bank, the shop had bought the right to sell goods to credit card holders without regard to the question whether the customer was complying with the terms of the contract between himself and the bank. Hence the shop assistant was not induced by a false representation that the defendant's credit standing at the bank gave her authority to use the card, since the state of the customer's credit with the bank was a matter for the customer and the bank, and did not concern the shop. The appeal would be allowed.

The court allowed the appeal with reluctance because the defendant's dishonest intention was manifest. If the decision was right, the bank had by its contractual arrangements opened a gateway to fraud. It was open to Parliament to frame legislation specifically to deal with credit card fraud.

R v LAMBIE [1981] 1 All ER 332 (Court of Appeal: CUMMING-BRUCE LJ, STOCKER and SMITH JJ). *Metropolitan Police Comr v Charles* [1977] AC 177, HL, 1976 Halsbury's Abridgment para. 651 distinguished.

Theft Act 1968, s. 16 now replaced by Theft Act 1978.

620 **Offences against the person—proposed law reform**

The Criminal Law Revision Committee in their 14th report, *Offences Against the Person* (1980, Cmnd. 7844), have made proposals for changes in relation to offences against the person. They propose a re-definition of murder and involuntary manslaughter and that, subject to some changes, the defences of provocation and diminished responsibility should be retained. They also favour the retention of the offence of infanticide as a separate offence, but subject to re-definition. They recommend that killing by consent should continue to be treated as murder and that terrorist crimes should not be classified as a special category of offence. Other recommendations include the abolition of the offence of causing death by reckless driving and the replacement of the offences of causing grievous bodily harm, unlawful wounding and causing actual bodily harm. The committee do not, however, favour a statutory definition for the offence of assault. They suggest that the statutory offences relating to the obstruction etc of railways should be modified so as to apply to interference with road or air traffic and that the offences of false imprisonment, kidnapping, child stealing and abduction should be replaced by new offences. The common law rules relating to voluntary intoxication and the defence of self-defence, it is suggested, should be put into statutory form.

621 **—— taking hostages**

See para. 1319.

622   **Offences relating to the administration of justice—proposed reform**

The Law Commission has published a report (Law Comm. 96) on offences relating to interference with the course of justice. It recommends a number of changes and a codification of the law. A draft bill to give effect to these changes is appended to its report. It proposes, inter alia, the abolition of certain common law offences: perverting (or attempting, conspiring or inciting the perverting of) the course of justice; embracery; personating a juror; disposing of a corpse with intent to obstruct or prevent an inquest; perjury at common law; and subornation of perjury. In the Bill, it proposes a new statutory offence of perjury and the offence of making false statements in unsworn evidence. Other offences would include the fabrication, concealment and destruction of evidence; the use of threats and bribes to suppress evidence; improper persuasion in relation to judicial proceedings; improper agreements to influence the outcome of proceedings; publication of false statements alleging corrupt conduct in relation to proceedings; publication of statements intended to produce miscarriage of justice; use of blackmail against parties to proceedings; reprisals of various sorts relating to proceedings; interference with investigations or prosecutions for arrestable offences; suppression of information relating to offences by bribes or threats; false implication of offences; false identification of self as driver of motor vehicle; wrongful pleading to criminal charge; false statement in documents prepared for criminal investigations; escape from lawful custody; and use of threats and bribes to induce pleas at trial.

623   **Offensive weapon—possession—intent to use for purpose of intimidation**

The defendant, on being refused entry to a nightclub, produced a carving knife. He was subsequently charged with carrying an offensive weapon contrary to the Prevention of Crime Act 1953, s. 1 which provides that an offensive weapon is any article made or adapted for use for causing injury to the person or intended for such use. The trial judge directed the jury that the knife was an offensive weapon if they were to find that the defendant intended to use it for the purpose of intimidation. The defendant was convicted and appealed on the ground of misdirection of the jury. *Held*, with reference to an offence under s. 1 the use of "intimidation" was to be avoided unless the evidence disclosed that it was the defendant's intention to cause injury by shock. The appeal would be allowed.

R v RAPIER (1979) 70 Cr App Rep 17 (Court of Appeal: LAWTON LJ, PARK and PETER PAIN JJ).

624   **Perjury—evidence—necessity for confirmation**

See *R v O'Connor*, para. 697.

625   **Perverting the course of justice—attempt—factors to be considered**

In giving judgment in an appeal against conviction for attempting to pervert the course of public justice, the Court of Appeal *held*, the offence was a substantive offence which consisted of conduct which had a tendency, and was intended, to pervert the course of justice. It was not an inchoate offence and the jury ought not to be directed to assess the conduct of the accused in terms of proximity to an ultimate offence, but should be left to consider the tendency and the intention of the accused. Thus, an attempt to fabricate evidence by alleging assault by police officers was an attempt to pervert the course of justice notwithstanding that the plan of the accused had not been pursued to a final successful conclusion. The jury had been correctly directed and the appeal would accordingly be dismissed.

R v MACHIN [1980] 1 WLR 763 (Court of Appeal: LORD WIDGERY CJ, EVELEIGH LJ and O'CONNOR J).

626   **Prevention of crime—use of force reasonable in circumstances**

See *Farrell v Secretary of State for Defence*, para. 2989.

**627	Prevention of terrorism—supplemental temporary provisions**

The Prevention of Terrorism (Supplemental Temporary Provisions) (Amendment) Order 1980, S.I. 1980 No. 1336 (in force on 27th October 1980), substitutes a new Schedule for the Prevention of Terrorism (Supplemental Temporary Provisions) Order 1976, Sch. 1, 1976 Halsbury's Abridgment para. 664. The Schedule lists the ports which do not require the approval of an examining officer as to their use by ships and aircraft travelling between Great Britain, Northern Ireland, the Republic of Ireland or any of the Channel Islands or the Isle of Man. The new list adds Pembroke Dock to the list of seaports and hoverports and omits Hull (Leconsfield) from the list of airports.

**628	——— temporary provisions—continuance**

The Prevention of Terrorism (Temporary Provisions) Act 1976 (Continuance) Order 1980, S.I. 1980 No. 406 (in force on 25th March 1980), continues in force the temporary provisions of the Prevention of Terrorism (Temporary Provisions) Act 1976, 1976 Halsbury's Abridgment para. 662, for a period of twelve months from 25th March 1980.

**629	Public nuisance—conspiracy to effect—elements of offence— danger or risk to public**

The appellant was convicted of conspiracy to effect a public nuisance, the escape of a patient from the lawful custody of Broadmoor Hospital. At the trial the judge had directed the jury that it was enough for the Crown to prove that there had been an intention that the patient should escape, and that it was not necessary to prove that, had the escape succeeded, the patient would have been an actual danger to the public at large. On appeal against conviction *held*, a person, such as the patient, who was subject to hospital and restriction orders without limit of time under the Mental Health Act 1959, ss. 65, 60 was obviously a potential danger to the public whilst in custody, and an actual danger when at large. The court was concerned with the potential danger to the public which would become a real or actual danger if, and when, the objective of the conspiracy was achieved. The appeal would accordingly be dismissed.

R v SOUL (1980) 70 Cr App Rep 295 (Court of Appeal: LORD WIDGERY CJ, ROSKILL LJ and CAULFIELD J). *R v Madden* [1975] 3 All ER 155, CA, 1975 Halsbury's Abridgment para. 757 distinguished.

**630	Public officer—powers—use by police officer of parking space designated for disabled**

See *George v Garland*, para. 2163.

**631	Public order—control of processions and demonstrations**

The government has published a Green Paper, *Review of the Public Order Act 1936 and related legislation* (Cmnd. 7891, 1980), setting out in detail possible changes in the statutory provisions and seeking comments on them. It is suggested that there should be a requirement that organisers of a demonstration should give advance notice to the police; and that this requirement might extend to both processions and static demonstrations. Where informal discussions following such notice do not result in "ground rules" acceptable to all on the basis upon which the event could proceed, the police might have a reserve power to impose conditions where there was a risk of disorder. This reserve power would be linked to a stringent public order test. Only if the imposition of such terms seemed unlikely to deter disorder would the police be able to apply for a ban on the event.

**632	Road traffic offences**

See ROAD TRAFFIC.

633   **Robbery—appropriation—requirements of appropriation**

In a case where the defendant snatched a handbag from a woman's grasp and the bag was dropped, he ran off empty-handed. The question arose in subsequent proceedings against the defendant under Theft Act 1968, s. 8 for robbery, as to whether the bag had been "appropriated" within s.3 of the Act. *Held*, s. 3 defined "appropriation" as the assumption by a person of the rights of an owner. Appropriation took place at the moment the defendant, acting with an intention to deprive the woman of the bag, snatched it from her grasp so that she no longer had physical control of it. In doing so the defendant was trying to exclude the woman from her exclusive claim to the bag, and was trying to treat the bag as his. Such an action was an unlawful assumption of the rights of the owner.

    CORCORAN v ANDERTON (1980) 71 Cr App Rep 104 (Queen's Bench Division: EVELEIGH LJ and WATKINS J).

634   **Sentencing**

See SENTENCING.

635   **Sexual offences—Criminal Law Revision Committee Report—recommendations**

The Criminal Law Revision Committee have published a working paper on sexual offences (HMSO, 1980). The committee proposes that the offence of rape should remain substantially in its present form but that the presumption that a boy under 14 years is incapable of having sexual intercourse (and therefore of committing rape) should be abolished. Other proposals include the retention of two separate offences of unlawful sexual intercourse with young girls, the more serious being with a girl under 13 years and the less serious being with a girl under 16 years. It is suggested that consensual anal intercourse between a man and a woman should no longer be an offence where the woman has attained a certain age. The age of consent for acts of sexual indecency with a girl should remain at 16 years. The existing offences penalising sexual relations with severely sub-normal persons should be replaced by a "scheme" whereby a county court order might be obtained restraining a named man from associating with a defective man or woman; breach of the order would constitute contempt of court. The committee further suggests that consideration be given to the creation of an offence penalising sexual intercourse or acts of indecency in public. The committee recommends the repeal of the Sexual Offences Act 1956 ss. 17, 19, 20 and their replacement by an offence of abducting a girl under 16 years from her parent or guardian against his will with intent to have sexual intercourse with her.

636   **Theft—appropriation of property belonging to another—handler of stolen goods**

The defendant was convicted of theft after dealing with stolen property. His offer to plead guilty to handling had been refused, and he appealed, contending that he could not be said to have appropriated the property when it had already been appropriated by the person who stole it originally. *Held*, when the actions of a handler amounted to a dishonest assumption by him of the rights of an owner with the intent permanently to deprive, the handler would also be guilty of theft.

    R v SAINTHOUSE [1980] LS Gaz R 707 (Court of Appeal: LORD LANE CJ and PHILLIPS and WOOLF JJ).

637   —— —— **knowingly tendering obsolete banknotes at bureau de change**

The appellant purchased some foreign banknotes which he knew were obsolete. He exchanged them for cash at a bureau de change in a department store and received an amount equal to the value of the valid banknotes currently in use. He was charged with obtaining property by deception contrary to the Theft Act 1968, s. 15, and alternatively theft contrary to s. 1. On his conviction for theft, he appealed, contending that there had been no appropriation of property belonging to another since the cashier had handed over the money voluntarily, and at that moment, it was his property and not that of the store. *Held*, a person who offered foreign bank notes in exchange for cash was representing the notes to be genuine and valid as currency in their country of origin. The money remained the property of the store when it was handed over and it was the appellant's intention to deprive the owner permanently of that money. Accordingly the appeal would be dismissed.

R v WILLIAMS [1980] Crim LR 589 (Court of Appeal: LORD LANE CJ, COMYN and McNEILL JJ).

638 —— —— requirements of appropriation

The defendant was shopping in a supermarket. She changed the price tags of one item and subsequently bought that item at a lower price than originally marked. She was later charged with theft under Theft Act 1968, s. 1 (1) and the question arose as to whether the defendant had appropriated the property within the meaning of s. 1 (1). *Held*, the provisions of s. 1 (1) had to be read together with s. 3 which provided that any assumption by a person of the rights of an owner amounted to appropriation. In changing the price tags the defendant had assumed the rights of an owner and the operation was therefore an appropriation.

ANDERTON v WISH [1980] Crim LR 319 (Queen's Bench Division sitting in Manchester: LORD WIDGERY CJ, ROSKILL LJ and HEILBRON J). *R v McPherson* [1973] Crim LR 191 approved.

639 —— forfeiture order—partnership property—validity

The Court of Appeal quashed a forfeiture order made under the Powers of Criminal Courts Act 1973, s. 43 in respect of a lorry which was owned by the defendant and another jointly, on the ground that such orders should only be made in simple, uncomplicated cases.

R v TROTH [1980] RTR 389 (Court of Appeal: EVELEIGH LJ, WIEN and DRAKE JJ).

640 Throwing corrosive fluid with intent to disable—intention to disable permanently

The appellant was convicted of throwing corrosive fluid with intent to disable contrary to the Offences against the Person Act 1861, s. 29. He appealed contending that the trial judge had failed to direct the jury that in a charge under s. 29 the prosecution had to prove that the appellant had intended to disable permanently. *Held*, the word "disablement" covered both permanent and temporary disablement. The consequence of throwing corrosive liquid was uncontrollable and incalculable and the legislature would not have intended that a person who threw corrosive liquid should avoid conviction on the basis that he intended to cause only a minor injury. Accordingly the appeal would be dismissed.

R v JAMES (1979) 70 Cr App Rep 215 (Court of Appeal: EVELEIGH LJ, WIEN and DRAKE JJ).

641 Unlawful eviction—defence

A landlord changed the lock on the front-door of his house whilst tenants who occupied a flat in the house were away. When they returned they were refused entry by the landlord and he was subsequently charged with unlawful eviction of a residential occupier, contrary to the Protection from Eviction Act 1977, s. 1 (2). The landlord claimed that the section afforded a defence, in that he believed the tenants had ceased to reside in the house. The trial judge directed the jury that, for the purposes of the section, the landlord's belief had to exist at the time of the tenants' return, and that the landlord had no reasonable cause for such a belief. The landlord was found guilty and appealed. *Held*, the judge had erred in deciding the questions as to time and existence of the landlord's belief which were questions for the jury and accordingly the conviction would be quashed.

R v DAVIDSON-ACRES [1980] Crim LR 50 (Court of Appeal: CUMMING-BRUCE LJ, PHILLIPS and MICHAEL DAVIES JJ).

642   Unlawful wounding—physical injury not foreseen—whether malicious act

The defendant was convicted of malicious wounding under the Offences against the Person Act 1861, s. 20, after injuring a man by firing a shot at a bush with the intention of compelling him to come out of hiding. His appeal was unsuccessful, as it was found that although he had not foreseen the risk of causing personal injury, his act had been reckless and the wounding was therefore malicious. On the defendant's further appeal, *held*, the defendant was guilty of malicious wounding if he had been reckless. However, the defendant's inability to foresee the consequences of his act was inconsistent with recklessness and, accordingly, the offence was not proved. The appeal would be allowed.

FLACK v HUNT (1979) 123 Sol Jo 751 (Queen's Bench Division: BROWNE LJ and WATKINS J). *R v Stephenson* [1979] 2 All ER 1198, CA, 1979 Halsbury's Abridgment para. 589 applied.

CRIMINAL PROCEDURE

Halsbury's Laws of England (4th edn.), Vol. 11, paras. 89–480, 611–810

643   Articles

Access to Prosecution Witnesses, T. M. S. Tosswill (chance of defence lawyer to interview potential prosecution witnesses): 130 NLJ 254.

Admissibility of Sexual History Evidence and Allegations in Rape Cases, Jocelyne A. Scutt: 53 Australian Law Journal 817.

Bail Act 1976: Two inconsistencies and an Imaginary Offence, Neil Cameron (refusing to hear bail applications, making bail continuous to trial and "offence" of breaking bail conditions): 130 NLJ 382.

Bail Applications by Remand Prisoners, Paul Cavadino: 130 NLJ 661.

Changing Guilty Pleas in Magistrates' Court, Tony Radevsky: 130 NLJ 82.

Costs on Conditional Discharge: A Question of Jurisdiction, Jonathan Teesdale: 130 NLJ 671.

Criminal Trial and the Disruptive Defendant, Graham Zellick: 43 MLR 1.

Cross-Examination and Natural Justice, Richard Macrory: 130 NLJ 824.

Documents considered by Justices prior to committal proceedings (in the light of *R v Colchester Stipendiary Magistrates, ex parte Beck* [1979] 2 WLR 637, 1979 Halsbury's Abridgment para. 1777): 124 Sol Jo 404.

Evidence and the Co-Accused, Alec Samuels: 130 NLJ 849.

Giving Reasons, Brian Harris (discussion of the growing pressure for reasons to be given at all stages of the criminal process, from the refusal of bail, through conviction, the imposition of imprisonment and the refusal of parole): 144 JP Jo 424.

"Guilty But" Pleas, Nicholas Yell: 144 JP Jo 349

The Hostile Witness in the Magistrates' Court, Alec Samuels: 144 JP Jo 497.

Juries and Corroboration, Robert Munday: 130 NLJ 352.

Lessons to be learned from the Wilkinson Case, C.P.G. Chavasse (discussion on *R v Wilkinson* (1979) 123 Sol Jo 825, 1979 Halsbury's Abridgment para. 668): 129 NLJ 1248.

A Pre-trial Trial?, R. B. L. Prior: 130 NLJ 700.

Should the Prosecution Have the Right to Appeal, Alec Samuels: 130 NLJ 104.

Some Problems of Evidence Obtained by Hypnosis, L. Haward and A. Ashworth: [1980] Crim. LR 469.

The Social Inquiry Report—The Law and the Practice, Alec Samuels: 144 JP Jo 350.

644   Appeal—appeal against sentence—right of appeal—order dealing with suspended sentence—total term less than six months

On conviction by magistrates, the appellant was committed to the Crown Court for sentence. He was sentenced to one month's imprisonment and a previous suspended sentence was brought into effect to run consecutively, making a total of three months' imprisonment. On appeal against the sentence, the question arose whether the court had jurisdiction to hear the appeal. *Held*, the Criminal Appeal Act 1968, s. 10 (3) (a) provided for a right of appeal against sentence where the term was six months or more. Section 10 (1) (c) provided for a right of appeal where the court had made an order as to an existing suspended sentence. The general policy of the Act was that a court should look at the whole of a sentence. Therefore, under s. 10 (3), when a suspended sentence was brought into effect in addition to a sentence for a substantive offence, then even though the total sentence was less than six months, the appellant was entitled to appeal against the whole of the sentence and not merely against the suspended sentence.

R v WILSON [1980] 1 All ER 1093 (Court of Appeal: LAWTON LJ, CHAPMAN and WOOLF JJ).

645 —— appeal by prosecution—death of prosecutor before appeal heard—whether appeal lapsed

The chief constable of a police force issued instructions, similar to those issued by other chief constables, that informations laid by the police in magistrates' courts should be laid by the chief inspector of the force. The chief inspector laid informations against the respondents alleging certain offences. The justices found that there was no case to answer and dismissed the informations. The chief inspector appealed against their decision and asked them to state a case. He entered into a recognisance to prosecute the appeal without delay, as he was called on by law to do when requesting the justices to state a case. Before the appeal came on for hearing the chief inspector died. The respondents contended that the appeal lapsed upon his death, as the recognisance to prosecute was personal. *Held*, the chief inspector was acting in a representative capacity for the chief constable or the police force, since he was merely obeying, as was his duty, the instructions validly given by the chief constable. The real prosecutor was either the chief constable or the police force. Accordingly, as the chief constable was before the court as prosecutor, the court had jurisdiction to hear the appeal.

HAWKINS v BEPEY [1980] 1 All ER 797 (Queen's Bench Division: BROWNE LJ and WATKINS J). Dicta of Lush J in *R v Truelove* (1880) 5 QBD 336, DC, at 340, Lord Parker CJ in *R v Burt, ex parte Presburg* [1960] 1 All ER 424 at 428 and Lord Denning MR in *R v Metropolitan Police Commissioner* [1968] 1 All ER 763, CA, at 769, applied.

646 —— leave to appeal—refusal—direction as to computation of sentence

At a sitting of the Court of Appeal LORD WIDGERY CJ issued the following Practice Note ([1980] 1 All ER 555).

In 1970 the then Lord Chief Justice, Lord Parker CJ, found it necessary to issue a reminder of the power, both of the full court and of the single judge, when refusing an application for leave to appeal, to direct that part of the time, during which a person was in custody after lodging his application, should not count towards sentence: see the Practice Note [1970] 1 All ER 1119, [1970] 1 WLR 663.

The power was then being exercised only rarely at the single judge stage and the reminder was necessary due to the serious delays caused to meritorious appeals by the huge number of hopeless appeals which had also to be considered. It led immediately to an improvement in the situation.

A similar reminder is necessary now. Again, meritorious appeals are suffering serious and increasing delays, due to the lodging of huge numbers of hopeless appeals. Again, the power at the single judge stage is being rarely used.

In order to accelerate the hearing of those appeals in which there is some merit, single judges will, from 15th April 1980, give special consideration to the giving of a direction for loss of time, whenever an application for leave to appeal is refused. It may be expected that such a direction will normally be made unless the grounds are not only settled and signed by counsel, but also supported by the written opinion of counsel. Advice on appeal is, of course, often available to prisoners under the legal aid scheme. Counsel should not settle grounds, or support them with written advice, unless he considers that the proposed appeal is properly arguable. It would, therefore, clearly not be appropriate to penalise the prisoner in such a case, even if the single judge considered that the appeal was quite hopeless.

It is also necessary to stress that, if an application is refused by the single judge as being wholly devoid of merit, the full court has power, in the event of renewal, both to order loss of time, if the single judge has not done so, and to increase the amount of time ordered to be lost if the single judge has already made a direction, whether or not grounds have been settled and signed by counsel. It may be expected that this power too will, as from 15th April 1980, normally be exercised.

Steps will be taken to see that the terms of this Practice Note, which is made after consultation both with those Lords Justices who habitually preside in this court and with the judges, are brought to the attention of prisoners who contemplate lodging a notice of appeal.

647 —— verdict unsafe or unsatisfactory—denial of chosen representative

A club treasurer was charged with the theft of club money. He instructed a solicitor who had previously acted for the club. At the trial, upon discovery of this fact, the judge ordered the discharge of the jury and began a new trial with a different solicitor for the treasurer. Counsel remained the same. Upon conviction the treasurer appealed on the ground that he had been denied the representative of his choice, and had therefore made a bad witness so that the verdict was unsafe or unsatisfactory. *Held*, the solicitor had completed all the work and preparation before the trial had commenced and the fact of his absence from court was not a proper ground for holding the verdict unsafe or unsatisfactory. The conviction would be upheld.

R v Gregson (1980) 124 Sol Jo 497 (Court of Appeal: Lord Lane CJ, Park and Anthony Lincoln JJ).

648 —— —— power to substitute conviction for alternative offence

The defendant was convicted of murder. The sole question for the jury was whether the defendant was guilty of murder or whether he was guilty of manslaughter by reason of diminished responsibility. A consultant psychiatrist gave evidence for the defendant that, as a result of brain damage suffered in a motor accident, the defendant had responded to provocation received on the night of the killing in a grossly exaggerated way. A medical officer gave evidence for the prosecution that the defendant was not suffering from any abnormality of mind. The medical officer's evidence was subsequently discredited and the prosecution accepted that at the time of the offence the defendant was suffering from diminished responsibility. On appeal by the defendant, the question was whether a verdict of manslaughter could be substituted for the one of murder. *Held*, the court had to consider whether the jury must have been satisfied of sufficient facts to prove the defendant guilty of manslaughter, as they must have been satisfied of facts which proved that the homicide was neither justifiable nor excusable, and the fact that they rejected the defence of diminished responsibility because of the defective medical evidence was accordingly irrelevant. The court accordingly had jurisdiction under the Criminal Appeal Act 1968, s. 3 to substitute a conviction of manslaughter for the jury's verdict. The appeal would be allowed.

R v Spratt [1980] 2 All ER 269 (Court of Appeal: Lord Widgery CJ, Ackner LJ and O'Connor J). *R v Deacon* [1973] 1 WLR 696, CA, distinguished.

649 Arrest—failure to give reasons—validity of arrest

Following a car accident the defendant was breathalysed and was requested to give a blood specimen. He was not informed of the result but was subsequently arrested and convicted of driving with a blood alcohol level above the prescribed limit. He appealed contending that at the time he had not been informed of the true reason for his arrest and that it was consequently invalid. *Held*, a defendant should be informed of the true reason for his arrest unless the circumstances were such that the defendant must know the general nature of the alleged offence. The defendant knew of the reason for his arrest and in the circumstances it was not necessary for a police officer specifically to inform him of the reason. The defendant had been lawfully arrested and the appeal would be dismissed.

R v GRANT [1980] Crim LR 245 (Court of Appeal: SHAW LJ, CHAPMAN and DRAKE JJ).

650   —— power to stop, search and detain—suspected theft of car

A police officer was assaulted by the driver of a vehicle whilst detaining him for questioning regarding the ownership of the car. The driver was charged with assaulting a constable of the Metropolitan Police in the execution of his duty, contrary to the Police Act 1964, s. 51 (1), but contended that the officer's attempt to detain him merely for questioning was unlawful and he was therefore not acting in the execution of his duty. The officer contended that a constable was authorised by the Metropolitan Police Act 1839, s. 66 to stop, search and detain anyone who might reasonably be suspected of having or conveying anything stolen or unlawfully obtained. *Held*, the words in s. 66 "stop, search and detain" necessarily involved the detention of a suspect whilst a search was taking place or questions were answered. The power of search and questioning under the section existed whether a crime had been committed or not, and whether or not an arrest was to be made. As the driver had admitted that the car was stolen, the officer was entitled under s. 66 to make further inquiries and was within the execution of his duty when he was assaulted.

DANIEL v MORRISON [1980] Crim LR 181 (Queen's Bench Division: WALLER LJ and PARK J). Dictum of Lord Goddard CJ in *Willey v Peace* [1951] 1 QB 94 at 97 applied.

651   —— use of force in making arrest—meaning of "force"

See *Swales v Cox*, para. 653.

652   —— —— reasonableness of force used

A man brought an action for damages for injury and damage to his property caused during his arrest for a minor driving offence, carried out by a number of police officers. *Held*, when exercising their powers of arrest, police officers should only use such force as was reasonable in the circumstances. It was necessary to take into account such factors as the nature of the offence, the relative strength and numbers of people involved on each side and the place where the arrest occurred. It rested with the police to show that they had complied with the law. In the instant case excessive force had been used and the plaintiff would be awarded damages.

ALLEN v METROPOLITAN POLICE COMR (1980) Times, 25th March (Queen's Bench Divison: MAY J).

653   —— validity of arrest—need to demand entry to premises to make an arrest

Two police officers were observing the house of a man whom they suspected of being involved in a burglary. They saw him approaching the house and shouted that they were police officers. He ran away and the officers pursued him to a house nearby. He entered the house by a back door and unsuccessfully tried to prevent the officers from entering. On entering they found the defendant, the owner of the house, barring their way. He was subsequently charged with obstructing police officers in the execution of their duty. During proceedings two questions arose: (i) whether the police were empowered under the provisions of the Criminal Law Act 1967, s. 2 (6) to enter premises where there had been no prior demand and refusal to enter; (ii) whether an entry to premises by opening a closed door amounted to an entry by force. *Held*, (i) Parliament in the Criminal Law Act intended to provide a comprehensive code on the rights of an officer to enter a place in circumstances when he suspected that an arrestable offence had been or was about to be committed, and the code was an extension of the common law. The code was that he might enter without qualification, but not that he might use force without qualification. If force was to be used it was governed by the words "if need be" in s. 2 (6). In certain circumstances, as in the present case, the use of force did not need to be preceded by a request and refusal of permission. (ii) Force meant the application of energy to a door. If a door was open and it was necessary to use energy to open it further then force had been used, and furthermore the turning of a door handle when the door was closed was also an application of force.

SWALES v COX (1980) Times, 19th November (Queen's Bench Division: DONALDSON LJ and HODGSON J).

654   **Bail—application for bail—previous applications for bail refused—duty of justices to consider all matters before court on previous occasion**

While the defendant was on bail, he committed a number of offences. He was arrested and pending trial was remanded in custody. He applied for bail twice, but on each occasion the justices refused to grant bail under the Bail Act 1976, s. 4 as they were satisfied, in accordance with the 1976 Act, Sch. 1, Part 1, para. 2, that there were substantial grounds for believing that he would commit an offence if released on bail and would fail to surrender at the expiration of the bail period. The defendant made a third application for bail but as there had been no change in the circumstances of the case the justices refused to consider the facts which had been before the court on previous occasions. The defendant applied for an order of mandamus directing the justices to hear the full facts supporting the application and to determine the application for bail. *Held*, although the court had a duty under s. 4 to consider granting bail on every application, a previous refusal of bail by a court was a finding that the court was satisfied that one or more of the exceptions in Sch. 1 to the granting of bail existed. The justices considering a renewed application for bail had no duty to reconsider matters previously considered but should confine themselves to circumstances which had since occurred or to matters not brought to the attention of the court on the previous occasion, The application would accordingly be refused.

R v NOTTINGHAM JJ, EX PARTE DAVIES [1980] 2 All ER 775 (Queen's Bench Division: DONALDSON LJ and BRISTOW J).

655   ————— **refusal by High Court—jurisdiction of Crown Court**

The accused, who had been committed for trial, was refused bail by a Crown Court judge who held that, as bail had already been refused by a High Court judge, he had no jurisdiction to hear a fresh application by virtue of RSC Ord. 79, r. 9 (12) which provides that in such circumstances no application may be made to "any other judge". *Held*, r. 9 (12) referred to any other judge in the High Court and did not affect the jurisdiction of the Crown Court, whose jurisdiction in relation to bail remained quite distinct from that of the High Court, even though exercised by the same judges: the jurisdiction was that of the court, not of the individual judges. However, since the accused had been convicted and sentenced no order would be made.

R v CROWN COURT AT READING, EX PARTE MALIK [1981] 1 All ER 249 (Queen's Bench Division: DONALDSON LJ and McNEILL J).

656   ————— **police power to grant bail—delay in granting bail—delay in charging and bringing before court**

The applicants were arrested and taken into police custody on a Tuesday morning. By the following Thursday morning neither of them had been charged or brought before a magistrate and accordingly their solicitor applied for a writ of habeas corpus. On Friday morning the police explained to the court that although they had had sufficient evidence upon which to charge the applicants since Tuesday they had delayed making charges so as to avoid having to grant bail because inquiries into further possible charges were more easily effected if the applicants remained in custody. They did, however, intend to charge the applicants that afternoon and bring them before a magistrate on Saturday morning, four days after their arrest. The court stayed the writ upon an undertaking from the police to complete the making of charges within $1\frac{1}{2}$ hours. This was done and the applicants were released on bail. The hearing continued to complete consideration of the matter. *Held*, (i) Principle (d) of the Judges' Rules 1964 was mandatory and required that as soon as there was enough evidence to prefer a charge an arrested person must without delay be charged or informed that he might be prosecuted. The principle was subject to no qualification, and although there might be strong grounds for amending the rule this would have to be done in a constitutional manner and not by modification in practice. (ii) The Magistrates' Courts Act 1952, s. 38 (4), was also explicit and imperative in its terms; an arrested person had to be bailed or brought before a court as soon as practicable, and 48 hours was unmistakably the maximum period of detention permissible in right of an arrest in the absence of special statutory provision. In the circumstances the applicants were fully justified in making their application.

RE SHERMAN AND APPS (1980) Times, 9th December (Queen's Bench Division: DONALDSON LJ and HODGSON J).

657 Committal for sentence—request to re-open plea—discretion of Crown Court

See *R v Inner London Crown Court, ex parte Sloper*, para. 734.

658 Committal proceedings—function of committal proceedings—discretion of prosecution to call witnesses

See *R v Grays JJ, ex parte Tetley*, para. 1845.

659 —— order of certiorari—when order may be granted

The defendant was charged with conspiring to defraud his creditors. At the committal proceedings, his counsel sought to cross-examine a witness, who was alleged to be a creditor, concerning the progress of a civil claim against the defendant. The magistrate ruled that such questions were inadmissible but issued a subpoena duces tecum against the alleged creditors. When those witnesses failed to supply the court with any material documents the magistrate refused to put pressure on them to do so, even though the documents might have shown that they were not creditors. The defendant was committed for trial and applied for an order of certiorari to quash the decision. *Held*, the court could only issue prerogative orders at the end of committal proceedings where the error of the magistrate amounted to a refusal to exercise jurisdiction and not where the matter complained of merely concerned the exercise of judicial discretion. The magistrate had not refused to exercise his jurisdiction and the application would be refused.

R v WELLS STREET STIPENDIARY MAGISTRATES, EX PARTE SEILLON [1980] LS Gaz R 93 (Queen's Bench Division: LORD WIDGERY CJ and PARK J).

660 Conspiracy—conspiracy to steal—accomplices convicted of conspiracy to rob—admissibility of convictions as evidence

At his trial for conspiracy to commit theft, contrary to the Criminal Law Act 1977, s. 1, the defendant submitted that the scheme for the theft had been abandoned without any agreement to carry it out being reached. The judge allowed the prosecution to rely on the conviction of his accomplices for robbery as evidence of the conspiracy to commit theft. The defendant was convicted. On his appeal, *held*, conspiracy to commit theft was not merely a lesser form of conspiracy to rob. The two were different agreements, so that evidence of a conspiracy to rob had no relevance to a conspiracy to commit theft. The evidence of the robbery should have been ignored but the judge had failed to direct the jury to that effect. The evidence allowed the jury to infer that the scheme had not been abandoned and thus undermined the defendant's whole case. The appeal would be allowed.

R v BARNARD (1979) 70 Cr App Rep 28 (Court of Appeal: LAWTON LJ, TUDOR EVANS and MCNEILL JJ).

661   Costs—allowances payable to witnesses

The allowances payable to witnesses in respect of costs are determined administratively. The amounts payable under the costs in Criminal Cases (Allowances) Regulations 1977, 1977 Halsbury's Abridgment para. 624, regs. 7–11, have been determined by the Home Secretary and published in Home Office circular 11/1980. The new rates apply with effect from 22nd February 1980. The financial loss allowance payable to an ordinary witness in respect of necessary absence which does not exceed four hours may not exceed £7 unless he necessarily loses more than half a day's remuneration or the expense necessarily incurred exceeds £7; in other instances the allowance may not exceed £14 a day. Subsistence allowance for an ordinary witness is 80p (absence up to five hours), £1.65 (absence of five to ten hours), or £3.40 (absence over ten hours); overnight subsistence allowance is £26.35 (within 5 miles of Charing Cross) or £23.05 (elsewhere). The overnight allowance for expert and professional witnesses is £22.95 (within 5 miles of Charing Cross) or £19.65 (elsewhere). The loss allowance for a seaman losing his ship is £14. A travelling allowance of 7.7p a mile is allowed for the use of a motor car; but where a substantial saving of time results or the use of a car is otherwise reasonable the rates prescribed in Home Office circular 147/1979 apply. In Home Office circular 11/1980 it is also stated that the Home Secretary considers that where the court is of the opinion that a parent necessarily attends for the purpose of the case the parent may be paid allowances in accordance with the 1977 Regulations, reg. 13 (2).

662   The amounts payable to witnesses for travelling allowance in respect of the use of private vehicles was increased as from 28th April 1980. For motor cycles the amounts, where a substantial saving of time is effected or where otherwise reasonable, are for cycles of engine capacity 251–500 c.c., 8.6 p a mile; for cycles of 501 c.c. and over, 9.8 p a mile; for motor cars, in the same circumstances, the rates under Home Office circular 147/1979 apply. Where such circumstances do not apply the rates for motor cycles are 4.8 p a mile (engine capacity 150 c.c. or less), 6.3 p a mile (151–250 c.c.) and 8.4 p a mile (over 250 c.c.) and the rate for motor cars is 8.4 p a mile. See Home Office circular 42/1980 and *Law Society's Gazette*, 21st May 1980, p. 518.

663   —— award out of central funds—prosecution costs—Crown Court

The following Practice Direction ([1980] 2 All ER 336) has been given by LORD LANE CJ at the sitting of the Court of Appeal.

Paragraph 4 (a) of the Practice Direction concerning allowance and disallowance of costs out of central funds in criminal cases in the Crown Court of 7th February 1977 ([1977] 1 All ER 540, [1977] 1 WLR 181, 1977 Halsbury's Abridgment para. 627) requires the court to have regard to the principle that an order will normally be made for prosecution costs in the Crown Court to be paid out of central funds, unless the proceedings have been instituted or presented without reasonable cause. It has become the practice to assume that such an order has been made unless the court orders to the contrary.

That practice will no longer prevail. An application for costs is to be made by the prosecution in each case. This will serve to remind the court that where proceedings have been instituted or continued when they should not have been, the court has a discretion not to order the costs of the prosecution to be borne by central funds.

This Practice Direction takes effect from Monday, 30th June 1980.

664   —— discretion of Crown Court—application for certiorari— jurisdiction

A motorist who was convicted on twenty-one informations concerning road traffic offences appealed against one conviction and all the fines. The conviction was quashed and the fines considerably reduced and the prosecutor was ordered to pay the motorist's costs. On an application for judicial review on the ground that the Crown Court had wrongly exercised its jurisdiction to make an order for costs, the question also arose as to the Divisional Court's jurisdiction to entertain the application. *Held*, the discretion as to costs given to the Crown Court under the Crown Court Rules 1971, r. 10 (2), had to be exercised judicially, and as there was no question that the offences were trivial or that the case should never have been brought, there was no possible ground for awarding costs against the prosecutor. In relation to the question of jurisdiction the court's power under the Courts Act 1971, s. 10 (5) to control the Crown Court by an order of certiorari was not limited to matters of jurisdiction, and therefore the order for costs would be quashed.

R v LEWES CROWN COURT, EX PARTE CASTLE [1980] RTR 381 (Queen's Bench Division: WALLER LJ and PARK J). *David v Commissioners of Metropolitan Police* [1962] 1 All ER 491, DC, and *R v Exeter Crown Court, ex parte Beattie* [1974] 1 All ER 1183, DC, 1974 Halsbury's Abridgment para. 4, applied.

665   —— **taxation of costs—method of calculation of fees for court attendance—Law Society statement**

The Special Committee of the Law Society on Remuneration has published its views on the implications of the decision of Goff J in *R v Wilkinson* [1980] 1 All ER 597, 1979 Halsbury's Abridgment para. 668. The committee, pending the findings of further research, continues to regard 1,000 chargeable hours per annum as the norm for a solicitor. The committee will publish notional salary figures (including pension provision) for guidance in estimating costs. In relation to criminal proceedings in the Crown Court, it regards £10,000 as an appropriate salary for a partner working in a large city or town and £9,000 for a partner working elsewhere. The committee advises that an estimate of interest in clients' accounts should be made (based on the previous year and with subsequent trends in mind) and that this, less an amount for investment income surcharge, should be deducted from overheads before apportioning the overheads between the fee-earners. For costs purposes, articled clerks should be regarded as part-time fee-earners. See the Law Society Gazette, 23rd April 1980, p. 393.

666   **Criminal Law Act 1977—commencement**

The Criminal Law Act 1977 (Commencement No. 7) Order 1980, S.I. 1980 No. 487 brings into force on 12th May 1980 ss. 38 and 39 of the Act, which contain provisions relating to the execution of warrants of arrest and the service of summonses and citation throughout the United Kingdom. Provisions of certain enactments are repealed by the order.

667   The Criminal Law Act 1977 (Commencement No. 9) Order 1980, S.I. 1980 No. 1632 brings into force on 1st December 1980 s. 40, Schs. 7 (part), 13 (part) of the Act, which relate to the transfer of fine orders.

668   **Crown Court—appeal—joinder of informations—consent of defendant**

The defendant was convicted in the juvenile court on two informations involving allegations of arson which were tried together. On his appeal to the Crown Court, the defendant refused to consent to the informations being tried together, although he had not objected at the trial. *Held*, the Crown Court trying an appeal by way of rehearing stood in the same position as a juvenile or magistrates' court. The Crown Court in its appellate capacity could not order that two informations be tried together without the consent of the defendant and the defendant was not estopped from subsequently objecting because of his actual or implied consent to the joinder in the juvenile court.

SEDWELL v JAMES [1980] Crim LR 110 (Crown Court at Reading: JUDGE PIGOT). *Brangwynne v Evans* [1962] 1 WLR 267, *Aldus v Watson* [1973] QB 902 applied.

669   **Crown's immunity from prosecution—nomination of fictitious individual as defendant**

See *Barnett v French*, para. 735.

670   **Defence—judge's duty to put defence to jury—plea of self-defence**

Canada
A convicted murderer appealed against his conviction on the ground, inter alia, that
the trial judge, in directing the jury, had not tied the defence of self-defence to the
particular facts. *Held*, the judge had failed to instruct the jury that, in considering the
defence, if the accused had used more force than a reasonable man would have
considered necessary, it was not a good defence to murder, but that they could still
bring in a verdict of guilty of manslaughter. The appeal would accordingly be
allowed, the conviction quashed and new trial ordered.
        R v Deegan [1979] 6 WWR 97 (Court of Appeal of Alberta).

671   **Deportation order—recommendation for deportation—relevance
        of previous convictions**

See *R v Secretary of State for Home Department, ex parte Santillo*, para. 1507.

672   **Evidence—admissibility—admissions made by defendant when
        suffering from hypoglycaemia**

In a case concerning indecent assault, during the course of the trial, the defence
submitted that statements made by the defendant to the police were inadmissible
because he was a diabetic and suffered from hypoglycaemia at the time of the
admissions, which caused severe impairment of judgment. It was held that due to
the effect of his condition on the defendant's state of mind, such statements would be
excluded.
        R v Powell [1980] Crim LR 39 (Crown Court at Wakefield: Judge Randolph).

673   **—— —— confession—oppression**

A man was arrested and detained at a police station, ostensibly for an arrestable
offence, for fifty hours, during which he was asked some seven hundred questions
and made a written confession to allegations of corruption, a non-arrestable
offence. He was not charged until twelve months later. The defence appealed
against his conviction on the ground that the evidence was wrongly admitted
because it was obtained by oppression, or alternatively that it should have been
excluded in the exercise of the judge's discretion because the circumstances were
unfair. *Held*, the arrest and the detention thereafter were unlawful in that the
accused had not been charged, or warned that he might be charged, in accordance
with the Judges' Rules principle (d), nor had he been brought before a court within
forty-eight hours as he should. He had made incriminating statements which were
not borne out by the evidence, indicating that they were not made voluntarily.
Even if the court had reached the conclusion that they were voluntary the evidence
would have been excluded anyway because the detention was unfair.
        R v Hudson (1980) Times, 29th October (Court of Appeal: Waller LJ, Tudor
Evans and Glidewell JJ).

674   **—— —— —— record certified by accused**

The accused was arrested and interrogated in accordance with the Judges' Rules. He
made certain admissions which were the only evidence against him at the trial. The
Crown adduced evidence of the interview and successfully sought to put a
contemporaneous record of it, signed by the accused, as an exhibit. The accused
appealed. *Held*, although such a document was neither an aide memoire nor a
statement within the Judges' Rules, r. 4, it was a record certified by the accused of his
interview with the police and was admissible as an exhibit subject to the overriding
discretion of the judge to exclude it.
        R v Todd (1980) Times, 6th November (Court of Appeal: Lord Lane CJ,
Caulfield and Butler-Sloss JJ).

675   —— —— **deposition of minor—failure to comply with Oaths Act**

A wife was charged with the murder of her husband and at her trial her sixteen-year-old son was called to give evidence for the prosecution. While taking the oath the boy did not hold the Testament as required by the Oaths Act 1978, s. 1. The trial judge subsequently directed the jury to treat the boy's evidence as unsworn evidence of a person of tender years and to ignore it because of lack of corroboration. The wife was convicted and applied for leave to appeal on the ground that the verdict was unsafe and unsatisfactory inter alia on the ground of misdirection in relation to the boy's evidence. *Held*, the words in s. 1 were directive, so that even where there was a failure to comply with the provisions, the oath was not necessarily invalidated. The trial judge's directions on the boy's evidence were wrong because the pre-requisites of the Children and Young Persons Act 1933, s. 38, which allowed the reception of a child's unsworn evidence, were not satisfied. Since the boy was an unsatisfactory witness, the judge would have been justified in telling the jury to disregard his evidence and the application would be refused.

R v CHAPMAN [1980] Crim LR 42 (Court of Appeal: ROSKILL and ORMROD LJJ and BRISTOW J).

676   —— —— **discretion of judge to exclude evidence on grounds of unfairness**

See *R v Willis*, para. 691.

677   —— —— **privilege—statement to legal aid officer**

Canada

In a case where the defendant was charged with obtaining a quantity of groceries by false pretences using two worthless cheques, the information given by him to an officer of a local legal aid centre when applying for legal aid, was held to be privileged, and unless that privilege was waived the information given was inadmissible at the defendant's trial. Furthermore, the relationship between the legal aid officer and the defendant was analogous with that of a solicitor and his client.

R v LITTLECHILD (1979) 108 DLR (3d) 340 (Court of Appeal of Alberta).

678   —— —— **statement by defendant—self-serving statements**

The defendant was convicted of burglary. At his trial the judge refused to allow oral and written exculpatory statements made by him to the police, containing an alibi, on the ground that they were self-serving. On appeal, *held*, although a self-serving statement was not evidence of the facts alleged, it ought to be admitted in evidence as showing the initial reaction of the defendant when questioned by the police about a suspected crime. If, during his trial, the defendant did not go into the witness box to support that account by his own evidence, the trial judge was entitled to draw the attention of the jury to such a failure provided he did not suggest that the failure amounted to any evidence upon which the prosecution could rely. In the present case the jury was faced with a strong case against the defendant and as there had been no explanation coming from him the appeal would be dismissed.

R v MCCARTHY (1980) 71 Cr App Rep 142 (Court of Appeal: LAWTON and DUNN LJJ and HEILBRON J). *R v Pearce* (1979) 69 Cr App Rep 365, 1979 Halsbury's Abridgment para. 672 applied.

679   —— —— **telephone tapping**

See *R v Hennessey*, para. 767.

680   —— **alibi notice as prosecution evidence—guidelines**

On an appeal against a conviction for robbery, the court noted with concern the common practice at the Central Criminal Court of making an alibi notice part of the prosecution case. The primary purpose of an alibi notice was to warn the prosecution that an alibi might be relied on. Prosecuting counsel should consider most carefully before taking this course. If they put in an alibi notice they should be prepared to prove it rather than rely on the consent of defending counsel. Circumstances might arise where it would be before the jury as part of the prosecution case when it ought not to be.

R v WATTS (1980) 71 Cr App Rep 136 (Court of Appeal: LAWTON LJ, BOREHAM and COMYN JJ).

681   ——burden of proof—application for order to inspect bank account—whether notice required

The defendants were charged with offences of knowingly living wholly or in part on the earnings of prostitution contrary to the Sexual Offences Act 1956, s. 30. The police officers concerned wished to inspect the defendants' bank accounts and successfully made an ex parte application for orders under the Bankers' Books Evidence Act 1879, s. 7. The defendants were informed that the bank had been served with the orders and they subsequently sought an order of certiorari to quash the orders on the grounds that (i) the magistrate gave insufficient consideration to the evidence before him on the ex parte application; (ii) the orders did not relate to accounts concerned in any criminal proceedings and (iii) the orders were not limited in time. *Held*, s. 7 was to be used for the relief of banks and any other use was to be limited as much as possible. It was important in making such orders that they did not extend beyond the true purposes of the charges involved. In the present case it was not clear what evidence had been given before the magistrate and although there was nothing in s. 7 to say that an application could not be made ex parte, there was much to be said for notice being given in such circumstances. Further the orders should have been limited in time. The application would be granted and the orders would be quashed.

R v MARLBOROUGH ST. METROPOLITAN STIPENDIARY MAGISTRATE, EX PARTE SIMPSON [1980] Crim LR 305 (Queen's Bench Division: LORD WIDGERY CJ and WIEN J). *Williams v Summerfield* [1972] 2 All ER 1334 applied.

682   ——character—character of accused—imputation on witnesses' character

The defendants, C and M, were charged with causing grievous bodily harm contrary to the Offences Against the Person Act 1861, s. 18. At the trial the prosecution applied for leave to call evidence of C's previous convictions on the ground that during his evidence imputations had been made against prosecution witnesses within the Criminal Evidence Act 1898, s. 1 (f) (ii). The judge ruled in favour of the submission and subsequently M made an unsworn statement from the dock so as to prevent his previous convictions from being admitted in evidence. Both defendants were convicted and appealed on the ground that their evidence was merely a denial of the charges and that the judge did not warn defence counsel that the allegations made were of such a nature as to render C liable to cross-examination as to his records. *Held*, evidence of C's previous convictions was admissible since his defence amounted to more than a mere denial of the charge, as it involved imputations on the police. The judge need not warn defence counsel in every case of the risk of previous convictions being admitted as a result of imputations made against prosecution witnesses. It was not necessary in this case and the appeal would be dismissed.

R v McGEE AND CASSIDY (1979) 70 Cr App Rep 247 (Court of Appeal: EVELEIGH LJ, WIEN and DRAKE JJ).

683   ——confession—determination of admissibility on voir dire—judge's power to reconsider his ruling

At a trial within a trial to determine the admissibility of certain written confession statements signed by the accused, the trial judge ruled that the statements were voluntary and admissible and the trial then proceeded in the presence of the jury. During cross-examination a police officer gave certain evidence, which counsel for the accused regarded as inconsistent with the evidence he had given at the voir dire and which strengthened his earlier submissions that the statements were not voluntary. The judge however refused to reconsider his ruling. On appeal against conviction, *held*, the judge had been wrong to rule that he had no power to consider the relevance of evidence, given after the trial within the trial, upon the issue of whether the statements were not voluntary and therefore inadmissible. He had a duty to exclude inadmissible evidence from the jury's consideration. It was however only in rare and unusual cases that further evidence later emerged which might cause the judge to reconsider and judges should continue to discourage counsel from making submissions of law founded on a tenuous evidential base.

On the facts of the present case nothing had emerged which should have led the judge to rule that the prosecution had not proved that the statements were voluntary and the appeal would accordingly be dismissed.

R v WATSON [1980] 2 All ER 293 (Court of Appeal: CUMMING-BRUCE LJ, THOMPSON and SMITH JJ). Dictum of Lord MacDermott in *R v Murphy* [1965] NI 138 followed.

684　　　　―――― ――― ――― **subsequent function of jury**

At the appellant's trial on a charge of unlawful wounding the only evidence against him was a confession made to the police. His defence was that the confession was untrue: he claimed that he had been induced to make it by the promise of bail. The judge conducted a trial within a trial and ruled that the confession was admissible. However, he failed to direct the jury as to the possible effect of the alleged inducement on the voluntary nature of the confession. He further omitted specifically to invite them to determine its truthfulness. The appellant was convicted and appealed. *Held*, the judge's ruling on the voir dire only decided the question of admissibility. It was for the jury to decide all questions of fact including, if the confession was admitted, whether there had been an inducement and whether it was voluntary. It was also for the jury, after a proper direction from the judge, to assess its probative value. In the present case the judge's direction was inadequate and the appeal would be allowed.

R v McCARTHY (1980) 70 Cr App Rep 270 (Court of Appeal: WALLER LJ, MILMO and KENNETH JONES JJ). *Chan Wei Keung v Queen* [1967] 2 AC 160, [1967] 1 All ER 948, PC, followed; *R v Burgess* [1968] 2 QB 112, [1968] 2 All ER 54n, CA, applied.

685　　　　―――― **corroboration—sexual offence—distressed condition of victim**

Australia

On a charge of assault with intent to commit rape the trial judge admitted evidence of the victim's distressed state. On appeal, *held*, after an extensive review of the authorities, the judge was not in error in admitting the evidence nor in classifying it as potentially corroborative of the victim's testimony in view of, inter alia, the fact that it amounted to much more than evidence of an upset state at the time of making a complaint.

PETERSON v R (1979) 27 ALR 641 (High Court of Australia).

686　　　　―――― **cross-examination—credibility of witness—duty of defence counsel**

The appellant was one of three convicted of rape. At the trial he was the first to give evidence. The judge ruled that it was the duty of succeeding defence counsel to cross-examine him by putting to him evidence of their clients whenever it differed from his evidence. The appellant appealed claiming that the judge had been wrong to hold that it was part of the duty of defending counsel to suggest that his evidence was untruthful by way of cross-examination, thus exposing any conflicts between the defendants. *Held*, if it was suggested that a witness was not telling the truth, cross-examination gave him an opportunity of explaining or expanding on the evidence which he had given. Accordingly, it was the duty of defence counsel to inform him through cross-examination that the veracity of his evidence was challenged and in what respects it was not accepted. In this respect there was no difference between the duty of defending and prosecuting counsel. The appeal would be dismissed.

R v FENLON (1980) 71 Cr App Rep 307 (Court of Appeal: LORD LANE CJ, PARK and ANTHONY LINCOLN JJ). *Browne v Dunn* (1893) 6 R 67, HL applied.

687   —— **defence of automatism—necessity for medical evidence**

The defendant, a diabetic, was charged with driving without due care and attention contrary to the Road Traffic Act 1972, s. 3. He raised the defence of automatism but called no supporting evidence regarding his diabetic condition. He was acquitted and the prosecution appealed. *Held*, once careless driving had been proved it was for the defendant to show facts supporting the defence of automatism. Medical evidence was not essential to prove automatism but the defence would rarely succeed without it. The defendant had failed to take sufficient precautions to deal with his condition before driving and it was wrong in such circumstances to allow the defence. The appeal would be allowed.

MOSES v WINDER [1980] Crim LR 232 (Queen's Bench Division: ROSKILL LJ and CAULFIELD J).

688   —— **defendant's admission as to use of controlled drug—whether evidence of unlawful possession**

The defendants were questioned by the police in relation to the death of a drug addict. They made oral and written admissions as to the type of drugs they used and were charged with unlawful possession of those drugs contrary to the Misuse of Drugs Act 1971, s. 5 (1). *Held*, these statements were sufficient to provide prima facie evidence of the nature of the substances which had been in their possession.

R v CHATWOOD [1980] 1 All ER 467 (Court of Appeal: BRIDGE LJ, FORBES and SHELDON JJ). *Bird v Adams* [1972] Crim LR 174, DC approved.

689   —— **evidence in law—meaning of documents made evidence in law**

See *Attorney-General's Reference (No. 2 of 1980)*, para. 594.

690   —— **evidence irregularly obtained—judge's discretion to exclude evidence**

See *R v Trump*, para. 2352.

691   —— **evidence obtained by police infiltration—judge's discretion to exclude evidence**

The appellant was convicted of conspiracy to supply drugs which were controlled under the Misuse of Drugs Act 1971. A police officer had infiltrated amongst the alleged conspirators by pretending that he wished to be supplied with cocaine. By means of telephone conversations he succeeded in obtaining evidence of the existence of a conspiracy to which the appellant was a party. Subsequently, when the appellant supplied the drugs, he was arrested. He appealed against the conviction claiming that the trial judge had wrongly exercised his discretion in refusing to exclude the evidence of a police officer who had infiltrated the alleged conspiracy; he further put forward the defence of entrapment. *Held*, the appellant, by his own admissions, had provided clear evidence of a conspiracy to supply drugs during his telephone conversations with the police officer. By merely asking the appellant to supply the cocaine, the officer had not encouraged him to commit a crime. The trial judge was bound to admit the evidence and had not wrongly exercised his discretion. Furthermore, following the authorities, there was no defence of entrapment in English law. Accordingly, the appeal against conviction would be dismissed.

R v WILLIS (1978) 68 Cr App Rep 265 (Court of Appeal: LAWTON and GEOFFREY LANE LJJ and GOFF J). *R v Birtles* [1969] 1 WLR 1047, CA applied.

692   —— expert evidence—conflicting medical evidence—assessment by court

In an action for damages for personal injury there was conflicting medical evidence and the judge accepted that given by a witness for the defendant. The plaintiff appealed on the ground that the court should have made its own assessment of the medical evidence. *Held*, although the demeanour of medical experts giving evidence was not as important as when evidence was given by other witnesses, it was material for the purpose of weighing the value of the evidence. The trial judge therefore had an advantage over the appellate court which should be slow to interfere with the judge's findings on such evidence, although not to the same extent as in the case of evidence given by ordinary witnesses.

JOYCE V YEOMANS (1980) Times, 11th December (Court of Appeal: WALLER and BRANDON LJJ and SIR DAVID CAIRNS).

693   —— harassment of residential occupier—evidence of previous conviction—admissibility

See *R v Shepherd*, para. 1708.

694   —— identification—photographic identification—use of photographs in trial

Three men were verbally abused in a cafe and when they left, were followed and attacked. The police showed the men an album containing 900 photographs of all persons in the area with criminal records. Two of the men picked out the appellant as one of the assailants. At the appellant's trial, on a charge of wounding with intent to cause grievous bodily harm, the prosecution produced the album of photographs to the jury reasoning that it was a striking coincidence that two of the men had picked out the same photograph. On appeal against conviction *held*, the appellant's conviction would be quashed. It was clear that the jury had been made aware, by the use of the photograph album, that the appellant had a criminal record, and may have taken that fact into account when deciding whether or not to convict. Although this did not per se always lead to quashing a conviction, the present case was founded on visual identification unsupported by corroborative evidence.

R v LAMB (1980) 71 Cr App Rep 198 (Court of Appeal: LAWTON LJ, DUNN and HEILBRON JJ).

695   —— —— proper approach for the court

A police constable identified the defendant, whom he had had the opportunity of inspecting for fifteen minutes in a good light some six weeks earlier, in a room where he expected to find the defendant and where the defendant was the only person not in uniform. The defendant contended on appeal that his conviction could not stand, having regard to the circumstances of the purported identification. *Held*, in view of the high quality of the original observation the circumstances of the identification were irrelevant and the conviction would be upheld.

McSHANE V NORTHUMBRIA CHIEF CONSTABLE [1980] RTR 406 (Queen's Bench Division: LORD WIDGERY CJ and PARK J).

696   —— Judges' Rules—confession—defendant not informed before interrogation of right to speak to solicitor

The defendant was convicted of theft although there had been insufficient evidence save his admissions made to a police officer. The defendant claimed that the interview was conducted with only one officer present and his repeated requests to telephone a solicitor were refused. The officer involved stated that the defendant's accusations were untrue but he admitted that he had not taken the initiative in notifying the defendant of his right to telephone a solicitor before questioning. The defendant claimed that this amounted to a breach of the Administrative Directions on Interrogation and the Taking of Statements, para. 7, appended to the Judges' Rules 1964. *Held*, para. 7 presupposed an initial request to telephone a solicitor before questioning. In the absence of a person in custody having first raised the matter with the officer concerned, para. 7 placed no obligation on the officer before questioning him to tell him that he might telephone a solicitor if he wished to do so.

R v KING [1980] Crim LR 40 (Court of Appeal: LAWTON LJ, TUDOR EVANS and McNEILL JJ).

697 —— perjury—necessity for confirmation of evidence

In a case concerning an appeal against a conviction of perjury on the ground of a misdirection as to the requirements of the Perjury Act 1911, s. 13, it was *held* that s. 13 required that there should be more than the evidence of one person that the statement alleged in the indictment to be false was in fact untrue. Once the falsehood was proved by further evidence there was then no requirement for corroboration, in the common law sense, that the person charged knew that what he was saying was false.

R v O'CONNOR [1980] Crim LR 43 (Court of Appeal: ROSKILL LJ, BRISTOW and HOLLINGS JJ).

698 —— receiving stolen goods—receiver's knowledge—admissibility

See *Attorney-General's Reference (No 4 of 1979)*, para. 598.

699 —— report of police interview—report edited—admissibility

In a case concerning the trial of three men for murder and robbery it was admitted during cross-examination by the prosecution that the text of police interviews with the defendants had been edited. *Held*, where a record of a police interview had been taken, it was to form part of the police report to the prosecuting solicitor and was then to be included in instructions to prosecution counsel. The police were not to edit the records as the whole tone of the interview might be misrepresented by omitting an intimidatory passage which might vitiate a subsequent admission.

R v PENFOLD (1979) 71 Cr App Rep 4 (Court of Appeal: SHAW LJ, O'CONNOR and COMYN JJ).

700 —— similar facts—handling stolen goods—admissibility

The defendant was charged with handling stolen goods contrary to the Theft Act 1968, s. 22. During the trial the prosecution, relying on s. 27 (3) of the Act, adduced evidence to the effect that he had had in his possession, within the preceding year, similar stolen goods. Section 27 (3) provides that where a person is being proceeded against for handling stolen goods, evidence showing that he had had in his possession stolen goods from any theft taking place not earlier than twelve months before the offence charged is admissible for the purpose of proving that he knew or believed the goods to be stolen. The summing up included a direction on the doctrine of recent possession. After an objection by defence counsel it was withdrawn in brief terms. The defendant was convicted and appealed on the grounds of misdirection regarding the direction on recent possession and on the inadequacy of the withdrawal. *Held*, s. 27 (3) enabled otherwise irrelevant and inadmissible evidence to be introduced on a charge of handling stolen goods, but it had to be strictly construed. It was not designed to allow evidence to be given of what was, in effect, another offence of handling stolen goods committed before the offence charged. The law in general terms, save in very special circumstances, excluded evidence of previous offences. It was the judge's duty to ensure that nothing was introduced into the prosecution's case which was not permitted by law. Matters prejudicial to the defendant had been introduced and for that reason the conviction was unsatisfactory and would be quashed.

R v BRADLEY (1979) 70 Cr App Rep 200 (Court of Appeal: SHAW LJ, O'CONNOR and COMYN JJ).

701 —— —— indecent assault—admissibility

In a case where the defendant was convicted of indecent assault, a question of admissibility of evidence of similar circumstances concerning the defendant arose.

The Court of Appeal stated that evidence of similar facts that did not include evidence disclosing the commission of offences similar to that charged might be admissible where the surrounding circumstances were so similar to those in the offence charged as properly to be described as "striking".

R v BARRINGTON (1980) Times, 3rd December (Court of Appeal: DUNN LJ, PHILLIPS and DRAKE JJ).

702   —— submission of no case to answer—whether sufficient evidence to justify conviction

A motorist was charged with driving without due care and attention contrary to the Road Traffic Act 1972, s. 3 after an accident caused by a blue Range Rover. The motorist admitted that he owned a blue Range Rover and that he was in the vicinity at the relevant time but submitted before the magistrates that there was no case to answer. This was rejected and he appealed against conviction. *Held*, there was clearly some evidence to justify a finding of fact that the driver of the vehicle was the defendant. As the sufficiency of that evidence was a question of fact for the magistrates the appeal would be dismissed.

SCRUBY v BESKEEN [1980] RTR 420 (Queen's Bench Division: ROSKILL LJ and CAULFIELD J).

703   —— tape recordings—jury listening to tapes while in retirement— use of two-way radio—whether material irregularity

In a case where the defendant was charged with blackmail, there was evidence consisting of tape recordings. A two-way radio was used so that the recordings could be played in the courtroom and listened to by the jury when they had retired. On the question whether this constituted a material irregularity, *held*, in order to assess the evidence, the jury had to listen to the tapes. It was not practicable for them to come back into court each time they wished to hear a recording. What was done was done on the order of the court and with the parties' consent. No other method could have been adopted and there was no material irregularity.

R v DEMPSTER (1980) 71 Cr App Rep 302 (Court of Appeal: LORD LANE CJ and PARK and LINCOLN JJ).

704   —— trade or business records—information recorded in computer print-out—personal knowledge of information supplied

Stolen bank notes were found to have previously been in the possession of the owner of a burgled house by means of a computer print-out which identified their serial numbers. Evidence suggested that three notes found in the appellant's possession were from the same series and he was convicted of burglary. He appealed against conviction contending that the information recorded in the print-out was not a trade or business record compiled from information supplied by any person who had or could reasonably be supposed to have had personal knowledge of the matters dealt with in the information they supplied, and hence was not admissible as evidence under the Criminal Evidence Act 1965, s. 1 (1). *Held*, the serial numbers were recorded purely by the operation of the machine, which also recorded those numbers of notes which had been rejected as defective. Hence only the machine could be said to have had knowledge of the rejected notes' serial numbers. Accordingly they were not in the personal knowledge or mind of anyone and the print-out was not admissible in evidence. Further, the conviction could not be upheld by application of the proviso to the Criminal Appeal Act 1968, s. 2 (1) on the ground that no miscarriage of justice had occurred. The appeal would be allowed.

R v PETTIGREW (1980) 71 Cr App Rep 39 (Court of Appeal: LORD WIDGERY CJ, BRIDGE LJ and WOOLF J).

705   —— witness—credibility—attack on police evidence

While cross-examining police witnesses counsel for a man accused of assaulting a policeman alleged that a written confession had been improperly obtained. He failed to provide substantiating evidence. *Held* that, it was improper for counsel in making an attack on the honesty of the police to fail to call the defendant to substantiate the allegations by giving specific evidence.

R v CALLAGHAN (1979) 69 Cr App Rep 88 (Court of Appeal: WALLER LJ, LAWSON and JUPP JJ). Dicta of Lord Goddard CJ in *R v O'Neill and Ackers* (1950) 34 Cr App Rep 108 at 111 applied.

706   WALLER LJ, referring to *R v Callaghan*, para. 705, in which he observed that it was improper for counsel in making an attack on the honesty of the police to fail to call the defendant to substantiate the allegations by giving specific evidence, stated that there was an aspect of the problem which did not then occur to him. A client might require a challenge to be made to a police officer but refuse to go into the witness box to support that challenge because of his very bad record. If the client insisted that such a challenge be made, having been warned that his refusal would probably provoke a very strong comment from the judge, counsel then had to carry out his instructions. Such a case should, however, be wholly exceptional.

See Times, 20th February 1980.

707   —— —— **whether witness should remain out of court**

A car dealer pleaded not guilty to contravening the Trade Descriptions Act 1968, s. 1 (1) by making false representations as to a car's mileage at a car sale. Before evidence was adduced he sought leave for his son, whom he employed in his business and who he stated made the false representations, to remain in court throughout the prosecution case. The justices refused the application and the car dealer sought an order of certiorari to quash the justices' decision. *Held*, it was general practice that witnesses, other than experts, were to remain out of court until they were required to give evidence. The son was a potential defence witness and the justices had not erred in their decision. The application would be refused.

R v BEXLEY JJ, EX PARTE KING [1980] RTR 49 (Queen's Bench Division: WALLER LJ and PARK J).

708   **Indictment—alternative offences—validity of conviction**

The defendants were charged with conspiring to contravene the Immigration Act 1971. The indictment contained, in addition to conspiracy, counts of "harbouring" contrary to the 1971 Act, s. 25 (2). The conspiracy charge was subsequently not proceeded with and the defendants were convicted of harbouring. They appealed against the conviction on the grounds that harbouring was a summary offence and they had not elected before the magistrates to be tried on indictment. *Held*, the offence of harbouring was made an offence triable only summarily by the Criminal Law Act 1977, s. 15. Although committal proceedings in the present case started before the section came into operation no proceedings had been taken in relation to any offence under the 1971 Act, s. 25 (2) until after the date of commencement of the 1977 Act by which time they could not properly be joined in the indictment as they were then offences triable only summarily. The appeal would be allowed.

R v MEHET [1980] Crim LR 374 (Court of Appeal: EVELEIGH LJ, BRISTOW and McNEILL JJ).

709   —— **amendment—addition of further count**

The defendant was charged with burglary, contrary to the Theft Act 1968, s. 9 (1) (a). The cost of the damage caused amounted to £34.50. He was committed for trial on that charge only. The prosecution successfully applied to the recorder of the court to add to the indictment a count of damage to property, contrary to the Criminal Damage Act 1971, s. 1 (1), to which the defendant pleaded guilty and was convicted. His plea of not guilty to burglary was accepted. The defendant appealed against the conviction on the ground that the addition of the count was unlawful since, under the Criminal Law Act 1977, s. 23, justices could not commit a defendant on a charge or criminal damage where the damage involved did not exceed £200. *Held*, it was not unlawful to add to an indictment a charge on which the justices could not commit the defendant for trial. The added count was, in accordance with the Administration of Justice (Miscellaneous Provisions) Act 1933, s. 2 (2), to be founded on facts or evidence disclosed in an examination or evidence taken before a justice. The court had inherent jurisdiction to ensure that the additional count was not unfair. The addition of the count in the present case was neither unlawful nor unfair and the appeal would be dismissed.

R v CONSIDINE (1979) 70 Cr App Rep 239 (Court of Appeal: DONALDSON LJ, THOMPSON and BUSH JJ). *R v Nisbet* [1972] 1 QB 37 applied.

710 —————— **whether indictment defective**

The defendant was charged with wounding with intent. The judge told the jury that they could find him guilty of wounding with intent or of unlawful wounding. They returned a verdict of unlawful wounding, but even after a majority direction on the charge of wounding with intent the requisite majority could not be achieved. A second count was then added to the indictment charging him with unlawful wounding, and the defendant was convicted. On appeal, *held,* since the jury had not found the defendant not guilty of the offence charged in the original indictment, the Criminal Law Act 1967, s. 6 (3), did not permit them to find him guilty of the lesser offence on the indictment as it stood. The question was whether the judge was right to allow the addition of a second count. He could only do so if the indictment was defective. It was too narrow to regard "defective" as confined to such a defect as would render the indictment liable to be quashed. No injustice resulted to the defendant from the amendment, which merely removed a technical impediment, and the appeal would be dismissed.

R v COLLISON (1980) 71 Cr App Rep 249 (Court of Appeal: DUNN LJ and THOMPSON and HEILBRON JJ).

711 ——— **duplicity—theft of various goods**

In a case concerning the theft of various items from different departments of a shop, counts in the indictment each charged the theft of more than one item from different departments. It was *held* that the counts were not bad for duplicity. It was legitimate to charge in a single count one activity, although that activity might involve more than one act.

R v WILSON (1979) 69 Cr App Rep 83 (Court of Appeal: BROWNE LJ, LAWSON and PHILLIPS JJ). *Jemmison v Priddle* [1972] 1 QB 489 applied.

712 ——— **joinder of counts—validity**

The defendant was charged on an indictment containing four counts which were paired. They related to robbery on a shop and on the owner of the shop and the carrying of firearms. It was conceded that it was a case where the evidence admissible in connection with one of the robberies was not admissible in connection with the other although they were not dissimilar in character. The trial judge refused an application to sever the indictment and he directed the jury to consider the counts separately although there was some evidence which was common to both pairs of counts. The jury convicted on one pair of counts and acquitted on the other pair. On an application for leave to appeal on the ground that the counts should have been severed because it was not a similar fact case, *held,* there was no reason within the statutory provisions applicable why the two robbery counts together with the allocated firearms counts should not have been joined and tried together. There was no injustice where a jury was told that the evidence on one pair of counts was not evidence on the other pair. Further the trial judge had not misdirected the jury and accordingly leave to appeal would be refused.

R v BLACKSTOCK (1980) 70 Cr App Rep 34 (Court of Appeal: ROSKILL LJ, THOMPSON and GIBSON JJ).

713 Legal aid

See LEGAL AID AND ADVICE.

714   Magistrates' courts

See MAGISTRATES.

715   Plea—counsel asking judge's view of sentence and plea

Whilst giving judgment on an appeal against sentence, LAWTON LJ observed that defending counsel could not and should not, except in wholly exceptional cases, expect to be given guidance by a judge about the sentence which may be imposed. Counsel going to see the judge behind the scenes almost as a matter of course was bad practice.

R v COWARD (1980) 70 Cr App Rep 70 (Court of Appeal: LAWTON LJ, BRISTOW and HOLLINGS JJ).

716   —— plea of guilty—whether plea unequivocal—duty of judge not to accept plea

The defendant was charged with burglary and alternatively the theft of goods valued at £25. He was advised by counsel to plead not guilty. When he was arraigned he pleaded not guilty to burglary but guilty to theft. Counsel requested the count of theft to be put again to the defendant because a possible defence had been disclosed and the defendant had not precisely understood the proceedings. The judge ruled that the defendant had entered an unequivocal plea of guilty to theft and he was sentenced to imprisonment. He appealed. *Held*, the essential starting point was whether the plea was unequivocal. In the majority of cases the word "guilty" would have indicated that the plea was unequivocal. When the defendant was unrepresented the court took care to see that he was aware of the elements of the crime to which he was pleading guilty. This principle should be maintained even when the defendant was represented, as in this case. The appeal would be allowed and the conviction quashed.

R v HALLIWELL [1980] Crim LR 49 (Court of Appeal: EVELEIGH LJ, PHILLIPS and MICHAEL DAVIES JJ).

717   —— plea of not guilty—plea of guilty to lesser charge—effect of plea not being accepted

A driver pleaded not guilty to reckless driving, the only count in the indictment, but guilty to careless driving. The prosecution rejected that plea. The driver was tried and acquitted of reckless driving. The charge of careless driving was not left to the jury but the trial judge sentenced him on the basis of his earlier plea of guilty. The driver appealed on the ground that once the prosecution had rejected his plea of not guilty, his plea of guilty had to be treated as withdrawn. *Held*, once a defendant pleaded not guilty to the only count in an indictment, and the prosecution rejected his plea of guilty to a lesser offence, that plea of guilty had to be treated as withdrawn. Under the Road Traffic Act 1972, s. 3A, it was open to the judge to leave to the jury not only the offence of reckless driving but also the offence of careless driving. It was a fundamental error not to do so. The appeal would be allowed and the conviction quashed.

R v THOMPSON [1980] Crim LR 188 (Court of Appeal: EVELEIGH LJ, WIEN and DRAKE JJ). *R v Hazeltine* [1967] 2 QB 857 applied.

718   Prerogative order—certiorari—application to High Court—jurisdiction—whether matter relating to trial on indictment

Two police officers were committed for trial charged with assault occasioning actual bodily harm. Before the trial, solicitors for the defence requested information as to whether any of the jury panel had criminal convictions. The prosecuting solicitor refused their request, but the judge subsequently ordered that the chief constable be supplied with a list of the panel and that he supply the solicitors for the defence and prosecution with full details of any criminal proceedings recorded against any member of the panel. The chief constable applied for certiorari for the judge's order to be quashed, but the Divisional Court held that it had no jurisdiction to entertain the application. On appeal, *held*, LORD DENNING dissenting, a review of the judge's order would involve reviewing the jurisdiction of the Crown Court in a matter relating to trial on indictment and the Divisional Court's jurisdiction to do that was excluded by the express exception in the Courts Act 1971, s. 10 (5). The appeal would, accordingly, be dismissed.

Their Lordships, however, expressed serious doubts as to whether there should be any jury vetting at all, and stated that such vetting was unconstitutional.

R v SHEFFIELD CROWN COURT, EX PARTE BROWNLOW [1980] 2 All ER 444 (Court of Appeal: LORD DENNING MR, SHAW and BRANDON LJJ).

719   Previous conviction—conditional discharge—admissibility of conviction in subsequent disciplinary proceedings

A complaint of misconduct was referred to the Statutory Committee of the Pharmaceutical Society of Great Britain in respect of two of its members who had been conditionally discharged following convictions of criminal offences. The Committee ruled that it did not have jurisdiction to hear the complaint in view of the provisions of the Powers of the Criminal Courts Act 1973, s. 13 (3) which provides that the conviction of an offender who is placed on probation or discharged absolutely or conditionally shall in any event be disregarded for the purposes of any enactment or instrument which imposes any disqualification or disability upon convicted persons or authorises the imposition of any such disqualification or disability. The Committee also decided that it would be contrary to the maxim that no one should be punished twice for the same offence. On an application by the Pharmaceutical Society for an order of certiorari to quash the ruling, *held*, according to s. 13 there was nothing to prevent the allegation of misconduct being supported by proof of the facts as found by the criminal court. Further, the Pharmacy Act 1954, s. 8 provided that where a person had been convicted of an offence, the Committee was required to consider whether it was such as to render a member unfit to be registered. The committee could not take the conviction simpliciter as the basis of its decision, but there was no question of the member being punished twice, for while the facts might be the same before the court and the tribunal, the conviction was a finding of an entirely different nature. Further, the Committee was not a court of competent jurisdiction to which the maxim could apply. Accordingly the application would be granted.

R v STATUTORY COMMITTEE OF THE PHARMACEUTICAL SOCIETY OF GREAT BRITAIN, EX PARTE PHARMACEUTICAL SOCIETY OF GREAT BRITAIN (1980) Times, 13th November (Queen's Bench Division: LORD LANE CJ and WEBSTER J).

720   Prosecution—Director of Public Prosecutions—requirement that details of certain cases be made known to him

Under the Prosecution of Offences Regulations 1978, reg. 6 (2), 1978 Halsbury's Abridgment para. 747 chief officers of police are requested to supply information relating to certain cases to the Director of Public Prosecutions. The Director has specified the following cases as falling within that class: (1) offences against the Perjury Act 1911, s. 1, and the Criminal Justice Act 1967, s. 89; subornation of those offences and conspiracy and incitement to commit them; (2) conspiracy and attempt to pervert or defeat the course of justice; (3) conspiracy to manufacture controlled drugs; large-scale conspiracy to supply controlled drugs in large amounts; (4) large-scale conspiracy to contravene the immigration laws; (5) causing death by reckless driving where the deceased is a close relative of the accused; (6) rape where one woman is raped by more than one man on the same occasion and where one man rapes several women; (7) offences against the Sexual Offences Act 1956, s. 7, as amended by the Mental Health Act 1959, s. 127; (8) kidnapping; (9) robbing involving the use of firearms where injury is caused; (10) large-scale robbery involving property or money exceeding £250,000 in value; (11) arson involving grave damage to public property; (12) coinage offences except those that are trivial; (13) criminal libel; (14) conspiracy, attempt or incitement to commit offences listed at heads (6)–(13) above; and (15) offences in relation to the Backing of Warrants (Republic of Ireland) Act 1965 where the order is resisted under s. 2 (2) of the Act.

See the booklet entitled *The Prosecution of Offences Regulations 1978* published by the
Director of Public Prosecutions.

721   —— duty to enforce the law—Metropolitan Police Commissioner

See *R v Metropolitan Police Comr, ex parte Blackburn*, para. 2155.

722   —— private prosecution—Crown Court—right of prosecutor to appear in person

A private prosecution was brought by the complainant against a company alleging
offences under the Trade Descriptions Act 1968, the Theft Act 1968 and the
Companies Act 1948. The company was indicted and at the pre-trial review the
complainant appeared in person and claimed to represent the Crown. He contended
that as a litigant in person he was entitled to conduct the prosecution in the Crown
Court himself. *Held*, he was not a litigant in person before the Crown Court and
was not entitled to act as an advocate because once the indictment was signed the
proceedings continued in the name of the Sovereign. Secondly, the public interest
required that the prosecution in the Crown Court be impartial and subject to the
constraint necessary to ensure a fair trial. Therefore the complainant would not be
allowed to address the jury, call or examine witnesses, cross-examine defence
witnesses or address the court.

  R v GEORGE MAXWELL (DEVELOPMENTS) LTD [1980] 2 All ER 99 (Crown Court
at Chester: JUDGE DAVID).

723   Search warrant—extent of authorisation—whether warrant may be used twice

In a case concerning the use of the same search warrant obtained under the Obscene
Publications Act 1959, s. 3 (1), on more than one occasion, for the seizure of
publications and films from a shop, it was held that the intention of the section had
been for such a warrant to authorise only one entry, search and seizure.

  R v ADAMS [1980] 1 All ER 473 (Court of Appeal: CUMMING-BRUCE LJ, PHILLIPS
and MICHAEL DAVIES JJ).

724   Trial—direction to jury—self defence

See *R v Shannon*, para. 612.

725   —— discretion of trial judge—voluntary absence of accused—jurisdiction of judge to dismiss counsel

An accused absconded during his trial. Counsel's instructions were that the accused
would give evidence and that witnesses were available. The judge concluded that
the absence was voluntary and rejected an application to discharge the jury and order
a new trial. However, although both counsel and the solicitor for the accused
wished to continue their representation, they were prevented from doing so by
judicial order, the judge having ruled that the accused's instructions were deemed to
have been withdrawn. The accused was convicted and sentenced in his absence.
On appeal, *held*, a trial judge should not involve himself in questions of professional
conduct and etiquette. The judge's decision prevented counsel exercising his
discretion, and it prejudiced the fairness of the trial. The verdict was unsafe and
unsatisfactory and the conviction would be quashed.

  Their Lordships considered that both branches of the profession needed further
guidance from their professional bodies concerning their professional duties in cases
where an accused absconded.

  R v SHAW [1980] 2 All ER 433 (Court of Appeal: DONALDSON LJ, KILNER
BROWN and WOOD JJ).

726   —— offence triable either on indictment or summarily—election of mode of trial—jurisdiction of justices

The defendant was charged with theft and appeared before the justices without legal representation. He elected to be tried before the justices and pleaded not guilty. The case was adjourned so that the attendance of witnesses could be arranged. He sought legal advice and was advised to elect for trial before the Crown Court. It was then agreed with the prosecution that committal proceedings should take place on the adjourned date without the attendance of witnesses. On the adjourned date the justices refused to allow the defendant to change his election and as no witnesses were present the case was adjourned again. At the next hearing the defendant applied to the justices to be allowed to address them on the question as to whether they should permit him to be put to his election again. They refused to hear the application on the ground that they had no jurisdiction to do so where a previous application had been refused. The defendant sought an order of mandamus requiring the justices to hear and determine his application to be put to his election again. *Held*, the justices had erred in their decision. They had the power to hear the application, but whether they did so or not was a matter for their discretion. The application would be granted and the case remitted to the justices for them to decide whether it was right for them to consider the application.

R v SOUTHAMPTON CITY JJ, EX PARTE ROBINS [1980] LS Gaz R 459 (Queen's Bench Division: EVELEIGH LJ and WATKINS J).

727   —— summing up—several defendants charged with same offence—separate summings-up—possibility of unfairness

The appellant was one of several convicted of conspiracy to obtain money by deception, and forgery. On appeal it was contended that the trial judge had been in error in summing up the cases of all the defendants separately, since they had been so prejudiced as to make the verdicts against them unsatisfactory. *Held*, separate summing-ups were likely to lead to unfairness. The jury's verdicts against earlier defendants in the indictment might make it difficult for the jury fairly to review the evidence of a witness who had already been believed, when considered against that of a later defendant who had alleged that the witness should not have been believed. This was particularly common when the defences were "cut throat," ie exculpatory and inculpatory in nature. The appeal would be allowed.

R v WOODING (1979) 70 Cr App Rep 256 (Court of Appeal: LAWTON LJ, TUDOR EVANS and McNEILL JJ).

728   —— trial by jury—right of accused to elect trial by jury—young accused

A person aged sixteen years appeared in a juvenile court charged with an offence triable summarily or by jury. The case was adjourned and by the date of the adjourned hearing the defendant had turned seventeen. *Held*, as the defendant was seventeen when his trial began he was entitled to elect trial by jury.

R v ST ALBANS CROWN COURT, EX PARTE GOODMAN (1980) Times, 16th December (Queen's Bench Division: ACKNER LJ).

729   —— —— series of offences—right of accused to elect for trial by jury

The Criminal Law Act 1977, s. 23 (1) provides that where an offence is charged under the Criminal Damage Act 1971 and the value involved in the damage is less than £200 the offence shall be triable only summarily. Section 23 (7) creates an exception by providing that s. 23 (1) does not apply where the offence charged is one of two or more offences which appear to the court to constitute or form part of a series of two or more offences of the same or a similar character, committed on the same occasion.

The appellant, who was charged with obstructing a police officer in the course of his duty and causing criminal damage to his trousers, claimed that she had a right to elect for trial by jury on the ground that the offences formed part of a series of two or more offences of the same or a similar character. *Held*, although the two offences arose out of the same incident, they were not of the same or similar character and could not be described as a "series" of offences. Accordingly, the appellant had no right to elect for trial by jury.

RE PRESCOTT (1979) 70 Cr App Rep 244 (Court of Appeal: ORMROD, BROWNE and EVELEIGH LJJ). Dicta of Lord Pearson in *Ludlow v Metropolitan Police Commissioner* [1971] AC 29 at 39 applied.

730 —— trial within a trial—admissibility of evidence

See *R v Watson*, para. 683; *R v McCarthy*, para. 684.

731 Variation of order—Crown Court—time limit for variation

An employee was convicted of various offences involving dishonesty against his employer. He was sentenced to imprisonment and a criminal bankruptcy order was made against him under the Powers of Criminal Courts Act 1973, s. 39. The order was made in the sum of £35,000 which was specified as being a lump sum in respect of all the offences and, contrary to s. 39 (3) (a), was not apportioned between the offences. Two months later the trial judge purported to rectify the order by apportioning the sum into amounts attributable to each offence. The employee appealed against the order contending that the original order was void because it failed to comply with s. 39 and that the amendment contravened the Courts Act 1971, s. 11 (2) as it was a variation of the order made more than twenty-eight days after the original order was made. *Held*, it was in the judge's inherent jurisdiction to remedy a mistake in an inchoate order. He had not "varied" the order under s. 11 (2) and was therefore not required to make the alteration within twenty-eight days of the original order. The alteration had been properly made and the appeal would be dismissed.

R v SAVILLE [1980] 1 All ER 861 (Court of Appeal: LORD WIDGERY CJ, BRIDGE LJ and WOOLF J). *R v Michael* [1976] 1 All ER 129, 1975 Halsbury's Abridgment para. 667 applied. *R v Menocal* [1979] 2 All ER 510, HL, 1979 Halsbury's Abridgment para. 593 distinguished.

CROWN PROCEEDINGS

Halsbury's Laws of England (4th edn.), Vol. 11, paras. 1401–1580

732 Article

The Death of Habeas Corpus, Charles Blake: 130 NLJ 772.

733 Certiorari—application to quash order of Crown Court—when order may be granted

See *R v Wells Street Stipendiary Magistrates, ex parte Seillon*, para. 659.

734 —— —— whether excess of jurisdiction by Crown Court

The defendant was charged with an offence under the Theft Act 1968, s. 25. He made a written confession, pleaded guilty and was committed by the justices to the Crown Court for sentence. On the request of his counsel the Crown Court agreed to re-open the plea and the case was remitted to a stipendiary magistrate who declined to accept it. On an application for certiorari to quash the decision to remit the case, or an order of mandamus directing the magistrate to hear and determine the case, *held*, as the case was one of committal for sentence, the Crown Court had jurisdiction to re-open the question of the plea even where it was unequivocal. The Crown Court had not acted in excess of its jurisdiction and the application for certiorari would be refused, but an order for mandamus would be granted directing the justices and not the magistrate to hear and determine the case.

R v INNER LONDON CROWN COURT, EX PARTE SLOPER (1978) 69 Cr App Rep 1 (Queen's Bench Division: LORD WIDGERY CJ, KILNER BROWN and ROBERT GOFF JJ). *R v Mutford and Lothingland, ex parte Harber* [1971] 2 QB 291 applied.

735　Criminal proceedings—nomination of individual as defendant—nomination of fictitious defendant

Due to the Crown's immunity from prosecution, a principal transport officer in the Department of the Environment was nominated as defendant in respect of a motoring offence committed by the Department. He appealed against his conviction on the ground that, because of his position within the Department, he was likely to acquire a long record of motoring convictions of which he was not guilty. *Held*, dismissing the appeal, there were no grounds for overturning the conviction. However there was no reason why the practice, at one time adopted in analogous cases before the criminal courts, of nominating a fictitious defendant "John Doe", should not also be adopted by the Crown for the purposes of criminal proceedings, in order to overcome this problem.

BARNETT V FRENCH (1980) Times, 22nd December (Queen's Bench Division: DONALDSON LJ and KILNER BROWN J).

736　Judicial review—application—appropriate division of High Court

See *Heywood v Board of Visitors of Hull Prison*, para. 5.

737　Prerogative orders—immigration appeal—appeal to adjudicator available—whether mandamus and certiorari lie

See *R v Chief Immigration Officer, Gatwick Airport, ex parte Kharrazi*, para. 1497.

CUSTOMS AND EXCISE

Halsbury's Laws of England (4th edn.), Vol. 12, paras. 501–1100

738　Anti-dumping and countervailing duties—revocation and suspension of duties

The Anti-Dumping Duty (Temporary Suspension) Order 1980, S.I. 1980 No. 35 (in force on 18th January 1980), suspends for a further period of three months the anti-dumping duty imposed by the Anti-Dumping Duty (No. 2) Order 1977, 1977 Halsbury's Abridgment, para. 748, on certain stainless steel in so far as it consists of products covered by the ECSC Treaty, originating in Spain.

739

The Anti-Dumping Duty (Revocation) Order 1980, S.I. 1980 No. 279 (in force on 4th March 1980), removes the anti-dumping duty on imports of certain stainless steel originating in Spain imposed by the Anti-Dumping Duty (No. 2) Order 1977, 1977 Halsbury's Abridgment para. 748. The 1977 Order and a number of temporary suspension Orders are revoked. Any duty paid on or after 11th April 1979 must be repaid.

740　Appointment of ports

The following table lists the enactments which define certain limits of ports and provide for the establishment of new ports for customs and excise purposes.

Ports	Relevant Statutory Instruments (1980)	Effect	New Ports
Boston, Humberside, Scarborough and Whitby	486	Redefines limits	Humber
Bristol Channel and Cardigan Bay	1367	Defines limits in Cardigan Bay, Bristol Channel, Barnstaple Bay and Severn Estuary	Fishguard (incorporating the former port of Cardigan); Milford Haven (incorporating the former port of Milford); the revised port of Barnstaple includes the former port of Bideford
Colchester, Orwell Haven, Lowestoft, Great Yarmouth and King's Lynn and Wisbech	483	Defines limits	Orwell Haven, King's Lynn and Wisbech and Great Yarmouth
Folkestone, Dover, Ramsgate, Whitstable and Medway	484	Redefines limits	—
London	482	Redefines limits	—
Padstow, Penzance, St. Mary's, Falmouth, Fowey, Plymouth, Dartmouth, Teignmouth and Exeter	1368	Redefines limits	Falmouth (incorporating the former port of Truro)
Tees and Hartlepool, Sunderland, Tyne, Blyth and Berwick	485	Defines limits (Appointment of the Port of Tyne Order, 1970 revoked)	Tees and Hartlepool
Weymouth, Poole, Solent, Littlehampton, Shoreham and New Haven	1369	Defines limits	Solent (incorporating the former ports of Southampton, Portsmouth and Cowes)
Liverpool, Mostyn, Holyhead and Caernarfon	1879	Defines limits; ports of Liverpool and Caernarfon redefined	Mostyn (incorporating the former port of Chester); Holyhead, incorporating the former port of Chester
Preston, Fleetwood, Heysham and Workington	1882	Defines limits	Heysham (incorporating the former ports of Lancaster and Barrow in Furness); revised port of Workington incorporates the former ports of Workington, Whitehaven, Maryport and Carlisle).

741   Car tax

The Car Tax (Isle of Man) Order 1980, S.I. 1980 No. 182 (in force on 1st April 1980), provides for modification of various provisions relating to car tax following the agreement between the United Kingdom and the Isle of Man whereby both countries are to be treated as a single area for the purposes of that tax.

742   **Commissioners of Customs and Excise—designation order**

The European Communities (Designation) Order 1980, S.I. 1980 No. 865 (in force on 26th June 1980 except for article 2 (b) which came into force on 18th July 1980), designates the Commissioners of Customs and Excise to exercise powers conferred by the European Communities Act 1972, s. 2 (2), to make regulations in relation to the payment by the Commissioners of Customs and Excise to the Intervention Board for Agricultural Produce of sums equivalent to amounts paid to them as the monetary compensation amounts charged on imports in the United Kingdom from other member states of the European Economic Community and to excise matters of the European Communities.

743   **Community law—free movement of goods—quantitative restrictions between member states—whether price freeze a measure of equivalent effect**

See *Cases 16–20/79: Openbaar Ministerie v Joseph Danis*, para. 64.

744   **Community transit—penalties and sanctions for breach of rules**

The Customs and Excise (Community Transit) Regulations 1980, S.I. 1980 No. 762 (in force on 2nd July 1980), provide a penalty and a sanction of forfeiture of goods for breaches of Council Regulation (EEC) 222/77 and Commission Regulation (EEC)223/77 relating to the transit of goods within the Community. The regulations also give the Commissioners of Customs and Excise the power to require goods moving under the internal or external Community transit procedure within the United Kingdom to be moved by routes specified by them.

745   **Control of movement of goods**

The Control of Movement of Goods Regulations 1980, S.I. 1980 No. 761 (in force on 2nd July 1980), prescribe the procedure for the movement within the UK of imported goods which are to be cleared at an approved place other than at their port of importation or place of landing and goods for exportation which are presented for customs examination prior to their movement to the port or place of exportation at a place approved for such examination.

746   **Customs and excise airports—designated aerodromes**

See para. 178.

747   **Customs duties—ECSC unified tariff**

The Customs Duties (ECSC) Order 1980, S.I. 1980 No. 67 (in force on 23rd January 1980), amends the Customs Duties (ECSC) (No. 2) Order 1977, 1977 Halsbury's Abridgment para. 1177, to provide for exemption from customs duty up to and including 31st December 1980 for ECSC goods originating in the territory of Southern Rhodesia at the date of the order. This is in accordance with a Decision of the representatives of the governments of the member states of the ECSC meeting within the Council on 21st January 1980.

The order provides that the rules to be applied for determining whether goods originate in Southern Rhodesia shall be those applying to the Overseas Countries and Territories of the EEC contained in Council Decision (EEC) 76/568.

This order revoked by Customs Duties (ECSC) (No. 2) Order 1980, S.I. 1980 No. 1999 (in force on 1st January 1981).

748   **—— Greece**

The Customs Duties (Greece) Order 1980, S.I. 1980 No. 1911 (in force on 1st January 1981, except for art. 4 which comes into force on 6th April 1981), provides for reductions in the customs duties between the United Kingdom and Greece pursuant to Greece's accession to the European Economic Community. The reduction of duty in respect of all products listed in Schedule 1 is 10 per cent. The reduction of duty on products covered by the Community's common organisation of the market in beef and veal, which are listed in Schedule 2, is 20 per cent. The Order also further amends the Customs Duties (Greece) (No. 3) Order 1977, 1977 Halsbury's Abridgment para. 768, by providing that no customs duty is charged under it on the importation into the United Kingdom of any goods to which articles 2 and 4 of this order apply.

749   —— reliefs—quota relief

The Customs Duties (Quota Relief) Order 1980, S.I. 1980 No. 245 (in force on 1st March 1980), provides for the administration of the United Kingdom's share of the tariff quota opened for the period of 1st March 1980 to 30th June 1980 by the EEC, under the provisions of Commission Regulation (EEC) 438/80, providing exemption from customs duty on import into the United Kingdom for home use of rum, arrack and tafia originating in various African, Caribbean and Pacific States.

The application of the general provisions of the Customs Duties Quota Relief (Administration) Order 1976 is modified, so as to require that an application for relief from duty must be accompanied by the necessary origin documents and to ensure that relief from customs duty is restricted to goods entered for home use.

750

The Customs Duties (Quota Relief) (No. 2) Order 1980, S.I. 1980 No. 905 (in force on 1st July 1980), provides for the administration of the United Kingdom's share of the tariff quota opened for the period of 1st July 1980 to 30th June 1981 by the EEC, providing exemption from customs duty on import into the United Kingdom for home use of rum, arrack and tafia originating in various African, Caribbean and Pacific states. The order modifies the application of the general provisions of the Customs Duties Quota Relief (Administration) Order 1976, 1976 Halsbury's Abridgment para. 753, so as to require that an application for relief must be accompanied by the necessary origin documents and to ensure that relief is restricted to goods entered for home use for both customs duty and excise duty purposes.

751

The Customs Duties (Quota Relief) (Paper, Paperboard and Printed Products) (Amendment) Order 1980, S.I. 1980 No. 479 (in force on 24th April 1980), increases the duty-free quotas which the United Kingdom is entitled to open, under Protocol No. 1 to the Agreements between the EEC and Sweden, Norway and Finland, for folding boxboard.

752

The Customs Duties (Quota Relief) (Paper, Paperboard and Printed Products) (Amendment No. 2) Order 1980, S.I. 1980 No. 1303 (in force on 23rd September 1980) amends the Customs Duties (Quota Relief) (Paper, Paperboard and Printed Products) Order 1979, 1979 Halsbury's Abridgment para. 753, by increasing the duty-free tariff quota which the United Kingdom is entitled to open for a certain type of coated mechanical printing paper from Finland.

753

The Customs Duties (Quota Relief) (Paper, Paperboard and Printed Products) Order 1980, S.I. 1980 No. 1884 (in force on 1st January 1981), provides for the opening during 1981 of duty-free tariff quotas for these products originating in Austria, Iceland, Sweden, Switzerland, Norway and Finland.

754

The Customs Duties (ECSC) (Quota Relief) Order 1980, S.I. 1980 No. 665 (in force on 14th May 1980), provides for the opening of a tariff quota, within which customs duty will be reduced to two per cent, of 40,000 tonnes of certain tinplate and certain other products known as tin-free steel, imported into the United Kingdom from countries which are not member states of the ECSC. Goods do not constitute part of the quota if they are imported for the purpose of being exported to member states of the EEC in the same state as the goods were in when imported into the United Kingdom.

755　　The Customs Duties (ECSC) (Quota and Other Reliefs) (Amendment) Order 1980, S.I. 1980 No. 1800 (in force on 28th November 1980), amends the Customs Duties (ECSC) (Quota and Other Reliefs) Order 1979, 1979 Halsbury's Abridgment para. 757, such that it no longer applies to certain iron and steel products originating in Argentina.

756　　The Customs Duties (ECSC) (Quota and Other Reliefs) (Amendment No. 2) Order 1980, S.I. 1980 No. 1867 (in force on 5th December 1980), amends the Customs Duties (ECSC) (Quota and Other Reliefs) Order 1979, 1979 Halsbury's Abridgment para. 757, such that it no longer applies to certain steel products except those originating in those countries listed in Sch. 3 to 1979 Order.

757　　Customs Duties (ECSC) (Quota and Other Reliefs) (No. 2) Order 1980, S.I. 1980 No. 2032 (in force on 1st January 1981), revokes and replaces the Customs Duties (ECSC) (Quota and Other Reliefs) Order 1980, which would otherwise have come into force on the same date, but remains unpublished. The order provides for reliefs from customs duty on certain iron and steel products originating in certain developing countries.

758　　—— —— —— **agricultural levy relief**

See para. 54.

759　　**Excise duty—refund**

The Customs and Excise (Repayment of Customs Duties) Regulations 1980, S.I. 1980 No. 1825 (in force on 1st January 1981), substitute the words "excise duty" for the words "duty of customs or excise" in the Customs and Excise Management Act 1979, s. 123 (1).

760　　—— **reliefs**

The Excise Duties (Relief on Small Consignments) Regulations 1980, S.I. 1980 No. 1012 (in force on 15th August 1980), provide for the admission into the United Kingdom without payment of excise duty of certain small non-commercial consignments of goods sent from abroad by a private individual to another private individual in the United Kingdom for the personal or family use of the recipient. Effect is given to Council Directives (EEC) 74/651, as amended by 78/1034, and 78/1035. The regulations restrict the relief that may be given in respect of tobacco products, alcoholic beverages, perfumes and toilet waters to the quantities of those goods set out in the Schedule. These reliefs first came into force on 1st January 1979, but until now have been allowed on an extra-statutory basis.

761　　**Export of goods—control**

The Export of Goods (Control) (Amendment) Order 1980, S.I. 1980 No. 1370 (in force on 8th October 1980), further amends the Export of Goods (Control) Order 1978, 1978 Halsbury's Abridgment para. 813, by removing cocoa products and certain non-ferrous waste and scrap from the goods subject to export control under Sch. 1, Part 1, Group A. The order also alters the descriptions of cryptographic equipment, radio receivers and radio transmitters which are subject to export control under Group 3F of Part II of Schedule 1. Control of the radio receivers and transmitters is extended to exports to all destinations. The order also includes among the goods which are subject to export control in Group 3H of Part II of Schedule 1 certain maraging steel alloy and certain high strength aluminium alloy.

762　　—— —— **Iran**

The Export of Goods (Control) (Iran Sanctions) Order 1980, S.I. 1980 No. 735 (in force on 30th May 1980), is made under the Import, Export and Customs Powers (Defence) Act 1939 s. 1 and prohibits, subject to certain exceptions, the export of embargoed goods to Iran for delivery to a person in Iran. All goods are embargoed except for specified foodstuff, medical products and other specified products if sold or supplied for medical or surgical purposes.

The principal exceptions are goods exported pursuant to, or in furtherance of a contract made before the date on which the order came into operation, ships and aircraft on scheduled journeys or exported after temporary importation and goods licensed under the order.

763   Finance Act 1980

See para. 2328.

764   Hydrocarbon oil duties—heavy oil for road fuel—recovery of rebate—procedure

The Customs and Excise Commissioners brought an action in the High Court against a civil engineering company, contending that it had contravened the Hydrocarbon Oil (Customs and Excise) Act 1971, s. 10 (3), by using heavy oil on which a rebate had been obtained as fuel for vehicles adapted for use on roads without paying to the commissioners an amount equal to the rebate. They sought a declaration that the amount of the rebate be paid to them under s. 11 (1), which provides that a person who uses heavy oil in contravention of s. 10 (3) is liable to a penalty of three times the value of the oil or £100, whichever is the greater; and the commissioners may recover from him an amount equal to the rebate on like oil at the rate in force at the time of the contravention. The company applied to have the action struck out on the ground that the High Court had no jurisdiction to entertain it since the two parts of s. 11 (1) had to be read together so that the "amount equal to the rebate" which the commissioners sought to recover was a pecuniary penalty for a customs offence additional to the penalties specified in s. 11 (1) and was recoverable only in the magistrates' court within three years under the Customs and Excise Act 1952, s. 283 (1). *Held*, the second part of s. 11 (1) was not to be construed as an additional penalty but as providing a separate method by which the commissioners could recover an amount equal to the rebate. Such proceedings could be brought in any court, including the High Court. Accordingly the commissioners were entitled to the declaration sought.

CUSTOMS AND EXCISE COMRS v GEORGE WIMPEY & CO LTD [1980] 3 All ER 102 (Court of Appeal: LORD DENNING MR, WALLER and DUNN LJJ).

Hydrocarbon Oil (Customs and Excise) Act 1971, ss. 10 (3), 11 (1), now Hydrocarbon Oil Duties Act 1979, ss. 12 (2), 13 (1). Customs and Excise Act 1952, s. 283 (1), now Customs and Excise Management Act 1979, s. 147 (1).

765   Isle of Man Act 1979—excise warehousing

The Excise Warehousing Regulations 1979, etc. (Amendment) Regulations 1980, S.I. 1980 No. 992 (in force on 1st September 1980), provide for the removal of goods, subject to excise duty, to the Isle of Man, without payment of duty, from warehouses and certain licensed or registered premises within the United Kingdom, primarily for the purpose of warehousing in the Island, thus restoring the position which existed before the coming into force of the Isle of Man Act 1979.

766   Offence—importation of prohibited goods—burden of proof

The defendants were charged with an offence contrary to the Customs and Excise Act 1952, s. 304 (a) in that they knowingly and with intent to evade the importation prohibition were concerned in dealing with cocaine. Though there was evidence at the trial that the defendants had been dealing with cocaine, there was no evidence of importation. The prosecution submitted, however, that where a substance was the subject of a prohibition against importation, then any person found dealing with that substance was ipso facto dealing with the substance in circumstances in which there had been an evasion of the prohibition of importation. They also submitted that under s. 290 (2) of the Act the burden of proof had shifted to the defence. The defendants were convicted and appealed. *Held*, in order for there to be an evasion of a prohibition it had to be shown that the prohibited act had been committed. In order to establish that there had been an intention to evade a prohibition against importation by dealing with particular goods, it was for the prosecution to establish a link between the actus of the offence and the particular prohibited importation before s. 290 could operate. The conviction would be quashed.

R v WATTS AND STACK (1979) 70 Cr App Rep 187 (Court of Appeal: BRIDGE LJ, FORBES and SHELDON JJ).

1952 Act, s. 304 now Customs and Excise Management Act 1979, s. 170.

767   —— —— degree of knowledge required

The appellant was convicted of being knowingly concerned in the fraudulent evasion of the prohibition of the importation of a controlled drug contrary to the Customs and Excise Act 1952, s. 304. He appealed against his conviction on the grounds that he had not been aware that drugs were being smuggled into the country, but that he thought that the goods were "blue" films. *Held,* since the appellant knew that he was importing goods which were prohibited under s. 304, it was sufficient to justify his conviction, even if he was not aware of their precise nature.

The court also decided, in the course of hearing a connected appeal, that the trial judge had ruled correctly in refusing to allow the cross-examination of a police informer suspected of telephone tapping; such questions were "fishing" and should have been dealt with before the trial for the purpose of preparing the defence.

R v HENNESSEY (1978) 68 Cr App Rep 419 (Court of Appeal: LAWTON LJ, JONES and SMITH JJ). *R v Hussain* [1969] 2 All ER 1117, CA applied.

1952 Act, s. 304 now Customs and Excise Management Act 1979, s. 170.

768   —— —— effect of Community law

The appellants, who had imported pornographic material from an EEC member state, were convicted on count 13 of the indictment of fraudulently evading the prohibition on the importation of indecent or obscene articles, contrary to the Customs Consolidation Act 1876, s. 42 and the Customs and Excise Act 1952, s. 304. One of them was also convicted on count 15 of having obscene articles for gain, contrary to the Obscene Publications Acts 1959 and 1964, s. 2 (1). On appeal, the appellants contended that the prohibition imposed by s. 42 was contrary to the EEC Treaty, art. 30, which prohibits quantitative restrictions on imports. The House of Lords referred to the European Court of Justice questions on the interpretation of arts. 30 and 36, which provides that prohibitions or restrictions on imports may be justified on the grounds of, inter alia, public morality. However, such prohibitions or restrictions must not constitute a means of arbitrary discrimination or a disguised restriction on trade between member states. The European Court of Justice held that the prohibition imposed by s. 42 constituted a quantitative restriction within art. 30. However, a prohibition on the importation of indecent or obscene articles could be justified on the ground of public morality within art. 36 and if it were so justifiable, the enforcement of the prohibition could not, in the absence of a lawful trade in the goods in the member state, constitute a means of arbitrary discrimination or a disguised restriction on trade within art. 36. On receipt of this judgment the House of Lords *held,* the jury having found by the verdict on count 15 that the imported articles which were also the subject of count 13 were of such a character as to fall under the prohibition under the Obscene Publications Acts 1959 and 1964 of trading in them for gain in England, as well as under the prohibition of importation under the Customs Consolidation Act 1876, it followed that in the present case there was not an arbitrary discrimination or disguised restriction on trade within art. 36. The appeal would be dismissed.

LORD DIPLOCK considered that in a criminal court upon indictment it could seldom be a proper exercise of the presiding judge's discretion to seek a preliminary ruling before the facts of the alleged offence have been ascertained. It is generally better that the question be decided by him in the first instance and reviewed if necessary through the hierarchy of the national courts.

R v HENN AND DARBY [1980] 2 All ER 166 (House of Lords: LORD WILBERFORCE, LORD DIPLOCK, LORD SALMON, LORD FRASER OF TULLYBELTON and LORD

SCARMAN). Decision of the Court of Appeal [1978] 3 All ER 1190, 1978 Halsbury's Abridgment para. 1217 affirmed.

Customs and Excise Act 1952, s. 304, now Customs and Excise Management Act 1979, s. 170.

For proceedings on the reference to the European Court of Justice, see para. 1168.

769   Valuation of goods for customs purposes

See paras. 1117–1121.

770   Value added tax

See VALUE ADDED TAX.

DAMAGES AND COMPENSATION

Halsbury's Laws of England (4th edn.), Vol. 12, paras. 1101–1300

771   Articles

Damages for Injury to a Building, W. V. H. Rogers: 124 Sol Jo 383.
Products Liability: The Chain of Indemnity, Richard Lewis: 130 NLJ 739.
Third Party Damages: The Present Position, Tony Radevsky; 130 NLJ 874.

772   Assessment—fraudulent   misrepresentation—entitlement   to consequential damages

See *Siametis v Trojan Horse (Burlington) Inc*, para. 1990.

773   Award—appeal against award in nuisance action—injunction in lieu of damages

See *Kennaway v Thompson*, para. 1631.

774   Breach of contract—condition for payment to third party—whether sum recoverable in action by party to contract

See *Woodar Investment Development Ltd v Wimpey Construction UK Ltd*, para. 495.

775   —— contract for lease of land—date of assessment of damages

In June 1974 the defendant company agreed to take a lease of two lots on the plaintiff landowner's industrial estate. The owner was to construct premises in accordance with the agreement and the lease was to be taken up within a fortnight after the practical completion of the premises as certified by the owner's architect. The company began to occupy the premises in July 1974 but a certificate of completion was only received in September 1975. Meanwhile, the company contended that the building was not in accordance with the agreement, which the owners denied. By May 1975 the company had purported to rescind the contract and vacated the premises and later gave notice of termination of any periodical tenancy subsisting between the parties. The premises remained vacant until January 1976 when they were taken on short-term licences. By September 1977 both premises had been disposed of on long-term leases. The owners issued a writ claiming damages for breach of contract but there was a dispute as to the date from which damages were to be assessed. *Held*, the general rule governing the assessment of damages for breach of contract applied. Where a party suffered a loss by reason of breach of contract he was to be placed in the same situation with respect to damages as if the contract had been performed. There was no evidence that the owner had acted unreasonably during the transaction and therefore if any damages were sustained they were to be assessed as at September 1977, being the date the owners completed reletting the property on a permanent basis.

TECHNO LAND IMPROVEMENTS LTD v BRITISH LEYLAND (UK) LTD (1979) 252 Estates Gazette 805 (Chancery Division: GOULDING J).

776   Measure of damages—personal injury—negligence—loss of earning capacity

See *Floyd v Bowers*, para. 2062.

777   —— remoteness

Owners of a ship employed managers whom they supplied with operating funds at the beginning of each month. Certain accounts were more than expected and the managers made demands for payment and arrested the ship for sums allegedly owing to them. The owners secured release of the ship by putting up a bank guarantee which they obtained by increasing their overdraft substantially. Heavy interest charges were incurred as a result. The owners contended that as the arrest had been wrongful they were entitled to damages from the managers and in particular to compensation for the interest charges. The matter went to arbitration, the umpire stated a case for consideration by the court and the managers appealed against the court's finding. *Held*, the owners were entitled to recover the ordinary bank charges for obtaining the guarantee but they were not entitled to recover the heavy interest charges which had only been incurred because they operated on overdraft. Such charges did not flow naturally and foreseeably from the wrongful arrest and were consequently too remote to generate a right to compensation. The managers' appeal would be allowed.

THE BORAG (1980) Times, 3rd January 1981 (Court of Appeal: LORD DENNING MR, SHAW and TEMPLEMAN LJJ). Decision of Mustill J [1980] 1 Lloyd's Rep 111 reversed.

778   Penalty—carrying charges incurred due to late nomination of vessel

Under a contract for the sale of maize, it was agreed that all carrying charges at loading incurred due to late arrival and/or late nomination of the vessel should be as per terms of the contract. Clause 6 provided that the buyers should nominate the vessel ten days prior to the date of shipment. Clause 13 provided for the extension of the shipping period on the buyers' application on specified payments being made. The buyers were late in nominating a vessel. The sellers claimed the payments under cl. 13 as representing the carrying charges which had been incurred at loading due to late nomination of the vessel. The buyers argued that the charges were penalties and did not constitute a genuine pre-estimate of the damages since they were quite distinct from the real cost of storage. The dispute was referred to arbitration. The Board of Appeal of GAFTA found in favour of the sellers but stated the award in the form of a special case. *Held*, cl. 13 was not a provision whereby the parties had agreed that in the event of late arrival and/or late nomination a specified sum should be paid; it was a clause giving the buyers an option to apply for an extension of the shipping period on specific terms. The specified scale of charges represented the price to be paid for the extension. Thus the charges specified were not penalties.

THOS. P. GONZALEZ CORPN v F. R. WARING (INTERNATIONAL) (PTY) LTD [1980] 2 Lloyd's Rep 160 (Court of Appeal: MEGAW, SHAW and WALLER LJJ). Decision of Ackner J [1978] 1 Lloyd's Rep 494, 1978 Halsbury's Abridgment para. 857 affirmed.

779   Personal injury—calculation of award—loss of ability to perform housekeeping duties

The plaintiff, a housewife of thirty-four with two young children, was seriously injured as a result of the defendants' negligence and became permanently disabled in one arm. Her claim for damages against the defendants included a claim for loss of ability to do housework both during the pre-trial period and in the future. The plaintiff did not employ any domestic help during the pre-trial period as her family helped her with housework. The plaintiff's claim was treated as a separate head of damage and the award was assessed on the basis of the estimated cost of employing necessary domestic help. The defendants appealed against the part of the plaintiff's total award which represented damages for loss of housekeeping ability. *Held*, (i) in respect of the claim for future loss, the correct measure of damages was the estimated cost of employing domestic help during the plaintiff's life expectancy. The amount of award was not affected by the fact that she might not employ domestic help but try to cope herself. (ii) Damages for the pre-trial period had to be assessed not as a separate head but as part of the general damages for pain, suffering and loss of amenity. The court had to examine the plaintiff's actual loss and consider how her difficulties in doing housework had increased due to her injury. Therefore, the cost of domestic help could not be included since she did not employ any such help. However, assessing damages on the basis of actual loss resulted in the same total award as originally made. The appeal would be dismissed.

DALY v GENERAL STEAM NAVIGATION CO LTD [1980] 3 All ER 696 (Court of Appeal: ORMROD, BRIDGE and TEMPLEMAN LJJ).

780   —— —— loss of future earnings—effect of supervening injury

In 1973 an employee injured his back after a fall which was caused by a breach of statutory duty by his employer. In 1976 he began to suffer pain as a result of a neck injury sustained in 1956. A medical report showed that the neck pain, which was unrelated to the 1973 injury, made him totally unfit for work whilst the 1973 injury was only "somewhat disabling". The employee successfully claimed that the 1976 neck condition should not diminish his damages for loss of future earnings payable in respect of the 1973 injury. On appeal by the employer, *held*, when a person was injured by two separate tortious acts, damages for the first injury were not reduced as a result of the second injury unless the supervening injury reduced the disability from the first injury or shortened the person's life expectancy. However, in this case, the supervening injury of 1976 was caused by a non-tortious act. It would be unjust to require the employer to pay damages in excess of the loss which his tortious act caused. Accordingly the appeal would be allowed and the damages reduced to the extent that loss of future earnings was due to the disability arising in 1976.

JOBLING v ASSOCIATED DAIRIES LTD [1980] 3 All ER 769 (Court of Appeal: STEPHENSON and ACKNER LJJ and DAME ELIZABETH LANE).

781   —— deduction in respect of supplementary benefit

It has been held that supplementary benefit should be deducted from damages awarded to a plaintiff in a personal injury case. It had already been held that unemployment benefit had to be deducted (see *Nabi v British Leyland (UK) Ltd* [1980] 1 All ER 667, CA, 1979 Halsbury's Abridgment para. 800); as both types of benefit were receivable as of right, there was no ground for distinguishing them.

PLUMMER v P. W. WILKINS & SON LTD [1981] 1 All ER 91 (Queen's Bench Division: LATEY J). *Foxley v Olton* [1964] 3 All ER 248 and *Basnett v J & A Jackson Ltd* [1976] ICR 63, 1976 Halsbury's Abridgment para. 784, not followed.

782   Personal injury or death—quantum of damages

Examples of awards of damages in personal injury or fatal accident cases are arranged in the following order. Cases involving more than one injury are classified according to the major injury suffered.

Death	Nervous disorders	Neck and shoulders
Brain damage and paralysis	Burns	Back and trunk
Multiple injuries	Skin diseases	Arms and hands
Internal injuries	Head	Legs and feet

DEATH

783　　*Death*

General damages: £8,000. Pipe fitter, 43, married with 2 children, was killed in a car accident. Claims made under Law Reform (Miscellaneous Provisions) Act 1934 and Fatal Accidents Acts. *Tiplad v Anderson*, 23rd January 1980 (Queen's Bench Division: Russell J).

784　　General damages: £4,400. Married woman, scientist, killed in a car accident. Son, 17, daughter, 15, and mother, 81, lost care and attention of the deceased. Daughter had to go to a boarding school instead of day school. Claim under Fatal Accidents Acts. £3,000 awarded for daughter's boarding expenses, and £800, £250 and £350 awarded for loss of care and attention to the daughter, the son and the mother respectively. *Knowles v Craig*, 8th February, 1980. (Queen's Bench Division: Mais J.)

785　　General damages: £27,500 (agreed). Labourer, 48, died after developing mesothelioma (through contact with asbestos) in the course of employment, leaving widow and children, two of whom were minors. Above sum includes £18,500 for loss of future earnings. *Clark v Dicks Eagle Insulation Ltd*, 25th March 1980 (Queen's Bench Division: Willis J).

786　　General damages: £30,491. Building contractor, 27, married, killed in a car accident after sustaining shock and haemorrhages due to multiple injuries. He was survived by his widow, 22 and son, 4. Damages were originally assessed at £60,982 from which £20,327 were deducted for the plaintiff's contributory negligence. From the remaining £40,655, a further sum of £10,164, as 25 per cent of the remainder, was deducted for the plaintiff's failure to wear a seat belt. Multiplier agreed at 15. *Fletcher v Collins*, 15th May 1980 (Queen's Bench Division: Griffiths J).

787　　General damages: £55,000. Service layer, 23, was electrocuted when he came into contact with a live cable while extracting a gas service pipe from under a road. He left a widow aged 26 and a one year old son. The award comprised £49,000, under the Law Reform (Miscellaneous Provisions) Act 1934, and £6,000 under the Fatal Accidents Acts. *Benson v Biggs Wall & Co.*, 19th June 1980 (Queen's Bench Division: Peter Pain J).

788　　General damages: £6,225. Landscape gardener, 20, was killed in an accident in which he was held to be 50 per cent to blame. Much of his earnings were spent on his girl friend whom he planned to marry in 21 months. Claim made under the Law Reform (Miscellaneous Provisions) Act 1934. The above sum is 50 per cent of £12,450, made up of £9,400 (£15,000 less £5,600 under the Gourley rule on tax) for loss of future earnings at £1,250 with a multiplier of 12; £1,800 for loss of earnings up to the date of the trial and £1,250 for loss of expectation of life. A claim for maintenance of the deceased's girl friend was rejected. *Rooke v Higgins*, 4th July 1980 (Queen's Bench Division: Chapman J).

789　　General damages: £47,761. Construction worker, 54, was fatally injured when he fell from a 21 foot wall. He left a widow, 38, five sons aged 8 to 24 and two daughters aged 20 and 17. The deceased was earning £100 a week and contributing between £60 and £70 towards family expenses. Widow was earning £5,000 a year which she had to give up to look after the children. The award comprised £1,250 under the Law Reform (Miscellaneous Provisions) Act 1934 and £46,511 under the Fatal Accidents Acts. *Devlin v McAlpine Ltd*, 29th July 1980 (Queen's Bench Division: Peter Pain J).

BRAIN DAMAGE AND PARALYSIS

790   *Brain*
General damages: £95,368·50. Apprentice draftsman, 21, single, sustained serious injuries when a lorry collided with his car. He was held to be 10 per cent negligent. Severe blow across eyebrows, brain damage, fracture of lower end of left humerus at elbow joint with fracture of left ulna and subluxation of left radial head. Traumatic amnesia for 3 months and present ability to read reduced to that of a 10 year old. The above sum represents 90 per cent of the total award and includes the apportioned sum of £72,868·50 for loss of future earnings. *Hornby v South Cambridgeshire District Council*, 23rd January 1980 (Queen's Bench Division: Wien J).

791   General damages: £199,500 (agreed). Man, 20, passenger in car which collided with a motor cycle. Suffered severe head injury and was unconscious for 2 months. Fractures of 6th rib and left scapula. His chances of recovery from the head injury are low which necessitates his living in a sheltered home and reduces his life expectancy. The award was made up of £42,000 for pain, suffering and loss of amenity; £60,000 for loss of future earnings, worked out at £4,000 per annum with a multiplier of 15; £78,210 towards future costs for sheltered home and £19,290 for care in unit. *Muller v Barton*, 23rd April 1980 (Queen's Bench Division: Peter Pain J).

792   *Paraplegia*
General damages: £125,440. Milkman, 21, married, was driving his milk float which was crushed when it hit a fallen tree. Fracture and dislocation of 4th thoracic vertebra, fractures of 5th and 6th thoracic and 3rd lumbar vertebrae. Total paraplegia from 4th thoracic vertebra which means he will have to spend rest of his life in a wheelchair. Potential to better his position lost. The award was made up as follows: pain and suffering and loss of amenity £35,000 (agreed), loss of future earnings £45,500, value of wife's services £37,440 and cost of conversion of house and car £7,500. *Staddon v Steward*, 17th January 1980 (Queen's Bench Division: Bristow J).

MULTIPLE INJURIES

793   *Multiple injuries*
General damages: £1,250. Executive director, 62, injured in a car accident. Sustained fracture and bruising of nose, bruising and sprain of left ankle and foot, laceration of lip requiring sutures and superficial abrasion of right leg. Developed pain in the lower back and was unable to attend work for three weeks. *Hurst v Matthews*, 21st July 1980 (Queen's Bench Division: O'Connor J).

794   General damages: £306,300. Post graduate student, 32, was knocked down by a car and suffered extensive damage to his leg, hemi pelvis, penis, scrotum and sphinctera. There was also exposure of and loss of function of muscles controlling bladder, crushing of prostate, exposure of right rectum, strangulation of bowels, skin grafts to stump of leg, infection of left leg, bruising and laceration of shoulder, pain, suffering and loss of sexual function, loss of fertility and marriage prospects. The above award consists of £122,000 for loss of future earnings, £97,500 for future care and medical attention, £60,000 for pain, suffering and loss of amenity, £3,400 for loss of pension, £10,000 for cost of conversion of his house, £10,000 for any general contingencies and £3,400 for pecuniary loss after accident. *Watson v Murphy*, 7th November 1980 (Queen's Bench Division: Stocker J).

795   General damages: £24,288. A spastic, married woman and part-time worker, 41, was struck by a car. Large sub-dural haematoma requiring evacuation, brain damage needing surgical treatment, lip abrasions and laceration, loss of tooth, impairment of sense of smell, frequent micturition and deterioration in use of limbs. Tracheal stenosis with heavy breathing and 14 per cent risk of post traumatic epilepsy. The above award consists of £9,000 for pain, suffering and loss of amenity, and £15,288 for loss of future earnings. *Clee v Cooke*, 24th November 1980 (Queen's Bench Division: Park J).

796   General damages: £113,000. Girl, 15, was injured in a car collision sustaining depressed fracture of front-parietal bone with extradural haemorrhage, fracture of ribs and contusion of lung resulting in serious and permanent neurological defect with hemiplegic gait and gross spastic dysarthria. The above award comprised £30,000 for pain, suffering and loss of amenity, £35,000 for future loss of earnings and £48,000 for future care. *Kemmery v Dart*, 19th December 1980 (Queen's Bench Division: Milmo J).

INTERNAL INJURIES

797   *Asbestosis*
General damages: £52,500. Storeman, 49, contracted asbestosis when working with thermal lagging for an insulation company. Discomfort in breathing and likelihood of lung cancer. Sexual relations affected and life expectancy shortened. The award comprised £22,500 for pain, suffering and loss of amenity, and £30,000 for loss of future earnings. *Dove v Kitson Insulation Ltd*, 16th April 1980 (Queen's Bench Division: O'Connor J).

798   *Hernia*
General damages: £2,000. Warehouseman, 65, injured when the front wheel of a truck went through the floor of the lorry striking his lower abdomen. Hernia in right groin necessitating homeopathic operation. Abdominal pains caused by inflammation of the gall bladder which had to be removed. *Howe v Twindale Transport*, 17th April 1980 (Queen's Bench Division: Lloyd J).

799   General damages: £2,500. Hotel handyman, 63, suffered an inguinal hernia while attempting to lift cement bag weighing 110 lbs. He continued to work but five weeks later had to undergo an operation to have the hernia treated. He subsequently developed an infection which prolonged his convalescence and was unable to return to work. *Allardyce v Variety Inns Ltd.*, 29th July 1980 (Queen's Bench Division: Cantley J).

800   *Reproductive organs and kidney*
General damages: £2,000. Married woman, 43, suffered damage to kidney and was unable to bear more children due to negligent caesarean section. *Rushton v Somerset Area Health Authority*, 9th December 1980 (Queen's Bench Division: Park J).

NERVOUS DISORDERS

801   *Anxiety/apprehension*
General damages: £17,500. Diver, 36, found he was losing consciousness while diving due to an airpressure defect in his equipment. Became apprehensive about diving and developed a great fear of gas diving which restricted the depths at which he was able to dive. *Stokes v Northern Divers Ltd*, 8th October 1980 (Queen's Bench Division: Chapman J).

BURNS

802   *Burns*
General damages: £2,500. Apprentice boat builder, 22, single, was working on a roof top when the bitumen he was carrying spilled over him and caused him to fall

over 30 feet to the ground. Severe burns on arm and chest, requiring split skin grafts, scarring of thigh and stiffening of arm wrist. Loss of sensation to the skin which has become sensitive to the sun. *Cook v West*, 18th January 1980 (Queen's Bench Division: Kenneth Jones J).

803 General damages: £1,200. Labourer, 27, was working in a building when some hot bitumen spilled onto his left forearm causing severe burns. He had to have a skin graft on his arm and suffered a 30 per cent loss of grip of left hand and wasting of arm muscles owing to disuse. He was self conscious about his scar and suffered depression and nervous apprehension about returning to work. *Partenter v Permanite Ltd*, 7th February 1980 (Queen's Bench Division: Cantley J).

804 General damages: £5,880, £6,000, £22,857 and £800. Four oiltanker welders and fitters aged between 35 and 45 injured when the tanker caught fire. The first fitter who had burns on the face, upper chest, arms, hands and left knee was awarded £5,000 for pain, suffering and loss of amenity and £880 for loss of future earnings; the second fitter had burns on his face, neck, knees and hands and was awarded £5,500 for pain, suffering and loss of amenity and £500 for loss of future earnings; the third who had burns on his face, chest, shoulder, back and forearms was awarded £9,000 for pain, suffering and loss of amenity and £13,857 for loss of future earnings and the fourth, who suffered corneal oedema and superficial keratitis of both eyes was awarded £800 for pain, suffering and loss of amenity. *Stratford v Nicoverkern U.K. Ltd*, 14th July 1980 (Queen's Bench Division: Thompson J).

HEAD

805 *Head*
General damages: £1,500. Labourer, 58, fell to the ground while unloading pallets from a lorry. Received a head injury which caused traumatic subarachnoid bleeding, severe headaches for 3 months, discomfort below left collarbone and tingling in the left eyebrow. *Szmarhaj v Walls Meat Co Ltd*, 31st January 1980 (Queen's Bench Division: Milmo J).

806 General damages: £85,000. Student (17 at time of accident), now 22, suffered severe head injuries in a moped accident. Fracture of skull, brain damage, 50 per cent limitation of field of vision and scarring on face. Had epilepsy which is now under control and substantial diminution of hearing in the right ear. The above award was agreed and calculated at £25,000 for pain, suffering and loss of amenity and £60,000 for loss of future earnings at £4,000 with a multiplier of 15. *Dagnall v Campbell*, 17th July 1980 (Queen's Bench Division: Gower QC).

807 General damages: £75. Fitter, 59, was struck on the back of his head by a machine. Sustained lacerations and shock. *Kelly v London Transport Executive*, 30th October 1980 (Queen's Bench Division: Caulfield J).

808 General damages: £750. Glazier, 51, struck his head when a roof collapsed throwing him to the ground. Suffered depression, temporary shock and pain. *Cox v M Price Ltd*, 13th November 1980 (Queen's Bench Division: Michael Davies J).

809 *Head, face and finger*
General damages: £10,750. Naval officer, 58, married, was a passenger in a car which collided with a lorry. Severe concussion resulting in fractured vertebra requiring surgical stiffener, facial deformity and fracture of index finger causing permanent loss of grip. *Hedger v Bromley Demolition Ltd*, 22nd January 1980 (Queen's Bench Division: McNeill J).

810   *Head and neck*
General damages: £3,600.   Married woman, 72, was knocked down by a car. Suffered swelling on the back of her head, sprain to neck and bruising to spine and leg.   The above award was 80 per cent of £4,500 since the plaintiff was held 20 per cent contributorily negligent.   *Harvey v Spendley*, 28th November 1980 (Queen's Bench Division: Russell J).

811   *Head and rib*
General damages: £120,122.   Police constable, 34, was seriously injured in a car accident.   Fracture to the base of skull and ribs and laceration of jaw with numerous contusions and abrasions; unconscious for 2 days.   Continues to suffer from buzzing noises in ear, loss of hearing, dryness in mouth, loss of sensibility in tongue, persistent headaches, frequent depression and impairment of concentration, with risk of post traumatic epilepsy.   Remains permanently unable to obtain employment of similar nature or equivalent salary.   The above award consists of £25,000 for pain, suffering and loss of amenity, £86,842 for future loss of earnings by a multiplier of 16½, £1,880 for future loss of overtime by a multiplier of 10 and £6,400 for future loss of rent allowance by a multiplier of 10.   *James v Dyfed-Powys Police*, 31st July 1980 (Queen's Bench Division: Tudor Evans J).

812   *Head and thigh*
General damages: £10,000.   Detective sergeant, 37, was knocked down by a passing car while attempting to change tyre of his own car.   Sustained compound fracture to the right femur and cut in the occipital region.   The above includes £2,500 for loss of future earnings.   In addition to above £10,000, £37 for loss of no claims bonus under insurance policy and £10 for wife giving up part-time job to nurse the plaintiff were awarded.   *Darby v Letchford*, 28th March 1980 (Queen's Bench Division: Peter Pain J).

813   *Head and knee*
General damages: £35,458.   Detective constable, 44, injured in a motor car accident.   Injury to head with post traumatic amnesia and rupture of medial ligament of left knee.   Developed severe pains in head and abdomen.   His knee became unstable and could only be flexed up to an angle of 70 degrees.   Unable to attain pre-accident condition and had to become a private inquiry agent.   The award comprised £27,958 for loss of future earnings and £7,500 for pain, suffering and loss of amenity.   *Wilkins v Hillier*, 25th April 1980 (Queen's Bench Division: Michael Davies J).

814   *Skull*
General damages: £5,200.   Railway guard, 39, was injured when attempting to rescue a passenger.   Concussion, with fractured skull which led to serious headaches and loss of taste and smell.   He made good recovery in four months but was subsequently involved in another accident which left him medically unfit to continue his job.   He refused another job and his eye sight deteriorated a year after the second accident.   The judge awarded him £6,500 for pain, suffering and loss of amenity, reducing it by £1,300 for his contributory negligence assessed at 20 per cent.   *Harrison v British Railways Board*, 31st July 1980 (Queen's Bench Division: Boreham J).

815   *Skull and wrist*
General damages: £4,500 (agreed).   Married woman, 23, part-time factory worker, hit by a car.   Skull laceration and severe wrist laceration, causing swelling and disfiguration.   *Allibon v Williams*, 23rd January 1980 (Queen's Bench Division: Judge Lymbery QC).

816   *Face*
General damages: £11,500.   Female stable labourer, 24, was injured when a horse lashed out, kicking her violently in the face.   Suffered fracture of upper and lower

jaws, injury to orbit floor, $3\frac{1}{2}$ inch horizontal laceration across right cheek and depresssed scar with marked alteration in facial contour and noticeable facial palsy. *Lewty v Groos*, 5th November 1980 (Queen's Bench Division: Latey J).

817   *Face and knee*
General damages: £12,000 (agreed). Married woman, 26, was a passenger in a car which hit a kerb and collided with a tree. Concussion, fracture of nose, left femur and scapula and lacerations to forehead, upper lip and tongue; gross deformation of nose restricting breathing through right nostril, resulting in nasal operation and cosmetic surgery. Restriction in movement of left knee continuing causing her to walk with a limp. *Clarke v Bertrand*, 6th March 1980 (Queen's Bench Division: Chapman J).

818   *Eyes*
General damages: £87,500. Nepalese post graduate student, 32. Due to the wrongful administration of a drug he sustained a 75 per cent loss of visual function in both eyes with gross organic lesion on visual afferent pathway, depression of colour vision and bilateral optic atrophy. Plaintiff was a civil servant in his country and had the opportunity of being employed by the United Nations. The award comprised £32,500 for pain, suffering and loss of amenity, £50,000 (net) for loss of future earnings (based on earnings in Nepal at £3,275 with a multiplier of 15) and £5,000 (net) for loss of job opportunity. *Sharma v Rowland*, 30th October 1980 (Queen's Bench Division: Gibson J).

819   General damages: £15,000. Surveyor, 64, sustained substantial impairment to eyesight as a result of treatment received for pulmonary tuberculosis when he was prescribed daily dosages of 1300 to 1400 mg of Ethanbutol tablets and 100 mg Rymactacid antibiotic. *Edwarde v Hall & Bromley Area Health Authority*, 11th November 1980 (Queen's Bench Division: Michael Davies J).

NECK AND SHOULDERS

820   *Neck*
General damages: £1,250. Mill owner, 64, was thrown off his feet by an explosion due to a defective socket. The sprain exacerbated a pain he had already been experiencing before the accident and caused him to give up his hobby of gardening. *Webb v E & E Kaye Ltd*, 17th April 1980 (Queen's Bench Division: Stephen Brown J).

821   General damages: £2,500 (agreed). Storeman, 30, was thrown over a wheelbarrow. Sprained cervical spine and fractured base of the axis. Pain in his neck restricted its movement. He suffered from a pre-existing deformity to his neck and right shoulder. He also sprained certain ligaments, muscles and joints. *Burns v W. H. Cork Gully & Co*, 9th June 1980 (Queen's Bench Division: Stocker J).

822   General damages: £17,300. Draughtsman, 47, was injured in a car accident. Prior to the accident he underwent lumbar osteotomy, but he was still stooping. After accident he suffered ankylosing spondylitis in right cervical spine. Movement of his neck was restricted to nodding and a 20 degree rotation on either side, his head was immobile and was tilted down 20 degrees to the right. The above award consists of: £8,000 for pain, suffering and loss of amenity; £6,300 for future loss of earnings and £3,000 for loss of job opportunity. *Taylor v R C Beadle*, 24th June 1980 (Queen's Bench Division: Judge Oddie).

823   General damages: £1,500 (agreed). Head waitress, 47, slipped and fell at a shop door causing fracture of the neck and left femur, which did not unite for a considerable time and she consequently could not put any weight on her left hip.

Further she suffered a vascular necrosis and was unable to participate in ballroom dancing. *Reed v Martin The Newsagent Ltd*, 13th November 1980 (Queen's Bench Division: Russell J).

824   *Neck and shoulder*

General damages: £5,479·50. District nurse, 49, was injured in a car accident. Sustained a whiplash injury to her neck, sublaxation of left intervertebral joint. Pain in left shoulder and arm and weakness in grip for 3½ years. The above award consists of £3,500 for pain, suffering and loss of amenity and £1,979·50 (£2,079·50 less £100 industrial benefit received) for loss of earnings for 6 months. *Willsmer v Schopman*, 4th July 1980 (Queen's Bench Division: Judge Underhill QC).

825   *Shoulder*

General damages: £2,500. Labourer, 59, slipped on a greasy floor and fell, striking his left shoulder. Suffered contusions, developed capsulitis in his joint resulting in permanent stiffness of the right shoulder. Injury to the neck required support of a surgical collar. *Donovan v Mirror Group Newspapers Ltd*, 24th April 1980 (Queen's Bench Division: Michael Davies J).

826   General damages: £28,000 (agreed). Window cleaner, 46, fell from stairs injuring soft tissue to right shoulder and prolapsed intervertebral disc. His activities were restricted. *White v Greater London Council*, 14th November 1980 (Queen's Bench Division: Mais J).

827   General damages: £1,250. Lift surveyor, 46, fell from a ladder dislocating his left shoulder with spontaneous reduction. There was also tearing of capsular fibres of shoulder joint and traumatic supra-spinatus tendinitis. Loss of 5 degrees in internal rotation and loss of 70 per cent power in the shoulder. *Tait v Britain and Overseas Trading Ltd*, 14th November 1980 (Queen's Bench Division: Sheen J).

BACK AND TRUNK

828   *Back*

General damages: £15,850. Labourer, 45, sustained injury to his back when straining to support a heavy shelf in order to prevent injury to his fellow workers. Continuous discomfort at top of natal cleft, pain in right buttock and inability to stand upright. The above award was made up as follows: £6,850 for loss of future earnings, £8,000 (agreed) for pain and suffering and £1,000 for loss of prospects in the employment market. *Honeysett v Timothywhites Ltd*, 6th March 1980 (Queen's Bench Division: Woolf J).

829   General damages: £6,250 (agreed). Dock worker, 32, while unloading cargo, fell 6 foot onto a dock and injured his back. Spinal and back movement were restricted and low lumbar sacral strain was diagnosed. *Bowes v Convoys (London Wharves) Ltd*, 31st October 1980 (Queen's Bench Division: Tudor Evans J).

830   General damages: £1,000. Machine operator, 36, fell over an empty hand-truck, receiving bruises, ligamentous strain of back and scoliosis on his left side. Difficulty in sexual intercourse which aggravates back pain, causing marital disharmony. *Grant v SKF (UK) Ltd*, 5th November 1980 (Queen's Bench Division: Thompson J).

831   General damages: £900. Lorry driver, 48, fell to the ground and received traumatic bruising of tissues of lower part of back and left sacro-iliac. Suffered discomfort on forward flexion, tenderness on direct palpation, difficulty in lifting heavy objects. *Stylianides v A G Thames Holdings Ltd*, 6th October 1980 (Queen's Bench Division: Judge Fay QC).

832   General damages: £2,000 (agreed). Production instructor, married woman, 45, was knocked down by an electric truck. Suffered pains in her back and the injury activated a pre-existing minor congenital back anomaly, causing acute traumatic disc lesion which has not been completely symptom free. Intermittent headaches; cannot stoop or bend and she had to take a down-graded and lower-paid job. *Neale v Wall's Meat Co Ltd*, 29th July 1980 (Queen's Bench Division: Stocker J).

833   General damages: £24,500. Male nursing auxiliary, 46, injured his back while lifting a heavy bed. Suffered restriction of movement of the lower spine, tenderness at limbo-sacral junction and over spinous ligament and sacral iliac joint region. A supportive limbo-sacral corset had to be worn. Experiences considerable pain in sexual intercourse which has caused marital disharmony. The above award consisted of £8,000 for pain, suffering and loss of amenity and £16,500 for loss of future earnings. *Denton v S W Thames Regional Health Authority*, 26th November 1980 (Queen's Bench Division: Park J).

834   *Back and hip*
General damages: £2,500. Female pedestrian, 26, hit by car. Strained right sacroiliac joint causing prolonged pain and tenderness in that region, abrasion of right hip, and manipulation of lower back required. Back ache, impairment of general mobility and continuing inability to walk. *Williams v Robinson*, 7th March 1980 (Queen's Bench Division: Willis J).

835   *Back and knee*
General damages: £6,500. Clerk, 20, single, keen sportsman and excellent swimmer, was thrown off his motor-cycle when hit by a car. Compound fracture of right femur, right tibia and fibula. Permanent shortening by 2 cm of right lower limb causing backache, restriction of flexion of right knee resulting in arthritic changes which could increase in middle age. Unlikely to be a competitive swimmer. *Codley v Dawes*, 24th January 1980 (Queen's Bench Division: McNeill J).

836   *Back and spine*
General damages: £3,400 (by consent). Building contractor, 50, was passenger in a car involved in a collision. Twisted his back thereby exacerbating pre-existing degenerative changes in spine; lordosis on first 15 degrees of lumbar flexion and partial restriction of left lateral flexion. *Crawley v Hargreaves*, 3rd November 1980 (Queen's Bench Division: Mais J).

837   *Spine*
General damages: £11,000. Building labourer, 46, fell 50 ft to the ground through a gap in the scaffolding. Suffered compression fracture of the 3rd and 4th lumbar vertebrae causing them to collapse to about two thirds of their normal depth. Comminuted fracture of left femur, stiffness across lumbar spine and discomfort and cracking sensation in knee. Unsuitable for work on ladders and scaffolding. The above sum includes £5,000 for loss of future earnings. *Moore v Waltham Forest Roofing and Road Contractors*, 11th March 1980 (Queen's Bench Division: Chapman J).

838   General damages: £1,500. Driver, 36, while securing a drum on the back of a lorry, his foot went through a hole in the lorry floor so that he fell. Sustained contusion and jarring of spine base with possible fracture of the spinal process of first sacral vertebrae, causing him continuous pain when lifting heavy objects. *O'Connor v Bedfordia Plant Ltd*, 14th May 1980 (Queen's Bench Division: O'Connor J).

839   General damages: £6,000. Wellknown actress, 49, fell from a "frisky" camel, sustaining crush fracture to 10th and 11th thoracic vertebrae. She had to complete a television agreement to act under considerable physical distress and pain. There is a 75 per cent chance that she will suffer from spinal osteoarthritis within the next 20 to 25 years. Her pre-accident prospect was to go on acting until 85 and her annual earning at the time of the accident was £28,000. The above award comprised £3,500 for pain, suffering and loss of amenity and £2,500 for loss of future earnings. *Tutin v Mary Chipperfield Promotions*, 23rd May 1980 (Queen's Bench Division: Cantley J).

840   General damages: £11,500. Warehouse manager, 51, slipped and fell on some rubbish while loading plastic sheets. Suffered tenderness in both the lower lumbar and thoracic vertebrae, restriction of spinal mobility, weakening of right quadriceps muscles, narrowing of disc spaces and reduction in the intervertebral formina. The award comprised £4,000 for pain, suffering and loss of amenity and £7,500 for loss of future earnings. *Bruce v J. Hill (Veneers) Ltd*, 23rd May 1980 (Queen's Bench Division: Lawson J).

841   General damages: £42,500 (agreed). Lorry driver, 32, was thrown off his lorry. He sustained traumatic spondylosis of pedicles of 5th lumbar vertebra, fracture of transverse processes of 3rd and 4th vertebrae and bruising over right medial epicondyle causing swelling and pain. Back pain, restriction of spinal movement and pains in right arm during cold weather. Sexual capacity affected and substantial disadvantage in the open labour market. *Tracey v Farnis & Son Ltd*, 30th July 1980 (Queen's Bench Division: Stocker J).

842   General damages: £242,000 (agreed). Student, 20, injured when he was passenger in a car involved in an accident. Crush fracture of upper spine and loss of power and sensation below 6th cervical segment. He became a permanent tetraplegic and suffered impairment of his bodily functions. *Rowbottom v Gharret*, 13th October 1980 (Queen's Bench Division: Forbes J).

843   General damages: £3,000. Nursing auxiliary, 45, with previous back injury, tore fibrous tissue surrounding the intervertebral disc while at work, causing continued pain. *John v Enfield and Haringey Area Health Authority*, 12th December 1980 (Queen's Bench Division: Hodgson J).

844   *Spine and neck*
General damages: £45,000. Female doctor, 32, was injured in a car crash. Fracture of seventh cervical and first thoracic vertebrae with narrowing of intervertebral disc space. Cannot ride or drive. Scars on scalp, neck and chest. Unable to take examination in ophthalmology. The above award comprised £10,000 for pain, suffering and loss of amenity and £35,000 for loss of future earnings. *Griffiths v Newman*, 10th December 1980 (Queen's Bench Division: Park J).

845   *Spine and shoulder*
General damages: £1,440·90. Machine assistant, 58, thrown to the ground when a set of wooden steps on which he was standing, toppled. Tore a supra spinatus muscle tendon and all movements of the right shoulder were restricted by about 10 per cent. Unable to lift arm above his head, loss of forward extension and abduction in muscles between the shoulder blade and chest wall. £2,250 was awarded for pain, suffering and loss of amenity and £631·80 for loss of future earnings. From that total of £2,881·80, £1,440·90 was deducted for the plaintiff's contributory negligence assessed at 50 per cent. *Nedhurst v A. E. I. Cabbs Ltd*, 20th May 1980 (Queen's Bench Division: Jupp J).

846   *Spine and fingers*
General damages: £9,000. Electrician, 31, fell from a pole sustaining compression fracture of 1st vertebra and of transverse provess of 3rd vertebra resulting in

permanent back-ache; dislocation of interphalangeal joints, right-middle and ring-fingers. Suffered 50 per cent loss of grip. The plaintiff, as a member of a small village cricket club, was due to play in cup final shortly after the accident, but he could not take part in the match and thereafter lost considerable sporting pleasure for some years. *Saunders v South East Electricity Board*, 21st April 1980 (Queen's Bench Division: Michael Davies J).

847   *Chest and arm*
General damages: £3,000. Salesman, 43, sustained a whiplash injury to his cervical spine when his car collided with the defendant's lorry. Developed pain, which was exacerbated by anxiety, in the right side of his chest and in right arm. Five per cent risk of osteoarthritis developing in neck. *Carter v A. E. Drain (Transport) Ltd*, 17th April 1980 (Queen's Bench Division: Hodgson J).

848   *Hip*
General damages: £24,668. Van driver, 54, injured in car collision. Suffered bilateral rib fracture with posterior dislocation of left hip and partial left sciatic nerve palsy, and fracture of left patella with disruption of left quadriceps mechanism. Two month stay in hospital involving period of intensive care. Plaintiff's contributary negligence was assessed at 15 per cent. His award included £11,900 for pain, suffering and loss of amenity, £3,150 for loss of future earnings, £1,018 for loss of pension, £3,500 for loss of use of car, £5,000 for loss of job prospects and £100 towards payment for shoes. *Parkett v Thripp*, 13th February 1980 (Queen's Bench Division: Judge Michael Hawser, QC).

849   *Hip and ankles*
General damages: £6,000 (agreed). Architect, 48, suffered injuries when his motor-cycle collided with defendant's motor car. Comminuted fracture of right os-calcis, 5th metatarsal bone and left tibia; restriction in movement of right and left ankles, and pain and gross limitation of movement in right hip; he still limps and can only walk for 15 minutes at a time. The above sum is 50 per cent of £12,000 as the plaintiff's contributory negligence was assessed at 50 per cent. *Fraser v Jones*, 6th March 1980 (Queen's Bench Division: Judge Mark Smith).

850   *Hip and leg*
General damages: £16,000 (agreed). Housewife, 29, injured in a car collision. Constant discomfort in the hip, inability to climb and walk further than 100 yards and half inch shortening of the right leg. *Norman v Johns*, 25th January 1980 (Queen's Bench Division: McNeill J).

ARMS AND HANDS

851   *Elbow*
General damages: £1,500. Labourer, 36, slipped from a vehicle wheel and fell striking his left elbow on the vehicle door. Suffered fracture of end of left olecranon; pain continuing in elbow at the end of a day's work. *Hayden v Port of London Authority*, 26th March 1980 (Queen's Bench Division: Peter Pain J).

852   General damages: £4,500. Factory worker, 46, was injured while cleaning an extractor room. Laceration on back of head, abrasions to left elbow and shoulder and contusion of left elbow damaging ulnar nerve. Pain and stiffness to elbow still persisted. The above award was agreed to include interest and costs *Falconer v Carreras Ltd*, 21st October 1980 (Queen's Bench Division: Forbes J).

853   *Elbow and thumb*
General damages: £8,000. Handyman painter, 51, fell from a 20 foot ladder. Suffered compound fracture of left olecranon with lacerations over the tip of the elbow and injury to the left thumb. Spent 7 days in hospital and was unable to bathe

or dress himself for 3 months. Experienced pain when straightening his arm, the movement of which was restricted, and had difficulty in clenching his fist. The award comprised £7,500 for pain, suffering and loss of amenity and £500 for loss of future earnings. *Perrin v Ian William & Co Ltd*, 16th May 1980 (Queen's Bench Division: Sheen J).

854   *Hand*
General damages: £6,000 (agreed). Labourer, 39, injured when he fell from a cycle on a repaired road. Fracture of right scaphoid which caused continuous pain and throbbing in the wrist and loss of grip in right hand. He had to give up heavy manual workshop labour. *Brent v A. C. Lloyd Industrial Ltd*, 25th June 1980 (Queen's Bench Division: Gibson J).

855   *Fingers*
General damages: £17,500. Post office technician, 59, tried to open an extremely stiff gate which suddenly came free and trapped his right hand fingers. Crush to the terminal part exposing finger bone. Loss of function and pincer grip. Psychotic depression. *Grinshaw v Post Office*, 25th January 1980 (Queen's Bench Division: Wien J).

856   General damages: £3,000. Machine assistant, 20, had his right hand drawn into the machine, crushing index and middle fingers. At the time of the accident he was already partially disabled by the loss of half of his index finger. The index finger was amputated through the distal interphalangeal joint and remained tender requiring the use of a protective cover. Middle finger was heavily scarred. Overall grip of the right hand impaired which caused him embarrassment. The damages of £3,000 included £500 for diminished prospects in the open employment market. *Lyons v Cox*, 7th February 1980 (Queen's Bench Division: Judge Lewis Hawser QC).

857   General damages: £5,000. Experienced welder, 45, suffered serious injury to his left hand resulting in the shortening of his index and middle fingers to the level of distal interphalangeal joints. His gripping power was diminished. He has difficulty dressing and eating and has unsightly scars on left hand. *Mackay v Ozonair Engineering Co Ltd*, 5th December 1980 (Queen's Bench Division: Sheen J).

858   *Thumb*
General damages: £4,000. Electrician, left-handed, 33, trapped his left thumb between a crane frame and a rail container. Injured thumb was amputated and what remained of it became sore and tender and looked unsightly. He had to make use of his right hand but was unable to ride a motor cycle or maintain and repair his house: *Fernie v Port of London Authority*, 9th June 1980 (Queen's Bench Division: William Stabb QC).

LEGS AND FEET

859   *Leg*
General damages: £22,000. Barrister, 34, suffered severe comminuted fracture of right femur, fracture of tibia, concussion and amnesia. Shortening of right leg restricting its use and rendering it unfit for weight bearing. *Booth v Levene*, 25th January 1980 (Queen's Bench Division: Russell J).

860   General damages: £19,000. Horticulturalist, 27, was injured when his motorcycle collided with a car. Sustained fractures of his leg, foot and left forearm and injury to the pelvic region. Left leg had to be amputated up to his knee. *Roach v Beard*, 25th April 1980 (Queen's Bench Division: Mais J).

861   General damages: £3,500. Self-employed hardware goods supplier, 32, met with
car accident. Sustained compound fracture of right tibia and fibula with cuts and
abrasions. Scarring of right leg and mobility restricted for a period. *Batchelor v
Zylan Ltd*, 4th July 1980 (Queen's Bench Division: Woolf J).

862   General damages: £8,000 (agreed). Messenger, 62, was hit by a motor cycle.
Suffered fracture of lower left tibia, oblique fracture of lower side of leg with double
fracture of fibula, vertical split from fracture site down into ankle joint and stiffness
in knee with loss of flexion at ankle. Unable to carry out vigorous walking. *Burns
v Rollason*, 15th July 1980 (Queen's Bench Division: Judge Fay QC).

863   General damages: £4,500. Bank official, 35, fell over debris when trying to avoid
being hit by a crane. Wound in lower right leg and compound fracture of lower
right tibia and fibula. Suffered a 10 degree loss of angulation and was unable to
continue horse-riding. *Webster v McKay Demolition Ltd*, 16th October 1980
(Queen's Bench Division: Forbes J).

864   General damages: £5,000 (agreed). Security officer, 57, tripped over a protruding
obstacle and fractured his right femur. *Ash v Beechy Group Ltd*, 30th October 1980
(Queen's Bench Division: Gibson J).

865   General damages: £6,750. Unmarried secretary, 18 (now 22) was knocked down
and received fracture of left tibia and fibula with displacement of fragments resulting
in a grossly disfigured, scarred and swollen leg giving pain in cold weather.
Possibility of degenerative arthritis in ankle joint. Lost training opportunity in
hotel catering. The above award consists of £6,000 for pain, suffering and loss of
amenity, and £750 for prospective loss of employment due to imminent closure of
present workplace. *Smith v Byrne*, 18th December 1980 (Queen's Bench Division:
Milmo J).

866   *Leg and face*
General damages: £32,160. Lorry driver, 48, injured in an accident involving his
lorry. Suffered multiple lacerations on his face, deep laceration over left elbow
exposing underlying bone, comminuted fracture of the shaft of right femur and
laceration over right knee cap. The above award comprised £15,000 for pain,
suffering and loss of amenity and £17,160 for loss of future earnings. *Lincoln v
Hayman*, 21st July 1980 (Queen's Bench Division: Judge Tibber).

867   *Leg, arm and ankle*
General damages: £110,000. Baby, born in January 1972, suffered injuries during
delivery. Osteomyelitis of right tibia, septic arthritis in left shoulder, cellulitis of left
hand with general septicaemia resulting in permanent deformity of left leg and right
ankle and shortening of arm. The above award comprised £100,000 for pain,
suffering and loss of amenity and £10,000 for future loss. *Wallace v Essex Area
Health Authority*, 5th November 1980 (Queen's Bench Division: Caulfield J).

868   *Thigh (scar)*
General damages: £1,500. Girl, aged 11 (now 16) suffered infection following
administration of B C G injection without inquiry into her medical history. Ulcer
developed at injection site and she underwent treatment for several weeks at a T B
clinic which included application of streptomycin dressings and an operation under
anaesthetic for excision. Unsightly scar of 2 cm on thigh, exposed when wearing
short dresses; gave up dancing and ballet. *Chissick v Essex Area Health Authority*,
28th March 1980 (Queen's Bench Division: O'Connor J).

869   *Thigh and knee*
General damages: £4,000 (agreed). Driver, 46, was injured in a car collision.
Fracture of medial femoral condyle and tibia condyle of left knee; abrasions and

contusions of right shin, bruising and lacerations of left hand and fingers leaving scar on the back of left hand. *Fuller v McAlonan*, 1st December 1980 (Queen's Bench Division: Kenneth Jones J).

870   *Knee*

General damages: £600. Radio operator, 31, tripped over in ship and injured his knee which, when sitting and during cold weather, became stiff. An ice-skating enthusiast and became apprehensive about resuming skating. *Wallington v Sheaf Steam Shipping Co Ltd*, 5th March 1980 (Queen's Bench Division: Willis J).

871   General damages: £1,500. Salesman, 65, tripped over some equipment while helping his manager carry a mattress. Injured his right knee, straining the medial lateral ligament and tearing a cartilage. Knee swollen for 10 days and on medical advice he resumed work as a telephone salesman. *Jones v Howard Thompson Ltd*, 30th April 1980 (Queen's Bench Division: Woolf J).

872   General damages: £1,850. Heavy goods vehicle driver, 33, fell off a tractor trailer and twisted his right knee damaging the medial meniscus. He had to be cared for by his pregnant wife who also had another child to look after. Severe pains in leg interfered with his work for two years, after which a successful operation enabled him to resume his job. In addition to the above sum, £40 was awarded for the wife's services. *Hayles v Ilford Ltd*, 25th June 1980 (Queen's Bench Division: Gibson J).

873   General damages: £15,500 (agreed). Factory worker, 47, fell to the ground and injured the weight bearing surface of his femur. This resulted in effusion of fluid in left knee, restricting flexion and tenderness in inner aspect of that knee. He cannot resume former employment or garden; ¼-inch surgical scar in leg and likelihood of osteoarthritic degenerative changes. *Sullivan v H Tidd & Sons*, 5th November 1980 (Queen's Bench Division: Cantley J).

874   General damages: £2,500 (agreed). Storeman, 45, slipped and struck his knee on a tray, sustaining contusion of articular cartilage in retropatellar region of right knee, causing pain and discomfort during long walks and kneeling. *Johnson v British Leyland (UK) Ltd*, 2nd December 1980 (Queen's Bench Division: Phillips J).

875   *Knee and elbow*

General damages: £1,200. Mine quarry operator, 66, fell to the bottom of a bank, when a rope snapped, suffering partial ligament rupture of left knee joint and abrasion to right elbow and right side of scalp. The above award was held as contingent since negligence of the defendant was not established. *Southgate v Hall Aggregates Ltd*, 9th December 1980 (Queen's Bench Division: Gibson J).

876   *Knee and hand*

General damages: £12,000 (agreed). Married woman, 47, medical audiologist and researcher, caught her shoe in a hole in a paving stone and bruised her left knee; abrasion of right knee and swelling in metacarpal joints. Damage to articular cartilage of patella of right knee, loss of dexterity of left hand and damage to left little finger. *Clements v Brewer*, 17th October 1980 (Queen's Bench Division: Chapman J).

877   *Ankle and knee*

General damages: £7,500 (agreed). Heavy vehicle driver, 53, was injured in a car crash. Sustained severe compound fracture and dislocation of left ankle; and ligament injury with permanent limited movement of right knee. Continues to limp and cannot drive lorry or take long walks. *Buss v Powel*, 2nd December 1980 (Queen's Bench Division: Jupp J).

878   *Ankle and foot*
General damages: £1,450. Self-employed bricklayer, 42, fell from a ladder, fracturing talus and oscalcis in the right foot. Loss of movement in the ankle. *Wheeler v C. W. Copas*, 13th June 1980 (Queen's Bench Division: Chapman J).

879   *Foot*
General damages: £200. Butcher, 21, single. Stack of lamb fell on his foot fracturing shafts of 2nd, 3rd and 4th metatarsals. Pre-accidental diabetic condition caused ulcerating of foot with infection and cellulitis around toes. *Carter v Tesco's Stores Ltd*, 25th January 1980 (Queen's Bench Division: Sheen J).

880   General damages: £2,000. Female shop assistant, 31, injured when jars of jam fell off a shelf. Severe bruising of right foot which became swollen and tender. She was fitted with a below the knee plaster which had to be kept on for some months. *Hopwood v F. W. Woolworth & Co Ltd*, 9th June 1980 (Queen's Bench Division: Smith J).

881   —— **loss of deceased's future earnings—compensation for lost years—recovery for benefit of deceased's estate**
The plaintiff's son was killed as a result of the negligent driving of the defendant. He was awarded damages which included £1,750 for loss of expectation of life and £6,656 for loss of future earnings. The defendant appealed claiming that the plaintiff was not entitled to recover anything in respect of loss of future earnings and that the amount awarded for loss of expectation of life was too high. *Held*, MEGAW LJ dissenting, the right of the estate to recover for loss of future earnings depended on the Law Reform (Miscellaneous Provisions) Act 1934, s. 1 (2) (c) which provides that where a cause of action survives for the benefit of the estate of a deceased person, damages are to be calculated without reference to any loss or gain to the deceased's estate consequent on the death. The cause of action for negligence was vested in the deceased immediately before his death and survived under the section for the benefit of his estate. Accordingly the plaintiff was entitled to recover damages in respect of the same loss on the basis of *Pickett v British Rail Engineering* unless s. 1 (2) (c) had a contrary effect. The intention of the section was (i) that the survival of the right to recover damages in respect of gains to the estate would not be reduced by incidental gains and (ii) that damages in respect of losses the right of which to recover which was already vested in the deceased would not be increased by including incidental losses to the estate. Accordingly the section did not exclude the recovery, for the benefit of the estate of a deceased person, of damages for loss of future earnings. The appropriate amount for loss of expectation of life had to be a conventional figure to ensure uniformity. Although the figure had increased with inflation it was not appropriate that it should be reassessed separately. Since the figure had been assessed at £1,250 the previous award of £1,750 would be reduced by £500.
MEGAW LJ considered that s. 1 (2) (c) excluded from the calculation of damages any amount referable to future earnings, since dependants could claim compensation under the Fatal Accidents Act 1976 which might be substantially increased by reason of the earnings of the lost years.
GAMMELL v WILSON [1980] 2 All ER 557 (Court of Appeal: MEGAW and BRANDON LJJ and SIR DAVID CAIRNS). *Pickett v British Rail Engineering Ltd* [1979] 1 All ER 774, HL, 1978 Halsbury's Abridgment para. 861 applied.
For earlier proceedings in this case see 1979 Halsbury's Abridgment para. 808.
This decision has been affirmed by the House of Lords; see [1981] 1 All ER 578.

882   The plaintiff's two daughters, both doctors, died as a result of an aircraft accident. The plaintiff claimed damages from the airline on behalf of himself and his wife, as dependants of the deceased under the Fatal Accidents Acts 1846 to 1959, and for the benefit of the deceased's estates under the Law Reform (Miscellaneous Provisions) Act 1934. The defendants contended that the estates were not entitled to recover damages in respect of money that the deceased would have earned had they lived, by virtue of s. 1 (2) (c) of the 1934 Act. Section 1 (2) (c) provides that damages are to be calculated without reference to any gain to the deceased's estate consequent on the death. *Held*, in principle, a claim under the 1934 Act for the lost years could survive for the benefit of a deceased's estate. Nor was the deceased's estate prevented from recovering such damages by s. 1 (2) (c); as damages for loss of expectation of life were not within the meaning of the section, so neither were damages for lost earnings in respect of the same life. The section had to be construed as applying to those gains to the estate that arose as a result of the death itself and independently of the fact that the death was caused by the defendant's wrongful act. Accordingly, s. 1 (2) (c) did not prevent the estate's recovering damages for the lost years.

KANDALLA v BRITISH AIRWAYS BOARD (formerly BRITISH EUROPEAN AIRWAYS CORPN) [1980] 1 All ER 341 (Queen's Bench Division: GRIFFITHS J).

883   **Unliquidated damages—whether provable in company winding up**

See *Re Berkeley Securities (Property) Ltd*, para. 390.

DEEDS

Halsbury's Laws of England (4th edn.), Vol. 12, paras. 1301–1566

884   **Construction of deed—ambiguity—construction by court**

Property was conveyed to a husband and wife "in fee simple as beneficial joint tenants in common in equal shares" for £500. The substantial consideration for the conveyance was, in fact, the surrender by the wife of the lease of certain land which the vendor wished to develop. The question arose as to whether the language of the conveyance created a beneficial joint tenancy or a tenancy in common. *Held*, the words used were inconsistent. The principle laid down in *Slingsby's Case* (1587) 5 Co Rep 18b, provided that where there were two inconsistent provisions the earlier provision should prevail. There was also a rule that where there were unequivocal words conveying an estate to persons as joint tenants those words were not to be cut down unless they could be read as a qualification or proviso. To read the words as creating a tenancy in common the court would be required not only to strike out words but also to add them. Furthermore, where a husband and wife were purchasers there was a presumption that they intended the survivor to remain in the matrimonial home, and to achieve this they would have created a beneficial joint tenancy. The court would accordingly construe the conflicting words as creating a beneficial joint tenancy, and strike out the remaining words as inconsistent.

JOYCE v BARKER BROS (BUILDERS) LTD (1980) Times, 26th February (Chancery Division: VINELOTT J).

885   **Escrow—guarantee delivered in escrow—effect**

See *Barclays Bank Ltd v Thomas*, para. 1377.

886   **—— lease—lease and counterpart delivered in escrow—effective date of commencement**

The plaintiff landlords sought a declaration that a lease granted to the defendants commenced on the date when the counterpart was sent to the plaintiffs' solicitors. Both the lease and the counterpart were delivered in escrow. A year later both became unconditional when an outstanding term was satisfied. *Held*, the lease took effect from the date when the condition was satisfied and not from the original date of delivery.

ALAN ESTATES LTD v W G STORES LTD (1980) 254 Estates Gazette 989 (Chancery Division: JUDGE RUBIN). *Terrapin International Ltd v Inland Revenue Comrs* [1976] 2 All ER 461, 1976 Halsbury's Abridgment para. 2483 applied.

DEVELOPMENT LAND TAX

Halsbury's Laws (4th edn.), Vol. 5, Supp. paras. 300A–D

887   Finance Act 1980

See para. 2328.

888   Liability to tax—purchase notice—date of disposal and acquisition

The taxpayer company served a purchase notice requiring the council to purchase a plot of land. The council accepted the notice in December 1974, but compensation was not approved until August 1976. The question arose as to the date of disposal of the land for the purpose of assessing liability to development land tax, which was introduced on 1st August 1976.· The Crown argued that the relevant date was the date at which the compensation was agreed because the council was deemed, under the Town and Country Planning Act 1971, s. 181 (2), to be acquiring the land compulsorily so that the Development Land Tax Act 1976, s. 45 (4) applied to regulate the date of disposal. The taxpayer contended that such a fiction could not have been intended to apply to a statute which had not yet been enacted in 1971 and claimed that the relevant date was the date of the acceptance of the purchase notice, pursuant to s. 45 (2) of the 1976 Act. *Held*, the statutory fiction was to be resorted to for all purposes of compulsory purchase; there was nothing in the provision limiting its application, nor would any unjust, anomalous or absurd result follow from applying it to s. 45 (4). Accordingly the disposal took place in August 1976, and the company was liable to development land tax.

INLAND REVENUE COMRS V METROLANDS (PROPERTY FINANCE) LTD (1980) Times, 12th December (Chancery Division: NOURSE J).

DISCOVERY, INSPECTION AND INTERROGATORIES

Halsbury's Laws of England (4th edn.), Vol. 13, paras. 1–200

889   Disclosure of documents—use of documents disclosed by journalist—whether abuse of process of discovery contempt of court

The Home Office applied for an order against a solicitor, under RSC Order 52, r. 9, for relief for her alleged contempt of court in supplying to a journalist copies of documents which had been disclosed to her in response to orders for discovery in her capacity as a solicitor for her client in his action for damages against the Home Office, on his claim that he had spent six months of a prison sentence in a special control unit. *Held*, a person to whom the court granted an order for discovery of documents in legal proceedings impliedly undertook that the documents were not to be used except for the purposes of the action in which they were disclosed. Such an undertaking was not destroyed if the documents were read out in open court. However, a person, however, who permitted a journalist to study a disclosed document which had been read out in open court did not necessarily commit contempt of court, but whether such conduct amounted to contempt had to be judged in the light of all the surrounding circumstances including such matters as the purposes and extent of the disclosure to the journalist, its date in relation to the trial of the action and whether leave of the court should have been obtained before the disclosure was made. In the present case the solicitor was bound by the implied obligation and in disclosing the documents to a journalist she had not made use of them for the purpose of the action by her client against the Home Office and was guilty of contempt of court, but as she had acted in good faith no penalty would be imposed.

HOME OFFICE v HARMAN (1980) Times, 28th November (Queen's Bench Division: PARK J).

This decision has been affirmed by the Court of Appeal; see [1981] 2 WLR 310.

890　　Discovery in support of injunction—power to make order in aid of Mareva injunction—inspection of bank account

The Queen's Bench Division of the High Court has the power to make an order for discovery in support of a Mareva injunction where it is necessary to do so in order to ensure the proper and effective exercise of the Mareva jurisdiction.

The plaintiffs brought an action for conspiracy to defraud and for deceit against the defendants, all of whom were resident outside the jurisdiction. They issued a writ for damages against the defendants and a tracing order against a bank in respect of a sum of money which one of the plaintiffs had paid, under a mistake of fact induced by fraud, into the account of one of the defendants. Prior to the issue of the writ, the plaintiffs obtained a Mareva injunction against the defendants limited to the sum of damages claimed by the plaintiffs, and an injunction restraining the defendants from disposing of the money in the bank account. They also obtained an order for discovery of the amount standing in the account and if that money was no longer there, an order for disclosure of knowledge of its whereabouts. These orders were however discharged by a judge and the plaintiffs applied to have the injunctions continued and the orders restored.

Held, the defendants' contention that the court ought not to make orders for discovery in support of a Mareva injunction would be rejected. The court had the power to order discovery of particular documents and interrogatories under RSC Ord. 21, r. 7 and Ord. 26, r. 1 or alternatively, under the Supreme Court of Judicature (Consolidation) Act 1925, s. 45 (1). Where the asset in respect of which the injunction was sought was a bank account, the court could also exercise its power under the Bankers' Books Evidence Act 1879, s. 7 to allow the plaintiff to inspect and take copies of entries in the banker's books. Thus, where the remedy the plaintiff was seeking in an action was the restoration of property which in equity belonged to him, the court had the power not only to grant an interlocutory injunction restraining disposal of the property but also to make an interlocutory order directed towards discovery of the whereabouts of that property. Accordingly the injunctions would be continued and the orders restored.

A v C [1980] 2 All ER 347 (Queen's Bench Division: ROBERT GOFF J).

891　　Two men presented for payment to the plaintiff bank two cheques for a sum of one million dollars purported to be drawn on a Saudi bank. The plaintiff honoured the cheques and credited certain sums to the defendant's accounts at D bank. The cheques were however forged and the plaintiff recredited the Saudi bank thus losing one million dollars. The plaintiff wished to trace and follow the funds of which it had been fraudulently deprived and brought an action against the two men and D bank. The plaintiff obtained a Mareva injunction to prevent D bank from disposing of any of the moneys of the two men, who were out of the country and who had not been served, and then sought an order for discovery from D bank of all correspondence, vouchers, transfer applications, orders and internal memoranda relating to the moneys. *Held*, D bank had become innocently involved in the tortious or wrongful acts of the two men and was under a duty to assist the plaintiff by giving it full information. The bank's confidential relationship with its clients did not apply to concealing the fraud and iniquities of the wrongdoers. To enable justice to be done and trace the funds, discovery had to be made notwithstanding that the two men had not been served and that the order sought was wider in scope than any order which could be obtained under the Bankers' Books Evidence Act, 1879. The order would be granted subject to an undertaking that the information which the plaintiff received would be used only for the purposes of the action.

BANKERS TRUST CO v SHAPIRA [1980] 3 All ER 353 (Court of Appeal: LORD DENNING MR, WALLER and DUNN LJJ). Dictum of Lord Reid in *Norwich Pharmacal*

Co v Customs and Excise Comrs [1974] AC 133 at 175, *Initial Services Ltd v Putterill* [1968] 1 QB 396 and *A v C* [1980] 2 All ER 347, para. 890, applied.

For a discussion of this case see "When probity must outweigh privacy", Justinian: Financial Times, 9th June 1980.

892 Inspection—documents and property on premises controlled by defendant

South Africa

The plaintiff and its agent obtained a rule nisi restraining the defendants from using certain trade names in infringement of their trade mark. On the return day the plaintiff applied for an order confirming the rule nisi. *Held*, the plaintiff had made out a case of infringement of the trade mark insofar as there had been an unauthorised use of the mark which was likely to cause confusion. The order restraining the defendants from using the mark would therefore be confirmed, but the disclosure of documents would not be ordered because this would effectively enable the plaintiff to obtain discovery before the institution of the proceedings, which would be unjustifiable now that the element of urgency was no longer present. The court would also refuse to compel the defendants to reveal their sources of supply because the plaintiff had failed to prove that it bona fide believed in a right of action against the person whose name it sought to discover, nor that the defendants would be able to supply it with such information. In view of the court's opinion that the plaintiff would be entitled to an order for the delivery up of the infringing articles for the purpose of removal or destruction should it be successful at the trial, an order for the disclosure of the presence and place of storage of the goods would be ordered.

ROAMER WATCH CO SA V AFRICAN TEXTILE DISTRIBUTORS [1980] RPC 457 (Supreme Court of South Africa).

893 Production of documents—complaint of racial discrimination—confidential reports

A lecturer at a college claimed that he had been discriminated against in respect of promotions on grounds of his race. An issue arose as to the extent to which he was entitled to discovery of documents dealing with appointments and promotions in the college which took place prior to the Race Relations Act 1976 coming into force. *Held*, evidence relating to incidents which took place before the Act came into force was capable of being logically probative of the issues arising in an allegation that there was racial discrimination after the Act came into force.

SELVARAJAN V INNER LONDON EDUCATION AUTHORITY [1980] IRLR 313 (Employment Appeal Tribunal: SLYNN J presiding). *Mood Music Publishing Co Ltd v De Wolfe Ltd* [1976] 1 Ch 119, 1975 Halsbury's Abridgment para. 1463 applied.

894 —— medical report on plaintiff in personal injuries action—stay of proceedings

See *Hall v Avon Area Health Authority*, para. 2241; *Megarity v D J Ryan & Sons Ltd*, para. 2242.

895 —— non-disclosure on grounds of legal professional privilege—availability in criminal proceedings

A solicitor was instructed by the employees of the plaintiff company to acquire three "ready-made" companies to carry out business in the same field as that of the plaintiff. The plaintiff brought an action claiming that the employees and the solicitor conspired to injure the company by setting up business in competition with it and, further, inducing other employees to break their contracts with the plaintiff. By a notice of motion the plaintiff sought an order for discovery and production of documents relating to the incorporation and affairs of the three "ready-made" companies. The solicitor claimed legal professional privilege. *Held*, the privilege was lost by the criminal or fraudulent intent of the client, whether or not the solicitor was aware of that intent. It had to be determined whether the employees consulted the solicitor before the commission of a fraudulent act and the purpose of being helped, wittingly or unwittingly, in committing the fraud. If the employees and solicitors embarked on a fraudulent activity, which was apparent, communications made in the course of that activity were not entitled to privilege and had to be disclosed. The order would be granted.

GAMLEN CHEMICAL CO (UK) LTD v ROCHEM LTD (No. 2) (1979) 124 Sol Jo 276 (Court of Appeal: GOFF and TEMPLEMAN LJJ). *R v Cox and Railton* (1884) 14 QBD 153 and *Williams v Quebrada Railway, Land and Copper Co* [1895] 2 Ch 751 applied. For other proceedings see 1979 Halsbury's Abridgment para. 2696.

896　　　—— non-disclosure on grounds of privilege—confidential relationship between media and sources of information

During a strike at the plaintiff company, the defendant television company broadcast a television programme on the strike, basing it upon confidential and secret documents belonging to the plaintiff. Upon recovery of the documents the plaintiff discovered that they had been mutilated, making it impossible to identify their owner. The plaintiff therefore sought an order compelling the defendant to serve an affidavit of the name of the person responsible for supplying the documents. The basis of the application was the decision in *Norwich Pharmalco v Customs and Excise Comrs* [1973] 2 All ER 943 HL, that a person who becomes involved in the tortious acts of another, however innocently, is under a duty to assist persons injured by those acts by giving them full discovery and disclosure of the identity of the tortfeasor. The order was granted and the defendant appealed. Accepting that the documents had been obtained in breach of confidence it contended, inter alia, that the court had a discretion to refuse to order discovery where it would be in breach of some ethical or social value and that the confidential relationship between newspapers and other media of information and their sources of information was an ethical or social value and one which the court ought to protect by refusing to order any disclosure. The Court of Appeal dismissed the appeal and the defendant appealed to the House of Lords. *Held*, Lord Salmon dissenting, (1) the media of information and journalists who wrote for them had no immunity based on public interest which protected them from the obligation to disclose their sources of information in a court of law where the court in its discretion considered such disclosure was necessary; (2) the plaintiff was prima facie entitled to the relief sought based on the decision in the *Norwich* case, especially as the defendant had become actively involved in the tortious acts of the informer by mutilating the documents so as to prevent identity of their owner becoming known; (3) the remedy was discretionary however and there would be cases where there would be an element of public interest in protecting the revelation of the sources of information. However in the present case the balance of interests was strongly in favour of the plaintiff, and it would be a significant denial of justice not to allow the plaintiff its remedy.

BRITISH STEEL CORPORATION v GRANADA TELEVISION LTD [1980] 3 WLR 774 (House of Lords: LORD WILBERFORCE, VISCOUNT DILHORNE, LORD SALMON, LORD FRASER OF TULLYBELTON and LORD RUSSELL OF KILLOWEN). *A-G v Clough* [1963] 1 QB 773, *A-G v Mulholland; A-G v Foster* [1963] 2 QB 477 CA, *McGuiness v A-G of Victoria* (1940) 63 CLR and *Norwich Pharmacal Co v Customs and Excise Comrs,* cited, applied. Decision of Court of Appeal (1980) Times, 8th May affirmed.

897　　　—— —— privilege against self-incrimination

See *Rank Film Distributors Ltd v Video Information Centre,* para. 2181.

898　　　—— —— —— evidence wrongfully obtained

See *International Electronics Ltd v Weigh Data Ltd,* para. 1226.

899　　　—— —— records of child in care of local authority

The Court of Appeal has held that the principle in *Re D (Infants)* [1970] 1 All ER 1088, CA, applied in *D v NSPCC* [1977] 1 All ER 589, HL, 1977 Halsbury's Abridgment para. 916, that child case records were private, confidential and privileged should now be regarded as of general application, not only in wardship and custody cases, but also in personal injury cases.

The plaintiff had been in the defendant local authority's care from the age of six months to eighteen years. He now sought to bring an action in negligence or for breach of duty against the defendant on the grounds that his current psychological injuries and anxiety neurosis were caused by its breach of duty. A doctor's report gave a history of neglect and mismanagement and there was prima facie evidence in support of the plaintiff's claim to warrant production of his case notes. His application under the Administration of Justice Act 1970, s. 31 for the disclosure of such documents before commencing proceedings against the authority was however refused and his appeal dismissed by the Court of Appeal.

GASKIN v LIVERPOOL CITY COUNCIL [1980] 1 WLR 1549 (Court of Appeal: LORD DENNING MR, MEGAW and DUNN LJJ).

900   —— non-disclosure on grounds of public interest—documents concerning interests of foreign states

The plaintiffs and defendants were American companies with oil concessionary rights over the same area in the Persian Gulf. The plaintiffs had been granted the concession by the ruler of one state and the defendants by the ruler of another state. After much dispute as to the extent of each company's concession area, the plaintiffs were eventually successful in obtaining and transporting the oil to the United States. The defendants then claimed that the ruler of the first state had conspired with the plaintiffs in order to extend his territorial waters thereby depriving them of the oil. In an action begun by the plaintiffs in 1970 for alleged slander by the defendants, the latter were refused discovery of documents relating to the affairs of the ruler which were relevant to the action. On appeal, *held*, it was in the public interest of the United Kingdom that the contents of confidential documents of sovereign states, relating to an international territorial dispute between the states, should not be ordered to be disclosed by a private litigant without the consent of the states concerned. Such documents were immune from disclosure under the heading of public interest immunity. That immunity outweighed the public interest that justice should be administered on the basis of full disclosure of documents. Further, the court should not act as arbiters in the dispute between the two oil companies. The underlying issue in the action for slander was a dispute between two sovereign states about their territorial waters and the court should exercise its judicial restraint by not ordering discovery of the documents in question. The appeal would be dismissed.

BUTTES GAS AND OIL CO v HAMMER (No. 3) [1980] 3 All ER 475 (Court of Appeal: LORD DENNING MR, DONALDSON and BRIGHTMAN LJJ). *Hesperides Hotels Ltd v Muftizade* [1978] 2 All ER 1168, HL, 1978 Halsbury's Abridgment para. 424, applied.

901   —— —— statements made during internal police investigation

See *Neilson v Laugharne*, para. 2153.

902   —— non-disclosure on grounds of public interest and Crown privilege—documents owned by defendants' foreign subsidiaries

The plaintiffs owned a pipeline which they built to carry oil from Mozambique to Rhodesia following an agreement with the defendants. When Rhodesia unilaterally declared independence the British government made an order imposing sanctions to prohibit oil reaching Rhodesia. It was suggested that the defendants broke this oil embargo. The plaintiffs therefore issued a writ for damages for non-use of the pipeline in breach of contract and also alleged conspiracy to break the sanctions order. A date for arbitration was fixed. The plaintiffs wished to see certain documents belonging to the defendants' subsidiary companies in South Africa, Mozambique and Rhodesia, and brought a claim in the courts for discovery. This was refused by the Court of Appeal on the ground that the parent company had no power over the documents of its subsidiaries, in that the documents could not be said to be in the defendants' possession, custody or power within RSC Ord. 24, r. 3 as the defendants did not have an existing indefeasible legal right enforceable by action to demand possession forthwith from their subsidiaries. The Court gave leave however to appeal to the House of Lords.

Following the suggestion that the defendants had broken the sanctions order, a government inquiry was ordered into the supply of oil to Rhodesia in contravention of the prohibition. The defendants co-operated fully with the inquiry and the plaintiffs therefore sought a further order compelling full discovery of the transcripts of evidence given and all written submissions made to the inquiry. This too was refused by the Court of Appeal on the grounds that the defendants had given information to the inquiry on the implicit understanding that it was confidential, and that the inquiry itself was private; the application for discovery was outweighed by the public interest in confidentiality but leave to appeal would be granted.

The appeals were heard together. *Held*, their Lordships would dismiss the appeals. The decisions of the judge at first instance and those in the Court of Appeal were unanimous and it was inappropriate to grant leave to appeal to the House of Lords against such judgments. The circumstances giving rise to the disputes were quite exceptional and unlikely to recur. In relation to the subsidiaries' position in South Africa or Rhodesia, the evidence had been that it would have been a criminal offence for the subsidiaries to disclose their documents and thus those documents were not, and never had been, in "the power" of the defendants. In the application for the discovery of the documents made available to the inquiry, the Attorney-General had been given leave to assert on behalf of the Crown immunity from disclosure on the ground of public interest and their Lordships agreed that this assertion ought to prevail.

LONRHO LTD v SHELL PETROLEUM CO LTD [1980] 1 WLR 627 (House of Lords: LORD DIPLOCK, LORD EDMUND-DAVIES, LORD FRASER OF TULLYBELTON, LORD RUSSELL OF KILLOWEN and LORD KEITH OF KINKEL). Decisions of Court of Appeal [1980] 2 WLR 367 and (1980) Times, 13th March affirmed.

903   —— relevance of documents—patents

See *Wellcome Foundation Ltd v VR Laboratories (Aust) Pty Ltd*, para. 2096.

DISTRESS

Halsbury's Laws of England (4th edn.), Vol. 13, paras. 201–500

904   Distress for rates—application for order of committal—magistrates' discretion to make order

A Divisional Court of the Queen's Bench Division has held that a magistrates' court which refused to make a committal order against a ratepayer had exercised its discretion not to make the order upon a wholly unjustifiable basis and its decision would therefore be quashed.

The ratepayer had purchased property of a rateable value low enough for the property to be eligible for an improvement grant. The rating authority then increased the rates and no grant was therefore available. The ratepayer refused to pay the increased sum and a distress order was made in respect of the balance. There was insufficient distress and the authority applied for a committal order. The magistrates had, without inquiring into the ratepayer's ability to pay, made an order dismissing the application and remitting liability for the sum claimed on the ground that they had felt it unfair that the ratepayer should be expected to pay the rates.

R v OUNDLE and THRAPSTON JJ AND DELANEY, EX PARTE EAST NORTHAMPTONSHIRE DISTRICT COUNCIL [1980] RA 232 (Queen's Bench Division: DONALDSON LJ and WOOLF J).

905   —— charges

The Distress for Rates Order (Amendment) Order 1980, S.I. 1980 No. 2013 (in force on 12th January 1981), amends the Distress for Rates Order 1979, 1979

Halsbury's Abridgment para. 921, to provide for charges to be made where levy for distress is attempted but not made.

906   —— **non-occupation of part of premises**

See *Benwell Mansions Ltd v Westminster City Council*, para. 2302.

907   —— **warrant of commitment—whether issue of rateable occupation can be raised**

A woman was sentenced to three months' imprisonment by a magistrates' court for non-payment of rates. In reply to the local authority's demand for rates, she had maintained that she was not the rateable occupier; but she was not allowed to argue the point before the justices who, relying on *R v Camberwell Green JJ, ex parte Gravesande*, stated that she could not raise, at that stage, the substantive issue of liability for rates. The woman sought an order of certiorari to quash the sentence of three months' imprisonment passed upon her by the justices. *Held*, in proceedings to commit a person to prison for non-payment of rates, the person in question was not precluded, at that stage, from contending that he was not a rateable occupier.

R v Ealing JJ, ex parte Coatsworth (1980) Times, 1st March (Queen's Bench Division: Lord Widgery CJ and Griffiths J). Dictum of James LJ in *R v Camberwell Green JJ, ex parte Gravesande* [1973] RA 297, at 300 distinguished.

DIVORCE

Halsbury's Laws of England (4th edn.), Vol. 13, paras. 501–1352

908   **Articles**

Compelling Disclosure of "Invisible" Assets Upon Divorce, Bernard Berkovits (a discussion of the difficulty of ascertaining the true financial situation of the parties in awarding ancillary relief upon divorce): 130 NLJ 648.

Financial Provision: The "Clean Break" Principle, Margaret Rutherford: 130 NLJ 183.

Financial Provision: Development of the "Clean Break" Principle, Margaret Rutherford: 130 NLJ 720.

The "Three Year Bar" to Divorce, M. W. Bryan (discussion of Matrimonial Causes Act 1973, s. 3): 130 NLJ 319.

When is a Final Agreement and a Final Order Final?, Alec Samuels: 124 Sol Jo 599.

909   **Administration of Justice Act 1977—commencement**

The Administration of Justice Act 1977 (Commencement No. 7) Order 1980, S.I. 1980 No. 1981, brought into force, on 1st January 1981, the remaining provisions of the Act, i.e. s. 3 and Sch. 3, paras. 1–10, which relate to the enforcement, in one part of the United Kingdom, of maintenance orders made in another part.

910   **Application for financial provision—jurisdiction of court to dismiss application—consent of applicant**

In ancillary proceedings following a divorce the judge ordered that the matrimonial home which was owned jointly by the husband and wife should be held on trust for the wife subject to a charge on the proceeds of sale in favour of the husband, and that no order for periodical payments should be made. The order as finally drafted was unsatisfactory and the judge varied the clause concerning periodical payments, purporting to act under CCR Ord. 15, r. 12 which provided that an order would be amended in the event of clerical mistakes. The amended order stated that the wife's application for periodical payments for herself and children was dismissed. The wife appealed. *Held*, the Matrimonial Causes Act 1973, s. 23 gave the parties a statutory right to apply for one of the orders listed in the section, including periodical payments. That statutory right could not be taken away by the court unless the party concerned had consented to such an order. Accordingly, the judge had no jurisdiction to dismiss the claim either for the children, who were not represented, or for the wife since she had not consented to it. A claim could only be barred following an appropriate agreement between the parties. However, since the original hearing, a subsequent agreement had been reached whereby the husband had agreed to transfer his whole interest in the matrimonial home to the wife absolutely; she in turn had agreed to indemnify him in respect of all the debts which had arisen under the existing mortgage. Accordingly, a nominal order for periodical payments for the wife and children would be made, but in the event of the husband agreeing to indemnify the wife against liability for their outstanding partnership debts, the order would be dismissed. Further, the alteration which the judge had made under CCR Ord. 15, r. 12 introduced a major change and was outside the ambit of the rule. The appeal would be allowed.

CARTER v CARTER [1980] 1 All ER 827 (Court of Appeal: ORR, ORMROD and GOFF LJJ).

911   The Court of Appeal has held that there is no power to dismiss a wife's application for periodical payments without her consent, as that would deprive her of her right under the Matrimonial Causes Act 1973, s. 23 (1) which provides that a court could make an order for periodical payments on granting a decree of divorce or at any time thereafter.

The court stated that there were four ways of dealing with an application for periodical payments: by making a substantive order; by making a nominal order to enable the applicant to take advantage of the 1973 Act, s. 31 (empowering variation); by adjourning the application generally if the court did not wish to make any order at that time; and finally by dismissing the application where the applicant consented. It was undesirable to make an order in the form of "no order" because of the difficulty of interpreting subsequently whether that was tantamount to dismissal of the application or indicated the court's wish to keep the position open.

Minton v Minton [1979] 1 All ER 79, HL, 1978 Halsbury's Abridgment para. 970 had not decided that the court, of its own volition, could strike out an application and therefore *Dunford v Dunford* [1980] 1 All ER 122, CA, para. 951 had been decided per incuriam.

DIPPER v DIPPER [1980] 2 All ER 722 (Court of Appeal: ROSKILL, ORMROD and CUMMING-BRUCE LJJ).

912   —— **practice**

See para. 2212.

913   **Conduct of parties—financial provision**

In 1969, the marriage between the husband and wife was dissolved. There were two children and the wife applied for ancillary relief. The husband was ordered, inter alia, to make periodical payments of £1,000 per annum to the wife. Meanwhile, the husband remarried. From the date of the remarriage the wife constantly harassed them and on one occasion violently attacked the new wife. The husband ceased making payments to the wife and applied to the court under the Matrimonial Causes Act 1973, s. 31 (1) for a variation of the order, seeking to have the payments reduced to a nominal sum because of the wife's conduct. *Held*, on an application to vary an order for periodical payments the court could take into account conduct between the making of the original order and the hearing of the application to vary it; such conduct was part of "all the circumstances of the case" under the Matrimonial Causes Act 1973, s. 31 (7). Accordingly, conduct which was both "gross and obvious", rendering it repugnant to anyone's sense of justice to order one party to support another in such circumstances was relevant in considering the application. In the present circumstances, although the wife's conduct could not be ignored, as the daughter of the marriage was still in full time education, to which the wife was contributing, and it was unlikely that the wife would recover the arrears of maintenance due to her, the application would be dismissed. Accordingly, the payments would remain at the same amount but without deduction of tax.

J (HD) v J (AM) [1980] 1 All ER 156 (Family Division: SHELDON J). *Jones v Jones* [1975] 2 All ER 12, CA, *Wachtel v Wachtel* [1973] 1 All ER 829, CA, *Williams v Williams* [1963] 2 All ER 994, HL and dictum of Sir George Baker P in *W v W* [1975] 3 All ER 972, applied.

914   Custody—child already subject to care order—jurisdiction of divorce court

See *E v E and Cheshire County Council (Intervener)*, para. 1968.

915   —— interim order

See *Jenkins v Jenkins*, para. 1975.

916   —— —— exclusion of tenant from council home—emergency jurisdiction

See *B v B*, para. 1972.

917   —— joint custody order—practice

See para. 2218.

918   Decree absolute—court's power to delay decree

See *England v England*, para. 959.

919   —— validity of decree—consequences of irregularity

A husband and wife were married in 1933 and separated in 1966. After the separation the wife went to another city and never again met or corresponded with her husband who died in 1979. In 1970 the husband, with a view to reconciliation, employed a private detective to find his wife. The detective reported that he was unable to discover the whereabouts of the wife and the husband made no further attempt to contact her. In 1977 the husband filed a petition for divorce and applied for an order dispensing with service on the wife. He swore an affidavit stating that he had not seen his wife since 1966 and that he had instructed a detective to find her who had been unable to do so. On the basis of the affidavit and supporting documents, and without further inquiry, the registrar made an order dispensing with service. In late 1977 the decree nisi was pronounced and made absolute. The wife applied to set aside the order dispensing with service, the decree nisi and the decree absolute on the basis that inadequate inquiry had been made into her whereabouts and that had she known of the petition the grave financial hardship which it would cause her would have provided her with ample grounds for opposing it. *Held*, the inquiries made into the wife's whereabouts were quite inadequate as a basis for dispensing with personal service and consequently the subsequent decrees were voidable. Whether they would be set aside was within the court's discretion. The process was not barred by the husband's death. In the circumstances grave injustice had been done to the wife by reason of the irregularly obtained order dispensing with service and accordingly it should be set aside together with the subsequent decrees.

PURSE V PURSE (1980) Times, 20th December (Court of Appeal: SIR JOHN ARNOLD P, ORMROD and DUNN LJJ).

920   Divorce and nullity—recovery abroad of maintenance

See para. 1853.

921 Divorce county courts

The Divorce County Courts (Amendment) Order 1980, S.I. 1980 No. 790 (in force on 30th June 1980), amends the Divorce County Courts Order 1978, 1978 Halsbury's Abridgment para. 961 by designating Thanet and Trowbridge County Courts as divorce county courts and courts of trial for undefended matrimonial causes.

922

The Divorce County Courts (Amendment No. 2) Order 1980, S.I. 1980 No. 1217 (in force on 6th October 1980), amends the Divorce County Courts Order 1978, 1978 Halsbury's Abridgment para. 961. The 1980 Order designates the Bury St. Edmunds and Romford County Courts as divorce county courts and courts of trial and designates the Eastbourne County Court as a court of trial.

923 Domestic Proceedings and Magistrates' Courts Act 1978—commencement

See para. 1976.

924 Financial needs of parties—obligation of support—Law Commission report

The Law Commission has published a discussion paper entitled the Financial Consequences of Divorce: the Basic Policy (Law Commission No. 103), which considers criticism of the principle that marriage involves a life-long obligation of support, even after divorce. The paper also discusses the possibilities of a change in the law in this area.

925 Financial resources of parties—exercise of judge's discretion

The parties married in 1949. There was one child of the marriage, aged twenty-six. The husband, aged fifty-four, was a chartered accountant in the Civil Service. The wife, aged fifty-one, had worked substantially throughout the marriage. In 1977, the husband left and went to live with another woman. The wife was granted a decree nisi of divorce in 1978, an agreement having been reached between the parties that the matrimonial home, a flat, should be transferred to the wife and that the agreement be made a rule of court. The husband was subsequently ordered to make periodical payments to the wife. The husband appealed, contending that the order was over the one-third fraction, the wife had received all the capital of the family under the previous agreement, and the judge was wrong in not crediting the wife with some earning capacity. *Held*, the husband was living with the other woman in a joint household with no dependants and had no immediate housing problem. Further, the other woman had a considerable income of her own and, regarding the matter in the most limited way, this had to reduce his cost of living substantially. The wife, however, had had financial difficulties and would have to sell the flat and find a modest flat for herself and would need enough money to live on. If the capital were divided, the wife would be left with too little to house herself, and that would not really help the husband. It was quite reasonable for the wife to continue to make a home for the son whilst he was still a student, and it was very difficult for her to do more than earn very little. Taking all these factors into consideration, the judge's order was plainly within the ambit of his discretion and was not one with which the court could properly interfere. The appeal would be dismissed.

WARD v WARD AND GREENE [1980] 1 All ER 176 (Court of Appeal: ORMROD LJ and SIR DAVID CAIRNS).

For the power of the court to order the sale of a matrimonial home, and the procedure to be followed, see para. 952.

926 —— financial resources of cohabitee—investigation by registrar

A wife applied for ancillary relief. She appealed against a decision ordering the husband's cohabitee to file an affidavit of means. *Held*, under the Matrimonial

Causes Rules 1977, r. 77 (5) the registrar could require further affidavits from the spouses during ancillary relief proceedings. A co-respondent could be ordered to attend a hearing and give evidence but the rule did not give the court power to order a co-respondent to swear an affidavit. Clear words were required to make the rule applicable to a stranger to the lis. The judge had no jurisdiction to make the order in question and the appeal would be dismissed.

WYNNE V WYNNE AND JEFFERS [1980] 3 All ER 659 (Court of Appeal: BRIDGE, CUMMING-BRUCE and EVELEIGH LJJ). Decision of Bush J (1980) Times, 1st March affirmed

927 —— financial resources of husband—consent order—fraud

During divorce proceedings the husband swore an affidavit as to his financial resources and an order was made by consent for a lump sum payment to the wife. The husband subsequently admitted that the earlier account of his assets had been false. The consent order was set aside and the husband successfully appealed on the ground that the registrar had no jurisdiction to set aside the order. On the wife's appeal, *held*, the consent order was a final order and so it could normally only be set aside for fraud in a separate action. However in this case, when fraud was not in dispute, an action would serve no useful purpose and the order should be set aside.

ALLSOP V ALLSOP [1980] LS Gaz R 1068 (Court of Appeal: ORMROD and BRANDON LJJ).

928 —— financial resources of second wife

After her divorce, a wife applied for periodical payments for herself and the children of the marriage, and sought an order for the transfer of the matrimonial home. The husband had remarried, and in his affidavit of means failed to disclose any income or capital of the second wife. The wife asked the registrar to make an order requiring the second wife to file an affidavit of means relating to her capital and income. The registrar refused. On appeal by the wife, *held*, financial benefits derived by a husband from a second wife were relevant when assessing a husband's liability to a former wife and children. Information regarding how the means of the second wife were deployed within the husband's household had to be forthcoming in order for the court to discharge its duty properly under the Matrimonial Causes Act 1973, s. 25 (1). Further, the first wife did not have to show that gifts of money or property were made to the husband by the second wife before the means of the second wife became a relevant consideration. The appeal would be allowed.

WILKINSON V WILKINSON (1979) 123 Sol Jo 752 (Family Division: BOOTH J). *Grainger v Grainger* [1954] 2 All ER 665 considered.

929 Foreign proceedings—recognition

See CONFLICT OF LAWS.

930 Lump sum payment—applicability of the one-third rule

The Family Division of the High Court has held that the one-third rule was inappropriate when considering financial provision for a sixty-seven year old woman on the breakdown of her forty-year old marriage.

The husband owned a farm business and his assets were over £2 million. On his various farms he employed thirty-five people who all lived in the nearby village, and if forced to curtail his business, the ensuing redundancies would cause a social problem in the village. The court therefore ordered the sale of three farms, which could be sold without undue disruption to the business. The wife would therefore receive a lump sum of £375,000, which was considerably more than she needed, but which recognised her contribution in assisting to build up the husband's assets, without causing problems for the husband in realising that sum.

S v S (1980) Times, 10th May (Family Division: BALCOMBE J).

931 ——— contingent gratuity—whether financial resource likely in foreseeable future

The parties were divorced in 1977, having been married for thirteen years. The wife lived in a council house with the three young children of the marriage. In 1978, the wife applied for a lump sum payment, asking for a share in a contingent gratuity for which the husband, who was serving in the Royal Marines, would first become eligible in 1983. The registrar's refusal to consider the possibility of the husband's future gratuity was upheld on appeal. The wife further appealed, the husband contending that even if receipt of the gratuity was likely, he was not likely to have it in the foreseeable future. *Held*, on the facts, the expectation of the receipt of the gratuity was not unlikely and on the balance of probabilities the husband would receive it. Further, the husband was likely to have the gratuity in 1983, which was sufficiently proximate in time to be regarded as the foreseeable future for the purposes of a lump sum order under the Matrimonial Causes Act 1973, s. 25. Accordingly, the appeal would be allowed.

PRIEST V PRIEST (1979) 9 Fam Law 252 (Court of Appeal: ORR and CUMMING-BRUCE LJJ).

932 Maintenance and custody order—appeal—leave to appeal out of time—question of paternity raised

In a case where a father sought leave to appeal out of time against a custody and maintenance order in favour of the mother, made pursuant to the Guardianship of Minors Act 1971, s. 9, on the grounds that he was not the father of the child in question, *held*, where the matter was of extreme importance to the child and where an inexcusable delay had occurred justice must be done to the child, as well as to the would-be appellant. For the purpose of seeking maintenance under the Matrimonial Causes Act 1973 a distinction existed between a child who was a child of "one parent" and a child of "both parents", and although the mother had power to return to the court to seek maintenance, nevertheless the child would be treated as a second class and not a first class child of the family. In the present case, although the medical evidence had not been tested and it might be an issue, where there was such an inexcusable delay in the proceedings and the court had a discretion, the court had to consider the importance of the risk to the child in losing his legitimacy. Accordingly it would be wrong to grant leave to appeal out of time.

EDWARDS V EDWARDS (1980) 10 Fam Law 188 (Family Division: SIR JOHN ARNOLD P and HEILBRON J).

933 Maintenance order—element in respect of school fees—tax relief

See paras. 1581, 2219.

934 ——— reciprocal enforcement

See CONFLICT OF LAWS.

935 ——— registration

The Magistrates' Courts (Maintenance Orders Act 1950) (Amendment) Rules 1980, S.I. 1980 No. 1895 (in force on 1st January 1981) amend the Maintenance Orders Act 1950 (Summary Jurisdiction) Rules 1950 in consequence of provisions enabling a maintenance order made by an inferior or superior court in Scotland or Northern Ireland to be registered in the High Court or a magistrates' court respectively.

936 The Magistrates' Courts (Maintenance Orders Act 1958) (Amendment) Rules 1980, S.I. 1980 No. 1896 (in force on 1st January 1981), amend the Magistrates' Courts (Maintenance Orders Act 1958) Rules 1959 in consequence of provisions enabling a maintenance order made by an inferior or superior court in Scotland or Northern Ireland to be registered in the High Court or a magistrates' court respectively.

937   —— registration in magistrates' courts

See para. 2220.

938   Matrimonial causes—fees

The Matrimonial Causes Fees Order 1980, S.I. 1980 No. 819 (in force on 7th July 1980), prescribes the fees payable (i) in all matrimonial proceedings; (ii) in matrimonial proceedings pending in a divorce county court and (iii) in matrimonial proceedings pending in the High Court. All fees are payable in cash. The Matrimonial Causes Fees Order 1975, 1975 Halsbury's Abridgment para. 1139 is revoked.

939   —— rules

The Matrimonial Causes (Amendment) Rules 1980, S.I. 1980 No. 977 (in force on 5th January 1981), further amend the Matrimonial Causes Rules 1977, 1977 Halsbury's Abridgment para. 955 by (i) providing that injunctions and similar orders must be served personally on a respondent, not delivered to his solicitor; (ii) enabling the court to order the attendance of any person for examination before an application for ancillary relief is heard; (iii) requiring the respondent, when acknowledging service of a petition based on adultery, to admit to or deny adultery; (iv) making it clear that the requirement to state in the petition whether children other than children of the family have been born to the petitioner is limited to children living at the date of the petition and (v) restricting the requirement to state in the petition what arrangements, if any, have been made for the respondent's support, to petitions based on five years' separation.

940   The Matrimonial Causes (Amendment No. 2) Rules 1980, S.I. 1980 No. 1484 (in force on 5th January 1981), amend the Matrimonial Causes Rules 1977, 1977 Halsbury's Abridgment para. 955. The 1980 Rules require a respondent to an application for a variation order to file an affidavit containing full particulars of his property and income in answer to the application.

941   Matrimonial home—exclusion of spouse—custody application

See *L v L*, para. 1973.

942   —— property adjustment order—issue estoppel

See *Tebbutt v Haynes*, para. 1104.

943   —— —— jurisdiction of court to vary order

In ancillary proceedings following the parties' divorce, the court made a property adjustment order under the Matrimonial Causes Act 1973, s. 24 and ordered that the husband should receive a lump sum payment. The parties agreed a valuation but the property was sold for more than the agreed valuation. On an application by the husband for an adjustment of the distribution of the net proceeds of sale, *held*, the Matrimonial Causes Act 1973, s. 31 gave the court power to vary or discharge certain orders for financial relief. It was clear that the court had no jurisdiction to vary lump sum orders, or property adjustment orders as they were not mentioned in the section. Accordingly the application would be dismissed.

L v L (1980) Times, 13th November (Family Division: BALCOMBE J).

944   —— restraint on dealings with property—order for avoidance of disposition

A judge of the Family Division has held that the meaning of "consequential directions" in the Matrimonial Causes Act 1973, s. 37 (3) is restricted to directions requiring, for example, repayment of money paid under the conveyance. Its discretion to make directions consequential upon an order setting aside the disposition of matrimonial property under s. 37 (2), could not therefore be exercised to set aside or reduce a charge executed by the purchaser of the matrimonial property against a bank.

G v G (1980) Times, 7th October (Family Division: EASTHAM J).

945 —— settlement of property—court's power to order sale of property—Law Commission's recommendations

The court has no express power under the Matrimonial Causes Act 1973 to order a sale of property. The Law Commission has recommended that there should be an express power to order sale of property when the court makes an order for financial relief (except for unsecured periodical payments) in divorce, nullity and judicial separation proceedings. See Orders for Sale of Property under the Matrimonial Causes Act 1973, HC 369 (Law Com No. 99). The Law Commission further recommends that this power should be exercised according to the guidelines set out in s. 25 of the Act and that it should be available in cases where a third party has an interest in the property, subject to any representations by the third party. The orders for sale might be made in the form of suspended or conditional orders.

946 —— transfer of property—extension of time for appeal—court's jurisdiction to hear appeal against order

After a husband had left his wife, she continued to live in the matrimonial home with some of the children and paid off the mortgage without any assistance from the husband. The wife subsequently obtained a divorce and applied for a transfer of property order in respect of the matrimonial home. An order was made in the husband's absence transferring his share of the property to the wife. He was granted leave to appeal out of time from the order and the wife appealed. *Held*, the judge had jurisdiction under CCR Ord, 13, r. 5 to extend the time for appealing from the order. The Supreme Court of Judicature (Consolidation) Act 1925, s. 31 (1) (b) provided that no appeal should lie from an order allowing an extension of time for appealing against a judgment or order. There was no restriction to any particular court. Accordingly the present order came within the provisions of s. 31 (1) (b) and the court had no jurisdiction to hear the appeal. If the section did not apply, the court could only disturb the order if there had been an error of law. The husband was entitled to have proper notice of the proceedings to enable him to put forward his case, since it was found that he had reasonable grounds for appealing. Accordingly if the court had had jurisdiction there would have been no grounds for disturbing the judge's order. The appeal would be dismissed.

LOWE v LOWE [1980] LS Gaz R 130 (Court of Appeal: MEGAW and BRANDON LJJ).

947 —— —— financial obligations of parties

The wife was granted a decree of divorce. In her petition she applied for ancillary relief. The judge ordered the husband to pay £14 per week for the benefit of the child of the marriage. He further ordered that the matrimonial home be transferred to the wife. Since both parties planned to remarry, which would result in two family units with similar resources, the husband appealed on the grounds that, in the circumstances, the interest in the matrimonial home should be divided equally. *Held*, it would be wrong to deprive the husband of his interest in the former matrimonial home as it was now worth a substantial sum. Since both parties would be in a similar financial position after their respective remarriages and taking into account the increased value of the home, it should be held in equal shares on trust for sale, not to be sold until the child of the marriage attained a specified age, or with leave of the court. Accordingly, the appeal would be allowed.

MESHER v MESHER AND HALL (1973) [1980] 1 All ER 126 (Court of Appeal: DAVIES, CAIRNS and STAMP LJJ).

948   —— —— **order for sale**

The parties married in 1950, and there were two children of the marriage. In 1975, the husband left the wife for another woman, who had two children by a previous marriage. In 1977, the wife obtained a decree nisi of divorce on the ground of the husband's adultery. The husband married the other woman in 1978 and bought a house in their joint names. The former matrimonial home was valued at £52,000 with an equity of £48,000. In proceedings for ancillary relief, the judge ordered that the matrimonial home be sold immediately and a lump sum payment of £32,500 be paid out of the proceeds of sale to the wife. The wife appealed. *Held*, it was in the parties' children's best interests that they should remain in the home with the wife until the younger child attained eighteen years of age. Further, the mother would easily be able to acquire suitable smaller accommodation with her share of the proceeds when the postponed sale took place. The order would, accordingly, be varied to provide for sale a few months after the younger child's eighteenth birthday. The appeal would be allowed.

LAWTON LJ considered that the conduct of the parties might be of the greatest importance when making a property disposition order under the Matrimonial Causes Act 1973, s. 24. In the instant case, where the court was faced with admitted facts, it was not necessary for the wife to serve notice, pursuant to the Matrimonial Causes Rules 1977, r. 18 (1), alleging that conduct was a material factor.

BLEZARD V BLEZARD (1979) 9 Fam Law 249 (Court of Appeal: ORR and LAWTON LJJ).

949   —— —— **partial property adjustment—right of occupation**

The parties were divorced in 1978. There was one child of the marriage and both parties had a child by their former marriages. The husband was employed in Kuwait under a contract that had several years to run. It was subsequently agreed that the husband should transfer the matrimonial home, which was in his sole name, into the joint names of himself and his wife. The judge, however, made no provision as to the right of occupation of the house. The husband appealed. *Held*, in making no provision as to the right of occupation, the judge had left the parties to their rights under the Law of Property Act 1925, s. 30 and by so doing had deprived himself or his successor of his discretionary powers under the Matrimonial Causes Act 1973. This was an extremely unsatisfactory situation and the order was wrong in principle. In the circumstances, the wife would be granted leave to cross-appeal. It would be ordered that the wife should have the right to occupy the house until the youngest child was eighteen, when it should be sold and the proceeds divided equally among the parties. The wife's cross-appeal would accordingly be allowed.

RUSHTON V RUSHTON (1979) 9 Fam Law 218 (Court of Appeal: ORR, ORMROD and TEMPLEMAN LJJ). *Mesher v Mesher* [1980] 1 All ER 126, CA, para. 947 applied.

950   The parties were married in 1969 and had two children. The matrimonial home was purchased by the husband in their joint names. Since the breakdown of the marriage in 1975 the husband remained in the matrimonial home, looking after the two children. The wife subsequently remarried and took no further interest in the children. In proceedings concerning financial provision consequent upon the dissolution of the marriage an order allowing the husband to remain in the matrimonial home only until the children became of age was varied by the Court of Appeal to enable him to live in the house for the rest of his life. The court considered that a husband, whose wife on remarriage had a secure home, would be severely handicapped in acquiring a new home and employment after the children had reached the age of eighteen or completed their full-time education.

ESHAK V NOWOJEWSKI (1980) Times, 19th November (Court of Appeal: SIR JOHN ARNOLD P, OLIVER LJ and DAME ELIZABETH LANE).

951   —— —— **principle to be applied**

In 1978 a wife was granted a decree of divorce. In her petition she applied for financial provision for herself and the children and a property adjustment order in respect of the matrimonial home. The judge ordered, inter alia, that the matrimonial home be transferred to the wife and charged with payment to the husband of 25 per cent of the net proceeds of sale when sold, or on the death of the wife. He further ordered that periodical payments of a nominal sum should be paid to the wife. The husband appealed, contending that the home should be sold on the completion of the youngest child's education or on the wife's earlier remarriage and that he should be required to transfer to the wife only that amount of interest in the home as would be necessary for her future needs. The wife cross appealed, contending that the provision in the order for a charge on the matrimonial home should be struck out. *Held*, in accordance with the principle of the "clean break" the judge's order was correct, as both parties knew exactly where they stood. However the order would be amended so as to strike out the clause ordering the payment of the nominal sums. Accordingly both the appeal and the cross appeal would be dismissed.

DUNFORD v DUNFORD [1980] 1 All ER 122 (Court of Appeal: LORD DENNING MR, and EVELEIGH LJ). *Hanlon v Hanlon* [1978] 2 All ER 889, CA, *Minton v Minton* [1979] 1 All ER 79, HL, 1978 Halsbury's Abridgment para. 970, and *Jessel v Jessel* [1979] 3 All ER 645, CA, 1979 Halsbury's Abridgment para. 945 applied.

It was held in *Dipper v Dipper* [1980] 2 All ER 722, CA, para. 911, that the part of the decision which related to striking out the clause providing for periodical payments was per incuriam and should not be followed.

952　　—— —— procedure

ORMROD LJ, after dismissing a husband's appeal against an order for periodical payments (see para. 925), considered the procedure to be followed when making an application for the sale of a matrimonial home. The judge had suggested that the husband should issue a pro forma summons under the Married Women's Property Act 1882, s. 17 asking for sale. His Lordship stated that it was quite clear that s. 17 of the 1882 Act gave the court power to order a sale in proceedings between husband and wife in connection with property, and that the Law of Property Act 1925, s. 30 gave the court power to order a sale where there was a trust for sale; it could not matter what the nature of the proceedings were, but whether the circumstances were such as to bring the case within one or other of those Acts which gave the necessary power to the court to order the sale. The court had power to order sale of property under the Matrimonial Causes Act 1973, s. 24 without specific application under the 1882 Act or the 1925 Act.

WARD v WARD AND GREENE (NOTE) [1980] 1 All ER 176 (Court of Appeal: ORMROD LJ and SIR DAVID CAIRNS).

See also Practice Note (Matrimonial Property: Order for Sale) [1980] 1 WLR 4, which draws the attention of practitioners to the above decision.

953　　Nullity of marriage—foreign decree—recognition

See *Gwyn v Mellen*, para. 432.

954　　—— three-year restriction on presenting petition for divorce—proposed reform

The Law Commission has published a working paper (*Time Restrictions on Presentation of Divorce and Nullity Petitions*, working paper 76) on the restriction on presenting a petition for divorce within three years of marriage and the rule that nullity proceedings, in certain cases, must be brought within three years of the date of marriage. If change in the divorce law is to be made, the Law Commission identifies in particular three possibilities: outright abolition of the time restriction on the presentation of divorce petitions; the retention of a reduced time restriction, but allowing the court in specified circumstances to permit divorce within that period; or the retention of a reduced time restriction, but not permitting divorce under any circumstances within that period. The Law Commission suggests that the availability of divorce in the early years of marriage should not depend on whether or not the marriage is childless. The Law Commission suggests that the three-year time limit for bringing nullity proceedings under the Matrimonial Causes Act 1973,

s. 12, should be extended, in the court's discretion, where the petitioner was suffering from mental incapacity at the time of the marriage or became subject to such incapacity within three years of the marriage.

955   Periodical payments—variation of order—factors to be considered

The parties were divorced in 1976. A consent order was made in April 1977 giving the wife £1 per week maintenance on the basis that she was working and earned £30 per week. The husband earned £72 per week as a police officer. In February 1977, the wife stopped work because she was pregnant by another man. The child was born in August 1977 and the wife lived on social security benefits. The husband lived with another woman who gave birth to his child in October 1977. On application by the wife, her weekly sum was increased from £1 to £10. The husband appealed. *Held*, it was not right to state any principle as to what the situation should be in such circumstances. As the wife derived her sole income from social security benefits, the husband's payments would not make any difference to the amount which she would actually receive and the question was what would be fair in the circumstances. The payment of £10 per week was too much, as it left the husband with only just under £3 available after all his expenses were paid. A fair figure in all the circumstances would be £3 per week. The appeal would, accordingly, be allowed.

WAGNER v WAGNER (1979) 9 Fam Law 183 (Court of Appeal: ORMROD, WALLER and BRANDON LJJ).

956   Petition—leave to present petition within three years—exceptional hardship—considerations governing grant

The parties married in 1976. In 1978, the wife applied for leave to present a petition for divorce within three years of the marriage on the ground of exceptional hardship. She alleged that her health was seriously affected, that she had severe reactive depression, and that her career had suffered. The judge refused her application, and the wife appealed. *Held*, exceptional hardship was hardship which was more extensive and more serious than that which one would normally expect to follow from the events concerned. It was not necessary to show something quite abnormal in the consequences to the applicant. The wife was suffering more than normal hardship and the appeal would be allowed.

WOOLF v WOOLF (1979) 9 Fam Law 216 (Court of Appeal: ORMROD, WALLER and BRANDON LJJ).

957   Practice—matrimonial proceedings in magistrates' courts—rules

See para. 1851.

958   Prior financial agreement between parties—effect of agreement on courts' jurisdiction

The parties were married in 1967. By 1975, the marriage was in serious difficulties and the wife wished to leave the husband. The husband, a multi-millionaire, made it clear that he would not agree to her leaving with the four children of the marriage unless she had a proper and suitable home for them. As a result of negotiations between the parties' solicitors, a deed was executed under which the husband agreed to make certain capital provisions for the wife and to make periodical payments to the wife and to each of the four children. The parties were divorced in 1979, when the wife applied for all forms of ancillary relief. The judge decided that he could properly ignore the wife's undertaking not to ask for any further capital provision and so proceeded to assess a lump sum under the Matrimonial Causes Act 1973, s. 25. The husband appealed. *Held*, a wife could not, by her covenant, preclude herself from invoking the jurisdiction or preclude the court from the exercise of that jurisdiction, and the real question was therefore to determine the effect, if any, to be given to such a covenant. Regard had to be had to the conduct of both parties and to the fact that formal agreements arrived at with competent legal advice should not be displaced other than on substantial grounds. The wife had therefore to offer prima facie evidence of material facts which showed that justice required that she should be relieved from the effects of her covenant in the deed. Despite the disparity of bargaining power between the parties, regard had to be had to the use, if any, made of that disparity by the husband. In the instant case, as there was no evidence which reflected adversely on the husband's conduct in the negotiations and no adequate explanation of the wife's conduct, the appeal would be allowed.

EDGAR v EDGAR [1980] 1 WLR 1410 (Court of Appeal: ORMROD and OLIVER LJJ). *Hyman v Hyman* [1929] AC 601, HL and *Brockwell v Brockwell* (1975) Times, 11th November, CA, 1975 Halsbury's Abridgment para. 1120 applied.

959   Provision for children—adequacy—power of court to delay decree absolute until maintenance order made

A wife and two of her children were living on social security benefits and her husband was unemployed. In divorce proceedings, notwithstanding that he made a declaration of satisfaction as to the financial arrangements under the Matrimonial Causes Act 1973, s. 41, the judge made an order that the decree nisi was not to be made absolute until a maintenance order had been made. On appeal against that order, *held*, the court had power to delay the making absolute of a decree nisi in special circumstances. It was clear however, from *Cook v Cook* [1978] 3 All ER 1009, CA, 1978 Halsbury's Abridgment para. 975, that it was not against a child's interests to be supported by supplementary benefit, nor could a judge consider the public interest when making a decison under s. 41. The judge could not circumvent this decision by delaying the declaration of decree absolute on the ground that the children were being provided for out of public funds. The appeal would be allowed and the order set aside.

ENGLAND v ENGLAND (1979) 10 Fam Law 86 (Court of Appeal: ORR, CUMMING-BRUCE and BRANDON LJJ). *Cook v Cook*, cited, applied.

960   —— child of the family—meaning

The Court of Appeal has stated that, in interpreting "child of the family" within the provisions of the Matrimonial Causes Act 1973, s. 52, the court should look at the phrase broadly and ask objectively whether the child in question had been treated by the parties concerned as a child of their family.

RE M (A MINOR) (1980) 10 Fam Law 184 (Court of Appeal: ORR, ORMROD and WALLER LJJ).

961   —— effect of children on "clean break" principle

The Court of Appeal has held that the "clean break" principle as laid down in *Minton v Minton* [1979] 1 All ER 865, HL, 1978 Halsbury's Abridgment para. 970, is not applicable where there are young children, as the parties have to continue to co-operate because of the children. Further, that it does not apply where one party is earning and other is not; a "clean break" in such cases would mean people living on social security.

MOORE v MOORE (1980) Times, 10th May (Court of Appeal: SIR ROBERT MEGARRY V-C and ORMROD LJ).

EASEMENTS

Halsbury's Laws of England (4th edn.), Vol. 14, paras. 1–300

962   Articles

Easements and Public Policy, H. W. Wilkinson (the law in the light of the decision in *Nickerson v Barraclough* [1979] 3 All ER 312, 1979 Halsbury's Abridgment para. 984); 130 NLJ 204.

Easements in Gross, M. F. Sturley: 96 LQR 557.

963   **Water rights—water abstracted for agricultural use—effect of statutory provisions on easement**

Water Resources Act 1963, s. 23 provides that it is illegal after 30th June 1965, subject to certain exceptions, for any person to abstract water from any source except in pursuance of a licence granted under the Act by the appropriate river authority. Section 24 provides, however, that these provisions do not apply to anyone who abstracts less than 1,000 gallons if it did not form part of a continuous operation or a series of operations.

The plaintiff had been in continuous occupation of a farm since 1928 first as lessee and then as a freeholder, and since then had drawn water for agricultural use from a mill pond which formed part of a river. In 1977 the defendant purchased adjoining property whereby he became the owner of the bed of the pond and acquired the natural rights of a riparian owner. He subsequently challenged the plaintiff's right to abstract water from the pond. The plaintiff successfully sought a declaration that he had an easement to abstract water from the pond by prescription at common law and an injunction restraining the defendant from preventing him from drawing water from the pond. On appeal by the defendant. *Held*, (i) under the provisions of the Water Resources Act 1963 the plaintiff had acted illegally on every occasion he had abstracted water from the pond after June 1965 in that each abstraction of water formed part of a series of operations, the object of which was to help meet the water requirements of the farm for agricultural purposes. The plaintiff, therefore, could not rely on any abstraction of water carried out after June 1965, in order to establish an easement by prescription. (ii) The courts would not recognise an easement established by illegal activities but the 1963 Act did contain provisions which destroyed easements already acquired. An easement of water acquired before 1st July 1965 could not legally be used without a licence but it did not cease to be an easement if the licence had not been obtained. (iii) The plaintiff however, having at common law an easement to draw water from the pond for farming purposes, could apply for a licence under the 1963 Act and thereby lawfully exercise his easement.

The appeal would therefore be allowed to the extent that the injunction previously granted would be discharged and a further declaration substituted that future exercise of the easement would be governed by the Water Resources Act 1963.

CARGILL v GOTTS [1981]) 1 All ER 682 (Court of Appeal: LAWTON, BRANDON and TEMPLEMAN LJJ). Decision of H. E. Francis QC [1980] 1 WLR 521 reversed.

ECCLESIASTICAL LAW

Halsbury's Laws of England (4th edn.), Vol. 14, paras. 301–1435

964   **Church Representation Rules**

The Church Representation Rules (Amendment) Resolution 1980, S.I. 1980 No. 178 (in force on 1st May 1980), makes several miscellaneous amendments to the Church Representation Rules contained in the Synodical Government Measure 1969, Sch. 3.

965   **Deaconesses and Lay Workers (Pensions) Measure 1980**

The Deaconesses and Lay Workers (Pensions) Measure 1980 empowers the Church Commissioners to make payments for the provision or augmentation of pensions and related benefits for deaconesses, lay workers, their dependants and widows. The Measure received the royal assent on 20th March 1980 and came into force on that date.

Section 1 empowers the Church Commissioners to make payments to the Church of England Pensions Board for the purpose of providing or augmenting pensions for deaconesses and lay workers and their dependants and widows and any lump sums paid or payable to deaconesses and lay workers on their retirement from service. Any such sums are to be applied by the Board in such manner as it, in consultation with the Church Commissioners, thinks fit. Any such sum may be paid into the Church Workers Pension Fund. Section 2 deals with short title and extent.

966   Diocese in Europe Measure 1980

The Diocese in Europe Measure 1980 provides for the establishment of a Diocese in Europe, incorporating the former diocese of Gibraltar and the areas of Northern and Central Europe formerly within the ecclesiastical jurisdiction of the Bishop of London, and for the representation of the new Diocese in the General Synod of the Church of England. The Measure received the royal assent on 30th June 1980 and came into force on 2nd July 1980.

Section 1 provides that, at any time after the new Diocese is established, the General Synod may make provision by Canon in the form set out in Sch. 1 for the purpose of making provision for the Diocese to be represented in the Convocation of Canterbury and, accordingly, in the House of Bishops and the House of Clergy of the General Synod. This has been done by Amending Canon No. 8.

Section 2 provides for the amendment of the Church Representation Rules by Sch. 2 to provide for the representation of the Diocese in the House of Laity of the General Synod. Section 3 amends the Constitutuon of the General Synod, art. 8, in relation to the Diocese.

Section 4 empowers the Church Commissioners to pay to the bishop and any suffragan bishop of the Diocese a stipend and official expenses, and to provide or assist with the provision of suitable residences for such bishops. Measures relating to pensions and related benefits are extended to the Diocese by s. 5. Section 6 restricts the application of the Overseas and other Clergy (Ministry and Ordination) Measure 1967 to bishops and clergy of the Diocese. Section 7 deals with short title and commencement.

967   Faculty—building on disused burial ground—enlargement of church

The incumbent and churchwardens of a parish sought a faculty authorising the erection of an extension to the church on part of the churchyard, a disused burial ground. The extension was to comprise a choir vestry, two halls and other amenities. The petition was opposed by a number of parishioners, few of whom had any connection with the church as a place of worship, on the grounds that the proposed extension would impair the natural beauty of the churchyard and the church itself. On the question whether the faculty could be granted, *held*, the purpose of the faculty jurisdiction was to ensure the proper discharge of the Church's responsibility for the protection of historic buildings and churchyards forming part of the national or local heritage. All parishioners, regardless of their allegiance to the Church, had an interest in the proceedings and were entitled to have their representations considered by the court. Under the Disused Burial Grounds Act 1884, s. 3 it was unlawful to erect a building on a disused burial ground except for the purpose of enlarging a church. The purposes for which the new building was intended were closely connected with the religious activities of the church and the proposed enlargement therefore came within the provisions of s. 3. The proposed extension was necessary to meet the needs of the church in its adaptation to changing circumstances and the objections on environmental grounds were not sufficiently substantial to exclude authorisation of the scheme. The faculty would accordingly be granted.

RE ST. THOMAS, LYMINGTON [1980] 2 WLR 267 (Winchester Consistory Court: PHILLIPS Ch). *Re St Ann's, Kew* [1976] 1 All ER 461, 1976 Halsbury's Abridgment para. 922 followed.

968   ——church building—demolition pursuant to notice requiring works of repair

The local authority served a notice on the priest-in-charge of a church requiring the execution of works to obviate the danger caused by loose slates on the roof. He petitioned for a faculty to demolish the church pursuant to the Faculty Jurisdiction Measure 1964, s. 2 (4). *Held*, the notice was not one which fell within s. 2 (4) (iii) because that subsection contemplated that the local authority itself proposed to take the necessary action; nor did it fall within s. 2 (4) (iv) as a notice requiring the execution of works of repair under the Public Health Act 1961, s. 27, because s. 27 related to buildings which appeared to be seriously detrimental to the amenities of the neighbourhood due to their ruinous condition, not specifically to dangerous buildings. The court did not therefore have jurisdiction to grant a faculty for demolition under s. 2 (4).

RE ALL SAINTS', PLYMOUTH [1980] 3 WLR 876 (Exeter Consistory Court: CALCUTT Ch).

969 ────── use of electric candles

The vicar and churchwardens of a parish church petitioned for a faculty in respect of certain alterations to their church, which included, inter alia, the provision of candlesticks fitted with electric lamps. In fact, the proposed alterations had been carried out two years previously on an experimental basis. *Held*, although electric lights were a lawful form of illumination in churches, they should not normally be used in the form of imitation candles, if only because, so far as reasonably possible, the genuine and best articles should be used in the worship of God. Furthermore where a parish wished to try out an alteration the proper procedure was to ask the registrar for the Chancellor's consent to a temporary permission, which would be coupled with a time limit. The proposed scheme would therefore be authorised for six months only so that due consideration could be given to the individual alterations at a later date.

RE ST. ANDREW'S, DEARNLEY [1981] 2 WLR 37 (Manchester Consistory Court: SPAFFORD Ch).

970 ──── crucifix—petition to place crucifix behind pulpit—whether crucifix a memorial

The priest-in-charge and the churchwardens of a country church petitioned, inter alia, for a faculty authorising the placing of a memorial crucifix in the church on the wall behind the pulpit. A number of parishioners lodged objections to the proposals on the grounds that it would provide a precedent for further memorials, that to cover the walls of the church with memorials would detract from its beauty and that the church, not being a high church, there was no special need for a crucifix. *Held*, a crucifix was not a memorial, except to the crucified Christ and the appearance of the church would not become more "high church" because an additional crucifix was displayed within it. Furthermore, only persons of national fame who had a local association, or persons who performed particularly valuable services for the church could expect to have memorials to them placed in a church. Accordingly leave would be granted to place the crucifix where requested.

RE ST. MARY THE VIRGIN, SELLING [1980] 1 WLR 1545 (Commissary Court of the city and diocese of Canterbury: NEWEY COM. GEN.).

971 ──── jurisdiction—unconsecrated land forming part of curtilage of church—power to authorise sale

A strip of land immediately adjacent to a church was conveyed to the Ecclesiastical Commission with the land which became the site of the church itself. The church was consecrated but the strip was not, but both became vested in the incumbent. The strip, because of its proximity to the church, was classed as curtilage within the Faculty Jurisdiction Measure 1964, s. 7. The local authority wished to purchase the strip for the purpose of a canalside walk and to be held by them as a public open space under the Open Spaces Act 1906. The vicar and church-wardens petitioned for the grant of a faculty authorising the sale of the strip. Questions arose as to the form of, and parties to, the proposed conveyance and as to the disposition of the proceeds of sale. *Held*, the incumbent had the power, either at common law or under the New

Parishes Measure 1943, s. 17, to convey the strip to the local authority with the authority of a consistory court. The court was not restricted to authorising the sale under the procedure set out in s. 17. It could adopt the simpler procedure of authorising a sale at common law involving only the parties to the sale and the court, the latter directing the application of the proceeds of sale. The faculty would be granted.

RE ST MARY MAGDALENE CHURCH, PADDINGTON [1980] 1 All ER 279 (London Consistory Court: G. H. NEWSOM QC Ch). *Re St George's Church, Oakdale* [1975] 2 All ER 870, 1975 Halsbury's Abridgment para. 1169 not followed.

972   —— pipe organ—replacement by electrostatic organ—organ of historic importance—extension of church facilities

By a petition a faculty was sought to dismantle an existing pipe organ and replace it with an electrostatic organ in order to make provision for a new meeting room and other facilities. Although the petition was unopposed witnesses from the Diocesan Advisory Committee and the Council for Places of Worship were of the opinion that the organ was of historic and artistic importance and should be preserved. *Held*, the issues raised by the petition had to be determined in the context of the proposed scheme. Expert evidence confirmed that the electrostatic organ was not musically an inferior instrument and the price of preserving the existing organ was too high in view of the advantages to be gained by the proposed scheme of enlargement. Accordingly, a faculty would be granted when a petition had been lodged for the execution of works and on the condition that no work should be executed on the existing organ until an order authorising such works was made.

The judge ruled that in future the provisions of RSC Ord 38 would be adopted in the court so that reports of expert witnesses could be delivered before the hearing to interested parties.

RE ST. MARY'S, LANCASTER [1980] 1 WLR 657 (Blackburn Consistory Court: EDWARDS Ch).

973   Legal officers—fees

The Legal Officers' Fees Order 1980, S.I. 1980 No. 952 (in force on 1st October 1980), provides for the payment of value added tax in addition to the amount of any prescribed fee where tax is chargeable in respect of the service to which that fee relates. The order also increases fees fixed in 1974, 1975 and 1977, and abolishes certain fees.

974   Parochial fees

The Parochial Fees Order 1980, S.I. 1980 No. 948 (in force on 1st January 1981), amends the 1979 Order, 1979 Halsbury's Abridgment para. 988, by replacing the table of fees payable for certain matters in connection with baptisms, marriages and burials, for the erection of monuments in churchyards and for miscellaneous matters.

975   Pastoral scheme—scheme for union of two parishes—validity of scheme

The Church Commissioners made a scheme providing for the union of two parishes and benefices and making one of the parish churches redundant. The parishioners of the church appealed to the Privy Council on the grounds that the scheme was not in the pastoral interests of the parish. *Held*, cogent evidence of erroneous judgment on the part of the Commissioners was necessary before an appeal against such a scheme on the ground that it was not in the pastoral interests of the parish would be allowed. There was strong evidence for the union of the two parishes, but it did not necessarily follow that the church had to be declared redundant. It would be unjust to permit the scheme to go forward if it were shown that the parochial church council was misinformed on the question of the cost of maintaining the fabric of the church. If, however, after a full hearing, the scheme appeared to have been regularly made and to be made in the interests of the parishes affected by it and of the diocese, only in exceptional circumstances dependent on the facts of the case would an appeal be allowed. On the evidence, the scheme had been regularly made and was in the interests of all concerned. The appeal would accordingly be dismissed.

DAWSON V CHURCH COMRS (1980) 11th February (unreported) (Privy Council: LORD EDMUND-DAVIES, LORD SCARMAN and LORD LANE).

EDUCATION

Halsbury's Laws of England (4th edn.), Vol. 15, paras. 1–400

976   **Awards—entitlement—ordinarily resident in the United Kingdom—meaning**

Two students from Kenya who had been in the United Kingdom since 1976 applied for local authority awards. The question arose whether they were ordinarily resident throughout the preceding three years in the United Kingdom for the purposes of the Local Education Authority Awards Regulations 1979, reg. 13. *Held,* the words "ordinarily resident" should be given their natural and ordinary meaning in their context. The question that should be asked was why the applicant was in this country. If the answer was for a specific or limited purpose rather than the general purpose of living here, he would not be ordinarily resident. Applying this test to the two applicants, the purpose of one was to settle here, while that of the other was to study and then to leave. Therefore the former was ordinarily resident and hence eligible for an award and the latter was not.

R V BARNET LONDON BOROUGH COUNCIL, EX PARTE SHAH [1980] 3 All ER 679 (Queen's Bench Division: ORMROD LJ and KILNER BROWN and MCNEILL JJ).

This case was applied in *Cicutti v Suffolk County Council* [1980] 3 All ER 689, para. 977.

The 1979 Regulations have been consolidated; see para. 979.

977   An Italian student aged nineteen who had been at school in England since he was ten applied for a local authority award. The question arose whether he was ordinarily resident in the area of the authority within the Education Act 1962, s. 1 (1) (a), and whether he was ordinarily resident throughout the preceding three years in the United Kingdom for the purposes of the Local Education Authority Awards Regulations 1979, reg. 13. *Held,* in considering the term "ordinarily resident" a distinction had to be made between those who were resident for general purposes and others who were resident for a specific or special or limited purpose. The applicant's intention was a paramount consideration. In this case, it was clear that the applicant initially came to England to be educated here and subsequently formed the intention of remaining, living and working here. The intention to be considered was that existing during the three-year period specified in reg. 13 and during that period the applicant's intention was to remain permanently in this country. Accordingly, he was entitled to an award.

CICUTTI V SUFFOLK COUNTY COUNCIL [1980] 3 All ER 689 (Chancery Division: SIR ROBERT MEGARRY V-C). *R v Barnet LBC, ex parte Shah* [1980] 3 All ER 679, DC, para. 976 applied.

The 1979 Regulations have been consolidated; see para. 979.

978   —— **grants for Welsh language education**

The Grants for Welsh Language Education Regulations 1980, S.I. 1980 No. 1011 (in force on 15th August 1980), are made under the Education Act 1980, para. 983, s. 21, which makes provision for the Secretary of State to make grants in respect of expenditure incurred, or to be incurred in, or in connection with, the teaching of the Welsh language or the teaching in that language of other subjects. These Regulations are made in exercise of those powers.

979   —— mandatory awards

The Education (Mandatory Awards) Regulations 1980, S.I. 1980 No. 974 (in force on 1st September 1980), consolidate, with amendments, the Local Education Authority Awards Regulations 1979, 1979 Halsbury's Abridgment para. 992. The principal amendments increase awards and alter the figures in relation to the maintenance element, authorise the Secretary of State to designate, for the purposes of the Regulations, a first degree or comparable course provided jointly by an institution within, and one outside, the United Kingdom and take account of ordinary residence in the Channel Islands and the Isle of Man as well as the United Kingdom.

980   The Education (Mandatory Awards) (Amendment) Regulations 1980, S.I. 1980 No. 1149 (in force on 1st September 1980), amend the 1980 Regulations, supra, relating to sandwich courses and, in the case of such a course at Oxford or Cambridge University, take account of the fact that terms at those universities are shorter than those at other universities.

981   The Education (Mandatory Awards) (Amendment) (No. 2) Regulations 1980, S.I. 1980 No. 1247 (in force on 1st September 1980), further amend the 1980 Regulations, supra. The 1980 Regulations provided that a step-parent's income should be taken into account for the purpose of calculating the parental contribution. The present regulations reverse this and provide that only the other parent's income should be so taken into account.

982   The Education (Mandatory Awards) (Amendment) (No. 3) Regulations 1980, S.I. 1980 No. 1352 (for the purposes of Part II, in force on 15th September 1980, and for Part III, on 1st January 1981), further amend the Education (Mandatory Awards) Regulations 1980, supra.

Part II relates to refugees, defined by reference to the United Nations Convention relating to the Status of Refugees. Refugees are relieved of the normal requirement of three years ordinary residence in the British Islands before an award can be made. Part III relates to fees.

983   **Education Act 1980**

The Education Act 1980 amends the law relating to education. The Act received the royal assent on 3rd April 1980 and by S.I. 1980 Nos. 489. 959 came into force on the following days:

14th April 1980: ss. 22, 23, 35–37, 38 (1)–(3), (6), (7), Sch. 7 (part).

5th May 1980: ss. 1, 10 (5)–(7), 19–21, 24–26, 28–30, 32, 33 (1), (2), Schs. 1, 5, 6, 7 (part). Parts of ss. 12, 14 and 16 are also brought into force.

1st August 1980: ss. 31, 38 (5), Schs. 3, 7 (part) and those parts of ss. 12, 14 and 16 not already in force.

1st October 1980: ss. 6–9, 17, 18, 34, 38 (4), Schs. 2, 4, (although ss. 6–8 do not apply in relation to admissions to schools before the beginning of the autumn school term in 1982).

1st July 1982: ss. 10 (1)–(4), 11 (there are transitional provisions in connection with these sections, which concern school attendance orders).

Sections 2–5, 27, 33 (3) and part of Sch. 7 are to come into force on a day to be appointed.

The Act extends to England and Wales only, apart from s. 20 which extends to the whole of the United Kingdom, and ss. 23, 25, 31 (5), 33 which extend to Scotland. Sections 1–5 make fresh provision concerning the government of county, voluntary and maintained special schools. By s. 1 and Sch. 1 the managers of primary schools are to be styled "governors" and by s. 2 are to include teachers, head teachers and parents. Such governors are not, by virtue of any trust deed made before the coming into force of s. 2, to be regarded as ex officio trustees of property: s. 5. Section 3 makes provision for the grouping of schools under a single governing body and, by s. 4, the Secretary of State is empowered to make regulations as to the governors' proceedings and tenure of office.

Arrangements are to be made, under s. 6, for parents to express a preference for a particular school (except those excluded by s. 9), which must be complied with except in certain specified circumstances. Sections 10, 11 make consequential provisions as regards the naming of a school in a school attendance order. A right of appeal is given against any admission decisions (s. 7, Sch. 2). Annual publication of information as to schools and admission arrangements is required under s. 8.

Sections 12–14 change the provisions relating to proposals by the local education authority, or by the governors or promoters of a voluntary school, for the establishment, discontinuance or significant enlargement of the character or premises of the school. Section 15 makes provision for the procedure to be adopted when making proposals to reduce the number of pupils in a school, and s. 16, Sch. 3 contain supplementary provisions.

Section 17 requires the Secretary of State to operate an assisted places scheme at independent schools and, by s. 18, to make grants to pupils holding such places. Schedule 4 deals with the termination of participation agreements. Section 19, Sch. 5 relate to awards for higher and further education and, under s. 20 the Secretary of State is authorised to make grants in respect of industrial scholarships and, under s. 21, for education in Welsh.

Local authorities are empowered to provide school meals, milk and refreshment under s. 22 and similar provision is made in respect of Scotland under s. 23. Authorities are no longer under a duty to provide nursery schools: s. 24, s. 25 making similar provision for Scotland. Arrangements are to be made under s. 26, for educational services to be provided in day nurseries.

Section 27 confers powers for the making of school and further education regulations and ss. 28–30 relax the conditions subject to which the authorities may assist or arrange for education at non-maintained schools, supply clothing for physical training, provide recreational facilities, charge boarding fees, engage in educational research, organise educational conferences and assist universities.

New provisions are made for recoupment between authorities where one authority provides education for a pupil from another area: s. 31. The statutory provisions relating to the sharing of expenditure on educational expenditure for rate support grant schemes are amended under s. 32, Sch. 6.

The Sex Discrimination Act 1975 and the Race Relations Act 1976 apply to this Act by virtue of s. 33. Section 34 defines independent schools and ss. 35–38 relate to the exercise of powers to make orders and regulations, repeals and the commencement, citation and construction of the Act.

984   Grants for removing defence works—termination of grants

The Education Act 1944 (Termination of Grants) Order 1980, S.I. 1980 No. 660 (in force on 14th July 1980), terminates the payment of grants to local education authorities in respect of expenditure incurred in the removal of air-raid shelters and other defence works and repeals the Education Act 1944, s. 100 (1) (a) (iii).

985   Independent schools—assisted places scheme

The Education (Assisted Places) Regulations 1980, S.I. 1980 No. 1743 (in force on 17th November 1980), relate to the scheme for assisted places at independent schools required to be established by the Education Act 1980, s. 17, para. 983. Pt. II of the regulations deals with eligibility for selection for assisted places, Pt. III with the extent to which fees are to be remitted, Pt. IV with administrative arrangements and Pt. V with miscellaneous requirements including, inter alia, the information a school is required to publish about itself and the operation of the scheme at the school.

986   —— sex discrimination

The Sex Discrimination (Designated Educational Establishments) (Amendment) Order 1980, S.I. 1980 No. 1860 (in force on 1st January 1981), revokes so much of the Sex Discrimination (Designated Educational Establishments) Order 1975, 1975 Halsbury's Abridgment para. 1189 as relates to direct grant schools other than nursery schools. This is in consequence of the amendment of the definition of "independent school" by the Education Act 1980, s. 34 (1), para. 983, which has the effect that all direct grant schools, other than nursery schools, fall within the Sex Discrimination Act 1975, s. 22, Table, para. 2 and can therefore no longer be designated establishments under s. 24 of that Act.

987   Local education authority—area to which pupil belongs

The Education (Areas to which Pupils belong) Regulations 1980, S.I. 1980 No. 917 (in force on 1st August 1980), specify the circumstances in which pupils are to be treated as belonging, or not belonging, to particular areas for the purposes of the Education Act 1980, para. 983, ss. 8(3)(d), 31(1), (3) (4), 32.

The regulations also prescribe the period within which a local education authority must make a claim in respect of the cost of providing education for a pupil belonging to the area of another such authority if they are entitled under s. 31 of the Act to be recouped that cost.

988

The Education (Areas to which Pupils belong) (Amendment) Regulations 1980, S.I. 1980 No. 1862 (in force on 1st January 1981), make amendments to the Education (Area to which Pupils belong) Regulations 1980, para. 987, consequential upon the Local Government, Planning and Land Act 1980, para. 1819.

989   —— committee   members—pecuniary   interests—removal   of disability

See para. 1821.

990   —— reorganisation of schools—adjustment of catchment areas following increase in population

A local authority adjusted the catchment areas for secondary schools in the area to allow for a temporary increase in the school population. Two headmasters sought a declaration that their schools had been "reorganised" within the Burnham rules 1978, para. 5 (b) because the authority's action had led to significant increases or reductions in the number of children in the schools, and that their salary scales should be determined accordingly. *Held*, what the local authority had done was to curtail the increase in the number of children, not reduce the number, and such hypothetical increases and reductions were not covered by para. 5 (b). Further, the increase was principally the result of a natural increase in the population, not of the action of the local authority as envisaged by para. 5 (b). The declaration would be refused.

VAUGHAN V SOLIHULL METROPOLITAN BOROUGH (1980) Times, 26th November (Chancery Division: DILLON J).

991   —— statutory duty to provide transport for pupils—extent of duty

See *Myton v Wood*, para. 2041.

992   Provision of clothing—local education authority

The Education (Provision of Clothing) Regulations 1980, S.I. 1980 No. 545 (in force on 19th May 1980), revoke the Provision of Clothing Regulations 1948 as amended. The regulations allow a local authority to make a charge where it provides clothing under the Education (Miscellaneous Provisions) Act 1948, s. 5 otherwise than on loan. In conformity with s. 5 (6) (b), the sum charged is not to be such as to result in a parent's financial hardship nor is it to exceed the authority's costs.

993   Publication of school proposals

The Education (Publication of School Proposals) (No. 2) Regulations 1980, S.I. 1980 No. 658 (in force for all purposes mentioned in reg. 1 (2) (a) on 16th June 1980 and for all other purposes on 1st August 1980), are made under the Education Act 1980, para. 983, ss. 12 (1), 13 (1), 15 (3). The regulations prescribe the manner of publication of proposals for the establishment, discontinuance or alteration of schools by local education authorities, of proposals for the establishment or alteration of voluntary schools or of proposals for reductions in school places.

These regulations supersede the Education (Publication of School Proposals) Regulations 1980, S.I. 1980 No. 490 which made the like provision but erroneously referred to the 1980 Act, s. 15 (2) instead of s. 15 (3).

994   Rate support grants—adjustment of needs element

See para. 1828.

995   Schools—middle schools—whether primary or secondary schools

The Education (Middle Schools) Regulations 1980, S.I. 1980 No. 918 (in force on 1st August 1980), provide for the determination by the Secretary of State of the question whether a middle school should be deemed to be a primary or a secondary school for the purposes of proposals made under the Education Act 1980, para. 983, ss. 12, 13.

A middle school is deemed to be a primary or secondary school according to whether the age range of pupils below the age of 11 years for which it provides is greater or less than that of pupils above that age.

996   —— special schools—handicapped pupils—provision of meals and milk

The Handicapped Pupils and Special Schools (Amendment) Regulations 1980, S.I. 1980 No. 888 (in force on 1st August 1980), amend the Handicapped Pupils and Special Schools Regulations 1959 by substituting a new regulation for regulation 23, which relates to milk and meals for day pupils at non-maintained special schools.

997   Students' dependants—allowances

The Education (Students' Dependants Allowances) Regulations 1980, S.I. 1980 No. 1111 (in force on 1st September 1980), consolidate, with amendments, the Students' Dependants Allowances Regulations, 1979 Halsbury's Abridgment para. 1004. The regulations, inter alia, increase the amount prescribed as a student's requirements.

998   Teachers—employment of unqualified teacher—dismissal on availability of qualified teacher—whether dismissal unfair

In 1969 a part-time needlework teacher was employed by a local council. She was not a qualified teacher within the Schools Regulations 1959. In 1977, on the advice of the local council's legal department, the education officer terminated the teacher's contract of employment. The council contended that under the Schools Regulations 1959, reg. 18 (6), which provides that a person who is not a qualified teacher may be employed if, in the case of such appointment, no qualified teacher is available to give instruction, it was illegal for it to retain the services of an unqualified teacher once a qualified teacher was available. The teacher claimed compensation for unfair dismissal. The question arose (i) whether reg. 18 defined a state of affairs relating to the initial taking into employment or, (ii) whether it referred to a continuing state of affairs resulting in the employment of an unqualified teacher becoming immediately illegal on the availability of a qualified teacher for the post. *Held*, the word 'employment' in reg. 18 was to be construed in the context in which it appeared and it was equivalent to an 'appointment'. On its true construction an appointment was a taking into employment. Accordingly the only duty of the council under reg. 18 was to ensure that, at the time when an unqualified teacher was appointed, no qualified teacher was available. Furthermore the council had acted unreasonably in dismissing the teacher, since it had failed to seek outside legal advice. The dismissal was therefore unfair.

BIRMINGHAM CITY COUNCIL v ELSON (1979) 77 LGR 743 (Employment Appeal Tribunal: ARNOLD J presiding).

999   —— remuneration

The Remuneration of Teachers (Further Education) Order 1980, S.I. 1980 No. 247 (coming into operation on 22nd February 1980), introduces with effect from 1st April 1979 new scales of pay and other provisions relating to remuneration of teachers in further education establishments, set out in a document published by HMSO, entitled "Scales of Salaries for Teachers in Establishments for Further Education, England and Wales, 1979". This document gives effect to recommendations agreed by the Committee constituted under the Remuneration of Teachers Act 1965.

1000   The Remuneration of Teachers (Further Education) (Amendment) Order 1980, S.I. 1980 No. 966 (in force on 9th July 1980), amends the scales and other provisions relating to the remuneration of teachers in all establishments of further education maintained by local education authorities as set out in a document published by HMSO on 21st September 1979. The order has retrospective effect partly from 1st April 1979 and partly from 1st January and 1st April 1980.

1001   The Remuneration of Teachers (Further Education) (Amendment) (No. 2) Order 1980, S.I. 1980 No. 1611 (in force on 5th November 1980), amends the Document relating to the remuneration of teachers in establishments for further education maintained by local education authorities and of other such further education teachers on the staff of such authorities so as to give effect to recommendations made by, respectively, the appropriate Burnham Committee and by arbitrators appointed under the Remuneration of Teachers Act 1965, s. 3.

1002   The Remuneration of Teachers (Primary and Secondary Schools) (Amendment) Order 1980, S.I. 1980 No. 965 (in force on 9th July 1980), amends the scales and other provisions relating to the remuneration of teachers in primary and secondary schools maintained by local education authorities as set out in a document published by HMSO on 21st September 1979. The order has retrospective effect partly from 1st April 1979, and partly from 1st January 1980.

1003   The Remuneration of Teachers (Primary and Secondary Schools) (Amendment) (No. 2) Order 1980, S.I. 1980 No. 1197 (in force on 18th August 1980), amends the scales and other provisions relating to the remuneration of teachers in primary and secondary schools maintained by local education authorities set out in a document published by HMSO on 21st September 1979. The order has retrospective effect from 1st January 1980.

1004   The Remuneration of Teachers (Primary and Secondary Schools) (Amendment) (No. 3) Order 1980, S.I. 1980 No. 1331 (in force on 15th September 1980), amend the Document relating to the remuneration of teachers in maintained primary and secondary schools and of certain other teachers employed by local education authorities, so as to give effect to recommendations made, respectively by the appropriate Burnham Committee under the Remuneration of Teachers Act 1965, s. 2 and by arbitrators appointed in pursuance of the 1965 Act, s. 3.

1005   —— superannuation

See PENSIONS AND SUPERANNUATION.

ELECTIONS

Halsbury's Laws of England (4th edn.), Vol. 15, paras. 401–981

1006   **Election expenses—regulations**

The Representation of the People (Variation of Limits of Candidates' Election

Expenses) Order 1980, S.I. 1980 No. 375 (in force on 14th March 1980), increases the maximum amount of candidates' election expenses at local government elections (other than elections to the GLC), ward elections in the City of London and elections by liverymen in Common Hall.

1007   Electoral register—requirements

The Representation of the People (Amendment) Regulations 1980, S.I. 1980 No. 1031 (in force 15th August 1980), further amend the 1974 Regulations, 1974 Halsbury's Abridgment para. 1152 to make provision consequential to the enactment of the Representation of the People Act 1980, infra; to prescribe new forms for the return by occupiers as to residents and for service declarations; and to make various minor amendments.

1008   Representation of the People Act 1980

The Representation of the People Act 1980 makes various amendments to the Representation of the People Act 1949 relating to the registration of persons having a service qualification and the correction of electoral registers. The Act received the royal assent on 31st January 1980 and the Representation of the People Act 1980 (Commencement) Order 1980, S.I. 1980 No. 1030 brought into force, on 15th August 1980, ss. 1 and 3 of the Act and that part of the Sch. which relates to s. 1; and on 16th February 1981, s. 2 and the rest of the Sch.

Section 1 provides that persons with a service qualification may not be registered for electoral purposes unless they have made an appropriate service declaration. Section 2 enables a registration officer to amend the electoral register by including the name of any person shown in the electors' list, by inserting the date when a person will attain voting age or by giving effect to a decision following an objection regarding the electors' list. Section 3 and the Schedule contain provisions dealing with citation, repeals and commencement.

1009   Welsh forms

The Elections (Welsh Forms) Regulations 1980, S.I. 1980 No. 1032 (in force on 15th August 1980), substitute a new bilingual Form A (return by occupier as to residents) for the form prescribed in the Elections (Welsh Forms) Regulations 1975, Sch. 1, Pt. I, 1975 Halsbury's Abridgment para. 1220. The new form corresponds to the new form A which is substituted by Sch. 1 to the Representation of the People (Amendment) Regulations 1980, para. 1007, for use in England.

EMPLOYMENT

Halsbury's Laws of England (4th edn.), Vol. 16, paras. 501–1200

1010   Articles

The Contract of Employment, David Newell: 130 NLJ 419.

Employment and Restrictive Covenants, Ian G. C. Stratton: 130 NLJ 4.

Handling Redundancies: the Unanswered Questions, John Bowers: 124 Sol Jo 369.

Who is a Servant? A. N. Khan (differences between contract of service and a contract for services): 53 Australian Law Journal 833.

1011   Attachment of earnings order—employer's deductions

The Attachment of Earnings (Employer's Deduction) Order 1980, S.I. 1980 No. 558 (in force on 1st June 1980), provides that an employer making a deduction from a debtor's earnings under an attachment of earnings order may take an additional amount of 50p towards his administrative and clerical costs. The Attachment of

Earnings (Employer's Deduction) Order 1975, 1975 Halsbury's Abridgment para. 1466 is revoked.

1012   Baking industry—Christmas and New Year

The Baking and Sausage Making (Christmas and New Year) Regulations 1980, S.I. 1980 No. 1576 (in force on 6th December 1980), enable women who have reached the age of eighteen to be employed on specified Saturday afternoons and Sundays in December 1980 and January 1981 in the manufacture of meat pies, sausages or cooked meats, in the pre-packing of bacon, in the manufacture of bread or flour confectionary (including fruit pies but not biscuits), or in work incidental or ancillary to such work.

1013   Central Arbitration Committee—jurisdiction—equal pay

In order to meet the requirements of the Equal Pay Act 1970, a company increased the salaries of its female employees and introduced a revised salary structure no longer specifying different grades and rates of pay for men and women. Subsequent to the implementation of the Act, a job evaluation study was carried out and a grading structure was agreed, but there was no agreement on the appropriate rates of pay for each grade. The union complained to the Central Arbitration Committee under the Equal Pay Act 1970, s. 3, contending that because 70 per cent of the female employees were in the lowest grade, the pay structure was still discriminatory. The Central Arbitration Committee held that, although the pay structure was no longer overtly discriminatory, it was not satisfied with the company's attitude towards equal pay, and therefore determined what it considered to be a reasonable pay structure. The company applied for an order of certiorari to quash the decision on the ground that the Central Arbitration Committee had exceeded its jurisdiction. *Held*, in upholding a complaint that an agreement between the company and the trade union was discriminatory within s. 3, and in amending the agreement, the committee had exceeded its jurisdiction. For a complaint under s. 3 to succeed, there had to be a provision in the agreement applying specifically to men only or to women only and in the present case no such provision existed. The Committee had no power to embark upon a general wage review as it had purported to do. An order of certiorari would be granted to quash the decision.

R v Central Arbitration Committee, ex parte Hy-Mac Ltd [1979] IRLR 461 (Queen's Bench Division: Lord Widgery CJ, Browne LJ and Watkins J).

1014   Code of practice

See TRADE UNIONS.

1015   Continuity of employment—whether employee "absent from work" when not contractually bound to work

An employee claimed that she had been unfairly dismissed. The question arose as to whether she had been continuously employed for twenty-six weeks as required by the Employment Protection (Consolidation) Act 1978, s. 64 (1) (a). Her contract of employment provided that she worked sixteen hours one week and twelve hours the next, but in fact she often worked more than her contractual obligation. During the twenty-six weeks preceding her dismissal she had worked for at least sixteen hours in all but three weeks. The industrial tribunal held that there had been no break in the continuity of employment. On appeal, *held*, the employee had worked her contractual obligation during those three weeks and the question was whether for any part of the rest of the week she was to be regarded as "absent from work" within Sch. 13, para. 9 (1) (c) so that she was regarded as continuing in employment. "Absent from work" meant absent from work when under her contract she should normally be present, so para. 9 (1) (c) was not satisfied. There was no arrangement or custom by which she was regarded as continuing in her employers' employment during the part of the week when she was absent, so the appeal would be allowed.

CORTON HOUSE LTD V SKIPPER (1980) Times, 6th December (Employment Appeal Tribunal: SLYNN J presiding).

1016   Contract of employment—breach—repudiation of contract by employee—whether employer entitled to treat contract as automatically terminated

See *Rasool v Hepworth Pipe Co Ltd (No. 1)*, para. 3021; *London Transport Executive v Clarke*, para. 3013.

1017   —— contract of service or for services—availability of compensation for unfair dismissal

An employee, a sheet metal worker, was employed by a company in their factory. On joining the company he chose to be treated as self-employed. The company agreed, and no deductions were made from his pay for tax or national insurance. Further, he was not entitled to any holiday payments or sickness benefits from the company. His contract of employment was subsequently terminated and he complained of unfair dismissal to an industrial tribunal. The company appealed against a decision in his favour and contended that he was not an employee under a contract of service, but that he was self-employed under a contract for services, and an industrial tribunal, therefore, had no jurisdiction to hear the employee's complaint of unfair dismissal. *Held*, where an agreement was made that a person was to be treated by a company as self-employed, it did not follow that he had to accept that position and could not claim compensation for unfair dismissal as if he was an employee. Whether a person is employed under a contract of service, or self-employed under a contract for services was a question of law and not fact. The label with which parties described their relationship did not alter the true relationship, and the legal relationship between parties had to be classified not by appearance but by reality. The industrial tribunal had to look behind the description given to the relationship by the parties and decide, on the basis of all the evidence, whether the true legal relationship accorded with the label given to it. In the present case although both parties intended to call the agreement between them a contract for services and not a contract of employment within the Employment Protection (Consolidation) Act 1978, the true legal relationship was not that of a self-employed agent working independently of the company, in business on his own account. Furthermore the employee's conditions of employment, apart from being paid wages without any deductions and not being entitled to holiday or sick pay, were the same as those employees working under a contract of employment within the 1978 Act. The tribunal had not erred in its decision that the employee was employed under a contract of service and it had jurisdiction to hear his complaint of unfair dismissal. The appeal, therefore, would be dismissed.

YOUNG AND WOODS LTD V WEST [1980] IRLR 201 (Court of Appeal: STEPHENSON and ACKNER LJJ and SIR DAVID CAIRNS). *Marketing Investigations Ltd v Minister of Social Security* [1968] 3 All ER 732 applied. *Massey v Crown Life Insurance Co* [1978] IRLR 31, 1977 Halsbury's Abridgment para. 2946 distinguished.

1018   —— —— casual musicians

See *Midland Sinfonia Concert Society Ltd v Secretary of State for Social Services*, para. 2723.

1019   —— —— part-time musicians

Four musicians regarded themselves as self-employed players with a certain orchestra, but they wished to test their status as "part-time players" with the orchestra. They made originating applications to an industrial tribunal requiring a reference to determine the particulars of their employment with the orchestra under the Employment Protection (Consolidation) Act 1978, s. 11 (1) on the ground that the orchestra refused to provide them with a statement of the terms of their employment in accordance with the 1978 Act, s. 1. The musicians played with the orchestra whenever requested to do so but were entitled to reject any engagement offered. They were paid sessional fees and certain expenses but they were not taxed as employed persons in respect of their earnings from the orchestra and they all paid national insurance as self-employed persons. Further, they were not registered as suppliers for value added tax purposes. The industrial tribunal refused the applications on the ground that the musicians were not employees of the orchestra under a contract of service within the 1978 Act, s. 153. On appeal, *held*, whether a person was employed under a contract of service or was self-employed under a contract for services was a question of law and not fact. The label with which the parties chose to describe their relationship would not alter the true nature of the relationship and although the expression of their true intention was relevant it was not conclusive. Although while the musicians were at work there was some degree of control by the orchestra over them, that was not a decisive pointer to a contract of service and a tribunal was, in the circumstances, entitled to find the basis of the relationship moral and professional rather than contractual. Further, the facts showed that when playing for the orchestra each musician remained essentially a freelance musician pursuing his own profession as an instrumentalist, with his own individual reputation and skills and was accordingly providing his services as a person in business on his own account. The industrial tribunal had not erred in its decision and the appeal would be dismissed.

ADDISON v LONDON PHILHARMONIC ORCHESTRA LTD (1980) Times, 21st October (Employment Appeal Tribunal: WATERHOUSE J presiding). *Young & Woods Ltd v West* [1980] IRLR 201, CA, para. 1017, applied.

1020 —— —— whether police cadet an "employee"

See *Wiltshire Police Authority v Wynn*, para. 2160.

1021 —— date of termination—summary dismissal—employee suspended pending domestic appeal—effect of subsequent suspension

See *Savage v J Sainsbury Ltd*, para. 3031.

1022 —— existence of contract—sub-postmaster

The applicant, a sub-postmaster, owned a general store with a sub-post office inside. He engaged and paid assistants who worked in both the post office and the store. Under Post Office rules, the applicant had to carry out any special instructions issued by the Post Office, and his freedom to advertise was limited. He was not entitled to annual leave, sick pay or a pension, and he had to notify the head postmaster if he was absent for more than three days. On his complaint of unfair dismissal, an industrial tribunal found on a preliminary issue of law that he was not employed by the Post Office under a contract of service and that they had no jurisdiction to hear the complaint. The applicant appealed. *Held*, there was a substantial measure of control by the Post Office, but the matter had to be looked at as a whole. With regard to the facts that the applicant provided the premises and part of the equipment, he had the right to delegate and there was an element of risk of profit and loss, he was carrying on business on his own account and was not employed. The appeal would, accordingly, be dismissed.

HITCHCOCK v POST OFFICE [1980] ICR 100 (Employment Appeal Tribunal: SLYNN J presiding).

1023 —— illegality—failure of employee to disclose benefits received to Inland Revenue

An employee received £5 per week over and above her basic wage from which deductions for income tax and national insurance contributions were not made by the employer. An industrial tribunal refused to hear the employee's complaint of unfair dismissal on the ground that the contract was illegal in that it constituted a fraud on the Revenue. The employee appealed. *Held*, where an employee was paid a sum on which tax was not paid when it should have been, it made no difference whether or not the parties were ignorant that what they were doing was illegal. Ignorance of the law was no defence. The issue was not whether a reasonable person would have realised that the arrangement constituted a fraud. If this was wrong, where a contract was on the face of it legal, the question of knowledge of the parties became an important factor. The test to be applied was the subjective one of the parties' knowledge of its intended illegal performance. Further where there was an agreement to defraud the Revenue the whole agreement was illegal and no part of the agreement could be severed and the legal promises enforced. In the circumstances of the case the industrial tribunal had not erred in its decision and the appeal would be dismissed.

CORBY v MORRISON [1980] ICR 564 (Employment Appeal Tribunal: MAY J presiding).

1024   —— registered medical practitioner—suspension from register—whether contract terminated

See *Tarnesby v Kensington, Chelsea and Westminster Area Health Authority (Teaching)*, para. 1893.

1025   —— work to rule—action by employee to recover wages—whether employee ready and willing to perform contract—burden of proof

An employee worked to rule during an unofficial industrial dispute at his employer's power station. He was not paid for that period, as the employer was of the opinion that the employee was not performing his contract of employment. The dispute went to arbitration, and it was effectively ruled that the burden of proof was upon the employer to satisfy the court on the balance of probabilities that the employee was not ready and willing to perform his contract. The award that the employee was entitled to his pay was subsequently upheld. On appeal by the employer, *held*, if a party claimed under a contract, he had to prove that he was ready and willing to perform the contract. Accordingly, the judge arbitrator had misdirected himself on a fundamental part of the case where he held that it was for the employer to prove the employee's unwillingness to work. The appeal would be allowed, the award set aside and the case remitted for a new trial.

HENTHORN v CENTRAL ELECTRICITY GENERATING BOARD [1980] IRLR 361 (Court of Appeal: LAWTON, BRIDGE and SHAW LJJ).

1026   —— wrongful dismissal—damages

See *Gunton v Richmond-upon-Thames LBC*, para. 1027.

1027   —— —— effective date of termination

In a case when an employee was dismissed without compliance with the disciplinary code by the employers, it was held that although the dismissal was wrongful, it was nevertheless effective to bring the employment to an end. The question that arose was whether the wrongful dismissal of an employee put an immediate end to the contract of service or whether it operated as a repudiation which resulted in determination of the contract only when it was accepted by the employee. *Held*, SHAW LJ dissenting, generally an unaccepted repudiation did not terminate a contract and there was no reason why that doctrine should operate differently in the case of contracts of personal service. However, in cases of wrongful dismissal in breach of a contract of personal service the court should easily infer that the innocent party had accepted the repudiation.

Consequently, the period by reference to which damages should be assessed was a reasonable period from the date of the dismissal for carrying out the disciplinary procedure, plus one month for the expiration of a notional notice, the employee giving credit for salary received after the date of the dismissal.

GUNTON v RICHMOND-UPON-THAMES LONDON BOROUGH COUNCIL [1980] IRLR 321 (Court of Appeal: BUCKLEY, SHAW and BRIGHTMAN LJJ).

1028 **Dismissal—contract for full-time and part-time duties—termination of part-time duties—whether employee dismissed**

The employee was appointed as a full-time fireman. His contract incorporated conditions of service which permitted full-time firemen to volunteer for standby duties in return for a retaining fee. The Fire Brigades' Union subsequently decided that retained duty should be abolished and their proposals were accepted by firemen's employers generally. The employee was asked by his employers to agree to a variation of his contract abolishing his retained duties. He refused and his employers gave him three months' notice terminating his retained duties. The employee claimed that such action terminated his contract of employment and gave rise to an action for unfair dismissal. *Held*, the employee's contract was clearly divisible into two parts; the full-time duties were covered in one part and the retained duties in the other. Although there was only one contract, there was no reason why it was not severable so that the employee's retained duties could be terminated without terminating his full-time employment. As the employers had failed to obtain the employee's agreement to a variation in his contract, they had no option but to give him reasonable notice, which did not affect his full-time employment. Therefore, as the employee had not been dismissed, his claim failed.

LAND v WEST YORKSHIRE METROPOLITAN COUNTY COUNCIL (1980) Times, 5th November (Court of Appeal: LORD DENNING MR, BRIGHTMAN LJ and SIR GEORGE BAKER).

1029 **—— dismissal notice—date from which notice takes effect**

See *Brown v Southall & Knight*, para. 3028.

1030 **Dock workers—regulation of employment scheme**

The Dock Workers (Regulation of Employment) (Amendment) Order 1980, S.I. 1980 No. 1940 (in force on 1st February 1981), amends the Dock Workers (Regulation of Employment) Scheme 1947 as varied, which is set out in the Dock Workers (Regulation of Employment) Scheme 1967, Sch. 2, by giving effect to the Dock Workers (Regulation of Employment) (Amendment) Scheme 1980. The order applies the 1967 Scheme to work at the Port of Hunterston and provides for it to apply to the handling of ore and coal and other commodities at the Port, except certain specified work.

1031 **Employee—duty of confidentiality—duty of ex-housekeeper not to disclose details of employer's private life**

The plaintiff had employed the first defendant as her housekeeper for nine years prior to 1979. She was granted an injunction, ex parte, to prevent her ex-housekeeper from disclosing, and the second defendant newspaper from publishing, allegedly confidential information concerning the plaintiff's private life which had been disclosed to the first defendant during the course of her employment. An interlocutory application, inter partes, was, however, dismissed. On appeal by the plaintiff *held*, on the basis that the circumstances of the relationship between the plaintiff and the first defendant implied a duty of confidentiality, the question for the court was whether the proposed disclosures came within any exception to abide by that duty. The confidential information fell into two parts; alleged criminal conduct by the plaintiff and her alleged love affairs. Although the court might have applied different considerations to the latter, disclosure for the purposes of investigation into the commission of alleged criminal conduct was permissible. The information was however so interwoven as to be impossible to separate, and the injunction to prevent disclosure would accordingly be refused.

KHASHOGGI v SMITH (1980) 124 Sol Jo 149 (Court of Appeal: ROSKILL LJ and SIR DAVID CAIRNS). *Woodward v Hutchins* [1977] 2 All ER 751, 1977 Halsbury's Abridgment para. 1565, followed.

1032   **Employer—duty of care—dangers inherent in job—whether a duty to warn employees of dangers**

A caulker-riveter employed by the Ministry of Defence claimed damages in respect of personal injuries caused by vibration-induced white finger (VWF). *Held*, the caulker-riveter's contention, that the Ministry was negligent in failing to warn the caulker-riveters in its employ what the symptoms of VWF were, and to introduce a system of regular medical examinations, would be rejected. Medical evidence showed that the likelihood of such a serious case as this particular one was rare, and any warning or instruction concerning VWF was likely to cause alarm and unhappiness to the many for the sake of providing some advantage to the potential exceptional case. There was therefore no breach of duty by the Ministry to the caulker-riveter.

JOSEPH v MINISTRY OF DEFENCE (1980) Times, 4th March (Court of Appeal: MEGAW, EVELEIGH and BRANDON LJJ).

1033   —— —— **employee injured in payroll robbery—safety of employee**

The Court of Appeal has held that a company was not liable in negligence for failure to take reasonable care for the safety of an employee who was attacked and injured in a payroll robbery.

The wages had been snatched on a previous occasion and the company had issued instructions that the arrangements for collection of the payroll were to be varied as much as possible in relation to the vehicles used, routes and parking places. Contrary to its instructions the collection had settled into a routine pattern when the robbery had occurred. The company had accordingly done all that was reasonable and was not under a duty to employ a security firm to make the collection.

CHARLTON v FORREST PRINTING INK CO LTD [1980] IRLR 331 (Court of Appeal: LORD DENNING MR and WALLER and DUNN LJJ). Decision of Forbes J (1978) 122 Sol Jo 730, 1978 Halsbury's Abridgment para. 1066 reversed.

1034   **Employment Act 1980**

See para. 2949.

1035   **Employment Appeal Tribunal—costs—discretion to order payment of other party's costs**

The applicant, a teacher, complained that the local authority which employed her had discriminated against her by refusing or deliberately omitting to afford her promotion. The Commission for Racial Equality undertook her case and gave her assistance in prosecuting her claim before an industrial tribunal on terms that she would not herself incur any expense. The tribunal found in her favour and awarded her compensation. The authority gave notice of appeal but shortly before the hearing was due it abandoned the appeal. The applicant applied under the Employment Appeal Tribunal Rules 1976, r. 21 (1), for an order that the authority pay her costs. *Held*, although the authority's conduct in not withdrawing its appeal until the last moment was sufficient to merit an order against it, under r. 21 (1) the appeal tribunal's jurisdiction to order payment of the costs was limited to costs incurred by a party to the appeal. Since the costs had been incurred by the commission, which was not a party to the appeal, the tribunal had no jurisdiction to make the order sought.

WALSALL METROPOLITAN BOROUGH COUNCIL v SIDHU [1980] ICR 519 (Employment Appeal Tribunal: SLYNN J presiding).

1036   —— **jurisdiction—application for leave to appeal to Court of Appeal—power to extend time for application**

An industrial tribunal rejected the applicant's claim that he had been unfairly dismissed and his appeal was dismissed by the Employment Appeal Tribunal, which refused him leave to appeal to the Court of Appeal. On the last day of the period for applying to the Court of Appeal for leave to appeal under RSC Ord. 59, r. 14 (3), the applicant applied to the appeal tribunal for an extension of time in which to apply to the Court of Appeal. On the question whether the appeal tribunal had jurisdiction to extend the time under Ord. 59, r. 15, *held*, that rule gave to "the court below" the power to extend time for making an ex parte application under r. 14 (3), notwithstanding that the rules of the court below did not expressly so provide. The term "court" included tribunals from which a right of appeal lay to the Court of Appeal. Accordingly the Employment Appeal Tribunal had jurisdiction to extend the period for making an application.

TETHER v FINANCIAL TIMES LTD [1980] ICR 447 (Employment Appeal Tribunal: SLYNN J presiding).

1037 ⸺ ⸺ grounds for appeal

On appeal against a decision, a party to the proceedings sought to raise matters already conceded before an industrial tribunal and further to raise new issues. The question arose as to the jurisdiction of the Employment Appeal Tribunal to hear new points of law. *Held*, it was wrong on principle to allow a party to an appeal to raise matters that were conceded before a lower tribunal or seek to introduce new issues where those issues required further investigation of fact.

SECRETARY OF STATE FOR EMPLOYMENT v NEWCASTLE UPON TYNE CITY COUNCIL [1980] ICR 407 (Employment Appeal Tribunal: TALBOT J presiding). *GKN (Cwmbran) Ltd v Lloyd* [1972] ICR 214 applied.

1038 ⸺ ⸺ power to set aside agreement to compromise appeal

An appeal to the Employment Appeal Tribunal was withdrawn after an agreement had been reached. The employee subsequently applied for a review of the order withdrawing the appeal pursuant to the Employment Appeal Tribunal Rules 1976, r. 20 (1) (c) on the ground that he had been required to settle against his will and the interests of justice required such a review. *Held*, the Appeal Tribunal, as a body set up by statute, only had the powers given to it by statute, which did not include a power to set aside an agreement to compromise an appeal. Accordingly the application would be refused.

EDEN v HUMPHRIES AND GLASGOW LTD (1980) Times, 15th November (Employment Appeal Tribunal: SLYNN J presiding).

1039 ⸺ procedure—rules

The Employment Appeal Tribunal Rules 1980, S.I. 1980 No. 2035 (in force on 1st February 1981), replace, with some amendments, the Employment Appeal Tribunal Rules 1976, 1976 Halsbury's Abridgment para. 982. The rules prescribe the procedure relating to the institution hearing and disposal of an appeal in the Employment Appeal Tribunal, established to hear appeals from industrial tribunals in England, Wales and Scotland, and from the certification officer and to hear applications for compensation under the Employment Act 1980, s. 5 (2), para. 2949.

1040 Employment Protection (Consolidation) Act 1978—variation of limits

The Employment Protection (Variation of Limits) Order 1980, S.I. 1980 No. 2019 (in force on 1st February 1981), varies certain of the limits which are required to be reviewed annually by the Secretary of State under the Employment Protection (Consolidation) Act 1978, s. 148. The amount of guarantee pay payable under s. 15 (1) in respect of any day is increased from £8·00 to £8·75. The amount payable under s. 122 in respect of a debt due to an employee whose employer becomes insolvent is increased from £120 to £130. The amount of a "week's pay" for the purposes of calculating redundancy payments and basic and additional awards of compensation for unfair dismissal is increased from £120 to £130.

1041 Guarantee payments—exemption

The Guarantee Payments (Exemption) (No. 20) Order 1980, S.I. 1980 No. 1715 (in force on 22nd December 1980), excludes the employees of the Building and Allied Trades from the operation of the Employment Protection (Consolidation) Act 1978, s. 12 which relates to guarantee payments.

1042   Health and safety at work

See HEALTH AND SAFETY AT WORK.

1043   Industrial training—Construction Board

The Industrial Training (Construction Board) Order 1980, S.I. 1980 No. 1274 (in force on 26th September 1980), redefines the activities in relation to which the Construction Industry Training Board exercises its functions. The following Orders are revoked: S.I. 1973 No. 160, S.I. 1974 No. 2081, 1974 Halsbury's Abridgment para. 221.

1044   —— Engineering Board

The Industrial Training (Engineering Board) Order 1980, S.I. 1980 No. 1273 (in force on 26th September 1980), redefines the activities in relation to which the Engineering Industry Training Board exercises its functions. The following orders are revoked: S.I. 1971 No. 1530, S.I. 1974 No. 2082, 1974 Halsbury's Abridgment para. 1222.

1045   —— transfer of activities of establishments

The Industrial Training (Transfer of the Activities of Establishments) Order 1980, S.I. 1980 No. 586 (in force on 26th May 1980), transfers the activities of specified establishments for the purposes of the Industrial Training Act 1964 to other industrial training boards.

1046

The Industrial Training (Transfer of the Activities of Establishments) (No. 2) Order 1980, S.I. 1980 No. 1753 (in force on 31st December 1980), transfers the activities of specified establishments for the purpose of the Industrial Training Act 1964 to other industrial training boards.

1047   Industrial training levy

Levies have been imposed on employers in the following industries:

	Relevant Statutory Instruments (1980)
Air Transport and Travel	230
Carpet	1658
Ceramics, Glass and Mineral Products	1372
Chemical and Allied Products	878
Clothing and Allied Products	409
Construction Board	1545
Cotton and Allied Textiles	1291
Engineering	693
Food, Drink and Tobacco	378
Footwear, Leather and Furskin	1385
Furniture and Timber	1053
Hotel and Catering	595
Knitting, Lace and Net	292
Paper and Paper Products	620

	Relevant Statutory Instruments (1980)
Petroleum	150
Printing and Publishing	843
Road Transport	1292
Rubber and Plastics Processing	1
Rubber and Plastics Processing Industry	179
Shipbuilding	583
Wool, Jute and Flax	214

A right to appeal against an assessment is provided for.

1048   Industrial tribunal—costs

An employee was dismissed because of her persistent absence. She complained to an industrial tribunal that her dismissal was unfair and at the hearing was represented by her union's unqualified regional organiser. The tribunal found that the employee's claim was meritless and they made an order for costs on the basis that her complaint was frivolous and vexatious within the meaning of the Industrial Tribunals (Labour Relations) Regulations 1974, Sch., r. 10 (1). Furthermore as she was assisted by her union they ordered her to pay the employers' full costs to be taxed by the County Court registrar. The employee appealed against the order for costs. *Held*, although there was no evidence to support a finding that the employee had acted vexatiously in the sense that she had brought her claim out of spite or some improper motive, the industrial tribunal was justified in finding that she had acted frivolously in that her claim was misconceived and they were entitled to make an order for costs under the 1974 Rules. The High Court practice, however, of taking account of the fact that an employee was supported by her union when awarding costs was an inappropriate practice for industrial tribunals to adopt. The tribunal was to consider the means of the claimant and not the trade union when considering whether or not to order costs and the term of the order to be made. Accordingly the appeal would be allowed and the order for costs altered.

CARR V ALLEN-BRADLEY ELECTRONICS LTD [1980] ICR 603 (Employment Appeal Tribunal: WATERHOUSE J presiding). *E.T. Marler Ltd v Robertson* [1974] ICR 72, 1974 Halsbury's Abridgment para. 1830, applied.

For the Industrial Tribunals (Labour Relations) Regulations 1974, Sch., r. 10 (1) see now the Industrial Tribunals (Rules of Procedure) Regulations 1980, Sch. 1, r. 11, para. 1056.

1049   —— decision—award made in reliance on special knowledge of tribunal member

An industrial tribunal found a general manager of a company to have been unfairly dismissed. They declined however to make an award in respect of future loss on the ground, in reliance upon the specialised knowledge of a member of the tribunal, that he ought to have found new employment at a salary commensurate with his former salary. On appeal against the award *held*, although it was proper to rely on the personal knowledge and experience of a member, the tribunal ought to have brought that knowledge to the attention of the employee's counsel. Accordingly the case would be remitted for re-hearing.

HAMMINGTON V BERKER SPORTSCRAFT LTD [1980] ICR 248 (Employment Appeal Tribunal: TALBOT J presiding). *Wetherall v Harrison* [1976] 1 All ER 241, DC, 1975 Halsbury's Abridgment para. 2176 and *Dugdale v Kraft Foods Ltd* [1977] 1 All ER 454, EAT, 1976 Halsbury's Abridgment para. 995 applied.

1050   —— evidence—special knowledge of member of tribunal—matter relied on not put in evidence

See *Hammington v Berker Sportscraft Ltd*, para. 1049.

1051　　—— jurisdiction—adjudication complete—jurisdiction to hear application for extension of time to enter appearance

The employers failed to enter an appearance prior to the hearing of an employee's complaint of unfair dismissal, although they had received notice of the proceedings. The tribunal therefore made an award in the employers' absence. The tribunal refused the employers' request for a review on the ground that, in accordance with the Industrial Tribunal (Labour Relations) Regulations 1974, Sch., r. 3 (2), a respondent could only apply for a review if he had not received notice of the proceedings. The employers then applied for leave to enter an appearance out of time and relied on r. 3 (3) that their notice of appearance was deemed to include an application, under r. 12 (1), for an extension of time. The tribunal refused leave on the ground that it had already reached a decision and was functus officio to the proceedings. On appeal *held*, both r. 3 (3) and r. 12 (1) imposed no time limit upon when such an application could be made. Accordingly the tribunal had erred in holding that it had no jurisdiction. The application would therefore be remitted for the tribunal's consideration.

ST. MUNGO COMMUNITY TRUST v COLLEANO [1980] ICR 254 (Employment Appeal Tribunal: WATERHOUSE J presiding).

1052　　—— —— application for joinder of parties

Industrial tribunal decision:

MARSHALL v ALEXANDER SLOAN & CO LTD [1980] ICR 394 (unfair dismissal proceedings brought by employee; through help of Advisory, Conciliation and Arbitration Service (ACAS) parties reached settlement; issue whether tribunal had jurisdiction to hear unfair dismissal claim; application by employer to join ACAS as respondent to proceedings; question whether a tribunal had discretion under Industrial Tribunals (Labour Relations) Regulations 1974, Sch., r. 13 (1) to direct ACAS to be joined as a respondent; under r. 13 (1) the tribunal's discretion was limited to persons "directly interested" in the originating application; a person "directly interested" in an unfair dismissal claim was one who might have an award made against him; ACAS was not directly interested; application refused).

1053　　—— —— discretion to admit evidence

An employee was dismissed as a result of strike action and subsequently brought a claim against his employers for unfair dismissal and redundancy payments. During the proceedings the question of an industrial tribunal's discretion to refuse to admit documentary evidence which was otherwise admissible and probative, arose. *Held*, notwithstanding that industrial tribunals were not bound to follow the strict rules of evidence which applied in civil proceedings to which the Civil Evidence Act 1968 applied, there was no discretion in an industrial tribunal to refuse to admit evidence which was admissible and probative of one or more of the issues before it.

ROSEDALE MOULDINGS LTD v SIBLEY [1980] ICR 816 (Employment Appeal Tribunal: TALBOT J presiding).

1054　　—— —— power to determine—whether contract of employment contract of service or for services

See *Young and Woods Ltd v West*, para. 1017.

1055　　—— —— power to order hearing in private

An employee made a complaint to an industrial tribunal that she had been unfairly dismissed by her employers, a firm of solicitors. The employers applied for an order for the case to be heard in camera on the ground that confidential matters would be raised within the meaning of the Industrial Tribunals (Labour Relations) Regulations 1974, Sch., r. 6 (1) (b). The chairman of the industrial tribunal refused the employers' request that the application should be considered before the hearing and directed that it should be made to a full tribunal at the beginning of the case. The employers appealed, contending that under r. 12 (2) the industrial tribunal was bound to hear the application for a private hearing in advance of the hearing of the originating application. Rule 12 (2) provides that a party might, at any time, apply to a tribunal for directions on any matter arising in connection with the proceedings. *Held*, a decision on the question as to whether the whole or part of a hearing of an originating application should be in camera could be a direction within r. 12 (2). The time when such a direction should be given was a matter for the tribunal's discretion. The tribunal had not erred in deciding that the application should be heard at the start of the case. The appeal would be dismissed.

MILNE AND LYALL v WALDREN [1980] LS Gaz R 39 (Employment Appeal Tribunal: WATERHOUSE J presiding).

1056　——— procedure

The Industrial Tribunals (Rules of Procedure) Regulations 1980, S.I. 1980 No. 884 (in force on 1st October 1980), regulate the procedure of industrial tribunals for England and Wales in relation to all proceedings instituted on or after 1st October 1980 except those where separate Rules of Procedure, made under the provisions of any enactment, are applicable. These regulations revoke the Industrial Tribunals (Labour Relations) Regulations 1974, 1974 Halsbury's Abridgment para. 1834, as amended.

1057　——— ——— preliminary issue—question of law—desirability where facts in issue

See *Turley v Allders Department Stores Ltd*, para. 2577.

1058　Job Release Act 1977—continuation

The Job Release Act 1977 (Continuation) Order 1980, S.I. 1980 No. 937 (in force on 30th September 1980), continues in force until 29th September 1981 the Job Release Act 1977, s. 1, 1977 Halsbury's Abridgment para. 1072, which makes financial provision for job release schemes.

1059　Local employment—promotion—derelict land clearance areas

See para. 2866.

1060　Maternity pay—calculation—deduction of state maternity allowance

An employee had two separate contracts of employment for different jobs with different employers. On the question of the calculation of maternity pay, *held*, under the Employment Protection (Consolidation) Act 1978, s. 35 each contract of employment was to be considered separately. Under each contract the employee was entitled to nine-tenths of the weekly pay for the appropriate week, subject to the deduction of state maternity allowance. If there were two contracts of employment, the maternity allowance was to be deducted in the calculation of each payment made under the statute.

CULLEN v CREASEY HOTELS (LIMBURY) LTD [1980] ICR 236 (Employment Appeal Tribunal: SLYNN J presiding).

1061　——— entitlement—continuity of employment

An employee began working for her employers, a company, in 1970. In 1977 she was involved in a strike and was dismissed. On 4th July 1977 she was re-engaged and was given a standard contract which provided that employment with a "previous employer" was not counted as part of the employee's period of continuous service with the company. The employee ceased employment with the company on 30th March 1979 because she was pregnant. The company refused to give her any maternity benefits on the ground that she did not have the requisite two years' continuous service with them. She unsuccessfully complained to an industrial tribunal and on appeal, *held*, the effect of Employment Protection (Consolidation)

Act 1978, Sch. 13, para. 15 was that whilst the weeks that an employee was on strike did not count towards her continuous service, continuity was preserved. Furthermore, the employee's continuity of employment remained unaffected by a term in her new contract which stated that previous employment would not count as part of her continuous service. Accordingly the industrial tribunal had erred in its decision and the employee had the requisite period of continuous service for her to qualify for maternity pay. The appeal would be allowed.

HANSON V FASHION INDUSTRIES (HARTLEPOOL) LTD [1980] IRLR 393 (Employment Appeal Tribunal: TALBOT J presiding). *Clarke Chapman–John Thompson Ltd v Walters* [1972] ICR 83 applied.

1062 —— —— **continuity of employment until eleventh week before confinement—meaning**

An employee became pregnant and gave notice that she would cease to work at the eleventh week before the expected date of her confinement. The employee gave notice of her intention to return to work after the birth and was paid full maternity pay. In the event, due to a miscalculation, the employee left twelve weeks before her confinement and did not exercise her right to return to work. The employers claimed a rebate of the maternity pay from the Maternity Pay Fund. The rebate was refused on the grounds that the employer was not liable to make the payment because the employee had not fulfilled the requirement of continuing to be employed (whether or not she was at work) until the beginning of the eleventh week before the expected week of confinement, as provided for under the Employment Protection (Consolidation) Act 1978, s. 33 (3) (a). *Held*, it was wrong to state that an employee who had ceased work before the eleventh week was not entitled to maternity pay because she had not been continuously employed until that time. The words "continues to be employed" in s. 33 (3) (a) were to be read with "whether or not she is at work" which emphasised that a woman did not have to be physically at work until the eleventh week. The existence of a contract of employment did not depend upon what the employee did but on what the parties agreed to do. The employee was absent with her employer's consent and she was entitled to maternity pay. The employers would therefore be entitled to a rebate.

SATCHWELL SUNVIC LTD V SECRETARY OF STATE FOR EMPLOYMENT [1979] IRLR 455 (Employment Appeal Tribunal: LORD MCDONALD MC presiding).

1063 **National Dock Labour Board—increase of loans**

The National Dock Labour Board (Increase of Loans Limit) Order 1980, S.I. 1980 No. 1703 (in force on 6th November 1980), increases the limit which the National Dock Labour Board is permitted to have outstanding by way of principal loans to £30 million.

1064 **Racial discrimination**

See RACE RELATIONS.

1065 **Redundancy—amount of payment—calculation of weekly wage—average weekly rate of remuneration**

Industrial tribunal decision:

RESTON V LEYLAND VEHICLES LTD [1980] IRLR 376 (a redundancy situation arose in a company; five employees were made redundant and received redundancy payments calculated on the basis of wage rates in force at that time; the employees' contracts of employment were terminated in March; subsequently a wages increase was agreed, backdated to January; the employees claimed that they were entitled to redundancy payments calculated at the new rates; amount of redundancy payment had to be calculated in accordance with the amount of "week's pay" due under contract of employment in force on the date at which employment was terminated: wage negotiations were annual and there existed an implied term that any agreement reached would be backdated to January; the employees would be entitled to redundancy payments calculated at the new rate).

1066   —— cessation or diminution of business—employee's knowledge of such diminution

See *Lee v Nottinghamshire County Council*, para. 1068.

1067   —— continuity of employment—contracts for specific jobs over periods of years—whether each job governed by fixed term contract

An employee had completed thirty-one different jobs over a period of five years for the same company of ship repairers on a job-to-job basis. In between jobs he had claimed unemployment benefit. He decided that his future prospects of employment were poor considering the general decline in the industry, and after eight weeks without work, he claimed a redundancy payment. An industrial tribunal found that he had been continuously employed within the meaning of the Employment Protection (Consolidation) Act 1978, s. 81 (1), that there was a redundancy situation as the requirements of the employer's business for ship repairing work had diminished within the meaning of s. 81 (2) (b), but that he could not be deemed to have been dismissed as he had not been employed under fixed term contracts within the meaning of s. 82 (3) (b). On appeal, *held*, an employee who completed a number of jobs for the same employers but who claimed unemployment benefit in between jobs was not continuously employed, nor was there a redundancy situation, there being no evidence that he would not have been offered another job in due course. At the end of each job there was a discharge of the contract by performance and the industrial tribunal had been correct in holding that there was not a series of fixed term contracts, and that therefore the employee could not have claimed a redundancy payment on the basis that he was dismissed from his last job. The appeal would accordingly be dismissed.

RYAN v SHIPBOARD MAINTENANCE LTD [1980] ICR 88 (Employment Appeal Tribunal: KILNER BROWN J presiding).

1068   —— dismissal—fixed term contract—whether dismissal by reason of redundancy

The Redundancy Payments Act 1965, s. 1 (2) (b) provides that an employee is considered to be dismissed by reason of redundancy if the dismissal is attributable wholly or mainly to the fact that the requirements of that business for employees to carry out work of a particular kind have ceased or diminished or are expected to cease or diminish. Section 3 (1) (b) provides that an employee is taken to be dismissed by his employer if, where under his contract he is employed for a fixed term, that term expires without being renewed under the same contract.

In April 1975 a teacher was employed by a local authority as a lecturer for a period of one year at a college of further education. At the time of his appointment it was commonly known that there would be a general diminution in that sphere of employment due to the declining number of students accepted for courses at the college. His contract was renewed for one year and his employment terminated on 31st August 1977. He applied to an industrial tribunal seeking re-instatement or re-engagement alleging unfair dismissal or redundancy. On a question of the effect of the 1965 Act ss. 1 (2) (b) and 3 (1) (b), *held*, both sections were to be read together with the result that where an employee's fixed term contract was not renewed at the expiry of the term the employee was deemed to be dismissed by virtue of s. 3 (1) (b). Thereupon a redundancy situation arose within the meaning of s. 1 (2) (b). The court however was not concerned with the cause of dismissal but with s. 1 (2) and to see whether the dismissal was attributable to a redundancy situation and it was immaterial whether the employee knew that a redundancy situation would arise. The employee had accordingly been dismissed by reason of redundancy.

Lee v Nottinghamshire County Council [1980] ICR 635 (Court of Appeal: Lawton and Eveleigh LJJ and Sir Stanley Rees). Decision of Employment Appeal Tribunal [1979] ICR 818, 1979 Halsbury's Abridgment para. 1107 reversed.

Redundancy Payments Act 1965 ss. 1 and 3 now Employment Protection (Consolidation) Act 1978, ss. 81 and 83.

1069   —— —— re-engagement—change of ownership of business—distinction between transfer of business and transfer of assets

Due to a fall in demand for its products, a company sold one of its factories to another company, which took over all work in progress. The employees' contracts of employment were terminated, but they carried on working at the factory, doing the same sort of work, on no less favourable terms under new contracts with the other company. They claimed redundancy payments from the first company, which resisted the claims on the ground that the employees should not be taken to have been dismissed because there had been a change in the ownership of a part of the business within the Redundancy Payments Act 1965, s. 13 (1). *Held*, the question to be decided was whether there had been a change of ownership of part of the business, or merely a change of ownership of particular assets. The essential distinction between the two was that in the former case the business was transferred as a going concern, whereas in the latter case the assets were transferred to the new owner to be used in whatever business he chose. There was ample material in the facts as found to support the view that the factory was not transferred as a going concern. Accordingly, the employees were entitled to redundancy payments.

Melon v Hector Powe Ltd [1981] 1 All ER 313 (House of Lords: Lord Diplock, Lord Elwyn Jones, Lord Edmund-Davies, Lord Fraser of Tullybelton and Lord Keith of Kinkel). Decision of Court of Session [1980] IRLR 80 affirmed.

1965 Act, s. 13, now Employment Protection (Consolidation) Act 1978, s. 94.

1070   —— employer's duty to notify Secretary of State—special circumstances preventing compliance

Employees were made redundant after consultation between the employers and the union. The employers' attention had been drawn by means of various documents sent to them to their duty under the Employment Protection Act 1975, s. 100, to give sixty days' notice of redundancies to the Secretary of State, but they failed to do so. The employers subsequently applied for a rebate of the redundancy payments and the Secretary of State exercised his statutory powers to reduce the amount of the rebate. On the employers' complaint to an industrial tribunal, it was found that there were special circumstances within s. 100 (6) making it not reasonably practicable for the employers to give sufficient notice, in that the requirement had not been brought adequately to their attention. On appeal by the Secretary of State, *held*, ignorance of the obligation under s. 100 to notify or a failure to heed information relating to it could not constitute special circumstances under s. 100 (6) so as to make it not reasonably practicable to comply with the obligation. The appeal would be allowed.

Secretary of State for Employment v Helitron Ltd [1980] ICR 523 (Employment Appeal Tribunal: Slynn J presiding). *Union of Construction, Allied Trades and Technicians v H. Rooke & Son (Cambridge) Ltd* [1978] ICR 818, EAT, 1978 Halsbury's Abridgment para. 1130 applied.

1071   —— employer's insolvency—employee's right to remuneration

An employee realised that his employers were in financial difficulties and founded a new company of which he and two other employees were salaried directors. The new company did not start trading immediately and the employees continued to work for the employers. On the employers' insolvency the employee was dismissed without notice or payment in lieu of notice. The day after his dismissal the new company began trading and it was agreed that the employee would not draw any salary for the first six weeks on the basis that he would receive six weeks' salary in lieu of notice from the employers. The employee was never paid and subsequently sought an order requiring the Secretary of State to pay him six weeks' salary in lieu of notice out of the redundancy fund in accordance with the Employment Protection (Consolidation) Act 1978, s. 122. *Held*, when calculating the amount of an order against the Secretary of State under s. 122, the amount of the salary an employee should have received during the period of notice was to be reduced by the amount of the employee's earnings during that period. Although an employee setting up business on his own might not earn anything during the initial period because the demands of a new business required all receipts to be left in, it was necessary for a tribunal to consider whether, in leaving all the receipts in the business, the employee was nevertheless receiving benefits which ought to be taken into account in assessing his true loss. In the present case the sole reason for the employee not drawing any money was the expected payment in lieu of notice and, accordingly, it was wrong not to take into account the amount which he could reasonably have earned. The employee's application would fail.

SECRETARY OF STATE FOR EMPLOYMENT v JOBLING [1980] ICR 380 (Employment Appeal Tribunal: SLYNN J presiding). *Secretary of State for Employment v Wilson* [1978] ICR 200, EAT, 1977 Halsbury's Abridgment para. 1037 applied.

1072   —— notice—payment in lieu of notice

See *Secretary of State for Employment v Jobling*, para. 1071.

1073   —— offer of alternative employment—whether refusal reasonable

An employee, a catering manageress, was dismissed by reason of redundancy. She refused suitable alternative employment offered to her by her employer on the basis of an erroneous belief that another company was intending to employ her. On her application to an industrial tribunal for a redundancy payment, the question arose as to whether her refusal of the employer's offer of alternative employment was reasonable within the Employment Protection (Consolidation) Act 1978, s. 82. *Held*, the employee's conduct was to be judged subjectively at the time she made the decision to refuse the employer's offer of alternative employment. She had, in the circumstances, not acted unreasonably in refusing the employer's offer and would therefore be entitled to receive a redundancy payment.

EXECUTORS OF J. F. EVEREST v COX [1980] ICR 415 (Employment Appeal Tribunal: PHILLIPS J presiding).

1074   —— payment—calculation—normal working hours

Under an agreement incorporated into national working rules for the building industry, employers purchased annual holiday credit stamps from a management company with which they paid employees during their holiday periods. If the employee failed to claim his holiday credit before the appropriate date he lost the value of the stamps. An employee was dismissed without notice on the insolvency of his employers. He subsequently sought a declaration that he was entitled to the value of the holiday stamps which ought to have been purchased during the period of notice to which he was entitled under the Contracts of Employment Act 1972, as a debt owed by the Secretary of State in accordance with the Employment Protection Act 1975, s. 64. *Held*, the amount an employer was liable to pay an employee during the statutory period of notice under s. 64 was to be calculated in accordance with the 1975 Act, Sch. 5 and not on the principles applicable to assessing damages at common law. Schedule 5 provided that the amount payable should be assessed by dividing a week's pay by the number of working hours, if the employee was ready and willing to work but no work was provided for him by his employer. A "week's pay", however, meant the amount payable by the employer for a particular week's work. The value of the holiday stamps could not be included in a week's pay as money paid for a particular week's work under the contract of employment because, if the employee failed to take his holiday at the appropriate time, he forfeited the money. Such a claim by the employee, therefore, would fail.

SECRETARY OF STATE FOR EMPLOYMENT v HAYNES [1980] ICR 371 (Employment Appeal Tribunal: SLYNN J presiding).

Employment Protection Act 1975, s. 64 and Sch. 5 are now Employment Protection (Consolidation) Act 1978, s. 122 and Sch. 3 and 14 respectively.

1075 —— —— **exemption**

The Redundancy Payments (Exemption) Order 1980, S.I. 1980 No. 1052 (in force on 29th August 1980), excludes the application of the Employment Protection (Consolidation) Act 1978, s. 81 as respects those employees of the governing bodies of certain schools and of the Lancashire Council to whom the agreement specified in the Sch. applies.

1076 —— **protective award—when payable—matters to be considered**

In June 1978 a company decided to close one of its factories on 15th September 1978. The company simultaneously informed the employees, the relevant trade unions and the Department of Employment of its decision. The closure in fact took place in July 1978 and was accepted by three of the unions involved, which only represented a minority of the workforce. The other trade union complained to an industrial tribunal which found that the company had failed to comply with the consultation requirements of the Employment Protection Act 1975, s. 99 (3) (a). The company was ordered to pay remuneration for a period of seventy days beginning on the date of the actual closure in July. The employers appealed against the tribunal's calculation of the protected period. *Held*, the industrial tribunal had not erred in its decision in making a protective award under the 1975 Act, s. 101 (5) covering a period of seventy days in respect of the company's failure to begin consultations over the proposed redundancies with the union at the earliest opportunity. The tribunal had correctly calculated the ninety-day maximum protected period under s. 101 (5) from the date on which the dismissals occurred and correctly distinguished between this period and the ninety-day period referred to in s. 99 (3) which related to the period at which consultations must begin before the dismissals were to take place. In exercising its discretion in making a protective award and in determining the period of that award a tribunal had to consider the loss of days of consultation and the tribunal, in the case concerned, had correctly done so. The appeal would be dismissed.

GKN SANKEY LTD v NATIONAL SOCIETY OF METAL MECHANICS [1980] ICR 148 (Employment Appeal Tribunal: TALBOT J presiding). *Spillers-French (Holdings) Ltd v USDAW* [1980] 1 All ER 231, EAT, 1979 Halsbury's Abridgment para. 1106, applied.

1077 —— **re-engagement or reinstatement**

The Employment Protection (Consolidation) Act 1978, s. 84 (1) provides that if an employee's contract of employment is renewed or he is re-engaged under a new contract in pursuance of an offer made by his employer before the termination of his employment under the previous contract, and the renewal or re-engagement takes effect immediately on the ending of that employment, then the employee is not regarded as having been dismissed by reason of ending his employment under the previous contract.

During an industrial dispute employees of a company received letters terminating their contracts of employment but at the same time offering them re-engagement under new contracts of employment, subject to certain conditions. The employees returned to work and all except twenty-two were reinstated rather than re-engaged. Subsequently a redundancy situation arose and the twenty-two re-engaged employees were dismissed on the basis of the application of the last in, first out rule. They complained to a tribunal that they had been unfairly selected for redundancy and that they were entitled to redundancy payments. *Held*, the offer of re-engagement contained in the dismissal letter was an offer of re-engagement made before employment was terminated so as to meet the requirements of s. 84 (1). The employees' continuity of employment was protected and they would be entitled to redundancy payments. The intention of s. 84 was that if an employer indicated a general intention to re-engage an employee whom he proposed to dismiss and if that intention was followed up and ultimately ended in a resumption of employment then the employment would be considered as continuous.

SINGER CO (UK) LTD v FERRIER [1980] IRLR 300 (Employment Appeal Tribunal: LORD McDONALD MC presiding).

1078 Redundancy payments scheme—shipbuilding

The Shipbuilding (Redundancy Payments Scheme) (Great Britain) (Amendment) Order 1980, S.I. 1980 No. 630 (in force on 7th May 1980), amends the scheme established by the Shipbuilding (Redundancy Payments Scheme) (Great Britain) Order 1978, 1978 Halsbury's Abridgment para. 1142, for the payment of benefits to employees of British Shipbuilders who are made redundant or transferred to less well paid employment. The order raises the limit of weekly pay which is taken into account in the calculation of previous earnings.

1079 Sex discrimination

See SEX DISCRIMINATION.

1080 Suspension on medical grounds—remuneration

The Employment Protection (Medical Suspension) Order 1980, S.I. 1980 No. 1581 (in force on 18th August 1981), removes certain provisions from the list of specified provisions, relating to remuneration on suspension on medical grounds, in the Employment (Consolidation) Act 1978, Sch. 1. It also adds to the Schedule, the Radioactive Substances (Road Transport Workers) (Great Britain) (Amendment) Regulations 1975 and the Control of Lead at Work Regulations 1980, para. 1383.

1081 Termination of employment—whether employment terminated by agreement or dismissal

Employers granted a period of leave to an Indian employee who wished to return to India for a holiday. They gave their permission on condition that if she did not return to work on a specified date, for whatever reason, her contract of employment would be terminated. The employee signed a document to that effect and when she failed to return to work on the specified date, due to illness, her contract was terminated. She claimed that she had been unfairly dismissed and the employers subsequently appealed against an industrial tribunal decision in her favour. *Held*, the employee had been unfairly dismissed when her employment was terminated after her failure to return to work on the specified date, notwithstanding that upon being granted leave she was warned as to the consequences of failure to return and signed a document to that effect. There had to be a consensual agreement to terminate such a contract. A unilateral statement of intention, which was what the document amounted to, was insufficient. The appeal would therefore be dismissed.

MIDLAND ELECTRIC MANUFACTURING CO LTD v KANJI [1980] IRLR 185 (Employment Appeal Tribunal: TALBOT J presiding). *British Leyland (UK) Ltd v Ashraf* [1978] IRLR 330, 1978, Halsbury's Abridgment para. 1147 distinguished.

1082 Time off—union duties and activities—entitlement to pay during working hours

In a case concerning time off for trade union duties where a union meeting was arranged during working hours and a request by a union official for paid time off was refused, it was held that a tribunal, in determining whether an employee was entitled to paid time off to attend the meeting under the Employment Protection (Consolidation) Act 1978, s. 27 was to look at all the surrounding circumstances, including the agenda, of the meeting and whether in attending the meeting the employee was doing his duty as a union official concerned with industrial relations between the employer and employees. Where only a proportion of the time was spent on matters covered under s. 27 then only a proportion of the time was to be paid for.

RHP BEARINGS LTD V BROOKES [1979] IRLR 452 (Employment Appeal Tribunal: BRISTOW J presiding).

1083 Trade unions

See TRADE UNIONS.

1084 Unemployment and supplementary benefit—recoupment from employer

The Employment Protection (Recoupment of Unemployment Benefit and Supplementary Benefit) (Amendment) Regulations 1980, S.I. 1980 No. 1608 (in force on 24th November 1980), amend the 1977 Regulations by substituting the words "a benefit officer" for the words "the Supplementary Benefits Commission" in regulations 11 and 12, and by inserting a new paragraph requiring a written notice of determination made pursuant to regulation 11 (2) (b) to be served on the employee and on the Secretary of State.

1085 Unfair dismissal

See UNFAIR DISMISSAL.

1086 Wages—deductions—attachment of earnings order

See para. 1011.

1087 —— itemised pay statement—required particulars—whether tips part of gross wages

The Employment Protection (Consolidation) Act 1978, s. 8 provides that every employee has the right to be given by his employer at or before the time at which any payment of wages is made to him an itemised pay statement, in writing, containing (a) the gross amount of wages and (b) the amounts of any variable and any fixed deductions from that gross amount and the purposes for which they are made.

An employee was a waiter in a restaurant owned by his employers. In addition to his wages he was allowed to keep any tips given to him by customers. Out of this amount he had to pay a fixed weekly sum to the manager. The sum was not disclosed on his pay statements as part of his gross wages. Pursuant to the 1978 Act, s. 11 the employee applied to an industrial tribunal for a determination of what particulars ought to have been included in his itemised pay statement. *Held*, the tips paid to and kept by the employee were not wages within the meaning of s. 8. The employers did not know the precise sum involved and were therefore unable to include particulars of tips in wages itemised in pay statements as required by s. 8 (a). Further the payments to the manager were made in respect of the tips alone and were not deductions from the gross amount of the employee's wages. The employers were therefore not obliged to disclose it as a fixed deduction from wages under s. 8 (b).

COFONE V SPAGHETTI HOUSE LTD [1980] ICR 155 (Employment Appeal Tribunal: TALBOT J presiding).

1088 Wages Councils—Pin, Hook and Eye, and Snap Fastener Wages Council

The Pin, Hook and Eye, and Snap Fastener Wages Council (Great Britain) (Abolition) Order 1980, S.I. 1980 No. 1495 (in force on 18th November 1980), abolishes the Pin, Hook and Eye, Snap Fastener Wages Council (Great Britain).

ENVIRONMENT

1089   Conservation — European wildlife and natural habitats — convention

The member states of the Council of Europe have agreed a Convention on the Conservation of European Wildlife and Natural Habitats. The states agree to take appropriate and necessary legislative and administrative measures to ensure, inter alia: the conservation of the habitats of wild flora and fauna species (art. 4); the special protection of wild flora specified in App. I, and the deliberate picking etc. of such plants shall be prohibited (art. 5); the special protection of the wild fauna specified in App. II, particularly prohibiting all forms of deliberate capture, keeping and deliberate killing and the deliberate damage or destruction of breeding or nesting sites (art. 6); and to prohibit the disturbance of wild fauna at breeding times etc., the destruction or taking of eggs and the trading in such animals, alive or dead (art. 6). States are authorised in certain circumstances to make exceptions to these provisions (art. 9). The convention will enter into force three months after five states have expressed their consent to be bound by it, provided those states include at least four member states of the Council of Europe (art. 19).

1090   Control of pollution—special waste

The Control of Pollution (Special Waste) Regulations 1980, S.I. 1980 No. 1709 (in force on 16th March 1981), give effect to Council Directive (EEC) 78/319 which relates to toxic and dangerous waste. The regulations provide that waste falling within certain descriptions contained in Sch. 1 is to be regarded as special waste. Radioactive waste will be special waste if it has dangerous properties, other than radioactivity, which bring it within the descriptions contained in Sch. 1. A system of consignment notes is prescribed for use by those who produce, transfer for disposal or dispose of special waste, and local authorities may waive the requirement that they should be separately notified of the dispatch and disposal of every consignment. The Secretary of State is given a power to direct that specified special waste must be disposed of at any site where a disposal licence is in force under the Control of Pollution Act 1974 or which is used for the disposal of waste by a disposal authority. Producers, disposers or carriers who fail to comply with the regulations are made liable to prosecution.

1091   Gipsies—accommodation—local authority's duty to provide sites—liability as landlord for gipsy nuisance

See *Page Motors Ltd v Epsom and Ewell Borough Council*, para. 2070.

EQUITY

Halsbury's Laws of England (4th edn.), Vol. 16, paras. 1201–1500

1092   Articles

Annexation of Restrictive Covenants, G. H. Hewson, QC (in the light of *Federated Homes Ltd v Mill Lodge Properties Ltd* [1980] 1 All ER 371, para. 1095: [1980] JPL 371.

Enforcement of Restrictive Covenants, T. I. Bailey (in the light of *Federated Homes Ltd v Hill Lodge Properties Ltd* [1980] 1 All ER 371, para. 1095): 130 NLJ 531

Priorities—Equitable Tracing Rights and Assignments of Book Debts, D. W. McLauchlan: 96 LQR 90.

1093   Equitable assignment—assignment for value of future property—when beneficial interest passes

The plaintiffs traded as selling agents in the United Kingdom for the defendants, a company in Singapore. The plaintiffs issued a writ claiming that they were owed money by the defendants. However the writ was withdrawn after an assurance by the defendants that they would pay the plaintiffs on the conclusion of English arbitration proceedings for the recovery of a substantial sum owed to them by a purchaser. The sum was paid to the defendants' solicitors in England and the plaintiffs issued a writ and applied for a Mareva injunction. The injunction was granted ex parte. Subsequently a bank in Singapore, which claimed that a sum had already been assigned to them out of the moneys due to the defendants as a result of the arbitration proceedings, successfully applied for the injunction to be discharged. On appeal by the plaintiffs, *held*, although no notice of the assignment was given to the purchaser, the other party to the arbitration proceedings, it operated as a valid equitable assignment. Therefore when the defendants succeeded in the arbitration the sums assigned to the bank under the equitable assignment operated at once between the bank and the defendants and the promise to pay the plaintiffs was not effective against the equitable assignment. The appeal would be dismissed.

PHAROAH'S PLYWOOD CO LTD v ALLIED WOOD PRODUCTS CO (PRIVATE) LTD, BANK OF AMERICA NATIONAL TRUST & SAVINGS ASSOCIATION intervening, [1980] LS Gaz R 130 (Court of Appeal: LORD DENNING MR and ACKNER LJ). *Re Lind* [1915] 2 Ch 345 applied.

1094   **Equitable interest—securities acquired by English company with foreign bank loan—further advance obtained from English bank— charge executed over securities—priority**

The plaintiff foreign bank lent money to an English company to enable it to acquire securities in a foreign company. The Bank of England granted permission for the loan subject to certain conditions which included that the servicing of the loan and its eventual repayment were to be made out of the income or capital of the investments acquired by the company and the company agreed to observe all the conditions of the loan agreement. The company subsequently encountered financial difficulties and obtained credit facilities from the defendant English bank which was an authorised depositary, by executing a charge and depositing its securities with it. On appeal against the decision that (i) the loan agreement constituted an equitable charge in favour of the plaintiff bank and (ii) the transfer was void for infringing the Exchange Control Act 1947, ss. 16 (2) and 17 (2), *held*, (i) in order to determine whether a transaction gave rise to an equitable charge, it was necessary to ascertain the intention of the parties which could be express or implied. A binding obligation by a debtor to repay a debt out of a particular fund amounted to an equitable charge. On the construction of the loan agreement there was no obligation to repay the loan from the proceeds of the securities in any event, but merely an obligation to observe the requirements of the Bank of England and to repay the loan in an approved manner. Accordingly, since there was no specifically enforceable right the agreement was incapable of constituting an equitable charge in favour of the plaintiff bank. (ii) The transfer was void for infringing the 1947 Act, ss. 16 (2) and 17 (2), which provided, respectively, that an authorised depositary was prohibited from parting with a certificate relating to a foreign currency security which was in his custody, and that no person might do anything affecting his rights or powers in relation to certain securities, without Treasury permission. However, since it came within the provisions of Exchange Control Notice EC7 paras. 87 and 88 the securities had been validly charged to the defendant bank and the appeal would be allowed.

SWISS BANK CORPN v LLOYDS BANK LTD [1980] 2 All ER 419 (Court of Appeal: BUCKLEY, BRANDON and BRIGHTMAN LJJ). *English Sewing Cotton Co Ltd v Inland Revenue Comrs* [1947] 1 All ER 679 and dictum of Atkin LJ in *National Provincial and Union Bank of England v Charnley* [1924] 1 KB 499 applied. Decision of Browne-Wilkinson J [1979] 2 All ER 853, 1978 Halsbury's Abridgment para. 1965 varied.

Since 24th October 1979 all persons in or resident in the United Kingdom are exempted from the obligations under the Exchange Control Act 1947. See 1979 Halsbury's Abridgment paras. 1905–1917.

1095   Restrictive covenant—annexation of benefit—annexation by statute

In 1970 the owners of a site which included three areas of land, the red, green and blue land, obtained outline planning permission, valid for three years, to develop the site by erecting a certain number of dwellings on it. The blue land was later sold to the defendants. In a covenant contained in the conveyance, the defendants covenanted, in carrying out development on the blue land, not to build at a greater density than three hundred houses, so as not to reduce the number of houses the owners of the remaining red and green land might erect under the existing planning permission. By a series of transfers the plaintiffs became the owners of the red and green land. The transfers of the green land, but not of the red land, contained an unbroken chain of express assignments of the benefit of the restrictive covenant. In 1977, the plaintiffs obtained planning permission to develop the red and green land and discovered that the defendants had obtained new planning permission to develop the blue land at a higher density than permitted by the restrictive covenant. The plaintiffs brought an action to restrain the defendants. The defendants contended that if the covenant was capable of assignment and was not spent by the lapse of the 1970 planning permission, the benefit of it had not been transmitted to the plaintiffs. The benefit of the covenant had not been expressly or impliedly annexed to the retained land by the conveyance nor did the Law of Property Act 1925, s. 78 have the effect of annexing it. The judge found the benefit of the covenant had been assigned by the unbroken chain of assignments in relation to the green land and by virtue of the 1925 Act, s. 62, in relation to the red land. The injunction sought by the plaintiffs was granted. On appeal by the defendants, *held*, the parties had not intended to tie the restrictive covenant to the original planning permission. The covenant was not personal but assignable. Where there was a restrictive covenant which related to, or touched and concerned the covenantee's land, s. 78 (1) had the effect of annexing the benefit of the covenant to the land for the benefit of the convenantee and his successors in title. The covenant between the original owners and defendants had shown that the restrictive covenant was for the benefit of the retained land and that land had been sufficiently described for the purposes of annexation. The covenant related to, or touched and concerned, the land of the covenantee and the plaintiffs as his successors in title. Furthermore if a restrictive covenant was attached to land it was, prima facie, annexed to every part of the land including severed land and the plaintiffs as owners of the red and green land were entitled to enforce the covenant against the defendants. The appeal would therefore be dismissed.

FEDERATED HOMES LTD V MILL LODGE PROPERTIES LTD [1980] 1 All ER 371 (Court of Appeal: MEGAW, BROWNE and BRIGHTMAN LJJ).

1096   —— common vendor of several plots—covenants in varying terms—whether benefit passed to purchasers' successors in title

A large plot of land was divided into several plots and conveyed to various purchasers. Some of the conveyances contained covenants of indemnity to observe certain restrictions (e.g. on carrying on offensive trades), while others contained absolute covenants covering the same matters. The defendants, who were successors in title of one of the purchasers, began a pig farming business on their plot and the plaintiffs, successors in title of other purchasers, brought an action for breach of covenant. The defendants accepted that their land was subject to the covenants but denied that the benefit of the covenants had passed to the plaintiffs. *Held*, the benefit had passed if a scheme of development existed. However, the nature of and variation between the covenants entered into by the various purchasers precluded the establishment of such a scheme. The essence of a scheme was the reciprocity of obligations between the purchasers and the intention to create such reciprocity. It had to be shown that all plot-holders were subject to obligations enforceable by all the others. A covenant of personal indemnity such as was contained in some of the conveyances was inconsistent with an intention that the covenant should enure for the benefit of others. The benefit of the covenant was not vested in the plaintiffs.

KINGSBURY V L. W. ANDERSON LTD (1979) 40 P & CR 136 (Chancery Divison: BROWNE-WILKINSON J). *Elliston v Reacher* [1908] 2 Ch 374, *Brunner v Greenslade*

[1970] 3 All ER 833 and *Lund v Taylor* (1975) 31 P & CR 167, CA, 1976 Halsbury's Abridgment para. 1072 applied.

1097 —— **covenant running with land—annexation by statute**

See *Federated Homes Ltd v Mill Lodge Properties Ltd*, para. 1095.

1098 **Tracing property—discovery—payment of money induced by fraud—disclosure of bankers' books and correspondence**

See *Bankers Trust Co v Shapira*, para. 891.

1099 **Undue influence—licence ancillary to contract of employment—validity of licence**

See *Mathew v Bobbins*, para. 1716.

ESTOPPEL

Halsbury's Laws of England (4th edn.), Vol. 16, paras. 1501–1641

1100 **Election—purchase of land with trust funds—possession proceedings—trustees' claim barred**

See *Smith v Hobbs*, para. 2998.

1101 **Estoppel by conduct—claim for possession of house—occupant rendering unpaid services—whether assurances amount to estoppel**

The owners by inheritance of a dwelling house, after serving notices to quit on the defendant, the sole occupier of the house, brought a claim for possession against her. She had originally entered the house as a paid servant and subsequently remained in occupation rendering unpaid services to the family. During that time she was encouraged by members of the family to believe that she could regard the property as her home for the rest of her life. She contended that by virtue of these statements the owners were estopped from evicting her and further sought a declaration that she was entitled to occupy the house rent-free for the rest of her life. *Held*, once it was shown that the occupant had relied on the assurances given to her, the burden of proving that she acted to her detriment in staying on to look after the house and family without payment did not rest on her. In the absence of evidence to the contrary the court would infer that her conduct was induced by the assurances given and grant the declaration as sought. Further, expenditure of money on property was not a necessary element to establish proprietary estoppel. It was sufficient to raise the equity if the party to whom the assurance was given acted in good faith on it and it was for the courts to decide in what way the equity was to be satisfied.

GREASLEY V COOKE [1980] 1 WLR 1306 (Court of Appeal: LORD DENNING MR, WALLER and DUNN LJJ). *Reynell v Sprye* (1852) 1 De GM & G 600 and *Smith v Chadwick* (1882) 20 Ch D 27, CA applied.

1102 **Issue estoppel—issue decided in criminal proceedings—whether party estopped from bringing civil action relating to same issue**

Six men were convicted of the murders of twenty-one people by a bomb explosion. At their trial they had alleged that their confession statements had been induced by violence and threats from the police. In a "trial within a trial" the judge had found that they were voluntary statements made without police violence. The men's appeal against conviction was dismissed. They brought actions for assault against, inter alia, the police, and at first instance the judge dismissed the police application to strike out the statement of claim. On appeal by the police, the question for the court was whether the men were barred by issue estoppel or as an abuse of the process of court from bringing the actions. *Held,* GOFF LJ dissenting, on the question of issue estoppel, the appeal would be allowed. If the men were to be believed, they had a reasonable cause of action for damages against the police. The action itself was not therefore an abuse of process but was to be called an abuse in view of the "trial within a trial" and the jury's verdict. Estoppel per rem judicatam or issue estoppel was not an absolute bar to the matter in dispute being tried again. The party concerned could avoid the effect of the previous decision if he could prove that it had been obtained by fraud or collusion or if he could bring decisive new evidence which he could not have ascertained previously by reasonable diligence. Further, to operate as estoppel the previous decision had to be final.

The convicted men had contended that the evidence of three prison officers and of a doctor was fresh evidence, but counsel had admitted that he had had the prison officers' statements at the trial but had chosen not to call them. Further, the doctor's evidence could have been available at the trial had reasonable diligence been used. A "trial within a trial" was conclusive and created an issue estoppel sufficient to bar the convicted men's claims. On the facts it would not be fair or just to allow the decision to be reopened.

GOFF LJ held that the Crown as prosecutor at the trial and the police as tortfeasors by statute were not privies in interest for the purpose of the alleged issue estoppel and did not satisfy the doctrine of mutuality.

MCILKENNY V CHIEF CONSTABLE OF WEST MIDLANDS POLICE FORCE [1980] 2 All ER 227 (Court of Appeal: LORD DENNING MR, GOFF LJ and SIR GEORGE BAKER). *Duchess of Kingston's Case* [1775–1802] All ER Rep 623, dicta of Lord Reid, Lord Upjohn and Lord Wilberforce in *Carl-Zeiss Stiftung v Rayner and Keeler (No. 2)* [1966] 2 All ER at 550, 573 and 586, *Phosphate Sewage Co v Molleson* (1879) 4 App Cas 801, dicta of Lord Loreburn LC in *Brown v Dean* [1908–10] All ER Rep at 662, of Lord Halsbury LC in *Reichel v Magrath* (1889) 14 App Cas at 668 and of A L Smith LJ in *Stephenson v Garnett* [1898] 1 QB at 680 applied.

1103   **——plaintiff conceding issue on appeal—appeal dismissed by consent—whether plaintiff could raise issue in later action**

A company, a licensed moneylender, agreed to sell a property to the plaintiff and also finance the purchase. A contract of loan containing all the terms of the transaction was signed by both parties. Later the plaintiff unsuccessfully brought an action against the company. Questions arose as to whether the transaction amounted to a moneylending transaction within the Moneylenders Act 1927, s. 6 which provides that a loan must be evidenced by a note or memorandum in writing if it is to be valid. The plaintiff appealed but before the appeal was heard he decided to discontinue the action. The appeal was dismissed by consent, the plaintiff stating in the Court of Appeal that, even if he was able to succeed in showing that the requirements of s. 6 had not been complied with, he had to concede that the transaction was not a moneylending transaction within the section. A year later the plaintiff brought a second action against the company claiming that the debt was statute-barred under s. 13. The question arose as to whether the admission and content order made in the Court of Appeal gave rise to issue estoppel. *Held,* for the purposes of issue estoppel an issue was settled and founded on issue estoppel in subsequent proceedings if it was embodied in the terms of the judgment in the action because it was embodied in the decision of the court and also if it was embodied in an admission made in the face of the court or implied in a consent order. The concession made by the plaintiff in the Court of Appeal in the first action therefore founded an issue estoppel preventing the plaintiff from asserting in the second action that the transaction was a moneylending transaction.

KHAN V GOLECCHA INTERNATIONAL LTD [1980] 2 All ER 259 (Court of Appeal: BRIDGE, CUMMING-BRUCE and BRIGHTMAN LJJ). Dicta of Lush J in *Ord v Ord* [1923] All ER Rep 206 at 210 and of Lord Shaw in *Haystead v Taxation Comr* [1925] All ER Rep 56 at 62 applied. *Jenkins v Robertson* (1867) LR 1 SC & Div 17 distinguished.

1104   —— **property adjustment order—whether estoppel created**

In proceedings brought under the Matrimonial Causes Act 1973, s. 24, the plaintiff was adjudged to be entitled to the whole equitable interest of the matrimonial home of a husband and wife who were divorced. In subsequent proceedings for the transfer of the legal estate to her, she claimed, unsuccessfully, that the defendants, the husband and wife, were estopped from claiming a share in the equity of the house. On appeal, *held*, it was fundamental to the jurisdiction of the Family Division under s. 24 that the court should know over what property its discretion was to be exercised and the rights of interested parties. When these conditions were satisfied and an issue was decided against a party, that issue must be taken to have been conclusively decided against him and he could not reopen it, unless it would be fair and just to do so. Accordingly the defendants were estopped from claiming a share in the equity and the appeal would be allowed.

TEBBUTT v HAYNES (1980) Times, 28th October (Court of Appeal: LORD DENNING MR, BRIGHTMAN and GRIFFITHS LJJ). *McIlkenny v Chief Constable of the West Midlands* [1980] 2 All ER 227, CA, para. 1102, applied.

1105   **Promissory estoppel—bill of exchange—undertaking to forward cheque**

See *Aquaflite Ltd v Jaymar International Freight Consultants Ltd*, para. 260.

1106   —— **building contract—payment against certificate—contractor undertaking to obtain supporting document—whether entitled to terminate for non-payment despite failure to obtain**

Canada
A building contract provided for payments against architect's certificates. The contractor could terminate the contract on the owner's failure to pay a certified sum within seven days. After a certificate was issued the owner requested the contractor to secure formal execution of a supporting document by a subcontractor, which the contractor agreed to do. The date for payment passed without payment and without presentation of the formally executed document. The contractor gave notice of termination. Despite subsequent authorisation of payment the contractor purported to terminate the contract. The owner unsuccessfully sued for breach. On appeal, *held*, the contractor's conduct had led the owner to believe that he could delay payment pending presentation of the formally executed document. The contractor was estopped from exercising his strict contractual rights. The appeal would be allowed.

OWEN SOUND PUBLIC LIBRARY BOARD v MIAL DEVELOPMENT LTD (1979) 102 DLR (3d) 685 (Court of Appeal of Ontario).

1107   —— **ingredients of doctrine—detriment**

The wife of the tenant of a flat which was outside the scope of the Rent Acts suffered from severe physical and mental illness which was likely to be aggravated if she had to move. On a change of landlords the tenant was warned that he would have to give up possession. When the situation was explained to the landlord's representative the tenant was told that he could stay as long as he wished, but later he was given notice to quit. In possession proceedings he pleaded promissory estoppel. *Held*, nothing had been done, either by action or inaction, in reliance on the representation. Detriment was an essential ingredient of the doctrine of promissory estoppel, and as this was lacking possession would be ordered.

FONTANA NV v MAUTNER (1979) 254 Estates Gazette 199 (Chancery Division: BALCOMBE J). *Ajay v R T Briscoe (Nigeria) Ltd* [1964] 1 WLR 1326 applied.

1108   —— **lease—rent review clause—time limit**

See *James v Heim Gallery (London) Ltd*, para. 1746.

1109   —— mortgage   agreement—agreement   to   waive   mortgage
re-payments

Canada

The plaintiff conveyed his interests in a house to the defendant subject to two
mortgages in favour of third parties. The defendant executed a further mortgage in
favour of the plaintiff on the understanding that the mortgage repayments would be
waived by the plaintiff and granted to the defendant as a gift. The plaintiff
subsequently brought an action for payment of the mortgage debt. *Held*, the
transaction amounted to a contract whereby the plaintiff was bound to waive the
debt. The consideration for the contract was the defendant's assumption of the third
party mortgage debts. Further the plaintiff was estopped from withdrawing his
promise after the defendant had relied on it by accepting the conveyance and taking
possession of the house.

BOJTAR v PARKER (1979) 26 OR (2d) 705 (Court of Appeal of Ontario).

EUROPEAN COMMUNITIES

Halsbury's Laws of England (3rd edn.), Supp. Vol. 39A

1110   Articles

The Application of European Community Law in National Courts—Problems,
Pitfalls and Precepts, Joseph M. Steiner: 96 LQR 126.

Article 86—Some Recent Developments, Richard D. Hacker (a review of recent
decisions of the European Court of Justice): 130 NLJ 40.

EEC Directives and Public Bodies, K. F. W. Gumbley: 130 NLJ 1175.

EEC: Social Security for the Migrant Worker, Marilynne A. Morgan: 130 NLJ
731.

Interim Measures and Articles 85 and 86: A Stitch In Time, C. J. Sherliner (a
review of Case 792/79R: *Camera Care v EC Commission* [1980] 1 CMLR 334, para.
1143): 130 NLJ 931.

Reform of the Commission of the European Communities and its Services,
R. M. M. Wallace: 130 NLJ 39.

Tenancies of Immovable Property and the EEC, J. Kodwo Bentil: 124 Sol Jo 523.

1111   Budget

The European Parliament has approved the general budget of the European
Communities for the financial year 1980. The budget sets out the estimated revenue
of the Community, the calculation of the relative share of each member state's
contribution to the budget and details of the authorised expenditure for each of the
Community institutions. (OJ No. L242, 15.9.80.)

1112   The European Parliament has adopted the amending and supplementary budget No.
1 of the European Communities for the financial year 1980, para. 1111. The
supplementary budget sets out the estimated revenue of the Community, the
financing of the budget and a summary of the authorised expenditure for each of the
Community institutions. (OJ No. L364, 31.12.80.)

1113   —— payments to member states

Council Regulation (EEC) 2743/80 (OJ No. L284, 29.10.80) amends Council
Regulation (EEC) 1172/76, 1976 Halsbury's Abridgment para. 1140, which provides
for a financial mechanism consisting of payments from the budget of the Community
to member states in a special economic situation, in respect of certain provisions
relating to the United Kingdom.

1114   Council Regulation (EEC) 2744/80 (OJ No. L284, 29.10.80) establishes supplementary measures in favour of the United Kingdom in addition to the amounts which will be transferred to the United Kingdom in application of Council Regulation (EEC) 1172/76, 1976 Halsbury's Abridgment para. 1140, establishing a financial mechanism, as amended by Council Regulation (EEC) 2743/80, para. 1113, for the years 1980 and 1981.

1115   **Common agricultural policy**

See AGRICULTURE.

1116   **Common commercial policy—state-trading countries—import arrangements**

Council Regulation (EEC) 3286/80 (OJ No. L353, 29.12.80) lays down further common arrangements for imports into the Community of products from state-trading countries.

1117   —— **valuation of goods for customs purposes**

Council Regulation (EEC) 1224/80 (OJ No. L134, 31.5.80) amends Council Regulation (EEC) 803/68 on the valuation of goods for customs purposes. This follows the conclusion of an international agreement, under the General Agreement on tariffs and trade (GATT), concerning the valuation of goods for customs purposes in international trade. The regulation provides a method of determining the customs value of imported goods which is the price paid or payable for the goods when sold for export to the customs territory of the Community, known as the "transaction value" of the goods.

1118   Commission Regulation (EEC) 1495/80 (OJ No. L154, 21.6.80) implements certain provisions of Council Regulation (EEC) 1224/80, arts. 1, 3 and 8, para. 1117, on the valuation of goods for customs purposes.

1119   —— —— **accounting principles**

Commission Regulation (EEC) 1494/80 (OJ No. L154, 21.6.80) provides interpretative notes and generally accepted accounting principles for the purposes of the customs value of goods.

1120   —— —— **particulars to be disclosed on customs value of goods**

Commission Regulation (EEC) 1496/80 (OJ No. L154, 21.6.80) provides for documents to be furnished and particulars to be declared relating to the customs value of goods.

1121   —— —— **transitional provisions**

Commission Regulation (EEC) 1493/80 (OJ No. L154, 21.6.80) extends as a transitional measure the validity of certain regulations based on Council Regulation (EEC) 803/68 on the valuation of goods for customs purposes.

1122   **Common transport policy—inland waterways—statistical returns**

Council Directive (EEC) 80/1119 (OJ No. L339, 15.12.80) introduces provisions relating to statistical returns to be made by member states in respect of carriage of goods by inland waterways.

1123   —— **road transport—safety regulations—grounds for exemption**

In a case concerning a private undertaking which had contracted with a local municipal authority to collect the city's refuse and where the firm had failed to comply with Council Regulation (EEC) 543/69 on the harmonisation of certain road safety provisions, the European Court stated that the exclusion from the need to comply with the rules on hours of work given by art. 4 (4) to "vehicles which are used by other public authorities for public services" applied only to vehicles owned by or under the control of the public authority. The exemption did not extend to vehicles owned by a private enterprise which contracted to carry out work for the public authority.

Case 47/79: STÄDTEREINIGUNG K NEHLSEN KG, BREMEN v FREIE HANSESTADT BREMEN [1980] 2 CMLR 654 (European Court of Justice).

1124   —— —— tachographs—exemption from installation

See para. 2418.

1125   Community legislation—action by individual for failure to act— admissibility

In an action before the European Court against the Council and the Commission a Dutch company sought (i) a declaration under EEC Treaty, art. 175 that the defendant institutions had infringed the Treaty by failing to adopt a measure addressed to the company as it had requested and, (ii) compensation pursuant to art. 215 in respect of damage allegedly sustained as a result of that infringement. The defendant institutions claimed that the application for compensation was inadmissible in so far as it omitted to state the subject matter of the dispute and the grounds on which it was based, contrary to the Rules of Procedure, art. 38 (1). *Held*, where in an action for damages pursuant to art. 178 of the Treaty the legal basis of the Community's liability was disputed, as in the present case, the court would, in the interests of economy, determine the issue of liability as a preliminary question. Accordingly, although the company's application did not comply with the Rules of Procedure, in the circumstance of the case it was not automatically rendered inadmissible for that reason. However, the application would be dismissed since the only measure by which the defendant institutions could have satisfied the company's claim was a regulation, which was not an act which could be addressed to a natural or legal person within the meaning of art. 175.

Case 90/78: GRANARIA BV v EC COUNCIL AND EC COMMISSION [1979] ECR 1081 (European Court of Justice).

1126   —— decision — action for annulment — requirement of direct and individual concern

The minimum price for the sale of frozen beef by national intervention agencies is governed by Council Regulation (EEC) 805/68, as amended, and Commission Regulation (EEC) 2900/77. In 1978 a general notice of invitation to tender for the sale of frozen beef held in stock by an Italian intervention agency was published. A tender by an Italian company was refused on the basis of a Commission decision addressed to member states made under Regulation 2900/77, fixing the minimum selling price for frozen beef. An application for the annulment of the Commission decision was made. *Held*, (i) a Commission decision addressed to member states referring to invitations to tender for the sale of frozen beef held by intervention agencies was of direct and individual concern to all tenderers within the provisions of the EEC Treaty, art. 173. (ii) Article 184 of the Treaty conferred on an individual the right to challenge the validity of an act of a Community institution. The article applied to acts of institutions, which although they were not in the form of a regulation, produced similar effects and therefore could not be challenged under art. 173 by individuals other than by Community institutions and member states. A notice of invitation to tender was a general act determining the rights and obligations of individuals and therefore produced a similar effect to a regulation. Article 184 included, therefore, invitations to tender. (iii) Where an enabling Council regulation provided a procedure aimed at achieving a certain purpose, the adoption by the Commission of an amending regulation inconsistent with the ideas of the original regulation and resulting in benefits becoming available to a class outside those intended was not permitted. The decision would be annulled accordingly.

Case 92/78: SIMMENTHAL SpA v EC COMMISSION [1979] ECR 777, [1980] 1 CMLR 25 (European Court of Justice).

1127 —— directive—non-implementation—justification

In proceedings under the EEC Treaty, art. 169 the Commission claimed that Italy, by failing to implement within the prescribed time Council Directive (EEC) 75/410 on the approximation of the laws of member states relating to continuous totalising weighing machines, had failed to fulfil an obligation under the Treaty. The Italian government explained that the failure was due to political and parliamentary events. *Held*, it was well-established that a member state could not plead provisions, practices or circumstances existing in its internal system in order to justify a failure to comply with obligations and time limits under Community directives. Accordingly, Italy had failed to fulfil an obligation under the Treaty.

Case 93/79: RE WEIGHING MACHINES FOR CONVEYOR BELTS: EC COMMISSION v ITALY [1980] 2 CMLR 647 (European Court of Justice).

1128 —— —— time limit for implementation—effect of inconsistent national law

Council Directives (EEC) 73/173 and 77/728 provide for the approximation of national laws relating to the classification, packaging and labelling of solvents and varnishes respectively. An Italian company affixed to its containers labels conforming to the directives. The Italian government had not implemented the provisions of the directives, although in relation to the latter the time limit for implementation had not expired. Criminal proceedings were instituted against the company since it had not complied with the national legislation which was in some respects more stringent than the directives. A reference was made to the European Court for a preliminary ruling under EEC Treaty, art. 177 on the interpretation and application of the directives. *Held*, (i) after the expiration of the period fixed for the implementation of a directive, a member state could not apply its national law, in so far as it failed to comply with a directive, to a person who had complied with the requirements of the directive. (ii) A member state could not introduce into its national legislation conditions which were different from the directive in question. (iii) Where a directive provided for the harmonisation of measures to ensure the protection of the health of persons and established Community procedures to supervise its enforcement, there could be no recourse to the exemptions contained in EEC Treaty, art. 36. Accordingly, any restrictions on freedom of movement on those grounds had to be carried out in accordance with the procedure established by the directive. (iv) The national law of a member state could be enforced until the expiration of the period fixed for the implementation of a directive. Accordingly, Directive 77/728 could not confer any effect capable of being taken into consideration by the national court.

Case 148/78: PUBBLICO MINISTERO v RATTI [1979] ECR 1629, [1980] 1 CMLR 96 (European Court of Justice).

1129 —— liability of Community in damages

See Case 90/78: *Granaria BV v EC Council and EC Commission*, para. 1125.

1130 —— national law—power of member state to act unilaterally in area within Community competence

In 1977 the United Kingdom adopted, in implementation of certain international obligations, the Fishing Nets (North-East Atlantic) Order 1977, 1977 Halsbury's Abridgment para. 1313. In an action before the European Court pursuant to EEC Treaty, art. 170 France alleged that the United Kingdom had thus failed to fulfil its obligations under the Treaty. France claimed that the order had been adopted unilaterally in an area reserved for the competence of the Community and, further, that it had been brought into force contrary to the requirements of a Council resolution under which, pending the implementation of a common fisheries policy, the adoption of unilateral measures was subject to notification to and the approval of the Commission. *Held*, EEC Treaty, Annex II expressly included fisheries within the sphere of the common agricultural policy and the order in question had therefore been adopted in an area reserved for the competence of the Community. Accordingly, the bringing into force of the order was subject to all the relevant provisions of Community law, namely the particular Council resolution. Further, that resolution extended to any relevant measure emanating from a member state, as opposed to the Community, including measures adopted in compliance with international obligations. The adoption of the order thus constituted a breach by the United Kingdom of its obligations under the Treaty.

Case 141/78: RE FISHING NET MESH SIZES: FRANCE V UNITED KINGDOM [1979] ECR 2923, [1980] 1 CMLR 6 (European Court of Justice).

1131　　　—— —— **power of member state to exclude judicial review**

Council Directive (EEC) 72/159 relates to the provision of grants for agricultural development. A farmer was refused such a grant for work carried out on his land on the ground that the work did not relate exclusively to agricultural development. National law provided that any decision by the Minister relating to such a scheme would be final. The question for the European Court was whether such a provision was contrary to the directive. *Held*, the provisions of the directive made it clear that member states were to implement the measures laid down by the Community and were to determine on the basis of those conditions the extent to which such measures should be concentrated on certain regions. Member states were obliged to establish schemes which satisfied the Community conditions but were authorised to constitute them in accordance with the national law. Further, the directive contained no specific obligations to make judicial remedies available against administrative decisions relating to the grant or refusal of the advantages contemplated by the directive.

Case 152/79: LEE V MINISTER FOR AGRICULTURE [1980] 2 CMLR 682 (European Court of Justice).

1132　　　—— **notice of invitation to tender—status**

See Case 92/78: *Simmenthal SpA v EC Commission*, para. 1126.

1133　　　—— **regulation—action for annulment—requirement of direct and individual concern**

In the course of an earlier dispute relating to the calculation of export refunds fixed in national currency the European Court had held that in order for a monetary co-efficient to be applied in accordance with Commission Regulation (EEC) 1380/75, it was necessary to show that the refunds were fixed in units of account. Commission Regulation (EEC) 1837/78 was subsequently adopted providing that the co-efficient applied to refunds fixed in national currency and was applicable to operations for which customs formalities had been completed by a certain date. Sugar exporters applied under EEC Treaty, art. 173 for the annulment of the regulation on the ground that since it applied retroactively it deprived them of refunds which had already been awarded to them and was accordingly invalid. The Commission challenged the admissibility of the application on the ground that it did not comply with the provisions of art. 173. *Held*, art. 173 provided that a private individual was entitled to challenge a decision addressed to him even if it was in the form of a regulation. Regulations had general application and the purpose of art. 173 was to prevent the Community institutions from being able to bar an individual from instituting proceedings, by implementing legislation in the form of a regulation. The provisions in question were legislative measures and applied to refunds payable to all successful tenderers at a certain date. Accordingly the regulation was not of individual concern to the applicants, and the application would be dismissed..

Case 162/78: WAGNER GmbH V EC COMMISSION [1979] ECR 3467 (European Court of Justice). For earlier proceedings see [1978] ECR 1187, 1978 Halsbury's Abridgment para. 56.

1134   —— —— amending   regulation—powers   of   **Community** institutions

In two cases concerning the validity of Commission Regulation (EEC) 2604/77 imposing monetary compensatory amounts on certain cereals and products therefrom, the European Court of Justice stated that Community institutions were prohibited from amending the rules which enabled traders to protect themselves from the effects of any variations in the provisions providing for the common organisation of the produce market in question without providing transitional measures unless there was an overriding public interest to do so. This did not apply to preventing new rules from applying to the future effects of situations which arose under the earlier provisions in the absence of obligations entered into with public authorities.

Cases 12/78, 84/78: Re Monetary Compensatory Amounts for Durum Wheat: Italy v EC Commission; Tomadini SNC v Amministrazione Delle Finanze Dello Stato [1980] 2 CMLR 573 (European Court of Justice).

1135   —— —— —— requirement of consistency with first regulation

See Case 92/78: *Simmenthal SpA v EC Commission*, para. 1126.

1136   —— —— date of entry into force—retroactivity

A German national was refused permission to plant vines on her land on the ground that the land was unsuitable. During proceedings, Council Regulation (EEC) 1162/76 came into force prohibiting all new planting of vines for three years. She claimed that the regulation was not applicable in the case of an application lodged before its entry into force, particularly since her land was subsequently declared to be suitable. A reference was made to the European Court on the application of the regulation. *Held*, since the provisions expressly stated that no authorisations should be given for new planting "as from the date on which this regulation enters into force" the regulation was immediately applicable. Accordingly, it applied to applications for authorisation of "all new planting" made before its entry into force, irrespective of the suitability of the land, as determined by national law.

The court also considered the question of fundamental human rights in relation to the right to property. It stated that in protecting such rights the constitutional traditions common to the member states had to be considered. Restrictions upon the use of property in many spheres were authorised by the European Convention on Human Rights, Protocol, art. 1, to the extent that they protected the general interest.

Case 44/79: Hauer v Land Rheinland-Pfalz [1980] 3 CMLR 42 (European Court of Justice).

1137   —— —— statement of reasons

In the course of interpreting, under EEC Treaty, art. 177, a Commission regulation, the European Court *held*, that the requirement under art. 190 that a regulation should state the reasons on which it was based was satisfied when the statement of reasons explained in essence the measures which were being adopted; the statement of reasons could not be required to cover specifically all the details of the regulation. Accordingly, since the statement of reasons in the regulation in question set out as a whole the situation which led to its adoption and the general objectives which it sought to attain, the validity of the regulation could not be challenged on that ground.

Case 134/78: Firma E Danhuber v Bundesanstalt für Landwirtschaftliche Marktordnung [1979] ECR 1007 (European Court of Justice).

1138   **Companies—capital duty—basis of assessment**

A Danish limited company was formed by a memorandum of association under which the company's share capital was raised by the transfer of the assets of a commercial partnership. The partnership had previously been carried on by two of the company's founder members, who effected the transfer by way of contribution. The opening balance sheet of the company showed the value of the transferred assets as their written down value, as permitted by Danish law. The national tax authorities subsequently assessed the company to capital duty, as introduced by Council Directive (EEC) 69/335, on the actual value of the assets. The company claimed that, in accordance with art. 5 of the directive, which provides for deductions in respect of liabilities arising from a contribution, a deduction should have been made in respect of any tax which, by virtue of national legislation, might have subsequently become payable on the amount by which the actual value of the assets had been written down. Certain questions on the interpretation of art. 5 were referred to the European Court. *Held*, the objective of the directive was to encourage the free movement of capital within the Community by the harmonisation of national taxes on the raising of capital. The imposition of a uniform capital duty, at a uniform rate, implied that the basis of assessment was to be calculated in each member state in accordance with objective criteria, independent of national legislation. Thus, the duty was expressly payable on the actual value of the assets at the time they were contributed; no deduction could be made in respect of potential tax liabilities on those assets since such liabilities were, by definition, unascertainable at the time the actual value of the assets was to be calculated in order to provide the necessary basis of assessment.

Case 161/78: P. CONRADSEN A/S v MINISTRY FOR FISCAL AFFAIRS [1979] ECR 2221, [1980] 1 CMLR 121 (European Court of Justice).

For the implementation of the directive in the United Kingdom see the Finance Act 1973, ss. 47–50, Sch. 19.

1139   Competition policy—abuse of dominant position—contracts performed in non-member states—effect on trade between member states

A French performing rights society brought an action in France to recover royalties in respect of the public performance of the music for two films produced by the French defendant company and shown in certain non-member states. The music for the films had been composed by two French composers, who were members of the plaintiff society and had assigned to it the exclusive right to authorise or prohibit the public performance of their work anywhere in the world. The defendant company, which had commissioned the music for the films, claimed the copyright in the music and defended the action on the ground that the plaintiff society's condition of membership, namely that its members should execute a general assignment of their rights throughout the whole world for a long period, constituted an abuse of its dominant market position contrary to EEC Treaty, art. 86. The national court stayed the proceedings and referred to the European Court the question whether contracts entered into within the Community between Community nationals but performed in non-member states could affect trade between member states. *Held*, in determining whether the abuse by an undertaking of its dominant position in the Common Market was such as to affect trade between member states it was necessary to consider the consequences of that undertaking's conduct for the effective competitive structure in the common market. To this end there was no reason to distinguish either between production intended for sale within the common market and that intended for export or, with reference to the present case, between the provision of services (such as the management of copyrights) within or outside the common market: such activities could have the effect of partitioning the market, thereby restricting the freedom to provide services and thus affecting trade between member states.

Case 22/79: GREENWICH FILM PRODUCTION v SOCIETE DES AUTEURS, COMPOSITEURS ET EDITEURS DE MUSIQUE [1979] ECR 3275, [1980] 1 CMLR 629 (European Court of Justice). Joined Cases 6 and 7/73: *Institute Chemioterapico Italiano SpA v EC Commission* [1974] ECR 223, ECJ, 1974 Halsbury's Abridgment para. 1330 referred to.

1140   —— concerted practice—prosecution of infringers of copyright

See *British Leyland Motor Corpn Ltd v T I Silencers Ltd*, para. 508.

1141   **—— export prohibition agreement—infringement of Community law—intention**

A German car manufacturing company exported cars to its Belgian subsidiary for distribution in Belgium. Under the standard form distribution agreements entered into by the Belgian company and its dealers, the approved dealers undertook not to resell cars to non-approved dealers; however they remained free to sell to other approved dealers and to consumers throughout the Community. In 1975 the price of cars in Belgium was lower than in other member states, resulting in an increase in re-exports from Belgium, including sales to non-approved dealers. The Belgian company therefore sent circulars to its dealers, reminding them of the terms of their distribution agreements and prohibiting any further sales outside Belgium. The terms of the circulars, which remained in force for five months, were agreed to by the majority of dealers. By a decision addressed to the company and those dealers the Commission found that the circulars constituted an infringement of EEC Treaty, art. 85 (1), intentional on the part of the company. In an action for the annulment of that decision the company contended that the purpose of the circulars was merely to reiterate the terms of the distribution agreements. *Held*, the prohibition on export contained in the circulars exceeded the scope of the selective distribution system authorised by the Commission since no distinction was made between sales to approved and non-approved dealers. The circulars as agreed to by the dealers were prohibited by art. 85 (1) and the company was therefore guilty of an infringement of that provision. Further, by intentionally addressing the circulars to its dealers and requesting them to subscribe to the export prohibition the company had committed that infringement intentionally: it was irrelevant whether the company was aware that in so doing it was infringing art. 85 (1). The application for annulment would be dismissed.

Case 32/78: BMW Belgium SA v EC Commission [1980] 1 CMLR 370 (European Court of Justice).

1142   **—— notification of agreements**

See Case 30/78: *Distillers Co Ltd v EC Commission*, para. 1147.

1143   **—— powers of Commission—power to adopt interim measures**

In proceedings pursuant to EEC Treaty, arts. 85 and 86 the complainant undertaking, whose business was in jeopardy as a result of the alleged infringements, requested the Commission to adopt interim protective measures. The Commission refused, on the grounds that Council Regulation (EEC) No. 17, implementing arts. 85 and 86, only empowered the Commission to make interim recommendations and to adopt final decisions. The question of the extent of the Commission's powers was then referred to the European Court. *Held*, it was clear that in certain circumstances, namely where the practice of an undertaking in competition matters had the effect of injuring the interests of some member states, or of causing damage to other undertakings, or of unacceptably jeopardising the Community's competition policy, there might be a need to adopt interim protective measures. Further, although Regulation 17 conferred no express powers to take such measures, it was essential that the right of the Commission to take a final decision under art. 3 (1) of the regulation should be exercised in the most efficacious manner best suited to the individual circumstances. Accordingly, art. 3 (1) was to be interpreted as including the power to take interim measures to the extent to which they were indispensable in order to avoid the exercise of the right to make decisions from becoming ineffectual or illusory because of the action of certain undertakings. However, the exercise of this power was subject to certain requirements: interim measures were to be taken only in urgent cases to avoid a situation likely to cause serious or irreparable damage to the applicant or which was intolerable for the public interest; the measures taken were to be temporary and conservatory and restricted to the needs of the individual situation; their adoption was subject to the essential safeguards guaranteed to the parties by Regulation 17 and in particular the right to be heard; and the measures were to be adopted in such a form as to be subject to review by the European Court.

In his opinion the Advocate General considered that even by implication Regulation 17 conferred no power on the Commission to adopt interim measures. He expressed the view that such a power could be conferred only by a further act of the Council.

Case 792/79R: CAMERA CARE LTD v EC COMMISSION [1980] ECR 119, [1980] 1 CMLR 334 (European Court of Justice).

For a discussion of this case, see Wide gap separates UK-EEC legal systems, Justinian, Financial Times, 10th March 1980.

1144   —— —— —— practice

See para. 1153.

1145   —— —— power to conduct investigation on undertaking's premises

Information received by the EC Commission indicated that an English company was a party to certain agreements and concerted practices contrary to EEC Treaty, art. 85 (1). The Commission therefore adopted a decision under Council Regulation (EEC) No. 17, art. 14 (3) requiring the company to submit to an investigation on its premises. The decision provided that it was to be notified by being personally handed over to a company officer immediately before the investigation was to begin. The investigation was duly carried out. The company brought proceedings for the annulment of the decision and for the return of all copies of documents and notes taken during the investigation on the grounds, inter alia, (i) that the decision infringed art. 14 in that the Commission had not first attempted to carry out the investigation on the basis of a written authorisation under art. 14 (1); (ii) that by failing to give the company advance notification of the decision the Commission had infringed certain fundamental rights of the company; and (iii) that the decision did not contain a sufficient statement of reasons. *Held*, (i) there was nothing in art. 14 which indicated that a decision could be adopted under art. 14 (3) only if the procedure under art. 14 (1) had first been followed: the two methods of investigation were alternative, to be chosen by the Commission in the light of individual circumstances. (ii) Although fundamental rights were protected within the Community legal system, none had been infringed in the present case. (iii) The decision fully complied with the requirements of Regulation 17 as to its statement of reasons in so far as it stated the purpose and subject matter of the investigation and the date and place where it would be carried out. The application would therefore be dismissed.

Case 136/79: NATIONAL PANASONIC (UK) LTD v EC COMMISSION [1980] 3 CMLR 169 (European Court of Justice).

1146   —— restrictive trade agreements—de minimis rule—application

See Case 30/78: *Distillers Co Ltd v EC Commission*, para. 1147.

1147   —— —— exemption—requirement of notification

In an action before the European Court for the annulment of a decision adopted by the EC Commission pursuant to EEC Treaty, art. 85 the applicant company, a large producer of spirits, claimed, inter alia, that the agreements in question, although prohibited under art. 85 (1), should have been granted exemption under art. 85 (3). Although the agreements had been the subject of several communications between the Commission and the applicant they had never been formally notified under Council Regulation (EEC) No. 17 for the purpose of seeking exemption. The applicant further contended that in respect of one product its market share in the member states other than the United Kingdom was so small in relation to the sales of other spirits as to preclude the application of art. 85 (1). *Held*, (i) under Regulation No. 17, arts. 4 and 6 notification to the Commission of the agreements in respect of which exemption was sought was clearly a prerequisite of a decision being taken under art. 85 (3) of the Treaty. (ii) Although an agreement which affected the market only to an insignificant extent could thus escape the prohibition under art.

85 (1), this did not apply in the case of an agreement relating to a product of a large undertaking which was responsible for the entire production of that product. Both of the applicant's claims were therefore unfounded and the action would be dismissed.

Case 30/78: DISTILLERS CO LTD V EC COMMISSION [1980] 3 CMLR 121 (European Court of Justice).

1148   Contractual obligations—convention

The European Convention on the law applicable to contractual obligations was opened for signature on 19th June 1980. The Convention establishes uniform rules concerning the law applicable to contractual obligations in any situation involving a choice between the laws of different countries. (See OJ No. L266, 9.10.80.)

For a report on the Convention see also OJ No. C282 (31.10.80).

1149   Court of Auditors—annual report

The European Court of Auditors has published its annual report concerning the financial year 1979. The report covers the 1979 accounts for all bodies for which the Court is responsible for audit, except for the financial operation of the ECSC, and is divided into two parts: Part I includes comments arising from the accounts of the general budget of the Communities; Part II concerns the four European Development Funds. Further, Annex I to the report contains a statistical survey of financial information relating to the general budget of the Communities and to the European Development Funds. (See OJ No. C342, 31.12.80.)

1150   Customs duties—evasion of payment of duties—Community's investigative powers for enforcing collection of Community revenue

The Commission brought an action against a member state claiming culpable non-cooperation by that member state in refusing to obtain and communicate to the Commission information held by a national court as part of a file in a criminal investigation. The information, which was required by the Commission as part of its supervision of the proper payment of Community revenue by member states under Council Regulation (EEC) 2/71, in that it suspected fraudulent inter-state trading transactions affecting the payment of agricultural levies, was privileged under national law and non-communicable to outside parties. *Held*, the Commission was entitled to exercise its supervisory powers, which included investigation, relating to the collection and accounting of Community revenue, due from a member state in accordance with Regulation 2/71, as soon as the relevant monthly statement of account had been made by the member state. The power, however, of the Commission to be associated with such an investigation did not give the Commission any direct powers of investigation nor did it alter the power of a member state to intervene in a criminal investigation. National rules, therefore, which preserved the secrecy of information during criminal proceedings, even vis-à-vis the national administrative authorities, continued to operate against disclosure of such information in matters concerning Regulation 2/71.

Case 267/78: RE CRIMINAL PROCEDURE: EC COMMISSION V ITALY [1980] ECR 31, [1980] 3 CMLR 306 (European Court of Justice).

1151   European Assembly—United Kingdom representatives—pensions

See para. 2115.

1152   European Coal and Steel Community—quotas—iron and steel

Commission Decision (EEC) 2794/80 (OJ No. L291, 31.10.80) establishes a system of steel production quotas for undertakings in the iron and steel industry.

1153   European Commission—powers—competition policy—power to adopt interim measures—practice

The EC Commission has issued a Practice Note ([1980] 2 CMLR 369) relating to its power under Council Regulation No. 17, art. 3, to adopt interim measures. This follows the judgment of the European Court in Case 792/79R: *Camera Care Ltd v EC Commission*, para. 1143, in which the Court held that the Commission had the power to order, by formal decision, interim measures pending a final decision under art. 3 requiring an undertaking to terminate an infringement of EEC Treaty, arts. 85 or 86.

In its judgment that Court gave some guidance as to the exercise of this power and the Practice Note states that the Commission will act strictly in accordance with those principles. In particular, the Commission will not consider an application for interim measures unless proceedings have already commenced under Regulation No. 17 or the application is accompanied by a formal complaint; unreasonable delay may also be a ground for refusing an application. Further, there must appear to be a prima facie case of violation of arts. 85 or 86 before the application will be granted. However, any decision to grant or refuse interim measures will not affect the Commission's final decision as to whether there has been a violation of arts. 85 or 86. Where the Commission does order interim measures, in whatever form it considers appropriate, they may be reviewed either on the application of one of the parties or on the initiative of the Commission, should circumstances change. In appropriate cases the Commission may require the applicant to provide a suitable guarantee to indemnify the party subject to the interim decision, in the event of a final decision against the applicant, for any loss arising as a result of the interim measures.

The Commission will in due course be guided but not bound by its own decisions in similar cases.

1154   —— —— ——power to conduct investigation on undertaking's premises

See Case 136/79: *National Panasonic (UK) Ltd v EC Commission*, para. 1145.

1155   —— ——customs duties—investigative powers for enforcing collection of Community revenue

See Case 267/78: *Re Criminal Procedure: EC Commission v Italy*, para. 1150.

1156   European Court of Justice—procedure—application for compensation—form of application

See Case 90/78: *Granaria BV v EC Council and EC Commission*, para. 1125.

1157   —— reference by national court—discretion to refer

See *British Leyland Motor Corpn v T I Silencers Ltd*, para. 2210.

1158   —— ——jurisdiction

In a case concerning various national measures freezing agricultural prices, questions arose as to (i) the jurisdiction of the European Court in references for a preliminary ruling, and (ii) the compatibility of such national measures with Community provisions establishing a common organisation of markets in certain products. *Held*, (i) although, within the framework of proceedings brought under EEC Treaty, art. 177, it was not for the Court to give a ruling on the compatibility of rules of internal law with provisions of Community law, the Court was competent to supply a national court with any criteria of interpretation coming within Community law, enabling that court to determine whether such rules were compatible with Community measures. (ii) In sectors covered by a common organisation of the market, and where that organisation was based on a common price system, member states could no longer take action, through national provisions adopted unilaterally, affecting the machinery of price formation as established under the common organisation of the market.   Provision, however, of a Community agricultural regulation which introduced a price system applicable at the production and wholesale stages left member states free to take appropriate measures relating to price formation at the retail and consumption stages, on condition that they did not jeopardize the aims or functioning of the common organisation of the market in question.

Joined Cases 95 and 96/79: Procureur du Roi v Kefer and Delmelle [1980] ECR 103 (European Court of Justice).

1159   —— —— **pleadings**

See *Reinold Hagen v Fratelli D. & G. Moretti SNC*, para. 541.

1160   —— —— **public payments wrongly made—whether matter solely for national court**

In a case concerning a Dutch trader who dispatched to Dutch ships cruising in waters off Bermuda two consignments of frozen meat, in respect of which he had been mistakenly granted an export refund, as provided for by Council Regulations (EEC) 441/69 and 1957/69, and where on discovering their mistake the Dutch authorities demanded repayment of the export refund, the European Court *held*, inter alia, that the taxes payable to and the payments made from the Community budget were to be applied uniformly for all persons who met the conditions laid down in Community legislation for such payments.   That implied that there was to be no discrimination in respect of the procedural and substantive conditions on which traders and member states might claim their entitlements, including repayment of payments wrongly made.   Disputes in connection with the reimbursement of amounts collected for the Community were a matter for the national courts and were to be settled by them under national law in so far as no provisions of Community law were relevant.   Where there were such relevant Community provisions it was for the national courts to provide the legal protection following from their direct effect both where they created obligations for and gave rights to the citizen.   It was for the national legal system to determine the procedures for judicial proceedings to protect these rights, and they were to be as favourable as similar procedures concerning internal matters.

Case 265/78: H Ferwerda BV v Produktschap voor vee en Vlees [1980] 3 CMLR 737 (European Court of Justice).

1161   —— —— **when Court of Appeal is court of final appeal**

See *Reinold Hagen v Fratelli D. & G. Moretti SNC*, para. 541.

1162   —— **reference for preliminary ruling—insufficient facts on which questions could be drafted**

See *Church of Scientology of California v Comrs of Customs and Excise*, para. 2184.

1163   **Free movement of capital—capital duty—basis of assessment**

See Case 161/78: *P. Conradsen A/S v Ministry for Fiscal Affairs*, para. 1138.

1164   **Free movement of goods—customs duties—charges of equivalent effect—veterinary and public health inspections**

See Case 251/78: *Denkavit Futtermittel GmbH v Minister für Ernährung, Landwirtschaft und Forsten des Landes Nordrhein-Westfalen*, para. 1170.

1165   —— **ECSC unified tariff**

See para. 747.

1166   —— harmonisation of national provisions—Commission guidelines

The Commission has issued a communication concerning the consequences of the judgment given by the European Court in Case 120/78: *Rewe-Zentral AG v Bundesmonopolverwaltung für Branntwein* [1979] 3 CMLR 494, 1979 Halsbury's Abridgment para. 1214. The European Court, in defining the barriers to free trade prohibited by the EEC Treaty, arts. 30 et seq, gave the Commission some interpretative guidance enabling it to monitor more strictly the application of the Treaty rules on the free movement of goods. As a result the Commission has drawn certain conclusions in terms of policy and has set out a number of guidelines dealing with the matter. Accordingly, the Commission's work of harmonisation in this area will be directed mainly at national laws which have an impact on the functioning of the Common Market in so far as they give rise to barriers to trade but which are valid under the Treaty in accordance with the criteria laid down by the European Court. (See OJ No. C256, 3.10.80.)

1167   —— quantitative restrictions—copyright—validity of national rights under Community law

See *British Leyland Motor Corpn Ltd v T I Silencers Ltd*, para. 508.

1168   —— —— exemption on ground of public morality

In English criminal proceedings the appellants were convicted of being knowingly concerned in the fraudulent evasion of the prohibition of the importation of indecent or obscene material contrary to the Customs Consolidation Act 1876, s. 42 and the Customs and Excise Act 1952, s. 304. The material was imported from Holland but was of Danish origin. On appeal the appellants contended that the prohibition imposed by s. 42 of the 1876 Act was contrary to the EEC Treaty, art. 30, which prohibits quantitative restrictions on imports, and that s. 42 was therefore invalid. Their appeal was dismissed and on further appeal the House of Lords stayed the proceedings and referred to the European Court certain questions on the interpretation of arts. 30 and 36. Article 36 provides that prohibitions on imports may be justified on the ground, inter alia, of public morality. *Held*, the prohibition imposed by s. 42 constituted a quantitative restriction within art. 30. However, the effect of art. 36 was to empower a member state to determine, in accordance with its own scale of values, the requirements of public morality in its own territory and to impose prohibitions on imports justified on that ground; the fact that certain differences existed between the relevant domestic laws enforced in the different constitutional parts of a member state, as was the case in the United Kingdom, did not preclude that state from applying a unitary concept in regard to prohibitions imposed on imports. Further, despite those differences and the fact that the domestic laws contained certain, limited, exceptions, it was clear that the purpose and effect of the national legislation was that there was no lawful trade in indecent or obscene articles in the United Kingdom. Thus the prohibition imposed by s. 42 could not be regarded as a means of arbitrary discrimination or a disguised restriction on trade contrary to art. 36, since the purpose of that provision was to prevent restrictions, purported to be justified on one of the grounds defined in that article, from being used in such a way as to discriminate against goods originating in other member states or indirectly to protect certain national products.

Case 34/79: R v HENN AND DARBY [1980] 1 CMLR 246 (European Court of Justice).

Customs and Excise Act 1952, s. 304 now Customs and Excise Management Act 1979, s. 170.

For the proceedings in which the reference was made see [1979] 2 CMLR 495, 1979 Halsbury's Abridgment para. 1202.

For subsequent proceedings in the House of Lords see [1980] 2 All ER 166, para. 768.

1169   —— —— measures of equivalent effect—national price freeze

See Case 5/79: *Procureur Général v Buys*, para. 63.

1170   —— —— —— veterinary and public health inspections

German measures regulating the importation of feeding stuffs containing products of animal origin provided that such feeding stuffs could only be imported if a certificate from the competent authorities in the exporting country was produced confirming that the goods had undergone a process to destroy certain bacteria, and further, on importation the goods were subject to a fresh inspection by veterinary experts of the importing country. A trader who imported feeding stuffs into Germany contrary to these measures questioned their compatibility with EEC Treaty, arts. 30 and 36 concerning free movement of goods between member states, in particular the prohibition of measures having an effect equivalent to quantitative restrictions. *Held*, the concept of measures having an effect equivalent to quantitative restrictions, within the meaning of art. 30, applied to systematic veterinary and public health inspections carried out on intra-Community frontiers and also to obligations imposed on a trader to apply to be exempted from such domestic measures which were in themselves quantitative restrictions having equivalent effect. The measures in question fell within the prohibition under art. 30 unless they fell within the exception provided for in art. 36. Article 36 was not designed to reserve certain matters to the exclusive jurisdiction of member states. It only permitted national laws to derogate from the principle of free movement of goods to the extent to which such derogation was justified for the attainment of the objectives referred to in that article.

The Court pointed out that, in applying art. 100, on the approximation of laws within member states, Community directives which provided for the harmonisation of measures necessary to guarantee the protection of animal and human health, and which established procedures to check that they were observed, recourse to art. 36 was no longer justified and the appropriate checks had to be carried out and the protective measures adopted within the framework outlined by the harmonising directives.

Case 251/78: DENKAVIT FUTTERMITTEL GmbH v MINISTER FÜR ERNÄHRUNG, LANDWIRTSCHAFT UND FORSTEN DES LANDES NORDRHEIN-WESTFALEN [1979] ECR 3369, [1980] 3 CMLR 513 (European Court of Justice).

1171   —— —— —— prohibition on distillation for imported product

French legislation prohibited the distillation of imported raw material, with the exception of fresh fruit, other than apples, pears or grapes. The provisions only applied to imported raw material which was suitable for the purposes of the state monopoly in ethyl alcohol. However it did not apply to the national product which was reserved to the monopoly. A French distillery imported from Italy oranges steeped in alcohol which originated in a third country, but were prohibited from distilling them. In proceedings before the national court, it was held that the oranges in question were not fresh fruit and therefore fell within the prohibition on distillation. The court however stayed the proceedings, and referred questions to the European Court on the interpretation and application of EEC Treaty, arts. 10, 30 and 37. The measures provided, respectively, for free circulation of goods between member states of products coming from third countries, the abolition of quantitative restrictions on imports and the adjustment of commercial state monopolies to end discrimination with regard to the marketing of goods. *Held*, obstacles to intra-Community trade constituted measures which had an effect equivalent to quantitative restrictions unless those provisions were applied without discrimination to both imported and national products. Accordingly, the national provisions which prohibited the distillation of raw materials coming from another member state where they were in free circulation, when they did not apply to the national product, constituted a measure having an effect equivalent to a quantitative restriction within arts. 10 and 30. Furthermore, they were discriminatory with regard to the conditions of procuring and marketing the goods within art. 37. There were no grounds for drawing a distinction between the imported and the national products.

Case 119/78: SA DES GRANDES DISTILLERIES PEUREUX v DIRECTEUR DES SERVICES FISCAUX DE LA HAUTE-SAÔNE ET DU TERRITOIRE DE BELFORT [1979] ECR 975, [1980] 3 CMLR 337 (European Court of Justice).

1172   —— state aids—prohibition of discrimination

See Case 91/78: *Hansen GmbH & Co v Hauptzollamt Flensburg*, para. 1173.

1173   —— state monopolies—exercise of exclusive rights—prohibition of discrimination

A German company marketed in Germany spirits imported from other member states. Under the provisions of the relevant national legislation, tax was levied on both home produced and imported spirits. The company instituted proceedings in Germany against the national tax authorities contending that the sole effect of the system was that the burden of the subsidies granted by the state monopoly, in favour of domestically produced spirits, was borne by imported spirits. Such provisions were alleged to be contrary to the EEC Treaty, art. 37. Article 37 provides that member states are not to introduce any new measures relating to state monopolies which are discriminatory as between nationals of member states concerning the conditions under which goods are marketed, or which restrict the scope of provisions concerning the free movement of goods. The national court stayed the proceedings and referred certain questions on the interpretation of art. 37 and its relationship with arts. 92 and 93 relating to state aids to the European Court of Justice. *Held*, state measures, inherent in the exercise by a state monopoly, of a commercial character, of its exclusive right, were to be considered in the light of the requirements of art. 37 even where those measures concerned state aids as authorised by arts. 92 and 93. It was incompatible with art. 37 for a state monopoly to market a subsidised product at a low resale price, compared to the price of a similar product imported from other member states. Further, art. 37 conferred directly enforceable rights which national courts were to protect, in particular where individuals suffered financial consequences of such discrimination.

Case 91/78: HANSEN GmbH & CO v HAUPTZOLLAMT FLENSBURG [1980] I CMLR 162 (European Court of Justice).

1174   —— —— internal taxation—imported product unaffected—application of principle of non-discrimination

See Case 86/78: *SA des Grandes Distilleries Peureux v Directeur des Services Fiscaux de la Haute-Saône et du Territoire de Belfort*, para. 1209.

1175   Free movement of persons—deportation order—right of appeal

A French national, who was legally employed in Belgium, was suspected of being a prostitute and was threatened with expulsion from that country on refusal of a residence permit. She subsequently lodged an appeal with the Belgian authorities and questions arose on the interpretation of Council Directive (EEC) 64/221, arts. 8 and 9, on the co-ordination of special measures concerning the movement and residence of foreign nationals which are justified on grounds of public policy, security or health. *Held*, the directive imposed on member states the obligation to provide, for persons covered by the directive, protection by the courts which was not less than that which they made available to their own nationals as regards appeals against acts of the administration, including, if appropriate, suspension of the acts appealed against. There was however no obligation for member states to allow an alien to remain in their territory for the duration of the proceedings, so long as he was able to obtain a fair hearing and present his defence in full.

Case 98/79: PECASTAING v THE BELGIAN STATE [1980] 3 CMLR 685 (European Court of Justice).

1176   —— —— validity

In 1974 an Italian national, resident and employed in England, was sentenced to imprisonment and at the same time a recommendation for deportation was made. In 1978, on his release from prison, a deportation order was made. He applied for judicial review to quash the deportation order on the ground that Council Directive (EEC) 64/221, art. 9 had not been complied with. Under art. 9 a decision to expel a national of another member state is not to be taken until an opinion has been obtained from a competent authority of the host country. Questions arose as to the interpretation and effect of art. 9 and were referred to the European Court. *Held*, the directive conferred on individuals, rights which were enforceable by them in the national courts of member states. The phrase "competent authority" referred to any public authority independent of the administrative authority called upon to adopt one of the measures referred to by the directive and a recommendation for deportation made by a criminal court at the time of conviction under national legislation constituted an "opinion" within the meaning of the directive provided that all other conditions of the directive were met. However, a lapse of time amounting to several years between the recommendation for deportation and the decision by the administration to deport deprived the recommendation of its status as an "opinion" under the directive.

Case 131/79: R v SECRETARY OF STATE FOR HOME AFFAIRS, EX PARTE SANTILLO [1980] 2 CMLR 308 (European Court of Justice).

For further proceedings in the Court of Appeal, see para. 1507.

1177   —— entry by EEC national—limited leave to enter—compatibility with Community provisions

A Dutch national, who entered the United Kingdom with permission to stay for six months, was charged with knowingly remaining in the country after the expiry of the permitted period. He claimed that the initial grant of six months' leave to enter the United Kingdom and the requirement to extend it were inconsistent with the rights conferred on nationals of member states as provided by EEC Treaty, arts. 7 and 48 and Council Directive (EEC) 68/630. On a reference to the European Court for an interpretation of the words "entry visa or equivalent document" contained in art. 3 (2) of the directive, which prohibits member states from demanding such documents from Community workers, *held*, this provision covered any formality for the purpose of granting leave to enter the territory of a member state which was coupled with a passport or identity card check at the frontier, irrespective of the place or time at which the leave was granted, and of the form in which it was granted. Restrictions on the free movement of persons were only justified on the grounds of public policy, public security or public health in accordance with EEC Treaty, art. 48. Those restrictions did not constitute a condition precedent to the acquisition of the right to enter and reside in the United Kingdom, but merely provided the possibility of imposing restrictions on the exercise of a right to enter derived directly from the EEC Treaty. Accordingly, the grant of limited leave to enter and the requirement to extend it were incompatible with the Community provisions as being a prohibited "entry visa" under art. 3 (2).

Case 157/79: R v PIECK [1980] 3 CMLR 220 (European Court of Justice).

1178   —— extradition—agreement between member states

See para. 1253.

1179   —— prevention of entry into United Kingdom under national immigration rules—compatibility with Community provisions

See *Nijssen v Immigration Officer, London (Heathrow) Airport*, para. 1515.

1180   —— right of establishment—discriminatory nature of national legislation—validity

In a case where Italian legislation restricted the functions of customs agents to approved and registered agents who were required to have Italian nationality and residence within the customs district in which they acted, the Court of Justice stated that such legislation did not constitute measures equivalent to quantitative restrictions under EEC Treaty, arts. 30 and 34, but that the nationality requirement infringed art. 52 on the right of establishment. Furthermore, the retention on the statute book of a national legislative provision which, when read in terms of national law alone, required or permitted conduct which was contrary to Community law was, in itself, a violation of that Community law, even if all concerned recognised the priority of the Community law and applied that priority.

Case 159/78: Re Customs Agents: EC Commission v Italy [1980] 3 CMLR 446 (European Court of Justice).

1181 —— serving member of Armed Forces—whether "worker" within Treaty provisions

See *Re Narinder Singh Virdee*, para. 2434.

1182 Human rights—European Convention on Human Rights—status in relation to Community law

See *Surjit Kaur v The Lord Advocate*, para. 1469.

1183 Jurisdiction of national courts—convention jurisdiction—contract

In proceedings in Germany the plaintiff, domiciled in Germany, sought repayment of a loan made to the defendant, domiciled in Italy. In bringing the action in Germany the plaintiff relied upon an oral agreement with the defendant, effective under German law, under which Munich was fixed as the place of repayment. The court hearing the action stayed the proceedings and referred to the European Court the question whether such an informal agreement was capable of founding jurisdiction under the Convention on Jurisdiction and the Enforcement of Judgments 1968. *Held*, art. 2 of the Convention laid down the general rule of jurisdiction, that a person domiciled in a contracting state was to be sued in the courts of that state. Article 5, which provided that in disputes relating to a contract a defendant domiciled in a contracting state could be sued in the courts for the place of performance of the obligation in question, constituted an exception to the general rule, at the option of the plaintiff, justified by the existence of a direct link between the dispute and the court adjudicating on it. By contrast, art. 17, which provided for the exclusive jurisdiction of a court pursuant to the agreement of the parties in the prescribed form, put aside both art. 2 and art. 5 and dispensed with any objective connection between the legal relationship in dispute and the court designated. Thus, jurisdiction under art. 5 was distinct from that under art. 17 and was not subject to the same requirements of form.

Case 56/79: Zelger v Salinitri [1980] ECR 89, [1980] 2 CMLR 635 (European Court of Justice).

1184 —— —— —— breach of contract prior to convention—applicability of convention

In 1971 a French worker, resident in France, was engaged by a German company under a written contract to work independently in Germany. A clause in the contract provided that the German courts would assume jurisdiction over any disputes between the parties. The contract was terminated in the same year and in 1973 the worker commenced proceedings in a French court to recover arrears of pay. The court assumed jurisdiction on the ground that under French law clauses contained in contracts of employment conferring territorial jurisdiction were void. On the company's appeal the proceedings were stayed pending the ruling of the European Court on the interpretation of the Convention on Jurisdiction and the Enforcement of Judgments 1968 arts. 17 and 54 and its effect on clauses in contracts of employment conferring jurisdiction on national courts. The Convention came into force in 1973. *Held*, art. 17 provided that parties could agree that the courts of contracting states could have exclusive jurisdiction. Article 54 provided that the Convention applied only to legal proceedings instituted and to documents drawn up after its entry into force. Although the contract was broken before the entry into force of the Convention the proceedings were commenced afterwards. The provisions did not affect the rules of substantive law but sought to determine the jurisdiction of the courts in the intra-community legal order with regard to civil matters which did not exclude contracts of employment. Accordingly, the choice of jurisdiction clause was only relevant from the date when judicial proceedings were commenced and the national procedural rules were subject to the provisions of the Convention.

Case 25/79: SANICENTRAL GmbH v COLLIN [1979] ECR 3423, [1980] 2 CMLR 164 (European Court of Justice).

1185 —— —— **divorce proceedings**

In the course of divorce proceedings instituted in France, the French court ordered the husband to pay to the wife, pending divorce, a monthly maintenance allowance. On an application made by the wife a German court made an order for the enforcement of the maintenance order. This decision was subsequently set aside on the ground that the decision of the French court was an intervening measure granted during divorce proceedings and was accordingly concerned with litigation relating to the status of persons which fell outside the scope of the Convention on Jurisdiction and the Enforcement of Judgments 1968 by virtue of the provisions of art. 1 (2). On the question of the applicability of the 1968 Convention, *held*, although according to art. 1 the 1968 Convention extends to "civil and commercial matters" excluding those concerned with status or legal capacity of natural persons, and rights in property arising out of a matrimonial relationship, maintenance obligations fell within the concept of "civil matters". The Convention therefore applied to financial arrangements between spouses, before and after the divorce, which were fixed on the basis of their respective needs and resources so long as they were not related to property.

Case 120/79: DE CAVEL v DE CAVEL [1980] 3 CMLR 1 (European Court of Justice).

For earlier proceedings see Case 143/78: *De Cavel v De Cavel* [1979] 2 CMLR 547, ECJ, 1979 Halsbury's Abridgment para. 1230.

1186 **Liability of Community—non-contractual liability—compensation for damage arising from legislative measures introducing a production levy**

EEC Treaty, art. 215 provides that in the case of non-contractual liability the Community will in accordance with general principles common to the laws of member states, make good any damage caused by its institutions or by its servants, in the performance of their duties.

In a number of cases the applicants, producers of certain sweeteners, claimed that the European Community, represented by the Council and the Commission, should be ordered to pay to them compensation under EEC Treaty, art. 215 for the damage which they suffered as a result of the imposition of a production levy on certain sweeteners in pursuance of Council Regulation (EEC) 1111/77. The question arose as to the extent of the Community's liability to pay such damages under art. 215. *Held*, a finding that a legal situation resulting from a legislative measure by the Community involving economic policy was illegal, was insufficient by itself to involve the Community in liability under art. 215. The measure had to be initiated by a serious breach of a superior rule of law for the protection of the individual. In the context of Community legislation in which one of the chief features was the exercise of a wide discretion essential in the implementation of the common agricultural policy, the liability of the Community only arose in exceptional circumstances where the institution concerned had manifestly disregarded the limits on the exercise of its powers. Even though an action for damages under art. 215 constituted an independent action, it was nevertheless to be assessed having regard to the whole system of the legal protection of the individual set up by the Treaty.

Joined Cases 116 and 124/77: GR AMYLUM NV AND TUNNEL REFINERIES LTD V EC COUNCIL AND EC COMMISSION [1979] ECR 3497 (European Court of Justice); Case 143/77: KONINKLIJKE SCHOLTEN HONIG NV v EC COUNCIL AND EC COMMISSION [1979] ECR 3583 (European Court of Justice).

For earlier proceedings see Joined Cases 103 and 145/77: *Royal Scholten–Honig (Holdings) Ltd v Intervention Board for Agricultural Produce* [1978] ECR 2037, ECJ, 1979 Halsbury's Abridgment para. 61.

1187   —— —— compensation for damage arising from unlawful abolition of refunds

The European Court has held that there was an infringement of the prohibition of discrimination contained in EEC Treaty, art. 40 (3) where after a long period of equal treatment the refund for maize groats and meal used in brewing and those for quellmehl for breadmaking were abolished, while those for pre-gelatinised starch and maize starch were retained.

By Council Regulation (EEC) 1125/78 the refunds were reintroduced. Subsequently several applications were made by producers who claimed that the Community was liable to compensate them for loss suffered as a result of the absence of refunds, under EEC Treaty, art. 215 which provides that in the case of non-contractual liability the Community shall make good any damage caused by its institutions or its servants in the performance of their duties. *Held*, the prohibition of discrimination in the common organisation of the agricultural market was intended to protect the interests of the individual. In the present case, the disregard of that principle affected a limited and clearly defined group of commercial operators and the damage extended beyond the bounds of the economic risks inherent in the activities of the sector concerned. Since equality of treatment had been ended without sufficient justification, it was a manifest disregard of the limits of the Council's discretionary powers in relation to the common agricultural policy. Accordingly, the Community would be ordered to pay the producers the amounts equivalent to the production refunds which they would have been entitled to receive before their abolition.

Case 238/78: IREKS-ARKADY GmbH v EC COUNCIL AND EC COMMISSION; Joined Cases 261 and 262/78: INTERQUELL STÄRKE-CHEMIE GmbH KG & CO KG AND DIAMALT AG v EC COUNCIL AND EC COMMISSION; Joined Cases 241, 242 and 245–250/78: DGV, DEUTSCHE GETREIDEVERWERTUNG UND RHEINISCHE KRAFTFUTTER-WERKE GmbH v EC COUNCIL AND EC COMMISSION; Joined Cases 64, 113/76, 167, 239/78, 27, 28 and 45/79: P DUMORTIER FRERES SA v EC COUNCIL [1979] ECR 2955, 3045, 3017, 3091 (European Court of Justice).

1188   —— —— conversion rate for sterling—comparison with member states

A United Kingdom cattle breeder sought compensation under EEC Treaty, art. 215 for the loss which he allegedly had suffered as a result of Council Regulation (EEC) 2498/74 which prescribed the conversion rates of currencies for the purposes of the common agricultural policy. He contended that because the regulation fixed the representative rates in the United Kingdom at a lower rate than in Ireland (which used the same monetary system at that time) the prohibition of discrimination contained in EEC Treaty, art. 40 (3) had been infringed. *Held*, art. 215 provided that in the case of non-contractual liability the Community was to make good any damage caused by its institutions or its servants in the performance of their duties. Different price levels in different member states for agricultural produce under the common organisation of the agricultural markets could not in themselves result in damage for the purposes of an action for damages under art. 215. Those prices, even when combined with the intervention system of the common agricultural policy, did not constitute values which could be used as a basis for comparison with prices actually obtained by a producer on the market for the purpose of demonstrating that certain damage had been caused.

Case 49/79: POOL v EC COUNCIL [1980] 3 CMLR 279 (European Court of Justice).

1189   **Monetary Committee—report**

The Council and Commission have adopted the twenty-first report on the activities of the Monetary Committee which gives an account of the Committee's activities during the course of 1979. The report details the principal matters on which the Committee concentrated including: (i) surveillance of the functioning of the European Monetary System (EMS), (ii) the improvement in the co-ordination of economic policies in member states, and (iii) examination of the developments toward the convergence of policies in each member state with particular reference to monetary and exchange rate policies. (See OJ No. C166, 7.7.80.)

1190   Regional development measures—hydro-electric power and alternative energy sources

Council Regulation (EEC) 2618/80 (OJ No. L271, 15.10.80) institutes a specific Community regional development measure which contributes to improving security of energy supply in certain Community regions by way of improved use of new techniques for hydro-electric power and alternative energy sources.

1191   —— Ireland and Northern Ireland

Council Regulation (EEC) 2619/80 (OJ No. L271, 15.10.80) institutes a specific Community regional development measure which contributes to the improvement of the economic and social situation of the border areas of Ireland and Northern Ireland.

1192   —— shipbuilding industry

Council Regulation (EEC) 2617/80 (OJ No. L271, 15.10.80) institutes a specific Community regional development measure which contributes to overcoming constraints on the development of new economic activities in certain zones adversely affected by the restructuring of the shipbuilding industry.

1193   —— steel industry

Council Regulation (EEC) 2616/80 (OJ No. L271, 15.10.80) institutes a specific Community regional development measure which contributes to overcoming constraints on the development of new economic activities in certain zones adversely affected by the restructuring of the steel industry.

1194   Social policy—harmonisation of laws—employee protection

Council Directive (EEC) 80/987 (OJ No. L283, 28.10.80) provides for the approximation of the laws of the member states relating to the protection of employees in the event of the insolvency of their employer.

1195   —— health and safety at work

Council Directive (EEC) 80/1107 (OJ No. L327, 3.12.80) provides for the harmonisation of provisions and measures regarding the protection of workers with respect to chemical, physical and biological agents.

1196   —— principle of equal pay—application to employment in succession

The Court of Appeal referred to the European Court certain questions on the scope of EEC Treaty, art. 119, which lays down the principle that men and women should receive equal pay for equal work, and its application to the situation where a woman is employed in succession to a man. *Held*, the application of the principle contained in art. 119 depended on whether work done by a man and a woman respectively was "equal work" a qualitative concept which could not be restricted by a requirement of contemporaneity. Article 119, which was directly applicable in all member states, therefore applied to a situation such as that referred to by the Court of Appeal.

Case 129/79: MACARTHYS LTD v SMITH [1980] 2 CMLR 205 (European Court of Justice). Case 43/75: *Defrenne v Sabena* [1976] ECR 445, ECJ, 1976 Halsbury's Abridgment para. 1111 referred to.

For the proceedings in which the reference was made see [1979] 3 All ER 325, 1979 Halsbury's Abridgment para. 2501. For the subsequent decision of the Court of Appeal see [1980] 3 All ER 111, para. 2580.

1197   Social security—legislation—codification

The EC Council has published codified versions of Council Regulation (EEC)
1408/71 on the application of social security schemes to employed persons and their
families moving within the Community, and Council Regulation (EEC) 574/72 on
the implementation of Regulation 1408/71. (OJ No. C138, 9.6.80).

1198   The EC Council has updated the Declarations of the Member States provided for in
Council Regulation (EEC) 1408/71 on the application of social security schemes to
employed persons and their families moving within the Community. (OJ No. C139,
9.6.80.)

**1199   —— mineworker's pension—employment in different member
states—overlapping**

In a case concerning an Italian mineworker who had worked in France and Belgium
and who was invalided out with a Belgian invalidity pension to which he was
entitled under Belgian law alone, his entitlement to an apportioned French benefit
was only sustainable in France if his French and Belgian periods of employment were
aggregated under Council Regulation (EEC) 1408/71, art. 45. On a question of the
interpretation of Regulation 1408/71, art. 46 concerning the award of such benefits,
held, where the provisions of art. 46 were more favourable to the worker than the
national legislation alone, by virtue of which the worker received a pension, the
provisions of art. 46 were to be applied in their entirety.

Case 236/78: Fonds National de Retraite des Ouvriers Mineurs v Giovanni
Mura [1980] 3 CMLR 27 (European Court of Justice).

For other proceedings see Case 22/77: *Fonds National de Retraite des Ouvriers
Mineurs v Mura* [1977] ECR 1699, ECJ, 1978 Halsbury's Abridgment para. 1253.

**1200   —— national benefits—employment in different member states—
overlapping—applicability of national rules against overlapping
benefits**

A national court in the Netherlands referred a question to the European Court as to
the application of both Community and national rules, in relation to the overlapping
of national social security benefits. The question concerned the interpretation of
Council Regulation (EEC) 574/72, art. 46, including its heading, and its application
to Regulation 1408/71, art. 46, which it implements with regard to the calculation
of benefits in overlapping periods. *Held*, under Regulation 574/72, when a
compulsory insurance period completed under the legislation of one member state
coincided with a voluntary or optional insurance period under the legislation of
another member state, only the period completed under the compulsory insurance
was to be taken into account. For the purpose of the calculation of the actual
amount of benefit in accordance with Regulation 1408/71, art. 46 (2), the regulation
aimed to ensure that a voluntary or optional insurance period coinciding with a
compulsory insurance period was not to be taken into account for the purpose of the
aggregation of the periods. It followed that where there was no question of periods
coinciding because one body of legislation was one according to which the amount
of invalidity benefits was independent of the duration of the insurance periods or
periods of residence, Regulation 574/72 also allowed the worker the benefits
corresponding to any period of voluntary or optional insurance. Although
Regulation 574/72, art. 46 (2) appeared under the heading "Calculation of benefits
in the event of overlapping periods" it should be applied to all cases coming under
Regulation 1408/71, art. 46 (3) even when the periods did not coincide.
Accordingly, for the purpose of the application of that paragraph, the competent
institution could not take account of benefits corresponding to periods completed
under voluntary or optional insurance.

Case 176/78: Max Schapp v Bestuur van de Bedrijfsvereniging Voor Bank-
en Verzekeringswezen Groothandel en Vrije Beroepen [1979] ECR 1673,
[1980] 2 CMLR 13 (European Court of Justice).

1201 —— —— rules on equality of treatment for Community nationals— effect

On a reference from a French court the European Court was asked to interpret Council Regulation (EEC) 1408/71, art. 3 which provides for equality of treatment for Community nationals moving within the Community who wish to claim a national social security benefit. *Held*, the effect of art. 3 was to prohibit not only patent discrimination, based on the nationality of social security claimants, but also disguised discrimination which, by the application of other distinguishing criteria, produced the same result. Thus, with reference to the present case, the grant of the French allowance for women with children could not be refused on the ground that the claimant's children, Italian nationals, did not have French nationality.

Case 237/78: CAISSE REGIONALE D'ASSURANCE MALADIE V PALERMO [1980] 2 CMLR 31 (European Court of Justice).

1202 —— obligation to effect insurance under national law—application of Community provisions

Council Regulation (EEC) 1408/71, art. 45 provides that periods of relevant national insurance completed in different member states may be aggregated for the purpose of establishing a worker's right to social security benefits under the legislation of one member state. In the course of proceedings in Germany the question arose whether relevant insurance periods completed in two member states were to be aggregated for the purpose of determining a worker's obligation under German law to effect national insurance. On a reference to the European Court, *held*, the sole purpose of art. 45 was to determine the effect of insurance periods completed under the various national legal systems; it did not apply to the determination of the existence of an obligation to effect insurance laid down by national legislation, which was a matter exclusively for the appropriate national legal system.

Case 266/78: BRUNORI V LANDESVERSICHERUNGSANSTALT RHEINPROVINZ [1980] 1 CMLR 660 (European Court of Justice).

1203 —— schemes to employed persons and families moving within the Community

The text of the declaration made by the United Kingdom as provided for in Council Regulation (EEC) 1408/71, art. 5 on the application of social security schemes to employed persons and their families moving within the Community is replaced. (See OJ No. C241, 19.9.80.)

1204 —— sickness benefit—pensioners—entitlement to benefit provided in another member state—authorisation by competent institution

A Dutch court referred a question to the European Court in the context of earlier proceedings for further interpretation of Council Regulation (EEC) 1408/71, art. 22 with regard to the recovery of expenses for medical treatment incurred by a pensioner in a member state other than his state of residence. *Held*, the definition of the concept of worker in art. 1 (a) covered any person insured under the social security legislation of one or more member states whether or not he pursued a professional or trade activity. It followed that pensioners, irrespective of their occupation, came within the provisions of the regulations concerning workers by virtue of their insurance under a social security scheme unless they were subject to special provisions. Article 31 governed the entitlement to benefits in kind of those insured but not pursuing a professional or trade activity, which became necessary during a stay in a member state other than their normal place of residence. However art. 22 (1) (c) governed the entitlement to benefits in kind of an insured person who resided in one member state and asked the competent institution for authorisation to receive treatment in another member state. If the competent institution acknowledged that the medical treatment in question constituted an effective treatment of the sickness from which an individual suffered, it was bound by the obligations of the second subparagraph of art. 22 (2) not to refuse the authorisation referred to by that provision and required under art. 22 (1) (c). Further, the provisions of art. 22 (1) (c) referred to any benefit which the institution of a member state had the power to grant, even if it was not required to provide it under its legislation.

Case 182/78: Bestuur Van Het Algemeen Ziekenfonds Drenthe-Platteland v Pierik [1979] ECR 1977, [1980] 2 CMLR 89 (European Court of Justice).

For earlier proceedings see [1978] 3 CMLR 343, 1978 Halsbury's Abridgment para. 1259.

1205   —— —— **provision of medical or surgical care—extent of benefits**

A Belgian national who worked in the Netherlands was in receipt of invalidity benefit under Dutch law. Following the refusal by the Dutch department of social security to reimburse her for expenses incurred at a clinic in Belgium, questions arose on the interpretation of the words "sickness and maternity benefits" in Council Regulation (EEC) 1408/71, in order to determine whether the benefits received in respect of medical care given were covered by the provisions of that regulation. *Held*, the concept of "sickness and maternity benefits" was to be determined not according to the type of national legislation which contained the provisions giving those benefits, but in accordance with Community rules which defined the contents of those benefits. The regulation applied to all legislation concerning the branches of social security law set out in art. 4. Accordingly, all benefits provided in the case of sickness and maternity, including health care, were covered by the regulation, provided that the legislation in question related to a branch of social security which concerned them. Further, the regulation did not preclude a member state from granting social security benefits of a medical or surgical nature to a person who was in receipt of an invalidity pension under the law of that state but who resided in another member state.

Case 69/79: Jordens-Vosters v Bestuur van de Bedrijfsvereniging voor de Leder-en Lederverwerkende Industrie [1980] ECR 75, [1980] 3 CMLR 412 (European Court of Justice).

1206   **Taxation—capital duty—basis of assessment**

See Case 161/78: *P. Conradsen A/S v Ministry for Fiscal Affairs*, para. 1138.

1207   —— **internal taxation—principle of non-discrimination—right of national producers to defer payment of duty**

Under Irish law the payment of excise duty on home-produced spirits, beer and wine could be deferred, subject to the giving of financial security and payment of an additional duty. No such facility was granted in respect of similar imported products. The Commission brought proceedings against the Irish government under EEC Treaty, art. 169, alleging that Ireland was in breach of art. 95. Article 95 provides that member states shall not impose on imported products any internal taxation in excess of that imposed on similar domestic products. *Held*, the decisive criterion for the application of art. 95 was the actual comparative effect of the national system of taxation on domestic and imported products: it was necessary to compare not only the rates of tax imposed (which in the present case were identical), but also the basis of assessment and the rules for levying the duty. In the present case the discrimination in favour of domestic products which resulted from the right of Irish producers to defer payment of duty was not removed by the fact that that right was subject to conditions: those conditions were so trivial as to fail to compensate for the clear, albeit small benefit, which thus accrued to national producers. Ireland was therefore in breach of art. 95.

Case 55/79: Re Collection of Duty on Alcoholic Drinks: EC Commission v Ireland [1980] ECR 481, [1980] 1 CMLR 734 (European Court of Justice).

1208   —— —— —— **tax advantage in favour of domestic products**

Under Italian law home produced petroleum products are subject to an internal tax, which is charged at a reduced rate in respects of products manufactured from regenerated oils. All imported petroleum products are subject to the full rate of tax on crossing the Italian frontier, regardless of the type of manufacturing process used.

In proceedings under EEC Treaty, art. 169 the Commission claimed that Italy was thus in breach of art. 95, under which member states are prohibited from imposing on products imported from within the Community any internal taxation in excess of that imposed on similar domestic products. The Commission maintained that compliance with art. 95 required the abolition of the tax advantage in favour of domestic regenerated products. *Held*, in the present absence of any unification or harmonisation of the relevant national provisions Community law did not prohibit member states from granting tax advantages to certain products or certain classes of producers. However, the effect of art. 95 was that such advantages also had to be granted without discrimination to imported products which satisfied the same conditions as the domestic products which qualified for the advantage. Accordingly, by refusing the tax advantage to imported regenerated products which were identical to those produced in Italy, Italy was in breach of art. 95.

The Court pointed out that the purpose of art. 95 was to ensure that the Treaty provisions relating to the abolition of customs duties were not evaded or rendered nugatory by the discriminatory application of internal taxation to imported products.

Case 21/79: RE TAX RULES ON PETROLEUM PRODUCTS: EC COMMISSION v ITALY [1980] ECR 1, [1980] 2 CMLR 613 (European Court of Justice).

1209   —— —— —— **tax advantage in favour of imported products**

In France ethyl alcohol was produced by private undertakings but was sold to the state monopoly administration which marketed the product. Since 1974, producers had been permitted freely to dispose of the alcohol, upon payment of a "cash adjustment" sum to the state. As a result of legislation in 1977 ethyl alcohol contained in products imported into France was not subject to the payment, when it was identical to that which had been freed from the monopoly in France. The plaintiff undertaking brought an action against the French administrative authority contending that the obligation to pay a "cash adjustment" sum was contrary to the prohibition of discrimination by a state monopoly in respect of imports and exports between nationals of member states contained in EEC Treaty, art. 37 in that it penalised the home product. The national court stayed the proceedings and referred a question to the European Court on the interpretation and application of art. 37. *Held*, art. 95 governed the relationship between the imposition of internal taxation on imported products and national products, whether or not the latter was subject to a monopoly. Its provisions did not prohibit the imposition on national products of internal taxation in excess of that on imported products. Article 37 only related to activities connected with the specific business of the monopoly; it was not concerned with the incidence of internal taxation on products whether or not those products were subject to a monopoly. Accordingly, the powers of member states in relation to internal taxation on domestic products were not affected by arts. 37 and 95.

Case 86/78: SA DES GRANDES DISTILLERIES PEUREUX v DIRECTEUR DES SERVICES FISCAUX DE LA HAUTE-SAÔNE ET DU TERRITOIRE DE BELFORT [1979] ECR 897, [1980] 3 CMLR 337 (European Court of Justice).

1210   —— —— **taxation of imported products—indirect protection of similar domestic products**

In proceedings before the European Court pursuant to EEC Treaty, art. 169 the Commission sought a declaration that the United Kingdom, by levying excise duty on certain wines, had infringed art. 95. Article 95 (2) prohibits member states from imposing on products imported from within the Community any internal taxation of such a nature as to afford indirect protection to other products. The Commission alleged that a competitive relationship existed in the United Kingdom between wine and beer with a real possibility that one might be substituted for the other and that the national tax system was therefore discriminatory in that it afforded indirect protection to domestic beer. The United Kingdom denied the existence of any such competitive relationship. *Held*, in order for art. 95 (2) to apply it was sufficient to show that a particular fiscal system was capable of producing the effect of indirect protection for home-produced products; although factors which could be deduced from statistics concerning the operation of a particular fiscal system were relevant, the Commission could not be required to supply figures showing the precise situation as regards the effect of that system.

The Court found that the relevant United Kingdom legislation had a protective leaning with respect to beer and imported wine. However, in the absence of the Commission's opinion as to what should be the proper taxation relationship between two competing products, the Court felt unable to give a decision in the case which could then be evaluated with sufficient certainty. An interlocutory judgment was therefore given, under which the Commission and the United Kingdom government were required to re-examine and report on the subject matter of the action by 31st December 1980, after which the Court would give final judgment.

Case 170/78: EC COMMISSION v UNITED KINGDOM [1980] ECR 481 (European Court of Justice).

1211　　—— value added tax—calculation

Commission Decision (EEC) 80/774 (OJ No. L222, 23.8.80), concerning the calculation of the value added tax resources basis for 1979 pursuant to Council Regulation (EEC) 2892/77, authorises the United Kingdom to exclude certain transactions and to use approximate estimates to calculate the basis for certain other transactions.

1212　　—— —— transport of goods and ancillary services—interpretation

A Dutch undertaking engaged in the transport of goods operated a cash-on-delivery service in respect of which it charged a separate fee, a cash-on-delivery commission. Under Council Directive (EEC) 67/228 value added tax is compulsorily payable on, inter alia, the service of transporting goods "and ancillary services". The question arose as to whether the cash-on-delivery system constituted a service ancillary to the transport of goods and thus whether the commission was subject to value added tax. On a reference to the European Court on the interpretation of "ancillary services" *held*, in providing that the common system of value added tax was compulsorily applicable to certain services, namely those contained in Annex B, the directive sought to harmonise the legislation of member states governing value added tax so as to achieve neutrality in competition within the Community. Accordingly, where a carrier contracted to perform two services, namely the transport of the goods and the collection of their price, the performance of which was inseparable, it was necessary to treat the collection of the price as a service ancillary to the transport of the goods in order to assure equality of treatment in all member states between the various modes of transport. Further, Annex A, Point 10 provided that member states were to refrain, as far as possible, from exempting the services listed in Annex B from value added tax; the ancillary service could therefore be exempted only in exceptional cases which justified the consequent adverse effect on neutrality in competition.

Case 126/78: NV NEDERLANDSE SPOORWEGEN v SECRETARY OF STATE FOR FINANCE [1979] ECR 2041, [1980] 1 CMLR 144 (European Court of Justice).

1213　　Treaties

The European Communities (Definition of Treaties) (ECSC Decision of 18th March 1980 on Supplementary Revenue) Order 1980, S.I. 1980 No. 1090 (in force on 29th July 1980), declares the Decision of the Representatives of the Governments of the Member States of the European Coal and Steel Community, meeting within the Council, of 18th March 1980 (Cmnd. 7930) to be a Community Treaty as defined in the European Communities Act 1972, s. 1 (2). This decision allocates to the ECSC supplementary revenue totalling 28 million European Units of Account for the financial year 1980.

1214   The European Communities (Definition of Treaties) (International Railway Tariffs Agreements) Order 1980, S.I. 1980 No. 1094 (in force on 7th August 1980), declares the European Coal and Steel Community Agreements with Switzerland and Austria of 1956 and 1957, and certain other agreements to be Community Treaties as defined in the European Communities Act 1972, s. 1 (2).

1215   The European Communities (Definition of Treaties) (Multilateral Trade Negotiations) Order 1980, S.I. 1980 No. 191 (in force on a day when, in respect of each Treaty specified in the Sch. Pt I, the Treaty enters into force for the EEC, that date to be notified in the London, Edinburgh and Belfast Gazettes), declares that the agreements listed in the Schedule are to become Community Treaties as defined in the European Communities Act 1972, s. 1 (2).

1216   The European Communities (Definition of Treaties) (Second ACP–EEC Convention of Lomé) Order 1980, S.I. 1980 No. 1077 (in force on a day when, in respect of each treaty specified in the Schedule, on the date on which the treaty enters into force for the United Kingdom that date to be notified in the London, Edinburgh and Belfast Gazettes), declares the Second ACP–EEC Convention of Lomé and related agreements are to become Community Treaties as defined in the European Communities Act 1972 s. 1 (2).

1217   —— **agreements between member states and third countries**

Council Decision (EEC) 80/1045 (OJ No. L307, 18.11.80) authorises the prolongation or tacit renewal of certain trade agreements concluded between member states and third countries.

1218   Council Decision (EEC) 80/1046 (OJ No. L307, 18.11.80) authorises the tacit renewal or continued operation of certain treaties of friendship, trade and navigation treaties, and similar agreements concluded between member states and third countries.

1219   Council Decision (EEC) 80/1186 (OJ No. L361, 31.12.80) on the association of the overseas countries and territories with the Community aims to facilitate the economic and social development and to strengthen the economic structures of the countries listed, in particular by developing trade, economic relations and agricultural and industrial co-operation between the Community and those countries.

1220   —— —— **effect of Community law**

On 1st January 1977 Ireland extended her exclusive fishery limits to 200 nautical miles from the base line. Subsequently the defendant, the master of a Spanish trawler, was charged with having on board nets with undersized mesh whilst fishing within the exclusive Irish fishery limits. The applicable Irish legislation, equivalent to the Sea Fisheries Act 1968, s. 6, makes such action an offence punishable by a fine and forfeiture of any fish and fishing gear found on the vessel. The defendant contended that the London Fisheries Convention 1964, in force between Spain and the nine member states, which defines the features of a fisheries system up to twelve miles from the base line, created for him antecedent rights maintained by Community law, in particular, EEC Treaty, art. 234 on the compatibility, with the EEC Treaty, of agreements concluded between member states and third countries. Questions arose as to the interpretation and effect of art. 234. *Held*, the purpose of art. 234 was to lay down, in accordance with the principles of international law, that the application of the Treaty did not effect the rights of non-member states under a prior agreement and the obligation thereunder. Furthermore as it was to remove any obstacle to the performance of agreements previously concluded with non-member states which the accession of a member state to the Community might present, it could not have the effect of altering the nature of the rights which would flow from such agreements. It followed, inter alia, that art. 234 neither had the effect of conferring upon individuals who relied upon an agreement concluded prior to the entry into force of the Treaty or the accession of the member state concerned, rights which the national courts of the member states had to uphold, nor of adversely affecting the rights which individuals derived from such an agreement.

Case 812/79: A-G v BURGOA (1980) Times, 20th October (European Court of Justice).

1221   —— —— Second Lomé Convention

Council Regulation (EEC) 3225/80 (OJ No. L347, 22.12.80) on the conclusion of the second ACP-EEC Convention signed at Lomé on 31st October 1979, sets out the Convention in full. The Convention comes into force on 1st January 1981, and is to promote trade between the African, Caribbean and Pacific States and the Community. Provisions are made for increased industrial, agricultural, financial and technical cooperation between the contracting parties.

1222   —— Convention on the suppression of terrorism

See para. 1253.

EVIDENCE

Halsbury's Laws of England (4th edn.), Vol. 17, paras. 1–400

1223   Articles

Discovery, Experts' Reports and RSC Order 38, Geoff Holgate: 130 NLJ 421.
Is the Oath out of Date? Tony Radevsky: 130 NLJ 397.
Tribunal Evidence, Carolyn Yates: [1980] Conv 137.

1224   Admissibility—documents—bankers' books

See *R v Andover JJ, ex parte Rhodes*, para. 209; *Barker v Wilson*, para. 210.

1225   —— evidence given to inspectors investigating company's affairs—public interest

See *London and County Securities Ltd v Nicholson*, para. 376.

1226   —— evidence wrongfully obtained—relevancy to matters in issue

The plaintiffs brought a patent action against the defendants. The defendants obtained an Anton Piller order for the disclosure and production of certain documents by the plaintiffs. At the hearing of the action, the trial judge gave judgment but was informed, before making an appropriate order, that during the course of the action the Court of Appeal had given a majority judgment which might materially have affected the Anton Piller order. The plaintiffs argued that, in view of the Court of Appeal's decision, the Anton Piller order ought never to have been made and that it should be discharged. They contended that there should be a retrial because the documents, which were forgeries, need never have been disclosed since they would have tended to incriminate their witnesses. The order was obtained ex parte, without service of any of the evidence on which it was obtained; the evidence would have made it clear that fraud was being alleged and service of it would have given the plaintiffs an opportunity to object on the ground of self-incrimination. *Held*, throughout the hearing the parties and the court had proceeded on the basis that the Anton Piller order had been properly made. The documents produced were relevant to the issues in the case and were therefore admissible in evidence; the court was not concerned with how the evidence was obtained. The judgment would be perfected, and the requests for discharge of the order and for a retrial would be refused.

INTERNATIONAL ELECTRONICS LTD v WEIGH DATA LTD (1980) Times, 13th March (Chancery Division: GRAHAM J). *Kuruma Son of Kaniu v R* [1955] AC 197 applied.

For the Court of Appeal decision referred to, see *Rank Film Distributors Ltd v Video Information Centre*, para. 2181.

1227   —— **expert evidence—evidence disclosed by another party pursuant to a summons for directions**

It has been held that a party in an action may put in evidence, under RSC Ord. 38, r. 42, any expert report disclosed to him by another party pursuant to an order made on the summons for directions. A report so disclosed was, by virtue of RSC Ord. 25, r. 3 (a) disclosed in accordance with Ord. 38, Part IV and could therefore be put in evidence.

MALLICK V ALLIED SCHOOLS AGENCY LTD (1980) Times, 4th March (Court of Appeal: LORD DENNING MR, WALLER and DUNN LJJ).

1228   **Criminal cases**

See CRIMINAL PROCEDURE.

1229   **Cross-examination—affidavit—discretion of court to refuse cross-examination on contents**

See *Re A Debtor (No. 37 of 1976) (Liverpool), ex parte Taylor v The Debtor*, para. 227.

1230   **Evidence (Proceedings in Other Jurisdictions) Act 1975— Guernsey**

The Evidence (Proceedings in Other Jurisdictions) (Guernsey) Order 1980, S.I. 1980 No. 1956 (in force on 10th January 1981), extends to the Bailiwick of Guernsey certain provisions of the Evidence (Proceedings in Other Jurisdictions) Act 1975, 1975 Halsbury's Abridgment para. 1460, subject to modifications. The order also extends the Evidence (European Court) Order 1976, 1976 Halsbury's Abridgment para. 1176, to the Bailiwick of Guernsey so that evidence for proceedings before the European Court of Justice may be taken at the request of that Court by certain specified courts in the Bailiwick of Guernsey.

1231   **Expert evidence—disclosure of reports—medical negligence**

In an action for damages for medical negligence the judge ordered that there should be no mutual disclosure of medical reports, pursuant to RSC Order 38, r. 37, under which disclosure should be ordered unless there is sufficient reason for not doing so. The paragraph further provides for situations when the court might consider disclosure inappropriate, including allegations of medical negligence. The plaintiff appealed on the ground that rule 37 merely provided illustrations and that even though this was a case of medical negligence it was open to the court to order disclosure. *Held*, the purpose of rule 37 (2) was to prevent the effective disclosure of the defendant's proofs of evidence in cases such as medical negligence where the expert needed such information in order to found his opinion. The paragraph went further than merely to provide illustrations, and the reports should not be disclosed.

RAHMAN V KIRKLEES AREA HEALTH AUTHORITY [1980] 1 WLR 1244 (Court of Appeal: ORMROD and CUMMING-BRUCE LJJ).

1232   —— —— **validity of order for disclosure**

In an action for damages arising out of a collision, the question arose as to whether an order should have been made for the mutual disclosure of actuarial reports and for the calling of actuarial evidence if such reports were not agreed. *Held*, it was for the parties to decide what evidence to call and for the judge to rule as to its admissibility. While the number of expert witnesses could be limited, there was nothing to prevent judges from considering actuarial evidence and it could not be said that such evidence would confuse them. Accordingly, having regard to RSC

Ord. 38, rr. 36, 38 which related to restrictions on adducing expert evidence, the order had been correctly made.

SULLIVAN V WEST YORKSHIRE PASSENGER TRANSPORT EXECUTIVE (1980) Times, 28th June (Court of Appeal: STEPHENSON, ACKNER LJJ and SIR DAVID CAIRNS). RSC Ord. 38, rr. 36, 38 amended: S.I. 1980 No. 1010, para. 2234.

1233   Letters of request—German Democratic Republic

Under a convention signed by this country and the German Democratic Republic in Berlin on 28th February 1980 an English court may by letter of request ask the Ministry of Justice in the Republic to take evidence or cause it to be taken. The convention prescribes the particulars which must be included in the letter of request and the manner in which it must be executed. Provision is also made for evidence to be taken directly by a consular officer. Reciprocal arrangements are made so that the German authorities may address letters of request, in England and Wales, to the Senior Master.

The same convention provides procedures for the service in the Republic of judicial and extra-judicial documents by means of a request to the Ministry of Justice addressed and sent by a diplomatic mission or consulate. Reciprocal arrangements are also made for requesting the Senior Master to effect service.

The convention has not yet been ratified. See Convention regarding Legal Proceedings in Civil Matters (Cmnd. 7918).

1234   Magistrates' court—custody proceedings—evidence obtained other than in open court

See *Boatman v Boatman*, para. 1974.

1235   Oaths—fees

The Commissioners for Oaths (Fees) Order 1980, S.I. 1980 No. 70 (in force on 11th February 1980), increases the fees chargeable by commissioners for oaths and practising solicitors for taking affidavits and similar declarations from £1 to £2 and for marking exhibits from 40p to 50p. The increased amounts include value added tax where payable. The Commissioners for Oaths (Fees) Order 1975, 1975 Halsbury's Abridgment para. 1462 is revoked.

1236   Witness—expenses—professional witness

The professional witness allowances have been increased: see Home Office circular 80/60. The allowance may not exceed £20.80 where the professional witness attends on any day to give evidence in one case only and (i) the period during which he is necessarily absent from his place of residence or practice does not exceed four hours, and (ii) he does not employ a person to take care of his practice during his absence. Where, however, the professional witness necessarily incurs expense in the provision of a person to take care of his practice during his absence, or attends for a period exceeding four hours, or attends for more than one case, a higher allowance (not exceeding £41.60 a day) may be paid. See the *Law Society's Gazette*, 16th July 1980, p. 731.

EXECUTION

Halsbury's Laws of England (4th edn.), Vol. 17, paras. 401–700

1237   Attachment of debts—attachment of bank acount—foreign currency—whether foreign currency a debt

A debtor had sufficient foreign currency on deposit in an English bank account to satisfy a judgment given against him in England. His judgment creditors contended that the foreign currency was a debt which could be attached for their benefit. *Held*, under the Administration of Justice Act 1956, s. 38 and the County Courts Act 1959, s. 143 a sum standing to a person's credit in a deposit account was attachable for the purposes of the court's jurisdiction to attach debts. It was clearly settled that if a sum was payable in England in a foreign currency, the courts could give judgment for that sum in a foreign currency as a debt. Therefore, it followed that the debtor's foreign currency constituted a debt which was attachable under the court's jurisdiction.

The court outlined the procedure to be followed by a bank when a garnishee order was served in respect of an account containing foreign currency.

CHOICE INVESTMENTS LTD V JEROMNIMON (MIDLAND BANK LTD, GARNISHEE) [1981] 1 All ER 225 (Court of Appeal: LORD DENNING MR, BRIGHTMAN and GRIFFITHS LJJ). *Miliangos v George Frank (Textiles) Ltd* [1976] AC 443, HL, 1975 Halsbury's Abridgment para. 1916 applied.

1238 Charging order—chargeable property—beneficial interest under a trust for sale

A creditor obtained judgment for a debt but the debtor failed to make any payments under the judgment. The debtor and his wife held beneficial interests under a trust for sale in the matrimonial home. The creditor appealed against a refusal to make a charging order nisi in respect of the debtor's beneficial interest. *Held*, the previous position regarding charging orders under the Administration of Justice Act 1956, s. 35 (1) limited such orders to "an interest in land". Therefore, as held in *Irani Finance Ltd v Singh* [1971] Ch 59, CA, an order could not be imposed on land held jointly since a beneficial interest under a trust for sale was not "an interest in land". However, under the Charging Orders Act 1979, s. 2 (1) (a) (i) an order could be imposed on a judgment debtor's beneficial interest "under any trust". Therefore, although the debtor's interest in the matrimonial home was not an interest in land, it was a beneficial interest under a trust for the purposes of s. 2 (1) (a) (i). Accordingly an order under the 1979 Act could be made in respect of such an interest and the appeal would be allowed.

NATIONAL WESTMINSTER BANK LTD V STOCKMAN [1981] 1 WLR 67 (Queen's Bench Division: RUSSELL J).

1239 Charging Orders Act 1979—commencement

The Charging Orders Act 1979 (Commencement) Order 1980, S.I. 1980 No. 627 brought the whole of the Act (see 1979 Halsbury's Abridgment para. 1263) into force on 3rd June 1980.

1240 Exemption from execution—prescribed value

The Protection from Execution (Prescribed Value) Order 1980, S.I. 1980 No. 26 (in force on 18th February 1980), provides that wearing apparel and bedding not exceeding £100 in value and tools of trade not exceeding £150 are exempt from seizure in execution.

1241 Garnishee proceedings—discretionary power—whether undertaking "judgment or order"

The parties were divorced. In 1972, it was ordered, inter alia, that the husband should make periodical payments to the wife and to the only child of the marriage, and that he should undertake to pay the child's school fees until the child attained seventeen years. The order was varied in 1976. The husband subsequently undertook to pay certain arrears under the 1972 order and the child's school fees on the wife's undertaking to waive her rights under the 1976 order. The husband, however, failed to pay the arrears or the school fees and the wife consequently took out a garnishee summons against him. Under CCR Ord. 27, r. 1, a judgment creditor may take proceedings by way of garnishee to enforce a judgment or order for the payment of money. The judge held that the wife's undertaking released the husband from the obligations of the 1976 order, but that, in the circumstances, the husband's undertaking to pay the school fees was an integral part of the 1972 order. The judge ordered the garnishee, the husband's bank, to make a payment to the wife, exercising the wider discretion under Ord. 27, r. 10 that the court might make such an order as to repayment "as may be just". The husband appealed, contending that the undertaking embodied in the 1972 order was not a "judgment or order" within the meaning of Ord. 27, r. 1 and that it was not obtained by the wife, as the money for the school fees was not necessarily going to be paid to her. *Held*, Ord. 27, r. 10 did not apply as it dealt with instances where the garnishee disputed his liability to the judgment debtor. The question was therefore whether the case fell within Ord. 27, r. 1. On the authorities, it was appropriate in certain cases to treat an undertaking as being equivalent to an order for the purposes of CCR Ord. 27, r. 1 or the corresponding Rules of the Supreme Court; this was such a case, as the undertaking was clearly an integral part of the 1972 order. Further, the wife was the only person who could have brought the summons and she was obtaining the order in her own right, as she was going to pay the school fees for herself or on behalf of the child. The appeal would, accordingly, be dismissed.

GANDOLFO v GANDOLFO AND STANDARD CHARTERED BANK LTD (GARNISHEE) [1980] 1 All ER 833 (Court of Appeal: MEGAW and BROWNE LJJ and SIR STANLEY REES). *Milburn v Newton Colliery Ltd* (1907–8) 52 Sol Jo 317 and *Biba Ltd v Stratford Investments Ltd* [1973] Ch 281 applied.

EXECUTORS AND ADMINISTRATORS

Halsbury's Laws of England (4th edn.), Vol. 17, paras. 701–1591

1242   Articles

Dependants' Applications Under The Inheritance (Provision for Family and Dependants) Act 1975, Suman Naresh: 96 LQR 534.

A Mistresses' Charter, C. E. Cadwallader (rights of mistresses under the Inheritance (Provision for Family and Dependants) Act 1975): [1980] Conv. 46.

Treatment of Income in Probate Further Considered, R. Meads: 124 Sol Jo 197.

1243   Distribution of assets—residuary estate settled—rule in Howe v Earl of Dartmouth—whether applicable to real property

Canada

The rule in *Howe v Earl of Dartmouth* provides that where residuary personalty is settled on death for the benefit of persons who are to enjoy it in succession, the duty of the trustees is to convert all such parts of it as are of a wasting or future or reversionary nature, or consist of unauthorised securities, into property of a permanent and income-bearing character. The question arose whether this rule applied to a residuary gift of real property. *Held*, the purpose of the rule was to require the trustee of an estate settled in succession to deal even handedly between the life tenant and the remaindermen. However, its operation was confined to personalty and it had no application to real property. Any change in the rule should be made by the legislature, which could also enact the necessary transitional and protective provisions.

LOTTMAN v STANFORD (1980) 107 DLR (3d) 28 (Supreme Court of Canada). *Howe v Earl of Dartmouth, Howe v Countess of Aylesbury* (1802) 7 Ves 137 considered.

1244   Family provision—application out of time—when application allowed

See *Re Dennis, Dennis v Lloyd's Bank Ltd*, para. 2194.

1245   —— guidelines

See *Re Salmon, Coard v National Westminster Bank Ltd*, para. 2195.

1246   —— **person maintained by deceased otherwise than for full valuable consideration—shared accommodation**

The applicant, an old age pensioner, went to live with the deceased in her house in 1971. There was doubt whether he was merely a lodger or whether they were actually living together as man and wife. They shared accommodation in the house for eight years until the death of the deceased in 1979. Her estate was worth £17,303 and by her will was left entirely to her three children with no provision at all for the applicant. He sought to have provision made for him from her estate under the Inheritance (Provision for Family and Dependants) Act 1975, s. 1 (1) (e). The executors succeeded in having his application struck out as showing no reasonable cause of action and he appealed. *Held*, whether the applicant was dependent upon the deceased and was being maintained by her was a question of fact to be determined by weighing their respective contributions to the relationship. If there was any doubt about the balance tipping in favour of the deceased's being the greater contribution then the matter must go to trial. On the evidence before the court it was possible that the applicant was being maintained by the deceased before her death and accordingly he was entitled to apply for provision from her estate. The appeal would be allowed.

JELLEY V ILIFFE (1980) Times, 19th December (Court of Appeal: STEPHENSON, CUMMING-BRUCE and GRIFFITH LJJ).

1247   **Practice—non-contentious probate—fees**

The Supreme Court (Non-Contentious Probate) Fees (Amendment) Order 1980, S.I. 1980 No. 820 (in force on 7th July 1980), further amends the 1975 Order, 1975 Halsbury's Abridgment para. 1481 by increasing the fee for administering an oath and for each exhibit to £2 and 50p respectively. The fee for the production of documents is abolished.

1248   **Probate—grant—resealing—grants issued by courts of Zimbabwe**

See para. 2221.

EXTRADITION AND FUGITIVE OFFENDERS

Halsbury's Laws of England (4th edn.), Vol. 18, paras. 201–300

1249   **Articles**

Passage of Time and the Return of Fugitive Offenders, David Lloyd Jones: [1979] Crim LR 29.
Recent Developments in Extradition, A. N. Khan: 144 JP Jo 612.

1250   **Fugitive offender—application for habeas corpus—relevant offence**

The Fugitive Offenders Act 1967, s. 3 (1) (c) provides that an offence of which a person is accused or has been convicted in a designated Commonwealth country or a United Kingdom dependency is a relevant offence, if in any case, the act or omission constituting the offence would constitute an offence against the law of the United Kingdom if it took place within the United Kingdom, or, in the case of an extra-territorial offence, in corresponding circumstances outside the United Kingdom.

An Indian citizen, resident in Ghana, made false representations in Ghana in order to circumvent the exchange control restrictions. He obtained the authorisation of the national bank for the payment of foreign currencies made to him in Germany and the United States. On his arrival in the United Kingdom the Ghanaian Government requested his extradition on a charge of obtaining property by deception contrary to the criminal law of Ghana. A magistrate issued a warrant under the 1967 Act, s. 7 (5) committing him to custody to await extradition. He applied for a writ of habeas corpus on the ground that the committal was unlawful, in that there was no "relevant offence" within the meaning of s. 3 (1) (c) of the Act. *Held*, where a deception was made in the United Kingdom but the property was obtained outside the jurisdiction there was no offence under English law. Accordingly the extradition proceedings based on the relevancy of an offence of obtaining property by deception were, on the facts of the present case, misconceived and the application would succeed.

R v GOVERNOR OF PENTONVILLE PRISON, EX PARTE KHUBCHANDANI (1979) 71 Cr App Rep 241 (Queen's Bench Division: SHAW LJ and KILNER BROWN J). *R v Governor of Brixton Prison, ex parte Gardner* [1968] 2 QB 399 and *R v Harden* [1963] 1 QB 8 applied.

1251   —— extradition—Argentine

The Argentine Republic (Extradition) (Amendment) Order 1980, S.I. 1980 No. 185 (in force on 13th March 1980), applies the Extradition Acts 1870–1935 in the case of the Argentine Republic.

1252   —— —— Sweden

The Sweden (Extradition) (Amendment) Order 1980, S.I. 1980 No. 566 (in force on 19th May 1980), applies the Extradition Acts 1870 to 1935 in the case of the Kingdom of Sweden in accordance with the Extradition Treaty between the United Kingdom and Sweden signed at London on 26th April 1963, as amended by the Protocol signed on 6th December 1965, and as further amended by Notes exchanged at Stockholm on 19th February 1980.

1253   Suppression of terrorism—convention—agreement between member states of European Communities

An agreement has been reached by the member states of the European Communities on the application of the European Convention on the Suppression of Terrorism. The agreement will apply only until such date as all the member states of the European Communities have become parties, without reservation, to the Convention. Until that date, in relations between two member states which are parties to the Convention (where one, or both, has made a reservation to that Convention), the application of the Convention is made subject to the agreement. In relations between two member states of which one (or both) is not a party to the Convention, arts. 1–8 and 13 of the Convention apply subject to the provisions of the agreement. The agreement provides for parties to declare whether they intend to make use of the reservation under art. 13 of the Convention or (if the member state concerned is not a party to the Convention) to make a declaration reserving the right to refuse extradition in relation to offences listed in art. 1 of the Convention for the purpose of taking proceedings to prosecute such offences. The agreement was signed in Dublin on 4th December 1979 and will come into force three months after deposit of the instruments of ratification by all member states of the European Communities. The text of the agreement has been published as Cmnd. 7823.

1254   —— designated countries—Iceland

The Suppression of Terrorism Act 1978 (Designation of Countries) (No. 2) Order 1980, S.I. 1980 No. 1392 (in force on 12th October 1980), designates Iceland for the purposes of the Suppression of Terrorism Act 1978, 1978 Halsbury's Abridgment para. 1321 so that it becomes a convention country within the meaning of the Act. Iceland is a party to the European Convention on the Suppression of Terrorism.

1255   The Extradition (Suppression of Terrorism) (Amendment) (No. 2) Order 1980, S.I. 1980 No. 1525 (in force on 7th November 1980), applies the Extradition Acts 1870–1895 to Iceland. The order makes extraditable the offences mentioned in the European Convention on the Suppression of Terrorism, arts. 1, 2, in so far as they are not already extraditable.

1256 —— —— **Norway**

The Suppression of Terrorism Act 1978 (Designation of Countries) Order 1980, S.I. 1980 No. 357 (in force on 11th April), designates the Kingdom of Norway for the purposes of the Suppression of Terrorism Act 1978, 1978 Halsbury's Abridgment para. 1321 so that it becomes a convention country within the meaning of the Act. The Kingdom of Norway is a party to the European Convention on the Suppression of Terrorism.

1257 The Extradition (Suppression of Terrorism) (Amendment) Order 1980, S.I. 1980 No. 398 (in force on 11th April 1980), applies the Extradition Acts 1870–1895 to the Kingdom of Norway. The order makes extraditable the offences mentioned in the European Convention on the Suppression of Terrorism, arts. 1, 2, in so far as they are not already extraditable.

FIREARMS

Halsbury's Laws of England (4th edn.), Vol. 11, paras. 875–898

1258 **Definition—whether air rifle a firearm**

The two defendants were charged with being drunk and in possession of a loaded firearm contrary to the Licensing Act 1872, s. 12. The question arose on appeal by way of case stated, as to whether a loaded air rifle was a loaded "firearm" for the purposes of s. 12. *Held*, the modern meaning of "firearm" was wider than its dictionary definition. It was only the nature of the propellant that distinguished different types of firearms and the ordinary meaning of the word did include an air rifle.

SEAMARK V PROUSE [1980] 3 All ER 26 (Queen's Bench Division: LORD WIDGERY CJ and WOOLF J).

1259 **Fees**

The Firearms (Variation of Fees) Order 1980, S.I. 1980 No. 574 (in force on 1st July 1980), increases the fees for firearms certificates and shot gun certificates and in respect of the registration of firearms dealers and the new registration certificates issued to firearms dealers annually. The Order also extends an existing exemption relating to signalling devices. The Firearms (Variation of Fees) Order 1978, 1978 Halsbury's Abridgment para. 1329 is revoked.

1260 **Possession of firearms—application for certificate—meaning of "minor traffic offences"**

On an application form for a shotgun certificate the accused answered "no" to a question asking whether he had been convicted of any offence other than minor traffic offences. In fact, he had been convicted of driving without due care and attention, failing to give a breath test and driving with excess alcohol, and he was charged with making a false statement for the purpose of obtaining a shotgun certificate, contrary to the Firearms Act 1968, s. 26 (5). He was acquitted on the ground that the expression "minor traffic offences" was too vague and was not defined in the Act, or in the form, or in decided cases. On appeal, *held*, the offence under s. 26 (5) was directed at a person who made a statement which he knew to be false. The question was ambiguous and whether the accused's statement was false or not was a question of fact for the magistrates to decide.

OGSTON V MILLER (1980) Times, 31st October (Queen's Bench Division: DONALDSON LJ and FORBES J).

1261   —— possession without a certificate—exemption in respect of antiques

The defendant, a collector of military weapons, was charged with possessing firearms without a certificate contrary to the Firearms Act 1968, s. 1. The guns in question were made between 1905 and 1910 and were in full working order, capable of being fired. On the question whether they were antiques, therefore providing a defence under the 1968 Act, s. 58(2), *held*, it was a question of fact and depended on the articles in question. In the present case the firearms in question were manufactured in this century and were available for use in a war, and were therefore not antiques.

BENNETT V BROWN (1980) 71 Cr App Rep 109 (Queen's Bench Division: EVELEIGH LJ and WATKINS J). *Richards v Curwen* [1977] 3 All ER 426, 1977 Halsbury's Abridgment para. 1289 applied.

1262   —— —— nature of offence

It has been held that the Firearms Act 1968, s. 1 created an offence of possessing a firearm without a certificate. If an article in a person's possession was found to be a firearm, that person was guilty of an offence under s. 1 even though he did not know that the article was a firearm. Section 1 did not refer to a person's state of knowledge and the offence was one of absolute liability.

R V HUSSAIN (1980) Times, 20th November (Court of Appeal). *Warner v Metropolitan Police Commissioner* [1969] 2 AC 256, HL applied.

1263   —— —— whether rifle with rifling removed requires a firearm certificate

The Firearms Act 1968, s. 1 (1) makes it an offence to possess a firearm without a firearm certificate unless it is a shotgun, that is to say a smooth-bore gun with a barrel not less than twenty-four inches in length, not being an airgun, within s. 1 (3). "Firearms" are further defined in s. 57 of the Act.

A man owned a rifle with a barrel of more than twenty-four inches long which had had its rifling removed and had been rechambered to take different cartridges so that it became a smooth-bore gun. He was charged with possession of a rifle without a firearm certificate. The question arose as to whether it was possible to adapt a firearm requiring a firearm certificate so as to exclude it from the necessity of having such a certificate by reason of s. 1 (3). *Held*, the court had to consider the weapon solely in the context of s. 1 (3) and not s. 57. The removal of the rifling converted the weapon to a shotgun within s. 1 (3) and therefore no firearm certificate was required by the owner.

R V HUCKLEBRIDGE; A-G's REFERENCE (No. 3 OF 1980) [1980] 3 All ER 273 (Court of Appeal: LORD LANE CJ, BOREHAM and GIBSON JJ). Dictum of Lord Widgery CJ, dissenting in *Creaser v Tunnicliffe* [1978] 1 All ER 569 at 572, 1977 Halsbury's Abridgment para. 1290 applied. *Creaser v Tunnicliffe* not followed.

FIRE SERVICES

Halsbury's Laws of England (4th edn.), Vol. 18, paras. 401–600

1264   Fireman—occupier's duty of care towards fireman

See *Bermingham v Sher Bros*, para. 2051.

1265   Fire precautions—fire certificate—office premises—room used as office

Three rooms in a library building were used as offices. In proceedings under the Fire Precautions Act 1971, s. 9A, relating to the need for a fire certificate, *held*, if a room used for office purposes was separate and definable it could be part of a building used for office purposes and therefore office premises within the Offices, Shops and

Railway Premises Act 1963, s. 1 (2) (a), even though its area was not substantial in relation to the building as a whole. In such a case a means of escape in case of fire would be required.

OXFORDSHIRE COUNTY COUNCIL v CHANCELLOR MASTERS AND SCHOLARS OF OXFORD UNIVERSITY (1980) Times, 10th December (Queen's Bench Division: ACKNER LJ and SKINNER J).

1266   Pensions

See PENSIONS AND SUPERANNUATION.

FISHERIES

Halsbury's Laws of England (4th edn.), Vol. 18, paras. 601–1000

1267   Article

British Off-Shore Continental Shelf and Fishery Limit Boundaries: An Analysis of Overlapping Zones, C. R. Symmons: 28 ICLQ 703.

1268   Common organisation of fisheries—third country fishing

The Third Country Fishing (Enforcement) Regulations 1980, S.I. 1980 No. 754 (in force on 11th June 1980), make breaches of certain Community regulations relating to third country fishing offences under United Kingdom law where they occur within British fishery limits. They revoke and replace the 1979 Regulations, 1979 Halsbury's Abridgment para. 1299.

1269   The Third Country Fishing (Enforcement) (No. 2) Regulations 1980, S.I. 1980 No. 1198 (in force on 5th September 1980), make breaches of certain Community regulations relating to third country fishing offences under United Kingdom law where they occur within British fishing limits.

1270   Community provisions

See AGRICULTURE (COMMON AGRICULTURAL POLICY).

1271   Fishing vessels—grants

The Fishing Vessels (Acquisition and Improvement) (Grants) (Variation) Scheme 1980, S.I. 1980 No. 1973 (in force on 16th December 1980) varies the 1976 Scheme, 1976 Halsbury's Abridgment para. 1222, by substituting 1st January 1982 as the date by which applications must be approved for the payment of grants under the 1976 Scheme.

1272   —— manning requirements

See para. 2672.

1273   Herring—prohibition of fishing and landing

The Herring (Restrictions on Landing) Order 1980, S.I. 1980 No. 1657 (in force on 25th November 1980), prohibits the landing in the United Kingdom of herring caught in the North Sea and other waters surrounding the United Kingdom except where the herring is caught under licence granted by one of the Fisheries Ministers, the herring is caught in waters coming under the jurisdiction of another member state in compliance with Community law or they are permitted by-catches. The order implements Council Regulation (EEC) 754/80 in so far as it relates to total allowable catches for herring.

The Herring By-Catch (Restrictions on Landing) (No. 2) Order 1976, 1976 Halsbury's Abridgment para. 1231 and the 1979 Variation Order, 1979 Halsbury's Abridgment para. 1305 are revoked.

1274   The Irish Sea Herring (Prohibition of Fishing) Order 1980, S.I. 1980 No. 1480 (in force on 8th October 1980), prohibits fishing for herring from 8th October to 16th November 1980 in the area of the Irish Sea as defined by the order.

1275   The Irish Sea Herring (Prohibition of Fishing) Regulations 1980, S.I. 1980 No. 1479 (in force on 8th October 1980), which are made under the European Communities Act 1972, s. 2 (2), prohibit fishing for herring from the 8th October 1980 to the 16th November 1980 in the area of the Irish Sea as defined by the regulations.

1276   ## Import of Live Fish (England and Wales) Act 1980
The Import of Live Fish (England and Wales) Act 1980 makes provision for restrictions on the importation, keeping or release of certain species of live fish and shellfish or their live eggs or milt. The Act received the royal assent on 15th May 1980 and came into force on that date.

Section 1 empowers the Minister by order to forbid either absolutely, or, subject to a licence, the importation, keeping or release of live fish or the eggs of a species which is not native to England and Wales and which might compete with or harm the habitat of any freshwater fish, shellfish or salmon. A licence under this section may be granted subject to conditions and may be revoked or varied at any time. While an order is in force, certain authorised persons are empowered to enter and inspect land occupied by the holder of a licence, or any other land upon which they believe fish or eggs specified in the order are being kept: s. 2. Section 3 deals with offences and penalties under the Act, s. 4 with interpretation and s. 5 with citation and extent.

1277   ## Mackerel—prohibition
The Mackerel (Specified Western Waters) (Prohibition of Fishing) Order 1980, S.I. 1980 No. 478 (in force on 4th April 1980), prohibits fishing for mackerel from 4th April to 30th April 1980 in certain specified waters off the north and west coasts of Scotland. The order applies to all fishing boats including foreign vessels.

1278   ## Nets—mesh sizes
The Fishing Nets Order 1980, S.I. 1980 No. 1810 (in force on 19th December 1980), provides for the enforcement of certain provisions of Council Regulation (EEC) 2527/80, para. 72, laying down technical measures for the conservation of fishery resources. The provisions of the order cease to have effect on 20th December 1980.

The Fishing Nets (North East Atlantic) Order 1977, 1977 Halsbury's Abridgment para. 1313, as varied in 1978, 1978 Halsbury's Abridgment para. 1355, and in 1979, 1979 Halsbury's Abridgment para. 1307, is revoked.

1279   The Fishing Nets (No. 2) Order 1980, S.I. 1980 No. 1994 (in force on 20th December 1980), provides for the enforcement of certain provisions of Council Regulation (EEC) 2527/80, para. 72, laying down technical measures for the conservation of fishery resources, as extended by Council Regulation (EEC) 3458/80, para. 73.

The provisions of this order cease to have effect on 31st January 1981.

1280   ## Sea fish—conservation
The Sea Fish (Conservation) (Enforcement of Miscellaneous EEC Provisions) Regulations 1980, S.I. 1980 No. 1795 (in force on 19th December 1980), provide for the enforcement of certain provisions of Council Regulation (EEC) 2527/80, para. 72, laying down technical measures for the conservation of fishery resources. The provisions of the regulations cease to have effect on 20th December 1980.

1281   The Sea Fish (Conservation) (Enforcement of Miscellaneous EEC Provisions) (No. 2) Regulations 1980, S.I. 1980 No. 1997 (in force on 20th December 1980), provide for the enforcement of certain provisions of Council Regulation (EEC) 2527/80, para. 72, laying down technical measures for the conservation of fishery resources, as extended by Council Regulation (EEC) 3458/80, para. 73.
The provisions of these regulations cease to have effect on 31st January 1981.

1282   —— **landing and sale—restrictions**
The Immature Sea Fish Order 1980, S.I. 1980 No. 1808 (in force on the 19th December 1980), implements the United Kingdom's obligation to provide for the enforcement of Council Regulation (EEC) 2527/80, para. 72, laying down technical measures for the conservation of fishery resources. The provisions of the order cease to have effect on the 20th December.
The following orders are revoked: Mackerel (Regulation of Landing) Order 1974, 1974 Halsbury's Abridgment para. 1418; Immature Sea Fish Order 1979 and Immature Nephrops Order 1979, 1979 Halsbury's Abridgment paras. 1309 and 1308.

1283   The Immature Sea Fish (No. 2) Order 1980, S.I. 1980 No. 1985 (in force on 20th December 1980), implements the United Kingdom's obligation to provide for the enforcement of Council Regulation (EEC) 2527/80, para. 72, laying down technical measures for the conservation of fishery resources, as extended by Council Regulation (EEC) 3458/80, para. 73.
The provisions of this order cease to have effect on 31st January 1981.

1284   —— **prohibition of fishing methods**
The Specified Sea Fish (Prohibition of Fishing Methods) Order 1980, S.I. 1980 No. 1809 (in force on 19th December 1980), implements the United Kingdom's obligation to provide for the enforcement of Council Regulation (EEC) 2527/80, para. 72, laying down technical measures for the conservation of fishery resources, and in so doing revokes certain specified orders. The provisions of the order cease to have effect on 20th December 1980.

1285   The Specified Sea Fish (Prohibition of Fishing Methods) (No. 2) Order 1980, S.I. 1980 No. 1996 (in force on 20th December 1980), implements the United Kingdom's obligation to provide for the enforcement of Council Regulation (EEC) 2527/80, para. 72 laying down technical measures for the conservation of fishery resources, as extended by Council Regulation (EEC) 3458/80, para. 73.
The provisions of this order cease to have effect on 31st January 1981.

1286   **Sea Fish Industry Act 1980**
The Sea Fish Industry Act 1980 enables the White Fish Authority to impose a levy in respect of white fish and white fish products trans-shipped within British fishery limits. The Act received the royal assent on 30th June 1980 and came into force on that date.
Section 1 (1) extends the Sea Fish Industry Act 1970, s. 17, under which the White Fish Authority may impose on persons engaged in the white fish industry in the United Kingdom a levy in respect of white fish and white fish products landed in the United Kingdom, so as to permit the Authority to impose a levy on such persons in respect of white fish and white fish products trans-shipped within British fishery limits. Section 1 (2) provides that the Authority may not impose a levy more than once in respect of the same fish or fish products. Section 2 deals with citation and extent.

1287   **Sea fishing—industry—loans and grants—time limits**
The Sea Fish Industry Act 1970 (Relaxation of Time Limits) Order 1980, S.I. 1980 No. 1971 (in force on 16th December 1980), extends the time limits contained in certain provisions of the Sea Fish Industry Act 1970 to the end of 1981.

1288   —— licensing—western waters

The Sea Fishing (Specified Western Waters) (Manx and Channel Island Boats) Licensing Order 1980, S.I. 1980 No. 332 (in force on 7th April 1980), prohibits fishing for cod, haddock, whiting, plaice and sole in the area specified in Sch. 1 of the Order by British fishing boats registered in the Isle of Man or any of the Channel Islands unless such fishing is authorised by a licence granted by one of the fisheries Ministers. Fishing by boats of less than forty feet in length is excepted.

1289   The Sea Fishing (Specified Western Waters) Licensing Order 1980, S.I. 1980 No. 333 (in force on 7th April 1980), prohibits fishing for cod, haddock, whiting, plaice and sole in the area specified in Sch. 1 of the Order by British fishing boats registered in the United Kingdom, unless such fishing is authorised by a licence granted by one of the fisheries Ministers. Fishing by boats of less than forty feet in length is excepted.

1290   The Sea Fishing (Specified Western Waters) (Isle of Man) Licensing Order 1980, S.I. 1980 No. 334 (in force on 7th April 1980), prohibits fishing for cod, haddock, whiting, plaice and sole within the fishing limits of the Isle of Man but outside its territorial waters, by British fishing boats, unless such fishing is authorised by a licence granted by the Isle of Man Board of Agriculture and Fisheries. Fishing by boats of less than forty feet in length is excepted.

1291   —— restrictions on landing—western waters

The Sea Fishing (Specified Western Waters) (Restrictions on Landing) Order 1980, S.I. 1980 No. 335 (in force on 7th April 1980), prohibits the landing in the United Kingdom of cod, haddock, whiting, plaice and sole caught in the area specified in Sch. 1, Pt. 1 of the Order by British fishing boats of forty feet and over in length. The landing of sea fish caught under the authority of a licence granted by one of the fisheries Ministers of the Isle of Man Board of Agriculture and Fisheries, or caught in specified circumstances within the fishery limits of the Channel Islands is excepted. The landing of a by-catch is also excepted from the prohibition in certain circumstances.

1292   White Fish Authority—general levy

The Sea Fish Industry Act 1970 (Increase in Rate of Levy) Order 1980, S.I. 1980 No. 379 (in force on 14th March 1980), increases the maximum rate at which the White Fish Authority is empowered by the Sea Fish Industry Act 1970 to impose a general levy on persons engaged in the white fish industry. The maximum rate is raised from 2p to 5p per stone of white fish landed in the UK.

1293   The White Fish Authority (General Levy) (Amendment) Regulations 1979 Confirmatory Order 1980, S.I. 1980 No. 527 (in force on 8th May 1980), confirms, after modification, regulations made by the White Fish Authority further amending the White Fish Authority (General Levy) Regulations 1969 so as to increase the levy payable under those regulations.

1294   The White Fish Authority (General Levy) Regulations 1980 Confirmatory Order 1980, S.I. 1980 No. 1199 (in force on 16th August 1980), confirms regulations made by the White Fish Authority which supersede the White Fish Authority (General Levy) Regulations 1969, as amended. The regulations maintain the existing levy on firsthand sales of whte fish and their products landed. They also extend the levy to white fish and the products trans-shipped by way of sale.

1295   —— grants

The White Fish Authority (Research and Development Grants) Order 1980, S.I. 1980 No. 1972 (in force on 16th December 1980), raises to £6,500,000 the limit imposed by the Sea Fish Industry Act 1970 in relation to the aggregate amount of grants payable to the White Fish Authority for the purposes of research or experiment or in providing plants for processing white fish or making ice.

FOOD, DAIRIES AND SLAUGHTERHOUSES

Halsbury's Laws of England (4th edn.), Vol. 18, paras. 1001–1400

1296   Additives

The Miscellaneous Additives in Food Regulations 1980, S.I. 1980 No. 1834 (in force on 31st December 1980), replace the 1974 Regulations, 1974 Halsbury's Abridgment para. 1426. The regulations implement various Council Directives (EEC) concerned with emulsifiers, stabilisers, thickeners, gelling agents and antioxidants used in foodstuffs.

1297   Antioxidants in food

The Antioxidants in Food (Amendment) Regulations 1980, S.I. 1980 No. 1831 (in force on 31st December 1980), amend the 1978 Regulations, 1978 Halsbury's Abridgment para. 1367. The regulations implement Council Directive (EEC) 78/143 laying down specific criteria of purity for antioxidants which may be used in foodstuffs intended for human consumption.

1298   Butter—prices

The Butter and Concentrated Butter Prices (Amendment) Order 1980, S.I. 1980 No. 4 (in force on 28th January 1980), varies the Butter Prices Order 1978, as varied, and the Concentrated Butter Prices Order 1978, 1978 Halsbury's Abridgment paras. 1371–73. The principal changes are that the maximum retail prices of butter sold in certain rectangular packs of specific weights and of concentrated butter sold in packs of specified weights are increased. Those prices apply only in relation to metric units of weight.

1299   Chloroform in food

The Chloroform in Food Regulations 1980, S.I. 1980 No. 36 (in force on 1st April 1980), prohibit the sale and importation of food containing chloroform. The Regulations do not apply to food intended for export or to products whose chloroform content is controlled by the Medicines (Chloroform Prohibition) Order 1979.

1300   Emulsifiers and stabilisers in food

The Emulsifiers and Stabilisers in Food Regulations 1980, S.I. 1980 No. 1833 (in force on 31st December 1980), replace the 1975 Regulations, 1975 Halsbury's Abridgment para. 1546, as amended. The regulations implement the Council Directive (EEC) 78/612, laying down specific criteria of purity for emulsifiers, stabilisers, thickeners and gelling agents for use in foodstuffs, and Council Directive (EEC) 78/664, laying down specific criteria of purity for antioxidants which may be used in foodstuffs intended for human consumption.

1301   Food—labelling of food

The Food Labelling Regulations 1980, S.I. 1980 No. 1849 (in force on 1st January 1981 in respect of the transitional provisions, and in force on 1st January 1983 in respect of the remainder), supersede the Labelling of Food Regulations 1970, as amended, apart from those provisions relating to claims. The Regulations implement Council Directives (EEC) 77/94 and 79/112 relating to the labelling, presentation and advertising of foodstuffs for sale to the ultimate consumer. They also implement Council Directive (EEC) 76/766 relating to alcohol tables.

1302   Foodstuffs—materials in contact with food—approximation of laws

Council Directive (EEC) 80/590 determines the symbol that may accompany materials and articles intended to come into contact with foodstuffs, as provided for by Council Directive (EEC) 76/893, 1976 Halsbury's Abridgment para. 1254 (OJ No. L151, 19.6.80).

1303   Materials in contact with food

The Materials and Articles in Contact with Food (Amendment) Regulations 1980, S.I. 1980 No. 1838 (in force on 1st January 1981), amend the 1978 Regulations. The regulations implement Council Directive (EEC) 80/766, laying down the Community method of analysis for the official control of the vinyl chloride monomer level in materials and articles which are intended to come into contact with food, and implement Council Directive (EEC) 78/142 on the approximation of the laws of the member states relating to such materials and articles.

1304   Meat—premiums for non-marketing and dairy herd conversion schemes

The Non-Marketing of Milk and Milk Products and the Dairy Herd Conversion Premiums (Amendment) Regulations 1980, S.I. 1980 No. 124 (in force on 3rd March 1980), amend the Non-Marketing of Milk and Milk Products and the Dairy Herd Conversion Premiums Regulations 1977, 1977 Halsbury's Abridgment para. 70, by taking into account certain amending Council Regulations (EEC) and Commission Regulations (EEC).

1305   The Non-Marketing of Milk and Milk Products and the Dairy Herd Conversion Premiums (Amendment) (No. 2) Regulations 1980, S.I. 1980 No. 1394 (in force on 14th October 1980) further amend the 1977 Regulations, 1977 Halsbury's Abridgment para. 70 by including in the definition of "the Regulation of the Council" a reference to legislation which has further amended the Regulation there defined.

1306   —— preserving meat—meaning

See *Jaka Foods Group Ltd v Secretary of State for Industry*, para. 2913.

1307   Milk—prices

The Milk (Great Britain) Order 1980, S.I. 1980 No. 48 (in force on 1st February 1980), supersedes the Milk (Great Britain) Order 1977, 1977 Halsbury's Abridgment para. 1339, as amended. The order prescribes maximum prices for the sale in Great Britain of raw milk for heat treatment, increases the maximum retail prices of milk by $1\frac{1}{2}$p per pint and prescribes the maximum retail prices in metric units as well as in non-metric units.

This order has been revoked; see para. 1310.

1308   The Milk (Great Britain) (Amendment) Order 1980, S.I. 1980 No. 1175 (in force on 10th August 1980), amends the Milk (Great Britain) Order 1980, supra by increasing the maximum retail prices of milk on sale in Great Britain.

This order has been revoked; see para. 1310.

1309   The Milk (Great Britain) (Amendment) (No. 2) Order 1980, S.I. 1980 No. 1295 (in force on 1st September 1980) further amends the 1980 Order, para. A108 in relation to the maximum price for the sale of raw milk for heat treatment.

This order has been revoked; see para. 1310.

1310   The Milk (Great Britain) (No. 2) Order 1980, S.I. 1980 No. 2022 (in force on 1st January 1981), supersedes the Milk (Great Britain) Order 1980 as amended, supra.

The order increases by 1·276p per litre the maximum prices for the sale in Great Britain of raw milk for heat treatment with effect from 1st January 1981 and increases by 1½p per pint, and a corresponding amount per litre, the maximum retail prices of milk on sale in Great Britain with effect from 4th January 1981. An additional charge for Channel Islands and South Devon milk may be made at the rate of 3·014p per pint throughout the year.

1311   —— special designation

The Milk (Special Designation) (Amendment) Regulations 1980, S.I. 1980 No. 488 (in force on 1st May 1980), amend the Milk (Special Designation) Regulations 1977, reg. 8, 1977 Halsbury's Abridgment para. 1341, by providing that every producer's licence granted on or before 30th April 1985 will expire on that date and that every producer's licence granted after that date will expire at the end of the five year period during which the licence is granted.

These regulations have been revoked; see para. 1312.

1312   The Milk (Special Designation) (Amendment) (No. 2) Regulations 1980, S.I. 1980 No. 1863 (in force on 1st January 1981), further amend the Milk (Special Designation) Regulations 1977, 1977 Halsbury's Abridgment para. 1341, by providing that a dealer's licence may no longer be granted to use the special designation "Untreated". An untreated milk distributor's licence is introduced to use the special designation "Untreated", and may be granted to persons who obtain farm bottled milk pre-packed from a licensed producer and who re-sell such milk by retail. The regulations also provide that on or after 1st January 1982, the words "Raw Unpasteurised Milk" must be marked on retail containers of milk in relation to which the special designation "Untreated" is used, and also make changes to the conditions relating to the use of the special designations "Pasteurised", "Sterilised" and "Ultra Heat-Treated". Every producer's licence and untreated milk distributor's licence granted on or before 30th April 1985 will expire on that date and every such licence granted after that date but on or before 31st December 1990 will expire on 31st December 1990. Every producer's licence and untreated milk distributor's licence granted after 31st December 1990 will expire at the end of the five year period in which it is granted. The Milk (Special Designation) (Amendment) Regulations 1980, supra are revoked.

1313   Preservatives in food

The Preservatives in Food Regulations 1980, S.I. 1980 No. 931 (in force on 1st August 1980), amend the Preservatives in Food Regulations 1979, 1979 Halsbury's Abridgment para. 1331. The regulations specify additional foods which may contain the permitted preservatives, exclude canned fruit, fruit pulp and fruit purée from the list of specified foods, amend the method of analysis of treated citrus food and insert a new diagram of a modified Clevenger-type separator.

1314   Sale—sale of food unfit for consumption—statutory defence—warranty

A frozen chicken was sold to a local authority through a number of suppliers. The immediate supplier had bought it from the defendants, who had bought it under an invoice in which it was described under the brand name of the original suppliers. The invoice contained no written warranties. The chicken was unfit for human consumption and the authority laid an information against the immediate suppliers alleging an offence under the Food and Drugs Act 1955, s. 8 (1). The suppliers joined the defendants in accordance with s. 113. The information was dismissed on the ground that the defendants were entitled to rely on the provisions of s. 115 (1) to the effect that in any proceedings for an offence under the Act consisting of selling an article it was a defence to prove that the defendant purchased it as being an article which could lawfully be sold or otherwise dealt with or could lawfully be sold or dealt with under the name or description or for the purpose under or for which he sold or dealt with it, and with a written warranty to that effect, and that he had no reason to believe at the time of the commission of the alleged offence that it was otherwise, and that it was then in the same state as when he purchased it. It was held that the brand name in the invoice amounted to a warranty by virtue of s. 115 (5), which provides that a name or description entered in an invoice is to be deemed to be a written warranty that the article or substance to which the entry refers can be sold or otherwise dealt with under that name or description by any person without contravening the Act. On appeal by the authority, *held*, it was a necessary ingredient of a defence under s. 115 (1) that a defendant should prove that he had purchased the article as being one which could lawfully be sold under the name under which he sold it and that he had purchased it with a written warranty to that effect. The defence was available in any proceedings for an offence under the Act, which clearly included an offence under s. 8 (1). The entry of a name or description in an invoice was deemed by s. 115 (5) to be a written warranty that the article could be sold under that name without contravening the Act. The effect of s. 115 (5) was not limited to cases where the offence related to the name or description of the article only. The defendants had proved the necessary facts to establish a defence under s. 115 and the appeal would be dismissed.

ROCHDALE METROPOLITAN BOROUGH COUNCIL v FMC (MEAT) LTD [1980] 2 All ER 303 (Queen's Bench Division: LORD WIDGERY CJ and WOOLF J).

1315   Solvents in food

The Solvents in Food (Amendment) Regulations 1980, S.I. 1980 No. 1832 (in force on 31st December 1980), further amend the 1967 Regulations. The regulations implement Council Directive (EEC) 78/663, laying down specific criteria of purity for emulsifiers, stabilisers, thickeners and gelling agents for use in foodstuffs, and Council Directive (EEC) 78/664 laying down specific criteria of purity for antioxidants which may be used in foodstuffs intended for consumption.

1316   Welfare food

See paras. 2802, 2803.

FOREIGN RELATIONS LAW

Halsbury's Laws of England (4th edn.), Vol. 18, paras. 1401–1908

1317   Consular Fees Act 1980

See para. 423.

1318   Consular relations—diplomatic and consular privileges—seizure of United States embassy

The United States initiated proceedings against Iran before the International Court of Justice complaining of violation of, inter alia, the Vienna Convention on Diplomatic Relations 1961 and the Vienna Convention on Consular Relations 1963 in an incident involving the seizure of the United States embassy in Tehran and the holding of United States nationals hostage in the buildings. The government of Iran, alleged to have tolerated and encouraged the incident, pleaded that the incident represented only a marginal and secondary aspect of an overall problem involving more than 25 years' continual interference by the United States in the internal affairs of Iran. It was pleaded that the court could not validly examine this one aspect of a larger problem in isolation. In the course of making an order indicating provisional measures the court rejected this plea. It stated that the seizure of an embassy and consulates and the detention of internationally-protected persons as hostages could not be regarded as a "secondary" or "marginal" matter having regard to the importance of the principles involved and did not constitute an obstacle to the courts' taking cognizance of the application by the United States.

United States Diplomatic and Consular Staff in Tehran, Provisional Measures, Order of 15th December 1979, ICJ Reports 1979, 7.

1319   Convention—Convention against the Taking of Hostages

An International Convention against the Taking of Hostages was opened for signature in New York, 18th December 1979. The contracting parties undertake to create offences relating to the taking of hostages which will be punishable with penalties which are appropriate to the gravity of the offence. The offence is defined as the seizure or detention of another person under threat of killing, injuring or continuing to detain that person in order to compel a third party to do or to abstain from doing any act as a condition for the release of the hostage. An offence would also be committed by a person who attempts to commit any such act or who acts as an accomplice. The convention calls on the contracting party, in whose territory any such offence is committed, to do what it can to relieve the plight of the hostage and calls for co-operation between states in the prevention of such offences. Contracting parties are required to take appropriate measures to ensure that they have jurisdiction to deal with offences and, in appropriate circumstances, to ensure that the alleged offender may be extradited. If a state does not extradite an alleged offender it is required to ensure that he is prosecuted for the alleged offence. The convention will come into effect after twenty-two states have ratified or acceded to it. The United Kingdom has not ratified the convention, the text of which is set out in Cmnd. 7893.

1320   —— interpretation—use of travaux préparatoires

See *Fothergill v Monarch Airlines*, para. 197.

1321   —— Long-Range Transboundary Air Pollution

A Convention on Long-Range Transboundary Air Pollution was signed at Geneva, 13th–16th November 1979. The contracting parties have undertaken to endeavour to limit and, as far as possible, gradually reduce and prevent air pollution including long-range transboundary air pollution. They also have undertaken to develop without undue delay policies and strategies which serve to combat the discharge of air pollutants and to consult with parties which are exposed to a significant risk of long-range transboundary air pollution. The convention will enter into force after twenty-four states have ratified, accepted, approved or acceded to it. The United Kingdom has not ratified the convention. For the text of the convention, see Cmnd. 7885.

1322   Council of Europe—conservation

See para. 1089.

1323   —— convention on establishment

The European Convention on Establishment was signed in Paris in 1955 and came into force on 23rd February 1965. The aim of the convention is to establish a favourable basis for the treatment by one country of the nationals of another country (both countries being contracting parties to the convention) in the matters of entry, residence and expulsion. The nationals of one such country who are in the territory of another such country should, in general terms, be accorded treatment equal to that which the latter country accords to its own nationals in the exercise of private rights; judicial and administrative guarantees for individuals; the exercise of gainful occupations; in taxation, compulsory services, expropriation and nationalisation; and in certain other rights (e.g. in relation to education). Any existing restrictions vis-à-vis nationals of other countries must be "frozen" and then gradually phased out. A standing committee is established to formulate proposals to improve the practical implementation of the convention. At its 12th session in 1979 the standing committee adopted a commentary on the provisions of the convention intended to facilitate an understanding of them. The commentary, together with the text of the convention, has been published by the Council of Europe (Strasbourg, 1980) and is available from HMSO.

1324   —— European Highway Code

See para. 2368.

1325   —— missing persons

The Committee of Ministers of the Council of Europe on 20th April 1979 adopted a recommendation on the search for missing persons (Recommendation R (79)6). It recommends that governments of member states should each nominate a department for the reception of search applications etc. for missing persons and an office to serve as the centre for the exchange of information on an international level concerning such persons. It recommends that a missing person should have the right, once he or she is found, to refuse to have certain information disclosed to the applicant. The recommendation applies to missing persons who are minors, persons disappearing in suspicious circumstances, persons who may have had an accident and persons unable to provide for themselves by reasons of their physical state, their mental state or their poverty.

1326   Diplomatic and consular privileges and immunities—personal privileges

International law so far as it concerns diplomatic and consular officials (see the Vienna Convention on Diplomatic Relations 1961 and the Vienna Convention on Consular Relations 1963) provides its own means of defence against, and sanction for, illicit activities by members of diplomatic or consular missions: i.e. declaring an individual to be persona non grata and breaking off diplomatic relations. Accordingly, even if it were possible to prove that members of a diplomatic or consular mission had indulged in criminal activities in the host country this would not constitute to a charge that the host country had violated the canons of diplomatic and consular privileges and immunities

United States Diplomatic and Consular Staff in Tehran, Judgment, ICJ Reports, p. 3.

1327   —— Vienna Convention

Articles II and III of the Optional Protocols on the Compulsory Settlement of Disputes to the Vienna Convention on Diplomatic Relations 1961 and the Vienna Convention on Consular Relations 1963 provide that within two months after a party has notified its opinion to the other that a dispute exists, the parties may agree to "resort not to the International Court of Justice but to an arbitral tribunal" or to "adopt a conciliation procedure before resorting to the International Court of Justice". The International Court of Justice has ruled that these articles provide only that, as a substitute for recourse to the court, the parties may agree upon resort to arbitration or conciliation. The articles have no application unless recourse to arbitration or conciliation has been proposed by one of the parties to the dispute and the other has expressed its readiness to consider the proposal. Further, it follows that only then may the provisions in the articles regarding a two-month period come into play and operate as a time limit upon the conclusion of an agreement as to the establishment of the alternative procedure. The articles do not lay down a precondition of the applicability of the precise and categorical provision contained in art I establishing the compulsory jurisdiction of the court.

United States Diplomatic and Consular Staff in Tehran, Judgment, ICJ Reports 1980, p. 3 especially p. 26.

1328   European Communities

See EUROPEAN COMMUNITIES.

1329   European Convention on the Custody of Children

The Council of Europe has drawn up a Convention on the Recognition and Enforcement of Decisions concerning Custody of Children and of the Restoration of Custody of Children. The convention also includes within its scope decisions on rights of access. The convention requires contracting states to recognise decisions relating to custody in other contracting states and, where they are enforceable, to enforce them. Application for enforcement is made to a central authority in the state concerned. The grounds on which recognition or enforcement may be refused are specified and the convention also prescribes the relevant procedure. The convention is open to ratification etc by member states of the Council of Europe. The text of the convention has been published by the Council of Europe as European Treaty Series No. 105.

The United Kingdom has signed the convention but legislation will be necessary before it can be ratified. However, the United Kingdom reserved the right to refuse to return a child by allowing the British courts to determine whether the return would be in the child's best interests. See Home Office Press Release 20th May, 1980.

1330   Foreign Compensation Commission—distribution of compensation—China

The Foreign Compensation (People's Republic of China) (Registration) Order 1980, S.I. 1980 No. 1720 (in force on 5th January 1981), enables certain claims relating to property in the People's Republic of China owned by United Kingdom nationals or relating to debts owed on pensions payable by persons resident in the People's Republic of China to United Kingdom nationals to be registered with, and reported upon by, the Foreign Compensation Commission.

1331   Human rights

See HUMAN RIGHTS.

1332   Immunities and privileges—international organisations

The Eurocontrol (Immunities and Privileges) (Amendment) Order 1980, S.I. 1980 No. 1076 (in force on a day to be notified in the London, Edinburgh and Belfast Gazettes), amends the 1970 Order by conferring exemption from income tax on the officers of Eurocontrol.

1333

The International Organisations (Immunities and Privileges) Miscellaneous Provisions Order 1980, S.I. 1980 No. 1096 (in force on 18th August 1980), makes amendments to certain orders mentioned in the Sch. thereto consequential upon the changes in terminology for duties of customs and excise introduced by the Finance (No. 2) Act 1975 and the Customs and Excise Management Act 1979.

1334

By an Exchange of Notes, 20th May 1980 (Cmnd. 8047), between the Government and the Inter-American Development Bank, certain exemptions from customs and excise duties have been extended to new staff members of the bank taking up appointments in the United Kingdom. The privileges are subject to conditions restricting the disposal of goods imported duty free and to general restrictions on imports and exports. They do not apply to citizens of the United Kingdom and colonies nor to permanent residents.

1335   —— —— INMARSAT

The INMARSAT (Immunities and Privileges) Order 1980, S.I. 1980 No. 187 (in force on a date to be notified in the London, Edinburgh and Belfast Gazettes), confers privileges and immunities on the International Maritime Satellite Organisation (INMARSAT), on representatives of its member states and signatories designated by its member states and on its officers and experts. The privileges and immunities are conferred in accordance with an agreement between the government of the United Kingdom and INMARSAT. The INMARSAT (Immunities and Privileges Order) 1979, 1979 Halsbury's Abridgment para. 1343 is revoked.

1336   Inter-American Development Bank

The Inter-American Development Bank (Further Payments) Order 1980, S.I. 1980 No. 1381 (in force on 9th September 1980), provides for further payments to the Bank.

1337   —— immunities and privileges

See para. 1334.

1338   International Court of Justice—exclusion of jurisdiction

In 1979 the Security Council of the United Nations adopted resolution 459 (1979) calling on Iran to release the personnel of the US embassy in Tehran who had been seized by militants, to provide them with protection and to allow them to leave the country. The resolution also, inter alia, requested the Secretary-General to lend his good offices for the immediate implementation of the resolution. Resolution 461 (1979) of the Security Council reinforced resolution 459. Early in 1980 the Secretary-General set up a commission to undertake a fact-finding mission to Iran. In subsequent proceedings brought by the United States against Iran in the International Court of Justice, the court ruled that neither the mandate given by the Security Council to the Secretary-General in resolutions 459 and 461 nor the setting up of the commission presented any obstacle to the courts considering the merits of the case

United States Diplomatic and Consular Staff in Tehran, Judgment, ICJ Reports, 1980, p. 3, especially at p. 24.

1339   —— power to indicate interim measures of protection

Article 41 of the Statute of the International Court of Justice empowers the court to indicate interim or provisional measures which ought to be taken to preserve the respective rights of either party to a dispute before the International Court of Justice. On an application to the court by the United States for a provisional measure calling upon the government of Iran, inter alia, to release United States nationals held hostage in the United States embassy in Tehran and to clear the premises of the embassy of all unauthorised persons, the government of Iran pleaded that since provisional measures were intended to protect the interests of the parties they could not be unilateral in nature. The court ruled that although, in indicating provisional measures, it had frequently done so with reference to both the parties the fact that the measures requested were unilateral did not preclude the court from entertaining the application. The court indicated provisional measures in an order dated 15th December 1979.

United States Diplomatic and Consular Staff in Tehran, Provisional Measures Order of 15th December 1979, ICJ Reports 1979, 7.

1340   International Labour Conference—conventions and recommendations—implementation

The government has announced that it fully supports the aims and principles of Convention 150 and Recommendation 158 adopted by the International Labour Conference at its 64th session in 1978. The convention sets out general principles to be applied to public administration activities in the field of national labour policy and the recommendation sets out in more detail the responsibilities of the labour administration system concerned with labour standards, labour relations, employment and research. The government proposes to ratify the convention and accept the recommendation on the basis of existing legislation. The government similarly intends to ratify Convention 151 and accept Recommendation 159 which are both concerned with the extension of trade union rights to employees in the public service. The acceptance of the recommendation is subject to a reservation that it is not the practice in the United Kingdom for recognition to be based on pre-established criteria. Current legislation and changes to it which are under consideration fully satisfy the requirements of the legislation. The government's decision and the text of the conventions and recommendations are published as Cmnd. 7786.

1341   International Monetary Fund—breach of exchange control—effect on letter of credit

See *United City Merchants (Investments) Ltd v Royal Bank of Canada (No. 2)*, para. 221.

1342   —— increase in subscription

The International Monetary Fund (Increase in Subscription) Order 1980, S.I. 1980 No. 1131 (in force on 1st August 1980), authorises an increase in the amount of the United Kingdom's subscription to the International Monetary Fund.

1343   Iran (Temporary Powers) Act 1980

The Iran (Temporary Powers) Act 1980 enables provisions to be made in consequence of breaches of international law by Iran in connection with or arising out of the detention of members of the embassy of the United States of America. This is in accordance with the decision on 22nd April 1980 of the Foreign Ministers of the member states of the European Communities. The Act received the royal assent on 15th May 1980 and came into force on 17th May 1980.

Section 1 empowers Her Majesty by Order in Council to make such provision in relation to contracts in any way relating to or connected with Iran, being either contracts for services or contracts for the sale, supply or transport of goods, as appear to be necessary or expedient; see para. 1344. This does not apply to contracts made before the date of the order, nor to contracts for financial services. The cases in which extra-territorial offences may be created are limited and provision is made for parliamentary control over Orders in Council exercising these powers.

Section 2 deals with short title, commencement and extent and provides for s. 1 to be terminated by Order in Council.

1344   —— trading sanctions

The Iran (Trading Sanctions) Order 1980, S.I. 1980 No. 737 (in force on 30th May 1980), made under the Iran (Temporary Powers) Act 1980, para. 1343, prohibits the making or performance of contracts for the sale, supply or transport of embargoed goods from the United Kingdom, or from any territory to which the order extends, to Iran.

All goods are embargoed except specific foodstuffs, medical products and other specified products if sold or supplied for medical or surgical purposes.

Contracts made before the 30th May 1980 are excluded.

1345   —— —— exports

See para. 762.

1346   Protection of Trading Interests Act 1980

The Protection of Trading Interests Act 1980 provides protection from requirements, prohibitions and judgments imposed or given under the laws of countries outside the United Kingdom and affecting the trading or other interests of persons in the United Kingdom. The Act received the royal assent on 20th March 1980 and came into force on that date.

Section 1 provides a number of means by which the Secretary of State may counter measures which are taken or proposed to be taken by or under the law of overseas countries for regulating or controlling international trade, and which are or would be damaging to the trading interests of the United Kingdom. (i) He may make orders specifying the measures concerned; (ii) he may make further orders requiring persons in the United Kingdom who carry on business there to notify him of any requirements or prohibitions imposed or threatened to be imposed on them under such measures; and (iii) he may prohibit compliance with such measures. International trade is widely defined to include any business activity.

Section 2 provides that, where a person in the United Kingdom has been or may be required to produce to a court, tribunal or authority of an overseas country commercial documents outside that country or to furnish commercial information, the Secretary of State may give directions prohibiting compliance with that requirement. The section specifies the circumstances in which a direction may be given, which are broadly comparable to the circumstances in which a United Kingdom court would refuse a request made by an overseas court for evidence under the Evidence (Proceedings in Other Jurisdictions) Act 1975.

Section 3 provides penalties for failure to comply with requirements imposed under ss. 1, 2. It provides for a maximum fine of £1,000 on summary conviction and for an unlimited fine on conviction on indictment.

Section 4 provides that, in proceedings under the Evidence (Proceedings in Other Jurisdictions) Act 1975, United Kingdom courts must not comply with a request made by a court of an overseas country when the Secretary of State has given a certificate that the request infringes United Kingdom jurisdiction or is otherwise prejudicial to United Kingdom sovereignty.

Section 5 provides that judgments for multiple damages given in civil proceedings by courts of overseas countries are not enforceable in the United Kingdom. It further provides that judgments given in overseas countries based on competition laws which have been specified by an order made by the Secretary of State are not enforceable in the United Kindom.

Section 6 concerns United Kingdom citizens, United Kingdom corporations and other persons carrying on business in the United Kingdom who, under foreign judgments for multiple damages, have paid an amount on account of the damages. Qualifying defendants may recover back so much of the amount paid as exceeds the part attributable to compensation, subject to certain exceptions. It also permits courts in the United Kingdom to entertain such proceedings even if the defendant is not within the jurisdiction of the court. Section 7 concerns the enforcement in the United Kingdom of overseas judgments under provisions corresponding to s. 6. Citation, interpretation, repeals and extent are dealt with by s. 8.

1347　Recognition of new governments—change in United Kingdom practice

The Lord Privy Seal in a written answer to a parliamentary question has stated that the practice whereby the government made and announced a decision formally recognising a foreign government which had come to power unconstitutionally had become a political liability and would be abandoned. Many other countries did not accord recognition to governments. In accordance with such practice, the government would decide the nature of its dealings with régimes which came to power unconstitutionally in the light of its assessment of whether they were able of themselves to exercise effective control of the territory of the state concerned, and seemed likely to continue to do so. See the *Daily Telegraph*, 26th April 1980.

1348　State immunity—Guernsey

The State Immunity (Guernsey) Order 1980, S.I. 1980 No. 871 (in force on 21st July 1980), extends the State Immunity Act 1978, 1978 Halsbury's Abridgment para. 1421, with specified modifications, to the Bailiwick of Guernsey.

1349　State succession—treaty rights and obligations

The Vienna Convention on the Succession of States in respect of Treaties (Cmnd 7760) has been signed by 20 nations. It covers succession in respect of part of the territory of a state, the position of newly independent states (for example in relation to multi-lateral and bilateral treaties; and provisional application), the uniting and separating of states and the settlement of disputes under the convention. The convention will come into force on the 30th day after the deposit of the 15th instrument of ratification. The convention is open to accession by any state. The United Kingdom has not signed the convention.

1350   United Nations Industrial Development Organisation

The constitution of the United Nations Industrial Development Organisation was adopted on 8th April 1979. The primary objective of the organisation is the promotion and acceleration of industrial development in the developing countries with a view to assisting in the establishment of a new international economic order. The organisation will also promote industrial development and co-operation on global, regional, national and sectoral levels. The principle organs of the organisation are the general conference, the Industrial Development Board and the secretariat. The organisation will have an Industrial Development Fund financed in part by voluntary contributions. The organisation will be based in Vienna. The organisation enjoys legal personality in the territory of each of its member states and all necessary privileges and immunities. The constitution has not been ratified by the United Kingdom. See Cmnd. 7861, 1980.

1351   Vienna Convention on Diplomatic Relations—violation—seizure of embassy

See *Re United States Diplomatic and Consular Staff in Tehran*, para. 1318.

FORESTRY

Halsbury's Laws of England (4th edn.), Vol. 19, paras. 1–100

1352   Importation of trees—restrictions

The Import and Export of Trees, Wood and Bark (Health) (Great Britain) Order 1980, S.I. 1980 No. 449 (in force on 1st May 1980), made by the Forestry Commissioners, revokes the Importation of Forest Trees (Prohibition) (Great Britain) Order 1965 and the Importation of Wood and Bark (Prohibition) (Great Britain) Order 1977, 1977 Halsbury's Abridgment para. 111. The order implements Council Directive (EEC) 77/93, which prohibits the import into the EEC of certain pests harmful to forest trees and prescribes controls on the movement of forest trees, wood and isolated bark. In addition the order prescribes controls in respect of the import of genetically manipulated material and in respect of direct trade in forest trees, wood and isolated bark with countries outside the EEC.

1353   Tree pests—control

The Tree Pests (Great Britain) Order 1980, S.I. 1980 No. 450 (in force on 1st May 1980), is made by the Forestry Commissioners under the Plant Health Act 1967 and relates to the control of non-indigenous tree pests. The order prohibits, except under licence, the keeping or disposal of such pests, trees and plants infected with such pests and tree pests subjected to genetic manipulation. It also provides for powers of entry, examination, sampling and marking and powers for the destruction or treatment of plants or wood carrying tree pests. Persons having information relating to pests are bound to disclose that information and provision is made for offences and penalties in connection with the order.

FRIENDLY SOCIETIES

Halsbury's Laws of England (4th edn.), Vol. 19, paras. 101–400

1354   Benefit—increase of limits

The Friendly Societies (Limits of Benefits) Order 1980, S.I. 1980 No. 1142 (in force on 1st September 1980), increases the limits on the amounts which a member of a registered friendly society or branch may be entitled to receive from any one or more of such societies or branches under non-tax exempt business.

1355   Chief Registrar of Friendly Societies—annual report

In Part I of the Report of the Chief Registrar of Friendly Societies for 1978 (Friendly Societies, Industrial Assurance Companies and General), the registrar noted that, at the beginning of the year, there were 7,638 societies (including branches) registered under the Friendly Societies Act 1974, and that there were 7,421 societies on the register at the end of the year. No dispute was formally referred to him under the 1974 Act, s. 77 (1) during the year but 26 summonses were issued against seven working men's clubs and their officers for failing to submit annual returns in due time.

At the end of the year there were 12 industrial assurance companies one of which was registered under the Industrial and Provident Societies Act 1965. During 1978, 1,334 new complaints were handled relating to industrial assurance policies (compared with 1,557 in 1977). Only two summonses were taken out in the year against industrial assurance companies.

1356   Fees

The Friendly Societies (Fees) Regulations 1980, S.I. 1980 No. 1750 (in force on 1st January 1981), increase the fees to be paid for matters to be transacted, and for the inspection of documents, under the Friendly Societies Act 1974.

1357   Life assurance premiums—income tax relief—change of rate

The Friendly Societies (Life Assurance Premium Relief) (Change of Rate) Regulations 1980, S.I. 1980 No. 1947 (in force on 20th January 1981), authorise registered friendly societies (other than collecting societies) to amend prescribed or approved schemes adopted in accordance with the 1977 Regulations pursuant to a change in the authorised percentage rate.

FUEL AND ENERGY

Halsbury's Laws of England (4th edn.), Vol. 16, paras. 1–490 and Vol. 19, paras. 401–600

1358   Euratom—health and safety standards—ionising radiation

Council Directive (Euratom) 80/836 (OJ No. L246 17.9.80) amends Directives laying down the basic safety standard, for the health protection of the general public and workers against the dangers of ionising radiation.

1359   Fuel and electricity—control of heating

The Fuel and Electricity (Heating) (Control) (Amendment) Order 1980, S.I. 1980 No. 1013 (in force on 1st October 1980), amends the Fuel and Electricity (Heating) Order 1974, S.I. 1974 No. 2160, by substituting 19°C for 68°F as the temperature above which, subject to the provisions of the amended order, premises must not be heated by the use of electricity or fuel.

1360   Gas—quantities—metric units

The Gas (Metrication) Regulations 1980, S.I. 1980 No. 1851 (in force on 1st April 1981), amend the Gas Act 1972, the Gas Safety Regulations 1972, the Gas Quality Regulations 1972, the Gas (Declaration of Calorific Value) Regulations 1972 and the Gas (Meter) Regulations 1974, 1974 Halsbury's Abridgment para. 1498, by substituting for quantities expressed in imperial units quantities expressed in metric units.

1361 Gas Act 1980

The Gas Act 1980, which supersedes the Energy Act 1976, s. 13, amends the British Gas Corporation's obligation to supply under the Gas Act 1972, Sch. 4, para. 2. The Act received the royal assent on 30th June 1980 and came into force on that date.

Section 1 amends the Corporation's general obligation, under Sch. 4 para. 2, so that they are not obliged to supply any premises with more than 25,000 therms per annum. Charges for supply in excess of 25,000 therms are not to be subject to the restrictions on undue discrimination or preference in the 1972 Act, ss. 24 (1), 25 (5). The proviso to s. 25 (6), that a special agreement for the supply of gas may only be entered into when the tariffs in force are not appropriate, is not to apply to a special agreement for a minimum supply to any premises of more than 25,000 therms per annum. Section 1 also provides that the Energy Act 1976, s. 13 is to cease to have effect. Section 2 deals with citation and extent.

1362 National Radiological Protection Board—constitution

The National Radiological Protection Board (Constitution Amendment) Order 1980, S.I. 1980 No. 970 (in force on 31st July 1980), increases to twelve the maximum membership of the Board.

1363 Nuclear installations—Jersey

The Nuclear Installations (Jersey) Order 1980, S.I. 1980 No. 1527 (in force on 3rd November 1980), extends to the Bailiwick of Jersey, with specified exceptions, adaptations and modifications, those provisions of the Nuclear Installations Act 1965, as amended, which relate to the duty in respect of the carriage of nuclear matter, to the right to compensation for breach of that duty and to the bringing and satisfaction of claims and certain ancillary provisions.

1364 Passenger cars—fuel consumption—tests—transfer of functions

The Transfer of Functions (Passenger Car Fuel Consumption Tests) Order 1980, S.I. 1980 No. 1719 (in force on 11th December 1980), transfers to the Minister of Transport the functions of the Secretary of State under the Energy Act 1976, s. 15 and the Passenger Car Fuel Consumption Order 1977, 1977 Halsbury's Abridgment para. 1376.

1365 Radioactive substances—smoke detectors—exemption

The Radioactive Substances (Smoke Detectors) Exemption Order 1980, S.I. 1980 No. 953 (in force on 7th August 1980), exempts persons conditionally from registration under the Radioactive Substances Act 1960, ss. 1 and 3, in respect of the keeping and use of radioactive material consisting of smoke detectors incorporating closed sources possessing limited radioactivity. It also excludes conditionally from ss. 6 (1), 6 (2) and 7 (1) of that Act certain descriptions of radioactive waste arising directly or indirectly from the keeping or use of smoke detectors exempted from the order.

The Radioactive Substances (Fire Detectors) Exemption Order 1967 is revoked and re-enacted with certain amendments.

GIFT AND ESTATE TAXATION

Halsbury's Laws of England (4th edn.), Vol. 19, paras. 601–926

1366 Articles

Capital Transfer Tax—Interests in Possession, O. P. Wylie: 106 Taxation 307.
CTT: Treatment of Free Loans, Barry McCutcheon: 130 NLJ 282
Relief for Woodlands, Barry McCutcheon: Taxation 22nd–29th December 1979.

1367　Capital transfer tax—double taxation relief—arrangements—Netherlands

The Double Taxation Relief (Taxes on Estates of Deceased Persons and Inheritances and on Gifts) (Netherlands) Order 1980, S.I. 1980 No. 706 (made on 21st May 1980), gives effect to the Convention signed at the Hague on 11th December 1979, which provides relief from double taxation in relation to capital transfer tax and taxes of a similar character imposed by the Netherlands.

1368　—— interest in possession—whether affected by power of accumulation

Under the terms of a settlement, trustees held the capital and income of the trust fund for such of the settlor's daughters as attained twenty-one or married under that age, subject to a power of accumulation vested in the trustees. All had attained twenty-one by February 1974 and in 1976 the trustees made an appointment in favour of one of the daughters. The Revenue claimed that the trustees were liable to capital transfer tax under the Finance Act 1975, Sch. 5, para. 6 (2) since the daughter was not entitled to an "interest in possession" before the appointment was made. The trustees contended that her interest became an interest in possession in February 1974. *Held*, LORD SALMON and LORD RUSSELL dissenting, "interest in possession" bore its ordinary natural meaning of a present right to present enjoyment of property. The daughter did not acquire an interest in possession on reaching twenty-one as the enjoyment of any income from the trust fund depended on the trustees' decision as to the accumulation of income. The appointment was therefore subject to capital transfer tax.

PEARSON v INLAND REVENUE COMRS [1980] 2 WLR 872 (House of Lords: VISCOUNT DILHORNE, LORD SALMON, LORD RUSSELL OF KILLOWEN, LORD KEITH OF KINKEL and LORD LANE). Decision of Court of Appeal [1979] 3 All ER 7, 1979 Halsbury's Abridgment para. 1384 reversed.

1369　—— settled property—interest in possession—excluded property

Under a settlement, a fund was held on trust for the two infant children of the settlor as the trustees might appoint on discretionary trusts for the children's benefit. The settlor's children were resident and domiciled outside the United Kingdom. The trustees appointed Treasury Stock to be held on the trusts of the settlement on 22nd March. On 25th March they appointed the trust fund into two equal parts to pay the income of each to the children with remainder over. There was thus no interest in possession in the stock before the appointment of the 25th, but in consequence of the appointment the two children became entitled to interests in possession of the whole of the stock. The Revenue claimed that by reason of the appointment on the 25th an occasion of charge to capital transfer tax arose under the Finance Act 1975, Sch. 5, para. 6 (2), which provided that a capital distribution was made out of settled property where, at the time when no interest in possession subsisted in it, a person became entitled to an interest in possession in the whole or part of the property comprised in the settlement. The taxpayer contended that, as the stock became excluded property on the appointment, within the meaning of Sch. 7, para. 3 relating to Government securities in foreign ownership, there was no liability to tax. *Held*, as the stock was not excluded property immediately before the appointment, Sch. 7, para. 3 could not apply to nullify the occasion of a charge arising under Sch. 5, para. 6 (2). The creation of interests in possession created a liability to capital transfer tax.

PORTER v INLAND REVENUE COMRS [1979] TR 125 (Chancery Division: BROWNE-WILKINSON J).

1370　—— —— settled property income yield

The Capital Transfer Tax (Settled Property Income Yield) Order 1980, S.I. 1980 No. 1000 (in force on 15th August 1980), alters the designated rates of yield for the purposes of the Finance Act 1975, Sch. 5, para. 3. For the higher rate calculation it now prescribes the yield published for irredeemable British Government Stocks in the Financial Times—Actuaries Share Indices.

1371   Estate duty—gift inter vivos—gift transferred to company in exchange for shares—valuation of gift

The deceased bought £99,687 British Gas stock and the following scheme was devised to lessen the amount of estate duty payable on her death. A private company was incorporated with a capital of £100 divided into a hundred shares of £1 each. The plaintiffs, the deceased's two nephews, were subscribers to the company's memorandum of association. On 10th August 1971 the deceased transferred to each of the plaintiffs £49,843 of the stock. On the same day, the plaintiffs appointed themselves the directors of the company and were each allotted one £1 share ("the subscribers' shares") at a premium of £999. The plaintiffs transferred their respective holdings of Gas Stock to the company at a value of £49,000 each, in consideration of the issue of forty-nine shares in the company to each of them. At an extra-ordinary general meeting the "subscribers' shares" were designated as ordinary shares and the remainder were converted into preference shares. Shortly after the death of the deceased, the company was put into a member's voluntary liquidation and the liquidator repaid the preference shares at par and paid the remaining funds of the company to the plaintiffs as the holders of the two ordinary shares. By an originating summons the plaintiffs claimed against the Inland Revenue a declaration that, in ascertaining their liability to estate duty in respect of the gift of Gas Stock, the value in each case should be taken as the value of the preference shares in the company to which the Gas Stock had been converted, which was £48 and not £49,095, the value of each Gas Stock holding on the date they were transferred to the company. The plaintiffs contended that by virtue of the Finance Act 1957, s. 38 (1) the property to be treated as the gift was the preference shares which they had received in substitution for the property in the gift, which at the date of the deceased's death were only worth par or less. The Revenue contended that s. 38 (1) was subject to s. 38 (3) and that since the plaintiffs had voluntarily divested themselves of their Gas Stock holdings for a consideration worth less than their value on the date of transfer, the value of each holding as at that date was the value of the property in the gift made by the deceased for the purposes of estate duty under s. 38 (3). *Held*, the preference shares in the company were consideration for the transfer of the Gas Stock and those shares constituted "any property" within s. 38 (15). They therefore fell to be valued as they would have been for the purposes of estate duty chargeable on the death of the deceased, had she died immediatedly before the plaintiffs transferred their share of the Gas Stock to the company. The valuation of the gift was made on the basis of a sale in the open market. On such a valuation the shares were worth less than the value of the Gas Stock and accordingly under s. 38 (3) the value of the gift for the purpose of estate duty was the value of each holding of the Gas Stock by the plaintiffs i.e. £49,095. The plaintiffs' claim would therefore fail.

BATTLE v INLAND REVENUE COMRS [1980] STC 86 (Chancery Division: BALCOMBE J).

In respect of deaths after 12th March 1975, estate duty is replaced by capital transfer tax; see now Finance Act 1975.

1372   —— property passing on death—settled property—insurance policy—duty to accumulate income

Scotland

The deceased effected policies of assurance on his own life for the benefit of his children. The policies were assignable for valuable consideration. On the deceased's death in 1971 the assurance company paid a sum in respect of each policy to his executors, which they held in trust for the named beneficiaries. An assessment to estate duty was made under the Finance Act 1894, s. 2 (1) (b) (iv), on the ground that the policies had been held by the deceased on trust to accumulate any income which might have arisen during the existence of the trust. On appeal against the assessment, *held*, it was conceivable that a situation could have arisen in which the policies might have been converted into cash during the deceased's lifetime. If this had occurred, the deceased would have been under a duty to invest the money received and to accumulate the income for the benefit of the beneficiaries; the income would not have fallen to be paid to the beneficiaries as it arose. Thus, although in fact no income had arisen from the policies, a duty to accumulate income on the part of the deceased would be implied and accordingly the proceeds of the policies were liable to estate duty under s. 2 (1) (b) (iv).

WILL v INLAND REVENUE COMRS [1980] STC 507 (Inner House). *Royal Bank of Scotland v Inland Revenue Comrs* [1977] STC 121, 1977 Halsbury's Abridgment para. 1382 followed.

In respect of deaths after 12th March 1975, estate duty is replaced by capital transfer tax; see now Finance Act 1975.

1373　Finance Act 1980

See para. 2328.

1374　Relief for business property—relevant business property—binding contract for sale of property

It is sometimes the practice for partners or shareholder directors of companies to enter into an agreement whereby, in the event of the death before retirement of one of them, the deceased's personal representatives are obliged to sell and the survivors are obliged to purchase the deceased's business interest or shares, funds for the purchase being frequently provided by means of appropriate life assurance policies. Such an agreement, requiring as it does a sale and purchase and not merely conferring an option to sell or buy, is a binding contract for sale within the Finance Act 1976, Sch. 10, para. 3 (4); thus there is no entitlement to relief for business property: statement of practice No. SP12/80.

GIFTS

Halsbury's Laws of England (4th edn.), Vol. 20, paras. 1–100

1375　Gift inter vivos—gift of valuable stock—gift exchanged for shares in company—valuation of gift for purposes of estate duty

See *Battle v Inland Revenue Comrs*, para. 1371.

GUARANTEE AND INDEMNITY

Halsbury's Laws of England (4th edn.), Vol. 20, paras. 101–400

1376　Guarantee—construction—effect of debtors' breach of contract

The plaintiff shipbuilders contracted to build a ship. The contract was guaranteed by the defendants who undertook to pay "any sums due" under the contract in the event of the buyers' default. The purchase price was payable in five instalments and a default by the buyers in paying the second instalment gave the plaintiffs the right to rescind the contract and recover damages from the buyers. The buyers defaulted in paying the second instalment and the plaintiffs rescinded the contract and claimed under the guarantee. The trial judge gave judgment for the plaintiffs which was affirmed by the Court of Appeal. On further appeal the defendants contended that the effect of the plaintiffs' rescission was to terminate the contract and destroy their right to recover the second instalment and replace it with a remedy in damages, which could not be recovered from the defendants as they were not "sums due" under the contract. *Held,* (i) notwithstanding the notice of cancellation by the plaintiffs, the buyers remained liable for the payment of the second instalment. The liability arose before the rescission and the defendants remained liable under the guarantee for the buyers' default. (ii) In any event, the defendants were liable in damages to the plaintiffs for payment because the object of the guarantee was to enable the plaintiffs to recover the amount due irrespective of the position between the plaintiffs and the buyers. The appeal would accordingly be dismissed.

HYUNDAI HEAVY INDUSTRIES CO LTD v PAPADOPOULOS [1980] 2 All ER 29 (House of Lords: VISCOUNT DILHORNE, LORD EDMUND-DAVIES, LORD FRASER OF TULLYBELTON, LORD RUSSELL OF KILLOWEN and LORD KEITH OF KINKEL). Decision of Court of Appeal [1979] 1 Lloyd's Rep 130, 1979 Halsbury's Abridgment para. 1395 affirmed. Dicta of Dixon J in *McDonald v Denny Lascelles Ltd* (1938) 48 CLR at 476, Parker J in *Chatterton v Maclean* [1951] 1 All ER 761, at 764 and Lord Reid, Lord Diplock and Lord Simon in *Moschi v Lep Air Services* [1972] 3 All ER 393, at 398, 403, 407, applied.

1377 —— **guarantee delivered in escrow—effect**

The plaintiff bank sought to recover, against the defendant, money alleged to be due under a guarantee made in 1974. The defendant denied liability on the ground, inter alia, that the guarantee had been delivered in escrow and had never become binding. As a result of the defendant's contention the plaintiff claimed in the alternative under an earlier guarantee of 1973. The defendant contended, inter alia, that the bank having alleged that the 1974 guarantee was one upon which it could sue, it could not be allowed to go back on it. *Held,* if the 1974 guarantee, which was to have replaced all earlier guarantees, had been delivered in escrow, it could not possibly have had the legal effect of discharging anything beforehand since it had no effect unless certain conditions were met. Further the bank was entitled to go back on something which it had alleged because it had never been the law that if a person put something in the pleadings he was thereafter precluded automatically from putting an alternative and inconsistent claim or defence on the pleading also. The bank was entitled to recover the full amount claimed from the defendant under the 1973 guarantee.

BARCLAYS BANK LTD v THOMAS [1979] 2 Lloyd's Rep 505 (Queen's Bench Division: PARKER J).

1378 **Indemnity—creation of rights of indemnity—implied indemnity—enforceability**

Hong Kong

The administrator of a church mission was the registered holder of shares in a national bank. The certificates were stolen and later a firm of stockbrokers, acting in good faith, presented the certificates to the bank together with the "duly completed transfer deeds" under cover of letters signed in the firm's name requesting the bank to give effect to the transfers in favour of W and to issue new certificates in W's name. The bank failed to check the transferor's signature and new certificates were issued to W who had forged the administrator's signature. W subsequently sold the shares. The administrator proved the forgeries and obtained judgment against the bank which in turn obtained judgment against the firm of stockbrokers for an indemnity in respect of its liability to the administrator, on the basis that the stockbrokers' request in their letters amounted to an implied warranty that the documents presented by them were genuine. The stockbrokers appealed. *Held,* the principle that a person doing an act at the request of another was entitled to an indemnity if the act was not apparently illegal in itself and was done without default, but injured a third party, was not limited to a request made by a party for his own benefit. Default on the part of the person doing the act negating the application of the principle only arose in the event of dishonesty, lack of good faith or failure to comply with the request. The principle applied to the request of the stockbrokers who had promised to indemnify the bank if by acting on the request the bank caused damage to a third party, and the bank by acting on the request had accepted that promise which had therefore become a contractual indemnity. Whether a warranty was to be implied was a question of fact, but where a stockbroker requested the

registration of a share transfer which a company was under an administrative duty
to effect if the documents were genuine, the sound conduct of business required that
the company should be entitled to rely on the documents submitted.   There was
therefore implied in the stockbrokers' request a warranty that the transfer deeds were
genuine and they were in breach of that warranty.   Accordingly the appeal would
be dismissed.

YEUNG V HONG KONG AND SHANGHAI BANKING CORPN [1980] 2 All ER 599
(Privy Council: VISCOUNT DILHORNE, LORD SALMON, LORD ELWYN-JONES, LORD
SCARMAN and LORD LANE).   *Sheffield Corpn v Barclay* [1905] AC 392, HL applied.

HEALTH AND SAFETY AT WORK

Halsbury's Laws of England (4th edn.), Vol. 20, paras. 401–801

1379   Article

Safety and Dismissal: Dismissal and Safety, Alec Samuels (justification of dismissal
on ground of breach of safety rule): 130 NLJ 395.

1380   Animal products—metrication

The Health and Safety (Animal Products) (Metrication) Regulations 1980, S.I. 1980
No. 1690 (in force on 1st January 1981), amend the Wool, Goat-hair and Camel-
hair Regulations 1905, the Horsehair Regulations 1907, and the Hides and Skins
Regulations 1921, by substituting measurements expressed in metric units for
measurements not so expressed.   The amendments do not relate to plant which was
in existence immediately before the coming into operation of the regulations if the
dimensions of that plant complied with the then existing requirements.

1381   Articles for use at work—leasing arrangements

The Health and Safety at Work etc. Act 1974, s. 6 provides for the general duties of
manufacturers and others in relation to articles and substances for use at work.

The Health and Safety (Leasing Arrangements) Regulations 1980, S.I. 1980 No.
907 (in force on 8th August 1980), modify s. 6 so as to provide for cases where an
article is supplied under a lease for use at work.   In the case of the first lease of an
article, provision is made corresponding to that already existing under s. 6 (9) where
the finance is provided under a hire-purchase agreement.   The duties on the supplier
of an article are imposed on the person providing the finance and the regulations set
out the circumstances in which the modification applies.   In the case of further leases
to the same customer, where the article remains in the customer's possession and
certain other conditions are satisfied, no duty arises as the duty under s. 6 will have
arisen on the first transaction.

1382   Celluloid and cinematograph film—storage—exemptions

See para. 2263.

1383   Control of working environment—exposure to lead

The Control of Lead at Work Regulations 1980, S.I. 1980 No. 1248 (in force on
18th August 1981), impose requirements for the protection of employees who may
be exposed to lead at work and of other persons who may be affected by such
work.   The regulations require any work which may expose persons to lead to be
assessed to determine the nature and degree of that exposure and for adequate
measures to be taken to control it and to prevent the spread of contamination by lead
from the work place.   The regulations also provide, in appropriate cases, for the
monitoring and for the medical surveillance of employees including biological
tests.   The regulations apply in relation to any work with lead to which the Health
and Safety at Work etc. Act 1974 applies and supersede existing provisions, listed in

Schedules 1 and 2 which are repealed or revoked. A Code of Practice approved by the Health and Safety Commission under the 1974 Act, s. 16 (1) gives practical guidance on the regulations.

1384   **Employer—duty of care—duty to fence machinery—employee incorrectly replacing defective guard—liability of employer**

The plaintiff was employed as a trainee horizontal milling machine operator. The guard on the machine did not enclose the whole cutting surface (except that necessarily exposed for the milling operations) as required by the Horizontal Milling Machine Regulations 1928, reg. 3. In changing the cutter, the plaintiff replaced the guard incorrectly and was subsequently injured as a result. He brought an action against the defendant employer for breach of statutory duty and negligence, which was dismissed at first instance on the ground that the accident had been caused, not by the breach of statutory duty but by the incorrect replacement of the guard. On appeal, *held*, the accident would have occurred had the guard complied with the 1928 Regulations and was therefore not caused by a breach of statutory duty. Nor was there a breach of the common law duty of care as the plaintiff had known that he was not allowed to change the cutter himself and that a tool-cutter was available to do so. The appeal would accordingly be dismissed.

     LINEKER v RALEIGH INDUSTRIES LTD [1980] ICR 83 (Court of Appeal: ORMROD LJ and SIR DAVID CAIRNS).

1385   **—— duty to provide safe access to place of work—extent of duty**

In wintry weather conditions an employer gritted a path across the factory car park, but not the rest of the car park. An employee fell and injured her back whilst walking across the car park to the path. On the question whether the employer was in breach of his statutory duty to provide safe means of access to the place of employment under Factories Act 1961, s. 29 (1), *held*, the car park was access to the factory and it was obvious that employees would have to walk across the car park to the path. The employer should have taken precautions in wintry conditions to grit not only the footpath but also the rest of the car park. In failing to do so the employer was in breach of his statutory duty under the 1961 Act and would be liable to the employee for damages.

     WOODWARD v RENOLD LTD [1980] ICR 387 (Queen's Bench Division: LAWSON J). *Thomas v Bristol Aeroplane Co Ltd* [1954] 1 WLR 694 distinguished.

1386   **—— occupier of factory—employer's liability for employees' breach—availability of defence to occupier who has taken all reasonable steps to prevent breach**

The defendant employers, who were occupiers of a factory, were charged under the Factories Act 1961, s. 155 (1) with contravention of the Construction (Working Places) Regulations 1966. The people responsible for the breaches were the employees and the employers successfully claimed that they were entitled to rely on the defence provided by s. 155 (2) of the Act. Under that subsection, an occupier is not guilty of an offence unless it is proved that he has failed to take all reasonable steps to prevent the contravention. However, his liability in respect of the same matters by virtue of some other provision is unaffected. The Health and Safety Executive inspectors appealed. *Held*, the breaches had been committed by the employees who had a duty to comply with the Regulations under reg. 3 (2). The employers had a separate duty as employers to comply with the Regulations under reg. 3 (1). Therefore, if the concluding words of s. 155 (2) were applied to the present case, it followed that the employers' liability for the breaches by virtue of some other provision, that is, reg. 3 (1), remained unaffected. Their duty under reg. 3 (1) as employers thus prevented them from relying on the defence that would otherwise have been available to them as occupiers of the factory who had taken all reasonable steps to prevent the breach. The appeal would accordingly be allowed.

     DAVIES v CAMERONS INDUSTRIAL SERVICES LTD [1980] 2 All ER 680 (Queen's Bench Division: BRIDGE LJ and WOOLF J).

1387   Factory—definition—hospital workshop

In an action for damages for personal injuries by a hospital employee, the question arose whether the premises on which he was injured, a hospital workshop used for the repair of hospital equipment, was a factory within the Factories Act 1961, s. 175 (1). That subsection defines a factory as premises in which persons are employed in manual labour in, inter alia, the making of an article or part of an article or the altering or repairing of an article. *Held*, having regard to the nature of the workshop and the work carried out there, it was prima facie a factory and there was nothing in the 1961 Act to show that its provisions were clearly not applicable to the hospital workshop and the processes carried on there. Accordingly, it could not be inferred that Parliament did not intend the Act to apply to it.

BROMWICH V NATIONAL EAR NOSE AND THROAT HOSPITAL [1980] 2 All ER 663 (Queen's Bench Division: CANTLEY J).

1388   Health and Safety at Work etc. Act 1974—commencement

The Health and Safety at Work etc. Act 1974 (Commencement No. 5) Order 1980, S.I. 1980 No. 208, brought into force on 17th March 1980 the following paragraphs of Sch. 6, Part I of the Act: para. 4 (b) which raises the maximum penalties for contravention or failure to comply with the Building Regulations to £400 and £50 per day on which the default continues after conviction and para. 5 (b), (c) which relates to the power of the Secretary of State to make Building Regulations enabling a local authority to dispense with or relax the Building Regulations in respect of its own projects in its own area.

1389

The Health and Safety at Work etc. Act 1974 (Commencement No. 6) Order 1980, S.I. 1980 No. 269, brought into force on 17th March 1980 the increased penalties prescribed in Sch. 7, para. 7 of the Act, for contravention of certain provisions of the Building (Scotland) Act 1959.

1390   Heavy load—whether employee required to carry heavy load— meaning of "required"

An employee worked as a manageress of a bakery. There was a shortage of staff and the delivery trays of fresh bread had not been unloaded. The employee rang head office explaining the situation and was told to manage as best she could and if she needed any help in lifting the trays she should ask a customer to assist her. In serving a customer she lifted one of the trays and as a result suffered back injuries. She unsuccessfully claimed damages for personal injuries and loss suffered as a result of the accident. On appeal it was held that, in order for there to be a breach of statutory duty under the Offices, Shops and Railway Premises Act 1963, s. 23 which provided that a person, in the course of his employment, should not be required to lift any load likely to cause him injury, the employee had to show that she had been "required" to lift such a load. The word "required" carried with it the connotation that the employee could not have performed her task adequately, in the circumstances, in any manner which would not have necessitated lifting the weight she did. In the present case the employee was not so "required" and accordingly the appeal would be dismissed.

BLACK V CARRICKS (CATERERS) LTD [1980] IRLR 448 (Court of Appeal: MEGAW and SHAW LJJ and SIR PATRICK BROWNE).

1391   Notification of accidents and dangerous occurrences

The Notification of Accidents and Dangerous Occurrences Regulations 1980, S.I. 1980 No. 804 (in force on 1st January 1981), impose duties on persons responsible for the activities of persons at work and on self-employed persons to report to the enforcing authority under the Health and Safety at Work etc. Act 1974 accidents resulting in the death of or major injury to persons arising out of or in connection with that work. Dangerous occurrences as defined in Sch. 1 are also required to be reported. The regulations require certain particulars of accidents at work reported to the Department of Health and Social Security to be sent to the Health and Safety Executive and require records to be kept of accidents, dangerous occurrences and of certain claims made in relation to industrial diseases. Repeals and revocations are listed in Sch. 5.

1392   Petroleum—conveyance by road—exemptions

The Petroleum (Consolidation) Act 1928 (Conveyance by Road Regulations Exemptions) Regulations 1980, S.I. 1980 No. 1100 (in force on 28th August 1980), enable the Health and Safety Executive to grant exemptions from any requirement or prohibition imposed by any provision of certain regulations made under the Petroleum (Consolidation) Act 1928, s. 6 and relating to the conveyance by road of petroleum spirit and certain other dangerous substances. The Executive may attach conditions to any exemption and may only grant an exemption if it is satisfied that the health and safety of persons who are likely to be affected by the exemption will not be prejudiced in consequence of it.

1393   Safety signs

The Safety Signs Regulations 1980, S.I. 1980 No. 1471 (in force on 1st January 1981 for the purposes of new signs and colours and on 1st January 1986 for all other purposes), provide that safety signs for persons at work and colours in strips identifying places where there is danger to their health or safety must comply with Standard number BS5378: Part I: 1980 issued by the British Standards Institution. The regulations also provide that certain safety signs are not to be used at places of work except to provide specified health or safety information or instruction, and that signs used for regulating traffic at places of work are to be the appropriate signs under the Road Traffic Regulation Act 1967.

1394   Statutory provisions—enforcing authority

The Health and Safety (Enforcing Authority) (Amendment) Regulations 1980, S.I. 1980 No. 1744 (in force on 29th December 1980), amend the 1977 Regulations, 1977 Halsbury's Abridgment para. 1397 by excluding from the activities for which local authorities are responsible the maintenance or repair of motor vehicles, the enforcing authority for which is the Health and Safety Executive.

HIGHWAYS, STREETS AND BRIDGES

Halsbury's Laws of England (4th edn.), Vol. 21

1395   Compulsory purchase order—green belt land—motorway—consent of minister—validity

The Green Belt (London and Home Counties) Act 1938, s. 6 (1) makes provision for the acquisition of green belt land by a highway authority for use for the purpose of its statutory powers. Where land is to be compulsorily purchased the consent of a minister is required to initiate the procedure. Section 6 (3) provides that before giving his consent the minister must consider any objections to the proposed scheme.

A large area of green belt land was to be acquired for the purposes of a new motorway scheme. The Minister of Transport obtained the consent of the Secretary of State to proceed with the compulsory purchase of the land. The consent was challenged on the ground that he ought to have investigated the question of the need for a motorway. *Held*, although the Secretary of State had "to consider any objections" he was not required to investigate those objections further since the inquiry which had previously been conducted had established a need for a motorway. Accordingly there had been no breach of s. 6 (3) and the consent was valid.

Lovelock v Minister of Transport (1980) 40 P & CR 336 (Court of Appeal:

LORD DENNING MR, WALLER AND DUNN LJJ). Dicta of Lord Denning in *Pyx Granite Co Ltd v Ministry of Housing and Local Government* [1958] 1 QB 554 at 572, CA and of Lord Diplock in *Bushell v Secretary of State for the Environment* [1980] 2 All ER 608, HL, para. 24 applied.

1396 Cycle racing
See paras. 2345, 2346.

1397 Highway—duty to maintain—duty to prevent straying dogs
In order to reduce the number of road accidents caused by straying dogs, a local authority designated certain roads and appointed a dog-catcher. However, an accident was caused by a group of dogs, as a result of which a motorist was killed. His widow claimed damages from the authority for negligence and breach of statutory duty in failing to maintain the highway and in failing to prevent the obstruction of the highway. *Held,* if a duty of care existed, there was no breach of it by the authority, as it had taken measures to reduce the hazard. Failure to take effective measures to reduce the number of straying dogs could not be a failure to maintain the highway, as the presence of dogs was too transient a danger. Dogs crossing the road could not be regarded as an obstruction. The claim would be dismissed.

ALLISON V CORBY DISTRICT COUNCIL [1980] RTR 111 (Queen's Bench Division: PETER PAIN J).

1398 —— obstruction—mobile snack bar parked in layby—whether "pitching a stall"
The defendant owned a mobile snack bar which he regularly parked in a layby. The snack bar was towed by a separate van. Customers parked in the layby and along the side of the road. The defendant was charged with wilfully obstructing the highway, contrary to the Highways Act 1959, s. 121 (1) and with pitching a stall on the highway, being a hawker or other itinerant person, contrary to s. 127 (c). The case was dismissed and the prosecution appealed. *Held,* selling refreshments on the highway was unreasonable and the defendant's action had caused an interruption of free passage on the highway and fell within s. 121 (1). Further the defendant was a "hawker" for the purpose of s. 127 (c) and an offence had been committed because the snack bar was a "stall" as it could be detached from the towing vehicle and had been "pitched" on the layby for extended periods of time. The appeal would be allowed.

WALTHAM FOREST LONDON BOROUGH COUNCIL V MILLS [1980] Crim LR 243 (Queen's Bench Division: WALLER LJ and PARK J). Dictum of Lord Parker CJ in *Pitcher v Lockett* (1966) 64 LGR 477 at 479 applied.

1399 Highways Act 1980
The Highways Act 1980 consolidates the Highways Acts 1959 to 1971 and related enactments, with amendments to give effect to recommendations of the Law Commission. The Act received the royal assent on 13th November 1980 and came into force on 1st January 1981. A table showing the destination of enactments consolidated is set out on pages 315–331 following.

DESTINATION TABLE

This table shows in column (1) the enactments repealed by the Highways Act 1980, and in column (2) the provisions of that Act corresponding to the repealed provisions.

In certain cases, the enactment in column (1), though having a corresponding provision in column (2), is not, or is not wholly, repealed, as it is still required, or partly required, for the purposes of other legislation.

(1)	(2)	(1)	(2)
National Parks and Access to the Countryside Act 1949 (c 97)	Highways Act 1980 (c 66)	Highways Act 1959 (c 25)	Highways Act 1980 (c 66)
		s 18 (2)	s 126 (2), (3)
		(3)	(2)
s 111†	See s 344 (1)–(4)	19	Sch 23, para 3
		20 (1)	s 106 (1), (7)
Highways Act 1959 (c 25)		(2)	(2), (7)
		(3)	106 (8), 107 (1)
s 1 (1), (2)	s 1 (1), (2)	(4)	106 (8), 107 (2)
(3)	Rep., 1972 c 70, s 272 (1), Sch 30	(5)	106 (8), 107 (3)
		(6)	106 (5)
(4)	s 1 (4)	(7)	107 (4)
2	2	21–25	Rep., 1972 c 70, s 272 (1), Sch 30
3	5		
4, 5	Rep., 1972 c 70, s 272 (1), Sch 30	26 (1), (2)	s 24 (1), (2)
		(3)	(4)
6	s 3	27 (1)	25 (1)
7 (1), (2)	10 (1), (2)	(1A), (1B)	(2), (3)
(3)–(7)	(4)–(8)	(2), (3)	(4), (5)
8	11	28 (1)	26 (1)
9 (1)	14 (1), (3)	(2)	(4)
(2), (3)	(6), (7)	(3)	(1), (3)
(4)	(4)	(4), (5)	(5), (6)
10 (1)	6 (1), Sch 23, para 1	29 (1), (2)	Rep., 1972 c 70, ss 188 (7) (a), 272 (1), Sch 21, para 9 (1), Sch 30
(2)	6 (2), (3)		
(3), (4)	(4), (5)	(3)	s 26 (2)
(5), (6)	(7), (8)	(4), (5)	Rep., 1972 c 70, ss 188 (7) (a), 272 (1), Sch 21, para 9 (1), Sch 30
11 (1)	16 (3)		
(2)	(4), (10)	30 (1)	s 27 (1)
(3)–(7)	(5)–(9)	(2), (3)	Rep., 1980 c 65, ss 1 (7), 194, Sch 7, para 2 (2), Sch 34, Part VII
(8)	16 (10), 106 (6)		
12	17	(4), (4A), (5), (5A), (6)	s 27 (2)–(6)
13 (1)	1 (1), 18 (1)	31–33	28–30
(2), (3)	18 (3), (4)	34 (1)–(3)	31 (1)–(3)
(4)–(6)	(6)–(8)	(4)	(5), (7)
14	19	(5)	(4)
15 (1)	20 (1), (2)	(6)	(6), (7)
(2)–(5)	(3)–(6)	(7)	(7)
(6)	(8)	(8)–(11)	(8)–(11)
16 (1)	21 (1), (2)	(12)	(7)
(2)–(4)	(3)–(5)	35–37	32–34
17 (1)	20 (7), 22 (1)	38 (1)	——
(2)	Rep., S.I. 1970 No 1681, art 5 (3), Sch 4		
(3), (4)	s 22 (3), (4)		
18 (1)	125 (1), (2)		
(1), proviso	(3)		

† Not repealed

(1) Highways Act 1959 (c 25)	(2) Highways Act 1980 (c 66)	(1) Highways Act 1959 (c 25)	(2) Highways Act 1980 (c 66)
s 38 (2)	s 36 (2)	s 61	s 57
(3)	—	62 (1)	59 (1)–(3)
(4)	36 (3)	(2)	(4), (5)
(5)	(4), (5)	(3)	(2)
(6)	(6), (7)	(4)	(6)
(7)	(2)	63 (1)	60 (1)
39	37	(2), (3)	(3), (4)
40 (1)	38 (1), (2)	(4)	(2)
(2)–(5)	(3)–(6)	(5)	12 (4), 60 (5)
41	39	64 (1), (2)	62 (1), (2)
42	Rep., 1963 c 33, ss 16 (2), 93 (1), Sch 6, para 16, Sch 18, Part II	(2), proviso	(3)
		(3), (4)	(4), (5)
		65, 66	64, 65
43	s 40	67 (1), (2)	66 (1), (2)
44 (1)	41 (1)	(2A), (3)	(3), (4)
(2)	(2)–(4)	(3A)	(5)
(3)	(2)–(4)	(4)–(6)	(6)–(8)
45	Rep., 1972 c 70, s 272 (1), Sch 30	(7)	Rep., 1972 c 79, s 272 (1), Sch 30
46	s 43 (1), (3)	68	s 68
47	44	69 (1)–(3)	69
48 (1), (2)	45 (1), (2)	(4)	Rep., 1972 c 70, s 272 (1), Sch 30
(2), proviso	(3)	69A, 70, 71	s 70–72
(3)	(4)	72 (1)	73 (1)
(3), proviso	(5)	(2)	(2), (3)
(4)–(6)	(6)–(8)	(3)–(12)	(4)–(13)
(6), proviso	(9)	73 (1)	74 (1)
(7), (8)	(10), (11)	(2)	(2), (3)
(8A), (9)	(12)	(3)–(11)	(4)–(12)
49–52	46–49	(12)	12 (4), 74 (13)
53 (1)	50 (1)	74, 75	Rep., 1972 c 70, s 272 (1), Sch 30
(2)	(2), (3)	76 (1)	s 75 (1)
(3)	(2)	(2)	Rep., 1971 c 41, ss 74, 86 (2), Sch 12
54, 55	51, 52	(3)	s 75 (2), (3)
56 (1), (2)	53 (1), (2)	(4)	Rep., 1972 c 70, s 272 (1), Sch 30
(3)	(3), (4)	77, 78	s 76, 77
(4), (5)	(5), (6)	79	91
57 (1)	54 (1), (2)	80	78
(2)	(3)	81 (1)	79 (1), (2)
58 (1)	55 (1)	(2)–(5)	(3)–(6)
(2)	(2), (3)	(6)	(7), (8)
(3), (4)	(4), (5)	(7)–(9)	(9)–(11)
59 (1)	—	(10)	(12), (13)
(2), (3)	56 (1), (2)	(11)–(14)	(14)–(17)
(4), (5)	(4), (5)	82 (1)	96 (1), (2)
(6)	Rep., 1980 c 65, s 194, Sch 34, Part VII	(2)–(6)	(3)–(7)
(7)–(10)	s 56 (7)–(10)	(6), proviso	(8)
60 (1)	Rep., 1971 c 23, s 56 (4), Sch 11, Part IV	(7), (8)	(9), (10)
(2)	s 56 (3)	83, 84	Rep., 1966 c 42, s 43 (2), Sch 6, Part II
(3)–(5)	Rep., 1971 c 23, s 56 (4), Sch 11, Part IV		

(1)	(2)	(1)	(2)
Highways Act 1959 (c 25)	Highways Act 1980 (c 66)	Highways Act 1959 (c 25)	Highways Act 1980 (c 66)
s 85 (1)–(3)	s 80 (1)–(3)	s 112 (5)	s 120 (3)
(4), (5)	(4)	(6), (7)	(4), (5)
86	81	113 (1)–(3)	121 (1)–(3)
87 (1), (2)	82 (1), (2)	(4)	(4), (5)
(3)	(3), (4)	(5)	(6)
(4), (5)	(5), (6)	114, 115	122, 123
(6)	(7), (8)	116 (1)–(6)	130 (1)–(6)
88 (1)	83 (1)	(7), (8)	Rep., 1972 c 70, s 272 (1), Sch 30
(2)	(2), (3)		
(3)	(4)	(9)	s 130 (7)
89–91	84–86	117	131
92 (1)–(3)	87 (1)–(3)	118 (1)	133
(4)	(4)–(6)	(2)	Rep., 1972 c 70, ss 188 (7) (a), 272 (1), Sch 21, para 35, Sch 30
(5)	(7)		
93–94	88–89		
95–96	Rep., 1980 c 65, ss 1 (7), 194, Sch 7, para 7, Sch 34, Part VII	119 (1)	s 134 (1)
		(2)–(5)	(3)–(6)
		(5A)	(7)
97	s 90	(6)	(11)
98	92	120 (1)	136 (1), (2)
99 (1)–(3)	93 (1)–(3)	(2), (3)	(3), (4)
(4)	(4), (5)	(4)	Rep., S.L.(R.)A. 1977
(5), (6)	(6), (7)	121, 122	s 137, 138
100	94	123	141
101 (1)	95 (2)	124 (1)	143 (1)
(2)	(1)	(2)	Rep., 1974 c 7, s 42 (2), Sch 8
(2), proviso	(2)		
(3)–(5)	(3)–(5)	(3)	s 143 (2), (3)
(6)	(6), (7)	(4)	(4)
(7), (8)	(8), (9)	(5)	(1)–(3)
102	99	125	145
103 (1), (1A)	100 (1), (2)	126 (1)	147 (1), (2)
(2)	100 (3), 301 (2)	(2)	Rep., 1980 c 65, ss 1 (7), 194, Sch 7, para 2 (5), Sch 34, Part VII
(3), (4), (4A), (5)	100 (4)–(7)		
(6)	(9)	(3), (4)	s 147 (3), (4)
103A	102	(5)	(6)
104	Rep., 1971 c 41, ss 74, 86 (2), Sch 12	(6)	(1), (2)
		127	148
105–107	s 103–105	128 (1)	149 (1)
108 (1)	116 (1)	(2)–(4)	(4)–(6)
(2)–(9)	(3)–(10)	129 (1)–(3)	150 (1)–(3)
(10)	(2)	(4)	(6)
109, 110	117, 118	130 (1)–(3)	151 (1)–(3)
111 (1)	119 (1)	(4)	(1)
(1), proviso	(2)	131 (1)	152 (1), (7)
(2)–(8)	(3)–(9)	(2)–(5)	(2)–(5)
112 (1)	120 (2)	(6), (7)	(8), (9)
(2)	(1)	(8)	(6)
(3), (4)	Rep., 1972 c 70, ss 188 (7) (a), 272 (1), Sch 21, para 32 (3), Sch 30	(9)	(7), (9)
		(10)	Rep., 1972 c 70, s 272 (1), Sch 30
		132 (1)–(6)	s 153 (1)–(6)

(1)	(2)	(1)	(2)
Highways Act 1959 (c 25)	Highways Act 1980 (c 66)	Highways Act 1959 (c 25)	Highways Act 1980 (c 66)
s 132 (7)	Rep., 1972 c 70, s 272 (1), Sch 30	s 151 (3), (4)	s 176 (7), (8)
(8)	s 153 (7)	152 (1)	178 (1)
(9)	Rep., 1972 c 70, s 272 (1), Sch 30	(2)	(2), (3)
133	Rep., 1972 c 70, s 272 (1), Sch 30	(3), (4)	(4), (5)
134 (1)	s 154 (1)	153 (1)–(5)	179 (1)–(5)
(2), (3)	(3), (4)	(6)	179 (1), 180 (1)
(4)	(1)	154 (1)	180 (1)
(5)	Rep., S.L.(R.)A. 1977	(2)–(6)	(3)–(7)
135 (1)–(4)	s 155 (1)–(4)	155	Rep., 1971 c 41, s 86 (2), Sch 12, but see Sch 23, para 7 (1)
(4A)	(1)		
(5)	(5)	156 (1)–(4)	s 185 (1)–(4)
136 (1)	156 (1), (2)	(5)	(1)
(2)–(8)	(3)–(9)	157 (1)	186 (1)
(9), (10)	(10)	(1), proviso	(2)
(11)	(2)	(2)	(3)
137 (1)	157 (1), (2)	(3)	Rep., 1972 c 70, ss 188 (7) (a), 272 (1), Sch 21, para 50 (3), Sch 30
(2)	(3), (4)		
(3)	157 (5), (6), 328		
	(4)	(4)–(8)	s 186 (4)–(8)
(4), (5)	157 (7), (8)	(9)	(1), (3), (5), (7)
(6)	157 (9), 158 (5), 159 (6)	158	187
	159 (1)–(5)	159 (1)–(5)	188 (1)–(5)
138	160 (1), (3)–(5)	(6)	(6), (7)
139 (1)	(6)	(7)	(8)
(1), proviso	(7)	(8)	(1), (9)
(2)	157 (9), 158 (5), 159 (6), 160 (8)	160, 161	190, 191
(3)		162 (1)	192 (1), (2)
140 (1)–(4)	161	(2)	(3)
(5)		163 (1)	193 (1)
141	162	(2)	Rep., 1972 c 70, ss 188 (7) (a), 272 (1), Sch 21, para 55 (2), Sch 30
142 (1)–(4)	163 (1)–(4)		
(5)	(1)		
143 (1)–(3)	164 (1)–(3)	(3), (4)	s 193 (2), (3)
(4), (5)	(1)	(5)	(2)
144 (1)–(3)	165 (1)–(3)	(6)	(4)
(4)	(4), (5)	(7)	Rep., 1972 c 70, ss 188 (7) (a), 272 (1), Sch 21, para 55 (5), Sch 30
145	Rep., 1961 c 64, s 86 (3), Sch 5, Part II		
146 (1)	s 171 (1)	164	s 194
(2)	(3)	165 (1)–(3)	195
(3) (5)	(5)–(7)	(4)	Rep., 1972 c 70, ss 188 (7) (a), 272 (1), Sch 21, para 57 (3), Sch 30
147 (1)	172 (1)		
(1), proviso	(2)		
(2), (3)	(3), (4)	166 (1)	s 196 (1), (2)
(4)	(5)	(2)	(3)
(5)	(1)	(3)	(4), (6)
148–150	173–175	(4)	(5)
151 (1)	176 (1)–(4)	(5), (6)	(7), (8)
(2)	(5), (6)		

(1) Highways Act 1959 (c 25)	(2) Highways Act 1980 (c 66)
s 167 (1)–(6)	s 197 (1)–(6)
(7)	(7), (8)
(8)	Rep., 1972 c 70, ss 188 (7) (a), 272 (1), Sch 21, para 59 (6), Sch 30
168–172	s 198–202
173 (1)	203 (1), 204 (1)
(2)	Rep., 1972 c 70 ss 188 (7) (a), 272 (1), Sch 21, para 65 (2), Sch 30
(3)	s 203 (1), 204 (2)
174 (1)	205 (1), (2)
(2)	(3)
(2), proviso	(4)
(3), (4)	(5), (6)
175–180	206–211
181 (1)–(4)	212
(5)	Rep., 1980 c 65, s 194, Sch 34. Part VII
182–184	s 213–215
185 (1)	216 (1)–(3)
(2)	(4)
186	217
187	Rep., 1972 c 70, ss 188 (7) (a), 272 (1), Sch 21, para 68, Sch 30
188	s 218
189–191	Rep., 1972 c 70, s 272 (1), Sch 30
192 (1)	s 219 (1)
(2)	(2), (3)
(3)	(4), (6)
(4), (5)	(5), (6)
193 (1)	220 (1), (2)
(2)–(5)	(3)–(6)
(6)	(7), (8)
(7)	(9)
194	221
195 (1)	222 (1)–(3)
(2)	(4)
196 (1)	223 (1)
(2)	(2), (3)
(3)–(5)	(4)–(6)
197	224
198 (1)	225 (1)
(2)	(2), (3)
199	Rep., 1960 c 64, s 76, Sch 6
200, 201	s 226, 227
202 (1)	228 (1), (2)
(2), (3)	(6), (7)

(1) Highways Act 1959 (c 25)	(2) Highways Act 1980 (c 66)
s 203 (1)	s 229 (1), (2)
(2), (3)	(3), (4)
204 (1)	230 (1), (2)
(2)–(5)	(3)–(6)
205	231
206 (1), (2)	232 (1), (2)
(2), proviso	(3)
(3)	(4)
(4)–(7)	(5)–(8)
(8)	Rep., 1972 c 70, s 272 (1), Sch 30
(9)	s 232 (2), (5), (6), (9)
207	233
208 (1)	234 (1)–(3)
(2), (3)	(4), (5)
209–211	235–237
212	Rep., S.L.(R.)A. 1977
213 (1), (2)	s 203 (2), (3)
(3)	
(4)	Rep., 1972 c 70, s 272 (1), Sch 30
(5), (6)	s 203 (4), (5)
214 (1)	238 (1), 239 (1)
(2)	238 (1), 239 (3)
(3)	249 (1), Sch 18, Part I
(4)	239 (5)
(5), (6)	Rep., 1973 c 26, ss 22 (8), 86, Sch 3
(7)	Rep., 1973 c 26, s 86, Sch 3
(8)	s 238 (1), 239 (6)
(9)	Rep., 1971 c 41, ss 44 (8), 86 (2), Sch 12
(10)	s 238 (2), 239 (5)
215 (1)	238 (1), 239 (2)
(2)	238 (1), 239 (4)
(3)	249 (1), Sch 18, Part I
(4)	Rep., 1971 c 41, ss 44 (8), 86 (2), Sch 12
216	s 249 (2), Sch 18, Part II, para 2
217	238 (1), 241
218	238 (1), 242
219	238 (1), 243
220	238 (1), 244
221	238 (1), 245, 247 (1)
222 (1)–(4)	247 (1)–(4)
(5)	Rep., 1973 c 26, s 86, Sch 3
(6)	s 261 (1), (6)
(7)	(5), (6)

(1)	(2)	(1)	(2)
Highways Act 1959 (c 25)	Highways Act 1980 (c 66)	Highways Act 1959 (c 25)	Highways Act 1980 (c 66)
s 222 (8)	Rep., 1961 c 33, ss 40 (3), 41, Sch 5	s 245	Rep., 1972 c 70, s 272 (1), Sch 30
(9)	s 247 (5)	246 (1)	s 280 (1)
(10)	Rep., 1973 c 26, s 86, Sch 3	(2)	Rep., 1980 c 65, ss 1 (7), 194, Sch 7, para 6 (4), Sch 34, Part VII
(11)	s 247 (6)		
223	254, Sch 23, para 14 (1)	(3)	s 280 (2)
224 (1)	255 (1)	(4)	Rep., 1972 c 70, s 272 (1), Sch 30
(2)	(2), (3)		
(3)	(4)	247	Rep., 1972 c 70, s 272 (1), Sch 30
(4)	(5), (6)		
(5)	(7)	248	s 281
225	Rep., 1973 c 26, s 86, Sch 3, S.I. 1970 No 1681, art 5 (3), Sch 4	249, 250	283, 284
		251 (1), (1A), (1B)	8 (1)–(3)
		(2), (3)	(4), (5)
226 (1)	s 263 (1), (2)	252 (1)	286 (1), (3)
(2)–(4)	(3)–(5)	(2)	(2)
227 (1)	264 (1)	(3)	(4)
(2)	(3)	253	288
228 (1)	265 (1), (2)	254	Rep., 1971 c 41, ss 64 (4), 86 (2), Sch 12
(2)–(10)	(3)–(11)		
229 (1)	266 (1), (2)	255	s 293
(2)	(3), (4)	256 (1)	294 (1)
(3)	(5)	(2)	(2), (3)
(4)	(6), (7)	(3), (4)	(4), (5)
(5)–(7)	(8)–(10)	257 (1), (2)	295 (1), (2)
230	267	(3), (4)	Rep., S.L.(R.)A. 1977
231 (1)	268 (1), (2)	258, 259	s 296, 297
(2), (3)	(3), (4)	260	298 (1)
232	Rep., 1972 c 70, s 272 (1), Sch 30	261	———
233 (1), (2)	s 271 (1), (2)	262, 263	303, 304
(3)	(3), (4)	264 (1)	305 (1), (7)
(4)–(6)	(5)–(7)	(2)–(4)	(2)–(4)
234	Rep., 1972 c 70, s 272 (1), Sch 30	(5)	Rep., 1980 c 65, s 194, Sch 34, Part VII
235 (1)	s 272 (1)	(6)	s 305 (5)
(2)	(3)	265–272	306–313
(3)	Rep., 1971 c 41, ss 8 (2), 86 (2), Sch 12	273–275	315–317
		276	Rep., S.I. 1971 No 1292, r 24, Sch 3
(4)–(6)	s 272 (5)–(7)		
(7)	Rep., 1966 c 42, s 43 (2), Sch 6, Part II	277, 278	s 318, 319
		279	302
236	———	280 (1)	320
237, 238	s 273, 274	(2)–(4)	Rep., 1980 c 65, ss 1 (7), 194, Sch 7, para 8 (1), Sch 34, Part VII
239 (1), (2)	275		
(3)	Rep., 1972 c 70, s 272 (1), Sch 30	281–283	s 321–323
240, 241	s 276, 277	284 (1)	324 (1)
242	Rep., 1972 c 70, s 272 (1), Sch 30	(2)	Rep., 1971 c 41, ss 14 (10), 86 (2), Sch 12
243	s 279		
244	Rep., S.L.(R.)A. 1977	(3), (4)	s 257 (4)

(1)	(2)	(1)	(2)
Highways Act 1959 (c 25)	Highways Act 1980 (c 66)	Highways Act 1959 (c 25)	Highways Act 1980 (c 66)
s 284 (5)	Rep., 1971 c 41, ss 17 (3), 86 (2), Sch 12	s 304	
285	s 325	305	s 337
286 (1)	—	306	Rep., S.L.(R.)A. 1977
(2)	326 (1)–(3), Sch 23, para 11	307	s 338
		308	339 (1)–(3)
(3)–(6)	326 (6)–(9)	309, 310	See s 340 (1)
287	327	311	Rep., S.L.(R.)A. 1974
288	Rep., 1980 c 65, ss 1 (7), 194, Sch 7, para 8 (2), Sch 34, Part VII	312 (1), (2)	
		(3)	Rep., 1963 c 33, ss 16 (2), 93 (1), Sch 6, para 70, Sch 18, Part II
289	s 341	(4)	Rep., S.L.(R.)A. 1974
290	Rep., 1972 c 70, s 272 (1), Sch 30	(5)	Rep., 1972 c 70, s 272 (1), Sch 30
291 (1), (2)	Rep., 1963 c 33, ss 16 (2), 93 (1), Sch 6, para 67, Sch 18, Part II	(6)	See Sch 23, para 11
		(7)	Rep., 1972 c 70, s 272 (1), Sch 30
		(8)	
(3)	s 10 (9)	313 (1)	
(4)–(12)	Rep., 1963 c 33, ss 16 (2), 93 (1), Sch 6, para 67, Sch 18, Part II	(2)	Sch 23, para 12 (1)
		(3)	Rep., 1963 c 33, s 93 (1), Sch 18, Part II
292	Rep., 1972 c 70, s 272 (1), Sch 30	(4)	s 345 (3)
293 (1)–(4)	s 344 (1)–(4)	Sch 1, para 1–4	Sch 1, para 1–4
(5)	325 (2)	para 4A, 4B	para 5, 6
(6), (7)	344 (5), (6)	para 5	para 7
294	328	para 6	para 8 (1)
295 (1)	12 (4), 329 (1)	para 6A	para 9
(2)	329 (2)	para 7, 8	para 10, 11
(3)	Rep., 1963 c 33, s 93 (1), Sch 18, Part II	para 8A, 8B, 9	para 12–14
(4)	s 329 (3)	para 10	para 15 (1)
(4A)	Rep., 1963 c 33, s 93 (1), Sch 18, Part II	para 11	para 16
		para 12	
(5)	s 329 (4)	para 13	Rep., S.I. 1979 No 571, art. 3 (1), Sch
(6)	Rep., 1973 c 37, s 40 (3), Sch 9	2, para 1	Sch 2, para 1 (1)
		para 2–5	para 2–5
(7), (8)	—	3, 4	3, 4
296, 297	s 330, 331	5	23, para 3 (2)
298	Rep., 1961 c 63, s 1 (6)	6	Rep., 1972 c 70, s 272 (1), Sch 30
299	s 333	7	Sch 6
300 (1)	334 (1)	8	Rep., 1972 c 70, s 272 (1), Sch 30
(1A)	20 (9)	9, para 1, 2, 2A	Sch 9, para 1–3
(2)	334 (2), (3)	para 3–9	para 4–10
(3)–(5)	(4)–(6)	10–13	10–13
(5A)	(7), (8)	14, Part I	15
(6), (6A), (7), (7A), (7B), (8)	(9)–(14)	Part II	Rep., 1972 c 70, ss 188 (7) (a), 272 (1), Sch 21, para 95 (5), Sch 30
301	Rep., 1967 c 9, s 117 (1), Sch 14, Part I		
302, 303	s 335, 336		

(1)	(2)	(1)	(2)
Highways Act 1959 (c 25)	Highways Act 1980 (c 66)	Road Traffic and Roads Improvement Act 1960 (c 63)	Highways Act 1980 (c 66)
Sch 15	Sch 16		
16, 17	21, 22	s 18 (1)	s 158 (1), (2)
18	s 305 (7)	(2)	157 (9), 158 (3)–(5), 159 (6), 326 (4)
19	Rep., 1972 c 70, s 272 (1), Sch 30		
20	Rep., 1963 c 33, s 93 (1), Sch 18, Part II	(3), (4)	Rep., 1963 c 33, ss 14 (1), 93 (1), Sch 18, Part II
21	Rep., 1972 c 70, s 272 (1), Sch 30	19 (1)	s 285 (1), (2)
22	See s 340 (1)	(2)–(6)	(4)–(8)
23	Rep., S.L.(R.)A. 1977	(7)	Rep., 1963 c 33, ss 14 (2), 93 (1), Sch 18, Part II
24, para 1–3		19A (1)	s 285 (1), (2)
para 4	Sch 23, para 2	(2)	(4)–(8)
para 5–11	———	20	332
para 12 (1)		23 (1)	329 (1)
para 12 (2)	Sch 23, para 9 (1), (2)	Private Street Works Act 1961 (c 24)	
para 12 (3)	para 9 (3)		
para 12 (4)	Rep., 1980 c 65, s 194, Sch 34, Part VII	s 1	
para 13–17	———	2 (1)	Sch 23, para 12 (1)
para 18 (1)	———	(2)	para 12 (1), (2)
para 18 (2)	Omitted; see Law Com. No 100, para 24	(3)	———
para 18 (3)	———	(4)	Sch 23, para 12 (3)
para 19–21	———	3 (1)–(4)	———
para 22 (1)	Sch 23, para 10 (2)	(5)	s 345 (3)
para 22 (2)	para 10 (4)	Land Compensation Act 1961 (c 33)	
para 23	———		
para 24	See Sch 23, para 13 (1), (3)	s 40 (1)†	307 (2), (3)
para 25–28	———	Highways (Miscellaneous Provisions) Act 1961 (c 63)	
para 29	Sch 23, para 4		
para 30 (1)–(3)	para 5 (1)–(3)	s 1 (1)	———
para 30 (4)	———	(2), (3)	58 (1), (2)
para 30 (5)	Sch 23, para 5 (4)	(4)	
para 31–33	———	(5)	58 (3)
para 34, 35	Sch 23, para 22, 23	(6)	
para 36	———	(7)	58 (4)
para 37	Sch 23, para 21	(8)	See Sch 23, para 8
25	Rep., S.L.(R.)A. 1974	2 (1)	s 10 (3)
26	Rep., 1963 c 33, s 93 (1), Sch 18, Part II	(2)	63
		3 (1)	106 (3), (7)
Town and Country Planning Act 1959 (c 53)		(2)	106 (5), (6), 107
		4 (1), (2)	43 (2), (3)
s 48 (1)	s 248 (1)	(3)	(2)
(2)	Rep., S.L.R. Act 1960		
49	s 272 (1)		

† Not repealed

(1)	(2)
Highways (Miscellaneous Provisions) Act 1961 (c 63)	Highways Act 1980 (c 66)
s 5 (1), (2)	s 98 (1), (2)
(3)	(10)
6 (1)	101 (1)
(2)	(2), (3)
(3)	101 (4), 294 (5), 339 (1)–(3)
(4), (5)	101 (5), (6)
7	Rep., 1976 c 57, s 81 (1), Sch 2
8 (1)	s 149 (2), (3)
(2)	(3)–(6)
9	150 (4), (5)
10 (1)	154 (2)
(2)	(1), (3), (4), 294 (1), (5)
11 (1)	228 (2), (6)
(2)	(3), (4), (6)
(3)	(5)
12	Rep., S.L.(R.)A. 1974
13	Rep., 1971 c 41, s 86 (2), Sch 12
14 (1)–(5)	s 256 (1)–(5)
(6)	256 (6), 334 (2), (3), Sch 12, Part II
(7)	256 (7)
15	
16 (1)–(3)	
(4)	Rep., 1980 c 65, ss 1 (7), 194, Sch 7, para 8 (2), Sch 34, Part VII
17 (1), (2)	
(3)	s 345 (3)
Public Health Act 1961 (c 64)	
s 2 (3)†	67 (5), 166 (5), 287 (6), 300 (1)
3†	345 (3)
43	67 (1)–(4)
44 (1)–(4)	287 (1)–(4)
(5)	287 (5), 310
46	166 (1)–(4)
47 (1), (2)	230 (7)
(3)	338 (1), (4)–(6)
48 (1)–(4)	180 (2)–(5)
(5)	(1)
49 (1)	300 (1)
(2)	300 (2), 325 (1), (2)

(1)	(2)
Public Health Act 1961 (c 64)	Highways Act 1980 (c 66)
s 49 (3)	s 300 (1)
(4)	186 (1)
50	203 (2), 219 (1)
Sch 1, Part III*	Sch 8
3†	
Recorded Delivery Service Act 1962 (c 27)	
Sch 1, para 1†	s 322 (2), Sch 15, para 5 (*b*)
Transport Act 1962 (c 46)	
Sch 2, Part I*	219 (4) (*i*), 329 (4)
Pipe-lines Act 1962 (c 58)	
s 19	160 (1), (5), (6)
Water Resources Act 1963 (c 38)	
s 5†	254 (4), 276, Sch 1, para 11
London Government Act 1963 (c 33)	
s 9 (6)†	158 (1)–(4)
14 (1)	157 (1)–(8), 158 (1)–(4), (6), 159 (1)–(3)
(2)	285
(3)	157 (5), (6)
(4)	159 (4)
16 (1)	1 (3)
(2)	179 (1) and *passim*
(3)	24 (3)
(4)	(2)
(5)	298 (2)
(6)	
17 (1)–(3)	Rep., 1969 c 35, s 47 (2), Sch 6
(4)	s 269
(5)	264 (2), (3)
(6)	Rep., 1969 c 35, s 47 (2), Sch 6
18 (1)	s 7 (1), Sch 23, para 1
(1A)	7 (2)

† Not repealed   * Repealed in part

(1) London Government Act 1963 (c 33)	(2) Highways Act 1980 (c 66)
s 18 (2)	s 7 (3), (4)
(3)–(7)	(5)–(9)
Sch 5, Part II, para 6	158 (1)–(4), 326
	(4)
para 7	285 (1)
para 8	(1), (2), (4)–(8)
6, para 1	1 (2)
para 2	2
para 3	Rep., 1972 c 70, s 272
	(1), Sch 30
para 4	s 11
para 5 (1)	6 (1)
para 5 (2)	(5)
para 6	18 (8)
para 7	—
para 8	24 (1)
para 9, 10	Rep., 1972 c 70, s 272
	(1), Sch 30
para 11	s 31 (7)
para 12	34
para 13 (1)	Rep., 1972 c 70, s 272
	(1), Sch 30
para 13 (2)	s 36 (2)
para 14–17	Rep., 1972 c 70, s 272
	(1), Sch 30
para 18 (1), (2)	s 45 (7), (8)
para 18 (3)	(12)
para 19	47 (2)
para 20	Rep., 1971 c 23, s 56
	(4), Sch 11, Part IV
para 21–25	Rep., 1972 c 70, s 272
	(1), Sch 30
para 26	s 80 (4)
para 27	95 (1)
para 28	116 (2)
para 29	Rep., 1972 c 70, s 272
	(1), Sch 30
para 30	s 130 (2)
para 31–34	Rep., 1972 c 70, s 272
	(1), Sch 30
para 35	s 157, 158 (5), 159
	(6), 326 (4)
para 36	159 (1)–(5)
para 37	160 (1)
para 38–41	Rep., 1972 c 70, s 272
	(1), Sch 30
para 42	Rep., 1971 c 41, s 86
	(2), Sch 12
para 43	Rep., 1972 c 70, s 272
	(1), Sch 30
para 44	Rep., 1971 c 41, s 86
	(2), Sch 12
para 45	s 186 (1), (3), (5), (7)

(1) London Government Act 1963 (c 33)	(2) Highways Act 1980 (c 66)
Sch 6, para 46–52	Rep., 1971 c 70, s 272
	(1), Sch 30
para 53 (1)	s 204 (1)
para 53 (2)	—
para 53 (3)	204 (2)
para 54	Rep., 1972 c 70, s 272
	(1), Sch 30
para 55	—
para 56	s 232 (2), (5), (6)
para 57	Rep., 1972 c 70, s 272
	(1), Sch 30
para 58	Rep., 1973 c 26, s 86,
	Sch 3
para 59	s 254 (2)
para 60	271 (1)
para 61	Rep., 1972 c 70, s 272
	(1), Sch 30
para 62	s 275
para 63 (1)	Rep., 1972 c 70, s 272
	(1), Sch 30
para 63 (2)	s 286 (2)
para 64, 65	Rep., 1972 c 70, s 272
	(1), Sch 30
para 66	s 326 (3)
para 67	—
para 68	329 (1)
para 69–71	Rep., 1972 c 70, s 272
	(1), Sch 30
para 72	Sch 1, para 3
para 73	para 11
para 74, 75	6, Part I
para 76, 77	
para 78	See Sch 23, para 13
9, Part II, para 5*	See Sch 24, para 11
11, Part I, para 33†	s 67 (5), 166 (5),
	285 (6), 300
	(1)
para 37	67 (5), 285 (6)

Highways (Amendment) Act 1965 (c 30)	Highways Act 1980 (c 66)
s 1	150 (1)–(3), (6)
2 (1)	—
(2)	345 (3)

Compulsory Purchase Act 1965 (c 56)	Highways Act 1980 (c 66)
s 39 (2)†	213
Sch 6*	247 (6)

† Not repealed * Repealed in part

(1)	(2)	(1)	(2)
New Towns Act 1965 (c 59)	Highways Act 1980 (c 66)	Countryside Act 1968 (c 41)	Highways Act 1980 (c 66)
s 48 (3)	s 219 (4) (i)	s 28 (1)	s 146 (1)
		(2)	(2), (3)
Local Government Act 1966 (c 42)		(3), (4)	(4), (5)
		(4A)	(2)–(5)
s 27 (1)	272 (2)	(5)	
(2)	12 (3)	29 (1)	134 (4)
(3), (4)	(1), (2)	(2)–(5)	135
28 (1)–(4)	97	(6)	134 (2)
(5)		(7), (7A)	(8)–(10)
(6)	Rep., 1972 c 70, s 272 (1), Sch 30	(8)	Rep., 1971 c 41, s 86 (2), Sch 12
29 (1), (2)	s 301 (1), (2)	(9)	
(3)	Rep., 1980 c 65, ss 1 (7), 194, Sch 7, para 6 (6), Sch 34, Part VII	43 (1)†, (2)†	s 113 (5)
		(5)†	(6)
		46 (1)†	See s 344 (1)–(4)
(4)	s 301 (3), 329 (1)	47 (5)	See s 146
30	98	50 (3)†	See Sch 23, para 13 (2)
31 (1), (2)	270 (3), (4)	Sch 3, Part I*	s 26 (1), 118 (1), (2), 119 (1), (6), 147 (7), 326 (5), Sch 6
(3)	(5), (6)		
(4)	(1)–(6)		
(5)	(1)	**Town and Country Planning Act 1968 (c 72)**	
32 (1)	270 (1)		
(2)	(2)–(6)	Sch 9, para 9	36 (2)
(3)	(7)	**Transport Act 1968 (c 73)**	
33	9		
34 (1)	329 (1)	s 51 (5)†	219 (4) (i), 329 (4)
(2)		130 (6) (e)	285 (3)
39†	344 (7)	139 (1)*	262 (1), (3)
40 (1)†	325	(2)*	(4)
40 (2)†	326 (2)	140	239 (5)
44 (2)†	345 (3)	Sch 16, para 7 (2) (f)	219 (4) (i), 329 (4)
Road Traffic Regulation Act 1967 (c 80)		**Transport (London) Act 1969 (c 35)**	
Sch 6*	285 (3)	s 17 (5)†	157 (5)
8, para 2†	265 (10), 329 (1)	29 (1)–(3)	15 (2)–(4)
Criminal Justice Act 1967 (c 80)		(4)	7 (2)
		(5)	
Sch 3, Part I*	131 (3), 134 (5) (a), 137 (1), 138, 148, 151 (3), 155 (2), 161, 163 (4), 172 (5)	(6)	15 (5)
		31 (1)	160 (2)–(5)
		(2), (3)	(6), (7)
		(4)	157 (9), 158 (5), 159 (6), 160 (8)
National Loans Act 1968 (c 13)		(5), (6)	160 (1)
		34 (1)	62 (5)
s 6 (1)*, (2)†	225 (3)	Sch 3, para 1 (2) (g)†	219 (4) (i), 329 (4)

† Not repealed   * Repealed in part

(1)	(2)	(1)	(2)
Post Office Act 1969 (c 48)	Highways Act 1980 (c 66)	Highways Act 1971 (c 41)	Highways Act 1980 (c 66)
Sch 4, para 65 (1)	——	s 7 (2), (3)	s 129 (3), (4)
para 65 (2)	s 157 (9), 158 (5), 159 (6)	8 (1)	272 (1)
para 65 (3)	334 (1)	(2)	——
para 65 (4)	(2), (3)	9	See s 340 (2)
para 65 (5)–(7)	(4)–(6)	10 (1), (2)	s 108 (1), (2)
para 69	(2), (3)	(3)	(6)
para 93 (1) (xv)	178 (5), 254 (6), Sch 6, para 3 (3)	11 (1)	106 (4), (7)
		(2)	106 (8), 108 (4)
Courts Act 1971 (c 23)		(3), (4)	108 (5), (6)
		(5)	106 (8), 107 (1)
Sch 1, para 1†	73 (4), 176 (5), 188 (4), 193 (4), 194 (3), 195 (2), 196 (7), 315, 317	(6)	106 (8), 107 (2)
		(7)	106 (8), 107 (3)
		12 (1)	108 (3), Sch 1
8, Part II, para 36 (1)	56 (3)	(2)	107 (4)
para 36 (2), (3)	116 (8), (9)	(3), (4)	109
9, Part I*	73 (4), 176 (5), 188 (4), 193 (4), 194 (3), 195 (2), 196 (7), 315, 317	(5), (6)	111 (1)
		13 (1)–(3)	110 (1)–(3)
		(4)	339
Part II*	56 (2)	(5)–(8)	110 (4)–(7)
		14 (1)	——
Highways Act 1971 (c 41)		(2)	Sch 1, para 17
		(3), (4)	para 18 (1), (2)
s 1 (1)	1 (1), 14 (1)	(5), (6)	para 19 (1), (2)
(2), (3)	14 (3), (4)		
(4), (5)	(6), (7)	(7), (8)	para 20, 21
(6)	12 (4)	(8A)	——
2 (1)	124 (1), (2)	15 (1)	Sch 1, para 8 (2), 15 (2)
(2)	(2), (3)		
(3)	(4)	(2)	para 8 (3), 15 (3)
(4)	(2), (5)		
(5), (6)	(6), (7)	(3)	s 14 (5)
(7)	Cf. s 329 (1)	(4)	18 (1), (5)
3 (1)	s 125 (1), (2)	16	14 (4), 108 (3), 124 (8), Sch 2, para 1 (2)
(2)	(3)		
(3)	Sch 1	17 (1), (2)	324 (2), (3)
(4)	s 125 (4)	(3)	——
4 (1)	126 (1)	18 (1)	35 (1), (2)
(2)	(2), (3)	(2)–(4)	(3)–(5)
(3)	(4)	(5)	(6), (7)
5	127	(6)	(8), (9)
6	128, 310	(7)–(11)	(10)–(14)
7 (1)	129 (1), (2)	19 (1)	66 (3)
		(2)	(5)
		(3)	(8)
		(4)	(3)
		20	70
		21	94 (2)
		22 (1)	——
		(2), (3)	100 (1), (2)
		(4)	100 (3), 300 (2)
		(5)–(8)	100 (4)–(7)
		(9)	(9)

† Not repealed　　　　　　　　　　* Repealed in part

(1) Highways Act 1971 (c 41)	(2) Highways Act 1980 (c 66)	(1) Highways Act 1971 (c 41)	(2) Highways Act 1980 (c 66)
s 22 (10), (11)	s 300 (1), (2)	s 47 (5)	s 261 (4)
(12)	339	(6)–(9)	250 (4)–(7)
(13)	100 (8), 300 (3)	48	251
23 (1)	102	49 (1)–(4)	252
(2)	62 (3)	(5)	261 (2)
24 (1)	23	50	Rep., 1971 c 78, s 292, Sch 25
(2)	126 (4)		
25 (1)	300 (1)	51 (1)	s 249 (1), Sch 18, Part I
(2)	———	(2)	249 (2), Sch 18, Part II, para 1
26 (1)–(8)	112 (1)–(8)		
(9)	(2), (5)	(3)	249 (1), (2), Sch 18, Part I
27 (1)–(4)	113 (1)–(4)	(4)	249 (3)
(5)	113 (5), (6), 342	(5)	249 (2), Sch 18, Part II, para 2
(6)	113 (7)		
(7)	113	52 (1), (2)	260 (1), (2)
28 (1)	114 (1), (4)	(3)	(3), (4)
(2)–(4)	(2)–(4)	(4)	(3), (4)
29	272 (1)	53 (1)–(3)	257 (1)–(3)
30 (1)–(3)	115 (1)–(3)	(4)	———
(4)	(4), (5)	54, 55	258, 259
(5)	(6)	56	See s 340 (2)
(6)	272 (1)	57 (1), (2)	s 4 (1), (2)
(7), (8)	115 (7), (8)	(3)	4 (3), 24 (1)
31	139, 310	(4)	Rep., 1972 c 70, s 272 (1), Sch 30
32	140, 310		
33	155 (1), (3)	(5), (6)	s 4 (4), (5)
34 (1)	165 (4), (5)	58	8 (2), (3)
(2)	See s 340 (2)	59	Rep., 1972 c 70, s 272 (1), Sch 30
35	s 167, 310		
36	168, 310	60	s 278
37	174	61	See destinations of 1971 c 41, Sch 9
38 (1)–(14)	177, 310		
(15)	———	62	s 14 (2), 18 (2)
39	176 (8)	63 (1)	21 (1)–(3)
40 (1)–(17)	184, 310	(2), (3)	22 (1), (2)
(18)	———	64 (1)–(3)	289
41 (1)–(5)	181 (1)–(5), 310	(4)	———
(6)–(11)	182	65, 66	290, 291
(12)–(16)	181 (6)–(10)	67	292, 310
42	183	68 (1)	41 (1)–(4)
43 (1)–(10)	142	(2)	(5)
(11)	141 (1)	69	Rep., 1972 c 70 s 272 (1), Sch 30
44 (1)–(5)	240 (1)–(5)		
(6)	238 (2), 240 (6)	70 (1)	s 130 (5), (6)
(7)	238 (1)	(2)	134 (6), (7)
(8)	———	71 (1)	162
45 (1)–(3)	247 (1)–(3)	(2)	171 (6)
(4)	261 (1), (6)	(3)	293 (4)
(5)	262 (2), (4)	(4)	297 (2), (3)
(6)	247 (6)	72 (1)	Sch 1, para 16
46	248 (2)–(4)		
47 (1), (2)	250 (1)		
(3)	250 (2), 261 (1)		
(4)	250 (3), 261 (3)		

(1)	(2)	(1)	(2)
Highways Act 1971 (c 41)	Highways Act 1980 (c 66)	Highways Act 1971 (c 41)	Highways Act 1980 (c 66)
s 72 (2)	Sch 12, para 3	Sch 5	s 252 (1)
73 (1)	——	6	Sch 19
(2)	s 329 (1)	7	Rep., 1971 c 78, s 292, Sch 25
74		8	Sch 20
75	See s 340 (2)	9, para 1	s 334 (1)
76 (1)	See Sch 23, para 13 (2)	para 2	20 (9)
(2)	Sch 23, para 13 (3)	para 3	334 (2)
77	Rep., 1971 c 78, s 292, Sch 25	para 4	(6)
78 (1)	See s 340 (2)	para 5	(7), (8)
(2)	Rep., 1971 c 78, s 292, Sch 25	para 6, 7	(9), (10)
79	s 327	para 8	——
80 (1)	314 (1), (3)	para 9	334 (12), (13)
(2)	(2)	para 10	(14)
(3)	312	10	Sch 5, Part II
81 (1)	305 (1)–(5), (7)	11, para 1–4	——
(2)	(6)	para 5	Sch 23, para 7
(3)	307 (1)–(3)	para 6–8	——
(4)	(4)	12	——
82 (1)	326 (2)	13	Sch 1, Part I
(2)	(5), (6)	**Civil Aviation Act 1971 (c 75)**	
(3)	325		
83	——	Sch 5, para 5 (m)	s 178 (5), 254 (6), Sch 6, para 3
84 (1)	——		(3)
(2)	112 (1), 329 (1)	para 5 (ee)	290 (9)
(3)	250 (8)	**Town and Country Planning Act 1971 (c 78)**	
(4)	See Sch 23, para 18		
(5)		s 16 (c)	See Sch 24, para 20 (a) (iii)
85	Rep., 1980 c 65, ss 1 (7), 194, Sch 7, para 8 (2), Sch 34, Part VII	20†	s 232 (9)
86	——	Sch 23, Part II*	21 (1), 22 (1), (2), 36 (1) (d), 125 (1), (2), (4), 126 (1), 184 (3), 262 (1), 272 (1), Sch 5, Part II, Sch 23, para 3 (1)
87 (1)–(5)		Sch 24, para 2†	166 (3), 329 (1)
(6)	s 345 (3)	**Banking and Financial Dealings Act 1971 (c 80)**	
Sch 1, para 1, 2	Rep., 1972 c 70, s 272 (1), Sch 30		
para 3	s 80 (1)	s 4 (1)†	323
para 4 (1)	268 (1)	**Gas Act 1972 (c 60)**	
para 4 (2)	(4)		
para 5, 6	Sch 1, para 2, 3	Sch 4, para 1 (6)*	——
para 7	para 9		
para 8	para 3		
para 9–11	para 1–3		
para 12	para 1		
para 13	para 5, 6		
para 14	——		
para 15	para 10		
para 16	para 12, 13		
para 17	——		
2	s 100		
3	Sch 14		
4	17		

† Not repealed   * Repealed in part

(1)	(2)
Local Government Act 1972 (c 70)	Highways Act 1980 (c 66)
s 179 (4)†	s 18 (8), 30, 43 (1), (2), 47 (4), (8), 50 (2), 72 (3), 96 (5), (7), 134 (7), 300 (1)
187 (1)	1 (2)
(2)	42 (1), (2), 50 (2), (3)
(3) (b)	134 (7)
(4), (5)	42 (3)
(6)	6 (6)
(7)	61
(8)	12 (4), 42 (2)
188 (1)	—
(2)	130 (1)
(3), (4)	—
(5)	203 (3)
(6)	35 (1), (3), (4), (6), (7), (9), (10)
(7), (8)	—
Sch 14, para 40†	166 (1), 287
20	Sch 7
21, para 1 (1)	s 1 (2)
para 1 (2)	(4)
para 2	2
para 3	5
para 4	3
para 5	—
para 6 (1)	6 (1)
para 6 (2)	(5)
para 7	25 (2), (3)
para 8	26 (1), (3)
para 9	—
para 10-12	27-29
para 13 (1)	31 (7)
para 13 (2)	31 (6)
para 14	34
para 15	36 (1), (6), (7)
para 16	38 (5)
para 17	40
para 18 (1)	45 (4), (6)
para 18 (2), (3)	(7), (8)
para 18 (4), (5)	(12)
para 19 (1)	47 (1)
para 19 (2)	(3)
para 20	50 (2)
para 21	64 (4)
para 22	66 (6), (7)
para 23	69
para 24	72 (2)

(1)	(2)
Local Government Act 1972 (c 70)	Highways Act 1980 (c 66)
Sch 21, para 25	s 75 (1)
para 26	79 (3)
para 27	80 (4)
para 28 (1)	95 (1)
para 28 (2)	(3)
para 29	116 (3)
para 30 (1)	118 (1), (5)
para 30 (2)	(7)
para 31	119 (1), (3), (5)
para 32 (1)	120 (2)
para 32 (2)	(1)
para 32 (3)	—
para 32 (4)	120 (3)
para 32 (5)	—
para 33	121 (1)
para 34 (1)–(4)	130 (1)–(4)
para 34 (5)	(6)
para 35	133
para 36	134 (7)
para 37	143 (1)–(3)
para 38	147 (1), (2)
para 39	151 (1)
para 40 (1), (2)	153 (1), (2)
para 40 (3)	(3), (4), (6), (7)
para 41	154 (1)
para 42	156 (2)
para 43	163 (1)
para 44 (1)	164 (3)
para 44 (2)	(1)
para 45	172 (1)–(4)
para 46	173 (1)
para 47	175
para 48 (1)	179 (1), (2)
para 48 (2)	179 (1), 180 (1)
para 49 (1)	180 (1)
para 49 (2)	(3), (4), (7)
para 50 (1)	186 (1)
para 50 (2)	(3)
para 50 (3)	—
para 50 (4)	186 (5), (7)
para 50 (5)	(1), (3), (5), (7)
para 51	188 (1)
para 52-54	190-192
para 55 (1)	193 (1)
para 55 (2)	
para 55 (3), (4)	193 (2)
para 55 (5)	
para 56 (1), (2)	194 (1), (2)
para 56 (3)	(5), (6)
para 57 (1)	195 (1)

† Not repealed

(1)	(2)
Local Government Act 1972 (c 70)	Highways Act 1980 (c 66)
Sch 21, para 57 (2)	s 195 (3)
para 57 (3)	——
para 58	196 (8)
para 59–64	197–202
para 65 (1)	204 (1)
para 65 (2)	——
para 65 (3)	204 (2)
para 66 (1), (2)	205 (4), (5)
para 67	210 (2)
para 68	——
para 69 (1)	219 (4)
para 69 (2)	(6)
para 70	220 (1), (2)
para 71	223 (6)
para 72 (1)	——
para 72 (2)	224 (3)
para 73	——
para 74 (1)	232 (2), (5), (6)
para 74 (2)	——
para 75	237 (1)
para 76 (1)	203 (3)
para 76 (2), 77	——
para 78	254 (2)
para 79	——
para 80	263 (5)
para 81	264 (1)
para 82	265 (10)
para 83	272 (5)
para 84, 85	273, 274
para 86	286 (1)
para 87	295
para 88	——
para 89	329 (1)
para 90, 91	330, 331
para 92	——
para 93 (1)	Sch 9, para 1
para 93 (2)	para 2, 3
para 93 (3)	para 9
para 94	12, para 1
para 95	15
para 99	s 43 (2)
para 100 (1)	146 (2)–(5)
para 100 (2)	134 (8)–(10)
29, para 4 (1)†	59 (1), 193 (3), 205 (3), 211 (1), 212 (4), 216 (1), 295 (1), 321, Sch 9, para 4, Sch 15

(1)	(2)
Land Compensation Act 1973 (c 26)	Highways Act 1980 (c 66)
s 20 (10)	s 272 (1)
22 (1)	238 (1), 246 (1)
(2), (3)	246 (2), (3)
(4)	(5)
(5)	247 (1)–(3)
(6)	246 (4)
(7)	246 (6), 247 (6), 261 (1), (6)
(8)	6 (1)
(9)	250 (1)
(10)	246 (7)
(11)	Applied to Scotland
23	s 282
24 (1)–(5)	253
(6)	Applied to Scotland
25	s 272 (1)
74 (1) (a)	See Sch 24, para 23 (e)
78 (5)	s 262 (1), (2)
87 (3)	See Sch 24, para 23 (i)
(4)†	s 262 (2)
Water Act 1973 (c 37)	
s 9†	254 (4), 276, 290, 339 (1)–(3), Sch 1, para 3, 11
14 (2)†	290
Sch 6, para 11†, 13†	218
8, para 70	100 (5), (6)
para 71	264 (3)
Local Government Act 1974 (c 7)	
s 6 (8)*	——
40 (1)	12 (1), (2)
(2)–(4)	13
Sch 1, Part II, para 6*	272 (4)
6, para 12	——
7, para 2	12 (1), (2)
Local Land Charges Act 1975 (c 76)	
Sch 1*	35 (5), 73 (12), 74 (13), 79 (16), 87 (7), 177 (11), 224 (1), 223 (4), 305 (6)

† Not repealed   * Repealed in part

(1)	(2)
Community Land Act 1975 (c 77)	**Highways Act 1980 (c 66)**
s 7†, 41†	See Sch 23, para 14 (1)
Local Government (Miscellaneous Provisions) Act 1976 (c 57)	
s 1	s 144 (1)–(5)
2 (1)–(3)	169 (1)–(3)
(4)	
(5)–(8)	169 (4)–(7)
(9)	
3 (1), (2)	170 (1), (2)
(3)	
4 (1)–(3)	171 (2)–(4)
(4)	(6)
(5)	Sch 22
5	s 132
6 (1)–(4)	189, Sch 23, para 10 (1), (3)
(5)	
44 (1)*	144 (6), 169 (4), 170 (3), 171 (2); see also Sch 24, para 27 (c) (ii)
Sch 2*	
Land Drainage Act 1976 (c 70)	
s 17 (7)†	329 (1)
116 (1)†	339 (1)–(3)
Sch 7, para 2	Sch 1, para 3
para 7	s 339 (1)
Statute Law (Repeals) Act 1977 (c 18)	
Sch 2†	247 (5), 254 (1)

(1)	(2)
Criminal Law Act 1977 (c 45)	**Highways Act 1980 (c 66)**
s 28 (2)†, (7)† 31 (5)†, (6)†, (9)†	s 292 (4), 297 (3), 46, 73 (6), 74 (6), 79 (10), 136 (3), 141 (3), 152 (4), 153 (5), 155 (4), 173 (2), 175, 176 (7), 178 (4), 179 (3), 180 (4), 194 (4), 195 (3), 196 (6), 303
Sch 6*	134 (5) (b)
Interpretation Act 1978 (c 30)	
s 14†	326 (1)
Transport Act 1980 (c 34)	
s 45†	See Sch 23, para 15
Magistrates' Courts Act 1980 (c 43)	
Sch 7, para 29	s 329 (1)
Local Government, Planning and Land Act 1980 (c 65)	
Sch 7, para 1 (2)	24 (4)
para 2 (1)	26 (2)
para 2 (2) (b)	27 (2)
para 2 (3)	(4), (5)
para 2 (4)	120 (3), (5)
para 3 (1)	212 (1)
para 3 (3)	305 (1), (2)
para 5	124 (2)–(7); and cf. s 329 (1)
para 6 (5)†	Sch 8 para 4

† Not repealed   * Repealed in part

1400   New street byelaws—extension of operation

The New Street Byelaws (Extension of Operation) Order 1980, S.I. 1980 No. 457 (made on 27th March 1980), extends until 31st March 1983 the period of operation of certain new street byelaws which were made before the coming into operation of the Highways Act 1959 under enactments repealed by that Act.

1401   Public inquiries—procedure—rights of objectors to motorway scheme

See *Bushell v Secretary of State for the Environment*, para. 24.

1402   Public path—stopping-up order—matters to be disregarded—temporary obstructions

A public path had become overgrown. On some parts there were sizeable trees and shrubs, including a pine tree and a laurel hedge growing across the path. The local authority made a public path extinguishment order. In deciding not to confirm the order the Secretary of State disregarded the obstructions in view of Highways Act 1959, s. 110 (6), which provides that any temporary circumstances preventing or diminishing the use of the path by the public are to be disregarded. On an application for his decision to be quashed, *held*, an obstruction which seemed permanent but which was unlawful and likely to be removed could be regarded as temporary. The trees and shrubs which were blocking the path were temporary circumstances and had been properly disregarded.

R v SECRETARY OF STATE FOR THE ENVIRONMENT, EX PARTE STEWART (1979) 39 P & CR 534 (Queen's Bench Division: PHILLIPS J).

1403   Right of way—footpath—obstruction—discretion of authority to protect rights of public

A landowner erected a barrier across a footpath on his land and marked it "private". Local residents contended that the footpath was a highway under the Highways Act 1959 because it had been used by the public as of right, without interruption, for at least twenty years. The local highway authority was asked to exercise its duty under the 1959 Act, s. 116 (1) to assert and protect the rights of the public to use and enjoy the footpath. After a local public inquiry the authority decided that it was only under a duty to act under s. 116 (1) if it was satisfied that there was a public right of way to be asserted in respect of a highway and that it could not be established whether the footpath was public or private. The residents applied for an order of mandamus requiring the authority to fulfil its duty under s. 116 (1). *Held*, on the correct interpretation of s. 116 (1) a highway authority was under a duty to assert and protect the rights of the public to the use and enjoyment of a highway only if it was satisfied that it was beyond serious dispute that the path was a highway within the meaning of the Act. In the present case there existed a serious dispute on the matter and the highway authority was under no duty to act under s. 116. The application would accordingly be dismissed.

RE GUYER'S APPLICATION [1980] 2 All ER 520 (Court of Appeal: STEPHENSON and ACKNER LJJ and SIR DAVID CAIRNS).

1404   —— —— —— duty of highway authority to remove obstruction

A path, which was a public right of way, was obstructed by the owners of houses built adjacent to the path. Between 1969 and 1977 the local parish council made repeated efforts to persuade the county council as highway authority to exercise its powers under the Highways Act 1959 to remove the obstructions. In January 1977 the county council served removal notices on the houseowners who then proposed that if the public right of way over the path was extinguished, they would provide an alternative path. The parish council opposed the proposal; the county council took no action as a result of which the parish council applied for an order compelling the county council to perform its duty under the 1959 Act. *Held,* under the 1959 Act, s. 116 (6), if a parish council complained about an obstruction, the highway authority had a duty to take proper proceedings. The court could not interfere in such matters unless satisfied that an authority acted unreasonably in view of its duties under the 1959 Act. The county council failed to take any action because it was influenced by the convenience of the houseowners' proposals. In being so influenced, the council was acting in the interests of the people who had obstructed the path and not those who should have been enjoying a right of way over it. No reasonable authority could have acted that way in view of its duty under the 1959 Act, s. 116. Accordingly an order of mandamus would be granted against the county council.

R v SURREY COUNTY COUNCIL, EX PARTE SEND PARISH COUNCIL (1979) 40 P & CR 390 (Queen's Bench Division: LORD WIDGERY CJ, GEOFFREY LANE LJ and ACKNER J). Dicta of Lord Reid in *Padfield v Minister of Agriculture, Fisheries and Food* [1968] AC 997 at 1029, 1030 applied.

1405   Road—meaning of "road"—vehicles on road in private housing estate

Residents on a private estate considered that the driving of cars and buses on a road in the estate was dangerous. Police prosecutions were not instituted on the basis that the road was not a "road" within the Road Traffic Act 1972, s. 196 (1) which provides that a "road" is any highway and any road to which the public has access. The residents, in an action against the local Commissioner of Police, sought a declaration that he was not precluded from prosecuting alleged road traffic offences on the road by reason of s. 196 (1). *Held,* although the evidence established that the public had access to the road and that therefore the road was a "road" within the meaning of s. 196 (1) the declaration sought would be refused on the ground that such a declaration fettered the Commissioner's discretion in prosecuting alleged offences.

ADAMS v METROPOLITAN POLICE COMR [1980] RTR 289 (Queen's Bench Division: JUPP J). *Harrison v Hill* 1932 JC 13 and *Ottway v Jones* [1955] 2 All ER 585 applied.

HIRE PURCHASE AND CONSUMER CREDIT

Halsbury's Laws of England (4th edn.), Vol. 22, paras. 1–400

1406   Article

The Consumer Credit Act: Where We Are Now, R. G. Lawson (summary of implementation of the 1974 Act): 130 NLJ 408.

1407   Conditional sale agreement—accelerated payment clause— validity

The defendant entered into a conditional sale agreement with a finance company. She paid the deposit but none of the instalments and the company claimed payment under the accelerated payment clause. The defendant contended that the clause was void under the Hire-Purchase Act 1965, s. 29, since it interfered with her right under s. 27 (1) to terminate the agreement at any time before the final payment fell due. *Held,* if the seller elected to call for accelerated payment and gave the necessary notice which expired without the buyer having paid off the arrears, the accelerated payment, which was the final payment under the conditional sale agreement, fell due for the purposes of s. 27 (1). Consequently, the right to terminate under s. 27 (1) came to an end. Until the sum under the accelerated payment clause became due, the right to terminate was expressly recognised and although that right was lost thereafter, the loss occurred after the time specified in s. 27 (1). Accordingly the clause was not void for restricting the right to terminate. Nor was it a penalty clause but a genuine pre-estimate of what the company would lose because of the early termination of the agreement. Accordingly the defendant was liable under the clause.

WADHAM STRINGER FINANCE LTD v MEANEY [1980] 3 All ER 789 (Queen's Bench Division: WOOLF J).

1408   Consumer credit—advertisements

The Consumer Credit (Advertisements) Regulations 1980, S.I. 1980 No. 54 (in force on 6th October 1980), govern advertisements published by persons carrying on consumer credit businesses, consumer hire businesses and businesses in the course of which credit secured on land is provided to individuals. They also apply to certain advertisements published by credit-brokers. The information to be given in different categories of advertisement are prescribed in Pt. II. Part III contains provisions relating to the form of advertisements.

1409   The Consumer Credit (Advertisements) (Amendment) Regulations 1980, S.I. 1980 No. 1360 (in force on 6th October 1980), exempt from the requirements of the Consumer Credit (Advertisements) Regulations 1980 (the principal regulations), para. 1408, certain advertisements where the creditor is a body specified in the Schedule to the Consumer Credit (Exempt Agreements) Order 1980, para. 1413. The regulations make it clear that the exemptions from the principal regulations apply only in so far as the advertisement relates to matters specified in those regulations.

1410   —— —— exemptions

The Consumer Credit (Exempt Advertisements) Order 1980, S.I. 1980 No. 53 (in force on 6th October 1980), extends the categories of advertisements which are exempt from the provisions of the Consumer Credit Act 1974, Pt. IV (which relates to seeking credit or hire business).

1411   The Consumer Credit (Exempt Advertisements) (Amendment) Order 1980, S.I. 1980 No. 1359 (in force on 6th October 1980), makes it clear that the exemptions from the Consumer Credit Act 1974, Pt. IV provided for in the Consumer Credit (Exempt Advertisements) Order 1980, para. 1410, apply only to advertisements in so far as they relate to consumer credit agreements or consumer hire agreements specified in that order and to advertisements which would fall within certain paragraphs of that order if they were to relate to consumer credit agreements or consumer hire agreements.

1412   —— "credit token"—meaning

It fell to be determined whether an unsolicited plastic card purporting to be a credit account card for a chain of shoe shops was a "credit token" within the meaning of the Consumer Credit Act 1974, s. 14 (1), which defines it as a card given to an individual by a person carrying on a consumer credit business who undertakes that on production of the card he will supply goods and services on credit. The card stated that it was available for immediate use, the sole requirement being a signature, means of identification and a bank account. That was in fact not true. *Held*, the fact that none of the statements was true did not absolve the card from being what it purported to be. On the face of it the shoe shop undertook that on production of the card, goods or services would be supplied. The card was therefore a credit token and to send such cards to potential customers was an offence contrary to the 1974 Act, s. 51(1).

ELLIOTT v DIRECTOR GENERAL OF FAIR TRADING [1980] 1 WLR 977 (Queen's Bench Division: LORD LANE CJ and WOOLF J).

1413 —— exempt agreements

The Consumer Credit (Exempt Agreements) Order 1980, S.I. 1980 No. 52 (in force on 28th April 1980), supersedes the Consumer Credit (Exempt Agreements) Order 1977, 1977 Halsbury's Abridgment para. 1415, as amended, and provides that certain consumer credit and consumer hire agreements shall be exempt agreements for the purposes of the Consumer Credit Act 1974. The agreements include certain agreements secured on land where the creditor is a specified body, certain agreements where the number of payments to be made by the debtor does not exceed the number specified, certain agreements where the rate of the total charge for credit is a rate which does not exceed minimum lending rate plus 1 per cent or 13 per cent, whichever is the higher, and certain agreements having a connection with a country outside the United Kingdom. Consumer hire agreements are exempt where the owner is a statutory corporation supplying electricity, gas or water and the subject of the agreement is a meter used in connection with that supply, and where the owner is the Post Office or the Kingston upon Hull City Council and the subject of the agreement is telecommunications equipment other than equipment forming part of an internal telephone system.

Certain changes are made by the new order. The principal changes are that the scope of the exemption covering certain agreements for the alteration of premises is slightly widened; certain agreements connected with building and related insurance contracts or with mortgage protection or indemnity insurance and certain agreements under which the only charge for credit is interest are made exempt; a further body is now specified in the Schedule.

1414 —— quotations

The Consumer Credit (Quotations) Regulations 1980, S.I. 1980 No. 55 (in force on 6th October 1980), prescribe the form and content of quotations in which persons carrying on consumer credit businesses, consumer hire businesses and businesses in the course of which credit secured on land is provided to individuals give prospective customers information about the terms on which they are prepared to do business. The circumstances in which such quotations are to be provided are also prescribed. With certain exceptions, the regulations apply when the proposed transaction would be an agreement regulated by the Consumer Credit Act 1974 or an agreement secured on land. A quotation must be provided in response to a request for written information made in writing, orally on the trader's premises or, in certain circumstances, by telephone.

1415

The Consumer Credit (Quotations) (Amendment) Regulations 1980, S.I. 1980 No. 1361 (in force on 6th October 1980), exempt from the requirements to provide quotations found in the Consumer Credit (Quotations) Regulations 1980 (the principal regulations), para. 1414, certain cases where the request is made to a creditor which is a body specified in the Schedule to the Consumer Credit (Exempt Agreements) Order 1980, para. 1413. The regulations also make it clear that the exemptions from the principal regulations apply only in so far as the request relates to the matters specified in those regulations.

1416   —— sex discrimination—refusal to grant woman credit without guarantee—validity

The Court of Appeal has held that a retailer who refused to provide a married woman with credit facilities unless her husband entered into a guarantee, and who admitted that a man in the same circumstances would not have been required to produce such a guarantee, was guilty of discrimination against a woman contrary to the Sex Discrimination Act 1975, s. 29 (1) (b).

QUINN v WILLIAMS FURNITURE LTD (1980) Times, 18th November (Court of Appeal: LORD DENNING MR and O'CONNOR LJ).

1417   —— total charge for credit

The Consumer Credit (Total Charge for Credit) Regulations 1980, S.I. 1980 No. 51 (in force on 28th April 1980), which supersede the Consumer Credit (Total Charge for Credit) Regulations 1977, 1977 Halsbury's Abridgment para. 1417, make provision for ascertaining the true cost to debtors of credit provided or to be provided under actual or prospective consumer credit agreements. They prescribe the items which are to be treated as entering into the true cost of the credit to the debtor and provide for the calculation of the rate of the total charge as an annual percentage rate. The regulations also contain provisions dealing with assumptions which must be made for calculations in cases where relevant factors cannot be quantified at the time when the calculations are to be made. The new regulations make a number of changes, the principal change being that certain insurance premiums are not to be included in the total charge for credit.

1418   Consumer Credit Act 1974—commencement

The Consumer Credit Act 1974 (Commencement No. 6) Order 1980, S.I. 1980 No. 50 brings into force, on 6th October 1980, the following provisions of the 1974 Act, 1974 Halsbury's Abridgment para. 1597: for certain purposes Part IV of the Act (which relates to seeking business); s. 151 (1), (2) (which apply certain provisions of Part IV relating to advertisements published for the purposes of certain ancillary credit business). These provisions are not to apply to any advertisement published before 6th October 1980.

1419   Extortionate credit bargain—application to reopen bargain—rate of interest

The Consumer Credit Act 1974, s. 138 provides that a credit bargain is extortionate if it requires a debtor to make payments which are grossly exorbitant. It further provides that regard should be had to interest rates prevailing at the time the bargain was made, and various other factors. In relation to the debtor these include his experience, business capacity and the degree and nature of any financial pressure on him. In relation to the creditor these include the degree of risk accepted by him having regard to the value of any security provided. Section 139 provides that a court may re-open a credit bargain if it thinks it just.

The defendant failed to complete a contract of sale in time and risked forfeiting his deposit if he failed to complete within one month. He was unable to obtain a loan from his bank since he had already overdrawn and had signed a legal charge on the property to cover the overdraft. The plaintiff agreed to lend him £20,500 for three months with interest equal to the rate of 48 per cent per annum. The terms also included a legal charge on the property and the agreement was concluded within a few hours to enable the defendant to complete. The defendant applied to have the bargain reopened on the ground that it was extortionate. *Held,* the documents which the defendants had signed clearly indicated the terms of the agreement and in view of defendant's experience in business it was unlikely that he would have entered into the agreement if he was unaware of them. The plaintiff had accepted a considerable degree of risk in lending such a large sum at such short notice without making inquiries about the defendant's financial position. Further, since the defendant had failed to disclose several material facts relevant to his financial situation the court did not think it just to reopen the bargain.

A KETLEY LTD V SCOTT (1980) Times, 25th June (Chancery Division: FOSTER J).

1420 Licensing—Director-General of Fair Trading—annual report

The Annual Report of the Director-General of Fair Trading 1979 (HC 624) discloses that 11,886 new applications for standard licences (Consumer Credit Act 1974) were made in 1979 and 23,261 licences were issued. Many new applications are dealt with within a few weeks and at the end of 1979 the number of applications awaiting decision was 7,069 (at the end of 1978, 19,193). The licences in force in respect of different categories of business at the end of 1979 were: consumer credit, 36,498; consumer hire, 18,535; credit brokerage, 63,731; debt adjusting and debt counselling, 28,442; debt collecting, 11,095; and credit reference agency, 2,413. Those with a permit to canvass off trade premises, debtor–creditor-supplier agreements or regulated hire agreements, 23,888. During the year 2,006 applications to vary licences were granted (out of a total of 2,210 applications) and 7,415 notifications were received of changes in particulars of licensees.

HOUSING

Halsbury's Laws of England (4th edn.), Vol. 22, paras. 401–900

1421 Articles

Increase of Rent by Housing Associations and Variation of Terms of Secure Tenancies, P. H. Pettit: 130 NLJ 1060.

Unit Housing: The Issue of "Reasonable Cost", David Morgan (recent cases on interpretation of "reasonable cost" in relation to Housing Act 1957, ss. 9, 16, 39): [1979] Conv. 414.

1422 Assistance for home purchase—limits

The Home Purchase Assistance (Price Limits) Order 1980, S.I. 1980, No. 1371 (in force on 1st October 1980), prescribes the limits on the purchase price of property in different parts of England and Wales in respect of which finance assistance is available for first-time purchasers under the Home Purchase Assistance and Housing Corporation Guarantee Act 1978.

1423 Assistance for house purchase and improvement—loans by local authorities—increase in mortgage limits

The government has announced that the maximum sums which may be advanced by local authorities on mortgages for house purchase and improvements are to be increased from £13,000 or £15,000 in Greater London to £25,000. See 124 Sol Jo 315.

1424 —— qualifying lender

The Assistance for House Purchase and Improvement (Qualifying Lenders) Order 1980, S.I. 1980 No. 1636 (in force on 11th November 1980), adds Save and Prosper

Pensions Limited to the list of qualifying lenders under the Housing Subsidies Act 1967, Pt. II.

1425　　The Assistance for House Purchase and Improvement (Qualifying Lenders) (No. 2) Order 1980, S.I. 1980 No. 2040 (in force on 16th February 1981), adds Home Reversions Ltd to the list of qualifying lenders under the Housing Subsidies Act 1967, Pt. II.

1426　　**Clearance area—compulsory purchase—compensation—owner-occupier supplement—calculation**

See *Khan v Birmingham City Council*, para. 409.

1427　　**Homeless persons—duties of local authority—duty to provide accommodation—responsibility of other housing authorities**

Housing (Homeless Persons) Act 1977, s. 5 provides that a local housing authority is under a duty to house homeless persons within its area, but this obligation does not arise where the applicant does not have a local connection with the area and has a connection with another area.

A family who had been living for many years in council property in Slough were, as a result of their undesirable conduct, evicted by the local housing authority. The family subsequently applied for accommodation as they were homeless. The authority found that they were homeless intentionally under the Housing (Homeless Persons) Act 1977 and having no temporary accommodation available arranged with a guest house in another local housing authority area, Ealing, to accommodate the family for two weeks. Before the expiry of the two weeks the family applied to Ealing housing authority for accommodation.

The authority, having made all the appropriate inquiries, found that the family was homeless unintentionally and therefore had a duty under the Act to house the family indefinitely unless it was possible to pass that obligation back to the original housing authority, Slough, under s. 5 (3) which, after they had notified the original housing authority of the family's application for accommodation, they claimed they could do. Questions arose, inter alia, as to the effect of s. 5. *Held*, the effect of the section was that if a local housing authority, having been satisfied that a person who applied to them for accommodation was homeless unintentionally and had a local connection with another housing authority area, notified the other authority under the 1977 Act that the application had been made, then the notified authority was under a duty to secure that accommodation became available for that person indefinitely, notwithstanding that the notified authority had previously determined that he was homeless intentionally. It was apparent that the effect was that one local housing authority could reverse another's decision on the question whether an applicant's homelessness was intentional, while at the same time disclaiming all responsibility for providing accommodation for him.

R v SLOUGH BOROUGH COUNCIL, EX PARTE EALING LONDON BOROUGH COUNCIL [1981] 1 All ER 601 (Court of Appeal: LORD DENNING MR, SHAW and TEMPLEMAN LJJ).

1428　　**———— duty to provide temporary accommodation—successive applications**

The applicant applied for, and was granted, temporary accommodation under the Housing (Homeless Persons) Act 1977. On the termination of that accommodation, he made another application for temporary accommodation. *Held*, a person who was granted temporary accommodation could not, when use of that accommodation was terminated, rely solely upon the same matters as he relied on in support of his earlier application or the termination or threat of termination of the previous temporary accommodation as the basis for a further application. It could not have been Parliament's intention that the Act should be used by someone who was not entitled to permanent accommodation to obtain the continuous use of temporary accommodation. The application would fail.

DELAHAYE v OSWESTRY BOROUGH COUNCIL (1980) Times, 29th July (Queen's Bench Division: WOOLF J).

1429 —— —— inquiries as to homelessness

Upon eviction from council housing for non-payment of rent, the plaintiff and his family entered into temporary accommodation provided by the council under their obligations under the Housing (Homeless Persons) Act 1977. The council had concluded that as the plaintiff had become homeless intentionally their duty was to give him advice and assurance and temporary accommodation until such time as he had had reasonable opportunity to secure his own accommodation. The plaintiff and his family found temporary accommodation in the private sector, and when forced to leave, made an application to the council for emergency housing assistance. The council's housing officer concluded that his homelessness was a continuance of the earlier state of homelessness and only advice was given to the plaintiff. On application to the court for various declarations and orders, the question for the court, inter alia, was whether the council were correct in assuming that the plaintiff's homelessness was a continuation of the earlier homelessness. *Held,* when the plaintiff had found his own accommodation the original homelessness came to an end and he became a person who could once again become homeless within the 1977 Act s. 1. The council could not therefore assume that his homelessness was a continuance of the earlier homelessness.

YOUNGS v THANET DISTRICT COUNCIL (1980) 78 LGR 474 (Chancery Division: JUDGE MERVYN DAVIES).

1430 —— —— intentional homelessness—cohabitee's conduct

A woman lived with a farm labourer who had been provided with a house on the farm. Both lived there until he voluntarily terminated his employment and his employer, the farm owner, took possession of the house. The labourer applied under the Housing (Homeless Persons) Act 1977 for accommodation but the local housing authority considered that both were intentionally homeless as he had voluntarily given up his job. The woman subsequently unsuccessfully applied for accommodation under the Act making it clear that the labourer would share any accommodation given to her. In an application by the woman for judicial review of the decision of the local housing authority that she had become intentionally homeless within the meaning of the Act, s. 17, *held,* the statutory test for intentional homelessness required the local housing authority to have regard for the "family unit" and s. 16 made it clear that it was the policy of the Act to keep families together where possible. There was no express provision in the Act which provided that where a man and a woman cohabited, appearing to form a "family unit", if one became homeless intentionally, the other should also be so treated. The fact however that the Act required consideration of the family unit as a whole indicated that it was reasonable for a housing authority to look at the family as a whole and, where the conduct of one member was such that he should be regarded as having become homeless intentionally, to assume in the absence of contrary evidence that was conduct to which other members were party. In the present case the applicant had acquiesced in her cohabitee's decision to terminate his employment knowing that the accommodation was tied and the council had not erred in taking the view that she was intentionally homeless. The application would accordingly be dismissed.

LEWIS v NORTH DEVON DISTRICT COUNCIL [1981] 1 All ER 27 (Queen's Bench Division: WOOLF J).

1431 —— —— —— duty to children of intentionally homeless families

A local authority passed a resolution that assistance with alternative housing would not be provided under the Children and Young Persons Act 1963, s. 1 where the family was intentionally homeless within the meaning of the Housing (Homeless Persons) Act 1977. The validity of this resolution was challenged in the courts.

Under the Children Act 1948, s. 1 the local authority has a duty to receive children into care where the parents are unable to provide proper accommodation. They have a further duty under the 1963 Act, s. 1 to make such "assistance in kind" as is necessary to promote the welfare of children by diminishing the need to keep them in care. *Held*, by analogy with the National Assistance Act 1948, s. 12 (2) "assistance in kind" included accommodation. The placing of a child with its parents in accommodation was therefore within the powers of the local authority under the 1963 Act. In deciding whether the child's welfare required that some attempt be made to keep the family together, it would be unfair to disregard the children of intentionally homeless parents. The resolution was therefore ultra vires and invalid in so much as it sought to differentiate between children according to the conduct of their parents.

A-G (ON THE RELATION OF TILLEY) v WANDSWORTH LONDON BOROUGH COUNCIL (1980) Times, 21st March (Chancery Division: JUDGE MERVYN DAVIES).

This decision has been affirmed by the Court of Appeal; see (1981) 125 Sol Jo 148.

1432 ———— —— duty to provide temporary accommodation for reasonable period

A family left their council flat in circumstances which led the council to regard the flat as abandoned. The flat was subsequently relet. Four months later, the husband asked the council for the keys to the flat, explaining that he and his family had had no intention of giving it up. A housing officer made inquiries and concluded that the family were intentionally homeless. Temporary accommodation was arranged for them for fourteen days. The wife, who was pregnant, was then taken ill, and the housing officer reluctantly agreed to allow an extra day for a medical certificate. The certificate arrived on the fifteenth day stating that the wife was unable to search for accommodation. The housing officer refused to extend the period, but after an interim injunction the family were allowed to stay pending a decision in the husband's present action for, inter alia, a mandatory injunction either requiring the council to allow him and his family to return to the flat or requiring the council to secure accommodation for them. *Held*, the court could only intervene if the council had misdirected themselves and had reached a decision that no reasonable council could have reached. The housing officer had made adequate inquiries, and her conclusion that the family was intentionally homeless was not unreasonable. However, the council's duty under the Housing (Homeless Persons) Act 1977, s. 4 (3) was to give the family a reasonable time to find another home. The fourteen day limit which the council was applying was insufficient and, by failing to consider in relation to the family what the period of temporary accommodation should have been, the council had not discharged their duty under s. 4 (3). The family were accordingly entitled to damages, but no other order would be made on the council's assurance that the family would not be evicted from their present temporary accommodation.

LALLY v KENSINGTON AND CHELSEA ROYAL BOROUGH (1980) Times, 27th March (Chancery Division: BROWNE-WILKINSON J).

1433 ——— ——— —— voluntary termination of tenancy

An application for a mandatory injunction against a local authority to secure accommodation under the Housing (Homeless Persons) Act 1977 until the hearing of the action was dismissed by the Chancery Division. Following a fire causing comparatively minor damage to a family's flat, the landlady had asked the family to stay elsewhere until repairs had been effected. The family had stayed with relatives and then voluntarily terminated their tenancy or licence to occupy the flat. The court *held*, the authority had been entitled to find that the family had made themselves intentionally homeless and had made sufficient inquiries as to their homelessness before making its decision.

MILLER v WANDSWORTH LONDON BOROUGH COUNCIL (1980) Times, 19th March (Chancery Division: WALTON J).

1434 A young woman deliberately surrendered the tenancy of her council flat and thereafter took a short term tenancy of another flat which she had to leave after a possession order was made against her. On the question as to whether the local housing authority had a duty under the Housing (Homeless Persons) Act 1977 to provide her with permanent accommodation, it was held that the woman had become intentionally homeless within the meaning of the 1977 Act, s. 17 by deliberately surrendering the tenancy of her council flat and the council were therefore under no duty to provide her with permanent accommodation. "International homelessness" included a deliberate act or omission in respect of accommodation other than that last occupied.

DYSON v KERRIER DISTRICT COUNCIL [1980] 3 All ER 313 (Court of Appeal: MEGAW and BRIGHTMAN LJJ and SIR PATRICK BROWNE).

1435 ——— ——— person with no local connection with any housing authority

The Court of Appeal was faced with the question whether when a woman, accompanied by her young son, from a foreign country was homeless both in Great Britain and in her country of origin, a local authority was bound under the Housing (Homeless Persons) Act 1977 to secure accommodation for her. *Held*, there was nothing in the Act limiting the authority's duty to a person with a "local connection". The Act applied to any person who had no accommodation in Great Britain. The only condition was that the person was in Great Britain lawfully. The local authority was under an obligation to inquire as to whether a person had a "priority need" and whether his homelessness was unintentional. If he had a priority need and his homelessness was unintentional the authority was under a duty to secure that person permanent accommodation available in Great Britain. In the present case the applicant's homelessness was unintentional and the authority was under a duty to provide her with accommodation.

R v HILLINGDON LONDON BOROUGH COUNCIL, EX PARTE STREETING [1980] 3 All ER 413 (Court of Appeal: LORD DENNING MR, WALLER and DUNN LJJ). *R v Bristol City Council, ex parte Browne* [1979] 3 All ER 344, 1979 Halsbury's Abridgment para. 1434, *De Falco v Crawley Borough Council* [1980] 2 WLR 664, CA, 1979 Halsbury's Abridgment para. 1433, *R v Inhabitants of Eastbourne* (1803) 4 East 103 applied. Decision of Divisional Court of the Queen's Bench Division (1980) Times, 28th February affirmed.

1436 **Housing Act 1980**

The Housing Act 1980 gives security of tenure, and the right to buy their homes, to tenants of local authorities and other bodies and makes other provisions with respect to those and other tenants. It also amends the law relating to house finance in the public sector and restricts the discretion of the court in making orders for possession of land. The Act received the royal assent on 8th August 1980 and ss. 90–105, 108, 112, 113, 120, 122–127, 130, 131, 133–135, 137–140, 150, 151, 152 (2) and 153–155 came into force on that date. Sections 1–50 came into force on 3rd October 1980. For other ss. now in force see below:

	date brought into force	brought into force by S.I. 1980 No.
s. 121	1st October 1980	1406
ss. 80–89, 110, 111, 114, 116 (1) (part), (2), 128, 129, 132, 136, 141 (part), 143–146, 148, 152 (1) (part), (3) part)	3rd October 1980	1406
ss. 56–58	6th October 1980	1466
ss. 78, 79, 118	20th October 1980	1557
ss. 107 (part), 147, 152 (1) (part), (3) (part)	27th October 1980	1557
s. 115	11th November 1980	1693
ss. 51–55, 59 (1), (2), 60–77, 149, 152 (1) (part), (3) (part)	28th November 1980	1706

	date brought into force	brought into force by S.I. 1980 No.
ss. 106, 107 (part), 109, 152 (1) (part), (3) (part) ss. 116 (1) (part), 117, 119, 141 (part), 142, 152 (3) (part)	15th December 1980 on a day or days to be appointed	1781

Part I: Public Sector Tenants
Part I deals with public sector tenants' rights.

The right to buy. Sections 1–27 confer rights on secure tenants to buy their houses and flats and to have a mortgage. With certain limited exceptions contained in s. 2, Sch. 1, a secure tenant of at least three years' standing is given the right to buy the freehold of his home if it is a house and a long lease if it is a flat and to a first mortgage to enable him to do so: s. 1. Sections 3, 4 define "house", "flat" and "dwelling house" and provide for joint tenants and members of a family occupying the dwelling house otherwise than as joint tenants to join in the purchase. Sections 5, 12 provide for the notices claiming exercise of the right to buy and to a mortgage. The price which is payable is arrived at by valuing the property on certain assumptions and subtracting the discount to which the tenant is entitled: ss. 6, 7. The purchaser is under an obligation to repay the discount if he sells again within five years: s. 8. The amount which a purchaser is entitled to leave outstanding on the mortgage is calculated in accordance with s. 9 and the landlord must serve a notice on the tenant giving the purchase price and how it is arrived at: s. 10. A tenant has the right to have the value determined by a district valuer under s. 11. Sections 13, 14 make provisions consequent upon a change in the secure tenant or the landlord after a notice claiming the right to buy or to a mortgage has been served. Sections 15, 16, Sch. 2 set out the terms on which the property is to be sold, including under ss. 17, 18 the terms of the mortgage deed. Sections 19, 20, 21, 22 relate to dwelling houses in National Parks and areas of outstanding natural beauty, registration of title, costs and notices. The Secretary of State is given a power of intervention, under s. 23, where it appears to him that the tenants have or may have difficulty in exercising the right to buy effectively and expeditiously. He may also make orders, pursuant to his right under s. 23, vesting the freehold or long leases of the dwelling houses in tenants who have claimed to exercise the right to buy: s. 24. Sections 25, 26 and 27 relate to statutory declarations, the power of the Secretary of State to amend or repeal local Acts and interpretation.

Security of tenure and rights of secure tenants. Sections 28, 29 provide that, subject to certain exclusions outlined in s. 49, Sch. 3, there is to be security of tenure for tenants and licensees of local housing authorities, new town corporations, the Development Board for Rural Wales and certain housing associations and other bodies. On death there is provision for one succession by a member of a tenant's family: ss. 30, 31. The court may grant possession orders against secure tenants only on the grounds set out in Sch. 4. It must assess the reasonableness of the order in most cases, and in some cases satisfy itself that suitable alternative accommodation will be available: ss. 32–34. Sections 35–41 deal with the terms of secure tenancies and ss. 42–45 provide for consultation with secure tenants on questions of housing management. Section 46 empowers the Secretary of State, with the consent of the Treasury, to make contributions to the cost of arrangements for assisting transfers and exchanges for secure tenants. Sections 47, 48 provide for the application of the Act to existing tenancies and licences, and ss. 49, 50 relate to interpretation.

Part II: Private Sector Tenants
Part II deals with privately rented housing and amends the Rent Act 1977.

Sections 51–55 make provision for shorthold tenancies: landlords will be able to let at fair rents for fixed terms of between 1–5 years at the end of which they will have the right to regain possession. Tenants will have security during the term of letting. Sections 56–58 and Sch. 5 introduce assured tenancies: approved landlords will be able to let new tenancies outside Rent Act protection, but the Landlord and Tenant Act 1954, Pt. II (renewal and continuation of tenancies) will apply in modified form to such lettings. Section 59 and Sch. 6 amend the Rent Act 1977 in respect of the management and procedures of rent officers. Section 60 reduces the normal period before fair rents can be re-registered and alters the phasing of rent increases accordingly. The date of registration, rather than the date of application, is the date on which a rent registration takes effect: s. 61. Section 62 allows for cancellation of a registered rent in certain additional circumstances. The 1977 Act, ss. 48 and 50 are repealed by s. 63. All controlled tenancies are to be converted into regulated tenancies: s. 64. Section 65 makes changes to the provisions relating to lettings by resident landlords and s. 66, Sch. 7 amend the provisions governing letting by temporarily absent owner-occupiers and owners of retirement homes. Section 67 adds a new Case (lettings by servicemen) to the 1977 Act, Sch. 15, Pt. II. Sections 68, 69 relate to rent agreements and restricted contracts with tenants having security of tenure. Section 70 reduces the registration period for rents under restricted contracts and s. 71 provides for the cancellation of rents registered by rent tribunals, while s. 72 deals with the administrative arrangements for those tribunals. Section 73 relates to dwellings forming part of Crown Estate or belonging to Duchies. Under ss. 74, 77, Schs. 9, 10 the provisions relating to housing association tenancies in the 1977 Act are amended. Section 75 modifies the court's discretion in possession cases with regard to the imposition of conditions about the payment of rent and arrears, and gives the deserted spouse of a statutory or protected tenant the right to participate in possession proceedings. Section 76 extends the succession rights of widows to widowers. Section 78 clarifies the circumstances in which a premium may be charged for the grant or assignment of certain long tenancies, whilst s. 79 provides that certain deposits do not constitute unlawful premiums.

Part III: Tenant's Repairs and Improvements
Part III deals with tenant's repairs and improvements both in the public and private sectors.

  Section 80 enables certain bodies to take on the repairing obligations in short leases under the Housing Act 1961, s. 32, without leave of the court. Sections 81–84 provide that certain secure, protected and statutory tenants may make improvements to their homes with consent. Section 85 relates to interpretation.

Part IV: Jurisdiction and Procedure
Sections 86–88 provide that any proceedings under Pts. I, III may be dealt with by a county court. The court may stay or suspend the operation of certain possession orders. Section 89 restricts to fourteen days the period for which a court can postpone the coming into effect of a possession order in most cases where there is a mandatory right to possession of any land.

Part V: Amendment of Pt. V of Housing Act 1957
Section 90 relaxes the requirement on local authorities under the 1957 Act, s. 91. Section 91 introduces a new s. 104 into that Act, containing a power for local authorities to dispose of interests in land. The power is subject to Ministerial consent and conditions to consent are dealt with in s. 92. Sections 93–95 are provisions dealing with the acquisition of land for subsequent disposal or other purposes and the granting by local authorities of options to purchase houses.

Part VI: Housing Subsidies
Sections 96–103, Sch. 11, introduce a new system of housing subsidy in England and Wales for local housing authorities, new town corporations and the Development Board for Rural Wales to replace the interim system in the Housing Rents and Subsidies Act 1975. Section 104 relates to the transitional town development subsidy and s. 105 to interpretation.

Part VII: Housing; financial and related provisions
Sections 106–109, Schs. 12, 13 deal with housing repairs and improvements and ss. 110–116, Sch. 14 are concerned mainly with mortgages (local authority and other). A ninety per cent rate of subsidy is payable to local authorities towards the standard amounts of rent rebates and rent allowances: s. 117. Sections 118, 119, Sch. 15 amend the Housing Finance Act 1972, Pt. II to widen eligibility for rent rebates and rent allowances.

Part VIII: Housing Associations and the Housing Corporation
Sections 120, 121 relate to the borrowing powers and grants to and by the Housing Corporation. Sections 122, 123 give all registered housing associations power to sell properties subject to the revised consent powers of the Housing Corporation. Sections 124–126, Sch. 15 relate to the accountancy and audit procedures of registered housing associations. Registered housing associations are now allowed to provide houses for sale as well as for letting: s. 127. Section 128 provides for the circumstances in which a housing association can be removed from the register. The Housing Act 1974, ss. 19, 20 are amended by s. 129, Sch. 17 to extend an inspector's power to requisition information from a registered housing association's agents. Section 130 provides for subsidies to enable housing associations to improve houses with a view to sale, and s. 130 (4), Sch. 18 make amendments to the 1974 Act, Pt. III to allow housing association grants to be paid on housing association shared ownership schemes and on other schemes. Any surplus rental income is required to be accounted for separately in a Grant Redemption Fund: s. 131. Section 132 makes provision for the amendment of the rules of a registered housing association and s. 133 relates to interpretation.

Part IX: General
Part IX comprises provisions relating to housing accounts, service charges and other matters.

Section 134 provides for the repeal of the Housing Rents and Subsidies Act 1975, s. 1 (3), and thus enables local authorities to transfer credit balances arising on their Housing Revenue Accounts to their general rate funds. Local authorities may now keep a separate Housing Repairs Account: s. 135. Section 136, Sch. 19 relates to the service charge payable by tenants of flats and replace and extend the Housing Finance Act 1972, ss. 90–91A. Section 137 relates to the avoidance of certain unauthorised disposals and s. 138 to displacement of residential occupiers by housing authorities. Housing co-operatives are dealt with in s. 139, Sch. 20. Section 140 excludes certain shared ownership leases from the enfranchisement provisions of the Leasehold Reform Act 1967, which is further amended by s. 141, Sch. 21. Leasehold Valuation Tribunals are to be established to settle valuation disputes arising under the 1967 Act: s. 142, Sch. 22. The Landlord and Tenant Act 1927, s. 20 is amended by s. 143. The penalties for a landlord's failure to disclose his identity or give notice of assignment are increased: s. 144, and the penalties for offences in relation to houses in multiple occupation are revised: ss. 145–147, Sch. 23. The Secretary of State may pay pensions to presidents and vice-presidents of rent assessment panels: s. 148. Section 149 enlarges a local authority's power to deal with disrepair affecting the comfort of an occupying tenant.

Sections 150–155, Schs. 25, 26 relate to interpretation; regulations and orders, amendments, transitional provisions, repeals, commencement, expenses and receipts and short title, extent etc.

For orders and regulations made under this Act, see paras. 1449–1457, infra.

1437 Housing action area—acquisition of land—local authority's undertaking not to acquire if repairs effected

See *Varsani v Secretary of State for the Environment*, para. 411.

1438 Housing finance—rent allowance subsidy

The Housing Finance (Rent Allowance Subsidy) Order 1980, S.I. 1980 No. 31 (in force on 8th February 1980), fixes the amount of rent allowance subsidy payable to a local authority for 1980–81 at 100 per cent of the authority's standard amount of rent allowances for the year.

1439 Improvement areas—approved expenditure

The Approved Expenditure (Housing Act 1969 Part II) Order 1980, S.I. 1980 No. 857 (in force on 22nd July 1980), increases to £400 the amount per dwelling which is to be taken into account in calculating the maximum approved by local authorities under Pt. II of the 1969 Act in respect of general improvement areas towards which contributions may be paid by the Secretaries of State.

1440   The Approved Expenditure (Housing Act 1974 Part IV) Order 1980, S.I. 1980 No. 855 (in force on 22nd July 1980), increases to £400 the amount per dwelling which is to be taken into account in calculating the maximum approved expenditure by local authorities under Pt. IV of the 1974 Act in respect of housing action areas towards which contributions may be paid by the Secretaries of State.

1441   **Improvement and repair grants—amount of grant—appropriate percentage**

The Grants by Local Authorities (Appropriate Percentage and Exchequer Contributions) Order 1980, S.I. 1980 No. 1735 (in force on 15th December 1980), prescribes the percentage which is to be the appropriate percentage of the cost of works to be carried out for the purpose of determining the amount of a grant for the improvement or repair of a dwelling or house in multiple occupation under the Housing Act 1974, Part VII, as amended by the Housing Act 1980, s. 107, Sch. 12, para. 1436. Also specified are the percentages of grants which may be contributed by the Secretary of State.

1442   **—— eligible expense limits**

The Grants by Local Authorities (Eligible Expense Limits) Order 1980, S.I. 1980 No. 1736 (in force on 15th December 1980), increases the limits on the amount of the estimated expense of the works to be carried out which is eligible to be taken into account when an application for a grant for the improvement or repair of a dwelling or house in multiple occupation under the Housing Act 1974, Pt. VII, as amended by the Housing Act 1980, s. 107, Sch. 12, para. 1436, is approved. Also raised are the maximum eligible amounts specified in the 1974 Act, Sch. 6, Pt. I, in relation to standard amenities. This has the effect of increasing the maximum eligible expense for intermediate grants. The limits for the repairs element of intermediate grants are also increased.

1443   **—— increased amounts**

The Grants by Local Authorities Order 1980, S.I. 1980 No. 856 (in force on 22nd July 1980), increases the maximum eligible amounts specified in Housing Act 1974, Sch. 6, Pt. I in relation to standard amenities. The order also increases to £2,000 the maximum eligible expense for works of repair or replacement for the purpose of an intermediate or repairs grant.

1444   **—— repairs**

The Grants by Local Authorities (Repairs) Order 1980, S.I. 1980 No. 1737 (in force on 15th December 1980), prescribes a higher percentage of the element of the estimated expense of works to be carried out with the assistance of an improvement grant which may consist of works of repair and replacement, where the application relates to a dwelling in need of works of repair of a substantial and structural character. The expression "old dwellings" in the Housing Act 1974, ss. 71, 72, as amended by the Housing Act 1980, s. 107, Sch. 12, para. 1436 is defined. Limits of rateable value of dwellings within which repairs grants are available to owner-occupiers are specified.

1445   **—— repayment where work not completed—interest on outstanding repayment**

The Housing Act 1974, s. 82 (6) provides that where an instalment of an improvement grant is paid before the completion of the works and the works are not completed within twelve months from the payment of the instalment, the amount of the grant already paid becomes repayable and carries interest from the date it was paid by the local authority until repayment. By a decision of a county court registrar, the repayment was to be made to the local authority in instalments. Interest was only awarded down to the date of judgment, on the basis that the local authority's right to interest merged in the judgment and no interest was payable after judgment. On appeal by the local authority, *held*, the doctrine of merger applied only to contract and covenant, and could not override the provision of a statute, which in this case clearly provided that the debt should continue to carry interest until the date of repayment.

EALING LONDON BOROUGH COUNCIL V EL ISAACS [1980] 2 All ER 548 (Court of Appeal: MEGAW and TEMPLEMAN LJJ and SIR PATRICK BROWNE). *Re Sneyd* (1883) 25 Ch D 338 distinguished.

1446   Improvement notice—whether practicable to comply with requirements of notice at reasonable expense—matters to be considered

The Court of Appeal has held that a dwelling which has only shared use of an internal water closet and bathroom is a dwelling which is "without one or more of the standard amenities" within the meaning of the Housing Act 1974, s. 89, so that a local authority is entitled to serve on the owner an improvement notice under that section. In assessing whether it is practicable to comply with the requirements of the improvement notice at reasonable expense within s. 91 (2) (a), the court must make a realistic approach to the value of the dwelling-house as a saleable asset in the hands of the owner and must therefore have regard to the presence of tenants and their rights of continued occupation and their effect on the market value. In this case, the expenditure the owners would be required to make in improving the dwellings was unreasonable and the improvement notices would be quashed.

FFF ESTATES LTD V HACKNEY LONDON BOROUGH COUNCIL [1980] 3 WLR 909 (Court of Appeal: STEPHENSON and ACKNER LJJ and DAME ELIZABETH LANE).

1447   Local authority housing—management and control—notice to quit—reasons

On the basis of complaints received over a number of years concerning a tenant occupying a council house, the local housing authority served a notice to quit on the tenant. The tenant failed to comply with the notice, and the authority instituted proceedings against him claiming possession of the house. The tenant disputed the authority's entitlement to an order for possession, contending that the decision to institute proceedings against him was arrived at in circumstances amounting to bad faith or abuse of power. He further contended that it was the duty of the authority to give him a fair hearing. *Held*, bad faith meant dishonesty. Where such an allegation was made, it had to be particularised and there was nothing in the evidence which suggested any basis for an allegation of dishonesty on the part of the authority. If an authority was guilty of bad faith then a decision to issue a notice to quit would be quashed and similarly if it was shown that the authority took into account material factors irrelevant to the issue at hand. However, it was not for the court to tell the authority what it was it ought to do in relation to the making of its decisions provided that the authority stayed within the limits of fair dealing. It was not generally a requirement that an authority when giving notice to a tenant to quit should give its reasons why it had arrived at that decision, nor was it generally a duty of the authority to give the tenant concerned the opportunity to make representations about that matter. On the basis of the evidence submitted, the authority had not acted unfairly, and was entitled to the order sought.

SEVENOAKS DISTRICT COUNCIL V EMMOTT (1979) 39 P & CR 404 (Court of Appeal: MEGAW, BROWNE and BRIGHTMAN LJJ). *Cannock Chase District Council v Kelly* [1978] 1 WLR 1, 1977 Halsbury's Abridgment para. 1432 applied.

1448   —— recovery of possession of controlled housing—notice to quit

A local authority sought possession of a council flat because the tenant was in arrears with the rent. The tenant did not comply with the notice to quit and applied to the rent tribunal to fix a fair rent for the flat and to defer operation of the notice to quit. In an appeal against a possession order it fell to be determined (i) whether the "restricted contract" provisions of the Rent Act 1977 applied to tenancies or licences to occupy granted by the local authority; (ii) if so, whether the tenant was therefore entitled to the benefit of security of tenure under the 1977 Act, s. 104, which prevented the notice to quit taking effect pending the determination of the application to the rent tribunal, or whether he was deprived of such benefit by the Housing Act 1957, s. 158 (1), which provided that nothing in the 1977 Act could prevent a local authority obtaining possession for the purpose of exercising its powers under any enactment relating to housing; (iii) whether the claim for possession failed on the ground that the notice to quit did not comply with the Notice to Quit (Prescribed Information) (Protected Tenancies and Part VI Contracts) Regulations 1975, 1975 Halsbury's Abridgment para. 2036.

Held, (i) the "restricted contracts" provisions applied to local authority licences or tenants notwithstanding that this would qualify the general right of local authorities under the 1957 Act, s. 111 (1) to make such reasonable charge for the tenancy or occupation of their houses as they thought fit. In the present case the tenant had been given the right to occupy the flat in consideration of a weekly rent which included a payment for heating so the agreement came within the definition of a restricted contract in s. 19 (2) of the 1977 Act. (ii) In seeking possession the local authority were exercising their powers of general management under the 1957 Act, s. 111 (1) and therefore the 1977 Act, s. 104 could not prevent the authority from obtaining possession of the flat. (iii) The effect of the 1977 Act, Sch. 24, para. 8 and the 1975 Regulations was that any notice to quit a dwelling let under a restricted contract was required to contain all the information set out in the Sch. to the Regulations. The present notice to quit failed to contain that information and was therefore invalid and ineffective to determine the tenancy.

LAMBETH LONDON BOROUGH COUNCIL v UDECHUKA (1980) Times, 30th April (Court of Appeal: ROSKILL, BRANDON and ACKNER LJJ).

1449   —— **right to buy—designated regions**

The Housing (Right to Buy) (Designated Regions) Order 1980, S.I. 1980 No. 1345 (in force on 3rd October 1980), designates in respect of dwelling-houses in National Parks or areas of outstanding natural beauty situated in England a region comprising the Park or area in which the dwelling-house is situated and, so far as not situated in the Park or area, the county in which it is situated, for the purposes of the Housing Act 1980, s. 19, para. 1436. Special provision is made for the area designated as an area of outstanding natural beauty by the Wye Valley Area of Outstanding Natural Beauty (Designation) (England) Order 1971, and for the Isles of Scilly.

1450   The Housing (Right to Buy) (Designated Rural Areas and Designated Regions) (Wales) Order 1980, S.I. 1980 No. 1375 (in force on 3rd October 1980), designates rural areas in Wales for the purpose of the Housing Act 1980, s. 19, para. 1436. It also designates in respect of dwelling-houses in National Parks, areas of outstanding natural beauty, or rural areas so designated, situated in Wales, a region comprising the Park or area in which the dwelling-house is situated and, so far as not situated in that Park or area, the county in which it is situated.

1451   —— —— **maximum discount**

The Housing (Right to Buy) (Maximum Discount) Order 1980, S.I. 1980 No. 1342 (in force on 3rd October 1980), prescribes £25,000 as the maximum discount to which a person exercising the right to buy under the Housing Act 1980, para. 1436 may be entitled.

1452   —— —— **prescribed statutory notice—forms**

The Housing (Right to Buy) (Prescribed Forms) (No. 1) Regulations 1980, S.I. 1980 No. 1391 (in force on 3rd October 1980), prescribe the form of notice to be used by a secure tenant claiming to exercise the right to buy under the Housing Act 1980, para. 1436 and the forms of notices to be used by the landlord to admit or deny the tenant's right to buy.

1453   The Housing (Right to Buy) (Prescribed Forms) (No. 1) (Welsh Forms) Regulations 1980, S.I. 1980 No. 1620 (in force on 1st December 1980), prescribe Welsh versions of the form of notice to be used by a secure tenant claiming to exercise the right to buy under the Housing Act 1980, para. 1436 and the forms of notices to be used by the landlord to admit or deny the tenant's right to buy. The forms may be used only in relation to a house or flat situated in Wales.

1454   —— —— **right to a mortgage—costs**

The Housing (Right to Buy) (Mortgage Costs) Order 1980, S.I. 1980 No. 1390 (in force on 3rd October 1980), specifies £50 as the maximum amount which a person exercising the right to a mortgage in connection with the exercise of the right to buy under the Housing Act 1980, para. 1436 may be charged towards the costs of the mortgage.

1455   —— —— —— **mortgage limit**

The Housing (Right to Buy) (Mortgage Limit) Regulations 1980, S.I. 1980 No. 1423 (in force on 3rd October 1980), provide for the calculation of the tenant's available income and specify the appropriate factor by which it must be multiplied to arrive at the limit which applies under the Housing Act 1980, para. 1436 to a mortgage for a tenant who is exercising his right to buy under the Act and is entitled to a mortgage.

1456   —— —— —— **statutory notice—forms**

The Housing (Right to Buy) (Prescribed Forms) (No. 2) Regulations 1980, S.I. 1980 No. 1465 (in force on 10th October 1980), prescribe the form of notice to be used by a secure tenant who is exercising the right to buy under the Housing Act 1980, para. 1436, for the purpose of claiming the right to a mortgage.

1457   The Housing (Right to Buy) (Prescribed Forms) (No. 2) (Welsh Forms) Regulations 1980, S.I. 1980 No. 1930 (in force on 30th January 1981), prescribe a version in Welsh of the form of notice for use by a secure tenant claiming to exercise his right to a mortgage under the provisions of the Housing Act 1980, Part I, Chapter I, para. 1436 concerning the right to buy. The form may be used only in relation to a house or flat situated in Wales.

1458   —— **sale of land and houses**

A new general consent to the disposal of land and houses by local authorities in England was granted on 3rd September 1980 under the Housing Act 1957, s. 104 as added by the Housing Act 1980, s. 92. The new consent introduces discount sharing arrangements similar to the provisions in the Housing Act 1980. If a purchaser resells his house within five years he will be able to sell at current market value; but the discount will have to be repaid on a sliding scale reducing from 100 per cent in the first year to 20 per cent in the fifth year. Local authorities are able to offer a discount of up to 30 per cent on vacant houses and flats to special groups of buyers (i.e. persons moving to take up a new job, first-time buyers, those who have recently left armed forces accommodation, tied accommodation or accommodation in a slum clearance area). Local authorities, using their discretionary powers to sell to sitting tenants are able to count for discount purposes any period the purchaser spent as a tenant of another local authority, new town or a housing association. Local authorities have also been given a general consent for the disposal of housing land. See Department of the Environment press notice 358, dated 3rd September 1980.

1459   **Rent rebate and rent allowance schemes**

The Rent Rebate and Rent Allowance Schemes (England and Wales) Regulations 1980, S.I. 1980 No. 730 (in force on 1st July 1980), increase the maximum rebate and maximum allowance permitted under the Housing Finance Act 1972, Sch. 3, para. 14. They are increased to £25 in the Greater London Council area and £23 elsewhere for any week in a rebate or allowance period beginning on or after 1st July 1980.

1460   The Rent Rebate and Rent Allowance Schemes (England and Wales) (No. 2) Regulations 1980, S.I. 1980 No. 1555 (in force on 7th November 1980, except reg. 6 which comes into force on 24th November 1980), further vary provisions relating to rent rebates and rent allowances permitted under the Housing Finance Act 1972, Schs. 3 and 4. The needs allowance specified in Sch. 3, para. 8 is increased and certain sums are to be disregarded in ascertaining income in accordance with Sch. 3, para. 9. Schedule 3, para. 12 is varied to increase deductions for non-dependants used in calculating the amount of rebate or allowance.

1461   The Rent Rebates and Rent Allowances (Student) (England and Wales) Regulations 1980 S.I. 1980 No. 1141 (in force on 1st September 1980), further amend the Rent Rebates and Rent Allowances (Student) (England and Wales) Regulations 1976, 1976 Halsbury's Abridgment para. 1380. They raise to £10 the amount prescribed as the deduction to be made in calculating the rent which is eligible to be met by a rent rebate or a rent allowance under Part II of the Housing Finance Act 1972, as amended, in the case of tenants who are students in receipt of certain awards or grants from public funds for the purpose of their full time further education.

1462   **Rent rebates—tenants of transferred dwellings**

The Rent Rebate (Transfer of Greater London Council Housing Accommodation) Regulations 1980, S.I. 1980 No. 341 (in force on 1st April 1980), are made in consequence of the transfer of certain dwellings from the Greater London Council to local authorities. Most of these dwellings are transferred under the Greater London Council (Transfer of Land and Housing Accommodation) Order 1980, para. 1833. The regulations enable local authorities to continue to pay to a tenant of a transferred dwelling the amount of rent rebate (subject to modifications due to change of circumstances) formerly granted by the Greater London Council until such time as the tenant would be entitled to a greater rebate under the local authority's rebate scheme or until one year from the transfer, whichever is the earlier. Corresponding provision is made for tenants of transferred dwellings who receive rent allowances under the Housing Finance Act 1972, s. 19 (8A), (10).

1463   **Thermal insulation—homes insulation scheme—grant—amount**

The Homes Insulation Grants Order 1980, S.I. 1980 No. 1062 (in force on 26th August 1980), prescribes the maximum percentages of the cost of insulation works, and money sums payable as grant. In the case of persons of pensionable age who are in receipt either of a supplementary pension, or grant or rate rebate or a rent allowance the amount is 90 per cent and £90. In other cases it is 66 per cent and £65.

1464   —— —— —— **revised scheme**

The Homes Insulation Scheme 1978, 1978 Halsbury's Abridgment para. 1489, has been amended by the Homes Insulation Scheme 1978 Amendment (No. 1) 1979 which has been published as App. A to Department of the Environment circular 27/79. The amendments to the scheme list the loft insulation materials which must be used if grant is to be paid. Subject to transitional provisions, listed products must normally be used after 1st November 1979. From the same date tenants of local authorities, new towns and/or housing associations become eligible for a grant. Changes have also been made in the administrative rules. The text of the 1978 scheme as amended is set out in App. B to the circular.   Circular 60/78 of the Department of the Environment ceases to have effect.

1465   Transfer of housing—transfer to London boroughs

See *Brent London Borough Council v GLC*, para. 1835.

1466   Unfit house—notice requiring repair—specifications

A local authority served a notice on the owners of a house under the Housing Act 1957, s 9 (1A), requiring them to repair it and bring it up to a reasonable standard. The owners appealed and the preliminary point was raised that the notice was too vague and indeterminate and did not sufficiently specify the work to be done.   The judge quashed the notice and the local authority appealed.   *Held*, only in very rare cases where the content of the notice was so vague that the owner could not know what the cost of repairs would be with regard to the major requirements of the notice should the court exercise its power to quash a notice without hearing the evidence.   The owner need not be told precisely what he had to do; the test was that the notice should contain sufficient information in its schedule to enable the building owner to have the work costed out.   As the schedule satisfied these requirements, the appeal would be allowed and the notice restored.

CHURCH OF OUR LADY OF HAL v LONDON BOROUGH OF CAMDEN (1980) 255 Estates Gazette 991 (Court of Appeal: STEPHENSON and OLIVER LJJ and SIR DAVID CAIRNS).

HUMAN RIGHTS

Halsbury's Laws of England (4th edn.), Vol. 18, paras. 1625–1722

1467   Articles

Computers and Privacy, The New Council of Europe Convention, Andrew Evans: 130 NLJ 1067.

Individual Rights and Telephone Tapping by the Police, J. Kodwo Bentil: 124 Sol Jo 451.

Right to Consult a Solicitor, P. Collins and Keith Vaughan: 130 NLJ 952.

1468   Elections—right to vote—failure to allow non-residents to vote

A complaint was made to the European Commission for Human Rights that a citizen of the United Kingdom who had taken up employment with the European Communities and was resident in Brussels was not allowed to vote in parliamentary elections.   The Commission stated as she had chosen to take up residence abroad her situation could properly be distinguished from that of persons permanently resident in the United Kingdom.   The Commission was accordingly satisfied that the restrictions on her right to vote were not arbitrary so as to constitute a violation of her rights to a free expression by secret ballot in the choice of the legislature contrary to the European Convention on Human Rights, Protocol 1, art. 3.   The Commission also ruled that there was no direct comparison between the situation of the applicant and that of other categories such as diplomats and servicemen stationed overseas (who were entitled to vote in parliamentary elections) so as to found a complaint of discrimination.   The Commission declared the application inadmissible.

X v UNITED KINGDOM (Application 7730/76), Decisions and Reports 15, p. 137.

1469   European Convention on Human Rights—Community and national law—status of Convention

Scotland

An Indian mother of three British-born patrial children contended that certain provisions of the Immigration Act 1971 and her subsequent deportation from the United Kingdom violated the European Convention on Human Rights, art. 8 relating to the right to family life, and the 4th Protocol to the Convention, art. 3 relating to expulsion. The question arose as to the status of the Convention in relation to both Community and national law. *Held*, (i) the court was not entitled to have regard to the Convention either as an aid to the construction or interpretation of a statute or otherwise. The Convention was irrelevant in legal proceedings in the United Kingdom, unless and until its provisions had been incorporated or given effect to in national legislation. To suggest otherwise was to confer upon the Convention, concluded by the Executive, an effect which only an Act of the legislature could achieve. (ii) The European Court of Justice did not deal with fundamental rights as such but only where they arose under the EEC Treaty and had a bearing on Community law. The Convention itself was therefore not part of Community law and not enforceable by the United Kingdom courts under the European Communities Act 1972, s. 2. (iii) Furthermore, a claim based on a non-economic right contained in the Convention brought in a United Kingdom court by a plaintiff who was not a Community national, had no factor connecting it with any of the situations envisaged by Community law and therefore did not fall to be governed by Community law. The provisions of the Convention were not linked to any of the documents referred to in the EEC Treaty, art. 177 and consequently it was not open to a national court to refer to the European Court under art. 177 any question, not otherwise linked to Community law, of interpretation of the Convention.

SURJIT KAUR v THE LORD ADVOCATE [1980] 3 CMLR 79 (Outer House). Dicta of Diplock LJ in *Salomon v Comrs of Customs and Excise* [1967] 2 QB 116 at 143 applied. *R v Chief Immigration Officer, Heathrow Airport, ex parte Salamat Bibi* [1976] 3 All ER 843, 1976 Halsbury's Abridgment para. 258; *Malone v Metropolitan Police Comr* [1979] 2 WLR 700, 1979 Halsbury's Abridgment para. 2093; *H. P. Bulmer Ltd v Bollinger SA* [1974] 2 CMLR 108, 1974 Halsbury's Abridgment para. 1320; Case 175/78: *R v Saunders* [1979] 2 All ER 267, 1979 Halsbury's Abridgment para. 1220 considered.

1470   ——obligations of contracting parties—whether obligation to secure compliance with Convention by non-contracting parties

Letters sent by registered post from the United Kingdom to the Soviet Union by the applicant included materials relating to human rights. The Soviet authorities either refused to deliver, or "lost" the mail. They stated that compensation for the loss of registered packages would not be paid when the postal service was used for activities incompatible with domestic legislation of the USSR. The Post Office (in the United Kingdom) would not accept responsibility for the mail after it had been passed to another postal authority. The applicant complained to the European Commission of Human Rights that the government of the United Kingdom had failed to take sufficient measures to protect its correspondence from interference by the Soviet authorities and had failed to secure its right for respect for its correspondence in accordance with the European Convention on Human Rights, art. 8 and its right to impart information "regardless of frontiers" as guaranteed by art. 10. The European Commission, in declaring the complaint inadmissible, stated that art. 1 of the Convention could not be interpreted as giving rise to an obligation on a contracting party to secure that non-contracting states, acting within their own jurisdiction, respect the rights and freedoms guaranteed by the convention even when their failure to do so had adverse effects on persons within the jurisdiction of the contracting party. Further, that although art. 10 guaranteed the right to receive and impart information "regardless of frontiers" this did not imply any right to intervention in respect of acts of a non-contracting state for which the contracting state was in no way responsible; it merely implied that the contracting state must, in the exercise of its jurisdiction, itself respect this right.

BERTRAND RUSSELL PEACE FOUNDATION LTD v UNITED KINGDOM (Application 7597/76) Decisions and Reports 14, p. 117.

1471   European Court of Human Rights—jurisdiction—renewal of right of individual petition

In a written reply to a Parliamentary question, the Prime Minister has stated that the right of individual petition to the European Commission of Human Rights is to be extended for a further five years terminating on 1st January 1986. See Times, 26th November 1980.

1472   Right to fair and public hearing—hearing within a reasonable time

The European Commission of Human Rights has stated that the "reasonable time" within which the European Convention on Human Rights, art 6 (1) requires a trial to be heard begins when the suspicions resting on the applicant has an important effect on his situation; see *Hätti v Federal Republic of Germany, Application 618/73*. In considering the application of this doctrine to English criminal proceedings the European Commission commented that an applicant's position may be significantly affected as soon as suspicion against him was seriously investigated and the prosecution case compiled.

X v UNITED KINGDOM (Application 6728/74), Decisions and Reports 14, p. 26.

1473   Right to family life and home—deportation—compatibility with Convention

See *Surjit Kaur v The Lord Advocate*, para. 1469.

1474   Right to freedom of thought, conscience and religion—freedom of religion—limitation on grounds of public health

See *Panesar v Nestlé Co Ltd*, para. 2277.

1475   Right to liberty and security of person—deprivation of liberty— arrest—right to communicate with lawyer

Trinidad and Tobago

On a question of construction of the 1962 Constitution of Trinidad and Tobago, the Privy Council held that the right of a police detainee, under s. 2 (ii) (c) of the Constitution, to communicate with a legal adviser of his own choice without delay is a right independent of any rights enjoyed under the common law at the commencement of the Constitution. Further, it is also an existing right protected under s. 1 of the Constitution as the right to consult a lawyer had become a matter of settled practice before the Constitution was made.

THORNHILL v A-G OF TRINIDAD AND TOBAGO [1980] 2 WLR 510 (Privy Council: LORD DIPLOCK, VISCOUNT DILHORNE, LORD EDMUND-DAVIES, LORD SCARMAN and LORD LANE).

1476   Right to peaceful enjoyment of property—Community law imposing restrictions on new planting of trees—compatibility with Convention

See Case 44/79: *Hauer v Land Rheinland-Pfalz*, para. 1136.

1477   Right to trial by jury—Jamaican constitution—whether right entrenched in constitution

See *Stone v R*, para. 340.

HUSBAND AND WIFE

Halsbury's Laws of England (4th edn.), Vol. 22, paras. 901–1178

1478 Articles

The Domestic Violence and Matrimonial Proceedings Act 1976: An Evaluation, Moira Wright: 130 NLJ 127.

Matrimonial Statistics 1978, Susan Maidment: 129 NLJ 1252.

Towards an Adjustive Jurisdiction for Cohabitees?, S. J. Parker (discussion of jurisdiction on cohabitees and domestic violence): 124 Sol Jo 471.

1479 Abortion—wife seeking legal abortion—power of husband to prevent

See *Re Simms and H*, para. 1954.

1480 Consumer credit—sex discrimination—refusal to grant wife credit without husband's guarantee—validity

See *Quinn v Williams Furniture Ltd*, para. 1416.

1481 Divorce

See DIVORCE.

1482 Financial provision—lump sum—order effectively requiring sale of matrimonial home

The parties had separated in 1977. The wife was living in a council house with the four children of the family and was wholly maintained by social security. The husband was living in the matrimonial home, which was valued at £11,000 with an equity of £5,000. The wife had a one-third interest in the matrimonial home. On application by the wife, the husband was ordered to make periodical payments for the wife and children and ordered to pay the wife a lump sum of £2,000 within six months. The husband appealed against a decision upholding the registrar's order for a lump sum payment. *Held*, in the circumstances, ordering the husband to make an immediate payment of £2,000 inevitably meant that the matrimonial home would have to be sold at once, as he could not possibly raise any sum by way of loan on the house. There was no evidence whatsoever that the husband could obtain other accommodation once that house was sold. Requiring the husband to sell the house was bound to cause him a large degree of hardship and to give the wife an unfair advantage over him. Accordingly, an order that the husband hold the property subject to a charge of one-third of the net proceeds of sale, not to be enforceable until the husband either sold the property or died, would be substituted for the lump sum order. The appeal would be allowed.

CHINNOCK v CHINNOCK (1979) 9 Fam Law 249 (Court of Appeal: ORMROD and WALLER LJJ).

1483 Maintenance order—adjournment of proceedings—notice of adjournment

See *Unitt v Unitt*, para. 1852.

1484 —— duration of order

In a case where a husband was found to have constructively deserted his wife, the husband appealed against the quantum of an order directing him to pay his wife maintenance of £18 per week. *Held*, under the Matrimonial Proceedings (Magistrates' Courts) Act 1960, s. 2 (1) (b) the magistrates' court had the power to make an order directing the husband to pay to the wife "such weekly sum as the court considers reasonable in all circumstances of the case". The court was therefore entitled to qualify the duration of the order, as well as the amount payable. The court had to consider all the relevant factors of the case, in particular the earning capacity of the wife. On the evidence given, the sum of £18 per week was sufficient to enable the wife to seek training and obtain satisfactory employment but a time limit of a year would be set and after that date maintenance was to be assessed on an entirely different basis. The appeal would be allowed and the order amended accordingly.

KHAN v KHAN [1980] 1 All ER 497 (Family Division: SIR JOHN ARNOLD P and WATERHOUSE J). Dictum of Sir George Baker P in *Chesworth v Chesworth* (1973) 118 Sol Jo 183 approved.

1485　—— variation by justices—discretion to admit evidence—witness present during hearing

A husband applied to the justices for an order reducing the amount of maintenance which he had been ordered to pay his wife. He contended that she was cohabiting with and being maintained by another man, H. The wife denied this. At the hearing no order was made excluding H from the court, and he was present throughout. However, during the proceedings, the justices refused to allow the wife, who was unrepresented, to call H as a witness in support of her case. The order sought was made and the amount of maintenance payable reduced to a nominal sum. The wife appealed against the order on the ground that the justices were wrong in law or, alternatively, had exercised their discretion wrongly, in refusing to allow her to call H as a witness. *Held*, witnesses in matrimonial proceedings in magistrates' courts were not under any obligation to leave the court unless an order excluding them had been made. If an application was made, the appropriate course for the justices would be to exclude the witnesses unless they were satisfied that it would not be a suitable step to take in the circumstances. If a party was unrepresented and they thought the case was one in which a witness should be excluded, they should suggest to that party that he should make an application to that effect. If a witness remained in court after an order excluding him had been made and his evidence was offered to the court, the justices had a discretion to admit it. The discretion remained unaffected by the Magistrates' Courts Act 1952, s. 57, which gave justices power to exclude witnesses from the hearing. No order had been made requiring H to withdraw from the court and the justices had exceeded their powers by excluding his evidence which might have affected their decision in respect of the maintenance order. The appeal would be allowed and a rehearing would be ordered.

TOMLINSON v TOMLINSON [1980] 1 All ER 593 (Family Division: SIR JOHN ARNOLD P and WOOD J).

1486　Matrimonial home—domestic violence—danger of physical injury

A wife applied, under the Domestic Proceedings and Magistrates' Courts Act 1978, for an order to exclude her husband from the matrimonial home. She complained that her husband had violently assaulted her four months previously, but gave evidence of the husband's subsequent good behaviour. The justices refused to make the order on the ground that immediate danger of being physically injured was a requirement under s. 16 (3) of the 1978 Act. They accordingly made a personal protection order under s. 16 (2) and attached a power of arrest to it. The wife appealed. *Held*, the word "danger" in s. 16 (3) was not qualified and the justices had erred in adding "immediate" to that subsection. Further, the attachment of a power of arrest was inconsistent with their refusal to make an exclusion order. It was also inappropriate in a domestic case not to hear both sides, and the justices had been unwise to make the order without hearing evidence from the husband. The appeal would be allowed, and the case remitted to the justices.

McCARTNEY v McCARTNEY [1981] 2 WLR 184 (Family Division: SIR JOHN ARNOLD P and EWBANK J).

1487　—— —— exclusion of one party—custody issue pending

The parties married in 1958. In 1978, the wife, who was living in a home for battered wives with the youngest of the four children of the marriage, petitioned for divorce. She applied for an order to enable her to return to the matrimonial home, a council house, where the husband lived with two of their older children. The judge ordered that the husband should vacate the matrimonial home within seven days and dismissed an application by the husband for custody of the youngest child. The husband appealed. *Held*, the issue of custody of the youngest child had to be decided before the issue of occupation of the matrimonial home. Accordingly, the order would be quashed on the husband undertaking not to return to the matrimonial home pending a hearing on the issue of custody. The appeal would be allowed.

WOOD v WOOD (1979) 9 Fam Law 254 (Court of Appeal: ORR and ORMROD LJJ).

1488 ——— —— non-molestation injunction—power of arrest—committal for contempt for breach of injunction

A county court judge committed a husband to prison for contempt of court for breach of an injunction restraining him from molesting his wife, to which a power of arrest was attached under the Domestic Violence and Matrimonial Proceedings Act 1976, s. 2 (1). The wife had made no application for committal. The husband appealed, contending that the judge had no jurisdiction to make the order for committal. *Held*, CCR Ord. 46, r. 28 (6) provided that the judge before whom a person arrested was brought pursuant to s. 2 (4) might exercise his power to punish that person for disobedience to the injunction. Rule 28 (8) provided that, in relation to a person who was in custody under an order and warrant in Form 412, Ord. 25, r. 70 (discharge of person in custody) was to have effect as if the order and warrant were issued at the instance of the person who made the application for the injunction under s. 2 (1). It was therefore not necessary for the wife to apply for the committal and the judge had jurisdiction to make the order if the facts justified it. In this case they did not and the appeal would be allowed.

BOYLAN v BOYLAN (1980) Times, 3rd October (Court of Appeal: ORMROD, EVELEIGH and TEMPLEMAN LJJ).

1489 ——— —— parties unmarried—whether living together in same household as husband and wife

Halsbury's Laws (4th edn.), Vol. 22, paras. 1104, 1118

The parties, who were not married, had been living together for several years. The woman had adopted the man's surname, and the tenancy of their two-roomed flat was in their joint names. In 1979, the relationship deteriorated and the man began sleeping in the sitting room. The woman refused to cook for him or to wash his clothes. They did not speak to each other and kept their rooms locked. They shared the rent and the cost of electricity. The woman applied for an order restraining the man from assaulting, molesting or otherwise interfering with her, and an order that he should leave the flat. The judge held that he had no jurisdiction, as the parties were not living together in the same household as husband and wife within the meaning of the Domestic Violence and Matrimonial Proceedings Act 1976, s. 1 (2). On appeal, *held*, s. 1 (2) applied where a man and woman were living together in the same household as man and wife. It was impossible to say that the parties were living separately in a flat with only two rooms. The appeal would be allowed.

ADEOSO v ADEOSO [1980] 1 WLR 1535 (Court of Appeal: ORMROD LJ and DAME ELIZABETH LANE). *Davis v Johnson* [1979] AC 264, HL, 1978 Halsbury's Abridgment para. 1522 applied.

1490 ——— —— welfare of children

Following a decree nisi the wife applied for an order against the husband excluding him from the matrimonial home and for interim custody of the children. The judge refused to make the exclusion order until the question of custody was determined. He therefore adjourned the applications pending welfare reports on the children. On appeal *held*, the decision on the matter of custody had to precede a decision as to who should occupy the matrimonial home. There was evidence to doubt the mother's capacity to care for the children and the judge was correct in adjourning the applications accordingly.

SMITH V SMITH (1978) 10 Fam Law 50 (Court of Appeal: ORR, ORMROD and TEMPLEMAN LJJ).

1491   —— right of occupation—purported surrender of tenancy by one spouse—right of other spouse to remain in occupation

A husband, who lived with his wife and son, was the tenant of a house under a weekly protected tenancy. The wife was treated violently by her husband and after she had been in hospital he refused to allow her back into the house. W and her brother subsequently lived with the husband in the house. The husband purported to surrender the tenancy and asked the landlord to accept W as a tenant. The landlord agreed and gave W a rent book. The husband left the house, and W and her brother continued to live there. W asked the wife to remove certain furniture belonging to her. The wife refused to do so and applied under the Matrimonial Homes Act 1967 for an order that the husband allow her into the matrimonial home. The judge found that the purported surrender of the husband's tenancy and the reletting was a sham, the parties having known that the real intention was that the husband should continue to be the tenant and occupy the premises to the exclusion of the wife. The landlord, however, was not a party to the sham. Further, in law, the wife was still in occupation of the house, as she had been evicted by the husband and had always wished to return. He made a declaration that the wife was entitled to remain in the house and that the husband, W and her brother should leave. W appealed. *Held*, (i) a transaction was only a sham if all the parties to the transaction in question were parties to it. In the present case since the landlord had not been a party to the sham, the surrender was not void on that basis. (ii) A tenancy could be surrendered by operation of law, or expressly by deed or in writing. In the present case there was no valid express surrender of the tenancy as there had been no deed and nothing in writing. (iii) For a surrender of a tenancy by operation of law there had to be a delivery of possession by the tenant and acceptance of possession by the landlord. There was no valid surrender if the wife remained in occupation. Whether an evicted wife remained in occupation of the house in law depended on similar considerations as those that applied where a statutory tenant had left a house but asserted a continuing right to occupation. The wife's rights against the husband were not dependent on the registration of a charge under the Matrimonial Homes Act 1967 as there had been no effective surrender of the tenancy. The wife had not voluntarily gone out of occupation but had been evicted, and although her intention to return to the house was conditional on not living with the husband, this was not, where a wife had been violently treated, sufficient to destroy the intention to return. The judge had not erred in holding that the wife remained in occupation and that the purported surrender was invalid. Accordingly the husband remained a protected tenant and W had no rights against the wife. The appeal would be dismissed.

HOGGETT V HOGGETT (1979) 39 P & C R 121 (Court of Appeal: ORR and ORMROD LJJ and SIR DAVID CAIRNS). *Snook v London and West Riding Investments Ltd* [1967] 2 QB 786; *Miles v Bull* [1968] 3 All ER 632; *Collins v Claughton* [1959] 1 All ER 95; *Brown v Brash* [1948] 1 All ER 922 applied.

1492   —— unmarried couple—purchase of house in joint names—trust for sale—purpose of trust

See *Re Evers' Trust, Papps v Evers*, para. 2997.

1493   —— wife's unregistered interest—position of mortgagee

See *Williams and Glyn's Bank Ltd v Boland; Williams and Glyn's Bank Ltd v Brown*, para. 2012.

1494   Matrimonial relief—husband's property—right of wife to occupy

A wife returned from a long visit abroad to find her husband living, with his
mistress, in a house he had bought in her absence. She filed a petition for divorce
and in those proceedings sought to take up residence in part of the house. There
were no children of the marriage. *Held*, the court had no jurisdiction to grant an
order directing the husband to let the wife live in the house. The house was not the
matrimonial home and the court could not imply that the wife had been granted an
occupational licence to live there by the husband. Even if the court had jurisdiction,
as a matter of discretion the order would be refused as the wife was employed and
had rented reasonable accommodation for herself.

S v S (1980) 124 Sol Jo 219 (Family Division: FRENCH J). *Gurasz v Gurasz*
[1969] 3 All ER 822, CA distinguished.

**1495   Practice—leave to appeal—property adjustment order—leave to
appeal out of time—matters to be considered**

A husband was ordered to transfer his interest in the matrimonial home (involving
a sum in excess of £10,000) to the wife outright, and in return the wife's claim for
periodical payments was dismissed and she made certain undertakings. The
husband's application for leave to appeal out of time against the order was refused.
The husband appealed. *Held*, having regard to the amount of money at stake and to
the facts that the delay was not serious in itself, the wife was not in any way
prejudiced by the delay, and the husband was not at fault, the appeal would be
allowed.

JOHNSON v JOHNSON (1980) 10 Fam Law 19 (Court of Appeal: ORR and ORMROD
LJJ). *Lane v Esdaile* [1891] 1 AC 210, HL distinguished.

IMMIGRATION

Halsbury's Laws of England (4th edn.), Vol. 4, paras. 974–1033

1496   Articles

Immigration Appeals, K. Nathan: 130 NLJ 1084.
Immigration—Humane Interpretation, A. N. Khan (significance of immigration
officer's stamp on non-patrial's passport in the light of recent cases): 123 Sol Jo 847.
Marriage and Immigration: Are the New Rules Unlawfully Discriminatory?,
David Bonner: 130 NLJ 696.
Status of Returning Residents under the Immigration Rules, Zahir H. Chowdhury:
131 NLJ 344.

**1497   Admission for temporary purposes—student—meaning of "a full-
time course of study"**

The applicant, an Iranian national aged thirteen, was enrolled for a three-year "O"
level course at an English school. When interviewed by the immigration officer,
the applicant said that he intended to remain in the United Kingdom for up to ten
years so as to complete his education by taking "A" levels and going on to
university. The immigration officer refused him leave to enter the United
Kingdom, not being satisfied that he intended to leave the United Kingdom when
his studies were completed as required by the Statement of Changes in Immigration
Rules (1980), r. 22. The applicant was allowed to enter temporarily. He had a
right of appeal to an adjudicator but could not exercise that right so long as he was
in the United Kingdom, and Iranian law now forbade a student to leave Iran under
the age of eighteen years. The applicant unsuccessfully applied for leave to apply for
judicial review, for an order of certiorari quashing the refusal of leave to enter the
United Kingdom and for an order of mandamus directing the immigration officer
to consider the applicant's claim fully and to admit him into the United Kingdom.
On appeal, *held*, WALLER LJ dissenting, the words "a full-time course of study" in

r. 22 should be interpreted as meaning a full-time course of study such as a boy of the applicant's age could reasonably be expected to follow through to its completion, such as the attainment of a degree even though he had not yet been accepted for a place at university. He could be admitted for an appropriate period depending on the length of the course of study and on his means. He should then apply for extensions from time to time under r. 98. The words should not be confined to the course of study for which the applicant had been accepted.

On the question whether the case was one where mandamus or certiorari would lie, WALLER LJ dissenting, the immigration officer had misdirected himself in point of law and acted ultra vires. The applicant had a remedy by way of an appeal to an adjudicator, but the availability of appeal did not debar the court from quashing an order by prerogative writ. In the instant case, the remedy by way of appeal was useless, as the applicant, once sent back to Iran, would be unable to return to the United Kingdom if his appeal was successful. The appeal would accordingly be allowed, the refusal of entry quashed and the case ordered to be reconsidered.

R v CHIEF IMMIGRATION OFFICER, GATWICK AIRPORT, EX PARTE KHARRAZI [1980] 3 All ER 373 (Court of Appeal: LORD DENNING MR, WALLER and DUNN LJJ).

1498   Appeal—appeal against decision on facts—power of Immigration Appeal Tribunal

A sponsor declared to an entry clearance officer in Pakistan that the applicants were his wife and sons. The officer had disbelieved the sponsor but the adjudicator believed him. The appeal tribunal decided that the adjudicator was wrong and refused the applicants leave to enter. On appeal the question for the court was whether the tribunal, when hearing an appeal from an adjudicator, was limited to considering points of law. *Held*, if, after hearing the adjudicator's decision on the facts, the tribunal found, on the evidence, that the facts were incorrect, it had the power and duty to review and reverse the decision based on those facts. The appeal tribunal had not erred therefore in restoring the decision of the entry clearance officer and the appeal would accordingly be dismissed.

R v IMMIGRATION APPEAL TRIBUNAL, EX PARTE BI (1980) Times, 25th April (Court of Appeal: STEPHENSON, BRIGHTMAN LJJ and DAME ELIZABETH LANE).

1499   —— appeal against refusal to grant judicial review and prerogative orders

See *R v Chief Immigration Officer, Gatwick Airport, ex parte Kharrazi*, para. 1497.

1500   —— application for extension of leave made after expiry of leave— refusal—jurisdiction to hear appeal

The applicant was given leave to enter the United Kingdom as a visitor for one month. He subsequently applied for an extension of stay after the expiry of his limited leave, under the Immigration Act 1971, to enter or remain in the United Kingdom. The application was made whilst an appeal was pending following the refusal of a similar earlier application which was made in time. Both applications for an extension of stay were refused by the Secretary of State. In his written decision he concluded that the applicant was entitled to appeal against the decision under the Immigration Act 1971, s. 14 (1), to the independent appellate authorities established under the Act, within fourteen days. This statement was mistaken in the light of later decisions in the cases of *R v Immigration Appeal Tribunal, ex parte Subramaniam* [1976] 3 All ER 604, CA, 1976 Halsbury's Abridgment para. 245, and *Suthendran v Immigration Appeal Tribunal* [1976] 3 All ER 611, HL, 1976 Halsbury's Abridgment para. 246. Questions arose as to whether, by acting on the Secretary of State's mistaken statement, an estoppel was raised conferring jurisdiction upon the immigration appellate authorities to consider the appeal lodged by the applicant. *Held*, the statement by the Secretary of State regarding the right to appeal under s. 14 (1) was incorrect. An appeal could only be made if the refusal was made during the actual time in which the applicant had limited leave to enter. An estoppel was not created by relying on the Secretary of State's mistake. It was impossible to confer jurisdiction on an appeal tribunal except by statute.

BALBIR SINGH V SECRETARY OF STATE FOR THE HOME DEPARTMENT [1978] Imm AR 204 (Court of Appeal: LORD DENNING MR, BRIDGE and TEMPLEMAN LJJ).

1501 **—— refusal of entry clearance—whether special voucher an entry clearance**

The Immigration Act 1971, s. 13 (2) provides that a person who, on an application duly made, is refused an entry clearance may appeal to an adjudicator against the refusal. Section 33 (1) provides that an "entry clearance" includes a visa, entry certificate or other document which, in accordance with the Immigration Rules, is to be taken as evidence of a person's eligibility for entry into the United Kingdom.

In 1968 the Government restricted the number of East African Asians holding United Kingdom passports allowed to enter the United Kingdom. A certain number of special quota vouchers were issued to the heads of families or dependent relatives. In 1973 the applicant's father successfully applied for such a voucher. At the time the applicant was married to an Indian national and was therefore not a dependent member of the family entitled to an entry certificate. In 1976 the applicant applied to the entry clearance office at Bombay for a voucher to enable her to join her family in the United Kingdom. The application was refused and the applicant sought an order of mandamus directed to the entry clearance officer to entertain her application for a special quota voucher. Questions arose as to whether a special quota voucher amounted to an entry clearance and the right to appeal on the refusal of such a voucher. *Held*, for the purposes of s. 13 (2) and 33 (1) a special quota voucher was not to be taken as evidence of a person's eligibility to enter the United Kingdom but was itself the factual basis which entitled a person to enter. The vouchers were documents which dispensed with the necessity for a holder to adduce further evidence of eligibility to enter, in contrast with holders of other entry documents who might be required to satisfy immigration officers that they were entitled to enter the country. A special quota voucher did not fall within s. 33 (2) and there was therefore no right of appeal against a refusal to grant such a voucher under s. 13 (2). The application for an order of mandamus would be refused.

R V BOMBAY ENTRY CLEARANCE OFFICER, EX PARTE AMIN [1980] 2 All ER 837 (Queen's Bench Division: LORD LANE CJ, GRIFFITHS and WEBSTER JJ).

1502 **Commission for Racial Equality—power to make investigation into control of immigration**

A judge of the Queen's Bench Division has held that the Commission for Racial Equality (CRE) has the power to conduct a formal investigation to inquire into the arrangements for the enforcement of the Immigration Act 1971 with special reference to the equality of treatment afforded to persons of different racial groups seeking to enter the United Kingdom.

The CRE's duty under the Race Relations Act 1976, s. 43 (1) (b) was to promote equality of opportunity and good relations, between persons of different racial groups generally. Under s. 48 it had the power to make formal investigations in connection with those duties. An inquiry into the control of immigration could be beneficial for promoting good relations. The court would reject the Home Office's contention that Parliament had not intended the CRE to have the power to embark upon such an investigation, and that such a power would substantially interfere with the manner of discharge by the Crown of the functions of government. In any event, the CRE had only extremely limited powers against the Crown. Its ability to require persons to furnish information was limited, without the authorisation of the Secretary of State under s. 50 (1) of the Act, and without his co-operation the investigation would be incomplete.

HOME OFFICE V COMMISSION FOR RACIAL EQUALITY (1980) Times, 15th October (Queen's Bench Division: WOOLF J).

1503   **Deportation—appeal—petition to European Commission for Human Rights—relevance of European Convention**

An immigrant applied for a stay of deportation pending the presentation and prosecution of a petition to the European Commission of Human Rights, arguing that there was a prima facie case that article 8 of the Convention for Human Rights had been breached. *Held*, although there was an arguable case that the article had been breached there were still a number of preliminary steps to be taken before the case could come before the European Court of Human Rights. The Commission had not requested a stay of deportation and it could not be said that the Home Secretary had acted unreasonably in failing to grant one. Further, the Convention did not have the force of law here and so there was no obligation on the Home Secretary to consider whether his actions were in contravention of the Convention.

R v Secretary of State for the Home Department, ex parte Fernandes (1980) Times, 21st November (Court of Appeal: Waller, Ackner and Watkins LJJ). *R v Chief Immigration Officer, Heathrow Airport, ex parte Bibi* [1976] 3 All ER 843, 1976 Halsbury's Abridgment para. 258, CA, applied.

1504   —— **status of European Convention on Human Rights to Community and national law**

See *Surjit Kaur v The Lord Advocate*, para. 1469.

1505   —— **recommendation for deportation—defendant living on social security**

The accused was convicted of shoplifting and recommended for deportation, the judge having treated as a detriment to the country the fact that the accused had been living on social security. On appeal, *held*, the potential detriment to the country of the continued presence of the offender was a relevant consideration but the fact that the accused had been living on social security was not a detriment within the guidelines.

R v Serry (1980) Times, 31st October (Court of Appeal: Ormrod LJ, Lloyd and Bingham JJ). *R v Caird* (1970) 54 Cr App Rep 499, and *R v Nazari* (1980) 71 Cr App Rep 87, CA, applied.

1506   —— **guidelines for making recommendation**

In a case concerning the proposed deportation of four immigrants who had been convicted of, or pleaded guilty to, offences committed in the United Kingdom, questions arose as to the considerations relevant on recommending deportation under the Immigration Act 1971, s. 6. Section 6 provides that any court having power to sentence a convicted person for the offence in question may recommend him for deportation unless it commits him to be sentenced or further dealt with for that offence by another court. *Held*, Parliament's intention in s. 6 was that a proper and full inquiry should take place before a recommendation was made which was likely to result in a deportation order. The following guidelines were suggested for courts making a recommendation for deportation under s. 6. (i) The court should consider whether a recommendation was justified by the potential detriment to the country of the continued presence of an offender. The more serious the crime, or the longer the criminal record, the more obvious it was that a recommendation should be made. (ii) The court should not concern itself with the political systems and administration of justice in other countries. It was for the Home Secretary to decide whether returning an offender to his country of origin would have unduly harsh consequences. In the case of a short sentence, however, a court might have to decide whether to make a recommendation and if it were satisfied on the evidence that it would be unduly harsh to return the offender to his country of origin, then the court might feel impelled, in fairness to the accused, not to recommend deportation. (iii) The court should also consider the effect of a recommendation for deportation upon others not before the court, in particular the family of the offender.

R v Nazari (1980) 71 Cr App Rep 87 (Court of Appeal: Lawton LJ, Boreham and Comyn JJ).

1507 —— —— relevance of previous convictions—whether deportation procedure in conformity with Community law

An Italian national, resident and employed in England, was sentenced to imprisonment and at the same time a recommendation for deportation was made. On his release from prison such an order was made. In the course of proceedings brought by the Italian for judicial review to quash the deportation order, a Divisional Court of the Queen's Bench Division stayed the proceedings and referred certain questions to the European Court. The questions related to the interpretation and application of Council Directive (EEC) 64/221, art. 9 which provides that a decision to expel a national of another member state is not to be taken until an opinion has been obtained from a competent authority of the host country. On the resumption of proceedings following the decision of the European Court, the court held that the procedure for deportation in the United Kingdom did not breach any provision of Community law and in recommending deportation the existence of previous convictions was an important factor for consideration. The deportation order was therefore valid. The Italian appealed. *Held*, it was difficult to reconcile the provisions of art. 9 with the deportation procedures in the United Kingdom. In order to do so it had to be said that the Central Criminal Court was a "competent authority of the host country" and that court had expressed its opinion by recommending the deportation of the Italian. The Home Secretary was the "administrative authority" which ordered the deportation and he had before him the opinion of the competent authority which was sufficient for him to act upon. Further, although the rules of natural justice required the Home Secretary to take into account every relevant factor when considering whether to make a deportation order, he was not bound to hold a hearing or to disclose to the deportee all the matters, including new factors, which were available to him if the case for deportation was already so strong that the new factors simply reinforced it. The deportation order was therefore valid and the appeal would be dismissed.

R v SECRETARY OF STATE FOR THE HOME DEPARTMENT, EX PARTE SANTILLO [1981] 2 WLR 362 (Court of Appeal: LORD DENNING MR, SHAW and TEMPLEMAN LJJ). Decision of Divisional Court of the Queen's Bench Division [1980] 3 CMLR 212, affirmed.

For the decision of the European Court see [1980] 2 CMLR 308, para. 1176.

1508 Detention order—validity

The father of the applicant minor had successfully applied under the British Nationality Act 1948, s. 7 for the registration of the applicant as a United Kingdom citizen. It subsequently emerged that he was not his son and the applicant was ordered to be detained as an illegal immigrant. He contended that since he was a citizen of the United Kingdom by virtue of his registration he could only be deprived of that citizenship under s. 20 (2) following an inquiry conducted in accordance with s. 20 (6) and (7). *Held*, s. 20 of the Act only applied if a person had become a citizen of the United Kingdom by registration or naturalisation. In the present case since there were reasonable grounds for believing that the appellant was not the person who had been registered and the appellant could not rebut that presumption, he was not a citizen of the United Kingdom and the section did not apply. Accordingly the detention was not unlawful and the appeal would be dismissed.

R v SECRETARY OF STATE FOR THE HOME DEPARTMENT, EX PARTE AKHTAR [1980] 2 All ER 735 (Court of Appeal: MEGAW, TEMPLEMAN LJJ and SIR PATRICK BROWNE). *R v Secretary of State for the Home Department, ex parte Sultan Mahmood (Note)* [1980] 3 WLR 312, CA, 1978 Halsbury's Abridgment para. 263, *R v Secretary of State for the Home Department, ex parte Hussain* [1978] 1 WLR 700, CA, 1977 Halsbury's Abridgment para. 1486 applied. Decision of Divisional Court of the Queen's Bench Division [1980] 1 All ER 1089 affirmed.

1509 Entry—appeal against refusal—whether new evidence admissible

Immigration Appeal Tribunal decision:

VISA OFFICER, KARACHI v MOHAMMAD [1978] Imm AR 168 (applicant refused visa to visit family for three months because visa officer not satisfied he intended to stay only for a limited period; on appeal adjudicator allowed new evidence to show applicant was landowner and therefore had incentive to return after visit ended; visa officer appealed on ground that new evidence not admissible; tribunal dismissed appeal; adjudicator entitled to receive fresh evidence if relevant and if referred to facts in existence at time of decision appealed against).

1510 —— application by dependant—dependent parent—step-parent

Immigration Appeal Tribunal decision:

BIBI BAGAS v ENTRY CLEARANCE OFFICER, BOMBAY [1978] Imm AR 85 (applicant refused entry to join her two stepsons as their dependent parent; tribunal upheld decision on grounds that "parent" did not include step-parent except where the step-parent sought admission together with the natural parent).

1511 —— —— existence of family unit overseas—admission of whole family for settlement

Immigration Appeal Tribunal decision:

STEWART v ENTRY CLEARANCE OFFICER, KINGSTON, JAMAICA [1978] Imm AR 32 (appeal from adjudicator's decision refusing application by appellant for entry into United Kingdom to join parents residing there; appellant, Jamaican citizen, aged 18, mother of illegitimate child, residing with unmarried brother aged 21 in home rented by parents; father of child provided negligible support; 2 younger sisters granted entry certificates; appellant applied for entry to join parents as their dependent daughter under HC 79 para 44; appellant had not formed a family unit with the child's father and accordingly was still part of the original family unit overseas with her brother; however since he did not qualify for admission under the provisions, the appellant did not qualify because the whole family were not being admitted for settlement).

1512 —— —— whether "necessarily dependent" upon sponsor

Immigration Appeal Tribunal decision:

CHAVDA v ENTRY CLEARANCE OFFICER, BOMBAY [1978] Imm AR 40 (widow, three sons and daughter, Commonwealth citizens, applied for entry certificates for settlement in United Kingdom as dependants of widow's eldest son; refused on ground that family was not "necessarily dependent" on the sponsor son as three sons had not sought employment as able to live on money sent by sponsor; three sons abandoned appeal before tribunal; persons could not obtain entry as dependants by deliberately divesting themselves of assets and means of support; appeals of sons would have failed; widow's and daughter's appeal allowed as widow unable to compel sons to seek employment and therefore were "necessarily dependent" on sponsor in United Kingdom). *R v Secretary of State for Home Affairs, ex parte Hosenball* [1977] 3 All ER 452 at 459, 463, 465–6, 1977 Halsbury's Abridgment para. 11 applied.

1513 —— control of entry through Republic of Ireland

The Immigration (Control of Entry through Republic of Ireland) (Amendment) Order 1980, S.I. 1980 No. 1859 (in force on 1st January 1981), amends the Immigration (Control of Entry through Republic of Ireland) Order 1972, art. 4. The order provides that nationals of Greece who enter the United Kingdom in the circumstances specified in art. 4 are prohibited from taking up employment but may pursue an occupation for reward.

1514 —— entry by Community national—immigration rules—compatibility with principle of free movement of persons within EEC

See *R v Pieck*, para. 1177.

1515   —— —— refusal on ground that likely to become a charge on public funds—validity under Community law

Immigration Appeal Tribunal decision:

NIJSSEN V IMMIGRATION OFFICER, LONDON (HEATHROW) AIRPORT [1978] Imm AR 226 (applicant, EEC national, refused leave to enter United Kingdom on ground that likely to become a charge on public funds, as during three years' previous residence had been in regular receipt of supplementary benefit; applicant contended immigration rules were in breach of EEC provisions relating to free movement of persons within EEC, and sought reference to European Court of Justice; tribunal dismissed his appeal; on admitted facts there was nothing to show that applicant genuinely sought employment in United Kingdom; therefore he was not a worker and not entitled to rely on provisions relating to free movement of workers within EEC; reference to European Court refused).

1516   —— entry by distressed relative

Immigration Appeal Tribunal decision:

VISA OFFICER, ISLAMABAD V BASHIR [1978] Imm AR 77 (applicant, thirty year-old blind Pakistani citizen, refused entry (as a distressed relative), as not being a near relative of a person already settled in United Kingdom, that person being his father; tribunal upheld decision; near relatives defined in immigration rules as brothers, sisters, aunts and uncles and did not include sons and daughters).

1517   —— entry clearance—meaning

See *R v Bombay Entry Clearance Officer, ex parte Amin*, para. 1501.

1518   —— entry for purpose of setting up business—financial requirements

The Statement of Changes in Immigration Rules (HC 394) includes a requirement (in para 35) that a person entering the country for the purpose of setting up business here must be prepared, inter alia, to invest £100,000 for this purpose. The Minister of State has indicated this financial requirement would not be applied to consultants in overseas law. See the LS Gaz, 5th November 1980, p. 1082.

1519   —— fiancé—entry certificate granted in error—subsequent refusal of leave to enter

The applicant, an Indian citizen, obtained an entry certificate as a fiancé under HC 79, para. 48, as amended. The entry certificate was apparently granted in error because his fiancée, who was settled in the United Kingdom, was under sixteen and thus unable to marry. Subsequently, on the applicant's arrival in the United Kingdom, leave to enter was refused. The applicant's appeal to an adjudicator was dismissed. On further appeal, the Immigration Appeal Tribunal found that the entry certificate was not obtained by misrepresentation which, under HC 79, para. 12 (a), precluded entry, but that the immigration procedures were manipulated by relatives who knew that the fiancée was unable to marry before the age of sixteen. The tribunal dismissed the applicant's appeal by invoking HC 79, para. 63 (b) under which leave to enter may be refused if the refusal seems right on the ground that the person's exclusion is conducive to the public good if, for example, in the light of his character, conduct or association it is undesirable to give him leave to enter. The applicant sought orders of certiorari and mandamus. *Held*, the tribunal had not erred in its decision to invoke para. 63 (b). The examples given in para. 63 (b) were not exclusive and if the applicant were to be admitted it would contravene immigration regulations made by the Secretary of State and approved by Parliament. It was in the public interest that this should not occur and the application would be refused.

R v IMMIGRATION APPEAL TRIBUNAL, EX PARTE AJAIB SINGH [1978] Imm AR 59 (Queen's Bench Division: LORD WIDGERY CJ, TALBOT and BOREHAM JJ).

1520   —— legality of entry—failure to disclose marital status—duty to disclose material change of circumstances

In 1973, when the applicant was fifteen years old, he applied to enter the United Kingdom as a dependant of his father. The entry certificate was granted in 1975, when he was eighteen. He married early in 1976 and in March of that year he left for the United Kingdom while his wife remained in Pakistan. Under the Statement of Immigration Rules for Control on Entry 1973, para. 39, indefinite leave to enter can be granted to an unmarried and fully dependent son under twenty-one. Paragraph 10 of the Rules provide that leave to enter can be refused if there has been a material change of circumstances after the issue of the entry certificate which has removed the basis of the entrant's claim to admission. On his arrival in the country, the applicant was not asked whether he was married and he did not volunteer the information. Two years later, when his wife and child applied to join him, inquiries into his circumstances were made and he was detained as an illegal immigrant. The Court of Appeal dismissed his appeal against the refusal of a writ of habeas corpus. On further appeal, *held*, an alien who sought entry into the United Kingdom was under a positive duty to disclose to the immigration officer any material change of circumstances after the issue of the entry certificate. This duty of candour arose whether or not the entrant was questioned by the officer, and, on general principles of law, deception could arise from conduct accompanied by silence as to a material fact. In the present case, the applicant had not revealed the fact of his marriage which was a clear change of circumstances most material to the immigration officer's decision. It was one thing to seek to enter as a dependent child and quite another to enter as the head of a household and prospective family, even if there was to be a interim period of dependency. The Home Office therefore had reasonable grounds for deciding that the applicant's leave to enter had been obtained by deception and his appeal would be dismissed.

ZAMIR v SECRETARY OF STATE FOR THE HOME DEPARTMENT [1980] 2 All ER 768 (House of Lords: LORD WILBERFORCE, VISCOUNT DILHORNE, LORD SALMON, LORD FRASER OF TULLYBELTON and LORD RUSSELL OF KILLOWEN). Decision of the Court of Appeal, sub nom *R v Secretary of State for the Home Department, ex parte Zamir* [1980] 1 All ER 1041 affirmed. *R v Secretary of State for the Home Department, ex parte Mango Khan* [1980] 2 All ER 337, CA, para. 1521 disapproved.

1521   In 1972, applications were made for the applicant and the rest of his family to join his father in the United Kingdom. They were given entry certificates in 1978. In July 1978, the applicant married and in August he and his family entered the country whilst his wife remained in Pakistan. He was then aged twenty-two. Under the Statement of Immigration Rules for Control on Entry 1973, indefinite leave to enter can be granted to an unmarried and fully dependent son under twenty-one. On arrival at Heathrow, the applicant was granted indefinite leave to enter without being asked his age or marital status, though it was evident from his passport that he was over twenty-one. His wife was given an entry clearance to join him in May 1979. When she arrived at Heathrow the applicant admitted to the immigration authorities that he had married after he had received his entry certificate. Three weeks later, he was arrested and detained as an illegal immigrant. His application for a writ of habeas corpus was refused and he appealed. *Held*, the question was whether the grant of indefinite leave to enter in August was void, voidable or valid. If the officer had granted leave under a fundamental mistake due to the applicant's fraud or misrepresentation, the leave was void. If the applicant had not been guilty of any fraud or misrepresentation and the mistake was that of the immigration officer alone, the leave was validly granted. From the facts, the applicant had not been guilty of any fraud or misrepresentation. There had been a change of circumstances since 1972 which might have been a ground under the rules for refusing leave to enter. However, the applicant had been under no duty to disclose that change to the immigration officer unless she had asked him. By failing to ask any questions she seemed to have ignored any change of circumstances or to have waived any objection on those grounds. There had been no duty of disclosure on the applicant, and as there had been no deception on his part, leave had been validly granted. Accordingly he had been wrongly detained as an illegal entrant and his application would be granted.

R v SECRETARY OF STATE FOR THE HOME DEPARTMENT, EX PARTE MANGOO KHAN [1980] 2 All ER 337 (Court of Appeal: LORD DENNING MR, LAWTON and ACKNER LJJ).

This decision was disapproved in *Zamir v Secretary of State for the Home Department*, para. 1520.

1522   —— —— failure to disclose material fact on entry

In a case where two brothers successfully applied for entry certificates to the United Kingdom from Pakistan to join their father who had settled in this country, they failed to inform the Home Office of their father's death before the entry certificates were issued. After their arrival in the United Kingdom they were detained pending deportation and applied for writs of habeaus corpus on the ground that they had entered the country legally with valid entry clearances for settlement. *Held*, the case fell within the Statement of Immigration Rules for Control on Entry 1973, para. 10 (a), as there had been suppression of a material fact. The brothers were under a duty to inform the Home Office of their father's death before their arrival in the United Kingdom. The application would be refused.

R v SECRETARY OF STATE FOR THE HOME DEPARTMENT, EX PARTE IQBAL [1980] Crim LR 308 (Queen's Bench Division: LORD WIDGERY CJ and WIEN J).

1523   —— permission to stay obtained by fraud—entrant's knowledge of fraud

In a case where an Indian citizen was granted leave to enter the United Kingdom in order to marry a resident, the leave to enter was held to be void because of the fraudulent misrepresentations made by her fiancé that he intended to marry her when he did not so intend. It was immaterial that the fraud was committed by another party and unknown to the entrant.

R v SECRETARY OF STATE FOR THE HOME DEPARTMENT, EX PARTE IBRAHIM (1980) Times, 29th March (Queen's Bench Division: EVELEIGH LJ and WATKINS J). *R v Secretary of State for the Home Department, ex parte Hussain* [1977] 1 WLR 700, 1977 Halsbury's Abridgment para. 1486 and dicta of Megaw LJ in *R v Secretary of State for the Home Department, ex parte Khan* [1978] 1 WLR 1466, 1977 Halsbury's Abridgment para. 1479 applied. *R v Secretary of State for the Home Department, ex parte Mangoo Khan* [1980] 2 All ER 337, CA, para. 1521 distinguished.

1524   —— returning resident—evidence of status—admissibility

In a case where an application for entry under HC 79, para. 51, as a returning resident, was refused by an immigration officer because the applicant had not substantiated his contention that he was a "returning resident", it was held that additional evidence supporting the applicant's claimed status would be relevant and admissible on an appeal against the refusal.

R v IMMIGRATION APPEAL TRIBUNAL, EX PARTE ABDUL RASHID [1978] Imm AR 71 (Queen's Bench Division: LORD WIDGERY CJ, CUMMING-BRUCE LJ and PARK J).

1525   —— temporary admission—concealment of material facts—false representation made as to position of husband

Immigration Appeal Tribunal decision:

QURASHA BEGUM v IMMIGRATION OFFICER, LONDON (HEATHROW) AIRPORT [1978] Imm AR 158 (applicant obtained visa for eight months from visa officer whom she told that her husband was a United Kingdom passport holder, was in United Kingdom and would return to Pakistan with her at end of her visit; she was in fact a widow and immigration officer refused entry as she also had one-way ticket only; tribunal dismissed her appeal; where evidence of misrepresentation or concealment of material facts immigration officer entitled to refuse entry, regardless of whether visa officer had been influenced by her false representations).

1526 —— —— —— **pregnancy**

Immigration Appeal Tribunal decision:

FARIDA BEGUM v IMMIGRATION OFFICER, LONDON (HEATHROW) AIRPORT [1978] Imm AR 107 (citizen of Pakistan granted visa to visit United Kingdom for three months to attend brother's wedding; immigration officer refused entry on ground that she had concealed material fact of her pregnancy and fact that child would be born during proposed visit; visa invalid as had withheld information from visa officer; immigration officer entitled properly to refuse her entry as not satisfied she was genuinely seeking entry for stated purpose of her visit; appeal dismissed).

1527 —— —— **likelihood of overstay—whether relevant consideration**

Immigration Appeal Tribunal decision:

DIN v ENTRY CLEARANCE OFFICER, KARACHI [1978] Imm AR 56 (applicant, non-patrial United Kingdom passport holder, refused entry for six months to visit grandchildren on ground that, by reason of his passport, unlikely to be deported if outstayed permitted visit; tribunal allowed his appeal; in absence of intention of male fides in his application, United Kingdom passport an irrelevant consideration when determining whether he intended staying longer than proposed limit).

1528 —— —— **wife of student—sex discrimination**

See *Kassam v Immigration Appeal Tribunal*, para. 2586.

1529 **Harbouring an illegal immigrant—meaning of "harbouring"**

Two appeals against conviction on charges of harbouring illegal immigrants contrary to the Immigration Act 1971, s. 25 (2) were heard together. In the first case it was contended that a person could not harbour another unless there was an intention to impede prosecution or apprehension. In the second case it was further argued that by virtue of the Matrimonial Homes Act 1967 and the Domestic Proceedings and Magistrates' Courts Act 1978 a man could not evict his wife from the home without leave of the court. Therefore he could not be guilty of harbouring his own wife, notwithstanding that she was an illegal immigrant, because she had a right to live in the matrimonial home. *Held*, "harbour" was to be given its ordinary meaning: if the applicants knew that the persons to whom they gave shelter were illegal immigrants then they were harbouring those persons. Further, there was no reason in principle why a husband who knew his wife was an illegal immigrant should not apply to the court for an order for her eviction. The appeals would be dismissed.

R v MISTRY; R v ASARE [1980] LS Gaz R 69 (Court of Appeal: ROSKILL and ORMROD LJJ and BRISTOW J).

1530 —— **whether summary offence**

See *R v Mehet*, para. 708.

1531 **Immigration rules—amendment**

The practice to be followed in the administration of the Immigration Act 1971 for regulating the entry and stay in the United Kingdom of non-patrials is contained in statements of the rules laid by the Secretary of State before Parliament. A statement of Changes in Immigration Rules was so laid before Parliament by the Home Secretary on 20th February 1980. The rules as changed, with effect from 1st March 1980, are set out in that document which has been published as HC 394 and replace the statements laid before Parliament in January 1973 (as subsequently amended). The rules include transitional provisions in Section Three (paras. 157–162). Section One of the rules (paras. 2 to 83) relates to control on entry and Section Two (paras. 84 to 156) relates to control after entry. The rules are subject to disapproval by resolution of either House of Parliament within 40 days from their laying: Immigration Act 1971, s. 3 (2).

1532   Merchant seaman—service on British ship—approved employment "here"—removal of time limit and conditions of stay

Immigration Appeal Tribunal decision:

DE SOUZA V SECRETARY OF STATE FOR THE HOME DEPARTMENT [1978] Imm AR 1 (appeal against refusal of adjudicator to remove time limit and conditions attached to appellant's stay in United Kingsom; appellant, Indian citizen, merchant seaman employed on British ship; claimed that his service from 1969–1977 constituted ordinary residence and that he had been in approved employment "here" within HC 80 para. 28; although appellant's service and payment of tax and National Insurance contributions implied that employment approved, the rules related to employment "here", ie in the United Kingdom; Immigration Act concerned with regulation of entry into and stay in United Kingdom; appellant employed at sea and had only been given limited leave to enter during periods of leave; appeal dismissed).

1533   Registration with police—fees

The Immigration (Registration with Police) (Amendment) Regulations 1980, S.I. 1980 No. 451 (in force on 1st May 1980), increase the fees payable where aliens (other than EEC nationals) are required to register with the police.

INCOME TAXATION

Halsbury's Laws of England (4th edn.), Vol. 23, paras. 1–1701

1534   Articles

Benefits-in-kind—The Use and Transfer of Assets, K. R. Tingley: Taxation 14 June 1980 p. 294.

The Legality of Extra-Statutory Concessions, John Alder (Inland Revenue tax concessions): 130 NLJ 180.

Non-Resident: United Kingdom Trade, E. C. D. Norfolk: [1980] BTR 70 (the liability of a non-resident to United Kingdom taxation in respect of United Kingdom trading profits).

Revenue Enquiries, Tony Foreman (Inland Revenue powers to obtain information): Taxation, 9th February 1980, p. 526.

To Incorporate or Not, Robert P. Burrow, A. J. Shipwright (fiscal considerations in carrying on a business): 124 Sol Jo 123.

Transfer of Assets Overseas, Tony Foreman (the law in the light of *Vestey v IRC* [1979] 3 All ER 976, HL, 1979 Halsbury's Abridgment para. 1505): Taxation 8th March 1980.

United Kingdom Ventures: Branch or Subsidiary? Robert P. Burrow and A. J. Shipwright (fiscal and commercial implications for a non-resident company wishing to carry on business in UK): 124 Sol Jo 319.

Worse than the Spanish Inquisition?: the Rossminster Case, A. J. Shipwright (discussion on *IRC v Rossminster* [1980] 1 All ER 80, 1979 Halsbury's Abridgment para. 1532): 124 Sol Jo 227.

1535   Appeal—appeal against assessment—costs

In response to a parliamentary question regarding the policy of the Customs and Excise and the Inland Revenue in respect of costs in the High Court and superior courts of appeal, the Minister of State at the Treasury has stated that he did not think it right that, as a matter of course, tax cases should be treated differently from other cases. He added that both departments exercised a discretion on matters of costs and were willing, in appropriate circumstances and in particular where they were themselves appealing against adverse decisions, to consider waiving their claims to costs or making other arrangements. Influential factors included the risk of financial hardship to the other party and whether the case was one of significant interest to taxpayers as a whole, turning on a point of law in need of clarification. If the departments concerned were to come to an arrangement of this nature, they would expect to do so in advance of the hearing and following an approach by the taxpayer involved. See 124 Sol Jo 207.

1536   Assessment—payments made under covenant out of earned income—whether investment income

The taxpayer and his wife executed two deeds covenanting to pay £2,200 annually to their respective parents. The question arose as to whether the payments made under the covenants were to be assessed as the investment income of the taxpayer. *Held*, by the provisions of the Income and Corporation Taxes Act 1970, s. 457, as amended by the Finance Act 1971, payments made out of earned income under deeds of covenant were to be assessed as investment income and might be subject to a surcharge over the ordinary rates of tax, under the Finance Act 1971, s. 32.

ANG V PARRISH (INSPECTOR OF TAXES) [1980] STC 341 (Chancery Division: WALTON J).

1537   —— separate assessment of husband and wife—taxpayer assessed in respect of wife's income

The taxpayer appealed by way of case stated against a decision of the General Commissioners that he was liable to income tax in respect of his wife's income, contending that he had applied for separate assessment under the Income and Corporation Taxes Act 1970, s. 38, and hence was not liable to tax on his wife's income. He produced a letter which he had sent to the tax inspector requesting separate assessment. *Held*, the letter was never put before the General Commissioners and hence could not give rise to any question of law as to the correctness of their decision. In any event, the letter did not comply with the requirements of s. 38 as to manner and form. The appeal would be dismissed.

HOTTER V SPACKMAN (INSPECTOR OF TAXES) (NOTE) [1980] STC 552 (Chancery Division: DILLON J).

1538   Avoidance—artificial transactions in land—acquisition of land with purpose of realising gain from disposal—liability to tax of beneficial owners of part of interest in land

The taxpayers were minority shareholders of a group of companies. The majority shareholder used the group's facilities to acquire land with the object of realising gains from its disposal. The taxpayers objected and the majority shareholder therefore declared himself a trustee of a share of his interest in the land for the taxpayers. He then embarked on a tax avoidance scheme to which the taxpayers were not a party. The taxpayers received their share of the proceeds of sale of the land during the two years 1970–71, and 1971–72. The Revenue assessed them to tax under the Income and Corporation Taxes Act 1970, s. 488 for the year 1970–71 on the whole of their sums received. The taxpayers appealed, contending, inter alia, that (i) the majority shareholder had not acquired the land solely for gain and the taxpayers had not been concerned in any scheme in respect of that land, thus s. 488 (2) did not apply; (ii) if s. 488 (2) was satisfied, their liabilty to tax in the year 1970–71 was limited to income received in that year. *Held*, (1) on the facts it was clear that the land had been acquired by the majority shareholder with the sole or main object of realising a gain by its disposal. That the taxpayers were concerned in the scheme was confirmed by the declarations of trust made by the majority shareholder, and the scheme effected enabled a gain to be realised by the taxpayers, and thus satisfied s. 488 (2). (ii) Although most of the gains accruing to the taxpayers were actually received by them in the year 1971–72, it could not be said that those gains were not realised by them in the year 1970–71 as that was the year in which the taxpayers were given rights as beneficiaries under a trust affecting the proceeds of the sale of the land. It followed therefore that the taxpayers were liable to tax in the year 1970–71 on the whole of their share of the gains which they had received from the majority shareholder.

WINTERTON V EDWARDS (INSPECTOR OF TAXES) [1980] 2 All ER 56 (Chancery Division: SLADE J).

1539 ——— ——— **opportunity of realising gain provided by taxpayer**

A family settlement was created by the taxpayer, a United Kingdom resident, with trustees resident in Guernsey. In 1972 the trustees set up two Guernsey companies which purchased land from subsidiary companies of a company controlled by the taxpayer, for sums exceeding those originally paid by the subsidiaries but substantially lower than its value should planning permission be granted. Planning permission was granted and the taxpayer's company bought back the land at a greatly increased price. Substantial parts of the purchase price were left outstanding as loans repayable by instalments on certain contingencies. The taxpayer was assessed to income tax for 1973–74 on the basis that the capital gains that had accrued to the Guernsey companies on the sale of the land fell to be taxed as his income by virtue of the Income and Corporation Taxes Act 1970, s. 488, which provides that where land is acquired with the sole or main object of realising a gain from its disposal, a person who enables a gain to be realised is to be taxed as if it were his income. The taxpayer contended that the fact that the sale to the Guernsey companies was at market value prevented the section from applying. *Held*, the taxpayer's contention was incorrect. The disposal of the land at full market value to the Guernsey companies did not prevent s. 488 from applying. His liability depended on whether he was caught by s. 488 (8) as having provided the Guernsey companies directly or indirectly with an opportunity of realising a gain. The commissioners had found as a fact that he had obtained gains for those companies. Although they had not expressly found that he had provided them with the opportunity of realising those gains, this was implicit in their finding, and there was no need to remit the case for a further finding.

Section 488 (3) provided for the whole gain to be treated as income which arose when the gain was realised and that it was chargeable to tax for the period in which it was realised. In view of the sale agreement whereby only a small part of the purchase price was at the disposal of the Guernsey companies on the completion of the sales, it was unreal to say that in 1973–74 the Guernsey companies realised a gain of the total purchase price less the cost of the acquisition of the land and the expenses of its sale. It was doubtful whether the value of the Guernsey companies' rights in future years to receive sums were capable of valuation. A gain was not realised until it could be effectively enjoyed or disposed of and the assessment would be reduced.

YUILL v WILSON (INSPECTOR OF TAXES) [1980] STC 460 (House of Lords: VISCOUNT DILHORNE, LORD SALMON, LORD EDMUND-DAVIES, LORD RUSSELL OF KILLOWEN and LORD KEITH OF KINKEL). Decision of the Court of Appeal [1979] 2 All ER 1205, 1979 Halsbury's Abridgment para. 1504 reversed.

1540 ——— **establishment of overseas partnership—validity of partnership**

The taxpayer, a well-known United Kingdom television personality, wished to exploit his talents abroad. In anticipation of substantial earnings overseas a tax saving scheme was devised whereby he entered into partnership with a Bahamian company, ninety-five per cent of the profits payable to the taxpayer and five per cent to the company. Under its memorandum of association the company was authorised to carry out "all kinds of financial commercial transactions or other operations". The objects of the partnership agreement was to enter into the business, inter alia, of exploiting television consultants and advisers, publicity agents and providers of public services. The source of all the partnership's income was the taxpayer's income earned in America and no overseas earnings of the taxpayer were remitted to the United Kingdom. The taxpayer was assessed to tax on the basis that his share of the partnership's profit was in reality the profits of his trade, business or vocation. On appeal by the taxpayer the General Commissioners held that a genuine partnership had existed between the taxpayer and the company. As the income arose from possession outside the United Kingdom, within the Income and Corporation Taxes Act 1970, s. 109 (2), tax was chargeable under Sch. D, Case V. It was however derived from the carrying on by the taxpayer of his profession in partnership, within s. 122 (2) (b), and he was chargeable to tax in respect of the income, under s. 122 (3) (b), only to the extent to which it had been received by him in the United Kingdom. Their decision was upheld by the judge and the Court of

Appeal. On appeal to the House of Lords, the Crown contended, inter alia; (i) there was no partnership between the taxpayer and the company in respect of the taxpayer's activities, as a limited company could not perform those activities and acts done by one partner which another partner could not perform were not acts done for the partnership; (ii) that the company had no power under the memorandum of association to carry on the business of a partnership. *Held* (i) the purpose of the agreement was not for both parties to be television entertainers but to exploit and procure engagements for such performers. It did not matter that the taxpayer was one of those performers. (ii) It was within the company's power to enter into the partnership since the business of the partnership was a form of financial operation, or, if not, it came within "other operations", those words having been inserted ex abundanti cautela to cover any kind of such activity if not covered by the words "financial commercial trading". Therefore the partnership was a valid one and the taxpayer's income derived therefrom was not liable to United Kingdom tax on earnings which were not remitted to the United Kingdom.

NEWSTEAD (INSPECTOR OF TAXES) v FROST [1980] 1 All ER 363 (House of Lords: LORD DIPLOCK, VISCOUNT DILHORNE, LORD SALMON, LORD FRASER OF TULLYBELTON and LORD KEITH OF KINKEL). Decision of Court of Appeal [1979] 2 All ER 129, CA, 1978 Halsbury's Abridgment para. 1557 affirmed.

1541 ⸻ **power of commissioners to require information—notice requiring information about unidentified transactions—validity of notice**

The Inland Revenue Commissioners served on the taxpayers notices pursuant to the Income and Corporation Taxes Act 1970, s. 490, requiring them to give certain particulars. The taxpayers sought a declaration that the notices were void since, as they required particulars of unidentified transactions or arrangements, the only provision under which they could be issued was s. 490 (2) (c) and in the form in which they were issued they were outside the powers conferred by that subsection. They also contended that the notices were worded with such obscurity that they were inordinately burdensome and oppressive. *Held*, the notices were valid. Section 490 (2), which was a corollary to the commissioners' power under s. 490 (1) to require any person to furnish such particulars as they thought necessary, defined the recipient's duty, including the duty under s. 490 (2) (c) to furnish particulars as to whether or not he had taken part in transactions or arrangements of a specified character. "Particulars" in this context was synonymous with information and was not limited to details of specfic transactions or arrangements. The precision of expression required in a taxing statute was not necessary in a statutory notice and there was no evidence that the notices were unintelligible or oppressive.

ESSEX v INLAND REVENUE COMRS [1980] STC 378 (Court of Appeal: BUCKLEY, SHAW and BRIGHTMAN LJJ). Decision of Slade J [1979] STC 525, 1979 Halsbury's Abridgment para. 1506 affirmed.

1542 ⸻ **sale of securities "cum dividend"—basic rate liability**

The taxpayer successfully appealed against his assessment to income tax at the basic rate in respect of notional income deemed to arise under the Income and Corporation Taxes Act 1970, s. 30, as amended, on the sale of securities "cum dividend". On the Crown's appeal on the ground that the section was directed at avoidance of basic rate income tax as well as avoidance of excess liability, *held*, such an interpretation of s. 30 would involve a radical change in the law for which clear words would be required. The appeal would be dismissed.

McCARNEY (INSPECTOR OF TAXES) v FREILICH [1981] STC 79 (Chancery Division: GOULDING J).

1543 ⸻ **transaction in securities—receipt of abnormal amount by way of dividend**

The taxpayers were the sole shareholders in five property companies which had substantial profits available for distribution. To avoid liability to income tax and surtax which would have arisen on distribution the taxpayers entered into certain transactions. They sold their shares in the five companies to E and then disposed of the right to receive future instalments of the purchase price of the shares to G. Finally, the five companies paid an abnormal dividend to E. The Crown contended that the sale by the taxpayers of their shares in the five companies was a transaction whereby E subsequently received an abnormal amount by way of dividend and accordingly the taxpayers had obtained, or were in a position to obtain, a tax advantage in the circumstances of the Income and Corporation Taxes Act 1970, s. 461, para. C, and therefore s. 460 of that Act applied to them. The Crown also sought to rely on s. 461, para. D, contending that the consideration received by the taxpayers on the sale of their shares in the five companies was received "in connection with the distribution of profits" of those companies and that the five companies were companies to which para. D applied since they were under the control of not more than five persons on the date on which the tax advantage was received and which was therefore the date relevant for determining whether para. D. applied to those companies. These contentions were rejected and the Crown appealed. *Held*, TEMPLEMAN LJ dissenting, (1) the word "whereby" in para. C imported some causal connection, but it was for the court to determine whether a sufficient causal link existed between the transactions under consideration and the subsequent receipt of the abnormal dividend. On the facts, it was impossible to hold that there was sufficient causal link between the sale of the shares in the five companies to E and the declaration of dividends by the companies. The fact that E acquired the whole of the share capital of the companies with large undistributed profits did not by itself afford sufficient ground for holding that such acquisition was the cause of subsequent distribution of those profits by the companies. Therefore para. C did not apply to the transactions in question. (ii) The relevant date for determining whether para. D applied to the transactions was the date of distribution of profits. The Crown had not established that at that date the five companies were companies to which para. D applied and therefore it could not assert that the circumstances in para. D applied to the transactions. Thus s. 460 did not apply to the transactions and the appeal would be dismissed.

INLAND REVENUE COMRS V GARVIN [1980] STC 295 (Court of Appeal: BUCKLEY, TEMPLEMAN and DONALDSON LJJ). Decision of Slade J [1979] STC 98, 1979 Halsbury's Abridgment para. 1507 affirmed.

1544   A taxpayer's company (A) owned valuable properties which it sold at a net profit of £244,000. The taxpayer sold his shares in A to an investment company (B) for £233,409 to be paid in instalments, and then sold his right to receive those instalments to a further investment company (C), a wholly owned subsidiary of B, for £233,409. A then paid a dividend of £260,500 to its new parent company B. Pursuant to the Income and Corporation Taxes Act 1970, ss. 460, 461, the Commissioners of Inland Revenue issued the taxpayer with a notice to counteract the tax advantage and the taxpayer appealed. *Held*, the phrase "a transaction whereby any other person subsequently receives an abnormal amount by way of dividend" was to be given a wide meaning, both as a whole and in regard to its individual components. On the facts the taxpayer received his money in consequence of the series of operations, the transaction, whereby B received an abnormal dividend and accordingly his appeal would be dismissed.

EMERY V INLAND REVENUE COMRS [1981] STC 150 (Chancery Division: NOURSE J).

1545   —— —— **tax advantage**

The taxpayers entered into a scheme designed to avoid the payment of tax on the sale of land owned by a company wholly owned by them. In order to achieve this, a series of transactions took place, at the end of which the taxpayers received interest-free loans equivalent to the profit made from the sale of the land. The loans were repayable to a company owned by them and of which they were the directors. The Crown contended that they were liable to tax by virtue of the Income and Corporation Taxes Act 1970, s. 460, on the basis that they had obtained a tax advantage in consequence of a transaction in securities or the combined effect of two or more such transactions, in the circumstances provided for in s. 461, para. D, that in connection with the distribution of the profits of a company they received a consideration representing the value of assets which were or would have been available for distribution by way of dividend. *Held,* it was clear that the taxpayers had received a sum without paying tax on it and had thereby obtained a tax advantage. In connection with the distribution of profits by the company which originally owned the land, they received without paying or bearing tax a consideration which represented the value of assets which would have been available for distribution to them by way of dividend, but for the steps taken by that company. Hence para. D applied. The advantage was obtained in consequence of the combined effect of two or more transactions in securities within the definition of "transactions in securities" in s. 467 (1), notwithstanding that not all the transactions involved fell within the definition. Accordingly, by the receipt of loans repayable to a company which they controlled, the taxpayers secured a tax advantage in circumstances which brought them within the scope of s. 460, and the Revenue was entitled to counteract that advantage.

WILLIAMS v INLAND REVENUE COMRS [1980] STC 535 (House of Lords: LORD DIPLOCK, VISCOUNT DILHORNE, LORD SALMON, LORD RUSSELL OF KILLOWEN and LORD KEITH OF KINKEL). Decision of the Court of Appeal [1979] STC 598, 1979 Halsbury's Abridgment para. 1572 affirmed on different grounds.

1546 Capital allowance—corresponding Northern Ireland grants

The Capital Allowances (Corresponding Northern Ireland Grants) Order 1980, S.I. 1980 No. 1071 (in force on 25th August 1980), supersedes the Capital Allowances (Corresponding Northern Ireland Grants) Order 1978, S.I. 1978 No. 53, and applies to grants made under agreements entered into on or after 1st April 1980 but before 1st April 1983.

1547 —— industrial building or structure—meaning

The question arose whether depots where heavy plant and machinery hired out by the taxpayer were repaired and refurbished were "industrial buildings or structures" within the Capital Allowances Act 1968, s. 7 (1) (e), which defines them as buildings in use for the purpose of a trade which consists in, inter alia, the subjection of goods or materials to any process. *Held,* the depots were not being used for the subjection of goods to "any process" since a process connoted a continuous and regular action carried on in a definite manner. The essence of the repair work was that it was individual to the particular defect of a particular item. Accordingly, the depots were not industrial buildings or structures within s. 7 (1) (e).

VIBROPLANT LTD v HOLLAND (INSPECTOR OF TAXES) [1980] STC 671 (Chancery Division: DILLON J). *Ellerker (Inspector of Taxes) v Union Cold Storage Co Ltd* [1939] 1 All ER 23, *Inland Revenue Comrs v Leith Harbour and Docks Comrs* (1942) 24 Tax Cas 118 and *Kilmarnock Equitable Co-operative Society Ltd v Inland Revenue Comrs* (1966) 42 Tax Cas 675 followed.

1548 —— machinery and plant—meaning of plant—electrical installation

The taxpayer company contended that the whole expenditure on the electrical installation in a building used as a department store was capital expenditure on the provision of machinery or plant for the purposes of the trade within the Finance Act 1971, s. 41 (1). The Crown conceded that part of the expenditure was on the provision of plant, but disallowed certain items of expenditure including transformers, switchgear, specially designed light fittings, conduits and cables and window panels, lighting and sockets. The company contended that the installation should be regarded as a single item of plant, or, alternatively, that some of the disallowed items qualified as plant. The Special Commissioners rejected their first contention and determined that some of the disallowed items were plant. On appeal by the company, *held,* (i) in determining whether a structure was plant, the question was whether it was something by means of which a business was carried on, or merely the place within which it was carried on. In the present case, the question was whether the department store would have been a complete building and usable for any purpose without the electrical installation or whether the installation could be regarded as something added to a building otherwise complete and as something employed in the carrying on of the activity of the taxpayer's retail trade. The department store was patently incomplete as a setting for any trading activity without a reticulation system for electric current. Hence the claim that the electrical installation as a whole was plant failed. (ii) Although the meaning of the word "plant" and the principles and criteria to be applied in deciding whether expenditure was expenditure on the provision of plant were questions of law, the application of that meaning and of those principles and criteria to any given set of circumstances was largely, if not entirely, a matter of degree and therefore of fact. There was no error of principle in the commissioners' approach and the appeal would be dismissed.

COLE BROS LTD v PHILLIPS (INSPECTOR OF TAXES) [1980] STC 518 (Chancery Division: VINELOTT J). *Imperial Chemical Industries of Australia and New Zealand Ltd v Federal Comr of Taxation* (1970) 120 CLR 396 followed.

1549   —— —— installation of false ceilings

The taxpayer company, who traded as caterers, installed false ceilings in the restaurant premises from which it operated. They were a permanent installation and provided cladding and support for services used by the company for carrying on its trade. The company claimed capital allowances under the Finance Act 1971, s. 41 in respect of the expenditure incurred, contending that it constituted captial expenditure on the provision of plant. On appeal by the Crown from the decision of the General Commissioners, *held*, in determining whether something was plant a "functional test" had to be applied, namely, whether it performed a function in the actual carrying out of the trade. In the present case, the primary function of the ceilings was to provide cladding for the services. They were not part of the means by which the company provided services to its customers. Accordingly, the expenditure did not qualify for the allowances and the appeal would be allowed.

HAMPTON (INSPECTOR OF TAXES) v FORTES AUTOGRILL LTD [1980] STC 80 (Chancery Division: FOX J). *Benson (Inspector of Taxes) v Yard Arm Club Ltd* [1979] STC 226, CA, 1978 Halsbury's Abridgment para. 1563 followed.

1550   Certificates of tax deposit

A new Prospectus (Series 5) for certificates of tax deposit was introduced on 31st July 1980 and applies to all deposits received on or after that date. The Prospectus introduces two new features. Firstly there is provision for the payment of an interest supplement over the standard rate of interest during the initial months of a deposit, at the rate in force at the time of the investment. Secondly various tax and other liabilities against which certificates of tax deposit may be applied are now specified in a Schedule to the Prospectus with provision for additions to the Schedule from time to time: H M Treasury Press Release dated 29th July 1980.

1551   —— rates of interest

The Treasury announced in a press release on 29th August 1980 that after 1st September 1980 the rate of interest applicable to deposits accepted under the Prospectus (series 5) dated 31st July 1980 and applied in payment of a scheduled liability would be 15 per cent. The rate of interest on deposits withdrawn for cash would be $11\frac{1}{2}$ per cent. An interest supplement, which is only payable in respect of a deposit applied in payment of a scheduled liability, of 2 per cent would be paid in respect of the first three months of a deposit. A nil rate of bonus would apply to deposits held for more than six months and applied in payment of a scheduled liability. After 1st September 1980 these rates will apply to deposits under earlier Prospectuses (series 1 to 4) which reach the second or fourth anniversary of deposit, as applicable, in accordance with the terms and conditions set out therein. Interest supplement is not payable on deposits made under earlier Prospectuses and bonus arrangements do not apply to deposits made under series 1 and 2.

1552   Child allowance—entitlement—evidence

The taxpayer, a citizen of the Republic of the Yemen, claimed child allowances in respect of his children and a number of dependent relatives. At a hearing before the commissioners he gave evidence in person and submitted a number of documents. However, the commissioners concluded that he had not been able to substantiate his claim to any of the reliefs. The taxpayer required the commissioners to state a case for the High Court. *Held*, the evidence provided had been unsatisfactory and as there was no question of law involved in the case and the court had no jurisdiction to reach any different findings of fact the appeal would be dismissed.

TALIB v WATERSON (INSPECTOR OF TAXES) (NOTE) [1980] STC 563 (Chancery Division: BROWNE-WILKINSON J). *Mohsin v Edon (Inspector of Taxes) (Note)* [1978] STC 163, 1978 Halsbury's Abridgment para. 1569 followed.

1553   Child benefit—exemption of foreign child benefit

Under the Income and Corporation Taxes Act 1970, s. 219 (1) social security benefits are exempted from income tax; similarly under s. 219 (2) child benefit is exempted from income tax. By extra-statutory concession foreign benefits, which correspond to social security benefits, have also been exempted (see Inland Revenue booklet IR 1 (1976) A26) and this exemption is to be extended to foreign benefits corresponding to child benefit, with effect from 4th April 1977, so long as the exemption for the United Kingdom benefit subsists: Inland Revenue Press Release dated 8th January 1980.

1554   Construction industry—sub-contractors—tax deduction scheme

The Income Tax (Sub-contractors in the Construction Industry) Regulations 1980, S.I. 1980 No. 1135 (in force on 11th August 1980), amend the Income Tax (Sub-contractors in the Construction Industry) Regulations 1975, 1975 Halsbury's Abridgment para. 1773 by (i) making provisions regarding the calculation of any repayment due to a sub-contractor, (ii) providing for the inclusion of a business name on the sub-contractor's certificate and (iii) specifying the requirements which an applicant must satisfy to qualify for a sub-contractor's certificate.

1555   —— —— —— certificate of exemption—statutory condition requiring employment in United Kingdom for three years—power to dispense with requirement

The taxpayer left his business as an electrical subcontractor in October 1975 to work abroad. He returned to England two years later and recommenced his business. In February 1978 he applied for an exemption certificate under the Finance (No. 2) Act 1975, Sch. 12, Part I, para. 2, his previous certificate having expired. The certificate was refused on the ground that he had not been employed, in the United Kingdom, for the requisite three years. The taxpayer appealed, contending that the Revenue had a discretion to waive the condition under para. 3 (2) and that in the circumstances it was reasonable for it to do so. The General Commissioners accepted the contention and allowed the appeal. On appeal by the Crown, *held*, para. 3 (2) did not give the Revenue power to waive the conditions in Sch. 12, Pt. I but only the requirements of para. 3 (1). Further, the General Commissioners did not have the power to review a decision under para. 3 (2) because s. 70 (6) expressly excluded from the Commissioners' jurisdiction any power to make such a review. The appeal would therefore be allowed.

COOPER (INSPECTOR OF TAXES) v SERCOMBE [1980] STC 76 (Chancery Division: FOX J).

1556   —— —— —— conditions on grant of certificate

The Finance (No. 2) Act 1975, s. 69 requires a contractor on paying a sub-contractor to deduct a sum equal to the standard rate of tax, unless that sub-contractor is an excepted person by virtue of a tax certificate issued to him under s. 70. Schedule 12 provides that a certificate can only be issued where, throughout the three year period ending with the date of the application for a certificate, the sub-contractor has been employed as a holder of an office or employment or as a person carrying on a trade, profession or vocation.

In a case where a man was employed as a sub-contractor in the building industry and applied for a certificate under s. 70, it was held that where the three year period preceding his application included a year during which he was unemployed but nevertheless actively seeking work, he was not entitled to a certificate. "Employed" in Sch. 12 was not to be regarded purely on a master and servant relationship basis, but it was tantamount to "engaged in". In order to show that a person was employed in a trade during a period of inactivity it had to be shown that he was carrying on that trade before that period.

PHELPS (INSPECTOR OF TAXES) v MOORE [1980] STC 568 (Chancery Division: BROWNE-WILKINSON J).

1557 ——— ——— ——— excluded operations

The Income Tax (Construction Operations) Order 1980, S.I. 1980 No. 1171 (in force on 7th August 1980), excludes certain operations from the scope of the construction industry tax deduction scheme.

1558 ——— ——— tax repayments—amount payable

The taxpayer who was self-employed, did not hold a sub-contractor's certificate pursuant to the Finance (No. 2) Act 1975 s. 70. In the year 1977–1978 deductions were made by contractors from payments made to the taxpayer on account of income tax pursuant to s. 69 of the Act. He was subsequently assessed to income tax under Sch. D, Case I in respect of his profits for the year 1977–1978. In January 1978 the taxpayer claimed repayment of the deductions under the Income Tax (Sub-Contractors in the Construction Industry) Regulations 1975 reg. 13 (1) (a) which provides that if the total of the sums deducted in any year exceeds the aggregate of the income tax payable by the sub-contractor for that year on the profits or gains of the trade the sub-contractor shall be entitled to repayment of the excess. The taxpayer contended that only the tax which had become due and payable on 1st January should be deducted from the repayments. On appeal by the Crown, *held*, the word "payable" was not used in the sense of "due and payable" and referred to the amount payable in toto for the whole year. The appeal would be allowed.

WOODCOCK (INSPECTOR OF TAXES) v BONHAM [1980] STC 336 (Chancery Division: WALTON J).

1559 Corporation tax—directors' fees

Directors' fees are normally assessable under Schedule E. However where a company has the right to appoint a director to the board of another company, provided the director hands over to the first company any fees or other emoluments received in respect of the directorship and the first company agrees to accept liability on the fees, those fees are treated as income of the company and not of the director. Where the first company is chargeable not to corporation tax but to income tax (for example, if it is a non-resident company not trading through a branch or agency in the United Kingdom) and agrees to accept liability, tax is deducted at the basic rate of income tax from the fees. With effect from 6 April 1980, this practice will be extended to cases where the first company has no formal right to appoint the director to the board but the director is nevertheless required to (and does) hand over the fees to that company, provided it is:—

(a) a company resident in the United Kingdom liable to United Kingdom Corporation tax or, if non-resident, is trading through a branch or agency in the United Kingdom so that its income is chargeable to corporation tax under the Income and Corporation Taxes Act 1970, s. 246 (2); and

(b) not a company over which the director has control. For this purpose "control" has the meaning given to it by s. 534 of the 1970 Act, but in determining whether the company is controlled by the director the rights and powers of his spouse, his children and their spouses and his parents, will also be taken into account.

This concession will be included in due course in the Board's published list of extra-statutory concessions: Inland Revenue Press Release dated 20th March 1980.

1560　　　—— **group relief—restriction where arrangements exist whereby person controls one company but not another—meaning of "arrangements"**

Under the Income and Corporation Taxes Act 1970, s. 258, certain reliefs from corporation tax to which one company was entitled could be deducted when computing the profits of another company in the same group. For the purposes of such group relief, two companies were treated as members of the same group if not less than 75 per cent of the ordinary share capital of one company was owned by the other. Group relief was excluded by the Finance Act 1973, s. 29 (1) (b) (ii) where arrangements existed under which a person controlled one company but not the other.

Two companies, A Ltd and B Ltd, devised a scheme whereby A Ltd's excess capital allowances would be used to reduce B Ltd's tax liability. A Ltd had one subsidiary, X Ltd; B Ltd had two subsidiaries, Y Ltd and Z Ltd. The articles of association of all three subsidiaries were amended as part of the scheme; no amendments were required to be made to A Ltd or B Ltd's articles. As a result of various dealings in the shares of the three subsidiaries, B Ltd and X Ltd became members of the same group within the 1970 Act, s. 258. In addition, A Ltd and B Ltd had equal control of Z Ltd; Y Ltd and Z Ltd had equal control of X Ltd. X Ltd then bought a ship and agreed to its excess capital allowances being deducted from B Ltd's profits. The Inland Revenue contended that the 1973 Act, s. 29 (1) (b) (ii) excluded group relief since arrangements existing under B Ltd's articles of association were "arrangements" within s. 29. *Held*, the word "arrangements" in s. 29 had to be widely defined and not confined to relationships having contractual force. However, according to the dictionary meaning, it had to be construed as referring to dealings which were combined for a particular purpose. On that basis, B Ltd's articles could not be "arrangments" within s. 29: they remained unchanged throughout and were not in any ordinary sense part of the combination of dealings necessary under the scheme. Accordingly, s. 29 (1) (b) (ii) did not apply and B Ltd was entitled to group relief.

PILKINGTON BROTHERS LTD v INLAND REVENUE COMRS (1980) Times, 23rd December (Chancery Division: NOURSE J).

1561　　　—— **liability to tax—whether national political organisation an "unincorporated association"**

It has been held that the Conservative Party is not an "unincorporated association" within the definition of a company in the Income and Corporation Taxes Act 1970, s. 526 (5), and its profits are not therefore chargeable to corporation tax under s. 238 (1) of the Act.

The court held that the commissioners' finding, that the Central Office funds held by the Party Treasurer were owned by the members of the unincorporated association comprising all the members of the local constituency associations together with the Conservative members of both Houses of Parliament, was misconceived. The funds were accordingly liable to bear income tax chargeable, under s. 114, on the treasurer as the person "receiving or entitled to the income".

CONSERVATIVE AND UNIONIST CENTRAL OFFICE v BURRELL (INSPECTOR OF TAXES) [1980] STC 400 (Chancery Division: VINELOTT J).

1562　　　—— **profits—apportionment to particular accounting period**

On an appeal by the taxpayer against an assessment to corporation tax made by reference to the profits from the relevant transactions in each accounting period, *held*, the Income and Corporation Taxes Act 1970, s. 129 (2), provided that, for the purpose of computing the profits of a particular accounting period, profits or gains or losses or apportioned parts of them might be aggregated. However, this provision did not make the Crown bound by law to apportion the profits on a time basis; the word "necessary" emphasised that apportionment was only applicable if there was no better method available of ascertaining the profits of a particular accounting period. In this case, the mode of computation used by the Crown was a better method and the appeal would be dismissed.

MARSHALL HUS & PARTNERS LTD V BOLTON (INSPECTOR OF TAXES) [1981] STC 18 (Chancery Division: GOULDING J).

1563   Costs—cost in tax cases—policies of Inland Revenue and Customs and Excise

See para. 1535.

1564   Discretionary trust—charge to additional rate

A company registered and resident in Jersey was the sole trustee of a discretionary settlement made to provide for the settlor's daughter and family, who were domiciled and resident in the United Kingdom. The trustee had power to apply the income of the trust fund for the benefit of the beneficiaries and to accumulate the income. The trust fund included ordinary shares in United Kingdom companies for which dividends had been received by the trustee. The trustee was assessed to income tax at the additional rate under the Finance Act 1973, s. 16 (1) on the distributions from the companies resident in the United Kingdom. The trustee appealed against assessment on the ground that s. 16 (1) was not applicable to the income in question. On its true construction s. 16 (1), he contended, applied only to income which was chargeable to tax at the basic rate; the trustee was outside the United Kingdom and thus was not entitled to tax credit in respect of the relevant dividends under the Finance Act 1972, s. 86 (5). Therefore, under s. 87 (5) (a) of the 1972 Act, no assessment could be made on him in respect of income tax at the basic rate on the amount of the relevant dividends. *Held*, the phrase in s. 16 (1) "in addition to being chargeable to income tax at the basic rate" had no further function other than to make it clear that the charge at the additional rate was not to supersede the charge, if any, to tax at the basic rate. The trustee was accordingly properly chargeable to tax at the additional rate notwithstanding that he was not chargeable to tax at the basic rate.

INLAND REVENUE COMRS V REGENT TRUST CO LTD [1980] STC 140 (Chancery Division: SLADE J).

1565   Double taxation relief

Double taxation relief arrangements have been made with the following countries:

	Relevant Statutory Instruments (1980)
Australia	707
Bangladesh	708
Canada	709, 780, 1528
Cyprus	1529
Denmark	1960
Egypt	1091
Finland	710
Gambia	1963
Japan	1530
Luxembourg	567
Netherlands	1961
New Zealand	1531
Norway	711, 712, 1962
Sri Lanka	713
Sweden	1532
United States of America	568, 779

1566   Evasion—grant of amnesty—rights of other taxpayers to bring action declaring amnesty unlawful

See *R v Inland Revenue Comrs, ex parte National Federation of Self-Employed and Small Businesses Ltd*, para. 8.

1567   Exemption—charities—donations by one charity to another— donations accumulated by recipient charity

Two companies, a charitable trust and a foundation, were registered as charities and set up to work in tandem. The trust made large donations to the foundation, which were added by the foundation to its capital. The trust successfully claimed exemption from tax under the Income and Corporation Taxes Act 1970, s. 360 (1) and the Finance Act 1965, s. 35 (1) in respect of the donations, on the ground that they were an application of its income and gains for charitable purposes. The Revenue appealed. *Held*, a charitable corporation which, acting intra vires, made an outright transfer of money applicable for charitable purposes to any other charity in such a manner as to pass to the transferee full title to the money had to be taken, by the transfer itself, to have applied such money for charitable purposes, unless the transferor knew or ought to have known that the money would be misapplied by the transferee. The trust had, therefore, applied the money for charitable purposes and was entitled to exemption without having to show how the money was dealt with by the foundation. The appeal would be dismissed.

INLAND REVENUE COMRS v HELEN SLATER CHARITABLE TRUST LTD [1980] 1 All ER 785 (Chancery Division: SLADE J).

1568   Extra statutory concession—foreign emoluments

By statutory concession the reimbursement of travelling expenses to and from the United Kingdom of persons working in the United Kingdom who are in receipt of "foreign emoluments", are exempt from tax. However persons not domiciled in the United Kingdom who are employed by Irish companies are not entitled to this concession, because emoluments from employment with an Irish company do not fall within the definition of "foreign emoluments" contained in the Income and Corporation Taxes Act 1970, s. 181, Sch. 12, Part III, para. 3 (3). The Inland Revenue are to extend the concession to such persons with effect from 6th April 1980 and the Irish Revenue Commissioners have agreed to amend their own practice in line with the United Kingdom concession: Inland Revenue Press Release dated 2nd May 1980.

1569   —— long service testimonials

The Inland Revenue have reviewed the published extra-statutory concession under which they do not seek to charge tax in respect of awards made to directors and employees as testimonials to mark long service, which take the form of tangible articles of reasonable cost, when the relevant period of service is not less than twenty years, and no similar award has been made to the recipient within the previous ten years. From 1st July 1980 an article will be taken to be of reasonable cost when the cost to the employer does not exceed £10 per year of service: Inland Revenue Press Release dated 2nd July 1980.

1570   Finance Act 1980

See para. 2328.

1571   Interest—excess interest as distribution—limit

See para. 1606.

1572   —— interest on overdue tax—limit

In the observations by the Government on the Third Report from the Select Committee on the Parliamentary Commissioner for Administration, Session 1977–

78, Cmnd. 7803, the government states that it accepts in principle the changes recommended by the Select Committee in the arrangements for payment of interest on tax paid late. The government has stated that it is ready at an appropriate time to introduce legislation to raise the de minimis limit for charging interest from £10 to £20 and to change the statutory payment date from 6th July to 1st December.

1573   —— purchase of cum-dividend securities—liability to tax on proportion of interest attributable to period prior to date of purchase

The Court of Appeal has held that a purchaser of securities is assessable to tax on the interest accrued on those securities before the date of purchase where the purchase is a purchase cum-dividend.

The taxpayer purchased Government stock, the sale price for which included an additional amount representing unpaid interest which had accrued from the last previous dividend date. He was assessed to tax on this instalment and the Court of Appeal upheld the assessment on the basis of the decision in *Wigmore v Thomas Summerson and Sons Ltd*, that it was the purchaser, and not the vendor, of securities who was liable to tax on any part of the sale price representing the apportioned interest for the period since the last previous dividend date.

SCHAFFER v CATERMOLE (INSPECTOR OF TAXES) [1980] STC 650 (Court of Appeal: LAWTON, BRIDGE and SHAW LJJ). Decision of Goulding J [1979] STC 670, 1979 Halsbury's Abridgment para. 1537 affirmed. *Wigmore v Thomas Summerson and Sons Ltd* [1926] 1 KB 131 followed.

1574   —— relief for increase in value of stock—meaning of trading stock

Scotland

A company claimed relief under the Finance (No. 2) Act 1975, s. 54 for increases in value of its trading stock, in respect of flats which it had purchased and not yet resold. Under Sch. 10, para. 16 (1) "trading stock" does not include land and the Crown contended that the flats were "land" within the definition contained in the Interpretation Act 1889, s. 3. The Special Commissioners upheld the company's claim and the Crown appealed. *Held*, dismissing the appeal, the word "land" in para. 16 (2) did not have the extended meaning given to it in the Act of 1889 and did not include buildings.

INLAND REVENUE COMRS v CLYDEBRIDGE PROPERTIES LTD [1980] STC 68 (Inner House).

Interpretation Act 1889, s. 3 now Interpretation Act 1978, Schs. 1, 2, paras. 4 (1), 5 (b).

In the Inland Revenue Board's view this decision is limited to the particular facts of the case. It is considered, therefore, that stock relief is not due under Sch. 10 or under the Finance Act 1976, Sch. 5 in respect of buildings held together with the underlying land (unlike the flats in this case), unless they are held as part of the trading stock and sold after being developed: Inland Revenue Press Release dated 25th February 1980.

1575   Judicial review—mandamus—application by taxpayer to amend case stated—availability of remedy

A taxpayer applied to the Queen's Bench Divisional Court for judicial review, seeking an order of mandamus requiring the Special Commissioners to amend a case stated by them. The question at issue was what was the appropriate court to which to resort for relief in cases of this kind. *Held*, the Queen's Bench Divisional Court had residual jurisdiction exceptionally over the supervision of such matters as the validity of, or errors in, proceedings and could interfere by means of prerogative orders. However, where there was a specialised jurisdiction available to remedy the injustice complained of, the court should not intervene. A case such as this should proceed in the Chancery Division, which dealt with cases stated in regard to tax matters.

R v INLAND REVENUE COMRS, EX PARTE EMERY (NOTE) [1980] STC 549 (Queen's Bench Division: DONALDSON LJ and COMYN J).

1576　Life assurance—long term policies—cancellation—repayment of stamp duty

Repayment of stamp duty is to be allowed where long term life policies have been cancelled pursuant to the Insurance Companies Act 1974, ss. 65 and 66. If it is shown to the satisfaction of the Inland Revenue Commissioners that, under s. 66 (4) (a) a notice of cancellation has operated within the previous six months to rescind a contract of insurance, then any ad valorem duty paid on the instrument securing such contract will be repaid by the Commissioners, provided that the instrument is given up to be destroyed. Where an insurance company is permitted, pursuant to the Finance Act 1956, s. 38, to pay duties in bulk, rather than on the issue of each individual policy, any duties which are repayable may be deducted in the next periodical accounts required to be delivered to the commissioners: Inland Revenue Press Release dated 10th January 1980.

1577　Pay As You Earn—application to cases with foreign element

An overseas company carried out activities on the installation of platforms and pipelines in both United Kingdom and foreign areas of the North Sea designated for the purposes of the Continental Shelf Act 1964. It employed both British and foreign employees and the question arose whether it was required by the Income and Corporation Taxes Act 1970, s. 204, to deduct tax on the emoluments paid to all its employees. Section 204 provides that on the making of any payment of any income assessable to income tax under Schedule E, income tax is to be deducted by the person making the payment. *Held*, it was undisputed that all the employees were liable to Schedule E tax on their emoluments. Section 204 applied where the duties of the employment were carried out within the United Kingdom, whether the employer was foreign or not. Although the designated areas of the North Sea were not part of the United Kingdom, the Finance Act 1973, s. 38, provided for exploration activities in a designated area to be treated as a UK trade. Hence s. 204 extended to the emoluments paid by the company.

CLARK (INSPECTOR OF TAXES) v OCEANIC CONTRACTORS INCORPORATED [1980] STC 656 (Chancery Division: DILLON J).

1578　—— limits on pay

The Income Tax (Employments) (No. 10) Regulations 1980, S.I. 1980 No. 505 (in force on 1st June 1980), raise the limit of weekly or monthly pay above which an employer has to operate the Pay As You Earn scheme for every employee, to take into account the increased income tax allowances proposed for 1980/81.

1579　Petroleum Revenue Tax Act 1980

The Petroleum Revenue Tax Act 1980 received the royal assent on 31st January 1980 and came into force on that date. Section 1 has effect in relation to chargeable periods ending on or after 31st December 1979 with s. 2 (1), (2) having effect in relation to tax charged for any such period and s. 2 (3) having effect from 1st January 1980. The Act provides that payments on account of tax are to be made in advance of the making of an assessment: s. 1. Section 2 (1), (2) provides for the bringing forward of the date from which interest is payable on unpaid and overpaid tax and s. 2 (3) for the altering of the rate at which such interest is payable. Section 3 deals with the short title, construction and commencement.

1580　Relief—child relief—entitlement—reduction where child entitled to his own income—effect of payments under deed of covenant

The taxpayer's son was a student between 1974 and 1977; his local authority awarded him a grant and assessed the taxpayer to a voluntary parental contribution which varied each year. By deed of covenant in 1975 the taxpayer undertook to pay his son a certain sum each year for seven years. In addition, he paid his son the difference, if any, between the covenanted payment and the relevant amount of parental contribution. The covenanted payments were taken into account when assessing the taxpayer's entitlement to child relief for 1974–1977. He contended that the payments were part of an educational endowment held by his son and should be disregarded. *Held*, under the Income and Corporation Taxes Act 1970, s. 10 (5) proviso, income to which a child was entitled as holder of an educational endowment did not affect his parent's entitlement to child relief. However, if the taxpayer had simply paid the parental contribution instead of executing a deed, such voluntary and unenforceable payments would not have been income to which his son was entitled, whether or not received as holder of an educational endowment. The position was not altered by showing that the son was entitled to income by virtue of the taxpayer's binding deed of covenant: the covenant did not relate to education in any way but was regarded by both as covering in whole or part the parental contribution. Accordingly the covenanted payments did not fall within the 1970 Act, s. 10 (5) proviso.

GIBBS (INSPECTOR OF TAXES) v RANDALL [1981] STC 106 (Chancery Division: GOULDING J).

1581   —— —— school fees paid under maintenance order

A Practice Direction has been issued by the Family Division of the High Court concerning tax relief on school fees, which are part of a child's maintenance paid under a maintenance order and which are paid direct to the school (see para. 2219). The Inland Revenue have issued a statement of practice SP 15/80, in which it is stated that the onus will be on the parties themselves to produce evidence, where requested, that the person receiving the school fees has agreed to act as agent for the child and that the contract for the payment of the fees (which will most easily be proved if in writing) is between the child (not the spouse making the payments) and the school.

1582   —— interest—interest on a loan—interest paid by guarantor of loan

The taxpayer and his wife held the entire issued share capital of a company which was partly financed by a bank overdraft guaranteed by the taxpayer and his wife. They were called on to implement the guarantee and subsequently discharged their liability by paying off the overdraft and the interest on it. The taxpayer contended that the interest was interest on a loan and therefore eligible for relief under the Finance Act 1974, Sch. 1, para. 9. *Held*, the liability of a guarantor of a loan which arose on a demand to meet the guarantee could not be described as a loan or arising in any way out of a loan made to him. His liability was to make good the default of another for that other's debt and to make good the liability of that other for interest on that debt. Hence the interest paid in this case was not interest on a loan within Sch. 1, para. 9 and the taxpayer was not entitled to relief.

HENDY (INSPECTOR OF TAXES) v HADLEY [1980] 2 All ER 554 (Chancery Division: VINELOTT J).

1583   —— —— —— main residence

The taxpayer, the licensee and tenant of a public house in Essex, purchased property in Wales with the assistance of a building society mortgage. It was the only property that he had ever purchased, it was furnished and equipped as a home and the taxpayer and his wife spent a few days every month there. He claimed tax relief in respect of the interest paid on the mortgage, pursuant to the Finance Act 1974, Sch. 1, para. 4 (1), which restricted the availability of such relief to the purchase of a house which was "used as the only or main residence" of the taxpayer or a dependent relative. *Held*, if someone lived in two or more places, the question which he used as his principal or more important residence could not be determined solely by reference to the way in which he divided his time between the two. Although it was clear that the house in Wales was not his "only" residence, taking all the factors into account the taxpayer used it as his principal residence and was therefore entitled to relief.

FROST (INSPECTOR OF TAXES) v FELTHAM [1981] STC 115 (Chancery Division: NOURSE J).

1584   —— **life assurance—change of rate**

The Industrial Assurance (Life Assurance Premium Relief) (Change of Rate) Regulations 1980, S.I. 1980 No. 1948 (in force on 20th January 1981), authorise industrial assurance companies and collecting societies to amend prescribed or approved schemes adopted in accordance with the 1977 Regulations, 1977 Halsbury's Abridgment para. 1558 pursuant to a change in the authorised percentage rate.

1585   —— **life insurance premiums—policies issued in connection with superannuation schemes**

The Inland Revenue have issued a Press Release dated 6th March 1980 concerning an extra statutory concession. Life assurance premium relief is normally allowable only in respect of "qualifying" policies, i.e. those which satisfy the conditions laid down in the Taxes Acts. As regards life assurance policies issued in connection with sponsored superannuation schemes, however, the Income and Corporation Taxes Act 1970, s. 19 (4) (b) allows relief on premiums paid even though the policies may not be "qualifying", and s. 393 (2) (b) similarly protects the policyholder from any charge to tax in respect of gains on the surrender etc. of a policy. The Finance Act 1971, Sch. 14 repealed these provisions with effect from 6th April 1980, as part of the series of measures introducing the new tax code for superannuation. The Inland Revenue intend to continue with the protection, however, by means of an extra statutory concession. This concession came into effect on 6th April 1980 and will be reviewed in five years' time. The concession will not apply in the case of a policy issued in connection with a retirement benefits scheme established on or after 6th April 1980.

1586   —— **mortgage interest—overlapping loans in year of marriage**

The Inland Revenue have issued a Press Release dated 24th September 1980 in which they have clarified the position under the Finance Act 1974, Sch. 1, para. 6, where, because of a change of residence on marriage, there is an overlap of mortgage loans.

Firstly, by a statement of practice SP10/80, where two people, each buying a property before marriage with the aid of a loan, buy a new property in joint names on marriage which will be used as their new joint only or main residence and sell their existing properties, the bridging loan provisions in para. 6 will be regarded as applying to all three properties. This means that relief will continue to be available within a period of twelve months from the date of the new loan (or such further period as the Board may direct in the particular circumstances) for interest within the normal ceiling limits on both existing loans whether or not the relevant property continues to be used as that owner's only or main residence; and for interest on the new joint loan as if no interest were payable on either of the existing loans.

Secondly an extra-statutory concession extends relief to the situation where one spouse goes to live in the other's home, which is being purchased under a mortgage, and sells his or her own property. No relief is available under para. 6 for the interest on the property being sold, between the date it is vacated and the date of sale. But the concession allows for such relief provided the property is sold within twelve months from the date it is vacated. Furthermore such interest will be disregarded in determining the relief due on interest payable on the new matrimonial home.

1587   —— **relief for increase in value of stock—"major alteration" in conduct of trade—onus of proving right to relief**

Scotland

During the accounting period ended 30th April 1976 the taxpayer company undertook an agency for a Japanese manufacturing company which resulted in its making a number of changes in its trading practices, in particular by increasing its trading stock by 80 per cent. The taxpayer company claimed stock relief in respect of the increase but omitted to provide information upon which a stock valuation for the purposes of relief could be made. *Held*, (i) whether the changes in the company's conduct of its trade amounted to a "major alteration" so as to bring the matter within the Finance Act 1976, Sch. 5, para. 23 (1) was a matter of fact and degree. (ii) The onus was on the taxpayer company to show that it was entitled to the relief and the amount of that relief. Accordingly the company, in neglecting to provide information upon which a valuation could be made under para. 23 (3), had failed to discharge this onus and was not entitled to the relief.

D I K TRANSMISSIONS (DUNDEE) LTD v INLAND REVENUE COMRS [1980] STC 724 (Inner House).

1588   —— relief in respect of loss in trade

The Inland Revenue have issued a Statement of Practice No. SP 2/80 relating to losses arising under Case V of Schedule D. There is no statutory authority for relief of Case V losses, apart from that provided by the Finance Act 1974, s. 23 (2), but deficiencies of income from lettings of overseas property, including caravans and houseboats, may in practice be carried forward for set-off against future income from the same property. This Statement has been issued to make it clear that this practice applies whether the owner of the property is an individual or a company, as the index of Statements issued prior to 1978 may have given rise to confusion on this point.

1589   Schedule D—accrued interest from bank deposit account—basis of assessment

The taxpayer opened a bank deposit account from which he earned interest. For two years he was assessed to tax on income which actually arose during those years. In the third year he was assessed on an amount of income equal to that arising in the second year. He appealed stating that his income for the third year should not have been computed by reference to his income in the second year on which he had already paid tax. *Held*, the Income and Corporation Taxes Act 1970 s. 119 provided that the measure of income tax on which tax was to be computed under Schedule D Case III was "the full amount of the income arising within the year preceding the year of assessment." Section 120 modified that principle by providing that (a) as respects the year of assessment in which the income first arose tax should be computed on the amount of income arising in that year; (b) where the income first arose on some day in the year preceding the year of assessment, tax should be computed on the amount of the income of the year of assessment. However s. 120 (1) (a), (b) was not applicable to the third and subsequent years of assessment from the year in which income first arose and the appeal would be dismissed.

BEESE v MACKINLAY (INSPECTOR OF TAXES) [1980] STC 228 (Chancery Division: VINELOTT J).

1590   —— benefits in kind—double taxation

The Inland Revenue interpret the Income and Corporation Taxes Act 1970, s. 284 (2) as though the provisos included an exemption by reference to the provision of accommodation giving rise to a charge under the Finance Act 1977 s. 33. This concession is not formally published, see memorandum by the Council of the Law Society, para. 7, LS Gaz 13.

1591   —— profits—allowable deductions—capital or revenue expenditure—payment under guarantee—contract of indemnity

H, a partner in a firm of accountants, executed in his own name a guarantee of a loan by a bank to one of the firm's clients. He alone was liable for any loss arising out of it. Subsequently he died, and when the bank demanded payment of £14,000 the remaining partners paid it and were indemnified by H's estate. On the question whether this payment was a deductible expense for the purposes of income taxation assessment, *held*, where a payment by a partnership was a proper disbursement wholly and exclusively laid out for the purposes of the partnership trade, that payment was a deductible expense for income tax purposes. An indemnity by a partner only affected the distribution of the partnership profits and losses and did not affect liability to income tax.

BOLTON (INSPECTOR OF TAXES) v HALPERN AND WOOLF [1981] STC 14 (Court of Appeal: ORMROD, EVELEIGH AND TEMPLEMAN LJJ). Decision of Oliver J [1979] STC 761, 1979 Halsbury's Abridgment para. 1555 reversed.

1592   ——— ——— ——— expenditure on repairs

A spectators' stand at a football stadium had become unsafe and was demolished and replaced by a new one in almost the same position and of approximately the same capacity. The club claimed that the erection of the new stand constituted repairs and that consequently the expenditure was an allowable deduction in computing profits under Income and Corporation Taxes Act 1970, s. 130 (d), and alternatively that the expenditure was incurred on the provision of plant within Finance Act 1971, s. 41. *Held*, repair was restoration by renewal or replacement of subsidiary parts of a whole. The club premises comprised a number of distinct parts with distinct functions. The stand was one part and its replacement was not the repair of a larger entity. Nor was the stand plant as it did not perform any function in the actual processes which constituted the club's trade.

BROWN (INSPECTOR OF TAXES) v BURNLEY FOOTBALL AND ATHLETIC CO LTD [1980] STC 424 (Chancery Division: VINELOTT J). Dictum of Buckley LJ in *Lurcott v Wakely & Wheeler* [1911] 1 KB at 924 applied.

1593   ——— ——— ——— provision of residential accommodation above office

The taxpayer, a chartered surveyor, repaired and decorated a flat above his office in order that he might stay there overnight when working late. The taxpayer was seventy years old and found travelling home at night difficult. He unsuccessfully claimed that his expenditure on the flat was an allowable deduction in computing his profits. On appeal by the taxpayer, *held*, the expenditure was not incurred "wholly and exclusively" for his professional purposes, within the meaning of the Income and Corporation Taxes Act 1970, s. 130 (a), and the furnishings were not "plant" used in his profession within the meaning of the Finance Act 1971, s. 41 (1) (a). The appeal would be dismissed.

MASON v TYSON (INSPECTOR OF TAXES) [1980] STC 284 (Chancery Division: WALTON J).

1594   ——— ——— ——— trade expenses

An associated company of the taxpayer company obtained loans from a bank which were secured partly by a floating charge on its undertaking and all its property and partly by a guarantee by a subsidiary of the associated company, by a mortgage of its land and a floating charge on its undertaking. At the same time, the taxpayer company charged a property to the bank to secure the liabilities of the subsidiary company to the bank. Subsequently a receiver of the associated and the subsidiary companies was appointed by the bank. The taxpayer company sold the charged property to a purchaser for £40,000. A deposit of £5,000 was paid to the bank by virtue of its mortgage and the purchaser mortgaged the property back to the taxpayer company to secure the repayment of the balance of £35,000. The bank then took a sub-charge on the mortgage to the taxpayer company and on the debt of £35,000 due thereunder and required that the instalments due under the mortgage to the taxpayer company should be paid into an account at the bank to secure the liabilities of the subsidiary company to the bank. By this arrangement, the whole of the £40,000 together with interest of £1,920 was paid into the account. The taxpayer company claimed that in computing its taxable profits it was entitled to deduct the sum claimed by the bank under the charge because the charge given and the loss incurred thereunder was wholly and exclusively for the purpose of its trade within the Income and Corporation Taxes Act 1970, s. 130 (a), and such a loss was expenditure of a revenue nature. The General Commissioners found as a fact that the interests of all three companies were considered together when decisions were made, including the decision that the taxpayer company should give security. They upheld the taxpayer company's claim and the Crown appealed. *Held*, in view of the commissioners' finding, the payment to the bank by the taxpayer company in discharge of the subsidiary's liabilities could not be said to have been made "wholly and exclusively" for the purposes of the taxpayer company's trade. On payment of the sum to the bank by the taxpayer company in discharge of the subsidiary's liabilities, the subsidiary became immediately liable to refund the sum to the taxpayer company. Thus in return for the payment to the bank the taxpayer company acquired an asset in the nature of a loan from the subsidiary. The payment was therefore capital in nature. It followed that the sum did not fall to be deducted in computing the taxpayer company's profits and the appeal would be allowed.

GARFORTH (INSPECTOR OF TAXES) v TANKARD CARPETS LTD [1980] STC 251 (Chancery Divison: WALTON J).

1595   A parent company, in order to support its French subsidiary company which had been making losses, acquired a 100 per cent interest in the subsidiary and seconded to it one of its employees to provide technical and marketing expertise. The parent company successfully claimed a deduction of the sum it had paid to the employee as wages and expenses against its liability to corporation tax. The Crown appealed. *Held*, the sum paid to the employee was an allowable deduction if it was expended wholly and exclusively for the purpose of the parent company's trade, notwithstanding that it would, of necessity, benefit the subsidiary to some extent. The test was a subjective one, the question being what was the object of the person making the disbursement and not what was the effect of the disbursement when made; in all cases that was a pure question of fact. In the instant case, the commissioners had found as a fact that the object of the expenditure was to further the parent's business in France and not that of the subsidiary. Accordingly, the appeal would be dismissed.

ROBINSON (INSPECTOR OF TAXES) v SCOTT BADER CO LTD [1980] STC 241 (Chancery Division: WALTON J). Dicta of Romer LJ in *Bentleys, Stokes & Lowless v Beeson* [1952] 2 All ER 82 at 84–87 applied.

1596   —— —— **capital or revenue receipts—sale of properties acquired for investment**

The appellant purchased a number of properties as investments. He then formed a group of companies as property investment companies and acquired various sites for development. Those developments were subsequently sold and the companies went into liquidation. The appellant contended that those sales should not be subject to corporation tax on the ground that the proceeds were the realisation of an investment rather than trading receipts. On appeal, *held*, LORD SCARMAN dissenting, the activities of the appellant clearly indicated an investment purpose. The initial intention was to create investments and not to proceed with an immediate sale after development. The Commissioner's reference to the group's original aim "to create investments for retention where possible, or where not possible for turning to account by way of trade" was inconsistent with the whole history of the group. Further, they had made no finding nor had any evidence of a trading intention at any stage of the transaction. It followed that the sale of the properties was not a sale in the course of trade, but a realisation of capital. The appeal would be allowed.

SIMMONS (AS LIQUIDATOR OF LIONEL SIMMONS PROPERTIES LTD) v INLAND REVENUE COMRS [1980] STC 350 (House of Lords: LORD WILBERFORCE, VISCOUNT DILHORNE, LORD SALMON, LORD SCARMAN and LORD ROSKILL). Decision of Court of Appeal [1979] STC 471, 1979 Halsbury's Abridgment para. 1575 reversed.

1597   —— —— **profit or gain arising or accruing from any property in the United Kingdom**

The taxpayer, who lived in Canada, was the wife of a man who had been convicted and sentenced for robbery, had escaped from prison and had been recaptured. After his recapture his wife made an agreement with an English newspaper to provide her life experiences for publication. In return she was to receive a sum of money to be paid in London. She was assessed to tax under Sch. D, Case VI on the basis that, under the Income and Corporation Taxes Act 1970, s. 108, the money amounted to a profit or gain arising or accruing from any property whatsoever in the United Kingdom. Her appeal against assessment was unsuccessful and on further appeal the question for the court was, inter alia, whether the profit derived from property in the United Kingdom. *Held*, the taxpayer had property in England, namely choses in action, the right to receive a sum of money from the English newspaper. She had no property in Canada as she had only the information that she gave to the newspaper reporter, and that was not a species of property known to English law. The appeal would accordingly be dismissed.

ALLOWAY V PHILLIPS (INSPECTOR OF TAXES) [1980] 3 All ER 138 (Court of Appeal: LORD DENNING MR, WALLER and DUNN LJJ). Decision of Brightman J [1979] STC 452, 1979 Halsbury's Abridgment para. 1565, affirmed.

1598 —— —— trade receipt—compensation for unremunerated work

The taxpayer was a diamond merchant broker whose client transferred to another broker before the taxpayer became entitled to any commission. The taxpayer received a payment from the competitor "in lieu of damages". His income tax was assessed on the basis that the payment was a trading receipt, and he appealed successfully against the assessment. The Crown appealed against the finding of the commissioners that the payment was ex gratia and not compensation for work done or loss of future profits. *Held*, taking into account the fact that the payment was conditional on the accrual to the competitor of the anticipated profits, on the evidence the payment was compensation for the taxpayer's unremunerated work or for loss of anticipated profits. The Crown's appeal would therefore be allowed.

ROLFE (INSPECTOR OF TAXES) v NAGEL [1980] STC 585 (Chancery Division: BROWNE-WILKINSON J). *London and Thames Haven Oil Wharves Ltd v Attwooll (Inspector of Taxes)* (1967) 43 Tax Cas 491 and *McGowan (Inspector of Taxes) v Brown and Cousins (trading as Stuart Edwards)* [1977] STC 342, 1977 Halsbury's Abridgment para. 1560, applied.

1599 —— stock relief—meaning of trading stock

See *Inland Revenue Comrs v Clydebridge Properties Ltd*, para. 1574.

1600 Schedule E—emoluments from office or employment—beneficial loans

The Income Tax (Official Rate of Interest on Beneficial Loans) Order 1980, S.I. 1980 No. 439 (in force on 6th May 1980), amends the Finance Act 1976, s. 66 (1) (b). Section 66 provides, inter alia, that where the interest paid on a beneficial loan for the year is less than the official rate of interest, then an amount equal to the cash equivalant of the benefit of the loan for that year is chargeable to tax. This order increases the official rate of interest from 9 per cent to 15 per cent.

1601 —— —— car benefits

The Income Tax (Cash Equivalents of Car Benefits) Order 1980, S.I. 1980 No. 889 (in force on 6th April 1981), prescribes new cash equivalents on which directors and higher paid employees are chargeable to income tax under the Finance Act 1976, s. 64 in respect of the benefit of a car made available for private use due to their employment. Higher paid employees are those earning at least £8,500 a year. The 1980 Order replaces the Income Tax (Cash Equivalents of Car Benefits) Order 1978, 1978 Halsbury's Abridgment para. 1561.

1602 —— —— meaning of "office"

At the request of the Department of the Environment, the taxpayer, a chartered civil engineer, acted from time to time as an inspector to conduct independent public inquiries and to make reports thereon. He was remunerated for those services by fees on a daily basis. In an appeal against an assessment to tax under Schedule E, the question for the court was whether the fees were an emolument of an "office" under the Income and Corporation Taxes Act 1970, s. 18. *Held*, "office" could be described as a post, not necessarily of a permanent, prolonged or indefinite nature, which had an existence independent of the person occupying it and which was not limited to the tenure of one person. The taxpayer thus did not hold any office in respect of any of the public inquiries he had been appointed to conduct, as each appointment was personal to the taxpayer and effective only for the purpose of the particular inquiry to which it related. Each appointment thus lacked the essential characteristics of independent existence and continuance necessary to an "office". The fees would therefore be assessed under Schedule D.

EDWARDS (INSPECTOR OF TAXES) v CLINCH [1980] STC 438 (Court of Appeal: BUCKLEY, ACKNER and OLIVER LJJ). Dictum of Rowlatt J in *Great Western Railway Co v Bater (Surveyor of Taxes)* (1920) 8 Tax Cas at 253 applied. Decision of Walton J [1979] 1 All ER 648, 1978 Halsbury's Abridgment para. 1613 reversed.

1603   **—— exemption from tax—lump sum retirement benefits—standard capital superannuation benefit**

The "old code" legislation governing tax approval of retirement benefit schemes is to be repealed with effect from 6th April 1980; thus lump sums paid after 5th April 1980 from schemes which are "closed" or "frozen" and which have not sought approval under the new code in the Finance Act 1970 will no longer in law be exempt from tax under Schedule E. For the same reason lump sums received or receivable from schemes of this type will cease, on 6th April 1980, to be deductible when calculating the Standard Capital Superannuation Benefit (SCSB) relief, for the purpose of tax charged on terminal payments under the Income and Corporation Taxes Act 1970, s. 187. However it is proposed to continue, by extra statutory concession, these exemptions after 6th April 1980, subject to the following condition.

Where terminal payments are made to employees within s. 187, SCSB relief may be available as an alternative to the current £10,000 exemption limit, where this is to the recipient's advantage. This is intended to enable an individual with little or no benefit from a pension scheme to receive as large a lump sum tax free as could be obtained from an approved scheme. It is for this reason that the SCSB relief is abated by the amount of tax free lump sum actually received or receivable from approved retirement benefit schemes. It would not be reasonable to allow lump sums to be received tax free by concession if they are not to be taken into account in calculating the SCSB relief. This concession will therefore be conditional on the individual concerned giving up his right to receive unabated SCSB relief to which he may become entitled: Inland Revenue Press Release dated 15th January 1980.

1604   **—— income arising from scholarship—exemption**

A trust was set up by a company to provide scholarships for children of employees. The Revenue claimed that the directors and higher-paid employees were liable to be taxed under the Finance Act 1976, s. 61, arguing that the Income and Corporation Taxes Act 1970, s. 375, which provided an exemption from tax on income arising from a scholarship, did not apply, distinguishing between the "income" received by the scholarship holder, and the "cash equivalent" which was taxable as an emolument of the parent employee. *Held*, the awards were "income arising from a scholarship" and, considering the purpose of the statute, Parliament could not have intended to nullify the unqualified exemption in s. 375 by introducing a scheme of assessing notional sums. Accordingly, the employees were not liable to tax under Schedule E.

WICKS v FIRTH (INSPECTOR OF TAXES) [1981] STC 28 (Chancery Division: GOULDING J).

1605   **—— payments on retirement from office or employment**

The taxpayer retired in 1976 when he was sixty-two, after twenty-four years' service. Under the terms of his company pension scheme, the trustees of the scheme could amend its terms with the company's consent. The scheme was amended in 1972 and on retirement the taxpayer became entitled to a permanent life pension and a temporary pension payable until he reached sixty-five. Payments by way of temporary pension were made after deduction of tax under the Income and Corporation Taxes Act 1970, s. 181, Schedule E. The taxpayer unsuccessfully contended that the payments were not taxable as pension payments since they were not made under an approved pension scheme to which he had agreed. On appeal, *held*, in view of the amendment provision in the pension scheme, changes to the scheme were binding on all persons beneficially interested under the trust, even though made after they joined the company. On the basis of the General Commissioners' original findings of fact, which were not open to question by the court, the payments were at all times treated as pension payments. As they were pension payments, they were taxable. The appeal would be dismissed.

ESSLEMONT v ESTILL (INSPECTOR OF TAXES) [1980] STC 620 (Court of Appeal: BUCKLEY, BRIDGE and CUMMING-BRUCE LJJ). Decision of Oliver J [1979] STC 624, 1979 Halsbury's Abridgment para. 1570 affirmed.

1606   Schedule F—excess interest as distribution—limit

The Income Tax (Excess Interest As Distributions) Order 1980, S.I. 1980 No. 114 (in force on 31st January 1980), amends the Finance Act 1974, s. 35 (1). It increases from 12 per cent to 17 per cent per annum the limit provided by the Income and Corporation Taxes Act 1970, s. 285 above which interest paid by close companies to directors and directors' associates is to be a distribution chargeable to Schedule F income tax by the 1970 Act, s. 232.

1607   Small maintenance payments—increase of limits

The Income Tax (Small Maintenance Payments) Order 1980, S.I. 1980 No. 951 (in force on 1st September 1980), amends the Income and Corporation Taxes Act 1970, s. 65 (1), by increasing the limit for small maintenance payments from which income tax is not to be deducted at source. The limits for payments for the maintenance of a party to a broken marriage are now £33 weekly or £91 monthly. The limits for payments for the benefit, maintenance or education of a person under twenty-one are now £18 weekly or £78 monthly. The order applies to all payments under orders made after 31st August 1980, to payments under orders varied or revived after that date which fall due after the variation or revival and to payments falling due after 5th August 1981 under orders in force at 31st August 1980.

INDUSTRIAL AND PROVIDENT SOCIETIES

Halsbury's Laws of England (4th edn.), Vol. 24, paras. 1–200

1608   Credit unions—authorised banks—termination of powers of chief registrar

The Credit Unions (Authorised Banks) (Termination of Powers of Chief Registrar) Order 1980, S.I. 1980 No. 736 (in force on 21st May 1980), terminates the powers of the chief registrar of friendly societies to designate as an authorised bank for the purposes of the Credit Unions Act 1979 any body corporate or partnership carrying on the business of banking, or to vary or revoke the order by which such designation was made.

1609   —— restrictions on registration—exemption from insurance requirements

The Credit Unions (Insurance against Fraud etc.) Regulations 1980 prescribe exceptions to the cover which a policy of insurance against fraud or other dishonesty of the officers or employees of a credit union must provide in order to comply with the compulsory insurance requirements of the Credit Unions Act 1979, s. 15, and substitute a scale of the minimum amount of such cover by reference to the aggregate value of share subscriptions and other deposits received and not repaid by a credit union, in place of the fixed amounts stated in that section. The regulations (which are not published as a statutory instrument) came into force on 1st October 1980 and are obtainable from HMSO.

1610 Credit Unions Act 1979—commencement

The Credit Unions Act 1979 (Commencement No. 2) Order 1980, S.I. 1980 No. 481 brings into force on 1st October 1980 s. 15 of the Act which contains provisions as to insurance against fraud or other dishonesty.

1611 Fees—credit unions

The Industrial and Provident Societies (Credit Unions) (Amendment of Fees) Regulations 1980, S.I. 1980 No. 1752 (in force on 1st January 1981), increase the fees payable in connection with matters to be transacted and for the inspection of documents under the Industrial and Provident Societies Act 1965 and 1967 and the Credit Unions Act 1979. The regulations apply only in relation to societies registered as credit unions under the Industrial and Provident Societies Act 1965.

1612 —— industrial and provident societies

The Industrial and Provident Societies (Amendment of Fees) Regulations 1980, S.I. 1980 No. 1751 (in force on 1st January 1981), increase the fees to be paid for matters to be transacted and for the inspection of documents under the Industrial and Provident Societies Acts 1965 and 1967. They supersede the 1979 Regulations 1979 Halsbury's Abridgment para. 1580 and amend the regulations of 1965 and 1967.

INDUSTRIAL ASSURANCE

Halsbury's Laws of England (4th edn.), Vol. 24, paras. 201–400

1613 Accounts and statements—prescribed forms

The Industrial Assurance Companies (Accounts and Statements) Regulations 1980, S.I. 1980 No. 1820 (in force on 1st January 1981), replace the Industrial Assurance (Companies Forms, etc.) Regulations 1968. They prescribe the forms of revenue account, abstract of actuary's report and statements of business to be prepared by insurance companies in respect of their industrial assurance business.

1614 Insurance Companies Act 1980

See para. 1647.

1615 Tax relief on premiums—retention by premium payer—change of rate

See para. 1584.

INJUNCTIONS

Halsbury's Laws of England (4th edn.), Vol. 24, paras. 901–1200

1616 Articles

The Mareva Injunction: Preserving the Fruits of Success, E W H Christie: 1 BLR 155.

The "Mareva" injunction—Recent developments, Frank Meisel: [1980] LMCLQ 38.

1617   **Anton Piller order**

See PRACTICE AND PROCEDURE.

1618   **Domestic violence**

See HUSBAND AND WIFE.

1619   **Interlocutory injunction—balance of convenience—likelihood of damage to both parties**

See *Athlete's Foot Marketing Associates Inc v Cobra Sports Ltd*, para. 2927.

1620   —— **injunction to restrain action in furtherance of a trade dispute**

See TRADE UNIONS.

1621   —— **injunction to restrain infringement of copyright—grounds for refusal**

See *Who Group Ltd v Stage One (Records) Ltd*, para. 504.

1622   —— **order made with consent of defendant—effect of subsequent change in the law**

The plaintiff company, which was the registered proprietor of a trade mark, obtained a consent order restraining the defendants from dealing with the infringing goods. The defendants sought to have this order set aside in the light of a change in the law resulting from a subsequent decision. *Held*, a subsequent change in the law was an insufficient reason to upset a consent order where there was no allegation of fraud or mistake. Even if such a change was a sufficient reason there was insufficient evidence on the facts to show that the recent decision completely covered the present case.

CHANEL LTD v F. W. WOOLWORTH (1980) Times, 28th October (Chancery Division: FOSTER J).

Leave to appeal from this discision has been refused by the Court of Appeal; see [1981] 1 All ER 745.

1623   **Mandatory injunction—injunction requiring owners of ship to issue bill of lading**

See *The Anwar Al Sabar, Gulf Steel Co Ltd v Al Khalifa Shipping Co Ltd*, para. 2597.

1624   **Mareva injunction—circumstances in which injunction may be granted**

The plaintiff was the owner of cargo on a vessel owned by the defendant, a Greek company, which sank while on a time charter resulting in the complete loss of cargo. The plaintiff successfully applied, ex parte, for a Mareva injunction preventing the defendant from disposing of the proceeds of an insurance policy and the defendant applied for it to be set aside. *Held*, the plaintiff had not produced sufficient evidence of agency to show that he was, as undisclosed principal, the charterer of the vessel. Further, he had failed to advance an arguable case on its merits in view of the defendant's cogent evidence showing lack of personal fault. It would be unjust to expose foreign shipowners to having their assets frozen merely on the prima facie evidence of loss of cargo. Such use of the Mareva injunction would imperil its continued existence.

The court also stated that, on the basis of the judgment in the *Angel Bell*, the defendant would be allowed to repay a bank overdraft, an obligation which had arisen in the ordinary course of business, even though the transaction might not ultimately be enforceable.

BAKARIM v VICTORIA P, SHIPPING CO LTD, THE TATIANGELA [1980] 2 Lloyd's Rep 193 (Queen's Bench Division: PARKER J). *Iraqi Ministry of Defence v Arcepey Shipping Co SA (Gillespie Brothers and Co Ltd intervening), The Angel Bell* [1980] 1 All ER 480, para. 1630 followed.

1625   —— **defendant an English national domiciled in England—jurisdiction to grant injunction**

The plaintiff transferred a flat to the defendant on the terms that he would renovate it to a certain value and pay to the plaintiff £2,000. The defendant failed to pay the sum and it subsequently emerged that the flat had been purchased by a third party and the defendant had gone abroad. The plaintiff applied for a Mareva injunction to prevent the defendant from dealing with the proceeds of sale otherwise than by paying them into a bank account within the jurisdiction and keeping them separate from other moneys. It was contended that a Mareva injunction could not be granted against an English national domiciled in England. *Held,* since the essence of a Mareva injunction was the risk that assets would be removed from the jurisdiction or disposed of within the jurisdiction, there was no reason why it should be confined to a foreigner or a foreign based defendant. However, it was essential that there should be a real risk of assets being removed from the jurisdiction which would result in stultifying any judgment that the plaintiff might obtain. The defendant's nationality, domicile and place of residence were relevant in determining whether there was such a risk. Further, a plaintiff was required to show that there would be a danger of default if assets were removed from the jurisdiction and that the balance of convenience would be in favour of granting an injunction. In the present case, the injunction would be continued since it was not known whether the defendant would return to the jurisdiction, although it was open to him to apply to vary or discharge it.

BARCLAY-JOHNSON v YUILL [1980] 3 All ER 190 (Chancery Division: SIR ROBERT MEGARRY V-C). *Third Chandris Shipping Corpn v Unimarine SA* [1979] 2 All ER 972, 1979 Halsbury's Abridgment para. 1594, and *Chartered Bank v Daklouche* [1980] 1 All ER 205, para. 1627, applied. *The Agrabele* [1979] 2 Lloyd's Rep 117, 1979 Halsbury's Abridgment para. 1597, not followed.

1626   The Court of Appeal has affirmed the principle in *Barclay-Johnson v Yuill* [1980] 3 All ER 190, para. 1625, that Mareva injunction relief is not confined to foreign based defendants.

The court granted a Mareva injunction against the defendants, partners in a London firm, in respect of a claim by the plaintiff for £34,000. The defendants had maintained that they were resident in England, although they had not given their home addresses, and the court was apprehensive that they would remove their assets from the jurisdiction.

PRINCE ABDUL RAHMAN BIN TURKI AL SUDAIRY v ABU-TAHA [1980] 3 All ER 409 (Court of Appeal: LORD DENNING MR, WALLER and DUNN LJJ).

1627   —— **defendant within jurisdiction—circumstances in which court will grant injunction**

The husband and wife were Lebanese citizens in business in the Persian Gulf. Due to financial difficulties, the husband's firm's account with the plaintiff bank became heavily overdrawn. When several outstanding trade debts had been paid, the husband deposited them in his personal account and later gave the cash to his wife. She transferred the money to accounts in her name in London and later came to England. The bank brought an action against the husband and wife claiming damages for fraud and conspiracy and applied for a Mareva injunction restraining the husband and wife from disposing of the money in England. An injunction was granted, but on the wife's application it was discharged. On appeal by the bank, *held,* an English court had jurisdiction to grant a Mareva injunction against both the husband and the wife. With regard to the husband, since fraud and conspiracy were pleaded against him, there was a cause of action which was justiciable in England and a writ could be served on him outside the jurisdiction under RSC Ord. 11. With regard to the wife, although she was at present within the jurisdiction and could be served accordingly, she was likely to leave at short notice. Accordingly, both the husband and the wife came within the ambit of a Mareva injunction. The appeal would be allowed, and the injunction restored.

THE CHARTERED BANK v DAKLOUCHE [1980] 1 All ER 205 (Court of Appeal: LORD DENNING MR, EVELEIGH LJ and SIR STANLEY REES). *The Siskina* [1977] 3 All ER 803, HL, 1977 Halsbury's Abridgment para. 1579 distinguished.

1628   —— **discovery in aid of injunction**

See *A v C*, para. 890.

1629   —— **personal injuries claim—effect of inability to give cross-undertaking in damages**

The plaintiffs were granted a Mareva injunction to prevent an aircraft from being removed from the jurisdiction. The plaintiffs were the widow, children and executors of a man killed when hit by the propeller of a light aircraft which, at the time of the accident, was in England for servicing. The plaintiffs anticipated making a fatal accident claim against the pilot and the Nigerian company who employed him, and obtained the injunction when they realised that the Nigerian company had no other assets in England. On appeal against a judge's decision to discharge the injunction, the questions for the court were whether (i) a Mareva injunction could be granted in respect of a personal injury action and, (ii) the injunction should be refused because the widow was legally aided and could not therefore give a satisfactory undertaking as to damages if their anticipated action failed. *Held*, (i) there was no difference in principle between commercial activities and personal injury or other causes of action in relation to the issue of a Mareva injunction. (ii) A legally-aided plaintiff was not to be in any worse position by reason of being legally-aided than any other person would be. The issue of an injunction depended upon the balance of justice and convenience. On the facts of the case, the appeal would be allowed and the injunction would be restored.

ALLEN v JAMBO HOLDINGS LTD [1980] 2 All ER 502 (Court of Appeal: LORD DENNING MR, SHAW and TEMPLEMAN LJJ).

1630   —— **variation—circumstances in which court will grant variation**

The plaintiffs were owners of cargo on a vessel owned by the defendants, a Panamanian company. The vessel sank resulting in a complete loss of cargo and the plaintiffs commenced proceedings against the defendants claiming substantial damages in respect of the lost cargo. Although the defendants had no assets within the jurisdiction, they were expecting to recover the proceeds of an insurance policy on the vessel. The plaintiffs obtained a Mareva injunction restraining the defendants from disposing of the anticipated proceeds of the policy. Subsequently, a third party was given leave to intervene in the action. They claimed that they had lent money to the defendants for the purpose of buying the ship, and that they had executed documents whereby they had been given a mortgage over the vessel and had been assigned an insurance policy in respect of the vessel. In an action between the plaintiffs and the interveners on the issue, judgment was given for the interveners and they then applied to the court for an order varying the injunction so that the loan could be repaid out of the insurance moneys. *Held*, the purpose of a Mareva injunction was to prevent foreign parties from removing assets from the jurisdiction. However, this did not preclude a variation to the injunction if the court was satisfied that the assets were required for a purpose which did not conflict with the policy underlying the Mareva jurisdiction. The plaintiffs were not to be given the status of a judgment creditor before judgment had been given. Further, there was no reason why the defendants should not be allowed to repay the loan owed to the interveners which had arisen in the ordinary course of business, since they were not seeking to avoid their responsibilities to the plaintiff should they ultimately obtain judgment. Accordingly, the Mareva injunction granted would be qualified.

IRAQI MINISTRY OF DEFENCE v ARCEPEY SHIPPING CO SA (GILLESPIE BROTHERS AND CO LTD intervening), THE ANGEL BELL [1980] 1 All ER 480 (Queen's Bench Division: ROBERT GOFF J). *Cretanor Maritime Co Ltd v Irish Marine Management Ltd, The Cretan Harmony* [1978] 3 All ER 164, CA, 1978 Halsbury's Abridgment para. 1637 applied.

1631   Nuisance—continuing nuisance—public interest—whether injunction appropriate

In a case where the owner of a house was refused an injunction but granted considerable damages under the Chancery Amendment Act 1858, for the nuisance caused by the noise of the activities of a motor boat club, the owner appealed, seeking an injunction restraining the club from such activities. *Held*, the provisions of the Chancery Amendment Act 1858 conferred on the courts a jurisdiction to award damages instead of an injunction but this had not altered the settled principles upon which the Court of Equity interfered by way of injunction. In cases of continuing actionable nuisance the jurisdiction so conferred was to be exercised only in very special circumstances. Public interest did not prevail over private interest in considering the question of damages or an injunction and the court was bound by the principles enunciated in *Shelfer v City of London Lighting Co* [1895] 1 Ch 287 indicating the circumstances in which such damages would be awarded. In the present case by awarding the owner damages his legal rights had been severely curtailed. It followed that the appeal would be allowed and an injunction restraining the club from any of their activities causing a nuisance would be granted.

KENNAWAY v THOMPSON [1980] 3 All ER 329 (Court of Appeal: LAWTON and WALLER LJJ and SIR DAVID CAIRNS). *Shelfer v City of London Electric Lighting Co* [1895] 1 Ch 287, CA, followed.

1632   Restraint of legal proceedings—continuation of legal proceedings abroad

See *Castanho v Brown & Root (UK) Ltd*, para. 2206.

1633   Trespass to land—injunction to restrain—prohibitory and mandatory injunctions

See *John Trenberth Ltd v National Westminster Bank Ltd*, para. 2988.

INSURANCE

Halsbury's Laws of England (4th edn.), Vol. 25, paras. 1–1000

1634   Article

Reinstatement or Market Value, J. W. Williams (level of indemnity following total destruction of property): 1 Business Law Review 41.

1635   Accident insurance—accidental death—death from respiratory failure after excessive drinking

Canada

The insured, who had been drinking heavily, died from respiratory failure after losing consciousness in a position in which her breathing was impeded. A claim was made under a policy which provided for payment upon the death of the insured as a result of an injury caused by an accident. *Held*, the insured's death was accidental. An unintended result was accidental even though it resulted from deliberate acts unless it was known or should have been known that those acts were likely to cause the result.

CNA Assurance Co v MacIsaac (1979) 102 DLR (3d) 160 (Supreme Court of Nova Scotia, Appeal Division).

1636 ——— exception for loss caused while insured intoxicated—whether necessary that intoxication is the cause of the loss

Canada

An exclusion clause in an accident insurance policy excluded "death caused directly or indirectly wholly or in part while the insured was under the influence of intoxicants". The insured was killed in a road accident whilst intoxicated. It was established that the other driver was wholly at fault and that there was no causal connection between the insured's condition and the accident. On the question of whether the insurer's liability was excluded by the clause, *held*, the proper interpretation of "caused" was "effected" or "brought about". Thus the condition of being "under the influence" had to be causally connected with the accident. In any case the language used was ambiguous and thus had to be construed as against the insurer, who was therefore liable under the policy.

Astro Tire and Rubber Co of Canada Ltd v Western Assurance Co (1979) 97 DLR (3d) 515 (Court of Appeal of Ontario).

1637 Fidelity insurance—fraudulent dealings by company directors—liability of insurer

Canada

In a case where a company was insured against any loss caused by dishonest acts of its employees it was held that the insurance company was not liable to the company for any fraudulent action implemented by the directors. Such an insurance policy was intended to protect the company from the dishonesty of its employees and not to protect the company's creditors from the dishonesty of its directors.

Clarkson Co Ltd v Canadian Indemnity Co (1979) 25 OR (2d) 281 (High Court of Ontario).

1638 Fire insurance—assignee of mortgagor insuring premises—entitlement of mortgagee to proceeds of insurance

Canada

A mortgagor's assignee insured the mortgage property for the whole value rather than the value of his own limited interest. The property was destroyed and the mortgagor foreclosed the mortgage. The insurance proceeds were paid to the assignee of the mortgagor's interest. The mortgagee claimed a proportion of the proceeds. *Held*, where an insurance policy disclosed the intention of the holder of a limited interest to insure more than that limited interest, the insured was entitled to recover the entire value. However, the amount exceeding the insured's actual loss was held by him on trust for the holders of other interests in the insured property. The mortgagee was accordingly entitled to a proportion of the proceeds.

Battersby v Lenhoco Enterprises Ltd (1980) 109 DLR (3d) 330 (Court of Appeal of Saskatchewan).

1639 ——— excepted perils—property looted and damaged due to rioting—liability of insurers

The plaintiffs owned businesses in Beirut, Lebanon. They insured their property with the defendants by means of standard fire insurance policies, which were subject to a special condition clause. The clause provided that the insurance did not cover any loss or damage suffered in consequence of civil war, revolution, military or usurped power, or any act of any person acting in connection with an organisation acting against the Government. During political unrest in the city, the plaintiffs' premises were damaged causing them financial loss which they sought to recover from the defendants. The defendants claimed that although prima facie the losses fell within the cover conferred by the policy, they were relieved from liability by one or more of the exceptions. *Held*, the exception would be construed in the narrower sense in that it related to the acts of members of terrorist organisations in furtherance of their organisations' aims. The words formed part of the description of the organisation and were not descriptive of the acts which constituted the excepted perils. Accordingly the defendants were covered by the exceptions and the plaintiffs' claims under all the policies would fail.

SPINNEY'S (1948) LTD v ROYAL INSURANCE CO LTD [1980] 1 Lloyd's Rep 406 (Queen's Bench Division: MUSTILL J). *Curtis & Sons v Mathews* [1919] 2 KB 825, *Drinkwater v The Corporation of The London Assurance* (1770) 2 Wils 363 and *Rogers v Whittaker* [1917] 1 KB 942 considered.

1640   —— imminent peril—loss caused by steps taken to avert risk

Canada
Damage was caused at a manufacturing plant as the result of water being poured onto an overheated pressure tank, in an effort to cool it down, and the consequent rupture of the tank. The manufacturers claimed under an insurance policy which covered damage caused by fire or explosion. The judge dismissed the claim, finding that no explosion had occurred. The manufacturers appealed. *Held*, the word "explosion" was to be given its ordinary meaning so as to include an eruption without a chemical reaction, and on the facts there had been an explosion. Even if there had been no explosion, the damage had been caused by steps taken in an emergency to avoid the insured risk and the loss would have been recoverable.

CANADIAN GENERAL ELECTRIC CO LTD v LIVERPOOL AND LONDON AND GLOBE INSURANCE CO LTD (1980) 106 DLR (3d) 750 (Court of Appeal of Ontario).

1641   —— lessor covenanting with lessee to insure premises—fire caused by lessee's negligence—liability of lessee

Canada
The Supreme Court of Nova Scotia has held, that where a lessor has covenanted, with the lessee, to insure the leased premises against fire, he is precluded from asserting a claim for loss by fire against the lessee or against his individual employees, notwithstanding that the fire was caused by the negligence of the lessee's employees.

GREENWOOD SHOPPING PLAZA LTD v NEIL J. BUCHANAN LTD (1979) 99 DLR (3d) 289 (Supreme Court of Nova Scotia).

1642   —— wilful act of insured—liability of insurer

Canada
Under a fire insurance policy the term "insured" extended to the relatives of the named insured living with him in the same house. The policy did not cover damage caused by a criminal or wilful act or omission by the insured. The son of the named insured set fire to the house causing severe damage to the property. The insurance company denied liability on the ground that the loss occurred as a result of a wilful act of the insured within the meaning of the exemption clause. *Held*, where there was more than one person insured under a policy, the insured whose wilful act was referred to in the exemption clause meant the person making the claim. Accordingly, in the present case, the exemption clause did not apply and the insurance company was liable.

RANKIN v NORTH WATERLOO FARMERS MUTUAL INSURANCE CO (1979) 25 OR (2d) 102 (Court of Appeal of Ontario).

1643   General business—transfer between insurers

The Insurance (Transfer of General Business) Regulations 1980, S.I. 1980 No. 956 (in force on 1st September 1980), implement Council Directive (EEC) 73/239, art. 21. They enable an insurer with the approval of the Secretary of State to transfer to another insurer all or some of its portfolio of policies relating to non-life business. In the case of Lloyds, the regulations apply to transactions between members and non-members but not to internal transactions among members.

1644   **Indemnity—double insurance—exclusion clause—contribution**

The plaintiffs insured a firm of solicitors against any claim for damages made against them during the period of the insurance in the conduct of the business. The policy provided that written notice should be given of any occurrence which might subsequently give rise to a claim against them; such notice having been given, any subsequent claim should be deemed to have been made during the subsistence of the policy. The policy also contained a clause excluding the plaintiffs' liability to indemnify the solicitors if they were already entitled to indemnity under any other policy. On 24th March, the day that the policy expired, the solicitors gave written notice of an occurrence which might give rise to a claim against them in the future. On 30th April, the defendant issued a certificate referring to a policy (the master policy) by which the solicitors were insured against all loss arising from any claims made against them from midnight on 24th March. The master policy provided that the solicitors should not be indemnified in respect of any loss arising out of an occurrence which had already been notified under any other prior insurance. The plaintiffs claimed that this was a case of double insurance and that they were entitled to a contribution from the defendant. *Held*, the two clauses were clearly distinguishable from each other and on their true construction the solicitors were covered by the first mentioned policy and not by the master policy. The claim made was deemed to have been made before midnight on 24th March and before the solicitors were insured by the master policy. The plaintiffs' claim to contribution would fail.

NATIONAL EMPLOYERS MUTUAL GENERAL INSURANCE ASSOCIATION LTD v HAYDON [1980] 2 Lloyd's Rep 149 (Court of Appeal: STEPHENSON, BRIDGE and TEMPLEMAN LJJ). Decision of Lloyd J [1979] 2 Lloyd's Rep 235, 1979 Halsbury's Abridgment para. 1610 reversed.

1645   **Insurance Brokers (Registration) Act 1977—commencement**

The Insurance Brokers (Registration) Act 1977 (Commencement No. 3) Order 1980, S.I. 1980 No. 1824, brings into force, on 1st December 1981, those provisions of the Act not yet in force, i.e. ss. 22–24.

1646   **Insurance Brokers Registration Council—election scheme**

The Insurance Brokers Registration Council Election Scheme Approval Order 1980, S.I. 1980 No, 62 (in force on 1st March 1980), approves an election scheme made in 1979 by the Insurance Brokers Registration Council, under the Insurance Brokers Registration Act 1977, 1977 Halsbury's Abridgment para. 1590. The scheme is set out in the schedule to the order.

1647   **Insurance Companies Act 1980**

The Insurance Companies Act 1980 extends the Insurance Companies Act 1974 to Northern Ireland and amends that Act with respect to the functions of the Industrial Assurance Commissioner. The Act received the royal assent on 1st May 1980 and came into force on 1st June 1980: S.I. 1980 No. 678.

Section 1 extends the 1974 Act as amended, to Northern Ireland. Section 2 and Sch. 1 provide for amendments of that Act. Schedule 1, Pt. I contains the amendments that are directly consequential on the extension of the Act. The majority of these are attributable to the continued existence of a separate system of company law in Northern Ireland. Schedule 1, Pt. II contains the amendments needed to provide for new unified arrangements for making and depositing returns about industrial assurance business.

Section 3 and Sch. 2 extend relevant statutory instruments to Northern Ireland with modifications. The extended instruments are listed in Sch. 2, Pt. I, and Pt. II contains the modifications. Special provision is made for the Insurance Companies (Deposits) Regulations 1978 which were made under Acts applying only in Great Britain. The relevant enabling powers in the parent Acts are therefore extended.

Section 4 and Schs. 3–6 deal with consequential amendments, transitional provisions and repeals and s. 5 provides that the Act is to extend to Northern Ireland.

1648   Insurance companies—accounts and statements

The Insurance Companies (Accounts and Statements) Regulations 1980, S.I. 1980 No. 6 (in force on 1st January 1981), prescribe the form and content of company accounts made under the Insurance Companies Act 1974, s. 13 (1). Provision is made for certain information to be noted on the accounts or annexed to the accounts in a statement or report and for certificates to be given by certain persons. The Regulations make provision as to audit and prescribe the form and contents of any statement of ordinary long term business prepared by the company under s. 14 (3) of the Act, any abstract of an actuary's report made under s. 14 of the Act and the form and contents of the annual statement of prescribed general business prepared by company under s. 16 of the Act. For an actuary to be appointed to a company under s. 15 of the Act he must possess certain prescribed qualifications.

The Insurance Companies (Accounts and Forms) Regulations 1968, as amended, are revoked.

1649   —— valuation of assets

The Insurance Companies (Valuation of Assets) (Amendment) Regulations 1980, S.I. 1980 No. 5 (in force on 15th February 1980), enable insurance companies to elect subject to certain conditions, for the purposes of actuarial investigations under the Insurance Companies Act 1974, ss. 14, 34, to use the book value of their assets instead of the value determined in accordance with the Insurance Companies (Valuation of Assets) Regulations 1976, 1976 Halsbury's Abridgment para. 1504.

1650   Insurance policy—mistake as to name—correction

See *Nittan (UK) Ltd v Solent Steel Fabrications*, para. 1992.

1651   Marine insurance—Inchmaree clause—latent defect in hull

The owners of a vessel brought a claim under their insurance policy, maintaining that the sinking of the vessel was caused by a latent defect in the hull. The policy contained an Inchmaree clause, which provided that the policy covered loss or damage to the vessel directly caused by any latent defect in the hull, but that should the vessel's class be changed, cancelled or withdrawn then the policy would automatically terminate. The underwriters contended that the defect in the hull was caused by either ordinary wear and tear or by defect in design, both of which, they claimed, were uninsured perils. They also contended that the vessel had lost its class, due to its having been grounded a few days before the sinking. The vessel was classed with Bureau Veritas, whose rules provided that in the event of grounding the classification certificate would lose its validity and arrangements should be made for surveying the vessel as soon as possible. *Held*, the vessel had not lost its class. Although the grounding had resulted in the vessel's classification certificate losing its validity until such time as the vessel was surveyed again, this was not tantamount to the vessel losing its class, but meant that there was a possibility of the vessel losing its class should the requirements for surveying not be complied with. The defect in the hull was a latent defect and was covered by the Inchmaree clause. The sinking had occurred long before the end of the vessel's normal life and could not be said therefore to be the result of normal wear and tear. Recovery for defective design was not precluded by the Inchmaree clause and the fracture which had opened up in the hull and caused the vessel to sink, was the result of the defective design of part of the hull. The owners' claim would therefore succeed.

THE CARIBBEAN SEA, PRUDENT TANKERS LTD SA v THE DOMINION INSURANCE CO LTD [1980] 1 Lloyd's Rep 338 (Queen's Bench Division: ROBERT GOFF J).

1652   —— losses for which insurers liable—perils of the seas

Australia

A ship sank in relatively calm waters. The owners claimed under an insurance policy which insured the ship, inter alia, against "perils of the seas". The insurance company contended that the loss of the ship was due to its unseaworthiness, or, alternatively negligence on the part of the ship's crew. The company appealed against an adverse decision of the Supreme Court of South Australia on the ground that the court had failed to recognise that the onus of proving seaworthiness lay on the owners. *Held*, (i) under the Australian equivalent to the Marine Insurance Act 1906, Sch. 1, r. 7 "perils of the seas" referred to fortuitous accidents or casualities of the seas. Losses caused by natural actions of the elements were not to be considered as fortuitous casualties as they could be foreseen. It was, however, no longer law that an extraordinary action alone constituted a fortuitous casualty. It was possible that if an accident causing damage occurred in a calm sea, the consequential loss was not attributable to the ordinary course of the elements. (ii) It was for the insured to prove that a loss was caused by "perils of the seas". The burden of proof was discharged when they gave evidence to the effect that a sinking had occurred as a result of a fortuitous event. The insured would only find it necessary to show a ship's seaworthiness in order to prove his case if there was no direct evidence of loss due to a fortuitous event and sought to establish, by inference, a case of loss due to an unascertained peril of the sea. (iii) Although the insurer, the company, had to show that the insured ship was unseaworthy, the insurer did not have to prove the question of unseaworthiness when it arose in relation to whether or not loss was caused by perils of the seas. There was no presumption of unseaworthiness unless, in the absence of any other evidence as to the condition of the ship or the cause of loss, the ship sank in calm waters soon after the policy was attached or the ship left port. In the present case the claim that the ship was unseaworthy was rejected and it was correct to infer that the loss was due to a peril of the sea even though the peril was unidentifiable. The appeal would be dismissed.

SKANDIA INSURANCE CO LTD v SKOLJAREV (1979) 26 ALR 1 (High Court of Australia). Dictum of Lord Halsbury LC in *Hamilton, Fraser & Co v Pandorf & Co* (1887) 12 App Cas 518 at 524–5 and of Scrutton LJ in *La Compania Martiartu v Royal Exchange Assurance Corporation* [1923] 1 KB 650 at 657 approved.

1653   Motor insurance—indemnity—accident resulting in personal injury—disclaimer of liability to indemnify

The plaintiff's car was insured by the defendants. The policy provided that if the defendants should disclaim their liability to indemnify the plaintiff, legal proceedings had to be instituted within twelve months of the disclaimer or the claim would be deemed to have been abandoned. In August 1970, the plaintiff was driving when his car was involved in a collision in which one of the plaintiff's passengers was severely injured. When the passenger claimed damages for her injuries, the defendants refused to meet the claim because the plaintiff was in breach of his policy conditions at the time of the accident. The plaintiff's solicitors wrote to the defendants questioning their decision. The defendants replied, in March 1971, that they were not prepared to reconsider their decision concerning indemnity. The passenger subsequently obtained judgment in default of appearance. In 1975, the plaintiff's solicitors re-opened correspondence with the defendants, having heard that damages in the passenger's action were to be assessed. In 1976, judgment was entered for a sum of damages for the passenger. The plaintiff claimed a declaration that he was entitled to be indemnified by the defendants. *Held*, the defendants, by their letter of March 1971, clearly disclaimed any liability to the plaintiff for any claim to an indemnity under the policy; they did not at any time repudiate the contract. The plaintiff's claim was made in 1971, as it was possible to have a claim for indemnity against a potential liability long in advance of any claim by a third party being agreed or determined. The defendants were entitled to disclaim liability in certain circumstances under the contract of insurance, and they had disclaimed liability more than twelve months before the plaintiff had instituted legal proceedings. Accordingly, the plaintiff's application for a declaration would be dismissed.

WALKER v PENNINE INSURANCE CO LTD [1980] 2 Lloyd's Rep 156 (Court of Appeal: ROSKILL and BRIGHTMAN LJJ and SIR DAVID CAIRNS). Decision of Sheen J [1979] 2 Lloyd's Rep 139, 1979 Halsbury's Abridgment para. 1625 affirmed.

1654 —— personal injury—insurer's obligation to pay for medical treatment—increase in medical charges

See para. 2021.

1655 —— —— limitation of insurer's liability

The plaintiff's son was severely injured in a motor accident in British Honduras and later died. The plaintiff, as the executor of his son's estate, brought an action in British Honduras against the driver responsible and recovered a consent judgment for $175,000 with interest and costs, but the driver was unable to pay. In a direct action in England against the driver's insurers, it was held that the insurers' liability was limited to $4,000, the monetary limit for compulsory third party insurance under an ordinance of British Honduras. The plaintiff appealed. *Held*, the wording of the ordinance was clear and unambiguous, and on its true construction the amount recoverable was limited to $4,000. The appeal would be discussed.

HARKER v CALEDONIAN INSURANCE CO (1980) Times, 4th March (House of Lords: LORD DIPLOCK, LORD EDMUND-DAVIES, LORD FRASER OF TULLYBELTON, LORD RUSSELL OF KILLOWEN and LORD KEITH OF KINKEL). Decision of the Court of Appeal [1979] 2 Lloyd's Rep 193, 1979 Halsbury's Abridgment para. 1626, affirmed.

1656 —— use of uninsured vehicle—meaning of "use"

See *Bennett v Richardson*, para. 2394; *Leathley v Tatton*, para. 2395.

1657 Non-disclosure of material fact—defence—further and better particulars

See *Butcher v Dowlen*, para. 2147.

1658 Professional indemnity insurance—solicitors—Law Society group scheme—validity

See *Swain v Law Society*, para. 2814.

INTOXICATING LIQUOR

Halsbury's Laws of England (4th edn.), Vol. 26, paras. 1–500

1659 Drunkenness—person found drunk in possession of a loaded air rifle—whether a "firearm"

See *Seamark v Prouse*, para. 1258.

1660 Licences—fees

The Licensing (Fees) (Variation) Order 1980, S.I. 1980 No. 1543 (in force on 1st January 1981), substitutes new fees for the various fees chargeable by justices clerks under the 1978 Order, 1978 Halsbury's Abridgment, para. 1676 in respect of matters arising under the Licensing Act 1964.

1661 Licensed Premises (Exclusion of Certain Persons) Act 1980

The Licensed Premises (Exclusion of Certain Persons) Act 1980 empowers the courts to make orders excluding certain categories of convicted persons from licensed premises. The Act received the royal assent on 30th June 1980 and came into force on that date.

Section 1 (1) provides that where a person is convicted of an offence committed on licensed premises, if the court is satisfied that he resorted to violence or offered or threatened to resort to violence, it may make an exclusion order prohibiting him from entering those premises or any other specified premises without the express consent of the licensee of the premises or his servant or agent. Section 1 (2) provides that an exclusion order may be made only in addition to any sentence which is imposed in respect of the offence or in addition to a probation order or an order discharging him absolutely or conditionally. Section 1 (3) provides that the order is effective for a period of not less than three months and not more than two years.

Section 2 provides that anyone who enters premises in breach of an exclusion order is liable on summary conviction to a fine not exceeding £200, or to imprisonment for a term not exceeding one month or both. When a person has been convicted, the court may terminate or vary the exclusion order if it thinks fit.

Section 3 provides that a licensee or his servant or agent may expel anyone from his premises who has entered or whom he reasonably suspects of having entered in breach of an exclusion order and may demand the help of a constable to expel anyone whom the constable reasonably suspects of having entered in breach of such an order. Section 4 contains definitions and supplemental provisions and s. 5 deals with short title, citation and extent.

1662　Licensing (Amendment) Act 1980

The Licensing (Amendment) Act 1980 amends the Licensing Act 1964 in relation to the grant of special hours certificates and the extension of existing on-licences to additional types of liquor. The Act received the royal assent on 17th July 1980 and came into force on that date, except for ss. 2, 3, which come into force on a day to be appointed.

Section 1 amends the Licensing Act 1964, s. 37 relating to the upgrading of on-licences. Section 2 amends the 1964 Act, s. 76 relating to permitted hours under special hours certificates. Section 3 adds a new s. 81A, imposing conditions restricting hours under special hours certificates, and s. 81B, concerning appeals against decisions relating to special hours certificates. Section 4 deals with the short title, commencement and extent of the Act.

1663　Licensing hours—exemptions—special order of exemption—special occasion—relevant factors

A Divisional Court of the Queen's Bench Division has confirmed the principles laid down in *Martin v Spalding* [1979] 2 All ER 1193, DC, 1979 Halsbury's Abridgment para. 1634 as to the approach licensing justices should take when considering applications for extensions of permitted hours under the Licensing Act 1964, s. 74 (4). The justices should ask themselves three questions: (i) whether the occasion is capable of being a special occasion; (ii) if so, whether it is in fact a special occasion in the locality in which the licensed premises are situated; (iii) whether, as a matter of discretion, the application should be granted. All three questions must be answered in the affirmative if the application is to be granted. The court also produced three guidelines for consideration in border-line cases: (i) the occasion could be special from the national or local point of view; (ii) the more frequently the occasion occurred the less it would be likely to be a special occasion; (iii) an occasion created by the licensee solely for the purposes of the licensed premises was unlikely to be capable of being a special occasion (this did not include a registered sports club which created sporting occasions which were celebrated by the club).

Thus, an application by the police for an order of certiorari to quash an order of the justices granting the extension of permitted hours on Bank Holiday weekends would be dismissed. There was nothing in the evidence to show that the justices had misdirected themselves and it was impossible for the court to say that the days in question were incapable of being special occasions.

R v CORWEN JJ, EX PARTE EDWARDS [1980] 1 All ER 1035 (Queen's Bench Division: LORD WIDGERY CJ, SHAW LJ, PARK, KILNER BROWN and WOOLF JJ).

1664　——renewal of licence—jurisdiction to impose new conditions

A hotel licensee applied to the licensing justices for renewal of his music and dancing licence. In accordance with a policy decision made by the justices to restrict the hours of music and dancing in the area, the licence was renewed but with terms restricting the hours of music and dancing to 1 a.m. He sought an order of certiorari to quash the renewal restricted to 1 a.m. and an order of mandamus requiring the justices to renew the original licence in its entirety. *Held*, the licensing justices were entitled to adopt a general policy regarding the granting of music and dancing licences in their area but each application for a licence had to be considered separately on its merits and whether in any particular case there were facts which took it out of the general policy. Further the provisions of the Public Health Acts Amendment Act 1890, s. 51 (2) and the Licensing Act 1964, s. 3 (2), dealing with the granting and renewal of such licences, made it clear that justices were not required automatically to renew the licence on the same terms. They could alter the terms of the licence and in particular restrict the permitted hours for music and dancing. The order sought would therefore be refused.

R v TORBAY LICENSING JJ, EX PARTE WHITE [1980] 2 All ER 25 (Queen's Bench Division: LORD WIDGERY CJ, EVELEIGH and WIEN JJ). *R v Torquay Licensing JJ, ex parte Brockman* [1951] 2 All ER 656 applied.

JUDGMENTS AND ORDERS

Halsbury's Laws of England (4th edn.), Vol. 26, paras. 501–587

1665   **Article**

Foreign Currency Judgments in Tort: An Illustration of the Wealth–Time Continuum, J. A. Knott: 43 MLR 19.

1666   **Declaratory judgment—jurisdiction—prosecution for unlawful lottery—civil proceedings**

See *Imperial Tobacco Ltd v A-G*, para. 258.

1667   **Drawing up—bespeaking orders—Chancery Division**

See para. 2190.

1668   **Finality of order—conditional order—jurisdiction of court to extend time for compliance**

In an action commenced by writ, the plaintiff issued a summons for directions and an order was made that the defendants comply with a request for further and better particulars of their defence and counterclaim within twenty-one days. The defendants failed to comply and the court extended time with a conditional order, so that in default the defence and counterclaim would be struck out and judgment entered for the plaintiff. The particulars were not served by the requested date, but were handed to the plaintiff's solicitor three days later. Meanwhile the defendants issued a summons asking for an order extending the time for service of the further and better particulars. The judge granted the extension order. On appeal the question for the court was whether a judge had jurisdiction, where a conditional order had been made and time allowed to run out, without that order being properly complied with, to grant a further extension of time. *Held*, a court had jurisdiction to extend the time where a conditional order had been made and not complied with. However the jurisdiction to extend the time was a power to be exercised cautiously and with due regard to the necessity of maintaining the principle that orders were to be complied with and not ignored. It was a matter of discretion for the Master or judge in chambers to decide whether the necessary relief should be granted. On the facts of the particular case the judge had been entitled to grant the relief sought and to exercise his discretion in the way he did. The appeal would therefore be dismissed.

SAMUEL v LINZI DRESSES LTD [1980] 1 All ER 803 (Court of Appeal: ROSKILL and LAWTON LJJ and SIR STANLEY REES). *Whistler v Hancock* (1878) 3 QBD 83 not followed; dictum of Lord Denning MR in *R v Bloomsbury and Marylebone County Court, ex parte Villerwest Ltd* [1976] 1 All ER 897 at 900, 1975 Halsbury's Abridgment para. 583 applied.

1669   Foreign judgments—reciprocal enforcement

See CONFLICT OF LAWS.

1670   Garnishee order—foreign currency in English bank account—enforceability of order against foreign currency

See *Choice Investments Ltd v Jeromnimon (Midland Bank Ltd), Garnishee*, para. 1237.

1671   Judgment debt—foreign currency in English bank account—whether foreign currency a debt

See *Choice Investments Ltd v Jeromnimon (Midland Bank Ltd), Garnishee*, para. 1237.

1672   —— interest—rate

The Judgment Debts (Rate of Interest) Order 1980, S.I. 1980 No. 672 (in force on 9th June 1980), increases to 15 per cent per annum the rate of interest on judgment debts under the Judgments Act 1836, s. 17.

1673   Judgment in default of appearance—plaintiff precluded from entering judgment due to nature of claim—court's power to grant plaintiff leave to enter judgment

By RSC Ord. 13, r. 6 where a writ is indorsed with a claim of a description not mentioned in rr. 1 to 4 of the order then, where the defendant enters no appearance, the plaintiff may not enter judgment in default of appearance, but may proceed with the action as if the defendant had entered an appearance. The plaintiff's writ was indorsed with a claim for a Mareva injunction to restrain the defendant from removing assets out of the jurisdiction. A claim for an injunction does not fall within rr. 1 to 4, thus the plaintiff could not proceed to judgment without abandoning the injunction, with the result that the defendant could defeat the purpose of Mareva proceedings by declining to enter an appearance. *Held*, the court had an inherent jurisdiction to control its own process, in particular to prevent any abuse of that process. The defendant's attempt to defeat the purpose of the Mareva injunction by declining to enter an appearance was such an abuse and leave would be granted to the plaintiff to enter judgment in default of appearance.

THE VENUS DESTINY, STEWART CHARTERING LTD v C & O MANAGEMENTS SA [1980] 1 All ER 718 (Queen's Bench Division: ROBERT GOFF J).

1674   Order to do an act—requirement for order to specify time after service or some other time within which act must be done—act to be done "within ten days"—validity of order

The plaintiff claimed a sum of money from the defendants and on 27th February 1979 both parties were ordered to serve a list of documents on the other "within fourteen days thereafter". The defendants failed to do so and at a hearing on 2nd November an order was made in their absence providing that unless they complied with the original order "within ten days" their defence would be struck out. The order was not served on the defendants' solicitors until 12th November and on 14th November judgment was entered for the plaintiff. The defendants contended that the order of 2nd November was invalid. *Held*, under RSC Ord. 42, r. 2 (1) an order requiring a person to do an act must specify the time after service of the order or "some other time" within which the act must be done. The requirements laid down by the RSC regarding the content of orders had to be strictly observed. Therefore, although Ord. 42, r. 3 provided that a court order took effect when made, an order simply requiring action "within ten days" did not specify "some other time" within the meaning of Ord. 42, r. 2 (1) and was invalid.

VAN HOUTEN V FOODSAFE LTD (1980) Times, 7th February (Court of Appeal: LORD DENNING MR, SHAW LJ and SIR DAVID CAIRNS).

1675 Precedent—decision on facts—whether elevated to principle of law

The plaintiff and defendant collided in a road accident. On a question of liability the trial judge reluctantly relied on *Clarke v Winchurch* [1969] 1 All ER 275, CA as laying down the principle that a driver who moved forward slowly was entitled to emerge blind from a minor road, and accordingly found against the plaintiff. On appeal, *held*, there was ample authority concerning the dangers of elevating decisions on the facts in particular cases into principles of law. The judge was not bound by *Clark v Winchurch*, which laid down no principle of law. As the judge had noted that, but for that decision, he would have apportioned the blame equally, the appeal would be allowed and judgment given for the plaintiff for half the agreed damages.

WORSFOLD V HOWE [1980] 1 All ER 1028 (Court of Appeal: MEGAW, BROWNE and DONALDSON LJJ).

1676 Summary judgment—time limit for counterclaim

See *CSI International Co Ltd v Archway Personnel (Middle East) Ltd.*, para. 2568.

JURIES

Halsbury's Laws of England (4th edn.), Vol. 26, paras. 601–700

1677 Jurors—allowances—financial loss, travelling and subsistence allowances—revised rates

The Lord Chancellor has announced that the following rates are payable to jurors in the High Court, the Crown Court or a county court in respect of financial loss, travelling and subsistence allowances (with effect from 21st January 1980).

Financial loss allowance. Where the period over which earnings or benefit are lost or additional expense is incurred is not more than four hours—£7.00. Where that period exceeds four hours—£14.00. This sum may be exceeded where the juror has served for more than ten days and the court so directs: but the payment may not exceed £28.00.

Travelling allowance. For a motor cycle (engine not exceeding 150 cc)—3.5 p per mile; or (engine 150–245 cc) 4.4 p per mile; or (engine 245–500 cc) 5.6 p per mile; or (engine exceeding 500 cc) 7.2 p per mile; or (engine exceeding 500 cc and use resulting in a substantial saving in time or being otherwise reasonable) 7.8 p per mile.

For use of a private motor-car—7.6 p per mile. But, if a substantial saving of time is made or use is otherwise reasonable, at a rate not exceeding (engine not exceeding 1000 cc), 14.1 p per mile; or (engine 1000–1750 cc) 16.4 p per mile; or (engine exceeding 1750 cc) 18.7 p per mile. In addition, where passengers otherwise eligible for allowance are carried, a supplement of 2 p per mile for the first passenger and 1 p per mile for each additional passenger. Where use of the car results in substantial saving of time or is otherwise reasonable, parking fees are refundable.

Subsistence allowances. For absence not exceeding five hours—80 p; for five to ten hours—£1.65; over ten hours—£3.40; overnight (within five miles of Charing Cross)—£26.35; overnight (elsewhere)—£23.05.

See (1980) LS Gaz 58.

1678 —— **discharge of jury after trial—evidence by juror on deliberations—admissibility on appeal**

New Zealand

A jury, having deliberated for nearly eleven hours, returned a unanimous verdict of guilty on three defendants charged with arson. When the verdict was given there was a disturbance in the court resulting in the foreman having to repeat the jury's unanimous verdict of guilty. At that time the judge noted that there was no sign of distress or dissent from the jurors. Subsequent to the discharge of the jury, a juror swore an affidavit setting out purported irregularities and misunderstandings which occurred during the deliberation. The defendants appealed against the conviction on the ground that there had been a miscarriage of justice arising from the length of the jury's retirement. The question arose as to the admissibility of the affidavit as evidence. *Held*, in the circumstances the length of the jury's deliberation was reasonable. When a verdict was delivered in the sight and hearing of all the jury without protest, their assent to it was conclusively inferred. Furthermore the courts had consistently declined to receive affidavits from jurors purporting to disclose what took place during deliberation. The rule would be upheld in the interests of safeguarding the impartiality of and confidence in the jury system. Accordingly the affidavit would not be received by the court to support the defendants' grounds of appeal.

R v PAPADOPOULOS [1979] 1 NZLR 621 (Court of Appeal).

1679 —— **disclosure of jury room secrets—whether publication of disclosure contempt of court**

See *A-G v New Statesman and Nation Publishing Co Ltd*, para. 467.

1680 **Jury vetting—Attorney-General's statement**

The Attorney-General has drawn up revised guidelines on jury checks.

No check is to be made against the records of police special branches except on the Attorney-General's authority and such checks will not be authorised in cases involving so-called strong political motives, except in terrorist cases. In cases involving security, checks will only be authorised where national security is involved and where the court is expected to sit in camera. In no other type of case will such checks be authorised.

Except where, and in so far as, it may be necessary to confirm the identity of a member of the panel against whom the initial checks had raised doubts, checks are not to be made which go beyond checks on criminal records or those of police special branchees.

The judge's authority for access is not required, as all parties to proceedings have a statutory right to inspect the jury panel under the Juries Act 1974, s. 5 (2). However the judge and defence counsel will be informed when a check is authorised.

The result of an authorised check is sent to the DPP who will then decide what information ought to be brought to the attention of prosecuting counsel.

A defence counsel may make a request to the A-G through the DPP for assistance in obtaining information relative to its right of peremptory challenge, and chief constables are also prepared to consider a request relating to checks on criminal records if approved by the DPP. See [1980] 3 All ER 785.

1681 —— **exclusion of disqualified jurors—necessity**

The Court of Appeal has held that some jury vetting is necessary if persons disqualified under the Jurors Act 1974 are to be excluded from juries.

Before the applicant's trial, the police checked against local criminal records the names of the persons summoned to attend the Crown Court to form a jury panel, and had supplied prosecuting counsel with particulars of convictions of those on the panel. The applicant appealed for leave to appeal against conviction on the ground that counsel had wrongly used those particulars for the purpose of asking some members of the panel, not disqualified by their convictions, to stand by for the Crown. *Held*, leave to appeal would be refused. As it was a criminal offence to serve on a jury if disqualified, the police were entitled to search the records to check if there were any disqualified persons on the panel in order to prevent the commission of an offence. Other convictions which did not amount to disqualifications would also be revealed and there was no reason why such information should not be passed on to prosecuting counsel, who might consider that for example a juror with a conviction for burglary was unsuitable to sit on a jury trying a burglar.

R v MASON [1980] 3 All ER 777 (Court of Appeal: LAWTON LJ, BOREHAM and BALCOMBE JJ). *Mansell v The Queen* (1857) 8 E & B 54 followed.

1682   —— **validity**

See *R v Sheffield Crown Court, ex parte Brownlow*, para. 718.

1683   **Retirement to consider verdict—overnight stay in hotels— desirability**

See *R v Wooding*, para. 727.

LAND CHARGES

Halsbury's Laws of England (4th edn.), Vol. 26, paras. 701–900

1684   **Rating surcharge—mortgage—priority of surcharge as registered charge**

See *Westminster City Council v Haymarket Publishing Ltd*, para. 2307.

1685   **Registration—effect of failure to register—estate contract**

For consideration a farmer granted his son a ten year option to purchase his farm. The option was not registered. A family quarrel resulted in the farmer executing a conveyance of the farm to his wife for consideration in order to defeat the option. The son gave notice exercising the option and issued a writ claiming specific performance and damages. *Held*, (i) as the option had been granted for consideration it was contractually enforceable against the farmer who was therefore liable in damages for his breach. (ii) The option was void against the farmer's wife under the Land Charges Act 1925, s. 13 (2), as she was a purchaser of the legal estate for money or money's worth. No inquiry was necessary under s. 13 (2) into the bona fides of the purchaser or the adequacy of the consideration paid. Specific performance and damages from the wife would be refused.

MIDLAND BANK TRUST CO LTD v GREEN [1981] 1 All ER 153 (House of Lords: LORD WILBERFORCE, LORD EDMUND-DAVIES, LORD FRASER OF TULLYBELTON, LORD RUSSELL OF KILLOWEN, and LORD BRIDGE OF HARWICH). Decision of Court of Appeal [1979] 3 All ER 28, 1979 Halsbury's Abridgment para. 1657 reversed.

1686   —— **equitable charge affecting land—registration under Companies Act 1948—effect**

See *Property Discount Corporation Ltd v Lyon Group Ltd*, para. 381.

LAND REGISTRATION

Halsbury's Laws of England (4th edn.), Vol. 26, paras. 901–1490

1687   **Chief Land Registrar—annual report**

The report of the Chief Land Registrar for 1979–80 has been published and is available from HMSO. The registrar notes that over the previous ten years compulsory registration of land has been extended from 43 per cent of the population in England and Wales to 74 per cent. During 1979–80 there were 378,883 first registrations (417,080 in 1978–79) and a total of 2,204,850 transactions. Applications for first registrations (other than dispositionary leases) averaged 64·9 days to process in 1979–80 (61·3 days in 1978–79), transfers of part averaged 67·1 days (63·7 days in 1978–79) and other dealings averaged 24 days (20·8 days in 1978–79). Applications for office copies of the register in straightforward cases usually were issued on the working day following receipt and searches of the whole of the land in a registered title were usually completed on the day of receipt. During the year payment was made in respect of 120 applications for indemnity. The Land Charges Department dealt with most certificates of search within 24 hours of application and usage of the telephone search service continued to increase (over 12 per cent of all applications for full searches in 1979–80).

1688 District registries—areas served

The Land Registration (District Registry) Order 1980, S.I. 1980 No. 1499 (in force on 1st December 1980), replaces the 1979 Order, 1979 Halsbury's Abridgment para. 1660. A new district land registry is constituted at Peterborough and responsibility for the registration of titles in various areas is transferred.

1689 Entries in register—indemnity covenants

In the case of applications completed after 29th February 1980, where there is a transfer of registered land containing indemnity covenants in respect of restrictive or positive covenants already set out on the register or contained in a deed of which a copy is bound up in the certificate, the words of covenant will not be set out (as previously) in a separately bound-up document. A note will instead be entered in the proprietorship register stating that the transfer to the proprietor contains a covenant to observe and perform the covenants in the particular conveyance or other deed referred to in the charges register and of indemnity in respect thereof. Where the transferee has not covenanted to observe and perform the original covenants the note will merely state that the transfer to the proprietor contains a covenant of indemnity in respect thereof. There is no change in procedure where a transfer contains fresh positive covenants or indemnity covenants in respect of positive covenants previously set out in the land or charge certificate by means of a separately bound document. It remains the intention that details of positive covenants which are contained in the conveyance to an applicant for first registration be entered on the register; but it is not practicable for this to be implemented at present. See statement from the Chief Land Registrar, (1980) LS Gaz 43.

1690 Unregistered interest in property—position of mortgagee claiming possession

See *Williams and Glyn's Bank Ltd v Boland; Williams and Glyn's Bank Ltd v Brown,* para. 2012.

LANDLORD AND TENANT

Halsbury's Laws of England (3rd edn.), Vol. 23, paras. 985–1746

1691 Articles

Business Tenancies: The Effect of Dilapidations on New Rents, M. Barnes: 130 NLJ 969.

Clear the Way, Landlord, Trevor M. Aldridge (discussion on *Hilton v James Smith and Sons (Norwood) Ltd* (1979) 251 Estates Gazette 1063, CA, 1979 Halsbury's Abridgment para. 1690.)

Covenant Against Assignment, H. W. Wilkinson (law in the light of *Bocardo SA v S & M Hotels Ltd* [1979] 3 All ER 737, CA, 1979 Halsbury's Abridgment para. 1687): 130 NLJ 19.

Implied Tenancies—The Die Hard Doctrine, R. N. Judd (common law presumption of a tenancy from payment and acceptance of a sum): 130 NLJ 58.

Order for Possession, Audrey Harvey (security of tenure of local authority tenants): 130 NLJ 8.

Possession Proceedings, Henry E. Markson (recent decisions covering the questions of claiming interim payments, serving notice of breach of covenant, and applying to set aside a possession order): 124 Sol Jo 538.

Postponing or Suspending a Possession Order, John Alder: 124 Sol Jo 283.

Problems of Assignment, S. Farren (law in the light of the decision in *Old Grovebury Manor Farm Ltd v W. Seymour Plant Sales and Hire Ltd (No. 2)* [1979] 3 All ER 504, CA, 1979 Halsbury's Abridgment para. 1691): 130 NLJ 130.

Remedies of Tenant for Breach of Landlord's Covenant to Repair, P. F. Smith: 131 NLJ 330.

Rent Act Law: Recent Developments, D.M. Bows and E.O. Bowne (meaning of "member of the family"): 124 Sol Jo 197.

Rent Reviews: A Framework for Valuers, P. M. Clarke: [1980] JPL 565.

Repair, Renewal and Improvement, P. F. Smith (scope of lessee's obligations): [1979] Conv 429.

Shorthold: Repeating the Rent Acts, Peter Robson and Paul Watchman: 124 Sol Jo 367.

1692   Agricultural tenancies

See AGRICULTURE.

1693   Assured tenancy—approved bodies

The Assured Tenancies (Approved Body) (No. 1) Order 1980, S.I. 1980 No. 1694 (in force on 4th December 1980), approves the Abbey Housing Association Ltd as a body which may grant an assured tenancy under the Housing Act 1980, s. 56, para. 1436.

1694   Business tenancy—agreement to surrender—validity

A clause in a lease of business premises prohibited assignment without consent unless the tenant first offered to surrender the lease to the landlord. The tenant made an offer to surrender which he later withdrew as the landlord's offer was unsatisfactory, and the landlord brought an action for specific performance. The tenant counterclaimed for a declaration that the agreement was rendered void by the Landlord and Tenant Act 1954, s. 38, which rendered void agreements purporting to preclude applications and requests under Part II of the Act, and for a declaration that he was entitled to assign without consent. *Held*, the question was whether the agreement in fact operated to prevent a tenant from making an application under Part II. This would be the inevitable result of surrender, so the agreement was void, and the action for specific performance would fail. However, the clause was not itself invalidated because it only covered an offer to surrender, therefore the machinery for offering to surrender before assignment still applied, and the second declaration sought by the tenant would be refused.

ALLNATT LONDON PROPERTIES LTD v NEWTON (1980) Times. 26th November (Chancery Division: SIR ROBERT MEGARRY VC). *Joseph v Joseph* [1967] Ch 78, CA, applied.

1695   —— application for new tenancy—earlier judgment for forfeiture—subsisting application for relief—whether tenancy terminated

A company, which held business premises under a lease from the defendants, granted an underlease of part of the premises to the plaintiff. The defendants, who were the plaintiff's landlords for the purposes of the Landlord and Tenant Act 1954, Pt. II, served on the plaintiff a notice under Pt. II of the Act terminating his tenancy. The plaintiff served a counter notice under the Act claiming a new tenancy. The company subsequently successfully claimed forfeiture of the underlease and judgment for possession was entered for them. However, a claim for relief against forfeiture by the plaintiff, and the assessment of damages, was adjourned generally on the plaintiff undertaking to make quarterly payments to the company, and execution of the judgment for possession was stayed meanwhile. On the plaintiff's application to the court for the grant of a new tenancy under the 1954 Act, the defendants asked the court to dismiss the plaintiff's originating summons on the ground that when it was issued the plaintiff had no tenancy to which Pt. II of the Act applied, as his underlease had come to an end by forfeiture within s. 24 (2). *Held*, the right to apply for relief against forfeiture was part of the process of forfeiture and until that process was completed by the application for relief being determined, the tenancy could be restored by the grant of relief and could not be said to have come to an end. Further, there had been no undue delay in seeking relief. The plaintiff was therefore entitled to apply to the court for a new tenancy under s. 24 (1), notwithstanding the judgment for forfeiture, and his originating summons was accordingly valid.

MEADOWS v CLERICAL AND GENERAL LIFE ASSURANCE SOCIETY [1980] 1 All ER 454 (Chancery Division: SIR ROBERT MEGARRY V-C). *Dendy v Evans* [1910] 1 KB 263 applied.

1696   —— —— interim rent—factors to be taken into consideration

After an application by a business tenant for a new tenancy under Part II of the Landlord and Tenant Act 1954, the landlord issued a summons asking the court to determine the interim rent payable while the tenancy continued by virtue of that Act. *Held*, the rent should be assessed in the light of the circumstances prevailing at the beginning of the continuation period and with reference to the rent payable under a hypothetical yearly tenancy of the premises tempered by reference to the actual previous rent. Comparable rents were examined and reductions made to allow for the fact that the hypothetical yearly tenancy lacked the security of tenure enjoyed by a normal shop tenancy of a term of years, and also to allow for a stringent user clause in the lease. The court refused to make any reduction for a reservation of a right of entry in favour of the landlord nor for the fact that a shopping centre had recently been constructed nearby because these circumstances were not regarded as adverse.

RATNERS (JEWELLERS) LTD v LEMNOLL LTD (1980) 255 Estates Gazette 987 (Chancery Division: DILLON J). *English Exporters (London) Ltd v Eldonwall Ltd* [1973] 2 Ch 415 followed.

1697   —— —— landlord's intention to demolish or reconstruct

The landlords of business premises resisted a claim for a new lease on the ground, as provided by Landlord and Tenant Act 1954, s. 30 (1) (f), that they intended to demolish and reconstruct the premises and could not reasonably do so without obtaining possession. The judge decided that they had satisfied the requirements of s. 30 (1) (f) but decided in favour of the tenants the question whether s. 31A (1) (a) was applicable. Section 31A (1) (a) provides that the court cannot hold that the landlord could not reasonably carry out the work without obtaining possession if the tenant agrees to give access, and, given access, the landlord could reasonably carry out the work without obtaining possession and without interfering substantially with the use of the premises for the purpose of the tenant's business. On appeal, *held*, in deciding in the tenant's favour the judge had taken into account the future of the business after completion of the work, which he was precluded from doing by the decision of the Court of Appeal in *Redfern v Reeves*. However, the landlords did not need to obtain possession as they were entitled under the tenancy agreement to enter to carry out the work and consequently could not rely on s. 30 (1) (f).

PRICE v ESSO PETROLEUM CO LTD (1980) 255 Estates Gazette 243 (Court of Appeal: MEGAW and TEMPLEMAN LJJ and SIR PATRICK BROWNE). *Redfern v Reeves* (1978) 37 P & CR 364, 1978 Halsbury's Abridgment para. 1705 followed. *Heath v Drown* [1973] AC 498 applied.

1698   —— —— **termination date for new tenancy**

The tenants, stamp dealers, occupied a series of stalls in part of a large office complex. The company owning the office complex required more space for its staff and as a result served notices on the tenants, determining all the tenancies. The tenants subsequently served notices asking for new tenancies. The question arose as to the duration of the new tenancies. *Held*, courts determining the duration of new business tenancies under the Landlord and Tenant Act 1954, s. 33 should, rather than nominating the length of the term, direct that when the matter was finally disposed, the term of the lease to be executed should be a term ending on a specified date.

WARWICK & WARWICK (PHILATELY) LTD v SHELL (UK) LTD; CHIPPERFIELD V SHELL (UK) LTD (1980) 125 Sol Jo 99 (Court of Appeal: CUMMING-BRUCE, GRIFFITHS and O'CONNOR LJJ).

1699   —— —— **variation of terms**

The tenants of part of an office block applied for a new tenancy under the Landlord and Tenant Act 1954, Part II. The landlords wished to replace the existing service charges by comprehensive variable contributions under a scheme which was designed to shift from the landlords to the various tenants the financial burden of providing services and maintaining the structure and condition of the whole building. The shift in burden was to be allowed for in the new rent. At first instance the landlords' proposals were approved. The tenants appealed. *Held*, while there was now a tendency in the case of new lettings to cover all outgoings by the tenants' obligations (the "clear rent" basis), a variation of terms on an application under the 1954 Act had to satisfy various tests, in particular whether the tenant would be adequately compensated by the consequential adjustment of open market rent. In the present case the landlords' term introduced a radical change in the balance of rights and responsibilities, advantage and detriment, security and risk, and the tenants were justified in rejecting it. The appeal would be allowed.

O'MAY v CITY OF LONDON REAL PROPERTY CO LTD [1980] 3 All ER 466 (Court of Appeal: BUCKLEY, SHAW and BRIGHTMAN LJJ). Decision of Goulding J (1979) 249 Estates Gazette 1065, 1979 Halsbury's Abridgment para. 1677 reversed.

1700   —— —— **when time for giving notice of application expires**

See *Dodds v Walker*, para. 2847.

1701   —— —— **whether new tenancy new asset for tax purposes**

See *Bayley (Inspector of Taxes) v Rogers*, para. 301.

1702   —— **occupation for business purposes—consent of landlord to business use**

A landlord let a flat and a garage to a company. The company covenanted to use the garage for standing a private car only and the flat as a private dwelling. After the lease expired, the company continued to pay rent and became yearly tenants under the terms of the lease. The landlord then assigned the reversion to the plaintiff. For several years, the company had used the garage for storing samples and for garaging company cars used for conveying customers. The landlord had known of these practices and had never objected. The plaintiff, however, served notice to quit and brought an action for possession of the premises. The company contended that it occupied the garage for the purposes of a business so that the Landlord and Tenant Act 1954, Pt. II applied, and the notice to quit was ineffective because it was not in the form required by s. 25 of the Act. The judge found in favour of the company on the ground that it was using the garage for business purposes notwithstanding the covenant, and that the use had been consented to within the meaning of s. 23 (4), which sufficed to bring the tenancy within Pt. II. The plaintiff appealed. *Held*, the use for business purposes of the cars kept in the garage and the storage of samples there constituted a breach of the covenant. For the purposes of s. 23 (4), a distinction had to be drawn between acquiescence and consent, as mere acquiescence would not be sufficient. Acquiescence arose out of a passive failure to do anything whereas consent was based on an act of demonstration. The only implied consent which might serve was some positive action which showed affirmation. The landlord had acquiesced in the company's activities but no positive approval or permission had been given at any time. The landlord had not, therefore, consented, and the tenancy had not been brought within Pt. II. The notice to quit was effective and the appeal would be allowed.

BELL V ALFRED FRANKS AND BARTLETT CO LTD [1980] 1 All ER 356 (Court of Appeal: MEGAW, SHAW and WALLER LJJ).

1703   **Covenant—common areas subject to lessor's control—implied covenant to maintain services**

Australia

The plaintiff tenant entered into a written agreement with the defendant landlord for the lease of a licensed restaurant situated on the sixth floor of a building. When the tenant entered into possession access to the sixth floor was provided by four lifts and two escalators. The lease provided that the common areas, which included the lifts and escalators, should at all times be subject to the control of the lessor, and that the tenant should have the use of these, subject to the covenants, terms and conditions of the lease. After a year, the landlord ceased operating the escalators beyond the second floor and provided a reduced passenger-operated lift service since he claimed that the full service was operating at a financial loss. The tenant claimed that there was an implied covenant that the service would be maintained and the landlord had therefore committed a breach of the covenants of the lease. He applied for a mandatory injunction to compel the landlord to restore the services. *Held*, the tenants were entitled to the use of the lifts and escalators in substantially the same state and to the same extent as they were when the lease was executed. A covenant would be implied to this effect, both upon the terms of the lease itself and in order to give business efficacy to the agreement, since a licensed restaurant could only be operated satisfactorily on the sixth floor of a building if the public were afforded easy access. Further, the landlord had derogated from his grant by drastically reducing this access. Accordingly, a mandatory injunction would be granted ordering the landlord to restore the services to the restaurant since damages would not be an adequate remedy.

KARAGGIANIS V MALLTOWN PTY LTD [1979] 21 SASR 381 (Supreme Court of South Australia). *Reigate v Union Manufacturing Co (Ramsbottom) Ltd* [1918] 1 KB 592, CA and *Browne v Flower* [1911] 1 Ch. 219 applied; *Attorney-General v Colchester Corporation* [1955] 2 QB 207 distinguished.

1704   **—— covenant against assignment without consent—vesting order made on appointment of new trustees—breach**

The defendant was the lessee of premises under an under-lease containing a covenant against assignment without consent. He executed a declaration of trust of the premises in favour of himself and the plaintiff. He subsequently disappeared, and the plaintiff, who wished to acquire the freehold under the Leasehold Reform Act 1967, obtained an order appointing herself and her solicitor trustees of the declaration of trust and vesting in them the property subject to the trust. In an interlocutory application to discharge the order insofar as it vested the underleased premises in the new trustees, the head lessors contended that the court vesting order operated as an assignment and should not have been made without their consent. *Held*, on the wording of the covenant against assignment, it was clear that before a breach of the covenant could occur there had to be an assignment made by the lessee himself. The vesting order was a transfer of the legal estate which took effect by operation of law, and was not an assignment, nor was it effected by the lessee himself, who had disappeared. The application would accordingly be dismissed.

MARSH V GILBERT (1980) 256 Estates Gazette 715 (Chancery Division: NOURSE J).

1705   —— **covenant to pay service charge—power of landlord to require interim sums in advance**

Under a long lease of a flat made in 1965, the landlords covenanted with the tenants, inter alia, to keep the demised premises in repair and pay the water rates. The tenants covenanted to pay a contribution to the landlord in respect of outgoing expenses and liabilities incurred by the landlord in the previous year. The lease further provided for the payment, in advance, of interim sums on account of the contribution, to be paid into a separate bank account maintained by the landlords' managing agents. The questions arose whether (i) the interim sums were a service charge to which the Housing and Finance Act 1972, s. 91 (1) applied, (ii) the landlords were entitled to payment in advance, and (iii) the landlords were entitled to recover the cost of borrowing the money required by them to meet their obligations under the lease, if they were not entitled to advance payments. *Held* (i) on the terms of the lease the contributions were a service charge. (ii) On the true construction of s. 91 (1) (b), a service charge was only recoverable from a tenant once the landlord had either defrayed the cost or incurred liability to pay the cost. Therefore the landlords were not entitled to require the interim payments to be made in advance. Further, the court could not uphold the landlords' contention that the payments had been held by their managing agents as shareholders or on trust. (iii) There was no provision in the lease for the contributions to include the interest paid by the landlords on money they would be obliged to borrow in order to carry out their obligations. Nor could a term be implied that, in the event of supervening legislation rendering the advance payment of a service charge unlawful, the tenant would then be obliged to pay such interest. The doctrine of implying a term to give efficacy to an agreement did not apply where there had been a disturbance to contractual arrangements by a statute.

FROBISHER (SECOND INVESTMENTS) LTD v KILORAN TRUST CO LTD [1980] 1 All ER 488 (Chancery Division: WALTON J).

1706   **Forfeiture—breach of covenant to resell property to owner on termination of employment—validity**

Canada
In a case where an employee agreed to purchase a house from his employer on condition that he resold the house to his employer on termination of his employment with him, *held*, such an agreement was enforceable even where the employee was made redundant. Furthermore the employee would be unable to claim relief against forfeiture as the agreement was perfectly reasonable in the circumstances.

ATHABASCA REALTY CO LTD v GRAVES (1979) 106 DLR (3d) 473 (Court of Queen's Bench of Alberta).

1707   —— **relief—order for possession of part of leased premises only**

The tenant of ground floor and basement premises allowed the sub-tenant of the basement to use it for immoral purposes, in breach of covenant. The landlord claimed forfeiture of the lease and the question arose as to whether the court had jurisdiction to grant relief in respect of part only of the leased premises. *Held*, where the two parts of the demised property were physically separated and the breaches complained of were committed on one part only, it was possible to grant relief in respect of part of the premises only, therefore an order for possession of the basement only would be made.

GMS SYNDICATE LTD v GARY ELLIOTT LTD [1981] 1 All ER 619 (Chancery Division: NOURSE J). *Dumpor's case* (1603) 4 Co Rep 119b applied.

1708   **Harassment of residential occupier—evidence of previous conviction—admissibility**

Landlords who were husband and wife, were charged with harassing their tenants. Evidence of the landlords' previous conviction of harassment of the same tenants was admitted at the trial and they were convicted. They appealed against conviction on the ground that the evidence had been wrongly admitted. *Held*, evidence of the facts which resulted in the previous conviction was relevant in so far as it could be an indication of the landlords' intentions towards the tenants. However, it was probable that knowledge of the previous conviction would lead the jury to infer that on similar facts the landlords intended to evict the tenants. The earlier decision was similar to evidence of an opinion as to the landlords' intention and was inadmissible for the purpose of proving the offence. Further, if it was assumed that reference to the conviction could have been made in cross examination under the Criminal Evidence Act 1898, s. 1 (i) (ii) such evidence should have been excluded because the jury could have inferred that it was evidence of the probability that the landlords committed the offence and not simply evidence of the their credibility.

R v SHEPHERD (1980) 71 Cr App Rep 120 (Court of Appeal: EVELEIGH LJ, BRISTOW and McNEILL JJ). Dictum of Lord Sankey LC in *Maxwell v Director of Public Prosecutions* [1935] AC 309, HL followed.

1709   Housing Act 1980

See para. 1436.

1710   Lease—doctrine of frustration—applicability

By a lease in 1974 the landlords let to the tenants a purpose-built warehouse for a term of ten years, expiring on 31st December 1983. The only access to the warehouse was by a public highway, along which the landlords purported to grant a right of way to the tenants for all purposes connected with the occupation of the premises. In May 1979 the local authority ordered the closure of the highway because of the unsafe condition of a derelict warehouse which was a "listed" building. The Secretary of State for the Environment subsequently granted consent for its demolition and the estimated date for the completion of the demolition was January 1981, when the street would be reopened. The closure would then have lasted twenty months. On the closure of the highway the tenants ceased to pay the rent and the landlords subsequently applied for summary judgment under RSC Ord. 14 for the outstanding sum. The question of the application of the doctrine of frustration to leases and agreements for leases of land arose. *Held* LORD RUSSELL OF KILLOWEN dissenting, the doctrine of frustration was developed by the law as an expedient to escape from injustice where such would have resulted from the enforcement of a contract in its literal terms after a significant change in the circumstances surrounding that contract. The law was founded on comprehensive principles: compartmentalism, particularly if producing an anomaly, led to the injustice of different results in fundamentally analogous circumstances. To deny the extension of the doctrine of frustration to leaseholds would produce a number of undesirable anomalies. Although a lease was not inherently unsusceptible to the application of the doctrine of frustration, the cases in which it was properly applicable were rare and such cases belonged to the class where the question arose as to which of the two innocent parties had to bear the loss as a result of circumstances for which neither party was to blame. Furthermore, the doctrine of frustration, in its application to leases of land, had to be applied with proper regard to the fact that a grant of a legal estate was involved. In the present case the tenants had failed to raise a triable issue and the doctrine would therefore not apply.

NATIONAL CARRIERS LTD v PANALPINA (NORTHERN) LTD [1981] 1 All ER 161 (House of Lords: LORD HAILSHAM OF ST MARYLEBONE LC, LORD WILBERFORCE, LORD SIMON OF GLAISDALE, LORD RUSSELL OF KILLOWEN, and LORD ROSKILL). *Cricklewood Property & Investment Trust Ltd v Leighton's Investment Trust Ltd* [1945] AC 221, HL, considered.

1711   ——escrow—lease and counterpart delivered in escrow—effective date of commencement

See *Alan Estates Ltd v W G Stores Ltd*, para. 886.

1712   —— option to purchase property—condition precedent—default—effect

Canada

A lease provided for an option to purchase the property provided that the lessee duly and regularly paid the rent. He later fell into arrears and the lessor brought a distress action to recover the unpaid rent. The lessee paid the outstanding rent and upon the lessor's refusal to allow the exercise of the option brought an action for specific performance of the option. *Held,* the lessee had saved the lease by paying the rent, but due and regular payment was a condition precedent to the option and the action would therefore be dismissed.

NORTH CENTRAL EXPRESSWAYS LTD v MACCROSTIE (1979) 96 DLR (3d) 637 (Court of Queen's Bench of Saskatchewan).

1713   —— renewal—construction of clause—perpetual renewal

A seven year lease contained a renewal clause which provided that upon certain conditions the landlord would grant a new lease and that such a new lease would contain a like covenant for renewal for a further term of seven years. The landlord sought a declaration that the renewal clause did not amount to a covenant for perpetual renewal and that the lease could be renewed twice only. *Held,* the court was against construing a lease as perpetually renewable unless a contrary intention had been unequivocally expressed therein. On the facts no such intention was expressed and the declaration sought would be made.

MARJORIE BURNETT LTD v BARCLAY (1980) Times, 19th December (Chancery Division: NOURSE J).

1714   Leasehold enfranchisement or extension

See LEASEHOLD ENFRANCHISEMENT OR EXTENSION.

1715   Licence—contractual licence—specific performance—appropriateness of remedy

See *Verrall v Great Yarmouth Borough Council,* para. 469.

1716   —— licence ancillary to contract of employment—undue influence—validity of licence

A tenant occupied a flat as a protected tenant under the Rent Acts and contended that he had been induced to enter into an agreement for a licence at will. The tenant was employed by a company, owners of the flat, who in 1965 allowed him to occupy the flat at a low rent. In 1973 the company came under new management with a new housing policy. They wanted to abolish protected tenancies and substitute licences with no protection. The tenant signed an agreement providing that the licence could be determined at any time by the company and would automatically be determined on the tenant ceasing to be employed by the company. In 1978 the tenant was made redundant and the licence was terminated with two months' notice. The company claimed possession of the flat and on appeal the question arose as to whether the licence was invalid due to the "undue influence" exercised by the company in inducing the tenant to enter into the agreement. *Held,* although the tenant had a protected tenancy it was not absolutely secure in that it was dependent on his continued employment by the company. In the circumstances the terms of the licence were not unfair and it would be wrong to set aside such an agreement for inequality of bargaining power of the parties. Such a licence however, was not to be used to get round the Rent Acts. As a result of modern legislation it could not be said that the relationship of master and servant or landlord and tenant put the master in a dominant position so as to give rise to a presumption of undue influence. An order for possession would therefore be made.

MATHEW v BOBBINS (1980) Times, 21st June (Court of Appeal: LORD DENNING MR, WALLER and DUNN LJJ).

1717 Mobile home—agreement offered by owner to occupier—validity of terms

The Mobile Homes Act 1975, ss. 1–3 provide that it is the duty of the owner of a caravan site to offer to enter into a written agreement with the occupiers of mobile homes on the site for a term of at least five years. The agreement is to contain all terms and conditions of the occupation.

The owners of a carvan park, in purported compliance with ss. 1–3, offered to enter into an agreement with the occupiers of mobile homes pitched there. The agreement provided by cl. 2 (d) that the owners should have the right to move the mobile home for the purpose of better management of the park. Clause 3 (1) stated that the occupier was to pay a pitch fee to the owners but the amount of the fee and the date from when it was payable were omitted. Clause 3 (5), (6) and (12) were undertakings by the occupier to repair and maintain the mobile home and gave the owners the right to enter onto the pitch and carry out repairs if the occupiers had failed to do so. Further, by cl. 6 (c) the owners were entitled to receive a commission from the occupiers if the occupiers assigned the agreement without selling to the assignee or disposing of the mobile home otherwise than by sale. The occupiers, in rejecting the draft agreement, applied to the court under s. 4 (5) of the Act, which provides that where an owner has offered to enter into an agreement as required by s. 1, but the occupier is dissatisfied with one or more of the terms offered, he may apply to the court for relief under s. 4 (7). The judge, acting under s. 4 (7), determined the pitch fee and the date from which it was payable. That date was also determined as the commencement date of the agreement. The disputed clauses proposed by the owners were approved. The occupiers appealed. *Held*, the agreement was not a draft agreement complying with s. 1 (4) since blank spaces relating to crucial matters had not been filled in. The application should therefore have been made under s. 4 (1) (a), which provided that where an owner had failed without reasonable excuse to make an offer as required by s. 1, an occupier could apply to the court for relief under s. 4 (2) (a). However, on the basis that it was an application under s. 4 (5), the appeal would be determined in accordance with s. 4 (7). The court had to apply the same criteria in determining a dispute under s. 4 (7) as it was required to apply by s. 4 (2) (a). It had to determine the dispute about the particular terms of the agreement by ensuring that such terms and conditions complied with s. 3 and were reasonable.

(i) The appeal would be dismissed in so far as it related to cl. 3 (1). A judge had the power to order a retrospective date for the commencement of an agreement if it was reasonable to do so. (ii) The appeal would be allowed in that clauses 2 (d) and 6 (d) extended the rights of the owners beyond the scope of the Act and were therefore inconsistent with the Act and would be deleted. (iii) In relation to clause 3 (5) and (6) a limitation on the right of access onto the occupiers' pitch would be added to cl. 3 (12) in order to clarify the provision.

GRANT V ALLEN [1980] 1 All ER 720 (Court of Appeal: STEPHENSON, EVELEIGH and BRANDON LJJ).

1718 Notice to quit—validity—possession by local authority of controlled housing

See *Lambeth LBC v Udechuka*, para. 1448.

1719 Protected shorthold tenancy—notice to tenant—form of notice

The Protected Shorthold Tenancies (Notice to Tenant) Regulations 1980, S.I. 1980 No. 1707 (in force on 28th November 1980), prescribe the form of notice to be served on the tenant by the landlord before the tenancy can become a protected shorthold tenancy under the Housing Act 1980, s. 52.

1720 Protected tenancy—claim for possession—requirement for premises to be let as a separate dwelling

In 1936 a penthouse comprising a maisonette and a self-contained flat was let at a low rent for a term expiring on 29th September 1978. In 1973 the whole lease was assigned to the person who occupied the flat. The new tenant then sub-let the maisonette for a term expiring on 28th September 1978. When the head lease expired, the tenant claimed protection by virtue of the Landlord and Tenant Act 1954 in respect of the whole penthouse on the ground that it had been let to him as a separate dwelling. The head landlord contended that the 1954 Act did not apply since the penthouse had been divided into separate dwellings by the sub-lease. The tenant claimed that the Act applied because he intended to occupy the penthouse as a single dwelling in the future. *Held*, the 1954 Act protected the tenant if his tenancy would have been protected under the Rent Act 1968 if it had not been at a low rent. A person was entitled to protection under the 1968 Act if the premises were let to him as a separate dwelling and he was in residential occupation of them. The court was required by the 1954 Act, s. 22 (3) to determine whether property or part of property was let as a separate dwelling by reference to how it was being used when the head lease expired; the tenant's intentions were irrelevant. As the penthouse had been divided into two separate dwellings with separate occupants by 29th September 1978, the tenant was not protected in respect of the whole penthouse. However, under the Rent Act 1968 he would have been regarded as being in residential occupation of the flat which was clearly let to him as a separate dwelling on 29th September 1978. Accordingly, he was protected in respect of the flat but not the whole penthouse.

REGALIAN SECURITIES LTD V RAMSDEN [1980] 2 All ER 497 (Court of Appeal: LORD DENNING MR, BRIDGE and OLIVER LJJ).

The Rent Act 1968 has been consolidated by the Rent Act 1977.

1721 —— **dwelling house let with other land—whether agricultural land**

In 1972 a bungalow and an area of pasture land of more than two acres were demised to the tenants. Until 1973, the land was used for recreational purposes. From 1976 it was not used at all, except for the yearly cutting of hay to fulfil obligations under the lease. In 1978 the tenants applied for a declaration that the tenancy was a protected tenancy. *Held*, under the Rent Act 1977, s. 6, a tenancy was not protected if the dwelling house was let together with land other than the site of the dwelling house. This was subject to s. 26, under which any land or premises let together with a dwelling house was to be treated as part of the dwelling house unless it consisted of agricultural land exceeding two acres in extent. The question was whether the land in this case was agricultural land. The General Rate Act 1967, s. 26 (3) (a), defined it as land used as arable meadow or pasture land only, but not land kept or preserved mainly or exclusively for purposes of sport or recreation. To come within the definition, land had to be "used" as a meadow or pasture for the purpose of growing grass for grazing or for being cut. This was not so in this case, as the grass was being cut simply to comply with the lease. Further, the land was "kept or preserved" exclusively for the purpose of recreation until 1973. Thereafter it was not used for any purpose at all, but so far as it was kept or preserved for anything, it was for recreation. Hence the land was not agricultural land and the tenants were protected.

BRADSHAW V SMITH [1980] LS Gaz R 432 (Court of Appeal: MEGAW and TEMPLEMAN LJJ and SIR PATRICK BROWNE).

1722 —— **exceptions—resident landlord—tenant's rights after death of landlord**

Under the Rent Act 1977, s. 12 (1) (c) a tenancy of a dwelling house is not a protected tenancy if, inter alia, at all times since the tenancy was granted, the interest of the landlord under the tenancy has belonged to a person who, at the time he owned that interest, occupied, as his residence, part of that dwelling house. Certain periods are, however, to be disregarded for the purposes of s. 12 (1) (c), including, under Sch. 2, para. 1, a period of up to twelve months in which the landlord's interest becomes vested in his personal representatives. It fell to be determined whether non-resident landlords, the personal representatives of the deceased landlord, who served a notice to quit during the disregarded period, could obtain an order for possession when the disregarded period had expired. The personal representatives contended that the notice to quit ended the common law tenancy and that thereafter the tenant was a trespasser and could not therefore become a protected tenant if the landlords failed to satisfy the test of residence at the end of the twelve month period. *Held*, Sch. 2, para. 3 provided that during a disregarded period no order for possession could be made other than an order which might have been able to have been made if the tenancy was a regulated tenancy. Thus, during the disregarded period the tenant was protected against everyone except a resident landlord who could show a continuous chain of resident landlords broken only by any relevant disregarded period. At the end of the disregarded period the security of the tenant depended on the qualification of the landlord. The position had therefore to be examined at the end of that period: if the landlord was resident and no notice to quit had become effective, the tenant was a contractual tenant; if the landlord was resident and the notice to quit had expired the tenant was holding over after the determination of a contractual tenancy; if the landlord was not resident and no notice to quit had become effective, the tenant was a protected tenant; if the landlord was not resident and notice to quit had become effective, the tenant was a statutory tenant. The personal representatives' contention would accordingly be rejected.

LANDAU v SLOANE; MIGDALSKI v CORVIN [1980] 2 All ER 539 (Court of Appeal: STEPHENSON, BRIDGE and TEMPLEMAN LJJ).

This decision has been reversed by the House of Lords; see [1981] 2 WLR 349.

1723　　Ten months after the death of the resident landlord, her brother who was sole executor and sole beneficiary, went into occupation. No vesting assent was made during the period of twelve months which was to be disregarded by virtue of Rent Act 1977, Sch. 2, para. 1 (c), in determining whether there was a resident landlord. On the tenant's claim to be fully protected, *held*, as the executor was absolutely entitled to the property it belonged to him both before and after any assent and he satisfied the requirements of the Act once he went into occupation. The tenant's claim would fail.

BEEBE v MASON (1980) 254 Estates Gazette 987 (Court of Appeal: STEPHENSON, BRIDGE and TEMPLEMAN LJJ).

1724　　—— **matrimonial home—purported surrender of tenancy—validity of surrender**

See *Hoggett v Hoggett*, para. 1491.

1725　　—— **notice to quit—prescribed information**

The Notices to Quit (Prescribed Information) Regulations 1980, S.I. 1980 No. 1624 (in force on 28th November 1980), replace the Notices to Quit (Prescribed Information) (Protected Tenancies and Part VI Contracts) Regulations 1975, 1975 Halsbury's Abridgment para. 2036. The regulations prescribe the information to be contained in a notice to quit, given on or after 28th November 1980, to determine a tenancy of premises let as a dwelling.

1726　　—— **unlawful eviction—defence**

See *R v Davidson-Acres*, para. 641.

1727　　**Recovery of possession—dwelling-house let on regulated tenancy—suitable alternative accommodation**

The defendant was a protected tenant of a flat in London, owned by a charitable trust. The defendant's social and religious life centred in London but he worked in Luton. The trustees wished to sell the flat with vacant possession. They offered the defendant alternative accommodation in Luton and sought a possession order. The question arose whether the alternative accommodation was "reasonably suitable to the needs of the tenant as regards character" as required by the Rent Act 1977, Sch. 15, Part IV, para. 5 (1) (b). *Held*, "character" in para. 5 (1) (b) was confined to the character of the property and did not include consideration of the tenant's leisure activities or proximity to friends. It was impossible to say that the accommodation offered was not such that the defendant could live there in reasonably comfortable conditions suitable to the style of life he had been living in London. In the circumstances it was reasonable to grant a possession order.

SIDDIQUI V RASHID [1980] 1 WLR 1018 (Court of Appeal: STEPHENSON AND DUNN LJJ and SIR DAVID CAIRNS). *Redspring Ltd v Francis* [1973] 1 WLR 134, CA applied.

1728   —— —— —— proximity to place of work

The defendant, a freelance clothes designer, was the statutory tenant of a furnished flat in the area in which most of her customers were situated. The premises fell into disrepair and the local authority served notices on the landlords requiring the repairs to be carried out. The landlords served notice to quit and brought an action for possession contending that they had offered the defendant alternative accommodation which was reasonably suitable for her as regards proximity to her place of work. The claim was dismissed. On appeal, *held*, the Rent Act 1977, s. 98 provided that an order for possession might be made subject to certain limitations contained in Sch. 15, paras. 4 and 5 (1), which included a condition that the accommodation was to be reasonably suitable to the needs of the tenant as regards proximity to place of work. Although the defendant did work in other areas, most of her customers were drawn from the area in which her original flat was situated, and there was no reason why a "place of work" could not include an area. The alternative accommodation was situated outside that area and accordingly was not suitable. The appeal would be dismissed.

YEWBRIGHT PROPERTIES LTD V STONE (1980) 40 P & CR 402 (Court of Appeal: MEGAW, BRANDON and OLIVER LJJ).

1729   —— non-payment of rent—application to set aside judgment—delay on part of tenant

The plaintiffs, owners of a block of flats, let a flat to a tenant for a term expiring in March 1978. In July 1973, the tenant granted a lawful sub-tenancy to the defendant. In February 1978, the defendant went abroad on business and did not return until July 1979. He made no attempt during that time to ensure that the rent was paid when it fell due. In April 1979, the plaintiffs successfully applied for an order for possession on the ground of non-payment of rent. In June 1979, the plaintiffs entered into possession, removed the defendant's furniture and changed the locks. They then granted a seventy-five year lease of all the flats in the block to a property company. The defendant returned to England in July and applied under CCR, Ord. 37 to have the judgment set aside. The judge granted his application, and the plaintiffs appealed. *Held*, as a general principle it would be wrong to maintain a judgment against a party who had no knowledge of the proceedings or of the judgment. There was no delay on the defendant's part in that he took steps as soon as he knew of the judgment against him. However, delay over all was a factor to be taken into account, and, in the circumstances, any reasonable landlord would suppose that the flat had been abandoned and that he was entitled to seek possession. Further, where a third party (in the instant case, the property company) had intervened, its rights ought to weigh heavily with the judge. There was a real threat to the company's interest and the judge in setting aside the order had made an order which no court could reasonably have made if consideration had been given to all the relevant factors. The appeal would be allowed.

RHODES TRUST V KHAN (1979) 123 Sol Jo 719 (Court of Appeal: MEGAW and SHAW LJJ). *Grimshaw v Dunbar* [1953] 1 QB 408 applied.

1730   —— prior representation by landlord—promissory estoppel

See *Fontana NV v Mautner*, para. 1107.

1731   —— resident landlord—furnished tenancy

In order to get possession of a flat the resident landlord had to show that the tenancy, which commenced before the Rent Act 1974 and under which the rent included a payment for furniture, was a furnished tenancy and consequently a restricted contract within the Rent Act 1977, s. 19. The Rent Act 1968, s. 2 (3), provided that the amount of rent attributable to the use of furniture had to form a substantial proportion of the whole rent. The conclusion of the deputy county court judge that in 1974 the value of the furniture did not form such a proportion, and that therefore the tenancy was protected, was upheld on appeal.

MANN v CORNELLA (1980) 254 Estates Gazette 403 (Court of Appeal: ORR and ORMROD LJJ and SIR ROBERT MEGARRY V-C).

1732 —— service of summons—necessary parties to proceedings

Trinidad and Tobago

In a case concerning the interpretation of the Summary Ejectment Ordinance of Trinidad and Tobago, ss. 3–5, concerning the procedure for bringing an action against an occupier of premises who refused to quit and deliver up possession of land on the expiration of the interest or term, it was *held* that a complaint or summons need only be served on the person in actual occupation, and not on a non-occupying tenant, who was not a necessary party to the proceedings.

ISAAC v FRANCIS [1980] 1 WLR 40 (Privy Council: LORD FRASER OF TULLYBELTON, LORD SCARMAN and SIR CLIFFORD RICHMOND).

The equivalent English provisions were contained in the Small Tenements Recovery Act 1838, s. 1, now repealed by the Rent Act 1965.

1733 Regulated tenancy—procedure

The Regulated Tenancies (Procedure) Regulations 1980, S.I. 1980 No. 1696 (in force on 28th November 1980), modify the procedure to be followed by rent officers on applications for the registration of rents and by rent officers and rent assessment committees on applications for certificates of fair rent. The existing procedure is in the Rent Act 1977, Schs. 11, 12. The modifications to Sch. 11 (applications for registration of rent) are broadly the same as those in the Housing Act 1980, Sch. 6, para. 1436, which will not now be brought into operation, but differ in that they do not require the rent officer to supply an applicant with information or documents already supplied. The modifications to Sch. 12 (certificates of fair rent) generally follow the changes to Sch. 11 and enable rent officers to deal with applications more quickly, particularly in the case of unoccupied dwellings.

1734 Rent—clause fixing amount for part of term only—certainty

A lease for a term of twenty-one years provided for a yearly rent of £250 during the first seven years and thereafter for "such rent as may be agreed" between the lessor and lessee. On the question whether the agreement was void for uncertainty and the lease void for failure of consideration, *held*, in the absence of agreement and in the absence of anything in the lease which indicated that the rent should change, a term could be implied that the rent should remain the same.

KING v KING (1980) 255 Estates Gazette 1205 (Chancery Division: NOURSE J).

1735 —— fair rent—jurisdiction of rent assessment committee— unreasonable decision

In a case where a landlord made an application under the Rent Act 1977, s. 69 for a certificate of fair rent, the rent assessment committee failed to supply any reasons for reaching its decision and disregarded the landlord's evidence concerning proposed repairs to the property in question. The landlord appealed on the grounds that, (i) the committee should have considered all the evidence before it and, (ii), the committee had given insufficient reasons for their decision contrary to the Tribunals and Inquiries Act 1958, s. 12. *Held*, (i) there was nothing in the 1977 Act empowering the committee to take into account proposed repairs in reaching an assessment under s. 69. During the course of such assessments however, committees were entitled to use their own knowledge and experience, having considered all the evidence. (ii) The court had the power to compel any tribunal, to which the 1958

Act, s. 12 applied, to give sufficient reasons by mandamus, or in an appeal, by remission of the case to the tribunal. On the facts the committee had failed to fulfil its duty under s. 12 and the case would be remitted to the committee for further consideration.

GUPPY'S PROPERTIES LTD v KNOTT (1979) 124 Sol Jo 81 (Queen's Bench Division: SIR DOUGLAS FRANK QC). *Mountview Court Properties Ltd v Devlin* (1970) 21 P & CR 689 applied.

1736 —— rent assessment committees—procedure

The Rent Assessment Committees (England and Wales) (Amendment) Regulations 1980, S.I. 1980 No. 1699 (in force on 28th November 1980), amend the Rent Assessment Committees (England and Wales) Regulations 1971, which regulate the procedure to be followed by rent assessment committees when a reference is made to them by the rent officer under the Rent Act 1977, Pt. IV. The amendments are consequent on the Housing Act 1980, para. 1436 and the Regulated Tenancies (Procedure) Regulations 1980, para. 1733. The 1971 regulations are disapplied when rent assessment committees are exercising the functions formerly conferred on rent tribunals under the Rent Act 1977 and on the Lands Tribunal by the Leasehold Reform Act 1967.

1737

The Rent Assessment Committees (England and Wales) (Rent Tribunal) Regulations 1980, S.I. 1980 No. 1700 (in force on 28th November 1980), replace the Furnished Houses (Rent Control) Regulations 1946, paras. 4–10, following the repeal by the Housing Act 1980, s. 152, Sch. 26, para. 1436, of the Rent Act 1977, s. 84 (b), which enabled the Secretary of State to make regulations with regard to proceedings before rent tribunals. These regulations deal with the procedure to be followed by rent assessment committees when carrying out the functions formerly conferred on rent tribunals and now carried out by them under the 1980 Act, s. 72.

1738 —— rent regulation—cancellation of registration

The Rent Regulation (Cancellation of Registration of Rent) Regulations 1980, S.I. 1980 No. 1698 (in force on 28th November 1980), prescribe the procedure to be followed when an application is made jointly by the landlord and tenant for the cancellation of the registration of a rent under the Rent Act 1977, s. 73, as amended by the Housing Act 1980, s. 62, para. 1436, so that an application for cancellation may also be made where the dwelling-house is not for the time being subject to a regulated tenancy. Provision is also made for the service of notifications by the rent officer in such a case. The Rent Regulation (Cancellation of Registration of Rent) Regulations 1972 are revoked.

1739 —— —— forms

The Rent Act 1977 (Forms etc.) Regulations 1980, S.I. 1980 No. 1697 (in force on 28th November 1980), supersede the Rent (Agriculture) (Rent Registration) Regulations 1978 and the Rent Regulation (Forms etc.) Regulations 1978, 1978 Halsbury's Abridgment paras. 1755, 1744. They also replace the Furnished Houses (Rent Control) Regulations 1946, paras. 11, 12. They prescribe the forms to be used for the purposes of various provisions of the Rent (Agriculture) Act 1976 and the Rent Act 1977. The main changes in the forms reflect the amendments made to those Acts by the Housing Act 1980, para. 1436. Certain forms previously prescribed are not repeated. Four new forms have been prescribed; an application for cancellation of a registered rent where there is no regulated tenancy; notices to be given by rent officers to landlords and tenants on the receipt of applications for the registration of fair rents; and the application for the cancellation of a rent registered by a rent tribunal. The fee payable for a certified copy of an entry in the register kept by rent officers and in the register kept by the president of rent assessment panels is increased to 50p.

1740   —— review clause—construction of clause

A lease of business premises provided for a rent review on specified dates. The new rent was to be the rack rental market value of the premises, which was the amount agreed to be the best rent at which the premises might reasonably be expected to be let in the open market as a whole for a term not exceeding five and a half years. The question arose whether, in assessing the rack rental market value, account was to be taken of any possibility of the tenancy being continued or renewed under the Landlord and Tenant Act 1954, Part II. *Held*, under the review clause, the parties were to envisage the premises being put on the market as a whole for a term not exceeding five and a half years, and then to decide what was the best rent at which they could be expected to be let. A bidder would be likely to have in mind the possibility that a new tenancy might be granted under the 1954 Act at the end of the term and increase his bid accordingly. To take account of the possibilities under the 1954 Act was not to assess the rent for a term longer than five and a half years, but to assess it for a term of five and a half years, one of the possbilities of which was that it might be continued or renewed. Accordingly, in assessing the rack rental market value, account should be taken of the provisions of the 1954 Act.

SECRETARY OF STATE FOR THE ENVIRONMENT V PIVOT PROPERTIES LTD [1980] LS Gaz R 1182 (Court of Appeal: LAWTON and BRIGHTMAN LJJ and SIR PATRICK BROWNE). Decision of Phillips J (1979) 39 P & CR 386 affirmed.

1741   —— —— —— notice of increase—validity of counternotice

A rent review clause provided that the increased rental was to be the sum specified in a notice from the landlord unless either the parties agreed or a valid counternotice was served by the tenant requiring determination by a third party. Time was expressed to be of the essence in the rent review procedure. The landlord served a valid notice specifying a rental and this was followed by a letter from the tenant's solicitors. Negotiations between the parties continued after expiry of the period allowed for service of the counternotice and eventually broke down. It fell to be decided whether the solicitor's letter was a valid counternotice. *Held*, the solicitor's letter was ambiguous as to whether determination by a third party was being demanded and was not therefore a valid counternotice. Consequently, upon expiry of the period for service of the counternotice and in the absence of agreement between the parties, the rental was that specified in the landlord's notice. Continued negotiation by the landlord was not a sufficiently clear representation to the tenant that the landlord had waived the requirement of a counternotice and did not estop the landlord from disputing its validity.

OLDSCHOOL V JOHNS (1980) 256 Estates Gazette 381 (Chancery Division: M WHEELER QC).

1742   —— —— no machinery for arbitration in default of agreement—rectification

Due to the mistake of the lessor the rent review clause in a renewed lease was executed without provision for arbitration in default of agreement. The lessor claimed rectification. *Held*, rectification would be granted because the contract was concluded on the basis that such a provision was included, the tenant being aware of the lessor's mistake and failing to draw his attention to it. The arbitrator should determine the rent at such amount as it would have been reasonable for the parties to have agreed under the lease, not at the market rent.

THOMAS BATES AND SON LTD V WYNDHAM'S (LINGERIE) LTD (1980) Times, 25th November (Court of Appeal: BUCKLEY, EVELEIGH and BRIGHTMAN LJJ). *A. Roberts and Co Ltd v Leicestershire County Council* [1961] Ch 555, applied. Decision of Michael Wheeler QC (1979) 39 P & CR 517 reversed in part.

1743   —— —— provision for open market rent—non-compliance by lessor with procedural provisions—whether clause inoperative

A rent review clause in a lease provided an adequate formula for determining an increased rental as well as a specific procedure for putting the formula into

operation. Strict compliance with time limits was stipulated. The landlord failed
to follow the specified procedure. *Held*, where there was a clearly expressed
requirement of strict compliance with a procedure then that procedure had to be
followed or the power to review was lost. The old rental would continue for the
remainder of the lease.

WELLER V AKEHURST (1980) Times, 29th November (Chancery Division: FOX
J). *United Scientific Holdings Ltd v Burnley Borough Council* [1978] AC 904, 1977
Halsbury's Abridgment para. 1673 followed.

1744   —— —— **time limit**

A lease made in 1961 contained a rent review clause: This provided for an
assessment of a higher rent for the period from 25th June 1975 onwards to be made
by the lessor and submitted for the lessee's approval on or before 25th December
1974. In the event of failure to agree on or before the date appointed (in respect of
which time was to be deemed to be of the essence) the new rent was to be fixed by
an independent surveyor appointed by the parties; failing agreement as to such
appointment by 25th January 1975 (time again being deemed to be of the essence)
it was to be fixed by an independent surveyor appointed by the president of the
Royal Institution of Chartered Surveyors. Thus time was expressed to be of the
essence for the subsequent procedures but not for the "trigger" notice itself. The
lessor did not give that notice to the lessee until January 1975. *Held*, time was not
of the essence for that purpose and consequently the lessor was not out of time.

AMHERST V JAMES WALKER GOLDSMITH & SILVERSMITH LTD (1980) 254 Estates
Gazette 123 (Court of Appeal: MEGAW and EVELEIGH LJJ and SIR DAVID CAIRNS).
United Scientific Holdings Ltd v Burnley Borough Council [1977] 2 All ER 62, HL,
1977 Halsbury's Abridgment para. 1673 followed.

1745   —— —— —— **non-compliance**

In a case where an underlease provided a rent review clause the lessor served notice
for a rent review after the specified date in the clause. The question arose as to the
importance of time limits specified in rent review clauses. *Held*, time was, prima
facie, not of the essence of a rent review clause. It was however of the essence in
certain circumstances, namely (i) if it was expressly so provided by the parties in the
clause itself (ii) if there was some clear inter-relation of the rent review clause with
a break clause or, (ii) if there was some contra indication from surrounding
circumstances.

AL SALOOM V SHIRLEY JAMES TRAVEL SERVICE LTD [1980] LS Gaz R 296
(Chancery Division: JOHN MILLS QC). *United Scientific Holdings Ltd v Burnley
Borough Council* [1977] 2 All ER 62, 1977 Halsbury's Abridgment para. 1673
applied.

1746   A rent review clause in a business premises lease provided a procedure for increasing
the rental which operated to certain time limits. In 1972 the landlords served notice
on the tenants of their intention to review the rental. The tenants replied claiming
that as the notice was out of time under the review procedure it was invalid and
consequently the rent could not be reviewed again until the expiry of the then
current seven year rental period just begun. The landlords ceased to insist upon a
review and the tenants, believing they would continue to enjoy a low rental,
expended money on their business. Following the decision of the House of Lords
in *United Scientific Holdings Limited v Burnley Borough Council* [1977] 2 All ER 62,
1977 Halsbury's Abridgment para. 1673, the landlords renewed their 1972 notice
by letter dated October 1977. The tenants disputed the landlords' right to claim
increased rent prior to October 1977 on the basis that by their actions, and in
particular by not pursuing the matter in 1972 or for five years thereafter, the
landlords had waived their rights of review and under the doctrine of promissory
estoppel could not then reassert them. *Held*, by their actions the landlords had
merely acknowledged that under the law as it then appeared their notice was invalid
and they could not enforce a review of rent, but this did not amount to a promise or
representation on their part not to enforce a review should it become legally possible

for them to do so. Accordingly there was no basis upon which they could be estopped from asserting their rights and they were entitled to recover the rent increase from the beginning of the rent period in 1972.

JAMES V HEIM GALLERY (LONDON) LTD (1979) 256 Estates Gazette 819 (Court of Appeal: BUCKLEY, SHAW AND OLIVER LJJ). Decision of Judge Thomas (1979) 39 P & CR 155 reversed.

1747 Rent and repair—recovery of rent—breach of covenant by landlord—tenant's right to equitable set-off

A lease provided that the landlords undertook to do certain repairs. Such works were to commence within three months of the signing of the lease. The tenants failed to pay any rent and no repairs were carried out. The landlords brought an action claiming the arrears of rent. The tenants counter-claimed damages in respect of the landlords' breach of their undertaking to repair the premises. They further contended that their obligation to pay rent had been suspended as soon as the landlords had become in breach of their undertaking, and that they were entitled to set off their claim for damages against the landlords' claim for rent. *Held*, the tenants' obligation under the lease to pay rent and the landlords' obligation to carry out repairs were separate obligations. The tenants' obligation was not removed or altered by any breach by the landlords of their undertaking. There were no grounds for treating an obligation to pay rent as an obligation different in kind from that imposed by other contracts. A claim for unliquidated damages was capable of being set off against a claim for rent provided that there was a sufficiently close connection between the two claims. As there was a close connection between the claims the tenants' counter-claim for damages would be capable in law of constituting a valid equitable set-off against the landlords' claim for rent.

MELVILLE V GRAPELODGE DEVELOPMENTS LTD (1979) 39 P & CR 179 (Queen's Bench Division: NEILL J). *Taylor v Webb* [1937] 2 KB 283, dicta of Lord Denning MR in *Henriksens Reden A/S v THZ Rolimpex* [1973] 3 All ER 589, CA, and *Federal Commerce & Navigation Co Ltd v Molena Alpha Inc* [1978] 3 All ER 1066, CA, 1978 Halsbury's Abridgment para. 2607 applied.

1748 Secure tenancy—exceptions—student lettings

The Secure Tenancies (Designated Causes) Regulations 1980, S.I. 1980 No. 1407 (in force on 3rd October 1980), designate certain courses of further education for the purposes of the Housing Act 1980, Sch. 3, para. 11. Under that provision, a tenancy is not a secure tenancy if it was granted to enable the tenant to attend a course so designated.

1749 ——— notice requiring secure tenant to give up possession—form of notice

The Secure Tenancies (Notices) Regulations 1980, S.I. 1980 No. 1339 (in force on 5th September 1980), prescribe the form of the notices which have to be served on a secure tenant under the Housing Act 1980, para. 1436, before the court can entertain proceedings for possession of a dwelling house let under a secure tenancy or for the termination of a secure tenancy.

1750 Statutory tenancy—limited company—provision of dwelling for director

Under an agreement with the defendant company the owner of a flat let it for occupation by a director of the company. The agreement was signed by the director as director tenant. The tenant's covenants were more suitable to a personal tenant than a corporation. On expiry of the contractual tenancy it was claimed that a statutory tenancy had come into existence but an order for possession was made. On appeal, *held*, a limited company could not on termination of its contractual tenancy acquire a statutory tenancy either for itself or for a residential occupier. The possession order would be upheld.

FIRSTCROSS LTD v EAST WEST (EXPORT/IMPORT) LTD (1980) 255 Estates Gazette 355 (Court of Appeal: STEPHENSON and DUNN LJJ and SIR STANLEY REES). *Hiller v United Dairies (London) Ltd* [1934] 1 KB 57, CA, and *Dando (SL) Ltd v Hitchcock* [1954] 2 QB 317, CA, applied.

1751   —— **occupation of dwelling house as residence—property owned by company—whether in effect owned by owner of company**

In 1964 the plaintiff purchased a property, with his own money, which he had conveyed into the name of a company, in which he owned all the shares. He let the property, and in 1978 sought possession, under the Rent Act 1977, Sch. 15, Case 9, on the ground that the property was reasonably required for occupation by himself and his family. The company transferred the property to him by way of a deed of gift so as to enable him to claim, for the purposes of Case 9, that he did not become a landlord by purchase on any day after 23rd March 1965, because he had acquired the property as a gift. The county court judge made an order for possession, and on appeal the question for the court was whether the plaintiff was a landlord who had become a landlord by purchasing the house after 23rd March 1965. *Held,* the plaintiff had paid the purchase price of the property in 1964 and the company was a mere nominee. Thus, when he re-acquired the property in 1978 he was already the landlord by virtue of the 1964 purchase, and the application of Case 9 was not therefore excluded. The order for possession would stand and the appeal would be dismissed.

EVANS v ENGELSON (1979) 253 Estates Gazette 577 (Court of Appeal: ORMROD and CUMMING-BRUCE LJJ and SIR DAVID CAIRNS).

1752   —— **right of succession—member of tenant's family—whether married man a member of family of mistress**

A person is entitled to remain in occupation of a dwelling-house as a statutory tenant by succession, pursuant to the Rent Act 1977, s. 2 (1), Sch. 3, para. 3, if he is a member of the family of the original tenant. It fell to be determined whether the defendant, a married man who had lived with his mistress for nearly twenty years, was a member of her family. *Held,* OLIVER LJ dissenting, notwithstanding that the parties had retained their own names and that the defendant had not divorced his wife and married his mistress, their relationship was a permanent and stable association. In the light of the facts the ordinary man would consider the defendant to be a member of his mistress's family, and accordingly there would be a declaration to that effect.

WATSON v LUCAS [1980] 3 All ER 647 (Court of Appeal: STEPHENSON and OLIVER LJJ and SIR DAVID CAIRNS). *Dyson Holdings Ltd v Fox* [1975] 3 All ER 1030, CA, 1975 Halsbury's Abridgment para. 2771, applied.

1753   **Surrender of tenancy—validity—matrimonial home—wife remaining in occupation**

See *Hoggett v Hoggett*, para. 1491.

LAW REFORM

1754   **Articles**

Royal Commission on Legal Services (1) Benson and the Criminal Bar, Michael Hill; (2) Criminal Legal Services—Gifts or Millstones, Michael King: [1980] Crim LR 75 & 84.

1755   County court—interest on judgments
See *Ealing London Borough Council v El Isaacs*, para. 1445.

1756   Criminal law—attempt—Law Commission proposals—proposed statutory offence
See para. 568.

1757   —— juvenile offenders—proposals for strengthening the law relating to juvenile and young adult offenders
See para. 603.

1758   —— offences relating to the administration of justice—proposed reform
See para. 622.

1759   —— sexual offences—Law Revision Committee's recommendations
See para. 635.

1760   Divorce—financial provision—power of court to order a sale of property—Law Commission's recommendations
See para. 945.

1761   —— nullity of marriage—proposed reform on three-year restriction on presenting petition
See para. 954.

1762   Legal aid—costs—charging order on matrimonial home
See *Hanlon v Law Society*, para. 1790.

1763   Prison service—reform of internal organisation
See para. 2255.

1764   Public order—control of processions and demonstrations
See para. 631.

1765   Road traffic—drinking and driving—proposals for reform
See para. 2363.

1766   Taxation—interest on overdue tax—proposed increase in limit
See para. 1572.

1767   Town and country planning—proposals for improving planning appeals system
See para. 2862.

1768   Wills—making and revocation—Law Reform Committee's recommendations
See para. 3143.

LEASEHOLD ENFRANCHISEMENT OR EXTENSION

Halsbury's Laws of England (3rd edn.), Vol. 23, Supp. paras. 1747–1845

1769   **Acquisition of freehold—long tenancy at low rent—meaning of low rent**

A lease dated July 1945 was granted for a term of forty and one half years at a rent of £100 per annum and in consideration of a premium of £500. The tenant acquired the lease in 1973. In 1978 the tenant gave notice to the landlords of his claim to acquire the freehold of the property in question under the Leasehold Reform Act 1967, s. 4 (1) on the basis of the lease creating a "low rent tenancy". The issue to be decided was whether at the commencement of the lease the rent "exceeded two-thirds of the letting value of the property (on the same terms)"; only if it did not could the tenant's claim succeed. The county court found in favour of the tenant and the landlords appealed. *Held*, in determining the letting value of a property any premium lawfully obtainable as consideration for granting a lease must be taken into account in addition to the rent obtainable on the open market for the property on the terms of the lease. Taking such premium into account in the case before the court showed the rent at the commencement of the tenancy as being less than two-thirds of the letting value of the property and consequently the tenant was entitled to obtain the freehold. The appeal would be dismissed.

MANSON V DUKE OF WESTMINSTER (1980) 125 Sol Jo 16 (Court of Appeal: STEPHENSON, BRANDON LJJ and SIR DAVID CAIRNS).

1770   **—— occupation of house by tenant as his residence—interruption of occupation**

From December 1973 the applicants were tenants of a house on a long lease at a low rent, subject to a mortgage. From August to November 1974 they were abroad. In October 1975 they again went abroad, leaving caretakers in the house and asking estate agents to sublet it, although it was not in fact sublet. The mortgage instalments fell into arrears and in December 1976 the mortgagees took possession. The applicants returned in January 1977 and in March 1977 received the keys, while agreeing that the mortgagees remained in lawful possession. In September 1977 they again became lawful mortgagors in possession. They did not reoccupy the house until May 1979, because until then it was unfit for habitation. In December 1978 they gave notice under the Leasehold Reform Act 1967 of their desire to acquire the freehold, and the question arose whether they had been occupying the house as their residence for the last five years or for periods amounting to five years in the last ten years within the 1967 Act, s. 1. *Held*, between December 1976 and September 1977 the applicants had not been occupying the house "in right of the tenancy" within s. 1 but by permission of the mortgagees; accordingly, they had not been occupying it as their residence during that time. Section 1 clearly contemplated periods when the residential occupation was interrupted, but it had to be applied strictly. Going away for a short holiday did not involve a break in occupation, but once the tenant was not physically in occupation the onus was on him to show that he had taken steps to maintain occupation. In this case, the applicants' arrangements about subletting had been such as to make them cease to occupy the house as their residence. Hence they were not entitled to acquire the freehold.

POLAND V EARL CADOGAN [1980] 3 All ER 544 (Court of Appeal: MEGAW, WALLER and EVELEIGH LJJ).

The period specified in the 1967 Act, s. 1, has been reduced to three years: Housing Act 1980, s. 141, Sch. 21.

LEGAL AID AND ADVICE

Halsbury's Laws of England (4th edn.), Vol. 11, paras. 751–779; (3rd edn.), Vol. 30, paras. 901–1036

1771   Costs—criminal proceedings—payment to witnesses out of Central Fund

See para. 661.

1772   —— unassisted party—award out of Legal Aid Fund—costs of counterclaim

The plaintiffs, part-time entertainers, sought declarations that contracts which they had entered into with the defendants, their managers, had been induced by oppression and fraud and were not binding on them. They also claimed an account of all sums received by the defendants on their behalf. The defendants obtained legal aid and in their defence denied all the plaintiffs' allegations. A year later, one of the defendants obtained an extension of his legal aid certificate entitling him to counterclaim against the plaintiffs. At the trial the defendant added an alternative counterclaim for remuneration on a quantum meruit basis. The dispute was subsequently settled in the plaintiffs' favour, but due to the financial position of the defendants, the plaintiffs had to accept judgment for £2,000. The plaintiffs had incurred costs in excess of £6,000, but the costs could not be recovered from the defendants as they were legally aided with nil contributions. In addition, the company which had paid money to the defendants on the plaintiffs' behalf were claiming a repayment of £8,000. Accordingly, the plaintiffs sought an order for costs against the Legal Aid Fund under the Legal Aid Act 1974, s. 13. The judge ordered payment of the plaintiffs' costs of the counterclaim and directed that in taxing those costs, the costs incurred after the date of the counterclaim on issues common to both claim and counterclaim should be divided equally between the two. The Legal Aid Fund appealed. *Held*, where it was ordered that a claim and counterclaim be dismissed or allowed with costs, the rule of taxation was that the claim should be treated as if it stood alone, and the counterclaim should bear only the amount by which the costs of the proceedings had been increased by it. In the instant case, the plaintiffs' costs would have been incurred even if the claim had stood alone, and although the counterclaim for remuneration on the basis of quantum meruit did raise a new issue, it was unlikely that it involved the plaintiffs in any significant increase in their costs. The Legal Aid Fund was not a party to the proceedings and the judge's order was made pursuant to the statutory power under s. 13 and not in exercise of the inherent jurisdiction of the court. The costs incurred in connection with the claim could never be appropriated to the counterclaim, either wholly or by apportionment, so as to become part of the costs of the counterclaim. In effect, the judge had inadvertently ordered the fund to pay part of the plaintiffs' costs of the claim and the appeal would, accordingly, be allowed.

MILLICAN v TUCKER [1980] 1 All ER 1083 (Court of Appeal: BUCKLEY and DONALDSON LJJ). *Saner v Bilton* (1879) 11 Ch D 416 applied.

1773   —— —— —— costs of interlocutory appeal

In proceedings in the Queen's Bench Division for damages for personal injuries, the plaintiff was granted a legal aid certificate in respect of the entirety of his proceedings. The defendants were not legally aided. The plaintiff's appeal against an interlocutory order requiring him to submit unconditionally to an examination by the defendants' medical adviser was authorised by the legal aid committee, but no separate legal aid certificate was issued in respect of the appeal. The interlocutory appeal was dismissed and it was ordered that, subject to any objection by the Law Society, the defendants' costs of the appeal be paid out of the legal aid fund. On the Law Society's objection to the order, *held*, an interlocutory appeal to the Court of Appeal in a Queen's Bench action amounted to "proceedings" between the assisted party and the unassisted party within the Legal Aid Act 1974, s. 13 (1). Accordingly, on the determination of such an appeal, the court had power under s. 13 (1) to order payment out of the legal aid fund of the successful unassisted party's costs of the appeal, since the "proceedings" had been "finally decided" in favour of the unassisted party within s. 13 (1). The order should stand.

MEGARITY v D. J. RYAN & SONS LTD (No. 2) [1980] 3 All ER 602 (Court of Appeal: LORD ROSKILL and ORMROD LJ).

This decision has been affirmed by the House of Lords; see [1981] 1 All ER 641. For previous proceedings, see [1980] 2 All ER 832, para. 2242.

1774　　—— —— —— meaning of "court of first instance"

A defendant, who was not receiving legal aid, appealed to a judge in chambers against an order of the district registrar. An order was made by the judge dismissing the defendant's appeal but ordering the legal aid fund to pay the costs of the appeal. By the Legal Aid Act 1974, s. 13 an order may be made against the fund in favour of an unassisted party in certain circumstances, but under s. 13 (3) no order is to be made in respect of costs incurred in a court of first instance; it was contended that a judge in chambers was a court of first instance. *Held*, a court of first instance was one which first heard and determined a case and which could make an order which was effective and operative unless reversed on appeal. An appellate court was one which could rehear a matter decided at first instance and which could reverse that decision. On this test, in the present case, the district registrar was the court of first instance and the judge in chambers was the appellate court; thus the order to the fund to pay the costs of the appeal would be upheld.

GAYWAYS LININGS LTD v TOCZEK (1980) Times, 1st March (Court of Appeal: LORD DENNING MR, SHAW and BRANDON LJJ).

This decision has been affirmed by the House of Lords; see [1981] 1 All ER 641.

1775　　Criminal proceedings

The Legal Aid in Criminal Proceedings (General) (Amendment) Regulations 1980, S.I. 1980 No. 661 (in force on 23rd June 1980), amend the Legal Aid in Criminal Proceedings (General) Regulations 1968, reg. 26, as amended, to correct an error in drafting.

1776　　The Legal Aid in Criminal Proceedings (General) (Amendment No. 2) Regulations 1980, S.I. 1980 No. 1651 (in force on 24th November 1980), amend the Legal Aid in Criminal Proceedings (General) Regulations 1968. The 1980 Regulations take account of the abolition of the Supplementary Benefits Commission and the transfer of its function to inquire into the means of an assisted person to the Secretary of State.

1777　　—— assessment of resources

The Legal Aid in Criminal Proceedings (Assessment of Resources) (Amendment) Regulations 1980, S.I. 1980 No. 1652 (in force on 24th November 1980), amend the Legal Aid in Criminal Proceedings (Assessment of Resources) Regulations 1978, 1978 Halsbury's Abridgment para. 1774. The 1980 Regulations take account of the abolition of the Supplementary Benefits Commission and the transfer of its function to inquire into the means of an assisted person to the Secretary of State.

1778　　—— transfer of ministerial responsibility

The Transfer of Functions (Legal Aid in Criminal Proceedings and Costs in Criminal Cases) Order 1980, S.I. 1980 No. 705 (in force on 1st July 1980), transfers certain functions of the Home Secretary to the Lord Chancellor. The functions in question are those under Part II of the Legal Aid Act 1974 and the Costs of Criminal Cases Act 1973 and the regulations made thereunder relating to legal aid in criminal proceedings and costs in criminal cases in England and Wales. The order also makes amendments to the functions incidental to and consequential on the transfer.

1779　　Legal advice and assistance

The Legal Advice and Assistance Regulations (No. 2) 1980, S.I. 1980 No. 1898 (in force on 1st January 1981), consolidate the Legal Advice and Assistance Regulations

1980, paras. 1780–1782, with minor amendments including amendments to take account of the Legal Aid Scheme 1980.

1780   —— assessment of resources—disposable income—allowances for dependants

The Legal Advice and Assistance (Amendment No. 2) Regulations 1980, S.I. 1980 No. 1628 (in force on 24th November 1980), further amend the Legal Advice and Assistance Regulations 1980, para. 1781, to take account of charges made by the Social Security Act 1980, para. 2761, which affect the allowances for a spouse, dependent child or dependent relative when assessing disposable income.

These regulations have been revoked: see now para. 1779.

1781   —— assistance by way of representation

The Legal Advice and Assistance Regulations 1980, S.I. 1980 No. 477 (in force on 28th April 1980) introduce assistance by way of representation as provided for by the Legal Aid Act 1979, 1979 Halsbury's Abridgments para. 1737. Such assistance may be approved on application by a solicitor by the appropriate area committee appointed by the Council of the Law Society or the appropriate local committee, but may be subject to certain conditions.

The regulations also consolidate the Legal Advice and Assistance Regulations 1973, as amended, with amendments, principally in relation to applications for advice and assistance. The table of maximum contributions previously contained in the Legal Aid Act 1974, s. 4 (3) is also set out.

These regulations have been revoked: see now para. 1779.

1782   —— charge on property recovered or preserved—exceptions

The Legal Advice and Assistance (Amendment) Regulations 1980, S.I. 1980 No. 1059 (in force on 25th August 1980) amend the 1980 Regulations, para. 1781, by extending the benefit of the £2,500 exemption from the statutory charge on property to various lump sum orders made under the Domestic Proceedings and Magistrates' Courts Act 1978 or under Acts amended by that Act and to lump sum orders payable to or for the benefit of a child under the Matrimonial Causes Act 1973. The regulations also reinstate disablement benefit and industrial death benefit in the list of exceptions to the statutory charge.

These regulations have been revoked: see now para. 1779.

1783   —— prospective cost

The Legal Advice and Assistance (Prospective Cost) Regulations 1980, S.I. 1980 No. 1119 (in force on 1st October 1979), increase from £25 to £40 the limit on the cost of legal advice and assistance under the Legal Aid Act 1974, ss. 1, 2, as amended by the Legal Aid Act 1979, which a solicitor may incur without obtaining the approval of the appropriate authority.

1784   Legal aid—assessment of resources

The Legal Aid (Assessment of Resources) Regulations 1980, S.I. 1980 No. 1630 (in force on 24th November 1980), consolidate, with amendments, the Legal Aid (Assessment of Resources) Regulations 1960 and subsequent amending regulations.

The main changes are that the assessment of resources is to be carried out by an officer authorised by the Secretary of State, that maintenance paid under a court order is not to be excluded from the assessment on the basis that it forms the subject matter of the dispute, that where a person is concerned in proceedings to a representative capacity the means of anyone who might benefit from the outcome may be taken into account and that, with a view to the discharge of a person's certificate, a committee may require the determination of current disposable income and capital outside the original period of computation.

The regulations also contain the rules for computing disposable income and disposable capital.

1785 —— —— **disposable income—determination by authorised officer**

The Legal Aid (General) (Amendment) Regulations 1980, S.I. 1980 No. 1629 (in force on 24th November 1980), amend the Legal Aid (General) Regulations 1971 to take account of the abolition of the Supplementary Benefits Commission and the transfer of its assessment of resources functions in respect of applications for legal aid to an officer authorised by the Secretary of State.

These regulations have been revoked; see para. 1786.

1786 —— **general**

The Legal Aid (General) Regulations 1980, S.I. 1980 No. 1894 (in force on 1st January 1981), consolidate with amendments the Legal Aid (General) Regulations 1971, the Legal Aid (Costs of Successful Unassisted Parties) Regulations 1964 and subsequent amending legislation. These regulations take into account the changes made by the Legal Aid Scheme 1980 and make other important amendments.

1787 —— **legal aid fund charge—effect of compromise**

The Legal Aid Act 1974, s. 9 (6) and (7) provides that sums remaining unpaid on account of a person's contribution to the legal aid fund in respect of any proceedings and, if the total contribution is less than the net liability of that fund on his account, a sum equal to the deficiency is to be a first charge for the benefit of the legal aid fund in respect of any property which is recovered for him in proceedings. Such property includes any rights under a compromise arrived at to terminate proceedings.

The plaintiff brought an action for breach of contract against a multinational company, having obtained a legal aid certificate from the Law Society to pursue the action. Heavy costs were incurred in the preparation of the case and the parties considered that a compromise was the best way of dealing with the matter. The company was prepared to pay the plaintiff £40,000 but the parties realised that the payment of that sum would attract the legal aid fund statutory charge under the Legal Aid Act 1974, s. 9 (6) and (7), resulting, after the payment of costs, in the plaintiff's bankruptcy. Subsequently a scheme was devised whereby £40,000 was to be paid to both the plaintiff's and the company's solicitors jointly. The solicitors, acting as the company's agents, were to buy up the plaintiff's debts and the company was to write them off. The solicitors were to reimburse themselves and the residue was to be paid to the plaintiff. The plaintiff informed the Law Society of the scheme shortly before a consent order containing the terms of the scheme was obtained. The Law Society claimed that the statutory charge had attached to the £40,000. The plaintiff, subsequently, successfully sought a declaration that the charge had not attached to that sum. On appeal by the Law Society, *held*, the court had to look at the concept underlying such a compromise and in the present case it was obvious that the £40,000 was to be used to pay off the plaintiff's debts at his request. It was therefore the subject of the statutory charge in favour of the legal aid fund. When money was paid to a party, or at his request to his creditors, it was plainly recovered "for him" within s. 9 (6). Furthermore, although the settlement had gone too far to be set aside, equity could intervene so as to hold that, if and in so far as the solicitors had intentionally deprived the fund of a charge for their own costs, they were themselves precluded from making any claims on the fund for those costs. The appeal would accordingly be allowed.

MANLEY v THE LAW SOCIETY [1981] 1 All ER 401 (Court of Appeal: LORD DENNING MR, ORMROD and O'CONNOR LJJ). Decision of Bristow J (1980) Times, 11th October, reversed.

1788 —— **taxation—application for review of taxation**

The plaintiff in an action for damages for personal injuries as a result of an accident was legally aided. His solicitors prepared a bill of costs for payment out of the legal aid fund. It included fees and expenses in respect of a visit with counsel to the scene of the accident, four years after the accident occurred. The taxing master disallowed the items on the ground that they were unreasonably incurred; the solicitors objected but the taxing master affirmed his decision. The solicitors then applied to the Law Society under the Legal Aid (General) Regulations 1971, reg. 23, for authority to apply for review of the taxation by a judge. Although the Law Society refused authority, the solicitors applied to a judge who refused to hear their application as it was not authorised by the Law Society. On appeal by the solicitors, *held*, under the Legal Aid Act 1974, Sch. 2, para. 4, legal aid taxation was on the common fund basis of a reasonable sum for costs reasonably incurred. In the absence of anyone to contest the amount of the bill, it was the taxing master's duty to protect the public interest and ensure that only reasonable expenditure was allowed. The taxing master decided quite properly that certain items should be disallowed. The solicitors could only apply for a review of taxation with the Law Society's authority which had been refused after careful consideration. Accordingly the appeal would be dismissed.

STORER V WRIGHT [1981] 2 WLR 208 (Court of Appeal: LORD DENNING MR, BRIGHTMAN LJ and SIR GEORGE BAKER). Decision of Neill J (1980) Times, 22nd July affirmed.

1789   **Legal Aid Act 1979—commencement**

The Legal Aid Act 1979 (Commencement No. 2) Order 1980, S.I. 1980 No. 476 brought into force on 28th April 1980 the remainder of Parts I (ss. 1–5) and III (ss. 11–14, Schs. 1 and 2) of the Act not already in force. These provisions relate to England and Wales.

1790   **Legal aid certificate—costs—charging order on matrimonial home**

In January 1972 a wife was granted a full legal aid certificate to enable her to pursue a suit for divorce, continue property proceedings and to apply for a non-molestation order. She was granted a decree of divorce and the matrimonial home was transferred to her absolutely. Costs amounted to £8,000 and a charge on the house was registered by the Law Society. The wife had difficulty maintaining the property and wished to buy a smaller house. She was informed that the Law Society had no power to register a charge on a replacement house. Her application for a declaration that she had not "recovered or preserved" any property within the Legal Aid Act 1974, s. 9 (6) by virtue of the proceedings for ancillary relief brought by her against her husband, was refused. On appeal the questions for the House of Lords were whether, (i) the legal aid fund was entitled to the charge, and to what extent and, (ii) there was a discretion as to its enforcement by the Law Society. *Held*, (i) the legal aid certificate had been made to cover the whole of the proceedings including the suit for divorce, for custody, access and the transfer of the matrimonial home. The legal aid fund was entitled to the charge where property was "recovered or preserved" under s. 9 (6), if ownership or transfer had been in issue in the proceedings as a matter of fact rather than of theoretical risk. On the facts of the present case the ownership of the whole house had been in issue and accordingly the house was property recovered by the wife in respect of her husband's interest and preserved to her in respect of her own. The whole house was therefore subject to the charge in favour of the legal aid fund. (ii) The Law Society had a discretion, as chargee, to postpone enforcement of the charge or accept a substitute charge on a replacement house. In considering how to exercise this discretion its duty was not only to the legal aid fund but to the legal aid scheme as a whole.

Their Lordships urged the legislative and executive authorities to make an urgent review of the problems raised in this case and to make any consequential amendments necessary.

HANLON V THE LAW SOCIETY [1980] 2 All ER 199 (House of Lords: LORD EDMUND-DAVIES, LORD SIMON OF GLAISDALE, LORD FRASER OF TULLYBELTON, LORD SCARMAN and LORD LOWRY). Decision of Court of Appeal [1980] 1 All ER 764 affirmed.

LIBEL AND SLANDER

Halsbury's Laws of England (4th edn.), Vol. 28, paras. 1–300

1791   Defence—fair comment—essentials of defence

Canada

In a libel action arising out of a newspaper editorial it was held that, in order to establish the defence of fair comment the subject matter had to be of public importance and was to be truthfully reported. In deciding whether comments made were fair, the court had to consider what an ordinary reader would understand from the facts as stated compared with what in fact did occur.

HOLT v SUN PUBLISHING CO LTD (1979) 100 DLR (3d) 447 (Court of Appeal of British Columbia). *Kemsley v Foot* [1952] AC 345 applied.

1792   —— privilege—qualified privilege—existence of express malice—circumstances under which judge should leave question to jury

Canada

The respondent alleged in two letters that the appellant had committed a deliberate and carefully calculated fraud in respect of a mortgage which he had executed on a house constructed by the appellant. The appellant had retained documents relating to an earlier mortgage which had been superseded, and registered a caution in respect of the existing mortgage which they had agreed would not be registered. The letters were written to a solicitor acting for a third party who had arranged to purchase the existing mortgage and to the appellant's solicitors. A libel action was commenced and it was found that the letters were written on occasions of qualified privilege. At first instance the question of malice was left to the jury. It was withdrawn on appeal and the company appealed. *Held*, qualified privilege existed to enable the respondent to protect his legitimate interests and created a presumption against malice. It was necessary to show more than a mere possibility of malice in order to override the privilege. Accordingly, the question of the existence of express malice, which alone would destroy the privilege, should not be left to the jury unless a probable case was made for it. In the present case there was insufficient evidence to raise a probability of malice. The respondent asserted an honest belief in the truth of his statement, since he was motivated by a desire to protect his interest in the house. The appeal would therefore be dismissed.

DAVIES AND DAVIES LTD v KOTT (1980) 98 DLR (3d) 591 (Supreme Court of Canada).

1793   Pleading—statement of claim—order requiring further and better particulars—television play

Canada

The defendants, a television company, broadcast a play based on recent political events. The plaintiff, a local politician, issued a statement of claim alleging that he had been defamed in the play. In the statement of claim he alleged that the defendants had defamed him by the combined effect of images and scenes, statements falsely attributed to him and others, and music and narration which together portrayed him as weak and irresolute and as having concealed from the public the true nature of certain negotiations. The defendants successfully applied for an order requiring the plaintiff to provide further and better particulars of the defamation alleged. The plaintiff appealed. *Held*, the plaintiff's assertion that the whole play was defamatory overstated the situation as regards a request for particulars. The whole play was to be taken into account in determining whether any particular episode was defamatory since it created a background against which episodes might be defamatory. The statement of claim should specify the defamatory episodes in detail. There was an analogy between a defamatory broadcast and defamatory passages in a book, and a similar method of particularisation of the episodes alleged to be defamatory should be adopted. The appeal would be allowed to the extent that the earlier order for particulars would be varied.

LOUGHEED V CANADIAN BROADCASTING CORPN (1979) 98 DLR (3d) 264 (Supreme Court of Alberta, Appellate Division).

LIBRARIES

Halsbury's Laws of England (4th edn.), Vol. 23, paras. 301–500

1794   Public Lending Right Act 1979—commencement

The Public Lending Right Act 1979 (Commencement) Order 1980, S.I. 1980 No. 83, brought the Act into force on 1st March 1980.

1795   —— scheme for administration

The Chancellor of the Duchy of Lancaster has published a consultative document as a basis for consultation prior to the drawing up of a scheme for the administration of the public lending right under the Public Lending Right Act 1979, s. 3. It is proposed that rights under the Act be registered with a Registrar of Public Lending Right. Once registered, a right will subsist for the life of the author and for 50 years after his death. No right will be claimable after an author has died. All books will be eligible except (it is proposed) books issued without charge, books in Crown copyright and books with more than three co-authors. The Central Fund will pay the administrative expenses of the registrar and his staff; it will also be used to reimburse the relevant local authorities; the residue of the fund will be available for distribution to those entitled under the scheme. Payment will be made on the basis of the amount available for distribution in any one year and the estimated number of occasions on which registered books are loaned. A ceiling of £1000 per £1 million available for distribution is proposed on the payments to any one author in any year. The registrar will arrange for a stratified random sample of approximately 70 libraries to supply him with information concerning loans.

It is proposed that registration should be made on application by the author after publication. The author will have to support his application with, inter alia, proof of identity, a copy of the title page of the book and documentary proof of authorship. He will also have to quote the relevant international standard book number. It is hoped that the scheme will be operational in 1982–83.

LIMITATION OF ACTIONS

Halsbury's Laws of England (4th edn.), Vol. 28, paras. 601–1000

1796   Article

Overriding the Time Bar in Personal Injury Actions, John Vickers: 130 NLJ 380.

1797   Limitation Amendment Act 1980

The Limitation Amendment Act 1980 makes various provisions regarding the limitation of actions and other miscellaneous matters. The Act received the royal assent on 1st May 1980 and came into force on 1st August 1980 except s. 8 which comes into force on a day or days to be appointed: s. 14.

Section 1 makes provision for the beginning of the limitation period in the case of certain contracts for a loan. Section 2 relates to stolen goods and provides that only a bona fide purchaser for value may raise a defence of limitation against the owner. Section 3 provides that time does not begin to run in favour of a tenant at will until the tenancy is actually determined. A licence may not be implied by law so as to defeat an occupier's claim to adverse possession and thereby prevent time running in his favour: s. 4.   Certain trustees may rely on a defence of limitation against a claim by a beneficiary more than six years after distribution of the trust property: s. 5.   Section 6 provides that a right of action which has been barred under the Limitation Act 1939 cannot be revived.   Section 7 postpones the beginning of the limitation period in the case of fraud or mistake.   Various provisions relating to the limitation period in the case of new claims in pending actions are contained in s. 8.   Section 9 provides that the 1939 Act applies to Admiralty actions. Miscellaneous supplementary provisions and repeals are contained in ss. 10–14 and Schs. 1, 2.

This Act has been consolidated in the Limitation Act 1980; see para. 1798.

1798   Limitation Act 1980

The Limitation Act 1980 consolidates the Limitation Acts 1939 to 1980.   It received the royal assent on 13th November 1980 and, except for s. 35, will come into force on 1st May 1981.   Section 35 will also come into force on that date to the extent (if any) that the Limitation Act 1939, s. 28, as substituted by the Limitation Amendment Act 1980, s. 8, is in force immediately before that date; but otherwise it is to come into force on a day or days to be appointed.   Tables showing the destination of enactments consolidated and the derivation of the new Act are set out on pages 434–440 following.

DESTINATION TABLE

This table shows in column (1) the enactments repealed by the Limitation Act 1980, and in column (2) the provisions of that Act corresponding to the repealed provisions.

In certain cases the enactment in column (1), though having a corresponding provision in column (2), is not or is not wholly repealed, as it is still required, or partly required, for the purposes of other legislation.

(1)	(2)	(1)	(2)
Limitation Act 1939 (c 21)	Limitation Act 1980 (c 58)	Limitation Act 1939 (c 21)	Limitation Act 1980 (c 58)
s 1	s 1 (2)	s 9 (1)	Rep., 1980 c 24, ss 3 (1), 13 (2), Sch 2
2 (1) (a)	2, 5	(2)	Sch 1, para 5
(b)	Rep., 1980 c 24, s 13, Sch 1, para 2, Sch 2	(3), (4)	para 6
(c)	s 7	10	para 8
(d)	9 (1)	11	s 27
proviso	Rep., 1975 c 54, s 4 (4), Sch 1, para 3	12	16
(2)	Rep., 1980 c 24, s 13, Sch 1, para 2, Sch 2	13	Rep., 1980 c 24, s 13, Sch 1, para 6, Sch 2
(3)	s 8	14	s 25 (1), (2)
(4)	24	15	26
(5)	Rep., 1980 c 24, s 13, Sch 1, para 2, Sch 2	16	17, 25 (3)
(6)	Rep., 1980 c 24, ss 9 (2), 13 (2), Sch 2	17	19
(7)	s 36 (1)	18 (1)–(4)	20 (1)–(4)
(8)	11 (2)	(5)	(5)–(7)
2AA	6	(6)	Rep., 1980 c 24, ss 9 (2), 13 (2), Sch 2
2A (1), (2)	11 (1), (2)	19 (1), (1A)	s 21 (1), (2)
(3)	1 (2), 11 (3)	(2), (3)	(3), (4)
(4), (5)	11 (4), (5)	20	22
(6)–(8)	14	20A	23
(9), (10)	11 (6), (7)	21	Rep., 1954 c 36, ss 1, 8 (3), Sch
2B (1)	1 (2), 12 (3)	22 (1)	s 28 (1)
(2), (3)	12 (1), (2)	proviso	
(4)	(2), (3)	(a)–(c)	(2)–(4)
(5)	(3)	(d)	Rep., 1954 c 36, s 8 (3), Sch
2C (1)	13 (1)	(e)	Rep., 1980 c 24, s 13 (2), Sch 2
(2)	13	(2)	s 28 (6)
2D	33	(3)	(5)
3	3	23 (1)	29 (1), (2) (a), (3)
3A	4	(2)	(2) (b)
4 (1)	Sch 1, para 10	(3)	(4)
proviso	para 11 (1), (2)	(4)	(5), (6)
(2)	para 10	(5)	(7)
(3)	s 15 (1)	24	30
proviso	Sch 1, para 12	25 (1), (2)	31 (1), (2)
5	paras 1–3	(3)	(3), (4)
6 (1)	para 4	(4)	(5)
(2)	s 15 (2)	(5)	(6)
proviso	Sch 1, para 13	proviso	Rep., 1980 c 24, ss 6 (3), 13 (2), Sch 2
(3)–(5)	s 15 (3)–(5)	(6)	s 31 (7)
7 (1)–(4)	18	proviso	Rep., 1980 c 24, ss 6 (3), 13 (2), Sch 2
8	Sch 1, para 9 / para 7	(7), (8)	s 31 (8), (9)

(1)	(2)
Limitation Act 1939 (c 21)	Limitation Act 1980 (c 58)
s 26 (1)–(4)	s 32 (1)–(4)
(5)	(1)
27 (1)	34 (1), (7) (*b*)
(2)–(6)	(2)–(6)
(7)	(7) (*a*)
28	35
29	36 (2)
30 (1)	37 (1), (2), (5)
(2), (3)	(3), (4)
(4)	(6)
31 (1)	37 (2), 38 (1), Sch 1, para 11 (3)
(2)	s 38 (2)
(3)	(3), (4)
(4)	(5), (6)
(5), (6)	(7), (8)
(7)	(9), (10)
32	9 (2), 39
33	——
34 (1)	——
(2)	Rep., S.L.R.A. 1980
(3)	s 41 (4)
(4)	Rep., S.L.R.A. 1950
Schedule	Rep., S.L.R.A. 1950
Mental Health Act 1959 (c 72)	
Sch 7, Part I†	s 38 (4)
Limitation Act 1963 (c 47)	
s 4 (1)	10 (1)
(2)	(2)–(4)
(3)	1 (2), 10 (5)
(4)	10 (5)
5	10 (5)
7 (7)	10 (5)
14 (1)	See Sch 2, para 2
15	——
16 (1)	——
(2), (3)	s 41 (4)
Limitation Act 1975 (c 54)	
s 1	See under 1939 c 21, ss 2A–2D above
2 (1)	s 28 (5), (6)
(2)	——

(1)	(2)
Limitation Act 1975 (c 54)	Limitation Act 1980 (c 58)
s 3 (1), (2)	——
(3)	Sch 2, para 3
(4)	——
4 (1), (2)	——
(3)	s 41 (4)
(4)–(6)	Rep., 1976 c 30, s 6 (2), Sch 2
Sch 1, para 1	s 11 (2)
para 2	38 (1)
para 3	39
para 4	——
2	
Fatal Accidents Act 1976 (c 30)	
Sch 1, para 3	12, 13 (1), 33 (2), (6), Sch 2, para 4
Civil Liability (Contribution) Act 1978 (c 47)	
s 7 (1)*	Sch 2, para 1
Sch 1, para 6	s 1 (2), 10
Limitation Amendment Act 1980 (c 24)	
s 1	6
2	4
3 (1)	——
(2)	Sch 1, para 6 (1) (*a*)
(3)	2, para 8
(4)	1, para 6 (2)
4	para 8 (4)
5 (1)	s 21 (2)
(2)	18 (1), 22
6 (1)	29 (7)
(2)–(4)	——
(5)	Sch 2, para 5
7	s 32
8	35
9	——
11	——
12 (1)	Sch 2, para 9
(2), (3)	——
13	——
14 (2), (3)	——
(4)	s 41 (3), Sch 2, para 6
(5)*	41 (4)

† Repealed in part   * Not repealed

(1)	(2)	(1)	(2)
Limitation Amendment Act 1980 (c 24)	Limitation Act 1980 (c 58)	Limitation Amendment Act 1980 (c 24)	Limitation Act 1980 (c 58)
Sch 1, para 1	——	Sch 1, para 9	s 31 (2), (5)
para 2 (a)–(c)	——	para 10 (a)	34 (7) (b)
para 2 (d)	s 24 (1)	para 10 (b)	(5) (b)
para 2 (e)	——	para 11	37 (2)
para 3 (a)	11 (4) (b)	para 12	——
para 3 (b), (c)	14 (2), (3)	para 13	38 (3), (4)
para 4	12 (2), (3)	para 14	——
para 5–7	——	para 15	9 (2), 39
para 8	23	2	——

TABLE OF DERIVATIONS

This table shows in the right-hand column the legislative source from which the sections of the Limitation Act 1980 in the left-hand column have been derived. In the table the following abbreviations are used:

1939 = The Limitation Act 1939 (2 & 3 Geo. 6 c. 21)
1963 = The Limitation Act 1963 (1963 c. 47)
1975 = The Limitation Act 1975 (1975 c. 54)
1976 = The Fatal Accidents Act 1976 (1976 c. 30)
1978 = The Civil Liability (Contribution) Act 1978 (1978 c. 47)
1980 = The Limitation Amendment Act 1980 (1980 c. 24)

NB. Sections 2A to 2D of the Limitation Act 1939 were inserted by section 1 of the Limitation Act 1975. This is not acknowledged in the Table.

Section of Act	Derivation
1	1939 ss. 1, 2A (3), 2B (1); 1963 s. 4 (3); 1978 Sch. 1 para. 6.
2	1939 s. 2 (1) (a).
3	1939 s. 3.
4	1939 s. 3A; 1980 s. 2.
5	1939 s. 2 (1) (a).
6	1939 s. 2AA; 1980 s. 1.
7	1939 s. 2 (1) (c).
8	1939 s. 2 (3).
9 (1)	1939 s. 2 (1) (d).
(2)	1939 s. 32; 1980 Sch. 1 para. 15.
10 (1)	1963 s. 4 (1); 1978 Sch. 1 para. 6.
(2), (3)	1963 s. 4 (2); 1978 Sch. 1 para. 6.
(4)	1963 s. 4 (2) (b); 1978 Sch. 1 para. 6.
(5)	1963 ss. 4 (3), (4), 5, 7 (7); 1978 Sch. 1 para. 6.
11 (1)	1939 s. 2A (1).
(2)	1939 ss. 2 (8), 2A (2); 1975 Sch. 1 para. 2.
(3)	1939 s. 2A (3).
(4)	1939 s. 2A (4); 1980 Sch. 1 para. 3 (a).
(5)	1939 s. 2A (5).
(6)	1939 s. 2A (9).
(7)	1939 s. 2A (10).
12 (1)	1939 s. 2B (2); 1976 Sch. 1 para. 3 (b).
(2)	1939 s. 2B (3), (4); 1976 Sch. 1 para. 3 (b); 1980 Sch. 1 para. 4 (a).
(3)	1939 s. 2B (1), (4), (5); 1976 Sch. 1 para. 3 (b); 1980 Sch. 1 para. 4.
13 (1)	1939 s. 2C (1), (2); 1976 Sch. 1 para. 3 (b).
(2), (3)	1939 s. 2C (2).
14 (1)	1939 s. 2A (6).
(2)	1939 s. 2A (7); 1980 Sch. 1 para. 3 (b).
(3)	1939 s. 2A (8); 1980 Sch. 1 para. 3 (c).

Section of Act	Derivation
15 (1)	1939 s. 4 (3).
(2)–(5)	1939 s. 6 (2)–(5).
(6), (7)	
16	1939 s. 12.
17	1939 s. 16.
18 (1)	1939 s. 7 (1); 1980 s. 5 (2).
(2)–(4)	1939 s. 7 (2)–(4).
19	1939 s. 17.
20 (1)–(4)	1939 s. 18 (1)–(4).
(5)–(7)	1939 s. 18 (5).
21 (1)	1939 s. 19 (1).
(2)	1939 s. 19 (1A); 1980 s. 5 (1).
(3)	1939 s. 19 (2).
(4)	1939 s. 19 (3).
22	1939 s. 10; 1980 s. 5 (2).
23	1939 s. 20A; 1980 Sch. 1 para. 8.
24 (1)	1939 s. 2 (4); 1980 Sch. 1 para. 2 (*d*).
(2)	1939 s. 2 (4).
25 (1), (2)	1939 s. 14 (1), (2).
(3)	1939 s. 16.
26	1939 s. 15.
27	1939 s. 11.
28 (1)–(4)	1939 s. 22 (1).
(5)	1939 s. 22 (3); 1975 s. 2 (1).
(6)	1939 s. 22 (2); 1975 s. 2 (1).
29 (1)	1939 s. 23 (1).
(2) (*a*)	1939 s. 23 (1) (*a*).
(*b*)	1939 s. 23 (2).
(3)	1939 s. 23 (1) (*b*).
(4)	1939 s. 23 (3).
(5), (6)	1939 s. 23 (4).
(7)	1939 s. 23 (5); 1980 s. 6 (1).
30	1939 s. 24.
31 (1)	1939 s. 25 (1).
(2)	1939 s. 25 (2); 1980 Sch. 1 para. 9 (*a*).
(3), (4)	1939 s. 25 (3).
(5)	1939 s. 25 (4); 1980 Sch. 1 para. 9 (*b*).
(6)–(9)	1939 s. 25 (5)–(8).
32 (1)	1939 s. 26 (1), (5); 1980 s. 7.
(2)–(4)	1939 s. 26 (2)–(4); 1980 s. 7.

Section of Act	Derivation
33	1939 s. 2D.
34 (1)–(4)	1939 s. 27 (1)–(4).
(5)	1939 s. 27 (5); 1980 Sch. 1 para. 10 (*b*).
(6)	1939 s. 27 (6).
(7) (*a*)	1939 s. 27 (7).
(*b*)	1939 s. 27 (1); 1980 Sch. 1 para. 10 (*a*).
35	1939 s. 28; 1980 s. 8.
36 (1)	1939 s. 2 (7).
(2)	1939 s. 29.
37 (1)	1939 s. 30 (1).
(2)	1939 s. 30 (1) proviso, s. 31 (1); 1980 Sch. 1 para. 11.
(3)	1939 s. 30 (2).
(4)	1939 s. 30 (3).
(5)	1939 s. 30 (1).
(6)	1939 s. 30 (4).
38 (1)	1939 s. 31 (1); 1975 Sch. 1 para. 3.
(2)	1939 s. 31 (2).
(3), (4)	1939 s. 31 (3); Mental Health Act 1959 (c. 72) Sch. 7 Pt. I; 1980 Sch. 1 para. 13.
(5), (6)	1939 s. 31 (4).
(7)	1939 s. 31 (5).
(8)	1939 s. 31 (6).
(9), (10)	1939 s. 31 (7).
39	1939 s. 32; 1975 Sch. 1 para. 4; 1980 Sch. 1 para. 15.
40	[Transitional provisions, amendments and repeals]
41	Short title, commencement and extent.
(1), (2)	—
(3)	1980 s. 14 (4).
(4)	1963 s. 16 (3).
Sch. 1	
para. 1	1939 s. 5 (1).
2	1939 s. 5 (2).
3	1939 s. 5 (3).
4	1939 s. 6 (1).
5	1939 s. 9 (2).
6 (1)	1939 s. 9 (3); 1980 s. 3 (2).
(2)	1939 s. 9 (4); 1980 s. 3 (4).
7	1939 s. 8.
8 (1)–(3)	1939 s. 10 (1)–(3).
(4)	1939 s. 10 (4); 1980 s. 4.
9	1939 s. 7 (5).
10	1939 s. 4 (1), (2).
11 (1), (2)	1939 s. 4 (1); proviso.
(3)	1939 s. 31 (1).
12	1939 s. 4 (3), proviso.
13	1939 s. 6 (2), proviso.

Section of Act	Derivation
Sch. 2	
para. 1	1978 s. 7 (1).
2	—
3	1975 s. 3 (3).
4	1976 Sch. 1 para. 3.
5	1980 s. 6 (5).
6	1980 s. 14 (4).
7	—
8	1980 s. 3 (3).
9	1980 s. 12 (1).
Sch. 3	[Consequential amendments]
Sch. 4	[Enactments repealed]

1799   Parties—joinder of second defendant—action time-barred—date joinder takes effect—rule of practice

In 1973 the plaintiff was injured while travelling as a passenger in a car driven by S which collided with another car driven by the defendant. In 1975 the plaintiff issued a writ against the defendant claiming damages in negligence for personal injury. The defendant's insurers repudiated liability and the Motor Insurers Bureau (MIB) nominated another company as his insurers. In 1977 the plaintiff delivered his statement of claim and the defendant alleged in his defence contributory negligence on the part of S. Accordingly, in 1978 at the instance of the MIB the plaintiff applied to join S as second defendant and in 1979 the writ was amended to this effect. S entered an unconditional appearance and subsequently served a defence claiming that the plaintiff's cause of action was barred under the Limitation Act 1939, s. 21A as added by the Limitation Act 1975 s. 1. By summons he then applied for an order that, (1) the plaintiff's claim be struck out as being statute-barred, (ii) he cease to be a party to the proceedings since he had been improperly joined within the meaning of RSC Ord. 15 r. 6, and (iii) the claim be dismissed for want of prosecution. On appeal from the dismissal of his application, *held*, (i) the court would not exercise its discretion under s. 2D to override the limitation period imposed by s. 2A since the plaintiff had not been prejudiced by that section: he had a strong case against the first defendant and, further the MIB would be required to satisfy any judgment against him. The insurance position was relevant and it would be unrealistic and inequitable to disregard it. (ii) Although the entry of an unconditional appearance operated as a waiver of any irregularity in the process, the joinder, which was contrary to the rule of practice whereby the court will not allow the joinder of a defendant to an existing action if the claim is already statute-barred, should not be treated as a mere irregularity. There were two bases to the rule of practice: the joinder could either relate back to the date of the original writ or to the date of the amended writ. In the present case, if the relation-back theory was applied it would take away an accrued right of defence under the Limitation Acts which could not be waived by a merely procedural error such as entering an unconditional appearance. Alternatively, if the joinder took effect from the date of the amended writ the action was therefore statute barred, and S had a complete defence. On either view S had initially been properly joined by the order since it was not known whether he would rely on the limitation defence. However, as soon as he entered his defence, he became a person who had been improperly made a party or ceased to be a proper party within the meaning RSC Ord. 15, r. 6. (iii) The action against S would not be dismissed for want of prosecution. An order would be made that S would cease to be a party to the action.

LIFF V PEASLEY [1980] 1 All ER 623 (Court of Appeal: STEPHENSON and BRANDON LJJ). *Firman v Ellis* [1978] 2 All ER 851, CA, 1978 Halsbury's Abridgment, para. 1795, *Walkley v Precision Forgings Ltd* [1979] 2 All ER 548 HL, 1979 Halsbury's Abridgment para. 1761 applied.

1800   —— third party proceedings—action time-barred—effect on third party notice

An agreement was made whereby a land filling company accepted responsibility for, and agreed to release and indemnify a landowner "from and against all liability of whatsoever nature and howsoever caused" in return for permission to carry out filling operations on his land. Proceedings for damages were brought by G against the landowner after subsidence had occurred on adjoining land. In an application by the landowner to join the company as a third party in the action, *held*, such third party proceedings were not barred by the Limitation Act 1939, s. 21 even though six years had elapsed since the cause of action arose. A cause of action did not arise until the ascertainment of the fact and extent of the liability of the person who was to be indemnified. Accordingly, time did not begin to run against the landowner in favour of the company until the landowner's liability to G had been established and ascertained.

R. H. GREEN AND SILLEY WEIR LTD V BRITISH RAILWAYS BOARD (1980) Times,

8th October (Chancery Division: Dillon J). *County District Properties Ltd v Jenner Sons Ltd* [1976] 2 Lloyd's Rep 727 and *Post Office v Norwich Union Fire Insurance Ltd* [1967] 2 QB 363 applied.

1801   Personal injury—date of commencement of limitation period—plaintiff's knowledge—constructive knowledge

See *Common v Croft*, para. 1803.

1802   —— expiry of limitation period—court's discretion to override time limit

The plaintiff was injured at work on 4th August 1976. He was employed by the defendant company which formed part of the Norwest Holst group, only the group name being shown on the statement of his terms of employment and payslips. His solicitors, claiming damages on his behalf, were unable to discover the correct title of the employing company until July 1979, the reason for the delay being the fault of the company's insurers. The solicitors issued a summons in the county court on 17th August 1979, the three-year period of limitation having expired on 3rd August 1979. An application to have the action dismissed as time-barred was refused. On appeal, *held*, when the plaintiff was injured he did not know his employer's identity and could not before 17th August 1976 reasonably have been expected to acquire that knowledge. Consequently on 17th August 1979 the action was not time-barred. If, however, the action was time-barred the court would exercise its discretion, under Limitation Act 1939, s. 2D, to override the time limit. The provision was not to be construed restrictively as applying only to exceptional cases. There was ample evidence upon which the judge could have come to his decision. The claim was only fourteen days out of time and the defendants were in no worse position to defend it then they would have been had it been commenced on 3rd August 1979. The appeal would be dismissed.

Simpson v Norwest Holst Southern Ltd [1980] 2 All ER 471 (Court of Appeal: Lawton, Ormrod and Brightman LJJ). *Firman v Ellis* [1978] 2 All ER 851, 1978 Halsbury's Abridgment para. 1795 considered.

1803   In November 1975 the plaintiff was injured in a collision with the defendant's car. In April 1976 the plaintiff and the defendant were convicted of driving without due care and attention. The plaintiff issued a writ against the defendant in April 1979. The reasons for the delay were that the plaintiff had not discovered the defendant's identity until April 1976 and thought until 1979 that his conviction precluded him from pursuing a civil remedy. The defendant sought to have the plaintiff's action dismissed on the ground that it was statute-barred and that it would be inequitable to allow it to proceed. The defendant's summons was dismissed on the ground that the action came within the primary limitation period under the Limitation Act 1939, s. 2A because time ran from April 1976 when the plaintiff first had knowledge of the defendant's identity. On appeal by the defendant, *held*, the judge had not considered the effect of s. 2A (8), concerning the plaintiff's constructive knowledge. He could reasonably have been expected to make inquiries as to the defendant's identity on receipt of the summons. Hence s. 2A did not assist the plaintiff and the action was barred unless he could bring himself within s. 2D. The judge had been right to decide that, if he were wrong as to the action having been brought within the limitation period, he would exercise his discretion to allow the action to proceed. In considering the length of, and reasons for, the plaintiff's delay, he had correctly borne in mind that "delay" meant unlawful, culpable delay. The relevant delay was that which occurred from the date of expiry of the primary limitation period to the issue of the writ. The judge was not guilty of any error and the appeal would be dismissed.

Common v Croft [1980] LS Gaz R 358 (Court of Appeal: Stephenson and Ackner LJJ and Sir David Cairns).

Limitation Act 1939, s. 2A, now amended by Limitation Amendment Act 1980, s. 13 (1), Sch. 1.

1804 —— —— —— **extent of discretion**

The Limitation Act 1939, s. 2A provides that an action for personal injuries may not be brought after three years from the date on which the cause of action accrued. Section 2D provides that if the court considers that it would be equitable to allow an action to proceed, having regard to the degree to which (a) the provisions of s. 2A prejudice the plaintiff and (b) any decision of the court would prejudice the plaintiff, it may direct that the provisions are not to apply to the action.

A second cause of action was brought outside the limitation period after the plaintiff had failed to proceed with an action for the same cause of action brought within the limitation period. The question for the court was whether it should exercise its discretion under s. 2D and how far that discretion was unfettered. *Held*, the decision in *Walkley v Precision Forgings Ltd* had established that if a plaintiff commenced but did not proceed with an action for whatever reason, it was not open to him subsequently to take advantage of s. 2D because he was not prejudiced by the provisions of s. 2A, but by his own act, or failure to act in relation to the first action. In such cases the court did not have a discretion to override the limitation period and accordingly previous authority which conferred an unfettered discretion on the court was no longer binding.

The court also decided that in light of the restrictive interpretation of s. 2D, it should not exercise its discretion in favour of the renewal of a writ which was not served in time since it would deprive the defendant of the accrued benefit of the limitation period. In order to obtain an extension, it was necessary to comply with RSC Ord. 6, r. 8 which remained unaffected by s. 2D.

CHAPPELL v COOPER; PLAYER v BRUGUIERE [1980] 2 All ER 463 (Court of Appeal: ROSKILL and ORMROD LJJ and SIR DAVID CAIRNS). *Walkley v Precision Forgings Ltd* [1979] 2 All ER 548, HL, 1979 Halsbury's Abridgment, para. 1761 applied, *Firman v Ellis* [1978] 2 All ER 851, CA, 1978 Halsbury's Abridgment para. 1795 disapproved.

1805 —— —— —— **relevance of insurance position**

See *Liff v Peasley*, para. 1799.

LOCAL GOVERNMENT

Halsbury's Laws of England (4th edn.), Vol. 28, paras. 1001–1403

1806 **Local authority—contract for hire—repudiation by local authority committee—validity**

A political party arranged to book a hall for a private membership conference. The local authority subsequently cancelled the booking following a meeting of a local authority committee which considered the matter as an application for the use of the hall rather than on the basis that there was already a binding commitment. The party was awarded damages for breach of contract and the local authority appealed. *Held*, the committee had failed to take into account a relevant consideration, namely that there was a binding contract to let the hall, so its resolution was invalid and they were liable for breach of contract.

WEBSTER v NEWHAM LONDON BOROUGH COUNCIL (1980) Times, 22nd November (Court of Appeal: LORD DENNING MR, O'CONNOR and MEGAW LJJ). *Associated Provincial Picture Houses Ltd v Wednesbury Corporation* [1948] 1 KB 223, CA, applied.

1807 —— **duty of care—child in care**

A boy was remanded by a court into the care of a local authority after having caused a number of local fires. He was placed in a community home but the house parent in charge was not informed of the boy's fire-raising propensities by the social worker. Whilst at the home the boy set fire to a nearby church. The vicar and churchwardens brought an action for damages against the local authority, claiming that they were negligent in their failure to exercise proper supervision over the boy. *Held*, there was a duty of care owed by the local authority to the plaintiffs similar to that of a parent, having regard to its duty to the boy under the Children and Young Persons Act 1969, s. 24 (2). However a wide discretion existed limiting the duty of care owed by the local authority to others. In this case no information had been given about the boy and hence no discretion had been exercised and therefore the potential limitation of the scope of the duty of care did not exist. In the circumstances the duty of care owed by the local authority was that of a reasonable parent to control his child. The local authority had not acted reasonably in failing to warn the head of the home and accordingly the plaintiffs would be awarded damages.

VICAR OF WRITTLE v ESSEX COUNTY COUNCIL (1979) 77 LGR 656 (Queen's Bench Division: FORBES J). *Home Office v Dorset Yacht Co Ltd* [1970] AC 1004, HL and *Anns v Merton London Borough Council* [1978] AC 728, HL, 1977 Halsbury's Abridgment para. 2175 applied.

1808   —— —— **negligent misstatement—liability of authority**

Australia

A company wished to purchase some land for commercial development. It was important in relation to the nature of the scheme to determine whether any proposals for road alterations had been made by the local council. The company was told by a council officer, in response to oral inquiries, that no such proposals existed. The company sent in written inquiries but the reply contained no reference to any road widening scheme. Following the exchange of contracts, the company discovered that the land was affected by a road widening scheme. The company claimed damages for negligence contending that the council's misstatement was in breach of a duty owed by the council to the company. *Held*, on a majority decision, an adviser who held himself out as carrying on the business of giving advice had a common law duty to do so without negligence. This only applied where the adviser let it be known that he claimed to possess a skill generally shown by persons giving such advice. The council was, in the relevant sense, engaged in the supply of information relating to road alterations. However, the council was not liable in this case since, in relation to the oral inquiry, the inquirer failed to state that he intended to rely on the council's information without subsequently seeking confirmation. In relation to the written inquiry, the council was not statutorily obliged to answer the question and hence no liability arose from failure to do so. There was thus no breach of any duty of care owed to the company in respect of either the oral or the written statement.

L. SHADDOCK & ASSOCIATES PTY LTD v PARRAMATTA CITY COUNCIL [1979] 1 NSWLR 566 (Court of Appeal of New South Wales). *Hedley Byrne & Co Ltd v Heller & Partners Ltd* [1964] AC 465; *Mutual Life & Citizens' Assurance Co Ltd v Evatt* [1971] 1 All ER 150; *Howard Marine and Dredging Co Ltd v A Ogden & Sons (Excavations) Ltd* [1978] 1 QB 574, 1977 Halsbury's Abridgment para. 1896 applied.

1809   —— **duty to provide sites for gipsies—liability as landlords for gipsy nuisance**

See *Page Motors Ltd v Epsom and Ewell Borough Council*, para. 2070.

1810   —— **duty towards homeless persons—inquiries as to homelessness**

See *Youngs v Thanet District Council*, para. 1429.

1811   —— —— **persons with no local connections**

See *R v Hillingdon London Borough Council, ex parte Streeting*, para. 1435.

1812   —— —— **whether intentionally homeless**

See *Dyson v Kerrier District Council*, para. 1434.

1813   —— **expenses—resolution charging special expenses on part of area—validity of resolution**

As a result of local government reorganisation under the Local Government Act 1972, the Pontypridd Urban District Council was merged into the larger Taff Ely Borough Council which took over all of its functions and operations as from 1st April 1974. By a resolution made in March 1974 the Borough Council resolved in respect of the 1974/75 rating year to declare the expenses of a former District Council operation to be a special expense chargeable only on the community of Pontypridd. On an objection by a ratepayer, *held*, despite the fact that the Borough Council did not take over the operations of the District Council until 1st April 1974, the Local Government Act 1972 (Commencement No. 2) (Wales) Order 1973 entitled them to prepare or approve rates in respect of the 1974/75 rating year under provisions of the Local Government Act 1972 which by virtue of that order came into force on 1st January 1974. In preparing rates the Council could properly take into account expenses to be incurred as a result of the forthcoming merger. Under the Local Government Act 1972, s. 147 (3) the Council was entitled to declare any expenses incurred or to be incurred by them to be special expenses chargeable only upon such part of their area as they might specify. The objection would be rejected.

MURPHY v DISTRICT AUDITOR NO 6 AUDIT DISTRICT MID GLAMORGAN [1980] RA 263 (Queen's Bench Division: LORD LANE (CJ and WOOLF J).

1814   —— **Isles of Scilly**

The Isles of Scilly (National Assistance) Order 1980, S.I. 1980 No. 326 (in force on 1st April 1980), provides that the Council of the Isles of Scilly is a local authority for the purposes of the National Assistance Act 1948. The Isles of Scilly (National Assistance) Order 1948 is revoked.

1815   The Isles of Scilly (Children and Young Persons) Order 1980, S.I. 1980 No. 327 (in force on 1st April 1980), provides that the Council of the Isles of Scilly is a local authority for the purposes of the Children and Young Persons Act 1969.

1816   The Isles of Scilly (Local Authority Social Services) Order 1980, S.I. 1980 No. 328 (in force on 1st April 1980), provides that the Council of the Isles of Scilly is a local authority for the purposes of the Local Authority Social Services Act 1970.

1817   —— **powers—trust established to provide money for assisted places at independent schools—whether ultra vires**

The Local Government Act 1972, s. 137 provides that a local authority may incur expenditure which, in its opinion, is in the interests of its area or of its inhabitants, but a local authority may not incur any expenditure for a purpose for which it is authorised to make any payment by virtue of any other enactment.

In April 1978 a county council passed a resolution establishing a trust fund for the purpose of providing free or assisted places at independent schools. A payment of £1·12 million was made to the trust by the county council in order to pay the educational costs of children chosen to start schools in September 1978 through their seven year curriculum. A city council within the county sought a declaration that the county council had acted beyond their powers in passing the resolution and in making the payment to the trust because the money was to be applied over seven years. *Held*, the scheme was within the county council's powers although education was not one of its functions and it could not be challenged on any valid ground. Although expenditure pursuant to s. 137 (1) had to be incurred within the relevant year the purpose for which it had been incurred did not necessarily have to be carried out within that year. Furthermore when the trustees were given the sum of money to be applied by them for the prescribed payments in future years that constituted, then and there, the incurring of expenditure within the meaning of s. 137. The creation of the trust was purely incidental to the exercise of the county council's power to expend the sum as they desired to do and in doing so they had exercised their own powers exhaustively. There had been no ultra vires delegation of powers to the trustees who in carrying out the purposes of the trust were exercising their own powers in accordance with the general law of administering trust funds.

MANCHESTER CITY COUNCIL v GREATER MANCHESTER METROPOLITAN COUNTY COUNCIL (1980) Times, 11th July (House of Lords: LORD DIPLOCK, LORD EDMUND-DAVIES, LORD KEITH OF KINKEL, LORD SCARMAN and LORD ROSKILL). Decision of the Court of Appeal (1979) 78 LGR 71, affirmed.

1818   Inspection of local authority documents—right of new councillor to inspect documents of special committee of which he was a member

A report concerning the activities of certain police officers in Blackpool contained rumours, gossip and hearsay. The report was made available to the Lancashire police committee for their consideration. The contents of the report were leaked to the press, who published large parts of it. Several police officers brought successful actions for libel. Following local government elections the appellant was elected a councillor and appointed to the committee. Certain matters relating to the report remained outstanding. The clerk to the committee refused to disclose to the appellant those parts of the report which contained material damaging and potentially defamatory to third parties. At a special meeting the committee, acting on leading counsel's advice, resolved, by a substantial majority vote, not to disclose the whole of the report to new members. The appellant's application for judicial review to compel the clerk to provide him with the report was refused at first instance. On appeal, *held*, LORD DENNING MR dissenting, the question whether disclosure was necessary to enable the appellant to carry out his duties was one of necessity and reasonableness. Counsel had correctly directed the committee as to the appellant's right of access to the report and to the possibility that disclosure to new members, where not necessary, would not be protected by qualified privilege. The final decision as to whether something was necessary to enable a councillor properly to perform his duties lay with the committee, who had to take into consideration the possible ill-effects on innocent people of allowing the inspection of the report. The committee's decision was reasonable and had been democratically taken. The appeal would therefore be dismissed.

LORD DENNING MR held that publication to new members would be protected by qualified privilege. New members had a right at common law to see and inspect all the committee's documents relating to past and present affairs.

R v CLERK TO LANCASHIRE POLICE COMMITTEE, EX PARTE HOOK [1980] 2 All ER 353 (Court of Appeal: LORD DENNING MR, WALLER and DUNN LJJ). *Stuart v Bell* [1891] 2 QB 341, *Adams v Ward* [1916–17] All ER Rep 157, *R v Barnes Borough Council, Ex Parte Conlan* [1938] 3 All ER 226 and *Associated Provincial Picture Houses Ltd v Wednesbury Corpn* [1948] 1 KB 223 applied.

1819   Local Government, Planning and Land Act 1980

The Local Government, Planning and Land Act 1980 makes amendments relating to local government, planning and land to the Local Government Acts 1972 and 1974, the Town and Country Planning Act 1971 and other legislation. It also creates new substantive law in these areas. The Act received the royal assent on 13th November 1980. As to commencement provisions, see infra.

Part I (s. 1, Schs. 1–7) gives effect to proposals in the White Paper "Central Government Controls over Local Authorities" (Cmnd. 7634). It removes or relaxes certain controls affecting the exercise by local and other authorities of certain of their functions and relieves ministers of certain functions.

Part II (ss. 2–4) empowers the Secretary of State to issue a code of practice concerning the publication by specified authorities of information about the discharge of their functions and other matters. He may also direct certain bodies to publish such information.

Part III (ss. 5–23) deals with local authority direct labour organisations. It controls the power of authorities to enter into agreements to carry out construction and maintenance work for other bodies and regulates the way in which direct labour organisations carry out such work for their parent authorities. It obliges them to invite tenders in certain circumstances and requires separate accounts to be kept for direct labour organisations and certain conventions to be followed in their keeping. The Secretary of State is enabled to deprive authorities of the power to maintain direct labour organisations where a prescribed rate of return on capital has not been achieved. Authorities are required to publish reports on construction and maintenance work undertaken by them. Small direct labour organisations are exempted from the requirements of Part III.

Part IV (ss. 24–27) amends the Local Government Act 1972 in relation to allowances to members of local authorities. Councillors may receive financial loss allowance instead of attendance allowance for the performance of approved duties and local authorities may pay additional allowances to councillors with special responsibilities. The three-mile limit for the payment of subsistence allowance is abolished and the range of meetings in respect of which water authorities and certain joint bodies may pay allowances to their members is extended.

Part V (ss. 28–47) amends the General Rate Act 1967 so as to abolish the requirement for five-yearly revisions of rateable values. It alters the basis of valuation of certain hereditaments and enables the Secretary of State by order to specify in relation to a class of hereditaments the time by reference to which values are determined for the purposes of new valuation lists. Separate provision is made for the value to be ascribed to a hereditament in respect of which no time is specified. Fish farms are exempted from rates. Domestic rate relief is extended to more domestic and mixed hereditaments and the right to pay rates by instalments is extended to the occupiers of non-domestic hereditaments within certain rateable limits. Certain provisions for the rating of unoccupied property may be varied by the Secretary of State by order.

Part VI (ss. 48–68, Schs. 8–11) provides a new system for the distribution of rate support grants to local authorities, with a single block grant in place of the present needs and resources elements.

Part VII (ss. 69, 70) enables the Secretary of State to pay grants to local authorities granting rebates under the Rating (Disabled Persons) Act 1978 or providing caravan sites for gipsies.

Part VIII (ss. 71–85, Schs. 12, 13), empowers the Secretary of State by order to introduce a new system for the control of capital expenditure by local and other authorities. Ministers are under a duty to specify allocations of expenditure and provision is made for the use of capital receipts, for switching between years and between authorities, and for specific control over schemes of national and regional importance. The Secretary of State may issue directions in respect of levels of expenditure.

Part IX (ss. 86–92, Schs. 14, 15) deals with amendments to planning legislation. The distribution of planning functions made by the Local Government Act 1972 is amended to reduce the powers of county planning authorities. Powers are conferred for fees to be charged in respect of planning applications. The procedures for the approval or adoption of structure and local plans are modified and local planning authorities are enabled to repeal and replace structure plans. Further amendments relate to planning applications, decisions and planning appeals, the provisions of the Town and Country Planning Act 1971 relating to listed buildings, conservation areas, blight notices and tree preservation orders, and the allocation of functions in relation to advertisement control, waste land, orders stopping up or diverting footpaths and bridleways, and building preservation notices. The powers of compulsory acquisition of land conferred on local authorities by the 1971 Act are also amended.

Part X (ss. 93–100, Sch. 16) provides that the Secretary of State may designate areas in which land owned by public authorities which is underused may be recorded in a register. To that end, the Secretary of State is empowered to require information about such land. Under certain conditions the Secretary of State may direct that such land be offered for sale.

Part XI (s. 101, Sch. 17) repeals the Community Land Act 1975 and makes consequential and transitional provisions.

Part XII (ss. 102–111, Schs. 18–22) provides for the retention of the Land Authority for Wales, but replaces the functions under the Community Land Act 1975 with new powers and duties enabling it to make land available for development.

Part XIII (ss. 112–115) follows upon reports by the Select Committee on the Parliamentary Commissioner for Administration. It removes the present time limit for future claims for compensation under the Land Compensation Act 1973, Pt. I and enables new claims to be made in certain circumstances where the time limit has expired. It also removes the time limit on claims for home loss payments under the 1973 Act, Pt. III.

Part XIV (ss. 116–125, Schs. 23, 24) contains miscellaneous provisions about land. It re-enacts certain provisions of the Community Land Act 1975; gives the Secretary of State power to direct local authorities to assess the availability of land for residential development in their area; extends the powers of the Secretary of State in the Local Government Act 1966 and the Local Employment Act 1972 to make grants for the reclamation of derelict land; clarifies and extends the powers of the Crown contained in the 1975 Act, s. 37, to acquire and dispose of land; and provides for the removal from county councils of certain powers under the Town Development Act 1952.

Part XV (ss, 126–133, Sch. 25) deals with new towns. It enables the Secretary of State to require development corporations and the Commission for the New Towns to pay him sums of money, extends the power of corporations and the Commission to dispose of land, empowers the Secretary of State to reduce new town designated areas and enables the special arrangements for licensed premises in new towns to be ended.

Part XVI (ss. 134–172, Schs. 26–31) provides for the creation of new corporations to regenerate urban areas. The powers of such corporations are to be modelled on those of the new town development corporations and the provisions will allow them to be given powers of land assembly, planning, housing and industrial promotion. Each corporation will be established by order which will specify the powers granted and designate the area in which they are exercisable. These powers may include functions of housing authorities and local planning authorities.

Part XVII (ss. 173–178) deals with caravan sites and concerns the duty of local authorities to provide caravan sites for gipsies; the removal of unlawfully parked caravans and their occupants; the designation of areas for the purpose of making unauthorised camping unlawful; and exemptions from the requirement for site licences.

Part XVIII (s. 179, Sch. 32) provides for the establishment of enterprise zones within which special planning provisions will apply, and most non-domestic hereditaments will be exempt from rates.

Part XIX (ss. 180–197, Schs. 33, 34) deals with miscellaneous and general matters, including consequential amendments and repeals. It also provides for the abolition of the Clean Air Councils.

Commencement of the Act
The Act came into force on receiving the royal assent on 13th November 1980, subject to the following exceptions:

Part III: in force on a day or days to be appointed.

Part V: ss. 33, 34, 37, 44, Sch. 34 Pt. IX (part), have effect for any rate period beginning on or after 1st April 1981: S.I. 1980 No. 2014; s. 31 has effect for any rate period beginning on or after 1st April 1981; ss. 38–40 came into force on 13th December 1980; s. 29 (1)–(3), Schs. 33 (part), 34, Pt. IX (part) do not have effect for any rate period beginning before the first date on which new valuation lists come into force; Sch. 33 (part) does not have effect until the Secretary of State exercises the power conferred on him thereby; s. 45 (1)–(4) has effect for any rebate period beginning on or after 1st April 1981: S.I. 1980 No. 2014.

Part VI: s. 68 (2)–(6) in force on 11th December 1980: S.I. 1980 No. 1893. The commencing year for the purposes of this Part is the year beginning 1st April 1981: S.I. 1980 No. 1893.

Part VIII: ss. 72 (1), (2), 73, 74 came into force on 11th December 1980 for certain purposes; ss. 71 75 (5), 76, 84, Sch. 12 came into force on 11th December 1980:

S.I. 1980 No. 1893. Remainder of Part in force on 1st April 1981: S.I. 1980 No. 1893.

Part X: to be brought into force in the area of any district council or London borough council specified in the order: 31st December 1980 for specified areas: S.I. 1980 No. 1871.

Part XVII: 13th December 1980, except s. 173 (b) (13th December 1981) and s. 174 (13th February 1981).

1820   Officers—fees for inquiries

The Fees for Inquiries (Variation) (Amendment) Order 1980, S.I. 1980 No. 1612 (in force on 28th November 1980), further amends the 1968 Order by increasing from £70 to £105 the maximum fee payable daily under the Local Government Act 1972, s. 250 (4) for the services of an officer engaged in an inquiry held under that section.

1821   Pecuniary interests of members of committees of local education authority—removal of disability

The Secretary of State for the Environment and the Secretary of State for Wales have removed the disability on members of local education authorities, which results solely from the pecuniary interest which any member may have by reason of being the parent of a child in full-time education, with regard to consideration, discussion and voting on any question respecting the provision of school milk, meals or other refreshment, school transport, the charges to be made for such provision, or the re-imbursement of school travelling expenses. (The dispensation does not extend to questions relating solely to an individual member's own particular circumstances.) The dispensation embraces any committee, joint committee or sub-committee of a local education authority. The dispensation which is dated 16th January 1980 is published as an appendix to Department of the Environment circular 5/80, Welsh Office circular 8/80.

1822   Rate support grants

The Rate Support Grant Order 1979, S.I. 1980 No. 57 (in force on 17th January 1980), fixes and prescribes for the year 1980–81 the aggregate amount of the rate support grants payable to local authorities under the Local Government Act 1974, Part I; the division of the amount between the needs element, the resources element and the domestic element; the amount of supplementary grants payable to county councils for transport purposes and towards expenditure on national parks; and the amount by which rates on dwelling-houses are to be reduced in each rating area to take account of the domestic element.

1823

The Rate Support Grant (Amendment) Regulations 1980, S.I. 1980 No. 37 (in force on 1st April 1980), amend the Rate Support Grant Regulations 1979, 1979 Halsbury's Abridgment para. 1770 regarding the proportion of the needs element of the rate support grant payable to councils of non-metropolitan districts.

1824   —— increase

The Rate Support Grant (Increase) Order 1979, S.I. 1980 No. 58 (in force on 17th January 1980), increases the rate support grants for the financial year 1978-79.

1825

The Rate Support Grant (Increase) (No. 2) Order 1979, S.I. 1980 No. 59 (in force on 17th January 1980), further increases the rate support grants for the financial year 1979-80.

1826

The Rate Support Grant (Increase) Order 1980, S.I. 1980 No. 2048 (in force on 15th January 1981), further increases the rate suppport grants for the financial year 1979–80. These increases are referable to the increase in the level of costs since the grants for the year 1979–80 were first revised.

1827   The Rate Support Grant (Increase) (No. 2) Order 1980, S.I. 1980 No. 2049 (in force on 15th January 1981), increases the rate support grants for the financial year 1980–81. These increases are referable to the increase in the level of costs since the grants for the year 1980–81 were originally fixed.

1828   ——— needs element

The Rate Support Grants (Adjustment of Needs Element) Regulations 1980, S.I. 1980 No. 877 (in force on 24th July 1980), provide for the adjustment of the needs element of the rate support grants payable from 1st April in any year to a local education authority. The 1980 Regulations also amend the Rate Support Grants (Adjustment of Needs Element) Regulations 1976, 1976 Halsbury's Abridgment para. 1640 regarding their application to the financial years commencing in 1977, 1978 and 1979.

1829   ——— principles for multipliers

The Rate Support Grant (Principles for Multipliers) Order 1980, S.I. 1980 No. 2047 (in force on 15th January 1981), specifies the principles on which multipliers are to be determined for the purposes of the Local Government, Planning and Land Act 1980, ss. 49, 50, para. 1819.

1830   Travelling and subsistence allowances—revised rates

Revised rates of travelling and subsistence allowances payable to members of local authorities and other bodies under Part VIII of the Local Government Act 1972 came into operation on 4th December 1979 and are set out in an appendix to Department of the Environment circular 30/79 (Welsh Office circular 66/79) which cancels Department of the Environment circular 10/79. The rate for travel by public transport may not exceed the ordinary fare or any available cheap fare unless the body determines that first class rail fares may be paid (Appendix, Part 1, para. 1 (1)). Special rates are payable for travel by a member's own solo motor cycle (not exceeding 500 cc) (see Appendix, Part 1, para. 2 (1)). The rate for the use of a member's own private motor vehicle (other than such motor cycle) shall not exceed 6·8p per mile (Appendix, Part 1, para. 2 (2)) unless he can show that such travel (a) results in a substantial saving in his time, or (b) is in the interests of the body, or (c) is otherwise reasonable, when a higher rate may be paid. The higher rate may not exceed: (i) for the use of a solo motor cycle exceeding 500 cc, a motor cycle with side-car, or a tri-car not exceeding 500 cc, 7·8p per mile; (ii) for the use of a motor car not exceeding 500 cc, 12·9p per mile; and (iii) for the use of a motor car or tri-car (a) between 500 cc and 999 cc, 12·9p per mile, (b) between 999 cc and 1199 cc, 14·1p per mile, and (c) exceeding 1199 cc, 15·6p per mile (Appendix, Part 1, para. 2 (2)). Additional amounts may be paid in respect of certain passengers, fees for tolls, ferries or parking and garaging (in respect of overnight absences) (see Appendix, Part 1, para. 2 (3)). Travel by taxi may be reimbursed by the rate appropriate for travel by public transport, except in cases of urgency or where no public transport is reasonably available; in such instances the actual fare and any reasonable gratuity may be reimbursed (Appendix, Part 1, para. 3). The rate for the use of other hired vehicles may not exceed the rate applicable had the vehicle belonged to the member; the body may, however, approve a payment not exceeding the actual cost (Appendix, Part 1, para. 4). Provision is also made (see Appendix, Part 1, para. 5) for payments in respect of travel by air and by ship (see Appendix, para. 1 (1)). Subsistence allowances are at a rate not exceeding (i) for between four and eight hours, £3·66, (ii) for between eight and twelve hours, £6·43, (iii) for between twelve and sixteen hours, £9·10, (iv) for more than sixteen hours, £10·88, and (v) for overnight absence, £27·06 plus (in certain circumstances) a supplementary allowance of £3·44 (Appendix, Part 2, para. 1 (1)).

LONDON GOVERNMENT

Halsbury's Laws of England (4th edn.), Vol. 29, paras. 1–200

1831　Greater London Council—homesteading scheme—waiver of interest payments

See para. 1832.

1832　Housing—homesteading scheme—waiver of interest payments

The Department of the Environment announced in a press notice on 6th October 1980, that approval had been given to the Greater London Council, under the Housing Act 1980, s. 110 (12), for the council to waive interest payments on mortgages granted under their homesteading scheme for up to three years. The homesteading scheme of the Greater London Council concerns property in Greater London which is in need of essential repairs or improvements and the purchaser is entitled to a waiver of interest payments and deferment of capital repayment in return for carrying out the improvements or repairs.

1833　—— transfer of land and housing accommodation

The Greater London Council (Transfer of Land and Housing Accommodation) Order 1980, S.I. 1980 No. 320 (in force on 31st March 1980), provides for an agreed transfer of housing land and accommodation from the Greater London Council to certain London borough and district councils in whose respective areas the land and accommodation is situated. It includes the agreed terms on which the transfer is to take place and also certain consequential and supplemental provisions.

1834　—— —— rent rebates for tenants of transferred dwellings

See para. 1462.

1835　—— —— application to prevent transfer

The London Government Act 1963, s. 23 (3) permits the Minister, on request, to make an order transferring housing from the Greater London Council (GLC) to the London boroughs. Subsection (4) required the GLC to make a programme for housing transfers before 1st April 1970. Eight London boroughs applied for judicial review of the GLC's request for a transfer of land to them. This was refused and on appeal the boroughs contended that the Minister's powers to make the transfer were limited to those houses contained in the programme, and that the programme the GLC had made in January 1970 had exhausted the transfers that could be made. *Held*, the programme was valuable as a statement of intention and to require the GLC to review its housing needs. It was not a binding commitment and it had to remain open to the parties to make such transfers as the changing situation required. The boroughs had a right to make submissions to the Minister against any transfers. The appeal would accordingly be dismissed.

BRENT LONDON BOROUGH COUNCIL v GREATER LONDON COUNCIL (1980) Times, 14th October (Court of Appeal: LORD DENNING MR, BRANDON and ACKNER LJJ).

1836　—— —— loss of employment

The Greater London Council Housing (Compensation) Regulations 1980, S.I. 1980 No. 646 (in force on 13th June 1980), provide for the payment of compensation to or in respect of persons who suffer loss of employment or loss or diminution of emoluments, as a result of the transfer of land or housing accommodation by an order under the London Government Act 1963, s. 23 (3).

MAGISTRATES

Halsbury's Laws of England (4th edn.), paras. 201–600

1837　Articles

Magistrates and Audi Alteram Partem Principle, J. Kodwo Bentil: 124 Sol Jo 600. The Role of the Magistrates' Clerk in Summary Proceedings, Penny Darbyshire: 144 JP Jo 186.

1838　Bail—renewed application for bail—guidance

See *R v Nottingham JJ, ex parte Davies*, para. 654.

1839　Case stated—application for statement of case—question in issue not specifically stated—substantial compliance with statutory requirements

After a distress warrant was issued against them for non-payment of rates the applicants, who denied that they were in rateable occupation, applied to the justices to state a case "setting forth the facts and grounds of . . . determination including evidence upon which the justices made their findings of fact." The justices refused to state a case on the ground that the application failed to comply with the Magistrates' Courts Rules 1968, r. 65, as amended, in that there had been no proper identification of the question upon which the case was to be stated. An application for leave to apply for judicial review was refused. On appeal, *held*, although the provisions of r. 65 were to be enforced strictly they could be waived, if the interests of justice required it, where there had been a substantial compliance with the rules. In the present case the only question at the hearing had been whether the applicants were in rateable occupation, so the wording of the application was sufficient to alert the justices to what was in issue. The justices would be ordered to state a case.

R v Croydon JJ, ex parte Lefore Holdings Ltd [1980] 1 WLR 1465 (Court of Appeal: Lawton and Waller LJJ).

1840　———— time limit for application—compliance with statutory requirements—whether requirements mandatory or directory

A charge of theft was dismissed by magistrates who also refused an application to state a case for the opinion of the High Court. The magistrates decided that the application was not good because it merely stated that their decision was erroneous in point of law but did not clearly state the point of law, as required by the Magistrates' Court Rules 1968, r. 65 (1). As an application to state a case had to be made within twenty-one days from the magistrates' decision, they held that since the application was bad, the time limit could not be extended to correct the application. *Held*, the 1968 Rules, r. 65 (1) provided that an application to state a case "shall identify" the point of law on which the court's opinion was sought. The question was whether or not the provision was mandatory. Although the word "shall" was mandatory, it was important to consider the position realistically. Therefore, although the applicants failed to state the point of law within the twenty-one day time limit prescribed by the Magistrates' Courts Act 1952, s. 87, they should be allowed to correct the application within such reasonable time as the magistrates thought proper. Accordingly, an order would be granted requiring the magistrates to state a case for the court's opinion.

R v Bromley Magistrates' Court, ex parte Waitrose Ltd [1980] 3 All ER 464 (Queen's Bench Division: Waller LJ and Park J).

1841　A farmer was charged with putting down a poisonous substance with a view to killing birds contrary to s. 5 (1) (b) of the Protection of Birds Act 1954. He successfully raised a defence under s. 4 (2) (a), contending that his action was necessary to prevent damage to his crops. The prosecutor applied for a case to be stated for the opinion of the High Court. The application was made within the twenty-one day period prescribed by the Magistrates' Courts Act 1952, s. 87, but did not comply with the Magistrates' Courts Rules 1968, r. 65 (1) because it did not identify the question on which the opinion of the court was sought, and the farmer contended that the High Court consequently had no jurisdiction. *Held*, rule 65 (1) was directory, not mandatory, and did not go to the jurisdiction of the High Court to hear and adjudicate on a case stated. Any irregularities could be corrected before the hearing. On the question of the s. 4 (2) (a) defence, it was confined to the offence of killing or attempting to kill a bird, which was not the offence for which the farmer had been charged. The justices had been wrong to acquit but it would be inappropriate to remit the case to them with a direction to convict in view of the delay.

ROBINSON V WHITTLE [1980] 3 All ER 459 (Queen's Bench Division: DONALDSON LJ and BRISTOW J). *Moore v Hewitt* [1947] 1 KB 831 followed.

1842 Following an application for a case to be stated by the justices for the opinion of the Divisional Court, the applicant caused the justices' clerk to delay the issue of the draft case to the parties beyond the time limit of twenty-one days laid down by r. 65A of the Magistrates' Courts Rules 1968. *Held*, the 1968 rules were directory, not mandatory, and did not go to the jurisdiction of the court to adjudicate, but the court would exercise its discretion to refuse to adjudicate because the delay had been caused by the applicant himself.

PARSONS V F. W. WOOLWORTH & CO LTD [1980] 3 All ER 456 (Queen's Bench Division: DONALDSON LJ and BRISTOW J).

1843 ### Certiorari—certiorari to quash order of justices—magistrate apparently asleep during trial

In an application for judicial review on the ground that the presiding magistrate had appeared to be asleep and had refused to withdraw, the Divisional Court held that although the magistrate had not been asleep the accused's application was a genuine one, therefore on the principle that justice must be seen to be done the case would be remitted for trial by another bench.

R V WESTON-SUPER-MARE JJ, EX PARTE TAYLOR (1980) Times, 14th November (Queen's Bench Division: DONALDSON LJ and HODGSON J).

1844 ### Committal for trial—offence triable either way—value involved small—whether offence one of series of similar offences

The accused was charged with four offences including one of criminal damage which was within the limit prescribed by the Criminal Damage Act 1977 s. 23 (1) and therefore triable summarily, and three offences which were triable either way. The magistrates proceeded on the basis that the criminal damage charge was also triable either way because it came within s. 23 (7) (a) as one of a series of offences which were of the same or a similar character. The prosecution applied for an order of mandamus directing the magistrates to try the offence summarily. *Held*, in order to satisfy s 23 (7) (a) the offences should all be triable either way as well as being similar in fact and in law. The criminal damage charge had been adjudged to be summary and should therefore be tried separately.

R V HATFIELD JJ, EX PARTE CASTLE [1980] 3 All ER 509 (Queen's Bench Division: WALLER LJ and PARK J). *Ludlow v Metropolitan Police Comr* [1970] 1 All ER 567 applied.

1845 ### Committal proceedings—function of committal proceedings—discretion of prosecution to call witnesses

At committal proceedings the defendant was served with copies of four witnesses' written statements. The defendant gave notice that he wished those witnesses to give oral evidence. The prosecution refused to call those witnesses and the justices subsequently found that there was a prima facie case to answer and committed the defendant for trial. The defendant applied for an order of certiorari to quash the justices' decision on the ground that there had been a denial of natural justice and material irregularities in the conduct of the proceedings. *Held*, the function of committal proceedings was to ensure that no one stood trial unless a prima facie case had been made against him. As the onus was on the prosecution to show that such a prima facie case had been made out, they had the choice of deciding what witnesses would be called. There had been no irregularity in the committal proceedings and accordingly certiorari would be refused for no breach of the rules of natural justice had occurred.

R v GRAYS JJ, EX PARTE TETLEY (1979) 70 Cr App Rep 11 (Queen's Bench Division: LORD WIDGERY CJ, EVELEIGH LJ and KILNER BROWN J). *R v Epping and Harlow JJ, ex parte Massaro* [1973] 1 All ER 1011 applied.

1846　Decision of justices—judicial review—likelihood of bias

See *R v Smethwick JJ, ex parte Hands*, para. 10.

1847　Domestic proceedings—amendment of rules

The Magistrates' Courts (Amendment) (No. 2) Rules 1980, S.I. 1980 No. 1583 (in force on 1st February 1980), amend the Magistrates' Courts Rules 1968 consequent upon the coming into force of the Domestic Proceedings and Magistrates' Courts Act 1978, Pts. I, II, III. The amendments do not apply in relation to applications and orders made before the new provisions come into force.

1848　—— custody order—reasons for decision

On appeal from a custody order granted by justices who gave the reasons for their decision at considerable length, the President of the Family Division gave guidance to justices on how to implement the provisions of the Domestic Proceedings and Magistrates' Courts Act 1978, s. 84, under which rules may be formulated for the recording of reasons for decisions made in domestic proceedings. In making a decision on a custody matter the justices should set out the matters in dispute, then give an account of the reasoning which led them to their decision in a concise, realistic way.

HUTCHINSON v HUTCHINSON (1980) Times, 29th October (Family Division: SIR JOHN ARNOLD P and WOOD J).

1849　—— guardianship of minors

The Magistrates' Courts (Guardianship of Minors) (Amendment) Rules 1980, S.I. 1980 No. 1585 (in force on 1st February 1981), amend the Magistrates' Courts (Guardianship of Minors) Rules 1974, 1974 Halsbury's Abridgment para. 1737, consequent upon the coming into force on 1st February 1981 of certain provisions in the Domestic Proceedings and Magistrates' Courts Act 1978. The amendments do not apply in relation to applications made before the new provisions come into force.

The principal change is the omission of r. 10 which relates to proceedings against a person outside the United Kingdom for the variation etc. of certain guardianship orders. Provisions relating to such proceedings are inserted in the Magistrates' Court Rules 1968 by the Magistrates' Courts (Amendment) (No. 2) Rules 1980, para. 1847.

1850　—— justices' power to exclude witness from hearing—discretion to admit witness' evidence

See *Tomlinson v Tomlinson*, para. 1485.

1851　—— matrimonial proceedings

The Magistrates' Courts (Matrimonial Proceedings) Rules 1980, S.I. 1980 No. 1582 (in force on 1st February 1981), revoke and replace the Magistrates' Courts (Matrimonial Proceedings) Rules 1960 consequent upon the coming into force on 1st February 1981 of the main provisions of the Domestic Proceedings and

Magistrates' Courts Act 1978, Part I and the repeal by that Act of the Matrimonial Proceedings (Magistrates' Courts) Act 1960. The Rules do not apply in relation to applications and orders made before the new provisions come into force.

The Rules provide for, inter alia, the forms of applications on complaint, orders and notices in connection with matrimonial proceedings in magistrates' courts, the parties to applications for the variation or revocation of certain orders, the jurisdiction of the courts and the transfer of certain applications from one court to another having jurisdiction to hear them.

1852   —— **notice of adjournment**

In a case where a wife complained of her husband's desertion and wilful neglect to maintain, SIR JOHN ARNOLD P stated that a notice for an adjournment of a hearing should be treated like a service of a summons. Notice should be served under the Magistrates' Courts Rules 1968, r. 82, which provide that a summons must be served personally or by post at the last known place of abode.

UNITT v UNITT (1979) 124 Sol Jo 80 (Family Division: SIR JOHN ARNOLD P and WOOD J).

1853   —— **recovery abroad of maintenance—enforcement**

The Magistrates' Courts (Recovery Abroad of Maintenance) (Amendment) Rules 1980, S.I. 1980 No. 1584 (in force on 1st February 1981), amend the Magistrates' Courts (Recovery Abroad of Maintenance) Rules 1975, r. 7 (2), 1975 Halsbury's Abridgment para. 1132 in consequence of the coming into force of the Domestic Proceedings and Magistrates' Courts Act 1978, s. 57. The amendment does not apply in relation to orders made before s. 57 comes into force.

1854   **Election of trial by jury—series of offences—validity**

See *Re Prescott*, para. 729.

1855   **Evidence—evidence obtained from witness other than in open court—whether justice seen to be done**

See *Boatman v Boatman*, para. 1974.

1856   —— **lack of evidence—duty to draw inference from primary facts found**

The defendant was driving on a road about twenty feet wide. After a sharp bend, the car rolled over several times and was subsequently pushed off the road into a forestry track. No other vehicle was involved and the accident could not be attributed to any defect in the car or to the condition of the road surface. The defendant was charged with driving without due care and attention contrary to the Road Traffic Act 1972, s. 3. He gave no evidence or explanation of how the accident had occurred. The justices took the view that they were not entitled to speculate on the cause of the accident and in the absence of firm evidence, the prosecutor had not discharged the burden of proof. Accordingly, they dismissed the information. On appeal by the prosecutor, *held*, in the absence of any adequate explanation, the justices' duty of adjudication was to determine the inference to be drawn from the primary facts as found. In the present case there was an overwhelming inference that the defendant had not been driving with due care and attention. The justices had thus erred and the case would therefore be remitted to them with a direction to convict.

JARVIS v WILLIAMS [1979] RTR 497 (Queen's Bench Division: CUMMING-BRUCE LJ and NEILL J). *Wright v Wenlock* [1971] RTR 228, *Watts v Carter* [1971] RTR 232 and *Rabjohns v Burgar* [1971] RTR 234, applied.

1857   **Information—information laid but not served—fresh information served—when proceedings commenced**

Early in 1978, an information was laid against the defendant for an alleged offence under the Road Traffic Act 1972, s. 6 (1), of driving with a blood–alcohol concentration above the prescribed limit. The information was not served. The Criminal Law Act 1977, s. 15 came into operation on 17th July and provides that an offence under s. 6 (1) is triable only summarily and applies to proceedings commenced after that date. A fresh information was subsequently laid against him alleging the same offence. The applicant submitted that the proceedings against him had commenced before s. 15 had come into operation and that he was therefore entitled to trial by jury. His application was refused and he applied for judicial review of the decision. *Held*, the original information had no force and the information which gave rise to the proceedings was laid after s. 15 had come into operation. Accordingly, the justices had come to the right decision and the application for certiorari would be dismissed.

R v SOUTH WESTERN MAGISTRATES' COURT, EX PARTE BEATON [1980] RTR 35 (Queen's Bench Division: LORD WIDGERY CJ and LLOYD J).

1858   **Justices' clerks' assistants—qualifications**

The Justices' Clerks (Qualifications of Assistants) (Amendment) Rules 1980, S.I. 1980 No. 1897 (in force on 1st January 1981), amend the Justices' Clerks (Qualifications of Assistants) Rules 1979, Sch. 1, 1979 Halsbury's Abridgment para. 1784, by extending until 31st March 1981 the time for granting certificates of competence to certain justices' clerks' assistants with five years experience of court work prior to 31st December 1979.

1859   **Juvenile courts—power of magistrates to see witness before hearing**

See *Re W (a minor)*, para. 1962.

1860   **Licensing—fees**

See para. 1660.

1861   **Magistrates' Courts Act 1980**

The Magistrates' Courts Act 1980 consolidates certain enactments relating to the jurisdiction of, and the practice and procedure before, magistrates' courts and the functions of justices' clerks and connected matters. The Act, which includes amendments to give effect to the recommendations of the Law Commission, received the royal assent on 1st August 1980 and comes into force on a day to be appointed. Tables showing the destination of enactments consolidated and the derivation of the new Act are set out on pages 457–477 following.

DESTINATION TABLE

This table shows in column (1) the enactments repealed by the Magistrates' Courts Act 1980 and in column (2) the provisions of that Act corresponding to the repealed provisions.

In certain cases the enactment in column (1), though having a corresponding provision in column (2), is not, or is not wholly, repealed, as it is still required, or partly required, for the purposes of other legislation.

(1)	(2)
Justices of the Peace Act 1949 (c 101)	Magistrates Courts Act 1980 (c 43)
s 15 (1)-(3)	s 144 (1)-(3)
(7)	Sch 7, para. 5
(8)	\ 145 (5)
(9)	144 (4)
44 (1)‡	144 (5)
Magistrates' Courts Act 1952 (c 55)	
s 1 (1)	1 (1), (3), (8)
(2)	(2), (5), (8)
(3)	(6)
(4)	Rep., 1971 c 23, s 56 (4), Sch 11, Pt IV
(5)	1 (7)
2 (1)-(4)	2 (1)-(4)
(4A)	(5)
(5)	(7)
3 (1)	3 (1), (4)
(2)	(2), (4)
(3)	(3), (4)
(4)	Rep., 1972 c 70, s 272 (1), Sch 30
4 (1)	s 4 (1)
(2)	Rep., 1967, s 103 (2), Sch 7, Pt I
(3)	s 4 (3)
5	Rep., 1965, s 10 (3), Sch 2, Pt II
6	s 5
7 (1)	6 (1)
(2), (3)	(3), (4)
8	41
9-12	Rep., 1971 c 23, s 56 (4), Sch 11, Pt IV
13	s 9
14	10
15 (1)	11 (1)
(2)	13 (1), (5)
(3)	11 (2), 13 (2)
16	15
17	16
18, 19	Rep., 1977 c 45, s 65 (5), Sch 13
20, 21	Rep., 1969 c 54, s 72 (4), Sch 6
22	s 27

(1)	(2)
Magistrates Courts Act 1952 (c 55)	Magistrates Courts Act 1980 (c 43)
s 23	s 28
24, 25	Rep., 1977 c 45, s 65 (5), Sch 13
26 (1)	s 30 (1)
(2)	Rep., 1969 c 54, s 72 (4), Sch 6
(3)	s 30 (2)
(4)	Rep., 1976 c 63, s 12 (2), Sch 3
(5)	s 30 (3)
(6)	Rep., 1959 c 72, s 149 (2), Sch 8, Pt I
27	s 34
28 (1)	37 (1)
(2), (3)	Rep., 1961 c 39, s 41 (2), Sch 5
(4)	s 37 (2)
29	38
30	Rep., 1959 c 72, s 149 (2), Sch 8, Pt I
31 (1)	s 35
(2), (3)	
32	Rep., 1969 c 54, s 72 (4), Sch 6; 1977 c 45, s 65 (5), Sch 13
33	Rep., 1968 c 60, s 33 (3), Sch 3, Pt III
34	Rep., 1972 c 71, s 64 (2), Sch 6, Pt II
35	s 44
36	46
37	47
38 (1)	43 (1)
(1A)	(2)
(2)	(3)
(3)	Rep., 1976 c 63, s 12 (2), Sch 3
(4)	s 43 (4)
39	48
40	49 (1)-(4)
41	105
42	50
43	51
44	52
45	53

‡ Rep. by the Justices of the Peace Act 1979, s. 71(2), Sch. 3

(1) Magistrates' Courts Act 1952 (c 55)	(2) Magistrates' Courts Act 1980 (c 43)	(1) Magistrates' Courts Act 1952 (c 55)	(2) Magistrates' Courts Act 1980 (c 43)
s 46	s 54	s 75	s 94
47	55	76	95
48	56	77	97
49	57	78	98
50	58	79	99
51	Rep., 1957 c 55, s 12, Sch	80	100
		81	101
52	s 59	82	107
53	60	83 (1)–(3)	108
53A	62	(4)	Rep., 1957 c 55, s 12, Sch
54	63		
55	64	84	Rep., 1971 c 23, s 56 (4), Sch 11, Part IV
56 (1)	65 (1), (6)		
(1A)–(1D)	(2)–(5)	85 (1)	Rep., 1971 c 23, s 56 (4), Sch 11, Part IV
(2)	66 (1)		
56A	67	(2)	s 109 (1)
56B	68	(2A)	(2)
57 (1), (2)	69 (1), (2)	(3)	Rep., 1970 c 31, s 54 (3), Sch 11
(2A)	(3)		
(2B)	(7)	86	s 110
(3)	(4)	87	111
(4)	Rep., 1978 c 22, s 89 (2), Sch 3	88	112
		89 (1)	113 (1)
(5), (6)	s 69 (5), (6)	(1A)	(2)
58 (1)	71 (1)	(2), (3)	(3), (4)
(1A)	(2)	90	114
(1B)	(6)	91	115
(2)–(5)	(3)–(5)	92 (1)	116 (1), (3)
59	Rep., 1978 c 22, s 89 (2), Sch 3	(2)	(2)
		93	117
60 (1)–(3)	s 72 (1)–(3)	94	118
(3A)	(4)	95	119
(4)	(5)	96	120
61	73	97	Rep., 1976 c 63, s 12 (2), Sch 3
62	Rep., 1978 c 22, s 89 (2), Sch 3	98	s 121
		99	122
63	s 75	100	123
64	76	101	124
65	77	102 (1), (2)	125 (1), (2)
66	78	(3)	Rep., 1977 c. 45, s 65 (5), Sch 13
67	79		
68	80	(4)	s 125 (3)
69	Rep., 1967 c 80, s 103 (2), Sch 7, Pt I	103	126
		104	127 (1)
70 (1)	Rep., 1967 c 80, s 103 (2), Sch 7, Pt I	105 (1)	128 (1)
		(1A)	(2)
(2)–(5)	s 83	(2), (3)	(3), (4)
71	88	(3A)	(5)
72	89 (1)–(3)	(4), (5)	(6), (7)
72A	90	106	129
72B	91	107 (1)	132
73	96		
74	93		

(1)	(2)
Magistrates' Courts Act 1952 (c 55)	Magistrates' Courts Act 1980 (c 43)
s 107 (2), (3)	Rep., 1973 c 62, s 56 (2), Sch 6
(4)–(6)	Rep., 1961 c 39, s 41 (2), Sch 5
108	s 133
109	134 (1)–(6)
110	135
111 (1)	136 (1)
(2)	(2), (3)
112	137 (1)–(5)
113 (1)	138
(2)	Rep., 1967 c 80, s 103 (2), Sch 7, Pt I
114 (1) (a), (b)	s 139 (a), (b)
(c)–(e)	Rep., 1967 c 80, s 103 (2), Sch 7, Pt I
(f)	139 (c)
(2)	Rep., 1967 c 80, s 103 (2), Sch 7, Pt I
115	s 140
116 (1)	Rep., 1979 c 55, s 71 (2), Sch 3
(2), (3)	Rep., 1972 c 70, s 272 (1), Sch 30
117	Rep., 1972 c 70, s 272 (1), Sch 30
118 (1), (2)	s 141 (1), (2)
(3)	Rep., 1979 c 55, s 71 (2), Sch 3
(4)	s 141 (3)
119 (1)	Rep., 1964 c 42, s 41 (8), Sch 5
(2)	Rep., 1963 c 39, s 52 (2), Sch 6
(3)–(7)	Rep., 1964 c 42, s 41 (8), Sch 5
(8)	s 134 (7)
(9)	Rep., 1964 c 42, s 41 (8), Sch 5
120 (1)	Rep., 1968 c 69, s 8 (2), Sch 5, Pt II
(2)	Rep., 1964 c 42, s 41 (8), Sch 5
121 (1)	Rep., 1979 c 55, s 71 (2), Sch 3
(2)	Rep., 1978 c 22, s 89 (2), Sch 3
(3)	Rep., 1968 c 69, s 8 (2), Sch 5, Pt II
122	s 145 (1)–(3)
123	147
124	148
125	Rep., 1977 c 45, s 65 (5), Sch 13

(1)	(2)
Magistrates' Courts Act 1952 (c 55)	Magistrates' Courts Act 1980 (c 43)
s 126 (1)–(3)	s 150 (1)–(3)
(4)	Rep., 1972 c 70, s 272 (1), Sch 30
(5), (6)	s 150 (4), (5)
(7)	Rep., 1967 c 58, s 10 (2), Sch 3, Pt III
(8), (9)	s 150 (6), (7)
(10)	
127 (1)	Rep., 1971 c 48, s 11 (8), Sch, Pt I
(2)	Rep., 1977 c 45, s 65 (5), Sch 13
128	s 151
129	Rep., 1971 c 23, s 56 (4), Sch 11, Pt IV
130	s 152
130A	153
131	See Sch 8, para 8
132 (1)	Rep., S.L. (R.) A 1974
(2)–(5)	————
133 (1)	
(2)	s 155 (3), (4), (6)
(3)	
Sch 1	Rep., 1977 c 45, s 65 (5), Sch 13
2 para 1, 2	Sch 3 para 1
para 3	para 2
para 4, 5	para 3
para 6	Rep., 1971 c 23, s 56 (4), Sch 11, Pt IV
para 7–10	Sch 3 para 5–8
3 para 1, 2	4 para 1, 2
para 3	Rep., 1977 c 45, s 65 (5), Sch 13
para 4	Sch 4 para 3
4	6
5	See Sch 8, para 8
6	————

(1)	(2)
Magistrates' Courts Act 1957 (c 29)	Magistrates' Courts Act 1980 (c 43)
s 1 (1), (2)	s 12 (1), (2)
(2) proviso	(3)–(5)
(3)	12 (6), 13 (4)
(4)	Rep., 1965, c 55, s 1 (1), Sch
(5)	s 12 (7)
2	Rep., 1960, c 16, s 267 (1), Sch 18, Pt I
3	s 104
4	13 (5)
5	34 (1)
6 (1), (2)	————

(1)	(2)
Magistrates' Courts Act 1957 (c 29)	Magistrates' Courts Act 1980 (c 43)
s 6 (3)	s 155 (6)
(4)	——
Maintenance Orders Act 1958 (c 39)	
s 16 (1)	93 (3)–(8)
(2)	——
20 (6)	59 (3), (4)
23 (2)*	155 (6)
Mental Health Act 1959 (c 72)	
Sch 7 Part I†	30 (1)
Legitimacy Act 1959 (c 73)	
s 5 (2)	——
Criminal Justice Act 1961 (c 39)	
s 1 (5)†	——
8 (3)	36 (1)
41 (4)†	——
42 (2)*	155 (6)
Sch 4†	37 (1), 150 (1)
6†	——
Children and Young Persons Act 1963 (c 37)	
s 27 (1), (2)	103 (1), (2)
(3)	28, 103 (3)
(4)	103 (4)
65 (3)*	103 (4)
(5)*	155 (6)
Administration of Justice Act 1964 (c 42)	
s 11 (1), (2)	66 (2), (3)
(3), (4)	70 (1), (2)
(5)	66 (5), 70 (3)
38 (1)*	66 (5), 70 (3)
41 (7)*	155 (6)
Sch 3 para 20 (2)	144 (2)
22 (3)	137 (6)
(5)	——

(1)	(2)
Criminal Procedure (Attendance of Witnesses) Act 1965 (c 69)	Magistrates' Courts Act 1980 (c 43)
Sch 2 Part I†	s 145 (1) (e)
Criminal Justice Act 1967 (c 80)	
s 1	6 (2)
2 (1)–(8)	102 (1)–(8)
(9)	28, 102 (9)
(10)	102 (10)
3	8 (1)–(8)
4	6 (5)
5	8 (9)
6 (1)	4 (2)
(2)	——
19	42
20†	37 (1), 38
22 (5)*	113 (4)
24 (1)	1 (4)
(2)	13 (3)
(3), (4)	14 (1), (2)
(4A)	(3)
(5)	145 (4)
(6)	14 (4)
26 (1)	11 (3)
(2), (3)	(4)
28	2 (6)
29 (1)	Sch 3 para 2 (c)
(2)	para 8
(3)	para 4 (1)
30 (a)	10 (3)
(b)	30 (1)
33†	49
36 (1)†	8 (10), 150 (1)
44 (1)	——
(2)–(5)	82 (1)–(4)
(6)	(5), 83 (1)
(7)	(6)
(8), (9)	84 (1), (2)
(10), (11)	85
44A	86
45	87
50†	——
56 (4)	38
89 (1)†, (2)*	106
90 (1)†	84 (3)
94	114, Sch 6, Pt II
104 (4)*	150 (6)
106 (2) (b)†	Applied to Scotland
(3)*	s 155 (6)

† Repealed in part   * Not repealed

(1)	(2)	(1)	(2)
Criminal Justice Act 1967 (c 80)	Magistrates' Courts Act 1980 (c 43)	Courts Act 1971 (c 23)	Magistrates' Courts Act 1980 (c 43)
Sch 6 para 9	s 10 (3)	Sch 8 para 48 (b)†	s 38
para 10	30 (1)	para 52	85 (2)
para 11	37	9 Pt I†	108 (1), (2)
para 12	38		
para 13	83 (1)	**Maintenance Orders (Reciprocal Enforcement) Act 1972 (c 18)**	
para 17	120 (4)		
para 18	121 (2), (3)	s 22 (2) (b)	____
para 19	135 (1)		
para 20	136 (1)	**Local Government Act 1972 (c 70)**	
Justices of the Peace Act 1968 (c 69)		s 216*	149
		Sch 27 para 16	3 (4), 150 (1)
s 8 (3)*	155 (6)		
Sch 3 para 8	141 (3)	**Criminal Justice Act 1972 (c 71)**	
Children and Young Persons Act 1969 (c 54)		s 41	142
		44	24 (1)
s 6 (1)	24 (1)	45	4 (4)
(1A)	(2)	50	89 (1)
(2)	Rep., 1977 c 45, s 65 (5), Sch 13	66 (7)*	155 (6)
(3)	s 24 (3)	Sch 5†	6 (4), 24 (1), 139
10 (3)	6 (6)		
61	146	**Costs in Criminal Cases Act 1973 (c 14)**	
73 (5)*	155 (6)		
Sch 4 para 4		Sch 1 para 1	30 (3)
Administration of Justice Act 1970 (c 31)		**Guardianship Act 1973 (c 29)**	
s 1 (6) (b)*	144 (2)	s 9 (2) (b)	59 (2)
12 (1)	92 (1)		
(2)	(1), (2)	**Social Security Act 1973 (c 38)**	
28 (1)†	92 (3)		
30 (1)†, (2)†		Sch 27 para 85†	92 (1)
41 (6)	89 (1), (2)		
42	87 (1)	**Powers of Criminal Courts Act 1973 (c 62)**	
50	150 (4)		
51 (1)	150 (4)	s 35 (5)	40 (1)
(3)†		57 (1)*	40 (2)
54 (6)*	155 (6)	59 (1)*	155 (6)
Courts Act 1971 (c 23)		Sch 5 para 4	38
		para 5	76 (1)
s 7 (1)	7	para 7	135 (1)
Sch 8 para 2*	111 (4), 120 (5)	para 16	11 (3)
para 34	1 (2) (e), 37 (1), 38, 109 (2), 110, 113 (1), (3), 145 (1) (c), (e), Sch 3, para 5	para 34	24 (3)

† Repealed in part   * Not repealed

(1)	(2)
Legal Aid Act 1974 (c 4)	Magistrates' Courts Act 1980 (c 43)
Sch 4 para 3	s 92 (1)
Criminal Procedure (Scotland) Act 1975 (c 21)	
s 326 (2)	12 (8)
463 (1) (b)†	Cf. s 155 (2) (a)
Bail Act 1976 (c 63)	
Sch 2 para 14	6 (3)
para 15	6 (4)
para 16	41
para 17	30 (2)
para 18	43 (1)
para 19	43 (2)
para 20	43 (3)
para 21	——
para 22	113 (1), (2)
para 23	113 (4)
para 24	117
para 25	118 (2)
para 26	128 (1), (2)
para 27	128 (4), (5)
para 28	129 (2)–(4)
para 29	150 (1)
para 35	42 (1)
Criminal Law Act 1977 (c 45)	
s 14	——
15 (1) (b)	45 (1)
(3) (a)	——
16 (1)–(3)	17 (1)
(4)	(2)
18	127 (2)–(4)
19	18
20	19
21	20
22	21
23 (1)–(7)	22 (1)–(7)
(8)	22 (8), Sch 7, para 71 (b)
(9), (10)	22 (9), (10)
24	23
25	25
26	26
27	31 (1)–(3)

(1)	(2)
Criminal Law Act 1977 (c 45)	Magistrates' Courts Act 1980 (c 43)
s 28 (1)–(4)	s 32 (1)–(4)
(5), (6)	(6), (7)
(7)	(9)
(8)†	(5)
29	33 (1)
30 (4)	45 (3)
31 (5) (a)*, (6)*, (9)*	78 (4), (5)
32 (2)	34 (3)
34	29
35	24 (2)
36 (2)–(8)	81 (1)–(7)
(9)†	(8)
41	130
42	131
45	39
58 (1)	36 (1)
(4)	24 (3)
(6)	24 (4), 36 (2)
59	Sch 4 para 1
60 (1)	s 40 (1)
(2)	See Sch 8, para 3 (3)
61 (1)	s 143 (1), (3)
(2)	(2)
(3)–(5)	(4)–(6)
63 (2)†	Applied to Scotland
65 (2)*	s 31 (4), 32 (9), 33 (2)
(10)†	155 (5), (6)
Sch 2	——
3	Sch 1
4	2
5 para 1 (2) (a), (b)	s 32 (5)
para 1 (3)*	(8)
7 para 1	90, 91
8	Sch 5
12†	s 2 (4), (5), 8 (1), (3), (8), 10 (4), 14 (1), (3), 27, 28, 38, 44, 82 (4), 86, 111 (2), 121 (3), 128 (6), 133 (2), 142 (4), 153, Sch 3, para 2, 7
14 para 2	⎫
para 3 (1)†	⎬ See Sch 8
para 4	⎪
para 5†	⎭

† Repealed in part   * Not repealed

(1)	(2)	(1)	(2)
Domestic Proceedings and Magistrates' Courts Act 1978 (c 22)	Magistrates' Courts Act 1980 (c 43)	Justices of the Peace Act 1979 (c 55)	Magistrates' Courts Act 1980 (c 43)
s 75	s 52, 67 (4)	s 2 (1)*	s 150 (1)
76	60	(2)*	1 (8), 2 (1), (3), 3
77	62		(4), 97 (1),
78	63 (3), (4)		116 (3), 150
79	65		(1)
80	67, 68	33 (1)*	66 (4)
81 (1)	69 (2)	41 (1)*	1 (8), 2 (1), (3), 3
(2)	(3), (7)		(4), 97 (1),
82 (1)	71 (1)		116 (3), 150
(2)	(2), (6)		(1)
(3)	(3)	Sch 2 para 7	52, 67 (4)
83	72	para 8	———
84	74	para 9	139
85	61	para 14	87 (4)
90 (3)*	155 (6)		
Sch 1 para 5†	⎱	Child Care Act	
para 6, 7	⎰ See Sch 8	1980 (c 5)	
2 para 15	59 (2)	———	
para 21	66 (2)	Sch 5 para 5	65 (1)
		Protection of Trading Interests Act 1980 (c 11)	
Protection of Children Act 1978 (c 37)		———	
———		s 8 (5)†	———
s 2 (2)	s 103 (4)	(6)*	Sch 1 para 24

† Repealed in part   * Not repealed

TABLE OF DERIVATIONS

This table shows in the right hand column the legislative source from which the sections of the Magistrates' Courts Act 1980 in the left hand column have been derived. In the table the following abbreviations are used:

1949 (c. 101)	=	Justices of the Peace Act 1949 (12, 13 & 14 Geo. 6. c. 101).
1952	=	Magistrates' Courts Act 1952 (15 & 16 Geo. 6 & 1 Eliz. 2. c. 55).
1957 (c. 29)	=	Magistrates' Courts Act 1957 (5 & 6 Eliz. 2. c. 29).
1958 (c. 39)	=	Maintenance Orders Act 1958 (6 & 7 Eliz. 2. c. 39).
1959 (c. 72)	=	Mental Health Act 1959 (7 & 8 Eliz. 2. c. 72).
1959 (c. 73)	=	Legitimacy Act 1959 (7 & 8 Eliz. 2. c. 73).
1960 (c. 12)	=	Distress for Rates Act 1960 (8 & 9 Eliz. 2. c. 12).
1961 (c. 39)	=	Criminal Justice Act 1961 (9 & 10 Eliz. 2. c. 39).
1963 (c. 37)	=	Children and Young Persons Act 1963.
1964 (c. 42)	=	Administration of Justice Act 1964.
1965 (c. 69)	=	Criminal Procedure (Attendance of Witnesses) Act 1965.
1967 (c. 80)	=	Criminal Justice Act 1967.
1968 (c. 69)	=	Justices of the Peace Act 1968.
1969 (c. 19)	=	Decimal Currency Act 1969.
1969 (c. 54)	=	Children and Young Persons Act 1969.
1970 (c. 31)	=	Administration of Justice Act 1970.
1971 (c. 3)	=	Guardianship of Minors Act 1971.
1971 (c. 23)	=	Courts Act 1971.
1972 (c. 18)	=	Maintenance Orders (Reciprocal Enforcement) Act 1972.
1972 (c. 70)	=	Local Government Act 1972.
1972 (c. 71)	=	Criminal Justice Act 1972.
1973 (c. 14)	=	Costs in Criminal Cases Act 1973.
1973 (c. 18)	=	Matrimonial Causes Act 1973.
1973 (c. 29)	=	Guardianship Act 1973.
1973 (c. 38)	=	Social Security Act 1973.
1973 (c. 62)	=	Powers of Criminal Courts Act 1973.
1974 (c. 4)	=	Legal Aid Act 1974.
1975 (c. 21)	=	Criminal Procedure (Scotland) Act 1975.
1975 (c. 72)	=	Children Act 1975.
1976 (c. 63)	=	Bail Act 1976.
1977 (c. 45)	=	Criminal Law Act 1977.
1978 (c. 22)	=	Domestic Proceedings and Magistrates' Courts Act 1978.
1978 (c. 37)	=	Protection of Children Act 1978.
1979 (c. 55)	=	Justices of the Peace Act 1979.
1980 (c. 5)	=	Child Care Act 1980.
1980 (c. 11)	=	Protection of Trading Interests Act 1980.
R (followed by a number)	=	The recommendation set out in the paragraph of that number in the Appendix to the Report of the Law Commission (Cmnd. 7887).

Section of Act	Derivation
1 (1)	1952 s. 1 (1).
(2)	1952 s. 1 (2); 1971 (c. 23) Sch. 8 para. 34 (2).
(3)	1952 s. 1 (1).
(4)	1967 (c. 80) s. 24 (1).
(5)	1952 s. 1 (2).
(6)	1952 s. 1 (3).
(7)	1952 s. 1 (5).
(8)	1952 s. 1 (1), (2); 1979 (c. 55) ss. 2 (2), 41 (1).
2 (1)	1952 s. 2 (1); 1979 (c. 55) ss. 2 (2), 41 (1).
(2)	1952 s. 2 (2).
(3)	1952 s. 2 (3); 1979 (c. 55) ss. 2 (2), 41 (1).
(4)	1952 s. 2 (4); 1977 (c. 45) Sch. 12.
(5)	1952 s. 2 (4A) (inserted by 1977 (c. 45) Sch. 12).

Section of Act	Derivation
2 (6)	1967 (c. 80) s. 28.
(7)	1952 s. 2 (5).
3 (1)	1952 s. 3 (1).
(2)	1952 s. 3 (2).
(3)	1952 s. 3 (3).
(4)	1952 s. 3 (1)–(3); 1972 (c. 70) Sch. 27 para. 16 (1), (2); 1979 (c. 55) ss. 2 (2), 41 (1).
4 (1)	1952 s. 4 (1).
(2)	1967 (c. 80) s. 6 (1).
(3)	1952 s. 4 (3).
(4)	1972 (c. 71) s. 45.
5 (1)	1952 s. 6 (1).
(2)	1952 s. 6 (2).
6 (1)	1952 s. 7 (1).
(2)	1967 (c. 80) s. 1.
(3)	1952 s. 7 (2) (substituted by 1976 (c. 63) Sch. 2 para. 14).
(4)	1952 s. 7 (3); 1972 (c. 71) Sch. 5; 1976 (c. 63) Sch. 2 para. 15.
(5)	1967 (c. 80) s. 4.
(6)	1969 (c. 54) s. 10 (3).
7	1971 (c. 23) s. 7 (1).
8 (1)	1967 (c. 80) s. 3 (1); 1977 (c. 45) Sch. 12.
(2)	1967 (c. 80) s. 3 (2).
(3)	1967 (c. 80) s. 3 (3); 1977 (c. 45) Sch. 12.
(4)	1967 (c. 80) s. 3 (4).
(5)	1967 (c. 80) s. 3 (5).
(6)	1967 (c. 80) s. 3 (6).
(7)	1967 (c. 80) s. 3 (7).
(8)	1967 (c. 80) s. 3 (8) (inserted by 1977 (c. 45) Sch. 12).
(9)	1967 (c. 80) s. 5.
(10)	1967 (c. 80) s. 36 (1).
9 (1)	1952 s. 13 (1).
(2)	1952 s. 13 (2).
(3)	1952 s. 13 (3).
10 (1)	1952 s. 14 (1).
(2)	1952 s. 14 (2).
(3)	1952 s. 14 (3); 1967 (c. 80) s. 30, Sch. 6 para. 9.
(4)	1952 s. 14 (4); 1977 (c. 45) Sch. 12.
11 (1)	1952 s. 15 (1).
(2)	1952 s. 15 (3).
(3)	1967 (c. 80) s. 26 (1); 1973 (c. 62) Sch. 5 para. 16.
(4)	1967 (c. 80) s. 26 (2), (3).
12 (1)	1957 (c. 29) s. 1 (1).
(2)	1957 (c. 29) s. 1 (2).
(3)	1957 (c. 29) s. 1 (2) proviso (i).
(4)	1957 (c. 29) s. 1 (2) proviso (ii).
(5)	1957 (c. 29) s. 1 (2) proviso (iii).
(6)	1957 (c. 29) s. 1 (3).

Section of Act	Derivation
12 (7)	1957 (c. 29) s. 1 (5).
(8)	1975 (c. 21) s. 326 (2).
13 (1)	1952 s. 15 (2).
(2)	1952 s. 15 (3).
(3)	1967 (c. 80) s. 24 (2).
(4)	1957 (c. 29) s. 1 (3).
(5)	1952 s. 15 (2) proviso (b); 1957 (c. 29) s. 4.
14 (1)	1967 (c. 80) s. 24 (3); 1977 (c. 45) Sch. 12.
(2)	1967 (c. 80) s. 24 (4).
(3)	1967 (c. 80) s. 24 (4A) (inserted by 1977 (c. 45) Sch. 12).
(4)	1967 (c. 80) s. 24 (6).
15 (1)	1952 s. 16 (1).
(2)	1952 s. 16 (2).
16	1952 s. 17.
17 (1)	1977 (c. 45) s. 16 (1) to (3).
(2)	1977 (c. 45) s. 16 (4).
18 (1)	1977 (c. 45) s. 19 (1).
(2)	1977 (c. 45) s. 19 (2).
(3)	1977 (c. 45) s. 19 (3).
(4)	1977 (c. 45) s. 19 (4).
(5)	1977 (c. 45) s. 19 (5).
19 (1)	1977 (c. 45) s. 20 (1).
(2)	1977 (c. 45) s. 20 (2).
(3)	1977 (c. 45) s. 20 (3).
(4)	1977 (c. 45) s. 20 (4).
20 (1)	1977 (c. 45) s. 21 (1).
(2)	1977 (c. 45) s. 21 (2).
(3)	1977 (c. 45) s. 21 (3).
21	1977 (c. 45) s. 22.
22 (1)	1977 (c. 45) s. 23 (1).
(2)	1977 (c. 45) s. 23 (2).
(3)	1977 (c. 45) s. 23 (3).
(4)	1977 (c. 45) s. 23 (4).
(5)	1977 (c. 45) s. 23 (5).
(6)	1977 (c. 45) s. 23 (6).
(7)	1977 (c. 45) s. 23 (7).
(8)	1977 (c. 45) s. 23 (8).
(9)	1977 (c. 45) s. 23 (9).
(10)	1977 (c. 45) s. 23 (10).
23 (1)	1977 (c. 45) s. 24 (1).
(2)	1977 (c. 45) s. 24 (2).
(3)	1977 (c. 45) s. 24 (3).
(4)	1977 (c. 45) s. 24 (4).
(5)	1977 (c. 45) s. 24 (5).

Section of Act	Derivation
24 (1)	1969 (c. 54) s. 6 (1); 1972 (c. 71) s. 44, Sch. 5.
(2)	1969 (c. 54) s. 6 (1A) (inserted by 1977 (c. 45) s. 35).
(3)	1969 (c. 54) s. 6 (3); 1973 (c. 62) Sch. 5 para. 34; 1977 (c. 45) s. 58 (4).
(4)	1977 (c. 45) s. 58 (6).
25 (1)	1977 (c. 45) s. 25 (1).
(2)	1977 (c. 45) s. 25 (2).
(3)	1977 (c. 45) s. 25 (3).
(4)	1977 (c. 45) s. 25 (4).
(5)	1977 (c. 45) s. 25 (5).
(6)	1977 (c. 45) s. 25 (6).
(7)	1977 (c. 45) s. 25 (7).
26 (1)	1977 (c. 45) s. 26 (1).
(2)	1977 (c. 45) s. 26 (2).
27	1952 s. 22; 1977 (c. 45) Sch. 12.
28	1952 s. 23; 1963 (c. 37) s. 27 (3); 1967 (c. 80) s. 2 (9); 1977 (c. 45) Sch. 12.
29 (1)	1977 (c. 45) s. 34 (1).
(2)	1977 (c. 45) s. 34 (2).
(3)	1977 (c. 45) s. 34 (3).
(4)	1977 (c. 45) s. 34 (4).
(5)	1977 (c. 45) s. 34 (5).
30 (1)	1952 s. 26 (1); 1959 (c. 72) Sch. 7 Pt. I; 1967 (c. 80) s. 30 (b), Sch. 6 para. 10.
(2)	1952 s. 26 (3) (substituted by 1976 (c. 63) Sch. 2 para. 17).
(3)	1952 s. 26 (5); 1973 (c. 14) Sch. 1 para. 1.
31 (1)	1977 (c. 45) s. 27 (1).
(2)	1977 (c. 45) s. 27 (2).
(3)	1977 (c. 45) s. 27 (3).
(4)	1977 (c. 45) s. 65 (2).
32 (1)	1977 (c. 45) s. 28 (1).
(2)	1977 (c. 45) s. 28 (2).
(3)	1977 (c. 45) s. 28 (3).
(4)	1977 (c. 45) s. 28 (4).
(5)	1977 (c. 45) s. 28 (8), Sch. 5 para. 1 (2) (a) and (b).
(6)	1977 (c. 45) s. 28 (5).
(7)	1977 (c. 45) s. 28 (6).
(8)	1977 (c. 45) Sch. 5 para. 1 (3).
(9)	1977 (c. 45) ss. 28 (7), 65 (2).
33 (1)	1977 (c. 45) s. 29.
(2)	1977 (c. 45) s. 65 (2).
34 (1)	1952 s. 27 (1); 1957 (c. 29) s. 5.
(2)	1952 s. 27 (2).
(3)	1952 s. 27 (3); 1977 (c. 45) s. 32 (2).
35	1952 s. 31 (1).
36 (1)	1961 (c. 39) s. 8 (3); 1977 (c. 45) s. 58 (1).
(2)	1977 (c. 45) s. 58 (6).

Section of Act	Derivation
37 (1)	1952 s. 28 (1); 1961 (c. 39) Sch. 4; 1967 (c. 80) s. 20, Sch. 6 para. 11; 1971 (c. 23) Sch. 8 para. 34 (1).
(2)	1952 s. 28 (4); 1967 (c. 80) Sch. 6 para. 11.
38	1952 s. 29; 1967 (c. 80) ss. 20, 56 (4), Sch. 6 para. 12; 1971 (c. 23) Sch. 8 para. 34 (1); 1973 (c. 62) Sch. 5 para. 4; 1977 (c. 45) Sch. 12.
39 (1)	1977 (c. 45) s. 45 (1).
(2)	1977 (c. 45) s. 45 (2).
(3)	1977 (c. 45) s. 45 (3).
(4)	1977 (c. 45) s. 45 (4).
(5)	1977 (c. 45) s. 45 (5).
(6)	1977 (c. 45) s. 45 (6).
40 (1)	1973 (c. 62) s. 35 (5); 1977 (c. 45) s. 60 (1).
(2)	1973 (c. 62) s. 57 (1).
41	1952 s. 8; 1976 (c. 63) Sch. 2 para. 16.
42 (1)	1967 (c. 80) s. 19 (1); 1976 (c. 63) Sch. 2 para. 35.
(2)	1967 (c. 80) s. 19 (2).
43 (1)	1952 s. 38 (1); 1976 (c. 63) Sch. 2 para. 18.
(2)	1952 s. 38 (1A) (inserted by 1976 (c. 63) Sch. 2 para. 19)
(3)	1952 s. 38 (2); 1976 (c. 63) Sch. 2 para. 20.
(4)	1952 s. 38 (4).
44 (1)	1952 s. 35 (1) (as re-numbered by 1977 (c. 45) Sch. 12).
(2)	1952 s. 35 (2) (added by 1977 (c. 45) Sch. 12).
45 (1)	1977 (c. 45) s. 15 (1) (b).
(2)	1977 (c. 45) s. 15 (5).
(3)	1977 (c. 45) s. 30 (4).
46	1952 s. 36.
47	1952 s. 37
48	1952 s. 39.
49 (1)	1952 s. 40 (1); 1967 (c. 80) s. 33.
(2)	1952 s. 40 (2).
(3)	1952 s. 40 (3).
(4)	1952 s. 40 (4).
(5)	1967 (c. 80) s. 33.
50	1952 s. 42.
51	1952 s. 43.
52	1952 s. 44; 1978 (c. 22) s. 75; 1979 (c. 55) Sch. 2 para. 7.
53 (1)	1952 s. 45 (1).
(2)	1952 s. 45 (2).
(3)	1952 s. 45 (3).

Section of Act	Derivation
54 (1)	1952 s. 46 (1).
(2)	1952 s. 46 (2).
55 (1)	1952 s. 47 (1).
(2)	1952 s. 47 (2).
(3)	1952 s. 47 (3).
(4)	1952 s. 47 (4).
(5)	1952 s. 47 (5).
(6)	1952 s. 47 (6).
(7)	1952 s. 47 (7).
(8)	1952 s. 47 (8).
56	1952 s. 48.
57	1952 s. 49.
58 (1)	1952 s. 50 (1).
(2)	1952 s. 50 (2).
59 (1)	1952 s. 52 (1).
(2)	1952 s. 52 (2); 1973 (c. 29) s. 9 (2); 1978 (c. 22) Sch. 2 para. 15.
(3)	1952 s. 52 (3); 1958 (c. 39) s. 20 (6).
(4)	1952 s. 52 (4); 1958 (c. 39) s. 20 (6).
60	1952 s. 53; 1978 (c. 22) s. 76.
61 (1)	1978 (c. 22) s. 85 (1).
(2)	1978 (c. 22) s. 85 (2).
62 (1)	1952 s. 53A (1). ⎫
(2)	1952 s. 53A (2). ⎪
(3)	1952 s. 53A (3). ⎪
(4)	1952 s. 53A (4). ⎬ inserted by 1978 (c. 22) s. 77.
(5)	1952 s. 53A (5). ⎪
(6)	1952 s. 53A (6). ⎪
(7)	1952 s. 53A (7). ⎭
63 (1)	1952 s. 54 (1).
(2)	1952 s. 54 (2).
(3)	1952 s. 54 (3); 1978 (c. 22) s. 78 (1).
(4)	1952 s. 54 (4) (substituted by 1978 (c. 22) s. 78 (2)).
(5)	1952 s. 54 (5).
64 (1)	1952 s. 55 (1).
(2)	1952 s. 55 (2).
(3)	1952 s. 55 (3).
(4)	1952 s. 55 (4).
(5)	1952 s. 55 (5).
65 (1)	1952 s. 56 (1). ⎫
(2)	1952 s. 56 (1A). ⎪
(3)	1952 s. 56 (1B). ⎬ substituted by 1978 (c. 22) s. 79; amended by
(4)	1952 s. 56 (1C). ⎪ 1980 (c. 5) Sch. 5 para. 5; R3.
(5)	1952 s. 56 (1D). ⎭
(6)	—

Section of Act	Derivation
66 (1)	1952 s. 56 (2).
(2)	1964 (c. 42) s. 11 (1); 1978 (c. 22) Sch. 2 para. 21.
(3)	1964 (c. 42) s. 11 (2).
(4)	1964 (c. 42) s. 9 (1); 1979 (c. 55) s. 33 (1).
(5)	1964 (c. 42) ss. 11 (5) and 38 (1).
67 (1)	1952 s. 56A (1).
(2)	1952 s. 56A (2).
(3)	1952 s. 56A (3).
(4)	1952 s. 56A (4). inserted by 1978 (c. 22) s. 80; "commission
(5)	1952 s. 56A (5). area" in s. 56A (4) defined in 1952 s. 44, 1978
(6)	1952 s. 56A (6). (c. 22) s. 75 and 1979 (c. 55) Sch. 2 para. 7.
(7)	1952 s. 56A (7).
(8)	1952 s. 56A (8).
68 (1)	1952 s. 56B (1).
(2)	1952 s. 56B (2).
(3)	1952 s. 56B (3).
(4)	1952 s. 56B (4). inserted by 1978 (c. 22) s. 80.
(5)	1952 s. 56B (5).
(6)	1952 s. 56B (6).
(7)	1952 s. 56B (7).
69 (1)	1952 s. 57 (1).
(2)	1952 s. 57 (2) (substituted by 1978 (c. 22) s. 81 (1)).
(3)	1952 s. 57 (2A) (inserted by 1978 (c. 22) s. 81 (2)).
(4)	1952 s. 57 (3).
(5)	1952 s. 57 (5).
(6)	1952 s. 57 (6).
(7)	1952 s. 57 (2B) (inserted by 1978 (c. 22) s. 81 (2)).
70 (1)	1964 (c. 42) s. 11 (3).
(2)	1964 (c. 42) s. 11 (4).
(3)	1964 (c. 42) ss. 11 (5) and 38 (1).
71 (1)	1952 s. 58 (1); 1978 (c. 22) s. 82 (1).
(2)	1952 s. 58 (1A) (inserted by 1978 (c. 22) s. 82 (2)).
(3)	1952 s. 58 (2) (substituted by 1978 (c. 22) s. 82 (3)).
(4)	1952 s. 58 (3).
(5)	1952 s. 58 (4).
(6)	1952 s. 58 (1B) (inserted by 1978 (c. 22) s. 82 (2)).
72 (1)	1952 s. 60 (1).
(2)	1952 s. 60 (2).
(3)	1952 s. 60 (3) (substituted by 1978 (c. 22) s. 83).
(4)	1952 s. 60 (3A) (substituted by 1978 (c. 22) s. 83).
(5)	1952 s. 60 (4); 1978 (c. 22) s. 83.
73	1952 s. 61.
74 (1)	1978 (c. 22) s. 84 (1).
(2)	1978 (c. 22) s. 84 (2).
75 (1)	1952 s. 63 (1).
(2)	1952 s. 63 (2).
(3)	1952 s. 63 (3).

Section of Act	Derivation
76 (1)	1952 s. 64 (1); 1973 (c. 62) Sch. 5 para. 5.
(2)	1952 s. 64 (2).
(3)	1952 s. 64 (3).
77 (1)	1952 s. 65 (1).
(2)	1952 s. 65 (2).
78 (1)	1952 s. 66 (1).
(2)	1952 s. 66 (2).
(3)	1952 s. 66 (3).
(4)	1952 s. 66 (4); 1977 (c. 45) s. 31 (5) (a), (6), (9).
(5)	1952 s. 66 (5); 1977 (c. 45) s. 31 (5) (a), (6), (9).
79 (1)	1952 s. 67 (1).
(2)	1952 s. 67 (2).
(3)	1952 s. 67 (3).
80 (1)	1952 s. 68 (1).
(2)	1952 s. 68 (2).
(3)	1952 s. 68 (3).
81 (1)	1977 (c. 45) s. 36 (2).
(2)	1977 (c. 45) s. 36 (3).
(3)	1977 (c. 45) s. 36 (4).
(4)	1977 (c. 45) s. 36 (5).
(5)	1977 (c. 45) s. 36 (6).
(6)	1977 (c. 45) s. 36 (7).
(7)	1977 (c. 45) s. 36 (8).
(8)	1977 (c. 45) s. 36 (9).
82 (1)	1967 (c. 80) s. 44 (2).
(2)	1967 (c. 80) s. 44 (3).
(3)	1967 (c. 80) s. 44 (4).
(4)	1967 (c. 80) s. 44 (5); 1977 (c. 45) Sch. 12.
(5)	1967 (c. 80) s. 44 (6).
(6)	1967 (c. 80) s. 44 (7).
83 (1)	1952 s. 70 (2); 1967 (c. 80) s. 44 (6), Sch. 6 para. 13.
(2)	1952 s. 70 (3).
(3)	1952 s. 70 (4).
(4)	1952 s. 70 (5).
84 (1)	1967 (c. 80) s. 44 (8).
(2)	1967 (c. 80) s. 44 (9).
(3)	1967 (c. 80) s. 90 (1).
(4)	1967 (c. 80) s. 90 (2).
85 (1)	1967 (c. 80) s. 44 (10).
(2)	1967 (c. 80) s. 44 (11) (substituted by 1971 (c. 23) Sch. 8 para. 52).
86 (1)	1967 (c. 80) s. 44A (1). ⎫
(2)	1967 (c. 80) s. 44A (2). ⎪
(3)	1967 (c. 80) s. 44A (3). ⎬ inserted by 1977 (c. 45) Sch. 12.
(4)	1967 (c. 80) s. 44A (4). ⎪
(5)	1967 (c. 80) s. 44A (5). ⎭
87 (1)	1967 (c. 80) s. 45 (1); 1970 (c. 31) s. 42.

Section of Act	Derivation
87 (2)	1967 (c. 80) s. 45 (2).
(3)	1967 (c. 80) s. 45 (3).
(4)	1967 (c. 80) s. 45 (4); 1979 (c. 55) Sch. 2 para. 14.
88 (1)	1952 s. 71 (1).
(2)	1952 s. 71 (2).
(3)	1952 s. 71 (3).
(4)	1952 s. 71 (4).
(5)	1952 s. 71 (5).
(6)	1952 s. 71 (6).
89 (1)	1952 s. 72 (1); 1970 (c. 31) s. 41 (6); 1972 (c. 71) s. 50.
(2)	1952 s. 72 (2); 1970 (c. 31) s. 41 (6).
(3)	1952 s. 72 (3).
(4)	—
90 (1)	1952 s. 72A (1). ⎫
(2)	1952 s. 72A (2). ⎬ substituted by 1977 (c. 45) Sch. 7 para. 1.
(3)	1952 s. 72A (3). ⎭
91 (1)	1952 s. 72B (1). ⎫
(2)	1952 s. 72B (2). ⎬ substituted by 1977 (c. 45) Sch. 7 para. 1.
(3)	1952 s. 72B (3). ⎭
92 (1)	1970 (c. 31) s. 12 (1), (2); 1973 (c. 38) Sch. 27 para. 85; 1974 (c. 4) Sch. 4 para. 3.
(2)	1970 (c. 31) s. 12 (2).
(3)	1970 (c. 31) s. 28.
93 (1)	1952 s. 74 (1).
(2)	1952 s. 74 (2).
(3)	1952 s. 74 (3). ⎫
(4)	1952 s. 74 (4). ⎪
(5)	1952 s. 74 (5). ⎬ substituted by 1958 (c. 39) s. 16 (1).
(6)	1952 s. 74 (6). ⎪
(7)	1952 s. 74 (7). ⎪
(8)	1952 s. 74 (8). ⎭
94	1952 s. 75.
95	1952 s. 76.
96 (1)	1952 s. 73 (1).
(2)	1952 s. 73 (2).
(3)	1952 s. 73 (3).
97 (1)	1952 s. 77 (1); 1979 (c. 55) ss. 2 (2), 41 (1).
(2)	1952 s. 77 (2).
(3)	1952 s. 77 (3).
(4)	1952 s. 77 (4).
98	1952 s. 78.
99	1952 s. 79.
100	1952 s. 80.

Section of Act	Derivation
101	1952 s. 81.
102 (1)	1967 (c. 80) s. 2 (1).
(2)	1967 (c. 80) s. 2 (2).
(3)	1967 (c. 80) s. 2 (3).
(4)	1967 (c. 80) s. 2 (4).
(5)	1967 (c. 80) s. 2 (5).
(6)	1967 (c. 80) s. 2 (6).
(7)	1967 (c. 80) s. 2 (7).
(8)	1967 (c. 80) s. 2 (8).
(9)	1967 (c. 80) s. 2 (9).
(10)	1967 (c. 80) s. 2 (10).
103 (1)	1963 (c. 37) s. 27 (1).
(2)	1963 (c. 37) s. 27 (2).
(3)	1963 (c. 37) s. 27 (3).
(4)	1963 (c. 37) ss. 27 (4), 65 (3); 1978 (c. 37) s. 2 (2).
104	1957 (c. 29) s. 3.
105 (1)	1952 s. 41 (1).
(2)	1952 s. 41 (2).
106 (1)	1967 (c. 80) s. 89 (1).
(2)	1967 (c. 80) s. 89 (2).
107	1952 s. 82.
108 (1)	1952 s. 83 (1); 1971 (c. 23) s. 56 (2), Sch. 9 Part I.
(2)	1952 s. 83 (2); 1971 (c. 23) s. 56 (2), Sch. 9 Part I.
(3)	1952 s. 83 (3).
109 (1)	1952 s. 85 (2).
(2)	1952 s. 85 (2A) (inserted by 1971 (c. 23) Sch. 8 para. 34 (4) (b)).
110	1952 s. 86; 1971 (c. 23) Sch. 8 paras. 2 and 34 (1).
111 (1)	1952 s. 87 (1).
(2)	1952 s. 87 (2); 1977 (c. 45) Sch. 12.
(3)	1952 s. 87 (3).
(4)	1952 s. 87 (4); 1971 (c. 23) Sch. 8 para. 2.
(5)	1952 s. 87 (5).
(6)	1952 s. 87 (6).
112	1952 s. 88.
113 (1)	1952 s. 89 (1); 1971 (c. 23) Sch. 8 para. 34 (1); 1976 (c. 63) Sch. 2 para. 22 (a).
(2)	1952 s. 89 (1A) (inserted by 1976 (c. 63) Sch. 2 para. 22 (b)).
(3)	1952 s. 89 (2); 1971 (c. 23) Sch. 8 para. 34 (1).
(4)	1952 s. 89 (3); 1967 (c. 80) s. 22 (5); 1976 (c. 63) Sch. 2 para. 23.
114	1952 s. 90; 1967 (c. 80) s. 94 (1).
115 (1)	1952 s. 91 (1).
(2)	1952 s. 91 (2).
(3)	1952 s. 91 (3).

Section of Act	Derivation
116 (1)	1952 s. 92 (1).
(2)	1952 s. 92 (2).
(3)	1952 s. 92 (1); 1979 (c. 55) ss. 2 (2), 41 (1).
117 (1)	1952 s. 93 (1). ⎫
(2)	1952 s. 93 (2). ⎬ (substituted by 1976 (c. 63) Sch. 2 para. 24).
(3)	1952 s. 93 (3). ⎭
118 (1)	1952 s. 94.
(2)	1952 s. 94 proviso (added by 1976 (c. 63) Sch. 2 para. 25).
119 (1)	1952 s. 95 (1).
(2)	1952 s. 95 (2).
(3)	1952 s. 95 (3).
120 (1)	1952 s. 96 (1).
(2)	1952 s. 96 (2).
(3)	1952 s. 96 (3).
(4)	1952 s. 96 (4); 1967 (c. 80) Sch. 6 para. 17.
(5)	1952 s. 96 (5); 1971 (c. 23) Sch. 8 para. 2.
121 (1)	1952 s. 98 (1).
(2)	1952 s. 98 (2); 1967 (c. 80) Sch. 6 para. 18.
(3)	1952 s. 98 (3); 1967 (c. 80) Sch. 6 para. 18; 1977 (c. 45) Sch. 12.
(4)	1952 s. 98 (4).
(5)	1952 s. 98 (5).
(6)	1952 s. 98 (6).
(7)	1952 s. 98 (7).
(8)	1952 s. 98 (8).
122	1952 s. 99.
123 (1)	1952 s. 100 (1).
(2)	1952 s. 100 (2).
124	1952 s. 101.
125 (1)	1952 s. 102 (1).
(2)	1952 s. 102 (2); 1960 (c. 12) Sch. 2.
(3)	1952 s. 102 (4).
126	1952 s. 103.
127 (1)	1952 s. 104.
(2)	1977 (c. 45) s. 18 (1).
(3)	1977 (c. 45) s. 18 (2).
(4)	1977 (c. 45) s. 18 (3).
128 (1)	1952 s. 105 (1) (substituted by 1976 (c. 63) Sch. 2 para. 26).
(2)	1952 s. 105 (1A) (substituted by 1976 (c. 63) Sch. 2 para. 26).
(3)	1952 s. 105 (2).
(4)	1952 s. 105 (3) (substituted by 1976 (c. 63) Sch. 2 para. 27).
(5)	1952 s. 105 (3A) (substituted by 1976 (c. 63) Sch. 2 para. 27).
(6)	1952 s. 105 (4); 1977 (c. 45) Sch. 12.
(7)	1952 s. 105 (5).
129 (1)	1952 s. 106 (1).

Section of Act	Derivation
129 (2)	1952 s. 106 (2); 1976 (c. 63) Sch. 2 para. 28.
(3)	1952 s. 106 (3) (substituted by 1976 (c. 63) Sch. 2 para. 28.)
(4)	1952 s. 106 (4) (added by 1976 (c. 63) Sch. 2 para. 28).
130 (1)	1977 (c. 45) s. 41 (1).
(2)	1977 (c. 45) s. 41 (2).
(3)	1977 (c. 45) s. 41 (3).
(4)	1977 (c. 45) s. 41 (4).
(5)	1977 (c. 45) s. 41 (5).
131 (1)	1977 (c. 45) s. 42 (1).
(2)	1977 (c. 45) s. 42 (2).
(3)	1977 (c. 45) s. 42 (3).
132	1952 s. 107 (1).
133 (1)	1952 s. 108 (1).
(2)	1952 s. 108 (2); 1977 (c. 45) Sch. 12.
(3)	1952 s. 108 (3).
(4)	1952 s. 108 (4).
(5)	1952 s. 108 (5).
134 (1)	1952 s. 109 (1).
(2)	1952 s. 109 (2).
(3)	1952 s. 109 (3).
(4)	1952 s. 109 (4).
(5)	1952 s. 109 (5).
(6)	1952 s. 109 (6).
(7)	1952 s. 119 (8).
135 (1)	1952 s. 110 (1); 1967 (c. 80) Sch. 6 para. 19.
(2)	1952 s. 110 (2).
136 (1)	1952 s. 111 (1); 1967 (c. 80) Sch. 6 para. 20.
(2)	1952 s. 111 (2).
(3)	1952 s. 111 (2).
137 (1)	1952 s. 112 (1).
(2)	1952 s. 112 (2).
(3)	1952 s. 112 (3).
(4)	1952 s. 112 (4).
(5)	1952 s. 112 (5).
(6)	1964 (c. 42) Sch. 3 para. 22 (3).
138	1952 s. 113 (1).
139	1952 s. 114 (1) (a), (b), (f); 1972 (c. 71) Sch. 5; 1979 (c. 55) Sch. 2 para. 9.
140	1952 s. 115.
141 (1)	1952 s. 118 (1).
(2)	1952 s. 118 (2).
(3)	1952 s. 118 (4) (substituted by 1968 (c. 69) Sch. 3 para. 8).
142 (1)	1972 (c. 71) s. 41 (1).
(2)	1972 (c. 71) s. 41 (2).
(3)	1972 (c. 71) s. 41 (3).

Section of Act	Derivation
142 (4)	1972 (c. 71) s. 41 (4); 1977 (c. 45) Sch. 12.
(5)	1972 (c. 71) s. 41 (5).
143 (1)	1977 (c. 45) s. 61 (1).
(2)	1977 (c. 45) s. 61 (2).
(3)	1977 (c. 45) s. 61 (1).
(4)	1977 (c. 45) s. 61 (3).
(5)	1977 (c. 45) s. 61 (4).
(6)	1977 (c. 45) s. 61 (5).
144 (1)	1949 (c. 101) s. 15 (1); R2.
(2)	1949 (c. 101) s. 15 (2); 1964 (c. 42) Sch. 3 para. 20 (2); 1970 (c. 31) s. 1 (6) (b).
(3)	1949 (c. 101) s. 15 (3).
(4)	1949 (c. 101) s. 15 (9).
145 (1)	1952 s. 122 (1); 1965 (c. 69) Sch. 2 Part I; 1971 (c. 23) Sch. 8 para. 34 (1), (5).
(2)	1952 s. 122 (2).
(3)	1952 s. 122 (3).
(4)	1967 (c. 80) s. 24 (5).
(5)	1949 (c. 101) s. 15 (8).
146 (1)	1969 (c. 54) s. 61 (1).
(2)	1969 (c. 54) s. 61 (2).
(3)	1969 (c. 54) s. 61 (3).
(4)	1969 (c. 54) s. 61 (4).
(5)	1969 (c. 54) s. 61 (5).
147 (1)	1952 s. 123 (1).
(2)	1952 s. 123 (2).
(3)	1952 s. 123 (3).
148 (1)	1952 s. 124 (1).
(2)	1952 s. 124 (2).
149	1972 (c. 70) s. 216.
150 (1)	1952 s. 126 (1); 1961 (c. 39) Sch. 4 ("fine"); 1979 (c. 55) s. 2 ("London commission area"); 1972 (c. 70) Sch. 27 para. 16 (4) and 1979 (c. 55) ss. 2 (2) and 41 (1) ("petty sessions area"); 1967 (c. 80) s. 36 (1) ("committal proceedings"); 1976 (c. 63) Sch. 2 para. 29 ("bail in criminal proceedings"); RI ("petty-sessional courthouse").
(2)	1952 s. 126 (2).
(3)	1952 s. 126 (3).
(4)	1952 s. 126 (5); 1970 (c. 31) ss. 50 and 51 (1).
(5)	1952 s. 126 (6).
(6)	1952 s. 126 (8); 1967 (c. 80) s. 104 (4).
(7)	1952 s. 126 (9).
151 (1)	1952 s. 128 (1); 1960 (c. 12) Sch. 2.
(2)	1952 s. 128 (2); 1960 (c. 12) Sch. 2.
(3)	1952 s. 128 (3).
152	1952 s. 130.
153	1952 s. 130A (inserted by 1977 (c. 45) Sch. 12).

Section of Act	Derivation
154	—
155 (1)	—
(2)–(6)	1952 s. 133 (2); 1957 (c. 29) s. 6 (3); 1958 (c. 39) s. 23 (2); 1961 (c. 39) s. 42; 1963 (c. 37) s. 65 (4), (5); 1964 (c. 42) s. 41 (6), (7); 1967 (c. 80) s. 106 (2), (3); 1968 (c. 69) ss. 6 (1), 8 (3); 1969 (c. 54) s. 73 (4), (5); 1970 (c. 31) s. 54; 1972 (c. 71) s. 66 (7); 1973 (c. 62) ss. 58, 59; 1975 (c. 21) s. 463; 1977 (c. 45) ss. 63, 65 (10); 1978 (c. 22) s. 90 (2), (3).
(7)	—
Sch. 1	1977 (c. 45) Sch. 3; 1980 (c. 11) s. 8 (5), (6).
Sch. 2.	1977 (c. 45) Sch. 4.
Sch. 3	
para. 1 (1)	1952 Sch. 2 para. 1.
(2)	1952 Sch. 2 para. 2.
2	1952 Sch. 2 para. 3; 1967 (c. 80) s. 29 (1); 1977 (c. 45) Sch. 12.
3 (1)	1952 Sch. 2 para. 4.
(2)	1952 Sch. 2 para. 5.
4 (1)	1967 (c. 80) s. 29 (3).
(2)	1967 (c. 80) s. 36 (1).
5	1952 Sch. 2 para. 7; 1971 (c. 23) Sch. 8 para. 34 (1).
6	1952 Sch. 2 para. 8.
7	1952 Sch. 2 para. 9 (substituted by 1977 (c. 45) Sch. 12).
8	1952 Sch. 2 para. 10; 1967 (c. 80) s. 29 (2).
Sch. 4.	
para. 1	1952 Sch. 3, para. 1; 1977 (c. 45) s. 59.
2	1952 Sch. 3, para. 2.
3	1952 Sch. 3, para. 4.
Sch. 5.	1977 (c. 45) Sch. 8.
Sch. 6	
Part I	1952 Sch. 4, Part I; 1969 (c. 19) s. 10 (1); Magistrates' Courts Fees (Decimalisation) Order 1971 (1971/188).
Part II	1952 Sch. 4, Part II; 1967 (c. 80) s. 94.
Part III	1952 Sch. 4 Part III.
Sch. 7.	—
Sch. 8	—
Sch. 9	—

1862   Magistrates' courts—forms

The Magistrates' Courts (Forms) (Amendment) Rules 1980, S.I. 1980 No. 511 (in force on 12th May 1980), amend the Magistrates' Courts (Forms) Rules 1968 by providing that certain particulars regarding bail decisions no longer have to be recorded in the court register. The particulars concerned relate to the date of the last bail or custody decision, if any, and the stage reached in proceedings.

1863   ——rules

The Magistrates' Courts (Amendment) Rules 1980, S.I. 1980 No. 510 (in force on 12th May 1980), amend the Magistrates' Courts Rules 1968 so as to enable the reasons for a bail decision to be entered in a separate part of the court register from that in which the particulars of the decision are entered. Various amendments are also made to the 1968 Rules in consequence of the coming into force of the Criminal Law Act 1977, s. 39 (1), para. 666.

1864   Magistrates' courts committees

The Magistrates' Courts Committees (Constitution) (Amendment) Regulations 1980, S.I. 1980 No. 1258 (in force on 18th October 1980 for the purpose of appointments taking effect on that date, otherwise on 1st December 1980), amend the 1973 Regulations so as to alter the formula which ensures that the number of members of a Magistrates' Courts Committee for a non-Metropolitan county or Metropolitan district does not exceed thirty-five.

1865   Maintenance orders—registration—orders for maintenance of children

See para. 2220.

1866   —— —— orders for payments to spouses

See para. 2220.

1867   Petty sessional divisions—Cambridgeshire

The Petty Sessional Divisions (Cambridgeshire) Order 1980, S.I. 1980 No. 381 (in force on 1st April 1980, except for Sch. 2, para. 2 which came into force on 14th March 1980), provides for the reorganisation of petty sessional divisions in respect of the areas comprised in the existing divisions of Arrington and Melbourn, Bottisham, Caxton, Linton and Newmarket.

1868   —— Gloucestershire

The Petty Sessional Divisions (Gloucestershire) Order 1980, S.I. 1980 No. 213 (in force on 1st March 1980, except for Schedule, para. 2, which came into force on 19th February 1980), provides for the divisions of Berkeley and Dursley to be combined into a new petty sessional division of Berkeley and Dursley and for the divisions of Gloucester (City) and Gloucester County to be combined into a new petty sessional division of Gloucester. The order also provides for the parish of Randwick to be transferred to the petty sessional division of Stroud.

1869   —— Hereford and Worcester

The Petty Sessional Divisions (Hereford and Worcester) Order 1980, S.I. 1980 No. 940 (in force on 1st August 1980), provides for the petty sessional divisions of Hereford (Borough) and Worcester (Borough) to be renamed as the City of Hereford and the City of Worcester respectively.

1870   Powers—power to alter decision—time limit

A Divisional Court of the Queen's Bench Division has held that where a defendant has been found guilty in his absence, under the Magistrates' Courts Act 1952, s. 15

(1), the magistrates are prohibited from reconsidering their finding if the application is made more than 28 days from the date of the conviction having regard to the Criminal Justice Act 1972, s. 41 (4), as amended by the Criminal Law Act 1977, Sch. 12. Little hardship would be caused by this decision as under the 1952 Act, s. 15 (3), the justices could only proceed in the defendant's absence if the defendant knew his case was being heard. There was therefore no excuse for the defendant not to apply within the 28 day period.

R v MAIDSTONE JJ, EX PARTE BOOTH (1980) Times, 17th May (Queen's Bench Division: LORD LANE CJ and WOOLF J).

1871 Probation and after-care areas

See PRISONS.

1872 Trial—offence triable either on indictment or summarily—withdrawal of evidence—substitution of summary offence

In two cases involving the determination of the mode of trial under the Criminal Law Act 1977, s. 23, the prosecution offered no evidence on indictable offences and substituted charges which were triable only summarily. On an application for judicial review, it was argued that the court's consent should have been obtained before the prosecution withheld evidence, and that there had been an abuse of the process of the court. It was also contended that in one of the cases which involved criminal damage, evidence should have been heard as to the value of the damaged property. *Held*, the rule that the court's consent was required before no evidence was offered did not apply to committal proceedings where the justices had no depositions on which to base their decision. Although the justices did have a power to prevent an abuse of process it had to be used sparingly, and there was no objection to a lesser offence being charged provided the powers of the justices were appropriate. Further, there was no necessity for the court to hear evidence as to the value of damaged property, although it had a discretion to do so. The application would be dismissed.

R v CANTERBURY AND ST AUGUSTINE JJ, EX PARTE KLISIAK; R v RAMSGATE JJ, EX PARTE WARREN (1980) Times, 18th November (Queen's Bench Division: LORD LANE CJ and WEBSTER J).

MARKETS AND FAIRS

Halsbury's Laws of England (4th edn.), Vol. 29, paras. 601–716

1873 Pedlars' certificate—variation in fee

The Pedlars' Certificates (Variation of Fee) Order 1980, S.I. 1980 No. 580 (in force on 30th June 1980), increases from £1·25 to £7 the fee payable in England and Wales for a pedlar's certificate under the Pedlars Act 1871.

MEDICINE, PHARMACY, DRUGS AND MEDICINAL PRODUCTS

Halsbury's Laws of England (4th edn.), Vol. 30, paras. 1–1000

1874 Abortion—form of notification

The Abortion (Amendment) Regulations 1980, S.I. 1980 No. 1724 (in force on 1st March 1981), further amend the Abortion Regulations 1968 by substituting a revised form of notification.

1875   —— **medical termination of pregnancy by registered medical practitioner—participation by nurses—legality**

The Abortion Act 1967, s. 1 (1), provides a defence to the criminal offence of abortion only when a pregnancy is terminated by a registered medical practitioner. The question arose whether it was necessary for a registered medical practitioner personally to perform each and every action needed to perform an abortion by induction, or whether participation in the process by nurses was permissible. *Held*, statutes could be divided into two categories; firstly, those which referred to acts being done by a registered medical practitioner or by a person acting in accordance with his directions, and secondly, those which referred to acts being done by a registered medical practitioner only. The 1967 Act fell into the latter category. In the case of an abortion by induction, the continuous act of administering the abortifacient drug, from the moment the process was started until the foetus was expelled, had to be done by the registered medical practitioner personally for the defence to be available. It was not sufficient for that act to be done by a nurse when the registered medical practitioner was not present, even if detailed instructions were given.

ROYAL COLLEGE OF NURSING OF THE UNITED KINGDOM v DEPARTMENT OF HEALTH AND SOCIAL SECURITY (1980) Times, 10th November (Court of Appeal: LORD DENNING MR, BRIGHTMAN LJ and SIR GEORGE BAKER). Decision of Woolf J (1980) 124 Sol Jo 615 reversed.

This decision has been reversed by the House of Lords; see [1981] 1 All ER 545.

1876   **Appeals to Privy Council against erasure from register—rules of procedure**

The Judicial Committee (Medical Rules) Order 1980, S.I. 1980 No. 873 (in force on 1st August 1980), contains the Rules governing procedure for all appeals to Her Majesty in Council under the Medical Act 1978.

1877   **Dangerous drugs—offences**

See CRIMINAL LAW.

1878   **Dentists—qualifications—recognition for qualifications of Community nationals**

The Dental Qualifications (EEC Recognition) Order 1980, S.I. 1980 No. 703 (in force on 1st June 1980), which is made under the European Communities Act 1972, amends the Dentists Act 1957, taking into account provisions of Council Directive (EEC) 78/687, 1978 Halsbury's Abridgment para. 1224 relating to the right of establishment of dentists and their freedom to provide dental services.

1879   **General Medical Council—disciplinary committee—appeal to Privy Council against committee's decision**

An appeal to the Privy Council, against the decision of the disciplinary committee of the General Medical Council to suspend the plaintiff's registration for twelve months, following his criminal conviction on charges of obtaining money by deception, has been dismissed. The court held it would not interfere with the decisions of professional disciplinary bodies as to the proper sentences to be imposed in cases of professional misconduct. That principle applied equally when matters complained of also constituted criminal offences which had already been punished under the criminal law.

LAUD v GENERAL MEDICAL COUNCIL (1980) Times, 8th March (Privy Council: LORD SALMON, LORD RUSSELL OF KILLOWEN and LORD KEITH OF KINKEL).

1880   —— **fitness to practise committees—constitution**

The General Medical Council (Constitution of Fitness to Practise Committees) Rules Order of Council 1980, S.I. 1980 No. 861 (in force on 1st August 1980), provides for the constitution of the Health Committee, Preliminary Proceedings Committee and Professional Conduct Committee.

1881   —— Health Committee

The General Medical Council Health Committee (Procedure) Rules Order of Council 1980, S.I. 1980 No. 859 (in force on 1st August 1980), provides for the reference of cases to the Committee and for the procedure to be followed before the Committee.

1882   —— Preliminary Proceedings Committee and Professional Conduct Committee

The General Medical Council Preliminary Proceedings Committee and Professional Conduct Committee (Procedure) Rules Order of Council 1980, S.I. 1980 No. 858 (in force on 1st August 1980), provides for the reference of cases to these Committees, for the procedure to be followed and rules of evidence to be observed before the Professional Conduct Committee and for the manner in which the Preliminary Proceedings Committee are to discharge their functions. The order also provides for the exercise of new powers conferred on the Committees by the Medical Act 1978.

1883   —— —— proceedings before the committees—legal assessors

The General Medical Council (Legal Assessors) Rules 1980, S.I. 1980 No. 941 (in force on 1st August 1980), regulate the functions of legal assessors appointed under the Medical Act 1978, when advising the Professional Conduct Committee, the Health Committee and the Preliminary Proceedings Committee on questions of law arising in the proceedings before those Committees.

1884   —— registration—fees

The General Medical Council (Registration (Fees) Regulations) Order of Council 1980, S.I. 1980 No. 1779 (in force on 1st January 1981), prescribe the fees payable to the General Medical Council under the Medical Acts 1956–78 in respect of the making of entries in the register of medical practitioners and increase the annual retention fee from £10 to £15 with effect from 1st May 1981. The regulations also provide for a scrutiny fee to be payable by overseas qualified medical practitioners who apply for registration.

1885   —— Registration Committee

The General Medical Council (Fraud or Error in Relation to Registration) Rules Order of Council 1980, S.I. 1980 No. 860 (in force on 1st August 1980), provides for the delegation by the Council to their Registration Committee of their functions under the Medical Act 1978, s. 10, in relation to fraudulent or erroneous registration.

1886   Medical Act 1978—commencement

The Medical Act 1978 (Commencement No. 3) Order 1980, S.I. 1980 No. 868 brought into force on 1st August 1980 the following provisions of the Medical Act 1978 which are concerned with professional conduct and fitness to practise: ss. 6–14, Schs. 3, 4 and 6, paras. 18 (3), 23 (3), (4), 47, 54, 57, 60, 61 (and s. 31 (1) so far as it relates to these paras.).

1887

The Medical Act 1978 (Commencement No. 4) Order 1980, S.I. 1980 No. 1524 brings into force on 1st December 1980 the following provisions, which relate largely to the registration of practitioners with overseas qualifications: ss. 18–21, 31 (1) (part), (2) (part), Schs. 6 (part), 7 (part). The whole of the Act is now in force.

1888   Medical, nursing and dental qualifications—recognition—Greece

The Medical, Nursing and Dental Qualifications (EEC Recognition) (Greek Qualifications) Order 1980, S.I. 1980 No. 1721 (in force on 1st January 1980), amends relevant legislation governing the medical, nursing or dental profession, to take into account Community legislation relating to the right of establishment of doctors, nurses and dentists and their freedom to provide services, so as to include therein Greek professional qualifications.

1889   Medical practitioners—emergency treatment of road accident victim—increase in charges

See para. 2021.

1890   —— medical partnership agreement—covenant restricting doctor's right to practise—validity

A restrictive covenant in a medical partnership agreement preventing a former partner from practising within a specified radius for five years after leaving the practice has been held unenforceable.

The court refused to grant an injunction to restrain the defendant from acting in breach of the covenant for, inter alia, the following reasons: (1) Such a restriction prevented a doctor from giving medical care to the patients allocated to him for that purpose by the family practitioner committee and was therefore contrary to public policy. (2) As the restraint was an independent restriction imposed only on the defendant and not on the other partners, it was unreasonable. (3) By agreeing to the covenant the defendant had given valuable consideration for being taken into the partnership and the National Health Service Act 1946, s. 35 (4) (now the National Health Service Act 1977, s. 54 (1), Sch. 10) operated to make that a sale of part of the goodwill of the partnership. Under s. 35 (1) where a medical practitioner was entered on any list of medical practitioners undertaking to provide general medical services it was unlawful subsequently to sell the goodwill, or part of the goodwill, of the medical practice of that practitioner, and accordingly the agreement was made unlawful.

HENSMAN V TRAILL (1980) 124 Sol Jo 776 (Queen's Bench Division: BRISTOW J).

1891   —— negligence

See NEGLIGENCE.

1892   —— operation—action for trespass to the person—whether patient consented to operation

The plaintiff suffered pain from a post-operative scar on her leg and was referred to the defendant doctor's clinic for treatment. As a regular practice, the defendant explained to his patients that an operation to relieve the pain would cause numbness over an area larger than the scar area and might result in a temporary loss of muscle control. The first operation was unsuccessful and after a second identical operation in 1975, which involved no greater risk than the first, the plaintiff lost all control over her leg; in addition, she still felt pain from the scar area. She blamed the defendant for the loss of control over her leg and claimed that (i) the operations were a trespass to her person, a battery, on the ground that she did not consent to them since the procedure and likely outcome were not explained to her and (ii) the defendant was in breach of his duty to inform her properly about the operations and had he done so, she would not have consented to them. *Held*, (i) in an action for trespass to the person, the consent of the injured party was a defence if the consent was real. There was nothing to suggest that the defendant had not followed his usual practice of explaining in broad terms the nature of the operation and its implications. Accordingly, the plaintiff's consent was real and a defence to the action. (ii) Once a plaintiff had given real consent, a claim for failure to perform a duty to inform should be based on negligence, not trespass; however, no allegations of negligence were ever made against the defendant. In any event, the evidence showed that the defendant had fulfilled his duty by giving the plaintiff such information as he did since there was no foreseeable risk that the whole leg would be damaged. Moreover, it was probable that the plaintiff would have consented to the operations whatever she had been told. The plaintiff's claim would be dismissed.

CHATTERTON v GERSON [1980] 3 WLR 1003 (Queen's Bench Division: BRISTOW J).

1893 ——— suspension from register—whether contract of employment terminated

A registered medical practitioner was employed under a contract with a hospital board as a psychiatrist at a hospital. In 1969 he was found guilty of infamous conduct and was suspended from the register for twelve months. The hospital board informed him that it regarded his contract of service as frustrated and therefore at an end. He brought an action for a declaration that his employment should have been continued or had been continued. *Held*, BRANDON LJ dissenting, by the provisions of the Medical Act 1956, the plaintiff ceased to be a fully registered practitioner when he was suspended from the register and accordingly by s. 28 (1) it became unlawful for him to continue to hold his appointment after the suspension. His appointment was no more than his contract of service and therefore that contract came to an end on his suspension. The declaration would be refused.

TARNESBY v KENSINGTON, CHELSEA AND WESTMINSTER AREA HEALTH AUTHORITY (TEACHING) [1980] ICR 475 (Court of Appeal: ROSKILL, BRANDON and BRIGHTMAN LJJ). Decision of Neill J (1978) 123 Sol Jo 49, 1979 Halsbury's Abridgment para. 1819 affirmed. *Reilly v R* [1934] AC 176, PC applied.

1894 Medical termination of pregnancy

See paras. 1874, 1875.

1895 Medicinal products

The Medicines (Intra-Uterine Contraceptive Devices) (Termination of Transitional Exemptions) Order 1980, S.I. 1980 No. 1467 (in force on 2nd October 1980), appoints the 31st October 1980 as the day upon which the transitional exemptions under the Medicines Act 1968 cease to have effect in relation to intra-uterine contraceptive devices.

1896 Medicines—fees

The Medicines (Fees) Amendment Regulations 1980, S.I. 1980 No. 16 (in force on 7th February 1980), reiterate that on an application for the grant of a product licence for two or more medicinal products of the same pharmaceutical form and consisting of the same active ingredients but of different strengths, a fee of the standard amount (at present £150) is payable for each different strength in excess of one, in addition to any fee that is otherwise payable on the application.

1897 ——— licences and certificates—fees

The Medicines (Fees) Amendment (No. 2) Regulations 1980, S.I. 1980 No. 1126 (in force on 1st September 1980), further amend the 1978 Regulations, 1978 Halsbury's Abridgment para. 1878. The regulations increase the amount of capital fees payable upon the grant, renewal and valuation of product licences, manufacturer's licences and wholesale dealer's licences.

1898 ——— prescription only—exemption

The Medicines (Prescription Only) Amendment Order 1980, S.I. 1980 No. 24 (in force on 10th February 1980), postpones to 11th February 1981 the termination of a temporary exemption from the restriction, imposed by the Medicines Act 1968, s. 58 (2) (b), on the administration of prescription only medicines. The exemption relates to the administration of certain injectible medicinal products to humans by certain persons in the course of a business, where the person administering the product in question could have done so lawfully before 11th August 1978, otherwise than in accordance with a prescription.

1899   The Medicines (Prescription Only) Order 1980, S.I. 1980 No. 1921 (in force on 30th January 1981), consolidates, with amendments, the Medicines (Prescription Only) Order 1977, 1977 Halsbury's Abridgment para. 1831, and its amending instruments, 1978 Halsbury's Abridgment paras. 1882, 1883, 1979 Halsbury's Abridgment paras. 1825, 1826, and para. 1898 supra. The order specifies the descriptions and classes of medicinal products which can only be supplied or sold against a prescription given by a doctor, dentist, veterinary surgeon or veterinary practitioner.

1900   —— **sale or supply**
The Medicines (General Sale List) Amendment Order 1980, S.I. 1980 No. 7 (in force on 31st January 1980), makes further amendments to the general sale list.

1901   The Medicines (General Sale List) Order 1980, S.I. 1980 No. 1922 (in force on 30th January 1981), consolidates, with amendments, the provisions of the Medicines (General Sale List) Order 1977, 1977 Halsbury's Abridgment para. 1832, and its amending instruments, 1979 Halsbury's Abridgment para. 1823 and para. 1900, supra. The order specifies descriptions and classes of medicinal products including veterinary drugs which can with reasonable safety be sold or supplied by automatic machines, or otherwise than by or under the supervision of a pharmacist.

1902   The Medicines (Pharmacy and General Sale—Exemption) Order 1980, S.I. 1980 No. 1924 (in force on 30th January 1981), consolidates, with amendments, provisions granting exemption from the Medicines Act 1968, ss. 52, 53, which restrict the sale of certain medicinal products to registered pharmacies by or under the supervision of pharmacists, or to other places fulfilling specified statutory requirements.

1903   The Medicines (Sale or Supply) (Miscellaneous Provisions) Regulations 1980, S.I. 1980 No. 1923 (in force on 30th January 1981), consolidate, with amendments, the provisions of the Medicines (Sale or Supply) (Miscellaneous Provisions) Regulations 1977 and its amending instruments, 1977 Halsbury's Abridgment, para. 1833, 1978 Halsbury's Abridgment para. 1884. The limits on the pack size of medicinal products on a general sale list has also been changed.

1904   —— —— **veterinary drugs**
The Medicines (Exemptions from Restrictions on the Retail Sale or Supply of Veterinary Drugs) (Amendment) Order 1980, S.I. 1980 No. 283 (in force on 31st March 1980), amends the Medicines (Exemptions from Restrictions on the Retail Sale or Supply of Veterinary Drugs) Order 1979, 1979 Halsbury's Abridgment para. 1827, by replacing all the schedules in that order with updated new schedules.

1905   —— —— —— **exemption**
The Medicines (Exemptions from Restrictions on the Retail Sale or Supply of Veterinary Drugs) (Amendment) (No. 2) Order 1980, S.I. 1980 No. 1650 (in force on 1st December 1980), further amends the Medicines (Exemptions from Restrictions on the Retail Sale or Supply of Veterinary Drugs) Order 1979, 1979 Halsbury's Abridgment para. 1827. It replaces the schedule to that order and provides for certain additional exemptions from the restrictions in the Medicines Act 1968. s. 52.

1906   **Midwives—rules**
The Midwives Rules Approval Instrument 1980, S.I. 1980 No. 1468 (in force on 1st November 1980), supersede the Midwives Rules 1955 to 1962 and the Midwives

(Amendment) Rules 1974, 1974 Halsbury's Abridgment para. 2138. The new rules specify the minimum educational requirements for direct entrants and reduces from age twenty to seventeen, the lower age limit for such entrants. They further provide for longer training periods, new courses for teachers of midwifery and update certain procedural rules of the Central Midwives Board.

1907   Nurses—participation in abortion—legality

See *Royal College of Nursing v Department of Health and Social Security*, para. 1875.

1908   —— rules

The Nurses (Amendment) Rules Approval Instrument 1980, S.I. 1980 No. 1974 (in force on 2nd January 1981), further amends the Nurses Rules 1969 by replacing rr. 14 and 16.

1909   —— training and discipline—fees

The Nurses and Enrolled Nurses (Amendment) Rules Approval Instrument 1980, S.I. 1980 No. 1837 (in force on 2nd January 1981), approve the Nurses (Amendment) Rules 1980 and the Enrolled Nurses (Amendment) Rules 1980 set out in Schs. 1 and 2 thereof. Consequently the Nurses Rules 1969 and the Enrolled Nurses Rules 1969 are amended by, inter alia, (i) the introduction of defined minimum and maximum training periods, (ii) the provision of the Council with power to ban student or pupil nurses from training whose training has been discontinued (associated with professional disciplinary action), and the provision of such banned nurses with power to apply for the removal of such ban, (iii) the introduction of definitions of breaks and interruptions in training and the reduction to five years in the period of validity of any previous incomplete training, (iv) an increase in the size of the Disciplinary Committee, (v) provision for allegations of misconduct against visiting EEC nurses to be dealt with in accordance with the procedure for registered nurses, (vi) making fees payable by persons trained outside the United Kingdom the same as those payable by persons trained in England and Wales, (vii) revision of the means of admission to the roll.

1910   Nurses, midwives and health visitors—central board—membership

The Nurses, Midwives and Health Visitors Act 1979 (Membership of Central Council) Order 1980, S.I. 1980 No. 894 (in force on 1st November 1980), prescribes the initial membership of the United Kingdom Central Council for Nursing, Midwifery and Health Visiting as twenty-three.

1911   —— national board—membership

The Nurses, Midwives and Health Visitors Act 1979 (Membership of National Boards) Order 1980, S.I. 1980 No. 895 (in force on 15th September 1980), prescribes the initial number of members for each of the National Boards for Nursing, Midwifery and Health Visiting set up in England, Wales, Scotland and Northern Ireland under the Nurses, Midwives and Health Visitors Act 1979.

1912   Nurses, Midwives and Health Visitors Act 1979—commencement

The Nurses, Midwives and Health Visitors Act 1979 (Commencement No. 1) Order 1980, S.I. 1980 No. 893 brings into force the following provisions on 15th September 1980: ss. 5, 7 (1) and (7) (a) (insofar as it relates to the Finance Committee and s. 7 (5)), 23 (1)–(3), Sch. 2, paras. 3 (1) (b), (2), 4 (1), (2), 5, 6 (1) (a), (3)–(6), 7, 8 and Sch. 6. Sections 19 (3) (a), (4), (5), 20 and Sch. 4 are brought into force so far as they relate to National Boards. The Order brings into force the following provisions on 1st November 1980: ss. 1, 3 (1) and (4) (a) (insofar as it relates to the Finance Committee and s. 3 (2)), Sch. 1 (except para. 6 (2)), Sch. 2, Part I and, so far as not already in force, ss. 19 (3) (a), (4), (5), 20 and Sch. 4.

1913   Opticians—registration and enrolment—fees

The General Optical Council (Registration and Enrolment Rules) (Amendment) Order of Council 1980, S.I. 1980 No. 1936 (in force on 1st April 1981), approves rules scheduled to the General Optical Council (Registration and Enrolment Rules) Order of Council 1977, 1977 Halsbury's Abridgment para. 1840 which increase with effect from 1st April 1981 the fees payable to the General Optical Council by ophthalmic and dispensing opticians and bodies corporate carrying on business as opticians for registration, retention and other purposes.

1914   Pharmaceutical society—disciplinary proceedings—jurisdiction of statutory committee—jurisdiction to consider previous conviction

See *R v Statutory Committee of the Pharmaceutical Society of Great Britain, ex parte Pharmaceutical Society of Great Britain*, para. 719.

1915   Pharmacies—registration of premises—fees

The Medicines (Pharmacies) Application for Registration and Fees) Amendment Regulations 1980, S.I. 1980 No. 1806 (in force on 1st January 1981), amend the 1973 Regulations by increasing the fees for registration of premises at which a retail pharmacy business is, or is to be, carried on, the subsequent retention fees and the penalty for failure to pay retention fees.

1916   Poisons

The Poisons (Amendment) Rules 1980, S.I. 1980 No. 127 (in force on 17th March 1980), amend the Poisons Rules 1978 by deleting certain diamines and their compounds from the Rules. These deletions are consequential on the deletion of these substances from the Poisons List by the Poisons List Order 1980, para. 1917.

1917   —— list

The Poisons List Order 1980, S.I. 1980 No. 126 (in force on 17th March 1980), amends the Poisons List Order 1978, 1978 Halsbury's Abridgment para. 1830 by deleting from Pt. II those diamines and their compounds specified in it.

1918   Private hospital premises—applications for controlled works

The Health Services (Authorisation) Regulations 1980, S.I. 1980 No. 1214 (in force on 7th September 1980), prescribe the form to be used and the fee payable in connection with applications for authorisations for controlled works in respect of hospital premises under the Health Services Act 1976, Pt. III, as amended by the Health Services Act 1980, para. 2027. The regulations also make provision for the procedure in connection with applications, the procedure at hearings and the making of decisions by the Secretary of State.

1919   —— appointment and powers of inspectors

The Health Services (Inspectors) Regulations 1980, S.I. 1980 No. 1202 (in force on 8th August 1980), replace the Health Services Board (Inspectors) Regulations 1977, 1977 Halsbury's Abridgment para. 1846. The regulations deal with the appointment and powers of entry and inspection granted to inspectors appointed for the purposes of the Health Services Act 1976, Pt. III.

1920   —— definition

The Health Services (Hospital Premises and Notification) Regulations 1980, S.I. 1980 No. 1192 (in force on 12th August 1980), revoke the Health Services Board (Hospital Premises) Regulations 1977, 1977 Halsbury's Abridgment para. 1943. The regulations prescribe the classes of premises which are to be "hospital premises" for the purpose of the Health Services Act 1976, s. 14. They also amend the Health

Services Board (Authorisation and Notification) Regulations 1977, 1977 Halsbury's Abridgment para. 1847 by substituting a new form of notice in consequence of the new definition of "hospital premises" and by making other minor amendments.
    These regulations have been revoked; see para. 1921.

1921   —— notifiable works or change—prescribed form of notice

The Health Services (Notification) Regulations 1980, S.I. 1980 No. 1201 (in force on 8th September 1980), revoke the Health Services Board (Authorisation and Notification) Regulations 1977, 1977 Halsbury's Abridgment para. 644 and the Health Services (Hospital Premises and Notification) Regulations 1980, para. 1920. The regulations prescribe the form to be used for notices which are required to be given to the Secretary of State under the Health Services Act 1976, Pt. III, by a person proposing to make an application for planning permission for notifiable works or a notifiable change in hospital premises.

1922   Professions supplementary to medicine—registration

The Professions Supplementary to Medicine (Registration Rules) (Amendment) Order of Council 1980, S.I. 1980 No. 968 (made on 11th July 1980), approves rules made by the Council for Professions Supplementary to Medicine. The rules increase the fee payable under the Professions Supplementary to Medicine Act 1960 by persons applying for registration under that Act who are required to take an examination.

1923   Veterinary surgeons—Commonwealth and foreign practitioners—fees

The Veterinary Surgeons (Examination of Commonwealth and Foreign Candidates) (Amendment) Regulations Order of Council 1980, S.I. 1980 No. 999 (made on 16th July 1980), increase the fees payable by persons holding certain Commonwealth or foreign qualifications in veterinary surgery for sitting the whole or part of the statutory examination of the Royal College of Veterinary Surgeons.

1924   —— qualifications—recognition for qualifications of Community nationals

The Veterinary Surgeons Qualifications (EEC Recognition) Order 1980, S.I. 1980 No. 1951 (in force on 21st December 1980), which is made under the European Communities Act 1972, amends the Veterinary Surgeons Act 1966, taking into account provisions of Council Directives (EEC) relating to the right of establishment of veterinary surgeons and their freedom to provide veterinary services.

1925   —— restrictions on practice by unqualified persons

The Veterinary Surgeons Act 1966 (Schedule 3 Amendment) Order 1980, S.I. 1980 No. 1003 (in force on 17th July 1980), amends the Veterinary Surgeons Act 1966, Sch. 3, Pt. II. Section 19 of the Act contains restrictions on the practice of veterinary surgery by unqualified persons subject to the exceptions in Sch. 3, Pts I and II. By amending Pt. II, the order prohibits the removal by unqualified persons of any part of a deer's antlers while the antlers are in velvet, except in an emergency for the purpose of saving life or relieving pain.

1926   Veterinary surgeons and veterinary practitioners—registration—fees

The Veterinary Surgeons and Veterinary Practitioners (Registration) (Amendment) Regulations Order of Council 1980, S.I. 1980 No. 2004 (made on 22nd December 1980), further amend the Veterinary Surgeons and Veterinary Practitioners Registration Regulations 1967 by increasing the fees payable in respect of the registration and retention of names in, or the restoration of names to, the registers kept by the Royal College of Veterinary Surgeons.

MENTAL HEALTH

Halsbury's Laws of England (4th edn.), Vol. 30, paras. 1001–1305

1927   Court of Protection—fees

The Court of Protection (Amendment) Rules 1980, S.I. 1980 No. 1164 (in force on 1st October 1980), amend the Court of Protection Rules 1960, rr. 87–95 by substituting new fees instead of the percentage previously charged on the estate of each patient. From 1st October 1980 a commencement fee of £50 will be taken on the commencement of proceedings in the Court of Protection, except in respect of small estates. An annual administration fee will also be charged on the income of patients under the Court's management. A fee of £50 or one quarter per cent of value will also be taken on certain specified transactions. The fees on an order and on an attendance of an officer as a witness will no longer be taken. Minor changes in financial limits for simplified procedure and in a rate of interest payable on default of a receiver are also made. The Court of Protection (Amendment No. 2) Rules 1975, 1975 Halsbury's Abridgment para. 2259 are revoked.

1928   —— order for execution of will—court's discretion not to make interested person a respondent

A patient at a nursing home was suffering from senile mental deterioration. She made a will but subsequently went through a ceremony of marriage with a nurse, thereby revoking the will. The Court of Protection took control of her affairs and the Official Solicitor, as receiver, successfully applied for an order for the execution of a new will in the same terms. The patient's husband appealed against the order on the ground that as an interested party he should have been given notice of the application. *Held*, under the Court of Protection Rules 1960, rr. 12, 21 (2), the Court of Protection had a discretion as to who was to be given such notice. It should normally be given where a person would be adversely affected but in this case notice was reasonably withheld in view of the patient's age and the consequent urgency of the case. This course offered the fairest solution because the patient's husband retained the right to make an application under the Inheritance (Provision for Family and Dependants) Act 1975 after her death. The appeal would be dismissed.

RE DAVEY [1980] 3 All ER 342 (Chancery Division: FOX J).

1929   Hospital order—withdrawal of undertaking to admit patient—court's powers

A hospital order made under the Mental Health Act 1959 may be frustrated if the hospital subsequently withdraws its undertaking to admit the patient. If no alternative is arranged before the 28 days during which the place of safety direction is extant have elapsed, the defendant must be released. The Home Secretary has expressed the view in Home Office circular 80/66 that magistrates may by means of an addendum to Form 35 of the Magistrates' Courts (Forms) Rules 1968 request that the clerk be informed promptly if it appears that the defendant might not be admitted to hospital. The magistrates may then, under their powers under the Criminal Justice Act 1972, s. 41 (as amended) vary the original sentence in an appropriate way. See the LS Gaz, 16th July 1980, p. 731.

MINES, MINERALS AND QUARRIES

Halsbury's Laws of England (4th edn.), Vol. 31, paras. 1–1000

1930   Coal industry—redundant workers—concessionary coal

The Redundant Mineworkers and Concessionary Coal (Payments Schemes) (Amendment) Order 1980, S.I. 1980 No. 434 (in force on 1st April 1980), makes further changes in the Redundant Mineworkers Payments Schemes scheduled to the Redundant Mineworkers and Concessionary Coal (Payments Schemes) Orders 1973 and 1978, 1978 Halsbury's Abridgment para. 1897. A new table of basic weekly benefit for those who become redundant on or after 6th April 1980 is added to the 1978 scheme. The minimum amount below which the rate of basic weekly benefit shall not be reduced to take account of certain social security and other benefits is raised to £7·37.

1931   The Redundant Mineworkers and Concessionary Coal (Payments Schemes) (Amendment No. 2) Order 1980, S.I. 1980 No. 835 (in force on 23rd June 1980), makes further changes in the Redundant Mineworkers Payments Scheme scheduled to the Redundant Mineworkers and Concessionary Coal (Payments Schemes) Order 1978, 1978 Halsbury's Abridgment para. 1897. The 1978 Scheme provides for benefits to certain coal industry employees made redundant between 25th March 1978 and 29th March 1981. The principal change made is the substitution of new provisions governing lump sum payments for those made redundant on or after 23rd June 1980 and before 29th March 1981, by the addition of art. 14A. A new system of calculating payments is substituted, the minimum qualifying age of those made redundant is reduced from thirty-five to twenty-one years and the requirement of not less than ten years coal industry employment is abolished. The previous provision for lump sum payments, under art. 14 of the 1978 Scheme, is retained to govern the making of such payments after 22nd June 1980 to coal industry employees made redundant before that date.

1932   The Redundant Mineworkers and Concessionary Coal (Payments Schemes) (Amendment No. 3) Order 1980, S.I. 1980 No. 1984 (in force on 22nd December 1980), extends the Redundant Mineworkers Payments Scheme and the Concessionary Coal Scheme, both scheduled to the Redundant Mineworkers and Concessionary Coal (Payments Schemes) Order 1978, 1978 Halsbury's Abridgment para. 1897, to certain employees made redundant in the coke industry. The period of eligibility under the schemes is extended for employees in the coal and coke industries so as to include those redundant before 1st April 1984. For a man redundant after 22nd October 1980, the order changes the date by reference to which his weekly pay is calculated for the purpose of determining the amount of any lump sum benefit payable; the date of redundancy notice will in most cases apply instead of the date of redundancy itself.

1933   **Coal Industry Act 1980**

The Coal Industry Act 1980 increases the limit on the borrowing powers of the National Coal Board and amends the law with respect to loans to the Board. It also makes new provision for grants by the Secretary of State to the Board and provides a new limit for those grants and for grants to the Board and other persons under certain existing powers; it amends the Coal Industry Act 1977, 1977 Halsbury's Abridgment, para. 1362, and increases the limit on grants by the Secretary of State to the Board under the Coal Industry Act 1973. The Act received the royal assent on 8th August 1980 and came into force on that date.

Section 1 increases the aggregate amount of borrowing by the Board to £3,400 million, which may be increased by order to £4,200 million. Restrictions on temporary borrowing are amended. Section 2 enables the Secretary of State to make loans to the Board out of moneys provided by Parliament and provides for the repayment of, and payment of interest on, such loans. Under s. 3 he has a power to make grants to the Board to reduce or eliminate any group deficit on the consolidated profit and loss account of the board. These grants are not to exceed £525 million, which may be increased by order to £590 million: s. 4. Section 4 also defines the period in respect of which grants may be paid under s. 3, under the Coal Industry Act 1973, s. 8 (in respect of coking coal) and under the Coal Industry Act 1977, ss. 2, 3 (for promoting the sale of coal to Electricity Boards and in connection with stocks of coal and coke). Section 5 repeals the Coal Industry Act 1977, s. 8 (power to make regional grants). Section 6 enables grants under the Coal Industry Act 1977, s. 6 (in connection with pit closures) to be made up to the Board's financial year 1983–84, subject to a new limit, for the period 1978–79 to 1983–84 of £170 million, and extends the 1977 Act, s. 6 to enable grants to be made towards transfer and other allowances paid by the Board to mineworkers who transfer from one pit to another.

Section 7 extends the qualifying period for schemes for payments to redundant mineworkers under the Coal Industry Act 1977, s. 7 to the end of March 1984 and fixes the limit on such payments for the period from 1978–79 to 1983–1984 at £220 million. Section 8 amends the Coal Industry Act 1975, s. 1 (2) by increasing the limit on grants made under the pneumoconiosis compensation scheme from £100 million to £107 million. Sections 9, 10, 11 relate to administrative expenses, interpretation, citation, repeals and extent.

1934   Health and safety—coal mines—breathing apparatus

The Coal and Other Mines (Fire and Rescue) (Amendment) Regulations 1980, S.I. 1980 No. 942 (in force on 1st August 1980), amend the provisions of the Coal and Other Mines (Fire and Rescue) Regulations 1956, relating to the testing of suits of breathing apparatus. The requirement that a suit should be tested for leakage by being immersed in water when fully distended under pressure and examined closely for leakage is replaced by a requirement simply to have it tested while it is fully distended under pressure.

1935   —— mines and quarries—fee for approval and testing of plant

The Mines and Quarries (Fees for Approvals) Regulations 1980, S.I. 1980 No. 1233 (in force on 22nd September 1980), provide for the fixing and determination of fees to be payable to the Health and Safety Executive in respect of approval and testing of plant, apparatus and substances for use in mines and quarries. The amount of the fee varies as respect approval according to the nature of the plant, apparatus or substance and different fees are payable for original approvals, renewals and variations of approvals. These fees are set out in Sch. 1. An additional fee is payable for any testing carried out by the Executive's staff. The fee for the testing of explosives and detonators is set out in Sch. 2, Pt. 1 and varies in amount with the nature of the test. Fees for other testing are to be determined under Sch. 2, Pt. II where a formula is prescribed for this purpose.

1936   Ironstone Restoration Fund

The Ironstone Restoration Fund (Rates of Contribution) Order 1980, S.I. 1980 No. 249 (in force on 1st April 1980), revokes and re-enacts with amendments the Ironstone Restoration Fund (Rates of Contribution) Order 1978, 1978 Halsbury's Abridgment para. 1905. It prescribes the full and reduced rates of contributions payable by ironstone operators towards the Ironstone Restoration Fund in respect of ironstone extracted on or after 1st April 1971 and the sums deductible from payments made under mining leases and mineral rights orders in respect of full rate contributions.

1937

The Ironstone Restoration Fund (Standard Rate) Order 1980, S.I. 1980 No. 250 (in force on 1st April 1980), prescribes at a standard rate of £871 per acre as the rate of payments to be made to ironstone operators in respect of the restoration of worked ironstone land in compliance with conditions of a planning permission. The Ironstone Restoration Fund (Standard Rate) Order 1979, 1979 Halsbury's Abridgment para 1845 is revoked.

1938   National Coal Board—borrowing powers

The Coal Industry (Borrowing Powers) Order 1980, S.I. 1980 No. 1101 (in force on 31st July 1980), increases the overall limit on the amount which the National Coal Board is empowered to borrow, temporarily or otherwise, under the Coal Industry Act 1965, s. 1, as amended, to £2,600 million.

1939   Offshore installations—life-saving appliances

The Offshore Installations (Life-saving Appliances and Fire-fighting Equipment) (Amendment) Regulations 1980, S.I. 1980 No. 322 (in force on 1st April 1980), amend the Offshore Installations (Life-saving Appliances) Regulations 1977, 1977 Halsbury's Abridgment para. 1862 and the Offshore Installations (Fire-fighting Equipment) Regulations 1978, 1978 Halsbury's Abridgment para. 1907 by substituting a new table of rates for the examination of life-saving appliances, higher than those previously set out. These regulations revoke the Offshore Installations (Life-saving Appliances and Fire-fighting Equipment) (Amendment) Regulations 1979, 1979 Halsbury's Abridgment para. 1847.

1940   —— well control

The Offshore Installations (Well Control) Regulations 1980, S.I. 1980 No. 1759 (in force on 1st January 1981), prohibit the carrying on of drilling operations or certain workover operations on offshore installations, unless they are carried on by persons in the immediate charge of a driller and under the general supervision of a drilling supervisor.

1941   Opencast coal—compensation—rate of interest

The Opencast Coal (Rate of Interest on Compensation) Order 1980, S.I. 1980 No. 44 (in force on 18th February 1980), increases the rate of interest payable under the Opencast Coal Act 1958, s. 35 to 18 per cent per annum and revokes the Opencast Coal (Rate of Interest on Compensation) Order 1979, 1979 Halsbury's Abridgment para. 1848.

This order has been revoked, see para. 1942.

1942   The Opencast Coal (Rate of Interest on Compensation) (No. 2) Order 1980, S.I. 1980 No. 1365 (in force on 8th October 1980), decreases the rate of interest payable in addition to compensation under the Opencast Coal Act 1958, s. 35 from eighteen per cent to sixteen and a half per cent. The Opencast Coal (Rate of Interest on Compensation) Order 1980, para. 1941, is revoked.

This order has been revoked; see para. 1943.

1943   The Opencast Coal (Rate of Interest on Compensation) (No. 3) Order 1980, S.I. 1980 No. 1978 (in force on 8th January 1981), decreases the rate of interest payable in addition to compensation under the Open-cast Coal Act 1958, s. 35 from sixteen and a half per cent to fourteen and a half per cent per annum. The Opencast Coal (Rate of Interest on Compensation) (No. 2) Order 1980, supra is revoked.

1944   Pensions

See PENSIONS AND SUPERANNUATION.

1945   Petroleum—licences

The Petroleum (Production) (Amendment) Regulations 1980, S.I. 1980 No. 721 (in force on 14th June 1980), further amend the Petroleum Production Regulations 1976, 1976 Halsbury's Abridgment para. 1720. They describe the circumstances in which applications for licences for seaward areas may be made otherwise than by virtue of the invited application procedure prescribed by the 1976 Regulations. They also provide for an increase in the fee payable by applicants for production licences and for amendments to be made to the model clauses included in those licences. Changes are also made to the model clauses relating to royalty payments and deliveries.

MINORS

Halsbury's Laws of England (4th edn.), Vol. 24, paras. 401–900

1946   Articles

Child Abuse—Strengthening the Legal Framework, Jean Graham Hall and Barbara Mitchell: 144 JP Jo 3.

Children at Risk and Care Proceedings, S. Christie: 130 NLJ 280.

Custody—an approach to Specific Difficulties, Godfrey Gypps: 144 JP Jo 629.

Estoppel in Custody Cases, F. Graham Glover: 10 Fam Law 81.

Press Publicity in the Family Division: Roger Pearson (lawyers' use of publicity to trace missing children): 130 NLJ 73.

Protecting Children From Their Parents—Grounds For State Intervention, J. Graham Hall: 10 Fam Law 201.

The Airey Case, Susan Maidment (discussion on Airey's Case (1979) Council of Europe Press Release, 1979 Halsbury's Abridgment para. 1451): 10 Fam Law 69.

1947   Access—decision whether access should take place—position of welfare officer

ORR LJ, considering an appeal against an order that a father's access to his two young children be suspended until the court welfare officer considered that it was appropriate that access should take place, stated that it was wrong in all save possibly very exceptional cases, to place the decision as to whether access should take place in the hands of the welfare officer.

ORFORD v ORFORD (1980) 10 Fam Law 114 (Court of Appeal: ORR, ORMROD and BROWNE LJJ).

1948   —— paramountcy of child's welfare—mother refusing father all access—best interests of child

The parties were divorced and the mother had custody of their young daughter. An order was made for reasonable access to the child by the father and a supervision order was directed to a probation officer. Subsequently, a specific order was made for access on 23rd May and thereafter once a month. However, after 23rd May, when access took place, the mother refused to co-operate with the supervising officer and refused any further access by the father. She gave evidence to the effect that the child was upset by seeing her father on 23rd May and the judge decided to make no order for the time being, but kept the supervision order in effect. The father appealed. *Held*, it was in the child's best interests to keep in contact with her father, and the mother had not put forward any real grounds for refusing access to him. An order would be made that there should be access as and when the supervising officer thought right. It would be further ordered that the question of custody of the child should be reviewed at a future date. The appeal would accordingly be allowed.

V-P v V-P (1980) 10 Fam Law 20 (Court of Appeal: ORR and ORMROD LJJ).

1949   Adoption—adoption agencies—local authority as adoption agency—disclosure of information between departments

Prospective adopters of a child have been refused an order prohibiting a local authority from disclosing, to a councillor unconnected with the social services department, any information disclosed by them in confidence to that department. The Adoption Agencies Regulations 1976, 1976 Halsbury's Abridgment para. 1727 provide that all information disclosed to an adoption agency is confidential. Under reg. 2 an agency includes a local authority.

The court rejected the contention that the councillor was not entitled to disclosure because the adoption work had been delegated to a social services committee. The local authority's functions as an adoption agency could not be delegated and any member of the authority had an interest in adoption proceedings and was entitled to receive information in pursuance of a genuine concern in the matter. Any information provided by the potential adopters was not limited to the social services department, but was given to the local authority as a whole as the adoption agency.

R v BIRMINGHAM CITY DISTRICT COUNCIL, EX PARTE O (1980) Times, 26th March (Queen's Bench Division: EVELEIGH LJ and WATKINS J).

1950 —— **order—paramountcy of child's welfare**

The Court of Appeal has held that when making an order for adoption in respect of an application by a parent and a step-parent of a child, the court must pay sufficient regard to the Children Act 1975, s. 3 which provides that the court's duty is to promote the welfare of the child. The court may only refuse to grant an order under s. 10 (3) of the 1975 Act if it believes that the application by the parent and step-parent could be better dealt with by an order for custody under the Matrimonial Causes Act 1973, s.42 and not merely if it could be equally as well dealt with under s. 42. Section 3 of the 1975 Act is the primary section to consider in hearing an application and s. 10 (3) merely qualifies it.

RE D (MINORS) (1980) Times, 17th June (Court of Appeal: ORMROD, BRANDON LJJ and HOLLINGS J).

1951 —— **parental consent—dispensing with consent—persistent ill-treatment**

A child aged eleven months was admitted to hospital with bone fractures and other injuries. A doctor reported that the child had been the subject of severe and repeated assaults over a period of some three weeks prior to admission. A place of safety order was made, and the child was placed in the interim care of approved foster parents. A year later, in 1973, a full care order was made. The natural parents had access to the child, but their visits eventually stopped because of their bad effect on him. In 1977, the foster parents gave notice of their intention to adopt the child. In adoption proceedings the judge, having concluded that there had been "persistent ill-treatment" of the child by his natural parents (without hearing any oral evidence), made an adoption order in favour of the foster parents. The natural parents' consent to the adoption was dispensed with, under the Children Act 1975, s. 12. The natural parents appealed. *Held*, in the circumstances of the case, the judge was fully justified in concluding that there had been persistent ill-treatment of the child. Further, the judge had doubtless carefully considered whether the interests of the child were better served by his being with the foster parents. Accordingly, the appeal would be dismissed.

RE A (A MINOR) (1980) 10 Fam Law 49 (Court of Appeal: ORR, ORMROD and GEOFFREY LANE LJJ).

1952 **Child—abduction—press publicity**

See para. 2214.

1953 —— **child out of jurisdiction—order for return**

See para. 2215.

1954 —— **unborn child—appointment of guardian ad litem**

Canada

In a case where a father sought an injunction preventing his wife from having an abortion the court, prior to the proceedings, appointed a guardian ad litem for the unborn child.

RE SIMMS AND H (1979) 106 DLR (3d) 435 (Family Court of Nova Scotia).

1955 —— **welfare—parental disagreement on education—responsibility of court**

The Court of Appeal has held that the courts ought not to discharge their responsibilities by allocating to one parent, particularly the parent who does not have formal custody of the child, the liberty to choose the child's education. Where divorced parents are unable to agree on the education of their child, the court will decide the dispute on all the evidence, sworn and unsworn, put before it.

BENSON v BENSON (1978) 10 Fam Law 56 (Court of Appeal: ORMROD, WALLER and BRANDON LJJ).

1956   Child care—assumption of parental rights and duties—parent's consistent failure to discharge obligations—culpability of conduct

A divorced woman was inept at caring for her child and frequently asked social workers for assistance. At her request, the child spent several periods in the care of the council. The council passed a resolution assuming parental rights and duties in respect of the child under the Children Act 1948, s. 2 (1) (b) (v), on the ground that the mother had so consistently failed without reasonable cause to discharge the obligations of a parent as to be unfit to have the care of the child. On appeal by the mother against a decision of a juvenile court upholding the resolution, *held*, it had to be established by the council that the mother's failure to discharge the obligations of a parent demonstrated some element of culpability. Although she had consistently abrogated her parental obligations, she had recognised her inadequacy as a mother. Her conduct could not be shown to be blameworthy or culpable and the appeal would be allowed.

O'D v SOUTH GLAMORGAN COUNTY COUNCIL (1980) 78 LGR 522 (Family Division: SIR JOHN ARNOLD P and BUTLER-SLOSS J).

1957   —— —— —— degree of failure

The Family Division of the High Court has held that where a juvenile court is required to determine whether a local authority's resolution vesting in the authority parental rights in respect of a child is to continue, if the court wishes to see the child in private prior to the hearing it ought to do so without the social worker on the case being present if he is to give evidence for the authority. Further, in considering whether a parent has consistently failed without reasonable cause to discharge parental duties within the Children Act 1945, s. 2 (1) (b) (v), it is sufficient for the authority to prove failure to discharge those duties over a period of time appropriate to the matters arising in the particular case. It is not necessary to prove such failure over a substantial period of time.

W v SUNDERLAND BOROUGH COUNCIL [1980] 2 All ER 514 (Family Division: SIR JOHN ARNOLD P and BUTLER-SLOSS J). *Re D (Minors)* [1973] 3 All ER 1001 distinguished.

1958   —— care order—appeal—appeal by parents on behalf of child

A care order was made by a juvenile court in respect of a child under the Children and Young Persons Act 1969, s. 1. The question then arose whether the Crown Court had jurisdiction to hear an appeal against the order by the child's parents on its behalf, or whether only the child who was the subject of the order had a right of appeal. *Held*, the 1969 Act, s. 2 (12), gave a right of appeal to the Crown Court to "the relevant infant". Section 70 (2) gave the parent, on behalf of the child, the right to exercise certain rights of application given to the child in certain sections of the Act, but not including the right of appeal against a care order under s. 2 (12). However, to give efficacy to that provision, the parents would in fact have to prosecute the appeal. Therefore the Crown Court had jurisdiction to hear an appeal by a child brought on its behalf by its parents.

B v GLOUCESTERSHIRE COUNTY COUNCIL [1980] 2 All ER 746 (Queen's Bench Division: ACKNER LJ and JUPP J).

1959   —— duties of local authority towards children of intentionally homeless families

See *A-G, on the relation of Tilley v Wandsworth LBC*, para. 1431.

1960   **—— duty towards children in care—production of records of child in care of local authority**

See *Gaskin v Liverpool City Council*, para. 899.

1961   **—— proceedings—mistake by local authority**

In wardship proceedings instituted by a local authority the judge indicated that in a case where evidence introduced clearly and cogently put a different complexion on an issue the local authority ought to acknowledge its mistaken view and change its stance in the proceedings accordingly.

S-W v S-W (1980) Times, 5th December (Family Division: LATEY J).

1962   **—— —— practice of justices**

SIR JOHN ARNOLD P has stated that the practice of justices, who, before hearing a mother's application to terminate a resolution vesting parental rights in the local authority, see the child and the social worker who is to give evidence, is unfortunate and ought not to happen.

RE W (A MINOR) (1980) Times, 5th February (Family Division: SIR JOHN ARNOLD P).

1963   **—— responsibility of local authority for child's actions whilst in care**

See *Vicar of Writtle v Essex County Council*, para. 1807.

1964   **Child Care Act 1980**

The Child Care Act 1980 consolidates certain enactments relating to the care of children by local authorities or voluntary organisations and certain other enactments relating to the care of children. The Act received the royal assent on 31st January 1980 and comes into force on 1st April 1981, except for ss. 7, 64–67, Sch. 6 (part), which come into force on a day or days to be appointed: S.I. 1980 No. 1935. Tables showing the destination of enactments consolidated and the derivation of the new Act are set out on pages 496–506 following.

DESTINATION TABLE

This table shows in column (1) the enactments repealed by the Child Care Act 1980, and in column (2) the provisions of that Act corresponding to the repealed provisions

In certain cases, the enactment in column (1), though having a corresponding provision in column (2), is not, or is not wholly, repealed, as it is still required, or partly required, for the purposes of other legislation.

(1)	(2)	(1)	(2)
Children and Young Persons Act 1933 (c 12)	Child Care Act 1980 (c 5)	Children Act 1948 (c 43)	Child Care Act 1980 (c 5)
s 86 (1)	s 45 (1)	s 3 (3)–(5)	Rep., 1969 c 54, s 72 (4), Sch 6
(2)	Rep., 1969, c 54, s 72 (4), Sch 6	(6), (7)	s 4 (2), (3)
(3)	s 45 (2)	(8)	13 (1), (2), (5)
(4)	Rep., 1969 c 54, s 72 (4), Sch 6	4 (1)	5 (1)
87 (1)	s 47 (1), (2)	(2), (3)	(3), (4)
(2)	(1)	4A	6
(3)	(3)	4B	7
(4)	47 (4), 48 (1)	5	Rep., 1969 c 54, s 72 (4), Sch 6
(5)	Rep., 1963 c 37, s 14 (5), 64 (3), Sch 5	6 (1)	s 8 (1)
88 (1)	s 49 (1)–(3)	(2)	8 (2), 13 (6)
(2)	(4)	(3), (4)	Rep., 1969 c 54, s 72 (4), Sch 6
(3)	Rep., 1948 c 43, s 60 (3), Sch 4, Pt I	7	Rep., 1969 c 54, s 72 (4), Sch 6
(4)	s 49 (5)–(7)	8	Rep., 1959 c 72, s 10 (2), 149 (2), Sch 8, Pt II
89 (1)	Rep., 1969 c 54, s 72 (4), Sch 6	9	s 2 (6), 24 (4)
(2), (3)	s 54	10 (1)–(3)	9 (1)–(3)
(4)	Rep., 1948 c 29, s 62 (3), Sch 7	(4)	(4), (5)
92	s 56	11	17
93 (1)	59 (1), (2)	12 (1)	18 (1)
(2)	(4)	(1A)	(3)
102 (1) (c), (d)	52 (1)	(2)	(2)
(2)*	(2)	13	21
106 (2)†	86	14	22
107 (1)†	87 (1)	15, 16	Rep., 1969 c 54, s 72 (4), Sch 6
109 (3)*	91 (3)	17 (1)	s 24 (1)
Children Act 1948 (c 43)		(2)	(2), (3)
s 1 (1)–(3)	2 (1)–(3)	(3)	(4)
(3A)	13 (2)–(4)	18	25
(3B)	(7)	19	72
(4), (5)	2 (4), (5)	20	27
2 (1)–(4)	3 (1)–(4)	21	30
(5)	(5), (6)	22	26
(6)	4 (1)	23 (1)	45 (1), (2), 47 (1), (2), (4), 48 (1), 49 (1), (3)–(7)
(7)	3 (7)	(2)	47 (3)
(8)	5 (2)	(3)	Rep., 1969 c 54, s 72 (4), Sch 6
(9)–(11)	3 (8)–(10)	24 (1)	s 45 (1)
3 (1), (2)	Rep., 1975 c 72, s 108 (1) (b), Sch 4, Pt V		

* Not repealed   † Repealed in part

(1) Children Act 1948 (c 43)	(2) Child Care Act 1980 (c 5)
s 24 (2)	s 45 (1), (4)
(3)	(1)
25	Rep. 1969 c 54, s 72 (4), Sch 6
26 (1)	s 50 (1), (2), 87 (1)
(2), (3)	50 (3), (4)
(4)	50 (5), 87 (1)
(5)	50 (6), 54
(6)	Rep., 1952 c 55, s 132, Sch 6
(7)	Rep., 1949 c 101, s 46 (2), Sch 7, Pt II
(8)	Rep., 1968 c 49, s 95 (2), Sch 9, Pt I
27, 28	s 56
29 (1)–(8)	57
(9)	
30 (1)–(6)	58
(7)	Rep., 1968 c 49, s 95 (2), Sch 9, Pt I
31	s 60
32	59 (3), (4)
33 (1), (2)	62 (1), (2)
(3)	61 (1)
(4)	61 (2), 62 (3)
33A	63
34 (1)	28 (1), 69 (1)
(2)	28 (2), 69 (2)
(3)	28 (3), 69 (3)
35–37	Rep., 1958 c 65, s 40 (2), Sch 3
38 (1)	s 87 (1), Sch 5, para 1, 18
(2)	Rep., 1968 c 49, s 95 (2), Sch 9, Pt I
39–42	Rep., 1970 c 42, s 14 (2), Sch 3
43	s 71
44	Rep., 1968 c 49, s 95 (2), Sch 9, Pt I
45 (1), (1A)	s 78
(2) } 46 }	Rep., 1975 c 72, s 108 (1) (b), Sch 4, Pt X
47	Rep., 1958 c 55, s 67, Sch 9, Pt II
48	s 83
49	Rep., 1972 c 70, s 272 (1), Sch 30
50	Rep., 1971 c 3, s 18 (2), Sch 2
51 (1)	s 73 (1)
(2)	Rep., 1969 c 54, s 72 (4), Sch 6
(3)	s 73 (2)

(1) Children Act 1948 (c 43)	(2) Child Care Act 1980 (c 5)
s 52	Rep., S.L.R. (Consequential Repeals) Act 1965
53	Rep., 1971 c 3, s 18 (2), Sch 2
54 (1), (2)	Rep., 1969 c 54, s 72 (4), Sch 6
(3)–(7)	s 68
55 (1)	84
(2)	Rep., S.L.R. Act 1953
56 (1)–(3)	
(4)	Rep., 1968 c 49, s 95 (2), Sch 9, Pt I
57	
58	s 85 (1), (2)
59 (1)	87 (1)
(2)	Rep., 1969 c 54, s 72 (4), Sch 6
(3)	
(4), (5)	Rep., 1968 c 49, s 95 (2), Sch 9, Pt I
60 (1), (2)	
(3)	Rep., S.L.R. Act 1950
61	s 88
62 (1)	
(2)	Rep., S.L.R. Act 1950
(3)	s 91 (3)
Sch 1, Pt I	Sch 3
II	Rep., 1968 c 49, s 95 (2), Sch 9, Pt I
2, para 1–3	Rep., S.L.(R.) Act 1977
4 (1)	
4 (2)	Rep., S.L.(R.) Act 1977
(3)	
5, 6	Rep., S.L.(R.) Act 1977
7	
8 (1)	
(2)	Rep., S.L.R. Act 1953
(3)	
9	Rep., S.L.R. Act 1953
10	Rep., 1958 c 65, s 40 (2), Sch 3
11	Rep., S.L.R. Act 1953
12	
3	s 45 (1), 52 (1)
4	Rep., S.L.R. Act 1950

(1) Adoption of Children Act 1949 (c 98)	(2)
s 13†	s 87 (1)

* Not repealed   † Repealed in part

(1)	(2)	(1)	(2)
Maintenance Orders Act 1950 (c 37)	Child Care Act 1980 (c 5)	Children and Young Persons Act 1963 (c 37)	Child Care Act 1980 (c 5)
s 3 (1)†	s 55 (3)	s 60*	s 77 (3)
4 (1)†	55 (1), 91 (3)	Sch 3, para 38	13 (1), (2), (5)
(2)†	55 (2), 91 (3)	40 (1)	Sch 5, para 18
14	55 (4)	(2)	Applied to Scotland
27 (1)*, (2)*	(5)	**Criminal Justice Act 1967 (c 80)**	
Sch 1	Sch 2, para 1–5, 7	Sch 3, Pt I†	s 9 (4), 49 (4), 51 (4)
Magistrates' Courts Act 1952 (c 55)		**Health Services and Public Health Act 1968 (c 46)**	
s 56 (1) (b), (d)	5, para 5	s 64 (3) (a)†	Sch 5, para 19
Local Government Act 1958 (c 55)		65 (3) (b) (iv)	20
Sch 8, para 2 (1), (2)	s 53 (1), (2)	**Social Work (Scotland) Act 1968 (c 49)**	
(3), (5)	Rep., 1969 c 54, s 72 (4), Sch 6	Sch 8, para 17(1),(2)	s 2 (4),(5)
(4)	s 47 (1), 49 (1), (2)	19	87 (1)
Children Act 1958 (c 65)		**Children and Young Persons Act 1969 (c 54)**	
Sch 2†	—	s 24 (1)–(4)	10
Mental Health Act 1959 (c 72)		(5)	11 (1), (3)
Sch 7, Pt I*	s 56	(6)	(2)
Children and Young Persons Act 1963 (c 37)		(7)	12 (2)
s 1 (1)–(3)	s 1 (1)–(3)	(8)	(1)
(4)	Rep., 1969 c 54, s 72 (4), Sch 6	27 (1)	17
(5)	s 1 (4)	(2)	Rep., 1975 c 72, s 108 (1) (b), Sch 4, Pt III
30 (1), (2)	51 (1), (2)	(3)	s 19
(3)	51 (3), 52 (1), 54, 55, (1), (2)	(4), (5)	20
(4)	Sch 2, para 6	32 (1)†	16 (1)
(5)	s 51 (4)	(2)*	(2), (6)
(6)	87 (1)	(2A)*	(3), (6)
45	77 (1), (2)	(3)*, (4)*	(4), (5)
46	27 (1), (2)	35–42	31–38
47	23, Sch 4, para 3, 6	43 (1)–(3)	39
49 (1)	14	(4)–(6)	40
(2)	87 (1)	44, 45	41, 42
55	24 (5)	47, 48	43, 44
58	29, Sch 4, para 3, 6	49	21
		50	72
		58, 59	74, 75
		62 (1)	45 (1), (2), 47 (1), (2), (4), 48 (1), 49 (2)–(7)

* Not repealed   † Repealed in part

(1)	(2)
Children and Young Persons Act 1969 (c 54)	Child Care Act 1980 (c 5)
s 62 (2)	s 45 (3)
(3), (4)	46
(5), (6)	47 (1), (2)
(7)	48 (2)
(8)	87 (1)
63 (1)	79 (1)
(2)	70
(3)–(6)	79 (2)–(5)
64, 64A	80, 81
65 (1)	82
67*	83
69 (1)†	85 (1), (2)
(3)*, (4)*	(3), (4)
70 (1)†	87 (1)
(5)*	(2)
71*	88
73 (5) (a)*	91 (3)
(6)*, (7)*	(4), (5)
Sch 2	Sch 1
5, para 8	s 45 (1)
9 (1), (2)	47 (1)
(3)	(3)
10 (1)	49 (1)–(3)
(2)	(4)
(3)	(6)
11*	86
14	———
15	27 (1)
16	45 (1), (2), 47 (1), (2), (4), 48 (1), 49 (1), (3)–(7)
17 (1)	50 (1)
(2)	(4), (5)
19	71 (1)
20	73
21	68 (1)–(3)
22	87 (1)
50 (1)	51 (1)
(2)	(3)
(3)	Sch 2, para 6
(4)	s 51 (4)
51	77 (1)
52	14
70 (1)†	87 (1)
(5)*	(2)
73	2 (4)
Administration of Justice Act 1970 (c 31)	
Sch 1†	Sch 5, para 27

(1)	(2)
Local Authority Social Services Act 1970 (c 42)	Child Care Act 1980 (c 5)
Sch 1†	Sch 5, para 29
2, para 5	s 78
11 (1)	79 (1)
(2), (3)	(4), (5)
Courts Act 1971 (c 23)	
Sch 9, Pt I*	52 (1)
Local Government Act 1972 (c 70)	
Sch 23, para 3	s 87 (1), Sch 5, para 1, 18
29, para 16*	Sch 1, para 6
Matrimonial Causes Act 1973 (c 18)	
s 43 (8)	———
Sch 2, para 9	s 79 (5)
Social Security Act 1973 (c 38)	
Sch 27, para 12*	25 (2)
Powers of Criminal Courts Act 1973 (c 62)	
Sch 5, para 37*	44 (5)
Social Security (Consequential Provisions) Act 1975 (c 18)	
Sch 2, para 9	25 (2)
Nursing Homes Act 1975 (c 37)	
Sch 1, para 5	56
Children Act 1975 (c 72)	
s 56 (1)	13 (2)–(4), (7)
(2)	63
57	3, 4 (1), 5 (2)
58	6, 7
59	18 (1), (3)

* Not repealed   † Repealed in part

(1)	(2)	(1)	(2)
Children Act 1975 (c 72)	Child Care Act 1980 (c 5)	Criminal Law Act 1977 (c 45)	Child Care Act 1980 (c 5)
s 60–63	s 64–67	s 31 (5)*, (6)*	s 59 (4), 68 (5)
67	15	(7)	68 (5)
68 (4)*	16 (2)	Sch 6†	57 (5), 60 (2)
(5)*	(3), (6)		
(6)*, (7)*	(4), (5)		
71	81		
98 (1)–(4)	76		
(5)			
109 (2)*	91 (3)		
Sch 3, para 4	13 (1)	National Health	
5	5 (4)	Service Act 1977	
6	71 (1)	(c 49)	
42	14		
71	19, 20	Sch 15, para 9*	87 (1)
72	74 (1)		
73 (1) (a)		Domestic	
		Proceedings and	
Adoption Act 1976 (c 36)		Magistrates'	
		Courts Act 1978	
		(c 22)	
Sch 3, para 1 (a)	5 (2)		
(b)	3 (10)	Sch 2, para 3	47 (1), (4), 48 (1)
2	71 (1)	4 (a)	49 (1), (2), (4), (7)
3	73 (1)	(b)	(4)
12	74 (1)	5	87 (1)
13	79 (5)	8	50 (1), (5), 87 (1)
20	64 (6)	20	
21*	76 (1)	24	79 (5)

* Not repealed   † Repealed in part

TABLE OF DERIVATIONS

This table shows in the right hand column the legislative source from which the sections of the Child Care Act 1980 in the left hand column have been derived. In the table the following abbreviations are used:

1933 = The Children and Young Persons Act 1933 (1933 c. 12)

1948 = The Children Act 1948 (1948 c. 43)

1950 = The Maintenance Orders Act 1950 (1950 c. 37)

1963 = The Children and Young Persons Act 1963 (1963 c. 37)

1969 = The Children and Young Persons Act 1969 (1969 c. 54)

1975 = The Children Act 1975 (1975 c. 72)

Section of Act	Derivation
1 (1)	1963 s. 1 (1).
(2)	1963 s. 1 (2).
(3)	1963 s. 1 (3).
(4)	1963 c. 1 (5).
2 (1)	1948 s. 1 (1).
(2)	1948 s. 1 (2).
(3)	1948 s. 1 (3).
(4)	1948 s. 1 (4); Social Work (Scotland) Act 1968 (c. 49) ss. 95 (1), 97 (1), Sch. 8, para. 17 (1); 1969 s. 72 (3), Sch. 5, para. 73.
(5)	1948 s. 1 (5); Social Work (Scotland) Act 1968 (c. 49) ss. 95 (1), 97 (1), Sch. 8, para. 17 (2).
(6)	1948 s. 9.
3 (1)	1948 s. 2 (1); 1975 s. 57.
(2)	1948 s. 2 (2); 1975 s. 57.
(3)	1948 s. 2 (3); 1975 s. 57.
(4)	1948 s. 2 (4); 1975 s. 57.
(5)	1948 s. 2 (5); 1975 s. 57.
(6)	1948 s. 2 (5); 1975 s. 57.
(7)	1948 s. 2 (7); 1975 s. 57.
(8)	1948 s. 2 (9); 1975 s. 57.
(9)	1948 s. 2 (10); 1975 s. 57.
(10)	1948 s. 2 (11); 1975 s. 57.
4 (1)	1948 s. 2 (6); 1975 s. 57.
(2)	1948 s. 3 (6).
(3)	1948 s. 3 (7).
5 (1)	1948 s. 4 (1)
(2)	1948 s. 2 (8); 1975 s. 57; Adoption Act 1976 (c. 36) s. 73 (2), Sch. 3, para. 1.
(3)	1948 s. 4 (2).
(4)	1948 s. 4 (3); 1975 s. 108 (1), Sch. 3, para. 5.
6	1948, s. 4A; 1975 s. 58.
7 (1)	1948 s. 4B (1); 1975 s. 58.
(2)	1948 s. 4B (2); 1975 s. 58.
(3)	1948 s. 4B (3); 1975 s. 58.
8 (1)	1948 s. 6 (1).
(2)	1948 s. 6 (2).
9 (1)	1948 s. 10 (1).
(2)	1948 s. 10 (2).
(3)	1948 s. 10 (3).
(4)	1948 s. 10 (4); Criminal Justice Act 1967 (c. 80) s. 92, Sch. 3.
(5)	1948 s. 10 (4).
10 (1)	1969 s. 24 (1).
(2)	1969 s. 24 (2).
(3)	1969 s. 24 (3).
(4)	1969 s. 24 (4).

Section of Act	Derivation
11 (1)	1969 s. 24 (5).
(2)	1969 s. 24 (6).
(3)	1969 s. 24 (5).
12 (1)	1969 s. 24 (8).
(2)	1969 s. 24 (7).
13 (1)	1948 s. 3 (8); 1963 s. 64 (1), Sch. 3, para. 38; 1975 s. 108 (1), Sch. 3, para. 5.
(2)	1948 s. 1 (3A); 1975 s. 56 (1).
(3)	1948 s. 3 (8).
(4)	1948 s. 6 (2).
(5)	1948 s. 1 (3B); 1975 s. 56 (1).
14	1963 s. 49 (1); 1969 s. 72 (3), Sch. 5, para. 52; 1975 s. 108 (1), Sch. 3, para. 42.
15	1975 s. 67.
16 (1)	1969 s. 32 (1).
(2)	1969 s. 32 (2); 1975 s. 68 (4).
(3)	1969 s. 32 (2A); 1975 s. 68 (5).
(4)	1969 s. 32 (3); 1975 s. 68 (6).
(5)	1969 s. 32 (4); 1975 s. 68 (7).
(6)	1969 s. 32 (2); 1975 s. 68 (5).
17	1948 s. 11; 1969 s. 27.
18 (1)	1948 s. 12 (1); 1975 s. 59.
(2)	1948 s. 12 (2).
(3)	1948 s. 12 (1A); 1975 s. 59.
19	1969 s. 27 (3).
20 (1)	1969 s. 27 (4); 1975 s. 108 (1), Sch. 3, para. 71.
(2)	1969 s. 27 (5); 1975 s. 108 (1), Sch. 3, para. 71.
21	1948 c. 13.
22 (1)	1948 s. 14 (1).
(2)	1948 s. 14 (2).
23	1963 s. 47.
24 (1)	1948 s. 17 (1).
(2)	1948 s. 17 (2).
(3)	1948 s. 17 (2).
(4)	1948 ss. 9, 17 (3).
(5)	1963 s. 55.
25 (1)	1948 s. 18 (1).
(2)	1948 s. 18 (2); Social Security Act 1973 (c. 38) s. 100 (2) (c), Sch. 27, para. 12.
(3)	1948 s. 18 (3).
(4)	1948 s. 18 (4).
26	1948 s. 22.
27 (1)	1948 s. 20 (1); 1963 s. 46 (1); 1969 s. 72 (3), Sch. 5, para. 15.
(2)	1948 s. 20 (2); 1963 s. 46 (2).
(3)	1948 s. 20 (3).
28 (1)	1948 s. 34 (1).
(2)	1948 s. 34 (2).
(3)	1948 s. 34 (3).
29	1963 s. 58.
30	1948 s. 21; Transfer of Functions (Wales) Order 1970 (S.I. 1970/1536).
31	1969 s. 35.
32	1969 s. 36.

Section of Act	Derivation
33	1969 s. 37.
34	1969 s. 38.
35	1969 s. 39.
36	1969 s. 40.
37	1969 s. 41.
38	1969 s. 42.
39 (1)	1969 s. 43 (1).
(2)	1969 s. 43 (2).
(3)	1969 s. 43 (3).
40 (1)	1969 s. 43 (4).
(2)	1969 s. 43 (5).
(3)	1969 s. 43 (6).
41	1969 s. 44.
42	1969 s. 45.
43	1969 s. 47.
44 (1)	1969 s. 48 (1).
(2)	1969 s. 48 (2).
(3)	1969 s. 48 (3).
(4)	1969 s. 48 (4).
(5)	1969 s. 48 (5); Powers of Criminal Courts Act 1973 (c. 62) s. 56 (1), Sch. 5 para. 37.
(6)	1969 s. 48 (6).
(7)	1969 s. 48 (7).
(8)	1969 s. 48 (8).
45 (1)	1933 s. 86 (1); 1948 ss. 23 (1), 24 (1)–(3); 1969 s. 62 (1).
(2)	1933 s. 86 (3); 1948 s. 23 (1). •
(3)	1969 s. 62 (2).
(4)	1948 s. 24 (2).
46 (1)	1969 s. 62 (3).
(2)	1969 s. 62 (4).
47 (1)	1933 s. 87 (1), (2); 1948 s. 23 (1); Local Government Act 1958 (c. 55) s. 62, Sch. 8, para. 2 (4); 1969 ss. 62 (5), 72 (3), Sch. 5, para. 9 (2); Domestic Proceedings and Magistrates' Courts Act 1978 (c. 22) s. 89, Sch. 2, para. 3.
(2)	1933 s. 87 (1); 1948 s. 23 (1); 1969 s. 62 (6).
(3)	1933 s. 87 (3); 1948 s. 23 (2); 1969 s. 72 (3), Sch. 5, para. 9 (3).
(4)	1933 s. 87 (4); 1948 s. 23 (1); Domestic Proceedings and Magistrates' Courts Act 1978 (c. 22) s. 89, Sch. 2, para. 3.
48 (1)	1933 s. 87 (4); 1948 s. 23 (1); Domestic Proceedings and Magistrates' Courts Act 1978 (c. 22) s. 89, Sch. 2, para. 3.
(2)	1969 s. 62 (7).
49 (1)	1933 s. 88 (1); 1948 s. 23 (1); Local Government Act 1958 (c. 55) s. 62, Sch. 8, para. 2 (4); 1969 s. 72 (3), Sch. 5, para. 10 (1); Domestic Proceedings and Magistrates' Courts Act 1978 (c. 22) s. 89, Sch. 2, para. 4.
(2)	1933 s. 88 (1); Local Government Act 1958 (c. 55) s. 62, Sch. 8, para. 2 (4); 1969 s. 72 (3), Sch. 5, para. 10 (1); Domestic Proceedings and Magistrates' Courts Act 1978 (c. 22) s. 89, Sch. 2, para. 4.
(3)	1933 s. 88 (1); 1948 s. 23 (1); 1969 s. 72 (3), Sch. 5, para. 10 (1).
(4)	1933 s. 88 (2); 1948 s. 23 (1); Criminal Justice Act 1967 (c. 80) s. 92, Sch. 3; 1969 s. 72 (3), Sch. 5, para. 10 (2); Domestic Proceedings and Magistrates' Courts Act 1978 (c. 22) s. 89, Sch. 2, para. 4.
(5)	1933 s. 88 (4); 1948 s. 23 (1).
(6)	1933 s. 88 (4); 1948 s. 23 (1); 1969 s. 72 (3), Sch. 5, para. 10 (3).

Section of Act	Derivation
(7)	1933 s. 88 (4); 1948 s. 23 (1); Domestic Proceedings and Magistrates' Courts Act 1978 (c. 22) s. 89, Sch. 2, para. 4.
50 (1)	1948 s. 26 (1); 1969 s. 72 (3), Sch. 5, para. 17 (1); Domestic Proceedings and Magistrates' Courts Act 1978 (c. 22) s. 89, Sch. 2, para. 8.
(2)	1948 s. 26 (1).
(3)	1948 s. 26 (2).
(4)	1948 s. 26 (3), 1969 s. 72 (3), Sch. 5, para. 17 (2).
(5)	1948 s. 26 (4), 1969 s. 72 (4), Sch. 5, para. 17 (2); Domestic Proceedings and Magistrates' Courts Act 1978 (c. 22) s. 89, Sch. 2, para. 8.
(6)	1948 s. 26 (5).
51 (1)	1963 s. 30 (1); 1969 s. 72 (3), Sch. 5, para. 50 (1).
(2)	1963 s. 30 (2).
(3)	1963 s. 30 (3); 1969 s. 72 (3); Sch. 5, para. 50 (2).
(4)	1963 s. 30 (5); Criminal Justice Act 1967 (c. 80) s. 92, Sch. 3; 1969 s. 72 (3), Sch. 5, para. 50 (4).
52 (1)	1933 s. 102 (1) (c) (d); 1963 s. 30 (3); Courts Act 1971 (c. 23) s. 56 (2), Sch. 5.
(2)	1933 s. 102 (2).
53 (1)	Local Government Act 1958 (c. 55) s. 62, Sch. 8, para. 2 (1).
(2)	Local Government Act 1958 (c. 55) s. 62, Sch. 8, para. 2 (2).
54 (1)	1933 s. 89 (2); 1948 s. 26 (5); 1963 s. 30 (3).
(2)	1933 s. 89 (3); 1948 s. 26 (5); 1963 s. 30 (3).
55 (1)	1950 s. 4 (1); 1963 s. 30 (3).
(2)	1950 s. 4 (2).
(3)	1950 s. 3 (1).
(4)	1950 s. 14; 1963 s. 30 (4).
(5)	1950 s. 27 (1), (2).
56	1933 s. 92; 1948 ss. 27, 28; Mental Health Act 1959 (c. 72) ss. 19 (3) 149 (1), Sch. 7.
57 (1)	1948 s. 29 (1).
(2)	1948 s. 29 (2).
(3)	1948 s. 29 (3).
(4)	1948 s. 29 (4).
(5)	1948 s. 29 (5); Criminal Law Act 1977 (c. 45) s. 31 (1), Sch. 6.
(6)	1948 s. 29 (6).
(7)	1948 s. 29 (7).
(8)	1948 s. 29 (8).
58 (1)	1948 s. 30 (1).
(2)	1948 s. 30 (2).
(3)	1948 s. 30 (3).
(4)	1948 s. 30 (4).
(5)	1948 s. 30 (5); Minister for the Civil Service Order 1971 (S.I. 1971/2099).
(6)	1948 s. 30 (6).
59 (1)	1933 s. 93 (1).
(2)	1933 s. 93 (1).
(3)	1948 s. 32 (1).
(4)	1933 s. 93 (2); 1948 s. 32 (2); Criminal Law Act 1977 (c. 45) s. 31 (5), (6).
60 (1)	1948 s. 31 (1).
(2)	1948 s. 31 (2); Criminal Law Act 1977 (c. 45) s. 31 (1), Sch. 6.
61 (1)	1948 s. 33 (3).
(2)	1948 s. 33 (4).
62 (1)	1948 s. 33 (1).
(2)	1948 s. 33 (2).
(3)	1948 s. 33 (4).

Section of Act	Derivation
63 (1)	1948 s. 33A (1); 1975 s. 56 (2).
(2)	1948 s. 33A (2); 1975 s. 56 (2).
64 (1)	1975 s. 60 (1).
(2)	1975 s. 60 (2).
(3)	1975 s. 60 (3).
(4)	1975 s. 60 (4).
(5)	1975 s. 60 (5).
(6)	1975 s. 60 (6); Adoption Act 1976 (c. 36) s. 73 Sch. 3, para. 20.
(7)	1975 s. 60 (7).
65	1975 s. 61.
66	1975 s. 62.
67	1975 s. 63.
68 (1)	1948 s. 54 (3); 1969 s. 72 (3), Sch. 5, para. 21.
(2)	1948 s. 54 (4); 1969 s. 72 (3), Sch. 5 para. 21.
(3)	1948 s. 54 (5); 1969 s. 72 (3), Sch. 5 para. 21.
(4)	1948 s. 54 (6).
(5)	1948 s. 54 (7); Criminal Law Act 1977 (c. 45) s. 31 (5), (6), (7).
69	1948 s. 34.
70	1969 s. 63 (2).
71 (1)	1948 s. 43 (1); 1969 s. 72 (3), Sch. 5, para. 19; 1975 s. 108 (1), Sch. 3 para. 6; Adoption Act 1976 (c. 36) s. 73, Sch. 3, para. 2.
(2)	1948 s. 43 (2).
(3)	1948 s. 43 (3).
(4)	1948 s. 43 (4).
(5)	1948 s. 43 (5); Minister for the Civil Service Order 1968 (S.I. 1968/1656).
72	1948 s. 19; 1969 s. 50.
73 (1)	1948 s. 51 (1); 1969 s. 72 (3), Sch. 5, para. 20; Adoption Act 1976 (c. 36) s. 73 (2), Sch. 3, para. 3.
(2)	1948 s. 51 (2).
74 (1)	1969 s. 58 (1); 1975 s. 108 (1), Sch. 3, para. 72; Adoption Act 1976 (c. 36) s. 73, Sch. 3, para. 12.
(2)	1969 s. 58 (2).
(3)	1969 s. 58 (3).
(4)	1969 s. 58 (4).
75	1969 s. 59.
76 (1)	1975 s. 98 (1); Adoption Act 1976 (c. 36) s. 73 (2), Sch. 3, para. 21.
(2)	1975 s. 98 (2).
(3)	1975 s. 98 (3).
(4)	1975 s. 98 (4).
77 (1)	1963 s. 45 (1).
(2)	1963 s. 45 (2).
(3)	1963 s. 60.
78 (1)	1948 s. 45 (1).
(2)	1948 s. 45 (1A); Local Authority Social Services Act 1970 (c. 42) s. 14 (1), Sch. 2, para. 5.
79 (1)	1969 s. 63 (1); Local Authority Social Services Act 1970 (c. 42) s. 14 (1), Sch. 2, para. 11.
(2)	1969 s. 63 (3).
(3)	1969 s. 63 (4).
(4)	1969 s. 63 (5); Local Authority Social Services Act 1970 (c. 42) s. 14 (1), Sch. 2, para. 11.
(5)	1969 s. 63 (6); Local Authority Social Services Act 1970 (c. 42) s. 14 (1), Sch. 2, para. 11; Matrimonial Causes Act 1973 (c. 18) s. 54 (1), Sch. 2,

Section of Act	Derivation
	para. 11; Adoption Act 1976 (c. 36) s. 73 (2), Sch. 3, para. 13; Domestic Proceedings and Magistrates' Courts Act 1978 (c. 22) s. 89 (2), Sch. 2, para. 24.
80	1969 s. 64.
81	1969 s. 64A; 1975 s. 71.
82	1969 s. 56 (1).
83	1948 s. 48; 1969 s. 67.
84	1948 s. 55 (1).
85 (1)	1948 s. 58 (1); 1969 s. 69 (1).
(2)	1948 s. 58 (2); 1969 s. 69 (1).
(3)	1948 s. 61; 1969 s. 69 (3).
(4)	1969 s. 69 (4).
86	1933 s. 106 (2); 1969 s. 72 (3), Sch. 5, para. 11.
87 (1)	1948 s. 59 (1); Adoption of Children Act 1949 (c. 98) s. 13; Children Act 1958 (c. 65) s. 40 (1), Sch. 2; Social Work (Scotland) Act 1968 (c. 49) s. 95 (1), Sch. 8, para. 19; 1969 s. 72 (3), Sch. 5, para. 22; Local Government Act 1972 (c. 70) s. 195 (6), Sch. 23, para. 3.
(2)	1969 s. 70 (5).
88	1948 s. 61; 1969 s. 71.
89	Transitional provisions, consequential amendments and repeals.
90	Commencement.
91 (1)	Short title.
(2)	1950 s. 4; 1969 s. 73 (4).
(3)	1950 s. 4; 1969 s. 73 (5).
(4)	1969 s. 73 (6).
(5)	1969 s. 73 (7).
Sch. 1	1969 Sch. 2; Local Government Act 1972 (c. 70) ss. 251 (2), 272 (2), Sch. 29, para. 16.
Sch. 2	1950 Sch. 1; 1963 s. 30 (4).
Sch. 3	1948 Sch. 1 Part 1.
Sch. 4	Transitional provisions and savings.
Sch. 5	Consequential amendments.
Sch. 6	Repeals.

1965   **Children Act 1975—commencement**

The Children Act 1975 (Commencement No. 4) Order 1980, S.I. 1980 No. 1475 brings into force on 1st February 1981, Sch. 3, para. 80 of the Act, which amends the Guardianship Act 1973, s. 4.

1966   **Cruelty to children—wilful neglect**

See *R v Sheppard*, para. 582.

1967   **Custody—access—supervised access**

See para. 2217.

1968   **—— jurisdiction—child already subject to care order—whether jurisdiction of divorce court ousted**

In 1976, a juvenile court made care orders in respect of the parties' two children under the Children and Young Persons Act 1969, s. 1, committing the children into care. In 1977, the father filed a petition for divorce and applied for custody of the two children. The judge held that he had no jurisdiction to entertain the custody application while there were care orders in respect of the children. The father appealed. *Held*, the judge was wrong, as he certainly had jurisdiction to entertain an application by the father for custody as between himself and the mother, although the order might well have been made subject to the local authority care and control orders. There was no appreciable difference between the powers of a judge in the divorce court and the powers of a judge exercising wardship jurisdiction. The jurisdiction of the the divorce court was not ousted by the existence of the care orders, but on general principles the court would not entertain a custody application in such circumstances unless there were special reasons, which meant no more than strong reasons, which indicated that the welfare of the child required the court to take that course. The appeal would be allowed, and the matter referred back to the judge for him to look at the merits if so required by the father.

E v E and Cheshire County Council (Intervener) (1979) 9 Fam Law 185 (Court of Appeal: Ormrod, Browne and Bridge LJJ). *Re H (a minor)* [1978] 2 All ER 903, CA, 1978 Halsbury's Abridgment para. 1929 applied.

1969   **—— —— joint custody order—practice**

See para. 2218.

1970   **—— order—power to commit to care of local authority—power exercised without reference to authority or to parent—validity**

On the parties' divorce, their four young children were placed in the mother's custody. The father applied for questions of custody and access to be restored to the list. A county court judge, having heard oral evidence from the father and having seen the children himself, adjourned the case and made a care order in favour of the local authority. The local authority had not been given any notice, the judge had no evidence from the mother, and there were no affidavits in the case. The mother appealed. *Held*, the judge's order was very much against the interests of the mother and made without hearing any evidence from her; unless it was a purely interim order, the order was necessarily bad. Further, with reference to the Matrimonial Causes Act 1973, s. 43, the judge in fact had no jurisdiction to make the care order, as to make such an order without warning the local authority was to put an unreasonable burden on the authority. The case would be transferred to the High Court for the matters of custody and access to be determined.

M v M (1980) 10 Fam Law 18 (Court of Appeal: Orr and Ormrod LJJ).

1971   **—— —— reasons for decision—guidance**

See *Hutchinson v Hutchinson*, para. 1848.

1972   —— —— variation—exclusion of tenant from council home—emergency jurisdiction

Following the dissolution of a marriage the wife obtained custody of the children and became sole tenant of a council house. Owing to a breakdown in her health a crisis occurred in the family and the judge awarded interim custody pending custody proceedings to the father who moved into the council house. The mother subsequently wished to return home and challenged the decision on the ground that the court had no jurisdiction to interfere with her common law right as the tenant to occupy her home. *Held*, the decision was made strictly on an emergency basis and for the protection of the children. The court had power in these circumstances to order that the interim custodian should be allowed to enter the home to the exclusion of the tenant if necessary for the temporary protection of the children. The order would be upheld.

B v B [1981] 1 All ER 783 (Court of Appeal: CUMMING-BRUCE, DUNN and GRIFFITHS LJJ).

1973   —— paramountcy of child's welfare—child living with father in former matrimonial home

The parties, who had been married for three years, separated in 1978 when the wife left the matrimonial home, a council house. There was one child of the marriage. The husband continued to look after the child, who was cared for by an aunt during the day whilst he worked. The wife successfully applied for custody of the child. The judge further ordered that the husband should vacate the matrimonial home in order that the wife should live there. The husband appealed. *Held*, on balance, the child should be restored to her mother to see whether they could live together again and to preserve the mother–daughter relationship. The judge's order probably best served the interests of the child and the appeal would accordingly be dismissed.

L v L (1980) Times, 6th February (Court of Appeal: LORD DENNING MR, SHAW LJ and SIR DAVID CAIRNS).

1974   —— proceedings—evidence—magistrate obtaining evidence other than in open court—whether justice seen to be done

A wife appealed against a magistrates' order granting custody of the two children of the marriage to the husband. She appealed on the ground that the chairman of the bench had made inquiries personally to the headmaster of the school of one of the children, although the headmaster was not called to give evidence. In a letter to the appeal court, the magistrates' clerk said that the chairman had told him that the headmaster's information had not affected the order as she had not divulged the information to the other magistrates. *Held*, it was impossible to say that because the magistrates were unanimous in their decision, the chairman's communication with the headmaster was not important, as but for that communication she might have taken a different line in discussion with the other magistrates and a different decision would have resulted. Justice had not been seen to be done nor indeed had been done. The appeal would accordingly be allowed.

BOATMAN V BOATMAN (1980) 10 Fam Law 120 (Family Division: Sir JOHN ARNOLD P AND LINCOLN J).

1975   —— —— interim order

The court granted a mother's application for interim custody of a child, who had been snatched by her father, pending a further and fuller investigation into the matter. BRANDON LJ stated that the court did not view favourably an alteration in the care and control of a child made by one parent without reference to the other parent, and that the immediate return of the child to the parent from whom the child had been snatched should be ordered.

JENKINS V JENKINS (1979) 9 Fam Law 215 (Court of Appeal: ORMROD, WALLER and BRANDON LJJ).

1976   **Domestic Proceedings and Magistrates' Courts Act 1978—commencement**

The Domestic Proceedings and Magistrates' Courts Act 1978 (Commencement No. 4) Order 1980, S.I. 1980 No. 1478 brings into force on 1st February 1981 the following provisions: ss. 1–15, 19–27, 29 (3), (4), 31–39, 41–63, 72, Schs. 2 (part), 3 (part). The order also contains transitional provisions adapting certain provisions of the 1978 Act under s. 89 (4) in consequence of the partial operation of the Children Act 1975, and in particular in consequence of the fact that Part II of 1975 Act (which deals with the custody of children) is not yet in force.

1977   **Foster Children Act 1980**

The Foster Children Act 1980 consolidates certain enactments relating to foster children as they have effect in England and Wales. The Act received the royal assent on 31st January 1980 and came into force on 1st April 1981: S.I. 1980 No. 1935. Tables showing the destination of enactments consolidated and the derivation of the new Act are set out on pages 510–513 following.

DESTINATION TABLE

This table shows in column (1) the enactments repealed by the Foster Children Act 1980 and in column (2) the provisions of that Act corresponding to the repealed provisions.

In certain cases the enactment in column (1), though having a corresponding provision in column (2) is not, or is not wholly, repealed, as it is still required, or partly required, for the purposes of other legislation.

(1)	(2)	(1)	(2)
Children Act 1958 (c 65)	Foster Children Act 1980 (c 6)	Children Act 1958 (c 65)	Foster Children Act 1980 (c 6)
s 1	s 3 (1), (3)	s 8	s 13 (2)
2 (1)	1	9	19
(2), (3)	2 (1), (2)	10	14 (1)
(3A)	(3)	11	14 (2)
(4)	(4), (5)	12	17
(4A)	2 (6), Sch 1, para 5	13	18
(5)	Rep., 1959 c 72, s 149 (2), Sch 8, Pt II, and 1960 c 61, s 113 (2), Sch 5	14 (1) (a)	16 (1) (a)
		(b)	(b), (f)
		(c)	(d)
		(d)	(c)
(6), (7)	Rep., 1969 c 54, s 72 (4), Sch 6	(e)	(e)
2A (1)	s 3 (2)	(1A)	(2)
(2)	Sch 1, para 4 (3)	(2)	(3)
(3)	s 21	(2A)	(4)
3 (1)	5 (1), (2)	(3)	(5)
(2)	(1)–(3)	15	20
(2A)	Sch 1, para 4 (2)	16	————
(3)	s 5 (4)	17	2 (4), 22
(4)	6 (1)	18–36	Rep., 1958 c 5, s 59 (2), Sch 6
(5)	(4)	37 (1)	s 15 (1)
(5A), (5B)	(2), (3)	(1A), (1B)	(2), (3)
(6)	Rep., 1969 c 54, s 72 (4), Sch 6	(1C)	15 (4), 21
(7)	s 5 (5)	(2)	16 (1) (g), (3)
(8)	Sch 1, para 4 (1)	(3)	(5)
3A (1)	s 4 (1), 21	38	Rep., S.L.(R.)A. 1969
(2) (a)	4 (2)	39	————
(b)	21	40 (1)	————
4 (1)	8	40 (2)	Rep., S.L.(R.)A. 1969
(1A)	13 (1)	41	
(2)	9 (1)–(3)	Sch 1	Rep., 1958 c 5, s 59 (2), Sch 6
(3)	10 (1)		
(3A), (3B)	(2), (3)	2†	Sch 2, Pt I
(4)	(4)	3	Rep., S.L.(R.)A. 1969
(5)	9 (4), 10 (5)		
5 (1), (2)	11 (1), (2)	**Adoption Act 1958 (c 5)**	
(3)	9 (4), 10 (5)		
(4)	11 (3)	s 57 (1)*	s 22
(5)	Applies to Scotland	Sch 4*	22
6	s 7		
7 (1)	12 (1), (2)	**Mental Health Act 1959 (c 72)**	
(2)	(4)		
(3)	12 (3)		
(4), (5)	(5), (6)	Sch 7, Pt II†	2 (5)
(6)	Applies to Scotland		

† Repealed in part　　　　　　* Not repealed

(1)	(2)	(1)	(2)
Social Work (Scotland) Act 1968 (c 49)	Foster Children Act 1980 (c 6)	Local Authority Social Services Act 1970 (c 42)	Foster Children Act 1980 (c 6)
Sch 8, para 44 (1)	Applies to Scotland	Sch 1†	Sch 2, Pt I
(2)	s 2 (4)		
45	7 (1) (b), (d)	**Courts Act 1971 (c 23)**	
46	Applies to Scotland		
47 (1)	Applies to Scotland	Sch 9, Pt I†	s 14 (2)
(2)	s 2 (4)		
Children and Young Persons Act 1969 (c 54)		**Local Government Act 1972 (c 70)**	
s 51	3 (1), (3)	Sch 23, para 7	22
52 (1)	1		
(2)	2 (2) (c)	**Local Government (Scotland) Act 1973 (c 65)**	
(3)	(3)		
(5)	2 (6), Sch 1, para 5 (1)	Sch 27 Pt III, para 140*	22
53 (1)	———		
(2)	5 (1), (2)	**Children Act 1975 (c 70)**	
(3)	(3)		
(4)	Sch 1, para 4 (2)	s 95 (1)	3 (1)
(5)	s 5 (4)	(2)	Applies to Scotland
(6)	6 (1), (4)	(3)	s 3 (2), 21, Sch 1, para 4 (3)
(7)	(2), (3)		
54 (1)	8	(4)	6 (2), (3), Sch 1, para 4 (1)
(2)	13 (1)		
(3)	16 (1) (f)	96 (1)	4, 21
55 (1), (2)	9 (1)	(2)	16 (1) (a)
(3)	(2)	97 (1)	15 (2)–(4), 21
(4)	10 (1)–(3)	(2)	16 (1) (g)
(5)	11 (1)	Sch 3, para 16 (a)	1
56 (1) (a), (b)	7 (1) (b), (c)	(b)**	Sch 1, para 5
(1) (c), (d)	7 (1) (e), (f)	18	s 7 (1)
(2)	7 (2)	19, 20	16 (3)
57 (1)	16 (2)		
(2)	(4)	**Adoption Act 1976 (c 36) .**	
72 (5)	———		
Sch 4, para 10	Sch 1, para 2	Sch 3, para 5	2 (6)
16	———	6	7 (1) (f)
5, para 29	s 2 (4)		
30	19		
31	17 (1)		
32	22		
82	———		
7	———		

† Repealed in part　　　　　　* Not repealed
** Repealed prospectively by the Adoption Act 1976, s. 73 (4).

TABLE OF DERIVATIONS

This table shows in the right hand column the legislative source from which the sections of the Foster Children Act 1980 in the left hand column have been derived. In the table the following abbreviations are used:

1958 = The Children Act 1958 (1958 c. 65)

1968 = The Social Work (Scotland) Act 1968 (1968 c. 49)

1969 = The Children and Young Persons Act 1969 (1969 c. 54)

1975 = The Children Act 1975 (1975 c. 72)

1976 = The Adoption Act 1976 (1976 c. 36)

Section of Act	Derivation
1	1958 s. 2 (1); 1975 Sch. 3, para. 16 (a).
2 (1)	1958 s. 2 (2).
(2)	1958 s. 2 (3); 1969 s. 52 (2); Nursing Homes Act 1975 (c. 37) Sch. 2, para. 4.
(3)	1958 s. 2 (3A); 1969 s. 52 (3).
(4)	1958 s. 2 (4); 1968 Sch. 8, para. 44 (2); 1969 Sch. 5, para. 29.
(5)	Mental Health Act 1959 (c. 72) Sch. 7, Part II.
(6)	1958 s. 2 (4A); 1969 s. 52 (5); 1976 Sch. 3, para. 5.
3 (1)	1958 s. 1; 1969 s. 51; 1975 s. 95 (1).
(2)	1958 s. 2A (1); 1975 s. 95 (3).
(3)	1958 s. 1; 1969 s. 51.
4	1958 s. 3A; 1975 s. 96 (1).
5 (1)–(3)	1958 s. 3 (1), (2); 1969 s. 53 (2), (3).
(4)	1958 s. 3 (3); 1969 s. 53 (5).
(5)	1958 s. 3 (7).
6 (1)	1958 s. 3 (4); 1969 s. 53 (6).
(2), (3)	1958 s. 3 (5A), (5B); 1969 s. 53 (7); 1975 s. 95 (4) (a), (b).
(4)	1958 s. 3 (5); 1959 s. 53 (6).
7 (1)	1958 s. 6 (1); 1968 Sch. 8, para. 45; 1969 s. 56 (1); 1975 Sch. 3 para. 18; 1976 Sch. 3, para. 6.
(2)	1958 s. 6 (2); 1969 s. 56 (2).
8	1958 s. 4 (1); 1969 s. 54 (1).
9 (1)–(3)	1958 s. 4 (2); 1969 s. 55 (1)–(3).
(4)	1958 ss. 4 (5), 5 (3).
10 (1)–(3)	1958 s. 4 (3), (3A), (3B); 1969 s. 55 (4).
(4)	1958 s. 4 (4).
(5)	1958 ss. 4 (5), 5 (3).
11	1958 s. 5 (1), (2), (4); 1969 s. 55 (5).
12	1958 s. 7.
13 (1)	1958 s. 4 (1A); 1969 s. 54 (2).
(2)	1958 s. 8.
14 (1)	1958 s. 10
(2)	1958 s. 11; Courts Act 1971 (c. 23) s. 56 (2), Sch. 9, Part I.
15 (1)	1958 s. 37 (1).
(2)–(4)	1958 s. 37 (1A)–(1C); 1975 s. 97 (1).
16 (1)	1958 ss. 14 (1), 37 (2); 1969 s. 54 (3); 1975 ss. 96 (2), 97 (2).
(2)	1958 s. 14 (1A); 1969 s. 57 (1).
(3)	1958 ss. 14 (2), 37 (2); 1975 Sch. 3, paras. 19, 20.
(4)	1958 s. 14 (2A); 1969 s. 57 (2).
(5)	1958 ss. 14 (3), 37 (3).

Section of Act	Derivation
17	1958 s. 12; 1969 Sch. 5, para. 31.
18	1958 s. 13.
19	1958 s. 9; 1969 Sch. 5, para. 30.
20	1958 s. 15.
21	1958 ss. 2A (3), 3A (2) (*b*), 37 (1C); 1975 ss. 95 (3), 96 (1), 97 (1).
22	1958 s. 17; 1958 s. 2 (4A), Adoption Act 1958 (7 & 8 Eliz. 2, c. 5) s. 28 (1), 1969 s. 52 (5), Local Government Act 1972 (c. 70) Sch. 23, paras. 7, 8, Local Government (Scotland) Act 1973 (c. 65) Sch. 27, Pt. II, paras. 140, 142 (definitions of "local authority", "local authority in Scotland"); 1969 Sch. 5, para. 32 (definition of "place of safety").
23	[Transitional provisions, consequential amendments and repeals.]
24	[Citation, etc.]
Sch. 1,	
paras. 1, 3, 5	[Transitional provisions.]
para. 2	1969 Sch. 4, para. 10.
para. 4	1958 ss. 2A (2), 3 (2A), (8); 1969 s. 53 (4); 1975 s. 95 (3), (4) (*c*).
para. 6	1958 s. 2 (4A); 1969 s. 52 (5); 1975 Sch. 3, para. 16 (*b*).
Sch. 2	[Consequential amendments.]
Sch. 3	[Repeals.]

1978   Guardianship—access and custody orders—applications—procedure

See para. 2222.

1979   —— proceedings—magistrates' courts

See paras. 1847, 1851.

1980   Juvenile offenders—proposed reform of criminal law relating to juveniles and young adults

See para. 603.

1981   Maintenance—order—provision for payment direct to child—registration of order in magistrates' court

See para. 2220.

1982   —— —— registration in magistrates' courts—provision for payment direct to child—wording of order

See para. 2220.

1983   Surname—change by one parent—objection by other parent—proper approach by court

In dismissing an appeal by a mother, who was divorced and remarried, against an order that she must continue the use by the children of her first marriage of their father's surname, the Court of Appeal decided that a change of children's name after the divorce of the parents was important so far as the children's interests and welfare were concerned. The mere fact that the mother was divorced and had remarried was not a sufficent reason for changing the children's name. It was a matter of discretion for the judge to decide whether such a change was in the interests of the children, taking all the facts into account and not attaching decisive importance to the wishes of young children.

W v A [1981] 1 All ER 100 (Court of Appeal: LAWTON, BRIDGE and DUNN LJJ). Re WG (1976) 6 Fam Law 210, CA followed. Dicta of Ormrod LJ in D v B [1979] 1 All ER 92, CA, at 99, 100, 1978 Halsbury's Abridgment para. 1943 not followed.

1984   Wardship—access and custody orders—applications—procedure

See para. 2222.

1985   —— application for fostering with a view to adoption

A local authority applied for an order that a ward of court be placed with foster parents "with a view to adoption". *Held*, it was not desirable that the application should be made in such a form which effectively asked the court to prejudge a matter which should properly be considered on an application for leave to apply for adoption.

RE K (A MINOR) (1980) 124 Sol Jo 809 (Family Division: PURCHAS J). F v S (Adoption: Ward) [1973] Fam 203 applied.

1986   —— application for place of safety order in respect of ward—magistrates' court—jurisdiction

A boy, aged two, was a ward of court who had been living in a children's home. Care and control of the child was subsequently granted to his parents. The child went to live with his parents, but his health rapidly deteriorated. The local authority successfully applied for a place of safety order in respect of the child under the Children and Young Persons Act 1969, s. 28, and the child returned to live in the children's home. Under the wardship jurisdiction, the local authority applied to have the order granting care and control of the child to the parents varied. *Held*, a local authority should not be inhibited by the fact that a child was a ward of court from applying to a justice of the peace for a place of safety order under the 1969 Act. The application should only be made to protect the child, and before the order expired the High Court should be informed of the matter and an application made for directions under the wardship jurisdiction. In the instant case, the care order would be varied by granting care and control of the child to the local authority. The child would remain a ward of court.

RE B (A MINOR) [1980] LS Gaz R 94 (Family Division: DUNN J).

1987   —— **jurisdiction—care proceedings dismissed by magistrates— High Court's power to assume wardship jurisdiction**

A child was put into local authority care and a series of interim care orders were made in respect of him. The magistrates refused to grant a care order when the matter came before the juvenile court for a full hearing. The local authority immediately issued an originating summons seeking to make the child a ward of court. The parents asked the judge to decline jurisdiction on the ground that the matter had already been dealt with in the juvenile court. The judge refused and on appeal, *held*, the welfare of the child was the overriding consideration in deciding whether to assume jurisdiction. The local authority had felt sufficiently strongly about the decision of the juvenile court to issue the summons to protect the child, and the judge was correct not to decline jurisdiction at that stage. The appeal would be dismissed.

RE C (A MINOR) (1979) 10 Fam Law 84 (Court of Appeal: ORR, ORMROD and GEOFFREY LANE LJJ). *Re D* [1977] 3 All ER 788, CA, 1977 Halsbury's Abridgment para. 1890 applied.

1988   —— **proceedings—application for declaration of paternity— power of court to make declaration**

On the question whether a court in wardship proceedings had the power to make a declaration of paternity, *held*, although from time to time the court had to decide the issue of paternity in order to resolve other issues between the parties, the question of biological parentage had little effect on the problems which the court handled in wardship proceedings. There was no statutory power to grant a declaration of paternity as there was no analogy with the powers contained in the Matrimonial Causes Act 1973, s. 45 to grant by decree declarations of legitimacy, legitimation or the validity of the marriage. Nor was there power to grant a declaration under the wardship jurisdiction as such, for it was not directly relevant to the issues in those proceedings. If there was the power to grant such a declaration it would have to be found in the inherent jurisdiction of the court. There was no authority for such a proposition and the judge had no power to make such a declaration. Even on the presumption that the jurisdiction existed, it was discretionary and in the circumstances, the judge should have refused to make the order. A declaration of paternity in wardship proceedings was no more than a finding of fact formalised in an order of the court and made without reference to any specific legal issues between the parties. Its effect was to pre-judge issues and possibly endanger the interests of the child. In wardship the interests of the child were paramount and all decisions were to be taken in the light of those interests. The courts should proceed carefully where the question of paternity was raised. If it was raised there should be an order for the trial of the issue, but such an order should be made only if the court was satisfied that the determination of the issue would have a material bearing on the case and that it was in the child's interests that the question should be investigated.

RE J S (A MINOR) [1980] 1 All ER 1061 (Court of Appeal: ORR and ORMROD LJJ).

MISREPRESENTATION AND FRAUD

Halsbury's Laws of England (4th edn.), Vol. 31, paras. 1001–1137

1989   Contract for sale of goods—misrepresentation of foreign law

See *Andre & Cie SA v Ets Michel Blanc & Fils*, para. 2443.

1990   Fraudulent misrepresentation—action for damages—entitlement to consequential damages

Canada

In a case where the plaintiffs were fraudulently induced to purchase a business it was held that, where a person was induced by fraud to enter into a contract, he was entitled to recover damages from the fraudulent party for his loss on the transaction itself and all consequential losses incurred.

SIAMETIS v TROJAN HORSE (BURLINGTON) INC (1979) 25 OR (2d) 120 (High Court of Ontario). *Doyle v Olby (Ironmongers) Ltd* [1969] 2 All ER 119 applied.

1991   Negligent misrepresentation—claim for damages—whether provable in company's winding up

See *Re Berkeley Securities (Property) Ltd*, para. 390.

MISTAKE

Halsbury's Laws of England (4th edn.), Vol. 32, paras. 1–100

1992   Mistake as to name—correction—insurance policy

An insurance company made a mistake in the name of a company in an exclusion clause in the products liability section of an insurance policy. The judge held that there was no case for rectification and that the insurers must put up with their mistake. On appeal, *held*, in construing a document the court was at liberty to correct a misnomer, so that people could not take advantage of it even though it was not a mistake which required the equitable remedy of rectification.

NITTAN (UK) LTD v SOLENT STEEL FABRICATIONS (1980) Times, 24th October (Court of Appeal: LORD DENNING MR, BRIGHTMAN and GRIFFITHS LJJ). *Whittam v W. J. Daniel & Co. Ltd* [1962] 1 QB 271, 277 applied.

1993   Mistake of fact—obsolete banknotes tendered at bureau de change—value of current banknotes given

See *R v Williams*, para. 637.

1994   Rectification—lease—rent review clause—no machinery for ascertaining rent in default of agreement

See *Thomas Bates and Son Ltd v Wyndham's (Lingerie) Ltd*, para. 1742.

MONEY AND MONEYLENDERS

Halsbury's Laws of England (4th edn.), Vol. 32, paras. 101–400

1995   Exchange control—contract contrary to Peruvian exchange regulations—enforceability

See *United City Merchants (Investments) Ltd v Royal Bank of Canada (No. 2)*, para. 221.

1996   **Foreign investment—protection—agreement with Jordan**

An agreement has been concluded with the government of Jordan relating to the promotion and protection of investments. Each government undertakes to encourage and create favourable conditions for nationals and companies of the other country to invest in its territory. Such investments, and the returns therefrom, will not be accorded less favourable treatment than the investments and returns of nationals or companies of any third state. The governments undertake not to expropriate or nationalise, directly or indirectly, such investments except for a public purpose related to the relevant country's internal needs and against prompt, adequate and effective compensation. The governments also guarantee the free transfer of such capital and returns on it (subject to the exercise of existing powers in exceptional financial or economic circumstances). The agreement provides for access to the International Centre for the Settlement of Investment Disputes by nationals and companies in dispute with a government under the terms of the agreement. The agreement was signed in Amman on 10th October 1979 and will come into force one month after the exchange of instruments of ratification or approval. The text of the agreement has been published as Cmnd. 7818.

1997   **—— —— agreement with Sri Lanka**

An agreement has been concluded with the government of Sri Lanka relating to the promotion and protection of investments. Each government undertakes to encourage and create favourable conditions for nationals and companies of the other country to invest in its territory. Such investments, and the returns therefrom, will not be accorded less favourable treatment than the investments and returns of nationals and companies of any third state. The governments undertake not to expropriate or nationalise, directly or indirectly, such investments except for a public purpose related to the relevant country's needs and against prompt, adequate and effective compensation. The governments also guarantee the free transfer of such capital and returns on it (subject to the exercise of lawful powers in exceptional financial and economic circumstances). The agreement provides for the reference of disputes to the International Centre for Settlement of Investment Disputes. The agreement was signed in Colombo on 13th February 1980 and will enter into force on the exchange of instruments of ratification. The text of the agreement has been published as Cmnd. 7984.

1998   **International Monetary Fund—increase in subscription**

See para. 1342.

1999   **Loan—no obligation to repay from specified fund—interest to lender in property**

See *Swiss Bank Corpn v Lloyds Bank Ltd*, para. 1094.

2000   **Loans by Public Works Loan Commissioners—increase of limit**

The Local Loans (Increase of Limit) Order 1980, S.I. 1980 No. 664 (in force on 10th May 1980), increases the limit on lending by the Public Works Loan Commissioners to local authorities and other eligible borrowers from £3,000 million to £6,000 million.

2001   **Overseas Development and Co-operation Act 1980**

See para. 343.

2002   **Premium savings bonds—maximum permitted holding**

The Premium Savings Bonds (Amendment) Regulations 1980, S.I. 1980 No. 452 (in force on 21st April 1980), further amend the Premium Savings Bonds Regulations 1972 by increasing the maximum permitted holding of premium savings bonds from 3000 to 10,000 bond units.

2003   —— purchase

The Premium Savings Bonds (Amendment) (No. 2) Regulations 1980, S.I. 1980 No. 767 (in force on 7th July 1980), amend the Premium Savings Bonds Regulations 1972 so as to permit the purchase of bonds on behalf of a mentally disordered person by his receiver. They also provide that the date on which a repayment warrant is issued in respect of a bond is, for the purpose of determining whether any other sum such as a prize is payable in respect of that bond, deemed to be the date on which the bond is repaid.

2004   Savings certificates

The Savings Certificates (Amendment) Regulations 1980, S.I. 1980 No. 45 (in force on 4th February 1980), amend the 1972 Regulations to provide that the maximum permitted holding of the 19th Issue of National Saving Certificates, which will be on sale from 4th February 1980 at a purchase price of £10 per certificate unit, will be 150. Certificates of the 18th Issue will not be issued after 3rd February 1980.

2005   The Savings Certificates (Amendment) (No. 2) Regulations 1980, S.I. 1980 No. 1614 (in force on 17th November 1980), amend the Savings Certificates Regulations 1972 to enable the issue of the second index-linked issue of the National Savings Certificate, which will be on sale from 17th November 1980 at a purchase price of £10 per unit certificate. These index-linked certificates may only be held by a person who is aged sixty years or over. Index-linked certificates of the earlier Retirement issue may still only be held by men aged sixty-five years or over and women aged sixty years or over except that it will now be possible, subject to the 1972 Regulations, for Retirement issue certificates to be transferred to men aged sixty years or over. The regulations also provide for the maximum permitted holding of certificates of the second index-linked issue to be 300 unit certificates.

2006   The Savings Certificates (Amendment) (No. 3) Regulations 1980, S.I. 1980 No. 1986 (in force on 12th January 1981), amend the Savings Certificates Regulations 1972 by increasing the maximum permitted holding of the 19th Issue of National Savings Certificates from 150 (purchase price £1,500) to 500 (purchase price £5,000).

2007   Trading funds—Her Majesty's Stationery Office

The HMSO Trading Fund Order 1980, S.I. 1980 No. 456 (in force on 1st April 1980), directs that the operations of Her Majesty's Stationery Office, with specified exceptions, shall be financed as from 1st April 1980 by means of a trading fund established with public money, instead of by means of annual votes and appropriations. It imposes a limit on the sums which may be issued to the fund out of the National Loans Fund.

MORTGAGE

Halsbury's Laws of England (4th edn.), Vol. 32, paras. 401–1052

2008   Local authority mortgages—increase in mortgage limits

See para. 1423.

2009   Mortgage agreement—agreement to waive mortgage repayments—promissory estoppel

See *Bojtar v Parker*, para. 1109.

2010   Mortgage of ship—priority over maritime lien

See *Bankers Trust International Ltd v Todd Shipyard Corpn*, para. 2627.

2011   Mortgagee—duty of care—exercise of power of sale

See *Bank of Cyprus (London) Ltd v Gill*, para. 2049.

2012   —— remedies—action for possession—effect of unregistered interest of mortgagor's spouse

The House of Lords has affirmed the decision of the Court of Appeal in *Williams and Glyn's Bank Ltd v Boland*; *Williams and Glyn's Bank Ltd v Brown* [1979] 2 WLR 550, 1979 Halsbury's Abridgment para. 934. The House of Lords held that the wives who were equitable tenants in common with their husbands by virtue of having contributed to the purchase price, although only the husbands' names appeared as registered proprietors on the register had "overriding interests" in the land within the meaning of the Land Registration Act 1925, s. 70 (1) (g), to which any charges on their houses would be subject.

Their Lordships considered that a spouse, living in a house, had an "actual occupation" capable of conferring protection as an "overriding interest" within s. 70 (1) (g); further, notwithstanding that the interests of the wives were equitable interests capable of being overreached and therefore "minor interests" within s. 3 (xv) (a) of the Act, once associated with actual occupation they acquired the status of overriding interests and were also interests "subsisting in reference" to the land within s. 70. Accordingly the wives were entitled to resist the claims for possession brought by the bank as mortgagee.

WILLIAMS AND GLYN'S BANK LTD v BOLAND; WILLIAMS AND GLYN'S BANK LTD v BROWN [1980] 2 All ER 408 (House of Lords: LORD WILBERFORCE, VISCOUNT DILHORNE, LORD SALMON, LORD SCARMAN and LORD ROSKILL). Decision of Court of Appeal [1979] 2 WLR 550, 1979 Halsbury's Abridgment para. 1934 affirmed.

2013   Priority—securities required by company with foreign bank loan—further advance obtained from English bank—charge executed over securities

See *Swiss Bank Corpn v Lloyds Bank Ltd*, para. 1094.

2014   Registration of charges—building agreement providing for grant of lease—mortgage of interest under agreement—whether creates equitable charge affecting land

See *Property Discount Corpn Ltd v Lyon Group Ltd*, para. 381.

NATIONAL HEALTH SERVICE

Halsbury's Laws of England (3rd edn.), Vol. 27, paras. 981–1186

2015   Area health authority—takeover of functions—validity of minister's action

See *R v Secretary of State for Social Services, ex parte Lewisham, Lambeth and Southwark London Borough Councils*, para. 11; *National Health Service (Invalid Direction) Act 1980*, para. 2030.

2016   Boards of Governors

The National Health Service (Preservation of Boards of Governors) Amendment Order 1980, S.I. 1980 No. 1193 (in force on 12th August 1980), amends the National Health Service (Preservation of Boards of Governors) Order 1979, 1979

Halsbury's Abridgment para. 1936. The order applies to preserved Boards the provisions for the funding and financial control of health authorities substituted in the National Health Service Act 1977 by the Health Services Act 1980, and the provisions for the giving of directions by the Secretary of State contained in s. 13 of the 1977 Act.

2017   Charges—dental and optical charges

The National Health Service (Dental and Optical Charges) Amendment Regulations 1980, S.I. 1980 No. 352 (in force on 1st April 1980), amend the National Health Service (Dental and Optical Charges) Regulations 1978, 1978 Halsbury's Abridgment para. 1984, by increasing the charges for the supply of certain dental appliances and the provision of dental treatment under the National Health Service Act 1977.

2018   The National Health Service (Dental and Optical Charges) Amendment (No. 2) Regulations 1980, S.I. 1980 No. 987 (in force on 1st October 1980), amend the National Health Service (Dental and Optical Charges) Regulations 1978, 1978 Halsbury's Abridgment para. 1984. In particular they prescribe that no charge is payable by a patient for the exceptional attendance by a dentist at his surgery in order to provide emergency treatment.

2019   —— drugs and appliances charges

The National Health Service (Charges for Drugs and Appliances) Amendment Regulations 1980, S.I. 1980 No. 264 (in force on 1st April 1980), further amend the National Health Service (Charges for Drugs and Appliances) Regulations 1974, 1974 Halsbury's Abridgment para. 2216, increasing the charges specified for the supply of drugs and certain appliances under the National Health Service Act 1977, increasing the sums prescribed and altering the period of validity for the grant of pre-payment certificates of exemption from those charges, increasing the allowance for exemption from those charges on grounds of low income, and correcting errors.

These regulations have been revoked: see para. 2020.

2020   The National Health Service (Charges for Drugs and Appliances) Regulation 1980, S.I. 1980 No. 1503 (in force on 1st December 1980), revoke the 1974 Regs, 1974 Halsbury's Abridgment paras. 2214, 2216; the 1975 Regs, 1975 Halsbury's Abridgment paras. 2318, 2319; the 1976 Regs, 1976 Halsbury's Abridgment para. 1800; the 1979 Regs, 1979 Halsbury's Abridgment para. 1937 and the 1980 Regs, para. 2019. The regulations consolidate with amendments the provisions for the making and recovery of charges for drugs and appliances (other than dental or optical appliances) supplied under the National Health Service Act 1977 and formerly contained in the 1974 Regs as amended. The principal amendments increase the charges specified for the supply of drugs and certain appliances and the sums prescribed for the grant of pre-payment certificates of exemption from those charges.

2021   —— hospital charges

The Road Traffic Accidents (Payments for Treatment) (England and Wales) Order 1980, S.I. 1980 No. 111 (in force on 1st April 1980), increases the hospital charges payable under the Road Traffic Act 1972 for the treatment of road accident victims to £1,250 for each person treated as an in-patient and £125 for each person treated as an out-patient. The order also increases charges payable to doctors or hospitals for emergency treatment given to road accident victims. See 1979 Halsbury's Abridgment para. 1943.

2022   —— remission of charges

The National Health Service (Remission of Charges) Amendment Regulations 1980, S.I. 1980 No. 1659 (in force on 1st December 1980), amend the 1974 Regulations, 1974 Halsbury's Abridgment para. 2253 to take account of amendments made by the Social Security Act 1980, para. 2761, to provisions of the Supplementary Benefits Act 1976 referred to in those regulations.

2023 Dental services

The National Health Service (General Dental Services) Amendment Regulations 1980, S.I. 1980 No. 986 (in force on 1st October 1980), make minor amendments to the National Health Service (General Dental Services) Regulations 1973, relating to the lists of dentists undertaking to provide dental services, the Statement of Dental Remuneration and to the treatment and other services which may be provided.

2024 Health authorities—directions

The National Health Service Functions (Directions to Authorities) Regulations 1980, S.I. 1980 No. 1204 (in force on 14th August 1980), direct Regional and Area Health Authorities to exercise the Secretary of State's functions with respect to authorising hospital accommodation to be made available on part payment and allowing authorised hospital accommodation and services to be made available for private patients. The directions in the National Health Service Functions (Directions to Authorities) Regulations 1974, 1974 Halsbury's Abridgment para. 2238 are revoked in relation to authorising hospital accommodation and services for private patients. Provision is also made in respect of functions exercisable by the preserved Boards of Governors of teaching hospitals.

2025 Health Service Supply Council

The Health Service Supply Council (Establishment and Constitution) Order 1980, S.I. 1980 No. 796 (in force on 14th July 1980), provides for the establishment and constitution of a special health authority for the purpose of exercising, on behalf of the Secretary of State and health authorities in England, functions relating to policy, arrangements and information concerning supplies for the national health service. The order also provides for the number of members to be appointed to the Council and for financial arrangements relating to the Council.

2026

The Health Service Supply Council Regulations 1980, S.I. 1980 No. 797 (in force on 14th July 1980), provide for the appointment and term of office of members of the Health Service Supply Council and for the procedure of and the appointment of officers for, and reports to the Secretary of State by, that special health authority.

2027 Health Services Act 1980

The Health Services Act 1980 makes provisions regarding the local administration of the National Health Service, the use of health service facilities by private patients and various other related matters. The Act received the royal assent on 8th August 1980 and came into force on that date, except s. 14, which came into force on 8th September 1980 (S.I. 1980 No. 1257) and ss. 16, 21, 25 (2), Schs. 4, 5, 7 (part), which come into force on a day or days to be appointed.

Section 1 and Sch. 1, Part I empower the Secretary of State to establish district health authorities in place of area health authorities or to redesignate area health authorities as district health authorities. Section 2 and Sch. 1, Part II modify the duty of each area or district health authority to establish a Family Practitioner Committee for its own area or district. Section 3 enables certain general medical services to be made available to local authorities. Area or district health authorities may make grants to local authorities towards their expenditure on services of common interest: s. 4. Health authorities may take part in activities to raise funds for health service purposes: s. 5. Section 6 deals with the provision of public money to health authorities and their financial duties. Section 7 relates to services provided by relatives of doctors providing general medical services. Section 8 abolishes the Central Health Services Council.

Section 9 and Sch. 2 remove the restrictions on the Secretary of State's power to authorise the private use of health service facilities under the National Health Service

Act 1977 and abolish the Health Services Board. Section 10 restates the general power to allow the private use of health service facilities under the 1977 Act, but prevents such power from being used to duplicate the power of authorisation preserved by s. 9. Section 11 prevents the power of authorisation from being used to interfere with the provision of health service facilities.

Sections 12–15 and Sch. 3 amend the provisions of the Health Services Act 1976 relating to the control of private hospital development. Section 12 increases to 120 the number of beds which a private hospital may have before an authorisation is required to carry out specified construction work. Certain work is exempt from the need for authorisation: s. 13. Section 14 amends the notification procedure under the 1976 Act, s. 14 so as to restrict its application to specified hospital premises. Section 15 and Sch. 3 make minor consequential amendments to the 1976 Act.

Section 16 and Sch. 4 extend the scope of various enactments relating to the registration of nursing homes and private hospitals.

Sections 17–19 amend provisions of the National Health Service Act 1966 relating to the General Practice Finance Corporation. Section 17 enables the Corporation to acquire general practice premises and lease them to medical practitioners. Section 18 increases the Corporation's borrowing powers and provides for further increase. The Corporation itself may pay the remuneration and allowances of its members: s. 19.

Section 20 empowers certain pharmacists to dispense drugs and medicine to hospital dentists. Section 21 amends powers under the National Health Service Act 1977 to make regulations regarding the arrangements for providing pharmaceutical services.

Sections 22–26 and Schs. 5–7 contain miscellaneous supplementary provisions, amendments and repeals.

2028 Inquiry—witness—expenses—reimbursement from public funds

The Parliamentary Under Secretary for Health and Social Security has stated, in reply to a parliamentary question, that the Department of Health and Social Security advised that the legal expenses of a witness might be met from public funds where there was a formal inquiry under the National Health Service Act 1977, s. 84, or by a health authority, if the chairman of the inquiry ruled that it was essential for him to be legally represented, no other source of re-imbursement was available, it would be unreasonable to expect him to meet the expense himself, and the authority conducting the inquiry was satisfied that the costs were reasonable. See 124 Sol Jo 482.

2029 Medical practitioners—prescribed experience

The National Health Service (Vocational Training) Amendment Regulations 1980, S.I. 1980 No. 1900 (in force on 8th January 1981), amend the National Health Service (Vocational Training) Regulations 1979, 1979 Halsbury's Abridgment para. 1944, by substituting a later date for that immediately before which a post may be approved so as to count as an "educationally approved post" for the purposes of reg. 5 of those regulations which relates to certificates of prescribed experience for the purposes of the National Health Service Act 1977, ss. 30, 32.

2030 National Health Service (Invalid Direction) Act 1980

The National Health Service (Invalid Direction) Act 1980 gives temporary effect to an instrument purporting to be a direction given by the Secretary of State for Social Services. The Act received the royal assent on 20th March 1980 and came into force on that date.

This Act is passed in consequence of a decision of Woolf J (*R v Secretary of State for Social Services, ex parte Lewisham, Lambeth and Southwark London Borough Councils* (1980) Times, 26th February, para. 11), in which he held that a purported direction dated 1st August 1979 of the Secretary of State under the National Health Service Act 1977, s. 86, was invalid. The Secretary of State has arranged for the members of the relevant authority to resume their functions from 1st April 1980. Section 1 of the Act gives effect to the invalid instrument for the period 1st August 1979 to 31st March 1980. Section 2 deals with short title.

2031   Private hospital premises

See MEDICINE, PHARMACY, DRUGS etc.

2032   Superannuation

See PENSIONS AND SUPERANNUATION.

NEGLIGENCE

Halsbury's Laws of England (3rd edn.), Vol. 28, paras. 1–120

2033   Abstraction of underground water—abstraction in excess of statutory limit—right of action

See *Re National Capital Commission*, para. 3123.

2034   Causation—congenital disabilities—whether question of causation triable as preliminary issue

A drug was marketed by the defendant manufacturers as a test for pregnancy. It was taken by women some of whom gave birth to children with congenital malformations. Results of research which were published did not disprove that the drug could cause abnormalities in children and it was eventually withdrawn from the market. Actions were brought in negligence alleging that the drug had caused malformations in children. On appeal, the manufacturers contended that the issue of causation should be tried as a preliminary issue. *Held*, in determining the issue of causation it was necessary to consider the statistical reports and evidence in order to discover whether the mothers had taken other drugs which might have caused any disabilities in their children. In determining the issue of negligence, it was necessary to consider how far the manufacturers should have been aware of the reports before marketing the drugs. The two issues were inextricably linked and the issue of causation would not be tried as a preliminary issue to the main action. Accordingly the appeal would be dismissed.

HYMAN AND WILLIAMS V SCHERING CHEMICALS LTD (1980) Times, 10th June (Court of Appeal: LORD DENNING MR and DUNN LJ).

2035   Contributory negligence—collision between vehicles—apportionment of liability

See *Worsfold v Howe*, para. 1675.

2036   Duty of care—auditors

See *Simonius Vischer & Co v Holt & Thompson*, para. 471.

2037   —— berthing a ship—duty to ensure safe berth

See *The Neapolis II, Alberta Shipping Ltd v The Briton Ferry Stevedoring Co Ltd*, para. 2594.

2038   —— building inspector—duty to inspect foundations

The owners of a block of flats sued the architects for negligent design and supervision following the appearance of serious cracks in the structure of the flats. Judgment was entered for the owners of the flats and the architects claimed against the local authority as joint tortfeasors for negligent building inspection. The local authority's building inspector, realising the dangers inherent in a London clay subsoil planted with trees, had specified foundations six inches deeper than the conventional depth. Both he and the architects had seen the problem as one of settlement of the subsoil, not of heave, and did not foresee the shrinkage resulting from trees dying of Dutch elm disease. The damage caused in the early years had been found to have been caused by the trees removed at the time of construction of the flats and in later years by the removal of diseased elms. The architects contended that the building inspector was negligent in not requiring the foundations to be deeper. *Held*, the building inspector was under a duty to take reasonable care to secure that the building complied with regulations requiring the foundations to be constructed so as to safeguard the building from shrinking. He had a duty to decide, in the light of his knowledge, whether there was a risk of the foundations being inadequate. He had made that decision negligently in that he had not taken reasonable care in the context of building regulations. The local authority were therefore jointly liable for the damage resulting from the initial heave, and for the recurring damage.

In relation to the damage resulting from the trees which died from Dutch elm disease, the test was not whether the events causing the damage were foreseeable, but whether the local authority could reasonably foresee the type of damage suffered. The cracks in the building could have been foreseen as a consequence of a failure to provide sufficiently deep foundations and the authority was therefore jointly liable for the damage consequential upon the felling of the elm trees.

ACRECREST LTD v W. S. HATTRELL & PARTNERS (1979) 252 Estates Gazette 1107 (Queen's Bench Division: SIR DOUGLAS FRANK QC). *Smith v Leech Brain & Co Ltd* [1961] 3 All ER 1159, *H Parsons (Livestock) Ltd v Uttley Ingham & Co Ltd* [1978] 1 All ER 525, CA, 1977 Halsbury's Abridgment para. 821, followed.

2039   The plaintiff, the owner of a house, sued the defendant local authority for damages in respect of structual damage to his property due to settlement. The plaintiff had purchased the house from the assignees of a person who had built the house on land acquired from the local authority. The local authority's building inspector had employed consultant engineers to carry out a site investigation and, following their advice, had made a routine inspection of the site and advised the builder as to the foundations. *Held*, the inspector armed with the technical advice and following it with reasonable care was under a duty only to ensure that the foundations were built in accordance with requirements. The action would therefore be dismissed.

STEWART v EAST CAMBRIDGESHIRE DISTRICT COUNCIL (1979) 252 Estates Gazette 1105 (Queen's Bench Division: SIR DOUGLAS FRANK QC). *Anns v Merton London Borough Council* [1977] 2 All ER 492, HL, 1977 Halsbury's Abridgment para. 2175 considered.

2040   —— driver—duty owed to passenger alighting from public service vehicle

See *Edwards v Rigby*, para. 2975.

2041   —— education authority—duty to provide transport for pupils— liability for negligence of independent contractor

The plaintiff attended a special school for retarded pupils situated a few miles from his home. The local education authority had made a contract with a taxi firm to send a taxi to take the plaintiff to and from school. The taxi driver dropped the plaintiff in a lay-by of a busy road which the plaintiff had to cross to reach home and he was severely injured by a van while crossing the road. The owner and driver of the taxi and the van respectively and the county council were held liable in negligence. On appeal the question arose as to the liability of the local education authority for the taxi driver's negligence in leaving the plaintiff on the wrong side of the road. *Held*, the Education Act 1944, s. 55, provided that a local education authority was under a duty to make arrangements for the provision of transport in order to facilitate the attendance of pupils at schools. A person who employed an independent contractor was not liable for his negligence unless he was under a duty which he could not delegate. The duty of a local education authority was to take such care of each pupil as a reasonably careful father would take for his own children. Accordingly the authority were not liable and their appeal would be allowed.

MYTON v WOOD (1980) Times, 12th July (Court of Appeal: LORD DENNING MR, WALLER and DUNN LJJ).

2042 —— employer—employee injured in payroll robbery

See *Charlton v Forrest Printing Ink Co Ltd*, para. 1033.

2043 —— engineer

Canada

The owner of a building site asked a professional engineer for a copy of a soils report which he had made at the request of the architect. The report was based on examination of shallow test holes on the site. Although the engineer told the architect that a deep soil test was necessary he signed a letter to the owner describing his examination of the test holes and stating his opinion of the load bearing capacity of the soil without indicating that the examination was inadequate as a basis for judging that capacity. *Held*, he was under a duty of care to the owner to inform him of the inadequacy of the test.

SURREY (DISTRICT) v CARROLL-HATCH & ASSOCIATES LTD (1979) 101 DLR (3d) 218 (Court of Appeal of British Columbia). *Hedley Byrne & Co Ltd v Heller & Partners Ltd* [1964] AC 465, HL, applied.

2044 —— highway authority—duty to prevent straying dogs

See *Allison v Corby District Council*, para. 1397.

2045 —— joint participants in crime—act done in connection with crime—existence of duty of care between participants

Three men spent an evening drinking together. Two of them then committed a burglary and attempted to escape in a car belonging to the third man. While doing so they were involved in an accident in which one of them, the passenger, was injured. He brought an action in negligence against the driver and against the car owner, on the ground that he had permitted the driver to use the car. *Held*, in certain circumstances, as a matter of public policy, the law might not recognise that a duty of care was owed by one participant in a crime to another in relation to an act done in the course of the commission of the crime. On the facts, the defendants did not owe a duty of care to the plaintiff during the burglary or while trying to escape.

Alternatively, in the circumstances of the present case of burglars who had been drinking and were fleeing in a get-away car, the defendants were entitled to rely on the maxim volenti non fit injuria.

ASHTON v TURNER [1980] 3 All ER 870 (Queen's Bench Division at Liverpool: EWBANK J). *Godbolt v Fittock* (1963) 63 SR (NSW) 617 and *Smith v Jenkins* (1970) 44 ALJR 78 applied.

2046 —— local authority—responsibility for child's actions whilst in care

See *Vicar of Writtle v Essex County Council*, para. 1807.

2047 —— medical practitioner—injury following tests

Canada

The patient, who was suffering from impaired circulation in his upper limbs, was sent to a radiologist for tests. In the course of the tests a quantity of neurologically toxic contrast medium was inadvertently introduced into the patient's spinal cord, thus rendering him paraplegic. The patient had not been warned of the risks of paralysis and he brought an action for damages against the radiologist for trespass to the person and negligence. His claim was dismissed. On appeal, *held*, the patient's consent to the tests had not been negatived because there had been no actual misdescription or misrepresentation, and so the claim of trespass was not substantiated. The allegation of negligence would also fail because the specific risk of paralysis was not generally known among the medical profession at the time and so the usual tests of foreseeability and avoidability could not be applied. Neither was the maxim res ipsa loquitur applicable in view of the substantial evidence by way of explanation that was available. Accordingly, the appeal would be dismissed.

McLean v Weir and Goff [1980] 4 WWR 330 (Court of Appeal of British Columbia).

2048 —— —— patient's consent to operation

See *Allan v New Mount Sinai Hospital*, para. 2990; *Chatterton v Gerson*, para. 1892.

2049 —— mortgagee—exercise of power of sale—duty of mortgagee

The defendant bought a hotel for £210,000. The plaintiff bank made him an advance by way of overdraft in order to pay off the money he had borrowed to buy the hotel. The facility was available for one year only and was secured by a legal charge on the property. At the end of the year the bank agreed not to apply a penal rate of interest on the outstanding loan if the defendant would sell the hotel immediately. The defendant did not do so and the bank commenced proceedings for possession. A third party made an offer of £200,000 for the hotel but withdrew it after he had made an inspection. The bank formally took possession, and decided to close the hotel and sell it following an unfavourable report by a firm of hotel consultants. The same third party then made an offer of £125,000 which was accepted. He subsequently sold the hotel for £225,000. The bank brought an action claiming the remainder of the money owed to it. The defendant counterclaimed alleging that the bank had failed to take reasonable care in exercising its power of sale, as a result of which the hotel had been sold at less than the market value. *Held*, a mortgagee was entitled to sell at any time and was not obliged to wait on a rising market or for a market to recover (although he could not sell without taking proper steps to secure the best available price at the time in question). The defendant had been given the opportunity to sell the hotel as a going concern and could not reasonably complain of the plaintiff's decision to close it. Further, the bank had taken professional advice before making their decision. The allegations of negligence accordingly failed.

Bank of Cyprus (London) Ltd v Gill [1980] 2 Lloyd's Rep 51 (Court of Appeal: Stephenson, Eveleigh and Brandon LJJ). Decision of Lloyd J [1979] 2 Lloyd's Rep 508 affirmed.

2050 —— nervous shock—road accident—parent's shock from seeing injured family in hospital

A mother was informed that her family had been injured in a car accident. She immediately went to the hospital where she saw her family and learnt that her youngest child was dead. There was no dispute that the accident had been caused by the defendant's negligence and the mother claimed damages for nervous shock. On appeal against the dismissal of her claim, *held*, the risk of the mother being severely affected by what she heard and saw was as great a risk as if she had been in or near the collision and accordingly the risk of injury by shock to the mother was not too remote to be a foreseeable consequence of the defendant's negligent driving. Further, the relationship between the mother and the defendant was sufficiently close so that carelessness might be likely to cause damage, and therefore prima facie a duty of care arose. However, considerations of policy limited the scope of duty to those on or near the highway at or near the time of the accident caused by the defendant's negligence and the court would not extend the boundaries of liability any further. The appeal would therefore be dismissed.

McLoughlin v O'Brian (1980) Times, 6th January 1981 (Court of Appeal: Stephenson, Cumming-Bruce and Griffiths LJJ). *Hambrook v Stokes Bros* [1925] 1 KB 141, CA, applied.

2051   —— occupier—whether duty to provide fireman with means of access and egress

Scotland

A widow brought an action against the occupiers of a warehouse for negligently failing to take reasonable care to adopt and maintain adequate fire precautions. Her husband, a fireman, had died from suffocation whilst fighting a fire in the warehouse. The ceiling of the first floor, made of untreated cardboard, had suddenly ignited causing a rush of smoke and hot gases up to the second floor blocking the staircase. On a question of whether the occupiers owed a duty of care to the fireman to provide a fire-screen separating the stairs from the rest of the first floor *held*, an occupier did not owe the same duty of care to a fireman as he did to a worker. The circumstances in which a worker and a fireman entered a building were very different. It would impose an impossible burden on an occupier if he had to take reasonable care to provide firemen with an escape route which would continue to be adequate throughout the firefighting. The firemen were a skilled and disciplined force, aware of the danger of being trapped in the building. The occupiers thus did not owe the firemen the duty to provide them with means of access and egress.

BERMINGHAM v SHER BROS (1980) 124 Sol Jo 117 (House of Lords: LORD DIPLOCK, VISCOUNT DILHORNE, LORD SALMON, LORD FRASER OF TULLYBELTON and LORD KEITH OF KINKEL).

2052   —— oil companies—duty to children—lead content of fuel

The infant plaintiffs brought an action in negligence against an oil company claiming damages and an injunction restraining oil companies from using organo-lead additives in their petroleum for motor vehicles. *Held*, the company had adhered in full to the regulations made by the Secretary of State under the Control of Pollution Act 1974 relating to the maximum permitted amount of lead per litre of fuel. Hence, what it had done was expressly permitted by subordinate legislation authorised by statute and the company had not therefore failed in its duty to the children. To decide otherwise would create a different and inconsistent policy from that of Parliament.

BUDDEN v BP OIL LTD; ALBERT-SPEYER v BP OIL LTD (1980) 124 Sol Jo 376 (Court of Appeal: MEGAW, BRIDGE and CUMMING-BRUCE LJJ).

2053   —— owner of motor vehicle—loan to inexperienced driver

Canada

The defendant lent his motorcycle to the plaintiff, who lost control of it and was seriously injured. In an action for negligence, *held*, the defendant was negligent, as he knew or ought to have known that the plaintiff did not have sufficient experience or knowledge to operate the motorcycle safely, and did not give him any adequate warning of the risks involved or any instructions on how to operate the motorcycle so as to minimise the risk. The maxim volenti non fit injuria did not apply as the plaintiff had no knowledge of the risk involved. However, the plaintiff was guilty of contributory negligence as he rode the motorcycle knowing of his own lack of proficiency. The fault would be apportioned ninety per cent to the plaintiff and ten per cent to the defendant.

STERMER v LAWSON (1979) 107 DLR (3d) 36 (Court of Appeal of British Columbia). Decision of Supreme Court of British Columbia (1978) 79 DLR (3d) 366, 1978 Halsbury's Abridgment para. 2013 reversed in part.

2054   —— prison officer—liability of officer for negligence of prisoner

Canada

The plaintiff was severely injured when the car in which she was a passenger, driven by the defendant W and owned by the defendant M left the road. W was an inmate of a minimum security penal institution, and at the time of the accident had held a temporary day pass from the institution, which had been authorised by the defendant S. The plaintiff successfully sued W for damages, but the trial judge dismissed the action against M and S. On appeal *held*, in granting a temporary absence to W, S was acting bona fide in the exercise of the discretion conferred on him by statute and S owed the plaintiff no duty of care in relation to the implementation of that discretion. In any case, S could not have reasonably forseen that if he granted W a temporary pass that W would, by his negligent driving, injure the plaintiff.

TOEWS v MACKENZIE (1980) 109 DLR (3d) 473 (Court of Appeal of British Columbia).

2055   —— **surgeon—duty to disclose risks inherent in operation**

Canada

An orthopaedic surgeon decided to perform an operation on the plaintiff, who had suffered a slipped disc. Following an inquiry by the plaintiff as to the seriousness of the operation, the surgeon informed the plaintiff that he would be well after ten days. The plaintiff gave his consent to the operation being performed. Subsequently, the plaintiff's symptoms reappeared and after a further operation, he suffered permanent damage. He brought an action for trespass against the person and negligence claiming that the surgeon had failed to disclose to him the risks involved in such an operation. The claim was allowed on appeal. On appeal by the surgeon, *held*, in obtaining a patient's consent to treatment, a doctor had to answer any specific questions asked by a patient concerning the risks involved. Further, he had to disclose to him the nature of the proposed operation, its gravity, any material risks and any special or unusual risks involved. However, the scope of the duty of disclosure had to be decided in relation to the circumstances of each case. In the present case, the risks involved were not great and there was no evidence which indicated that specific questions had been asked about the risks involved. Accordingly the appeal would be allowed.

HOPP v LEPP [1980] 4 WWR 645 (Supreme Court of Canada).

2056   **Foreseeability—nervous shock—road accident—shock resulting from sight of injured family**

See *McLoughlin v O'Brian*, para. 2050.

2057   **Negligent misstatement—statement made by local authority—existence of duty of care—liability of authority**

See *L. Shaddock & Associates Pty Ltd v Parramatta City Council*, para. 1808.

2058   —— **statement made by structural engineers—liability**

See *Independent Broadcasting Authority v BICC Construction Ltd*, para. 485.

2059   **Product liability—defective towing coupling—liability of owner and driver of vehicle and manufacturer of coupling**

The plaintiff's husband and son were killed in a road accident in 1972 when their car was struck by a trailer which had become detached from a Land Rover when a faulty coupling snapped. The Land Rover was owned by the first defendant and had been driven by his employee, the second defendant. The defective coupling had been manufactured by the third defendant and sold to the fourth defendant who had supplied it to the first defendant. The plaintiff claimed damages in tort against all the defendants. The first defendant brought third party proceedings against the fourth defendant on the ground that the coupling was not fit for the purpose for which it was sold under the Sale of Goods Act 1893, s. 14. The fourth defendant brought proceedings against the third defendant for negligent misrepresentation and breach of warranty. At first instance the first and second defendants were found liable in tort and the third defendant for faulty manufacture. The fourth defendant was found not liable in tort and, although in breach of s. 14, not liable to indemnify the first defendant because of the latter's own negligence. On appeal, *held*, the first and second defendants were negligent in not noticing the defective coupling and were accordingly liable to the plaintiff. The fourth defendant was liable to indemnify the first defendant to the extent that it was twenty-five per cent liable to the plaintiff in damages, on the ground that the damage sustained was a natural consequence of the breach of warranty, there being no break in the chain of causation between the warranty and the accident. The fourth defendant could not recover from the third defendant however, as the fourth defendant had not relied on any representation made by the third defendant, who had not, in fact, warranted the goods either. Although the third defendant had been negligent in manufacturing a defective towing coupling, the fourth defendant was not within the narrow limits of those who were sufficiently proximate between the wrongdoer and the person suffering damage as to be able to recover economic loss. They could not therefore recover damages for their financial loss in being liable to indemnify the owner.

LAMBERT V LEWIS [1980] 1 All ER 978 (Court of Appeal: STEPHENSON, ROSKILL and LAWTON LJJ). Decision of Stocker J [1978] 1 Lloyd's Rep 610, 1978 Halsbury's Abridgment para. 2026, reversed in part.

Sale of Goods Act 1893, s. 14 now Sale of Goods Act 1979, Sch. 1, para. 6.

2060 ——supplier of goods—duty to third parties—adequacy of warning

Canada

A supplier sold retreaded tyres to a road haulage company, but warned the company of their unsuitability for usage on heavy goods vehicles. The warning was ignored and subsequently a fatal accident occurred. The question arose as to whether, despite the warnings of the unsuitability of the tyres, the supplier owed a duty to other road users. *Held*, where the supplier of a product knew that the user intended to put it to a use that would endanger third parties, the supplier owed a duty to those persons not to sell the product. The supplier was not absolved from liability by issuing a warning about the product if he nevertheless sold the product, knowing that it would be put to an unsuitable use.

GOOD-WEAR TREADERS LTD V D & B HOLDINGS LTD (1979) 98 DLR (3d) 59 (Supreme Court of Nova Scotia, Appeal Division).

2061 Standard of care—education authority—provision of transport for pupils

See *Myton v Wood*, para. 2041.

2062 ——parental responsibility for children—whether parents negligent

Canada

The plaintiff, a child, lost the sight of one eye when he was shot by a boy aged thirteen with an air rifle. The negligence of the boy was conceded and his parents were found to be negligent in leaving the gun and ammunition readily accessible to their son who would naturally be attracted by the rifle. Prior to the injury in his right eye the plaintiff had only poor vision in his left eye and so the accident left him seriously disabled. The judge calculated the award by estimating that the plaintiff's earning capacity had been reduced by 25 per cent. The parents appealed against the findings of negligence and the plaintiff cross-appealed on the quantum of damages. *Held*, the judge had correctly applied the law to the facts and the appeal against liability would be dismissed. On the question of damages a more appropriate figure for the reduction in earning capacity would be 50 per cent, and general damages for the loss of the eye should be increased in view of the serious disability and consequent loss of amenities. The cross-appeal would therefore be allowed and the award of damages increased.

FLOYD V BOWERS (1979) 106 DLR (3d) 702 (Court of Appeal of Ontario). Decision of High Court of Ontario (1978) 21 OR (2d) 204, 1979 Halsbury's Abridgment para. 1985 varied.

2063　　—— **profession of special skill—doctor**

An obstetrician was sued in negligence for the brain damage suffered by a baby he had delivered by Caesarean section following a forceps examination. At first instance he was held liable in negligence and damages were awarded against him. The decision was subsequently reversed by the Court of Appeal and on appeal to the House of Lords, their Lordships emphasised their disagreement with suggestions in the Court of Appeal that an error of clinical judgment by a doctor was not the same thing as negligence. The test of an error of judgment in such a case was the standard of care of the ordinary skilled man exercising and professing to have a particular skill. Accordingly an error of judgment might or might not have been negligent. Their Lordships, nevertheless, affirmed the majority decision of the Court of Appeal, in reversing the first instance decision that the obstetrician was negligent, in that there was insufficient evidence of the negligence disclosed. It was held that the trial judge's conclusion of fact that the defendant had pulled too long and too hard was primarily an inference from the primary facts and as no issue of credibility was involved his conclusion was open to reassessment by an appellate court; consequently the Court of Appeal had been entitled to reject his finding of negligence.

WHITEHOUSE V JORDAN [1981] 1 All ER 267 (House of Lords: LORD WILBERFORCE, LORD EDMUND-DAVIES, LORD FRASER OF TULLYBELTON, LORD RUSSELL OF KILLOWEN and LORD BRIDGE OF HARWICH). Decision of the Court of Appeal [1980] 1 All ER 650, 1979 Halsbury's Abridgment para. 1986 affirmed. *The Hontestroom* [1927] AC 37, HL, and *Powell v Streatham Manor Nursing Home* [1935] AC 243, HL, applied. Doctrine formulated in *Bolam v Friern Hospital Management Committee* [1957] 2 All ER at 121 approved.

2064　　—— **safety provisions at ice hockey game**

Canada

A spectator at a game of ice hockey was hit in the eye by a flying hockey stick, whilst standing at the side of the ice rink. He brought an action, for damages, in negligence against the ice rink owners. The court held that the owners were in breach of their duty to take reasonable care but that the spectator was contributorily negligent. On appeal by the owners, *held*, there was screen protection at both ends of the rink and the goal areas. The spectator had chosen to stand in an unguarded place in order to have a better view of the game and the owners were not therefore liable for his injury.

KLYNE V TOWN OF INDIAN HEAD (1979) 107 DLR (3d) 692 (Court of Appeal of Saskatchewan). Decision of Court of Queen's Bench of Saskatchewan [1978] 6 WWR 743, 1979 Halsbury's Abridgment para. 152, reversed.

2065　　**Statutory duty—breach of statutory duty—particulars of breach— degree of particularity required**

See *Richardson v National Coal Board*, para. 2149.

NORTHERN IRELAND

Halsbury's Laws of England (4th edn.), Vol. 8, paras. 1637–1647

2066　　**Northern Ireland Act 1974—extension of interim period**

The Northern Ireland Act 1974 (Interim Period Extension) Order 1980, S.I. 1980 No. 993 (in force on 14th July 1980), extends until 16th July 1981 the period specified in the Northern Ireland Act 1974, s. 1 (4) for the operation of the temporary provisions for the government of Northern Ireland contained in Sch. 1 to the 1974 Act.

2067   Northern Ireland (Emergency Provisions) Act 1978—continuance

The Northern Ireland (Emergency Provisions) Act 1978 (Continuance) Order 1980, S.I. 1980 No. 1049 (in force on 25th July 1980), continues in force the temporary provisions of the 1978 Act (except s. 12 and Sch. 1, which relate to the detention of terrorists) for a period of six months from 25th July 1980.

2068   The Northern Ireland (Emergency Provisions) Act 1978 (Continuance) (No. 2) Order 1980, S.I. 1980 No. 1938 (in force on 25th January 1981), continues in force the temporary provisions of the Northern Ireland (Emergency Provisions) Act 1978 (except s. 12 and Sch. 1 relating to the detention of terrorists) for a period of six months from 25th January 1981.

NUISANCE

Halsbury's Laws of England (4th edn.), Vol. 34, paras. 301–400

2069   Abstraction of underground water—abstraction in excess of statutory limit—right of action

See *Re National Capital Commission*, para. 3123.

2070   Adoption of nuisance—nuisance created by gipsies—liability of landowner

A company bought an action for damages against the local borough council on the ground, inter alia, of nuisance, caused by gipsy encampments on their land, which was leased from the borough council. Five years had elapsed before other sites were found for the gipsies, who had then moved off the company's leased land. Orders for possession had been obtained but the county council, who had a statutory duty to provide adequate sites for gipsies, had persuaded the borough council not to enforce them. The issue for the court to decide was the extent of liability of the borough council, as a landlord, for unauthorised use for purposes which caused a nuisance. *Held*, an occupier of land was liable for the acts of a trespasser causing nuisance if he continued or adopted the nuisance. Notwithstanding the pressure put upon the borough council by the Department of the Environment and the county council, not to move gipsies needlessly, the borough council had power under the Caravan Sites and Control of Development Act 1960, s. 24 to provide sites, but had not considered the possibility. Nor was it reasonable to take five years to find a solution and the council, in failing to take steps to move the gipsies, had adopted the nuisance. They were thus liable for any loss suffered by the company due to the presence of the gipsies.

PAGE MOTORS LTD V EPSOM AND EWELL BOROUGH COUNCIL (1980) 124 Sol Jo 273 (Chancery Division: BALCOMBE J).

2071   Continuing nuisance—award of damages—appeal—injunction granted in lieu of damages

See *Kennaway v Thompson*, para. 1631.

2072   Public nuisance—criminal proceedings—elements of offence

See *R v Soul*, para. 629.

2073   Statutory nuisance—abatement—whether vacant possession of premises sufficient

The tenants of a council house alleged that the state of the house constituted a statutory nuisance within the Public Health Act 1936, s. 92 (1). Justices ordered that the defects were to be remedied. The tenants were rehoused by the local authority and the house was left vacant. On appeal, the local authority contended that by virtue of the premises having been left vacant the nuisance had been abated. The house was subsequently demolished but the court was asked to deal with the matters arising out of the case as many similar cases would be affected by the decision. *Held*, where premises were found to be a statutory nuisance within s. 92 (1) by reason of being in such a state as to be prejudicial to health, a nuisance was not abated by the owner obtaining and keeping possession of them. To abate a statutory nuisance something had to be done to the premises. Where an owner was a local authority and intended to demolish the premises concerned, that fact was to be taken into consideration by the court when drawing up the nuisance order. The appeal would be dismissed.

LAMBETH LONDON BOROUGH COUNCIL v STUBBS (1980) Times, 15th May (Queen's Bench Division: WALLER LJ and BROWN J). Dicta of Lord Widgery CJ in *Nottingham District Council v Newton* [1974] 1 WLR 923 at 930, 1974 Halsbury's Abridgment para. 2399 and *Northern Ireland Trailers Ltd v Preston Corporation* [1972] 1 WLR 203 applied.

2074   —— nuisance order—duty of justices

See *Lambeth London Borough Council v Stubbs*, para. 2073.

OPEN SPACES AND HISTORIC BUILDINGS

Halsbury's Laws of England (4th edn.), Vol. 34, paras. 401–1000

2075   Articles

The Ancient Monuments and Archaeological Areas Act 1979, G. Bennett: (1980) LS Gaz 1009.

Listed Buildings—Planning Law and Planning Reality, P. H. Morgan and S. M. Nott: 1980 JPL 715.

2076   Green belt land—compulsory purchase order—motorway—consent of minister—validity

See *Lovelock v Minister of Transport*, para. 1395.

2077   Listed buildings—criteria for listing certain buildings

The Secretary of State for the Environment announced in a press notice of 12th November 1980, the criteria which he applies in selected buildings of 1914–39 for inclusion in the statutory list of buildings of architectural or historic interest. The criteria are: (1) Selection by building style (a) classical (b) modern and (c) vernacular. (2) Selection by building type (a) churches, chapels and other places of public worship (b) cinemas, theatres, hotels and other places of public entertainment (c) commercial and industrial premises (including shops and offices) (d) schools, colleges and educational buildings (e) flats (f) houses and housing estates (g) municipal and other public buildings (h) railway stations, airport terminals and other places associated with public transport (i) miscellaneous. (3) Selection should reflect the work of the principal architects of the period.

2078   National Heritage Act 1980

The National Heritage Act 1980 establishes a National Heritage Memorial Fund for providing financial assistance for the acquisition, maintenance and preservation of land, buildings and objects of outstanding historic and other interest, to make new provision in relation to the arrangements for accepting property in satisfaction of capital transfer tax and estate duty; and to provide for payments out of public funds in respect of the loss of or damage to objects loaned to or displayed in local museums and other institutions. The Act received the royal assent on 31st March 1980, and comes into force on a day or days to be appointed.

Section 1 provides for the establishment of the National Heritage Memorial Fund to be administered by a body corporate comprising Trustees appointed by the Secretary of State and the Chancellor of the Duchy of Lancaster ("The Ministers"). Provision as to the status, tenure of office, expenses, staff and proceedings of the Trustees is made in Sch. 1. Section 2 provides for payments into the Fund. The powers of the Trustees to make loans and grants out of the Fund and to spend money otherwise than by making grants and loans, are contained in ss. 3, 4. By s. 5 the Trustees are permitted to accept gifts of money or other property but there are restrictions on the retention of such property. Any money in the Fund not required to meet current expenditure may be invested: s. 6. Under s. 7 the annual reports and accounts of the Trustees must be laid before Parliament.

Section 8 provides that the Ministers may reimburse the Inland Revenue Commissioners for the tax foregone in respect of property accepted in satisfaction of capital transfer tax and outstanding estate duty (s. 13 extends this to any interest on such tax or duty). By s. 9 the Ministers then have control over the disposal of that property and are required to lay before Parliament an annual statement giving particulars of disposals (by s. 11 such conveyances and transfers are exempt from stamp duty). Section 10 concerns receipts and expenses in respect of property accepted in satisfaction of tax under s. 8 and disposed of under s. 9.

Section 12 transfers from the Treasury to the Ministers certain functions relating to the acceptance of property by the Commissioners and makes their acceptance subject to the agreement of the Ministers. Ministerial functions exercisable under ss. 8–12 may be transferred to the National Heritage Memorial Fund Trustees by Order in Council approved in draft by both Houses of Parliament: s. 14. The National Land Fund is abolished by s. 15.

Section 16 makes provision for either of the Ministers to indemnify certain institutions or bodies where an object is lent to another institution or body on terms approved by him and the Treasury, and the object is lost or damaged while on loan.

Any sums received by the Ministers for making payments under the Act are to be made out of moneys provided by Parliament and sums received are to be paid into the Consolidated Fund: s. 17. Section 18 provides for commencment of the Act and s. 19 relates to interpretation, repeals (contained in Sch. 2) and the scope of the Act.

PARLIAMENT

Halsbury's Laws of England (4th edn.), Vol. 34, paras. 1001–1506

2079   **House of Commons—Members' Fund**

The Resolution of the House of Commons, dated 4th December 1980 (S.I. 1980 No. 1899), passed in pursuance of the House of Commons Members' Fund Act 1948, s. 3, varies from 1st December 1980 the maximum annual amounts of the periodical payments which may be made out of the House of Commons Members' Fund under the House of Commons Members' Fund Act 1939.

2080   **Members of Parliament—register of members' interests—Select Committee Report**

The Select Committee on Members' Interests has made a report (HC 337, Session 1979–80). The Register of Members' Interests was available for inspection from 14th January 1980. Five members had not declared their interests. They have concluded that a member who sponsors a function in the Palace of Westminster from which sponsorship he receives a taxable benefit should declare the source of the benefit. The receipt of a gift in relation to a member's parliamentary duties, other than from overseas (to which category 7 applies), should be registered under category 5 (b) (financial sponsorships); and that the register should record (for the present Parliament) sponsored overseas visits undertaken since the commencement of the Parliament.

2081   Official Report of Parliamentary Debates—references in court proceedings

The House of Commons has given general leave for reference to be made in court proceedings to the Official Report of Parliamentary Debates and to reports and evidence of committees. The House has also passed a motion that, notwithstanding its resolution of 21st April 1837, it would not entertain any complaint of contempt of the House or breach of privilege in respect of the publication of reports of evidence given by witnesses before select committttees meeting in public before such evidence should have been reported to the House. See *The Times*, 1st November 1980.

2082   Statutes—royal assent

During 1980 sixty-eight public general Acts and two ecclesiastical Measures received the royal assent. Of the Acts, twelve related to Scotland, and two to Northern Ireland. Of the remainder, eight were consolidation Acts.

PARTNERSHIP

Halsbury's Laws of England (3rd edn.), Vol. 28, paras. 925–1169

2083   Articles

Fiduciary Duty on Dissolution, Henry E. Markson: 130 NLJ 825.
Offences by Partners, J. Edmondson (liabilities of partners for offences of other partners): 144 JP Jo 188.

2084   Partner—fiduciary duties of partners—duty to inform partner of change in facts

Canada
The plaintiff and defendant companies were parties to a joint development venture. The defendant proposed that it should purchase the plaintiff's interest and that the partnership should be terminated, as planning permission for development had been refused. This statement was true when made, but subsequently the defendant had reason to believe that the planning authority would give its approval. It did not reveal this information to the plaintiff, who later brought an action to set aside the termination of partnership agreement. *Held*, the defendant owed a fiduciary duty to disclose all material facts, and was therefore bound to disclose the information to the plaintiff. Accordingly the agreement would be set aside.
Hogar Estates Ltd in Trust v Shebron Holdings Ltd (1979) 25 OR (2d) 543 (Supreme Court of Ontario).

2085   —— two separate firms each with same two partners—whether knowledge of one partner's client's affairs can be imputed to other partner

Scotland
The owner of a farm indicated to his solicitor, a partner in a firm of solicitors, that he was expecting an offer from a potential purchaser through another firm of solicitors, but that he wished to consider the offer before acceptance. The owner's solicitor, contrary to his instructions, sent an offer to sell the farm to the potential purchaser's solicitors and contracts were exchanged on the parties' behalf. The two firms of solicitors were in fact partnerships of the same two solicitors, one representing the owner and the other the purchaser. The owner refused to complete on the ground that the fact that he had not instructed his solicitor to send out the offer was known to the purchaser's solicitor. *Held*, whilst notice to one partner of any matter relating to the partnership's affairs operated as notice to the partnership, this did not apply to the affairs of the clients of the partnership. Accordingly, the

relevant knowledge of the owner's solicitor could not be imputed to the purchaser's solicitor. The purchaser could therefore take advantage of the offer ostensibly made on the owner's behalf.

CAMPBELL V MCCREATH 1975 SC 81 (Outer House).

2086   **Partnership agreement—covenant in deed of partnership— restraint of trade—validity**

See *Geraghty v Minter*, para. 2914; *Hensman v Traill*, para. 1890.

2087   **Partnership bank account—cheque drawn on account by one partner—liability of other partner**

See *Ringham v Hackett*, para. 262.

PATENTS AND INVENTIONS

Halsbury's Laws of England (3rd edn.), Vol. 29, paras. 1–338

2088   **Application—description filed in foreign language without trans- lation—filing date of application—discretion to permit late filing of translation**

Under the Patents Rules 1978, r. 20 (1) (a) all documents other than drawings, whether making up an application or replacing such documents, must be in the English language. By r. 113 (1) any document which is in a foreign language must be accompanied by a translation in English. The applicants filed an application with a description in German on 14th November 1978. The English translation was not filed until 17th November 1978 and the applicants were informed that the filing date of their application was the 17th November. *Held*, the filing date of the application was 14th November 1978 because, for the purposes of establishing the filing date, the description need not comply with r. 20 (1) (a). However, the application would be refused as it did not comply with r. 113 (1). Further, although there was a discretion to extend the time for filing the translation required by r. 113 (1), it should not be exercised on the facts in the instant case.

ROHDE AND SCHWARZ'S APPLICATION [1980] RPC 155 (Patent Office).

2089   **—— opposition—amendment of notice—effect of transitional provisions**

An application was originally opposed by two individuals. Their contentions were rejected, and one of the opponents appealed. After the appointed day for the coming into operation of the Patents Act 1977, the appellant was allowed to amend his notice of opposition to refer to documents said to anticipate the claimed invention. The respondent claimed that such an amendment should not have been allowed since no issue had been joined on the amended notice of opposition before the appointed day, and accordingly the effect of the transitional provisions contained in Sch. 4, para. 4 of the Act was that the ground of opposition must be taken to have abated immediately before the appointed day. *Held*, Sch. 4, para. 17 provided that issue was joined on a notice of opposition to the grant of a patent under the Patents Act 1949, s. 14 when the applicant for the patent filed a counter statement setting out the grounds on which the opposition was contested. In the present case, the original notice of opposition had been put in and a counter statement had been filed before the appointed day and accordingly issue had been joined. It had been correct to allow the amendment since it would have been admitted under the old law, and the appeal would proceed on that basis.

STANDARD OIL COMPANY (FAHRIG AND OTHERS' APPLICATION) [1980] RPC 359 (Patents Court: WHITFORD J).

2090   —— —— anticipation—semi-synthetic penicillin

See *Beecham Group Ltd's (Amoxycillin) Application*, para. 2092.

2091   —— —— conversion to patent of addition—right of appeal

In opposition proceedings, an application to convert the application in suit to one for a patent of addition to a cited patent was considered at the same time as the opposition. The application to convert was successful and the opponents appealed. *Held*, the propriety of the decision to allow the conversion could not be raised by way of appeal. There was no provision in the Patents Act 1949 for an appeal by an opponent as there was no provision for such an opposition. The appeal would be dismissed, and the hearing would proceed on the basis that the application was to proceed as a patent of addition.

HAUNI-WERKE KORBER & CO KG's PATENT OF ADDITION [1980] FSR 121 (Chancery Division: WHITFORD J).

2092   —— —— obviousness—test of obviousness

The applicants held a basic patent and a patent of addition on semi-synthetic penicillins. They subsequently developed a compound, known as Amoxycillin, which was found to be orally absorbed in humans exceptionally well, showing an improvement in blood-level concentration over previous compounds developed by them. Their application in respect of Amoxycillin was opposed on the grounds of obviousness and anticipation. *Held*, TEMPLEMAN LJ dissenting, (i) it was sufficient to found an objection of obviousness if it could be shown that it would appear to anyone skilled in the art but lacking in inventive capacity that to try the step or process in question would be worthwhile. However, that approach depended on there being extant some recognised problem or need. If the skilled man had no such problem or need in mind, the mere selection of the line of research could itself demonstrate that he possessed some inventive capacity. The evidence did not suggest that a higher blood level was an objective which the applicants had particularly in mind or that there was any reason to expect it. Accordingly, an inventive capacity had been shown and the obviousness objection would fail. (ii) The applicants' patent of addition did not reveal that Amoxycillin would necessarily prove suitable for treatment of humans. Accordingly, the anticipation objection would fail.

BEECHAM GROUP LTD's (AMOXYCILLIN) APPLICATION [1980] RPC 261 (Court of Appeal: BUCKLEY, BROWNE and TEMPLEMAN LJJ). *May and Baker's Patent* (1948) 65 RPC 255 and *Flour Oxidizing Co Ltd v Carr & Co Ltd* (1908) 25 RPC 428 followed.

2093   —— priority date—application under International Convention

In a case involving a patent application where priority was being claimed from the date of a Japanese application, the question arose as to whether the claim was fairly based on the matter disclosed in the Japanese application, pursuant to the Patents Act 1949, s. 5 (4). *Held*, "matter disclosed" included anything relevant in the foreign application which could form the subject of a patent application and which, in the absence of evidence to the contrary, could be regarded as something for which protection in the foreign country had been sought; it was not only the actual claim in the foreign application which should be compared with that in the United Kingdom application. The claim in the instant case was entitled to the priority date of the Japanese application.

CANON KK's APPLICATION [1980] RPC 133 (Patents Appeal Tribunal: GRAHAM J). *Kopat's Patent* [1965] RPC 404 applied.

2094   —— publication of application—meaning of "publication"

By the Patents Act 1977, s. 16 (1) the Comptroller must publish an application as soon as possible after the end of the prescribed period, unless the application is withdrawn or refused before preparations for its publication have been completed by the Patents Office. Under the Patents Rules 1979, r. 28 the Comptroller may determine when the technical preparations for publication are to be treated as having been completed. The applicants were informed that the application was expected to be published on 24th October 1979 (i.e. a few days after the prescribed period) and technical preparations were to be treated as having been completed on 25th July 1979. On 28th August 1979 the applicants requested withdrawal of the application; the Patents Office decided that the request had been filed too late, but agreed that the request was received before the specification of the application was in such a form that it could have been sent to the printers. *Held*, the Patents Office were entitled to refuse the request, as it had been filed after technical preparations for its publication had been completed. The fact that the specification was not ready for printing was not relevant, as for the purposes of s. 16 and r. 28 "publication" was not synonymous with "printing" but, according to s. 130 (1), required only that the application should be made available to the public.

PIERCE CHEMICAL COMPANY'S APPLICATION [1980] RPC 232 (Patents Court: GRAHAM J).

2095   Comptroller-General of Patents—annual report

The 97th report of the Comptroller-General of Patents, Designs and Trade Marks has been published as HC 580. It discloses that in 1979 there were 44,666 applications for United Kingdom patents. Of these 1,050 were filed under the Patents Act 1949; these were all divisional applications from applications filed before 1st June 1978. The 43,616 applications under the Patents Act 1977 included 326 applications originally filed, searched and published under the Patent Co-operation Treaty which have been perfected into United Kingdom applications and 62 applications originally searched and published by the European Patent Office and converted into United Kingdom applications. During the year, 3,082 applications under the European Patent Convention and 220 applications under the Patent Co-operation Treaty were filed at the Patent Office for onward transmission to the relevant international authority. Some 203,276 patents were renewed; this figure is almost unchanged from 1978. There were 5,111 applications for the registration of designs in 1979; 36 fewer than in 1978. The number of trade marks registered in the year, 10,036, was also lower than in 1978 but at much the same level as in 1977. The number of trade mark renewals in 1979 was 14,379 (57 per cent of the total due) and the report notes the continuance of the apparent trend towards a lower rate of renewal.

2096   Infringement—action for infringement—discovery of documents

Australia

In an action for infringement of a patent, and a counterclaim for its revocation, the judge ordered discovery of documents relating to research on the claimed invention. The proprietor of the patent sought to have the order set aside on the ground that evidence of experimental work carried out in England was irrelevant to the proceedings in Australia unless it could be shown that the state of the art in England was substantially the same as it was in Australia. *Held*, all relevant documents which might directly or indirectly enable the parties to advance their own case or damage that of their opponent would be discoverable, and their admissibility or otherwise at the trial would be immaterial. The experiments carried out in England were relevant to assist the defendant in examining the alleged invention against the background of the state of the art in Australia. Accordingly the appeal would be dismissed.

WELLCOME FOUNDATION LTD v VR LABORATORIES (AUST) PTY LTD (1980) 29 ALR 261 (Federal Court of Australia). *Compagnie Financiere et Commerciale du Pacifique v Peruvian Guano Co* (1882) 11 QBD 55 at 63 applied.

2097   —— inspection of property and documents

See *Roamer Watch Co SA v African Textile Distributors*, para. 892.

2098   —— interlocutory injunction—whether designs dictated by function

The plaintiffs, proprietors of registered designs for moulds for producing wax candles in the shape of various kinds of fruit, sought an interlocutory injunction preventing the defendants from manufacturing similar moulds. *Held*, the plaintiffs had to establish that the features of their registered designs were not dictated solely by function, but infringement of their registered designs would, in any case, be difficult to prove in view of the restricted degree of originality in such commonplace articles as fruit. The application, therefore, would be refused.

CONSTABLE V CLARKSON [1980] FSR 123 (Court of Appeal: BRANDON and BRIGHTMAN LJJ). *American Cyanamid Co v Ethicon Ltd* [1975] AC 396, 1974 Halsbury's Abridgment para. 2459 applied.

2099   International Patent Co-operation Treaty—regulations

The Assembly of the International Patent Co-operation Union adopted a revision of the Regulations under the Patent Co-operation Treaty on 1st May 1979 (see Cmnd. 7783). Rules 15, 16, 47 and 57 have been amended and a new rule, r. 96, has been added. Rule 96 contains a schedule of fees which are expressed in Swiss francs. The basic fee for an international application (not more than 30 sheets) is now Fr. 325 (if more than 30 sheets, an additional charge of Fr. 6 per sheet in excess of 30 is made); the designation fee is Fr. 78; the handling fee is Fr. 100; and the additional handling fee is Fr. 100.

2100   The Assembly of the Patent Co-operation Union adopted amendments to the Regulations under the Patent Co-operation Treaty on 16th June 1980. The amendments take effect from 1st October 1980 and 1st January 1980 and have been published by HMSO as Cmnd 8078.

2101   Restoration of lapsed patent—application—filing of renewal fee

The proprietors' patent lapsed through failure to pay the renewal fee. Eleven months later the renewal fee for the following year was filed. Consequently the Patent Office informed the proprietors that the patent had lapsed the year before. Meanwhile the Patents Act 1977 had come into force and, as by that time the patent had been lapsed for over a year, an application for restoration could not be entertained, unless the filing of the renewal fee could be regarded as an application. *Held*, a person would only file a renewal fee if he thought the patent was still in force; thus he could not be said to have intended to apply for restoration of the patent when filing the fee.

DYNAMICS RESEARCH AND MANUFACTURING INC'S PATENT [1980] RPC 179 (Patents Appeal Tribunal: WHITFORD J).

2102   —— patent lapsed before commencement of Patents Act 1977— preservation of right to restoration under Patents Act 1949

A patent lapsed in April 1978 because of failure to pay the renewal fee. In April 1979, the proprietors applied for restoration of the patent and the question arose whether the case should proceed under the Patents Act 1977, which had come into force on 1st June 1978, or under the Patents Act 1949, because the patent had lapsed before 1st June 1978. *Held*, the application fell to be dealt with under the 1949 Act. A patent which lapsed before 1st June 1978 by reason of failure to pay a renewal fee was not an "existing patent" within the 1977 Act, s. 127 (7), and hence the 1977 Act did not apply to it. The Interpretation Act 1978, s. 16 (1), provided that where an enactment was repealed, the repeal did not, unless the contrary intention appeared, affect any right or privilege accrued under that enactment. The proprietors had accrued before the commencement of the 1977 Act the right under the 1949 Act, s. 27, to have the patent restored if they complied with the requirements of the 1949 Act. Since the 1977 Act did not show any contrary intention, that right survived the repeal of s. 27 and proceedings could continue as if s. 27 remained in force.

CONVEX LTD'S PATENT [1980] RPC 423 (Court of Appeal: BUCKLEY, ACKNER and OLIVER LJJ). *Free Lanka Insurance Co Ltd v Ranasinghe* [1964] AC 541, PC applied.

2103   Revocation of patent—appeal against revocation—need for leave to appeal

Proceedings for revocation of a patent were brought under the Patents Act 1949, s. 33. A question arose on the interpretation of the transitional provisions contained in the Patents Act 1977, Sch. 4, as to whether the patentees required leave to appeal to the Court of Appeal. By para. 6 (1) (a) of Sch. 4 where an application has been made under s. 33 before the "appointed day" under the 1977 Act, any appeal or further appeal must be prosecuted under the old law; and under the old law no leave to appeal was required. By para. 11 (6) of Sch. 4, s. 97 (3) of the 1977 Act applies to any decision of the Patents Court on an appeal, instituted on or after the appointed day, from a decision of the Comptroller under s. 33. Section 97 (3) provides that leave to appeal to the Court of Appeal must be obtained for an appeal under the section. In the instant case the application was made before the appointed day and the patentees appealed to the Patents Court after the appointed day. *Held*, there was a direct conflict between paras. 6 (1) (a) and 11 (6) as to whether leave to appeal was required. As a person should not be deprived of a vested right unless legislation clearly and unequivocally deprived him of that right, para. 6 (1) (a) should prevail over para. 11 (6). Thus leave to appeal was not required.

STANDARD BRANDS' PATENT [1980] RPC 187 (Court of Appeal: BUCKLEY, GOFF LJJ and SIR DAVID CAIRNS).

2104   Rules

The Patents (Amendment) Rules 1980, S.I. 1980 No. 137 amend the Patent Rules 1978, 1978 Halsbury's Abridgment para. 2075, so as to increase from 6th May 1980, with certain exceptions mentioned below, the fees payable under the Patents Act 1977. The exceptions are fees payable for the sealing of a patent under the Patents Act 1949 in respect of which the complete specification was accepted on or after 27th February 1980 but before 6th May 1980 and fees for the renewal of a patent in respect of any year beginning on or after 6th May 1980; these fees are increased on 27th February 1980.

2105

The Patents (Amendment No. 2) Rules 1980, S.I. 1980 No. 498 amend the Patents (Amendment) Rules 1980, para. 2104, so as to prevent the fee payable on a request for the sealing of a patent under the Patents Act 1949 being increased on 6th May 1980 from £20 to £25. Further, persons who, on or after 27th February 1980, requested the sealing of such a patent in respect of which the complete specification had not been accepted before that date, and who have already paid a fee of £25, are to have the sum of £5 remitted to them.

2106

The Patents (Amendment No. 3) Rules 1980, S.I. 1980 No. 1146 (in force on 1st September 1980), further amend the Patents Rules 1978, 1978 Halsbury's Abridgment para. 2075. They extend the period within which an application for a patent must comply with the Patents Act 1977 and the 1978 Rules as amended from three years and six months to four years and six months. The rules also make corresponding extensions in relation to applications for European patents (UK) and international applications for patents.

2107

The Patents (Amendment No. 4) Rules 1980, S.I. 1980 No. 1783 (in force on 5th January 1981), further amend the Patents Rules 1978, 1978 Halsbury's Abridgment para. 2075. The rules amend certain time limits and other requirements for filing documents in the Patents Office.

PENSIONS AND SUPERANNUATION

2108 Article

Assessment of Pensions Loss on Unfair Dismissal, D. G. Ballantine: 130 NLJ 516.

2109 Appeal Tribunals—posthumous appeals

The Pensions Appeal Tribunals (Posthumous Appeals) Order 1980, S.I. 1980 No. 1082 (in force on 1st September 1980), modifies the Pensions Appeals Tribunals Act 1943 so as to make provision for appeals, to a Pensions Appeal Tribunal or appropriate court in the case of Scotland and Northern Ireland, to be brought or continued under the Act after the death of a claimant. Provision is also made for the modification of restrictions in relation to the Secretary of State's powers to pay awards following decisions in the appeals.

2110 —— rules

The Pensions Appeal Tribunals (England and Wales) Rules 1980, S.I. 1980 No. 1120 (in force on 1st September 1980), consolidate and amend the Pensions Appeal Tribunals (England and Wales) Rules 1971, as amended. The amendments include modifications to provide for the carrying on of appeals after the death of the original claimant. An appeal which has been struck out after having been on the deferred list for a year may not be brought again without leave and the payment of the Tribunal's fees and expenses are now to be determined by the Lord Chancellor with the consent of the Minister for the Civil Service.

2111 British Transport—pensions

The British Transport (Pensions of Employees) Order 1980, S.I. 1980 No. 1351 (in force on 30th September 1980), provide for certain changes in connection with pension schemes in the nationalised transport sector which are desirable in consequence of the Transport Act 1980, Pt II, which provides for the transfer of the undertaking of the National Freight Corporation to a successor company. Article 4 amends certain provisions of the British Transport (Pensions of Employees) (No. 1) Order 1969 so that those provisions will be applicable in circumstances where employees are members of pension schemes which are not the responsibility of their employing body by virtue of transport legislation enacted subsequently to the 1969 Order. Article 5 regulates the position of Members of the Corporation's pension schemes who become members of pension schemes for which the British Railways Board are responsible so as to avoid duplication of membership. Articles 6–8 provide for the payment of transfer values in such circumstances, for certain consequential matters and for the determination of questions.

2112 Children's pensions—earnings limit

The Superannuation (Children's Pensions) (Earnings Limit) Order 1980, S.I. 1980 No. 1610 (in force on 24th November 1980), revokes the Superannuation (Children's Pensions) (Earnings Limit) (No. 2) Order 1979, 1979 Halsbury's Abridgment para. 2040. The order increases the financial limit on emoluments received during training, excluding premium returns by children over sixteen, from £694 to £808 per year.

2113 Coal industry—mineworkers' pension scheme—limit on contributions

The Mineworkers' Pension Scheme (Limit on Contributions) Order 1980, S.I. 1980 No. 433 (in force on 25th March 1980), amends the National Coal Board (Finance) Act 1976, s. 2 (3) (b) by increasing the maximum aggregate of payments by the Secretary of State to the National Coal Board to reimburse expenditure incurred towards reducing or eliminating deficiencies in the Mineworkers' Pension Scheme to £41,080,000.

2114   Deaconesses and Lay Workers (Pensions) Measure 1980

See para. 965.

2115   European Assembly—United Kingdom representatives—pensions

The European Assembly (United Kingdom Representatives) Pensions Order 1980, S.I. 1980 No. 1450 (in force on 12th December 1980), is made under the European Assembly (Pay and Pensions) Act 1979, s. 4, 1979 Halsbury's Abridgment para 1191, and makes provision for the pensions payable to, or in respect of, persons who have ceased to be representatives to the Assembly of the European Communities for the United Kingdom constituencies. The benefits provided are similar to those conferred on Members of the House of Commons. Generally, the pension entitlement for representatives who have served for at least four years will be one-sixtieth of their pensionable salary in the last year of service for each year of service, subject to a limit on the number of years service. Part of the pension may be converted into a lump sum.

2116   Firemen—pensions

The Firemen's Pension Scheme (Amendment) Order 1980, S.I. 1980 No. 273 (in force on 1st April 1980), amends the Firemen's Pension Scheme 1973 with effect from the dates specified in art. 2. The order clarifies certain provisions in the 1973 Scheme concerning the accrued pensions of firemen's widows. It also makes amendments in relation to a fireman's absence from duty due to an offence, the earnings limit on repayment of contributions and flat-rate national insurance modifications.

2117   The Firemen's Pension Scheme (Amendment) (No. 2) Order 1980, S.I. 1980 No. 1587 (in force on 1st December 1980), modifies the Firemen's Pension Scheme 1973 in relation to pensionable pay for certain firemen's pension purposes over the period of 1978 and 1979.

2118   The Firemen's Pension Scheme (Amendment) (No. 3) Order 1980, S.I. 1980 No. 1615 (in force on 24th November 1980), amends the Firemen's Pension Scheme Orders 1948 to 1973 in relation to awards or payments to a person who has ceased to be a member of a fire brigade before certain specified dates. The main amendments are concerned with awards under those orders which are at present of specified amounts and which have been statutorily increased. The present order ensures that the amounts of those awards will increase automatically in line with pension increases under the Social Security Pensions Acts 1975.

2119   Gas industry—superannuation scheme—winding up

The Gas (Superannuation Scheme) (Winding Up) Regulations 1980, S.I. 1980 No. 1782 (in force on 1st January 1981), provide for the winding up of the pension schemes listed in the Schedule which provided superannuation benefits for the employees of the former gas undertakings specified therein.

2120   Local government—superannuation

The Local Government Superannuation (Amendment) Regulations 1980, S.I. 1980 No. 216 (in force on 25th March 1980), further amend the 1974 Regulations, 1974 Halsbury's Abridgment para. 2502. The regulations provide for the discontinuance of the modification of the local government superannuation scheme on account of flat-rate retirement pensions under the Social Security Act 1975, s. 28 for periods of employment after 31st March 1980.

2121   The Local Government Superannuation (Amendment) (No. 2) Regulations 1980, S.I. 1980 No. 233 (in force on 1st April 1980), further amend the 1974 Regulations, 1974 Halsbury's Abridgment para. 2502. The regulations provide for contributions to be made to authorities paying gratuities and allowances to ex-employees, and their widows and dependants, of certain local authorities and other bodies which ceased to exist in 1974.

2122　　The Local Government Superannuation (Amendment) (No. 3) Regulations 1980, S.I. 1980 No. 234 (in force on 1st April 1980), amend the Local Government Superannuation Regulations 1974, 1974 Halsbury's Abridgment para. 2502 by (i) providing that employees transferred to other local authorities under the Greater London Council Housing (Staff Transfer and Protection) Order 1979 will remain with the Greater London Council superannuation fund until 1st April 1981; (ii) enabling a "non-pensionable" addition to salary awarded to certain New Town employees to be disregarded for the purposes of the 1974 Regulations; (iii) providing for admission agreements to be made by certain employing bodies; (iv) providing that an employee making payments to avoid reduction of retiring allowance may, on becoming redundant, elect to pay the capital equivalent of any outstanding payments; (v) giving effect to successive relaxations for certain employees of Inland Revenue restrictions, on the return of superannuation contributions; (vi) extending the period during which applications may be made (a) for indirect service to be treated as non-contributing service and (b) for consent to purchase added years; (vii) providing that a female pensionable employee with no husband who gives notice that she wishes to receive certain pension benefits will not have her retiring allowance reduced in respect of service before 1st April 1972.

2123　　**National Freight Corporation—pensions**

The National Freight Corporation (Central Trust) (Amendment) Order 1980, S.I. 1980 No. 657 (in force on 10th June 1980), transfers to the National Freight Corporation (1978) Pension Fund responsibility for the payment of certain supplemental pensions which are at present paid, or due to be paid, by the NFC out of revenue. The rights of the recipients and potential recipients of these pensions are preserved.

The order also deletes provisions in the Trust Deed, constituting the NFC (1978) Pension Fund, which restrict pension schemes and arrangements which can be brought within the fund, to schemes and arrangements which could have been prescribed under the Transport Act 1978, s 19.

2124　　**National Health Service—superannuation**

The National Health Service (Superannuation) Regulations 1980, S.I. 1980 No. 362 (in force on 1st April 1980), consolidate with minor amendments the provisions of the National Health Service (Superannuation) Regulations 1961 to 1978 which provide for the superannuation of persons engaged in the National Health Service. The regulations also include improvements to the National Health Service superannuation scheme relating to the determination of final remuneration, the refunding of contributions, the reduction of pensions on re-employment and the introduction of a "no-detriment" clause to protect the rights of practitioners who would otherwise be adversely affected by the 1978 Regulations, para. 40, 1978 Halsbury's Abridgment para. 2100. The National Insurance (National Health Service Superannuation Scheme—Modification and Non-participation) Regulations 1976, 1976 Halsbury's Abridgment para. 1809 are revoked.

2125　　**—— —— war service**

The National Health Service (Superannuation) (War Service, etc.) Amendment Regulations 1980, S.I. 1980 No. 1949 (in force on 13th January 1981), amend the 1977 Regulations. They provide for the transfer of reckonable war service from the National Health superannuation scheme to certain other schemes, and vice versa, subject to certain conditions. Certain officers in public health service employment who were previously excluded may now apply under the 1977 Regulations to have their war service reckoned for benefit purposes.

2126 Occupational pension scheme—public service

The Occupational Pension Schemes (Public Service Pension Schemes) (Amendment) Regulations 1980, S.I. 1980 No. 288 (in force on 1st April 1980), further amend the Occupational Pension Schemes (Public Service Pension Schemes) Regulations 1978, 1978 Halsbury's Abridgment para. 2107, so as to add a further occupational pension scheme to the Schedule to those regulations.

2127 Official pensions—increase—review

The Pensions Increase (Review) Order 1980, S.I. 1980 No. 1302 (in force on 24th November 1980), increases the rate of public service pensions. Pensions beginning before 12th November 1979 are increased by 16·5 per cent and those beginning after that date are increased by between 8·3 per cent and 1·4 per cent. The order also increases certain deferred lump sums and makes provision for the amount by reference to which any increase in the rate of an official pension is to be calculated to be reduced by the amount equal to the rate of the guaranteed minimum pension entitlement deriving from the employment which gives rise to the official pension.

2128 Police—pensions

The Police Cadets (Pensions) (Amendment) Regulations 1980, S.I. 1980 No. 1260 (in force on 1st October 1980), amend the Police Cadets (Pensions) Regulations 1973 with effect from 1st April, 1980. Under Reg. 5 (3) (a) of the 1973 Regs. an ill-health pension payable to a police cadet is reduced by an amount calculated at an annual rate obtained by multiplying £1·70 by the number of years of pensionable service which the cadet is entitled to reckon. These regulations amend this by limiting the reduction to service before 1st April 1980.

2129

The Police Pensions (Amendment) Regulations 1980, S.I. 1980 No. 82 (in force on 1st March 1980), secure that the recent increase in police pay has effect for pension purposes from 1st September 1978. The levels of police pay recommended by the Committee of Inquiry on the Police (Cmnd. 7283) have been implemented in two stages by the Police (Amendment) Regulations 1978, 1978 Halsbury's Abridgment para. 2147, which have effect from 1st September 1978, and the Police (Amendment) Regulations 1979, 1979 Halsbury's Abridgment para. 2086.

2130

The Police Pensions (Amendment) (No. 2) Regulations 1980, S.I. 1980 No. 272 (in force on 1st April 1980 with effect from the dates specified in reg. 2), amend the Police Pensions Regulations 1973. They contain amendments clarifying the 1973 regulations, making it clear that, in the case of an officer who has elected to uprate his service before 1st April 1972 for a one-third or half rate widow's pension, or who transferred service into the Police Pensions Scheme after that date, and the service concerned amounted to less than a year, all the service concerned reckons towards the widow's accrued pension. Where a widow's accrued pension is calculated as a proportion of her husband's deferred pension, it is his gross deferred pension to which the calculation applies.

A further amendment ensures that officers transferred from the British Airports Authority Constabulary, who were fully paid up for widow's half rate pension when transferred, count all their previous service at half rate for the purpose of calculating a widow's accrued pension. Part III of the Schedule gives officers who have served before 7th August 1961 the right to payment of an ordinary pension after twenty-five years' pensionable service even though they have retired before reaching the age of fifty. Part IV fixes the earnings limit on repayment of contributions for the purposes of the Police Pensions (Amendment) (No. 2) Regulations, 1978 Halsbury's Abridgment para. 2114, reg. 23D, with effect from 6th April 1978.

Part V of the Schedule amends provisions in the 1973 Regulations concerned with flat-rate national insurance modifications. Part VI abolishes the earnings limit on repayment of contributions (referred to in Part IV), with effect from 6th April 1980, although transitional provision is made to extend the time limit for claiming an award under the 1973 Regulations, reg. 23D to allow advantage to be taken of the change in the earnings limit.

2131   The Police Pensions (Amendment) (No. 3) Regulations 1980, S.I. 1980 No. 1616 (in force on 24th November 1980), amend the Police Pensions Regulations 1973 and, in so far as they continue to have effect, the Police Pensions Regulations 1971. These regulations amend the 1971 Regulations, reg. 106 which provides for certain awards under those regulations to be increased by reference to the Pensions (Increase) Act 1971 and orders made thereunder, in that with the effect from 12th November 1979 the relevant orders are made under the Social Security Pensions Act 1975, s. 59. The amendments to the 1973 Regulations and the remaining amendments to the 1971 Regulations are concerned with awards under those Regulations which are at present of specified amounts. The amounts have been increased in line with the increases in pensions made by the Pensions (Increase) Act 1971 and the Social Security Pensions Act 1975.

2132   The Special Constables (Pensions) (Amendment) Regulations 1980, S.I. 1980 No. 1259 (in force on 1st October 1980), amend the Special Constables (Pensions) Regulations 1973 with effect from 1st September 1978. The effect of the amendment is to provide that awards under the 1973 Regulations which have to be calculated by reference to rates of pensionable pay of regular constables for any period after 31st August 1973 and before 1st May 1979, are to be calculated by reference to the higher rates of pensionable pay prescribed for that period by the Police (Pensions) (Amendment) Regulations 1980, para. 2129.

2133   The Police Pensions (Lump Sum Payments to Widows) Regulations 1980, S.I. 1980 No. 1485 (in force on 1st December 1980), provide for payment of a gratuity of £10 in the case of a policeman's widow in receipt of a discretionary increase in her police widow's pension, pursuant to the Police Pensions Regulations 1971, during the week beginning with 1st December 1980, if she is not entitled to a payment by virtue of the Pensioners' Lump Sum Payments Order 1980, para. 2753.

2134   Teachers—superannuation

The Teachers' Superannuation (Amendment) Regulations 1980, S.I. 1980 No. 919 (in force on 4th August 1980), further amend the Teachers' Superannuation Regulations 1976, 1976 Halsbury's Abridgment para. 944. Regulation 3 provides that the amendments are not to apply to certain persons who so elect. Parts II and III have retrospective effect from 1st January 1977 and 6th April 1978 respectively. The principal amendments include: maternity leave does not now have to be recorded as sick leave and is to be treated as reckonable service (reg. 501); the Pensions (Increase) Act 1971, s. 8 (2) (a) is to apply in respect of pensions under the 1976 Regulations (reg. 1 (2) (a)); fresh provisions as respects the calculation of transfer values (reg. 1 (2) (b)); the categories of part-time employment which may be treated as full time employment are extended (reg. 16); changes in calculating a repayment of superannuation contributions (reg. 21) and provisions relating to persons entitled to short term pensions on the death of a teacher (reg. 24).

2135   The Teachers' Superannuation (Amendment) (No. 2) Regulations 1980, S.I. 1980 No. 1043 (in force on 1st September 1980), amend the Teachers' Superannuation Regulations 1976, 1976 Halsbury's Abridgment para. 994. The regulations take effect from 1st April 1980.

2136   Universities—pensions

The Pensions Increase (Federated Superannuation System for Universities) (Amendment) Regulations 1980, S.I. 1980 No. 1869 (in force on 5th January 1981), further amend the definition of "relevant employment" contained in the Pensions Increase (Federated Superannuation System for Universities) Regulations 1972.

2137   **War—civilians' pensions**

The Personal Injuries (Civilians) Amendment Scheme 1980, S.I. 1980 No. 1102 (in force on 1st September 1980), amends the Personal Injuries (Civilians) Scheme 1976, 1976 Halsbury's Abridgment para. 1910, by making new provisions for posthumous awards to be made. The award may be either in the first instance or consequent upon an appeal from a rejection of a claim.

2138   The Personal Injuries (Civilians) Amendment (No. 2) Scheme 1980, S.I. 1980 No. 1103 (arts. 1, 3 in force on 14th September 1980 and the remainder on 24th November 1980), further amends the Personal Injuries (Civilians) Scheme 1976, 1976 Halsbury's Abridgment para. 1910. The scheme raises the maximum amount of annual earnings allowed in relation to unemployability allowance, makes amendments in relation to invalidity allowance and allowance for part-time treatment and also increases the rates of pensions and allowances in respect of disablement and death in the Second World War.

2139   The Personal Injuries (Civilians) Amendment (No. 3) Scheme 1980, S.I. 1980 No. 1950 (in force on 27th January 1981), further amends the Personal Injuries (Civilians) Scheme 1976, 1976 Halsbury's Abridgment para. 1910, by extending the period in which an allowance may be continued in respect of a child who is under nineteen at the discretion of the Secretary of State as if the child were still receiving full-time education for a period not exceeding thirteen weeks after he ceases to undergo such education and before the child reaches the age of nineteen. The definition of "student" is amended accordingly.

2140   —— **pensions committees**

The War Pensions Committees (Revocation and Reconstitution) Order 1980, S.I. 1980 No. 1685 (in force on 1st January 1981), revokes the 1975 Order, 1975 Halsbury's Abridgment para. 2525. The 1975 Order established war pensions committees for certain specified areas until 31st December 1980 and the present order reconstitutes those committees with minor amendments until 31st December 1985.

2141   —— **service pensions**

The Injuries in War (Shore Employments) Compensation (Amendment) Scheme 1980, S.I. 1980 No. 1731 (in force on 24th November 1980), provides that the maximum weekly allowance payable to ex-members of the Women's Auxiliary Forces who suffered disablement from their service overseas during the 1914–18 War is to be increased from £38 to £44·30 and that other allowances will be increased proportionately.

2142   The Naval, Military and Air Forces etc. (Disablement and Death) Service Pensions Amendment Order 1980, S.I. 1980 No. 1080 (in force on 1st September 1980), further amends the 1978 Order, 1978 Halsbury's Abridgment para. 2134 by adding new provisions for awards to be made after the death of the claimant in respect of any period before his death, whether the claim is in the first instance or consequent upon an appeal from a rejection of a claim.

2143   The Naval, Military and Air Forces etc. (Disablement and Death) Service Pensions Amendment (No. 2) Order 1980, S.I. 1980 No. 1081 (arts. 1, 3 in force on 14th September 1980 and the remainder on 24th November 1980), further amends the 1978 Order, 1978 Halsbury's Abridgment para. 2134. The order raises the maximum amount of annual earnings allowed in relation to unemployability allowance, makes amendments in relation to invalidity allowance and allowance for part-time treatment and also increases the rates of retired pay, pensions, gratuities and allowances in respect of disablement and death due to service in the forces during the First World War and after the start of the Second World War.

2144   The Naval, Military and Air Forces etc. (Disablement and Death) Service Pensions
Amendment (No. 3) Order 1980, S.I. 1980 No. 1955 (in force on 27th January
1981), further amends the 1978 Order, 1978 Halsbury's Abridgment para. 2134, by
extending the period in which an allowance may be continued in respect of a child
who is under nineteen at the discretion of the Secretary of State as if the child were
still receiving full-time education for a period not exceeding thirteen weeks after he
ceases to undergo such education and before the child reaches the age of nineteen.
The definition of "student" is amended accordingly.

PLEADING

Halsbury's Laws of England (3rd edn.), Vol. 30, paras. 1–78

2145   **Alternative claim—inconsistency of alternative—effect on
pleading**

See *Barclays Bank Ltd v Thomas*, para. 1377.

2146   **Defence—amendment—application to introduce issues not relevant to trial of action—whether amendment possible**

See *Reinold Hagen v Fratelli D. & G. Moretti SNC*, para. 541.

2147   —— **further and better particulars not available**

The plaintiff made a claim under her deceased husband's motor insurance policy and
the insurers raised as a defence the allegation that the deceased had not made
disclosure of previous driving offences. The master ordered that they should give
the plaintiff further and better particulars of the alleged offences. The insurers were
unable to comply and their defence was struck out. On appeal, *held*, the insurers'
suspicions did not entitle them to say that they had a defence without further and
better particulars. The appeal would be dismissed.

BUTCHER V DOWLEN (1980) Times, 17th October (Court of Appeal: STEPHENSON
and DUNN LJJ and SIR DAVID CAIRNS).

2148   —— **leave to amend—effect of amendment on plaintiff**

In an action concerning damages for the loss of cargo which failed to arrive at its
destination, the defence served admitted certain facts. The third defendant later
sought leave to amend the defence on the ground that it had been fraudulently
drafted by the first defendant. The plaintiff contended that this would cause
hardship as it had been induced by the defence not to try to obtain security for its
claim from the first defendant, which was now in liquidation. *Held*, although as a
general principle such amendments ought to be allowed to enable the main issue
between the parties to be decided, in this case the plaintiffs would be prejudiced in
a way which could not be compensated by the court if the amendment was
allowed. Further, the third defendant was not entirely free from responsibility for
the situation and accordingly the application for leave to amend would be rejected.

THE KYOAN MARU [1980] 2 Lloyd's Rep 233 (Queen's Bench Division: SHEEN J).

2149   **Particularity—breach of statutory duty—whether necessary to
particularise breach**

The plaintiff, a miner, was injured in a fall at the coal face and claimed damages for
personal injuries, pleading that the defendants were in breach of the statutory duty
imposed on them by the Mines and Quarries Act 1954, s. 48 (1), to keep his place of
work secure. The defendants obtained an order for delivery of particulars of the
breach and the plaintiff appealed. *Held*, the duty under s. 48 was not absolute but a
manager had to exercise care and skill of the highest degree. The admitted fall was

a prima facie breach of s. 48. It appeared that the defendants' primary purpose in seeking an order for particulars was that if they found that the plaintiff was relying on the fall alone he would be precluded from claiming that the defendants should have taken specific steps to prevent the fall. Although the purpose of particularity in pleadings was to prevent surprise at trial, it would be wrong to require the plaintiff to show how he proposed to rebut the defendants' case since he would be in a position to identify the weaknesses in the defendants' case only at the hearing of the action. The appeal would be allowed.

RICHARDSON V NATIONAL COAL BOARD (1980) 124 Sol Jo 313 (Court of Appeal: STEPHENSON, BRIDGE and TEMPLEMAN LJJ).

2150   **Statement of claim—further and better particulars—libel action**

See *Lougheed v Canadian Broadcasting Corpn*, para. 1793.

2151   **Time limit for pleading—counterclaim**

See *CSI International Co Ltd v Archway Personnel (Middle East) Ltd*, para. 2568.

POLICE

Halsbury's Laws of England (3rd edn.), Vol. 30, paras. 79–237

2152   **Assault on constable in execution of duty**

See CRIMINAL LAW.

2153   **Internal investigations—statements obtained during investigations—discovery**

The plaintiff left his home for a few days and during his absence the police obtained a search warrant. Two detectives entered his house and searched for drugs but found none. Soon after his return the plaintiff informed the police that his house had been burgled, but following several hours of questioning at the police station he withdrew this allegation. The plaintiff then went to solicitors and was granted legal aid. The solicitors wrote a letter before action to the Chief Constable who regarded himself as bound to cause an investigation to be held within the police force under the Police Act 1964, s. 49. Investigations proceeded and statements were taken from several persons but no cause was found for criminal or disciplinary proceedings against the detectives. The plaintiff however brought a civil action for damages against the police. His case depended almost entirely upon evidence contained in the statements obtained during the police internal investigation. The police objected to producing the statements on the grounds that it would be against public interest to do so and that they were subject to legal professional privilege. The county court upheld the objection and the plaintiff appealed. *Held*, (i) since criminal or internal disciplinary proceedings and not civil litigation had been the dominant purpose behind the police obtaining the statements there was no legal professional privilege. (ii) The court had a general discretion to order discovery which had to be exercised having regard to public interests. In the case in question the plaintiff was using legal aid to sue the police who appeared to have acted quite properly. His demand for production of the statements amounted to a "fishing expedition" to find evidence to back up his case. It would be against public interest to allow him to do that or to use statements in civil litigation which had been provided by the deponents for an entirely different purpose. Consequently the statements were accorded a class privilege and if the plaintiff had a case at all he would have to find his own witnesses and evidence. The appeal would be dismissed.

NEILSON V LAUGHARNE [1981] 1 All ER 829 (Court of Appeal: LORD DENNING MR, OLIVER and O'CONNOR LJJ).

2154   Law enforcement—dismissal of information laid by officer—death of officer before appeal heard—lapse of appeal

See *Hawkins v Bepey*, para. 645.

2155   Metropolitan Police Commissioner—duty to enforce the law against obscene publications—application for mandamus to compel performance of that duty

A private individual made an application for mandamus against the Metropolitan Police Commissioner requiring him, inter alia, to enforce, or secure the enforcement of, the law against those who illegally published or sold obscene material. The application was refused at first instance and on appeal, *held*, the Obscene Publications Act 1959 with its test of obscenity and defence of public good made law enforcement difficult. However, the Commissioner was doing the best he could in a difficult situation and the police were carrying out their duties in the best possible way with the resources at their command. There was therefore no justification for the court's interference and the appeal would be dismissed.

The court noted that the situation justified the attention of the Attorney-General, not only with a view to considering amending legislation, but also the initiation by him of proceedings.

R v METROPOLITAN POLICE COMR, EX PARTE BLACKBURN (1980) Times, 7th March (Court of Appeal: LORD DENNING MR, LAWTON and ACKNER LJJ). Decision of Divisional Court of the Queen's Bench Division (1979) Times, 1st December, 1979 Halsbury's Abridgment para. 2084 affirmed.

2156   Pay and allowances

The Police (Amendment) Regulations 1980, S.I. 1980 No. 405 (in force on 1st May 1980), amend the Police Regulations 1979, 1979 Halsbury's Abridgment para. 2091. Regulations 5, 6, 8, 11 increase, with effect from 1st February 1980, the supplementary rent allowances, the removal allowance and the bicycle allowance. Other amendments concern the calculation of pay and allowances.

2157   The Police (Amendment) (No. 2) Regulations 1980, S.I. No. 803 (in force on 1st August 1980), amend the Police Regulations 1979, 1979 Halsbury's Abridgment para. 2091. Regulation 4 increases, with effect from 1st July 1979, the London weighting payable to a member of the City of London or metropolitan police force and the corresponding supplement payable to a member of another police force who takes up residence as a university scholar within the City of London or the metropolitan police district. Regulation 5 increases, with effect from 1st September 1979, the dog handler's allowance payable where a dog owned by the police authority is kept and cared for by a member of a police force at his home. Regulation 6, which takes effect on 1st August 1980, amends the provisions about annual leave contained in Sch. 3 to the 1979 Regulations.

2158   The Police (Amendment) (No. 3) Regulations 1980, S.I. 1980 No. 1455 (in force on 1st November 1980) amend the Police Regulations 1979, 1979 Halsbury's Abridgment para. 2091. Regulations 4, 5 increase, with effect from 1st September 1980, the London allowances and the dog handlers allowance payable to members of a police force. Regulation 6 amends, with effect from 1st September 1980, Sch. 5 para 1 (5) of the 1979 Regulations. Regulation 8 substitutes, with effect from 1st September 1980, new pay scales for those contained in 1979 Regs., Sch. 5.

2159   Pensions

See PENSIONS AND SUPERANNUATION.

2160   **Police cadet—complaint of unfair dismissal—whether cadet an "employee"**

It was decided as a preliminary issue of law that a police cadet was an employee within the meaning of the Trade Union and Labour Relations Act 1974, s. 30 (1) and was therefore entitled to bring a complaint of unfair dismissal against a police authority. On appeal by the police authority, *held*, a police cadet was not an employee within s. 30 (1) but was a person being taught in the hope that he or she would then become a member of the force. Accordingly an industrial tribunal had no jurisdiction to entertain a complaint of unfair dismissal brought by a police cadet and the appeal would be allowed.

Wiltshire Police Authority v Wynn [1980] 3 WLR 445 (Court of Appeal: Lord Denning MR, Waller and Dunn LJJ). Decision of Employment Appeal Tribunal (1980) Times, 22nd February, reversed.

2161   **Police Negotiating Board Act 1980**

The Police Negotiating Board Act 1980 makes provision for the establishment of the Police Negotiating Board for the United Kingdom in place of the Police Council for the United Kingdom and confers certain functions on that Board. The Act received the royal assent on 20th March 1980 and came into force on 20th May 1980.

Section 1 provides for the establishment of the Board. It is to be composed of representaives of the police authorities and police staff associations and is to consider matters relating to hours of duty, leave, pay, pensions and conditions of service: s. 1 (1). Detailed arrangements for the establishment of the Board are to be made after consultations between the Secretary of State and the bodies represented on the Board, but the chairman and deputy chairman are to be appointed by the Prime Minister: s. 1 (2), (3). The Secretary of State is empowered to pay fees to the chairman and deputy chairman and to defray any expenses incurred by the Board: s. 1 (4). Subsection 1 (5) provides that the Police Council for the United Kingdom is to cease to exist.

Section 2 confers certain functions on the Board with respect to the making of regulations. Before making regulations under the Police Acts about matters with which the Board is concerned, the Secretary of State is required to have regard to any recommendation made by the Board and to furnish the Board with a draft of the regulations: s. 2 (1). The Board's constitution is to include suitable arrangements for reaching agreement on recommendations to the Secretary of State and for the reference of any dispute to arbitration: s. 2 (2).

Section 3 deals with citation, commencement, repeals and extent.

2162   **Powers—arrest—validity of arrest—need to demand entry to premises to make an arrest**

See *Swales v Cox*, para. 653.

2163   **—— police vehicles—use of parking space designated for the disabled**

A police officer, using a police car, parked in a space designated for the use of disabled persons under the Borough of Reading (Parking Places for Disabled Drivers) Order 1975, in order to make inquiries about a local robbery. He was charged with contravening the Order contrary to the Road Traffic Regulations Act 1967. He contended that his use of the parking space was exempt from the designated use by virtue of the 1975 Order, art. 11 (b) which provided that the restriction did not prevent parking enabling a police officer to perform his statutory powers or duties. Further under the Police Regulations 1971, reg. 22 he was obliged to carry out his duties promptly and attend all matters within the scope of his office as a police constable. *Held*, the Police Regulations 1971 set out the obligations of a police officer and should be regarded as statutory duties so that in parking a car in order to make inquiries, the police officer was performing statutory duties within art. 11 (b).

GEORGE v GARLAND [1980] RTR 77 (Queen's Bench Division: LORD WIDGERY CJ, EVELEIGH LJ and KILNER BROWN J).

2164 —— power to restrain where breach of the peace apprehended

See *Albert v Lavin*, para. 564.

2165 —— right of search—search of arrested person and removal of articles of clothing—whether police officer acting in execution of duty

See *Lindley v Rutter*, para. 566.

2166 —— whether obligation regarded as statutory duty

See *George v Garland*, para. 2163.

2167 Rest days—compensation for cancellation

A police constable had his rostered rest day cancelled and although he was given time off in lieu he was refused monetary compensation. The constable appealed. *Held*, the police authority acted within their powers under the Police (Amendment) Regulations 1975, reg. 26, since on a proper construction of reg. 26 the roster could be altered up to eight days before an allocated rest day without giving rights to compensation for its cancellation. The appeal would be dismissed.

STARBUCK v GOODSON (1980) Times, 13th December (Court of Appeal: LORD DENNING MR, ORMROD and O'CONNOR LJJ).

2168 Road traffic—power of constable in uniform to stop vehicle on road

See *Beard v Wood*, para. 2366.

2169 —— regulations—contravention by police officer—legality

See *Keene v Muncaster*, para. 2399.

PORTS, HARBOURS AND THE SEASHORE

Halsbury's Laws of England (3rd edn.), Vol. 35, paras. 1247–1311; Vol. 39, paras. 767–891

2170 Port health authority

See PUBLIC HEALTH.

2171 Port of London Authority—borrowing powers

The Port of London Authority (Borrowing Powers, etc) Revision Order 1980, S.I. 1980 No. 1068 (in force on 28th July 1980), amends the Port of London Act 1968 by increasing to £200 million the total amount of moneys which may be borrowed or raised by the Authority and outstanding at any one time as provided by that Act. The order also provides for the auditor of the Authority's annual accounts to be appointed by the Authority (instead of by the Minister) and removes the requirement for the audit fee to be agreed by the Minister.

2172   **Port of London (Financial Assistance) Act 1980**

The Port of London (Financial Assistance) Act 1980 provides financial assistance for and in connection with measures taken by the Port of London Authority to restore the profitability of their undertaking by reducing the number of persons employed by them. The Act received the royal assent on 30th June 1980 and came into force on that date.

Section 1 (1) enables the Minister of Transport, with the approval of the Treasury, to give financial assistance for measures to reduce the manpower of the Port of London Authority with a view to restoring the profitability of their undertaking and for the carrying on of their undertaking while such measures are being taken. Assistance may be given in the form of a grant, loan or guarantee: s. 1 (2). The Secretary of State may reimburse the National Dock Labour Board for any payments made by them to dock workers who become entitled to compensation from the Board in consequence of the measures taken under s. 1 (1): s. 1 (3). Payments under s. 1 (1), (3) are subject to a limit of £70 million: s. 1 (4).

Section 2 provides the short title for this Act.

POST OFFICE

Halsbury's Laws of England (3rd edn.), Vol. 30, paras. 238–362

2173   **Industrial relations machinery—duty to seek consultation with appropriate organisation—appropriateness of organisation—test to be applied**

A small independent trade union (TCOA) had negotiated terms and conditions of employment with the Post Office since 1921. TCOA combined to some extent with other Post Office employees' unions in the Council of Post Office Unions (COPOU) which consulted with management. Since 1969, Post Office policy, with the agreement of COPOU, had been to limit the number of trade unions by mergers in order to secure a stronger body for collective bargaining. For several years, negotiations had been carried out with a view to merging TCOA with another union of Post Office employees, but in 1979 TCOA voted overwhelmingly in favour of joining ASTMS. In 1980, TCOA became a section of ASTMS (ASTMS (TCO section)). COPOU refused to deal with ASTMS (TCO section) and the Post Office refused to recognise it. ASTMS (TCO section) unsuccessfully sought a declaration that it was an appropriate organisation with which the Post Office had a duty to seek consultation within the meaning of the Post Office Act 1969, Sch. 1, para. 11 (1) and an order for mandamus directed to the Post Office to seek such consultation. On appeal by ASTMS (TCO section), *held*, the right test was to consider the appropriateness of organisations to see whether they were appropriate for consultation on all the objectives stated in Sch. 1, para. 11 of the 1969 Act, one of which was the settlement by negotiation of conditions of employment of all Post Office employees, not just those in one section. The Post Office rightly considered that if it were to recognise ASTMS (TCO section), it would have to negotiate on the one hand with COPOU and then separately with ASTMS (TCO section), with all the dangers of subsequent disagreement. Further, more efficiency could be attained by having a few unions, members of COPOU, negotiating without any intrusion by an outside body like ASTMS. The Post Office took the view honestly, in good faith and on reasonable grounds that ASTMS (TCO section) was not an appropriate organisation within the meaning of the 1969 Act, and the appeal would accordingly be dismissed.

R v POST OFFICE, EX PARTE ASSOCIATION OF SCIENTIFIC, TECHNICAL AND MANAGERIAL STAFFS [1981] 1 All ER 139 (Court of Appeal: LORD DENNING MR, CUMMING-BRUCE and ACKNER LJJ). *Gallagher v Post Office* [1970] 3 All ER 712 disapproved.

2174   Postal services—value added tax—exempt supply—service of procuring postal delivery

See *BSN (Import and Export) Ltd v Customs and Excise Comrs*, para. 3067.

2175   Staff—sub-postmaster—contract of employment—whether contract of service or contract for services

See *Hitchcock v Post Office*, para. 1022.

POWERS

Halsbury's Laws of England (3rd edn.), Vol. 30, paras. 363–546

2176   Article

Widening the Investment Clause, F. Graham Glover (circumstances under which donee of power of appointment can enlarge the scope of the investment clause): 130 NLJ 182.

PRACTICE AND PROCEDURE

Halsbury's Laws of England (3rd edn.), Vol. 30, paras. 547–1036

2177   Article

Summons and Discretion, D. W. Fox and A. N. Khan (issue of summonses by magistrates): 144 JP Jo 7.

2178   Anton Piller order—application for discharge—privilege against self-incrimination—whether order wrongfully obtained—admissibility of documents in evidence

See *International Electronics Ltd v Weigh Data Ltd*, para. 1226.

2179   —— preservation of evidence—discretion to order inspection and removal of accounts

The plaintiff had an agreement with the defendant in respect of business placed by the plaintiff through the second defendant company. The accounts showed that a considerable sum in commission was due to the plaintiff and he subsequently issued a writ for the amount outstanding. After the writ had been served the plaintiff feared that documents in the company's possession, which contained details of relevant transactions, would be destroyed. He applied ex parte for an order permitting him to enter the company's premises in order to take custody of the documentary evidence. *Held*, DONALDSON LJ dissenting, since there was sufficient evidence to show that the plaintiff's fears were legitimate and that the documents were essential to his case he would be granted an "Anton Piller" order enabling him to take custody of the documents. This amounted to an order for the preservation of evidence which might be destroyed before the hearing.

YOUSIF V SALAMA [1980] 3 All ER 405 (Court of Appeal: LORD DENNING MR, DONALDSON and BRIGHTMAN LJJ). *Anton Piller KG v Manufacturing Processes Ltd* [1976] 1 All ER 779, CA, 1976 Halsbury's Abridgment para. 2623 applied.

2180   —— scope—availability in respect of matters not the subject of final relief

Australia
The Supreme Court of New South Wales has held, in a case concerning an infringement of copyright in sound recordings, that an Anton Piller order was available only in relation to recordings which were to be the subject of the final relief sought, notwithstanding that the defendants were persistent infringers of copyright in sound recordings.

EMI (AUSTRALIA) LTD V BAY IMPORTS PROPERTY LTD [1980] FSR 328 (Supreme Court of New South Wales).

2181   —— —— whether subject to privilege against self-incrimination

In an action by the plaintiffs for infringement of copyright the court made an Anton Piller order against the defendants for immediate seizure of infringing copies, immediate discovery of the relevant documents and immediate answers to interrogatories relating to the supply and sale of infringing copies. The defendants contended that they were entitled to claim privilege from giving discovery and answering questions on the ground that by so doing they would incriminate themselves for the purpose of the Copyright Act 1956, s. 21 under which the sale and supply of infringing material was a criminal offence. This contention was rejected at first instance and the defendants appealed. The plaintiffs contended that the privilege had been outmoded by the decision in *Riddick v Thames Board Mills Ltd* [1977] 2 All ER 677, CA, 1977 Halsbury's Abridgment para. 918, that where a party in a civil action was compelled to give discovery, the documents or answers could only be used for the purposes of that action. Alternatively, that there were several exceptions to the privilege and this fell within one of them. *Held*, LORD DENNING MR dissenting, the principle that no man should be compelled to incriminate himself was firmly entrenched in the law, and although the doctrine required reconsideration in the light of modern conditions it had not been abolished or modified by the decision in *Riddick's* case. Notwithstanding that if the claim of privilege to withhold discovery was available to defendants in copyright actions, it could have the effect of stultifying the copyright owner's effective remedy, any special exception to the availability of the privilege was to be provided by the legislature and not the courts. However this did not inhibit the making of orders ex parte requiring the defendants to permit search and seizure and the appeal would be allowed to the extent of deleting all requirements to answer questions and disclose documents.

LORD DENNING MR held that the court would not allow a defendant the benefit of the privilege where to do so would enable him to take advantage of his own fraud or wrongdoing so as to defeat the just claims of the plaintiff in a civil suit. In fairness to the plaintiffs the defendants should give discovery but their documents or answers should not be admissible in evidence against them in any criminal proceedings as in *Riddick's* case.

RANK FILM DISTRIBUTORS LTD V VIDEO INFORMATION CENTRE [1980] 2 All ER 273 (Court of Appeal: LORD DENNING MR, BRIDGE and TEMPLEMAN LJJ). *Anton Piller KG v Manufacturing Processes Ltd* [1976] 1 All ER 779, CA, *R v Garbett* (1847) 2 Car Kir 474, dicta of Bowen LJ in *Redfern v Redfern* [1886–90] All ER Rep at 528, of Du Parcq LJ in *Triplex Safety Glass Co Ltd v Lancegaye Safety Glass (1934) Ltd* [1939] 2 All ER at 617 and *Rio Tinto Zinc Corpn v Westinghouse Electric Corpn* [1978] 1 All ER 434, HL, 1977 Halsbury's Abridgment para. 1250, applied.

2182   In an action concerning the alleged passing off by the defendants of various garments as those of the plaintiffs, the plaintiffs sought an Anton Piller order. Compliance with the order by the defendants would involve the danger of self-incrimination, and the plaintiffs therefore undertook not to bring criminal proceedings against the defendants in respect of the matter. *Held*, the order would be granted and the undertaking incorporated into that order.

SNUGKOAT LTD V CHAUDHRY [1980] FSR 286 (Chancery Division: GRAHAM J). *Rank Film Distributors Ltd v Video Information Centre* [1980] 2 All ER 273, CA, para. 2181 considered.

2183 **Appeal—appeal against order granting third party leave to defend—right of appeal**

A colt was owned by the plaintiffs and his life was insured through third party brokers with the defendants, a firm of underwriters. The colt died during the period of the policy and the plaintiffs brought an action on the policy against the defendants for part of the sum assured. The defendants disputed the value of the colt and further contended that an extension of the policy enabling him to be covered by it whilst abroad had been made by the third party without their authority. The defendants asserted the latter claim against the third party in proceedings under RSC Ord. 16, by which they sought to be indemnified against any sum that they might be found liable to pay the plaintiffs. The plaintiffs' summons against the defendants under RSC Ord. 14 for leave to sign interlocutory judgment for damages and interest to be assessed, and the defendants' summons against the third party for directions were heard together. Subsequently the question arose as to whether the defendants could appeal against an order, not made under RSC Ords. 14 or 16, granting the third party leave to defend the third party claim. *Held*, under the provisions of the Supreme Court of Judicature (Consolidation) Act 1925, s. 31 (1) (c) there was no right of appeal from an order of a judge giving unconditional leave to defend an action. The order referred to in s. 31 (1) (c) did not have to be made under any RSC Order under which an action had been brought. The words were general. The essence of a third party claim was that it would be tried at the same time as one between plaintiff and defendant. On principle the same rule should apply to interlocutory judgments between defendants and third parties as between plaintiffs and defendants. No distinction should be drawn according to the particular form of words used in the judge's order granting the third party leave to defend and accordingly the court had no jurisdiction to hear an appeal against such an order.

MERINO v PILCHER [1980] LS Gaz R 296 (Court of Appeal: LAWTON and ORMROD LJJ).

2184 **—— appeal to Court of Appeal—amendment of notice of appeal—motion to refer case to European Court of Justice**

The taxpayer, an American body incorporated with the objective of propagating the religious faith scientology, unsuccessfully appealed against a value added tax assessment made under the Finance Act 1972, s. 2 on payments received relating to the sale of books. The taxpayer appealed to the Court of Appeal, amending the notice of appeal so as to include points relating to the application of certain provisions of the EEC Treaty not previously raised. The taxpayer subsequently sought a motion to refer to the European Court of Justice under art. 177 certain questions relating to Council Directive (EEC) 67/228. The motion was stood over pending argument on the appeal with a view to the motion being restored at such time as the need for a reference became apparent to the court. Before the Court of Appeal, *held*, both the appeal and the motion would be dismissed on the basis that there was insufficient factual foundation on which the questions could be drafted.

CHURCH OF SCIENTOLOGY OF CALIFORNIA v COMRS OF CUSTOMS and EXCISE [1981] STC 65 (Court of Appeal: STEPHENSON and OLIVER LJJ and SIR JOHN RAMSEY WILLIS).

For proceedings relating to the original motion to refer to the European Court of Justice see [1980] 3 CMLR 114. For earlier proceedings see [1979] STC 297, 1979 Halsbury's Abridgment para. 3027.

2185 **—— —— property adjustment order—application for leave to appeal out of time**

See *Johnson v Johnson*, para. 1495.

2186 **—— appeal to a Divisional Court of the Queen's Bench Division**

A Divisional Court of the Queen's Bench Division has stated that in cases where the facts are complicated, appeals and applications to the court should be made by way of case stated and not by way of prerogative order.

R v Felixstowe JJ, ex parte Baldwin (1980) Times, 22nd October (Queen's Bench Division: Donaldson LJ and McNeill J).

2187 —— notice of appeal—appeal out of time—when time begins to run

Malaysia

Under Malaysian law any person dissatisfied with an order made by a judge in chambers may apply to the court for the adjournment of the matter into open court to hear further argument which the judge may decline to do. An appeal to the Federal Court from an order made in chambers must be made within one month of the date on which the order was pronounced.

A judge in chambers adjudicated in favour of the appellants and the respondent applied for the matter to be adjourned in open court. Five weeks after the original determination the judge declined to hear further argument. The respondent therefore filed notice of appeal to the Federal Court. On a question of whether the notice was out of time, *held*, time for appealing to the Federal Court ran from the date on which the judge's decision not to hear further argument was communicated to the respondent and not from the date of the original order.

Bank of America National Trust and Savings Association v Chai Yen [1980] 1 WLR 350 (Privy Council: Lord Edmund-Davies, Lord Fraser of Tullybelton, Lord Russell of Killowen, Lord Keith of Kinkel and Lord Lane).

2188 Barristers

See BARRISTERS.

2189 Chancery Division—application for declaration—appropriate division of High Court

See *Heywood v Board of Visitors of Hull Prison*, para. 5.

2190 —— bespeaking judgments and orders

The following Practice Direction ([1980] 2 All ER 400) has been issued by Sir Robert Megarry V-C.

The attention of practitioners is drawn to the importance of bespeaking judgments and orders in the Chancery Division promptly in accordance with RSC Ord 42, r. 7. Rule 7 (2) provides that within seven days of the judgment being given or the order being made it should be bespoken and the necessary documents lodged. If this is not done, r. 7 (3) authorises the registrar to decline to draw up the judgment or order without the leave of the court.

It is recognised that it is not always practicable for there to be strict compliance with the seven days rule, especially where the court has directed that there should be minutes of order; and in such cases the registrars have always exercised their discretion under the rule. However, in too many cases delays of many weeks or months in bespeaking judgments or orders have been occurring without any apparent justification, sometimes to the prejudice of the litigants concerned.

I have therefore directed the Chancery registrars that if in future there appears to have been undue delay in bespeaking a judgment or order, then unless the registrar is satisfied that there is an adequate justification for the delay he should forthwith refer the matter to the Chief Registrar. Subject to any action that the Chief Registrar may take, he will then arrange for the case to be listed, normally before me on a Wednesday morning at 9.45 a.m., as an application in open court for leave to draw up the judgment or order notwithstanding the delay. On such an application, a full explanation of the delay must be before the court; and the court may direct affidavits to be filed. One of the matters that the court will consider is how the costs of the application should be borne, and whether steps should be taken under RSC Ord 62, r. 8 with a view to an order being made against the solicitors personally.

At present this direction does not apply to judgments or orders which are to be drawn up in district registries.

2191   —— companies—winding up—advertisement of petitions

The following Practice Note ([1980] 1 WLR 657) has been issued by VINELOTT J sitting in the Companies Court.

(1) During the period while the "London Gazette" was not being distributed on time OLIVER J and later DILLON J directed that petitioners might advertise either in a London or in a local newspaper according to the particular circumstances. The difficulties experienced by the "London Gazette" have happily been resolved and from today advertisements must be made in accordance with the Companies (Winding-up) (Amendment) Rules 1979, 1979 Halsbury's Abridgment para. 392 introduced on 1st April 1979.

(2) Experience shows that advertisements are still being made in the old form and not in the shorter form introduced by the new rules. The new rules *must* be observed and petitioners who do not advertise in the correct form may suffer the penalty of being required to re-advertise.

(3) Cases have arisen and are becoming more frequent in which a petition has been advertised less than seven days after it has been served on the company. The breach of these rules can cause serious injustice by unduly restricting the period within which a company may apply to restrain advertisement. I draw attention to this rule in the expectation that this will not occur in the future. If it does a petitioner may be deprived of part of his costs.

2192   —— costs—assessment in chambers—extension of monetary limit of costs assessed or settled in chambers

The following Practice Direction [1980] 3 All ER 704, [1980] 1 WLR 1386 has been issued by the direction of the Vice-Chancellor:

1. Since 1975 the limit of costs which may be assessed or settled in chambers by a master has been £500, with defined exceptions. This limit is now raised to £1,500.

2. Practice Direction (Costs: Assessment in Chambers) [1975] 3 All ER 224, [1975] 1 WLR 1202, 1975 Halsbury's Abridgment para. 2582 is amended accordingly.

2193   —— estimation of length of trial—necessity for case to be ready for date fixed—procedure for vacating allotted dates

The following Practice Direction [1980] 3 All ER 831 has been issued by Judge Blackett-Ord V-C sitting as a High Court judge.

1. The present practice of allotting fixed dates for all cases expected to last for a day or more depends for its working on the best possible estimates of length being supplied promptly to the court and on the cases being ready on the day. Attention is drawn to para. 2 of the Practice Direction of 5th May 1972 ([1972] 2 All ER 599, [1972] 1 WLR 723).

2. Delays are caused if one or more parties neglects to join in lodging a counsel's certificate of estimated length of trial. In this case any party who desires a hearing date may lodge his own certificate and apply by summons to the district registrar to arrange a date for trial. The district registrar will have authority to deal with the costs of the summons.

3. Solicitors are reminded that they are expected to make every effort to have cases ready by the dates fixed for trial. Dates once allotted will not be vacated unless (a) the case is settled, or (b) the leave of the Vice-Chancellor or his Honour Judge FitzHugh QC has been obtained.

4. If it becomes necessary to seek leave under para. 3 (b) above, the solicitor for the party seeking leave should forthwith apply (normally in writing) giving reasons to the Chief Chancery Clerk at the registry at which the case is listed to be heard.

The clerk will then get in touch with the Vice-Chancellor or Judge FitzHugh, who will either consent or direct the application (if it is to be pursued) to be made to him personally in chambers by counsel. The consent of all parties will not of itself be a sufficient reason for an application.

5. When a case is settled, the court should be informed as soon as possible, but no leave to vacate the date is needed, even if a consent order is sought. If a consent order is required, the case will be listed for a convenient motion day.

2194 —— family provision—application out of time—when application allowed

The testator's son applied under the Inheritance (Provision for Family and Dependants) Act 1975, s. 4 for leave to bring proceedings out of time, nineteen months after the time limit had expired. His claim was for a lump sum to pay capital transfer tax on an inter vivos gift made to him by the testator. His application was refused and he appealed. *Held*, it was relevant to consider whether the applicant had an arguable case. The 1975 Act was limited to provision for "maintenance," in respect of dependants other than the spouse, lump sums only being awarded when they would enable the dependant to discharge the cost of daily living of an income nature. In the circumstances, when the payment did not fall into that category and the applicant had already dissipated the first gift, the chances of success were very low. As the delay was also inexcusable and unexplained, the appeal would be dismissed.

RE DENNIS, DENNIS v LLOYD'S BANK LTD (1980) Times, 14th November (Chancery Division: BROWNE-WILKINSON J). *Re Salmon* [1980] 3 All ER 532, and *Re Coventry* [1979] 3 All ER 815, CA, 1979 Halsbury's Abridgment para. 1266 applied.

2195 —— —— time limit for application—extension of time—guidelines

The Inheritance (Provision for Family and Dependants) Act 1975, s. 4, provides that an application for an order shall not, except with the permission of the court, be made after the end of the period of six months from the date on which representation with respect to the estate of the deceased is first taken out.

In dismissing an application by a widow for an extension of time the Vice-Chancellor, while disclaiming any intention to lay down principles, identified the following six guidelines on the exercise of the court's discretion to extend the time. (i) The court's discretion was unfettered and was to be exercised judicially. (ii) The onus was on the plaintiff to establish sufficient grounds for the case to be taken out of the general rule. (iii) The court was to consider how promptly and in what circumstances the applicant had sought the permission of the court after the expiry of the time limit. (iv) It was material whether or not negotiations had been commenced within the time limit. (v) It was relevant to consider whether or not the estate had been distributed before a claim under the Act had been made or notified. (vi) It was relevant to consider whether a refusal to extend the time limit would leave the claimant without redress against anyone.

RE SALMON, COARD v NATIONAL WESTMINSTER BANK LTD [1980] 3 All ER 532 (Chancery Division: SIR ROBERT MEGARRY V-C).

2196 —— motions—revised procedure

The following Practice Direction ([1980] 2 All ER 750, [1980] 1 WLR 751) has been issued by the chief master of the Chancery Division by the direction of the Vice-Chancellor.

The judges of the Chancery Division have decided that as from 1st October 1980 the procedure for bringing motions in the Chancery Division should be revised. The new procedure is set out below. It is substantially on the lines of the proposals which were circulated in the profession for comment last year. The new procedure will apply until further notice, though it will be kept under review, and will, if necessary, be revised in the light of experience.

1   *Motion days*

Instead of the normal motion days being Tuesdays and Fridays, every weekday (except the last day of each sittings) will be a motion day.

2   *Motion judges*

(a) For each sittings, two judges will, as at present, be assigned to hear motions. One of these judges ("the motions judge") will sit to hear all motions, whether in Group A or Group B, on each court day for a period of two weeks. If the volume of motions requires it, the other judge ("the stand-by judge") or any other judge then available to assist with motions will hear such motions as the motions judge directs.

(b) Subject to this, the stand-by judge will hear such of the ordinary work of the Division (usually the short non-witness work hitherto heard by the motions judges on Mondays, Wednesdays and Thursdays) as may be required.

(c) At the end of the first two weeks, the motions judge and the stand-by judge will exchange functions for the ensuing two weeks, and so on until the end of the sittings. As at present, the Easter and Trinity Sittings will for this purpose be treated as a single sittings.

(d) Minor variations in these periods may be made from time to time, eg to equalise the burdens on the judges. Notices in the Term List or Daily Cause List will show the periods for which each judge will be motions judge and stand-by judge.

3   *Notices of motion*

Notices of motion will continue to be given for the same period as at present, though they may be given for any court day, whether or not a Tuesday or Friday, except the last day of each sittings.

4   *Listing motions*

(a) *Motions book.* As far as possible, all motions will be listed. For this purpose, the clerk to the motions judge for the time being will maintain a motions book.

(b) *Entry in motions book.* A motion will be entered in the motions book only if (i) two copies of the writ, (ii) two copies of the notice of motion and (iii) the best estimate of duration that counsel can give, signed by counsel for the applicant, are lodged with the clerk to the motions judge not later than 12 noon on the day before the date for which notice of motion has been given, or on the preceding Friday if the notice has been given for a Monday. If there is any difficulty in reaching the clerk to the motions judge, the documents may instead be lodged with the Clerk of the Lists (room 165), who will record the time of lodging and transmit the documents to the clerk to the motions judge.

(c) *Revised estimate of duration.* Counsel for the applicant must ensure that the clerk to the motions judge is at once informed of any material revision to an estimate of duration entered in the motions book. This applies equally to shortening, as where the parties come to terms or agree an adjournment, and lengthening, as where substantial last-minute affidavits are to be adduced. If a revised estimate is given orally, it should be confirmed in writing as soon as possible.

(d) *Short motions.* As soon as it becomes apparent that a motion will take less than five minutes to dispose of, as where terms have been agreed or the motion is to be stood over, the clerk to the motions judge should be informed and requested to mark the motion "short" in the motions book. This will not alter the sequence of motions in the book, but it will usually ensure that the motion will be taken before the more lengthy motions: see para. 6 below.

(e) *Daily Cause List.* Each motion duly entered in the motions book will be listed in the Daily Cause List for the day on which it is to be heard. Where possible, the motions judge will direct the later motions in the list to be marked "Not before" a stated time, though in view of the unpredictability of motions this will be done only where counsel for all parties have given the clerk to the motions judge telephone numbers which will make it possible for counsel to be in court on ten minutes' notice. There will be no warned list of motions, but information about motions listed for future days can be obtained from the clerk to the motions judge.

5   *Standing over and saving motions*

(a) *In court.* When a motion is stood over in court, or it is saved in court, the clerk to the motions judge will forthwith enter it in the motions book for the day for which it has been stood over or saved; and in due course the motion will be listed for that day.

(b) *Out of court.* If a motion is saved by agreement, or if by consent it is stood over before a registrar (see Practice Directions [1976] 2 All ER 198,]1976] 1 WLR 441, 1976 Halsbury's Abridgment para. 1939; [1977] 1 All ER 416, [1977] 1 WLR 228, 1977 Halsbury's Abridgment para. 2110), it will be entered in the motions book for the day for which it has been stood over or saved only when the clerk to the motions judge has been notified of this by the parties, and the documents mentioned in para. 4 (b) above have been lodged with him, if that has not already been done. Before arranging the future date, it will normally be advisable for the parties to consult the clerk to the motions judge in order to ascertain what other motions there will be on that date.

6 *Order of hearing*
The judge hearing motions will continue to exercise his discretion as to the order in which he hears them, so that he may, for instance, give priority to any application that he considers to be sufficiently urgent, as may be the case with some ex parte applications. Subject to this—
(a) Motions affecting the liberty of the subject will continue to take priority over all other motions;
(b) motions marked "short" in the motions book will usually be taken next. If it becomes apparent that a motion is not in fact "short", the judge will normally cease to hear it and let it resume its normal priority;
(c) all other listed motions will be heard in the order of listing, irrespective of the seniority (or juniority) of counsel;
(d) all unlisted motions will then be heard, according to the seniority (or juniority) of counsel as at present; but if the clerk to the motions judge or the registrar in court is informed that an unlisted motion is or has become "short" (see para. 4 (d) above) he will mention this to the judge, and the judge may take it after motions listed as "short" and before other listed motions;
(e) motions likely to last more than three hours will still normally be made motions by order unless the state of work permits the judge to deal with them as they arise;
(f) when another judge is available to assist with motions, the motions judge may transfer to him such motions as he considers appropriate, irrespective of priority;
(g) any motion which at the end of a day is part-heard will normally head the listed motions for the next court day, followed by any listed motions that have not been reached;
(h) the judge will usually give effect to any variation in this order of priority which is agreed by all who are affected.

7 *Ex parte motions*
The procedure under this practice direction will apply to ex parte motions. If it is desired to have an ex parte motion listed, two copies of the order sought should be lodged under para. 4 (b) (ii) above in place of a notice of motion. If the application is to be made otherwise than in open court, it can be listed under the applicant's name alone, without that of the defendant. Where it may be unjust to the defendant or some other party if the application is heard in public, the judge may exercise his discretion to sit otherwise than in open court. Where an application is very urgent and the motions judge is unable to hear it promptly, it may be heard, as at present, by any judge who is available, though the request for this must be made to the clerk to the motions judge, or, in default, to the Clerk of the Lists.

8 *Excepted motions*
This new procedure is intended to apply only to what may be called ordinary interlocutory motions made during the usual sittings. It does not apply to motions made during the vacations, nor to motions for judgment, or motions in the Patents Court, in the Companies Court, in bankruptcy, or in the revenue paper. In all these matters, the present procedure will remain unchanged. The same applies to originating motions, save that applications for directions as to the hearing of such motions which at present come before the judge hearing motions may be made under the procedure of this direction, with the originating notice of motion taking the place of the writ and notice of motion under para. 4 (b) above, and agreed directions may be given out of court under para. 9 below.

9 *Trade marks: agreed directions on originating motions*

(a) Certain proceedings by originating motion at present come before the judge hearing motions for directions as to the conduct of the proceedings. Where the parties are agreed as to the directions that should be given, then instead of being obliged to obtain those directions from a judge in court they may obtain them from a registrar of the Division out of court, subject to the registrar's discretion to require the application to be made in court. This is an extension of the procedure for agreed adjournments of motions by a registrar: see the Practice Directions cited in para. 5 above.

(b) Any application under this head must be made to the registrar in chambers either by counsel or solicitors for all parties, or else by counsel or solicitors for any party producing a consent or consents signed by counsel or solicitors representing all parties. The applicant must produce a document setting out the agreed directions and these, where appropriate, may include liberty to apply to the master if any further directions are required. On this being done, the registrar will give the necessary direction to the Clerk of the Lists for setting the matter down in the appropriate list for hearing. In simple cases it will not be necessary for any order to be drawn up.

(c) This procedure applies to the following proceedings: (i) any appeal from the Registrar of Trade Marks under RSC Ord. 100 from the refusal of an application to register a trade mark, or from his decision in opposition or rectification proceedings; (ii) any application for rectification of the register of trade marks under the Trade Marks Act 1938, s. 26, s. 27 or s. 32; and (iii) any case referred to the court by the Registrar of Trade Marks or the Board of Trade under s. 12 (2), s. 53 or s. 54 of that Act.

2197   Costs—criminal cases

See CRIMINAL PROCEDURE.

2198   —— interlocutory matters—counsel's fees

A new list of counsel's fees on interlocutory matters in accident cases has been agreed by the chief taxing master and the Senate. The following fees are regarded as properly allowable on taxation where the item has been dealt with fully; lower fees may, however, be appropriate where an item has not been dealt with comprehensively, was unusually simple or where more than one item was dealt with simultaneously. Any higher fee which has been agreed will have to be justified on taxation. The new scales became effective on 1st December 1979. See [1979] LS Gaz 1285.

	Personal Injury Cases	Running Down Cases
Statement of claim	£25	£18
Defence without counterclaim	£20	£15
Defence plain admission	£ 8	£ 8
Particulars, request and answers	£10	£10
Reply with or without defence to counterclaim	£15	£12
Third party notice (not to stand as statement of claim)	£15	£15
Interrogatories and answers	£20	£20
Advice on evidence	£25	£25
Opinion (including opinion on appeal)	£25	£25
Opinion on liability	£25	£25
Opinion on *quantum*	£25	£25
Opinion on liability and *quantum*	£35	£35
Notice of appeal to Court of Appeal and counternotice	£25	£25
Brief on summons before master	£20	£20

Conference fees

Queen's Counsel	£20 for first ½ hour £15	for each
		succeeding
Junior Counsel	£10 for first ½ hour £ 8	half hour

2199   —— liability of receiver appointed under debenture

See *Bacal Contracting Ltd v Modern Engineering (Bristol) Ltd*, para. 366.

2200   —— litigants in person

See paras. 2227, 2228.

2201   —— order for costs—difference between "costs" and "costs in any event"

In an interlocutory application for the continuation of an injunction restraining the defendants from certain activities, it was agreed between counsel before the proceedings commenced that the application ought to be dismissed and that the costs of the application should be the defendants'. The judge accordingly dismissed the application but inadvertently initialled the order for costs, which wrongly read "defendants' costs in any event". In an application for an order correcting the error, *held*, the words "in any event" would be deleted as a clerical error. Where, on an interlocutory application, the court intended one party to have the costs, the usual form of order was "costs in any event" and taxation would be delayed until the end of the proceedings. It was only in exceptional cases that the words "defendants' costs" or "plaintiffs' costs" were used, but where they were, the party concerned was entitled to an immediate taxation.

ALLIED COLLECTION AGENCIES LTD V WOOD (1980) 124 Sol Jo 498 (Queen's Bench Division: NEILL J).

2202   —— security for costs—counterclaim—when security for costs granted

The charterers of a vessel refused to load the cargo. The owners treated the charter as terminated and claimed damages for repudiatory breach. The charterers counterclaimed that the vessel had not been fit to load. The case was referred to arbitration and both parties applied for security for costs against the claim and counterclaim. On appeal by the owners against the refusal to order security for costs against the counterclaim, *held*, since both parties carried on business out of the jurisdiction and both were claiming as parties who had suffered damage in respect of the same matter they were entitled to be treated alike. The judge had misdirected himself in establishing that the fact that the same issues were likely to arise on both the claim and counterclaim was a decisive factor. It was not so decisive a factor as to exclude the exercise of discretion. Accordingly, the court would exercise its discretion to interfere with the decision. The appeal would be allowed and the charterers would be ordered to pay a similar amount to that payable by the owners by way of security for the costs of the counterclaim.

THE SILVER FIR, SAMUEL J COHL CO V EASTERN MEDITERRANEAN MARITIME LTD [1980] 1 Lloyd's Rep 371 (Court of Appeal: LAWTON LJ and SIR STANLEY REES). *Neck v Taylor* [1893] 1 QB 560, CA applied.

2203   —— —— quality of security—trust money

In an action for libel, following an order of security for costs, the question arose as to the quality of security required, because there was a possibility of trust money being involved. *Held*, a full and strict meaning would be given to the word "security" which must be truly secure. Money which was subject to a trust or from a charity would not be acceptable.

ORME V ASSOCIATED NEWSPAPERS GROUP LTD (1980) Times, 21st November (Queen's Bench Division: COMYN J).

2204 —— taxation—solicitor's duty towards client with unpaid bill of costs

See *Re Laceward Ltd*, para. 2808.

2205 —— taxation of costs "of and incidental to" an application—duty of taxing master to give reasons for decision

An order of court provided for the taxation of costs "of and incidental to" an application. In reviewing the costs, the taxing master took into account work done prior to the issue of the summons. On appeal *held*, under RSC Ord. 62, r. 28 (2), on a party and party taxation there were to be allowed "such costs as were necessary or proper for the attainment of justice or for enforcing or defending the rights of the party whose costs are being taxed". By r. 28 (4) on a taxation on the common fund basis, there was to be allowed "a reasonable amount in respect of all costs reasonably incurred" which referred to the "costs of and incidental to" the proceedings in question. It was important to identify the nature and the correct stage of the proceedings. It was clear that the words "incidental to" extended the ambit of the order. Accordingly, costs that would otherwise be recoverable were not be disallowed because they were incurred during preparations for negotiations and as incidental to them. Although the taxing master had been correct to disallow the objection he had not given adequate reasons for his decision in accordance with r. 34 (4) of the order which required him, on request, to give reasons for his decision on a review of costs and any special facts or circumstances relevant to it. It was not sufficient that he had taken "all relevant circumstances into account".

RE GIBSON'S SETTLEMENT TRUSTS, MELLORS v GIBSON [1981] 1 All ER 233 (Chancery Division: SIR ROBERT MEGARRY V-C). *SA Pêcheries Ostendaises v Merchants' Marine Insurance Co* [1928] 1 KB 750, CA, *Frankenburg v Famous Lasky Film Service Ltd* [1931] 1 Ch 428, CA, applied; *Re Fahy's Will Trusts* [1962] 1 All ER 73 not followed.

2206 Discontinuance of action—action for damages—court's power to prevent plaintiff from continuing foreign action

The plaintiff, a Portuguese worker, was rendered quadriplegic in an accident on board ship in an English port. His employers, the defendants, were a multi-national company with both American and United Kingdom associates. The plaintiff commenced proceedings for damages in England and the defendants made interim payments into court under RSC Ord. 29, r. 9. However, the plaintiff signed a power of attorney in favour of American lawyers, giving them full authority to enforce his claim in America on a contingency fee basis. The plaintiff's English solicitors therefore gave notice of discontinuance of action without leave, as they were entitled to do so under RSC Ord. 21, r. 2. The defendants' application for an injunction to restrain the plaintiff from commencing or continuing any further proceedings in America was granted on the ground that it was an abuse of process to use the mechanism of discontinuance without notice to improve the plaintiff's position in America whilst reserving the right to commence afresh in England. By a majority the Court of Appeal reversed this decision and on appeal by the defendants, *held*, the appeal would be dismissed. (1) Notwithstanding that it was illogical to treat an act which purported to terminate a process as an abuse of that process, the court had an inherent power to prevent a party from using the process to obtain an unjust advantage. Had leave been required to discontinue the action it would have only been granted subject to the repayment of moneys and an undertaking by the plaintiff not to issue a second writ in England. The notice of discontinuance had rightly been set aside, but leave to discontinue would be given pursuant to RSC Ord. 21, r. 3 (1). (2) To justify the grant of an injunction it had to be shown, inter alia, that the injunction would not deprive the plaintiff of a legitimate personal or judicial advantage available to him. The prospect of higher damages in America was a legitimate advantage and the Court of Appeal had properly discharged the injunction.

CASTANHO v BROWN & ROOT (UK) LTD [1980] 3 WLR 991 (House of Lords: LORD WILBERFORCE, LORD DIPLOCK, LORD KEITH OF KINKEL, LORD SCARMAN and LORD BRIDGE OF HARWICH). Decision of Court of Appeal [1980] 3 All ER 72 affirmed.

2207   **Dismissal of action—abuse of process of court—issue decided in earlier criminal proceedings**

See *McIlkenny v Chief Constable of West Midlands Police Force*, para. 1102.

2208   **Entry of appearance—unconditional appearance—action time-barred—effect of unconditional appearance**

See *Liff v Peasley*, para. 1799.

2209   **European Court of Justice—application for compensation—form of application**

See Case 90/78: *Granaria BV v EC Council and EC Commission*, para. 1125.

2210   **—— reference to European Court of Justice—power of English court to refuse reference**

In the course of hearing an application to strike out certain defences based on the EEC Treaty, to an action for infringement of copyright, WALTON J said that the effect of art. 177, under which national courts have a discretion to refer questions on the interpretation of the Treaty to the European Court, was not to exclude the jurisdiction of a national court to consider the validity of alleged defences based on the Treaty. There was no reason why such defences should be treated with any more caution than any other possible defence.

BRITISH LEYLAND MOTOR COPRN v T. I. SILENCERS LTD [1980] 1 CMLR 598 (Chancery Division: WALTON J).

2211   **Extension of time—conditional order—jurisdiction of court to extend time for compliance**

See *Samuels v Linzi Dresses Ltd*, para. 1668.

2212   **Family Division—application for ancillary relief—appointment for directions—pre-trial review**

The following Practice Direction ([1980] 1 All ER 592) has been issued by the Senior Registrar of the Family Division.

From 1st April 1980 by way of experiment in the Divorce Registry the substantive appointment for directions in all applications for property adjustment and lump sums will include a pre-trial review at which the registrar will consider the possibility of settlement of the case, or clarification of the issues. Where the case continues to be contested the registrar will give directions, particularly as to discovery, designed to elicit all necessary information but to save costs by excluding over-detailed requests for it.

With a view to achieving these objectives the following procedure should be followed in these cases:

1. The applicant's affidavit in support of the application should have annexed to it a list setting out the capital of the deponent, and any loans debts and other charges against capital. The list should also set out all the deponent's sources of income and the income from each source. A copy of this list with a similar list in respect of the respondent's means, set out on the same page, should be annexed to his affidavit. Where the deponent is employed he should exhibit his last three pay slips or, if he is the director of any company, the last three accounts of that company. Where the deponent is self-employed he should exhibit his accounts for the past three years or other appropriate information as to his means.

2. After affidavits have been filed, general mutual discovery should take place without order 14 days from the last affidavit, unless some other period is agreed, with inspection seven days thereafter.

3. Where a dispute arises as to the value of any property a valuation should be made by an agreed valuer or, in default of agreement, by an independent valuer

chosen by the President of the Royal Institution of Chartered Surveyors. The valuation should be produced at the appointment for directions and pre-trial review.

4. Any questionnaire should be delivered to the other side at least 21 days before the said appointment. At the pre-trial review directions will be given by the registrar as to what disputed items on discovery or in the questionnaire are to be dealt with. Where the registrar considers that to answer any question would entail considerable expense and that there is doubt whether the answer would provide any information of value, he may make the order for the question to be answered at the questioner's risk as to costs. The registrar may refuse to order an answer to a question if he considers that its value would be small in comparison with the property or income of the party to whom the question is addressed.

5. If after the pre-trial review there are relevant changes in the income or capital position of either party, these should be set out in an affidavit annexing a list of the changes as compared with the earlier list.

6. Where the issue of conduct is raised on the affidavits, the registrar will enquire whether it is being pursued and, if so, will order particulars to be given of the precise allegations relied on.

7. To ensure the success of this procedure it is essential that pre-trial reviews should be attended either by counsel or by a representative of solicitors who is fully conversant with the facts of the case.

2213   —— applications—"liberty to apply"—effect

The following Practice Direction ([1980] 1 All ER 1008) has been issued by the Senior Registrar of the Family Division.

Judges and registrars of the Family Division have found that there is misunderstanding among practitioners as to the meaning of the words "liberty to apply". In one sense there is always liberty to apply since the court can always be applied to by using the proper procedure, but it is emphasised that, except in a few special cases, the words "liberty to apply" do not give the right to apply to the court without using the procedures comprised in the Matrimonial Causes Rules 1977, r. 122 and in the Non-Contentious Probate Rules 1954, passim.

Under a summons for directions there is always liberty to apply for further directions without taking out a further summons. The court may give liberty to apply as to terms of compromise or as to the minor terms where property is settled. These examples are not exhaustive but, in general, applications should not be made under liberty to apply without using the procedures laid down by the rules referred to.

2214   —— children—abduction—press publicity

The following Practice Direction ([1980] 2 All ER 806) has been issued by the Senior Registrar of the Family Division.

In cases where a child has been abducted, a judge may consider that press publicity may assist in tracing that child.

The President is of the opinion that in such cases the judge should adjourn for a period of about ten minutes to enable representatives of the press to attend, so that the widest publicity may be given.

2215   —— —— order for return of child from outside jurisdiction—return by air

The following Practice Direction ([1980] 1 All ER 288) has been issued by the President of the Family Division with the concurrence of the Lord Chancellor.

Where a person seeks an order for the return to him of children about to arrive in England by air and desires to have information to enable him to meet the aeroplane, the judge should be asked to include in his order a direction that the airline operating the flight, and, if he has the information, the immigration officer at the appropriate airport, should supply such information to that person.

To obtain such information in such circumstances in a case where a person already has an order for the return to him of children, that person should apply to a judge ex parte for such a direction.

2216   —— counsel's fees—fees allowed on taxation

The following Practice Direction ([1980] 1 All ER 496) has been issued by the Senior Registrar of the Family Division.

The Senior Registrar of the Family Division, in consultation with the Senate of the Inns of Court and the Bar, has decided that the scale of fees set out hereafter would be proper to be allowed on taxation in respect of instructions and briefs delivered on or after 1st February 1980.

It is emphasised that the list is intended only to be a guide as to the broad range of fees applicable to the average 'weight' of each item of work, and higher or lower fees may be allowed in appropriate cases.

The items in the list are those most frequently found in the most common kind of case, but the list itself is not exhaustive. For example, it will be observed that brief fees relating to contested suits or to ancillary relief have not been dealt with, since it is considered that conditions vary too much for them to be included in a scale.

The Senior Registrar confirms his predecessor's view that, when, in circumstances which merit it, counsel gives an oral opinion in the course of a conference, his fee therefor may be substituted for the routine conference fee. The taxing officer will require to be satisfied that it was appropriate to have dealt with the matter orally. It should not be assumed that, as a matter of course, the fee given for such an oral opinion will be the same fee as for one in writing.

Answer (plain denial)	£8
Answer (with no cross-charge)	£15
Answer (with cross-charge)	£25–£35
Request for particulars	£10
Particulars	£10–£40
Reply (plain denial)	£8
Reply (other than a plain denial)	£15–£25
Advice on evidence	£15–£50
Opinion (comprehensive)	£25–£50
Opinion (limited)	£15–£25
Notice of appeal or counter-notice	£20–£30
★Affidavit (main)	£20–£50
★Affidavit (minor supporting)	£8–£15
Brief – registrar (procedural)	£25–£35
Brief – judge (ex parte injunction)	£25–£35
Brief – judge (injunction)	£30–£100
Brief – judge (uncontested application in chambers)	£30
Consultation (Queen's Counsel)	£20 first half hour £15 thereafter
Conference (junior counsel)	£10 first half hour £8 thereafter

★If drafted with other affidavits an omnibus fee may be allowed.

2217   —— custody—access—supervised access

The following Practice Direction ([1980] 1 All ER 1040, [1980] 1 WLR 334) has been issued by the President of the Family Division with the concurrence of the Lord Chancellor.

Where application is made to the court for access to be supervised, every effort should be made, before the matter comes before the court, to obtain the consent of a person likely to be agreeable to both parties to supervise the access. Mutual friends, unprejudiced relatives and godparents are examples of the classes of persons who should be approached.

Only when every effort has been made to enlist the help of such persons and has been unsuccessful should welfare officers and similar persons be involved. Application for such persons to supervise access should never be made without obtaining the consent of the person concerned and every effort should be made to avoid asking them to exercise supervision on Saturdays or Sundays.

In the few instances where it is necessary to ask that supervision should be carried out by welfare officers, the supervision should be confined to a very few occasions, the number of which should be specified in the order. Care must be taken to arrange a place of access which does not cause the welfare officer undue travelling difficulties.

2218 —— —— **joint custody order—right of parties to be heard**

The following Practice Direction ([1980] 1 All ER 784, [1980] 1 WLR 301) has been issued by the President of the Family Division with the concurrence of the Lord Chancellor.

It sometimes happens that the judge who is considering the arrangement for the children under s. 41 of the Matrimonial Causes Act 1973 is invited by one or both parties to make a joint custody order. Such orders are being sought more often now than formerly and variations of practice have been noticed in different parts of the country. With a view to securing uniformity of approach it is hereby directed as follows:

1. Where a petitioner and a respondent have reached an agreement as to which of them should have the care and control of the child, or children, and are further agreed that legal custody should be vested in the two of them jointly and only one of them appears on the appointment, the court ought not on that appointment to make an order which is inconsistent with the agreement. If the court is unwilling to make the agreed order, it should adjourn the matter to give each party the opportunity to be heard.

2. Where a petition contains a prayer for custody and the respondent has indicated in writing (in the acknowledgment of service or otherwise) that he (or she) wishes to apply for custody to be vested in the two of them jointly, the court should proceed on the basis that the question of custody is in issue, and should not make an order for custody, or joint custody, except with the agreement of both parties or after giving each of them the opportunity to be heard.

2219 —— **maintenance order including element in respect of school fees—tax relief—form of order**

The following Practice Direction [1980] 3 All ER 832, [1980] 1 WLR 1441 has been issued by the Senior Registrar of the Family Division with the concurrence of the Lord Chancellor.

Where a maintenance order to a child includes an element in respect of school fees, which is paid direct to the school (because, for example, it is feared that the other spouse might dissipate it), the Inland Revenue has agreed, subject to the condition hereafter set out, that tax relief will be given on that element. The wording of the order should be:

'That that part of the order which reflects the school fees shall be paid to the headmaster [or bursar or school secretary] as agent for the said child and the receipt of that payee shall be sufficient discharge.'

The school fees should be paid *in full* and should be paid out of the net amount under the maintenance order after deduction of tax. Certificates for the full tax deduction should continue to be provided to the other spouse (or other person referred to in r. 69 of the Matrimonial Causes Rules 1977, S.I. 1977 No. 344) in the normal way.

It is a condition of such an order being acceptable for tax purposes that the contract for the child's education (which should preferably be in writing) should be between the child (whose income is being used) and the school and that the fees are received by the officer of the school as the appointed agent for the child.

A form of contract which is acceptable to the Inland Revenue is as follows:

'THIS AGREEMENT is made between THE GOVERNORS OF . . . .
. . . . by their duly authorised officer . . . .
(hereinafter called "the school") of the first part, ... and the headmaster [or bursar or school secretary] of the second part, and (hereinafter called "the child") of the third part.

'WHEREAS it is proposed to ask the . . . . Court to make an order [or the

..... Court has made an order] in cause no .... that the father do make periodical payments to the child at the rate of £....... per annum less tax until the child completes full-time education [*or as the case may be*] and that that part of the order which reflects the school fees shall be paid to the headmaster [*or bursar or school secretary*] as agent for the said child and the receipt of that agent shall be a sufficient discharge.

'1. The child hereby constitutes the headmaster [*or bursar or school secretary*] to be his agent for the purpose of receiving the said fees and the child agrees to pay the said fees to the said school in consideration of being educated there.

'2. In consideration of the said covenant the headmaster [*or bursar or school secretary*] agrees to accept the said payments by the father as payments on behalf of the child and the school agrees to educate the child during such time as the said school fees are paid.'

2220   —— **maintenance orders—minors and spouses—registration in magistrates' court**

The following Practice Direction ([1980] 1 All ER 1007) has been issued by the Senior Registrar of the Family Division with the concurrence of the Lord Chancellor.

(a) Children's orders

Section 77 of the Domestic Proceedings and Magistrates' Court Act 1978, which came into operation on 1st November 1979, added a new s. 53A to the Magistrates' Court Act 1952. This makes provision, inter alia, for a magistrates' clerk to transmit payments under a maintenance order registered in his court, which provides for payment directly to a child, either directly to that child or to the person with whom the child has his home. It also provides that that person may proceed in his own name for variation, revival or revocation of the order and may enforce non-payment either in his own name or by requesting the magistrates to do so.

It is therefore no longer necessary for the High Court or the divorce county court when granting an application for registration to place on the order the wording required by the Practice Direction [1977] 3 All ER 942, 1977 Halsbury's Abridgment para. 952 and that direction is hereby cancelled.

The registration in a magistrates' court of an order made direct to a child entails a considerable amount of work. Accordingly, when the court is considering the form of an order where there are children, care should be taken not to make orders for payment direct where such orders would be of no benefit to the parties or where the parties would derive no immediate tax advantage.

(b) Nominal orders for spouses.

Applications for leave to register orders for nominal amounts in favour of spouses only should not be allowed and, except in special circumstances, leave to register should not be granted in respect of orders for maintenance pending suit and interim orders.

2221   —— **probate—resealing—grants issued by courts of Zimbabwe**

The following Practice Direction ([1980] 2 All ER 324, [1980] 1 WLR 553) has been issued by the Senior Registrar of the Family Division.

By virtue of an Ordinance enacted on 7th December 1979, provision was made for the recognition of any act done in Southern Rhodesia in reliance upon any law or purported law in operation in that country from 11th November 1965, onwards until its independence.

One of the effects of this provision is that grants of representation issued by the courts in Southern Rhodesia, irrespective of the date of issue, may once more be re-sealed in England and Wales under the Colonial Probates Act 1892.

Accordingly, the registrar's direction of 7th April 1970, Practice Direction (Rhodesian Grants: Resealing) [1970] 1 All ER 1248, [1970] 1 WLR 687, is hereby cancelled.

On 18th April 1980, Southern Rhodesia became an independent country known as Zimbabwe. Provision has been made in the Zimbabwe Act 1979 for the continued application of the Colonial Probates Act 1892 to grants issued by its courts on and after that date.

2222   —— wardship and guardianship proceedings—applications for custody or access

The following Practice Direction ([1980] 1 All ER 813) has been issued by the Senior Registrar of the Family Division with the approval of the President.

By a Practice Direction [1977] 3 All ER 944, [1977] 1 WLR 1226, 1977 Halsbury's Abridgment para. 925, it was provided that on an application in a matrimonial cause for an agreed custody order of for an order for access to a child where the only question at issue is the extent of such access, the application should in the first instance be made to a registrar, unless there are exceptional circumstances making it desirable for the matter to be brought before a judge for decision.

The judges of the Family Division are of the opinion, and it is accordingly hereby directed, that applications of like nature made in wardship and guardianship cases proceeding in the Principal Registry including applications for an agreed care and control order should be dealt with in the same manner.

2223   House of Lords—petitions for leave to appeal

A Procedure Direction ([1980] 2 All ER 688) has been issued by the Clerk of the Parliaments amending Directions as to Procedure Nos. 3 and 6. Direction No. 3 (i) (service of petition) now provides that where the Order of the Court of Appeal complained of is an Order refusing leave to appeal to that Court from a judgment of a lower court the House of Lords does not require an Order refusing leave to appeal to the House. Direction No. 6 (1) (a) (incompetent criminal petitions) now contains an exception in favour of cases of judicial review.

2224   Joinder of defendant—joinder after expiry of limitation period—date joinder takes effect

See *Liff v Peasley*, para. 1799.

2225   Lands Tribunal—application to state a case—jurisdiction of Lands Tribunal

See *R v Lands Tribunal, ex parte City of London Corpn*, para. 2287.

2226   Legal aid

See LEGAL AID AND ADVICE.

2227   Litigants in person—costs and expenses

The Litigants in Person (Costs and Expenses) Order 1980, S.I. 1980 No. 1159 (in force on 1st September 1980), applies to proceedings in the Employment Appeal Tribunal the provisions of the Litigants in Person (Costs and Expenses) Act 1975, so as to enable an award of costs made by the Tribunal to a litigant in person to include the same items of costs as a represented litigant can claim, including in particular costs for time spent preparing the case.

2228   Litigants in Person (Costs and Expenses) Act 1975—commencement

The Litigants in Person (Costs and Expenses) Act 1975 (Commencement No. 2) Order 1980, S.I. 1980 No. 1158, brought into force on 1st September 1980, that part of the Act not already in force.

2229   Payment into court—appropriation of payment—to whom interest payable

The High Court has held that where money was lodged into court as a condition of granting leave to defend under RSC Ord. 14, and the defendant appropriated part of the sum in satisfaction of the plaintiff's claim within the meaning of RSC Ord. 22

r. 8, the interest on the appropriated sum was not to be transferred, under the Supreme Court Fund Rules 1975, r. 27 (3), 1977 Halsbury's Abridgment para. 2639, to the Paymaster General. That requirement only applied where the plaintiff accepted the money paid into court in satisfaction of the claim. Hence where such a defendant was successful he was entitled to any such accrued interest.

SCHROEDER V ACCOUNTANT GENERAL [1980] 2 All ER 648 (Queen's Bench Division: WOOLF J).

2230   Preliminary trial of issue—causation—action in negligence

See *Hyman and Williams v Schering Chemicals Ltd*, para. 2034.

2231   Queen's Bench Division—land registration—production of register of title—procedure

The following Practice Direction [1980] 3 All ER 704, [1980] 1 WLR 1335 has been issued by the Senior Master of the Supreme Court, with the concurrence of the Chief Chancery Master.

The requirement that an application under the Land Registration Rules 1967, S.I. 1967 No. 761, should be made by summons is hereby revoked and such application may be made ex parte on affidavit.

Accordingly, the Practice Direction of 23rd June 1970 ([1970] 3 All ER 70, [1970] 1 WLR 1158) should be amended by deleting the words "should be made by summons pursuant to RSC Ord. 32, r. 1" and substituting therefor the words "may be made by an ex parte application".

2232   ——Masters' Practice Directions—commencement of proceedings

A Practice Direction ([1980] 3 All ER 822) has been issued by the Senior Master of the Supreme Court, regulating the consequential changes, occasioned by the new form of Writ of Summons, upon the practice to be followed in the Central Office.

Masters' Practice Directions 9, 9A–12 are replaced by Practice Directions 9 (issue of writ of summons), 9A (postal facilities for issue of writs, etc.), 9B (issue of originating summons), 10 (substituted service), 11 (service out of the jurisdiction), 12 (acknowledgment of service).

Direction 9 details the preparation of writ of summons for issue, acceptance of prescribed forms already adapted, the number of copies of writ to be prepared, the signing of the court copy, the preparation of forms of acknowledgment of service, the tendering of the writ for issue, and its issue, and concurrent writs. Direction 12 provides for the completion of acknowledgment of service, the requirements for due acknowledgment of service, the acknowledgment by a limited company or other body corporate, acknowledgment on one form by two or more defendants, the statement of intention to apply for a stay of execution, the statement of application for transfer of district registry action, the insertion of the address for service on the back page of the form of acknowledgment of service, the court procedure on receipt of acknowledgment of service, the amendment of acknowledgment of service and the acknowledgment of service of third party notice or other originating process.

In addition, the following Masters' Practice Forms are prescribed:

PF 4A	Praecipe for concurrent writ.
PF 9	Certificate of no acknowledgment of service.
PF 42	Praecipe for amended acknowledgment of service.
PF 120 (B 35)	Affidavit on application for substituted service.
PF 121 (H 19)	Order for substituted service.
PF 122 (B 36)	Affidavit of service of writ (personal).
PF 122A	Affidavit of service of writ on individual by post.
PF 122B	Affidavit of service of writ on individual by insertion through letter-box.
PF 122C	Affidavit of service of writ of summons on partnership by post.
PF 122D	Affidavit of service of writ on body corporate by post.

PF 122E   Affidavit of service of writ on body corporate by insertion through letter-box.
PF 123   Affidavit of service on a partner in a firm.
PF 124 (B 36A)   Affidavit of service on manager of partnership firm.
PF 125   Affidavit of service on officer of corporation (personal).
PF 126 (B 36C)   Affidavit of service on English limited company.
PF 127   Affidavit of service on foreign company registered in England.
PF 128   Affidavit of service of notice of writ on foreigner abroad.

For the full text of the forms see LS Gaz 18th June 1980, pp. 615 et seq, 130 NLJ 567 et seq.

2233   Rules of the Supreme Court

The Rules of the Supreme Court (Amendment) 1980, S.I. 1980 No. 629 (in force on 3rd June 1980 except r. 21 which comes into force on the day to be appointed for the coming into force of the Administration of Justice Act 1977, s. 3) amend the Rules primarily so as to (i) give procedural backing to the Protection of Trading Interests Act 1980, (ii) provide for the service of process under the Hague Convention on persons resident in independent Commonwealth countries, (iii) provide for the service of process on a State and for the recovery and enforcement of a default judgment against a State, (iv) permit the renewal of a writ of execution after its expiry, (v) amend the rules relating to charging orders in the light of the Charging Orders Act 1979, (vi) modernise the procedure for service in England and Wales of process originating abroad, (vii) authorise proceedings in accordance with the Fair Trading Act 1973, s. 85(7) to be begun by originating motion, (viii) provide for the re-registration of maintenance orders as soon as the Administration of Justice Act 1977, s. 3 is brought into force and (ix) provide for the enforcement of maintenance orders against persons resident in the Hague Convention countries.

2234   The Rules of the Supreme Court (Amendment No. 2) 1980, S.I. 1980 No. 1010 (in force on 1st October 1980 except rr. 1 and 14 which came into force on 11th August 1980) amend the Rules so as to (i) change the practice relating to further and better particulars, (ii) prevent discontinuance without leave once an interim payment has been made, (iii) provide for interest to be included in a payment into court in satisfaction of a claim, (iv) provide for automatic directions in personal injury actions, (v) allow the court to order payment on account of any damages or debt whatever the nature of the litigation, (vi) allow a defendant to offer to accept reduced liability where liability is ordered to be tried as a preliminary issue, (vii) require a writ of subpœna to be served no later than four days before the hearing unless the court directs otherwise, (viii) require the disclosure of all experts' reports in personal injury cases, unless sufficient reason is shown to the contrary, (ix) allow certain judgments and orders to be made "by consent" without judicial information, (x) provide for appeals by case stated under the Domestic Proceedings and Magistrates' Courts Act 1978 to be taken by a Divisional Court of the Family Division, (xi) revise the fixed costs allowable under Ord. 62, App. 3, (xii) require that certain particulars be included in the originating summons in wardship proceedings, and (xiii) require certain appeals from a magistrates' court in matrimonial proceedings to be heard by a single judge.

2235   The Rules of the Supreme Court (Amendment No. 3) 1980, S.I. 1980 No. 1908 (in force on 2nd January 1981), amend the RSC so as to, inter alia, broaden the scope of the notice to admit, transfer from the Divisional Court of the Queen's Bench Division to the Divisional Court of the Family Division the jurisdiction to hear appeals by case stated in care proceedings, to provide for appeals to the Court of Appeal from decisions of the Social Security Commissioners, to enlarge and clarify the power of taxing officers in relation to certificates of taxation, to increase the fixed costs recoverable under Ord. 62, App. 3, to simplify the procedure for releasing ships from arrest, to raise the size of the fund out of which money may be paid on an ex parte application, unless the Court directs otherwise, to revise Ord. 102 in the light of the Companies Act 1980 and to clarify the powers of the Court to specify a date for possession in proceedings under RSC 113.

2236   The Rules of the Supreme Court (Amendment No. 4) 1980, S.I. 1980 No. 2000 (rules 1–14 in force on 12th January 1981 and rules 15–23 on 2nd June 1981) make three major changes to the RSC. (1) They provide for a single judge to hear many of the appeals and applications in civil matters which are at present required to be heard by a Divisional Court; and conversely for certain appeals and applications in criminal matters to be heard in vacation by a Divisional Court rather than a vacation judge, as at present. The changes affect proceedings for judicial review (Ord. 53), habeas corpus (Ord. 54), case stated (Ord. 56), enforcement appeals (Ord. 94, r. 12) and applications and appeals under the Local Government Act 1972 Pt. VII (Ord. 98): these Rules rr. 1–14.

(2) All forms of originating process, not just writs of summons, must have the Royal Arms printed or embossed on them as from 2nd June 1981. (3) Where leave is given after 1st June 1981 for proceedings begun by writ to be served abroad, the document to be served must be a copy of the writ itself and not notice of the writ as required at present.

2237   **Service of process—concurrent writ—leave to serve writ out of jurisdiction—grounds on which leave granted**

The plaintiffs owned a cargo of crude oil shipped on a Liberian tanker under two bills of lading which provided that any disputes arising out of the bills of lading were to be governed by English law. A collision occurred between the tanker and a Greek vessel. Subsequently the plaintiffs claimed damages for the cargo lost and as the owners of the tanker had not elected to have the dispute referred to arbitration, the plaintiffs issued a writ against them. The plaintiffs were later granted leave under RSC Ord. 75 to issue a concurrent writ and serve notice of it on the owners of the Greek vessel. The latter applied for an order to set aside the leave granted. *Held*, the parties had agreed that any disputes arising under the bills of lading would be governed by English law and in seeking to do justice between all three parties it was desirable that there should be only one inquiry into the cause of the collision. That inquiry had been started by the plaintiffs in England and there was no other natural forum for the action. The application would be dismissed.

THE AEGEAN CAPTAIN [1980] 1 Lloyd's Rep 617 (Queen's Bench Division: SHEEN J).

2238   **—— service outside jurisdiction—action in tort—jurisdiction of English court**

See *Castree v E. R. Squibb & Sons Ltd*, para. 442.

2239   **—— —— discretion of court**

See *The Vikfrost, W & R Fletcher (New Zealand) Ltd v Sigurd Haarik Aksjeselskap*, para. 2614.

2240   **Stay of proceedings—jurisdiction—foreign contract with exclusive jurisdiction clause**

See *Trendtex Trading Corpn v Credit Suisse*, para. 322.

2241   **—— personal injuries claim—stay pending medical examination**

In a personal injuries action against a local health authority the plaintiff, who was fifty-two and a hospital employee, refused to undergo a medical examination by a surgeon nominated by the authority unless the examination was conducted in the presence of her own doctor. She appealed from an order that the action be stayed until she submitted unconditionally to an examination by the authority's surgeon. The judge found that the authority's request for such an examination was reasonable but without requiring supporting evidence, the condition put forward by the plaintiff was also reasonable. It was reasonable that a woman of fifty-two should be accompanied by her doctor at such a medical examination and that he should be present so as to protect her interests. Accordingly the judge, exercising his discretion, set aside the order. The authority applied to the Court of Appeal for leave to appeal against the judge's decision. *Held*, the court had to have substantial reasons before it was entitled to impose a condition that a plaintiff's doctor should be present at an examination, where that examination had been reasonably requested. It followed that the imposition of such a condition should not be the general practice. The fact that the plaintiff was a woman of fifty-two or that her doctor might be able to testify that the surgeon's report was inaccurate were not sufficient grounds for imposing such a condition. The judge had exercised his discretion on improper grounds. Leave to appeal would be granted and the appeal would be allowed.

HALL v AVON AREA HEALTH AUTHORITY [1980] 1 All ER 516 (Court of Appeal: STEPHENSON, WALLER and CUMMING-BRUCE LJJ). *Starr v National Coal Board* [1977] 1 All ER 243, 1976 Halsbury's Abridgment para. 1985 applied.

2242   In an action for damages for personal injuries, the defendants requested a medical examination of the plaintiff by their doctor. The plaintiff agreed on condition that a copy of the medical report be supplied to him. The defendants applied for a stay of the action until the plaintiff unconditionally submitted to the examination. *Held*, when a court was considering the terms, if any, on which a plaintiff should be required to undergo a medical examination, it should ensure fairness to both parties. That could now be achieved, not by the previous practice of imposing a condition on submitting to an examination, but by the operation of RSC Ord. 38, rr. 36-38, since under r. 37 a defendant had to make available at the stage of the summons for directions a copy of any report by his doctor on the plaintiff, if he wished to use it at the trial of the action, although he did not have to disclose any part of it containing an expression of opinion. It would be inconsistent if a plaintiff could, by imposing a condition to submitting to an examination, obtain details of matters to which he would not be entitled at a later stage. Accordingly, the order sought would be granted.

MEGARITY v D. J. RYAN & SONS LTD [1980] 2 All ER 832 (Court of Appeal: ROSKILL and ORMROD LJJ). *Clarke v Martlew* [1972] 3 All ER 764 not followed.

RSC Ord. 38, r. 37 has been substituted by RSC (Amendment No. 2) 1980, para. 2234.

2243   **Supreme Court fees**

The Supreme Court Fees Order 1980, S.I. 1980 No. 821 (in force on 7th July 1980), revokes the Supreme Court Fees Order 1975, 1975 Halsbury's Abridgment para. 2638, as amended and replaces the Schedule of fees contained in that order with a new Schedule. The sums payable in respect of the new fees are generally higher than those replaced.

2244   The Supreme Court Fees (Amendment) Order 1980, S.I. 1980 No. 1060 (in force on 4th August 1980), amends the 1980 Order, para. 2243, by adjusting the basis on which the fee for taking a cash account between solicitor and own client is calculated.

2245   **Supreme Court funds**

The Supreme Court Funds (Amendment) Rules 1980, S.I. 1980 No. 1858 (in force on 1st January 1981), amend the Supreme Court Funds Rules 1975, r. 35 (1), 1975 Halsbury's Abridgment para. 2639, by lowering the rate of interest allowed on money in a short term investment account from 15 per cent to $12\frac{1}{2}$ per cent per annum.

2246   **Transfer of proceedings—transfer between divisions of High Court—right to trial by jury in Queen's Bench Division where fraud alleged—right of defendant to require transfer**

An action was brought in the Chancery Division by a company against one of its directors, to whom it had made payments, alleging that she had not, nor had intended to, perform any services in respect of the payments, that the payments were made for no consideration, were made ultra vires the company and were effected by the defendant and her husband, another director, in breach of their fiduciary duties to the company, and that they had conspired together to have the money paid to her in breach of their duties to the company and had converted the sums to her use. Fraud was not mentioned in the statement of claim.. The company sought a declaration that the defendant had wrongfully misapplied the company's money, an order requiring her to pay an equivalent sum to the company as constructive trustee and damages for, inter alia, fraud. The defendant applied for the action to be transferred to the Queen's Bench Division on the ground that she was entitled under the Administration of Justice (Miscellaneous Provisions) Act 1933, s. 6 (1) (a), to have the action tried by jury in that division because a charge of fraud was in issue against her. *Held*, a litigant charged with fraud had the right to demand trial by jury if the action was brought in the Queen's Bench Division, but not if it was brought in the Chancery Division; he could not as of right demand the action to be transferred to the Queen's Bench Division. However, the court had a discretion under RSC Ord. 4, r. 3, to order the action to be transferred if it was appropriate to do so; that is, if the case was suitable for trial by jury and the interests of justice required the transfer to be made.

For a charge to fall within s. 6, it was not necessary specifically to use the word "fraud", but fraud had to be in issue between the parties, in that it was a question which had to be decided in order to determine their rights. In this case, no charge of fraud against the defendant was in issue within s. 6, since the company did not have to prove fraud in respect of any of the claims in the statement of claim. Even if a charge of fraud was in issue, the defendant had not established that the case was an appropriate one for the court in its discretion to order the action to be transferred. Accordingly, the application would fail.

STAFFORD WINFIELD COOK & PARTNERS LTD v WINFIELD [1980] 3 All ER 759 (Chancery Division: SIR ROBERT MEGARRY V-C). *Davy v Garrett* (1878) 7 Ch D 473, CA, *Everett v Islington Guardians* [1923] 1 KB 44, DC, *Barclays Bank Ltd v Cole* [1966] 3 All ER 948, CA, *Jenkins v Bushby* [1891] 1 Ch 488, CA and *Williams v Beesley* [1973] 3 All ER 144, HL applied.

2247   **Want of prosecution—dismissal of action—inordinate and inexcusable delay**

The defendants allegedly infringed the plaintiffs' patent for a number of years, and a meeting was arranged in 1965 in an attempt to resolve their differences. The plaintiffs issued a writ in 1972 but the summons for directions was not restored until 1979. The defendants' application to have the action struck out for want of prosecution, on the ground of acquiescence in view of the plaintiffs' considerable delay in proceeding with the action was granted. On appeal by the plaintiffs, *held*, although it was not clear whether the plaintiffs had agreed at the meeting to contact the defendants in any event, it had been incumbent on them to initiate litigation as soon as they were aware that the defendants were marketing a device which they claimed to be an infringement of their patent. Accordingly, delay occurring before the isssue of a writ was relevant, since the validity of the patent could have been determined at an early stage and the plaintiffs would not have suffered such prejudice. Further, due to a radical change in technology, that which had embodied the patent had been superseded, thereby increasing the defendants' difficulty in collecting relevant evidence and any witnesses were at a disadvantage with respect to their recollection of the facts. The judge had correctly exercised his discretion and the appeal would be dismissed.

THE HORSTMAN GEAR LTD v SMITHS INDUSTRIES LTD [1980] FSR 131 (Court of Appeal: BUCKLEY, BRIDGE and TEMPLEMAN LJJ). Decision of Graham J [1979] FSR

461, 1979 Halsbury's Abridgment para. 2170 affirmed. *Birkett v James* [1978] AC 297, 1977 Halsbury's Abridgment para. 2157 applied.

2248   Writ—renewal—cause of action statute-barred

See *Chappell v Cooper; Player v Bruguiere,* para. 1804.

2249   —— —— exceptional circumstances

In January 1976 a car accident occurred in which the driver was killed and the plaintiff, a passenger, was injured. In July 1976 the plaintiff's solicitors informed the deceased's insurers that the plaintiff intended to bring an action for damages for personal injuries. Negotiations took place and in September 1978 the plaintiff issued a writ naming the deceased's personal representatives as defendants. Negotiations continued between the insurer's solicitors and the plaintiff's solicitors in an attempt to reach a settlement. Delay occurred while the insurer's solicitors unsuccessfully attempted to find personal representatives. In September 1979 the plaintiff applied under RSC Ord. 15, r. 6A for the action to proceed. The writ was then out of time and on the plaintiff's application to renew it, *held,* there had been co-operation between the solicitors involved. If there had not been, the plaintiff would have applied to proceed sooner. Although an application could have been made as soon as it was apparent that personal representatives could not be found, negotiations had continued on the basis that the parties agreed that the case should proceed and neither party should take a technical point against the other. Consequently the delay was contributed to by the insurer's solicitors and an agreement that service of the writ be deferred would be implied. The application would be granted.

HARE V PERSONAL REPRESENTATIVES OF MOHAMMED YUNIS MALIK, DECEASED (1980) 124 Sol Jo 328 (Court of Appeal: ROSKILL and EVELEIGH LJJ).

PRISONS

Halsbury's Laws of England (3rd edn.), Vol. 30, paras. 1092–1231

2250   Imprisonment (Temporary Provisions) Act 1980

The Imprisonment (Temporary Provisions) Act 1980 makes provisions relating to the approval of accommodation for the detention of prisoners and the reduction in the number of people held in police custody. Provisions are also made regarding the detention in police custody of persons for whom the police are unable to secure a place in prison. The Act received the royal assent on 29th October 1980 and came into force on that date.

The Secretary of State may approve any place as a temporary place of detention for persons who would otherwise be detained in a prison, remand centre, Borstal institution or detention centre: s. 1. The powers of a magistrates' court to remand a person in custody in his absence are extended: s. 2. The Secretary of State may release a person who has been committed or remanded in custody if it is necessary to do so to make best use of the places available for detention: s. 3. Section 4 empowers the Secretary of State to instruct a magistrates' court not to commit a person to prison for non-payment of money or insufficient distress to satisfy a sum of money. Section 5 provides that specified offenders serving a prison sentence (other than a life sentence) or detained in a detention centre may be released not more than six months before their normal release date.

A person may be detained in police custody until a place in a prison, remand centre, Borstal institution or detention centre can be obtained for him: s. 6. Section 7 contains financial provisions. Section 8 provides that ss. 1–5 remain in force until 29th November 1980 unless continued in force by order (see paras. 2251, 2252) and enables lapsed provisions to be revived.

2251   —— **continuance**

The Imprisonment (Temporary Provisions) Act 1980 (Continuance) Order 1980, S.I. 1980 No. 1822 (in force on 29th November 1980), continues in force the Imprisonment (Temporary Provisions) Act 1980, ss. 1–5, para. 2250, for a period of one month from 29th November 1980.

2252   The Imprisonment (Temporary Provisions) Act 1980 (Continuance No. 2) Order 1980, S.I. 1980 No. 1998 (in force on 29th December 1980), continues in force the Imprisonment (Temporary Provisions) Act 1980, ss. 1–5, para. 2250, for one month from 29th December 1980.

2253   **Parole Board—annual report**

In 1979 local review committees considered 10,156 cases of prisoners serving determinate sentences with a view to suitability for parole and in 5,128 cases considered the prisoner to be suitable. Of these 5,128 cases, 1,925 were granted parole by the Home Secretary under the Criminal Justice Act 1976, s. 35; the Home Secretary also refused parole to 3,234 cases of the 5,028 regarded as unsuitable by local review committees without reference to the Parole Board. Of the 3,203 cases considered suitable for parole by the local review committees and referred to the Parole Board, the board recommended release in 2,488 cases; the board also recommended parole in 358 cases (out of 1,794) where the local review committees had regarded the prisoners as unsuitable. In all, the Home Secretary did not accept the recommendations of the Parole Board in 13 cases. See the Report of the Parole Board 1979 (HC 651). Appendices to the report include, inter alia, the criteria for selection for parole and the board's views on the giving of reasons for refusing parole.

2254   **Prison rules—correspondence between prisoner and legal adviser—legal proceedings**

The plaintiff prisoner complained that he had been assaulted by prison officers. His solicitor wrote to him with a view to lodging a petition with the European Commission of Human Rights but the letter was stopped by the governor. The plaintiff relied on the Prison Rules 1964, r. 37A (1), which provides that a party to legal proceedings may correspond privately with his legal adviser. *Held*, the proceedings in the European Commission were not legal proceedings because they exercised no judicial function. Even if they had been legal proceedings an applicant became a "party" only when his application was accepted by the Commission. As the prisoner was not a "party to any legal proceedings" the letters to and from his solicitor came within the normal rule in r. 33 (1) and could be read and examined by the governor.

GUILFOYLE v HOME OFFICE [1981] 2 WLR 223 (Court of Appeal: LORD DENNING MR, O'CONNOR LJ and SIR JOHN MEGAW).

2255   **Prison service—proposed reform**

In a statement to the House of Commons on the recommendations of the May committee of inquiry into the prison service, the Home Secretary has stated that the government intends to institute a major change in the position of the Prison Department in the Home Office and in its internal organisation. The department will be given wide delegated authority within the Home Office to manage its own staff and to control its own finance. A new post of deputy Director-General will be instituted. Membership of the Prisons Board will be expanded to include the four regional directors and two external non-executive members. An inspectorate will also be established. This will be headed by a Chief Inspector of Prisons and will be separate from the Prisons Department. The Chief Inspector will conduct regular inspections of prisons in England and Wales and will report to the Home Secretary. He may also be asked to conduct specific investigations. The Chief Inspector will be required to make annual reports which will be published. Other reports may be published as appropriate. See The Times, 1st May 1980.

2256   Probation and after-care areas

The Combined Probation and After-Care Areas (Cambridgeshire) Order 1980, S.I. 1980 No. 391 (in force on 1st April 1980), amends the Combined Probation and After-Care Areas Order 1974, 1974 Halsbury's Abridgment, para. 2679, to take account of the reorganisation of petty sessional divisions in Cambridgeshire effected by the Petty Sessional Divisions (Cambridgeshire) Order 1980, para. 1867.

This order has been revoked; see para. 2257.

2257   The Combined Probation and After-Care Areas (Cambridgeshire) (No. 2) Order 1980, S.I. 1980 No. 1162 (in force on 1st December 1980), amends the Combined Probation and After-Care Areas Order 1974, 1974 Halsbury's Abridgment para. 2679 by decreasing the number of justices on the Cambridgeshire Probation and After-Care Committee to sixteen. The following are revoked: S.I. 1976 No. 400, 1976 Halsbury's Abridgment para. 2004; S.I. 1977 No. 1863, 1977 Halsbury's Abridgment para. 2172; S.I. 1978 No. 1192, 1978 Halsbury's Abridgment para. 2244; S.I. 1980 No. 391, para. 2256.

2258   The Combined Probation and After-Care Areas (Hereford and Worcester) Order 1980, S.I. 1980 No. 1020 (in force on 1st August 1980), amends the Combined Probation and After-Care Areas Order 1974, 1974 Halsbury's Abridgment para. 2679 to take account of the renaming of the petty sessional divisions of Hereford (Borough) and Worcester (Borough) as the City of Hereford and the City of Worcester respectively.

2259   The Combined Probation and After-Care Areas (Buckinghamshire) Order 1980, S.I. 1980 No. 1261 (in force on 1st December 1980), amends the 1974 Order, 1974 Halsbury's Abridgment para. 2679, to vary the number of justices appointed by the justices for certain petty sessions areas to the Buckinghamshire Probation and After-care Committee. The total number of justices on the committee is reduced from 25 to 17.

PUBLIC AUTHORITIES AND PUBLIC OFFICERS

2260   Airports authority—statutory powers—exercise of power to prohibit access—validity

See *Cinnamond v British Airports Authority*, para. 186.

PUBLIC HEALTH

Halsbury's Laws of England (3rd edn.), Vol. 31, paras. 1–638

2261   Building regulations—inspection of building operations by local authority—duty of building inspector

See *Acrecrest Ltd v W. S. Hattrell and Partners*, para. 2038; *Stewart v East Cambridgeshire District Council*, para. 2039.

2262   —— prescribed fees

The Building (Prescribed Fees) Regulations 1980, S.I. 1980 No. 286 (in force on 1st April 1980), prescribe the fees payable to a local authority for passing or rejecting plans deposited with it in accordance with the Building Regulations 1976, 1976 Halsbury's Abridgment para. 2013 and for inspecting any building for which such plans have been deposited.

2263　Cinemas—storage of celluloid—exemptions

The Celluloid and Cinematograph Film Act 1922 (Exemptions) Regulations 1980, S.I. 1980 No. 1314 (in force on 31st October 1980), provide for the Health and Safety Executive to grant exemptions from any requirement or prohibition imposed by or under the 1922 Act or any order made under that Act. Conditions may be attached to such exemptions, which must only be granted if the health and safety of persons likely to be affected will not be prejudiced.

2264　Dangerous substances—restrictions on marketing and use

The Control of Pollution (Supply and Use of Injurious Substances) Regulations 1980, S.I. 1980 No. 638 (in force on 1st July 1980), give effect to Council Directive (EEC) 76/769, 1976 Halsbury's Abridgment para. 2017 as amended by Council Directive (EEC) 79/663, 1979 Halsbury's Abridgment para. 2182. The regulations relate to restrictions on the marketing and use of certain dangerous substances and preparations, particularly polychlorinated biphenyls and polychlorinated terphenyls.

2265　Local authority—statutory nuisance—abatement

See *Lambeth London Borough Council v Stubbs*, para. 2073.

2266　Pollution—international agreement

See para. 1321.

2267　—— lead content of petrol—duty of oil companies

See *Budden v BP Oil Ltd; Albert-Speyer v BP Oil Ltd*, para. 2052.

2268　Port health authorities

The following table lists the enactments which provide for the constitution of certain district councils as port health authorities for named ports.

Port District	Relevant Statutory Instruments (1980)
Colchester	1469
Faversham	1481
Folkestone	1063
Great Yarmouth	1104
Lancaster	609
Maldon	1497
Newhaven	1329
Penwith	1330
Teignmouth	1024
Weymouth	1320

2269　Public sewers—right to discharge trade effluent into sewers— whether discharge of effluent from launderettes "domestic sewage"

The plaintiff water authority claimed a sum of money from the defendants in respect of the discharge of effluent from nine different launderette premises. The plaintiff contended that the sum was due because the effluent was trade effluent within the Public Health (Drainage of Trade Premises) Act 1937, s. 14 (1), which, inter alia, defined trade effluent as not including domestic sewage. The defendants contended that the discharge was domestic sewage. *Held*, domestic sewage related to household activities on the premises, the domestic activities of those who worked there as opposed to the effects of the business activities. Everything produced in the course of a trade or business of a launderette was trade effluent. The sum was accordingly recoverable.

THAMES WATER AUTHORITY v BLUE AND WHITE LAUNDERETTES LTD [1980] 1 WLR 700 (Court of Appeal: STEPHENSON, EVELEIGH and BRANDON LJJ).

2270   Residential Homes Act 1980

The Residential Homes Act 1980 consolidates certain enactments relating to the registration, inspection and conduct of residential homes for disabled, old or mentally disordered persons and to the provision by district councils of meals and recreation for old people. The Act received the royal assent on 20th March 1980 and came into force on 1st August 1980: S.I. 1980 No. 947. Tables showing the destination of enactments consolidated and the derivation of the new Act are set out on pages 579–581 following.

DESTINATION TABLE

This table shows in column (1) the enactments repealed by the Residential Homes Act 1980, and in column (2) the provisions of that Act corresponding to the repealed provisions.

In certain cases the enactment in column (1), though having a corresponding provision in column (2), is not, or is not wholly, repealed, as it is still required, or partly required, for the purposes of other legislation.

(1)	(2)	(1)	(2)
Public Health Act 1936 (c 49)	Residential Homes Act 1980 (c 7)	Mental Health Act 1959 (c 72)	Residential Homes Act 1980 (c 7)
s 300 (1)* (2)*	s 4 (2), (3)	s 19 (2)	s 2 (9), 10 (1)
(3)*	3 (5)	(3)	
301*	4 (4)	20 (1)	2 (4)
302*	4 (5)	(2)	2 (5), 3 (2)
		(3)	See s 5 (1) (b)
National Assistance Act 1948 (c 29)		21 (1)	s 5 (1) (c)
		(2)	6 (3)
s 31 (1)–(3)	8 (1)–(3)	23 (1)	7 (1)
33 (1) proviso		147 (1)*	1 (3) (b), 10 (1)
35 (2)*, (3) (a)*, (c)*	8 (4)	154 (2)*	10 (2)
37 (1)	2 (1)	Sch 7, Part II†	
(2)	2 (2), (9)		
(3)	2 (3), (3) (1)	National Assistance Act 1948 (Amendment) Act 1962 (c 24)	
(4)	3 (2)		
(5), (6)	2 (6), (7)	s 1 (1)	8 (1)–(3)
(7)	7 (2)		
(8)	2 (8)	Health Services and Public Health Act 1968 (c 46)	
(9)	1 (2), 10 (1)		
38 (1)–(3)	3 (3)–(5)	s 45 (10)	See s 8 (1)
(4)	4 (1)		
(5)	3 (5), 4 (2)–(5)	Local Government Act 1972 (c 70)	
(6)	Rep., 1968 c 49, s 95 (2), Sch 9, Part 1		
		Sch 23, para 2 (8)	s 2 (9)
39	s 6 (1), (2)	(13)*	7 (1)
40 (1)	5 (1) (a), (b)		
(2), (3)	(2), (3)	Nursing Homes Act 1975 (c 37)	
55*	6 (4), (5)		
56 (3)*	7 (1)	Sch 1, para 4*	1 (3) (b)
63 (2)*	9, 10 (2)	6	1 (2) (b)
(3)*	9		
64 (1)*	1 (2) (a), 8 (5), 10 (1)	Criminal Law Act 1977 (c 45)	
66*	10 (2)		
		s 31 (5), (6)	2 (6)
Mental Health Act 1959 (c 72)		Sch 6†	2 (1), (5), 5 (3), 6 (5)
s 19 (1)	See against 1948, c 29, ss 37–40, above		

* Not repealed. † Repealed in part.

TABLE OF DERIVATIONS

This table shows in the right hand column the legislative source from which the sections of the Residential Homes Act 1980 in the left hand column have been derived. In the table the following abbreviations are used:

    1936 = The Public Health Act 1936
           (26 Geo. 5 & 1 Edw. 8. c. 49)
    1948 = The National Assistance Act 1948
           (11 & 12 Geo. 6. c. 29)
    1959 = The Mental Health Act 1959
           (7 & 8 Eliz. 2. c. 72)
    1968 = The Secretary of State for Social Services Order 1968
           (S.I. 1968/1699)
    1972 = The Local Government Act 1972
           (1972 c. 70)
    1977 = The Criminal Law Act 1977
           (1977 c. 45)

The derivation column does not acknowledge subsection (1) of section 19 of the Mental Health Act 1958 (c. 72), which provides that, subject to the provisions of that section and section 20 of that Act, sections 37 to 40 of the National Assistance Act 1948 (c. 29) shall apply in relation to residential homes for mentally disordered persons as they apply in relation to disabled person's or old persons' homes.

Section of Act	Derivation
1 (1)	—
(2)	1948 ss. 37 (9), 64 (1); 1968 Art. 5 (4); Nursing Homes Act 1975 (c. 37) s. 22 (1), Sch. 1, para. 6.
(3)	1959 ss. 19 (2), 147 (1); Nursing Homes Act 1975 (c. 37) s. 22 (1), Sch. 1, para. 4.
2 (1)	1948 s. 37 (1); 1977 s. 31 (1), Sch. 6.
(2)	1948 s. 37 (2); Fees for Registration of Nursing and Residential Homes (Variation) Order 1968 (S.I. 1968/102).
(3)	1948 s. 37 (3).
(4)	1959 s. 20 (1).
(5)	1959 s. 20 (2); 1977 s. 31 (1), Sch. 6.
(6)	1948 s. 37 (5); Decimal Currency Act 1969 (c. 19) s. 10 (1); 1977 s. 31 (5) (6).
(7)	1948 s. 37 (6).
(8)	1948 s. 37 (8); Decimal Currency Act 1969 (c. 19) s. 10 (1).
(9)	1948 s. 37 (2); 1959 s. 19 (2); 1972 s. 195 (6), Sch. 23, para. 2 (8).
3 (1)	1948 s. 37 (3).
(2)	1948 s. 37 (4); 1959 s. 20 (2).
(3), (4)	1948 s. 38 (1) (2).
(5)	1936 s. 300 (3) as applied by 1948 s. 38 (5); 1948 s. 38 (3).
4 (1)	1948 s. 38 (4).
(2)	1936 s. 300 (1) as applied by 1948 s. 38 (5).
(3)	1936 s. 300 (2) as applied by 1948 s. 38 (5).
(4)	1936 s. 301 as applied by 1948 s. 38 (5); Courts Act 1971 (c. 23), s. 56 (1), Sch. 8, para. 2.
(5)	1936 s. 302 as applied by 1948 s. 38 (5).
5 (1)	1948 s. 40 (1); 1959 ss. 20 (3), 21 (1); 1968 Art. 5 (4).
(2)	1948 s. 40 (2).
(3)	1948 s. 40 (3); 1977 s. 31 (1), Sch. 6.

Section of Act	Derivation
6 (1)	1948 s. 39 (1); 1968 Art. 5 (4).
(2)	1948 s. 39 (2).
(3)	1959 s. 21 (2).
(4)	1948 s. 55 (1).
(5)	1948 s. 55 (2); 1977 s. 31 (1), Sch. 6.
7 (1)	1948 s. 56 (3); 1959 s. 23 (1); 1972 s. 195 (6), Sch. 23, para. 2 (13).
(2)	1948 s. 37 (7).
8 (1)–(3)	1948 s. 31 (1)–(3); National Assistance Act 1948 (Amendment) Act 1962 (c. 24), s. 1 (1).
(4)	1948 s. 35; 1968 Art. 5 (4).
(5)	1948 s. 64 (1).
9	1948 s. 62 (2) (3).
10 (1)	1948 ss. 37 (9), 64 (1); 1959 ss. 8 (3), 19 (2), 147 (1), 149 (1), Sch. 7, Part II; Mental Health (Scotland) Act 1960 (c. 61), s. 113 (1), Sch. 4.
(2)	1948 ss. 63 (2), 66; 1959 s. 154 (2); Isles of Scilly (Mental Health) Order 1962 (S.I. 1962/42) Art. 3.
11	—
12	—
Sch. 1	—
Sch. 2	—

2271   Sports grounds—safety

The Safety of Sports Grounds (Designation) Order 1980, S.I. 1980 No. 1021 (in force on 1st January 1981), designates certain sports stadia as stadia requiring safety certificates under the Safety of Sports Grounds Act 1975.

RACE RELATIONS

Halsbury's Laws of England (4th edn.), Vol. 4, paras. 1034–1100

2272   Commission for Racial Equality—power to conduct formal investigations—procedure

In a case where a firm of estate agents was alleged to have discriminated against coloured people in the course of its business, questions arose as to the procedure adopted by the Commission for Racial Equality in the course of its formal investigation into the alleged discrimination. *Held*, an investigation carried out by the Commission was almost an administrative function and natural justice did not require the formality of a right to cross-examine witnesses upon whose evidence the Commission relied in reaching its decision to issue a non-discrimination notice. It was also open to the Commission to delegate the investigation largely to its employees and to act on their reports even though these were necessarily hearsay.

R v COMMISSION FOR RACIAL EQUALITY, EX PARTE COTTRELL AND ROTHON [1980] 3 All ER 265 (Queen's Bench Division: LORD LANE CJ and WOOLF J). Dictum of Scarman LJ in *Selvarajan v Race Relations Board* [1976] 1 All ER at 24, 1976 Halsbury's Abridgment para. 287 followed.

2273   Discrimination—report of Commission for Racial Equality

The Annual Report of the Commission for Racial Equality 1979 (HC 633) includes in App 11 some instances of complaints of racial discrimination which came before industrial tribunals and county courts. Where awards of compensation for injury to feelings have been identified separately from other heads of award, the amount awarded is shown in cases 10 and 12 (industrial tribunals) relating to discrimination in seeking employment as £75. An award of £50 was made in case 9 by an industrial tribunal when the applicant had refused an offer of £150 for settlement out of court. In case 7, an industrial tribunal awarded compensation of £315 (but this figure may have included a head of award in addition to injury to feelings) and an award of £135 in case 11 may similarly relate to more than one head. In case 15 the attitude of a landlord at a public house to the possible attendance of Pakistanis at a function to be held in a private room led to the organiser calling off the function; a county court judge sitting with assessors found that there had been a breach of the Race Relations Act and awarded nominal damages (£5). In case 16, a settlement was reached whereby two men whose bookings of functions at a hotel had been cancelled as a result of discrimination were awarded damages totalling £500.

2274   Employment—discrimination on racial grounds—discrimination by trade union

Certain employees complained of racial discrimination, contrary to the Race Relations Act 1976, ss. 1 and 11, by a trade union and their employer, a company. On a question of interpretation of those provisions, *held*, (i) the task of a tribunal in a case under ss. 1 (1) (a) and 11 (3) was to ask whether the employees had shown that the union had treated them on racial grounds less favourably than the union treated or would treat other persons in the way that it afforded them access to benefits or by refusing or deliberately omitting to afford the access to such benefits or by subjecting them to any other detriment. Insufficient support for the employees' request for their own union representative was not sufficient evidence indicating that there had been discrimination on the grounds of race contrary to the 1976 Act. (ii) If an employer kept apart one person from others on grounds of his race, contrary to s. 1 (2), that amounted to unlawful discrimination on the part of the employer. Where, however, the fact that all workers were of a particular racial group arose from the acts of those working in a particular department, the failure by the employer to intervene and to insist on workers of other racial groups entering that department, contrary to the wishes of the employees in the department to introduce their friends, did not constitute the act of segregating persons on racial grounds.

    Furniture, Timber and Allied Trades Union v Modgill; Pel Ltd v Modgill [1980] IRLR 142 (Employment Appeal Tribunal: Slynn J presiding).

2275   —— —— segregation

See *Furniture, Timber and Allied Trades Union v Modgill; Pel Ltd v Modgill*, para. 2274.

2276   —— selection for promotion

See *Walsall Metropolitan Borough Council v Sidhu*, para. 1035.

2277   —— selection of employees—indirect discrimination—whether restriction justifiable

An orthodox Sikh who, in accordance with his religion, wore an unshorn beard, applied for the post of maintenance engineer in a chocolate factory. His application was refused on the ground that the wearing of a beard was contrary to hygiene regulations. On his complaint under the Race Relations Act 1976, an industrial tribunal found that there had been indirect discrimination within s. 1 (1) (b) of the Act but that the employers had shown that their requirement in the interests of hygiene and safety was "justifiable". The applicant applied ex parte for leave to appeal from the Employment Appeal Tribunal's decision affirming the industrial tribunal's decision. *Held*, the applicant had a case for complaining that he had been indirectly discriminated against within s. 1 (1) (b) because the number of Sikhs who could comply with the condition imposed by the employers was smaller than in the case of other applicants. There was an exception in favour of the employer if he could show that the restriction was "justifiable" irrespective of the race of the individual. The employers proved that the rules were applied strictly in the interests of hygiene and were applied to persons of all races. The industrial tribunal, having made its findings of fact, held that the restriction about beards was "justifiable" within the meaning of the section. The question was one of fact and it could not be said that the industrial tribunal had erred in law or acted on a wrong principle. Further, there was no breach of the European Convention on Human Rights, art 9, relating to freedom of religion, as that was subject to such limitations as were necessary in the interests of public health. As no error of law had been established, the application for leave to appeal would be refused.

    Panesar v Nestlé Co Ltd [1980] ICR 144 (Court of Appeal: Lord Denning MR and Sir George Baker). *Singh v Rowntree Mackintosh Ltd* [1979] IRLR 199, 1979 Halsbury's Abridgment para. 2198 approved.

2278   —— victimisation of employee—whether justified

The Race Relations Act 1976, s. 2 (1) (c) provides that a person discriminates against another person if he treats that person less favourably in those circumstances than he treats or would treat others, and does so because that person has done something under or by reference to the Act in relation to the discriminator or another person.

    An employee was an interviewer at a job centre. Although he knew that his work was confidential he informed the local Council for Community Relations of incidents where prospective employees who were coloured were being discriminated against by employers. The employee was subsequently demoted. He complained to an industrial tribunal that he had been discriminated against by way of victimisation contrary to the 1976 Act, ss. 2 and 4. *Held*, the employee's disclosure of alleged discrimination was an act done "by reference" to the Act within the meaning of s. 2 (1) (c). Under s. 2 (1) it was necessary to look at the broad reason given by the employer for his treatment of an employee and ask whether other persons would have been treated in the same way. The reason for the employee's demotion was that he had disclosed information given to him in confidence as an employee and the employers would have taken the same view whoever had given confidential information to an outside body. The complaint would be dismissed.

KIRBY V MANPOWER SERVICES COMMISSION [1980] IRLR 229 (Employment Appeal Tribunal: SLYNN J presiding).

2279 Immigration

See IMMIGRATION.

RAILWAYS, INLAND WATERWAYS AND PIPELINES

Halsbury's Laws of England (3rd edn.), Vol. 31, paras. 639–1403

2280 Accidents—notice

The Railways (Notice of Accidents) Order 1980, S.I. 1980 No. 1941 (in force on 1st January 1981), supersedes the Railways (Notice of Accidents) Order 1965. The order applies to statutory railways and tramways and specifies certain classes of accidents on railways and railway premises which are to be reported to the Minister of Transport and contains provisions relating to the form and manner in which railway accidents are to be reported. Accidents involving trains on freight lines and accidents involving the permanent way and works of freight lines are included in the classes of reportable accidents.

RATING

Halsbury's Laws of England (3rd edn.), Vol. 32, paras. 1–272

2281 Article

Rateable Occupation by a Separated Husband, A. N. Khan (in the light of recent cases): 124 Sol Jo 24.

2282 Agricultural building—operation in connection with agriculture— use of hall by farmers' society

A society of farmers occupied a building for the purpose of marketing their produce, one third of which belonged to probationers who were not members. The society claimed that the hall should receive agricultural derating on the ground that it was an "agricultural building" used "in connection with" agricultural operations carried out on agricultural land within the Rating Act 1971, s. 4, and the General Rate Act 1967, s. 26, as amended. *Held*, the phrase "in connection with" in s. 26 meant "ancillary" to the agricultural operations, the test being whether the marketing operation was an independent business or enterprise. Since a substantial part of the produce sold came from non-members, it was not "ancillary" to the agricultural operations. Further, under s. 4 of the 1971 Act, agricultural land had to be occupied solely by members in order to be occupied solely in connection with agricultural operations. It was not, and therefore the hall was disqualified from being an agricultural building.

CORSER V GLOUCESTERSHIRE MARKETING SOCIETY LTD (1980) Times, 21st November (Court of Appeal: WALLER, ACKNER and WATKINS LJJ). *Eastwood Ltd v Herrod* [1971] AC 160, HL, and dictum of Lord Avonside in *Roxburgh Assessor v West Cumberland Farmers Trading Society Ltd* [1977] RA 298, at 307, applied.

2283   —— —— use of silos by grain merchants

Scotland

A company owned two silos used to store grain grown by its members. The grain was owned by the company and it also appointed agents to find suitable markets for the grain. The company appealed against a rating valuation of the two silos contending that they were agricultural buildings within the Rating Act 1971 as the buildings were used solely in connection with agricultural operations. *Held*, the silos were correctly entered on the valuation list because they were not agricultural buildings within the provisions of the 1971 Act. The company was a grain merchant employing agents to find markets for the grain and acting as storers of grain belonging to third parties. This was a separate enterprise from the agricultural operations carried out by the farmers and was more akin to commercial operations. The appeal would be dismissed.

LOWLAND CEREALS LTD v LOTHIAN ASSESSOR [1980] RA 85 (Lands Valuation Appeal Court).

2284   —— use of buildings for keeping or breeding livestock—fish farm

The Court of Appeal has held that a fish farm, used for the production and rearing of trout for consumption as food, does not comprise buildings which are used for keeping or breeding livestock within the Rating Act 1971, s. 2 (1). "Livestock" refers to domestic animals and birds which would ordinarily be regarded as livestock and did not include fish. Accordingly a fish farm does not fall within the exemption from rating afforded to agricultural buildings.

CRESSWELL (VALUATION OFFICER) v BOC LTD [1980] 3 All ER 443 (Court of Appeal: MEGAW, EVELEIGH and WATKINS LJJ).

Rating exemption for fish farms is now provided by the Local Government, Planning and Land Act 1980, s. 31, para. 1819.

2285   Amendment of rate—validity—proposal for alteration in valuation list—effect of failure to serve proposal on ratepayer

A rating authority made and published a rate and subsequently made an amendment to it in order to charge to the rate the premises of a company, in accordance with the General Rate Act 1967, s. 6 (2) (b), to bring the rate into conformity with a proposal to alter the valuation list made by the valuation officer. The company failed to pay the rates and a distress warrant was issued. On appeal, the company contended that the magistrates were wrong to do so. By virtue of the 1967 Act, s. 79 (1), the alteration in the valuation list should be deemed to have effect, in relation to the rate current at the date when notice of the proposal was served on the occupier, from the commencement of the period in respect of which the rate was made. The notice was not served on the company until twenty-eight days had expired and the company had lost the right of appeal; hence the demand for rates was invalid. *Held*, the rating authority had properly amended the rate in accordance with the provisions of s. 6 (2) (b) because of the proposal made by the valuation officer. Accordingly the magistrates were entitled to order the distress warrant and matters arising between the valuation officer and the ratepayer under s. 79 were irrelevant. The appeal would be dismissed.

PEBMARSH GRAIN LTD v BRAINTREE DISTRICT COUNCIL [1980] RA 136 (Queen's Bench Division: ROSKILL LJ and CAULFIELD J).

2286   Distress for rates

See DISTRESS.

2287   Lands Tribunal—application to state case—jurisdiction of Lands Tribunal

Rating assessments were made in respect of certain public houses based on valuations agreed between valuers acting for the owners and the valuation officer for the City of London Corporation. The Corporation was not party to the agreement and appealed against the assessments to the Lands Tribunal. At the hearing of the appeal, the Corporation unsuccessfully applied for disclosure of certain documents. The Corporation then asked the Tribunal to state a case for the decision of the Court of Appeal on the issue under the Lands Tribunal Act 1949, s. 3 (4). The tribunal decided that it did not have jurisdiction to state a case since it had not given a decision within s. 3 (4), only a decision on a procedural matter in interlocutory proceedings. *Held*, under s. 3 (4) a decision of the tribunal was final subject to the right of persons aggrieved by that decision to require the tribunal to state a case for the Court of Appeal. Under the 1949 Act, the Tribunal had jurisdiction not only to decide questions expressly referred to it but also questions of an interlocutory nature arising during the course of proceedings. When a tribunal member granted or refused an application, he made a final decision; the fact that it might be open to a person in changed circumstances to make a further application did not prevent the decision from being final. Therefore, as the tribunal had made a decision within s. 3 (4), an order would be granted requiring a case to be stated for the Court of Appeal.

R v Lands Tribunal, ex parte City of London Corpn [1981] 1 All ER 753 (Queen's Bench Division: Judge Newey).

2288 Local Government, Planning and Land Act 1980

See para. 1819.

2289 Local valuation court—whether "court" for purposes of protection from contempt

See *A-G v British Broadcasting Corpn*, para. 465.

2290 Payment of rates—payment by instalments—extent of ratepayer's right

The ratepayer received a rate demand for the year 1977/78 which informed him that he might pay by regular monthly instalments. In January 1977 he wrote to the rating authority seeking to pay by instalments. In November 1977 a distress warrant was issued and he appealed, relying on the General Rate Act 1967, s. 3 (4), which provides that where a rate is made for a period exceeding three months, the rating authority may declare that the rate shall be paid by instalments at specified times. He contended that this gave him the right to pay by instalments. He relied alternatively on s. 50, which provides that an occupier of a dwelling-house may by notice in writing to the rating authority given in accordance with Sch. 10, para. 1, elect to pay any rates in respect of that hereditament by instalments. *Held*, (i) Section 3 (4) gave the rating authority a discretion to charge rates by instalments but did not confer on the ratepayer any right to pay by instalments. (ii) Schedule 10, para. 1, required notice to be given to the rating authority between 1st February and 30th April in any year. Since the ratepayer's letter was sent in January, he could not therefore rely on s. 50. The appeal would be dismissed.

Hill v Camden London Borough Council [1980] RA 163 (Queen's Bench Division: Lord Widgery CJ and Woolf J).

The provisions as to payment of rates by instalments have been amended by the Local Government, Planning and Land Act 1980, s. 34, para. 1819.

2291 ———— prescribed rateable values

The Payment of Rates by Instalments (Prescribed Sums) Order 1980, S.I. 1980 No. 2011 (in force on 12th January 1981), prescribes maximum and minimum sums as rateable values of hereditaments for the purposes of the General Rate Act 1967, s. 50 (5), with effect from 1st April 1981. Hereditaments having a rateable value above or below the prescribed sums are no longer within s. 50 which enables the occupiers of certain hereditaments to pay rates by instalments.

2292   Payments in lieu of rates—transport boards—adjustment of payments

The Transport Boards (Adjustment of Payments) Order 1980, S.I. 1980 No. 494 (in force on 1st April 1980), decreases for rating years commencing on or after 1st April 1980, the standard amount which determines the contributions payable in lieu of rates by the British Railways Board.

2293   Precept—calculation of amount due

The Rate Product (Amendment) Rules 1980, S.I. 1980 No. 340 (in force on 1st April 1980), amend the Rate Product Rules 1974, 1974 Halsbury's Abridgment para. 2759. The methods of ascertaining the gross rate income and loss on collection are amended to take account of rebates granted under the Rating (Disabled Persons) Act 1978, ss. 1 and 2 and there is a minor amendment dealing with the auditor's certificate. The amendment applies for the determination of the product of a rate of one penny in the pound for the year beginning 1st April 1980 and any subsequent year.

2294   Rate demand note—contents

The Department of the Environment has published a code of practice called "Explaining the Local Authority Rate Bill" which sets out the basic contents of a rate demand note and supplementary information.

The basic contents should include the name and address of the rating authority, the name of any authority or parish for which a precept is issued, or on behalf of which a separate charge is levied, the poundage levied and the net poundage payable, the extent of relief for domestic and mixed hereditaments, the address, description (if necessary) and rateable value of the hereditament, the period of the rate and the amount payable, including any separate charge, and an explanation of the method of calculation and the methods of payment and reference to any entitlements.

The code also recommends that information about the make-up of the rate and the reason for the change in the last year also be published. See Department of the Environment Circular 14/80 (Welsh Office Circular 34/80).

2295   Rate rebate scheme

The Rate Rebate (Amendment) Regulations 1980, S.I. 1980 No. 1625 (in force on 24th November 1980), amend the statutory rate rebate scheme, provided for in the Rate Rebate Regulations 1978, 1978 Halsbury's Abridgment para. 2278. They provide for increases in the needs allowances, increases in the amounts to be deducted for non-dependants and increases in certain of the items to be disregarded in any week in a rebate period beginning after 23rd November 1980, and they add a further item to the items to be disregarded. They also provide for the increased amount of the residential occupier's earnings which is to be disregarded to be attributed, in certain circumstances, to his spouse. The regulations increase the maximum rebate from £4·50 to £6·75 in the GLC area, and from £3·20 to £4·80 elsewhere.

2296   Rate support grants

See LOCAL GOVERNMENT.

2297   Rateable occupation—occupation by spouse—husband and wife divorced—which spouse in rateable occupation

A local rating authority sought from a wife rates for the period 5th April 1974 to 24th June 1976 on the former matrimonial home. The premises had been registered in the Land Registry in the husband's name. In June 1972 the husband left but prior to this a caution was registered, pursuant to the Matrimonial Homes Act 1967, in respect of the premises in favour of the wife. A divorce ensued in September 1972 and the wife and children of the marriage remained in the former matrimonial home as licensees of the husband. The husband continued to use the garage for storage and as a workshop. No maintenance was payable to the wife but on 5th April 1974 the husband was ordered to transfer the premises to the wife on the understanding that she paid him certain sums of money on specified dates. The order was not fully complied with until 24th June 1976, when the premises were transferred to the wife. The rates were paid by the husband until 5th April 1974. The magistrates accepted the wife's contention that, for the period in question, the husband was in rateable occupation. The local authority appealed, contending that the wife was liable for rates because she occupied the premises by virtue of her right derived from the orders of the court made in the matrimonial proceedings which superseded everything that had gone before. *Held*, the magistrates had not erred in their decision. The evidence showed that the order had not been fully complied with until June 1976 and therefore the wife's position in relation to the property remained as it was before the order. On the evidence as a whole, including the fact that the husband had continued to use the garage during the period in question, the husband remained in beneficial occupation for the period in question. The appeal would be dismissed.

ENFIELD LONDON BOROUGH COUNCIL v WOOLLS [1979] RA 399 (Queen's Bench Division: LORD WIDGERY CJ, EVELEIGH LJ and KILNER BROWN J).

2298   In divorce proceedings the husband had been ordered to transfer the matrimonial home from his own sole ownership into his and his wife's joint names, the wife undertaking responsibility for the mortgage repayments and occupying the house as a home for herself and their children. The husband was required to pay maintenance. The wife appealed against a distress warrant issued against her in respect of the rates payable on the property for a period beginning on the date when the divorce became absolute, contending that her former husband ought to be deemed to be in rateable occupation. *Held*, a husband who left the matrimonial home but allowed his wife to occupy it rent free thereby discharging in part his obligation to maintain her and deriving benefit from the use, was deemed to be in rateable occupation. This principle did not extend, however, beyond the dissolution of the marriage, except where a father, after divorce, provided a home for his children in which the mother would also reside as the person having care and control of the children. In such a case the father would be in rateable occupation. However, the court would not extend this "legal fiction" to divorced fathers in respect of houses where their children happened to be living. In this particular case, the right to possession of the house had been vested in the wife by virtue of a court order by way of property adjustment. In no sense, either in fact or in law, could the former husband be said to have been in occupation.

ROUTHAN v ARUN DISTRICT COUNCIL [1980] RA 181 (Queen's Bench Division: DONALDSON LJ and BRISTOW J). *Charnwood District Council v Garner* [1979] RA 49, 1978 Halsbury's Abridgment para. 2283 disapproved. Dictum of Bridge J in *Mourton v London Borough of Hounslow* [1970] 2 All ER 564 applied.

2299   —— —— **husband and wife separated—which spouse in rateable occupation**

In 1974 a husband left his wife and two children, who remained in the matrimonial home. A maintenance order was made in 1975 and following a decree of judicial separation an order by consent was made in 1977 under which the husband was to transfer the whole of his beneficial interest in the property to trustees to hold on trust for sale for the benefit of the children. The rating authority sought a distress warrant against the husband at a time when the 1977 order had not been implemented. *Held*, the husband was rateable since he still had a beneficial interest in the property. The result of the non-implementation of the order was that the position continued as it was before; that is, that the husband maintained his wife pursuant to the maintenance order, allowed her to occupy the property with the children and paid the rent.

PRESTON BOROUGH COUNCIL v FLETCHER [1980] RA 177 (Queen's Bench Division: ACKNER LJ and MARS-JONES J).

2300   In 1974 a husband left his wife, who continued in sole possession of the matrimonial home, which was jointly owned by them. He owned most of the furniture, which he left in the house. He paid the rates until March 1976 and in December 1977 he filed a petition for divorce. No decree nisi had been obtained when the rating authority sought a distress warrant against the husband for 1976/77 and 1977/78. The husband had paid his wife no maintenance and had not discharged any of her liabilities since 1974. *Held*, the husband was liable for the rates. He had not discharged the onus on him to prove that he was no longer the notional occupier of the matrimonial home, because he retained an interest in it and no order or declaration had been made that he was no longer under an obligation to provide a home for his wife.

HARROW LONDON BOROUGH COUNCIL v BRADY [1980] RA 168 (Queen's Bench Division: DONALDSON LJ and BRISTOW J).

2301   From March 1978 the wife had lived with a man in premises of which they were joint tenants, having previously lived there alone. They married in July 1978 but in September 1978 the husband left. The wife continued to live there as sole tenant until March 1979. On the question whether the wife was the rateable occupier for the period October 1978 to March 1979, *held*, she was in rateable occupation because she was in actual occupation and had a legal interest in the property at all times.

ROBINSON v THANET DISTRICT COUNCIL [1980] RA 172 (Queen's Bench Division: ROSKILL LJ and CAULFIELD J).

2302   —— occupation of part of premises—closing order

The tenants of premises refused to pay rates on the ground that they were not in occupation of the basement as a result of a closing order which prohibited them from using it for any purpose other than one approved by the local authority. A distress warrant was issued and the tenants appealed. *Held*, although the tenants no longer physically occupied the basement, and would be liable to be fined if they did so, the closing order had not in itself ended occupation, therefore the tenants remained in rateable occupation.

BENWELL MANSIONS LTD v WESTMINSTER CITY COUNCIL (1980) 256 Estates Gazette 611 (Queen's Bench Division: ORMROD LJ and McNEILL J). Dictum of Goff J in *London Borough of Camden v Herwald* [1976] 2 All ER 808 at 810, 1976 Halsbury's Abridgment para. 865, DC, applied.

2303   —— unincorporated association—no appointment of trustees—liability of trustee by conduct

A Divisional Court of the Queen's Bench Division has held that the person controlling an unincorporated association for the relief of the poor and needy was a trustee by conduct and therefore in rateable occupation and liable to pay the rates on the premises used by the association.

The applicant had founded the association in 1973 and was responsible for its day to day management and control. He also signed all cheques on behalf of the association. Further, persons purporting to describe themselves as trustees were found not to have been validly appointed according to the Trustee Act 1925. The magistrates had issued a distress warrant and the court would refuse to quash their decision.

R v BRIGHTON JJ, EX PARTE HOWARD [1980] RA 222 (Queen's Bench Division: LORD LANE CJ and BOREHAM J).

2304   Rateable value—assessment—conditions affecting property—terms of lease—whether relevant

A ratepayer's lease of premises contained a provision that the ground floor was restricted to use as a launderette only. The first floor could only be reached by a ladder and trap door and was therefore of minimal use. The ratepayer appealed against a decision of the Lands Tribunal concerning assessment on the ground, inter alia, that the Lands Tribunal had failed to take into account, inter alia, the restriction as to use contained in the lease. *Held*, the general statutory obligations that would affect any letting of the premises were relevant but particular restrictions imposed upon the ratepayer by the terms of the lease were not. However the letting of the premises as a shop generally, not necessarily as a launderette, was something which could be, and had to be, considered in assessing the rent the hypothetical tenant would pay for the vacant hereditament. There had been no error of law on the part of the Lands Tribunal and the appeal would therefore be dismissed.

BYRNE V PARKER (VALUATION OFFICER) [1980] RA 45 (Court of Appeal: STEPHENSON, ORMROD and WALLER LJJ).

2305   Surcharge—unused commercial buildings

The Rating Surcharge (Suspension) Order 1980, S.I. 1980 No. 2015 (in force on 1st April 1981), suspends as from 1st April 1981 the General Rate Act 1967, ss. 17A, 17B which are concerned with the rating surcharge on unused commercial buildings. Rights accrued or liabilities incurred prior to 1st April 1981 are unaffected.

2306   —— —— exemption—industrial purposes

Garage premises comprising a car showroom, repair shops, fuelling area and offices were rated as commercial premises. The garage had remained vacant since 1975 and the local rating authority sought a rating surcharge from the owners. The owners claimed exemption under the Rating Surcharge (Exemption) Regulations 1974 on the ground that the premises were constructed as a factory or other premises of a similar character for use for industrial purposes. *Held*, the garage premises were constructed to supply the needs of the public seeking to buy cars, spare parts, fuel or services. They were not a factory but a retail establishment for the purposes of the 1974 Regulations and the surcharge sought would be payable.

POST OFFICE V OXFORD CITY COUNCIL [1980] 2 All ER 439 (Court of Appeal: STEPHENSON, BRIDGE and TEMPLEMAN LJJ). Decision of Divisional Court of the Queen's Bench Division [1979] RA 255, 1979 Halsbury's Abridgment para. 2222 reversed.

2307   —— —— surcharge registered as charge on land—land previously subject to mortgage—priority of charge

In January 1974, a company charged certain business premises by way of legal mortgage to a bank to secure payment of a sum owing to it. The General Rate Act 1967, ss. 17A, 17B, under which a rating surcharge is payable on unused commercial buildings, came into force in February 1974, and between that date and October 1975, the premises remained empty. In March 1976, the bank demanded payment of the sum owing to it. In April 1976, the local authority demanded payment of a rating surcharge under ss. 17A, 17B, and the rating surcharge, as a "charge on land" under s. 17B, was duly registered as a local land charge. The company failed to pay the bank or the surcharge. In July 1977, the bank, as mortgagees, sold the premises to the defendants. The local authority claimed payment of the surcharge and a declaration that the charge, as a registered local land charge, had priority over the defendants' interest in the land. *Held*, the words "charge on the land" in s. 17B naturally imported a charge on all the interests in the land. The charge was therefore a charge on all the interests in the premises including the bank's interest as mortgagees. As the defendants' interest was claimed from the bank the charge also had priority over their interest. The authority was entitled to the declaration sought.

WESTMINSTER CITY COUNCIL V HAYMARKET PUBLISHING LTD [1980] 1 All ER 289 (Chancery Division: DILLON J). Dicta of Jessel MR in *Birmingham Corpn v Baker* (1881) 17 Ch D 782 at 786 and of Fry LJ in *Guardians of Tendring Union v Dowton* [1891] 3 Ch 265 at 269 applied.

This decision has been affirmed by the Court of Appeal; see (1981) Times, 4th March.

2308 Unoccupied property—application for relief from rates on grounds of hardship—appeal—jurisdiction of Crown Court

An application was made under the General Rate Act 1967, Sch. 1, para. 3A, for relief from rates on an unoccupied office building on the grounds of hardship. It was refused by the local rating authority and the owners appealed to the Crown Court under the 1967 Act, s. 7. Section 7 provides that any person who is aggrieved by any neglect, act or thing done or omitted by the rating authority may appeal to the Crown Court. *Held*, the Crown Court had no jurisdiction to hear an appeal against a rating authority's refusal to give relief on the grounds of hardship. The giving of such relief was intended by Parliament to be discretionary and not subject to appeal. The appeal would be dismissed.

ABBEYGATE PROPERTIES LTD v IPSWICH BOROUGH COUNCIL [1980] RA 72 (Crown Court at Ipswich: JUDGE BERTRAND RICHARDS).

2309 —— commercial and industrial property—variation of current ceiling

The Unoccupied Property Rate (Variation of Current Ceiling) Order 1980, S.I. 1980 No. 2012 (in force on 1st April 1981), varies the current ceiling for unoccupied property rate from the whole of the amount of rates ordinarily payable to one half of that amount. The variation applies only to hereditaments other than houses.

2310 —— exemption—listed hereditament—part only of hereditament listed

The General Rate Act 1967, Sch. 1, para. 2 (c), provides that no unoccupied rates are payable in respect of a hereditament for any period during which it is included in a list compiled or approved under the Town and Country Planning Act 1971, s. 54. The ratepayers appealed against the issue of a distress warrant in respect of an unoccupied hereditament, part of which was listed under s. 54. *Held*, when part only of a hereditament was listed under s. 54, the hereditament was not exempt from unoccupied rates under Sch. 1, para. 2 (c). The appeal would be dismissed.

PROVIDENCE PROPERTIES LTD v LIVERPOOL CITY COUNCIL [1980] RA 189 (Queen's Bench Division: LORD LANE CJ and BOREHAM J).

2311 —— new house under construction in garden of existing house—planning permission requiring demolition of existing house—whether ratepayer prohibited by law from occupying new house

The ratepayer applied for, and obtained, planning permission to build a new house in the garden of his existing house, on the condition that he demolished the existing house within one month of the date of occupation of the new house. The rating authority served a completion notice mistakenly referring to the existing house. It then sought unoccupied rates on both houses. The ratepayer contended that (i) unoccupied rates on the new house were not payable as the completion notice was invalid; (ii) having regard to the condition of the planning permission, unoccupied rates were not payable on the existing house by virtue of the General Rate Act 1967, Sch. 1, para. 2 (a), which provides that no unoccupied rates are payable during the time the owner is prohibited by law from occupying it. *Held*, (i) the completion notice was valid and it clearly related to, and the ratepayer understood that it related to, the new house. (ii) The ratepayer was not prohibited by law from occupying the property as the condition in the planning permission did not prevent occupation until such time as it was demolished.

HENDERSON v LIVERPOOL METROPOLITAN DISTRICT COUNCIL [1980] RA 238 (Queen's Bench Division: LORD LANE CJ and WOOLF J).

2312 Valuation list—alteration—authority of local valuation court

A company owned and ran a railway hotel. Since 1971 the premises had been empty. The company made a proposal in respect of the valuation list to the effect that the assessment for the hotel should be deleted from the list on the grounds that it was incorrect, excessive and bad in law. The local valuation court directed that an alteration should be made to the list, reducing the gross and rateable value of the property. The local rating authority appealed, contending that the court's decision was wrong, and that in view of the form of the proposal, the court had no authority to reduce the value of the assessment, but only to have the entry removed or for it to remain. The contention was accepted by the Lands Tribunal and the company appealed. *Held*, since the words in the proposal "assessment should be deleted" were qualified with the ground that it was excessive, it meant that as an alternative to deletion the assessment could be reduced. The valuation court therefore had the authority to reduce the assessment and the appeal would be allowed.

LIVERPOOL CITY COUNCIL v BRITISH TRANSPORT HOTELS LTD (1979) 253 Estates Gazette 53 (Court of Appeal: MEGAW, SHAW and WALLER LJJ).

REAL PROPERTY

Halsbury's Laws of England (3rd edn.), Vol. 32, paras. 273–606

2313   Joint tenancy—severance—matrimonial home—effect of separation agreement providing for transfer of home

Canada

A husband and wife were joint tenants of the matrimonial home. They entered into a separation agreement which provided that the wife would join in a transfer of the home when the husband wished to sell. No sale was made before the death of the husband, who had remarried and had continued in occupation. On the second wife's application for determination of the parties' interests, *held*, the separation agreement had the effect of severing the tenancy.

PATERSON v PATERSON [1980] 2 WWR 683 (Court of Queen's Bench of Manitoba).

2314   —— —— severance by conduct

A freehold house was purchased by the defendant and his brother in 1947. The brothers and their mother lived there until 1962 when the latter died. The house was then converted into two self-contained maisonettes. The defendant and his wife occupied the ground floor and the brother and his wife the first floor. The defendant, at his own expense, built an extension to the ground floor and improved the bathroom on the first floor. The brother died and his wife, the plaintiff, sought a declaration that she was entitled to a half of the beneficial interest in the house. The defendant counterclaimed for possession. *Held*, the onus of establishing severance lay on the plaintiff. There was no written notice of severance and neither of the brothers had made clear any intention of ending the joint tenancy. The mere existence of two separate maisonettes was not inconsistent with continuance of the joint tenancy. The defendant was accordingly entitled to possession.

GREENFIELD v GREENFIELD (1979) 38 P & CR 570 (Chancery Division: Fox J). *Re Denny, Denny v Stokes* [1947] LJR 1029 and dictum of Page-Wood VC in *Williams v Hensman* (1861) 1 John & H 546 at 557 applied.

2315   Possession—summary proceedings—extent of court's jurisdiction

A group of university students occupied part of the university premises as a protest. On their failure to vacate the premises, the university issued a summons under RSC Ord. 113 claiming a possession order in respect of the whole of the university premises. Before the summons was heard the students vacated the premises but left a document threatening to take further action. The proceedings continued and on the question whether the court had jurisdiction to grant an order for possession of the whole premises or only that part of the premises actually occupied, *held*, RSC Ord. 113 merely supplemented the procedural law by providing a new procedure for seeking possession of land where it was not reasonably possible to identify every

wrongful occupier and did not affect the form of redress which the court had
jurisdiction to grant. It was open to the court to make a possession order extending
to the whole of a property although only part of it was adversely occupied. Since
there was a threat that the students might occupy other parts of the university, an
order would be granted to cover the whole of the university premises.

UNIVERSITY OF ESSEX v DJEMAL [1980] 2 All ER 742 (Court of Appeal: BUCKLEY,
SHAW and BRIGHTMAN LJJ).

2316   —— —— **triable issue**

On appeal against an order for possession made under CCR Ord. 26, it was contended
that the order did not apply because there was an issue as to whether there had been
an agreement to grant a lease. The appellants relied on a note on RSC Ord. 113, the
High Court equivalent to Ord. 26, in the Supreme Court Practice, to the effect that
the order normally applied only in virtually uncontested cases or in clear cases where
there was no issue or question to try. *Held*, the note was incorrect. Summary
proceedings should not come to an end by reason of the emergence of a triable
issue. When the court found that there was a triable issue, it could try it in the
course of dealing with the application. The appeal would be dismissed.

SHAH v GIVERT (1980) Times, 9th July (Court of Appeal: BRIDGE and LAWTON
LJJ).

RECEIVERS

Halsbury's Laws of England (3rd edn.), Vol. 32, paras. 607–792

2317   **Appointment—appointment by the court—receiver to manage
charity's affairs—extent of powers**

A school belonging to an educational charity was governed by articles made under
the Education Act 1944. The trustees of the charity were empowered to appoint
and remove governors of the school who in turn were vested with the general
conduct of the school's affairs including the appointment of a new headmaster. The
charity's affairs were in disarray and there was uncertainty as to which of the
governors had power to appoint a new headmaster. In proceedings brought by the
Attorney-General seeking a scheme the court appointed a receiver and manager of
the charity with powers to receive all assets, property and effects of the charity and
generally manage its affairs. Questions subsequently arose as to the receiver's powers
in relation to the appointment of a new headmaster and governors, and whether he
possessed similar powers to those of the trustees of the charity. *Held*, the power to
appoint persons to an office requiring the exercise of skill and judgment in the
discharge of the functions of that office did not confer on the appointor a power to
do indirectly that which the appointee was appointed to do directly. Although the
trustees had the power to appoint governors who directly appointed a headmaster,
they themselves did not have power to appoint a headmaster. It followed that the
receiver did not have power to appoint a headmaster. Further the remedy of
appointment of a receiver and manager of a charity was purely equitable and
permitted the court to adapt the receiver's functions to the needs of the particular
case. The power to manage the affairs of a charity effectively empowered the
receiver to conduct and control directly what could be done by him directly.

A-G v SCHONFELD [1980] 3 All ER 1 (Chancery Division: SIR ROBERT MEGARRY
V-C).

2318   —— **appointment under debenture—action carried on by receiver
after winding up of company—liability of receiver for costs of
action**

See *Bacal Contracting Ltd v Modern Engineering (Bristol) Ltd*, para. 366.

REGISTRATION CONCERNING THE INDIVIDUAL

Halsbury's Laws of England (3rd edn.), Vol. 32, paras. 793–887

2319   Census

The Census Order 1980, S.I. 1980 No. 702, provides for the taking of a census of the population of Great Britain on 5th April 1981. The order specifies the persons by whom and with respect to whom the census returns are to be made and sets out the particulars to be stated in the returns.

2320   —— regulations

The Census Regulations 1980, S.I. 1980 No. 897 (in force on 31st July 1980), provide for the appointment of officers and for the detailed arrangements necessary for the conduct of the census, directed to be taken by the Census Order 1980, para. 2319.

REVENUE

Halsbury's Laws of England (3rd edn.), Vol. 33, paras. 1–622

2321   Appropriation Act 1980

The Appropriation Act 1980 applies a sum out of the Consolidated Fund to the service of the year ending on 31st March 1981, appropriates the further supplies granted by Parliament and repeals certain Consolidated Fund and Appropriation Acts. The Act received the royal assent on 8th August 1980 and came into force on that date.

2322   Budget of the European Communities

See paras. 1111, 1112.

2323   Capital gains tax

See CAPITAL GAINS TAXATION.

2324   Capital transfer tax

See GIFT AND ESTATE TAXATION.

2325   Consolidated Fund Act 1980

The Consolidated Fund Act 1980 applies certain sums out of the Consolidated Fund to the service of the years ending on 31st March 1979 and 1980. The Act came into force on receiving the royal assent on 20th March 1980.

2326   Consolidated Fund (No. 2) Act 1980

The Consolidated Fund (No. 2) Act 1980 applies certain sums out of the Consolidated Fund to the service of the years ending on 31st March 1981 and 1982. The Act came into force on receiving the royal assent on 18th December 1980.

2327   Customs and excise

See CUSTOMS AND EXCISE.

2328   Finance Act 1980

The Finance Act 1980 grants and alters certain duties, amends the law relating to the National Debt and the Public Revenue and makes further provisions in connection with finance. The Act received the royal assent on 1st August 1980 and came into force on that date except as otherwise provided in each section. Section 47 and Sch. 10 came into force on 15th November 1980: S.I. 1980 No. 1546.

Part I Excise Duties

Section 1 and Schs. 1, 2 increase the excise duty on spirits, beer, wine, made-wine and cider with effect from 27th March 1980. The duty on tobacco products is increased from 29th March 1980: s. 2. The duty on hydrocarbon oil is increased from 26th March 1980: s. 3. Section 4 and Sch. 3 increase the annual rates of vehicle excise duty in Great Britain; in particular the duty on cars is increased to £60. Section 5 and Sch. 4 increase vehicle excise duty in Northern Ireland. As from 1st October 1980, the excise duty on gaming licences is altered by relating the duty payable to the profits of the premises concerned: s. 6 and Sch. 5. The duty on gaming machine licences is altered with effect from 1st October 1980: s. 7 and Sch. 6. As from 29th September 1980 the duty on bingo is increased: s. 8. Section 9 introduces a uniform definition of Scotch whisky and Irish whiskey. Section 10 amends provisions relating to surcharges or rebates on sums due in respect of excise duty.

Part II Value Added Tax

Sections 11 and 12 amend provisions regarding liability to be registered for value added tax and the termination of such liability with effect from 27th March 1980 and 1st June 1980 respectively. As from 1st June 1980 a deemed supply of business assets arises in certain circumstances when a person ceases to be taxable unless the tax on the deemed supply would not exceed £250: s. 13. The penalty for failing to pay overdue tax or furnish a tax return is increased: s. 14. As from 1st September 1980, clubs, associations and organisations may be registered in their own name and regulations may be made regarding the transfer of businesses so as to secure continuity of registration: s. 15. Provisions in connection with the use of computers are contained in s. 16. Section 17 makes provisions regarding the recovery and disclosure of information between EEC member states.

Part III Income Tax, Corporation Tax and Capital Gains Tax
Chapter 1 General

Section 18 charges income tax for the year 1980–81 at the basic rate of 30 per cent. Higher rates not exceeding 60 per cent will be chargeable on taxable income over £11,250. The lower rate of 25 per cent chargeable on the first £750 of a person's taxable income will be abolished. The investment income surcharge will be 15 per cent on investment income exceeding £5,500. The rate of corporation tax for the financial year 1979 will be 52 per cent: s. 19. The rate of advance corporation tax for the financial year 1980 will be 3/7: s. 20. The rate of corporation tax payable by small companies for the financial year 1979 will be 40 per cent on profits not exceeding £70,000 with marginal relief at 7/50 on profits between £70,000 and £130,000: s. 21. Section 22 deals with personal reliefs. A married man's allowance is increased to £2,145 and a single person's to £1,375; a wife's earned income relief also becomes £1,375. A married man's age allowance is increased to £2,895 and a single person's to £1,820 with a general limit on income for the full allowance of £5,900. Additional relief for widows and others in respect of children under their care is increased to £770. A widow is entitled to a new personal relief of up to £770 for the year of assessment in which her husband dies: s. 23. Increases in personal allowances and income tax thresholds for 1981–82 onwards are to be linked to the retail prices index: s. 24. Section 25 prescribes the tax allowances for 1981–82 in respect of children living abroad as being £165 for a child over sixteen at the commencement of the year of assessment, £135 for a child under sixteen but over eleven at that time and £100 for a child under eleven; the allowances are to be abolished after 1981–82. Section 26 provides that payments received in connection with specified gallantry awards are exempt from tax. The interest on a loan not exceeding £25,000 for the purchase of a private residence qualifies in full for tax relief: s. 27. Section 28 modifies the conditions to be satisfied for relief on interest payments after 26th March 1980 on money borrowed for investment in close companies. Section 29 reduces premium relief on life assurance policies to 15 per cent with effect from 6th April 1981. Certain life assurance policies do not qualify for premium relief: s. 30. The limits on relief for retirement annuity premiums are increased: s. 31. Unused relief on retirement annuity premiums may be carried forward: s. 32. Section 33 contains provisions relating to the approval of retirement annuity contracts for the purpose of premium relief. Annuities payable to former partners are deductible from the payer's investment income if the payments exceed a specified limit: s. 34. A pilots' benefit fund may be approved as a retirement benefits scheme: s. 35. Section 36 provides that income from the investment of certain superannuation funds is exempt from tax with effect from 6th April 1980. Section 37 grants income tax relief for losses on the disposal after 5th April 1980 of unquoted shares in prescribed trading companies. Certain incidental costs of obtaining loan finance incurred after 31st March 1980 are deductible when computing the profits of a trade, profession or vocation: s. 38. Section 39 grants relief for trade expenditure incurred after 31st March 1980 not more than one year before trading commences. Section 40 and Sch. 7 enable charges by way of recovery of stock relief to be deferred. Payments made after 31st March 1980 in addition to redundancy payments are eligible for relief although paid after permanent discontinuance of a business: s. 41. Grants to traders or investment companies under the Industry Act 1972, ss. 7, 8 are taxable: s. 42. Section 43 and Sch. 8 amend provisions relating to the tax deduction system in the construction industry. Section 44 and Sch. 9 abolish the power to apportion the trading income of a trading company or a company which is a member of a trading group. Restrictions on interest payments by a close company to directors are removed: s. 45. Provisions relating to profit sharing schemes are amended: s. 46. Section 47 and Sch. 10 grant tax reliefs when a director or employee obtains a right to acquire shares in a company under an approved savings-related share option scheme. Section 48 makes provisions with effect from April 1981 concerning the taxation of the benefit of cars and chauffeurs made available for private use by reason of employment. Section 49 amends provisions relating to the cash equivalent of certain benefits, other than cars, provided by reason of employment. The benefit of loans obtained by directors and higher-paid employees is exempt from tax if the cash equivalent of the benefit does not exceed £200 a year: s. 50. Minor amendments to provisions affecting benefits in kind are contained in s. 51. Section 52 provides for the taxation of settled funds for the maintenance of historic buildings in specified circumstances. Section 53 applies to property in such a settled fund forming part of an estate in relation to which an election has been made under the Income and Corporation Taxes Act 1970, s. 73. Expenditure incurred by traders after 31st March 1980 on charitable gifts is deductible when computing profits: s. 54. Income paid to a charity under covenant for over three years is eligible for tax relief: s. 55. Charitable payments of income under covenant not exceeding £3,000 in one year are not subject to higher rates of tax: s. 56. Section 57 modifies the restrictions on tax exemptions in favour of registered friendly societies and trade unions. Section 58 makes provisions regarding the reduced rate of tax payable by building societies. Interest paid after 20th November 1979 on ordinary deposit accounts by a trustee savings bank is taxable: s. 59 and Sch. 11. Section 60 specifies the circumstances when authorised unit trusts are not treated as companies for tax purposes. Section 61 amends provisions regarding the date for payment of tax and interest on unpaid tax. Interest on unpaid tax may be waived where the interest due does not exceed £30: s. 62. An overseas signatory to the International Maritime Satellite Organisation's Operating Agreement is exempt from tax on payments received under the Agreement: s. 63.

Chapter II Capital Allowances
First-year allowances may be made in respect of expenditure on providing machinery or plant for leasing providing each will be used exclusively for specified purposes: s. 64. Section 65 makes provisions regarding writing-down allowances for such leased assets when first-year allowances may not be made under s. 64. When a first-year allowance has been made under s. 64 but the assets are used other than for

specified purposes, excess relief may be recovered: s. 66. A claim for an allowance under s. 64 must be supported by a certificate containing prescribed information: s. 67. Sections 64–67 apply when machinery or plant is leased to two or more persons jointly in accordance with provisions contained in s. 68. Section 69 makes provisions regarding writing-down allowances for cars. Allowances for capital expenditure on machinery or plant for leasing in the course of a trade may be set-off against general income: s. 70. Capital allowances are available for trade expenditure incurred in altering or replacing certain premises used for quarantine purposes: s. 71. Sections 72, 73 and Sch. 12 contain commencement and transitional provisions and deal with interpretation. Section 74 and Sch. 13 grant 100 per cent capital allowances for expenditure on industrial and commercial buildings in enterprise zones to be designated by the Secretary of State. Full capital allowances are also available for expenditure incurred between 27th March 1980 and 26th March 1983 on small industrial buildings: s. 75 and Sch. 13. Where an industrial building is first used by a tenant, the initial allowance for expenditure is no longer deferred until commencement of the tenancy: s. 76.

Chapter III Capital Gains
The first £3,000 of an individual's net annual gain is exempt from tax: s. 77. The exemption for net gains by trustees is increased to £1,500: s. 78. Section 79 provides relief from capital gains tax for gifts between individuals. Section 80 introduces a restricted exemption from capital gains tax on the disposal after 5th April 1980 of a private residence, part of which has been let to a tenant. Authorised unit trusts and investment trusts are exempt from capital gains tax: s. 81. Section 82 grants relief when a trustee of maintenance funds for historic buildings is deemed to dispose of an asset comprised in the settlement. The consideration on disposal of an asset after 25th March 1980 includes money brought into account as the disposal value of machinery or plant when calculating writing-down allowances: s. 83. Section 84 contains provisions regarding traded options.

Part IV Capital Transfer Tax
Section 85 and Schs. 14, 15 increase the threshold for liability to £50,000 for chargeable transfers after 25th March 1980 and make transitional provisions. Section 86 provides that a transfer not exceeding £50,000 made after 25th March 1980 to a spouse domiciled abroad is exempt from tax; the exemption for small gifts made after 5th April 1980 is increased to £250 and the exemption for gifts to a charity made after 25th March 1980 is increased to £200,000. With effect from 27th March 1980, provisions regarding mutual transfers are amended by s. 87. Section 88 modifies the requirements to be satisfied by property in order to qualify for the exemptions granted to a settled fund for maintaining historic buildings. Section 89 and Sch. 16 impose a charge to tax when property forming part of such a settlement is used for unauthorised purposes. A transfer of settled property does not constitute a capital distribution if the property is transferred within thirty days to a maintenance fund for historic buildings: s. 90. Where tax charged on certain discretionary trusts is credited against the next charge, any excess credit may be carried forward: s. 91. Section 92 amends provisions in connection with the tax liability arising when the court makes an order under the Inheritance (Provision for Family and Dependants) Act 1975. Section 93 contains provisions regarding settlements in Scotland. Regulations may be made dispensing with the requirement to deliver accounts: s. 94.

Part V Stamp Duty
As from 6th April 1980, conveyances and transfers for a consideration not exceeding £20,000 are exempt from stamp duty and reduced rates apply up to a limit of £35,000: s. 95. The transfer of loan capital issued or raised by certain foreign bodies is not exempt from stamp duty: s. 96. Section 97 amends provisions regarding the duty payable on certain leases under which the lessee acquires the reversion. No stamp duty is payable on an instrument whereby property ceases to be comprised in a settlement if the property becomes part of a settled fund for maintaining historic buildings: s. 98. As from 6th April 1980, no stamp duty is payable on a charitable covenant for annual payments over a period which may exceed three years and can

only be terminated earlier with the payee's consent: s. 99. Reduced stamp duty is payable on the transfer of stock to a qualified dealer if he transfers the stock to a bona fide purchaser within two months: s. 100. Section 101 prescribes the circumstances when no duty is payable on the transfer of a unit in an authorised unit trust. Where property is conveyed in consideration of a debt which exceeds the value of the property, stamp duty is charged on the value of the property: s. 102. Section 103 repeals certain provisions regarding payment of stamp duty in Northern Ireland.

Part VI Oil Taxation
The rate of petroleum revenue tax is increased to 70 per cent: s. 104. Provision for the payment of tax in advance is contained in s. 105. If a participator in an oil field transfers his interest, the transferee is entitled to the participator's unused expenditure and loss relief: s. 106 and Sch. 17. Section 107 applies to an agreement between the United Kingdom and a foreign government for the exploration of oil in an area consisting of a United Kingdom designated oil field and a sector under the jurisdiction of the foreign country. Section 108 enables regulations to be made modifying the operation of various petroleum revenue tax provisions where a gas banking scheme is in force. Section 109 provides that the full cost of separating gas into its component streams is an allowable expenditure.

Part VII Development Land Tax
The development value realised on the disposal of an interest in land in an enterprise zone is exempt from tax if the disposal is made within ten years from the date when the land was designated an enterprise zone: s. 110. Charities are exempt from development land tax in relation to disposals made after 25th March 1980: s. 111. Section 112 repeals the Development Land Tax Act 1976, s. 39 with effect from 6th August 1980. Section 113 amends provisions relating to the payment of tax by instalments. A person who intends to begin a project for land development may elect to be assessed and taxed in advance in respect of the deemed disposal arising on commencement of the project: s. 114. A tax collector's certificate that interest is unpaid on outstanding tax is sufficient evidence that the sum is unpaid: s. 115. Section 116 makes miscellaneous amendments regarding development land tax.

Part VIII Miscellaneous and Supplementary
Section 117 and Sch. 18 grant certain tax reliefs to encourage the demerger of corporate trading activities. As from 1st April 1980, the trustees of the National Heritage Memorial Fund have the same tax exemptions as charities: s. 118. Section 119 contains provisions regarding the transfer of assets by the British Airways Board and the National Freight Corporation. Section 120 and Sch. 19 amend provisions relating to the National Savings Bank. Penalties are imposed for failing to comply with notices served under certain provisions of this Act: s. 121. Miscellaneous provisions and repeals are contained in s. 122 and Sch. 20.

2329   Income and corporation tax
See INCOME TAXATION.

2330   Petroleum revenue tax
See INCOME TAXATION.

2331   Repayment of tax—administrative practices
The Inland Revenue have issued a Statement of Practice SP 1/80 concerning instances where an assessment has been made and this shows a repayment due to the taxpayer. Repayment of the full amount is invariably made, but where the end of year check applied to Schedule E taxpayers shows an overpayment of £5 or less, an assessment is not made except at the taxpayer's request; for larger sums an assessment is automatically made. Where an employer has paid over more PAYE tax during the year than the amount shown on his returns, and it is not practicable to carry the excess forward to the next year, a repayment is not made automatically if the excess

is £5 or less. As regards payment of tax assessed, where a payment to the Collector exceeds the amount due, and the discrepancy is not noted before the payment has been processed, the excess is not repaid automatically unless it is greater than £1. For capital transfer tax, assessments which lead to repayments of sums overpaid are not initiated automatically by the Capital Taxes Office if the amount involved is £10 or less.

The aim of these tolerances is to minimise work which is highly cost-effective; they cannot operate to deny a repayment to a taxpayer who had claimed his full entitlement.

2332   Stamp duties

See STAMP DUTIES.

2333   Value added tax

See VALUE ADDED TAX.

ROAD TRAFFIC

Halsbury's Laws of England (3rd edn.), Vol. 33, paras. 623–1383

2334   Articles

The Meaning of Reckless Driving, Jonathan S. Fisher (the law in the light of *R v Davis* [1979] RTR 316, 1979 Halsbury's Abridgment para. 2313): 130 NLJ 205.
Reckless Driving Again, Jonathan Fisher: 130 NLJ 1057.
Traffic Warden and Voidable Endorsements, Jonathan Fisher: 130 NLJ 1037.

2335   Accident—apportionment of blame—effect of previous authority

See *Worsfold v Howe*, para. 1675.

2336   —— cost of full police report

The Home Office has stated that, with effect from 1st July 1980, the cost of a full accident report of a road traffic accident was increased from £12 to £16. At the same time, the cost of providing a copy of one statement was increased from £5·50 to £7, that of providing two or more statements from £8 to £10 and that of interviews from £13·50 to £15·50. The cost for abortive searches was increased from £4 to £6. See the Law Society Gazette, 2nd July 1980, front page.

2337   —— emergency and hospital treatment—increase in charges

See para. 2021.

2338   Breath test device—approval

The Home Secretary has made the Breath Test Device (Approval) (No 2) Order 1979 approving a device known as the "Alcolmeter" for the purposes of breath tests. A detachable tubular mouthpiece is attached to the device. On the front of the device there are two press buttons labelled "SET" and "READ", three oblong panels labelled "FAIL", "PASS" and "READY" and three round panels labelled "A", "B" and "BAT" below which are inscribed a lion's head and the inscription "LION alcometer S-L2". The order is not published in the S.I. series.

2339

The Home Secretary has approved the Alert device for use by the police in England and Wales for the purpose of carrying out breath tests. The device consists of a rigid plastic case with the inscription "DRAEGER A.L.E.R.T." on the front and a metal plaque on the side on which the device is described as "UK1".   On the front, there is an on/off switch and two groups of three labelled panels.   At the end of the case there is a rubber stud for the insertion of a detachable plastic mouthpiece. See the Breath Test Device (Approval) (No 1) Order 1980 (not published in the S.I. series).

2340   Careless driving—accident unexplained—duty of justices to draw inference from primary facts found

See *Jarvis v Williams*, para. 1856.

2341   —— defence of automatism—medical evidence

See *Moses v Winder*, para. 687.

2342   Carriage by road

See CARRIERS.

2343   Common transport policy

See EUROPEAN COMMUNITIES.

2344   Control books—failure to issue where tachograph installed

See *Concorde Express Transport Ltd v Traffic Examiner Metropolitan Area*, para. 2419.

2345   Cycle racing

The Cycle Racing on Highways (Special Authorisation) (England and Wales) Regulations 1980, S.I. 1980 No. 225 (in force on 14th March 1980), vary provisions of the Cycle Racing on Highways Regulations 1960 by increasing the maximum number of competitors who may take part in certain cycle racing events to be held in 1980.

2346   The Cycle Racing on Highways (Amendment) Regulations 1980, S.I. 1980 No. 1185 (in force on 12th September 1980), amend the provisions concerning the number of competitors taking part in certain races authorised under the Cycle Racing on Highways Regulations 1960.

2347   Disqualification—police index of disqualified drivers

An index of disqualified drivers has been established on the police national computer and is accessible to police forces in England, Wales and Scotland.   The information which is available is: the driver's personal details, the terminal date of the overall period of disqualification, the court by which the disqualification was imposed and the date of the hearing.   The index was compiled initially from information held at the Driver and Vehicle Licensing Centre and will be kept up to date by information supplied by the relevant police prosecuting force and supplemented by information from the centre.   See Home Office circular 46/1980.

2348   Driving or being in charge whilst unfit through drink or drugs—accident—inference of impaired ability to drive due to intoxication

The appellant drove into the back of an unlit stationary van which was parked beneath an illuminated street light.   He was arrested and a blood specimen revealed excess alcohol in his blood.   He was charged with driving with a blood–alcohol concentration above the prescribed limit contrary to the Road Traffic Act 1972, s. 6 (1) and of driving while unfit to drive through drink contrary to s. 5 (1).   He was convicted under s. 5 (1) and appealed against his conviction. *Held*, since the appellant had collided with a stationary van, which was plainly visible, for no apparent reason, it was open to the jury to infer that his ability to drive was impaired.   Further, since his blood–alcohol concentration was substantially above the prescribed limit the jury had been entitled to infer that such intoxication was responsible for the impairment of his ability to drive resulting in the accident. Although the applicant had successfully raised two technical defences to the charge under s 6 (1), it was impossible to know on which grounds the jury had acquitted on that charge and accordingly, there was no ground for upsetting the present conviction.

R v Hunt [1980] RTR 29 (Court of Appeal: Bridge LJ, Chapman and Lawson JJ).

2349   **—— arrest—failure to provide breath specimen—alternative charge—validity of arrest**

The appellant was arrested for driving when unfit to drive through drink or drugs under the Road Traffic Act 1972, s. 5. An officer at the police station asked him to provide a breath specimen, to which request he made no response. The officer then informed the appellant that he did not consider him to be unfit to drive although he might have a blood–alcohol content above the prescribed limit. A blood sample revealed excess alcohol and he was charged with contravening s. 6 (1) of the Act by driving with a blood–alcohol content which exceeded the prescribed limit. He was convicted and appealed on the ground that since he was not charged with the offence for which he had been arrested, the abandonment of the allegation ended the power of the police to require a blood specimen and to detain him further. *Held*, the appellant's contention was controverted by s. 9 (1) of the Act, since he remained a person who had been arrested under s. 5 (5) and had been given an opportunity to provide a breath specimen, as provided for in s. 8 (7). He fell within the provisions of s. 9 (1) even after he had been informed that he would not be charged under s. 5 (1). Accordingly the appeal would be dismissed.

R v Dixon [1980] RTR 17 (Court of Appeal: Shaw LJ, Kilner Brown and Wood JJ).

2350   **—— arrest by police on private property—validity of arrest**

See *R v Trump*, para. 2352.

2351   **—— blood or urine specimen—alternative charge—admissibility of specimen as evidence**

The vehicle driven by the defendant collided with another vehicle and he was arrested and taken to a police station. A police officer, pursuant to the procedure provided for by the Road Traffic Act 1972, s. 9, obtained with the defendant's consent a blood specimen for analysis. The defendant was charged with driving while unfit to do so through drink, contrary to s. 5 of the Act. During the trial it was found that when the blood specimen was given the police officer was only considering the possibility of prosecution under the 1972 Act, s. 6 for driving with excess alcohol in the blood. The question arose as to whether the evidence of the analysis was inadmissible upon prosecution under s. 5. *Held*, such evidence was specifically admissible under s. 7, the blood specimen having been given with the defendant's consent.

Tee v Gough [1980] Crim LR 380 (Queen's Bench Division: Bridge LJ and Caulfield J).

2352   **—— —— specimen irregularly obtained—admissibility of specimen as evidence**

The defendant did not stop when his car collided with another vehicle. At his home a police officer required him to provide a specimen of breath for a breath test which proved positive. He was arrested for driving when unfit to do so through drink contrary to the Road Traffic Act 1972, s. 5 (1). He was informed that if he failed to provide a blood or urine specimen he would be liable to imprisonment, a fine and disqualification. He provided a blood specimen which revealed an excessive concentration of alcohol in his blood and he was convicted of the offence. He appealed on the grounds that the evidence of alcohol should have been excluded since it was unlawfully obtained for a s. 5 offence, in that the sample was obtained consequent upon an unlawful arrest and improper threat. *Held*, although the specimen was not correctly obtained within s. 5 or with the defendant's consent as provided for by s. 7 of the Act and there was no obligation under the Act either to admit or to exclude the evidence of alcohol, it was subject to the judge's discretion to exclude evidence unlawfully obtained. In the light of the circumstances, such evidence would be treated as admissible and the appeal would be dismissed.

R v TRUMP [1980] Crim LR 379 (Court of Appeal: EVELEIGH LJ, WIEN and DRAKE JJ). *R v Sang* [1979] 2 All ER 1222, 1979 Halsbury's Abridgment para. 689 applied.

2353 Driving or being in charge with blood-alcohol concentration above prescribed limit—arrest—validity

A constable required a motorist under the Road Traffic Act 1972, s. 8 (1), to provide a breath specimen and warned him that he would be arrested if he refused. The motorist refused and attacked the constable. After a struggle the motorist was arrested for assaulting a constable in the execution of his duty. He was convicted of driving with a blood-alcohol concentration above the prescribed limit and appealed, contending that the arrest was unlawful as he had not been told the reason for it. *Held*, there had been a proper arrest under the 1972 Act, s. 8 (5), as the motorist had been told that if he refused to give a breath specimen he would be arrested, and it was clear that he was being arrested in connection with his refusal, notwithstanding that he was also arrested for assaulting a constable. The appeal would be dismissed.

GRANT v GORMAN [1980] RTR 119 (Queen's Bench Division: EVELEIGH LJ and WOOLF J). *R v Mayer* [1975] RTR 411, CA, 1975 Halsbury's Abridgment para. 2838 applied.

2354 See also *R v Grant*, para. 649.

2355 —— blood or urine specimen—accuracy

A motorist provided a specimen of blood pursuant to the Road Traffic Act 1972, s. 9, which revealed a high proportion of alcohol in his blood. One hour later a breath test proved negative, and he appealed against his conviction in the light of unchallenged evidence that the rate of destruction in the blood was such that the two tests were inconsistent with each other. He contended that the blood test was wrong or had been made on a sample from someone else. *Held*, although his argument was a valid one, the jury, who had heard all the evidence, had been satisfied of his guilt and the application would be refused.

R v GREEN [1980] RTR 415 (Court of Appeal: LORD WIDGERY CJ, BRIDGE and WOOLF J).

2356 —— —— failure to provide specimen—reasonable excuse

Scotland

A motorist was arrested following a positive breath test and taken to a police station. He was required to provide a specimen of urine or blood. He provided only one urine sample, as opposed to the two required under the Road Traffic Act 1972, s. 9, and refused to supply a blood sample when invited to do so. He was charged with failing to provide a specimen under s. 9 of the 1972 Act. He contended that he suffered from a fear of needles amounting to a phobia. He was convicted and appealed. *Held*, in order to constitute a reasonable excuse for failure to supply a specimen in accordance with s. 9 (3) an extreme mental condition had to exist. A fear of needles was not such a condition and the appeal would be dismissed.

GLICKMAN v MACKINNON 1978 SC 81 (High Court of Justiciary).

2357   —— —— —— **whether refusal to provide specimen amounts to failure**

The Road Traffic Act 1972, s. 9 provides that a failure to provide a specimen for a laboratory test constitutes an offence. On the question of whether a 'refusal' to provide a specimen amounted to a 'failure' to do so under s. 9, it was held that it was a question of fact. An agreement to provide a specimen subject to a condition amounted to a 'refusal' and therefore a 'failure' within s. 9.

PAYNE V DICCOX [1980] RTR 82 (Queen's Bench Division: EVELEIGH LJ and WOOLF J). *R v Reid* [1973] RTR 536 and *Pettigrew v Northumbria Police Authority* [1976] RTR 177, 1976 Halsbury's Abridgment para. 2140 applied.

2358   —— —— **specimen spilt—reliance on a second specimen**

The defendant provided a blood specimen for analysis in accordance with the Road Traffic Act 1972, s. 9. The specimen was accidentally spilt by a doctor and a further specimen was provided. The defendant was subsequently charged with driving or being in charge with a blood-alcohol concentration above the prescribed limit contrary to the 1972 Act, s. 6. On the question of whether the prosecution could rely on the analysis of the second specimen, *held*, the defendant had complied with s. 9 in giving a first specimen sufficient and suitable for analysis. The specimen did not cease to be so because it had been spilt by a doctor rendering it unsuitable for analysis. The prosecution would be unable to rely on the analysis of the second specimen.

BECK V WATSON [1980] RTR 90 (Queen's Bench Division: LANE LJ and ACKNER J). *Scott v Baker* [1968] 2 All ER 993, *R v Hyams* [1973] RTR 68 and *Ross v Hodges* [1975] RTR 55, 1975 Halsbury's Abridgment para. 2864 applied.

2359   —— **breath test—failure to provide—arrest by police on private property without lawful authority—validity of arrest**

Following a car accident in which the appellant was involved police officers went to his home where they were admitted by his son. The appellant refused to see them informing them through his son that they were trespassers and that he wished them to leave. The officers then entered the appellant's bedroom and requested him to take a breath test. He refused and was arrested. At the police station, he refused to provide breath, blood or urine samples. He was charged with failure to provide such specimens under the Road Traffic Act 1972, s. 8. The question for consideration was the infringement of the common law rights of a motorist who was required by a constable to undergo a breath test in accordance with s. 8 (2) and was charged with an offence because of his failure to do so. *Held*, the power which s. 8 (2) conferred on a constable to restrain the liberty of movement of a person required by him to take a breath test did not authorise him to enter a person's premises. In order to constitute a valid requirement, the constable had to be acting lawfully towards the person at the moment that he made the requirement. Accordingly, the constable was not acting lawfully if he was then committing the tort of trespass for which s. 8 (2) gave him no authority. Unless such conduct was authorised by statute, it was a serious violation of the common law rights of a driver to be forcibly detained or threatened, whether on his premises or at a police station, until he had taken a breath test.

MORRIS V BEARDMORE [1980] 2 All ER 753 (House of Lords: LORD DIPLOCK, LORD EDMUND-DAVIES, LORD KEITH OF KINKEL, LORD SCARMAN and LORD ROSKILL). Decision of Divisional Court of the Queen's Bench Division [1979] 2 All ER 290, 1979 Halsbury's Abridgment para. 2274 reversed.

2360   —— —— —— **validity of arrest**

A motorist agreed to provide a breath specimen but was prevented from doing so by his wife. The police officer arrested him for failure to provide a breath test specimen. He subsequently provided a blood specimen which revealed the presence of excess alcohol. He was charged with driving with excess alcohol in his blood in contravention of the Road Traffic Act 1972, s. 6 (1). He pleaded guilty to the offence and was convicted. He claimed that his arrest was unlawful as the circumstances had prevented him from providing the specimen. On his application for leave to appeal against conviction, *held*, since the police were not responsible for his failure to provide a breath specimen, it was impossible to say that the applicant had not failed to provide a specimen. Accordingly, in view of the motorist's admission and the evidence generally, there was no issue to leave to the jury. The application for leave to appeal would therefore be refused.

R v MILES [1979] RTR 509 (Court of Appeal: LORD WIDGERY CJ, GEOFFREY LANE LJ and ACKNER J). *Hoyle v Walsh* [1969] 1 All ER 38, *R v Kelly (HF)* [1972] RTR 447, CA and *R v Ferguson* [1970] RTR 395, CA applied.

2361   —— —— validity of test

A police constable saw a motorist commit a traffic offence and gave him a breath test on an Alcotest (R) 80 device. According to the manufacturer's instructions, the bag had to be inflated with a single breath. The motorist used several breaths as he suffered from bronchitis. The test was positive and the motorist was convicted of driving with excess alcohol in his bloodstream. He appealed against conviction, contending that the breath test was invalid due to the constable's failure to comply with the manufacturer's instructions. *Held*, the constable acted in good faith and the form of breath test was not a radical departure from the manufacturer's instructions. As the test was valid, the appeal would be dismissed.

SHERIDAN v WEBSTER [1980] RTR 349 (Queen's Bench Division: SHAW LJ and KILNER BROWN J).

2362   —— driving or attempting to drive—whether motorist driving

In a case where the defendant was charged with driving a vehicle having consumed alcohol in such quantity that the proportion in his blood exceeded the prescribed limit, contrary to the Road Traffic Act 1972, s. 6, it was held that, even though the defendant was walking some distance away from his car, he was still "driving or attempting to drive" within the meaning of the 1972 Act, s. 8 (1).

REGAN v ANDERTON [1980] Crim LR 245 (Queen's Bench Division: WALLER LJ and PARK J).

2363   —— offences—reform

The Department of Transport has issued a consultative document on the subject of drinking and driving as a preliminary step to taking action on the subject. The proposals include the merging of the present offences of driving with impaired ability and driving with excess alcohol in the blood. Breath testing would become the normal method of taking evidence of impairment but a person would have the right to opt for a blood (but not a urine) test before taking a breath test. The prescribed limit would be expressed in terms of breath rather than blood alcohol (40 microgrammes per 100 millilitres of breath) for purposes of breath tests. Proof of an offence should not be unreasonably dependent on procedural requirements; the specification of these would in any event be kept to the minimum. The power to require breath tests would be extended to persons in charge of motor vehicles (further views are sought on the possible removal of the present restrictions on requiring tests). Finally, the government seeks to introduce a special procedure for high risk offenders and to take further steps to deter the incidence of hit-and-run offences.

2364   Driving while disqualified—whether accused "driving" towed car

A motorist appealed against a conviction for driving while disqualified on the ground that steering a car while it was being towed did not constitute "driving". *Held*, the essence of "driving" was the use of the driver's controls in order to direct the movement of the car, the method of propulsion being irrelevant. Accordingly the appeal would be dismissed.

McQuaid v Anderton [1980] 3 All ER 540 (Queen's Bench Division: Lord Widgery CJ, Roskill LJ and Heilbron J). *R v MacDonagh* [1974] QB 448, 1974 Halsbury's Abridgment para. 2906, applied. Dicta of Lord Goddard CJ in *Wallace v Major* [1946] 2 All ER 87 at 88, 89 disapproved.

2365 Driving without due care and attention—evidence sufficient to justify conviction

See *Scruby v Beskeen*, para. 702.

2366 Duty to stop when required to do so—constable having no reason to suspect offence committed

A uniformed constable attempted to stop the defendant, who was driving a lorry, in order to ascertain whether the defendant had valid documents for the use of the lorry, and whether the lorry was in a lawful condition. The constable had no reason to suspect that the defendant was driving the lorry unlawfully. Justices dismissed an information alleging that the defendant had refused to comply with the requirements of the Road Traffic Act 1972, s. 159, on the ground that, as the constable had no reason to believe that an offence had been committed, he had no power to stop the lorry under s. 159. On appeal, *held*, under s. 159, a constable had the power to stop a motorist on the road provided that he was in uniform; the constable did not have to be acting in execution of a duty at common law. In the instant case, the constable was not acting capriciously and therefore had the power to stop the lorry under that section.

Beard v Wood (1979) Times, 6th February (Queen's Bench Division: Lord Widgery CJ and Wien J).

2367 —— meaning of "stop"

In a case where the defendant was charged with an offence of failing to stop when directed to do so by a traffic warden in the execution of her duty, contrary to the Road Traffic Act 1972, s. 22, it was held that an offence under s. 22 was committed when a driver who had stopped then proceeded in defiance of a command to remain stationary. That, however, did not mean that the driver had to remain stationary until he was ordered to proceed.

Kentesber v Waumsley [1980] Crim LR 383 (Queen's Bench Division: Eveleigh LJ and Watkins J).

2368 European Highway Code

With a view to promoting road safety and to ensuring that persons breaking traffic rules are treated uniformly throughout Europe, the Council of Europe has published *Guidelines concerning Offences to be included in a European Highway Code* (Strasbourg, 1979). These comprise General Principles (Chapter 1), Offences (Chapter 2), Procedure (Chapter 3) and Sanctions (Chapter 4). The offences are divided into: offences endangering the personal safety of others; breaches of the driver's essential duties (including serious cases of hit-and-run offences, driving without authorisation or without insurance) and minor offences. The sanctions envisaged include fines, imprisonment, deprivation of the right to drive, confiscation or immobilisation of vehicles and a points system leading (ultimately) to disqualification. The Council of Europe recommends that future legislation should follow these guidelines as far as possible.

2369 Goods haulage operators—qualifications

The Goods Haulage Operators (Certificates of Qualification) Regulations 1980, S.I. 1980 No. 1788 (in force on 21st December 1980), together with the Goods Vehicle Operators (Qualifications) (Amendment) Regulations 1980 (see para. 2372), implement Council Directive (EEC) 77/796 which is aimed at mutual recognition of diplomas, certificates and other evidence of formal qualifications for goods haulage operators and road passenger transport operators.

2370   Goods vehicles—international journeys—fees

The Goods Vehicles (Authorisation of International Journeys) (Fees) Regulations 1980, S.I. 1980 No. 615 (in force on 1st June 1980), consolidate, with amendments, the Goods Vehicles (Authorisation of International Journeys) (Fees) Regulations 1976, 1976 Halsbury's Abridgment para. 2149, as amended. The 1980 Regulations prescribe a fee of less than £45 for period permits valid for nine months or less and prescribe fees for permits issued on behalf of the Republic of Ireland in pursuance of a specified agreement.

2371   —— operators' licences

The Goods Vehicles (Operators' Licences) (Temporary Use in Great Britain) Regulations 1980, S.I. 1980 No. 637 (in force on 31st May 1980), consolidate, with amendments, the Goods Vehicles (Operators' Licences) (Temporary Use in Great Britain) Regulations 1975, 1975 Halsbury's Abridgment para. 2900, as amended. The 1980 Regulations modify the requirements of the Transport Act 1968, Part V regarding operators' licences in relation to Northern Ireland goods vehicles and certain foreign goods vehicles.

2372   —— operators' qualifications

The Goods Vehicle Operators (Qualifications) (Amendment) Regulations 1980, S.I. 1980 No. 1787 (in force on 21st December 1980), amend the Goods Vehicle Operators (Qualifications) Regulations 1977, 1977 Halsbury's Abridgment para. 2286. Together with the Goods Haulage Operators (Certificates of Qualification) Regulations 1980 (see para. 2369), these regulations implement Council Directive (EEC) 77/796 which is aimed at mutual recognition of diplomas, certificates and other evidence of formal qualifications for goods haulage operators and road passenger transport operators.

2373   —— plating and testing

The Goods Vehicles (Plating and Testing) (Amendment) Regulations 1980, S.I. 1980 No. 656 (in force on 1st June 1980), amend the Goods Vehicles (Plating and Testing) Regulations 1971 by increasing the fees payable for the replacement of plates, certificates and discs and for the examination, re-examination, re-testing and periodical testing of motor vehicles and trailers. The cancellation charge is also increased.

2374   Legal proceedings—requirement to give information as to identity of driver—failure to give information—validity of notice of requirement

The defendant was charged with contravening the Road Traffic Act 1972, s. 168 in that he had failed to comply with a requirement on behalf of a specified chief officer of police to give information as to the identity of a car driver alleged to be guilty of an offence. The requirement was in an official-looking printed notice, headed with the constabulary name and stating that the signatory, a superintendent, was authorised to make the requirement on behalf of the chief officer of police. At the trial the question arose as to the authenticity of the notice. *Held*, where justices were determining whether the prosecution had established the commission of an offence under s. 168 and were faced with the question of the authenticity of a notice all the evidence had to be examined in order to determine whether there was sufficient evidence from which an appropriate inference could be drawn. In the circumstances the notice, being produced from official sources and containing sufficient material, was valid.

PAMPLIN v GORMAN [1980] RTR 54 (Queen's Bench Division: LORD WIDGERY CJ, EVELEIGH LJ and KILNER BROWN J).

2375   **Licences—driving licence—causing or permitting an unlicensed person to drive a vehicle—employers' liability**

The defendants employed a van driver, ensuring beforehand that he held a valid driving licence. Three weeks after the expiry of his licence and without having renewed it, the employee drove the defendants' van. The defendants were charged with causing or permitting their employee to drive the van whilst not holding a valid driving licence, contrary to the Road Traffic Act 1972, s. 84 (2). *Held*, the prosecution had only to prove the granting of permission to drive the van and not that the defendants were aware of the deficiency in the driving licence. Hence the defendants should be convicted.

FERRYMASTERS LTD v ADAMS [1980] Crim LR 187 (Queen's Bench Division: WALLER LJ and PARK J). *Baugh v Crago* [1975] RTR 455, 1975 Halsbury's Abridgment para. 1899 followed.

2376   —— **heavy goods vehicles**

The Heavy Goods Vehicles (Drivers' Licences) (Amendment) Regulations 1980, S.I. 1980 No. 1733 (in force on 15th November 1980), amend the Heavy Goods Vehicles (Drivers' Licences) Regulations 1977, 1977 Halsbury's Abridgment para. 2291. The 1980 regulations introduce an exemption from heavy goods vehicle licensing in the case of vehicles being driven by members of the Armed Forces in the course of urgent work of national importance.

2377   The Heavy Goods Vehicles (Drivers' Licences) (Amendment) (No. 2) Regulations 1980, S.I. 1980 No. 1821 (in force on 5th January 1981), further amend the Heavy Goods Vehicles (Drivers' Licences) Regulations 1977, 1977 Halsbury's Abridgment para. 2291. The amendments relate to the qualifications of an applicant for a trainee driver's licence and the fees payable on application for a driving test and or issue of a driver's licence.

2378   —— **motor vehicles**

The Motor Vehicles (Driving Licences) (Amendment) Regulations 1980, S.I. 1980 No. 180 (in force on 17th March 1980), amend the Motor Vehicles (Driving Licences) Regulations 1976, 1976 Halsbury's Abridgment para. 2153 by increasing the fee for an appointment for a driving test to £10·30.

2379   The Motor Vehicles (Driving Licences) (Amendment) (No. 2) Regulations 1980, S.I. 1980 No. 1734 (in force on 15th November 1980), amend the Motor Vehicles (Driving Licences) Regulations 1976, 1976 Halsbury's Abridgment para. 2153. The 1980 regulations lower to seventeen the qualifying age for holding or obtaining a driving licence for certain classes of vehicles specified in the Road Traffic Act 1972, s. 96 in the case of members of the Armed Forces when using such vehicles in the course of urgent work of national importance.

2380   —— **prescribed disabilities—duty to investigate possible unfitness to drive**

A driver complained to the Parliamentary Commissioner for Administration that, as a person about whom prejudicial information had been passed to the Driver and Vehicle Licensing Centre, she should be supplied with the name of the informant. The centre had been provided with information suggesting that there were medical reasons why the driver might not be entitled to hold a driving licence. In consequence, the centre sought her permission to approach her doctor for information. The commissioner stated (Case C481/79, *Parliamentary Commissioner for Administration, Selected Cases 1980*, Vol. 2, HC 526) that he approved the centre's practice of investigating prima facie evidence from any source of a licence holder's possible unfitness to drive. He dismissed the complaint finding no cause to criticise their refusal to disclose the source of such evidence when it is received direct from a member of the public. The commissioner was informed that the source of information would be disclosed when the source was a public body, such as the police, the courts or a health authority.

2381 —— vehicle licence—duration and rate of duty

The Vehicle Licences (Duration and Rate of Duty) Order 1980, S.I. 1980 No. 1183 (in force on 17th September 1980), provides that a licence may be issued under the Vehicles (Excise) Act 1971 for six months instead of four months running from the beginning of any month and prescribes the rate of duty payable when taking out such a licence.

2382 Motor-cycles—protective helmets

The Motor Cycles (Protective Helmets) Regulations 1980, S.I. 1980 No. 1279 (in force on 20th September 1980), require every person driving or riding on a motor cycle when on a road to wear protective head gear and further prescribe certain types of helmet recommended as affording protection to persons on or in motor cycles from injury in the event of an accident. The following regulations are revoked: S.I. 1973 No. 180; S.I. 1974 No. 2000, 1974 Halsbury's Abridgment para. 2926; S.I. 1976 No. 2241, 1976 Halsbury's Abridgment para. 2163; S.I. 1977 Nos. 128, 129, 1977 Halsbury's Abridgment paras. 2299, 2300.

2383 —— sound level measurement certificate

The Motor Cycles (Sound Level Measurement Certificates) Regulations 1980, S.I. 1980 No. 765 (in force on 3rd July 1980), provide for the issue of a certificate to signify whether or not certain types of motor cycles comply with sound level requirements specified in Council Directive (EEC) 78/1015.

2384 —— —— fees

The Motor Cycles (Sound Level Measurement Certificates) (Fees) Regulations 1980, S.I. 1980 No. 766 (in force on 3rd July 1980), prescribe the fees payable for testing motor cycles in connection with the issue of a sound level measurement certificate.

2385 Motor vehicles—approval marks

The Motor Vehicles (Designation of Approval Marks) (Amendment) Regulations 1980, S.I. 1980 No. 582 (in force on 23rd May 1980), amend the Motor Vehicles (Designation of Approval Marks) Regulations 1979, 1979 Halsbury's Abridgment para. 2296 by designating an approval mark for safety belts and rear-view mirrors. Provision is also made for variations in both marks.

2386

The Motor Vehicles (Designation of Approval Marks) (Amendment) (No. 2) Regulations 1980, S.I. 1980 No. 2027 (in force on 15th February 1981), further amend the Motor Vehicles (Designation of Approval Marks) Regulations 1979, 1979 Halsbury's Abridgment para. 2229 by designating approval marks for certain glass panes, other than, inter alia, windscreens.

2387 —— construction and use

The Motor Vehicles (Construction and Use) (Amendment) Regulations 1980, S.I. 1980 No. 140 (in force on 5th March 1980), amend the Motor Vehicles (Construction and Use) Regulations 1978, 1978 Halsbury's Abridgment para. 2364 by prohibiting the use of a two-wheeled motor cycle first registered on or after 1st August 1981 if a sidecar is attached to the right or off-side of the motor cycle.

2388

The Motor Vehicles (Construction and Use) (Amendment) (No. 2) Regulations 1980, S.I. 1980 No. 139 (in force on 7th March 1980), amend the provisions of the Motor Vehicles (Construction and Use) Regulations 1978, 1978 Halsbury's Abridgment para. 2364 so as to require certain vehicles to be marked in accordance with the Motor Vehicles (Designation of Approval Marks) Regulations 1979, 1979 Halsbury's Abridgment para. 2296, thereby indicating that such vehicles satisfy requirements concerning the emission of gaseous pollutants.

2389   The Motor Vehicles (Construction and Use) (Amendment) (No. 3) Regulations 1980, S.I. 1980 No. 287 (in force on 8th April 1980), amend the Motor Vehicles (Construction and Use) Regulations 1978, 1978 Halsbury's Abridgment para. 2364 by making new provisions for the overall length of specified vehicles and extending the circumstances when a public service vehicle may draw a trailer.

2390   The Motor Vehicles (Construction and Use) (Amendment) (No. 4) Regulations 1980, S.I. 1980 No. 610 (in force on 30th May 1980), further amend the Motor Vehicles (Construction and Use) Regulations 1978, 1978 Halsbury's Abridgment para. 2364. The 1980 Regulations provide that seat belts (except those for disabled or young persons) fitted in any vehicle to which the 1978 Regulations, reg. 17 applies, may be marked with a designated approval mark in accordance with the Motor Vehicles (Designation of Approval Marks) Regulations 1979, 1979 Halsbury's Abridgment para. 2296, regs. 4 and 5.

2391   The Motor Vehicles (Construction and Use) (Amendment) (No. 5) Regulations 1980, S.I. 1980 No. 880 (in force on 28th July 1980), further amend the Motor Vehicles (Construction and Use) Regulations 1978, 1978 Halsbury's Abridgment para. 2364 by (i) providing that certain of the 1978 Regulations do not apply to a zero-rated motor vehicle made in Great Britain if it complies with certain international Conventions; (ii) providing that specified requirements relating to radio interference suppression and the construction of petrol tanks do not apply to a vehicle marked in accordance with the Motor Vehicles (Designation of Approval Marks) Regulations 1979, 1979 Halsbury's Abridgment para. 2296 and (iii) amending the requirements relating to wings on cars and the maintenance and operation of brakes on certain vehicles.

2392   The Motor Vehicles (Construction and Use) (Amendment) (No. 6) Regulations 1980, S.I. 1980 No. 1166 (in force on 8th September 1980), further amend the Motor Vehicles (Construction and Use) Regulations 1978, 1978 Halsbury's Abridgment para. 2364 by introducing new requirements relating to permissible sound levels and exhaust systems.

2393   The Motor Vehicles (Construction and Use) (Amendment) (No. 7) Regulations 1980, S.I. 1980 No. 1789 (in force on 24th December 1980), further amend the Motor Vehicles (Construction and Use) Regulations 1978, 1978 Halsbury's Abridgment para. 2364. The 1980 Regulations prescribe (i) the vehicles which are required to be fitted with a speedometer and (ii) the requirements regarding maintenance of speedometers to be complied with by specified vehicles.

2394   —— —— **meaning of "use"**
The defendant was sitting at the back of a van which he and his partner had hired for partnership business. The van, which had certain mechanical defects, was driven by his partner. The defendant was not insured to drive the vehicle. He was charged with using a defective vehicle contrary to various provisions of the Motor Vehicles (Construction and Use) Regulations 1973 and with using an uninsured vehicle contrary to the Road Traffic Act 1972, s. 143 (1). *Held*, a person could only be convicted of "using" a vehicle which he was not driving if he was the driver's employer. The partnership between the defendant and the driver did not make the defendant a "user" of the van. Therefore, as he was not using the van, he could not be liable as charged.
    BENNETT v RICHARDSON [1980] RTR 358 (Queen's Bench Division: LORD WIDGERY CJ and STOCKER J). *Garrett v Hooper* [1973] RTR 1 applied.

The 1973 Regulations have been replaced by the Motor Vehicles (Construction and Use) Regulations 1978.

2395   The defendant and two friends were looking at a car with a view to buying it. The owner was not there, but they managed to open the car. One of the friends sat in the driving seat while the defendant pushed the car. When it started, the defendant jumped into the passenger seat. He was at no time involved in driving the car. He was charged with using a motor vehicle on a road without there being in force an insurance policy or specified security in respect of third party risks, in contravention of the Road Traffic Act 1972, s. 143. The justices dismissed the information holding that since the defendant was not controlling the car he could not be said to be "using" it. On appeal by the prosecutor, *held*, the defendant was using the car directly for his own purposes, in that the car was set in motion as a joint enterprise. It was therefore irrelevant that someone else sat in the driver's seat. The case would be remitted to the justices with a direction to continue the hearing.

LEATHLEY V TATTON [1980] RTR 21 (Queen's Bench Division: GEOFFREY LANE LJ and ACKNER J). *Cobb v Williams* [1973] RTR 113, DC applied.

2396   —— **international circulation**

The Motor Vehicles (International Circulation) (Amendment) Order 1980, S.I. 1980 No. 1095 (in force on a date to be notified, except art. 10 (1) which came into force on 1st August 1980), amends the Motor Vehicles (International Circulation) Order 1975, 1975 Halsbury's Abridgment para. 2891. The 1980 Order gives effect to various provisions of the Vienna Convention on Road Traffic 1968 relating to the issue of international driving permits for travel abroad and licensing requirements in relation to visiting drivers. The order also increases the fees payable for international permits and certificates.

2397   —— **lighting**

The Road Vehicles Lighting (Amendment) Regulations 1980, S.I. 1980 No. 116 (in force on 28th February 1980), amend the Road Vehicles Lighting Regulations 1971 by allowing certain additional vehicles to carry coloured lamps and by modifying the requirements concerning the position of such lamps.

2398   The Road Vehicles Lighting (Amendment) (No. 2) Regulations 1980, S.I. 1980 No. 1855 (in force on 5th January 1981), further amend the Road Vehicles Lighting Regulations 1971 by permitting the use of a hazard warning device to warn road users of a temporary obstruction on any part of a road, instead of only on the carriageway of a road.

2399   —— —— **position of vehicle during hours of darkness—police permission to contravene regulations**

A Divisional Court of the Queen's Bench Division has dismissed an appeal by a police constable against his conviction of contravening the Vehicles (Construction and Use) Regulations 1973, reg. 115, which provided that no person was allowed, except with the permission of a uniformed police officer, to park his car on the wrong side of the road during the hours of darkness.

The uniformed policeman was on duty and was taking a statement from a proposed witness or defendant at the time he contravened the regulations. The court upheld the justices' conclusion that the policeman could not give himself permission to leave his car where he did, as the regulation envisaged that the person requesting permission should request it from another person.

KEENE V MUNCASTER (1980) 124 Sol Jo 496 (Queen's Bench Division: LORD LANE CJ and BOREHAM J).

The 1973 Regulations, reg. 115 now consolidated in the Vehicles (Construction and Use) Regulations 1978, reg. 123, 1978 Halsbury's Abridgment para. 2364.

2400 —— **removal and disposal**

The Removal and Disposal of Vehicles (Amendment) Regulations 1980, S.I. 1980 No. 169 (in force on 11th March 1980), increase the charges payable under the Removal and Disposal of Vehicles Regulations 1968, as amended. The charge for removing a vehicle from a motorway is now £30. The charge for removing a vehicle from a place not on a motorway is £29 in London and £27 elsewhere.

2401 —— **tests**

The Motor Vehicles (Tests) (Amendment) Regulations 1980, S.I. 1980 No. 616 (in force on 1st July 1980), amend the Motor Vehicles (Tests) Regulations 1976, 1976 Halsbury's Abridgment para. 2118 by increasing (i) the fee for issuing a duplicate test certificate to £1·00; (ii) the fee for examining a motor bicycle (without a sidecar) to £4·00 and (iii) the fee for examining any other vehicle to £6·70.

2402 —— **type approval**

The Motor Vehicles (Type Approval) (Great Britain) (Amendment) Regulations 1980, S.I. 1980 No. 879 (in force on 28th July 1980), amend the Motor Vehicles (Type Approval) (Great Britain) Regulations 1979, 1979 Halsbury's Abridgment para. 2308 by (i) modifying the type approval requirements for exhaust emissions; (ii) providing a new alternative prescribed requirement relating to rear-view mirrors and certain seat belts; (iii) prescribing type approval requirements for the brakes on certain vehicles and (iv) providing exemptions from the type approval requirements relating to external projections.

2403 The Motor Vehicles (Type Approval) (Great Britain) (Amendment) (No. 2) Regulations 1980, S.I. 1980 No. 1165 (in force on 8th September 1980), further amend the Motor Vehicles (Type Approval) (Great Britain) Regulations 1979, 1979 Halsbury's Abridgment para. 2308. The 1980 Regulations continue indefinitely the exemption relating to motor vehicles or parts constructed or assembled by persons not ordinarily engaged in the trade or business of manufacturing such motor vehicles or parts.

2404 The Motor Vehicles (Type Approval) (Great Britain) (Fees) Regulations 1980, S.I. 1980 No. 222 (in force on 1st April 1980), consolidate the Motor Vehicles (Type Approval) (Great Britain) (Fees) Regulations 1976, 1976 Halsbury's Abridgment para. 2177, as amended. The 1980 Regulations also provide for the payment of (i) revised fees for the examination of vehicles and the issue of documents in connection with the type approval scheme established under the Motor Vehicles (Type Approval) (Great Britain) Regulations 1979, 1979 Halsbury's Abridgment para. 2308, (ii) a partial fee when a vehicle or vehicle part is partially re-examined or when a type approval is modified following a minor design change and (iii) a cancellation charge if an application for an examination is withdrawn.

2405 The Motor Vehicles (Type Approval and Approval Marks) (Fees) Regulations 1980, S.I. 1980 No. 223 (in force on 1st April 1980), consolidate the Motor Vehicles (Type Approval and Approval Marks) (Fees) Regulations 1976, 1976 Halsbury's Abridgment para. 2176, as amended. The 1980 Regulations also provide for the payment of (i) revised fees for carrying out tests and issuing documents in connection with the type approval of vehicles and the authorisation of the application of approval marks to vehicles, as provided for in Community Regulations or Directives or in Regulations made by the United Nations Economic Commission for Europe, (ii) a partial fee when a vehicle or vehicle part is partially re-tested or when an approval or authorisation is modified following a minor design change and (iii) a cancellation charge if an application for a test is withdrawn.

2406 The Motor Vehicles (Type Approval) Regulations 1980, S.I. 1980 No. 1182 (in force on 9th September 1980), consolidate with amendments the Motor Vehicles

(Type Approval) Regulations 1973, as amended. The Minister of Transport must issue a type approval certificate if he is satisfied on application that (i) a vehicle or vehicle component conforms with certain information given in connection with the application and with requirements regarding design, construction, equipment and marking and that (ii) adequate arrangements have been made for conformity of production in the case of certain other vehicles and vehicle components. The following are revoked: S.I. 1973 No. 1199; S.I. 1974 No. 763, 1974 Halsbury's Abridgment para. 2853; S.I. 1978 No. 1832, 1978 Halsbury's Abridgment para. 2379; S.I. 1979 No. 1089, 1979 Halsbury's Abridgment para. 2307.

2407   Offence committed by Crown—Crown's immunity from prosecution—nomination of fictitious individual as defendant

See *Barnett v French*, para. 735.

2408   Parking place—designated space for the disabled—use of space by police vehicle

See *George v Garland*, para. 2163.

2409   —— excess charge—liability to pay excess charge

The defendant parked his car in a car park. By an order made under the Road Traffic Regulation Act 1967 a charge of 5p was payable on leaving a vehicle in the car park, by inserting a 5p coin in a machine to obtain a ticket to be displayed on the vehicle. An excess charge of £2 was to be paid in respect of a vehicle not displaying a ticket. The defendant did not have a 5p piece and left the car park without paying. He returned ten minutes later and purchased a ticket. An excess charge ticket had already been placed on his car. He refused to pay the excess charge and was subsequently charged with contravening the provisions of the order. On the question as to whether he had complied with the order by paying as soon as he was able to, *held*, the latest time at which the initial charge had to be paid was before the person parking the vehicle left the car park. It was insufficient to arrive at the car park without the appropriate coin and then to go off shopping, with the intention of returning and paying the charge afterwards.

RILEY v HUNT [1980] Crim LR 382 (Queen's Bench Division: BRIDGE LJ and CAULFIELD J).

2410   Public service vehicles

See TRANSPORT.

2411   Reckless driving—causing death—sentence—disqualification

See *R v Smith*, para. 2474.

2412   —— meaning of "reckless"

A motorist appealed against conviction on a charge of causing death by reckless driving on the ground that the recorder had erred in admitting the evidence of a police constable as an expert and not explaining the meaning of "reckless" to the jury. *Held*, a police constable could be heard as an expert as long as he kept within his reasonable expertise. On the question of the meaning of reckless, a driver was guilty of driving recklessly if he deliberately disregarded the obligation to drive with due care and attention or was indifferent as to whether or not he did so and thereby created a risk of an accident which a driver driving with care and attention would not create. Whether or not a motorist was driving in defiance of, or with indifference to, the proper standard was a question of inference for the jury on the evidence as to the manner in which the vehicle was driven and as to road conditions.

The original direction to the jury had been insufficient. However, the general explanation given to them when they had returned to ask for further guidance, was sufficient. The appeal would accordingly be dismissed.

R v MURPHY [1980] 2 WLR 743 (Court of Appeal: EVELEIGH LJ, BRISTOW and McNEILL JJ). *R v Oakley* [1979] RTR 417, CA, 1979 Halsbury's Abridgment para. 693, followed.

2413   *Scotland*
The respondent was charged with driving a motor cycle recklessly contrary to the Road Traffic Act 1972, s. 2 as substituted by the Criminal Law Act 1977, s. 50. The sheriff applied a subjective test, namely that a person could not be convicted unless it was shown that he knew that there were material risks in driving in a particular manner and he deliberately drove in that manner regardless of the consequences. On appeal by the Crown, *held*, the section did not indicate that such a test should be applied which would result in penalising only those who drove wilfully or deliberately in the face of known risks of a material kind. The quality of the driving in fact and not the state of mind or intention of the driver was the factor which should be considered. Accordingly before a person could be considered to have been driving recklessly his driving must have fallen far below the standard of the driving expected of a competent and careful driver and occurred in face of obvious dangers or in circumstances which showed a complete disregared for any potential danger which might result. The case would be remitted to the sheriff in order that a verdict might be given in light of the court's opinion since it was not evident that he had misdirected himself.
ALLAN v PATTERSON 1980 SLT 77 (High Court of Justiciary).

2414   —— **plea of guilty to careless driving—effect of rejection of plea**
See *R v Thompson*, para. 717.

2415   —— **test of recklessness—retaliation for grievance**
A motorist was acquitted of reckless driving contrary to the Road Traffic Act 1972, s. 2, the justices being of the opinion that his driving established no more than bad manners and retaliation for a grievance against the other motorist. On appeal, *held*, retaliation could never be a defence to bad driving and might well provide the necessary element of intention. The justices had therefore misdirected themselves and the appeal would be allowed.
JARVIS v NORRIS [1980] RTR 424 (Queen's Bench Division: DONALDSON LJ and WOOLF J).

2416   **Road—meaning of "road" for purpose of road traffic regulations**
See *Adams v Metropolitan Police Comr*, para. 1405.

2417   **Speed limits—exceeding limit—warning of prosecution—failure of defendant to hear warning—validity**
A motorist who was charged with driving at an excessive speed on a private road was given an oral warning of prosecution at the time of the offence, under the Road Traffic Act 1972, s. 179 (2) (a), but she failed to hear it. No further warning was given. Her conviction was quashed by the Crown Court on the ground that, to be effective, an oral warning must be heard and understood. On appeal by the prosecution, *held*, the obligation on the prosecution under s. 179 (2) (a) was to warn the accused so that he would have the prospective prosecution brought to his attention. Whether this had been done was a question of fact for the court, and accordingly the appeal would be dismissed.
GIBSON v DALTON [1980] RTR 410 (Queen's Bench Division: DONALDSON LJ and BRISTOW J).

2418   Tachographs—exemption from installation

The Community Road Transport Rules (Exemptions) (Amendment) Regulations 1980, S.I. 1980 No. 266 (in force on 31st March 1980), amend the Community Road Transport Rules (Exemptions) Regulations 1978, 1978 Halsbury's Abridgment para. 2400. The effect of the amendments is to exempt from the requirements of Council Regulations (EEC) 1463/70, which relates to the introduction of tachographs in road transport, vehicles which are used for the transport of live animals between farms and local markets, or for the transport of animal carcases or waste not intended for human consumption.

2419   —— installation compulsory under Community law—effect of national provisions on control books

The appellant company was convicted in the United Kingdom for failing to issue to a crew member an individual control book for the pupose of recording time keeping and distance travelled contrary to Council Regulation (EEC) 543/69 and the Transport Act 1968, s. 98 (4). The vehicles were fitted with tachographs in conformity with Council Regulation (EEC) 1463/70 which provides that the installation of such recording equipment is compulsory for certain road transport vehicles registered in a member state. On appeal against conviction, *held*, Council Regulation (EEC) 1463/70, art. 5 provided that the obligation to issue a control book did not apply to companies whose vehicles used tachographs. Accordingly, since the provisions requiring the installation of tachographs in vehicles were directly applicable, they replaced the earlier obligation to supply a control book to crew members whether or not there was equipment in the vehicle or in use in it.

CONCORDE EXPRESS TRANSPORT LTD v TRAFFIC EXAMINER METROPOLITAN AREA [1980] 2 CMLR 221 (Crown Court at Kingston-upon-Thames: JUDGE RUBIN). Case 128/78: *Re Tachographs: EC Commission v United Kingdom* [1979] 2 CMLR 45, ECJ, 1979 Halsbury's Abridgment para. 1159 considered.

For discussion of this case, see Tide of EEC law cannot be turned back, Justinian, Financial Times, 30th June 1980.

2420   Traffic Commissioners—nominations to panels

The Traffic Commissioners (Nominations to Panels) Regulations 1980, S.I. 1980 No. 916 (in force on 31st July 1980), revoke the Traffic Commissioners (Nominations to Panels) Regulations 1962 and make new provisions as to nominations to panels of persons from which appointment of persons to act as traffic commissioners may be made. They provide for nominations under the 1962 Regulations to continue until 31st March 1981 and for nominations as from that date to continue for three years.

2421   Traffic signs—temporary obstructions

The Traffic Signs (Temporary Obstructions) Regulations 1980, S.I. 1980 No. 1854 (in force on 5th January 1981), provide that two triangle signs may be placed on a road to warn traffic of a temporary obstruction on any part of the road, not only the carriageway. The Traffic Signs (Temporary Obstructions) Regulations 1966, as amended, are revoked.

2422   Transport operations—EEC regulations—exemption for the transport of milk

The Community Road Transport Rules (Exemptions) (Amendment) Regulations 1980, S.I. 1980 No. 2018 (in force on 31st December 1980), amend the Community Road Transport Rules (Exemptions) Regulations 1978, 1978 Halsbury's Abridgment para. 2400. The effect of the amendment is to extend until 31st December 1981 the conditional exemption from Council Regulation (EEC) 543/69 (relating to the ages, and the hours and conditions of work of, drivers in the road transport industry) for vehicles used for the transport of milk from farm to dairy and from dairy to farm.

ROYAL FORCES

Halsbury's Laws of England (3rd edn.), Vol. 33, paras. 1348–1866

2423   Army—serviceman charged with committing civil offence—plea in bar of trial—condonation of offence

The accused, a lance corporal in a tank regiment, wounded a trooper during a fight. The major commanding the accused's squadron told the accused that he was unlikely to be charged as a result of the incident, acting on information given informally by the adjutant. He was, however, subsequently charged under the Army Act 1955, s. 70, with committing a civil offence, that of wounding contrary to the Offences against the Person Act 1861, s. 20. The accused offered a plea in bar of trial on the ground that the offence had been condoned by his commanding officer under s. 134 of the Act. The judge-advocate ruled that as the major was not the commanding officer for the purposes of s. 134, the offence had not been condoned. The district court-martial convicted the accused, who appealed. *Held*, for the purposes of s. 134, the commanding officer of the accused was the officer commanding the tank regiment, so that the major could not lawfully condone the offence; he had not been properly authorised to do so by the commanding officer himself, and the adjutant had not been acting on behalf of the commanding officer. The appeal would be dismissed.

LAWTON LJ stated that the power was most unusual as it dispensed with the ordinary law of the land and considered that it could seldom be used under peacetime conditions.

R v BISSET [1980] I WLR 335 (Courts-Martial Appeal Court: LAWTON LJ, TUDOR EVANS and MCNEILL JJ).

2424   —— terms of service

The Army Terms of Service (Amendment) Regulations 1980, S.I. 1980 No. 746 (in force on 1st July 1980), further amend the Army Terms of Service Regulations 1967 1967 by altering the amount payable by a person exercising his right to claim discharge within three months of his engagement from £20 to seven days' gross pay.

2425   The Army Terms of Service (Second Amendment) Regulations 1980, S.I. 1980 No. 1494 (in force on 1st May 1981), further amend the 1967 Regulations by reducing from eighteen months to twelve months the notice required to be given by a man who has enlisted in regular army service for a term of more than twelve years and who wishes to transfer to the reserve or determine his service at the end of the twelve year period.

2426   Army, Air Force and Naval Discipline Acts—continuation

The Army, Air Force and Naval Discipline Acts (Continuation) Order 1980, S.I. 1980 No. 1074 (made on 28th July 1980), continues in force the Army Act 1955, the Air Force Act 1955 and the Naval Discipline Act 1957 until 31st August 1981.

2427   Imprisonment and detention—Air Force

The Imprisonment and Detention (Air Force) Rules 1980, S.I. 1980 No. 2005 (in force on 1st March 1981), consolidate the Imprisonment and Detention (Air Force) Rules 1956 as amended.

2428   —— army

The Imprisonment and Detention (Army) (Amendment) Rules 1980, S.I. 1980 No. 723 (in force on 1st July 1980), amend the 1979 Rules, 1979 Halsbury's Abridgment para. 2322. The Rules appoint the Independent Board of Visitors, established under the Naval Detention Quarters Rules 1973, the independent board of visitors for the purposes of the 1979 Rules.

2429   —— navy

The Naval Detention Quarters (Amendment) Rules 1980, S.I. 1980 No. 724 (in force on 1st July 1980), amend the 1973 Rules which provide for the inspection of naval detention quarters by an Independent Board of Visitors. These Rules alter the appointment, composition and general duties of the Board.

2430   Reserve Forces Act 1980

The Reserve Forces Act 1980 consolidates certain enactments relating to the reserve and auxiliary forces, and the lieutenancies, with amendments to give effect to a recommendation of the Law Commission. It also repeals certain obsolete enactments relating to the forces in question. The Act received the royal assent on 20th March 1980 and came into force on 20th April 1980. Tables showing the destination of enactments consolidated and the derivation of the new Act are set out on pages 617–638 following.

DESTINATION TABLE

This table shows in column (1) the enactments repealed by the Reserve Forces Act 1980, and in column (2) the provisions of that Act corresponding to the repealed provisions.

In certain cases the enactment in column (1), though having a corresponding provision in column (2), is not or is not wholly repealed, as it is still required, or partly required, for the purposes of other legislation.

(1)	(2)	(1)	(2)
City of London Militia Act 1662 (c 3)	Reserve Forces Act 1980 (c 9)	Royal Naval Reserve (Volunteer) Act 1859 (c 40)	Reserve Forces Act 1980 (c 9)
s 1	s 138 (1)	s 16, 17	Rep., S.L.(R.) Act 1975
		18	s 48
Militia Act 1802 (c 90)		19-22	Rep., 1957 c 53, s 137 (1), Sch 6
s 1-17	Rep., 1921 c 37, s 4 (1), Sch 2	23	Rep., 1875 c 60, s 5, Sch 1
18	s 137 (2)	24, 25	Rep., S.L.(R.) Act 1975
19-178 and Schs A-G	Rep., 1921 c 37, s 4 (1), Sch 2	Officers of Royal Naval Reserve Act 1863 (c 69)	
Naval Volunteers Act 1853 (c 73)		s 1	s 45
s 1-12	Rep., S.L.R. Act 1950	2	46
13-15	Rep., S.L.R. Act 1953	3	60
16	s 30 (1)	4, 5	Rep., S.L.R. Act 1893
17	30 (2)	6	Rep., S.L.R. Act 1875
18-20	Rep., S.L.R. Act 1950	7	—
21	s 30 (4)		
22-24	Rep., 1957 c 53, s 137 (1), Sch 6	Regulation of the Forces Act 1871 (c 86)	
		s 1	—
Royal Naval Reserve (Volunteer) Act 1859 (c 40)		2	Rep., S.L.R. Act 1883
		3-5	Rep., S.L.R. Act 1950
		6	s 117 (1)
s 1	s 1	7	Rep., 1882 c 48, s 29, Sch; 1882 c 49, s 54, Sch 2
2	50 (1), (2)	8	Rep., 1882 c 49, s 54, Sch 2
3	37 (1)-(3)	9	Rep., 1881 c 57, s 54, Sch
4	Rep., 1966 c 30, s 23 (7), Sch 2	10-13	Rep., S.L.R. Act 1950
5	s 17, 51	14	Rep., 1882 c 49, s 54, Sch 2
6	Rep., 1957 c 32, s 2 (2), Sch 2	15	Rep., 1881 c 57, s 54, Sch
7	s 55 (1)	16	Rep., S.L.R. Act 1966
8	53	17	Rep., 1892 c 43, s 28, Sch
9	Rep., 1957 c 32, s 2 (2), Sch 2	18	Rep., 1882 c 49, s 54, Sch 2
10	s 61	19	Rep., S.L.R. Act 1966
11, 12	Rep., 1957 c 53, s 137 (1), Sch 6	Schedule	Rep., S.L.R. Act 1963
13	s 37 (4), 56		
14	54 (1)		
15	(2)		

(1)	(2)	(1)	(2)
Merchant Shipping Act 1872 (c 73)	Reserve Forces Act 1980 (c 9)	Militia Act 1882 (c 49)	Reserve Forces Act 1980 (c 9)
s 1	—	s 52	Rep., 1973 c 65, s 237 (1), Sch 29
2–9	Rep., 1894 c 60, s 745, Sch 22	53	Rep., S.I. 1975 No. 156
10	Rep., S.L.R. Act 1950	54	Rep., S.L.R. Act 1964
11–16	Rep., 1894 c 60, s 745, Sch 22	Sch 1	Rep., 1972 c 70, s 272 (1), Sch 30
17	s 45	2	Rep., S.L.R. Act 1898
		3	Rep., 1921 c 37, s 4 (1), Sch 2
Militia Storehouses Act 1882 (c 12)			
s 1	Rep., S.L.R. Act 1898 Sch 8, para 7 (2)	Naval Enlistment Act 1884 (c 46)	
2		s 1	—
3	—	2	Rep., 1966 c 45, ss 11, 37 (2), Schs 2, 5
Militia Act 1882 (c 49)		3	Rep., 1960 c 61, s 113 (1), (2), Schs 4, 5
s 1	—	4	s 30 (3), (4)
2	Rep., S.L.R. Act 1898	5	Rep., S.I. 1964 No. 488
3–28	Rep., 1921 c 37, s 4 (1), Sch 2	Schedule	Rep., S.L.R. Act 1898
29	Rep., 1972 c 70, s 272 (1), Sch 30	Royal Naval Reserve Volunteer Act 1896 (c 33)	
30 (1)	s 133 (1)		
(2)	Rep., 1966 c 30, s 23 (6), (7), Schs 1, 2	s 1 (1)	s 49
(3)	s 133 (3)	(2)	Rep., S.L.R. Act 1908
(4)	136	2	Rep., 1957 c 53, s 137 (1), Sch 6
(5)	133 (4)	3	—
31	134		
32	135	Naval Reserve Act 1900 (c 52)	
33	Rep., 1918 c 19, s 1 (2), Sch; 1966 c 30, s 23 (7), Sch 2		
34 (1)	Rep., 1918 c 19, s 1 (2), Sch; 1966 c 30, s 23 (7), Sch 2	s 1 (1)	s 1 (1), 2 (1)
		(2)	2 (2)
		(3)	50 (3)
(2)	s 133 (5)	(4)	17, 37, 48, 51–54, 55 (1), 56, 61
(3)	Rep., 1918 c 19, s 1 (2), Sch; 1966 c 30, s 23 (7), Sch 2	2	—
35	Rep., 1918 c 19, s 1 (2), Sch; 1966 c 30, s 23 (7), Sch 2	Royal Naval Reserve Act 1902 (c 5)	
36	s 137 (1)	s 1	s 49
37–47	Rep., 1921 c 37, s 4 (1), Sch 2	2	—
48	Rep., 1972 c 70, s 272 (1), Sch 30	Naval Forces Act 1903 (c 6)	
49	Rep., 1921 c 37, s 4 (1), Sch 2; 1972 c 70, s 272 (1), Sch 30	s 1 (1)	Rep., 1966 c 30, s 23 (7), Sch 2
50	s 138 (2)–(4)	(2)	s 3, 17 (1), 48, 49, 51, 53, 54, 55 (1), 56
51	Rep., 1921 c 37, s 4 (1), Sch 2		

(1)	(2)
Naval Forces Act 1903 (c 6)	**Reserve Forces Act 1980 (c 9)**
s 2	Rep., 1948 c 25, s 1 (6)
3	Rep., 1957 c 32, s 2 (2), Sch 2
4	Rep., 1966 c 45, s 37 (2), Sch 5
5	s 1 (2), 2 (1)
6	—
Seamen's and Soldiers' False Characters Act 1906 (c 5)	
s 3	s 47
Territorial Army and Militia Act 1921 (c 37)	
s 1	Rep., 1953 c 50, s 44 (1), Sch 5
2	Rep., 1950 c 32, s 29 (1), Sch 3
3	Rep., 1955 c 20, s 5 (2), Sch 4
4	Sch 8 para 7 (1)
5 (1)	—
(2)	Rep., S.L.R. Act 1950
Sch 1	Rep., 1955 c 20, s 5 (2), Sch 4
2	Rep., S.L.R. Act 1950
Naval Reserve (Officers) Act 1926 (c 41)	
s 1	s 60
2	Rep., S.L.R. Act 1953
3	—
Royal Naval Reserve Act 1927 (c 18)	
s 1 (1)	Rep., 1957 c 32, s 2 (2), Sch 2
(2)	Rep., S.L.(R.) Act 1969
(3)	s 37 (3)
(4)	—
2	2 (2)
3	—
Royal Marines Act 1948 (c 25)	
s 1 (1)	s 3
(2)	Rep., 1966 c 30, s 23 (7), Sch 2

(1)	(2)
Royal Marines Act 1948 (c 25)	**Reserve Forces Act 1980 (c 9)**
s 1 (3)	Rep., 1948 c 64, s 60, Sch 6
(4)	s 55 (2)
(5)	
(6)	Rep., S.L.R. Act 1950
2	Rep., 1955 c 20, s 5 (2), Sch 4
3	
Recall of Army and Air Force Pensions Act 1948 (c 8)	
s 1	s 31 (1)–(4)
2 (1)	32 (1), (2)
(2)	(3)
(3)	(4), (5)
3 (1)–(3)	33 (1)–(3)
(4)	(4), (5)
4	31 (5)
5 (1)	31 (6)
(2)	
(3), (4)	(7)
6	
Schedule	Sch 2
Auxiliary and Reserve Forces Act 1949 (c 96)	
s 1–6	Rep., 1953 c 50, s 44 (1), Sch 5, Pt I Rep., S.L.(R.) Act 1976 *Passim*
7	s 2 (3), 57 (1)
8	57 (2)
9 (1)	(3), (4)
(2)	(5)
(3)	58
(4)	16 (1)
(5)	Sch 8 para 15 (1)
10 (1)	s 16 (2), Sch 8, para 15 (2)
(2)	Rep., 1966 c 30, s 23 (7), Sch 2
(3)	Sch 8 para 15 (1)
11 (1), (2)	s 17, 51
(3)	Rep., 1950 c 32, s 29 (1), (9), Sch 3; 1950 c 33, s 28 (1), Sch 3, Pt I
(4)	
12, 13	Rep., S.L.(R.) Act 1976
14, 15	Rep., S.L.(R.) Act 1977
16	s 16 (1), Sch 8, para 15 (1)
17 (1)	

(1)	(2)	(1)	(2)
Auxiliary and Reserve Forces Act 1949 (c 96)	Reserve Forces Act 1980 (c 9)	Army Reserve Act 1950 (c 32)	Reserve Forces Act 1980 (c 9)
s 17 (2)	Rep., S.L.(R.) Act 1977	s 13 (4), (5)	s 72 (3), (4)
(3)	s 57 (2)	14 (1)	73 (1), (2)
(4)	156 (3)	(2)–(4)	(3)–(5)
(5)	———	(5)	(6), (7)
18 (1)	———	(6)	Rep., S.L.(R.) Act 1977
(2)	Rep., 1953 c 50, s 44 (1), Sch 5	15 (1), (2)	s 74
(3)	Rep., 1950 c 32, s 29 (1), (9), Sch 3	(3)	Rep., 1971 c 33, s 77 (1), Sch 4, Pt II
Sch 1	Rep., S.L.(R.) Act 1977	16	s 75
2	Rep., S.L.R. Act 1953	17	76 (1)–(4)
Army Reserve Act 1950 (c 32)		18 (1)	77 (1)
s 1 (1), (2)	s 4	(2)	78 (1), (2)
(3), (4)	Rep., 1966 c 30, s 23 (7), Sch 2	(3)	(3)
(5)	s 4 (2)	(4)	76 (5)
2	Rep., S.L.(R.) Act 1977	(5)	77 (2); and cf. s 158 (3)
3 (1)–(3)	s 71	19–21	79–81
(4)	Rep., 1955 c 20, s 5 (1) Sch 8 para 17 (1)	22 (1)	84
4 (1)	Rep., S.L.(R.) Act 1977 Sch 8 para 17 (2)	(2)	Obsolete
(2)–(4)		23	s 64
(5)		24	63
5	Rep., 1966 c 30, s 23 (7), Sch 2	25	Rep., S.L.(R.) Act 1975
6 (1)	s 18 (1), Sch 8, para 16 (1)–(3), (8)	26	85
(2)	Rep., 1966 c 30, s 23 (7), Sch 2	27 (1)	s 86 (1), 155
(3)	Rep., 1962 c 10, s 3 (6)	(2), (3)	(2), (3)
(4)	s 18 (3), Sch 8, para 16 (9)	(4)	153
(5)	Sch 8 para 16 (3)	28 (1)	87, 156 (1), (2), Sch 8, para 16 (1), (2)
(6)	s 156 (1), (4), Sch 8, para 16 (10)	(2)	156 (3)
(7)	Rep., 1966 c 30, s 23 (7), Sch 2	(3)	Rep., 1955 c 20, ss 3, 5 (2), Sch 2, para. 13 (13), Sch 4
7	s 18 (2)	29 (1)	Rep., S.L.(R.) Act 1977
8 (1)	19 (1)	(2)	Rep., S.L.R. Act 1953
(2)	Sch 8 para 16 (7)	(3)	s 32 (1)
(3), (4)	s 19 (2), (3)	(4)	See Sch 8, para 1
9	Rep., 1966 c 30, s 23 (7), Sch 2	(5), (6)	Rep., S.L.(R.) Act 1977
10 (1), (2)	s 23 (1), (2) (a)	(7)	
(3)	Rep. S.I. 1973 No. 2163	(8), (9)	Rep., S.L.(R.) Act 1977
11	s 62	30	
12	82	Sch 1	Rep., 1966 c 30, s 23 (7), Sch 2
12A	Rep., 1960 c 61, s 113 (2), Sch 5	2	Sch 4
13 (1), (2)	s 72 (1), (2)	3	Rep., S.L.(R.) Act 1977
(3)	(1)	**Air Force Reserve Act 1950 (c 33)**	
		s 1	s 8
		2 (1)–(5)	68
		(6)	Rep., S.L.(R.) Act 1977
		3	s 71
		4 (1)	Sch 8 para 17 (3), (4)

(1)	(2)	(1)	(2)
Air Force Reserve Act 1950 (c 33)	Reserve Forces Act 1980 (c 9)	Air Force Reserve Act 1950 (c 33)	Reserve Forces Act 1980 (c 9)
s 4 (2), (3)	s 70	s 23	s 67
(4)	Rep., S.L.(R.) Act 1977	24	Rep., S.L.(R.) Act 1975
(5)	Sch 8 para 17 (5)	25	s 85
5	Rep., 1966 c 30, s 23 (7), Sch 2	26 (1)	86 (1), 155
6 (1)	s 20 (1), Sch 8, para 16 (4)–(6), (8)	(2), (3)	86 (2), (3)
		(4)	153
(2), (3)	Rep., 1966 c 30, s 23 (7), Sch 2	27 (1)	87, 156 (1), (2), Sch 8, para 16 (4), (5)
(4)	s 20 (2), Sch 8, para 16 (9)	(2)	156 (4)
(5)	Sch 8 para 16 (6)	(3)	(3)
(6)	s 156 (1), Sch 8, para 16 (10)	(4)	Rep., 1955 c 20, s 5 (2), Sch 4
(7)	Rep., 1966 c 30, s 23 (7), Sch 2	28	Rep., S.L.(R.) Act 1977
		29	Rep., S.L.(R.) Act 1976
7	Rep., 1955 c 20, s 3, Sch 4	30 (1)	Rep., S.L.(R.) Act 1977
8 (1)	s 21 (1)	(2)	s 32 (2)
(2)	Sch 8 para 16 (7)	(3)	Rep., S.L.(R.) Act 1977
(3)	s 21 (2), 69	(4)	See Sch 8, para 1
(4)	21 (3)	(5)	
9	Rep., 1966 c 30, s 23 (7), Sch 2	(6)	Rep., S.L.(R.) Act 1977
10 (1), (2)	s 23 (1), (2) (b)	31	
(3)	Rep., S.I. 1973 No. 2163	Sch 1	Rep., 1966 c 30, s 23 (7), Sch 2
11	s 66	2	Sch 4
12	82	3	Rep., S.L.(R.) Act 1977
12A	Rep., 1960 c 61, s 113 (2), Sch 5		
		Home Guard Act 1951 (c 8)	
13 (1), (2)	s 72 (1), (2)	s 1 (4)*	s 151
(3)	(1)	4 (3)†	151
(4), (5)	(3), (4)	(5)†	155
14 (1)	73 (1), (2)		
(2)–(4)	(3)–(5)	**Auxiliary Forces Act 1953 (c 50)**	
(5)	(6), (7)	s 1 (1)	s 5 (1), 9 (1)
(6)	Rep., S.L.(R.) Act 1977	(2)	5 (2), 9 (2)
15 (1), (2)	s 74	(3)	96 (3)
(3)	Rep., 1971 c 33, s 77 (1), Sch 4, Pt II	2 (1)	121 (1)
		(2)	
16	s 75	(3)	Rep., 1966 c 30, s 23 (7), Sch 2
17	76 (1)–(4)	(4)	s 122 (4)
18 (1)	77 (1)	(5)	121 (2)
(2)	78 (1), (2)	(6)	122 (2)
(3)	(3)	3	122 (1)
(4)	76 (5)	4	123 (2)
(5)	77 (2); and cf. s 158 (3)	5	123 (1)
19–21	79–81	6	124
22 (1)	84	7 (1)	125 (1)
(2)	Obsolete	(2)	Rep., S.I. 1964 No. 488

* Repealed in part   † Not repealed

(1) Auxiliary Forces Act 1953 (c 50)	(2) Reserve Forces Act 1980 (c 9)	(1) Auxiliary Forces Act 1953 (c 50)	(2) Reserve Forces Act 1980 (c 9)
s 7 (3)	s 125 (2)	s 26 (4)	Rep., 1966 c 30, s 23 (7), Sch 2
(4)	(3), (4)	(5)	Rep., S.L.(R.) Act 1977
(5)	(5), (6)	27 (1)	s 106 (1), (2)
(6)	Rep., S.I. 1964 No. 488	(2)	107
8 (1)	s 126 (1)	(3)	106 (4)
(2)	Rep., S.I. 1964 No. 488	(4)	Rep., 1971 c 33, s 77 (1), Sch 4, Pt II
(3)	s 126 (2)	(5)	s 106 (3)
9	127	28	108
10	128	29 (1)	109
11 (1)	88	(2)	Rep., 1968 c 60, s 33 (3), Sch 3, Pt I
(2)	89	(3)	s 109
(3)	90	30	Rep., 1955 c 20, s 5 (2), Sch 4
(4)	91	31 (1)–(3)	s 110
(5)	92	(4)	111
11 (6)	Sch 8 para 8	(5)	112
(7)	Rep., 1966 c 30 s 23 (3), (7), Sch 2	(6)	113
12 (1), (2)	s 94 (1)	(7)	Rep., 1955 c 20, s 5 (2), Sch 4
(3), (4)	(2), (3)	(8)	Applied to Scotland
13	95 (2)	32	s 114
14 (1)	96 (1)	33 (1), (2)	115
(2)	Rep., S.L.(R.) 1977	(3)	Applied to Scotland
(3)	s 96 (2)	34 (1), (2)	s 116 (1), (2)
15	97	(3)	(1), (2)
16	Rep., 1966 c 30, s 23 (7), Sch 2	(4)	Applied to Scotland
17 (1)	s 98	35	s 102
(2)	99	36 (1), (2)	93 (1)
(3)	Rep., S.L.(R.) Act 1977	(3)	(2)
18	s 100	37	119
18A	Rep., 1960 c 61, s 113 (2), Sch 5	38	152 (1)
19 (1)	s 40 (1), (2)	39	118
(2)	(3)	40	138 (5)
20 (1)	41 (1), Sch 8 para 18 (1)	41 (1)	120
(2)	41 (2), Sch. 8, para 18 (2)	(2)–(4)	Rep., 1966 c 30, s 23 (7), Sch 2
(3)	Sch 8 para 18 (1)	42 (1)	s 88, 91, 128 (4)
(4)	s 41 (3), Sch 8, para 18 (3)	(2)	154 (2)
(5)	42, Sch 8, para 18 (4)	(3)	(1)
21	Rep., S.L.(R.) Act 1977	(4)	155
22	s 43, Sch 8, para 18 (5)	(5)	153
23, 24	Rep., 1966 c 30, s 23 (7), Sch 2	43 (1)	156 (1), (2), Sch 7, para 8 (5)
25 (1)	s 22	(2)	156 (4)
(2)–(4)	Rep., 1966 c 30, s 23 (7), Sch 2	(3)	(3)
26 (1)	s 103	44	Rep., S.L.(R.) Act 1974
(2)	104	45	Rep., S.L.(R.) Act 1976
(3)	105	46 (1)	Rep., 1966, c 30, s 23 (7), Sch 2
		(2)	See Sch 8, para 1
		(3)	

(1)	(2)	(1)	(2)
Auxiliary Forces Act 1953 (c 50)	Reserve Forces Act 1980 (c 9)	Revision of the Army and Air Force Acts (Transitional Provisions) Act 1955 (c 20)	Reserve Forces Act 1980 (c 9)
s 46 (4)			
(5)			
(6)	Rep., S.L.(R.) Act 1977	Sch 2 para 14 (10)	s 78
47	Rep., S.L.(R.) Act 1976	para 14 (11)	80 (1)
	Rep., 1973 c 65, s 237 (1), Sch 29	para 14 (12)	81 (1), (2)
48 (1)	s 156 (5), (6)	para 14 (13)	84
(2)	112 (3)	para 14 (14)	87
49	See s 158 (3)	para 18 (1)	*Passim*
50		para 18 (2)	s 94 (2)
Sch 1 para 1, 2, 3–6	Sch 7 para 1, 2, 4–7	para 18 (3)	Rep., 1960 c 61 s 113 (2), Sch 5
para 7	para 8 (1)–(4)	para 18 (4)	s 106 (2), (4)
2	3	para 18 (5)	
3	Obsolete	para 18 (6)	112 (1), (2)
4	Rep., 1966 c 30, s 23 (7), Sch 2	para 18 (7)	114
5	Rep., S.L.(R.) Act 1974	para 18 (8)	116 (1), (2)
		para 18 (9)	119
Revision of the Army and Air Force Acts (Transitional Provisions) Act 1955 (c 20)		para 18 (10)	112 (3)
		para 18 (11)	Sch 3
Sch 2 para 11	s 32 (3)–(5)	Naval and Marine Reserves Pay Act 1957 (c 32)	
para 12			
para 13 (1)	Sch 8 para 10, and *passim*	s 1 (1)	s 59 (1)
para 13 (2)	s 71 (2), (3)	(2)	(3), (4)
para 13 (3)	18 (2)	(3)	(1)
para 13 (4)	19 (3)	2 (1)	
para 13 (5)	82 (1)	(2)	Rep., S.L.(R.) Act 1974
para 13 (6)	Rep., 1960, c 61, s 113 (2), Sch 5	Sch 1	s 59 (2), Sch 8, para 12
para 13 (7)	s 73 (2)–(7)	2	Rep., S.L.(R.) Act 1974
para 13 (8)	Rep., 1971 c 33, s 77 (1), Sch 4, Pt II	Army and Air Force Act 1961 (c 52)	
para 13 (9)	s 78		
para 13 (10)	80 (1)	Sch 2*	s 32 (5), Sch 8, para 16 (1), (2), (4), (5)
para 13 (11)	81 (1), (2)		
para 13 (12)	84		
para 13 (13)	87	Army Reserve Act 1962 (c 10)	
para 14 (1)	Sch 8 para 10, and *passim*		
para 14 (2)	s 71 (2), (3)	s 1, 2	Rep., 1966 c 30, s 23 (7), Sch 2
para 14 (3)		3 (1)	s 14 (1), Sch 1, para 3 (1)
para 14 (4)	21 (3)	(2)	Sch 1 para 3 (2)
para 14 (5)	82 (1)	(3)	para 1 (1)
para 14 (6)	Rep., 1960 c 61 s 113 (2), Sch 5	(4)	para 1 (2), 7
para 14 (7)	s 73 (2)–(6)	(5)	para 8
para 14 (8)	Rep., 1971 c 33, s 77 (1), Sch 4, Pt II	(6)	s 14 (4)
para 14 (9)	s 76 (1), (2)		

* Repealed in part

(1)	(2)
Army Reserve Act 1962 (c 10)	**Reserve Forces Act 1980 (c 9)**
s 4 (1)	Sch 1 para 2
(2)	s 14 (3)
(2A)	Sch 1 para 10
(3)	s 14 (5)
(4)	Sch 1 para 9
(5)	Rep., 1966 c 30, s 23 (7), Sch 2
5 (1)	Rep., 1966 c 30, s 23 (7), Sch 2
(2)	s 145 (1)
(3)	146 (1)
6 (1)	Rep., 1966 c 30, s 23 (7), Sch 2
(2)	s 14 (2)
(3)	——
7	——
8 (1)	——
(2)	See s 158 (3)
Sch 3	Sch 1 para 4–6
Navy Army and Air Force Reserves Act 1964 (c 11)	
s 1	Rep., 1969 c 23, s 1 (2)
2 (1)	s 34 (2)
(2)	(1)
(3)	35
(4), (5)	34 (3), (4)
(6)	145 (1), 146 (1)
(7)	34 (5), (6)
3 (1)	Sch 8 para 16 (2)
(2)	para 16 (5)
4 (1)	——
(2)	See s 158 (3)
Administration of Justice Act 1964 (c 42)	
s 18 (1), (2)	s 130 (2), (3)
Reserve Forces Act 1966 (c 30)	
s 1 (1)	s 3, 5 (1), 156 (1), Sch 8, para 5 (1) and *passim*
(2)	——
2 (1)	6 (1), (2)
(2)	(3)
3	——
4 (1)	14 (4)
(2), (3)	——

(1)	(2)
Reserve Forces Act 1966 (c 30)	**Reserve Forces Act 1980 (c 9)**
s 5 (1), (2)	s 10 (1), (2)
(3)	10 (6), 156 (4)
(4), (5)	10 (3), (4)
6 (1)	11 (1)
(2)	12 (1)
(3), (4)	11 (2), (3)
(5)	(4), (5)
(6)	13 (1)
(7)	12 (2)
7 (1)	16 (1), Sch 8, para 15 (1), 16 (1)–(6)
(2), (3)	11 (6)
8 (1)	14 (1)
(2)	15
9 (1)–(3)	26 (1)–(3)
(4)	27
(5)	145 (3), 146 (3)
(6)	26 (4)
(7)	(1)
10 (1), (2)	13 (2)
(3)	(3)
11	28
12	29
13 (1)	36 (1), 145 (3), 146 (3)
(2)	36 (2)
14 (1), (2)	65
(3)	72 (1), 95 (1)
(4)	Obsolete
(5)	s 117 (2)
15 (1)	83 (1), (2)
(2)	(3)
(3)	13 (4)
(4), (5)	101
16 (1)	38
(2)	39 (1)
(3)	39 (2), Sch 8, para 19
(4)	See Sch 8, paras 16–18
(5)	s 39 (3)
17 (1)	121 (1)
(2)	122 (3)
(3)	——
(4)	122 (4)
(5)	129 (1)
(6)	122 (5), 129 (2)
18 (1)	147 (1), 149 (1)
(2)	147 (2), (3), 149 (2), (3)
(3)	147 (4), (5), 149 (4)
(4)	147 (6), 149 (5)
(5)	147 (7), 149 (6)

(1)	(2)
Reserve Forces Act 1966 (c 30)	Reserve Forces Act 1980 (c 9)
s 18 (6)	s 147 (8), 149 (7)
(7)	147 (9), 149 (8)
(8)	147 (10), 149 (9)
(9)	149 (1)–(4), (6), (9)
19	Applied to Scotland
20 (1)	s 133 (2)
(2)	130 (2)
(3)	Rep., S.I. 1973 No 2163
21 (1)	s 6 (3), 117 (2), 156 (1)
(2)	156 (3)
(3), (4)	———
22 (1)	150 (1)
(2)	28 (3) (b), 65 (2) (b), 150 (2)
(3)	150 (1)
23 (1)	Sch 8 para 11, and *passim*
(2)	Sch 8 para 6
(3)	para 9
(4)	s 117 (3)
(5)	152 (2)
(6)	See against 1966 c 30, Sch 1, below
(7)	Rep., S.L.(R.) Act 1974
24	
25 (1), (2)	
(3)	s 158 (3)
Sch 1 para 1	30 (4)
para 2	17, 51
para 3	
para 4	3, 17 (1), 48, 49, 51, 53, 54, 55 (1), 56
para 5	Sch 8 para 15 (1)
para 6	s 17, 51
para 7	4 (2) (b)
para 8	Sch 8 para 16 (3), (8)
para 9	s 19 (1)
para 10	72 (2)
para 11	73 (2)
para 12	76 (1), (4)
para 13	Sch 8 para 16 (8)
para 14	s 21 (1)
para 15	72 (2)
para 16	73 (2)
para 17	76 (1), (4)
para 18	Sch 9 para 1
para 19	s 121 (1)
para 20	122 (4)
para 21	———

(1)	(2)
Reserve Forces Act 1966 (c 30)	Reserve Forces Act 1980 (c 9)
Sch 1 para 22	s 100 (3)
para 23	43, Sch 8, para 18
	(5)
para 24	106 (1), (2)
para 25	109
para 26	112 (3)
para 27–30	
para 31	Rep., S.L.(R.) Act 1976
para 32	See Sch 8, para 5 (1)
para 33	Sch 8 para (3)
para 34, 35	Sch 9 para 2 (b), 3
para 36, 37	para 5 (b), 6
para 38	
para 39	———
Sch 2	Sch 1 para 4
	Rep., S.L.(R.) Act 1974

Armed Forces Act 1966 (c 45)	
Sch 4*	s 32 (5), 34 (2), 47, 58 (a), Sch 8, para 16 (1), (2), (4), (5)

Criminal Justice Act 1967 (c 80)	
Sch 3, Parts I*, IV*	s 73 (5), 74, 76 (2), 107, 110 (1)

Ulster Defence Regiment Act 1969 (c 65)	
s 1 (1)	s 7
(2)	141
(3)	142
(4)	139
(5)	140
(6)	Rep., 1973 c 34, s 1 (2)
2 (1)	s 25 (2)
(2)	(1)
(3)	24, 26 (1)
(4)	10 (5)
(5), (6)	44
(7)	145 (2), 146 (2)
3 (1)	143
(2)	144
4 (1)	140 (3), 156 (1)
(2)	155
(3)	140 (3)
5, 6	———

* Repealed in part

(1)	(2)	(1)	(2)
Armed Forces Act 1971 (c 33)	Reserve Forces Act 1980 (c 9)	Ulster Defence Regiment Act 1973 (c 34)	Reserve Forces Act 1980 (c 9)
s 64 (2)	s 34 (2)	s 1 (3)	See Sch 8, para 5 (1)
69 (1)	74 (1) (*c*)	(4)	——
(2)	107 (*c*)	2	
76*	Applied to Scotland	**Northern Ireland Constitution Act 1973 (c 36)**	
Sch 3 para 6	s 156 (1)	s 36 (5)†	See s 132
Local Government Act 1972 (c 70)		**Statute Law (Repeals) Act 1977 (c 18)**	
s 216 (2)†	s 130 (2)	Sch 2*	s 14 (3), Sch 1, para 10
218 (1)	94 (2), 130 (1), Sch 8, para 13 (1)	**Criminal Law Act 1977 (c 45)**	
(2)	135 (1), 136	s 28 (2)†	s 144 (1) (i)
(3)	134	(7)†	(2) (*a*)
(4), (5)	Sch 8 para 13 (2)	31 (6)†	108
(6)	——	32 (1)†	144 (1) (iii)
(7)	Sch 8 para 13 (2)	**National Health Service Act 1977 (c 49)**	
(8)	s 130 (2), Sch 8, para 13 (2)	Sch 14 para 13 (1)*	Sch 2, para 2
270 (1)†	130 (2)		
Ulster Defence Regiment Act 1973 (c 34)			
s 1 (1)	s 7 (2), 156 (3)		
(2)	——		

* Repealed in part   † Not repealed

TABLE OF DERIVATIONS
This table shows in the right hand column the legislative source from which the sections of the Reserve Forces Act 1980 in the left hand column have been derived. In the table the following abbreviations are used:

1802 c. 90	= Militia Act 1802 c. 90
1802 c. 91	= Militia (Scotland) Act 1802 c. 91
1853	= Naval Volunteers Act 1853 c. 73
1859	= Royal Naval Reserve (Volunteer) Act 1859 c. 40
1863	= Officers of Royal Naval Reserve Act 1863 c. 69
1871	= Regulation of the Forces Act 1871 c. 86
1872	= Merchant Shipping Act 1872 c. 73
1882	= Militia Act 1882 c. 49
1884	= Naval Enlistment Act 1884 c. 46
1896	= Royal Naval Reserve Volunteer Act 1896 c. 33
1900	= Naval Reserve Act 1900 c. 52
1902	= Royal Naval Reserve Act 1902 c. 5
1903	= Naval Forces Act 1903 c. 6
1921	= Territorial Army and Militia Act 1921 c. 37
1926	= Naval Reserve (Officers) Act 1926 c. 41
1927	= Royal Naval Reserve Act 1927 c. 18
1948 c. 25	= Royal Marines Act 1948 11 & 12 Geo. 6 c. 25
1948 c. 8	= Recall of Army and Air Force Pensioners Act 1948 12, 13 & 14 Geo. 6. c. 8
1949	= Auxiliary and Reserve Forces Act 1949 c. 96
1950 c. 32	= Army Reserve Act 1950 c. 32
1950 c. 33	= Air Force Reserve Act 1950 c. 33
1951	= Home Guard Act 1951 15 & 16 Geo. 6 & 1 Eliz. 2. c. 8
1953	= Auxiliary Forces Act 1953 c. 50
1955	= Revision of the Army and Air Force Acts (Transitional Provisions) Act 1955 c. 20
1957	= Naval and Marine Reserves Pay Act 1957 c. 32
1962	= Army Reserve Act 1962 c. 10
1964	= Navy, Army and Air Force Reserves Act 1964 c. 11
1966	= Reserve Forces Act 1966 c. 30
1969	= Ulster Defence Regiment Act 1969 c. 65
1973	= Ulster Defence Regiment Act 1973 c. 34

The Table does not acknowledge the transfer of functions made by virtue of the Defence (Transfer of Functions) Act 1964 c. 15.
Effect is given to the Law Commission's recommendation at clause 158 (3) and Part II of Schedule 10.

Section of Act	Derivation
1 (1)	1859 s. 1; 1900 s. 1 (1).
(2)	1859 s. 1; 1903 s. 5.
2 (1)	1900 s. 1 (1); 1903 ss. 4 (2), 5.
(2)	1900 s. 1 (2); 1927 s. 2.
(3)	1949 s. 9 (1).
3	1903 s. 1 (2); 1948 c. 25 s. 1 (1).
4 (1)	1950 c. 32 s. 1 (1).
(2)	1950 c. 32 s. 1 (2), (5); 1966 s. 23 and Sch. 1 para. 7.
5 (1), (2)	1953 s. 1 (1), (2).
6 (1), (2)	1966 s. 2 (1).
(3)	1966 ss. 2 (2), 21 (1).
7 (1)	1969 s. 1 (1).
(2)	1969 s. 1 (1); 1973 s. 1 (1).
8 (1)–(3)	1950 c. 33 s. 1.
9 (1), (2)	1953 s. 1 (1), (2).

Section of Act	Derivation
10 (1)	1966 s. 5 (1).
(2)	1966 s. 5 (2).
(3)	1966 s. 5 (4).
(4)	1966 s. 5 (5).
(5)	1969 s. 2 (4).
(6)	1966 s. 5 (3).
11 (1)	1966 s. 6 (1).
(2)	1966 s. 6 (3).
(3)	1966 s. 6 (4).
(4), (5)	1966 s. 6 (5).
(6)	1966 s. 7 (2), (3).
12 (1)	1966 s. 6 (2).
(2)	1966 s. 6 (7).
13 (1)	1966 s. 6 (6).
(2)	1966 s. 10 (1), (2).
(3)	1966 s. 10 (3).
(4)	1966 s. 15 (3).
14 (1)	1962 s. 3 (1); 1966 s. 8 (1).
(2)	1962 s. 6 (2) and Sch., s. 8 (2).
(3)	1962 s. 4 (2); SL (Rep.) Act 1977 Sch. 2.
(4)	1962 s. 3 (6); 1966 s. 4 (1).
(5)	1962 s. 4 (3).
15	1966 s. 8 (2).
16 (1)	1949 ss. 10 (1), 17 (1); 1966 s. 7 (1).
(2)	1949 s. 10 (3).
17 (1)	1859 s. 5; 1903 s. 1 (2); 1949 s. 11 (4); 1966 s. 23 (6) and Sch. 1 para. 2.
(2), (3)	1859 s. 5 proviso 1; 1949 s. 11 (4); 1966 s. 23 (6) and Sch. 1 para. 2.
(4)	1859 s. 5 proviso 2; 1949 s. 11 (4); 1966 s. 23 (6) and Sch. 1 para. 2.
18 (1)	1950 c. 32 s. 6 (1).
(2)	1950 c. 32 s. 7; 1955 s. 3 and Sch. 2 para. 13 (3).
(3)	1950 c. 32 s. 6 (4).
19 (1)	1950 c. 32 s. 8 (1); 1966 s. 23 (6) and Sch. 1, para. 9.
(2)	1950 c. 32 s. 8 (3).
(3)	1950 c. 32 s. 8 (4); 1955 s. 3 and Sch. 2, para. 13 (4).
20 (1)	1950 c. 33 s. 6 (1).
(2)	1950 c. 33 s. 6 (4).
21 (1)	1950 c. 33 s. 8 (1); 1966 s. 23 (6) and Sch. 1, para. 14.
(2)	1950 c. 33 s. 8 (3).
(3)	1950 c. 33 s. 8 (4); 1955 s. 3 and Sch. 2, para. 14 (4).
22	1953 s. 25 (1); 1966 s. 23 (1).
23 (1)	1950 c. 32 s. 10 (1); 1950 c. 33 s. 10 (1).
(2)	1950 c. 32 s. 10 (2); 1950 c. 33 s. 10 (2).
24	1969 s. 2 (3).
25 (1)	1969 s. 2 (2).
(2)	1969 s. 2 (1).
26 (1)	1966 s. 9 (1), (7); 1969 s. 2 (3).
(2)	1966 s. 9 (2).
(3)	1966 s. 9 (3).
(4)	1966 s. 9 (6).

Section of Act	Derivation
27	1966 s. 9 (4).
28 (1), (2) (3)	1966 s. 11 (1), (2). 1966 ss. 11 (3), 22 (2).
29 (1), (2)	1966 s. 12 (1), (2).
30 (1) (2) (3) (4)	1853 s. 16. 1853 s. 17. 1884 s. 4. 1853 s. 21; 1884 s. 4; 1966 s. 23 (6) and Sch. 1, para. 1.
31 (1)–(4). (5) (6) (7)	1948 c. 8 s. 1 (1)–(4). 1948 c. 8 s. 4. 1948 c. 8 s. 5 (1). 1948 c. 8 s. 5 (3), (4).
32 (1) (2) (3) (4) (5)	1948 c. 8 s. 2 (1); 1950 c. 32 s. 29 (3); 1966 s. 23 (1). 1948 c. 8 s. 2 (1); 1950 c. 33 s. 30 (2); 1966 s. 23 (1). 1948 c. 8 s. 2 (2); 1955 s. 3 and Sch. 2, para. 11. 1948 c. 8 s. 2 (3); 1955 s. 3 and Sch. 2, para. 11. 1948 c. 8 s. 2 (3); 1955 s. 3 and Sch. 2, para. 11; Army and Air Force Act 1961 c. 52 s. 38 and Sch. 2; Armed Forces Act 1966 c. 45 s. 37 and Sch. 4.
33 (1)–(3) (4) (5)	1948 c. 8 s. 3 (1)–(3). 1948 c. 8 s. 3 (4). 1948 c. 8 s. 3 (4); Recorded Delivery Service Act 1962 c. 27 s. 1 (1).
34 (1) (2) (3) (4) (5), (6)	1964 s. 2 (2); 1966 s. 23 (1). 1964 s. 2 (1); Armed Forces Act 1966 c. 45 s. 37 (1) and Sch. 4; Armed Forces Act 1971 c. 33 s. 64 (2). 1964 s. 2 (4). 1964 s. 2 (5). 1964 s. 2 (7).
35 (1), (2)	1964 s. 2 (3).
36 (1) (2)	1966 s. 13 (1), (2). 1966 s. 13 (1), (2).
37 (1), (2) (3) (4)	1859 s. 3; 1900 s. 1 (4). 1859 s. 3; 1900 s. 1 (4); 1927 s. 1 (3). 1859 s. 13; 1900 s. 1 (4).
38	1966 s. 16 (1).
39 (1) (2) (3)	1966 s. 16 (2). 1966 s. 16 (3). 1966 s. 16 (5).
40 (1), (2) (3)	1953 s. 19 (1). 1953 s. 19 (2).
41 (1), (2) (3)	1953 s. 20 (1), (2). 1953 s. 20 (4).
42	1953 s. 20 (5).
43	1953 s. 22; 1966 s. 23 (6) and Sch. 1, para. 23.
44 (1) (2)	1969 s. 2 (5). 1969 s. 2 (6).
45	1863 s. 1; 1872 s. 17.

Section of Act	Derivation
46 (1), (2)	1863 s. 2.
47	Seamen's and Soldiers' False Characters Act 1906, c. 5 s. 3; Armed Forces Act 1966 c. 45 s. 37 (1) and Sch. 4.
48	1859 s. 18.
49	1896 s. 1 (1); 1902 s. 1; British Nationality Act 1948 c. 56 ss. 1 (2), 3 (2).
50 (1), (2)	1859 s. 2.
(3)	1900 s. 1 (3).
51	1859 s. 5; 1903 s. 1 (2); 1949 s. 11 (4); 1966 s. 23 and Sch. 1, para. 2.
52	1900 s. 1 (4).
53 (1), (2)	1859 s. 8; 1900 s. 1 (4); 1903 s. 1 (2).
54 (1), (2)	1859 s. 14; 1900 s. 1 (4); 1903 s. 1 (2).
(2)	1859 s. 15; 1900 s. 1 (4); 1903 s. 1 (2); Armed Forces Act 1966 c. 45 ss. 6, 14 (1); Armed Forces Act 1971 c. 33 s. 75 and Sch. 3, para. 7.
55 (1)	1859 s. 7; 1900 s. 1 (4); 1903 s. 1 (2).
(2)	1948 c. 25 s. 1 (4).
56	1859 s. 13; 1900 s. 1 (4); 1903 s. 1 (2).
57 (1)	1949 s. 9 (1).
(2)	1949 ss. 9 (2), 17 (3).
(3), (4)	1949 s. 9 (3).
(5)	1949 s. 9 (4).
58	1949 s. 9 (5); Armed Forces Act 1966 c. 45 s. 37 (1) and Sch. 4.
59 (1)	1957 s. 1 (1), (3).
(2)	1957 s. 1 and Sch. 1.
(3), (4)	1957 s. 1 (2).
60 (1), (2)	1863 s. 3; 1926 s. 1.
61 (1)	1859 s. 10; S.I. 1968/1656.
(2), (3)	1859 s. 10.
62 (1), (2)	1950 c. 32 s. 11.
63 (1), (2)	1950 c. 32 s. 24 (1), (2).
64	1950 c. 32 s. 23.
65 (1)	1966 s. 14 (1).
(2)	1966 ss. 14 (2), 22 (2).
66	1950 c. 33 s. 11.
67 (1), (2)	1950 c. 33 s. 23 (1), (2).
68 (1)–(5)	1950 c. 33 s. 2 (1)–(5).
69 (1), (2)	1950 c. 33 s. 8 (3), proviso.
70 (1)	1950 c. 33 s. 4 (2).
(2)	1950 c. 33 s. 4 (3).

Section of Act	Derivation
71 (1)	1950 c. 32 s. 3 (1); 1950 c. 33 s. 3 (1).
(2), (3)	1950 c. 32 s. 3 (2), (3); 1950 c. 33 s. 3 (2), (3); 1955 s. 3 and Sch. 2, paras. 13 (2), 14 (2).
72 (1)	1950 c. 32 s. 13 (1), (3); 1950 c. 33 s. 13 (1), (3); 1966 s. 14 (3).
(2)	1950 c. 32 s. 13 (2); 1950 c. 33 s. 13 (2); 1966 s. 23 (6) and Sch. 1, paras. 10, 15.
(3)	1950 c. 32 s. 13 (4); 1950 c. 33 s. 13 (4).
(4)	1950 c. 32 s. 13 (5); 1950 c. 33 s. 13 (5); Sri Lanka Republic Act 1972 c. 55 s. 1 (4).
(5)	1950 c. 32 s. 13 (3), (5); 1950 c. 33 s. 13 (3), (5).
73 (1)	1950 c. 32 s. 14 (1); 1950 c. 3 s. 14 (1).
(2)	1950 c. 32 s. 14 (1); 1950 c. 33 s. 14 (1); 1955 s. 3 and Sch. 2, paras. 13 (1), (7), 14 (1), (7); 1966 s. 23 (6) and Sch. 1, paras. 11, 16.
(3)	1950 c. 32 s. 14 (2); 1950 c. 33 s. 14 (2); 1955 s. 3 and Sch. 2, paras. 13 (7), 14 (7).
(4)	1950 c. 32 s. 14 (3); 1950 c. 33 s. 14 (3); 1955 s. 3 and Sch. 2, paras. 13 (1), (7), 14 (1), (7).
(5)	1950 c. 32 s. 14 (4); 1950 c. 33 s. 14 (4); 1955 s. 3 and Sch. 2, paras. 13 (1), (7), 14 (1), (7); Criminal Justice Act 1967 c. 80 s. 92 (1) and Sch. 3, Pts. I, IV.
(6)	1950 c. 32 s. 14 (5); 1950 c. 33 s. 14 (5); 1955 s. 3 and Sch. 2, paras. 13 (1), (7), 14 (1), (7).
(7)	1950 c. 32 s. 14 (5); 1950 c. 33 s. 14 (5); 1955 s. 3 and Sch. 2, para. 13 (1), (7).
74 (1)	1950 c. 32 s. 15 (1); 1950 c. 33 s. 15 (1); Criminal Justices Act 1967 c. 80 s. 92 (1) and Sch. 3, Pts. I, IV; Armed Forces Act 1971 c. 33 s. 69 (1).
(2)	1950 c. 32 s. 15 (2); 1950 c. 33 s. 15 (2); 1967 c. 80 s. 92 (1) and Sch. 3, Pts. I, IV.
75	1950 c. 32 s. 16; 1950 c. 33 s. 16.
76 (1)	1950 c. 32 s. 17 (1); 1950 c. 33 s. 17 (1); 1955 s. 3 and Sch. 2, para. 14 (9); 1966 s. 23 (6) and Sch. 1, paras. 12, 17.
(2)	1950 c. 32 s. 17 (2); 1950 c. 33 s. 17 (2); 1955 s. 3 and Sch. 2, paras. 13 (1), 14 (1), (9); Criminal Justice Act 1967 c. 80 s. 92 (1) and Sch. 3, Pts. I, IV.
(3)	1950 c. 32 s. 17 (3); 1950 c. 33 s. 17 (3).
(4)	1950 c. 32 s. 17 (4); 1950 c. 33 s. 17 (4); 1966 s. 23 (6) and Sch. 1, paras. 12, 17.
(5)	1950 c. 32 s. 18 (4); 1950 c. 33 s. 18 (4).
77 (1)	1950 c. 32 s. 18 (1); 1950 c. 33 s. 18 (1); 1955 s. 3 and Sch. 2, paras. 13 (1), 14 (1).
(2)	1950 c. 32 s. 18 (5); 1950 c. 33 s. 18 (5).
78 (1), (2)	1950 c. 32 s. 18 (2); 1950 c. 33 s. 18 (2); Army Act 1955 c. 18 s. 220 (1), (2); Air Force Act 1955 c. 19 s. 218 (1), (2); 1955 s. 3 and Sch. 2, paras. 13 (1), (9), 14 (1), (10).
(3)	1950 c. 32 s. 18 (3); 1950 c. 33 s. 18 (3); 1955 s. 3 and Sch. 2, para. 13 (9), 14 (10).
79	1950 c. 32 s. 19; 1950 c. 33 s. 19.
80 (1)	1950 c. 32 s. 20 (1); 1950 c. 33 s. 20 (1); 1955 s. 3 and Sch. 2, paras. 13 (1), (10), 14 (1), (11).
(2)	1950 c. 32 s. 20 (2); 1950 c. 33 s. 20 (2).
81 (1), (2)	1950 c. 32 s. 21 (1), (2); 1950 c. 33 s. 21 (1), (2); 1955 s. 3 and Sch. 2, paras. 13 (1), (11), 14 (1), (12).
(13)	1950 c. 32 s. 21 (3); 1950 c. 33 s. 21 (3); Armed Forces Act 1971 c. 33 s. 76.

Section of Act	Derivation
82 (1)	1950 c. 32 s. 12 (1); 1950 c. 33 s. 12 (1); 1955 s. 3 and Sch. 2, paras. 13 (5), 14 (5).
(2)	1950 c. 32 s. 12 (2); 1950 c. 33 s. 12 (2).
83 (1), (2)	1966 s. 15 (1).
(3)	1966 s. 15 (2).
84	1950 c. 32 s. 22 (1); 1950 c. 33 s. 22 (1); 1955 s. 3 and Sch. 2, paras. 13 (1), (12), 14 (1), (13).
85	1950 c. 32 s. 26; 1950 c. 33 s. 25.
86 (1)–(3)	1950 c. 32 s. 27 (1)–(3); 1950 c. 33 s. 26 (1)–(3).
87	1950 c. 32 s. 28 (1); 1950 c. 33 s. 27 (1); 1955 s. 3 and Sch. 2, paras. 13 (13), 14 (14).
88	1953 ss. 11 (1), 42 (1).
89	1953 s. 11 (2).
90	1953 s. 11 (3).
91	1953 ss. 11 (4), 42 (1).
92	1953 s. 11 (5); 1966 s. 23 (1).
93 (1)	1953 s. 36 (1), (2).
(2)	1953 s. 36 (3).
94 (1)	1953 s. 12 (1), (2).
(2)	1953 s. 12 (3); 1955 s. 3 and Sch. 2, para. 18 (2); Local Government Act 1972 c. 70 s. 218 (1); Local Government (Scotland) Act 1973 c. 65 s. 205 (4).
(3)	1953 s. 12 (4).
95 (1)	1966 s. 14 (3).
(2)	1953 s. 13.
96 (1)	1953 s. 14 (1).
(2)	1953 s. 14 (3).
(3)	1953 s. 1 (3).
97	1953 s. 15.
98 (1), (2)	1953 s. 17 (1).
99 (1), (2)	1953 s. 17 (2).
100 (1), (2)	1953 s. 18 (1), (2).
(3)	1953 s. 18 (3); 1966 s. 23 (6) and Sch. 1, para. 22.
101 (1)	1966 s. 15 (4).
(2)	1966 s. 15 (5).
102	1953 s. 35.
103	1953 s. 26 (1); 1966 s. 23 (1).
104	1953 s. 26 (2); 1966 s. 23 (1).
105	1953 s. 26 (3); 1966 s. 23 (1).
106 (1)	1953 s. 27 (1); 1966 s. 23 (6) and Sch. 1, para, 24.

Section of Act	Derivation
(2)	1953 s. 27 (1); 1955 s. 3 and Sch. 2, para. 19 (1), (4); 1966 s. 23 (6) and Sch. 1, para. 24.
(3)	1953 s. 27 (5).
(4)	1953 s. 27 (3); 1955 s. 3 and Sch. 2, para. 18 (1), (4).
107	1953 s. 27 (2); Criminal Justice Act 1967 c. 80 ss. 92, 106 (2)–(4) and Sch. 3, Pts. I, IV; Armed Forces Act 1971 c. 33 s. 69 (2).
108	1953 s. 28; Criminal Law Act 1977 c. 45 s. 31 (7).
109	1953 s. 29 (1), (3); 1966 s. 23 (6) and Sch. 1, para. 25.
110 (1)	1953 s. 31 (1); Criminal Justice Act 1967 c. 80 ss. 92, 106 (2)–(4) and Sch. 3, Pts. I, IV.
(2)	1953 s. 31 (2); 1955 s. 3 and Sch. 2, para. 18 (1); 1966 s. 23 (1).
(3)	1953 s. 31 (3).
111	1953 s. 31 (4); 1955 s. 3 and Sch. 2, para. 18 (1).
112 (1), (2)	1953 s. 31 (5); Army Act 1955 c. 18 s. 220 (1); Air Force Act 1955 c. 19 s. 218 (1); 1955 s. 3 and Sch. 2, para. 18 (1), (6).
(3)	1953 ss. 31 (5), 48 (2); 1955 s. 3 and Sch. 2, para. 18 (6), (10); 1966 s. 23 (6) and Sch. 1, para. 26.
113	1953 s. 31 (6).
114	1953 s. 32; 1955 s. 3 and Sch. 2, para. 18 (1), (7).
115 (1)–(2)	1953 s. 33 (1)–(2).
116 (1)	1953 s. 34 (1), (3); 1955 s. 3 and Sch. 2, para. 18 (1), (8).
(2)	1953 s. 34 (2), (3); 1955 s. 3 and Sch. 2, para. 18 (1), (8).
(3)	1953 s. 34 (4); Armed Forces Act 1971 c. 33 s. 76.
117 (1)	1871 s. 6.
(2)	1966 ss. 14 (5), 21 (1).
(3)	1966 s. 23 (4).
118 (1)	1953 s. 39 (1).
(2)	1953 s. 39 (2); 1966 s. 23 (1).
(3), (4)	1953 s. 39 (3), (4).
119	1953 s. 37 (1), (2); 1955 s. 3 and Sch. 2, para. 18 (1), (9).
120	1953 s. 41 (1).
121 (1)	1953 s. 2 (1); 1966 ss. 17 (1), 23 (6) and Sch. 1, para. 19.
(2)	1953 s. 2 (5).
122 (1)	1953 s. 3.
(2)	1953 s. 2 (6).
(3)	1966 s. 17 (2).
(4)	1953 s. 2 (4); 1966 ss. 17 (4), 23 (6) and Sch. 1, para. 20.
(5)	1966 s. 17 (6).
123 (1)	1953 s. 5 (1)–(3).
(2)	1953 s. 4.
124 (1)	1953 s. 6 (1).
(2)	1953 s. 6 (2); S.I. 1964/488; 1966 s. 23 (1).
(3)	1953 s. 6 (3).
125 (1)	1953 s. 7 (1).
(2)	1953 s. 7 (3).

Section of Act	Derivation
(3)	1953 s. 7 (4).
(4)	1953 s. 7 (4).
(5)	1953 s. 7 (5).
(6)	1953 s. 7 (5).
126 (1)	1953 s. 8 (1).
(2)	1953 s. 8 (3).
127 (1)–(4)	1953 s. 9 (1)–(4).
128 (1)–(3)	1953 s. 10 (1)–(3).
(4)	1953 ss. 10 (4), 42 (1).
129 (1)	1966 s. 17 (5); S.I. 1968/1656.
(2)	1966 s. 17 (6).
130 (1)	Local Government Act 1972 c. 70 s. 218 (1).
(2)	Administration of Justice Act 1964 c. 42 s. 18 (1); 1966 s. 20 (2); 1972 c. 70 ss. 216 (2), 218 (8), 270 (1).
(3)	1964 c. 42 s. 18 (2).
131 (1)–(3)	Local Government (Scotland) Act 1973 c. 65 s. 205 (1)–(3).
(4)	1973 c. 65 s. 205 (9), (10).
(5)	1973 c. 65 s. 205 (11).
132	Northern Ireland Constitution Act 1973 c. 36 s. 36 (5).
133 (1)	1882 s. 30 (1).
(2)	1966 s. 20 (1); Local Government (Scotland) Act 1973 c. 65 s. 214 and Sch. 27, Pt. II, para. 163.
(3)	1882 s. 30 (3).
(4)	1882 s. 30 (5).
(5)	1882 s. 34 (2); Local Government (Scotland) Act 1973 c. 65 s. 214 and Sch. 27, Pt. II, para. 12.
134	1882 s. 31; Local Government Act 1972 c. 70 s. 218 (3); Local Government (Scotland) Act 1973 c. 65 s. 205 (6).
135 (1)	1882 s. 32; Local Government Act 1972 c. 70 s. 218 (2); Local Government (Scotland) Act 1973 c. 62 s. 205 (5).
(2)	1882 s. 32.
136	1882 s. 30 (4); Local Government Act 1972 c. 70 s. 218 (2); Local Government (Scotland) Act 1973 c. 65 s. 205 (5).
137 (1)	1882 s. 36.
(2)	1802 c. 90 s. 18; 1802 c. 91 s. 13.
138 (1)	City of London Militia Act 1662 c. 3 s. 1; Administration of Justice Act 1964 c. 42 s. 18 (1).
(2)–(4)	1882 s. 50.
(5)	1953 s. 40.
139 (1), (2)	1969 s. 1 (4).
140 (1), (2)	1969 s. 1 (5).
(3)	1969 s. 4 (1), (3).
141	1969 s. 1 (2).
142	1969 s. 1 (3).
143 (1), (2)	1969 s. 3 (1).
144	1969 s. 3 (2); Criminal Law Act 1977 c. 45 s. 32 (1); Criminal Procedure (Scotland) Act 1975 c. 21 s. 193A.

Section of Act	Derivation
145 (1)	1962 s. 5 (2); 1964 s. 2 (6).
(2)	1969 s. 2 (7).
(3)	1966 ss. 9 (5), 13 (1).
146 (1)	1962 s. 5 (3); 1964 s. 2 (6).
(2)	1969 s. 2 (7).
(3)	1966 ss. 9 (5), 13 (1).
147 (1)	1966 s. 18 (1).
(2), (3)	1966 s. 18 (2).
(4), (5)	1966 s. 18 (3).
(6)	1966 s. 18 (4).
(7)	1966 s. 18 (5).
(8)	1966 s. 18 (6).
(9)	1966 s. 18 (7).
(10)	1966 s. 18 (8).
148 (1)	1966 s. 19 (1).
(2), (3)	1966 s. 19 (2).
(4)	1966 s. 19 (3).
(5)	1966 s. 19 (4).
(6)	1966 s. 19 (5).
(7)	1966 s. 19 (6).
(8)	1966 ss. 19 (7), 22 (2).
149 (1)	1966 s. 18 (1), (9).
(2), (3)	1966 s. 18 (2), (9).
(4)	1966 s. 18 (3), (9).
(5)	1966 s. 18 (4).
(6)	1966 s. 18 (5), (9).
(7)	1966 s. 18 (6).
(8)	1966 s. 18 (7).
(9)	1966 s. 18 (8), (9).
150 (1)	1966 s. 22 (1), (3).
(2)	1966 s. 22 (2).
151	1951 ss. 1 (4), 4 (3).
152 (1)	1953 s. 38.
(2)	1966 s. 23 (5).
153	1950 c. 32 s. 27 (4); 1950 c. 33 s. 26 (4); 1953 s. 42 (5).
154 (1)	1953 s. 42 (3).
(2)	1953 s. 42 (2).
155	1950 c. 32 s. 27 (1); 1950 c. 33 s. 26 (1); 1951 s. 4 (5); 1953 s. 42 (4); 1969 s. 4 (2).
156 (1)	Definitions: "home defence service", 1950 c. 32 s. 6 (6); 1950 c. 33 s. 6 (6); 1953 s. 43 (1); "man", 1950 c. 32 s. 28 (1); 1950 c. 33 s. 27 (1); 1953 s. 43 (1); 1966 s. 21 (1); Armed Forces Act 1971 c. 33 s. 75 and Sch. 3, para. 6; "permanent service", *passim*; "prescribed", 1950 c. 32 s. 28 (1); 1950 c. 33 s. 27 (1); 1953 s. 43 (1); 1966 s. 21 (1); 1969 s. 4 (1); "regular air force", 1966 s. 21 (1); "regular army", 1966 s. 21 (1); "Territorial Army", 1966 s. 1 (1).
(2)	1950 c. 32 s. 28 (1); 1950 c. 33 s. 27 (1); 1953 s. 43 (1).
(3)	1949 s. 17 (4); 1950 c. 32 s. 28 (2); 1950 c. 33 s. 27 (3); 1953 s. 43 (3); 1966 s. 21 (2); 1973 s. 1 (1).

Section of Act	Derivation
(4) (5)	1950 c. 32 s. 6 (6); 1950 c. 33 s. 27 (2); 1953 s. 43 (2); 1966 s. 5 (3). 1953 ss. 31 (8), 33 (3), 48 (1).
157	[Transitional provisions and savings, consequential amendments, and repeals.]
158 (1) (2) (3) (4)	[Citation.] [Northern Ireland.] 1966 c. 25 (3); [Law Commission's recommendation.] [Commencement.]
Sch. 1 para. 1 (1) (2) 2 (1), (2) 3 (1), (2) 4 5 6 7 8 9 10	 1962 s 3 (3). 1962 s. 3 (4). 1962 s. 4 (1). 1962 s. 3 (1), (2). 1962 s. 6 and Sch. para. 1; 1966 s. 23 (6) and Sch. 1, para. 39. 1962 s. 6 and Sch., para. 2. 1962 s. 6 and Sch., para. 3. 1962 s. 3 (4). 1962 s. 3 (5). 1962 s. 4 (4). 1962 s. 4 (2A); SL (Rep.) Act 1977, Sch. 2.
Sch. 2 para. 1 2 3	 1948 c. 8 Sch., para. 1. 1948 c. 8 Sch., para. 2; Mental Health (Scotland) Act 1960 c. 61 s. 113 ·(1) and Sch. 4; National Health Service Reorganisation Act 1973 c. 32 s. 57 and Sch. 4, para. 49; (E) National Health Service Act 1977 c. 49. s. 129 and Sch. 14, para. 13 (1); (S) National Health Service (Scotland) Act 1978 c. 29 s. 109 and Sch. 15, para. 10 (c). 1948 c. 8 Sch., para. 3.
Sch. 3 para. 1 (1)–(4) 2 (1)–(6) 3 (1)–(3) 4 (1), (2) (3) 5 6	 1950 c. 32 s. 3 (2); 1950 c. 33 s. 3 (2); 1953 s. 12 (2) and Sch. 2; Army Act 1955 c. 18 s. 2 (1)–(4); Air Force Act 1955 c. 19 s. 2 (1)–(4); 1955 s. 3 and Sch. 2, paras. 13 (2), 14 (2). 1950 c. 32 s. 3 (2); 1950 c. 33 s. 3 (2); 1953 s. 12 (2) and Sch. 2; Army Act 1955 c. 18 s. 2 (2) and Sch. 1; Air Force Act 1955 c. 19 s. 2 (2) and Sch. 1; 1955 s. 3 and Sch. 2, paras. 13 (2), 14 (2). 1950 c. 32 s. 3 (2); 1950 c. 33 s. 3 (2); 1953 s. 12 (2) and Sch. 2; Army Act 1955 c. 18 s. 18 (1)–(3); Air Force Act 1955 c. 19 s. 18 (1)–(3); 1955 s. 3 and Sch. 2, paras. 13 (2), 14 (2). 1950 c. 32 s. 3 (2); 1950 c. 33 s. 3 (2); 1953 s. 12 (2) and Sch. 2; Army Act 1955 c. 18 s. 19 (1) (2); Air Force Act 1955 c. 19 s. 19 (1), (2); 1955 s. 3 and Sch. 2, paras. 13 (2), 14 (2). 1950 c. 32 s. 3 (3); 1950 c. 33 s. 3 (3); 1953 s. 12 (2) and Sch. 2; Army Act 1955 c. 18 s. 61; Air Force Act 1955 c. 19 s. 61; 1955 s. 3 and Sch. 2, paras. 13 (2), 14 (2). 1950 c. 32 s. 3 (2); 1950 c. 33 s. 3 (2); 1953 s. 12 (2) and Sch. 2; Army Act 1955 c. 18 s. 198 (1)–(3); Air Force Act 1955 c. 19 s. 198 (1)–(3); 1955 s. 3 and Sch. 2, paras. 13 (2), 14 (2). 1950 c. 32 s. 3 (2); 1950 c. 33 s. 3 (2); 1953 s. 12 (2) and Sch. 2; Army Act 1955 c. 18 ss. 2 (5), 23 (1); Air force Act 1955 c. 19 ss. 2 (5), 23 (1); 1955 s. 3 and Sch. 2, paras. 13 (2), 14 (2).
Sch. 4	1950 c. 32 s. 13 (5) and Sch. 2; 1950 c. 33 s. 13 (5) and Sch. 2.
Sch. 5 para. 1 2 3	 1950 c. 32 s. 14 (5); 1950 c. 33 s. 14 (5); 1953 s. 27 (3); Army Act 1955 c. 18 s. 186; Air Force Act 1955 c. 19 s. 186. 1950 c. 32 s. 14 (5); 1950 c. 33 s. 14 (5); 1953 s. 27 (3); Army Act 1955 c. 18 s. 187; Air Force Act 1955 c. 19 s. 187. 1950 c. 32 s. 14 (5); 1950 c. 33 s. 14 (5); 1953 s. 27 (3); Army Act 1955 c. 18 s. 188; Air Force Act 1955 c. 19 s. 188.

Section of Act	Derivation
4	1950 c. 32 s. 14 (5); 1950 c. 33 s. 14 (5); 1953 s. 27 (3); Army Act 1955 c. 18 s. 189; Air Force Act 1955 c. 19 s. 189.
5	1950 c. 32 s. 14 (5); 1950 c. 33 s. 14 (5); 1953 s. 27 (3); Army Act 1955 c. 18 s. 190; Air Force Act 1955 c. 19 s. 190.
Sch. 6	
para. 1 (1)	1950 c. 32 s. 21 (1); 1950 c. 33 s. 21 (1); 1953 s. 34 (1); Army Act 1955 c. 18 s. 198 (1); Air Force Act 1955 c. 19 s. 198 (1).
(2)	1950 c. 32 s. 21 (1); 1950 c. 33 s. 21 (1); 1953 s. 34 (1); Army Act 1955 c. 18 s. 198 (4); Air Force Act 1955 c. 19 s. 198 (4).
(3), (4)	1950 c. 32 s. 21 (1); 1950 c. 33 s. 21 (1); 1953 s. 34 (1); Army Act 1955 c. 18 s. 198 (5); Air Force Act 1955 c. 19 s. 198 (5).
(5)	1950 c. 32 s. 21 (1); 1950 c. 33 s. 21 (1); 1953 s. 34 (1); Army Act 1955 c. 18 s. 198 (6); Air Force Act 1955 c. 19 s. 198 (6).
(6)	1950 c. 32 s. 21 (1); 1950 c. 33 s. 21 (1); 1953 s. 34 (1); Army Act 1955 c. 18 s. 198 (7); Air Force Act 1955 c. 19 s. 198 (7).
(7)	1950 c. 32 s. 21 (1); 1950 c. 33 s. 21 (1); 1953 s. 34 (1); Army Act 1955 c. 18 s. 198 (8); Air Force Act 1955 c. 19 s. 198 (8).
(8)	1950 c. 32 s. 21 (1); 1950 c. 33 s. 21 (1); 1953 s. 34 (1); Army Act 1955 c. 18 s. 198 (9); Air Force Act 1955 c. 19 s. 198 (9).
2	1950 c. 32 s. 21 (2); 1950 c. 33 s. 21 (2); 1953 s. 34 (2); Army Act 1955 c. 18 s. 199; Air Force Act 1955 c. 19 s. 199.
Sch. 7	
para. 1, 2	1953 s. 3 and Sch. 1; 1966 s. 17 (2); S.I. 1967/1857.
3	Local Government (Scotland) Act 1973 c. 65 s. 214 (2) Sch. 27, Pt. II, para. 114.
4–7	1953 s. 3 and Sch. 1; 1966 s. 17 (2); S.I. 1967/1857.
8	1953 s. 3 and Sch. 1, s. 43 (1); 1966 s. 17 (2); S.I. 1967/1857.
Sch. 8	
para. 1–4	[General.]
5 (1)	1966 s. 23 (6) and Sch. 1, para. 32; 1973 s. 1 (3).
(2)	1966 s. 1 (1).
(3)	1966 s. 23 (6) and Sch. 1, para. 33.
6	1966 s. 23 (2).
7 (1)	1921 s. 4 (1), (2).
(2)	Militia Storehouses Act 1882 c. 12 s. 2.
8	1953 s. 11 (6).
9	1966 s. 23 (3).
10	1955 s. 3 and Sch. 2, paras. 13 (1), 14 (1).
11	1966 s. 23 (1).
12	1957 s. 1 and Sch. 1.
13 (1)	Local Government Act 1972 c. 70 s. 218 (1).
(2)	1972 c. 70 s. 218 (4), (5), (7).
14 (1)	Local Government (Scotland) Act 1973 c. 65 s. 205 (4).
(2)	1973 c. 65 s. 205 (7), (8), (10).
15 (1)	1949 ss. 10 (2), 11 (3), 17 (1); 1966 ss. 7 (1), 23 (6) and Sch. 1, para. 5.
(2)	1949 s. 10 (3).
16 (1)	1950 c. 32 ss. 6 (1), 28 (1); 1955 s. 3 and Sch. 2, para. 13 (1); Army and Air Force Act 1961 c. 52 s. 38 and Sch. 2; 1966 s. 7 (1); Armed Forces Act 1966 c. 45 s. 37 and Sch. 4.
(2)	1950 c. 32 ss. 6 (1), 28 (1); 1955 s. 3 and Sch. 2, para. 13 (1); Army and Air Force Act 1961 c. 52 s. 38 and Sch. 2; 1964 s. 3 (1); 1966 s. 7 (1); Armed Forces Act 1966 c. 45 s. 37 and Sch. 4.
(3)	1950 c. 32 s. 6 (1), (5); 1966 ss. 7 (1), 23 (6) and Sch. 1, para. 8.
(4)	1950 c. 33 s. 6 (1), 27 (1); 1955 s. 3 and Sch. 2, para. 14 (1); Army and Air Force Act 1961 c. 52 s. 38 and Sch. 2; 1966 s. 7 (1); Armed Forces Act 1966 c. 45 s. 37 and Sch. 4.
(5)	1950 c. 33 ss. 6 (1), 27 (1); 1955 s. 3 and Sch. 2, para. 14 (1); Army and Air Force Act 1961 c. 52 s. 38 and Sch. 2; 1964 s. 3 (2); 1966 s. 7 (1); Armed Forces Act 1966 c. 45 s. 37 and Sch. 4.
(6)	1950 c. 33 s. 6 (1), (5); 1966 s. 7 (1).
(7)	1950 c. 32 s. 8 (2); 1950 c. 33 s. 8 (2).

Section of Act	Derivation
(8)	1950 c. 32 s. 6 (1); 1950 c. 33 s. 6 (1); 1966 s. 23 (6) and Sch. 1, paras. 8 and 13.
(9)	1950 c. 32 s. 6 (4); 1950 c. 33 s. 6 (4).
(10)	1950 c. 32 s. 6 (6); 1950 c. 33 s. 6 (6).
17 (1)	1950 c. 32 s. 4 (1).
(2)	1950 c. 32 s. 4 (5).
(3), (4)	1950 c. 33 s. 4 (1).
(5)	1950 c. 33 s. 4 (5).
(6)	1950 c. 33 s. 4 (2), (3).
18 (1)	1953 s. 20 (1), (3); 1966 s. 7 (1).
(2)	1953 s. 20 (2).
(3)	1953 s. 20 (4).
(4)	1953 s. 20 (5).
(5)	1953 s. 22; 1966 s. 23 (6) and Sch. 1, para. 23.
19	1966 s. 16 (3).
20	[General.]
Sch. 9	[Consequential amendments.]
Sch. 10	[Repeals.]

2431   Royal Air Force—terms of service

The Royal Air Force Terms of Service (Amendment) Regulations 1980, S.I. 1980 No. 747 (in force on 1st July 1980), amend the Royal Air Force Terms of Service Regulations 1977, 1977 Halsbury's Abridgment para. 2366. The regulations remove the twelve year limitation as the maximum period for which a recruit may be enlisted on a non-pensionable engagement and alter the amount payable by a person exercising his right to claim discharge within three months of attestation from £20 to seven days' gross pay.

2432   Royal Navy—terms of service

The Royal Navy Terms of Service (Amendment) Regulations 1980, S.I. 1980 No. 61 (in force on 1st April 1980), further amend the Royal Navy Terms of Service Regulations 1967 by extending the maximum period by which a person entered into naval service may extend his period of service from ten years to fifteen years.

2433

The Royal Navy Terms of Service (Amendment No. 2) Regulations 1980, S.I. 1980 No. 748 (in force on 1st July 1980), further amend the Royal Navy Terms of Service Regulations 1967 by altering the amount payable by a person exercising his right to claim a discharge within three months of his engagement from £20 to seven days' gross pay.

2434   Visiting forces—surrender of army deserter—surrender to visiting military authority—validity

A Kenyan Asian who held a British passport but was not a United Kingdom national, enlisted in the Indian Air Force. On marrying he deserted the air force in order to join his wife in England and because of her status as a United Kingdom national he was granted an entry certificate and found permanent employment. He was subsequently arrested and charged with deserting the Indian Air Force pursuant to the Visiting Forces Act 1952, s. 13, and surrendered to military custody. He applied for a writ of habeas corpus and, further, an order to refer to the European Court of Justice the question whether s. 13 of the 1952 Act was affected by EEC Treaty, art 48, which provides for the freedom of movement of workers. *Held*, to consider the issues raised it was necessary to decide whether the handover procedure under the 1952 Act was a criminal or civil process. The purpose of the handover procedure was trial by a foreign court with a view to punishment if guilt was established and the exercise of such powers was not merely to exclude the applicant from the United Kingdom, but was a step that assisted in the implementation of the domestic military law of a foreign state, and military law was analogous to criminal law. The free movement of workers of member states guaranteed by art. 48 was subject to limitations justified on grounds of public policy which included any matters covered by the criminal law of member states: article 48 was not intended to abolish the powers of the criminal courts and was therefore not intended to abolish the power of handover under the 1952 Act. Furthermore serving members of the Armed Forces under discipline could not be regarded as "workers" within the meaning of art. 48. The application would accordingly be dismissed.

Re Narinder Singh Virdee [1980] 1 CMLR 709 (Queen's Bench Division: Ackner LJ and Mars-Jones J). *R v Pentonville Prison Governor, ex parte Budlong* [1980] 1 All ER 701, 1979 Halsbury's Abridgment para. 1278; *Armand v Home Secretary and Minister of Defence of Royal Netherlands Government* [1943] AC 147, HL and Case 175/178: *R v Saunders* [1979] 2 CMLR 216, ECJ, 1979 Halsbury's Abridgment para 1220, considered.

SALE OF GOODS

Halsbury's Laws of England (3rd edn.), Vol. 34, paras. 1–321

2435 Article

Reservation of Title by the Unpaid Seller, Charles Lewis: [1980] LMCLQ 309.

2436 C.i.f. contract—appropriation—notice of appropriation—inter-office trading transactions—validity

See *Bremer Handelsgesellschaft mbH v Toepfer*, para. 475.

2437 —— non-delivery—application for extension of time for claim

See *Timmerman's Graan-en Maalhandel en Maalderij BV v Sachs*, para. 163.

2438 Consumer protection

See CONSUMER PROTECTION AND FAIR TRADING.

2439 Contract—breach—exclusion clause—pre-shipment inspection clause—effect on liability of seller

The sellers agreed to sell a quantity of bagged cement to the buyers. The contract contained a pre-shipment inspection clause which provided that the sellers should appoint one of two agencies to inspect the cement and packing and the loading; a certificate of pre-shipment inspection would absolve the sellers from liability for shortage or bursting of bags. The sellers accordingly appointed one of the agencies, which delegated the inspection to another firm. The agency then issued certificates which falsely stated that they had attended the inspection. On arrival, the cement bags were found to have opened during unloading. The dispute was referred to arbitration. The arbitrator found that the sellers were in breach of contract, but stated his award in the form of a special case, the question being whether the sellers were liable in view of the pre-shipment clause. *Held*, on any view, the certificates were to have some protective effect for the sellers. However, a contractual certificate was a certificate issued after an inspection by one of the two named agencies and not a certificate issued after an inspection carried out by another party which falsely stated that the named agency had attended. Even if a contractual certificate were given, it would not protect in circumstances where the goods were not of merchantable quality as a result of a latent defect in packing not discoverable on inspection. The clause was an exemption clause and had to be construed narrowly; there was no reference to the clause in the part of the contract dealing with packing and loading, and clear words would be necessary to protect against a breach such as existed in the instant case. The award would be remitted to the arbitrator for him to assess damages in the light of the judgment.

KOLLERICH & CIE SA V STATE TRADING CORPN OF INDIA [1980] 2 Lloyd's Rep 32 (Court of Appeal: MEGAW, SHAW and CUMMING-BRUCE LJJ). Decision of Parker J [1979] 2 Lloyd's Rep 442, affirmed.

The procedure for making an award in the form of a special case under the Arbitration Act 1950, s. 21 has ceased to have effect: Arbitration Act 1979, s. 1 (1). There is now a right of appeal to the High Court on any question of law arising out of an award made under an arbitration agreement: 1979 Act, s. 1 (2).

2440 —— force majeure and prohibition clauses—liability of seller

The sellers agreed to sell to the buyers a quantity of soya bean meal under a contract which contained a prohibition clause. The sellers purchased the meal from a third party. The American government imposed an embargo on the export of all soya bean meal except meal that was already on a lighter destined for an exporting vessel or meal which was already being loaded. The third party advised the sellers that they were invoking the prohibition clause in their contract as a result of the embargo. The sellers, in turn, invoked the prohibition clause in the contract with the buyers, but the buyers refused to accept their action without proof to justify it, stating that a total ban on export of soya bean meal had never been declared. The sellers failed to tender any proof and the buyers claimed damages. The sellers appealed against a decision that they were not protected by the prohibition clause. *Held*, as there was only a partial prohibition in that some goods could have been supplied, and since it was intended that the sellers should perform the contract by buying goods from a third party, there was no excuse for non-performance as the sellers had failed to show that performance had been prevented by the prohibition of export. The appeal would, accordingly, be dismissed.

BUNGE SA v DEUTSCHE CONTI HANDELSGESELLSCHAFT mbH [1979] 2 Lloyd's Rep 435 (Court of Appeal: LORD DENNING MR, ROSKILL and CUMMING-BRUCE LJJ).

2441   Under a contract for the sale of soya bean meal 1,500 tonnes were due for shipment in June 1973. A prohibition clause provided that the contract would be cancelled in the event of prohibition of export by the government of the country of origin. The sellers chartered a vessel to load the meal but restrictions were subsequently placed by the US government on the export of soya bean meal. The sellers failed to notify the buyers and only delivered 40 per cent of the full quantity. The buyers accepted, maintaining their contractual rights, and successfully claimed in respect of the non-delivery of the balance. On appeal by the sellers, *held*, in order to avail themselves of the prohibition clause, the burden of proof was on the sellers to show that there was a prohibition of export which had prevented them from fulfilling the contract. The prohibition was not absolute since it was provided that if goods were already destined for an exporting vessel or if loading had commenced, at the date of the prohibition, those goods could be exported under the previous licence provisions. The sellers had not discharged the burden of proof since they had not shown that there were no goods destined for an exporting vessel with which they could have fulfilled the contract. Accordingly, the appeal would be dismissed.

TOEPFER v SCHWARZE [1980] 1 Lloyd's Rep 385 (Court of Appeal: LORD DENNING MR, WALLER and CUMMING-BRUCE LJJ). Decision of Parker J [1977] 2 Lloyd's Rep 380, 1977 Halsbury's Abridgment para. 520 affirmed.

2442   It fell to be determined whether the sellers of a quantity of soya beans were in default when they failed to deliver the beans to the buyers because of a government embargo on the export of the beans. The sellers were not the shippers and had intended to fulfil the contract by appropriating to it goods brought in from other sources. The contract between the sellers and buyers incorporated GAFTA 100 provisions providing that government prohibitions and force majeure would have the effect, inter alia, of cancelling the contract. *Held*, the sellers were unable to trace a string back to the relevant shipper and show that shipment by him was impossible and could not therefore rely upon the prohibition clause. Further, they had failed to show that the goods intended to be appropriated by the shipper to the first trader in string were subject to delay because of force majeure. The sellers were accordingly in default.

BREMER HANDELSGESELLSCHAFT mbH v C. MACKPRANG JR [1980] 1 Lloyd's Rep 210 (Queen's Bench Division: ROBERT GOFF J).

2443   —— —— —— misrepresentation

The sellers agreed to ship quantities of US soya bean meal to the buyers. The contracts provided that in the case of any prohibition of export preventing fulfilment any unfulfilled portion of the contract should be cancelled. The American government restricted the export of soya bean meal. The sellers informed the buyers of the embargo and told them that only 40 per cent of the contracted quantities would be approved for export. The buyers accordingly agreed in writing to accept the 40 per cent in total fulfilment of the contracts, but subsequently contended that the sellers were in default in respect of the unfulfilled balance and claimed arbitration. The sellers were held liable in damages for misrepresenting the situation to the buyers. On appeal by the sellers, *held*, a misrepresentation of law did not give rise to a right to rescind, but a misrepresentation of foreign law, as in the instant case, was regarded as a representation of fact. The buyers were accordingly entitled to have the contracts rescinded notwithstanding the agreement under which they purported to accept 40 per cent of the contracted quantities in full satisfaction. Further, the sellers had not discharged the burden on them to prove that they could not have completed the deliveries under the contracts and they could not, therefore, rely on the prohibition clauses. The appeal would be dismissed.

ANDRE & CIE SA v ETS MICHEL BLANC & FILS [1979] 2 Lloyd's Rep 427 (Court of Appeal: LORD DENNING MR, LAWTON and GEOFFREY LANE LJJ). Decision of Ackner J [1977] 2 Lloyd's Rep 166, 1977 Halsbury's Abridgment para. 522 affirmed.

2444   —— requirement of inspection certificate for quality—letter of credit—effect

See *Ets. Soules & Cie v International Trade Development Co Ltd*, para. 477.

2445   —— stipulation as to time—default by seller—effective date of default

The sellers agreed to ship 300 tonnes of soya bean meal at a price of 158 US dollars per tonne. The contract provided that the notice of appropriation should be despatched by the shipper to the first buyer within ten days from the date of the bill of lading. Subsequent sellers were under the same obligation but if certain conditions were satisfied the notice of appropriation would be deemed to be in time. Export controls were imposed and the goods were not delivered. By telex on 11th July, the day after the notice of appropriation was due, the buyers gave the sellers seven days to agree that they were in default and to agree a market price for the goods or make a contractual tender. Failing the seller's agreement to this the buyers claimed arbitration. The market price for a tonne of meal was, on 10th July, 635 US dollars, and on 11th July, 585 US dollars. On 12th July the sellers gave notice of appropriation in respect of 40 tonnes only. The buyers were prepared to accept the 40 tonnes in part fulfilment of the contract on receipt of the shipping documents and proof that the notice of appropriation complied with the specified conditions. Neither the documents nor the proof were tendered. The buyers claimed that the sellers were in default in respect of the entire shipment. The sellers claimed that the buyers' telex of 11th July had extended by seven days the time within which the sellers could give notice of appropriation and therefore any damages awarded in respect of the 260 tonnes should be assessed by reference to the market price as at 18th July which was 475 US dollars. The sellers further claimed that the buyers had wrongfully refused to accept the shipping documents in respect of the 40 tonnes and that the damages for that amount should be assessed according to the market price at the date when they would have tendered the documents, which was 440 US dollars. The arbitrator found in favour of the buyers but stated as a special case the questions whether the sellers were liable to the buyers for non-fulfilment of the contract and if so what date was applicable for the calculation of damages. *Held*, the sellers were under an obligation to give notice of appropriation on or before 10th July. The notice given on 12th July was out of time as the sellers had not proved that specified conditions had been complied with. The buyers' telex did not amount to a repudiation which would free the sellers from what was otherwise a clear default, nor was it a variation of the contract in that the default date had already passed and since the documents had not been delivered within the seven-day period the date of default remained 11th July. The sellers were in default in respect of the entire consignment and damages would be calculated by reference to the market price on 10th July.

BUNGE GmbH v CCV LANDBOUWBELANG GA [1980] 1 Lloyd's Rep 458 (Court of Appeal: ROSKILL and ORMROD LJJ and SIR DAVID CAIRNS). Decision of Donaldson J [1978] 1 Lloyd's Rep 217, 1978 Halsbury's Abridgment para. 2413 affirmed.

2446   Defective goods—seller's duty of care—extent of duty

See *Good-Wear Treaders Ltd v D & B Holdings Ltd*, para. 2060.

2447   F.o.b. contract—buyer's notice of readiness to load—notice not given within time limit—whether buyers in default

An f.o.b. standard form contract of sale (GAFTA 119) provided that the buyers had to give fifteen days' notice of probable readiness of the vessel. The loading rates were such that the sellers were required to complete loading of the vessel within two and a half days not including Sundays. The shipment period expired on 30th June 1975 and notice was received by the sellers on 17th June. The questions for the court to decide were whether the buyers were in breach of contract and if so whether they were in breach of a condition entitling the sellers to rescind the contract. There was no doubt that the buyers were under a contractual obligation to give at least fifteen days' notice and, further, the notice had to be such that, after it expired, there was time, within the shipment period, for the goods to be loaded at the loading rates specified in the contract. The notice should therefore have been given before 13th June. The provision as to time was of the essence in the contract, therefore the sellers' obligation to deliver the goods not later than 30th June was a condition; thus the buyers' obligation to give sufficient notice to ensure that the sellers could fulfil their obligation must also be a condition.

BUNGE CORPN V TRADAX EXPORT SA [1980] 1 Lloyd's Rep 294 (Court of Appeal: MEGAW, BROWNE AND BRIGHTMAN LJJ). Decision of Parker J [1979] 2 Lloyd's Rep Lloyd's Rep 477, reversed. *Hong Kong Fir Shipping Co Ltd v Kawasaki Kisen Kaisha* [1961] 2 Lloyd's Rep 478 considered.

2448   —— carrying charges incurred due to late nomination of vessel—interest

See *Thos. P. Gonzales v F. R. Waring (International) (Pty) Ltd*, para. 778.

2449   Implied condition—fitness—breach—effect of negligence of buyer

See *Lambert v Lewis*, para. 2059.

2450   Non-acceptance—letter of credit—certificate of quality not in conformity with documents required under letter—buyer's right to reject goods

In a case concerning the sale of coffee where the goods were not in conformity with the original contract of sale and where the buyer opened an irrevocable letter of credit but the certificate of quality of the goods did not conform with the documents required under the letter of credit, the question arose whether the buyer was entitled to reject the goods. *Held*, on the authorities, parties to a contract of sale under which payment was to be made by means of a letter of credit could by subsequently agreeing to terms of the letter of credit which differed from those specified in the sale contract, vary their contractual obligation under the sale contract. Such a case could arise where the sale contract did not define the terms of the proposed letter of credit so that the letter as subsequently agreed might fill the contractual gap and so supplement the terms of the sale contract. In the present case the agreement so made was supported by consideration in that since the sale contract was silent to the terms of the letter of credit contemplated by the sale contract, the definition of these terms was a matter of mutual benefit and acceptance of the terms by each party was supported by consideration moving from the other. The letter of credit was binding and therefore the buyer would be entitled to reject the goods.

FICOM SA v SOCIEDAD CADEX LIMITADA [1980] 2 Lloyd's Rep 118 (Queen's Bench Division: ROBERT GOFF J).

2451   Price marking

See CONSUMER PROTECTION AND FAIR TRADING.

2452   Sale of stolen property—determination of title to goods—conflict of laws

See *Winkworth v Christie Manson & Woods Ltd*, para. 441.

SALE OF LAND

Halsbury's Laws of England (3rd edn.), Vol. 34, paras. 322–668

2453   Articles

Conveyancing Problems I, D. M. Bows and E. O. Bourne (exchange of contracts): 124 Sol Jo 3.

Damages for Delayed Completion, H. W. Wilkinson: 130 NLJ 108.

Effect of Delay in Completion, F. Graham Glover: 130 NLJ 1024.

Formation of Contracts in Conveyancing, Andrew Waite: 130 NLJ 774.

Pecuniary Compensation for Failure to Complete a Contract for the Sale of Land, A. J. Oakley: [1980] CLJ 58.

Relief Against Non-Disclosure of Defective Title, F. Graham Glover (discussion on *Faruqi v English Real Estates Ltd* [1979] 1 WLR 963, 1979 Halsbury's Abridgment para. 2361): 129 NLJ 1251.

Telephonic Exchange of Contracts, H. W. Wilkinson: 130 NLJ 295.

Title: Scope of Court's Inquiry, F. Graham Glover: 130 NLJ 26.

Unreasonable Delay—Something of a long-stop on the failure of a Notice to Complete?, Angela Sydenham: [1980] Conv. 19

2454   Completion—date of completion—contractual obligation—liability of vendor

The vendor agreed to complete the sale of his house to the defendant on 12th July 1977, and on the same day the defendant was to complete the sale of his house to the plaintiff. The vendor was unable to complete on the due date, as he was unable to raise sufficient money. The plaintiff had already vacated his home and was forced to rent accommodation until he obtained vacant possession of the defendant's house. In accordance with the Law Society's Conditions of Sale 1973, condition 19, the defendant gave the vendor notice to complete within twenty-eight days and completion took place on 11th August. The defendant's contract with the plaintiff was completed on that day and the plaintiff was let into possession. The plaintiff sued and was awarded damages against the defendant for the expenses incurred due to the delay in completion. The defendant served the vendor with a third party notice claiming indemnity. The questions for the court were (i) whether there had been a breach of contract on 12th July, or within a reasonable time thereafter, which could be remedied in damages; (ii) whether the service of a notice pursuant to condition 19 varied the original date for completion so that if completion took place before the new date, there was no breach of contract, it being accepted by the parties that if the vendor was in breach of contract he was liable to indemnify the plaintiff; (iii) whether the reason why the vendors delayed completion absolved them from liability. *Held*, Viscount Dilhorne dissenting, (i) the vendor committed a breach of contract by failing to complete on 12th July. Although a claim for specific performance of the contract would have been refused on the ground that the stipulation as to time was not of the essence of the contract, that was no ground for relieving the vendor or defendant from liability for failure to complete; (ii) a completion notice could only be served after the specified completion date had passed, at which time the innocent party had an accrued right to damages. The court would reject the argument that in serving a completion notice, the defendant had waived his accrued right; (iii) the vendor's inability to make the necessary financial arrangements and his deliberate decision not to complete afforded no defence. The vendor was thus liable to indemnify the defendant for damages paid to the plaintiff.

RAINERI V MILES (WIEJSKI, third party) [1980] 2 All ER 145 (House of Lords:
VISCOUNT DILHORNE, LORD EDMUND-DAVIES, LORD FRASER OF TULLYBELTON, LORD
RUSSELL OF KILLOWEN and LORD KEITH OF KINKEL). Decision of Court of Appeal
[1980] 3 All ER 763, 1979 Halsbury's Abridgment para. 2350 affirmed. Dictum of
Lord Parker of Waddington in *Stickney v Keeble* [1915] AC 386, 415, HL, *Tilley v
Thomas* (1867) LR 3 Ch App 61 and *Phillips v Lamdin* [1949] 2 KB 33 applied.

2455 —— notice to complete—validity—whether vendor ready and able
to complete

A contract for the sale of property, part of which was subject to a lease, provided for
completion on 2nd January 1979. When the purchasers failed to complete, the
vendors served notice on them in accordance with the Law Society's Conditions of
Sale 1973, requiring completion by 13th February 1979. The purchasers again
failed to complete. Meanwhile the vendors permitted a change in the lessee and user
of part of the property to be sold, in breach of covenant. On 15th February 1979
the purchasers requested a further extension of the completion date; the vendors
rescinded the contract on 19th February, but later agreed to consider an extension if
the purchase price was increased. The purchasers then claimed specific performance
of the contract; the vendors contended that the statement of claim showed no cause
of action and should be struck out. *Held*, in determining whether the claim should
be struck out, the court had to decide whether the notice to complete was valid and
if so, whether the subsequent negotiations prevented the vendors from treating the
contract as repudiated. (i) Under the contract, the notice was valid if the vendors
were ready and able to complete when it was served. The fact that they might have
failed in their duty to look after the property before completion by allowing a
breach of covenant, as claimed by the purchasers, did not affect their ability to
complete. Therefore, as the notice was valid, time was of the essence and the
purchasers were in fundamental breach of contract on 13th February 1979. (ii) The
vendors could only waive their contractual rights regarding such breach if they
showed unequivocally that they were not relying on those rights. However, their
action during negotiations after 13th February showed that they were relying on
their contractual right to rescind the existing contract whilst seeking a new contract
for an increased purchase price. Accordingly no cause of action had been shown and
the relevant parts of the purchasers' statement of claim would be struck out.

PROSPER HOMES LTD V HAMBROS BANK EXECUTOR AND TRUSTEE CO LTD (1979)
39 P & CR 395 (Chancery Division: BROWNE-WILKINSON J).

2456 Conditions of sale—Law Society's Contract and Conditions of
Sale

A new edition of the Law Society's Contract and Conditions of Sale was published
on 1st September 1980. These may be referred to as the "1980 Edition" to
differentiate them from earlier editions and revisions. Substantial changes have
been made and it is advisable for practitioners to refer specifically to the "1973
Revision" or the "1980 Edition" (rather than the "current" edition or revision) to
avoid ambiguity. The main changes are outlined in explanatory notes published in
the *Law Society's Gazette*, 3rd September 1980, pp. 837, 838.

2457 Contract—exchange of contracts—exchange by telephone—Law
Society guidelines

Following the Court of Appeal decision in *Domb v Isoz* [1980] 1 All ER 942, 1979
Halsbury's Abridgment para. 2355, the Law Society has suggested the formulae to
be used by solicitors when effecting an exchange of contracts by telephone or telex:
LS Gaz, 13th February 1980, p. 144.

Formula A (for use where one solicitor holds both signed parts of the contract)
reads as follows:
A completion date of .... 19... is agreed. The solicitor holding both parts of
the contract confirms that he holds the part signed by his client, which is identical to

the part he is also holding signed by the other solicitor's client and will forthwith insert the agreed completion date in each part.

Solicitors mutually agree that exchange shall take place from that moment and the solicitor holding both parts confirms that, as of that moment, he holds thenceforth the part signed by his client to the order of the other. He undertakes that day by first class post or hand delivery to send his signed part of the contract to the other solicitor, together, where he is the purchaser's solicitor, with a banker's draft or a solicitor's client account cheque for the deposit amounting to £......

Formula B (for use, in exceptional circumstance, where each solicitor holds his own client's signed part of the contract) reads as follows:

A completion date of ...... 19... is agreed. Each solicitor confirms to the other that he holds a part contract in the agreed form signed by his client and will forthwith insert the agreed completion date.

Each solicitor undertakes to the other thenceforth to hold the signed part of the contract to the other's order, so that contracts are exchanged at that moment. Each solicitor further undertakes that day by first class post or hand delivery to send his signed part of the contract to the other, together, in the case of the purchaser's solicitor, with a banker's draft or a solicitor's client account cheque for the deposit amounting to £.........

The Law Society suggests the following as an adequate record of the transaction:
Completion date of ...... 19... agreed.
Law Society's Exchange Formula A or B adopted [variations if any].
Banker's draft or a solicitors client account cheque for £......... to be paid.
Date and time of the conversation ....

2458   —— sale subject to survey—whether binding contract

In an action for specific performance of a contract for the sale of land, it was held that the agreement was binding notwithstanding the inclusion of the words "subject to survey". Both parties intended that the document should form a binding contract. The words "subject to survey" represented a suspensory condition and the document was a binding contract.

EE v KAKAR (1979) 40 P & CR 223 (Chancery Division: WALTON J).

2459   —— scope of "subject to contract" formula

The plaintiffs, as executors of the deceased's estate, negotiated the sale of a piece of land to the defendants on behalf of the legatee. They informed the defendants that the land would be offered to them and asked for a reply whether the offer which was "subject to contract" was acceptable. Negotiations were subsequently resumed when the defendants had raised the necessary money and the plaintiffs informed them that the legatee was prepared to proceed with the sale subject to certain conditions. Following an oral acceptance of the conditions a contract to sell was found. On appeal by the plaintiffs, *held*, the words "subject to contract" were effective throughout the negotiations. The parties could only dispense with the qualification if they both expressly agreed that it should be deleted or if such an agreement was to be necessarily implied. Accordingly the judge had been in error in finding that a contract had been concluded.

SHERBROOKE v DIPPLE (1980) 124 Sol Jo 345 (Court of Appeal: LORD DENNING MR, TEMPLEMAN and WATKINS LJJ). *Tevenan v Norman Brett (Builders) Ltd* (1972) 223 Estates Gazette 1945 applied.

2460   —— repudiation—whether rescission amounting to implied repudiation

See *Woodar Investment Development Ltd v Wimpey Construction UK Ltd*, para. 495.

2461   Conveyance—form of conveyance defective—plan

The Court of Appeal has strongly criticised "slapdash" conveyancing, in particular the use of inadequate and small scale survey plans or other drawings where the property transferred forms part of a larger building and/or land area.

SCARFE V ADAMS [1981] 1 All ER 843 (Court of Appeal: CUMMING-BRUCE, GRIFFITHS and O'CONNOR LJJ).

2462   Defect of quality—new building—builder's warranty—whether merged in conveyance

Canada

A contract for the sale of a new house by the builder contained a clause to the effect that he had disclosed all infractions and local authority orders requiring work to be done. After the property was conveyed to the purchaser damage occurred which was the consequence of a breach of the building byelaws. The purchaser claimed damages. *Held*, the clause amounted to an express warranty that the house was built in accordance with the byelaws unless the contrary was disclosed. Whether the warranty was merged in the conveyance depended on the parties' intention. In the present case the parties had not so intended. Consequently the purchaser's claim would succeed.

FRASER-REID V DROUMTSEKAS (1979) 103 DLR (3d) 385 (Supreme Court of Canada).

2463   Defect of title—good title—duty of solicitor to secure—liability of solicitor

See *Haberstich v McCormick & Nicholson*, para. 2812.

SENTENCING

Halsbury's Laws of England (4th edn.), Vol. 11, paras. 481–573

2464   Article

Sentencing Practice in Magistrates' Courts, Paul Softley: [1980] Crim LR 161.

2465   Appeal—examples

Examples of sentencing appeals are set out under the following headings:

OFFENCES AGAINST GOVERNMENT AND PUBLIC ORDER (Affray; Assaulting a police officer; Attempting to pervert the course of justice; Corruption; Making counterfeit coins).

OFFENCES AGAINST THE PERSON (Attempted murder; Manslaughter (diminished responsibility); Causing death by reckless driving; Causing grievous bodily harm; Attempting to cause grievous bodily harm; Wounding with intent; Inflicting grievous bodily harm; Assault occasioning actual bodily harm; Common assault).

SEXUAL OFFENCES AND OFFENCES AGAINST DECENCY AND MORALITY (Rape; Unlawful sexual intercourse; Incest; Indecent assault; Indecent assault on girl under 13; Buggery; Attempted buggery; Keeping a disorderly house; Living on earnings of prostitution; Possessing obscene articles for gain).

OFFENCES AGAINST PROPERTY (Robbery; Attempted robbery; Burglary; Theft; Conspiracy to steal; Abstracting electricity; Taking a motor vehicle without authority; Handling stolen goods; Obtaining property by deception; False accounting; Fraudulent trading; Carrying on a consumer credit business without a licence; Arson; Damaging property).

OFFENCES RELATING TO DRUGS (Possession of controlled drug; Being knowingly concerned in the fraudulent evasion of prohibition on importation of controlled drug; Conspiracy to supply drug).

DRIVING OFFENCES (Reckless driving).

OFFENCES AGAINST GOVERNMENT AND PUBLIC ORDER

2466   *Affray*
Sentence: 18 months' imprisonment. Divorced man, aged 26, with 2 children. Various employments, but unemployed at time of offence. Three previous findings of guilt and two previous convictions. Offences included larceny, burglary, assault on the police, assault occasioning actual bodily harm and affray. Placed on probation and served several terms of imprisonment varying from 3 to 12 months. One evening he went to a discotheque with a group of friends to seek revenge for an incident which had previously occurred there. There, they caused substantial chaos and damage, to the amount of £290. They also damaged some cars. The appellant was later seen by the police and admitted to being involved in the incident. Sentenced to 3 years' imprisonment. On appeal against severity of sentence since it was shown that the appellant had not been involved in the earlier incident and the part he had played in the latter incident was relatively minor, *held*, notwithstanding the appellant's previous record, the sentence was excessive as he had not been involved in planning the affray. Accordingly, it would be reduced to 18 months. *R v Hamilton*, 10th October 1980 (Court of Appeal: Waller LJ, Tudor Evans and McNeill JJ).

2467   *Affray; assault occasioning actual bodily harm*
Sentence: borstal training. Man, aged 19, living at home and in regular employment. One minor previous conviction. The appellant, D, and two others were out drinking when they came into conflict with another gang of young men who threatened them and assaulted one of their group. The appellant, D and a third man R, aged 30, later went back to take revenge on the gang. However, they mistook another four men for them and attacked them without warning. The latter were punched and kicked and one, who was stabbed by D, later required hospital treatment. The appellant produced a metal comb with a pointed handle and chased the men, threatening them with it. He and D were sentenced to borstal training and R to 18 months' imprisonment. On appeal, *held*, it was a gang fight in which the motive was revenge. Persons who behaved in such a manner, whether they had been wronged or not, had to expect an immediate custodial sentence. The appellant's plea of disparity of sentence would fail because it was clear that the trial judge had been deliberating on a 3 year prison sentence for D. The sentences imposed were all entirely appropriate. *R v Jones*, 21st July 1980 (Court of Appeal: Lord Lane CJ, Lawton and Shaw LJJ).

2468   *Assaulting a police officer*
Sentence: borstal training. Youth, aged 19. One previous conviction involving a motor vehicle. No history of violence or dishonesty. The appellant was one of a group of white youths who were arguing with a group of black youths outside a club. A police officer arrived on the scene and radioed for assistance while at the same time attempting to maintain the peace. The appellant rushed at the officer and struck him on the face. Up to that moment the officer had not been attacked by a member of either group. The appellant was arrested despite his violent struggles. Sentenced to borstal training and subsequent reports showed that he was responding well to treatment there. On appeal, *held*, anyone who became involved in brawls between different coloured factions had to expect a custodial sentence, and, if a police officer was assaulted in the course of the brawl it was right that a custodial sentence should be imposed even though the appellant's record was not serious. Accordingly, the borstal sentence would stand. *R v Parry*, 14th February 1980 (Court of Appeal: Lord Widgery CJ, Roskill LJ and Caulfield J).

2469   *Attempting to pervert the course of justice*
Sentence: 18 months' imprisonment consecutive to sentence currently being served (4 months' imprisonment for dishonesty and failure to pay fines). Man, aged 31. Twice married, with 4 children. Separated from second wife and living with another woman. Twenty-three previous findings of guilt and convictions mainly

for dishonesty and driving offences for which he was fined, put on probation and imprisoned. The appellant approached a man who was to be a prosecution witness at his forthcoming trial for attempted theft in 1978. He threatened to have the man killed if he gave evidence against him. When the appellant was subsequently interviewed, he denied that he had threatened the man who had not been intimidated. Sentenced as above. On appeal against severity of sentence, *held*, the gravity of the offence lay in the fact that the appellant had attempted to persuade a prosecution witness not to give evidence. The court had always recognised that an attempt to pervert the course of justice deserved to be punished. If the present offence had been planned rather than spontaneous the sentence would and should have been longer. The fact that the witness was a strong character who had not been intimidated did not carry much weight. The appeal would be dismissed. *R v Hill*, 31st March 1980 (Court of Appeal: Cumming Bruce LJ, Kilner Brown and Hollings JJ).

2470   *Corruption (16); theft (3) (2 tic)*
Sentence: 2 years' imprisonment concurrent 1 years' imprisonment concurrent (2 years in all). Married man, aged 27, with one child. One previous drink-driving offence. The corruption offences took place over a three year period when the appellant was employed at a prison initially as a joiner and then as an officer. He had been warned of the dangers of such work and against trafficking with prisoners but over that period supplied them with wines and spirits. The three counts of theft related to prison property valued at £97·50 and the two offences taken into consideration to prison property worth £125. Sentenced to 3 years' imprisonment. On appeal against severity of sentence, *held*, while the sentence imposed was not wrong in principle, as the appellant had confessed and pleaded guilty and as a 3 year sentence was above the maximum of 2 years for such offences, the sentence would be varied as set out above. *R v Sanderson*, 8th May 1980 (Court of Appeal: Lawton LJ, Michael Davies and Balcombe JJ).

2471   *Making counterfeit coins (2); possessing equipment for counterfeiting coins*
Sentence: 6 months' imprisonment suspended 2 years (8½ months' imprisonment served). Married man, aged 32 with 2 children. Various employments. Previous convictions but none for coinage offences. The appellant's house was searched by police officers in respect of another matter. There they found melting moulds and various other items of equipment used for counterfeiting coins as well as counterfeit sovereigns. The appellant admitted that the coins resembled real sovereigns, but contended that it had never been his intention to use them as counterfeit currency. On arrest, he admitted that he had started making the coins a year previously and after realising that his actions were unlawful destroyed most of them. Sentenced to 18 months' imprisonment concurrent on each count. On appeal on grounds that the sentence was excessive as he had no intention of passing off the coins as real currency, *held*, although such offences were very serious indeed the present offences were not that grave. Accordingly, as the appellant had already served a term of imprisonment, the sentence would be varied as set out above. *R v Thomas*, 12th May 1980 (Court of Appeal: Watkins LJ, Boreham and Hodgson JJ).

OFFENCES AGAINST THE PERSON

2472   *Attempted murder*
Sentence: 5 years' imprisonment. Married man, aged 34, with four children. No previous convictions for violence. Marital relations with his wife were strained. The appellant returned home drunk one day and had a violent quarrel with his wife in front of the children. He struck her on the head with two ornamental swords and when she ran out of the house he pursued her with a knife and repeatedly stabbed her with it. She was taken to hospital with thirteen knife wounds two of which had entered her chest cavity. She later recovered with the aid of emergency surgery and intensive care. Sentenced to 8 years' imprisonment. Since the trial the wife has

expressed a wish to be reconciled with the appellant who was behaving well in prison. On appeal, *held*, it was a very serious offence which could have easily resulted in a charge for murder. However, because of the wife's attitude the court would vary the sentence to 5 years' imprisonment. *R v Kelly*, 17th April 1980 (Court of Appeal: Roskill and Donaldson LJJ and Mustill J).

2473   *Manslaughter (diminished responsibility)*
Sentence: life imprisonment. Youth, aged 18, suffering from physical deformities. One previous conviction. Disturbed childhood, sent away from home by his father in 1977 and eventually put in care. Spent a year in a resettlement centre where he was assessed as immature and impulsive with little regard for the consequences of his actions. Returned home in 1978 and later that year killed a girl, aged 18, on a golf course after engaging in sexual activity with her. Cause of death was asphyxia through manual strangulation and suffocation by sand and vegetable matter. The victim's body was also bruised in various places. When the appellant was arrested on the following day he admitted to having killed her. He was charged with murder but the prosecution accepted a plea of manslaughter on grounds of diminished responsibility. The appellant was then aged 17 and the trial judge ordered him to be detained during Her Majesty's pleasure under the Children and Young Person's Act 1933, s. 53 (1). On appeal, *held*, that on the up to date medical reports before the court it was clear that both in the appellant's and public's best interests the proper sentence was one of life imprisonment. *R v Jones*, 11th February 1980 (Court of Appeal: Eveleigh LJ, Bristow and McNeill JJ).

2474   *Causing death by reckless driving*
Sentence: £1,000 fine (at £40 a week or 6 months' imprisonment in default), disqualification for 3 years. Man, aged 22, with no previous convictions and a good work record. He was driving along the A2 in Kent, in light traffic and in dry weather. He overtook a motor cyclist on the crest of a hill, cutting sharply in front of him and causing him to brake. The motor cyclist said the appellant was doing 80 m.p.h. The appellant continued edging into the centre of the road in an attempt to overtake two cars. He then attempted to pull in when he noticed two other cars coming in the opposite direction at the bend of the road. His car hit the kerb, skidded into the path of the oncoming traffic and hit the second car, killing the front seat passenger. Fined as above, and disqualified for 5 years. On appeal against the length of disqualification, *held*, it was a bad case of causing death by reckless driving. However, taking into account the appellant's previous good character and record, the period of disqualification would be reduced to 3 years. *R v Smith*, 5th February 1980 (Court of Appeal: Waller LJ, Milmo and Kenneth Jones JJ).

2475   Sentence: 9 months' imprisonment suspended 2 years. Fined £200 and disqualified for 1 year. Lorry driver, aged 30. No previous convictions. After drinking with friends the appellant was driving them home, when some servicemen provoked them. Later he returned to where they were and accelerated at about 25–30 mph and hit one of them, who was straggling the road with the others, killing him. He pleaded guilty and it was accepted that he had not intended to use his vehicle as a weapon. Sentenced to 2 years' imprisonment suspended 2 years, fined £500 and disqualified for 5 years. On appeal, *held*, the sentence called for an adjustment and would be varied as above. *R v Shooter*, 18th November 1980 (Court of Appeal: Shaw LJ, Milmo and Eastham JJ).

2476   *Causing grievous bodily harm; burglary*
Sentence: 7 years' imprisonment; 3 years' imprisonment concurrent. Single man, aged 20, self-employed window cleaner. Three previous findings of guilt, for burglary and theft for which he was conditionally discharged, sent to an attendance centre and received a supervision order. The appellant assisted a 76 year old widow by cleaning her windows free of charge and subsequently performed other household tasks for her. One morning at 3.30 a.m. he let himself into her house with a key, which he had previously taken, and demanded money from the widow. He then

attacked her, beating her on the head and neck, chest, backbone and other places, and left with £10 and some small trinkets. At the time of trial the victim was still in hospital. The appellant was sentenced as above. On appeal, *held*, such a vicious assault by a young man on an elderly lady who had been asleep at the time merited the sentence imposed which would remain as above. *R v Lord*, 3rd October 1980 (Court of Appeal: Lord Lane CJ, Stocker and Glidewell JJ).

2477 *Causing grievous bodily harm; causing actual bodily harm.*
Sentence: 3 years' imprisonment concurrent. Youth, aged 18, living with parents. Employed as a warehouseman. Two previous convictions for theft and conduct likely to cause a breach of the peace, both taking place at football match attendances. After a drinking session one day, while dressed as a punk rocker, the appellant got into an argument with a group of French students. He struck one of them in the eye causing an injury which required hospital treatment. There was also the possibility of a 60 per cent loss of vision in the victim's eye. The appellant claimed that the victim had kicked him but there was no medical evidence to substantiate this. The second offence was committed when the appellant was released on bail. It occurred at a football match disturbance. He punched a schoolboy in the mouth causing an injury which required stitches. Sentenced as above, the judge stating that a deterrent sentence was called for. The appellant appealed on the grounds of his good work record, the fact that the assaults were not premeditated and that borstal training would be a more appropriate sentence. *Held*, the offences were not acts of violence by an impulsive young man on one occasion but serious offences committed at football matches against which the public needed protection. The appeal would be dismissed. *R v McLean*, 21st April 1980 (Court of Appeal: Shaw LJ, Jupp and Mustill JJ).

2478 *Causing grievous bodily harm; unlawful wounding*
Sentence: immediate release (3¾ months' imprisonment served). Married man, aged 34, with one child. Self-employed garage proprietor, with no previous convictions. The victim, aged 49, had had an affair with the appellant's wife and she went to live with him. The appellant went to the victim's house and a fight ensued, the victim sustaining injuries to his face and two broken ribs. The wife returned home with the appellant. Two months later, another quarrel occurred during which the victim received a cut on his cheek bone. The appellant continued to threaten him and 5 months later the victim had a heart attack and died. Convicted of above offences and sentenced to 12 months' imprisonment and 2 years' imprisonment consecutive. At the appellant's trial it was not suggested that he was responsible for the victim's death as the latter had a bad heart and evidence showed that he would have died in any event. On appeal on grounds that he had been a happy family man of excellent character and that he and his wife were now reconciled, *held*, although a custodial sentence was called for, the short time the appellant had spent in prison was severe enough punishment and as a long sentence would jeopardise his business and family life the sentence would be varied to allow for his immediate release. *R v Martin*, 31st January 1980 (Court of Appeal: Cumming Bruce LJ, Mais and Smith JJ).

2479 *Attempting to cause grievous bodily harm; common assault*
Sentence: orders under the Mental Health Act 1959, ss. 60, 65. Man, aged 31. Unemployed on arrest. Six previous convictions for dishonesty, violence, breach of the peace and criminal damage for which he had been bound over, conditionally discharged, fined and put on probation. Most recent offence committed in 1976. The current offences were committed when the appellant was a voluntary patient at a sanatorium. He approached two male nurses in the dining room and attempted to pick a fight with one of them, telling the other that there was going to be a "knifing". Using a table knife, he pinned the nurse to a counter and threatened to kill him. His victim escaped and summoned help from another male nurse who the appellant also threatened to kill. When the nurse tried to calm him down the appellant lunged at him with the knife, striking his breast bone without penetrating

the skin. The appellant was overpowered and later told the police that he had intended to kill both men. Sentenced to 3 years' imprisonment and 12 months' imprisonment concurrent. Psychiatric reports had revealed a history of mental illness since the age of 20 but no local hospitals had considered him suitable for admission. Since conviction, subsequent medical reports had revealed that the appellant was a potentially dangerous schizophrenic in need of indefinite custodial care under secure conditions. On appeal, *held*, in view of the recent report the court would vary the sentence to a Mental Health Act 1959, s. 60 hospital order with a restriction order, without limit of time under s. 65 of the Act. *R v Carter*, 15th January 1980 (Court of Appeal: Cumming-Bruce LJ, Thompson and Smith JJ).

2480   *Wounding with intent*
Sentence: 8 years' imprisonment concurrent. Single man, aged 20, living with girlfriend and their child. Numerous short term jobs. Number of previous convictions, some for violence. The present offence arose when he gate crashed a party and started arguing with a young woman. When the hostess tried to intervene, he stabbed her in the ribs and stomach causing a serious abdominal wound which required hospital treatment. The appellant also lashed out at another girl and gave her flick knife wounds in the face, neck and forearm. On arrest, he denied the offences. Sentenced to concurrent terms of life imprisonment. On appeal, *held*, there was no medical report to indicate a mental or medical condition. While the offences were very grave and the appellant had a very bad record it was a big step to impose an indeterminate sentence on a man of his age. A fixed term of imprisonment was more suitable and the sentence would accordingly be varied to concurrent terms of 8 years' imprisonment. *R v Kelly*, 15th May 1980 (Court of Appeal: Watkins LJ, Boreham and Hodgson JJ).

2481   Sentence: 3 years' imprisonment. Divorced woman, aged 39, engaged to another man for 3 years. No relevant previous convictions. The appellant was asked by the victim if his mother could live with her in her flat. She agreed, but it later became apparent to her that it was a ruse to allow the victim into the flat. When she refused to let him in, he spread false rumours that they had been sleeping together. Her fiancé subsequently heard these rumours and broke off the engagement. That, together with domestic difficulties and the recent loss of a brother affected the appellant severely. She pleaded with the victim to stop spreading the rumours but he merely laughed. Later, in a restaurant, she again accused him of spreading the rumours and received the same response. She then got hold of a kitchen knife and stabbed the victim, almost completely severing his jugular vein. As a result he needed a transfusion of six pints of blood and medical reports showed that he would have died without surgery. Sentenced to 5 years' imprisonment. On appeal, *held*, though the offence was serious and the stabbing might have been fatal, in all the circumstances a more appropriate sentence would be 3 years' imprisonment. *R v Buck*, 13th June 1980 (Court of Appeal: Eveleigh LJ, Thompson and French JJ).

2482   *Inflicting grievous bodily harm*
Sentence: 6 months' imprisonment suspended 2 years, £250 fine and £154 costs. Single man, aged 20, employed as an apprentice fitter earning £39 per week. One previous conviction in 1978 for criminal damage for which he was bound over. The appellant had been drinking at a club and became involved in an incident with a rider of a motorcycle. Stepping out onto the road, he kicked at the motorcycle as it passed causing the rider to lose control and collide with an oncoming car. The rider was taken to hospital with a dislocated knee and fractured femur. The motorcycle (value £695) was extensively damaged and a write off. The car (value £2,200) was also badly damaged and a possible insurance write off. Sentenced to the above term of imprisonment and fined £1,000. The appellant had a good home record and an excellent report from his employers. On appeal against the severity of the fine, *held*, the judge had taken into account the damages the injured man would have probably been awarded by the Criminal Injuries Compensation Board and had tried to recoup public expenses by imposing such a fine. That was

the wrong approach to have taken as a fine imposed should be such as the judge considered proper punishment in all the circumstances of the case and that did not include any possible award from the Board. Accordingly, bearing in mind the appellant's previous good character and his modest wages, the fine of £1,000 was too severe. The offence could be adequately dealt with by a fine of £250. *R v Roberts*, 18th April 1980 (Court of Appeal: Lord Lane CJ, Griffiths and Webster JJ).

2483   Sentence: 75 hours' community service order. Youth, aged 18, of previous good character. Difficult family background. Employed as a tyre fitter and described by employer as honest and trustworthy. The appellant got involved in a disturbance in a public house. He threw a beer glass at a man which missed him and hit another man who was known to the appellant. The victim, who had not been involved in the disturbance, sustained a cut to his upper lip and wounds on his chin which required stitches. Sentenced to borstal training. On appeal, *held*, there was no reason why the appellant should have been sent to borstal. However, the victim's injury could not be overlooked and the probation officer's recommendation of community service was appropriate. As the appellant had been in custody for 7½ weeks, a community service order would be substituted for the sentence of borstal training. *R v McDiarmid*, 22nd April 1980 (Court of Appeal: Dunn LJ, Thompson and Heilbron JJ).

2484   Sentence: 12 months' imprisonment. Divorced man, aged 35, with two children. Seven previous spent convictions. Discharged from navy in 1963 for offence of causing actual bodily harm and sentenced to three months' imprisonment. In 1970, sentenced to six months' imprisonment for assault. Employed as a bouncer at a club. Following a violent incident, the defendant asked a youth involved to leave. The youth dropped a pint glass on the floor and the defendant assaulted him and knocked him to the ground. Sentenced to three years' imprisonment. On appeal as to the correct sentence when no weapon was used, *held*, although the appellant had severely injured the victim it was possible that the trial judge had paid too much attention to his previous convictions which should have been omitted in determining the present sentence. Accordingly the sentence would be varied to 12 months. *R v Fox*, 21st July 1980 (Court of Appeal: Lord Lane CJ, Lawton and Shaw LJJ).

2485   *Assault occasioning actual bodily harm*
Sentence: 4 months' imprisonment. Single woman, aged 19, living with parents. Greengrocer's assistant. One previous conviction when she was aged 16 for assaulting a policewoman. Has a tendency to be violent and aggressive. The appellant assaulted the proprietor of a public house when the latter told her to leave just after midnight one evening. She kicked the victim in the stomach and legs and punched her in the face knocking out a front tooth. Sentenced as above. On appeal against severity of sentence, *held*, it was a determined and vicious assault. Such an attack would have warranted a custodial sentence if it had been a male assailant as the courts were determined to stop this type of violence on people whose jobs exposed them to such risks. The same principles now applied to females who used violence and the sentence imposed would stand. *R v Williams*, 8th May 1980 (Court of Appeal: Lawton LJ, Michael Davies and Balcombe JJ).

2486   Sentence: immediate release (26 days' imprisonment served). Twins, aged 21. Previous good character and respectable family background. The twins went out drinking with the co-accused. As they left a public house a dispute arose with a man who had also been drinking and who started to swear at them. The co-accused threw stones at the man's dog and the twins joined in, one of them hitting the man in the stomach so that he fell to the ground. Then they both started kicking him in the back and legs. They were each sentenced to 4 months' imprisonment and the co-accused to 15 months' imprisonment. The shock of their sentence caused their father to have a heart attack and die and also adversely affected the health of their mother. On appeal, *held*, while their behaviour was disgraceful and merited the sentence imposed on them, the court would, on grounds of compassion, reduce the sentences to allow their release from the day they were granted bail. *R v Robinson; R v Robinson*, 20th August 1980 (Court of Appeal: Waller LJ, Wien and Mais JJ).

2487   Sentence: 9 months' imprisonment. £50 legal aid costs. Married man, aged 33, separated from wife and 2 children. Self employed mechanic. Nine previous convictions for offences of dishonesty and motoring offences for which he was fined, placed on probation and given a suspended sentence. A police officer saw the appellant and co-accused behaving suspiciously in a car park. When questioned, the appellant became abusive and attacked the officer, knocking him over the bonnet of a car. The co-accused then held the officer down while the appellant rained blows on his head and chest. Both men denied the charges. The appellant was sentenced as above and the co-accused was given a suspended sentence of 3 months' imprisonment, fined £100 and ordered to pay £50 legal aid costs. He had a relatively good character record with only one previous offence of drunkenness in 1969. On appeal against disparity of sentence, *held*, taking into consideration the parts both men had played and their records, it was impossible to say that the distinction in their sentences was not justified. The sentence imposed on the appellant was not wrong in principle and would stand. *R v Giannitto*, 16th June 1980 (Court of Appeal: Eveleigh LJ, Thompson and French JJ).

2488   Sentence: 9 months' imprisonment (immediate release as sentence already served). Married man, aged 25, separated from his wife. Two summary convictions for handling stolen goods, and deception for which he was conditionally discharged, and fined for offence of assault occasioning bodily harm. Unemployed at time of offence. The appellant was drinking with a friend in a pub when the latter damaged the premises with an axe. They were arrested, handcuffed together and put in a police van. A policeman accompanied them in the van and both men attacked him, kicking and hitting him. The friend also kicked the sergeant who came to the policeman's aid. Sentenced to 21 months' imprisonment. On appeal *held*, such an attack on a policeman was inexcusable. However, since the appellant had been drinking and his friend had started the trouble, a sentence of 9 months' imprisonment would be more appropriate. Accordingly, he would be released immediately as he had served the appropriate time. *R v Canny*, 20th August 1980 (Court of Appeal: Waller LJ, Wien and Mais JJ).

2489   *Common assault*
Sentence: immediate release (6 weeks' imprisonment served and then released on bail). Man, aged 22, living with girlfriend and their child. Eight previous convictions and four findings of guilt. The appellant and co-accused were at the seafront late one night. They saw two men walking past and the co-accused made a savage attack on the men. The appellant, who took a small part in the attack was sentenced to 6 months' immediate imprisonment. He was released on bail 6 weeks later and he returned to his job as a miner. On appeal, *held*, the offence warranted a custodial sentence. However, as the appellant had been out on bail for four months without trouble, public interest did not require his return to prison. The appeal would be allowed. *R v Worton*, 12th May 1980 (Court of Appeal: Lawton LJ, Michael Davies and Balcombe JJ).

SEXUAL OFFENCES AND OFFENCES AGAINST DECENCY AND MORALITY

2490   *Rape*
Sentence: 9 years' imprisonment. Married man, aged 27, with 3 children. Employed as a labourer and mechanic. Thirteen convictions since 1967 for burglary, theft, attempting to take a conveyance without authority and two sexual offences for which the appellant was imprisoned, fined and sent to borstal. The present offence involved a 13 year old girl who had run away from home. The appellant tried to lure her into his car, saying he was a police officer. He then forcibly dragged her into it and drove her to a disused shelter where he removed her clothes and violently raped her. In sentencing him to 12 years' imprisonment, the

judge said the appellant was a dangerous man who had shown little sign of remorse after violently raping a vulnerable girl in terrifying circumstances. On appeal, *held*, while it was an extremely bad case of rape, 12 years was a little excessive for a first rape sentence and would be varied to 9 years. *R v Cawser*, 28th January 1980 (Court of Appeal: Shaw LJ, Chapman and Drake JJ).

2491   (1) Rape and robbery; (2) Theft and handling stolen goods
Sentence: (1) 7 years' imprisonment concurrent (2) 9 months' imprisonment concurrent. Man aged 24, employed as an AA patrolman. A young woman was driving from London to Norfolk one evening when her car broke down. She summoned the AA's assistance and the appellant arrived. He suggested that she should park it for about ½ hour behind some petrol pumps in a fairly lonely area, in order to allow the engine to cool down. He left and returned 10 minutes later, wearing a hood with slits for the eyes, with a knife which he threatened to stick into her. He then dragged her from the car, pushed her on her knees, forced her to indulge in oral sex with him and then raped her. After that, he demanded her wallet and drove off with it. The theft and handling offence had occurred some time previously when the appellant was working with a recovery vehicle. He found some cassette tapes in a lorry and stole them, he later received a cassette player, which he knew to be stolen, from another person working on the lorry. He was arrested a week after the rape and admitted to having had intercourse with the victim but alleged that she was a consenting party. In sentencing him to concurrent terms of life imprisonment on (1) the judge said it was an appropriate sentence for a highway rape and robbery. Such an indeterminate sentence was required to protect other young women from the danger of cunning and sadistic attacks. There was no evidence that the appellant was mentally deranged. On appeal against the rape sentence, *held*, a life sentence for rape could be justified if the accused suffered from mental instability or a personality defect that could make him a danger to women. In the present case, as there was no evidence of mental disability, a sentence of life imprisonment was inappropriate. However, it was a bad case of rape where the appellant as an AA man, had been in a position of trust and accordingly a sentence of seven years' imprisonment would be substituted. *R v Owen*, 4th February 1980 (Court of Appeal: Waller LJ, Milmo and Kenneth Jones JJ).

2492   *Unlawful sexual intercourse (2); abduction*
Sentence: 15 months' imprisonment concurrent. Married man, aged 30. Mathematics teacher. He formed an association with one of his pupils when she was 14 and a virgin. He had sexual intercourse with her in 1978. In February 1979, after her parents expressed their disapproval of the affair, the appellant agreed to break off the association. He did not do so however and she became pregnant. In August 1979 they eloped to Scotland where they remained for a week. They then returned home and the appellant surrendered himself to the police admitting his guilt. Sentenced to a maximum term of 2 years' imprisonment for unlawful sexual intercourse and a similar concurrent term for abduction. He appealed contending that the maximum sentence was not appropriate for the offence which was not the worst of its type. *Held*, that submission was unsound as the charges related to offences taking place over a period of time coupled with abduction. They were deliberate acts and it was entirely open to the judge to have imposed consecutive sentences. However, although the offences were serious and committed by someone in a position of trust, as they fell short of the worst end of the possible spectrum of offences, the sentences would be varied to concurrent terms of 15 months' imprisonment. *R v Usher*, 18th April 1980 (Court of Appeal: Lord Roskill, Donaldson LJ and Mustill J).

2493   *Incest (4)*
Sentence: immediate release (8½ months' imprisonment served). Married man, aged 45, with four children. Employed as a mainslayer craftsman. One spent conviction for which he had been fined. No previous convictions for indecency. Had separated from his wife on various occasions. At time of offences was living with

the family. While his wife was in hospital, after taking a drug overdose, the appellant had sexual intercourse with his 15 year old daughter and committed the same offence on many occasions over a period of 8 months. Admitted offences and sentenced to 4 years' imprisonment. On appeal against sentence on the grounds that the daughter was promiscuous and had already had sexual intercourse with other men on a number of occasions, *held*, the girl's promiscuity mitigated the offence and the defendant would be released immediately. *R v Moores*, 3rd October 1980 (Court of Appeal: Watkins LJ, Thompson and Bush JJ).

2494 *Indecent assault*
Sentence: immediate release (3 months' imprisonment already served). Man, aged 39, with no previous convictions. Manager of a public house. The appellant became friendly with a girl he thought was aged 16 but whose actual age was 12. He admitted that he had fondled her breasts and other parts of her body but had done nothing more. As a result of the conviction for 2 counts of assault, for which he was sentenced to 12 months' imprisonment, the appellant was dismissed from his job and lost his home. He appealed against severity of sentence in view of his loss of job, the fact that he had voluntarily terminated his association with the girl before police inquiries had begun and the fact that the offences were of a relatively minor character. *Held*, indecent assault by a man of his age on a girl in her early teens was an offence which could not be overlooked. It was not a case for a suspended sentence but for a short term of immediate imprisonment. As the appellant had already served 3 months' imprisonment, the sentence would be varied as set out above. *R v Long*, 15th January 1980 (Court of Appeal: Lord Widgery CJ, Bridge LJ and Woolf J).

2495 Sentence: 12 months' imprisonment concurrent on 3 counts: 9 months' imprisonment concurrent on 2 counts: (12 months in all). Man aged 57, one son, separated from his wife. Various employments and at time of offences, self-employed. One previous conviction for indecent assault on girl aged 8. Little history of instability, but in middle years became obsessed with an interest in young girls between the ages of 8 to 13. Offences took place over a period of 4 years and involved fondling, kissing and touching their private parts. Sentenced to 12 months' imprisonment concurrent on 3 counts and 3 years' imprisonment concurrent on 2 counts consecutive to the 12 months (4 years in all). On appeal, *held*, the sentence imposed was too long since the appellant had not exposed himself to the girls in any way and the incidents did not seem to have affected them adversely. Accordingly the sentence would be reduced as above. *R v Freeman*, 21st July 1980 (Court of Appeal: Lord Lane CJ, Lawton and Shaw LJJ).

2496 *Indecent assault (2); unlawful sexual intercourse (6)*
Sentence: 12 months' imprisonment consecutive; 12 months' imprisonment concurrent. Man, aged 28, married with two children. No previous convictions for sexual offences. In 1977 he met two girls X and Y. X was just over 14 years of age and Y was just under that age. He formed a friendship with them and from 1977 to 1979 had sexual intercourse with X on several occasions and once with Y. Sentenced to consecutive terms of 12 months' imprisonment on the indecent assault counts and to 12 months' imprisonment concurrent on five of the unlawful sexual intercourse counts and to 12 months' imprisonment consecutive on the other unlawful sexual intercourse count (3 years' in all). On appeal on grounds that the total sentence was too severe, *held*, the offences fully merited a prison sentence as it was a case of a married man of responsible age setting out to attract young girls. Nevertheless, the total sentence imposed was longer than necessary and would be varied as set out above. *R v Sitton*, 16th June 1980 (Court of Appeal: Eveleigh LJ, Thompson and French JJ).

2497 *Indecent assault (3); theft (2)*
Sentence: 2 years' imprisonment consecutive on counts 1 and 2. 2 years' concurrent on count 3 (4 years); 12 months' imprisonment consecutive (2 years) on the second

where a further offence was committed the original terms should be activated unaltered unless it was unjust to do so. The offence committed in the present case was not trivial since the appellant conducted his business in such a way as to only narrowly escape committing a criminal offence and accordingly the sentence would remain. *R v Issacs*, 12th June 1980 (Court of Appeal: Lord Lane CJ, Boreham and Gibson JJ).

OFFENCES AGAINST PROPERTY

2505   *Robbery*

Sentence: 6 years' imprisonment. Married man, aged 42, with one daughter. Various jobs and eight previous convictions mainly for dishonesty for which he was fined and imprisoned. In 1968, a jeweller was attacked in his shop by men who escaped with £350 worth of silverware. He died later that day from head injuries. Four months later two men were convicted of his murder and the robbery. Their convictions for murder were quashed on appeal a year later. In 1978, the appellant confessed to the robbery, stating that it had been on his conscience for ten years. He gave the police further information about the crime which enabled them to arrest two other men. Sentenced to 8 years' imprisonment. Nine offences were taken into consideration which included five armed bank robberies involving £12,500. He appealed, contending that he had assisted the police and had thereby lived in considerable danger. *Held*, in view of the fact that his co-accused who were the ringleaders were sentenced to 7 years' imprisonment, the court would vary the appellant's to 6 years' imprisonment. *R v Barnes*, 20th March 1980 (Court of Appeal: Lord Widgery CJ, Eveleigh LJ and O'Connor J).

2506   *Robbery (2); burglary*

Sentence: 5 years' imprisonment concurrent. Youth, aged 17, unemployed. Four previous findings of guilt for burglary, criminal damage and possession of an offensive weapon for which he was fined, conditionally discharged and sent to an attendance centre. The appellant and three other youths broke into a house by forcing a window open. A woman, her baby and an au pair were asleep in the house, the woman's husband being away on business. The youths armed themselves with kitchen knives, bound the woman with a cord and ripped a bracelet and a gold watch off her wrists. They then attacked the au pair, placing a knife at her throat. After stealing from her, they ransacked the house, gagged the woman, cut the telephone wires and made off with £5,000 worth of property. When the youths were arrested shortly afterwards they admitted to the two offences and three of them, including the appellant received 5 years' imprisonment, the fourth, aged 16, was sent to borstal. On appeal, *held*, young people who engaged in armed robbery had to expect to be dealt with severely. The present case was one of the most dreadful the court had heard of, it was a premeditated robbery with violence being contemplated and used. The sentence imposed would therefore stand. *R v Lake*, 20th March 1980 (Court of Appeal: Ormrod LJ, Japp and Comyn JJ).

2507   *Attempted robbery; wounding with intent*

Sentence: 7 years' imprisonment concurrent. Man, aged 19, single, with one child. Expelled from school at 15. Various employments. Nine findings of guilt and two previous convictions mostly for motoring offences and including one for robbery for which he was fined, sent to borstal and imprisoned for short terms. One night, after drinking in a public house the appellant and the co-accused, aged 17, decided to follow a 50 year old man after closing time. They caught up with him at a solitary spot and the appellant threatened him with a dagger asking him for money. The man refused to give into their threats whereupon the appellant wounded him with a flick knife. The appellant then stabbed the victim again, both stabs penetrating the liver and endangering the victim's life. The appellant was sentenced to concurrent terms of 7 years' imprisonment and the co-accused to 3 years. On appeal, *held*, as the court could find no mitigating features from the shocking facts of the case, the sentence would stand. *R v Robinson*, 21st July 1980 (Court of Appeal: Lord Lane CJ, Lawton and Shaw LJJ).

2508   *Burglary*

Sentence: 2 years' imprisonment concurrent. Married man, aged 23. Previous convictions for burglary and theft for which he was sent to borstal and imprisoned. The appellant stole property valued at over £6,000 from a guesthouse. He threw some of the items into the sea and sold the jewellery for £900. On the same day he committed another burglary stealing a TV set and cash together worth £286. He also committed nine other offences of burglary and theft in 1978 which were taken into consideration. When he first appeared before the court on the above charges, the trial judge deferred judgment for 3 months stating that she intended to sentence him to 3 years' imprisonment. He was told that he was being given a chance to behave himself in the interim period. However, shortly afterwards he assaulted a barman in a public house. He was convicted of assault occasioning actual bodily harm and criminal damage. The appellant was then sentenced as above in respect of the two burglary charges. On appeal, *held*, it was a lenient sentence and would stand. The appeal would be dismissed. *R v Hope*, 14th January 1980 (Court of Appeal: Cumming-Bruce LJ, Thompson and Smith JJ).

2509   Sentence: 3 years' imprisonment. Man, aged 28, separated from wife. One child in care. A drug addict with seven previous convictions for dishonesty, burglary, violence and drug offences for which he was imprisoned and conditionally discharged. The current offence was committed whilst the appellant was on parole. He broke into a chemist's shop one night and stole a quantity of dangerous drugs and pharmaceutical preparations. He then took an overdose and went into hospital. The next day, the police found two bottles of the stolen drugs in his house. The appellant admitted the offence to the police and he was sentenced as above. He appealed on grounds that he had not committed the burglary for gain but in order to obtain drugs to commit suicide and promised to try and cure his addiction. *Held*, there was no reason for interfering with the sentence as his previous misconduct indicated that he would commit a similar offence if released. *R v Finch*, 8th February 1980 (Court of Appeal: Waller LJ, Milmo and Kenneth Jones JJ).

2510   Sentence: 18 months' imprisonment. Man, aged 35, living with girlfriend and her 3 children. Numerous convictions. Bad criminal record with 23 convictions for a variety of offences for which he was sent to approved school, borstal and imprisoned. Seven weeks before the instant offence he was fined £150 for committing burglary. With the 15 year old son of his girlfriend, the appellant drove into a town and broke into a radio and TV shop. When he realised that the burglar alarm might be operating, they left and returned to steal property worth £1,572. Sentenced to 18 months' imprisonment. The question arose on appeal as to how to deal with persistent offenders who set out to steal property with the intention of distributing it in the criminal underworld. *Held*, as this was a deliberate breaking and entering for the purpose of stealing substantial quantities of goods and the appellant had a bad criminal record, the sentence passed was appropriate. *R v Eastlake*, 21st July 1980 (Lord Lane CJ, Lawton and Shaw LJJ).

2511   Sentence: 9 months' imprisonment. Married man, aged 27, with one child. Left school at 16 and had been in various employments. One conviction in 1974 for which he was conditionally discharged. Broke into a shoe shop to steal money. Burglar alarm sounded and he was seen escaping by the police who found a metal case opener on the premises. Sentenced to 2 years' imprisonment. The judge held that it was a serious, planned professional burglary in view of the use of a metal bar to obtain access and the getaway car. On appeal against the severity of sentence, *held*, the burglary was of a minor type since it was not directed at a private house and he was after money and not goods. Since the appellant showed signs of not offending again, the sentence would be varied to 9 months. *R v McCann*, 21st July 1980 (Court of Appeal: Lord Lane CJ, Lawton and Shaw LJJ).

2512   Sentence: 6 months' imprisonment. First and second appellants, aged 21 and 20 respectively. Both had previous convictions for burglary, had been in borstal and had previous prison sentences. After drinking together, the two men broke into a working men's club and stole money and liquor. Sentenced to 18 months' imprisonment each. Trial judge was limited by Criminal Justice Act 1961, s. 3 to imposing either a 6 or 18 months' sentence. On appeal, *held*, a sentence of 12 months' would have been more appropriate, if the judge had not been restricted by the statutory provisions, since it was a comparatively trivial offence. However, in view of the alternative sentences provided for in s. 3, a trial judge should have chosen the lesser sentence of 6 months, and the appeal would be allowed to that extent. *R v Kelloe*; *R v Moorhouse*, 21st July 1980 (Court of Appeal: Lord Lane CJ, Lawton and Shaw LJJ).

2513   Sentence: 10 years' imprisonment concurrent. Bankruptcy order under Powers of Criminal Courts Act 1973, s. 39 for the sums of £25,000 and £46,000. Divorced man, aged 34, with 2 children. Employments of short duration in the building trade. Six findings of guilt and 22 previous convictions mainly for offences of burglary. Sentences included approved school, borstal training, fines, probation, suspended and deferred sentences and imprisonment. Last offences consisted of 10 for burglary and one attempted burglary with 37 cases taken into consideration. The appellant broke into a private house and stole jewellery worth £25,000, 2 months after his last offence. Two days later he raided a penthouse of a hotel and stole jewellery worth £46,000. When arrested, stated that he was a professional burglar and found the rewards of burglary attractive and worth the risks. Sentenced to concurrent terms of 10 years' imprisonment. On appeal *held*, the sentence imposed was correct since there was no hope of rehabilitating him or that he would be deterred by prison sentences. Further, it was difficult to understand why notice of the appellant's previous convictions were not served with the view to the imposition of an extended sentence. *R v Brewster*, 21st July 1980 (Court of Appeal: Lord Lane CJ, Lawton and Shaw LJJ).

2514   Sentence: 9 months' imprisonment, single man, aged 22. Orphaned and lacked stable home background. In employment. Five findings of guilt and 4 previous convictions, mostly for taking motor vehicles, but one for attempted burglary. Had been fined, put on probation, subject to a supervision order, detained at borstal, sent to an attendance centre and absolutely and conditionally discharged. Had begun voluntary community work. The appellant assisted 3 men remove 38 stolen television sets from a warehouse. He was not paid for his help and the sets were not recovered. The instigator of the offence received 2 years' imprisonment and the appellant was sentenced to 18 months. On appeal *held*, although it was a bad case of burglary, considering the sentence passed on the instigator, the appellant's culpability had been over estimated by the trial judge. Further, in view of the appellant's involvement in community work, the sentence would be reduced to 9 months. *R v Ingham*, 21st July 1980 (Court of Appeal: Lord Lane CJ, Lawton and Shaw LJJ).

2515   Sentence: 5 years' imprisonment (extended sentence). Man, aged 52. Twelve previous convictions with 8 terms of imprisonment. Last received 4 years' imprisonment for burglary and breach of a suspended sentence in 1976. Broke into a bungalow with the co-accused and stole £6,000 worth of property. Sentenced to 7 years' imprisonment, which was an extended sentence. The co-accused, who was aged 31, and had 10 previous convictions and a prison record, was sentenced to $4\frac{1}{2}$ years' imprisonment. On appeal on the grounds of disparity, *held*, in view of the co-accused's sentence, the sentence would be reduced as above, and would remain an extended sentence. *R v Bussell*, 31st October 1980 (Court of Appeal: Lord Lane CJ, Bristow and Butler-Sloss JJ).

2516   Sentence: 6 months' imprisonment. Married man, aged 20, with young baby. Had a record of dishonesty over the last 10 years. Had been in a detention centre for 3 months and in borstal, and had served a term of imprisonment. When aged 19, he kept watch outside while 2 youths broke into a house when the owner was out. They took £2,500 worth of property, including £1,000 cash. Appellant's share for keeping watch was £380. Sentenced to 18 months' imprisonment. In the interval between committing the offence and the sentence, he was sentenced to 6 months' imprisonment for other offences, and was released 2 months before the imposition of the present sentence. In mitigation it was contended no account had been taken of a social inquiry report which gave ground for cautious optimism. On appeal, *held*, the court had not made sufficient reduction for the intervening sentence and taking into account the inquiry report, the sentence would be varied as above. *R v Sebastenelli*, 3rd November 1980 (Court of Appeal: Ormrod LJ, Lloyd and Bingham JJ).

2517   *Burglary; taking a conveyance; obtaining pecuniary advantage by deception; breach of suspended sentence (theft)*
Sentence: 6 years' imprisonment; 3 years' imprisonment concurrent; 5 years' imprisonment concurrent; 18 months' imprisonment consecutive (7½ years in all). Man, aged 41, unemployed. Twelve previous convictions mainly for offences of dishonesty and driving offences for which he received suspended sentences, fines and 8 terms of imprisonment. Last released from prison in 1977. (1) The appellant broke into a garage and collected various articles, he was disturbed by a police patrol car and ran off without taking anything. (2) He took a car from the farm where he was working and drove it off. (3) Using a false name, he booked into an hotel with a girlfriend, stayed the night and left without paying the bill of £57. The 3 offences took place between July 1977 and August 1978. The 28 offences which were taken into consideration occurred in different parts of the country between June and August 1978 and were mainly offences of theft and deception involving a total sum of £1,000. The offence in respect of which the appellant received a suspended sentence was theft in November 1977. Sentenced as above. He appealed against severity of sentence. *Held*, while it was the court's duty to try and give offenders an opportunity to reform, it was also its duty to protect society against persistent offenders. The sentences imposed in the present case were suitable and would stand with the activated sentence running consecutively. *R v Newcombe*, 18th January 1980 (Court of Appeal: Cumming-Bruce LJ, Thompson and Smith JJ).

2518   *1. Burglary (3). 2. Failing to surrender to bail. 3. Breach of suspended sentence (2)*
Sentence: 1. 18 months' imprisonment concurrent; 2. 3 months' imprisonment concurrent; 3. 4 months' and 1 month imprisonment concurrent (18 months in all). Man, aged 20, living with girlfriend and their child. Various employments as labourer, packer and insulator. Unemployed on arrest. Three previous findings of guilt and 7 convictions mainly for dishonesty. The appellant went into a shop in a drunken state and was chased off the premises by the owner who later found his wallet containing £16 missing. The appellant was arrested shortly afterwards. He then broke into a closed building and stole a screwdriver worth 25 pence. The third offence involved breaking into a private house where nothing was stolen. The suspended sentences were in relation to four thefts. Sentenced to concurrent terms of 3 years' imprisonment for the burglaries, 3 months' imprisonment concurrent for not surrendering to bail, 3 months' imprisonment concurrent for the first 3 thefts and 1 month imprisonment concurrent for the fourth theft, each consecutive to the 3 years (3 years 4 months in all). On appeal, *held*, the appellant was a nuisance to society. However, because of the comparative triviality of the offences, the fact that they were committed while he was drunk and the fact that his girlfriend was standing by him, the court would vary the sentences as set out above. *R v Nicholson*, 17th April 1980 (Court of Appeal: Lord Lane CJ, Griffiths and Webster JJ).

2519   *Theft*
Sentence: immediate release (3 months' imprisonment served). Widowed man, aged 47, living with son. Of previous impeccable character. Worked as a loader with a road haulage firm. The appellant was seen taking a pair of jeans, valued at £12, from some cardboard boxes, and hiding them in the front of his boiler suit. When he was stopped by a foreman he threw the jeans away saying "there goes your evidence". He then asked the foreman if the matter could be forgotten. When interviewed by the police he admitted to the offence and showed great remorse.

Sentenced to 9 months' imprisonment, reference being made at the trial to the prevalence of theft at that particular haulage company. On appeal, *held*, the initial sentence was too long for a man of previous good character, and, as it was a comparatively small item, it would be varied as set out above. *R v Woolley*, 25th January 1980 (Court of Appeal: Shaw LJ, Chapman and Drake JJ).

2520   Sentence: 3 months' detention. Man, aged 18. One previous conviction for robbery, for which a suspension order, later varied to a care order, was made. Lived in a community home for 2 years. Appellant and co-accused followed a 71 year old lady and one of them pushed her to the ground, causing her minor injuries, and stole her bag which contained £8. The appellant was sentenced to 6 months' detention and the co-accused, who had previous convictions, mainly for motoring and one for burglary in 1971 was fined £500. On appeal against sentence on grounds of disparity. *Held*, although they were acting together, a sentence of more than 3 months at a detention centre was not justified unless there were very exceptional circumstances, and accordingly the sentence would be varied as above. *R v Mason*, 19th August 1980 (Court of Appeal: Waller LJ, Wien and Mais JJ).

2521   *Theft; obtaining property by deception; driving while disqualified*
Sentence: 15 months' imprisonment concurrent suspended 2 years (first and second offences); 6 months' imprisonment concurrent (9 months' imprisonment already served). Married man, aged 32, with 2 children. Labourer with construction company. Seventeen previous convictions, mainly for offences connected with motor vehicles for which he was fined, put on probation, sent to borstal and imprisoned. The appellant and two other men stole motorcars and, after changing their identities, sold them to unsuspecting customers. Three months later he was caught driving while disqualified and failed to stop at the request of the police. He later admitted the earlier offences to the police and asked for two similar cases to be taken into consideration. Sentenced to 2½ years' imprisonment on the first two offences and to 6 months concurrent on the third. On appeal *held*, although the sentences imposed could not be faulted, taking into consideration the fact that he had already served 9 months and his employers were willing to take him back, the court would vary the sentence as set out above. *R v Boyce*, 29th November 1979 (Court of Appeal: Shaw LJ, O'Connor and Comyn JJ).

2522   *Theft (shoplifting)*
Sentence: 6 months' imprisonment concurrent with the sentence of 18 months' imprisonment currently serving. Married man, aged 27. Said to be subnormal. Numerous previous convictions for dishonestly taking vehicles, motoring offences, criminal damage, theft and breach of sentence for which he was fined and imprisoned. The instant offence occurred when the appellant and his wife stole meat and dairy products to the value of £12 from a grocery store. The appellant was found to have £30 on his person. Six months later he and two others committed four shoplifting offences in four shops for which he was sentenced to 18 months. For the instant offence the appellant was sentenced to 6 months' imprisonment consecutive to those 18 months. On appeal *held*, despite his bad record, a 2 year sentence for five shoplifting offences was longer than necessary and the sentence would be varied as set out above. *R v Jones*, 14th January 1980 (Court of Appeal: Lord Widgery CJ, Bridge LJ and Woolf J).

2523   *Theft; false accounting*
Sentence: immediate release (5 months' imprisonment served). Married man, aged 46, with one son. Qualified as a solicitor at the age of 22. Partner in a firm until it was taken over in 1977, he then became a self employed property manager and consultant. No previous convictions. The appellant was appointed sole executor of a client's will in 1974 and granted probate on her death. In 1975 and 1976 certain distributions were made to residuary legatees. After a realisation account was produced, one of the legatees became suspicious and made inquiries. It transpired that certain building society accounts of the client had not been disclosed, the

appellant paying in some money in respect of the shortfalls. The matter was reported to the Law Society when it was discovered that a further building society account had not been revealed. The appellant had used the money for his own business purposes as he had been under financial difficulties at the time. He was struck off the Roll of Solicitors in 1978 and sentenced to concurrent terms of 18 months imprisonment. He appealed on grounds that the sentence was excessive, the offences had taken place four years previously, he had lost his professional standing of twenty years, and that he had repaid the full amount misappropriated plus compensation in 1977. *Held*, the offences were very serious and merited a custodial sentence. While the imposed sentence was not inappropriate, bearing in mind that the appellant's professional career was ruined the court would order his immediate release. *R v Simler*, 21st April 1980 (Court of Appeal: Shaw LJ, Jupp and Mustill JJ).

2524   *Theft (3); possession of controlled drug*
Sentence: 3 months' imprisonment consecutive on two charges of theft and 3 months' concurrent on third charge; 3 months' concurrent for drug offence; breach of suspended sentence of 3 months' imprisonment for theft which was activated and ordered to run consecutively (9 months' imprisonment in all). Man, aged 27. Seven previous convictions for theft, handling of stolen goods, criminal deception, burglary and one drug possession conviction. The thefts were of a bottle of whisky, £200 worth of goods from Woolworths and a watch band. The appellant was also found in possession of a plastic bag containing traces of cannabis resin. History of drug misuse which was said to be responsible for his criminal conduct. On appeal against severity of sentence, *held*, it was clear that the appellant was a persistent offender and it would be good for him to be kept away from drugs for a period. Accordingly the total sentence imposed was appropriate and would stand. *R v Isteed*, 17th June 1980 (Court of Appeal: Eveleigh LJ, Thompson and French JJ).

2525   *Theft; taking a conveyance without authority*
Sentence: 9 months' imprisonment concurrent consecutive to 3 years sentence being served. Man, aged 29. Numerous previous convictions from 1961 to 1978 which included several motoring offences, theft, burglaries and other offences of dishonesty for which he was fined, sent to approved school, put on probation, conditionally discharged and imprisoned. With some others, including a 10 year old boy, the appellant took a motor car and went on a joy ride. The appellant and the boy then stole a pair of jeans from a shop. Sentenced to 9 months' imprisonment consecutive on both charges (18 months in all). On appeal, *held*, as the two offences were the result of a single escapade consecutive sentences were inappropriate. They would be varied to run concurrently but consecutive to the 3 years he was already serving. *R v Deleito*, 7th August 1980 (Court of Appeal: Watkins LJ, Michael Davies and Stocker JJ).

2526   *Conspiracy to steal*
Sentence: 12 months' imprisonment. Man, aged 36. Many convictions up to 1973, most serious in 1963 for housebreaking for which he was sent to borstal. Since 1973 had not committed any offences. The conspiracy arose out of a series of thefts from lorries. The appellant observed a neighbourhood from the driving seat of a van while the co-accused looked for vehicles from which they could steal articles. They were arrested and admitted that they were involved in the operation although they had not stolen anything. Sentenced to 18 months' imprisonment. On appeal *held*, since the appellant had kept out of trouble for 5 years and work was available for him on his release from prison, the sentence would be reduced as above. *R v Duarte*, 19th August 1980 (Court of Appeal: Waller LJ, Wien and Mais JJ).

2527   *Abstracting electricity*
Sentence: 28 days' imprisonment; £750 fine or 28 days' imprisonment in default. Man, aged 31, of previous good character, save for minor motoring offences.

Director of 2 businesses. In 1979 obtained a device from a friend which he attached to the electricity meter in his house and caused it to go backwards. Charged with stealing £150 worth of electricity and sentenced to 12 months' imprisonment. On appeal it was contended that a sentence of immediate imprisonment would destroy his business, *held*, the deliberate stealing of electricity called for a sentence which would act as a deterrent to an offender. In the present case, that would be effected by varying the sentence as above. *R v Hodgkinson*, 23rd October 1980 (Court of Appeal: Lord Lane CJ, Bristow and Butler-Sloss JJ).

2528   *Taking a motor vehicle without authority*
Sentence: 12 months' imprisonment consecutive to sentence of 4 years currently being served (conspiracy to rob, driving while disqualified, possession of firearms, breach of suspended sentences). Man, aged 24. Two findings of guilt as a juvenile and six other convictions for numerous offences including arson, burglary and driving offences for which he was fined, sent to approved school and borstal, conditionally discharged and imprisoned. While on a day release scheme, the appellant and a fellow inmate went to visit relatives in the north of England. As they had no money, they took a car and used it to return to London, living in it for three days until arrested. Sentenced to 2 years' imprisonment to run consecutively to the 4 years being served (6 years in all). On appeal, *held*, while the sentence imposed was well deserved, the court would reduce it to 12 months making it 5 years in all. *R v Vitols*, 18th April 1980 (Court of Appeal: Lord Roskill, Donaldson LJ and Mustill J).

2529   Sentence: £50 fine and ordered to pay £150 towards the prosecution costs. Man employed as a coach driver. He was allowed to take the coach which he was driving at work to his home at the end of the day. The appellant drove his coach home and subsequently used it for a private journey to visit a friend. He stayed overnight and overslept with the result that the coach was not available for his employment. He was fined £50, disqualified for 12 months' and ordered to pay £150 towards the prosecution costs. He appealed against the order of disqualification on the grounds that there had been no allegation that he had driven dangerously or that he had been drinking and that he would be prevented from working. *Held*, since the appellant had incurred the penalties of being fined and having to pay the prosecution costs, it was not necessary to disqualify him in view of the fact that he had been made subject to a period of disqualification before his appeal was lodged. *R v Kingston* [1980] RTR 51 (Court of Appeal: Waller LJ, Kilner Brown and Neill JJ).

2530   *Taking a motor vehicle without authority; driving without insurance; driving while disqualified*
Sentence: 18 months' and 6 months' imprisonment concurrent. Eighteen previous convictions including offences connected with motor vehicles, for which he was sent to borstal. The appellant took a car and was stopped by the police. He was found to have been disqualified from driving and was not insured. The offence was committed within a month of his last borstal training. Sentenced to 18 months' imprisonment for taking the vehicle and 6 months' imprisonment consecutive for driving while disqualified. On appeal against sentence, *held*, the sentence of 18 months' imprisonment for taking the vehicle was correct. However, since the other offences arose out of the same incident, the six months' imposed would be ordered to run concurrently. *R v Kincaid*, 20th August 1980 (Court of Appeal: Waller LJ, Wien and Mais JJ).

2531   *Handling stolen goods*
Sentence: immediate release (4 months' imprisonment served). Married man, aged 25, of previous good character. Delivery driver with a good work record. The charges involved receiving stolen meat (and one instance of receiving stolen orange juice) over a 6 month period. The appellant's work as a delivery driver took him to a cold store where an employee offered him the opportunity of buying stolen goods cheaply. The goods were mainly cases of lamb at £40 a case which the

appellant bought at £15 and resold at £20 a case. The total value of the goods received was over £2000. Sentenced to concurrent terms of 12 months' imprisonment. The appellant's employer intimated to the court that it would re-employ him. On appeal, *held*, while the period of imprisonment was right in principle, taking into account the appellant's past good character, work record and the fact that he had served four months' imprisonment already, the sentence would be varied to allow for his immediate release. *R v Crawford*, 15th May 1980 (Watkins LJ, Boreham and Hodgson JJ).

2532 Sentence: immediate release (5½ months' served at Borstal). Single woman, aged 17, of previous good character. She asked at a bank for a sum of foreign currency (about £130) to be exchanged and gave a false name and address. The money was handed over to her and a few days later, she attempted to do the same thing at the same bank and was arrested as the money had been found to be stolen currency. Sentenced to borstal training. On appeal against sentence, *held*, a probation order would have been a more preferable sentence. However, as the defendant had already served 5½ months at Borstal, the sentence would be varied to permit her immediate release. *R v Ahmed*, 6th October 1980 (Court of Appeal: Waller LJ, Tudor Evans and McNeill JJ).

2533 Sentence: 3 months' imprisonment. First appellant, married man, aged 34. Barman of licensed premises managed by his wife. Previous convictions for road traffic offences, violence and offences relating to prostitution for which he was fined. Second appellant, married man aged 43, with 3 children. Proprietor of a general store/off licence. No previous convictions. Both admitted receiving stolen spirits, first appellant £262 worth and the second appellant £1,800 worth. Sentenced to 9 months' immediate imprisonment. On appeal, *held*, an immediate custodial sentence was appropriate but since neither appellant had previously been in custody, the sentence would be varied as above. *R v Burn*; *R v Shoukat*, 10th October 1980 (Court of Appeal: Waller LJ, Tudor Evans and McNeill JJ).

2534 Sentence: 7 days' imprisonment. Divorced woman, aged 36, with a 13 year old son and a young baby. Two previous shoplifting convictions for which she was fined and given a suspended sentence, and one for handling stolen goods for which she was fined. The appellant had a silver teapot which had been stolen by a third party. When she heard that he had been arrested she gave the teapot to another man, who was unaware that it was stolen, for safe keeping. The teapot was recovered and the appellant was sentenced to one month's immediate imprisonment. On appeal, *held*, normally, a sentence of one month's imprisonment was appropriate for such an offence. However, since the appellant had a young baby and she had been granted bail after a week in prison, the appeal would be allowed and she would not be sent back to prison. *R v Gough*, 10th October 1980 (Court of Appeal: Lord Lane CJ, Stocker and Glidewell JJ).

2535 Sentence: 6 months' imprisonment concurrent on two counts; 6 months' imprisonment consecutive on 1 count (12 months in all). Married man, aged 58, with 2 grown up children. Previous impeccable character. A tenant farmer since 1949 and also raised money for charity. Two counts were specimen charges relating to 2 bags of stolen animal feed. The third count related to a larger amount of animal feed. A load of 10 tons of animal feed for delivery to local farmers was found to be substandard and was required to be reprocessed. Before it was taken back, an agreement was reached whereby it was stolen and sold to the appellant, who paid £425 for what in its substandard condition was worth £1,122. Police went to the appellant's farm and found the load, and he admitted that he had received £3,000 worth of substandard feed over the last 5 years. Sentenced to 12 months' imprisonment concurrent on 2 specimen counts and 9 months' imprisonment consecutive on the third count. On appeal against the severity of sentence, *held*, imprisonment was the only appropriate way to deal with such an offence, in view of the fact that the appellant was an established farmer and was willing to take from the supplier's dishonest agents what they were willing to offer. However, the deterrent sentence imposed and its effect on other farmers who might act in the same way could be achieved by varying the sentence as above. *R v Stokes*, 12th June 1980 (Court of Appeal: Lord Lane CJ, Boreham and Gibson JJ).

2536   *Handling stolen goods (2); theft (2); handling stolen goods*
Sentence: 6 years' imprisonment, restitution order of £37,329; 18 months' imprisonment consecutive (theft) and 18 months' imprisonment concurrent (theft and handling) (7½ years in all). Married man, aged 39. Apprentice electrician and machinist. Five previous convictions mainly for burglary. Last released from a 7-year sentence in 1969 for burglary, theft and handling stolen property. A bank was robbed and £200,000 stolen. £37,324 was found in a safe deposit box belonging to the appellant and the notes were identified as belonging to the bank robbery. The second offence involved the theft of a car. The appellant then, under a false name, hired a caravan and failed to return it. Both the car and caravan were subsequently recovered outside his home. The second handling charge in the second indictment related to stolen postal orders found in the appellant's possession. Sentenced to 8 years' on the first indictment and a total of 18 months' imprisonment consecutive on the second indictment (9½ years in all). On appeal, *held*, the sentence would be varied as set out above. *R v Dewsnap*, 28th January 1980 (Court of Appeal: Cumming-Bruce LJ, Mais and Smith JJ).

2537   *Handling stolen goods (counts 1 & 2); obtaining property by deception (counts 13–14, 16–19); obtaining property on a forged instrument (count 15) (168 tic)*
Sentence: 12 months' imprisonment (counts 1 & 2); 15 months' imprisonment (counts 3–10, 12–14, 16 & 17); 18 months' imprisonment (counts 11, 15, 18 & 19) (18 months in all). Single woman, aged 27. Deprived background. Employed in shops and offices as a cleaner. Two previous convictions for shoplifting and theft for which she was imprisoned and fined. The appellant was supplied with stolen cheque books and cards (counts 1 & 2). Using a false name and forged signature (having substituted a false signature on the banker's card) she obtained money and goods valued at £6,225 from various banks and shops. The offences that were taken into consideration involved obtaining property by deception by the same method over a period of 19 months. Sentenced as above. On appeal, *held*, the sentence imposed was appropriate for the offences committed and it would not be altered. *R v Mocock*, 17th April 1980 (Court of Appeal: Dunn LJ, Thompson and Heilbron JJ).

2538   *Handling stolen goods (5); obtaining property by deception (5) (158 tic)*
Sentence: 3 years' imprisonment concurrent. Married man, aged 25. Previously employed as a fitter, mechanic, labourer and security guard for periods of short duration. Unemployed at time of arrest. Previous summary conviction and one spent conviction for theft for which he was fined and conditionally discharged. Appellant suggested to his brother, who was a postman that he should intercept any letters containing bank cards. He took 6 Barclaycards and passed them to the appellant and his wife, who obtained £3,800 worth of cash and goods at various places throughout Britain (158 offences were taken into consideration). A majority of the property was recovered. The brother was sent to borstal, the wife received a 6 months' suspended sentence and the appellant 4 years' imprisonment since he was clearly the ringleader. On appeal against sentence, *held*, since the recorder had stated that the brother would have been sentenced to 2 years' imprisonment had he been of full age the appellant's sentence was excessive and would be varied as above. *R v Iwasiw*, 11th November 1980 (Court of Appeal: Dunn LJ, Phillips and Drake JJ).

2539   *Obtaining property by deception*
Sentence: 15 months' imprisonment concurrent. Married man, with children. No previous convictions. He fell ill in 1975 and became unemployed. Remained unemployed until 1979 during which time he was entitled to sickness and unemployment benefit. However, over that period he also stated that his wife was

unemployed when she was in fact employed and in that way unlawfully obtained £1,100 in benefits. Sentenced as above. On appeal, *held*, although the appellant's family were in financial difficulties during the period of his illness and unemployment, his actions were a deliberate fraud on the social security system. Accordingly the imposed sentence was entirely proper and would stand. *R v Riley*, 14th January 1980 (Court of Appeal: Cumming-Bruce LJ, Thompson and Smith JJ).

2540   Sentence: 12 months' imprisonment concurrent. Widower, aged 57, with 2 sons. A qualified medical general practitioner earning a net income of £9,000 per annum. No previous convictions. Qualified in 1953 and employed to treat patients at a remand centre. The appellant obtained money from a local area health authority by submitting false claims for payment. He used three methods to defraud the authority: (1) by charging for injections he had not given or for more than he had given (counts 1, 2 & 3), (2) by claiming fees for night calls that he had not made either by inducing patients to say there had been a night visit or by forging their signatures (count 4), and (3) by making false claims for contributions towards his cleaning lady's wages. The offences were committed in 1975 and at the trial in 1979 the appellant was sentenced to 30 months' imprisonment. Although he had no real defence he fought the charges to the end. In the meantime his wife committed suicide. On appeal, *held*, bearing in mind the appellant's personal circumstances, the fact that his medical career was over and that there would inevitably be further disciplinary proceedings taken against him resulting in the possible loss of his pension rights, the court would vary the sentence as set out above. *R v Richards*, 17th April 1980 (Court of Appeal: Lord Lane CJ, Griffiths and Webster JJ).

2541   Sentence: 9 months' imprisonment concurrent. Company director, aged 40, no previous convictions. Started travel agency business and falsely represented that he possessed an air transport operator's licence although he had been informed that one would not be granted to him. Arranged flights for clients who paid money to him assuming that they were protected when he could not fulfil arrangements for their charter flights. Amount deposited was £18,600 of which he repaid approximately £16,000. Sentenced to 18 months' imprisonment concurrent on 6 counts of obtaining. On appeal, the question being the appropriate way of sentencing a small businessman who had started an honest business and had made dishonest representations when the business was in jeopardy, *held*, the present case was not in the nature of a "long firm fraud". The defendant had tried to run an honest business but had encountered difficulties. Further the amount involved was not substantial. He was a man of previous good character and the sentence would be varied to 9 months. *R v Murray*, 21st July 1980 (Court of Appeal: Lord Lane CJ, Lawton and Shaw LJJ).

2542   Sentence: 15 months' imprisonment concurrent. Married man, aged 37, with 3 children. No previous convictions. The appellant joined a company, which purported to install double glazing and carry out home improvements, as a freelancer and agent. The firm obtained deposits for work which they either did not carry out or did not complete. The appellant became involved in the dishonest practice and his personal gain amounted to £1,760. The trial was delayed to enable full-scale committal proceedings to take place. Sentenced as above, the judge taking into account this good work record since the offence and the delay. On appeal against sentence, *held*, the offence was serious involving more than one person. It was a calculated fraud upon the public and was not a case of sudden temptation. The sentence imposed was lenient and there were no grounds for interfering with it. *R v Burlinge*, 12th June 1980 (Court of Appeal: Eveleigh LJ, Thompson and French JJ).

2543   *1. Obtaining property by deception (3). 2. Obtaining property by deception (2); handling stolen goods*
Sentence: wife, 6 months' imprisonment concurrent; husband, 3 years' imprisonment concurrent. Husband and wife, aged 26 and 23 respectively, with 1 child. Husband had 4 findings of guilt and a previous conviction from 1968, mainly for dishonesty,

including burglaries, handling stolen goods, deception and forgery. Sentenced to terms of 4 years' imprisonment having previously undergone all forms of custodial sentence. Wife had a previous conviction for burglary in 1977 for which she was put on probation for 2 years (original sentence, 3 years' imprisonment). A large quantity of household goods was stolen from a house and stored in the appellants' flat. Husband pleaded guilty to receiving stolen property. The wife disposed of 3 items in an antique shop, the husband being present on 2 occasions. Approximately £3,000 worth of the property was recovered. Sentenced as above, the only mitigating factor being that the wife was pregnant. On appeal, *held*, in view of the fact that the wife had previously been convicted of a serious burglary and had had her sentence of 3 years reduced on appeal to probation, the sentence was merited, and the husband's sentence, in view of his criminal record, was proper. *R v Deegan and Deegan*, 3rd November 1980 (Court of Appeal: Ormrod LJ, Lloyd and Bingham JJ).

2544   *False accounting (4); theft (4)*
Sentence: 12 months' imprisonment concurrent on 2 counts, 2 years' imprisonment concurrent on the other counts (2 years' in all). Pakistani woman aged 33 with 2 children aged 10 and 12. Came to the UK in 1968. Previously employed as a bookmaker but unemployed at date of trial. Four previous convictions for dishonesty for which she was put on probation, fined and given a suspended sentence. During 1978/79 employed as general accounts clerk and falsified four of her employer's cheques so as to represent that certain sums of money had been paid out to fictitious persons, as a result of which she received £24,000. Sentenced as above. She contended in mitigation that her children were suffering as a result of her imprisonment. On appeal, *held*, the appellant had to pay the proper penalty for the offences committed and the sentences imposed were correct. *R v Nihalani*, 31st October 1980 (Court of Appeal: Lord Lane CJ, Bristow and Butler-Sloss JJ).

2545   *Fraudulent trading*
Sentence: 6 months' imprisonment. Pole aged 65, married with 2 children. No previous convictions. Had served in the army in Poland and in the Polish air force in England. Started a successful business career. In 1972 when the company became insolvent, he used its money to meet his gambling debts and defrauded creditors of £160,000. Sentenced to 12 months' imprisonment. Although he put forward no mitigating circumstances he was said to be in bad health and had been worrying about the matter since 1975. On appeal, *held*, the appellant was a compulsive gambler and used creditors' money to pay his debts, which constituted fraud. The sentence was therefore justified; however taking into account the appellant's health, and the fact that an immediate custodial sentence was inevitable in the case of fraud, the sentence would be varied as above. *R v Lichenstein*, 6th November 1980 (Court of Appeal: Lord Roskill, Eveleigh LJ and Kilner Brown J).

2546   *Carrying on a consumer credit business without a licence (6)*
Sentence: 2 months' imprisonment consecutive on each count (12 months' imprisonment in all), £2,400 fine. Man, aged 55, separated from his wife. Thirteen previous convictions mostly involving motor vehicles and 3 for unlawful possession of pension books and forgery, had been fined and served varying terms of imprisonment. At time of offence he ran a greengrocery and drapery business and lent money to customers at a high rate of interest which averaged 800 per cent per annum, without holding a licence as required by the Consumer Credit Act 1974, s. 39 (1). The appellant either issued his customers with a card and they repaid him weekly or he retained family allowance or pension books as security and required them to sign the forms in the books in advance authorising him to collect the money as agent. He pleaded guilty to 6 specimen counts and was sentenced to 5 months' imprisonment and fined £200 on each count (2½ years' imprisonment in all and £1,200 fine). On appeal against severity of sentence, *held*, in view of the fact that the appellant knew that he was breaking the law, the immediate sentence of imprisonment was justified. However, the sentence would be varied as above and

the fine would be increased as above. *R v Gurr*, 12th May 1980 (Court of Appeal: Lawton LJ, Davies and Balcombe JJ).

2547   *Arson*

Sentence: orders under the Mental Health Act 1959, ss. 60, 65. Youth, aged 17. Two previous convictions, one in 1976 for arson (conditional discharge) and the second in 1977 for motoring offences (care order and absolute discharge). Said to be an extremely disturbed boy who was a great risk to himself and others. Admitted to a psychiatric hospital in October 1979. There, he set fire to an ante room of a ward causing £1,250 worth of damage. He later confessed to the offence. Ordered to be detained for life under the Children and Young Persons Act 1933, s. 53 (2). Since his trial a place had been found for the appellant in a mental hospital. On appeal *held*, as all the requirements of the Mental Health Act 1959 had been complied with and a place had been found for the appellant in a suitable hospital, the court would vary the sentence to that set out above. *R v Wood*, 21st January 1980 (Court of Appeal: Shaw LJ, Chapman and Drake JJ).

2548   Sentence: 3 years' probation. Man, aged, 20. Educated at a school for maladjusted children. Unemployed since late 1979. History of epilepsy, now cured, and a drink problem. Very early one morning the appellant set fire to curtains in two separate maisonettes. In each case the fire was put out by the occupants. A month later, a police officer saw the appellant standing at the boot of a car in which he had started a fire. He ran off but was arrested. Later, he admitted to having set fire to both sets of curtains, to two rubbish bins and a Post Office letter box (the last three offences being taken into consideration). In a written statement, he said that the offences had been committed because he was depressed at having parted from his girl friend. Sentenced to 3 years' imprisonment. Said to be aware of the gravity of his offences and resigned to his sentence. Prison governor's report stated that the sentence had had positive effects on the appellant and a vacancy was available at a probation hostel. On appeal *held*, although the sentence was neither excessive nor wrong in principle, it would be varied by placing the appellant on probation for 3 years on condition that he resided at the hostel and subjected himself to the necessary psychiatric treatment. *R v Hoof*, 7th August 1980 (Court of Appeal: Watkins LJ, Michael Davies and Stocker JJ).

2549   *Arson; attempted murder (6); causing grievous bodily harm*

Sentence: 15 years' imprisonment concurrent. Man, aged 48, divorced. In 1976, sentenced to 3 years' imprisonment for offences of violence against his wife and son. Divorced by wife in 1978 while serving that sentence. When he came out of prison he went to his wife's flat. At the time, her son, two daughters and son-in-law were present. He let himself in carrying a long knife. He accused his wife of having put him in prison and bound and gagged all five of them and another daughter who had just arrived. He then set fire to the flat after blocking the front door with a sideboard. The six victims managed to escape through a window. One daughter jumped to the ground and suffered fractures. The son-in-law had burns covering 10 per cent of his body. The appellant was arrested on the following day and admitted to the offences. Sentenced as above. A social inquiry report described him as dangerous. On appeal, *held*, the sentence imposed was neither wrong nor excessive for the appalling offences he had committed. *R v Reid*, 19th February 1980 (Court of Appeal: Waller LJ, Milmo and Kenneth Jones JJ).

2550   *Damaging property (2)*

Sentence: £50 fine on each count (one month's imprisonment in default); £250 compensation plus prosecution and defence costs. Divorced man, aged 37. Had attended university. Since 1970 an exporter of cars. Owned property and occupied a house with two tenants. Difficulties arose between the appellant and the tenants and the appellant threw paint over their car on 2 occasions. Initially denied any involvement but pleaded guilty at the trial. Sentenced to one month's imprisonment concurrent, ordered to pay the tenants £250 compensation and to pay the prosecution's and his own costs. On appeal on the ground that the sentence was excessive for a man of previous good character, *held*, the proper sentence was a fine rather than imprisonment and the sentence would be varied as above. *R v Pecht*, 6th October 1980 (Court of Appeal: Watkins LJ, Thompson and Bush JJ).

2551   *Damaging property (2); wounding with intent*
Sentence: 6 months' imprisonment concurrent; 4 years' imprisonment concurrent. Man aged 34, with 2 spent convictions and employed as a bricklayer. No record of violence. He had been living with the victim and their 2 children for 7 years. The victim asked him to leave and while she was out of the house with a new male friend, he broke in and damaged a TV set and a window. He then took his 2 year old daughter away to his sister's house. He was later arrested and granted bail on condition he did not go near the house or contact the victim or the children. Three weeks later he went to the house and saw the victim holding one of his children. When she refused to hand the child over he stabbed her in the face several times with a broken bottle shouting "I'm going to kill you" and inflicting serious facial injuries. Sentenced to concurrent terms of 6 months' imprisonment for damaging property and to 6 years' imprisonment for the wounding. On appeal, *held*, it was a terrible attack that merited an immediate sentence of imprisonment. However, taking into account that he had no record of violence and that it was a domestic situation that gave rise to the trouble, a sentence of 4 years' imprisonment would be sufficient to deter the appellant and anyone else inclined to commit such an offence. *R v Lewis*, 18th February 1980 (Court of Appeal: Eveleigh LJ, Bristow and McNeill JJ).

Offences relating to drugs

2552   *Possession of controlled drug (3); supplying controlled drug (3)*
Sentence: borstal training. Youth, aged 19, troubled childhood. Good character with one irrelevant previous conviction. The police raided a house in Cambridge where the appellant was staying. They found 73 milligrammes of cannabis resin (count 1) which he admitted were his. They also found 49 grammes of cannabis resin (count 2) and 20 tablets of LSD (count 3) on the appellant. Cannabis and LSD were also found on two of his friends (the supplying counts). Sentenced to concurrent terms of 3 years' imprisonment, the judge stating that a deterrent sentence was needed due to the prevalence of that type of offence in the area. On appeal, *held*, as it was not a case in which there was a regular chain supply to the public at large but rather a supply on a limited basis amongst personal friends, a deterrent sentence was not called for. Bearing in mind that the appellant had spent 4 months in prison where he had been on good behaviour, and as a community service order was unrealistic, the appropriate sentence was one of borstal training and the sentence would be varied accordingly. *R v Sturt*, 24th March 1980 (Court of Appeal: Ormrod LJ, Chapman and Jupp JJ).

2553   *Being knowingly concerned in the fraudulent evasion of prohibition on importation of controlled drug*
Sentence: 6 years' imprisonment (E); borstal training (D). The first appellant E, divorced man, aged 31. A freelance musician, living in Holland with no previous convictions. The second appellant D, a Dutch girl, aged 21. Living with her parents in Amsterdam. A drug addict with no previous convictions. They arrived at Heathrow and in their luggage was found a suitcase with a false bottom. In it were plastic bags which contained 281·1 grammes of 90% diamorphine hydrochloride (heroin) at the street value of between £125,000 and £200,000. E admitted to the police that they had travelled together from Bangkok, that he had known that there was heroin in the suitcase and that he had intended to take it back to Amsterdam for his own use. E was sentenced to 6 years' imprisonment and D to 3 years' imprisonment. On appeal, *held*, as D was the younger partner and had been involved in an emotional relationship with E, the court would vary her sentence to one of borstal training. D's sentence would stand however in view of the pernicious and

dangerous trafficking involved in the case. *R v Echteld; R v De Vries*, 17th January 1980 (Court of Appeal: Shaw LJ, Chapman and Drake JJ).

2554   Sentence: 2 years' imprisonment. Nigerian man, aged 22, student. Stopped by customs officers at Heathrow after flying in from Lagos. His suitcase was found to have a false base in which was concealed 1·85 kilogrammes of cannabis. When questioned, he admitted that he had purchased the suitcase complete with the cannabis for about £40 and had brought it to England in order to finance his studies in Nigeria. He had managed to get a cheap flight over. Sentenced as above. On appeal on grounds of previous good character and the fact that he was not a professional smuggler and had no idea of the value of cannabis in this country, *held*, it was the type of deterrent sentence which, although severe for a person of his age, was appropriate for people who came to the UK on this sort of expedition whether privately or as carriers. The imposed sentence would therefore stand. *R v Egwuatu*, 28th January 1980 (Court of Appeal: Cumming-Bruce LJ, Mais and Smith JJ).

2555   *Conspiracy to supply drugs; possession of a controlled drug (2)*
Sentence: 6 months' imprisonment concurrent suspended for 2 years. Single man, aged 24, living with parents. Final year student at University, of previous good character. Police officers found cannabis resin and material for smoking cannabis in a suspect's house. The appellant arrived at the house later that day and tried to get away when he saw the police. He was restrained and searched and several small pieces of paper were found in his pocket. He then managed to break away and destroy them before the police caught up with him but later admitted that the pieces of paper contained LSD. When his room was searched, police found a tin containing traces of LSD, a bag containing two packets of 100 milligrammes and 385 grammes of cannabis resin, another with 6·9 grammes of cannabis resin and a pot containing cannabis resin. The appellant eventually admitted to dealing with cannabis resin through the suspect. He also admitted to buying cannabis resin at £330 a pound and selling it to the suspect at £512 a pound. The trial judge said that although the appellant had only been doing this for a short time it was a commercial undertaking and sentenced him to 12 months' imprisonment on the first offence and to concurrent terms of 3 months' imprisonment on the second offences. He appealed on the grounds that he had helped the police in their inquiries and was in his final year at university. *Held*, the appellant was an intelligent young man who chose to deal in drugs for his own gain. However, in view of the fact that he had helped the police and if he served his sentence his career propects would be ruined, the court would vary the sentence as set out above. *R v Zywina*, 22nd April 1980 (Court of Appeal: Lord Lane CJ, Griffiths and Webster JJ).

DRIVING OFFENCES

2556   *Reckless driving*
Sentence: 6 months' detention centre, concurrent. Man, aged 18, no previous convictions. Left school at 16, worked as an apprentice electrician. Does not drink or smoke; motor vehicles his main interest. When aged 17½ and unqualified, drove a car with "L" plates. He overtook a police car, ignored its directions to stop, and drove for 12 miles at high speed in built up areas, through an industrial estate and a private housing estate. He approached junctions without reducing speed and turned corners dangerously and also drove through a car park causing people to scatter. Eventually stopped, but when the police approached he started the car causing one officer to be thrown from the car bonnet. The latter suffered minor injuries. No suggestion that he had been drinking. Sentenced as above. On appeal against severity of sentence, *held*, although the appellant had a good work record, a sentence of detention was necessary to curb such behaviour. Accordingly the sentence imposed was not wrong in principle. *R v Bulman*, 12th June 1980 (Court of Appeal: Eveleigh LJ, Thompson and French JJ).

2557 —— **leave to appeal—refusal—effect on computation of sentence**

See para. 646.

2558 —— **right of appeal—order activating suspended sentence—total term less than six months**

See *R v Wilson*, para. 644.

2559 **Custodial sentences—restrictions imposed by overcrowding of prisons**

The Court of Appeal has stated that, in view of the problem of overcrowding in prisons, non-violent petty offenders should not be given custodial sentences except where absolutely necessary. Further, if there was no alternative to an immediate prison sentence, then it should be as short as possible.

Their Lordships allowed an appeal, against a six-month sentence, by a deputy manager of a supermarket, from which he had stolen goods worth £5. He had served two months of his sentence and was released immediately.

R v UPTON (1980) 124 Sol Jo 359 (Court of Appeal: LORD LANE CJ, GRIFFITHS and WEBSTER JJ).

2560 **Deportation—recommendation—principles**

See *R v Nazari*, para. 1506.

2561 **Deprivation of property used for crime—partnership property—validity**

See *R v Troth*, para. 639.

2562 **Outstanding offences—proper time for consideration**

Upon conviction of three offences under the Theft Act 1968 the accused asked for twenty-four offences to be taken into consideration. The magistrates committed him to the Crown Court for sentence, where the judge ruled that he could not now withdraw his request. On appeal, *held*, the proper time for the defendant to be asked if he wished other offences to be taken into consideration was at the court which was to sentence him, and the defendant should be asked personally, not merely through his counsel. However in the circumstances the sentencing judge had a discretion whether to take the offences into consideration.

R v DAVIES (1980) Times, 22nd November (Court of Appeal: DUNN LJ, DRAKE and PHILLIPS JJ).

2563 **Practice—counsel asking judge's view of sentence**

See *R v Coward*, para. 715.

2564 —— **uniformity of approach to length of sentences**

In considering an appeal against a three-year sentence for the fraudulent evasion of the prohibition on importation of herbal cannabis the Court of Appeal held that sentencing courts had to be particularly careful to examine each case to ensure that, if an immediate custodial sentence was necessary, the sentence was as short as possible, consistent only with the duty to protect the interests of the public and to punish and deter the criminal. The court could and should consider whether there was any compelling reason why a short sentence should not be passed. Although uniformity of sentence would be impossible, the aim was uniformity of approach.

R v BIBI [1980] 1 WLR 1193 (Court of Appeal: LORD LANE CJ, LAWTON and SHAW LJJ).

2565   Suspended sentence—powers of court—power to activate sentence

The Court of Appeal has stated that where a person under a suspended sentence commits another offence and the court sentencing him for the second offence has decided, in accordance with the power under the Powers of Criminal Courts Act 1973, s. 23 (d), to make no order with respect to the suspended sentence, a subsequent court has no power to deal with the same breach of the suspended sentence, but only with any further breach.

Thus, the defendant had been convicted of an offence and a community service order had been made in respect of him. He had admitted that a suspended sentence had been passed on him earlier. The court chose to make no order in respect of that suspended sentence. At the hearing for failure to comply with the community service order, the judge had activated the suspended sentence. The defendant appealed. *Held*, the judge had no jurisdiction to deal with the suspended sentence when dealing with the offence in respect of which the community service order had been made. The appeal would accordingly be allowed.

R v FOLAN [1980] 1 All ER 217 (Court of Appeal: WALLER LJ, LAWSON and JUPP JJ).

2566   Young offender—sentence—power of court to sentence while on parole

A young offender who was sentenced to eighteen months' imprisonment for offences committed while on parole appealed against sentence contending that since he was on parole, he was no longer serving a sentence within the meaning of the Criminal Justice Act 1961, s. 3(2). Accordingly s. 3(1) of the Act, which eliminated intermediate and short prison sentences for young offenders, was applicable and the court was barred from passing such a sentence. *Held*, a person released on parole had not had his sentence suspended, but was still serving a sentence of imprisonment within the meaning of s. 3(2). The references to supervision and licence in s. 3(2) dealt with special cases and had no application to the position of a person on parole.

R v MELLOR (1980) Times, 16th December (Court of Appeal).

SET-OFF AND COUNTERCLAIM

Halsbury's Laws of England (3rd edn.), Vol. 34, paras. 669–755

2567   Counterclaim—security for costs—when security for costs granted

See *The Silver Fir*, para. 2202.

2568   —— time limit for presentation

The plaintiffs appealed against a decision to allow the defendants to proceed with a counterclaim notwithstanding that judgment for the plaintiffs, under RSC Ord. 14, had been entered without a stay of execution. *Held*, an action was at an end when the plaintiffs' judgment had been satisfied, as it had been in this case upon the payment by the defendants of their debts to the plaintiffs. There was therefore no action by the plaintiffs in existence which could be the subject of a counterclaim by the defendants. The defendants therefore had no right or power to serve a counterclaim and the appeal would accordingly be allowed.

CSI INTERNATIONAL CO LTD v ARCHWAY PERSONNEL (MIDDLE EAST) LTD [1980] 3 All ER 215 (Court of Appeal: ROSKILL, EVELEIGH LJJ and WALTON J).

2569 Set-off against hire charge—sub-charterer's right to set-off against assignee of right to hire charge

A charterparty between the second plaintiff and the first defendant (L) provided that the second plaintiff had the right of withdrawal in the event of non-payment of the hire. L sub-chartered the vessel to the second defendant who agreed, inter alia, to advance funds to the master for ordinary disbursements, such sums then to be deducted from the payment of hire. L assigned to the second plaintiff all its rights under the sub-charter and the second defendant guaranteed payment of L's hire. The second plaintiff assigned all its rights to the first plaintiff. L failed to pay the hire and the first plaintiff claimed payment from the second defendant. The second defendant sought to set off its claim, in respect of certain sums expended under the sub-charter, against the first plaintiff's claim. *Held*, the amounts counterclaimed were payments made in order to enable the vessel to earn her hire and it would be unjust to allow the first plaintiff to recover the hire without giving credit for sums expended. The rule that an assignee took subject to equities did not mean that this was restricted to such set-offs as were equitable set-offs. Accordingly the sums could be set off against the first plaintiff's claim.

THE RAVEN, BANCO CENTRAL SA AND TREVELAN NAVIGATION INC v LINGOSS & FALCE LTD AND BFI LINE LTD [1980] 2 Lloyd's Rep 266 (Queen's Bench Division: PARKER J). *Newfoundland Government v Newfoundland Railway Co* (1888) 13 App Cas 199, PC applied.

2570 Set-off against rent—repairs covenant by landlord—tenant's right to equitable set-off

See *Melville v Grapelodge Developments Ltd*, para. 1747.

SETTLEMENTS

Halsbury's Laws of England (3rd edn.), Vol. 34, paras. 756–1141

2571 Class gift—compound gift for grandchildren born and unborn — time of ascertaining class

The terms of a settlement provided that a trust fund was to be held for the children of the settlor's son who, before the expiration of twenty-one years from the death of the survivor of the settlor or his son, attained the age of twenty-five, and for other children of the son living at the expiration of that period. When the eldest grandchild reached twenty-five the trustees issued an originating summons to determine whether the class of beneficiaries had closed in view of the rule in *Andrews v Partington* [1775–1802] All ER Rep 209, whereby the class closes upon the attainment of the specified age of one member of it. The trustees contended that the settlement provided for a compound class of the son's children with two qualifications, (i) children born in the settlor's lifetime attaining twenty-five within twenty-one years of the son's death and (ii) other children, of any age, alive twenty-one years after the son's death not qualifying under (i). As the rule did not apply to (ii), it could not apply to the whole gift. They also contended that the rule would be completely excluded if its application prevented one limb of the gift from having any operation save in improbable circumstances. *Held*, the rule could be excluded but it was insufficient if there were provisions which merely pointed to the exclusion of the rule if they were, nevertheless, capable of operating in conformity with it. There had to be complete incompatibility with the operation of the rule, and the fact that the rule did not apply to part of a compound class was insufficient to demonstrate any incompatibility of the rule with the other part or with the gift as a whole. Further, the exclusion of the rule did not depend on the improbability, but rather on the impossibility of circumstances and the reduction of the scope of (ii) to circumstances which were improbable but not impossible was insufficient to exclude the rule. The rule, therefore, applied and the class of persons entitled to a share under the settlement closed when the eldest grandchild reached twenty-five.

Re CLIFFORD'S SETTLEMENT TRUSTS; HEATON v WESTWATER [1980] 1 All ER 1013 (Chancery Division: SIR ROBERT MEGARRY V-C). *Andrews v Partington* [1775–1802] All ER Rep 209, dicta of Russell LJ in *Re Edmondson's Will Trusts* [1972] 1 All ER 444 at 449, and of Buckley J in *Re Wernher's Settlement Trusts* [1961] 1 All ER 184 at 188 applied.

SEX DISCRIMINATION

Halsbury's Laws of England (4th edn.), Vol. 16, paras. 771:2–771:38

2572   Articles

Four Years of the Equal Pay Act, John Bowers and Andrew Clarke: 130 NLJ 304.
The Question of Motive in Discrimination, H. Carty (in the light of *Ministry of Defence v Jeremiah* [1979] 3 All ER 883, 1979 Halsbury's Abridgment para. 2506): 130 NLJ 563.

2573   Advertisements—advertisements for job vacancy—whether reasonably understandable as indicating intention to discriminate

Industrial tribunal decision:

EQUAL OPPORTUNITIES COMMISSION v ROBERTSON [1980] IRLR 44 (proceedings against company in respect of series of advertisements for job vacancies; Commission alleged advertisements discriminatory within Sex Discrimination Act 1975, s. 38; s. 38 (1) read with s. 38 (2) provides that an advertisement is not unlawful if the intended act would itself not be unlawful; an advertisement has to be read as a whole according to what a reasonable person would find to be the ordinary meaning of words used in order to determine whether it is discriminatory; advertisements showed intention to discriminate by offering employment on different terms to men and women).

2574   Consumer credit—refusal to grant credit to married woman without guarantee—validity

See *Quinn v Williams Furniture Ltd*, para. 1416.

2575   Discrimination against contract worker—relief taxi cab driver—extent of statutory protection

A taxi cab firm allowed one of its drivers, E, to use a relief driver, R, for the night shift. On discovering that R was female the firm told E to dismiss her on the grounds that the work was unsuitable for a woman. R applied to an industrial tribunal for relief from unlawful discrimination on the grounds of her sex, pursuant to the Sex Discrimination Act 1975, s. 9. Alternatively she contended that the firm was an employment agency under the 1975 Act, s. 82, in that the firm found clients who would employ her as a driver, and had unlawfully discriminated against her within the meaning of s. 15. *Held*, R could not rely on either s. 9 or s. 15. (i) s. 9 only applied to work done by a person employed by another person who supplied work under a contract with the principal involving an obligation to supply the worker. There was no contractual agreement between E and the firm that E would supply others to do the driving and the work done by R was for E and not the firm as required by s. 9. (ii) The firm was not an employment agency within s. 82 as it did not provide services for the purpose of finding employment for R as clients contacted the firm who in turn contacted E, nor did the firm supply employers with workers.

RICE v FON-A-CAB [1980] ICR 133 (Employment Appeal Tribunal: SLYNN J presiding).

2576   **Discrimination by employment agency—whether taxi-cab firm employment agency**

See *Rice v Fon-a-cab*, para. 2575.

2577   **Dismissal—dismissal on grounds of pregnancy—whether dismissal discriminatory on grounds of sex**

An employee complained that she had been dismissed because she was pregnant. As she lacked the necessary continuous service required by the Trade Union and Labour Relations Act 1974 to bring a claim for unfair dismissal, she brought a complaint under the Sex Discrimination Act 1975. An industrial tribunal decided to try, as a preliminary issue, the question whether, if there was a dismissal on the ground of pregnancy, it was unlawful discrimination within the Sex Discrimination Act 1975, s. 1 (1). The tribunal concluded that such a dismissal was not unlawful discrimination and the employee appealed. *Held*, the tribunal had not erred in its decision. Section 1 required the court to compare men and women, and see that they were not treated unequally simply because they were men or women. In order to see whether a woman was treated less favourably than a man, the sense of s. 1 (1) was that like was to be compared with like and with a pregnant woman this was impossible. The only remedy of a woman dismissed on the ground of pregnancy was under the unfair dismissal provisions of the Employment Protection Act 1975, s. 34. The appeal would be dismissed.

     Turley v Allders Department Stores Ltd [1980] ICR 66 (Employment Appeal Tribunal: Bristow J presiding).

     Employment Protection Act 1975, s. 34 now Employment Protection (Consolation) Act 1978, s. 60.

2578   —— **dismissal on marriage to employee of rival agency—whether discrimination against married person**

See *Skyrail Oceanic Ltd v Coleman*, para. 3045.

2579   **Education**

See para. 986.

2580   **Equal pay—employment in succession—application of statutory provisions**

Four months after a man left his position as a stockroom manager a woman was appointed to the position at a lower wage. In the course of proceedings brought by the woman against her employers for equal pay under the Equal Pay Act 1970, s. 1 (2) (a) (i), as substituted by the Sex Discrimination Act 1975, s. 8 the Court of Appeal stayed the proceedings and referred certain questions to the European Court. The questions related to the interpretation and application of EEC Treaty, art. 119, which provides that men and women should receive equal pay for equal work. On the resumption of the proceedings following the decision of the European Court, *held*, the woman was entitled to succeed in her claim. Article 119, which had been held to apply to a situation such as the one in question, took priority over any inconsistent United Kingdom legislation by virtue of the European Communities Act 1972, s. 2.

     Macarthys Ltd v Smith (No. 2) [1980] 3 All ER 111 (Court of Appeal: Lord Denning MR, Lawton and Cumming-Bruce LJJ).

     For the proceedings in which the reference was made see [1979] 3 All ER 325, 1979 Halsbury's Abridgment para. 2501. For the decision of the European Court see [1980] IRLR 210, para. 1196.

2581   —— **job evaluation study—failure to implement—effect**

The Equal Pay Act 1970, s. 1 (2) (b), provides that where a woman is employed on work rated as equivalent with that of a man in the same employment if, apart from the equality clause (i) any term of her contract determined by the rating of the work is or becomes less favourable to her than a term of a similar kind in the contract under which the man is employed, such term of the woman's contract is treated as modified so as not to be less favourable, and (ii) at any time the woman's contract does not include a term corresponding to a term benefiting the man included in the contract under which he is employed and determined by the rating of the work, the woman's contract is treated as including such a term.

On a claim for equal pay by female employees, the employers contended that s. 1 (2) (b) did not apply when a job evaluation study had been carried out, but the pay structure had not been adjusted as a result. *Held*, once a job evaluation study had been undertaken and had resulted in a conclusion that the job of the woman had been evaluated under s. 1 (5) as of equal value with the job of the man, then the comparison of the respective terms of their contracts of employment was made feasible and a decision could be made whether modification under s. 1 (2) (b) (i) or treatment under s. 1 (2) (b) (ii) was called for. Accordingly, s. 1 (2) (b) applied notwithstanding that the employers had not accepted the scheme nor adjusted their pay structure.

O'BRIEN v SIM-CHEM LTD [1980] 3 All ER 132 (House of Lords: LORD DIPLOCK, VISCOUNT DILHORNE, LORD SALMON, LORD RUSSELL OF KILLOWEN and LORD KEITH OF KINKEL). Decision of the Court of Appeal [1980] 2 All ER 307, reversed.

2582   —— like work—job comparison—grading scheme

A female employee in a canteen at a grade 3 post made a complaint to an industrial tribunal that she did like work to that of a male canteen employee at a grade 1 post, and was therefore entitled to equal treatment. The tribunal ruled that notwithstanding that the differentials in pay between the grades were justified because of the differing degree of responsibility for stock control and for handling large sums of money, the employees were engaged in like work because they were both required by their contracts of employment to prepare, serve and sell food and clear away and clean the canteen. Her terms of employment were not to be regarded as less favourable than those of the male worker. On appeal, *held*, if the additional responsibility justified the grading difference, it also precluded their work from being like work. Accordingly, the tribunal had erred in law and its decision would be set aside.

CAPPER PASS LTD v ALLAN [1980] ICR 194 (Employment Appeal Tribunal: SLYNN J presiding).

2583   —— —— material difference other than sex

Three clerks were employed by a company. One post was successively filled by men who had been moved to the job because of age and ill-health. They were paid more than the rate for the job, retaining the rates they had been paid before appointment. A man was appointed to that job because of age and ill-health. He was given staff status and was paid the same as his predecessor. The other clerks were women who were paid less than the man. They sought a declaration that they were engaged on like work and hence entitled to equal remuneration under the Equal Pay Act 1970, s. 1. The employers relied on s. 1(3), contending that the variation was genuinely due to a material difference other than sex. *Held*, when an employer relied on s. 1(3) the questions to be considered were whether there was a material difference other than sex and whether the employer had proved on a balance of probabilities that the variation was due to the material difference. In this case, the employers had proved that the variation was due to the man's age and ill-health. The fact that his wages were the same as before his appointment and the same as his predecessor's did not prevent them being paid to him because of his age and ill-health. The declaration would be refused.

METHVEN v COW INDUSTRIAL POLYMERS LTD [1980] ICR 463 (Court of Appeal: STEPHENSON and DUNN LJJ and SIR STANLEY REES). Decision of the Employment Appeal Tribunal [1979] ICR 613, 1979 Halsbury's Abridgment para. 2504 affirmed.

2584 Eight male car drivers employed by the Ministry of Defence claimed equality with fifty-one female drivers who were paid more than they, despite being employed on like work. The situation arose in an attempt by the Ministry of Defence, prior to the introduction of the Equal Pay Act 1970, to eliminate any differentials in pay by upgrading the female drivers. When the 1970 Act came into force the female drivers remained in their higher grades and were therefore paid more than the male drivers. *Held*, under the 1970 Act, s. 1 (3) the employer had to prove that any variation in pay was genuinely due to a material difference, other than the difference of sex, between the employees in question. In determining this the court had to consider all the surrounding circumstances and in the present case the variation occurred, not because of a difference of sex, but because of a system adopted to eliminate the difference in pay between men and women, and the latter received extra pay on a personal basis because of circumstances special to them.

FARTHING V MINISTRY OF DEFENCE [1980] IRLR 402 (Court of Appeal: LORD DENNING MR, WALLER and DUNN LJJ).

2585 —— —— **reference to European Court**

A female part-time worker claimed that under the Equal Pay Act 1970, s. 1, she was entitled to the same hourly rate as a man who worked full-time and did like work. She claimed that an equality clause should be implied into her contract to that effect. An industrial tribunal dismissed her claim since it found that the difference in pay was due to a material difference, other than that of sex, as the employers had maintained a differentiation between part-time and full-time workers. The worker appealed, abandoning her claim under the Equal Pay Act, but contending that her employers were violating EEC Treaty, art. 119 and Council Directive (EEC) 75/117 which provide for equal pay for men and women for equal work. *Held*, the proceedings would be stayed pending the decision of the European Court on the construction and application of those provisions, particularly as to whether they were directly applicable where indirect discrimination was alleged.

JENKINS V KINGSGATE (CLOTHING PRODUCTIONS) LTD [1980] 1 CMLR 81 (Employment Appeal Tribunal: SLYNN J presiding).

2586 **Equal treatment—immigration rules—application of statutory provisions on sex discrimination**

It fell to be determined whether the Immigration Rules, para. 22, permitting a wife to be admitted to the UK for the duration of her husband's stay, but not expressly allowing a husband to stay for the period of his wife's authorised stay, offended against the provisions of the Sex Discrimination Act 1975. *Held*, s. 1 (1) of the Act provided that the provisions of the Act were conclusive as to the circumstances under which sex discrimination was unlawful. Therefore only circumstances specifically provided for in the Act could be subject to the provisions against unlawful sex discrimination. In giving leave to immigrants to enter or remain here, the Home Secretary could not be said to be providing facilities to a section of the public under s. 29 (1) of the Act. There was therefore no unlawful discrimination against the appellant by refusing to give him leave to remain here whilst his wife was a student.

KASSAM V IMMIGRATION APPEAL TRIBUNAL, [1980] 2 All ER 330 (Court of Appeal: STEPHENSON and ACKNER LJJ and SIR DAVID CAIRNS).

2587 —— **like work—women not allowed to transport dangerous chemicals**

A twenty-three year old woman was employed as a heavy goods vehicle driver. Her employers refused to allow her to transport certain chemicals because of the possible danger to women of child bearing age. An industrial tribunal dismissed her claim of unlawful sexual discrimination on the ground that although her employers' action was discriminatory, it was lawful because it was taken in the interests of her safety. On appeal by the employee, *held*, under the Sex Discrimination Act 1975, s. 51 (1) discriminatory action was not unlawful if it was taken to comply with an

Act passed before the 1975 Act. The Health and Safety at Work Act 1974, s. 2 required employers, so far as reasonably practicable, to protect their employees from risks to health and safety in connection with the transport of substances. Nevertheless, employers could not justify discrimination simply on the ground that there was a risk to health; all the circumstances of the risk involved and the measures necessary to eliminate it had to be considered. However, considerable evidence as to the danger of the chemicals to women of the employee's age had been given before the industrial tribunal. In view of such evidence, the tribunal would have found that the employers' action was necessary to comply with their duty under the 1974 Act. The appeal would be dismissed.

PAGE v FREIGHT HIRE (TANK HAULAGE) LTD [1981] 1 All ER 394 (Employment Appeal Tribunal: SLYNN J presiding). Dicta of Lord Denning MR in *Ministry of Defence v Jeremiah* [1979] 3 All ER 833, CA at 836, 1979 Halsbury's Abridgment para. 2506 applied.

2588   —— like work and redundancy—selection of redundant employees

Employers served notices of redundancy on three women who worked in their warehouse, without prior consultation with the women. The women claimed that they had been unfairly dismissed and unlawfully discriminated against on the ground of their sex. They also argued that they were entitled to equal pay with the men. An industrial tribunal dismissed their claims, accepting evidence that male employees carried out the heavier work in the warehouse whereas the women did lighter work, and it was the lighter side of the work that had diminished. The women's appeal was allowed and the case was remitted for a fresh hearing before a differently constituted industrial tribunal. The employers appealed. *Held*, within the warehouse there were two establishments, one manned by men, the other by women, and there was ground on which the industrial tribunal could have found that the women were not engaged on like work with the men and therefore not entitled to equal pay. There had been no unlawful discrimination as it had been quite reasonable for the employers to reduce their staff from those doing the lighter work. Further, the want of consultation did not necessarily make the dismissal unfair. The appeal would be allowed and the decision of the industrial tribunal restored.

NOBLE v DAVID GOLD & SONS (HOLDINGS) LTD [1980] ICR 543 (Court of Appeal: LORD DENNING MR, LAWTON and ACKNER LJJ). *Hollister v National Farmers' Union* [1979] ICR 542, CA 1979 Halsbury's Abridgment para. 2948 applied.

2589   Selection for appointment—discrimination against part-time female technician—burden of proof

Northern Ireland

A female employee was refused promotion by her employers, despite the fact that her qualifications were superior to those of the successful male applicant. The employee claimed that she had been discriminated against on the grounds of her sex contrary to provisions similar to the Sex Discrimination Act 1975. On the question of the burden of proof, *held*, where an act of discrimination had been established and one party to the act was male and the other party was female, prima facie that raised a case which called for an answer.

WALLACE v SOUTH EASTERN EDUCATION AND LIBRARY BOARD [1980] IRLR 193 (Court of Appeal of Northern Ireland). *Moberley v Commonwealth Hall (University of London)* [1977] IRLR 176, 1977 Halsbury's Abridgment para. 2545 applied.

2590   —— woman passed over for promotion—recommendation that employer take action to obviate effects of discrimination— provisions of recommendation

Where an industrial tribunal finds that a complaint of sex discrimination is well-founded, it is empowered under the Sex Discrimination Act 1975, s. 65 (1) (b) to make an order requiring the respondent to pay compensation to the complainant and under s. 65 (1) (c) to make a recommendation that the respondent take, within a specified period, action to obviate the adverse effect on the complainant of the act of discrimination. A tribunal found that a woman had been passed over for promotion on the grounds of her sex and awarded her compensation for four months future loss of salary under s. 65 (1) (b). It also made a recommendation under s. 65 (1) (c) that she should seriously be considered as the most suitable candidate for the position as soon as it fell vacant again and that in the alternative she should continue to receive the difference in salary until she was promoted to an equivalent job. The employers appealed on the ground that the recommendation was not for a specified period. *Held*, the intention of the legislation was that loss of wages should be dealt with under s. 65 (1) (b) and that a recommendation under s. 65 (1) (c) should not include matters relating to wages, but should deal with any other action intended to obviate the effect of the discrimination. The tribunal's recommendation under s. 65 (1) (c) would therefore be rescinded. In view of this rescission the tribunal would probably wish to reconsider the award under s. 65 (1) (b) and it would be remitted to the tribunal for this purpose.

    PRESTCOLD LTD V IRVINE [1980] ICR 610 (Employment Appeal Tribunal: SLYNN J presiding).

2591   **Social security—sickness benefit—effect of Sex Discrimination Act on Social Security Acts**

See *National Insurance Commissioner's Decision: R(S) 11/79*, para. 2760.

SHIPPING AND NAVIGATION

Halsbury's Laws of England (3rd edn.), Vol. 35

2592   **Articles**

    Cargo Dispute Resolution and the Hamburg Rules, C.W. O'Hare: 29 ICLQ 219.
    The Hague–Visby Rules and forum, arbitration and choice of law clauses, D. C. Jackson [1980] LMCLQ 159.

2593   **Admiralty jurisdiction**

See ADMIRALTY.

2594   **Berth—safety of berth—duty to ensure safe berth**

A number of shipping berths were situated alongside a wharf operated by the defendants. The berths were tidal and at low tide the bed at the foot of the quay wall dried out. At a point near the bottom of the wall was a culvert which discharged sewage and water; the top of the quay wall was painted white at that point. The discharge from the culvert made it dangerous to berth across it but the defendants had not put up any warning notices. When the plaintiffs' ship approached the wharf, no pilot was available to assist her to berth and the wharf manager had left. The ship's master moved her into a berth which obstructed the culvert. When the tide fell, there was a considerable discharge from the culvert due to very heavy rain; a depression was scoured in the river bed leaving part of the ship unsupported. The ship suffered damage which the plaintiffs claimed was due to the defendants' negligence. *Held*, (i) the defendants were aware of the danger of berthing a ship in front of the culvert and were negligent in failing to put up clear warning notices; (ii) the wharf manager was negligent in leaving without warning the ship's master about the culvert; (iii) the ship's master was not negligent in berthing the ship since he moved into a berth vacated by a ship which had been berthed by a pilot; moreover, the defendants had intended to allocate that particular berth to the plaintiffs' ship. Therefore, the damage was caused wholly by the defendants' negligence.

THE NEAPOLIS II, ALBERTA SHIPPING LTD v THE BRITON FERRY STEVEDORING CO LTD [1980] 2 Lloyd's Rep 369 (Queen's Bench Division: PARKER J).

2595   Bill of lading—foreign compensation clause—construction— application for stay of proceedings

See *The Kislovodsk*, para. 426.

2596   —— foreign jurisdiction clause—when proceedings in England should be stayed

See *The El Amria*, para. 428.

2597   —— lien clause—addition of lien clause to bill of lading

A judge in the Queen's Bench Division has granted to the charterers of a ship a mandatory injunction requiring the owners of the ship to issue the necessary bill of lading without the addition of an extra clause which the owners wished to add. The charterparty had provided for the owners to have a lien on the cargo for freight, dead freight and demurrage. The owners had refused to sign the bill of lading presented to them unless this clause was incorporated into the bill of lading. *Held*, the terms of the charterparty were effective to carry the owners' lien into the bill of lading. Further, a term in the charterparty that the master was to sign the bill of lading at such rate of freight as presented without prejudice to the charterparty, was to be interpreted as meaning that it was for the charterers, not the owners, to decide on the form of the bill of lading, provided that the bill of lading did not encroach on the rights conferred on the owners by the charterparty.

THE ANWAR AL SABAR, GULF STEEL CO LTD v AL KHALIFA SHIPPING CO LTD [1980] 2 Lloyd's Rep 261 (Queen's Bench Division: MUSTILL J).

2598   —— loss of goods—defences and immunities—rights of stranger to contract

Cargo was shipped to the consignees in Australia pursuant to a bill of lading which conferred certain defences and immunities on the carriers and in addition extended the same to independent contractors employed by them. Clause 17 of the bill of lading barred an action if not brought within a year after the goods should have been delivered. The cargo was stolen due to the negligence of the stevedores in Australia. The consignee brought an action against the stevedores after the year had elapsed, claiming that they could not escape liability by virtue of clause 17 because no consideration had moved from the stevedores and because the stevedores were in fundamental breach of their obligations and so the bill of lading ceased to operate after the goods had been unloaded. *Held*, the intent of the parties, in accordance with normal commercial practice, was that the stevedores should enjoy the benefit of contractual provisions in the bill of lading. An agency was found as a matter of fact, and from this it followed that consideration moved from the stevedores on the basis of established legal principles. Clause 17 was indistinguishable from an arbitration clause or forum clause and therefore it survived the breach even if it was repudiatory. Accordingly the stevedores were immune from liability.

PORT JACKSON STEVEDORING PTY LTD v SALMOND and SPRAGGON (AUSTRALIA) PTY, THE NEW YORK STAR LTD [1980] 3 All ER 257 (Privy Council: LORD WILBERFORCE, LORD DIPLOCK, LORD FRASER OF TULLYBELTON, LORD SCARMAN and LORD ROSKILL). *New Zealand Shipping Co Ltd v A M Satterthwaite & Co Ltd* [1974] 1 All ER 1015, 1974 Halsbury's Abridgment para. 504 followed.

2599   Carriage of goods by sea—damage to cargo—bill of lading signed by charterers' agents on behalf of master—liability of charterers

See *The Venezuela*, para. 2608.

2600   —— —— liability of carrier for fault of third party—effect of exemption clause

Frozen meat was shipped from New Zealand to England under a contract in which the carrier and his servants and agents disclaimed all liability, even in negligence, for any damage caused to the cargo. Owing to a shortage of time, new arrangements were made by the carriers for offloading the cargo. The work was entrusted to a third party. Delay caused by industrial action taken by the third party's employees led to much of the cargo going rotten. The cargo-owners claimed damages from the carriers, who denied liability. *Held*, the new arrangements did not amount to a new agreement but merely varied the original contract. The terms of the bill of lading all applied so far as they were applicable and the carrier could rely on the exemption clause.

THE ARAWA [1980] 2 Lloyd's Rep 135 (Court of Appeal: LORD DENNING MR, BRIDGE LJ and SIR DAVID CAIRNS). Decision of Brandon J [1977] 2 Lloyd's Rep 416, 1977 Halsbury's Abridgment para. 2568 reversed.

2601   —— freight—exclusion of liability

Canada

In a case where a carrier of goods by sea issued a bill of lading containing a clause which stated that contents of loaded lifts were unchecked but said to contain the correct contents as indicated, it was held that such a clause did not excuse the carrier from liability when, on unloading, there were fewer goods than indicated, unless the carrier proved that the goods were missing on loading.

COUTINHO, CARO & CO (CANADA) LTD v OWNERS OF THE VESSEL 'ERMUA' (1979) 100 DLR (3d) 461 (Federal Court of Canada, Trial Division).

2602   —— Hague Rules—application

The Hague Rules, art. III, r. 6 provides that the carrier and the ship are discharged from all liability in respect of loss or damage unless a suit is brought within a year after the date of delivery of the goods.

The question arose as to under what circumstances the Rules could be used. *Held*, the Hague Rules were designed for defence and not attack. Where they were used to defeat a cross-claim by charterers against the owners' claim for the balance of hire it might result in "undue hardship" to the charterers. The courts, therefore, had the power to grant charterers, in such circumstances, an extension of time for commencing arbitration proceedings under the Arbitration Act 1950, s. 27.

MOGUL LINE LTD v COMMERCE INTERNATIONAL INC (1980) Times, 19th April (Court of Appeal: LORD DENNING MR, TEMPLEMAN and WATKINS LJJ).

2603   —— —— —— Bermuda

The Carriage of Goods by Sea (Bermuda) Order 1980, S.I. 1980 No. 1507 (in force on 1st December 1980), extends to Bermuda, with certain modifications, the Carriage of Goods by Sea Act 1971 which gives effect to the Hague Rules 1924 relating to bills of lading.

2604   —— —— —— Hong Kong

The Carriage of Goods by Sea (Hong Kong) Order 1980, S.I. 1980 No. 1508 (in force on 1st February 1981), extends to Hong Kong, with certain modifications, the Carriage of Goods by Sea Act 1971 which gives effect to the Hague Rules 1924 relating to bills of lading.

2605   The Carriage of Goods by Sea (Hong Kong) (Amendment) Order 1980, S.I. 1980 No. 1954 (in force on 1st February 1981), amends the Carriage of Goods by Sea (Hong Kong) Order 1980, para. 2604. The meaning of the term "ship" is amended so as to exclude from the scope of the Hague Rules as applying to Hong Kong the lading system of junks and lorchas plying between Hong Kong and the mainland.

2606   Carriage of passengers by sea—Convention

The Carriage of Passengers and their Luggage by Sea (Interim Provisions) Order 1980, S.I. 1980 No. 1092 (in force on 1st January 1981), provides that, pending the coming into force internationally of the Athens Convention relating to the Carriage of Passengers and their Luggage by Sea 1974, the Convention shall, subject to modifications, have force of law in the United Kingdom in relation to certain contracts of carriage made on or after 1st January 1981. The order applies to contracts of international carriage made in the United Kingdom or such contracts under which the United Kingdom is the place of departure or destination and to contracts of carriage under which the places of departure and destination are in the area consisting of the United Kingdom, the Channel Islands and the Isle of Man and there is no intermediate port of call outside that area. The Unfair Contract Terms Act 1977, s. 28, which made temporary provision for contracts for the carriage of passengers and their luggage by sea, ceases to apply to any contract to which the order applies but continues to apply to any contract made before 1st January 1981.

2607   —— —— notice

The Carriage of Passengers and their Luggage by Sea (Interim Provisions) (Notice) Order 1980, S.I. 1980 No. 1125 (in force on 1st January 1981), requires a carrier, in relation to any contract of carriage to which the Carriage of Passengers and their Luggage by Sea (Interim Provisions) Order 1980, para. 2606 applies, to give to passengers notice of specified provisions of the Convention relating to the Carriage of Passengers and their Luggage by Sea 1974. Those provisions relate to valuables, the limit of the carrier's liability for death or personal injury and for loss of or damage to luggage (including a vehicle), and the notice to be given by the passenger in respect of loss or damage to luggage. Notice must be given by the carrier before departure and, where practicable, on the ticket itself.

2608   Charterparty—bill of lading signed by charterers' agents on behalf of master—parties to contract of carriage

By a charterparty the owners let their vessel to a transportation company. A term of the charter provided that the master was to sign the bills of lading as presented, without prejudice to the charterparty. The defendants subsequently time chartered the vessel from the company. It was a term of that charter that the charterers' agents were authorised to issue and sign bills of lading on the charterers' usual form on the master's behalf. The defendants had an agreement with agents which provided that the agents were to issue bills of lading on behalf of the defendants in the form presented by the defendants. The agents issued a bill of lading on the defendants' usual form in respect of the plaintiff's cargo which was carried on the vessel. The plaintiff alleged that it was damaged during the voyage and claimed damages. The defendants contended that the bill of lading had to be treated as having been signed by the master and that accordingly they were not the contracting party. *Held,* it was not necessary that all bills of lading signed during the time when the vessel was under a subcharterer had to contain evidence of contracts with the shipowners. It was open to the charterers to make contracts on their own behalf. The terms of the bill of lading provided that the carrier was anyone who operated a vessel carrying goods covered by a bill of lading. It was clear that the defendants were operating the vessel since they made the vessel available to carry the goods. If the defendants did not wish to contract as the carrier the bill of lading issued by them should have made it clear with which company a shipper was entering into a contract of carriage. Accordingly the defendants were parties to the contract of carriage as evidenced by the bill of lading.

THE VENEZUELA [1980] 1 Lloyd's Rep 393 (Queen's Bench Division: SHEEN J).

2609   —— construction—arrest of vessel—owner's failure to secure release of vessel

The terms of a charterparty provided that "the charterers will not suffer, nor permit to be continued, any lien or incumbrance incurred by them or their agents which might have priority over the title and interest of the owners in the vessel". While the vessel was under a subcharter for the carriage of cargo for a third party the charterers diverted the vessel from the port named in the bill of lading and discharged the cargo elsewhere. The cargo was then transhipped to its proper destination, where it was found to be contaminated. The vessel continued to trade under its original charter and was subsequently arrested by the receivers of the cargo in admiralty proceedings in rem against the vessel and her owners, based on the deviation and the failure to care for the cargo. The charterers refused to provide the security to procure the release of the vessel as required by the owners and contended that the owners' refusal to secure the release constituted a repudiation of the charter. The arbitrators found in favour of the owners and stated a special case for the decision of the court. *Held*, the arrest of the vessel was "a lien or incumbrance incurred by the charterers" amounting to a breach of the terms of the charterparty since it gave the person arresting the vessel a priority over the title and interest of the owners in the vessel. The liability to arrest arose from the charterers' orders to divert the vessel and was accordingly an incumbrance incurred by them. The owners, therefore had not repudiated the charterparty by refusing to secure the release of the vessel.

THE VESTLAND, RICHMOND SHIPPING LTD V VESTLAND [1980] 2 Lloyd's Rep 171 (Queen's Bench Division: MOCATTA J).

2610   —— demurrage—whether payable under two charters running concurrently

A vessel was let to charterers for a voyage from Sicily to Venezuela with a cargo of steel bars. The owners' rights to load a completion cargo were excluded but by a second charter a further cargo of steel coils was to be carried. The vessel arrived in Venezuela but berthed only three weeks later. The charterers accepted liability to pay demurrage for the delay but there was a dispute as to the amount. The owners contended that both charters should be read separately, resulting in the vessel being on demurrage under the first charter at the agreed rate of $3,000 per day and when, a few days later, the time period under the second charter expired, the vessel came on demurrage under that charter as well. The owners would thereafter be entitled to demurrage under both charters totalling $6,000 per day until the discharge of the steel coils was complete. The charterers contended that the two charters should be read together as one contract and they were therefore liable to pay only $3,000 per day for the whole period. *Held*, the second charter specifically mentioned the earlier charter and the intention was therefore that the provisions in both charters should be construed as if they had been contained in the same contract and the natural result of this was that the rate of demurrage payable would be $3,000 per day.

THE SEA PIONEER, SARMA NAVIGATION SA V SIDERMAR SpA [1979] 2 Lloyd's Rep 408 (Queen's Bench Division: LLOYD J).

2611   —— frustration—effect of strike—whether charterparty divisible

See *Pioneer Shipping Ltd v BTP Tioxide Ltd*, para. 483.

2612   —— hire—owner's right to withdraw ship failing punctual payment—whether charterer made payment in cash

In a case concerning the payment of hire under a time charter, the owners claimed that they were entitled, under the terms of the charter, to withdraw the vessel from the charterers' service as the hire had not been paid punctually. Due to the wording of a telex between an intermediate bank and the owners, the owners became entitled to the use of the money on the date of payment under the charter, 22nd January 1976, but interest on the payment was not payable until 26th January. The point in issue was whether this constituted "payment in cash" within the terms of the charter. The case went to arbitration and the arbitrator came to the conclusion that the owners had been paid in cash on 22nd January. This decision was reversed by the High Court, but on appeal to the Court of Appeal *held*, the arbitrator's decision would be restored. He had come to the conclusion that the owners had the unconditional right to the use of the money on 22nd because, under Italian banking law and practice, the credit transfers became irrevocable on that day. The fact that interest was not payable until 26th simply meant that, had the owners withdrawn the sum before that date, they might have been liable for a trifling sum in bank charges.

THE CHIKUMA, A/S AWILCO v FULVIA SpA DI NAVIGAZIONE (1980) Times, 7th June (Court of Appeal: LORD DENNING MR, WALLER and DUNN LJJ). Decision of Robert Goff J [1979] 1 Lloyd's Rep 367, 1979 Halsbury's Abridgment para. 2531 reversed. *Tenax Steamship Co Ltd v Reinante Transoceanica Navegacion SA (The Brimnes)* [1973] 1 All ER 769, distinguished.

This decision has been reversed by the House of Lords; see [1978] 1 All ER 652.

2613 ———— **time lost due to transhipment of cargo—recovery by owners of hire and transhipment costs**

The owners of a vessel let it to charterers under a time charter, cl. 8 of which provided that the master was to be under the order and directions of the charterers. Clause 15 provided that in the event of loss of time from any cause preventing the full working of the vessel, the hire would cease for the time thereby lost. The Hague Rules, which were incorporated in the charter, provided by art. 4 that the owners were exempted from liability for the act, neglect or default of the master in the navigation or management of the vessel. The vessel was refused entry to the Panama Canal on the ground that she exceeded the permitted draught. Delay occurred while part of the cargo was transhipped and reloaded at the other end of the canal. The charterers refused to pay hire for that period, contending that the vessel had been off hire and cl. 15 applied. The owners sought to recover the transhipment costs and the hire for the period of delay. The umpire found in favour of the owners but stated his award in the form of a special case. *Held*, if the vessel was fully efficient in herself, that is, fully capable of performing the service immediately required of her, she was not off hire, even though she was prevented from performing that service by some external cause, such as the refusal in this case to permit the vessel to pass through the canal. Accordingly the owners were entitled to be paid hire for the period of delay.

The question then arose whether the charterers could recover back the amount of the hire as damages. The master had failed to use reasonable care to comply with the charterers' orders as to loading under cl. 8, but the owners were entitled to rely on art. 4 to exempt them from the consequences of his failure. Additionally, the charterers had not suffered any damage by reason of the master's error in calculating the draught, because it had not been proved that it was his failure that caused the vessel to be refused entry.

Finally, the costs of transhipment were an ordinary expense incurred in the course of navigation and there was no ground on which the owners could recover them from the charterers.

THE AQUACHARM, ACTIS CO LTD v THE SANKO STEAMSHIP CO LTD [1980] 2 Lloyd's Rep 237 (Queen's Bench Division: LLOYD J). *Court Line Ltd v Dant & Russell Inc* (1939) Ll L Rep 212 applied.

2614 ———— **jurisdiction clause—conflicting clause in bill of lading—construction**

The owners let a vessel to the charterers. Under the charterparty any disputes arising from the agreement were to be referred to arbitration in Oslo. Subsequently the defendant bought the vessel and the charterers sub-chartered the vessel. The sub-charter provided that any dispute under the sub-charter would be referred to arbitration in London. A cargo of frozen meat was taken on in New Zealand to be shipped to Japan. The bill of lading stated that any dispute arising out of the contract for shipment of the meat would be determined by English law. On arrival of the vessel in Japan it was found that the meat was rotten. The plaintiffs, cargo owners and indorsees of the bill of lading, claimed damages from the defendant. The question arose as to whether, even if the case fell within the provisions of RSC Ord. 11, the court should as a matter of discretion refuse leave to serve notice of the writ out of the jurisdiction because none of the parties had any connection with

England. *Held*, the general rule was that where parties contractually agreed to a jurisdiction clause they would be held to their contract unless they could show very strong reasons why they should not be. In the present case it was obvious the parties wished that any disputes arising under the bill of lading would be governed by English law and there was no strong reason for the court to exercise its discretion and refuse leave to serve notice of the writ out of the jurisdiction. Further there was no inconsistency between the jurisdiction clause in the charter and the jurisdiction clause in the bill of lading in that although the charter provided for disputes between the owners and charterers to be referred to arbitration in Oslo this was not inconsistent with the provision in the bill of lading that disputes under a different contract between different parties were to be decided by the English courts.

THE VIKFROST, W & R FLETCHER (NEW ZEALAND) LTD v SIGURD HAAVIK AKSJESELSKAP [1980] 1 Lloyd's Rep 560 (Court of Appeal: MEGAW, LAWTON and BROWNE LJJ).

2615 —— "safe port"—vessel damaged—liability of charterers

A vessel was let to charterers by the owner under a time charter which provided that the vessel was not to enter any ice-bound port or where there was a risk that the vessel would not be able, on account of the ice, safely to enter or leave such a port. It further named safe sailing areas and provided that "loss of time caused by average" due to breach of the charter was to be accounted for by the charterers. The charterers, in accordance with the charter, paid the extra premium for breaching the provisions when the vessel sailed outside the areas named and suffered severe damage due to contact with ice. Repairs were made which resulted in expenditure and delay in respect of which the owners claimed against the charterers. The question arose as to whether on the facts and true construction of the charterparty, the charterers were liable for the repairs, even though they had paid the additional premium for breach of provisions of the charterparty. *Held*, "loss of time caused by average" included time wasted by the shipowner whilst the damaged vessel was being repaired, but if any extra expenditure arose from a breach, by the charterers, of an obligation to order the vessel only to safe ports, the cost of such repairs would fall on the charterers. In the present case the charterers were only permitted to order the vessel outside the safe sailing areas named, if the ports were safe, but this did not mean that the owners had impliedly agreed to take the risk that if the right was exercised the ports would prove to be unsafe, thereby relieving the charterers' liability for repairs to any damage caused. The charterers would therefore be liable for the cost of the repairs.

THE HELEN MILLER, ST VINCENT SHIPPING CO LTD v BOCK, GODEFFROY & CO [1980] 2 Lloyd's Rep 95 (Queen's Bench Division: MUSTILL J).

2616 —— time charter—breach of warranty of seaworthiness—grounds for repudiation

A company (MTC) chartered a vessel from her owners and subsequently sub-chartered it to another company (N). The charters were identical, providing a warranty of seaworthiness of the vessel. The vessel shipped a cargo of iodine and nitrates from Chile to Holland and on arrival it was found that the cargo had been severely damaged by seawater. The vessel went into dock for repairs causing N to lose a contract for the shipment of cargo back to Chile. The vessel was later involved in a collision with another vessel and ordered back to Chile for permanent repairs. The repairs were delayed and a survey of the vessel requested by N found that the vessel required extensive reconditioning. Subsequently N purported to terminate the sub-charter on the ground that it had been repudiated by MTC's conduct and applied to the court for a declaration that they were justified in taking such action. *Held*, although there was a breach of warranty of seaworthiness, where time had been lost to a promisee by events constituting a breach of contract and by events for which the promisor was not legally liable, the total amount of time lost was to be considered when deciding whether the promisee was discharged from further performance under the contract. In the present case, although N's enjoyment of the charter had been curtailed it had not been curtailed to such an extent as to make it possible to say that they had substantially lost the whole benefit of the charter. Further, in deciding whether MTC had repudiated the charter, the court had to consider not only MTC's conduct but also whether N could reasonably infer that the benefit of the contract would be substantially lost. The application would accordingly be dismissed.

THE HERMOSA [1980] 1 Lloyd's Rep 638 (Queen's Bench Division: MUSTILL J). *Federal Commerce & Navigation Co Ltd v Molena Alpha Inc* [1979] 1 All ER 307, 1978 Halsbury's Abridgment para. 2607 applied.

2617 —— —— **repudiation—measure of damages**

Under a time charter the owners let their Italian vessel to the charterers for three years. The owners were required to maintain the vessel. The charterers were traders in crude oil and, as the Italian coastal trade was in general reserved for vessels flying the Italian flag, the market rate for Italian vessels was higher than that for comparable vessels with no access to the Italian coastal trade. The vessel performed voyages both in the Italian coastal areas and elsewhere for fourteen months. The vessel was then found to be in need of substantial repairs. The owners decided not to repair her and the charterers treated the contract as at an end, although they did not take advantage of the offer of another Italian flag vessel, nor did they charter any other vessel. There was a substantial rise in the market after the breach. They sued for breach and repudiation of contract and the owners admitted liability. The arbitrators made an award of damages, based on the difference between the contract price of the vessel and the market price of hiring a similar vessel. They stated a special case as to whether the proper measure of damages was the difference between the contract and market prices or whether it was to be based on profits the charterers would have earned but for the wrongful withdrawal of the ship. *Held*, the normal measure of recovery in cases of premature wrongful repudiation of a time charter by the owners was the difference between the contract rate for the balance of the charter period and the market rate for the chartering of a substitute vessel. A charterer could only recover damages beyond the normal measure if the damages fell within the principle of *Hadley v Baxendale* (1854) 9 Exch 341. Thus, subject to the test of remoteness the charterer could only recover in respect of damages caused by the legal wrong. The charterers' decision not to take advantage of an available market nor to charter a substitute vessel was an independent decision made in their own business interests. There was therefore no reason for departing from the prima facie measure of damages and the arbitrators' award would be upheld.

THE ELENA D'AMICO, KOCH MARINE INC v D'AMICA SOCIETA DI NAVIGAZIONE ARL [1980] 1 Lloyd's Rep 75 (Queen's Bench Division: ROBERT GOFF J).

The procedure for making an award in the form of a special case has ceased to have effect: Arbitration Act 1979, s. 1 (1). There is now a right of appeal to the High Court on any question of law arising out of an award made under an arbitration agreement: s. 1 (2).

2618 **Code of safe working practices**

The Merchant Shipping (Code of Safe Working Practices) Regulations 1980, S.I. 1980 No. 686 (in force on 7th July 1980), require masters and other specified persons in UK merchant ships to make available to any seaman in the ship who requests it, a copy of the Department of Trade publication entitled "Code of Safe Working Practices for Merchant Seamen." The regulations require the master of any ship employing more than fifteen persons to display notices on the ship specifying the places where copies of the Code are kept. The regulations also require the owner to ensure, if possible, that the ship is provided with sufficient copies of the Code. Contravention of these requirements is made an offence.

2619 **Collision—apportionment of liability—negligence**

In a case concerning the collision of two cargo vessels where the navigation hazards of the port were known to the masters of both vessels and where there was clear visibility, it was held that a vessel altering her course resulting in a collision was negligent. However, failure by the vessel to sound her whistle on making the alteration did not constitute a breach of the Rules for Preventing Collisions at Sea.

Where there was clear visibility and favourable sea conditions a failure to make radar observations on the alteration of another vessel's course was not necessarily negligent particularly where it did not contribute to the collision.

THE THOMASEVERETT [1979] 2 Lloyd's Rep 402 (Queen's Bench Division: PARKER J).

This decision has been affirmed by the Court of Appeal; see [1981] 1 Lloyd's Rep 1.

2620   In a case concerning the collision of two vessels in a river in which the plaintiff's vessel was anchored, it was held that the plaintiff was not negligent in anchoring in good weather conditions and at an angle across the river whilst waiting for a pilot tug. The collision was due entirely to the indecision of the defendants in changing course and their general lack of appreciation of the situation.

THE ARYA ROKH [1980] 1 Lloyd's Rep 68 (Queen's Bench Division: SHEEN J).

2621   The plaintiffs' ship and the defendants' ship were navigating in dense fog. The master of each ship was aware of the presence of the other ship; each had course recorders and radar sets which were in use at the material times. The ships, which were on a steady bearing from each other, were travelling too fast in view of the restricted visibility. Minutes before a collision, the defendants' ship altered course slightly to starboard, reducing speed at the same time. A minute before collision the plaintiffs' ship turned to port; at the same time the defendants' ship turned hard to starboard. As soon as the plaintiffs' ship came into sight, the defendants' ship altered course to port, hitting the plaintiffs' ship. The plaintiffs claimed damages. *Held*, (i) neither ship was travelling at a safe speed in the fog so that proper and effective action could be taken to avoid a collision in accordance with the Collision Regulations, r. 6; (ii) the slight alteration of course by the defendants' ship was not large enough to be readily apparent on the plaintiffs' radar and the reduction of speed at the same time nullified any effect of the course alteration. Furthermore, as each ship was on a steady bearing from the other before the alteration, it was not sufficient to ensure that the ships passed at a safe distance; (iii) the Collision Regulations, r. 19 required a ship in the position of the plaintiffs' ship to avoid so far as possible an alteration to port. Therefore, the action taken by the plaintiffs' ship immediately before the collision was directly contrary to r. 19. In the circumstances, liability would be apportioned 55 per cent to the plaintiffs and 45 per cent to the defendants.

THE SANSHIN VICTORY [1980] 2 Lloyd's Rep 359 (Queen's Bench Division: SHEEN J).

2622   —— **collision in Swedish territorial waters—natural forum**

See *The Wellamo*, para. 437.

2623   **Continental shelf—protection of installations**

Orders have been made specifying a safety zone within a radius of 500 metres of the following offshore installations.

	Relevant Statutory Instruments (1980)	Revoking Statutory Instruments (1980)
9/13 Beryl "B" Template	1607	
21/1 Buchan A	1418	
Dixilyn-Field 97	1797	
Fulmar A	943	
Fulmar AD	758	
Norjarl	962	1426
Norjarl	1799	
Notroll	666	946
Notroll	1374	1606
Pentagone 84	961	1366
Pentagone 84	1417	
Pentagone 84	1798	
Venture II	960	1393

2624   Fishing vessels

See FISHERIES.

2625   Insurance

See INSURANCE (marine).

2626   Limitation of liability—owner's actual fault or privity

Canada
A collision at sea occurred due to the negligence of two inexperienced members of
the crew who had been left in charge of the navigation of the vessel. The owner of
the vessel claimed that his liability should be limited by virtue of the Canada
Shipping Act 1970, s. 647 (2), because the event occurred without his "actual fault
or privity". *Held*, by allowing the vessel to be left in such inexperienced hands and
thus creating a potentially dangerous situation the owner could not be said to have
been "without actual fault or privity" and he would not be entitled to claim the
benefit of the section.

KAUFMAN v VACCHER (1979) 106 DLR (3d) 658 (Federal Court of Appeal).

For the corresponding English legislation see the Merchant Shipping (Liability of
Shipowners and Others) Act 1958, s. 3 (2).

2627   Maritime lien—lien for repairs to ship—lien given by foreign law and recognised as maritime lien by English law—whether lien had priority over mortgage

Singapore
The High Court of Singapore held that in the distribution of the proceeds of sale of
a ship, a New York company of ship repairers, who were entitled under United
States law to a maritime lien, were entitled to take priority over the mortgagees of
the ship. On appeal to the Privy Council, *held*, LORD SALMON and LORD SCARMAN
dissenting, it was well-established that the question whether a particular class of
claim gave rise to a maritime lien was a matter to be determined by the law of the
lex fori. According to Singapore admiralty law, had the repairs been carried out in
Singapore the repairers would not have been entitled to a maritime lien for their
price. The mortagees therefore took priority and the appeal would be allowed.

BANKERS TRUST INTERNATIONAL LTD v TODD SHIPYARD CORPN, THE HALCYON
ISLE [1980] 3 All ER 197 (Privy Council: LORD DIPLOCK, LORD SALMON, LORD
ELWYN-JONES, LORD SCARMAN and LORD LANE).

2628   Merchant shipping—cargo ship—construction and survey

The Merchant Shipping (Cargo Ship Construction and Survey) Regulations 1980,
S.I. 1980 No. 537 (in force on 25th May 1980), revoke the Merchant Shipping
(Cargo Ship Construction and Survey) Rules 1965 and the Merchant Shipping
(Cargo Ship Construction and Survey) (Tankers and Combination Carriers) Rules
1975, 1975 Halsbury's Abridgment para. 3097, to the extent that they apply to UK
ships, and to ships registered in a country to which a Safety of Life at Sea Convention
applies while they are within the UK or its territorial waters. The 1965 Rules, as
amended, and the 1975 Rules will continue to apply to ships of non-Convention
countries while they are within UK ports. The 1980 Regulations re-enact the
provisions of those rules with modifications necessary to give effect to the
International Convention for the Safety of Life at Sea 1974 (Cmnd. 7874), and
the Protocol of 1978 relating to the International Convention for the Safety of Life
at Sea 1974 (Cmnd. 7346).

2629   —— dangerous goods

The Merchant Shipping (Dangerous Goods) (Amendment) Rules 1980, S.I. 1980
No. 789 (in force on 1st July 1980), amend the Merchant Shipping (Dangerous
Goods) Rules 1978, 1978 Halsbury's Abridgment para. 2619. The Blue Book and

the IMDG Code, referred to in the Rules, have now been further amended and the 1980 Rules make the necessary amendments (r. 1). Further provision is made as to the marking of dangerous goods carried aboard ships. The marking must remain identifiable on packages or receptacles surviving at least three months in the sea (r. 3). Rule 8 relates, inter alia, to the carriage of explosives and distress signals aboard ships carrying more than twelve passengers. The total weight of explosives is increased from 9 to 10 kilogrammes and the total weight of distress signals is reduced from 1016 to 1000 kilogrammes. These amendments give effect to the provisions of the International Convention for the Safety of Life at Sea 1974 (Cmnd. 7874).

2630   The Merchant Shipping (Dangerous Goods) (Amendment No. 2) Rules 1980, S.I. 1980 No. 1502 (in force on 10th November 1980), amend the Merchant Shipping (Dangerous Goods) Rules 1978, 1978 Halsbury's Abridgment para. 2619 in consequence of amendments made to the Blue Book referred to in the 1978 Rules.

2631   —— **deck officers—certification**

The Merchant Shipping (Certification of Deck Officers) Regulations 1980, S.I. 1980 No. 2026 (in force on 1st September 1981), consolidate with amendments the Merchant Shipping (Certification of Deck Officers) Regulations 1977, as amended, 1977 Halsbury's Abridgment para. 2603. The 1977 Regulations are revoked.

2632   —— **fees**

The Merchant Shipping (Fees) Regulations 1980, S.I. 1980 No. 270 (in force on 1st April 1980), revoke the Merchant Shipping (Fees) Regulations 1979, 1979 Halsbury's Abridgment para. 2555. The regulations prescribe increased fees for marine surveys and other services except for examinations for certificates of competency, certificates of service and copies of documents. Fees are prescribed for the examination for certificates of competency as a deck officer or as a marine engineer officer.

2633   The Merchant Shipping (Fees) (Amendment) Regulations 1980, S.I. 1980 No. 572 (in force on 25th May 1980), provide that fees to be paid in respect of any survey required by the Merchant Shipping (Cargo Ship Construction and Survey) Regulations 1980, para. 2628 are to be those prescribed by the Merchant Shipping (Fees) Regulations 1980, para. 2632, as amended by these regulations. The 1980 Fees Regulations are amended to make the fees which they prescribe payable in respect of such surveys, and to take account of regulations relating to radio and radar made under the Merchant Shipping Act 1979, ss. 21, 22 implementing the International Convention for the Safety of Life at Sea 1974 (Cmnd. 7874).

2634   The Merchant Shipping (Fees) (Amendment No. 2) Regulations 1980, S.I. 1980 No. 1143 (in force on 1st September 1980), further amend the Merchant Shipping (Fees) Regulations 1980, para. 2632 by prescribing increased fees in respect of examinations for certificates of competency for seafarers and for a certificate of competency as A.B.

2635   —— **fire appliances**

The Merchant Shipping (Fire Appliances) (Amendment) Rules 1980, S.I. 1980 No. 541 (in force on 25th May 1980), further amend the Merchant Shipping (Fire Appliances) Rules 1965 and apply to existing British ships (other than sea-going UK registered fishing vessels and pleasure craft less than 45 feet) and to other existing ships while they are within a port in the UK. Additional requirements are imposed on specified classes of existing ships which give effect to the provisions of the International Convention for the Safety of Life at Sea 1974 (Cmnd. 7874) and of the Protocol of 1978, Chap. II–2 relating to the 1974 Convention (Cmnd. 7346).

For the provisions with which new ships are required to comply, see the Merchant Shipping (Fire Appliances) Regulations 1980, para. 2636.

2636 The Merchant Shipping (Fire Appliances) Regulations 1980, S.I. 1980 No. 544 (in force on 25th May 1980), introduce requirements in respect of new UK ships and other new ships which are registered in a country to which the Safety of Life at Sea Convention 1974 applies while they are within the UK or its territorial waters. The requirements give effect to the 1974 Convention (Cmnd. 7874) and to the Protocol of 1978 relating to the 1974 Convention (Cmnd. 7346). The Regulations include the general requirements of the Merchant Shipping (Fire Appliances) Rules 1965, and make certain additional requirements relating to the provision of water for fire fighting, additional fire appliances, particular fire fighting equipment, deck foam systems and fire protection systems. Existing ships are required to comply with the requirements set out in the Merchant Shipping (Fire Appliances) (Amendment) Rules 1980, para. 2635.

2637 The Merchant Shipping (Fire Appliances—Application to Other Ships) Rules 1980, S.I. 1980 No. 687 (in force on 1st July 1980), require all tankers (other than UK tankers or specified chemical tankers) which operate a cargo tank cleaning procedure using crude oil washing to be provided with a specified type of fixed inert gas system and fixed tank washing machines when they are within a UK port. All other new tankers of 20,000 tonnes deadweight or over which are constructed or adapted to carry crude oil and petroleum products are also required to be provided with such a fixed inert gas system. Certain other existing tankers which are constructed or adapted to carry such cargoes are required to be provided with such a system from specified later dates.

2638 —— **foreign deserters**

The Merchant Shipping (Foreign Deserters) (Revocation) Order 1980, S.I. 1980 No. 699 (in force on 19th June 1980), revokes specified orders to the extent to which they provided for the apprehension and return their ship of deserters from merchant ships of the Netherlands, Greece, the Federal Republic of Germany and Denmark at ports in the Channel Islands, the Isle of Man or any colony. The provisions of the Merchant Shipping Act 1970, s. 89, which supersede the specified orders as far as they relate to the UK, cease to apply to Denmark, the Federal Republic of Germany, Greece and the Netherlands by virtue of the Merchant Shipping (Foreign Deserters) (Disapplication) Order 1980, para. 2640.

2639 The Merchant Shipping (Foreign Deserters) (Revocation) (Antigua) Order 1980, S.I. 1980 No. 700 (in force on 19th June 1980), provides for the revocation, in so far as they form part of the law of Antigua, of specified orders which provided for the apprehension and return to their ship of deserters from merchant ships of Denmark, Estonia, the Federal Republic of Germany, Greece, Japan, Latvia, the Netherlands and Romania.

2640 The Merchant Shipping (Foreign Deserters) (Disapplication) Order 1980, S.I. 1980 No. 716 (in force on 19th June 1980), provides that the Merchant Shipping Act 1970, s. 89, which prescribes the procedure for dealing in the UK with deserters from ships of certain foreign countries, is to cease to apply to Denmark, the Federal Republic of Germany, Greece and the Netherlands.

2641 —— **grain**

The Merchant Shipping (Grain) Regulations 1980, S.I. 1980 No. 536 (in force on 25th May 1980), repeal the Merchant Shipping (Safety Convention) Act 1949, s. 24 and the Merchant Shipping (Safety Convention) Act 1977, s. 1 (5) (which relate to the carriage of grain). They also revoke the Merchant Shipping (Grain) Rules 1965 to the extent that they apply to UK ships, and to ships registered in a country to which a Safety of Life at Sea Convention applies while they are within the UK or its territorial waters. The statutory provisions and the 1965 Rules continue to apply to ships of non-Convention countries whilst they are within UK ports. The 1980 Regulations apply to sea-going UK ships and to other Safety Convention ships while they are within the UK or its territorial waters when loaded with grain in bulk, and give effect to the International Convention for the Safety of Life at Sea 1974 (Cmnd. 7874), Chapter VI.

Ships to which the regulations apply must, when loaded in UK ports, comply with the loading arrangements set out in the Schedule. The Regulations require all new ships to carry a document of authorisation which states that the ship is capable of complying with the 1974 Convention requirements and incorporates certain grain loading information. Existing ships may produce specified documents which will constitute a document of authorisation. Ships which do not have such a document of authorisation must satisfy the Secretary of State as to the intended method of loading. The Secretary of State may grant exemptions from the loading requirements and approve equivalent fittings and provisions.

2642   —— hulls and watertight bulkheads

The Merchant Shipping (Closing of Openings in Hulls and in Watertight Bulkheads) Regulations 1980, S.I. 1980 No. 540 (in force on 25th May 1980), supersede the Merchant Shipping (Closing of Openings in Hulls and in Watertight Bulkheads) Rules 1965. They apply to UK passenger ships and include such requirements as appear to the Secretary of State to implement the provisions of the International Convention for the Safety of Life at Sea 1974 (Cmnd. 7874) for the closing of watertight doors and other contrivances, for their inspection, for practice drills and for relevant entries in the official log-book.

2643   —— life-saving appliances

The Merchant Shipping (Life-Saving Appliances) Regulations 1980, S.I. 1980 No. 538 (in force on 25th May 1980), revoke the Merchant Shipping (Life-Saving Appliances) Rules 1965 to the extent that they apply to UK ships and to other ships, registered in a country to which a Safety of Life at Sea Convention applies while they are within the UK or its territorial waters. The 1965 Rules will continue to apply to ships of non-Convention countries while they are within UK ports. The regulations re-enact the provisions of the 1965 Rules with additional requirements in respect of specified classes of ships. The additional requirements give effect to the Safety of Life at Sea Convention (Cmnd. 7874).

2644   —— light dues

The Merchant Shipping (Light Dues) Regulations 1980, S.I. 1980 No. 355 (in force on 1st April 1980), replace the Merchant Shipping (Mercantile Marine Fund) Act 1898, Sch. 2, as amended, relating to the charging of light dues. They are consequent on the coming into operation of the Merchant Shipping Act 1979, s. 36 (2), which substituted for the former provisions of s. 5 (2) of the 1898 Act (under which light dues were amended by Order in Council) a power of the Secretary of State to make regulations with respect to the amount and levying of such dues. All the provisions of Sch. 2, as amended, are re-enacted, but the scale of payments is increased by approximately 23 per cent.

2645   —— load line

The Merchant Shipping (Load Line) (Amendment) Rules 1980, S.I. 1980 No. 641 (in force on 9th June 1980), amend the Merchant Shipping Load Line Rules 1968, r. 30 (5), as substituted by the Merchant Shipping (Load Line) (Amendment) Rules 1975, 1975 Halsbury's Abridgment para. 3066, r. 2. The bodies who may approve stability information for the purpose of r. 30 in the case of certain ships over 100 metres in length are extended to include any assigning authority (as defined in the 1968 Rules, r. 2 (1)) which has assigned freeboards to the ship, as well as the Secretary of State. In all other cases, only the Secretary of State may approve this information. The Merchant Shipping (Load Line) (Amendment) Rules 1975, 1975 Halsbury's Abridgment para. 3066 are revoked.

2646   —— log books

The Merchant Shipping (Official Log Books) (Amendment) Regulations 1980, S.I. 1980 No. 533 (in force on 25th May 1980), further amend the Merchant Shipping (Official Log Books) Regulations 1972 by amending the entries required to be made in the official log book of ships registered in the UK in respect of musters and requiring entries to be made in respect of the testing and inspection of pilot hoists, in accordance with the provisions of the International Convention for the Safety of Life at Sea 1974 (Cmnd. 7874).

2647   —— marine engineer officers—certification

The Merchant Shipping (Certification of Marine Engineer Officers) Regulations 1980, S.I. 1980 No. 2025 (in force on 1st September 1981), consolidate with amendments the Merchant Shipping (Certification of Marine Engineer Officers) Regulations 1977, as amended, 1977 Halsbury's Abridgment para. 2611. The 1977 Regulations are revoked.

2648   —— medical scales

The Merchant Shipping (Medical Scales) (Merchant Ships and Other Vessels) (Amendment) Regulations 1980, S.I. 1980 No. 407 (in force on 21st April 1980), amend the Merchant Shipping (Medical Scales) Regulations 1974, 1974 Halsbury's Abridgment para. 3063 and the Merchant Shipping (Medical Scales) (Fishing Vessels) Regulations 1974, 1974 Halsbury's Abridgment para. 3064. The amended regulations require the carriage of certain vaccines and anti-toxin in those ships registered in the UK which are required to carry a qualified doctor. Certain other drugs have to be carried in other merchant ships and fishing vessels registered in the UK.

2649   —— musters

The Merchant Shipping (Musters) Regulations 1980, S.I. 1980 No. 542 (in force on 25th May 1980), revoke the Merchant Shipping (Musters) Rules 1965 to the extent that they apply to UK ships, and to ships registered in a country to which a Safety of Life at Sea Convention applies while they are within the UK or its territorial waters. The 1965 Rules continue to apply to ships of non-Convention countries while they are within UK ports. The regulations re-enact the provisions of the 1965 Rules with the minor modifications necessary to give effect to the International Convention for the Safety of Life at Sea 1974 (Cmnd. 7874). The regulations require the master of every ship to which the Regulations apply to prepare and maintain a muster list showing the emergency station of each crew member and the duties assigned to him in the event of an emergency and the signals calling crew to emergency stations. They also provide for the mustering and training of crew members in their emergency duties. The master is required to appoint emergency stations for passengers and to specify the emergency signal for passengers.

2650   —— navigational equipment

The Merchant Shipping (Navigational Equipment) Regulations 1980, S.I. 1980 No. 530 (in force on 25th May 1980), revoke the Merchant Shipping (Direction-Finders) Rules 1965 and the Merchant Shipping (Radar) Rules 1976, 1976 Halsbury's Abridgment para. 2395, to the extent that they apply to UK ships, and to ships registered in a country to which a Safety of Life at Sea Convention applies while they are within the UK or its territorial waters. The 1965 Rules will continue to apply to ships of non-Convention countries while they are within UK ports. The regulations re-enact the provisions of the 1965 and 1976 Rules. They require specified classes of ships of 500 tons or over to be provided, additionally, with a direction-finder, an echo sounder and gyro compass installation. The regulations implement the provisions of the International Convention for the Safety of Life at Sea 1974 (Cmnd. 7874), relating to the carriage of such navigational equipment.

2651 —— **navigational warnings**

The Merchant Shipping (Navigational Warnings) Regulations 1980, S.I. 1980 No. 534 (in force on 25th May 1980), revoke and re-enact the provisions of the Merchant Shipping (Navigational Warnings) Rules 1965. The regulations prescribe the nature of the information to be sent by the masters of UK ships on meeting with dangerous ice, a dangerous derelict or any other direct danger to navigation or a tropical storm or encountering sub-freezing air temperatures associated with gale force winds causing severe ice accretion on the superstructure of ships or winds of force ten or above on the Beaufort Scale for which no storm warning has been received. The authorities on shore to which the information is to be sent in addition to being sent to ships in the vicinity are also prescribed. The regulations include such requirements as appear to the Secretary of State to implement the provisions of the International Convention for the Safety of Life at Sea 1974 (Cmnd. 7874) relating to danger messages.

2652 —— **passenger ships—construction**

The Merchant Shipping (Passenger Ship Construction) Regulations 1980, S.I. 1980 No. 535 (in force on 25th May 1980), revoke the Merchant Shipping (Passenger Ship Construction) Rules 1965 to the extent that they apply to UK passenger ships and other sea-going passenger ships registered in a country to which a Safety of Life at Sea Convention applies while they are within the UK or its territorial waters. The 1965 Rules are re-enacted with modifications necessary to give effect to the International Convention for the Safety of Life at Sea 1974 (Cmnd. 7874). The modifications relate to stability information (regs. 9, 10, 11, Sch. 2), openings in the shell plating, and subdivision load line markings (regs. 19, 20, 23), fire protection in certain new passengers ships (Pt. V (A), and watertight subdivision bulkhead plating thicknesses and stiffener scantlings (Sch. 4, Pt. IV).

2653 —— **pilot ladders and hoists**

The Merchant Shipping (Pilot Ladders and Hoists) Regulations 1980, S.I. 1980 No. 543 (in force on 25th May 1980), revoke the Merchant Shipping (Pilot Ladders) Rules 1965, as amended, to the extent that they apply to UK ships, and to ships registered in a country to which a Safety of Life at Sea Convention applies while they are within the UK or its territorial waters. The 1965 Rules will continue to apply to ships of non-Convention countries while they are within UK ports. The regulations re-enact the provisions of those rules in respect of pilot ladders with the minor modifications necessary to give effect to the International Convention for the Safety of Life at Sea 1974 (Cmnd. 7874). The regulations do not require pilot hoists to be provided in ships but introduce requirements for them if they are provided.

The regulations require the owner of a ship to which the regulations apply to provide a pilot ladder which conforms to the specified requirements, and require the master of every such ship to ensure that each pilot ladder is efficient, kept in good condition and properly positioned and secured and, where necessary, that an accommodation ladder is available: reg. 6. Where a mechanical hoist is provided, the owner must ensure that it is of a type approved by the Secretary of State and conforms to the specified construction requirements. The master also has to ensure that there is a copy of the maintenance manual on board and the officer responsible for the maintenance of the hoist is required to maintain a record of the maintenance and repairs: reg. 7.

2654 —— **pilotage—Milford Haven**

The Milford Haven Pilotage Order 1980, S.I. 1980 No. 1304 (in force on 1st November 1980), supersedes the Milford Pilotage Order 1921, as amended, and establishes the new Pilotage Authority in place of Trinity House for the Milford Haven Pilotage District.

2655   —— —— Swansea

The Swansea Pilotage (Amendment) Order 1980, S.I. 1980 No. 903 (in force on 1st September 1980), amends the Swansea Pilotage Order 1921 and makes pilotage compulsory within the part of the Pilotage District which includes the approaches and entrance to the Port of Swansea.

2656   —— pilotage charges

The Pilotage Charges Regulations 1980, S.I. 1980 No. 1234 (in force on 3rd September 1980), prescribe the form in which lists of pilotage charges are to be made, the manner in which they are to be published, the scale of increase if the charges are not paid when they fall due, and the manner in which the Pilotage Commission may cancel or alter a list of charges.

2657   —— Pilotage Commission—provision of funds

The Pilotage Commission Provision of Funds Scheme 1980 (Confirmation) Order 1980, S.I. 1980 No. 1243 (in force on 1st October 1980), contained textual errors and has been revoked; see para. 2658.

2658   The Pilotage Commission Provision of Funds Scheme 1980 (Confirmation) (Amendment) Order 1980, S.I. 1980 No. 1350 (in force on 1st October 1980), confirms a scheme made and submitted to the Secretary of State under the Merchant Shipping Act 1979, s. 2, for imposing on pilotage authorities charges to provide funds for the Commission. The Scheme is set out in the Schedule. The Pilotage Commission Provision of Funds Scheme 1980 (Confirmation) Order 1980, para. 2657, is revoked.

2659   —— pilotage orders—applications

The Pilotage Orders (Applications) Regulations 1980, S.I. 1980 No. 1163 (in force on 1st September 1980), revoke and substantially re-enact, under the powers in the Merchant Shipping Act 1979, 1979 Halsbury's Abridgment para. 2567, s. 7, the Pilotage Orders (Applications) Rules 1964. Changes include (i) the notice of application for a Pilotage Order is not to be published until after the Secretary of State has approved publication; (ii) any person objecting to a notice of application must appear to the Secretary of State to have a substantial interest in the pilotage services in the area to which the application relates; (iii) a copy of the draft order is required to be sent to the bodies named, and the British Ports Association and the Pilotage Commission have been added to such bodies; (iv) the fees payable by an applicant for, and an objector to, a Pilotage Order, are increased.

2660   —— pilots—employment

The Employment of Pilots Regulations 1980, S.I. 1980 No. 1244 (in force on 15th September 1980), make provision for the passing and revocation of resolutions for the purposes of the Merchant Shipping Act 1979, s. 11, and for the recording of resolutions and of their revocation. Section 11 (2) provides that if a majority of licensed pilots for the district of a Pilotage Authority who are not employed by the Authority resolves that the Authority shall not be entitled to exercise the power to employ licensed pilots as pilots or assistants, the Authority is not entitled to exercise that power until the resolution is revoked by such a majority.

2661   —— radio installations

The Merchant Shipping (Radio Installations) Regulations 1980, S.I. 1980 No. 529 (in force on 25th May 1980), revoke and re-enact the provisions of the Merchant Shipping (Radio) Rules 1965. The regulations apply to sea-going UK ships which are radiotelegraph and radiotelephone ships, and to other such sea-going ships registered in a country to which a Safety of Life at Sea Convention applies while they are within the UK or its territorial waters. Subject to specified exceptions as to the time when some installations shall be provided, such ships which are cargo ships of 300 tons or more but less than 1600 tons must be provided with a radiotelephone or a radiotelegraph installation; cargo ships of 1600 tons or more and passenger ships must be provided with a radiotelegraph installation; and cargo ships of 300 tons or more and passenger ships must be provided with a VHF radiotelephone installation. The regulations implement the provisions of the International Convention for the Safety of Life at Sea 1974 (Cmnd. 7874) relating to the carriage of such installations.

2662   —— safety convention—certificates

The Merchant Shipping (Accepted Safety Convention Certificates) Regulations 1980, S.I. 1980 No. 532 (in force on 25th May 1980), provide for the acceptance for the purposes of the Merchant Shipping (Safety Convention) Act 1949, the Merchant Shipping Act 1964 and the Merchant Shipping (Safety Convention) Act 1977 of Convention Certificates issued under the International Convention for the Safety of Life at Sea 1974 (Cmnd. 7874) in respect of ships not registered in the UK.

2663   —— —— legislation—commencement

See para. 2676.

2664   —— —— —— modification

The Merchant Shipping (Modification of Merchant Shipping (Safety Convention) Act 1949 and Merchant Shipping Act 1964) Regulations 1980, S.I. 1980 No. 539 (in force on 25th May 1980), modify the references in the Merchant Shipping (Safety Convention) Act 1949 to the "life-saving appliances rules", the "radio rules" and the "rules for direction-finders." Those expressions will now mean, in relation to UK ships, or ships of countries party to the Safety of Life at Sea Convention 1974 whilst in the UK, the equivalent regulations made under the Merchant Shipping Act 1979, s. 21 in cases when those regulations apply. For other ships the expressions will continue to mean the rules for life-saving appliances made under the Merchant Shipping Act 1894, s. 427, or the radio rules or rules for direction-finders made under ss. 3, 5 respectively of the 1949 Act. The regulations also modify the references in the Merchant Shipping Act 1964 to "cargo ship construction and survey rules" to a similar extent.

2665   —— —— transitional provisions

The Merchant Shipping (Safety Convention) (Transitional Provisions) Regulations 1980, S.I. 1980 No. 531 (in force on 25th May 1980), provide that a country to which the International Convention for the Safety of Life at Sea 1960 applies is to be treated up to and including the 25th May 1981 for the purposes of the Merchant Shipping Act 1964 and the Merchant Shipping (Safety Convention) Act 1977, as if it were a country to which the International Convention for the Safety of Life at Sea 1974 applies. The regulations also provide for the continued acceptance for a limited time of certain certificates issued under the 1960 Convention in respect of ships not registered in the UK as if they had been issued under the 1974 Convention.

2666   —— South Australia

The Merchant Shipping (Confirmation of Legislation) (South Australia) Order 1980, S.I. 1980 No. 698 (in force on 19th June 1980), made under the Merchant Shipping Act 1894, s. 735, confirms an Act passed by the Legislature of South Australia to amend certain provisions of the South Australia Boating Act 1974–1978.

2667   —— sterling equivalents

The Merchant Shipping (Sterling Equivalents) (Various Enactments) Order 1980, S.I. 1980 No. 280 (in force on 21st March 1980), specifies the sterling amounts which are to be taken as equivalent to the amounts expressed in gold francs in the following enactments: Merchant Shipping (Liability of Shipowners and Others) Act 1958; Carriage of Goods by Sea Act 1971; Merchant Shipping (Oil Pollution) Act 1971; Merchant Shipping Act 1974, 1974 Halsbury's Abridgment para. 3067; Unfair Contract Terms Act 1977, 1977 Halsbury's Abridgment para. 540.

This order has been revoked; see para. 2668.

2668   The Merchant Shipping (Sterling Equivalents) (Various Enactments) (No. 2) Order 1980, S.I. 1980 No. 1872 (in force on 1st January 1981), specifies the sterling amounts to be taken as equivalent to the amounts expressed in gold francs in the following enactments: the Merchant Shipping (Liability of Shipowners and Others) Act 1958, the Carriage of Goods by Sea Act 1971, the Merchant Shipping (Oil Pollution) Act 1971, the Merchant Shipping Act 1974, the Unfair Contract Terms Act 1977 and the Merchant Shipping Act 1979. The Merchant Shipping (Sterling Equivalents) (Various Enactments) Order 1980, para. 2667 is revoked.

2669   —— tonnage

The Merchant Shipping (Tonnage) (Amendment) Regulations 1980, S.I. 1980 No. 282 (in force on 25th March 1980), in addition to some minor drafting amendments, amend the Merchant Shipping (Tonnage) Regulations 1967, reg. 11 (i) which relates to ships in which most deck spaces between the second and uppermost deck are excluded from the calculation of the gross tonnage. This exclusion is conditional on the tonnage mark and load lines being positioned below the lowest part of the second deck, thus limiting the loaded draught of the ship. In some ships, the second deck is stepped and the regulations empower the Secretary of State, at the request of the shipowner, to assign an equivalent deck line, intermediate between the higher and lower parts of the step, by way of substitution for the line through the lowest part of the second deck. The tonnage mark and load lines are then positioned in relation to this equivalent deck line, thus allowing a deeper loaded draught, while still excluding the spaces between the second and uppermost deck from being included in the calculation of the gross tonnage.

2670   The Merchant Shipping (Tonnage) (Amendment) Regulations 1980, S.I. 1980 No. 642 (in force on 9th June 1980), amend the Merchant Shipping (Tonnage) (Amendment) Regulations 1975, 1975 Halsbury's Abridgment para. 3102. The 1975 Regulations provided for the measurement and survey of certain ships for the purpose of ascertaining their tonnage, pursuant to the Merchant Shipping Act 1965, s. 1 (1) and the Merchant Shipping (Tonnage) Regulations 1967, to be undertaken by Lloyd's Register of Shipping, as well as by the Department of Trade. The 1980 Regulations enable the measurement and survey of any ship for this purpose to be undertaken by Lloyd's Register of Shipping and by four other authorised Classification Societies: the British Committee of Bureau Veritas; Det norske Veritas and Germanischer Lloyd, and the British Technical Committee of the American Bureau of Shipping.

These regulations have been revoked; see para. 2671.

2671   The Merchant Shipping (Tonnage) (Amendment No. 2) Regulations 1980, S.I. 1980 No. 744 (in force on 8th June 1980), amend the Merchant Shipping (Tonnage) (Amendment) Regulations 1975, 1975 Halsbury's Abridgment para. 3102, which provide for the measurement and survey of certain ships for the purpose of ascertaining their tonnage, pursuant to the Merchant Shipping Act 1965, s. 1 (1) and the Merchant Shipping (Tonnage) Regulations 1967, to be undertaken by Lloyd's Register of Shipping, as well as by the Department of Trade. Such measurements and surveys may now also be undertaken by four other authorised Classification Societies: British Committees of Bureau Veritas, Det norske Veritas and Germanischer Lloyd, and the British Technical Committee of the American Bureau of Shipping. The Merchant Shipping (Tonnage) (Amendment) Regulations 1980, para. 2670 are revoked.

2672   —— **United Kingdom fishing vessels—manning**

The Merchant Shipping (United Kingdom Fishing Vessels: Manning) Regulations 1980, S.I. 1980 No. 1227 (in force on 15th September 1980), make provision for the manning of United Kingdom fishing vessels. They supersede the Merchant Shipping Act 1894, s. 413, and the Merchant Shipping (Fishing Boats) Order 1948, as amended, which, however, continue to apply to fishing vessels which are not United Kingdom fishing vessels when sailing from any port in the United Kingdom. The main change in the manning provisions is in the description of the fishing vessels to which specific sections of the 1894 Act apply; the vessels are now described by reference to their length in metres, instead of to their gross tonnage. The 1894 Act, ss. 414, 416, relating to the granting of certificates of competency and registers of certificated skippers and second hands, are applied in relation to all United Kingdom fishing vessels which are subject to the manning requirements of these regulations. Exemptions may be granted by the Secretary of State. A maximum penalty of £1,000 on summary conviction is prescribed for offences under these regulations.

2673   **Merchant Shipping Act 1979—commencement**

The Merchant Shipping Act 1979 (Commencement No. 3) Order 1980, S.I. 1980 No. 354, brought into force on 1st April 1980 s. 36 (2) of the Act, which enables the Secretary of State to make regulations with respect to the amounts and levying of light dues. It also brings into effect certain consequential repeals in the Merchant Shipping (Mercantile Marine Fund) Act 1898.

2674   The Merchant Shipping Act 1979 (Commencement No. 4) Order 1980, S.I. 1980 No. 923, brought into force the following provisions of the Act on 4th July 1980: ss. 8 (1), (2), (4) and (6) (for certain purposes), 10, 13 (1) (for certain purposes), 46, 50 (3) and (4) (for certain purposes), Schs. 2 (part) and 7 (part). The order also brought into force the following provisions on 1st September 1980: ss. 7, 9, 11, 50 (4) (for certain purposes), Sch. 7 (part).

2675   —— **extension**

Certain provisions of the Merchant Shipping Act 1979, with necessary modifications, are extended to the following areas:

	Relevant Statutory Instruments (1980)
Belize	1509
Bermuda	1510
British Virgin Islands	1511
Cayman Islands	1512
Falkland Islands	1513
Guernsey	570
Hong Kong	1514
Isle of Man	1526
Jersey	569
Montserrat	1515
Pitcairn	1516
Saint Helena	1517
Sovereign Base Areas of Akrotiri and Dhekelia	1518
Turks and Caicos Islands	1519

2676   Merchant Shipping (Safety Convention) Act 1977—commencement

The Merchant Shipping (Safety Convention) Act 1977 (Commencement) Order 1980, S.I. 1980 No. 528 brought the Act into force on 25th May 1980.

2677   Offence committed by British subject on foreign ship—jurisdiction

See *R v Kelly*, para. 602.

2678   Oil pollution—Bermuda

The Prevention of Oil Pollution Act 1971 (Bermuda) Order 1980, S.I. 1980 No. 1520 (in force on 1st December 1980), extends to Bermuda those provisions of the Prevention of Oil Pollution Act 1971 that enable effect to be given to the International Convention for the Prevention of Pollution of the Sea by Oil 1954, as amended and enable measures to be taken for the prevention, mitigation or elimination of grave and imminent danger to the coast line or related interests from pollution or threat of pollution of the sea by oil, following upon a maritime casualty.

2679   ——— enforcement of convention

The Prevention of Oil Pollution (Enforcement of Convention) (Bermuda) Order 1980, S.I. 1980 No. 1521 (in force on 1st December 1980), empowers surveyors of ships to go on board any ship to which the International Convention for the Prevention of Pollution of the Sea by Oil 1954 applies while the ship is within a harbour in Bermuda, and to require production of any oil record book required to be kept in accordance with the Convention.

2680   ——— shipping casualties

The Prevention of Oil Pollution (Shipping Casualties) (Bermuda) Order 1980, S.I. 1980 No. 1522 (in force on 1st December 1980) applies the Prevention of Oil Pollution Act 1971 ss. 12 to 15, as extended to Bermuda, to ships not registered in Bermuda and which are outside the territorial waters of Bermuda, enabling action to be taken to prevent or reduce oil pollution which threatens Bermuda on a large scale as a result of a shipping casualty, and enabling persons unreasonably suffering loss or damage as a result of such action to recover compensation.

2681   —— convention countries

The Prevention of Oil Pollution (Convention Countries) (Additional Countries) Order 1980, S.I. 1980 No. 717 (in force on 19th June 1980), declares that the State of Qatar and Papua New Guinea have accepted the International Convention for the Prevention of Pollution of the Sea by Oil 1954.

2682   —— International Oil Pollution Compensation Fund—parties to Convention

The Merchant Shipping Act 1974, Pt. I, Sch. 1 gives effect in the UK to the International Convention on the Establishment of an International Fund for Compensation for Oil Pollution Damage (Cmnd. 7383). The International Oil Pollution Compensation Fund (Parties to Convention) Order 1980, S.I. 1980 No. 867 (in force on 1st August 1980), declares the states which are parties to the Convention and the countries in respect of which they are parties.

2683   Pollution—pollution by substances other than oil

The Merchant Shipping (Prevention of Pollution) (Intervention) Order 1980, S.I. 1980 No. 1093 (in force on 26th August 1980), gives effect to the Protocol relating to Intervention on the High Seas in Cases of Marine Pollution by Substances other than Oil 1973 (Cmnd. 6038). The Order applies the Prevention of Oil Pollution Act 1971, ss. 12–16, as modified by the Oil in Navigable Waters (Shipping

Casualties) Order 1971, with the modifications necessary to make them applicable in relation to pollution by substances other than oil in like manner as they apply to oil pollution. The 1971 Order is revoked.

2684   **Protection of Trading Interests Act 1980**

See para. 1346.

2685   **Protection of wrecks—restricted areas**

The Protection of Wrecks (Designation No. 1) Order 1980, S.I. 1980 No. 645 (in force on 6th June 1980), designates an area in the Goodwin Sands round the site of what is believed to be a wrecked vessel of historical and archaeological importance as a restricted area for the purposes of the Protection of Wrecks Act 1973.

2686   The Protection of Wrecks (Designation No. 1) Order 1980 (Amendment) Order 1980, S.I. 1980 No. 1306 (in force on 30th September 1980), amends the Protection of Wrecks (Designation No. 1) Order 1980, para. 2685, by redefining the centre of the site of an historic wreck in the area of the Goodwin Sands.

2687   The Protection of Wrecks (Designation No. 2) Order 1980, S.I. 1980 No. 1307 (in force on 30th September 1980), designates as a restricted area for the purposes of the Protection of Wrecks Act 1973 an area in the East Solent, round the site of what is, or may prove to be, the wreck of a vessel which is of historical and archaeological importance.

2688   The Protection of Wrecks (Designation No. 3) Order 1980, S.I. 1980 No. 1419 was made in error and has been revoked; see para. 2689.

2689   The Protection of Wrecks (Designation No. 4) Order 1980, S.I. 1980 No. 1456 (in force on 3rd October 1980), designates an area in the Isles of Scilly round the site of what is believed to be a wrecked vessel of historical and archaeological importance as a restricted area for the purposes of the Protection of Wrecks Act 1973. The order revokes the Protection of Wrecks (Designation No. 3) Order 1980, para. 2688, issued in error.

2690   **Salvage—agreement—arbitration clause—injunction res⸱ ⸱aining proceedings**

See *The Anna Maria*, para. 160.

2691   **—— award—claim in arbitration—court's power to ex⸱   ⸱ limit to make claim**

See *Sioux Inc v China Salvage Co, Kwangchow Branch*, para. 162.

2692   **——expenses of storing cargo—liability of cargo owne**   **2⸱**

A ship ran aground and her master, as agent for her owners and the ⸱ engaged a firm of salvors under the Lloyd's standard form of salva Salvage services were performed and the voyage was then abandonε owners refused to pay the expenses incurred by the salvors in off-load the salved cargo up to the date of the abandonment of the voyage, c the salvors' remedy was against the shipowners. In an action ag owners by the salvors, *held*, the essential issue was to whom the cargo by the salvors. When a salvor took possession of a cargo, his ob deliver it to the shipowners, since it was the latter's duty vis-à-vis tl under the charterparty to carry the goods to their destination unl voyage was abandoned or frustrated. The salvors' contention, that ι agreement they were bailees for the cargo owners and hε

reimbursement from them, was incorrect. Where, as here, the bailee's contractual duty had ended, the existence of a duty on his part to incur expenses, recoverable from the goods' owner, in keeping the goods bailed from damage or destruction, depended on there being an element of necessity that the bailee should so act in order to preserve the goods. There was no basis for finding that the salvors' conduct was founded upon any relevant emergency or necessity at the time of the arrival of the cargo at the place where it was stored. It was to the shipowners, as the persons primarily responsible for accepting delivery of the cargo when it was brought to the place of safety, that the salvors should look for the charges incurred by them.

CHINA-PACIFIC SA v THE FOOD CORPORATION OF INDIA, THE WINSON [1980] 3 All ER 556 (Court of Appeal: MEGAW, BRIDGE and CUMMING-BRUCE LJJ). Decision of Lloyd J [1979] 2 All ER 35, 1979 Halsbury's Abridgment para. 2580 reversed.

2693   —— salvage services—volunteers

A light vessel was in tow. During a storm the towing hawser parted from the tug M and the light vessel was left free to drift. The tug N, seeing what had happened, went to the assistance of the light vessel and managed to tow her to anchorage. Both the tugs had been employed by the defendants, the owners of the light vessel, under the UK Standard Conditions for towage. The plaintiffs, the owners and crew of the tug N, claimed a salvage reward in respect of their services. The defendants contended that they were not entitled to a salvage reward on the grounds that the light vessel was not in danger and the plaintiffs were not volunteers because the services which they rendered were rendered under the towage contract. *Held*, the light vessel had not been in danger and had the tug N offered her services on salvage terms, there was no doubt that the offer would have been refused. The risks incurred and the duties performed by the tug N were entirely within the scope of the towage contract and it could not be said that the crew were volunteers. They were employed to work aboard the tug whenever the tug was rendering towing services as she was on this occasion. The plaintiffs' claim for a salvage reward would, therefore, fail.

THE NORTH GOODWIN NO. 16 [1980] 1 Lloyd's Rep 71 (Queen's Bench Division: SHEEN J).

2694   Shipbuilding (Redundancy Payments) Act 1978—redundancy payments scheme

See para. 1078.

2695   Ship's manager—right to order arrest of ship—damages for wrongful arrest

See *The Borag*, para. 777.

2696   Statutory lien—arrest of vessel—lien or incumbrance incurred by charterers

See *The Vestland*, para. 2609.

SOCIAL SECURITY

Halsbury's Laws of England (3rd edn.), Vol. 27, paras. 897–980, 1187–1570

2697   Articles

Cohabitation in English Social Security and Supplementary Benefits Legislation, David Pearl: 9 Fam Law 232.

Supplementary Benefit Appeal Tribunal, Alec Samuels: 124 Sol Jo 265.

Supplementary Benefits and Education, W. T. West (meaning of "instruction of a kind given in schools" in the Supplementary Benefits Act 1976, s. 7 (1)): 124 Sol Jo 249.

2698 Accommodation—provision by local authority—charges

The National Assistance (Charges for Accommodation) Regulations 1980, S.I. 1980 No. 954 (in force on 24th November 1980), increase the minimum weekly amount which a person is required to pay for accommodation managed by a local authority, and the minimum weekly amounts required to be paid for that accommodation in respect of a child accompanying such a person according to whether the child is under the age of eleven or between the ages of eleven and sixteen. Also increased is the weekly sum which, in assessing a person's ability to pay for such accommodation, a local authority is, in the absence of special circumstances, to assume will be needed for personal requirements. The National Assistance (Charges for Accommodation) Regulations 1979, 1979 Halsbury's Abridgment para. 2589 are revoked.

2699 Attendance allowance—amendments

The Social Security (Attendance Allowance) Amendment Regulations 1980, S.I. 1980 No. 1136 (in force on 25th August 1980), amend the Social Security (Attendance Allowance) (No. 2) Regulations 1975, 1975 Halsbury's Abridgment para. 3107, and, as respects attendance allowance only, the Social Security (Claims and Payments) Regulations 1979, 1979 Halsbury's Abridgment para. 2611. An allowance is not payable when a person is in hospital. The 1975 Regulations, reg. 5A (special provision for satisfying the six months qualifying period in cases of relapse) applies to applications for review of awards of an allowance at the lower rate, as well as to claims. An award may cover a period of not more than six months since the expiry of a certificate relating to earlier attendance requirements, though that period precedes the date of claim. Provision is also made for non-disclosure to the claimant by the Attendance Allowance Board of medical information considered harmful to his health.

2700 —— entitlement—attention in connection with bodily functions

National Insurance Commissioner's decision:

R(A) 1/80 (claimant sixty-seven years old, suffered from diabetes mellitus and deficient circulation which led to bilateral amputation of legs below knee; unable to do any cooking; attention required by disabled person in connection with preparation of food was relevant matter to be taken into account when considering that person's requirements for attention in connection with his bodily functions under Social Security Act 1975, s. 35 (1)).

2701 —— —— claimant living in scheduled accommodation

National Insurance Commissioner's decision:

R(A)2/79 (claimant blind, 87 years old; lived in old persons' home provided and operated under National Assistance Act 1948, s. 21 (1) (a); paid from own resources full cost of accommodation; claim for attendance allowance; on construction of Social Security (Attendance Allowance) (No. 2) Regulations 1975, reg. 4, attendance allowance not payable when person living in accommodation provided in pursuance of 1948 Act, Pt. III other than s. 21 (1) (b) which was concerned with temporary accommodation; claimant lived in scheduled accommodation on a permanent basis; it was irrelevant that claimant liable to bear whole cost of accommodation provided).

2702 —— overpayment—whether claimant used due care and diligence

National Insurance Commissioner's decision:

R(A) 1/79 (claimant continued to receive attendance allowance in respect of daughter after daughter entered hospital; question whether repayment of resulting overpayment was required; ordinary rule of law was that money overpaid as result of mistake had to be repaid; in order to retain amount overpaid claimant had to show that she and any person acting for her used due care and diligence to avoid overpayment within Social Security Act 1975, s. 119; claimant's husband, who was acting for her, failed to ask local social security office for advice; accordingly, claimant had not used due care and diligence and repayment therefore required).

2703   Benefits

The Social Security (General Benefit, Claims and Payments) Regulations 1980, S.I. 1980 No. 1621 (in force on 24th November 1980), amend the Social Security (General Benefit) Regulations 1974, 1974 Halsbury's Abridgment para. 3086, and the Social Security (Claims and Payments) Regulations 1979, 1979 Halsbury's Abridgment para. 2611. Persons are excepted from disqualification for receiving benefit, and from suspension of payment of benefit, during imprisonment abroad if in similar circumstances in Great Britain they would be so excepted. Amendments are made concerning the suspension of payment of benefits pending the hearing of an appeal to the Commissioner. A new regulation is added to the 1974 Regulations concerning repayment by a person who has received payment of overpaid benefit on behalf of a beneficiary.

2704   —— finance

The Social Security (Financial Adjustments) Amendment Order 1980, S.I. 1980 No. 1408 (in force on 16th October 1980), amends the Social Security (Financial Adjustments) Order 1975, 1975 Halsbury's Abridgment para. 3144 so as to extend the cases in which an estimated basis may be used in ascertaining the amount of any adjustment falling to be made between the National Insurance Fund and money provided by Parliament. The cases specified are those in respect of payments of benefit or payments under the Pensioners' Payments and Social Security Act 1979 (Christmas bonus) which fall to be paid out of the National Insurance Fund and payments of benefit, in respect of all benefits under the Supplementary Benefits Act 1976 and certain benefits under the Social Security Act 1975, or Christmas bonus which fall to be made out of money provided by Parliament.

2705   —— knowingly making false statement for purpose of obtaining benefit—ingredients of offence

A claimant for benefit under the Social Security Act 1975 knowingly made a false statement on the claim form, relating to the date when he last worked. He was charged under s. 146 (3) with knowingly making a false representation for the purpose of obtaining benefit for himself. His purpose in making the false statement was merely to deceive his employer and he was unaware that his statement would affect the amount of benefit payable. *Held*, in order to prove an offence under s. 146 (3) it was not necessary to show that the false representation was made with the intention of obtaining benefit under the Act. It was sufficient to establish that the claimant made a representation which he knew to be false.

BARRASS V REEVE [1980] 3 All ER 705 (Queen's Bench Division: WALLER LJ and PARK J). *Stevens & Steed Ltd v King* [1943] 1 All ER 314 applied, *Moore v Branton* (1974) 118 Sol Jo 405, 1974 Halsbury's Abridgment para. 3091 not followed.

2706   —— married women and widows

The Social Security (Benefit) (Married Women and Widows Special Provisions) Amendment Regulations 1980, S.I. 1980 No. 1168 (in force on 11th August 1980), further amend the Social Security (Benefit) (Married Women and Widows Special Provisions) Regulations 1974, 1974 Halsbury's Abridgment para. 3085. They modify the Social Security Pensions Act 1975 so as to ensure that a woman does not derive increases of pension from any deceased husband to whom she was married when he died if subsequently, before she reaches pensionable age, she remarries. They also modify the Social Security Act 1975 in relation to the computation of the weekly rate of earnings-related addition to a widow's allowance to enable certain earnings of the widow's late husband while over pensionable age but not retired to be included in his reckonable weekly earnings. The Social Security (Earnings-Related Addition to Widow's Allowance) (Special Provisions) Regulations 1979, 1979 Halsbury's Abridgment para. 2608 are revoked.

2707 —— overlapping benefits

The Social Security (Overlapping Benefits) Amendment Regulations 1980, S.I. 1980 No. 1927 (in force on 5th January 1981), amend the Social Security (Overlapping Benefits) Regulations 1979, 1979 Halsbury's Abridgment para. 2597. The definitions of "personal benefit" and "Service Pensions Instrument" are amended. An allowance under the Job Release Act 1977 is added to the categories of personal benefit payable to the dependant by reference to which a dependency benefit payable for the same period is required to be adjusted.

2708 —— payment of benefits—mode of payment

Recommendations have been made that moves should be made towards the payment of social security benefits at fortnightly intervals and greater use be made of payments direct to bank accounts. (It has been suggested that supplementary benefits, family income supplement payments and payments to persons aged over 80 be excepted.) The Secretary of State for the Social Services has informed the Select Committee on Social Services that retirement pensioners will remain free to draw their pensions on a weekly basis from the post office and that there will be no compulsion on anyone to accept payment of a pension or other social security benefit through a bank account.

See Times, 13th March 1980.

2709 —— up-rating

The Social Security Benefits Up-rating Order 1980, S.I. 1980 No. 1245 (in force on 24th November 1980), is made consequent upon reviews under the Social Security Act 1975, ss. 125, 126A. It alters with effect from specified dates in the week beginning 24th November 1980 the rates and amounts of the benefits and increases of benefit (except age addition) specified in the 1975 Act, Sch. 4, Parts I, III, IV, V; the rates and amounts of certain benefits under the Social Security Pensions Act 1975, Part II, including increases of Category A or B retirement pension payable by reference to the increases of increments in guaranteed minimum pensions payable by virtue of s. 35 (6); and the rate of graduated retirement benefit under the National Insurance Act 1965. The order also increases the rates laid down in the Industrial Injuries and Diseases (Old Cases) Act 1975 for the maximum weekly rate of lesser incapacity allowance supplementing workmen's compensation and the weekly rate of allowance under the Industrial Diseases Benefit Schemes where disablement is not total.

2710 The Social Security Benefits Up-rating Regulations 1980, S.I. 1980 No. 1505 (in force on 24th November 1980), are made in consequence of the Social Security Benefits Up-rating Order 1980, para. 2709. They specify circumstances in which the rate of benefit which is awarded before the date from which altered rates become payable is not automatically altered by virtue of the Social Security Act 1975, Sch. 14, para. 2. They apply the provisions of the Social Security Benefit (Persons Abroad) Regulations 1975, reg. 5, which relates to persons who are absent from and not ordinarily resident in Great Britain when the weekly rate of certain benefits is increased, to the increases of benefit provided by virtue of the up-rating order. They amend the Social Security (Unemployment, Sickness and Invalidity Benefit) Regulations 1975, the Social Security (Non-Contributory Invalidity Pension) Regulations 1975 and the Social Security (Industrial Injuries) (Benefit) Regulations 1975, 1975 Halsbury's Abridgment paras. 3117, 3171 and 3154 so as to raise to £15 a week or £780 a year, as the case may be, the earnings limits in respect of work which a person in receipt of incapacity benefit to which those regulations apply may do in certain circumstances.

2711   Child benefit—claims and questions—determination

The Child Benefit (Determination of Claims and Questions) Amendment Regulations 1980, S.I. 1980 No. 15 (in force on 1st February 1980), amend the Child Benefit (Determination of Claims and Questions) Regulations 1976, 1976 Halsbury's Abridgment para. 2415, reg 18. Regulation 18 makes provision as to the date from which child benefit is payable to a person where another person, no longer entitled to benefit, had previously been awarded benefit. The regulations provide for payment of the amount by which the award to the person to whom benefit is payable exceeds the previous award to be made to that person entitled in respect of a period earlier than the week in which the claim for benefit is made.

2712

The Child Benefit (Determination of Claims and Questions) Amendment (No. 2) Regulations 1980, S.I. 1980 No. 1640 (in force on 24th November 1980), amend the Child Benefit (Determination of Claims and Questions) Regulations 1976, 1976 Halsbury's Abridgment para. 2415, by prescribing new time limits for appeals to local tribunals, and from such tribunals to a Commissioner. They insert a new regulation in the 1976 Regulations providing for the Social Security Act 1980, s. 15, para. 2761, requiring leave to appeal to a Commissioner from a decision of a tribunal which is unanimous, to apply to appeals under the Child Benefit Act 1975. A claimant must be informed of the effect of the provisions requiring such leave to appeal before he consents to a hearing by a local tribunal in the absence of one of its members. Provisions relating to suspension of benefit under a local tribunal award where notice of appeal is given to the Commissioner are amended. Amendment is also made to a provision whereby benefit is exempt from recovery as being overpaid if the Supplementary Benefits Commission certify that, but for the overpayment, more supplementary benefit would have been awarded.

2713   —— entitlement—claim for increase of sickness/invalidity benefit

National Insurance Commissioner's decision:

R(S) 3/80 (claimant incapable of work; claimed increase of sickness/invalidity benefit in respect of son; claim refused pursuant to Child Benefit Act 1975, s. 6 (1) because claimant had not claimed, and was therefore not entitled to, child benefit; Secretary of State subsequently accepted that certain other claims, including the present one, could be treated as a claim for child benefit; condition in s. 6 (1) was satisfied if by the time the question was determined such a claim had been made; claimant entitled to increase).

2714   —— —— extension

The Child Benefit (General) Amendment Regulations 1980, S.I. 1980 No. 1045 (in force on 24th November 1980), amend the Child Benefit (General) Regulations 1976, 1976 Halsbury's Abridgment para. 2418, so as to enable a school-leaver aged sixteen or over to continue to be treated as a child for a specified period, roughly the period of the final school holiday. Provision is made for a child not to be excluded from child benefit during the specified period notwithstanding that he is in receipt of financial support under the Employment and Training Act 1973 or receiving education by virtue of his employment or office. Payment of child benefit is excluded in respect of a child who has been awarded supplementary benefit. Where a person with whom a child is boarded out by a voluntary organisation claims child benefit on or after 24th November 1980, he is not to be treated for that purpose as contributing to the cost of providing for the child.

2715   —— —— meaning of "living with"

National Insurance Commissioner's decision:

R(F) 2/79 (claimant and wife divorced; order that children of marriage should remain in joint custody of claimant and wife, with care and control to wife; children attended boarding school at claimant's expense; spent part of holidays with claimant; question whether children were living with claimant at those times, within Child Benefit Act 1975, s. 3; "living with" should bear its ordinary and natural meaning;

does not necessarily involve exercise of de facto care and control; question should be decided on all relevant evidence; children were living with claimant at such times within meaning of s. 3).

2716　—— —— **parent of child—step-parent claiming increase in benefit after spouse's death**

National Insurance Commissioner's decision:

R(F) 1/79 (claimant's wife had child by previous marriage; wife had been divorced and child's father still living; on wife's death, child continued to live with claimant who claimed child benefit increase as a parent; claimant became step-father on marriage to child's mother although natural father still alive; claimant remained step-father after wife's death as his status relationship towards child was independent of his status relationship towards his wife as spouse; as step-father, claimant was "parent" within Child Benefit Act 1975 and entitled to increase of benefit claimed).

2717　—— **rates**

The Child Benefit and Social Security (Fixing and Adjusment of Rates) Amendment Regulations 1980, S.I. 1980 No. 110 (in force on 1st February 1980), amend the Child Benefit and Social Security (Fixing and Adjustment of Rates) Regulations 1976, 1976 Halsbury's Abridgment para. 2417, so as to enable a person though not a parent of the child to qualify for the increased rate of child benefit on the condition that he is not residing with a parent of the child. They also enable a person to qualify for the increase though he is entitled to an allowance in respect of the child at the lower rate under the Social Security Act 1975, s. 70 or to an amount at the lower rate under the Industrial Injuries and Diseases (Old Cases) Act 1975, s. 7 (3) (c).

2718　—— —— **up-rating**

The Child Benefit (Up-Rating) Regulations 1980, S.I. 1980 No. 1246 (in force on 24th November 1980), further amend the Child Benefit and Social Security (Fixing and Adjustment of Rates) Regulations 1976, 1976 Halsbury's Abridgment para. 2417, by providing for higher rates of child benefit.

2719　**Claims and payments**

The Social Security (Claims and Payments) Amendment Regulations 1980, S.I. 1980 No. 1943 (in force on 8th January 1981), further amend the Social Security (Claims and Payments) Regulations 1979, 1979 Halsbury's Abridgment para. 2611. The provision relating to disallowance of unemployment benefit being treated as disallowance of any further claim for a period expiring within twelve months is amended so as to exclude from its scope decisions disallowing unemployment benefit on grounds of failure to satisfy contribution conditions. Such a decision is to be treated, until the grounds for it cease to exist, as a decision disallowing any claim for unemployment benefit for a subsequent period.

2720　**Community provisions**

See EUROPEAN COMMUNITIES.

2721　**Contributions**

The Social Security (Contributions) Amendment Regulations 1980, S.I. 1980 No. 1975 (in force on 8th January 1981), further amend the Social Security (Contributions) Regulations 1979, 1979 Halsbury's Abridgment para. 2615. They prescribe a common earnings period for earnings derived from two or more employed earner's employments where the earnings fall to be aggregated and the earnings periods would otherwise be of different lengths. Persons to whom allowances are payable under the Job Release Act 1977 by virtue of a scheme implemented on or after 1st May 1979 are enabled to pay Class 3 contributions up to six years after the year in which the allowance ceased to be payable. For the purposes of entitlement to contributory benefit such contributions are to be treated as duly paid.　An employer may offset against further payments to the Collector of Taxes overpayments of primary Class 1 contributions to the extent only that he has reimbursed the employee.　The regulations also prescribe a new list of establishments and organisations of which, for the purposes of the Social Security Act 1975, Her Majesty's Forces are taken to consist.

2722　——categorisation of earners

The Social Security (Categorisation of Earners) Amendment Regulations 1980, S.I. 1980 No. 1713 (in force on 1st December 1980), amend the Social Security (Categorisation of Earners) Regulations 1978, 1978 Halsbury's Abridgment para. 2680.　They add new provisions which disregard for contribution purposes employment in, or as a civilian by, a visiting force to which a provision of the Visiting Forces Act 1952 applies except where the civilian is ordinarily resident in the United Kingdom; and employment as a member of an international headquarters or defence organisation designated under the International Headquarters and Defence Organisations Act 1964 except where the member is serving in Her Majesty's regular forces, or is a civilian ordinarily resident in the United Kingdom who is not a member of the pension scheme of his headquarters or organisation.

2723　——employed earners—whether casual musicians employed earners

Several musicians were employed individually to play for an orchestra society at irregular intervals for a particular performance or sequence of performances. Income tax was not deducted from their remuneration and each musician was expected to provide his own instruments.　The society contended that as the musicians were not employed earners, it was not liable for national insurance contributions in respect of their earnings.　*Held*, under the Social Security Act 1975, s. 2 (1) (a), an employed earner was a person gainfully employed under a contract of service.　However, in view of the facts, the musicians were each employed under a contract for services, not a contract of service.　Therefore, as they were not employed earners within s. 2(1)(a) the society was not liable for national insurance contributions.

MIDLAND SINFONIA CONCERT SOCIETY LTD v SECRETARY OF STATE FOR SOCIAL SERVICES (1980) Times, 11th November (Queen's Bench Division: GLIDEWELL J). *Addison v London Philharmonic Orchestra Ltd* (1980) Times, 21st October, EAT, para. 1019 applied.

2724　——re-rating

The Social Security (Contributions, Re-rating) Consequential Amendment Regulations 1980, S.I. 1980 No. 13 (in force on 6th April 1980), further amend the Social Security (Contributions) Regulations 1979, 1979 Halsbury's Abridgment para. 2615.　The regulations increase the percentage rates of secondary Class 1 contributions payable in respect of serving members of the forces and those mariners and registered dock workers excluded from the right to a redundancy payment conferred by the Employment Protection (Consolidation) Act 1978, s. 81 by reducing the amounts by which those contributions are abated.　The special rate of Class 2 contributions payable by share fishermen is also increased.

2725　Dependency benefit—amendments

The Social Security Benefit (Dependency) Amendment Regulations 1980, S.I. 1980 No. 585 (in force on 2nd June 1980), further amend the Social Security Benefit (Dependency) Regulations 1977, 1977 Halsbury's Abridgment para. 2667.　The Regulations re-prescribe and supersede certain provisions relating to entitlement to child's special allowance, guardian's allowance and increase of benefit in repect of dependent children, and to the conditions of such entitlement that the beneficiary is entitled to child benefit under the Child Benefit Act 1975, 1975 Halsbury's Abridgment para. 3119, in respect of the child or children concerned.　The 1977 Regulations provided for the beneficiary in prescribed circumstances to be treated as entitled to such child benefit and in other prescribed circumstances to be treated as not so entitled. The 1980 Regulations, in re-prescribing those provisions, apply them also to entitlement to increase of benefit in respect of a female person having care of such dependent children, an entitlement which is subject to the same condition. Regulations 6, 7 of the 1977 Regulations are revoked.

2726   The Social Security Benefit (Dependency) Amendment (No. 2) Regulations 1980, S.I. 1980 No. 827 (in force on 14th July 1980), substitute new provisions for those of the Social Security Benefit (Dependency) Regulations 1977, 1977 Halsbury's Abridgment para. 2667, reg. 13. In relation to a beneficiary who is over pensionable age, who has not retired from regular employment and whose contribution record is deficient, reg. 13 made provision for rates of increase of unemployment benefit, sickness benefit and invalidity pension in respect of his adult dependants and dependent children to be calculated by reference to the rate of increase of retirement pension to which he would have been entitled if he had so retired. The new reg. 13 makes provision for rates of increase of those benefits and invalidity pension in the same circumstances in respect of adult dependants to be calculated by reference to the percentage perscribed in the Social Security (Widow's Benefit and Retirement Pensions) Regulations 1979, 1979 Halsbury's Abridgment para. 2683, reg. 6 (3) (which makes similar prescription in relation to widow's benefit and retirement pensions).

2727   Determination of claims and questions

The Social Security (Determination of Claims and Questions) Amendment Regulations 1980, S.I. 1980 No. 1561 (in force on 24th November 1980), extend from six to twelve months the period specified in the Social Security (Determination of Claims and Questions) Regulations 1975, 1975 Halsbury's Abridgment para. 3133, reg. 17 (3), where disablement questions are referred to a single medical practitioner instead of to a medical board under the Social Security Act 1975, s. 111.

2728   The Social Security (Determination of Claims and Questions) Miscellaneous Amendments Regulations 1980, S.I. 1980 No. 1622 (in force on 24th November 1980), amend the Social Security (Determination of Claims and Questions) Regulations 1975 (the principal regulations), the Social Security (Attendance Allowance) (No. 2) Regulations 1975 and the Mobility Allowance Regulations 1975, 1975 Halsbury's Abridgment paras. 3133, 3107 and 3175 by prescribing new time limits for appeals to the adjudicating authorities under the Social Security Act 1975 and for review by the Secretary of State of a decision given by him under the 1975 Act, s. 93. A new regulation is inserted in the principal regulations which is concerned with applications for leave to appeal to a commissioner from a decision of a local tribunal which is unanimous. A claimant is to be informed of the effect of the provisions requiring such leave to appeal before he consents to a hearing by a local tribunal in the absence of one of its members. Another new regulation is inserted in the principal regulations concerning the right of appeal of a person other than the beneficiary who is required to repay overpaid benefit. The provision in the principal regulations requiring medical appeal tribunals hearing applications for leave to appeal to include in the record of their decision a statement of reasons is deleted. Amendment is made to a provision of the principal regulations whereby benefit is exempt from recovery as being overpaid if the Supplementary Benefits Commission certify that, but for the overpayment, more supplementary benefit would have been awarded.

2729   Earnings factor—revaluation

The Social Security Revaluation of Earnings Factors Order 1980, S.I. 1980 No. 728 (in force on 23rd June 1980), is made consequent upon a review under the Social Security Pensions Act 1975, s. 21, as amended by the Social Security Act 1979, s. 10 and the Social Security Act 1980, s. 3 (3), para. 2761. The order directs that the earnings factors relevant to calculating the additional component in the rate of any long-term benefit for the tax years specified in the Sch. to the order are to be increased by the percentage of their amount specified in the Sch. (so that their value is maintained in relation to the general level of earnings obtaining in Great Britain). The order also provides for the rounding of fractional amounts.

2730   Earnings-related supplement and addition—transitional provisions

The Social Security (Earnings-related Supplement and Addition) (Transitional) Regulations 1980, S.I. 1980 No. 1730 (regs. 1, 2 in force on 4th January 1981, reg. 3 on 3rd January 1982), provide that where there is entitlement to earnings-related supplement of unemployment benefit, sickness benefit or a maternity allowance in respect of a day which is not latter than 30th June 1982 and is part of a period of interruption of employment beginning earlier than 4th January 1981, the reduction made by Social Security (No. 2) Act 1980, s. 4 (1), para. 2762 is not to apply to the rate of that supplement. Where apart from the 1980 Act, s. 4 (2), there would be entitlement to earnings-related supplement in respect of a day which is not later than 30th June 1982 and is part of a period of interruption of employment beginning earlier than 3rd January 1982, the abolition of such supplement by s. 4 (2) will not apply. Provision is also made in connection with widows whose last or only husband died before 4th January 1981 or before 3rd January 1982.

2731   Family income supplement—appeals—rules

See para. 2770.

2732   —— claims and payments

The Family Income Supplements (Claims and Payments) Regulations 1980, S.I. 1980 No. 1438 (in force on 24th November 1980), consolidate with amendments provisions relating to the manner in which claims for, and payments of, family income supplements are to be made. Supplement officers are enabled to perform certain functions in relation to the extinguishment of the right to payment of benefit. The Family Income Supplements (Claims and Payments) Regulations 1971, as amended, are revoked.

2733   —— computation

The Family Income Supplements (Computation) Regulations 1980, S.I. 1980 No. 1167 (in force on 25th November 1980), specify the prescribed amount for any family and the weekly rate of benefit under the Family Income Supplements Act 1970 in accordance with the amendments made to that Act by the Child Benefit Act 1975. The prescribed amount is, if the family includes only one child, £67, and if the family includes more than one child, £67 plus £7 for each child additional to the first. The maximum weekly rate is, if the family includes only one child, £17, and if the family includes more than one child, £17 plus £1·50 for each child additional to the first. The Family Income Supplements (Computation) (No. 2) Regulations 1979, 1979 Halsbury's Abridgment para. 2628 are revoked.

2734   —— entitlement

The Family Income Supplements (General) Regulations 1980, S.I. 1980 No. 1437 (in force on 24th November 1980), consolidate with amendments miscellaneous provisions relating to entitlement to family income supplement. The principal amendments relate to functions conferred on supplement officers by the Social Security Act 1980, para. 2761, and on Social Security Commissioners by the Social Security Act 1979; the circumstances in which a person is to be treated as being or as not being engaged and normally engaged in remunerative full-time work; and the determination of claims and questions. The Family Income Supplements (General) Regulations 1971, as amended, are revoked.

2735   —— qualifications—full-time work

A Divisional Court of the Queen's Bench Division has granted an order of certiorari to quash a decision by the supplementary benefits appeal committee to reject the applicant's claim on the ground that he was not working, but ill, on the date of assessment and not therefore engaged or normally engaged in remunerative full-time work within the Family Income Supplements Act 1970, s. 1 (1) (a). *Held*, a man who was normally employed, but not actually working because of illness, was within s. 1 (1) (a).

R v Ebbw Vale and Merthyr Tydfil Supplementary Benefits Appeal Tribunal, ex parte Lewis [1981] 1 WLR 131 (Queen's Bench Division: Donaldson LJ and Kilner Brown J).

2736   —— transitional provisions

The Family Income Supplements (Transitional) Regulations 1980, S.I. 1980 No. 1023 (in force on 18th August 1980), make transitional provisions connected with the amendments made to the Family Income Supplements Act 1970 by the Social Security Act 1980 and brought into force on 24th November 1980 (see para. 2761).

Provision is made for questions relating to entitlement to family income supplement for periods beginning on or after 24th November 1980 which are determined before that day to be determined by the Supplementary Benefits Commission. Questions relating to entitlement for periods before that day but which are to be determined on or after that day are to be determined by a supplement officer. An appeal to a Supplementary Benefits Appeal Tribunal against a determination of the Commission may be brought after that day. A supplement officer will be a party to any proceedings in such an appeal against a determination of the Commission heard on or after that day. In other court or tribunal proceedings pending on 24th November 1980, the Secretary of State is substituted for the Commission.

2737   Industrial injury—accident arising out of and in the course of employment

National Insurance Commissioner's decision:

R (I) 2/80 (fireman injured playing football in grounds of fire service technical college in match organised by students in the evening after end of instruction; whether accident arising out of or in course of employment; fireman ordered to attend residential course at college went there in pursuance of contract of service; claimant had finished work for day and was playing for own recreation; hence was not playing football in course of employment).

2738   —— —— accident whilst walking across public highway to staff canteen

National Insurance Commissioner's decision:

R (I) 4/79 (bus driver taking permissible break during tour of duty; had accident whilst crossing public highway to reach staff canteen; claim for industrial injury benefit rejected; claimant had no duty to employers to rest and take refreshment in any particular place; walk across highway not in discharge of actual work employed to do).

2739   —— —— travelling from work in employer's transport

National Insurance Commissioner's decision:

R(I) 5/80 (claimant employed by CEGB; contract between employer and bus firm provided the latter would provide a passenger service for employees to and from a power station; claimant injured while travelling in bus proprietor's private car for part of return journey; under Social Security Act 1975, s. 53 (1) an accident happening while an employed earner is, with the express or implied permission of his employer, travelling as a passenger by any vehicle to or from his place of work is to be deemed to arise out of and in the course of his employment if at the time of the accident, the vehicle is being operated by or on behalf of some other person by whom it is provided in pursuance of arrangements made with his employer; only arrangement between firm and CEGB was the contract; owner of firm had not authorised the arrangement of carrying passengers in bus driver's car; claimant was not travelling in car with express or implied permission of employer; accordingly it was not an industrial accident and injury benefit was not payable).

2740   —— assessment of extent of disablement—matters to be taken into account—reasons for decision

National Insurance Commissioner's decision:

R(I)1/79 (claimant had no vision in left eye, for which he received war pension; injured right eye in industrial accident; two medical boards assessed disablement at 70 per cent and 80 per cent respectively for different periods; appeal tribunal reduced assessment to 55 per cent; claimant appealed; receipt of war pension not to be taken into account in assessing disablement; open to tribunal to reduce assessment below 100 per cent as tribunal had discretion under Social Security (Industrial Injuries) (Benefit) Regulations 1975, 1975 Halsbury's Abridgment para. 3154, reg. 2 (6); however, tribunal gave no reasons as to why assessment less than 100 per cent; tribunal also referred to war pension and claimant's partial sight without explaining how these facts affected assessment; decision erroneous in law on those grounds and therefore set aside).

2741   —— benefit

The Social Security (Industrial Injuries) (Benefit) Amendment Regulations 1980, S.I. 1980 No. 1631 (in force on 24th November 1980), amend the Social Security (Industrial Injuries) (Benefit) Regulations 1975, 1975 Halsbury's Abridgment para. 3154. Regulation 3 is amended to provide a new method of calculating the amount of injury benefit payable to persons who have not attained the age of sixteen. Regulation 37 is amended so as to except persons from disqualification for receiving benefit, and from suspension of payment of benefit, during imprisonment abroad if, in similar circumstances in Great Britain, they would be so excepted. Regulation 38 is amended so as to provide for the appointment by the Secretary of State of persons to receive and deal with sums payable by way of benefit during any period when a beneficiary is undergoing imprisonment or detention in legal custody. Regulation 39 is amended in relation to the suspension of payment of benefit pending appeals or references. Regulation 48, which is spent, is revoked.

2742   —— employed earners' employments

The Social Security (Employed Earners' Employments for Industrial Injuries Purposes) Amendment Regulations 1980, S.I. 1980 No. 1714 (in force on 1st December 1980), amend the Social Security (Employed Earners' Employments for Industrial Injuries Purposes) Regulations 1975, 1975 Halsbury's Abridgment para. 3161. They add provisions which provide that for industrial injuries purposes employment as a military or civilian member of a visiting force and employment as a member of a headquarters or defence organisation designated under the Headquarters and Defence Organisations Act 1964, s. 1, except, in either case, where a civilian is ordinarily resident in the United Kingdom, is not to be treated as employed earners' employment.

2743   —— prescribed diseases

The Social Security (Industrial Injuries) (Prescribed Diseases) Regulations 1980, S.I. 1980 No. 377 (in force on 15th April 1980), consolidate the Social Security (Industrial Injuries) (Prescribed Diseases) Regulations 1975, 1975 Halsbury's Abridgment para. 3164, as amended. The regulations prescribe, for the purposes of entitlement to industrial injuries benefit under the Social Security Act 1975, certain diseases and personal injuries (not caused by accident) by reference to the nature of the occupations of employed earners. The regulations also modify certain provisions of the Social Security Act 1975 and regulations made under that Act in their application to prescribed diseases and injuries.

2744   The Social Security (Industrial Injuries) (Prescribed Diseases) Amendment Regulations 1980, S.I. 1980 No. 1493 (in force on 15th December 1980), by making an addition to the diseases prescribed in the Social Security (Industrial Injuries) (Prescribed Diseases) Regulations 1980, para. 2743, Sch. 1, Part I, extend cover under the industrial injuries provisions of the Social Security Act 1975 to occupational vitiligo (depigmentation of certain areas of the skin) in the case of persons employed in employed earner's employment in occupations involving the use or handling of, or exposure to, certain chemicals. They also amend the 1980 regulations so as to remedy a minor omission.

2745   **—— —— occupational deafness—computation of time limits— test to be applied**

National Insurance Commissioner's decision:
     R(I) 2/79 (claimant employed in factory from 1950; continuously incapable of work due to sickness from 24th March 1975; received paid sick-leave to 20th February 1976, when claimant discharged on medical grounds; claimed disablement benefit on 17th February 1977; benefit refused because under Social Security (Industrial Injury) (Prescribed Diseases) Regulations 1975, reg. 40 (2) disablement benefit not payable in respect of claim for occupational deafness made more than twelve months after claimant had ceased to be employed in prescribed occupation; claimant appealed; time limit absolute and could not be extended for good cause; 1975 Regulations are directed to work done rather than contractual obligation to do it and "actual work" is test to be applied; no period of absence could be excluded from computation of ensuing twelve months; claimant therefore ceased to be employed on 24th March 1975 and benefit could not be paid).

2746   **—— —— —— prescribed occupation**

National Insurance Commissioner's decisions:
     R(I) 1/80 (claimant, riveter, used pneumatic percussive tool on rivets; argued that process constituted dressing or finishing of ingots within Social Security (Industrial Injuries) (Prescribed Diseases) Regulations 1975; rivet not ingot since latter was metal still in form of raw material whereas former was finished product ready for use; nor did process constitute dressing or finishing since those were processes completed before article ready for use; claim disallowed).

2747   R(I) 3/80 (claimant, driller in engineering, used grinder on cast metal; grinder, although a machine, was also a tool; question whether it was high-speed grinding tool within Social Security (Industrial Injuries) (Prescribed Diseases) Regulations 1975 not subject of absolute objective standard; grinder in this case was high-speed grinding tool and hence occupational deafness was prescribed in relation to claimant).

2748   **—— —— procedure where disease not prescribed**

National Insurance Commissioner's decision:
     R(I) 4/80 (claim for benefit disallowed on ground that claimant's disease not prescribed; although insurance officer had sought and received a medical report under National Insurance (Industrial Injuries) (Prescribed Diseases) Regulations 1959, reg. 25 (2), it was not necessary for him to deal with it under reg. 27 (2) by way of reference of the diagnosis question to a medical board, since medical report showed plainly that claimant not suffering from a prescribed disease). Decision R(I) 3/74 not followed.
     1959 Regulations now replaced by Social Security (Industrial Injuries) (Prescribed Diseases) Regulations 1980, para. 2743.

2749   **Invalidity benefit—non-contributory invalidity pension—entitle- ment—incapacity for normal household duties**

National Insurance Commissioner's decisions:
     R(S)9/79 (claim for non-contributory invalidity pension; question whether claimant incapable of performing normal household duties for 196 consecutive days

prior to relevant date; claimant subject to intermittent disablement and only incapable of performing such duties when affected by her disabilities; conceded that claimant incapable of paid work for preceding 196 days; paid work could not be equated with household duties; claimant who could only perform duties of paid employment for few days of working week would be virtually unemployable and therefore continuously incapable of paid work; housewife correspondingly disabled would be able to do housework on days when fit; pension not payable).

2750   R(S) 6/79 (claimant married woman suffering from thrombosis, cellulitus and swollen legs; able to move slowly and although had capacity to do some household tasks did not do so as exertion made her ill; test was whether she could perform her own normal household duties to any substantial extent without substantial assistance; on evidence presented, unable to do so, therefore entitled to non-contributory invalidity pension).

2751   R(S) 7/79 (claimant had mitral valve replacement some years earlier, suffered exhaustion but able to do most things not requiring considerable amount of exertion; received assistance from home help twice per week; claimed non-contributory invalidity pension on basis of incapacity for household duties; fact that claimant had home help did not establish that she was not reasonably to be expected to perform normal household duties to any substantial extent; further she could perform many household duties which, as a matter of common knowledge, normally arose in any household and did not call for sustained and considerable exertion; the pension was not therefore payable).

2752   Mobility allowance—entitlement—inability or virtual inability to walk

National Insurance Commissioner's decision:
      R(M) 1/80 (claimant suffered from agoraphobia; perfectly able to walk inside house but in practice unable to walk outside; question of inability to walk tied to physical condition of claimant and agoraphobia not a physical condition; claim disallowed).

2753   Pensioners' lump sum payments

The Pensioners' Lump Sum Payments Order 1980, S.I. 1980 No. 1169 (in force on 1st December 1980), provides for a lump sum payment of £10 to be made in respect of a person in whose case the provisions of the Pensioners' Payments and Social Security Act 1979, 1979 Halsbury's Abridgment para. 2648, ss. 1–3 are satisfied for a day in the week beginning Monday 1st December 1980.

2754   —— claims

The Pensioners' Lump Sum Payments (Claims) Regulations 1980, S.I. 1980 No. 71 (in force on 21st February 1980), prescribe the manner in which a claim for a lump sum payment under the Pensioners' Payments and Social Security Act 1979 is made for the purposes of s. 3 (7) of that Act.

2755   Re-adaptation benefit—iron and steel employees scheme

The European Communities (Iron and Steel Employees Re-adaptation Benefits Scheme) (Amendment) Regulations 1980, S.I. 1980 No. 1912 (in force on 4th January 1981), amend the European Communities (Iron and Steel Employees Re-adaptation Benefits Scheme) Regulations 1979, 1979 Halsbury's Abridgment para. 1233. The regulations permit payments to most unemployed redundant steel workers to continue to be made at the same level notwithstanding the reduction of the maximum weekly rate of earnings-related supplement by the Social Security (No. 2) Act 1980, s. 4 (1), para. 2762. A new method of calculation of payments under the scheme to supplement the current earnings of steel employees in certain circumstances is provided.

2756   Reciprocal arrangements—Austria

A new convention has been signed with Austria relating to the provision of
reciprocal arrangements in the field of social security (Cmnd 8048). This convention
will supersede the earlier conventions with Austria (Cmnd 5102 and Cmnd 6760).
The principle underlying the convention is that each country should treat the
nationals of the other in the same way as its own nationals. The convention
prescribes the law applicable to different categories of persons (arts. 5 to 9) and makes
express provision, inter alia, for sickness and maternity benefits (arts. 11, 12),
unemployment benefit (arts. 13–15), old age pensions (arts. 16–21), survivors'
pensions (art. 22), invalidity pensions (art. 23), industrial injuries and diseases benefits
(arts. 24, 25), death grant (arts. 26, 27), guardian's allowance (art. 28) and family
allowances (arts. 29–31). Instruments of ratification have not yet been exchanged.

2757   Sickness benefit—entitlement—absence abroad

National Insurance Commissioner's decision:
    R(S)4/80 (claimant, incapable of work, went to France to stay with daughter; visit
arranged before incapacity commenced; no treatment received abroad; claimant
disqualified under Social Security Act 1975, s. 82 (5) (a); claimant did not fall within
exceptions under Social Security Benefit (Pensions Abroad) Regulations 1975, reg.
2, the reciprocal convention with France, art. 15, or Council Regulation (EEC)
1408/71, art. 22 (1) (c) as he received no treatment abroad; nor did Regulation
1408/71, art. 22 (1) (a) apply as his condition did not necessitate immediate benefits,
i.e. benefits in kind such as assistance of local health service; claim disallowed).

2758   —— —— claimant participating in business—"work"

National Insurance Commissioner's decision:
    R(S)10/79 (claimant received sickness benefit for certain periods; also participated
in scrap metal business to extent of providing funds and discussing finances with
other partner; claimant convicted of offences relating to false representations made
in obtaining sickness benefit during same periods; evidence leading to that conviction
not before Commissioner and evidence actually before him inconsistent with any
grounds which would justify a conviction; participation in business was not "work"
for purposes of Social Security Act 1975, s. 17 (1); claimant had not failed to
establish that he was incapable of work during relevant periods and was entitled to
sickness benefit; in circumstances, conviction should not be regarded as proof that
offence had been committed).

2759   —— —— effect of foreign pension rights—overlapping of benefits

National Insurance Commissioner's decision:
    Decision CS 905/78: RE GERMAN RETIREMENT PENSION [1979] 3 CMLR 382
(claimant, sixty-eight, worked and paid insurance contributions in Germany for
four years; for the next thirty years he worked and paid contributions in the United
Kingdom; by virtue of Council Regulation (EEC) 1408/71, arts. 45 and 46 on
aggregation and apportionment he was entitled to a German pension after reaching
the age of sixty-five; for the purposes of the British social security system the
claimant had not retired but was incapable of work for two short periods; he
claimed sickness benefit; insurance officer contended the benefit was not payable
because of the provision on overlapping of benefits in the Social Security Regulations
1975, reg. 3 together with art. 12 (2) of the EEC Regulation precluded the payment
of both the German pension and the British sickness benefit; claimant entitled to the
benefit since art. 12 (2) was not applicable to the reduction of benefits payable under
national law alone).

**2760   —— —— increase for husband and child—increase only payable to
husband for wife and child—sex discrimination**

National Insurance Commissioner's decision:
    R(S)11/79 (claimant wife assumed role of breadwinner while husband cared for
child; husband capable of self-support; wife claimed increase in sickness benefit for

dependent husband and daughter; Social Security Act 1975, s. 44 provided increase would be payable to wife who resided with husband or contributed to his maintenance; s. 41 provided that increase would be payable to married woman residing with her husband for the benefit of child; both sections provided that increase would only be payable if husband was incapable of self-support; increase only payable to sick husband in respect of wife and child and not to sick wife in respect of her husband and child even where she was sole breadwinner; Sex Discrimination Act 1975, s. 51 provided that any act which re-enacted a provision of an act or an instrument made under an Act passed before the Sex Discrimination Act, was excluded from the provisions of that Act; ss. 44 and 41 were therefore applicable and wife not entitled to increase).

2761   Social Security Act 1980

The Social Security Act 1980 amends the law relating to social security and the Pensions Appeal Tribunals Act 1943. The Act received the royal assent on the 23rd May 1980 and certain provisions came into force on that date, the remaining provisions coming into force on specified days in 1980, with the exception of those relating to similar treatment for men and women and those relating to supplementary schemes for industrial injuries and diseases: S.I. 1980 No. 729.

Section 1 provides that, for the purpose of the annual up-rating reviews of benefit rates, the Secretary of State has regard only to prices in determining whether those rates have lost their value, although he continues to have regard to earnings in reviewing the retirement pensioners' earnings rule. The section also provides the dates from which any increase of benefit rates or public service pensions consequent upon a compulsory up-rating review need take effect.

Section 2, Sch. 1 makes various amendments to the Social Security Act 1975. These include amendments relating to similar treatment for men and women and take account, in relation to dependency additions, of Council Directive (EEC) 79/7 on Equal Treatment for Men and Women in Social Security. Further provisions concern the date on which attendance allowance may be claimed, the Social Security Act 1975, s. 96 (2), the time limit for giving notice of appeal from a decision of an insurance officer and a local tribunal, and the extension of the maximum time limit for the period to be taken into account in making an assessment by a single medical practitioner when giving a decision on a disablement question. Schedule 1, paras. 12–16 contains other amendments to the 1975 Act.

Section 3 makes various amendments to the Social Security Pensions Act 1975. In particular, regulations under ss. 9 (3), 21 of that Act, concerning the maximum additional component for a surviving spouse, and the revaluation of earnings factors, are now subject to negative instead of affirmative resolution procedure: s. 3 (1), (3). Certain persons may now be treated as having retired: s. 3 (2). The tax years to which optional revaluation at 12 per cent per annum (compound) applies are redefined: s. 3 (4), (8), (9). A number of miscellaneous amendments are made by s. 4. Section 5 provides for the contribution conditions for maternity grant to be replaced by prescribed conditions as to residence and presence in Great Britain if a confinement occurs, or is expected to occur, on or after an appointed date.

Section 6, Sch. 2, Pt. I, amends the Supplementary Benefits Act 1976. The changes include a revised legal structure under which designated supplementary benefit officers replace the Supplementary Benefits Commission as the initial determining authority in relation to claims for benefit. The Commission is abolished (s. 6 (2)), and regulation making powers replace provisions enabling matters to be dealt with on a discretionary basis.

Section 7 amends the Family Income Supplements Act 1970 by providing for the equal treatment of male and female members of couples who claim the supplement and by making other provisions in relation to supplementary benefits corresponding to the provision made by s. 6 (2). Section 8 contains powers to make transitional provisions.

Section 9, Sch. 3 provides for the setting up of a new advisory body on social security for Great Britain and Northern Ireland: the Social Security Advisory Committee. The National Insurance Advisory Committee is abolished. Section 10 provides for consultation with the new Committee on proposals for regulations. The circumstances in which requirements to consult Advisory Committees in connection with such proposals do not apply are specified by s. 11. Section 12 changes the title of National Insurance Commissioners to Social Security Commissioners. The tenure of office of a Commissioner is provided by s. 13. Section 14 provides for appeals on questions of law to the appropriate court from decisions of the Commissioners, with the leave of a Commissioner or of the appropriate court and from Northern Ireland medical appeal tribunals. No appeal lies to a Commissioner from a unanimous decision of a local tribunal except with the leave of a tribunal chairman or a Commissioner: s. 15.

Section 16 amends the Pensions Appeal Tribunals Act 1943 enabling, inter alia, provision to be made whereby an appeal can be brought or be continued by another person after the death of a claimant for pensions for disablement or death due to service in the armed services. Section 17 provides for the proof of a decision of an adjudicating authority in legal proceedings by a certified record of the decision. Section 18 concerns the computation of age in relation to specified enactments for the purposes of Scottish law. Financial provisions are contained in s. 19 and consequential and minor amendments of enactments in s. 20. Citation, interpretation, commencement, repeals and extent are provided by s. 21.

2762   Social Security (No. 2) Act 1980

The Social Security (No. 2) Act 1980 amends the law relating to social security for the purpose of reducing or abolishing certain duties to increase sums. The Act received the royal assent on 17th July 1980 and came into force on that date, except for the following provisions which, by S.I. 1980 No. 1025, come into force on the dates given in brackets: s. 3 and Sch. (part) (14th September 1980), s. 6 (24th November 1980), s. 4 (1) (4th January 1981), s. 5 (6th April 1981), s. 4 (2), 7 (7), Sch. (part) (3rd January 1982).

Section 1 (1) provides that if, in consequence of a review under the Social Security Act 1975, s. 125 in the tax year 1979–80, the Secretary of State is required to increase a specified sum, being certain benefits set out in s. 1 (2), he may reduce the increase by up to five per cent of that sum. Section 1 (4) provides that he may do likewise in consequence of a s. 125 review in the tax year 1980–81 or 1981–82 if he makes an affirmative resolution order providing that s. 1 (1) is to apply. Section 2 provides for the abolition of the compulsory up-rating of the amount which men under the age of seventy and women under the age of sixty-five who are entitled to a retirement pension may earn without their pensions being abated. Section 3 (1) alters the definition of period of interruption of employment in the 1975 Act, s. 17 (1) (d), so that less than four consecutive days of incapacity for work will not constitute a period of interruption of employment and so that any two periods of interruption of employment, whether periods of unemployment or incapacity, will not link to form one period of interruption of employment if they are separated by a period of more than eight weeks. Section 3 (3) reduces from thirteen to eight weeks the periods mentioned in the 1975 Act, ss. 28 (7) and 59 (4). Section 3 (4) enables regulations to be made prescribing a larger number of weeks than eight for any provision amended by s. 3 (1) or (3).

Section 4 provides for the reduction and abolition of the earnings-related supplement of unemployment benefit, sickness benefit and maternity allowance, and the earnings-related addition to widow's allowance. Section 5 provides for the abatement of unemployment benefit of persons who have attained the age of sixty and to whom payments by way of occupational pension in excess of a prescribed sum of not less than £35 per week are made.

Section 6 (1) provides, as respects any period for which the Supplementary Benefits Act 1976, s. 8 applies to a person, that is, a period for which he is without employment as a result of a stoppage of work due to a trade dispute at his place of employment, that for the purposes of that Act, except so far as regulations provide otherwise, certain payments which that person receives or could obtain are not to be disregarded; the weekly rate of any payment by way of supplementary pension or allowance which would be made to that person, or to another person whose resources fall to be aggregated with those of that person, will not be made if it is £12 or less and, if it is more than £12, will be at a weekly rate equal to the difference; and payments under the 1976 Act, s. 4 (cases of urgent need) will not be made to that person or to another person whose resources fall to be aggregated with those of that person. Section 6 (2), (3) make provision for the £12 sum to be increased or reduced. Section 7 is supplemental and with the Schedule provides for repeals. Section 8 deals with citation, commencement and extent.

2763   Social Security Advisory Committee—establishment—transitional provisions

The Social Security (Advisory Committees) Transitional Regulations 1980, S.I. 1980 No. 1874 (in force on 15th December 1980), make transitional provision in connection with the abolition, by the Social Security Act 1980, s. 9 (1), para. 2761, of the National Insurance Advisory Committee and the establishment of the Social Security Advisory Committee. The 1980 Act, s. 11 (1), which exempted certain proposals to make regulations from reference to the National Insurance Advisory Committee, is repealed.

2764   Social Security Commissioners—appeal to courts

The Social Security Commissioners (Appeals to the Courts) Regulations 1980, S.I. 1980 No. 1321 (in force on 24th November 1980), are concerned with applications for leave to appeal on a question of law from a decision of a Social Security Commissioner to the appropriate court, under the Social Security Act 1980, para. S1230, s. 14. They make provision for the selection of a Commissioner, other than the one against whose decision leave is sought to appeal, to determine the application for leave; for the procedure when the person who would otherwise have been entitled to apply for leave is a child or has become unable to act; for the time within which and the manner in which an application may be made; and for the hearing and determination of applications. Special provision is also made for cases where the Commissioner's decision is on a question of law referred by a medical appeal tribunal.

2765   —— reasons for decisions

The Tribunals and Inquiries (Social Security Commissioners) Order 1980, S.I. 1980 No. 1637 (in force on 24th November 1980), exempts Social Security Commissioners from the requirement, under the Tribunals and Inquiries Act 1971, s. 12 (1), to give reasons for their decisions in relation to applications for leave to appeal from a decision of a Commissioner and applications for leave to appeal to them from the decisions of local tribunals constituted under the Social Security Act 1975, appeal tribunals constituted under the Supplementary Benefits Act 1976 and medical appeal tribunals, and applications for leave to appeal to them against determinations by the Attendance Allowance Board.

2766   Supplementary benefit—aggregation of requirements and resources

The Supplementary Benefit (Aggregation) Regulations 1980, S.I. 1980 No. 982 (in force on 24th November 1980), contain provisions relating to the aggregation of requirements and resources for the purpose of entitlement to supplementary benefit under the Supplementary Benefits Act 1976, Sch. 1, para. 3, as amended by the Social Security Act 1980 (see para. 2761). Under these provisions, aggregation applies to couples who are married and living together in the same household, to unmarried couples who are living together as husband and wife otherwise than in prescribed circumstances, and in circumstances in which one person is responsible for, and a member of the same household as, a child under sixteen, or under nineteen and still at college or school, or in prescribed circumstances.

These regulations prescribe the circumstances in which married couples are to be treated as being, or not being, members of the same household; the circumstances in which a person is to be treated as being responsible for another person; dependants who are not to be treated as members of the household; the circumstances in which resources and requirements are to be aggregated; and circumstances in which persons are not an unmarried couple.

2767   The Supplementary Benefit (Aggregation, Requirements and Resources) Amendment Regulations 1980, S.I. 1980 No. 1774 (in force on 24th November 1980), amend and correct minor errors in the Supplementary Benefit (Aggregation) Regulations 1980, para. 2766, the Supplementary Benefit (Requirements) Regulations 1980, para. 2782, and the Supplementary Benefit (Resources) Regulations 1980, para. 2783.

2768   —— —— **payments made under affiliation and maintenance orders**

The House of Lords has held that weekly sums sent by fathers for the maintenance of their children under sixteen years and living with their mothers in the same household, are the "resources" of the child and have to be aggregated with those of the mother for the purpose of determining the amount of the mothers' weekly supplementary benefit under the Supplementary Benefit Act 1976.

In the first case, under a maintenance order the former husband was required to make payments direct to his child who was living with the claimant, the mother. Those payments to the child were taken into account in assessing the mother's entitlement to supplementary benefit and her benefit was accordingly reduced. In the second case, under an affiliation order the father made payments to the mother for the benefit of her illegitimate child, and account was also taken of this payment in assessing her supplementary benefit. Both mothers successfully appealed.

The Supplementary Benefit Commission was given leave to appeal to the House of Lords direct in both cases. *Held*, the amount of supplementary benefit to which a person was entitled under the Act was the amount by which his resources fell short of his requirements. Where a person had to provide for the requirements of another member of the household, their requirements could be aggregated. The fact of the fathers' payments did not mean that the mothers did not provide for their children's requirements. "Requirements" was to be given its ordinary meaning and included more than financial support. The appeal would accordingly be allowed.

Supplementary Benefits Commission v Jull; Supplementary Benefits Commission v Y [1980] 3 All ER 65 (House of Lords; Lord Wilberforce, Viscount Dilhorne, Lord Salmon, Lord Fraser of Tullybelton and Lord Russell of Killowen). Decisions of Woolf J (1980) Times, 21st March, and Comyn J (1980) Times 18th April, reversed.

The Supplementary Benefits Commission has been abolished: Social Security Act 1980, s. 6, Sch. 2, Pt. I, para. 2761.

2769   —— **appeals**

The Tribunals and Inquiries (Supplementary Benefit Appeal Tribunals) (Revocation) Order 1980, S.I. 1980 No. 1601 (in force on 24th November 1980), revokes the Tribunals and Inquiries (Supplementary Benefit Appeal Tribunals) Order 1977, 1977 Halsbury's Abridgment para. 2718, which provides for an appeal on a point of law from Supplementary Benefit Appeal Tribunals to the High Court, except in relation to decisions of Supplementary Benefit Appeal Tribunals recorded in writing before this Order comes into operation. New provisions concerning appeals from tribunals are made by the Supplementary Benefit and Family Income Supplements (Appeals) Rules 1980, para. 2770.

2770   —— —— **rules**

The Supplementary Benefit and Family Income Supplements (Appeals) Rules 1980, S.I. 1980 No. 1605 (in force on 24th November 1980), govern the procedure of appeal tribunals constituted under the Supplementary Benefits Act 1976, Sch. 4, as substituted by the Social Security Act 1979, provide for a right of appeal on a point of law from the tribunals to a Social Security Commissioner and for the procedure before the Commissioner. In relation to the procedure of tribunals, they replace the Supplementary Beneft (Appeal Tribunal) Rules 1971 and the Family Income Supplements (Appeal Tribunal) Rules 1971. The provisions relating to the Social Security Commissioners coincide with the ending, by the Tribunals and Inquiries (Supplementary Benefits Appeal Tribunals) (Revocation) Order 1980, para. 2769, of the right of appeal from the tribunals to the High Court.

Part I contains general provisions and makes provision for travelling and other allowances for persons attending oral hearings. Part II relates to appeals tribunals and provides for the time and manner of bringing appeals, for the time and place of tribunal hearings, for tribunal hearings and for tribunal determinations. Part III relates to appeals to a Social Security Commissioner and provides for a right of appeal to a Commissioner from decisions of a tribunal on a point of law, for applications for leave to appeal and for appeals to a Commissioner, for hearings before the Commissioner and for decisions of the Commissioner.

2771   —— claims and payments

The Supplementary Benefit (Claims and Payments) Regulations 1980, S.I. 1980 No. 1579 (in force on 24th November 1980), provide for the manner in which claims for and payments of supplementary benefit under the Supplementary Benefits Act 1976, as amended by the Social Security Act 1980, para. 2761, are to be made. Part I contains general provisions concerning interpretation and revokes the Supplementary Benefits (Claims and Payments) Regulations 1977, 1977 Halsbury's Abridgment para. 2711. Part II contains provisions relating to claims for supplementary benefit, including how claims are to be made and the forms and information required. Part III contains provisions concerning the payment of supplementary benefit, including time and manner of payment, information to be given and circumstances in which benefit may be paid in kind. Part IV contains miscellaneous provisions relating to persons unable to act or who have died, payments to persons under eighteen and payment of travelling expenses.

2772   —— deduction from damages for personal injuries

See *Plummer v P. W. Wilkins & Son Ltd*, para. 781.

2773   —— deductions and payments to third parties

The Supplementary Benefit (Deductions and Payments to Third Parties) Regulations 1980, S.I. 1980 No. 983 (in force on 24th November 1980), provide for the manner and circumstances in which supplementary benefit may be either deducted and subsequently paid to a claimant or paid direct to a third party.

Provision is made for the circumstances in which payment of benefit may be postponed, for regular payments to third parties for housing and fuel requirements, for regular payments to landlords on behalf of boarders, for payments to local authorities in respect of residential accommodation, for payment of certain accommodation charges, for payment of supplementary benefit to third parties, for payments to be made when entitlement to supplementary benefit ends, and for payment of single payments to third parties.

2774   —— determination of questions

The Supplementary Benefit (Determination of Questions) Regulations 1980, S.I. 1980 No. 1643 (in force on 24th November 1980), make provision for the determination of questions under the Supplementary Benefits Act 1976, as amended by the Social Security Act 1980, para. 2761.

Provision is made for the determination by benefit officers of questions relating to supplementary benefit, for notice of determinations made by benefit officers and for cases where particulars of the assessment are to be given. Provision is also made for review of determinations by benefit officers and for the reference by a benefit officer or appeal tribunal of specified questions for determination by authorities under the Social Security Act 1975. The duration of awards of pensions and allowances is specified, as is the date, to be determined by reference to the appropriate benefit week, on which entitlement to a pension or allowance is to begin, change or end. Payment of benefit is suspended pending review or appeal. The Supplementary Benefits (General) Regulations 1977, 1977 Halsbury's Abridgment para. 2709, as amended, are revoked.

2775   —— **duplication and overpayment**

The Supplementary Benefit (Duplication and Overpayment) Regulations 1980, S.I. 1980 No. 1580 (in force on 24th November 1980), contain provisions relating to the prevention of duplication of payments under the Supplementary Benefits Act 1976, s. 12, and recovery in cases of misrepresentation or non-disclosure under s. 20. The payments of income and benefits which may be abated or recovered are prescribed for the purposes of s. 12, and the benefits from which recovery may be made by deduction under s. 20 are prescribed. The Social Security Benefit (Dependency) Regulations 1977, 1977 Halsbury's Abridgment para. 2667, are amended.

2776   —— **entitlement—conditions**

The Supplementary Benefit (Conditions of Entitlement) Regulations 1980, S.I. 1980 No. 1586 (in force on 24th November 1980), contain provisions relating to the conditions upon which a person is to be entitled to supplementary benefit under the Supplementary Benefits Act 1976. Provision is made for persons abroad whose entitlement is to continue. "Employment" is defined and the manner in which registration is to be made is specified. Certain persons are exempted from the conditions of registration and availability for employment. The circumstances are prescribed in which persons are, or are not, to be treated as available for employment; in which persons are to be treated as, or as not, in remunerative full time work; in which persons are to be treated as receiving relevant education, and in which persons receiving relevant education are to be entitled to supplementary benefit. Provision is also made for directions to attend courses of instruction or training.

2777   —— —— **full-time remunerative employment—meaning**

The question arose whether the claimant, who ran a business from her home at a loss, was "engaged in full-time remunerative work" and was therefore excluded by the Supplementary Benefits Act 1976, s. 6, from entitlement to supplementary benefit. *Held*, in the context of s. 6, "remunerative" referred to work which was paid for, regardless of whether it resulted in a profit to the claimant. It was the character of the work which was being defined, not its economic result. Accordingly, the claimant was engaged in remunerative full-time work and was not entitled to supplementary benefit.

PERROT v SUPPLEMENTARY BENEFITS COMMISSION [1980] 3 All ER 110 (Court of Appeal: STEPHENSON and BRIGHTMAN LJJ and DAME ELIZABETH LANE).

2778   —— —— **help with removal expenses—cohabitation**

A complaint was made to the Parliamentary Commissioner for Adminstration by a husband that officials of the Department of Health and Social Security had assisted his estranged wife to remove furniture from the family home without his knowledge or agreement. The husband believed that his wife's motive in moving was to live with another man. The commissioner, in the course of his report (Case C282/79, *Parliamentary Commissioner for Administration, Selected Cases 1980*, Vol. 2, HC 526), referred to the criteria considered by the Supplementary Benefits Commission in determining whether a man and women are cohabiting for the purposes of supplementary benefit. Broadly speaking, the man must be living in the same household as the woman and will usually have no other home; the association must be adjudged stable; and in most cases one party would provide financial support for the other or there would be some sharing of household expenses. The commissioner found that the wife had been treated like any other supplementary benefit claimant who had decided to leave her husband and set up home on her own. The department indicated to the commissioner, however, that in future local offices acting in such cases would be instructed to seek confirmation, preferably from any solicitors involved, that there was no possibility of dispute between an estranged couple over the removal of household goods.

2779 —— —— meaning of "work"

The defendant was charged with having made representations for the purpose of obtaining supplementary benefit which he knew to be false contrary to the Supplementary Benefits Act 1976, s. 21. He contended that for the relevant period he had not "worked" as the money he had received was not remuneration but reimbursement for expenses incurred. *Held*, "work" did not necessarily mean "remunerative work" and whether the defendant's action was such as to make the declaration false was a question of fact.

CLEAR v SMITH [1980] Crim LR 246 (Queen's Bench Division: LORD WIDGERY CJ and WIEN J).

2780 —— miscellaneous

The Supplementary Benefit (Miscellaneous Amendments) Regulations 1980, S.I. 1980 No. 1649 (in force on 24th November 1980), amend and correct minor errors in the following regulations made under the Supplementary Benefits Act 1976, as amended by the Social Security Act 1980, para. 2761: Supplementary Benefit (Deductions and Payments to Third Parties) Regulations 1980, para. 2773; Supplementary Benefit (Transitional) Regulations 1980, para. 2786; Supplementary Benefit (Single Payments) Regulations 1980, para. 2784; and Supplementary Benefit (Duplication and Overpayment) Regulations 1980, para. 2775.

2781 —— payment in urgent cases

The Supplementary Benefit (Urgent Cases) Regulations 1980, S.I. 1980 No. 1642 (in force on 24th November 1980), provide for supplementary benefit by way of a single payment or a supplementary pension or allowance to be payable in urgent cases and modify the Supplementary Benefits Act 1976 accordingly. They also set out the circumstances in which a sum paid in such a case is not to be recovered. Part I contains general provisions. Parts II to IV set out the circumstances in which and items for which a single payment will be made and the circumstances in which an amount of pension or allowance to meet living expenses will be made. Part V relates to recovery of sums paid.

2782 —— requirements

The Supplementary Benefit (Requirements) Regulations 1980, S.I. 1980 No. 1299 (in force on 24th November 1980), provide for the determination of requirements for the purposes of determining the right to, and amount of, supplementary benefit under the Supplementary Benefits Act 1976, as amended by the Social Security Act 1980, para. 2761.

Part I contains general provisions affecting the interpretation of the Regulations. Part II relates to the determination of normal requirements and contains provisions specifying the items to which the category of normal requirements relates; varies the ordinary rates set out in the 1976 Act for the normal requirements of couples and householders; provides for the amounts of the normal requirements of other persons; sets out the conditions for the long-term rates for normal requirements; and modifies the amounts otherwise applicable for normal requirements, in certain cases of disqualification for unemployment benefit, for boarders and in special cases. Part III relates to the determination of additional requirements, such as heating. Part IV relates to the determination of housing requirements and contains provisions specifying the items to which the category of housing requirements relates, and providing for the determination of amounts applicable for those items, namely, rent, mortgage payments, maintenance and insurance, interest on loans for repairs and improvements, miscellaneous outgoings and items in special cases. Certain amounts are subject to restriction where they are excessive and to reduction in respect of lettings and housing contributions of non-dependants. Separate provision is made for a non-householder's contribution to housing expenses.

These regulations have been amended; see para. 2767.

2783   —— **resources**

The Supplementary Benefit (Resources) Regulations 1980, S.I. 1980 No. 1300 (in force on 24th November 1980), provide for the calculation of resources and determination of maximum capital resources for the purposes of determining the right to, and amount of, supplementary benefit under the Supplementary Benefits Act 1976, as amended by the Social Security Act 1980, para. 2761.

Part I contains general provisions affecting the interpretation of the Regulations, and sets out the circumstances in which persons may be treated as possessing resources which they do not in fact possess. Part II contains provisions for the calculation of capital resources and specifies the maximum for entitlement to benefit. Provision is made for such resources to be taken into account and the manner in which they are to be assessed. Certain capital resources are to be disregarded in the calculation and if, after the calculation, the claimant's capital resources in aggregate are less than the maximum for entitlement to supplementary benefit, then they are to be disregarded. Provision is also made for disregard of dependants' capital resources where the claimant's capital resources exceed that maximum. Part III contains provisions for the calculation of income resources. Earnings and any other income are to be taken into account on a weekly basis. Provision is made for the calculation of earnings, for which payments are to be treated as earnings, which are to be disregarded and which are to be deducted, and as to the amount of the weekly earnings as so calculated which are to be disregarded. Provision is also made for the calculation of any other income, and for the partial disregard of income resources of dependants.

These regulations have been amended; see para. 2767.

2784   —— **single payments**

The Supplementary Benefit (Single Payments) Regulations 1980, S.I. 1980 No. 985 (in force on 24th November 1980), provide for supplementary benefit to be payable by way of single payments of specified amounts to meet exceptional needs.

Part I defines "single payment", provides for the persons who are entitled to claim such payment, provides for the reduction or extinguishment of a payment if the claimant has available capital over £300, and prescribes the circumstances in which and items for which single payments will not be made. Part II relates to maternity needs, Part III to funeral expenses, Part IV to household expenses, Part V to housing expenses, Part VI to miscellaneous expenses, Part VII to items to which the categories of normal, additional and housing requirements relate, and Part VIII to discretionary payments. The amounts of the payments are specified in the Schedules.

2785   —— **trade disputes and recovery from earnings**

The Supplementary Benefit (Trade Disputes and Recovery from Earnings) Regulations 1980, S.I. 1980 No. 1641 (regs. 1–12 and 24 in force on 24th November 1980, remainder on 1st April 1981), make provision for certain aspects of the payment and recovery of supplementary benefit under the Supplementary Benefits Act 1976, as amended by the Social Security Act 1980, para. 2761, and as subject to the Social Security (No. 2) Act 1980, para. 2762, in cases where a member of the supplementary benefit assessment unit is, or the claimant has been, affected by a trade dispute.

Part I contains general provisions. Part II makes provision for supplementary benefit in urgent trade dispute cases (as the Supplementary Benefit (Urgent Cases) Regulations 1980, para. 2781 do not apply in trade dispute cases). Part III provides for the disregard of payments which a person receives or is entitled to obtain from a trade union by reason of being without employment up to the amount of the sum for the time being specified in the No. 2 Act, s. 6. Part IV makes provision for recovery by deductions from earnings of supplementary benefit paid to a claimant after his return to full-time employment following a trade dispute.

2786   —— **transitional provisions**

The Supplementary Benefit (Transitional) Regulations 1980, S.I. 1980 No. 984 (in force on 11th August 1980), make transitional provisions connected with the amendments made to the Supplementary Benefits Act 1976 by the Social Security Act 1980 and brought into force on 24th November 1980 (see para. 2761).

Provision is made for questions relating to entitlement to supplementary pension or allowance for periods after 24th November 1980 which are determined before that day to be determined by the Supplementary Benefits Commission. Questions relating to supplementary benefit for periods before that day but which are to be determined after that day to be determined by a benefit officer. A benefit officer may review any determination of the Commission. An appeal against a determination of the Commission may be brought after that day. A benefit officer is to be a party to any proceedings in an appeal against a determination of the Commission heard after that day. After that day, proceedings for the recovery of any sum which could have been taken before that day by the Commission may be taken by the Secretary of State. The Secretary of State is substituted for the Commission in any proceedings pending on that day, other than before Appeal Tribunals. Provision is made for payment of an additional amount of supplementary pension or allowance where after 24th November 1980 a person becomes entitled to less benefit than he would have been had the amendments not come into operation.

2787 Unemployment and sickness benefit—periods of interruption of employment—transitional provisions

The Social Security (Periods of Interruption of Employment) (Transitional) Regulations 1980, S.I. 1980 No. 1235 (in force on 14th September 1980), make transitional provisions in relation to the Social Security (No. 2) Act 1980, s. 3 (1), para. 2762, which amends the Social Security Act 1975, s. 17 (1), so that a "period of interruption of employment", instead of being any two days of either unemployment or incapacity for work within a period of six consecutive days, is to be either any two days unemployment within a period of six consecutive days or any four or more consecutive days of incapacity for work. These regulations provide that where 13th September 1980 is a day of incapacity for work forming part of a period of interruption of employment, that period is also to include 15th September, if it is also a day of incapacity, or 15th and 16th September, if they are also days of incapacity.

2788 Unemployment benefit—disqualification—whether claimant directly interested in trade dispute

National Insurance Commissioner's decisions:

R(U)5/79 (employer introduced separate bonus schemes for foundry workers and engineering workers; foundry workers' bonus payments rose as a result; engineering workers withdrew labour in pursuit of demands for new scheme; claimant, foundry worker, laid off by reason of stoppage; question whether claimant directly interested in trade dispute; claimant not directly interested in dispute as foundry workers would not be directly affected by any settlement reached; although foundry workers interested in dispute about bonus payments in general way, this was not direct interest; "directly interested" relates to dispute; unemployment benefit therefore payable to claimant).

2789
R(U)4/79 (claimant lost employment due to stoppage of work due to trade dispute; before end of dispute, claimant terminated employment and subsequently found another job; whether for period between leaving employment and finding another job claimant disqualified from receiving unemployment benefit because participating in or directly interested in trade dispute; claimant clearly disqualified up to date of leaving employment and disqualification, once imposed, could not be terminated because at some date after the stoppage commenced and disqualification was incurred the claimant ceased to participate in or be directly interested in trade dispute; hence claimant disqualified for period in question).

2790
R(U)8/80 (claimant laid off after continuous production halted by action of two out of five unions representing employees in annual wage negotiations; claimant a

member of one of three unions which had accepted employer's offer; negotiations conducted on basis that all unions should accept offer; claimant not entitled to unemployment benefit as directly interested in dispute because no separate negotiating).

2791 —— **entitlement—days of unemployment—effect of receipt of ex gratia payment on redundancy**

National Insurance Commissioner's decision:

R(U)1/80 (claimant employed by electricity board; claimant contractually entitled to 12 weeks' notice of termination of service; on redundancy agreed to accept state redundancy payment and ex gratia lump sum and to waive entitlement to notice; claimed unemployment benefit; under Social Security (Unemployment, Sickness and Invalidity Benefit) Regulations 1975, reg. 7 (1) (d), 1975 Halsbury's Abridgment para. 3117, a day in respect of which a person received a payment in lieu either of notice or of the remuneration he would otherwise have received is not to be treated as a day of unemployment; ex gratia payment did not include element as consideration for foregoing unexpired period of notice; payments were genuine redundancy payments and contained no element of payment in lieu of notice or remuneration; hence claimant entitled to benefit). *R v National Insurance Commissioner, ex parte Stratton* [1979] 2 All ER 278, CA, 1979 Halsbury's Abridgment para. 2677, applied.

2792 —— —— —— **effect of receipt of redundancy payment**

National Insurance Commissioner's decision:

R(U)7/80 (claimant employed in shipyard; due to reduction in staff, scheme between company and employees' trade union whereby union agreed to forego entitlement to 90 days' notice of redundancies, as provided by Employment Protection Act 1975, s. 99; employees who voluntarily accepted redundancy entitled to payment equal to remuneration they would have earned between date of leaving and end of 90 days' notification period; under Social Security (Unemployment, Sickness and Invalidity Benefit) Regulations 1975, reg. 7 (1) (d), a day in respect of which a person received payment in lieu either of notice or of the remuneration he would otherwise have received is not to be treated as a day of unemployment; payment was in consideration of giving up income recipient would have received under statutory provisions; nature of inducement to volunteer for redundancy was to offer safeguard against losing entitlement to 90 days' notice; immaterial whether payment equal to remuneration otherwise payable; hence claimant not entitled to benefit).

2793 —— —— —— **effect of receipt of severance payment on voluntary retirement**

National Insurance Commissioner's decision:

R(U) 2/80 (claimant employed by British Airways; entitled to 6 months' notice; severance scheme provided employees could retire early and be paid a capital lump sum determined by age and salary of employee; claimant retired early under severance terms and claimed unemployment benefit; under Social Security (Unemployment, Sickness and Invalidity Benefit) Regulations 1975, reg. 7 (1) (d), a day in respect of which a person received payment in lieu either of notice or of the remuneration he would otherwise have received is not to be treated as a day of unemployment; only factors determining amount of lump sum were amount of claimant's salary and his age; amount of notice to which he would have been entitled was not a factor taken into account in calculating the capital sum; accordingly no part of capital sum paid in lieu of notice or of remuneration and claimant entitled to benefit).

2794 —— —— —— **payment in lieu of notice**

National Insurance Commissioner's decision:

R(U) 4/80 (claimant employed in factory; claimant informed in January of intended closure and redundancies; agreed to accept redundancy terms of 4 weeks' wages per year of service and a week's pay to be calculated on an average of previous 13 weeks' prior to leaving; entitled to 12 weeks' notice; in April given 4 weeks' notice; agreed payment "in first and final satisfaction" in excess of statutory entitlement; claimed unemployment benefit; under Social Security (Unemployment, Sickness and Invalidity Benefit) Regulations 1975, reg. 7 (1) (d), a day in respect of which a person received a payment in lieu either of notice or of the remuneration he would otherwise have received is not to be treated as a day of unemployment; notice of intended closure in January not specific notice of termination of employment; payment was of a capital nature designed to compensate for loss of established asset; it was referable to the past and did not include payment in lieu of notice, or remuneration; hence claimant entitled to benefit). *R v National Insurance Commissioner, ex parte Stratton* [1979] 2 All ER 279, CA, 1979 Halsbury's Abridgment para. 2677 applied.

2795   —— —— **dismissal for misconduct—duty of tribunal to record material facts**

National Insurance Commissioner's decision:

R(U)3/80 (claimant dismissed for bad time-keeping and unsatisfactory work; disqualified from receiving unemployment benefit on grounds that he had lost employment through misconduct; local tribunal report recorded no single fact found to be material to decision; no indication of what conduct constituted misconduct; Social Security (Determination of Claims and Questions) Regulations 1975, reg. 12 (2) (b) placed a duty on a local tribunal to include in the record of every decision a statement of the grounds of such decision and of their findings on questions of fact material to the decision; claimant entitled to know why appeal failed so that on appeal those concerned were not left to speculate on the reasons; local tribunal decision set aside; case remitted for rehearing by a differently constituted tribunal).

2796   —— —— —— **period of disqualification**

National Insurance Commissioner's decision:

R(U) 3/79 (claimant dismissed from employment for being under influence of drink; insurance officer disqualified him from receiving unemployment benefit for six weeks on ground of misconduct; local tribunal, on majority decision, dismissed claimant's appeal; dissenting member noted proper dismissal procedure had not been followed; appeal dismissed, on evidence claimant showed signs of drink incompatible with proper performance of duties; tribunal not to concern itself with question of fair or unfair dismissal; six week period of disqualification not inappropriate).

2797   —— —— **effect of receipt of payment in lieu of notice**

National Insurance Tribunal decision:

R(U) 6/80 (claimant lost employment due to employer's insolvency and did not receive eight weeks' wages in lieu of notice to which he was entitled; received unemployment benefit and earnings-related supplement; applied under Employment Protection (Consolidation) Act 1978, s. 122, for payment in lieu of notice and received from Redundancy Fund sum representing eight weeks' wages less benefit paid in notice period; contended deduction constituted recovery within Social Security (General Benefit) Regulations 1974, reg. 13 (4) (a), (6), and hence entitlement to benefit should be extended by eight weeks; recovery meant recovery for the benefit of the National Insurance Fund; in absence of statutory provision enabling payment to be made out of Redundancy Fund to National Insurance Fund there was no recovery of benefit paid and accordingly terminal dates for payment of those benefits could not be extended).

2798   —— **increase for child dependants—undertaking to make contributions—power to review award**

National Insurance Commissioner's decision:

R(U)6/79 (claimant awarded unemployment benefit from July 1976 to October 1976 and from 17th November 1976 to 27th January 1977; received sickness benefit for intervening period; also received increase in respect of his two children who were not living with him; August 1976 and December 1976 gave undertakings to make contributions toward cost of maintaining children; claimant in breach of undertaking from 17th November 1976 to 20th January 1977; claimant argued that there was no power to review award of increase for children for period 17th November 1976 to 4th December 1976 because undertaking given in December 1976 could not operate retrospectively; undertaking given in December 1976 was merely in confirmation of August 1976 undertaking; earlier undertaking remained effective and was neither superseded nor destroyed by later one; award might therefore be reviewed).

2799   **Widow's benefit—entitlement—widow convicted of manslaughter of husband**

The applicant was convicted of the manslaughter of her husband. She subsequently applied for a widow's allowance under the Social Security Act 1975, s. 24. Her application was refused on the ground of public policy and she applied for an order for judicial review. *Held,* it was the nature of the crime and not the label attached to it which was the deciding factor as to whether the court should reject a claim on the ground of public policy. In this case, where it was plain that the applicant's act was deliberate, conscious and intentional, she was not entitled to benefit from it. The application would be refused.

R v CHIEF NATIONAL INSURANCE COMR, EX PARTE CONNOR [1981] 1 All ER 769 (Queen's Bench Division: LORD LANE CJ, GRIFFITHS and WEBSTER JJ). Decision of National Insurance Commissioner R(G) 2/79 affirmed.

2800   **Workmen's compensation—scheme—incapacity allowance—total or partial incapacity**

National Insurance Commissioner's decision:

R(I) 6/80 (claimant injured in 1939 and received workmen's compensation for partial incapacity; claim for incapacity allowance under Workmen's Compensation (Supplementation) Scheme 1966; claimant was totally incapable of work but was only partially disabled by relevant injury; under scheme, condition for major incapacity allowance was that, as result of relevant injury, claimant should be totally incapable of work; court's decision on Workmen's Compensation Acts relevant; since accident produced only partial incapacity, claimant only entitled to lesser incapacity allowance).

2801   —— **supplementation**

The Workmen's Compensation (Supplementation) (Amendment) Scheme 1980, S.I. 1980 No. 1556 (in force on 26th November 1980), amends the Workmen's Compensation (Supplementation) Scheme 1966 by making adjustments to the intermediate rates of lesser incapacity allowance consequential upon the increase in the maximum rate of that allowance made by the Social Security Benefits Up-rating Order 1980, para. 2709. The Scheme also makes transitional provisions consequent upon that order.

SOCIAL WELFARE

2802   **Welfare food**

The Welfare Food Order 1980, S.I. 1980 No. 1648 (in force on 24th November 1980), consolidates with amendments various orders relating to the welfare food scheme in Great Britain. The amendments take account of changes to certain provisions of the Supplementary Benefits Act 1976 made by the Social Security Act 1980, para. 2761. The principal matters dealt with in the 1980 Order include (i) a description of beneficiaries under the scheme and the welfare milk and vitamins to which each is entitled and (ii) the meaning of a family in special circumstances and how it is assessed for entitlement. The Welfare Food Order 1977, 1977 Halsbury's Abridgment para. 1016 as amended, is revoked.

2803   The Welfare Food (Amendment) Order 1980, S.I. 1980 No. 1836 (in force on 5th January 1981), amends the Welfare Food Order 1980, para. 2802 by increasing the price of children's vitamin drops and vitamin tablets for expectant and nursing mothers.

SOLICITORS

Halsbury's Laws of England (3rd edn.), Vol. 36, paras. 1–358

2804   **Articles**

A Fresh Look at Time Costing, David Harrowes: 130 NLJ 99.

An Assessment of the Master Policy Indemnity Insurance Scheme, C. G. Veljanouski and C. J. Whelan (discussion on Indemnity Insurance Scheme for Solicitors): 131 NLJ 328.

Damages for Breach of Contract—Solicitors and Mental Distress, Geoffrey Douglas [1980] LS Gaz 586.

Profits on Client Account Interest Revisited, Jeremy Cooper (recent developments on the question of whether solicitors should profit from their client accounts): 130 NLJ 644.

Solicitors' Negligence: Liability to Third Parties, FG: 124 Sol Jo 491.

Time to Reflect, David Leng: (determining solicitors' costs and the taxation of costs) 130 NLJ 432.

2805   **Authority—whether knowledge of one partner's client's affairs can be imputed to other partner**

See *Campbell v McCreath*, para. 2085.

2806   **Conduct in court—voluntary absence of accused—solicitor's discretion to continue to take part in case**

See *R v Shaw*, para. 725.

2807   **Costs—costs unnecessarily incurred—liability of solicitor to pay costs**

Canada

The plaintiff made an application for an order that the solicitor for the defendant pay the costs of the hearing personally on a solicitor and client basis. The court found that at the defendant's cross-examination by the plaintiff's counsel, the defendant's solicitor had been both unnecessarily loquacious and repetitive and had unduly interfered with the conduct of the examination. *Held*, for such an order to be made it was not necessary that the solicitor had been dishonest. Whilst mere mistake or error of judgment were not enough, conduct which involved a failure by the solicitor to fulfil his duty to the court and to realise his duty to aid in promoting in his own sphere the cause of justice, was sufficient. The order would accordingly be made.

SONNTAG V SONNTAG (1979) 24 OR (2d) 473 (Supreme Court of Ontario).

2808 —— non-contentious business—recovery—solicitor's duty to inform client of his rights

A judge of the Chancery Division has dismissed a petition for winding up a company on an alleged debt in respect of non-contentious business done by solicitors, on the ground that they had failed to inform the company of its rights to have the bill of costs taxed and to require the solicitors to obtain a certificate from the Law Society that the bill was fair and reasonable. The presentation of the petition constituted "proceedings" within the Solicitors Remuneration Order 1972, art. 3 (2). Furthermore, the court was satisfied that the debt relied upon was disputed upon substantial grounds and would refuse to sanction the petition for winding up on that ground also.

RE LACEWARD LTD [1981] 1 All ER 254 (Chancery Division: SLADE J). *Clement Davies v Inter GSA* (1979) 123 Sol Jo 505, CA, 1979 Halsbury's Abridgment para. 2695 applied.

2809 —— taxation—taxation after payment of bill of costs—time limit—separate bills

Under the Solicitors Act 1974, s. 70 (3) an order for taxation may be made at the instance of the party chargeable where the application is made before the expiration of twelve months from the payment of the bill. The defendant to an action brought by the plaintiff solicitors for non-payment of a bill of costs submitted that the bill should be taxed together with three others which had been settled more than twelve months before, on the basis that together they constituted one bill of costs. The plaintiffs conceded that the fourth bill was liable to taxation under s. 70 (3), as the application for taxation was made before the expiration of twelve months; but that all four were separate bills and thus the other three, which had been settled outside the time limit, could not be taxed. *Held*, where a solicitor submitted separate bills of costs from time to time during a protracted action, each one should be regarded as a final bill of costs in settlement of work done to date, where it was clear at the time that the solicitor intended them to be treated as such. Otherwise they should be treated as requests for payment on account, comprising one single bill. It was clear that the plaintiffs' intention had been that each bill was to be treated as a final settlement and therefore pursuant to s. 70 (3) the first three bills were not liable to taxation.

DAVIDSONS V JONES-FENLEIGH (1980) 124 Sol Jo 204 (Court of Appeal: ROSKILL and EVELEIGH LJJ).

2810 Documents—preparation by unqualified person—instrument relating to legal proceedings

The appellant was the founder of an association which offered counselling and assistance to individuals in divorce matters. He was not a qualified solicitor. Informations were laid against him in respect of a divorce petition and statement of arrangements which he had prepared. These documents were used in the divorce proceedings of a client. The appellant was convicted of drawing or preparing an instrument relating to legal proceedings in contravention of the Solicitors Act 1974, s. 22 (1) (b). On appeal, *held*, a divorce petition or statement of arrangements in divorce proceedings was an instrument relating to "any legal proceeding" within the meaning of the Act. The appeal would be dismissed.

POWELL V ELY (1980) Times, 22nd May (Queen's Bench Division: WALLER LJ and BROWN J).

2811 —— —— whether work done for fee

An association offered a house conveyancing service. All the work was done by members except drawing up the conveyance documents, which was done by the defendant, who was not a member but the association's "honorary conveyancer". The association received fees but no remuneration was paid to the defendant. On a charge under the Solicitors Act 1974, s. 22 (1), of preparing instruments of transfer, not being a qualified person, *held*, the defendant could not rely on the defence under

s. 22 (1) that the act was not done for or in expectation of any fee, since it was irrelevant that the fee was not paid to the person who actually prepared the instruments. Nor was it necessary that the fee should have been paid specifically for drawing up the documents. The work done by the defendant was the end of a series of actions by the association which constituted a composite unit in respect of which the fee was paid. Accordingly, it could not be said that the defendant had acted free of charge.

REYNOLDS v HOYLE (No. 2) [1980] LS Gaz R 819 (Queen's Bench Division: LORD LANE CJ and COMYN J).

For previous proceedings, see 1975 Halsbury's Abridgment para. 3213.

2812   Duty towards client—failure to secure good title to property—liability—assessment of damages

Scotland

In 1968 solicitors concluded a contract for the purchase of a cottage on behalf of the plaintiff. The solicitors knew, but did not inform the plaintiff that the title to the cottage was defective. The plaintiff sold the cottage three years later at a price £1,500 less than would have been offered had the title been good. The plaintiff brought an action for damages against the solicitors. *Held*, the sale of the cottage at a reduced price was a natural consequence of the solicitors' breach and they were accordingly liable in damages, the correct measure of which was the difference between the price the property would have fetched had the title been good and the price actually realised.

HABERSTICH v MCCORMICK AND NICHOLSON 1975 SC 1 (Court of Session). *Lake v Bushby* [1949] 2 All ER 964, *Pilkington v Wood* [1953] Ch 770 and *Ford v White* [1964] 1 WLR 885 distinguished.

2813   Insurance—professional indemnity insurance—double insurance

See *National Employers Mutual General Insurance Association Ltd v Haydon*, para. 1644.

2814   —— —— Law Society's group scheme—validity

The Solicitors Act 1974, s. 37 provides for a compulsory professional indemnity insurance scheme. The Council of the Law Society is empowered to make rules concerning indemnity and is empowered to withhold a practising certificate from any person who does not satisfy it that he was complying with the rules. The Solicitors' Indemnity Rules 1975, r. 2 provides that the Society should take out and maintain with authorised insurers a master policy and issue to solicitors certificates of insurance. Solicitors to whom the Rules applied should pay premiums payable by them under the master policy and certificate of insurance as soon as they fell due. The Society regarded the scheme as compulsory for all practising solicitors.

Questions arose as to the validity of the Solicitors' Indemnity Insurance Scheme introduced under the Rules and whether the Law Society was bound to account for any part of the commission received in respect of the premiums paid by individual solicitors pursuant to the scheme. *Held*, (i) the nature of the sanction for non-compliance with the Indemnity Rules afforded grounds for concluding that the wording of the power to make Indemnity Rules conferred by s. 37 should be construed narrowly. It was clear that the intention of the makers of the Rules was that the Society should enter into the agreement as a trustee, for persons ascertained and unascertained, to require the insurers to provide them with insurance. The argument that the proposed master policy as envisaged by the Rules did not involve the "taking out" of any insurance within the meaning of s. 37 (2) (b) was rejected and the challenge to the validity of the Rules would therefore fail. (ii) As regards the retention of the commission and accountability of the Society, the court had to proceed on the basis that the Rules were valid but that an agent or a trustee must account for the profit obtained. If the Society entered into a contract as trustee then as soon as the contract had been concluded there existed a fiduciary relationship between the Society and the solicitor. However, proof of a post-contract fiduciary relationship would not itself render the Society liable to account for the commissions paid, and it was not liable to account for them.

SWAIN V LAW SOCIETY [1980] 3 All ER 615 (Chancery Division: SLADE J).

2815   Lay observer—annual report

In the *Fifth Annual Report of the Lay Observer* 1979 (HC 507) the lay observer says that he shares the concern of his predecessor and of the Benson Commission that the Law Society lacks a system for bringing to the attention of the profession the lessons learnt from the investigation of complaints. He looks forward to the Law Society's proposed action on the subject. In considering the areas of professional practice principally likely to cause client dissatisfaction, the lay observer refers to the failure to keep the client informed of progress, and the absence of adequate estimates. The lay observer suggests that personal representatives should be required to account to their co-executors and administrators at suitable intervals and that, when work is to be handled by a legal executive or clerk, a partner should if possible introduce the client to the legal executive or clerk. He refers also to the failure of legally aided persons to understand the operation of the charge on property of damages recovered or preserved in proceedings and looks forward to the introduction of a leaflet explaining the charge which can be given to legally-aided persons. The lay observer also suggests that counsel's opinions should be so drafted as to satisfy the lay client that his case has been fully and fairly put to counsel by his solicitor and that counsel himself has understood the lay client's point of view. During the year the lay observer accepted 107 complaints for formal examination.

2816   Negligence—duty of care—formation of company

Canada

The defendant solicitor was instructed to form a company but failed to incorporate it properly. In an action for negligence he was held to be liable to his client for the latter's distress, inconvenience and aggravation, and to the company for the expenses incurred in remedying the deficiencies.

WOURNELL (PA) CONTRACTING LTD V ALLEN (1979) 100 DLR (3d) 62 (Supreme Court of Nova Scotia).

2817   Practice as solicitor—business for incorporating companies—whether constitutes unauthorised practice

Canada

The accused appealed against conviction of the offence of practising as a solicitor although not a member of the Law Society contrary to the provisions of a Canadian statute. He had established a business for incorporating companies, using prepared forms into which he inserted a suitable objects clause. If no form appeared suitable he had sent the client to a solicitor. He had not represented himself as a solicitor, nor given advice as to whether to incorporate or not. *Held*, by a majority decision, only acts which were to be done exclusively by solicitors were forbidden by the Act, and there was no express prohibition on such an activity. The purpose of the general prohibition was to protect the public from acts done by unqualified persons. The accused had not given legal advice and had not therefore contravened the Act. The appeal would be allowed.

R V NICHOLSON (1979) 96 DLR (3d) 693 (Supreme Court of Alberta).

2818   Professional misconduct—disciplinary proceedings—judicial review

See *Connor v Law Society of British Columbia*, para. 3.

2819   Professional privilege—production of documents—availability of privilege in criminal proceedings

See *Gamlen Chemical Co (UK) Ltd v Rochem Ltd (No. 2)*, para. 895.

2820   Qualifications—recognition of qualifications of Community nationals

See para. 247.

2821   Remuneration—non-contentious business

The Council of the Law Society has issued notes for guidance on what is a "fair and reasonable" charge for non-contentious business in accordance with art. 2 of the Solicitors Remuneration Order 1972. Reference is made to the importance of the time factor and the need to keep expense rates up to date. The notes include, as an appendix, specific yardsticks for value percentages for the conveyancing of domestic property, the conveyancing of property other than domestic property, the grant of a lease and non-contentious probate and the administration of estates. See (1980) LS Gaz, 15th October 1005, 1006.

SPECIFIC PERFORMANCE

Halsbury's Laws of England (3rd edn.), Vol. 36, paras. 359–529

2822   Contractual licence—order for specific performance—appropriateness of remedy

See *Verrall v Great Yarmouth Borough Council*, para. 469.

STAMP DUTIES

Halsbury's Laws of England (3rd edn.), Vol. 33, paras. 480–622

2823   Companies—duty on raising of capital—basis of assessment

See Case 161/78: *P. Conradsen A/S v Ministry for Fiscal Affairs*, para. 1138.

2824   Finance Act 1980

See para. 2328.

STATUTES

Halsbury's Laws of England (3rd edn.), Vol. 36, paras. 530–750

2825   Statute giving effect to international agreements—interpretation

See *Rothmans of Pall Mall (Overseas) Ltd v Saudi Arabian Airlines Corpn*, para. 195; *Fothergill v Monarch Airlines*, para. 197.

STOCK EXCHANGE

Halsbury's Laws of England (3rd edn.), Vol. 36, paras. 751–970

2826   Dealers in securities—code of conduct

The Council for the Securities Industry has issued the *Code of Conduct for Dealers in Securities* (May 1980). This is aimed at establishing standards of ethical behaviour to promote the effective functioning of the market and implements the European code of conduct relating to transactions in transferable securities. The code applies to all persons in the United Kingdom who as intermediaries engage in the business of arranging or undertaking transactions in transferable securities for investors. The code stresses the need to observe its spirit and the highest standards of professional conduct and complete integrity. It deals, inter alia, with conflicts of interest; the role of the dealer as agent; the making of a false market; dealings while shares are suspended by the Stock Exchange; the content of contract notes; compliance with the appropriate codes and rulings; the dealer's commission; the keeping of a separate account for each client; the content of an agreement to manage a client's investments; the keeping of records by a dealer and the auditing of his accounts; protection for the interests of clients from loss through negligence, etc.; and the need to assist in any formal inquiries.

2827   Licence fees

The Prevention of Fraud (Investments) Act Licensing (Amendment) Regulations 1980, S.I. 1980 No. 350 (in force on 1st April 1980), amend the Prevention of Fraud (Investments) Act Licensing Regulations 1944 by increasing the fees payable for a principal's licence and a representative's licence.

2828   Stockbroker—forged transfer of shares—knowledge—liability to indemnify bank

See *Yeung v Hong Kong and Shanghai Banking Corpn*, para. 1378.

TELECOMMUNICATIONS AND TELEVISION

Halsbury's Laws of England (3rd edn.), Vol. 36, paras. 971–1123

2829   Broadcasting—Channel Islands

The Independent Broadcasting Authority Act 1979 (Channel Islands) Order 1980, S.I. 1980 No. 189 (in force on 13th March 1980), extends the Independent Broadcasting Authority Act 1979 to the Channel Islands.

2830   Broadcasting Act 1980

The Broadcasting Act 1980 amends and supplements the Independent Broadcasting Authority Act 1973 in connection with the Independent Broadcasting Authority's (the IBA) functions and provision of a second television service (the Fourth Channel); it also provides for the broadcasting of television programmes in Wales and establishes a Broadcasting Complaints Commission. The Act received the royal assent on 13th November 1980 and ss. 1, 31, 32, 34, 36–39, 40 (1)–(3), 41, 40 (6) (in part) and Sch. 7 (in part) came into force on that date. Parts II, III, ss. 30, 33, 40 (4) (part), (6) (part), Schs. 1, 2, 6 (part), 7 (part) came into force on 1st January 1981, and ss. 17, 24, 28, 29, 40 (4) (part), Schs. 3, 5, 6 (part) on 1st February 1981: S.I. 1980 No. 1907. The remaining provisions come into force on days to be appointed.

Part I. Extension of duration of Authority's function
Section 1 extends the life of the IBA (which would otherwise expire on 31st December 1981) until 31st December 1996 and provides for a further extension of up to five years by order subject to the approval of Parliament.

Part II. Provision of second television service by Authority
Section 2 provides that programmes, other than advertisements, broadcast on the Fourth Channel are to be provided by the IBA themselves. The nature of the Fourth Channel and its relation to ITV are dealt with in s. 3. The IBA is to give the

channel a distinctive character of its own and to maintain a proper balance of subject matter between the two services. A subsidiary is to be formed for the purpose of obtaining and assembling material for the new channel: s. 4. Section 5 deals with advertisements and s. 6 makes provision in relation to rental payments. The content of annual reports is dealt with in s. 7.

Part III. The Fourth Channel in Wales
Section 8 provides that programmes (other than advertisements) broadcast on the Fourth Channel in Wales are to be provided by the Welsh Fourth Channel Authority established by s. 9. Provisions as to the Authority are contained in Sch. 1 and their functions, powers and duties in s. 10. Welsh programmes and advertisements on this channel are dealt with in ss. 11, 12. Section 13 and Sch. 2 modify certain provisions of the 1973 Act in relation to the IBA and under s. 14 the Welsh Authority is empowered to appoint advisory bodies for assistance. Provisions as to finances of the Authority, their accounts, audit and reports are contained in s. 15. Section 16 amends the 1973 Act in relation to rates of additional payments.

Part IV. The Broadcasting Complaints Commission
Sections 17–20 and Sch. 3 establish a Broadcasting Complaints Commission to consider complaints of unjust or unfair treatment in, and infringement of privacy in or in connection with, material included in programmes broadcast by the IBA or the BBC. Provision is also made in relation to the Commission's constitution, procedure and consideration of complaints. Section 21 deals with the publication of complaints and the Commission's findings. Section 22 confers a duty on the broadcasting bodies to publicise the Commission and their function and s. 23 provides for the making of annual reports by the Commission. Contributions towards the Commission's expenses are covered in s. 24 and s. 25 empowers the Secretary of State to make regulations in order to modify Part IV in relation to programmes broadcast on the Fourth Channel in Wales.

Part V. Other Provisions
Section 26 and Sch. 4 provide for rental payments to be made by local sound programme contractors and s. 27 enables the IBA to make grants to them. Section 28 and Sch. 5 deal with the provision of teletext services and s. 29 requires a code to be drawn up governing teletext transmissions. The Secretary of State may by order repeal Part III as from a specified date and modify Parts II, V accordingly: s. 30. Section 31 provides for the exclusion from programmes of opinions of the IBA, their subsidiary and programme contractors. Advisory committees for Scotland, Wales and Northern Ireland may be appointed under s. 32. The IBA's duties in relation to programme contracts are covered in s. 33; s. 34 disqualifies certain persons from being programme contractors and s. 35 deals with the training of persons employed by programme contractors. Local newspapers which have been adversely affected by a local radio are no longer entitled to acquire shareholdings in the radio company concerned: s. 36. Section 37 requires information as to television programme contracts and applications for such contracts to be furnished on request. Pensions and compensation to members of the IBA are dealt with in s. 38 and s. 39 relates to the computation of programme contractors' profits. Sections 40, 41 are concerned with interpretation, citation, extent and commencement and Schs. 6, 7 with transitional provisions and repeals.

2831　Interception of communications—warrants

The interception of communications may only be undertaken under warrant of the Home Secretary (in Scotland, the Secretary of State for Scotland) given under his own hand. In a command paper, *The Interception of Communications in Great Britain* (1980, Cmnd 7873), the Home Secretary has described the conditions on which warrants are granted, how they are obtained and the arrangements for the products of interception. To obtain a warrant the police and HM Customs and Excise must show that the offence in connection with which interception is requested is serious (as defined); normal methods of investigation either have been tried and failed or are inherently unlikely to succeed; and that there is good reason to think that interception would be likely to lead to an arrest and conviction. The conditions relating to the issue of a warrant by the security services are that there must be a major subversive, terrorist or espionage activity likely to injure the national interest; the probable product of the interception must be of direct use in compiling information necessary to the due functioning of the security service; and normal methods of investigation either have been tried and failed or are inherently unlikely to succeed. Similar conditions govern the issue of warrants to the police for counter-terrorist interceptions. Separate warrants are normally required for interceptions of mail and telephones. Except in instances of exceptional urgency warrants are granted in writing. They last for a maximum of two months but may be renewed thereafter on oral application. When interception is no longer required, the warrant is cancelled. Appropriate records of warrant are kept, in respect of England and Wales, by the Home Office. Interceptions are recorded and notes or transcripts made which are kept for a period of 12 months (sometimes longer). These are not tendered in evidence and there is no disclosure to private individuals, private bodies or domestic tribunals of any kind.

2832   Licences charges

The Wireless Telegraphy (Broadcast Licence Charges and Exemption) (Amendment) Regulations 1980, S.I. 1980 No. 798 (in force on 31st July 1980), amend the Wireless Telegraphy (Broadcast Licence Charges and Exemption) Regulations 1970, by substituting a new scale of fees for those licences related to the number of premises connected to the licensee's apparatus and by increasing certain fees prescribed by those regulations.

2833   The Wireless Telegraphy (General Licence Charges) (Amendment) Regulations 1980, S.I. 1980 No. 1850 (in force on 1st January 1981), increase the fees payable on the issue, renewal and variation of certain wireless telegraphy licences, other than television broadcast receiving licences and broadcast relay station licences. Fresh provision is also made for determining the fee payable on the issue and renewal of private mobile radio licences. The Wireless Telegraphy (General Licence Charges) Regulations 1968 are amended accordingly. The 1968 Regulations, reg. 5 (2) and the Wireless Telegraphy (General Licence Charges) (Amendment) Regulations 1978, 1978 Halsbury's Abridgment para. 2762, are revoked.

2834   —— exemptions

The Wireless Telegraphy (Exemption) Regulations 1980, S.I. 1980 No. 1848 (in force on 1st January 1981), exempt the installation and use of metal detectors and model control equipment from the requirement of a licence under the Wireless Telegraphy Act 1949 subject to the terms, provisions and limitations set out in the Schedule to the regulations.

2835   Television company—broadcast of programme based on confidential information—duty to inform injured party of source of information

See *British Steel Corpn v Granada Television Ltd*, para. 896.

THEATRES AND OTHER PLACES OF ENTERTAINMENT

Halsbury's Laws of England (3rd edn.), Vol. 37, paras. 1–132

2836   Cinemas—levy—collection

The Cinematograph Films (Collection of Levy) (Amendment No. 8) Regulations

1980, S.I. 1980 No. 1178 (in force on 21st September 1980), further amend the 1968 Regulations by prolonging to 1985 the liability on exhibitors of films to pay levy. The Cinematograph Films (Collection of Levy) (Amendment) Regulations 1970 are revoked.

2837　　—— —— distribution

The Cinematograph Films (Distribution of Levy) (Amendment No. 2) Regulations 1980, S.I. 1980 No. 1179 (in force on 21st September 1980), further amend the 1970 Regulations by prolonging to 1985 the time in respect of which the proceeds of the levy on exhibitors of films are to be distributed by the British Film Fund Agency to the makers of eligible films. The 1979 Regulations, reg. 3, 1979 Halsbury's Abridgment para. 2740 is revoked.

2838　　—— licence fees

The Fees for Cinematograph Licences (Variation) Order 1980, S.I. 1980 No. 1398 (in force on 1st November 1980), raises the maximum fees payable for the grant, renewal and transfer of licences issued under the Cinematograph Act 1909, s. 2 for the use of premises for the purpose of cinematograph exhibitions. The 1978 Order, 1978 Halsbury's Abridgment para 2765 is revoked.

2839　　—— multiple cinemas in one building—exhibitors' records

The Films (Exhibitors) (Amendment No. 2) Regulations 1980, S.I. 1980 No. 1819 (in force on 1st January 1981), substitute a new Second Schedule into the 1961 Regulations and revoke the 1972 Amendment Regulations and the 1970 Amendment Regulations, reg. 3 (3). They add to the prescribed exhibitors' records form a summary for completion by an exhibitor who carries on business at more than one cinema in the same building.

2840　　—— storage of celluloid—exemptions

See para. 2263.

2841　　Films—licence fees—exhibitors

The Films (Exhibitors) (Amendment) Regulations 1980, S.I. 1980 No. 1180 (in force on 1st October 1980), further amend the 1961 Regulations by increasing the fees payable in respect of applications for exhibitors' licences. The 1977 Regulations, 1977 Halsbury's Abridgement para 2760 are revoked.

2842　　—— —— renters

The Films (Renters' Licences) (Amendment) Regulations 1980, S.I. 1980 No. 1188 (in force on 1st October 1980), further amend the 1961 Regulations by increasing to £100 the fee payable for a renter's licence. The 1977 Regulations, 1977 Halsbury's Abridgment para 2761 are revoked.

2843　　—— registration fees

The Films (Registration) (Amendment) Regulations 1980, S.I. 1980 No. 1181 (in force on 1st October 1980), amend the 1970 Regulations by increasing the fees payable in respect of applications for the registration of all films, applications to amend the register, inspection of the register and applications for certified copies of entries in the register. The Regulations also differentiate between the fees payable in respect of a long film and a short film. The 1977 Regulations, 1977 Halsbury's Abridgment para 2762 are revoked.

2844　　Films Act 1980

The Films Act 1980 amends the enactments relating to the financing and exhibition of films. The Act received the royal assent on 17th July 1980 and except for s. 8

came into force on 20th July 1980. Section 8 comes into force on a day to be appointed.

Section 1 extends to the end of 1985 the existing power of the National Film Finance Corporation to acquire the copyright in any film and to make loans for the production or distribution of films on a commercially successful basis. The corporation is empowered until then to make loans or otherwise give financial assistance for preproduction purposes. The power of the Secretary of State is also extended in regard to the transfer of the Corporation's assets and liabilities and the cesser of their functions and his power to dissolve the Corporation is postponed until after the end of 1985.

Section 2 repeals the power of the Government to lend to the Corporation and extinguishes the liability of the Corporation to repay outstanding Government loans and interest. It empowers the Secretary of State to make a grant to the Corporation of £1 million and increases the aggregate amount that the Corporation may borrow from non-Government sources. In respect to the levy periods in the five years beginning with the coming into force of the section provision is made for the British Film Fund Agency to make payments to the Corporation in preference to other payments which it is authorised or required to make. The Corporation is no longer required to make payments in respect of preproduction work in accordance with arrangements approved by the Secretary of State.

Section 3 increases the maximum number of members of the Board of the Corporation from five to six. Section 4 provides that the levy on exhibitors is to be prolonged. Section 5 extends to the end of 1985 the obligation upon exhibitors to include a prescribed quota of British or Community films among the registered films shown. Section 6 provides that for the purpose of determining whether an exhibitor has shown the prescribed quota, where a person exhibits at more than one cinema in the same building the showing times at each of those cinemas are to be aggregated. Section 7 enables the Secretary of State, after consulting the Cinematograph Films Council, by order to suspend and reimpose the requirement for cinemas to show a prescribed quota of British or Community films. Section 8 enables the labour costs of a film registrable as British to include payments to citizens of other member states. The status of a film as British affects eligibility for payments from the proceeds of the levy on exhibitors as provided in s. 4. Section 9 and Sch. 1 deal with citation commencement, repeals and extent.

2845   **Music and dancing licence—renewal—jurisdiction to impose new conditions**

See *R v Torbay Licensing JJ, ex parte White*, para. 1664.

TIME

Halsbury's Laws of England (3rd edn.), Vol. 37, paras. 133–185

2846   **Airports shops—hours**

See para. 181.

2847   **Computation of time—calendar month running from an arbitrary date**

On 30th September 1978 the landlord of business premises served a notice to quit on the tenant, who, under the Landlord and Tenant Act 1954, s. 29 (3), then had four months from the date of the landlord's notice to apply for a new tenancy. Under the Interpretation Act 1889, s. 3 this meant four calendar months. The tenant did not serve his notice until 31st January 1979 and it was held to be out of time. On appeal, *held*, BRIDGE LJ dissenting, where the time within which a person was required to act was fixed by reference to a period of calendar months from the performance of another act which could be performed on any date in any month, one month elapsed on the corresponding day of the next month.   No account was to be taken of the fact that some months were shorter than others.   Accordingly, the date of expiry for service by the tenant lapsed on the 30th day of the fourth succeeding month, that was the 30th January, even though it was a calendar month of 31 days.   The tenant's appeal would be dismissed.

DODDS v WALKER [1980] 2 All ER 507 (Court of Appeal: STEPHENSON, BRIDGE and TEMPLEMAN LJJ).

2848   Summer time

The Summer Time Order 1980, S.I. 1980 No. 1089 (in force on 28th July 1980), provides for the periods of summer time in 1981 and 1982 during which the time for general purposes in the United Kingdom will be one hour in advance of Greenwich mean time.

TORT

Halsbury's Laws of England (3rd edn.), Vol. 37, paras. 186–280

2849   Abstraction of underground water—abstraction in excess of statutory limit—nature of cause of action

See *Re National Capital Commission*, para. 3123.

2850   Breach of criminal law—whether gives rise to action for damages—conspiracy

Oil companies supplied oil to the Southern Rhodesian Government in breach of an order imposing criminal penalties for such a breach.   A company which had entered into an agreement with the oil companies alleged that the breach helped prolong the existence of the illegal regime in Rhodesia which in turn damaged the company's business interests, giving rise to a right of action for damages.   Further, it alleged that agreement by the oil companies to commit the breach amounted to conspiracy and also gave rise to a right of action for damages.   *Held*, the general rule, that the remedy for breach of the criminal law was prima facie the criminal sanction and none other, applied in this case so as to avoid the possibility of multiplicity of actions.   Hence breach of the order gave rise to no civil remedy.   Also, since the acts done in combination were not done with intent to harm the company and were not themselves actionable, the tort of conspiracy was not committed.

LONRHO LTD v SHELL PETROLEUM (UK) LTD (1980) Times, 1st December (Queen's Bench Division: PARKER J).

This decision has been affirmed by the Court of Appeal; see (1981) Times, 7th March.

For previous proceedings, see *Lonrho Ltd v Shell Petroleum Co Ltd* [1980] 1 WLR 627, HL, para. 902.

2851   Conspiracy—agreement for company to give financial aid for purchase of own shares—whether gives rise to tortious liability

See *Belmont Finance Corpn v Williams Furniture Ltd (No. 2)*, para. 385.

2852   Conversion— determination of title to goods—conflict of laws

See *Winkworth v Christie Manson & Woods Ltd*, para. 441.

2853   —— order to deliver up goods—court's discretion in making order

See *Howard E. Perry & Co Ltd v British Railways Board*, para. 2854.

2854   —— **refusal to deliver up goods—liability where refusal to release goods induced by fear**

During a steel strike a quantity of steel belonging to a company was held up by the British Railways Board at certain depots. The board feared industrial action by the rail unions if attempts were made by either the company or the board to remove the steel. The company contended that this action amounted to wrongful interference with goods contrary to the Torts (Interference with Goods) Act 1977, s. 1, and claimed an order for delivery up of the steel and payment of damages. The board admitted that the company was entitled to possession of the steel but contended that (i) the new statutory tort of wrongful interference with goods under s. 1 did not include a mere refusal to deliver and further that there was no conversion if the reason for the refusal to release the goods was a genuine or reasonable fear and (ii) damages alone would be an adequate remedy as the board feared industrial action if the order for delivery up of the steel was to be made. *Held*, (i) it was a clear case of conversion. The board were denying the company most rights of ownership of goods, including the right of possession, for an indefinite period. Further a denial of the right of possession did not cease to be a denial by being accompanied by a statement that the company was entitled to possession which was being denied to it. The withholding of the steel was a wrongful interference with goods within the Act and the reason for withholding the goods provided no reasonable justification for doing so. (ii) If a plaintiff could easily replace the goods detained by purchasing them on the open market, then the payment of damages, out of which the price could be paid, would be adequate compensation. Steel was difficult to obtain and damages were poor compensation if failure of supplies caused a trader's insolvency. In exercising its discretion in making an order the court should not allow threats to one party, or one party's fears from such threats to dominate the decision. Litigants' rights were not to be curtailed by fears of disorder which included fears of unlawful assemblies and breaches of the peace. The order sought would accordingly be made.

HOWARD E. PERRY & CO LTD v BRITISH RAILWAYS BOARD [1980] 2 All ER 579 (Chancery Division: SIR ROBERT MEGARRY V-C).

2855   **Damages—appeal—injunction in lieu of damages**

See *Kennaway v Thompson*, para. 1631.

2856   **Location of tort—defective goods—service of process out of the jurisdiction**

See *Castree v E R Squibb and Sons Ltd*, para. 442.

TOWN AND COUNTRY PLANNING

Halsbury's Laws of England (3rd edn.), Vol. 37, paras. 281–816

2857   **Articles**

Compulsory Purchase and Planning Proceedings, Henry E. Markson: 124 Sol Jo 643.

Development Upon the Resumption of the Abandoned Use, Owen Watkin: [1980] JPL 226.

The Dormant Established Use, H. W. Wilkinson: 130 NLJ 490 (in the light of *Newbury District Council v Secretary of State for the Environment* [1980] 1 All ER 731, HL, para. 2881).

Maintenance, Improvement or Reconstruction of a Building, H. W. Wilkinson: 130 NLJ 876.

Parliamentary Ombudsman: Planning Cases, Henry E. Markson: 124 Sol Jo 587.

Planning Conditions Again, Henry E. Markson, (recent developments in planning law): 124 Sol Jo 488.

Planning Conditions Reviewed, Henry E. Markson: 124 Sol Jo 404.
Planning Errors, Henry E. Markson: 124 Sol Jo 571.
Planning Investigations, Henry E. Markson: 124 Sol Jo 263.
Planning Law and Undesirable Activities, H. W. Wilkinson: 130 NLJ 1099.
Prostitution and Planning Law, Alec Samuels: [1980] JPL 578.
Public Inquiries: Natural Justice, Henry E. Markson: 124 Sol Jo 436.
Public Inquiry Costs, Henry E. Markson: 124 Sol Jo 625.
Stop Notices, Henry E. Markson: 124 Sol Jo 56.
Use Classes, Henry E. Markson: 124 Sol Jo 783.

2858   Advertisements—control—outdoor advertising

The Department of the Environment has issued a consultation document on the relaxation of controls on outdoor advertising. It is proposed to add two categories, to those which may be displayed without the specific consent of the planning authority. These are: (1) illuminated advertisements on shops and "shop-like" premises, subject to certain specified limits on the number and size of the type of advertisement and the intensity of the illumination; and (2) temporary advertisements on hoardings around construction sites on which building operations are taking place, or are about to begin, in commercial or industrial areas of towns and cities, subject to certain specified limits on the size of advertisements and the duration of their display.

2859   Appeal—decision—reasons for decision misstatement of fact— validity of decision

In a case where an inspector's decision on a planning appeal contained a material misstatement of fact as to distances between the proposed and existing buildings, it was held that the decision was not vitiated because the misstatement was an obvious silly mistake.

ELMBRIDGE BOROUGH COUNCIL v SECRETARY OF STATE FOR THE ENVIRONMENT [1980] LS Gaz R 181 (Queen's Bench Division: BRISTOW J).

2860   —— —— whether perverse or disclosing errors of law

In 1976 a local planning authority refused to grant permission for the first floor of premises in a busy street to be used as solicitors' offices. Permission for such use of the ground floor had been granted in 1973. The decision of the Secretary of State to uphold the refusal was challenged as perverse and as disclosing errors of law. The court was unable to hold that the decision, which was based on the policies set out in the development plan and the need for preserving residential accommodation, was so unreasonable that no reasonable person could have reached it, or that there were errors of law on the face of the decision letter. Decision letters should not be subject to hypercritical analysis nor construed as if they were statutes.

SEARS BLOK v SECRETARY OF STATE FOR THE ENVIRONMENT (1980) 254 Estates Gazette 1195 (Queen's Bench Division: LLOYD J).

2861   ——inquiry—Secretary of State's refusal to adjourn inquiry— court's jurisdiction to quash decision

The Secretary of State refused an application to adjourn an inquiry requested by the applicants to allow them time to prepare their case against allowing certain developers to build a supermarket. The applicants applied, by notice of motion, to the High Court to quash the Secretary of State's decision contending, inter alia, that the refusal amounted to a breach of natural justice. The judge held that he had no jurisdiction to hear the notice of motion. On appeal, *held*, the refusal to adjourn the inquiry did not constitute a "decision of the Secretary of State on appeal" under the Town and Country Planning Act 1971, s. 36, relating to planning decisions, within the meaning of s. 242 (3) (b) which provided that only such decisions could be questioned in legal proceedings. Accordingly the judge had no jurisdiction to deal with the application. If there had been jurisdiction, however, there was no evidence that the Secretary of State's refusal was a breach of natural justice. Under the Town and Country Planning (Inquiries Procedure) Rules 1974, r. 10 (8), 1974 Halsbury's Abridgment para. 3213, an inspector had a wide and unfettered discretion to adjourn the inquiry as he thought necessary in the interests of justice to any objector to do so. The appeal would therefore be dismissed.

     CO-OPERATIVE RETAIL SERVICES LTD v SECRETARY OF STATE FOR THE ENVIRONMENT [1980] 1 All ER 449 (Court of Appeal: STEPHENSON and BRANDON LJJ). Dictum of Lord Denning MR in *Ostreicher v Secretary of State for the Environment* [1978] 3 All ER 82, CA at 86, 1978 Halsbury's Abridgment para. 10 applied.

2862   —— proposals for improving planning appeals system

The Department of the Environment published a consultation paper on 21st October 1980 (Press Notice 437) setting out proposals for speeding up the appeal system. The proposals include the transfer of all classes of appeal to inspectors; excepted classes would be limited to those which cannot be totally transferred and the Secretary of State would exercise his powers to direct "recovery" of appeals sparingly. Informal inquiries would be introduced as an experiment as a simpler and cheaper alternative to formal local inquiries and in other instances appeals by written representations would be encouraged rather than the holding of local inquiries. Where local inquiries are to be held, these would be arranged more promptly.

2863   Community land—authority—register of land holdings

The Land Authority for Wales (Register of Land Holdings) Regulations 1980, S.I. 1980 No. 1856 (in force on 13th January 1981), provide for the Land Authority for Wales to keep a register of its land acquisitions, holdings and disposals. They prescribe the kinds of land to be registered, the form of the register and the particulars to be contained in it. They also prescribe that the register of local extracts be available for public inspection.

2864   —— compulsory acquisition by public authorities

The Compulsory Acquisition by Public Authorities (Compensation) (Revocation) Order 1980, S.I. 1980 No. 1172 (in force on 6th August 1980), revokes the Compulsory Acquisition by Public Authorities (Compensation) Order 1976, 1976 Halsbury's Abridgment para. 2518, as amended, in relation to disposals of land after 5th August 1980. The 1976 Order altered the rules for assessing compensation when the authority from which land was acquired was exempt from development land tax by virtue of the Development Land Tax Act 1976, s. 39, Sch. 7, now repealed by the Finance Act 1980, para. 2328. For the purposes of tax liability when land is compulsorily acquired, the time of disposal is now determined in accordance with the Development Land Tax Act 1976, s. 45.

2865   —— Docklands Land Board—dissolution

The Docklands Land Board (Dissolution) Order 1980, S.I. 1980 No. 393 (in force on 1st April 1980), abolishes the Docklands Land Board and makes various consequential and transitional provisions. The Docklands Land Board Order 1977, 1977 Halsbury's Abridgment para. 2776 is revoked.

2866   Derelict land clearance areas

The Derelict Land Clearance Areas Order 1980, S.I. 1980 No. 1890 (in force on 31st December 1980), specifies as a derelict land clearance area the employment office area of Coalville. The Derelict Land Clearance Areas Order 1978, Sch., 1978 Halsbury's Abridgment para. 2779, is amended by substituting a new description of the map referred to in para. 1 of that order. The area delineated on the map is unchanged.

2867   Development—exceptions—improvement of dwelling—whether building operations amount to improvement or rebuilding

The appellant sought to avoid the need for planning permission in respect of development of land in the form of the erection of what was effectively a new building on the site of an existing building by completing the erection in stages, each stage of which could be said to be merely an improvement, thus not requiring permission. *Held*, in each case it was a matter of fact and degree whether the operation could properly be called improvement or whether it should be held to be rebuilding for which permission would be required. On the facts before the court the appellant would have to obtain permission.

LARKIN V BASILDON DISTRICT COUNCIL (1980) 256 Estates Gazette 389 (Queen's Bench Division: LORD WIDGERY CJ and MAY J). *Sainty v Minister of Housing and Local Government* (1964) 15 P & CR 432 followed.

2868   —— meaning—material change of use—holiday use of dwelling house

The purchaser of a dwelling house in a predominantly residential part of a seaside resort used it for holidays for himself and his family, for lending to members of his office staff and for letting for rent to family groups. It was left empty outside the holiday season. He was served with an enforcement notice alleging change of use from use as a private dwelling house to use for holiday lettings on a commercial basis. On appeal, the inspector stated that if the house was occupied by one family, whether on holiday or permanently, the use was residential and within the permitted use as a private dwelling house. The appeal was accordingly allowed. On further appeal, *held*, not every residential use was necessarily a use as a private dwelling house but the inspector had been entitled to conclude that the character of the use of the house, which was not a house that was being constantly let in short holiday lettings, had not been changed so substantially as to amount to a change of use.

BLACKPOOL BOROUGH COUNCIL V SECRETARY OF STATE FOR THE ENVIRONMENT (1980) 40 P & CR 104 (Queen's Bench Division: ACKNER LJ and JUPP J). *Birmingham Corpn v Minister of Housing and Local Government* [1963] 3 All ER 668 applied.

2869   —— permitted development—applications and appeals

The Town and Country Planning General Development (Amendment) Order 1980, S.I. 1980 No. 1946 (in force on 13th January 1981), amends the Town and Country Planning General Development Order 1977, 1977 Halsbury's Abridgment para. 2787. The amendments relate mainly to provisions added to the Town and Country Planning Act 1971 and to the Local Government Act 1972, Sch. 16 by the Local Government, Planning and Land Act 1980, s. 86, Sch. 15, para. 1819. The amendments are mainly concerned with procedural matters relating to the handling of planning applications and the making of appeals.

2870   —— —— use classes—holiday accommodation for mentally handicapped persons

Planning permission was given for use of a house as a hotel/guest house. Subsequently it was used to provide holiday accommodation for mentally handicapped persons. On appeal against an enforcement notice and refusal of planning permission the Secretary of State held that the new use fell within Class XIV of the Town and Country Planning (Use Classes) Order 1972, which covers use as a home or institution providing for the boarding, care and maintenance of children, old people or persons under disability, a convalescent home, a nursing home, a sanatorium or a hospital, and that consequently there had been a material change of use. On an application to quash his decision, *held*, the words home and institution connoted permanence. The present case did not fall within Class XIV and the decision would be quashed. The court emphasised that the purpose of the

1972 Order was only to define what was not development and had been used in the present case for a purpose for which it was not intended.

RANN v SECRETARY OF STATE FOR THE ENVIRONMENT (1979) 254 Estates Gazette 1095 (Queen's Bench Division: SIR DOUGLAS FRANK QC).

2871 —— —— **validity of enforcement notice**

Landowners erected a fence one metre higher than their planning permission allowed, and were served with an enforcement notice requiring them to dismantle the fence and returf the ground. In an action for non-compliance it was held that the notice was invalid because it exceeded what was necessary to remedy the breach. On appeal, *held*, the limit prescribed by the permission was not a mere limitation subject to which the permission was granted but it was part of the definition of the permitted development itself and accordingly the whole development had been carried out without permission. The planning authority was therefore entitled to require the removal of the fence so as to restore the land to its previous condition. Further, although the validity of an enforcement notice could be challenged before justices on the ground that the steps required were excessive, the challenge had to be confined to questions of validity and not be directed to the merits of the notice. Accordingly the appeal would be allowed.

ROCHDALE METROPOLITAN BOROUGH COUNCIL v SIMMONDS (1980) 256 Estates Gazette 607 (Queen's Bench Division: LORD LANE CJ, GRIFFITHS and WEBSTER JJ).

2872 —— **planning authority—Greater London**

The Town and Country Planning (Local Planning Authorities in Greater London) Regulations 1980, S.I. 1980 No. 443 (in force on 1st May 1980), prescribe the manner for dealing with applications for planning permission for the development of land in Greater London. In particular, the regulations prescribe the classes of development in specified areas for which the Greater London Council (GLC) is the local planning authority. Provision is made for applications for planning permssion for certain classes of development to be referred to the GLC and for the GLC to direct how such applications are to be dealt with. Provision is also made for applications for planning permission for development which would conflict with the Greater London development plan to be referred to the GLC or the Secretary of State. The Town and Country Planning (Local Planning Authorities in Greater London) Regulations 1978, 1978 Halsbury's Abridgment para. 2788 are revoked.

2873 —— **structure and local plans**

The Town and Country Planning Act 1971, s. 20 and Sch. 23, Part I (part), which deal with structure and local plans, have been brought into force with respect to the following areas on the following dates, and the provisions in the 1971 Act relating to development plans have been repealed.

Area	Date (1980)	Commencement Order No. (1980)	Repeal Order No. (1980)
Bedfordshire	8th February	41	40
Cambridgeshire	3rd September	1209	1210
Central and East Berkshire	12th May	575	576
Cleveland (Hartlepool)	24th April	458	459
Derbyshire	30th July	932	933
Kent	21st April	492	493
Mid Hampshire	27th October	1547	1548
North East Hampshire	17th November	1634	1635
Northamptonshire	25th February	101	102
Northumberland	16th October	1451	1452
Nottinghamshire	19th August	1098	1099
Salford (Brunswick)	22nd October	1559	1560
Salop	21st March	300	301
South East Dorset	4th March	174	175
South Glamorgan	29th February	65	66

Area	Date (1980)	Commencement Order No. (1980)	Repeal Order No. (1980)
South Wiltshire	28th August	1155	1156
South Yorkshire	19th January	2	3
Surrey	12th May	577	578
West Glamorgan	23rd October	1403	1404
West Sussex	11th July	828	829
West Yorkshire	9th August	963	964
Worcester City	24th April	460	461

2874   Enforcement notice—appeal to Secretary of State—decision given in appeal proceedings

On 8th June 1971 a local planning authority served an enforcement notice on the plaintiffs, to take effect thirty days later. Notice of appeal had to be given before the date on which the notice was to take effect. The plaintiffs purported to give notice of appeal to the Secretary of State by letter dated 28th June. The letter did not state the grounds of appeal nor the facts on which it was based. The Secretary of State stated that he could not entertain the appeal unless that information was provided. In a letter dated 11th August, he repeated that statement and added that he had no power to extend the time for appealing against the notice, which had expired, and hence no further action could be taken in the matter. On 19th October 1973 the Court of Appeal in *Howard v Secretary of State for the Environment* [1975] QB 235 decided that a notice of appeal against an enforcement notice did not have to contain the grounds of appeal and the facts on which it was based. The plaintiffs claimed a declaration that their letter of 28th June 1971 was a valid notice of appeal. *Held,* the Secretary of State's letter of 11th August 1971 amounted to a decision given in proceedings on an appeal against an enforcement notice within the Town and Country Planning Act 1971, s. 246 and that decision stood until reversed on appeal. As there had been no such appeal, the decision stood and could not be questioned in the present proceedings. The declaration would be refused.

WAIN v SECRETARY OF STATE FOR THE ENVIRONMENT (1978) 39 P & CR 82 (Queen's Bench Division: STOCKER J). *Button v Jenkins* [1975] 3 All ER 585, DC, 1975 Halsbury's Abridgment para. 3284 and *Chalgray Ltd v Secretary of State for the Environment* (1976) 33 P & CR 10, 1977 Halsbury's Abridgment para. 2796 applied.

2875   —— —— time limit for further appeal

An appeal against an enforcement notice was dismissed by a decision letter sent on 6th March 1979 and received on the following day. On an application to strike out a purported appeal to the High Court by notice given on 4th April 1979 (the time for appealing being 28 days) the question for the court was whether time ran from the date on which the letter was sent or from the date of receipt. *Held,* LLOYD J dissenting, the court was bound by authority to hold that time ran from the date on which the letter had been sent.

RINGROAD INVESTMENTS LTD v SECRETARY OF STATE FOR THE ENVIRONMENT (1979) 40 P & CR 99 (Queen's Bench Division: LORD WIDGERY CJ, FORBES and LLOYD JJ). *Minister of Labour v Genner Iron & Steel Co (Wollescote) Ltd* [1967] 3 All ER 278, DC, applied.

2876   —— validity of notice—time limit—time when breach of planning control occurred—distinction between carrying out of operations and change of use

In 1950 a local authority granted planning permission for the use of a worked-out quarry as a tip, subject to its surveyor's approval of the materials to be deposited. No formal selection of materials was made by the surveyor. Builders' rubble and other materials were deposited from about 1950 in breach of the condition. In 1976 the planning officer informed the new owners that only certain approved materials could be deposited and that deposit of any others would be a breach of planning control. The owners asked for formal approval of the tipping of builders' rubble but the local authority restricted approval to sand, soil, rock and clay. The owners were served with an enforcement notice alleging a breach consisting of the deposit of materials other than those approved. The notice was upheld by the Secretary of State and the owners appealed. *Held*, it was important to appreciate the distinction between development consisting of the carrying out of operations and development consisting of a change of use. In the present case the development consisted of a change of use, not the carrying out of operations. If no permission at all had been given, the breach would have taken place once and for all in about 1950 and the same would apply to non-compliance with the original condition. Enforcement action in 1976 was restricted to breaches taking place after 1963 and consequently the local authority had not been entitled to serve the notice.

BILBOE V SECRETARY OF STATE FOR THE ENVIRONMENT (1980) 254 Estates Gazette 607 (Court of Appeal: MEGAW and DONALDSON LJJ and SIR PATRICK BROWNE). Decision of Queen's Bench Divisional Court (1978) 248 Estates Gazette 229, 1978 Halsbury's Abridgment para. 2783 reversed.

2877   Local Government, Planning and Land Act 1980

See para. 1819.

2878   Local planning authorities—county matters

The Town and Country Planning (Prescription of County Matters) Regulations 1980, S.I. 1980 No. 2010 (in force on 13th January 1981), add to the definition of "county matter" in the Local Government Act 1972, Sch. 16, para. 32, by prescribing additional classes of operations and uses of land in connection with waste disposal for the purposes of that para.

2879   New Towns Act 1980

The New Towns Act 1980 increases the limit imposed by the New Towns Act 1965, s. 43 on the amounts which may be borrowed by development corporations and the Commission for the New Towns. The Act received the royal assent on 30th June 1980 and came into force on that date.

Section 1 of the Act increases the limit on borrowing imposed by the 1965 Act, s. 43 to £4,000 m. Section 2 deals with the short title and extent of the Act.

2880   Planning   permission — conditional   planning   permission — construction

A company wished to erect eighty dwellings on a large area of land. The sewage installation in the area was inadequate and consequently the planning authority was unwilling to grant planning permission for further developments until additional sewerage had been provided. An agreement was made between the company and the planning authority, in accordance with the Town and Country Planning Act 1971, s. 52, that planning permission would be granted subject to conditions. Permission was granted and a condition included providing that the proposed development had to commence not later than the expiration of three years from the date of the permission. Improvements to the sewage installations did not take place within the three year period and in effect there was never any time at which it was possible for the company to commence its development in accordance with the terms of the permission. The company sought a declaration as to the true construction of the agreement and planning permission. *Held*, the agreement made under s. 52 was binding on the company and its successors in title and clearly prevented the company from commencing any development until a contract for a new sewage installation had been entered into. It was also clear that the agreement merely stated what the council proposed to do, namely grant planning permission subject to a condition. The condition attached to the permission was not unreasonable or inconsistent with the terms of the agreement. The three year time limit for commencing development ran from the date of the grant of planning permission and any other interpretation would be contrary to the provisions of s. 41 of the Act regarding the duration of planning permission.

LAH AMES LTD V NORTH BEDFORDSHIRE BOROUGH COUNCIL (1979) 253 Estates Gazette 55 (Court of Appeal: BUCKLEY, BRIDGE and TEMPLEMAN LJJ).

2881 —— —— validity of condition

In 1962 a company was granted planning permission to use two hangars as warehouses for storing synthetic rubber on condition that the buildings were to be removed by the end of 1972. The buildings were not removed and the local authority served enforcement notices. They were quashed by the Secretary of State on the ground that the condition was void as being extraneous to the proposed use. The notices were restored by the Court of Appeal. On further appeal, *held*, the hangars had previously been used as repositories within the Town and Country Planning (Use Classes) Order 1950, Class X and, as it had not been proved that the use was abandoned, the company could, by virtue of Class X, have used the hangars as warehouses without obtaining planning permission. The existing use rights were not extinguished by the grant of planning permission however, as a new planning unit had not been created by the permission. In any event, the condition attached to the permission was invalid as it did not sufficiently relate to the change of use in respect of which permission was granted and was therefore unreasonable. The Secretary of State had held that the condition was not severable from the permission granted and that consequently the permission was void and the enforcement notices were therefore invalid. The Secretary of State was entitled so to hold, and accordingly the appeal would be allowed.

NEWBURY DISTRICT COUNCIL v SECRETARY OF STATE FOR THE ENVIRONMENT [1980] 1 All ER 731 (House of Lords: VISCOUNT DILHORNE, LORD EDMUND-DAVIES, LORD FRASER OF TULLYBELTON, LORD SCARMAN and LORD LANE). Decision of Court of Appeal [1979] 1 All ER 243, 1978 Halsbury's Abridgment para. 2781 reversed. *Mounsdon v Weymouth and Melcombe Regis Corpn* [1960] 1 All ER 538 applied; dicta of Havers J in *Horwitz v Rowson* [1960] 2 All ER 881 and of Lord Denning MR in *G Percy Trentham Ltd v Gloucestershire County Council* [1966] 1 All ER 701 at 703 disapproved.

2882 —— consultation—code of practice

In a written reply to a parliamentary question on 10th June 1980, the Secretary of State for the Environment said that a code of practice had been agreed to speed up consultations on planning applications and for listed building demolition consent. The code, which came into effect on 1st July 1980, applies to all authorities or bodies consulted on applications under arts 11, 12 and 15 of the Town and Country Planning General Development Order 1977, S.I. 1977 No. 289, to those bodies (specified in Department of the Environment circular 23/77) consulted on listed building demolition applications and to those consulted under the Town and Country Planning (Aerodromes) Directions 1972. The code also applies to other major national consultees regularly consulted on planning applications and to other authorities, persons or bodies regularly consulted on such applications. The highway authorities and the Ministry of Transport have agreed to observe the spirit of the code. (The code does not apply to (i) applications which have to be notified to parish, town or community councils (these will continue to be dealt with under the Local Government Act 1972); (ii) consultations under reg. 10 of the Town and Country Planning General Regulations 1976, S.I. 1976 No. 1419; nor (iii) occasional notification and consultation on planning applications carried out on a voluntary basis by local authorities.) The code requires a local planning authority, in appropriate circumstances, to give a consultee 28 days' notice of intention to determine an application and to take into account, in reaching its determination, any representations made by the consultee. The code specifies information to be given to a consultee and allows an extension of time (21 days) in exceptional circumstances to a consultee (on making application to that effect). See Department of the Environment Press Notice 229, dated 10th June 1980.

2883 —— outline permission—application for approval of reserved matters—time limit

In a case where outline planning permission had been given, the three-year period for applying for approval of reserved matters expired on a Sunday. The offices of the local authority were closed on Saturday and Sunday. As the applicant knew that no one would be available to receive the application during the weekend he handed it to an official at the offices on the following Monday. The authority contended that it was out of time. *Held*, in view of the closure of the offices on the Sunday, the time limit had been complied with.

R v Bromley London Borough, ex parte Sievers (1980) 255 Estates Gazette 359 (Queen's Bench Division: Shaw LJ and Kilner Brown J).

2884   Tree preservation—order—coppice

A farmer owned a small coppice primarily consisting of ash which had been clear felled on a rotational basis over twenty years or so, the wood being used for fencing. Following the refusal of permission for residential development a tree preservation order was made and confirmed. The order was challenged on the ground that it was not possible to make an order in respect of a coppice and alternatively that it was in practice impossible to reconcile an order with good management which required regular felling and regeneration. *Held*, there was no reason to exclude trees in a coppice from the power to make tree preservation orders. It should be possible to produce a practical scheme in the case of a coppice as in the case of any other group of trees or of a woodland.

Bullock v Secretary of State for the Environment (1980) 40 P & CR 246 (Queen's Bench Division: Phillips J). Dictum of Lord Denning MR in *Kent County Council v Batchelor* (1976) 33 P & CR 185 at 189, 1976 Halsbury's Abridgment para. 445 not applied.

2885   —— —— offence—whether knowledge of preservation order a necessary ingredient of offence

A tree feller was acquitted of cutting down a tree which, unknown to him, was subject to a tree preservation order, contrary to the Town and Country Planning Act 1971 s. 102 (1), on the ground that knowledge of the existence of the order was a necessary ingredient of the offence. The local authority appealed. *Held*, the object of a tree preservation order was to ensure that no protected tree should be destroyed without the consent of the local authority and on its true construction s. 102 (1) penalised such an act whether or not the tree feller knew of the existence of the order. Accordingly the appeal would be allowed.

Maidstone Borough Council v Mortimer [1980] 3 All ER 552 (Queen's Bench Division: Waller LJ and Park J). Dicta of Wright J in *Sherras v De Rutzen* [1895–9] All ER Rep 1167 at 1169 and of Lord Reid in *Sweet v Parsley* [1969] 1 All ER 347 at 350 applied.

2886   Waste land—maintenance—statutory offence of continuing or aggravating injury—whether positive act required

A Divisional Court of the Queen's Bench Division has held that a company, which failed to remove a trailer from vacant land, cannot be convicted of doing "anything which has the effect of continuing or aggravating the injury caused by the condition of the land", contrary to the Town and Country Planning Act 1971, s. 104 (2) because a positive act is required. There was no criminal offence under s. 104 (2) if, in response to a s. 65 notice, nothing at all was done.

Red House Farms (Thorndon) Ltd v Mid Suffolk District Council (1980) Times, 30th April (Queen's Bench Division: Donaldson LJ and Bristow J).

TRADE AND INDUSTRY

Halsbury's Laws of England (3rd edn.), Vol. 38, paras. 1–600

2887   Article

Industrial Espionage, A. M. Tettenborn: 130 NLJ 406.

2888   Assisted areas

The Assisted Areas (Amendment) Order 1980, S.I. 1980 No. 1110 (in force on 1st August 1980), further amends the Assisted Areas Order 1979, 1979 Halsbury's Abridgment para. 2790 by upgrading certain areas and annulling the provisions relating to the downgrading of certain areas.

2889   British Aerospace Act 1980

See para. 184.

2890   Competition Act 1980

The Competition Act 1980 provides for the abolition of the Price Commission and the investigation and control of practices which restrict competition or abuse a monopoly position. The Act received the royal assent on 3rd April 1980 and came into force by S.I. 1980 Nos. 497, 978 on the following dates:

4th April 1980: ss. 1, 11 (1), (2), (3) (part), 15 (2) (part), (5), 16, 17 (part), 19, 23, 31 (1), 32, 33 (1), (2), (4) (part), (5)–(8), Schs. 1, 2 (part).

1st May 1980: ss. 3 (7), (8), 12–14, 15 (1), 16, 17 (part), 18, 20–22, 24–30, 31 (3) (part) (4), 33 (3).

12th August 1980: ss. 2–10, 11 (3) (b), (f), 15 (2)–(5), 16, 17, 31 (2), (3) (part).

Section 33 (4) and Sch. 2 so far as they relate to the repeal of certain provisions of the Counter-Inflation Act 1973 and the Price Commission Act 1977 are to come into force on 1st January 2011.

Section 1 and Sch. 1 provide for the abolition of the Price Commission and the transfer of its functions to the Secretary of State.

Section 2 defines anti-competitive practice as conduct which has or is intended or is likely to have the effect of restricting, distorting or preventing competition. Section 3 empowers the Director General of Fair Trading to investigate activities which he considers may be anti-competitive and requires him to report on such investigation. He may also obtain and monitor an undertaking to remedy a practice reported as being anti-competitive: s. 4. If no satisfactory undertaking is in force, the Director General may refer the matter to the Monopolies and Mergers Commission: s. 5. Section 6 requires the Commission to investigate whether conduct is an anti-competitive practice and if so, whether it is against the public interest. Section 7 contains supplementary provisions regarding a competition reference to the Commission. The Commission must report to the Secretary of State on its conclusions: s. 8. If the Commission reports that a practice is against the public interest, the Director General may obtain and monitor an undertaking to remedy the position: s. 9. If no satisfactory undertaking is in force, the Secretary of State may make an order prohibiting the practice or remedying its effects: s. 10.

Section 11 enables the Secretary of State to refer to the Commission any matter relating to the efficiency and costs of, or possible abuse of a monopoly position by, nationalised industries and certain other bodies. If the Commission reports that conduct is against the public interest, the Secretary of State may make an order remedying its effects: s. 12. He may also require the Director General to investigate and report on any matter of major public concern relating to prices: s. 13.

The Comptroller General of Patents and Ministers responsible for agricultural marketing schemes may take appropriate action where the Commission has found that certain matters concerning patents, patent licences or agricultural marketing schemes are against the public interest: ss. 14, 15.

Certain material which would be against the public interest if published must be excluded from reports by the Director General or the Commission: s. 16. Provisions concerning the publication of reports are contained in s. 17. The Director General must give the public such advice and information concerning the Act as he considers appropriate: s. 18. Section 19 imposes restrictions on the disclosure of certain information obtained under the Act.

The Secretary of State may make grants to certain bodies which provide information on matters of interest to users of goods and services: s. 20.

Sections 21–30 contain various amendments to the Fair Trading Act 1973 and the Restrictive Trade Practices Act 1976.

Miscellaneous supplementary provisions and repeals are contained in ss. 31–33 and Sch. 2.

2891   —— anti-competitive practices

The Anti-Competitive Practices (Exclusions) Order 1980, S.I. 1980 No. 979 (in force on 12th August 1980), excludes certain types of conduct from being anti-competitive practices. Also excluded is the conduct of any person (other than a local authority) with an annual turnover in the United Kingdom of less than £5 million if he enjoys less than one quarter of a relevant market and if he is not a member of a group of interconnected bodies corporate with an annual turnover in the United Kingdom of £5 million or more, or which enjoys one quarter or more of the relevant market. For the purpose of enabling the Director General of Fair Trading to establish whether a person's conduct is so excluded, the Fair Trading Act 1973, ss. 44 and 46 are applied with modifications.

2892   —— bus operators

The Competition (Exclusion of Bus Operators) Order 1980, S.I. 1980 No. 981 (in force on 12th August 1980), excludes from the Competition Act 1980, s. 11 (3) (b), para. 2890 (which relates to the persons about whose affairs certain questions may be referred to the Monopolies and Mergers Commission) any person providing a bus service whose annual turnover from fares and subsidies is less than £1 million, unless he is associated with other persons providing bus services and their total annual turnover is £1 million or more.

2893   —— notices

The Competition (Notices) Regulations 1980, S.I. 1980 No. 980 (in force on 12th August 1980), prescribe the manner in which notices under the Competition Act 1980, ss. 3 (2), 4 and 9 (5) (b), para. 2890 are to be given and the method of proving these notices.

2894   Competition policy

see EUROPEAN COMMUNITIES.

2895   Development Councils—Apple and Pear Development Council

The Apple and Pear Development Council Order 1980, S.I. 1980 No. 623 (in force on 7th May 1980), consolidates, with amendments, the Apple and Pear Development Council Order 1966, as amended, which established a development council for the apple and pear growing industry in England and Wales. The order reduces the number of members of the Council, assigns to the Council additional powers and raises the maximum rate of annual charge which the Council may impose on growers.

The following orders are revoked: Apple and Pear Development Council Order 1966, as amended by subsequent orders in 1970, 1971 and 1975, 1975 Halsbury's Abridgment para. 59.

2896   The Apple and Pear Development Council (Amendment) Order 1980, S.I. 1980 No. 2001 (in force on 18th December 1980), amends the Apple and Pear Development Council Order 1980, para. 2895, by raising the maximum rate of annual charge for growers and by empowering the Council to make additional charges to cover their expenses in promoting production and marketing of standard products. The order also assigns to the Council an additional advisory function.

2897　Enterprise zones

H M Treasury has given such information about the enterprise zones referred to by the Chancellor of the Exchequer in his budget speech. The sites of the zones are expected to be up to 500 acres in size and will be in areas of physical and economic decay, where conventional government policies have not succeeded in regenerating self-sustaining economic activity. The selection of the areas will be made after consultation with local authorities. It is expected that there will be one enterprise zone in Scotland, are in Wales, one in Northern Ireland and three or four in England. The sites shortlisted are: Attercliffe, Sheffield; a site in Tyne and Wear; a site in Liverpool; Manchester and Salford docks/Trafford Park; Bilston, Wolverhampton; a site in London; Lower Swansea Valley; a Clydeside site; and a Belfast inner city site. The enterprise zones will be designated for an initial period of ten years, subject to renewal. New and existing firms in the areas will benefit from the following measures: exemption from development land tax; 100 per cent capital allowances on industrial and commercial property; exemption from general rates; simplification of planning procedures; exemptions from the requirements of industrial training boards; speedier handling of Customs warehousing and inward processing relief; a relaxed regime for "private" warehouses; the abolition of the remaining industrial development certificates; and a reduction to the bare minimum of the government's requests for statistical information. It is stressed that there will be no reduction in the standards needed to protect health and safety or to control pollution: Press Release, 26th March 1980.

2898　Export controls

See CUSTOMS AND EXCISE.

2899　Export guarantees and overseas investment

The Export Guarantees (Extension of Period) (No. 2) Order 1980, S.I. 1980 No. 366 (in force on 11th March 1980), extends the period under the Export Guarantees and Overseas Investment Act 1978, s. 5 to 26th March 1981.

2900

The Export Guarantees (Limit on Foreign Currency Commitments) Order 1980, S.I. 1980 No. 371 (in force on 12th March 1980), increases the limit on commitments in foreign currency applicable under the Export Guarantees and Overseas Investment Act 1978, s. 6 (2) to 15,000 million special drawing rights.

2901　Industry—financial assistance

The Financial Assistance for Industry (Increase of Limit) Order 1979, S.I. 1980 No. 109 (in force on 1st February 1980), increases the limit of the aggregate of the sums paid by the Secretary of State, and the liabilities of the Secretary of State under guarantees given, under the Industry Act 1972, s. 8 (6), (7), as amended by the Industry (Amendment) Act 1976, from £1,100 million to £1,350 million.

2902　Industry Act 1980

The Industry Act 1980 makes further provision in relation to the National Enterprise Board (NEB), the Scottish Development Agency, the Welsh Development Agency and the English Industrial Estates Corporation. The Secretary of State is authorised to acquire securities of, make loans to and provide guarantees for companies in which he acquires shares from the NEB and to provide an advisory service. The Act amends the Industry Acts 1972 and 1975. The requirement for a register of the financial interests of members of British Shipbuilders is removed. The Act received the royal assent on 30th June 1980 and came into force on that date.

Section 1 amends the Industry Act 1975, s. 2, the Scottish Development Agency Act 1975, s. 2 and the Welsh Development Agency Act 1975, s. 1. It provides that the NEB is to cease to have the function of extending public ownership and provides that the NEB and the Agencies are to cease to have the function of promoting industrial reorganisation and industrial democracy. The new function of the NEB and the Agencies are to dispose of assets held by them in order to promote private ownership. Section 2 empowers the NEB and the Agencies to transfer assets held or controlled by them to the Secretary of State, and extends his powers of direction to enable him to require them to transfer assets to him.

Section 3 empowers the Secretary of State to provide finance for companies transferred to him, and s. 4 provides for the making of payments by the NEB and the Agencies in reduction of their public dividend capital. Section 5 sets financial limits in relation to the NEB and the Agencies and in relation to the transferred companies. Section 6 reduces the existing limits on the acquisition of share capital by the NEB and the Agencies. The maximum number of members of the NEB is reduced by s 7. Section 8 deals with selective financial assistance under the Industry Act 1972. Under s. 9, the NEB and the Agencies are no longer able to furnish technical assistance outside the UK under the Overseas Aid Act 1966.

Section 10 governs the functions and status of the English Industrial Estates Corporation. Sections 11–15 provide for the transfer of land to the Corporation, membership of the Corporation, borrowing powers, Treasury guarantees and expenses.

Section 16 makes changes in relation to regional development grants. Section 17, Sch. 1 amends the Industry Act 1972, ss. 7, 8 inter alia to enable the Secretary of State to give guarantees where the liability is in foreign currencies. Section 18 empowers the Secretary of State to provide advisory services to those carrying on or proposing to carry on business. The provisions of the Industry Act 1975 relating to planning agreements and to the disclosure of information by companies are repealed by s 19. The obligation on the Secretary of State to keep a register of financial interests of members of British Shipbuilders is removed by s 20. Section 21, Sch. 2 deals with repeals and transitional provisions, and s. 22 with citation and extent.

2903   International trade—rubber supplies

The International Natural Rubber Agreement 1979 was concluded at Geneva on 6th October 1979. The agreement is intended to implement certain objectives of the United Nations Conference on Trade and Development, including, inter alia, a balanced growth between supply and demand for the product and stable conditions of trade. An International National Rubber Organisation is to be established which will have a council as its executive arm. To give effect to the purposes of the agreement a buffer stock will be set up so that supplies may be bought or sold on the world market in order to keep prices stable. The buffer stock is to be financed by members. The agreement has not been ratified by the United Kingdom. The text of the agreement has been published as Cmnd. 8018 (1980).

As to the powers of the EEC to negotiate and participate in the agreement on behalf of the member states see *Opinion 1/78 (EEC): Re The Draft International Agreement on Natural Rubber* [1979] ECR 2871, [1979] 3 CMLR 639, ECJ.

2904   Iron and steel—borrowing powers

The Iron and Steel (Borrowing Powers) Order 1980, S.I. 1980 No. 764 (in force on 23rd May 1980), specifies the maximum permissible limit on borrowing by the British Steel Corporation and the publicly-owned companies and investment by the Secretary of State in the British Steel Corporation as £5,500m.

2905   Local Government, Planning and Land Act 1980

See para. 1819.

2906   Monopolies and mergers—newspaper merger reference—public interest

The Secretary of State for Trade referred to the Monopolies and Merger Commission the proposed transfer of 75 per cent of the equity in Cox, Sons & Co Ltd, the publishers of the West Somerset Free Press, from Farnham Castle Newspapers Ltd to Bristol United Press Ltd, in which Associated Newspapers Group Ltd had a substantial shareholding and also significant indirect interests. In concluding that the proposed transfer might be expected to operate against the public interest, the commission followed the views expressed by the Royal Commission on the Press in its final report (Cmnd. 6810, 1977) that a case had been established against further concentration of ownership of local newspapers and said that it followed that there were prima facie reasons on public interests grounds against any individual acquisition of a local newspaper which would carry the concentration further. The royal commission had been particularly concerned by the prospect of further regional, rather than national, concentration. The Monopolies and Mergers Commission noted that if Associated Newspapers were, in some unforseen circumstances, to increase their shareholding in Bristol United Press this would not require the consent of the Secretary of State under the Fair Trading Act 1973. Apart from furthering the regional concentration of local newspapers, the commission said that the proposed transfer also would prevent the alternative prospect (which it viewed more favourably) of the newspaper being controlled by a small newspaper proprietor specialising in weekly newspapers but without any substantial newspaper interest in the area. See *Monopolies and Merger Commission: West Somerset Free Press and Bristol United Press Ltd* (HC 546).

2907   —— proposed conglomerate merger—factors to be taken into consideration

In the course of its report on the proposed merger between Blue Circle Industries Ltd and Armitage Shanks Group Ltd (Cmnd. 8039), the Monopolies and Mergers Commission made reference to its general approach to conglomerate mergers. In this context the report described (without attempting a formal definition of the term) conglomerate mergers as mergers between companies which did not produce similar products and were not actual or potential suppliers of each other. Such mergers led to the concentration of control of assets, but not, normally, to a concentration of market shares. The commission pointed out that its approach was governed by the Fair Trading Act 1973, ss. 72 (2), 84 (1), (2). Hence it was bound to consider the particular circumstances of the case and to judge what, in those circumstances, the particular effects of the merger situation were or might be expected to be. The commission could not judge a particular merger to be conglomerate and base a conclusion simply on that decision; it had to have regard to any possible effects adverse to the public interest. Nevertheless, the commission could not ignore the fact of a conglomerate merger. The type of business and the type of product of each of the parties were relevant. If, between the types, there were a certain degree of dissimilarity, this might create a possibility, or likelihood, of certain consequences adverse to the public interest. In considering whether such consequences might be anticipated, the commission would give primary attention to consequences which might restrict competition.

2908   —— references to Monopolies and Mergers Commission—value of assets

The Merger References (Increase in Value of Assets) Order 1980, S.I. 1980 No. 373 (in force on 10th April 1980), amends the Fair Trading Act 1973, s. 64 (1) (b). Section 64 provides that the Secretary of State may refer a merger to the Mergers and Monopolies Commission where, among other things, the value of the assets taken over exceeds the sum specified in s. 64 (1) (b). The order increases the sum specified from £5 million to £15 million.

2909   National Enterprise Board—financial limits

The Financial Limits (National Enterprise Board and Secretary of State) Order 1980, S.I. 1980 No. 1211 (in force on 9th August 1980), reduces from £3,000 million to £2,250 million the limit on the aggregate outstanding in respect of sums paid as public dividend capital and loans guaranteed by the National Enterprise Board. It also specifies the sum of £750 million as the limit of the financial obligations incurred by companies, of which control has been transferred to the Secretary of State, by the National Enterprise Board.

2910   Petroleum stocks

The Petroleum Stocks (Amendment) Order 1980, S.I. 1980 No. 1609 (in force on 1st January 1981), amends the Petroleum Stocks Order 1976, 1976 Halsbury's Abridgment para. 1317, by providing that stocks of crude liquid petroleum only count as stocks of light oil in respect of 47 per cent by weight of those stocks.

2911   Prices

See CONSUMER PROTECTION AND FAIR TRADING.

2912   Protection of Trading Interests Act 1980

See para. 1346.

2913   Regional development grant—qualifying premises—qualifying activities—preserving meat

The applicants wanted to build a plant where cooked meat imported from Denmark would be removed from sealed cans, sliced and packed into vacuum-sealed plastic containers before being transferred to shops for resale. On their application under the Industry Act 1972, s. 1, for a capital expenditure grant, the question arose whether the activity constituted "preserving meat" within the meaning of the Standard Industrial Classification. *Held*, the practical man, looking at the whole picture, would say that the meat was cooked and preserved in Denmark. When it reached England, in order to reduce it into units in which it could be sold, its level of preservation had to be reduced and its wholesome life shortened. This could not be said to amount to "preserving meat". The activity was thus not a qualifying activity within the 1972 Act, s. 2, and the application would be refused.

JAKA FOODS GROUP LTD V SECRETARY OF STATE FOR INDUSTRY [1980] LS Gaz R 52 (Queen's Bench Division: BRISTOW J).

2914   Restraint of trade—covenant in deed of partnership—validity

Australia

G and M entered into a written partnership agreement in order to carry on the business of insurance loss assessors. The agreement provided that, under cl. 3, each party had the right to terminate the partnership by giving not less than fourteen days' notice in writing. Clause 21 provided that should the partnership business be determined, G should not work as an insurance loss assessor within a radius of twenty miles for a period of three years. M, pursuant to cl. 3, gave G written notice of termination of the partnership. G subsequently assigned to M all his interests in the partnership. Clause 5 of this deed reserved and excluded from assignment the interests of the parties in the goodwill of the dissolved partnership. One month later G commenced business as an insurance loss assessor only two miles away. M subsequently sought and obtained an injunction to restrain the breach of cl. 21. G appealed contending that cl. 21 was invalid because it was unreasonable restraint of trade in that the clause could operate if the partnership was terminated through no fault of his own, but through the positive default of M. *Held*, by a majority decision, the validity of a covenant in restraint of trade had to be considered in the light of all surrounding circumstances. The fact that G was admitted as a partner and not merely employed as an insurance loss assessor did not, in itself, mean that M had any less right to protect his interest in the business. There was no apparent reason for regarding a covenant between partners more strictly than a similar covenant between an employer and employee. Goodwill could not be dealt with separately from the business with which it was associated. The benefit of a restrictive covenant formed part of the goodwill and enured for the benefit of the partnership. Hence, cl. 5 of the assignment did not affect M's right to protect the whole goodwill of the business. Clause 21 was not unreasonable as it was not injurious to the public, but protected the interests of the parties and the goodwill of the partnership. The appeal would be dismissed.

GERAGHTY V MINTER (1979) 26 ALR 141 (High Court of Australia). *Fitch v Dewes* [1921] 2 AC 158, *Scorer v Seymour Jones* [1966] 3 All ER 347, *Inland Revenue Commissioners v Muller & Co's Margarine Ltd* [1901] AC 217 applied. *Shell UK Ltd v Lostock Garage Ltd* [1977] 1 All ER 481, 1976 Halsbury's Abridgment para. 2588 followed.

2915   Trade statistics—census of production

The Census of Production (1981) (Returns and Exempted Persons) Order 1980, S.I. 1980 No. 1835 (in force on 31st December 1980), lays down certain provisions for the census of production to be taken in 1981.

TRADE DESCRIPTIONS

2916   Fabrics—misdescription

The Fabrics (Misdescription) Regulations 1980, S.I. 1980 No. 726, (in force on 23rd June 1980), prescribe the standards to which textile fabric must conform for the purposes of the Fabrics (Misdescription) Act 1913 if it is described as being resistant to ignition from smouldering cigarettes or lighted matches when used in combination with other upholstery materials.

2917   False trade description—car dealer's estimate of mileage—whether estimate a trade description

A motor dealer bought a car with a mileage of over 70,000 miles; the odometer recorded only 716 miles. A prospective buyer asked the dealer about the mileage; he replied that he did not know the true mileage but promised to make inquiries. Later, when completing an invoice with the buyer, the dealer said that in his opinion the mileage was probably about 45,000 miles. He wrote "estimated mileage 45,000 miles" on the invoice. His opinion, based on his professional knowledge and information in a guide to car prices, was accepted by the buyer as correct. When the estimate was shown to be incorrect the dealer was convicted of applying a false trade description to the car. On appeal, *held*, under the Trade Descriptions Act 1968, s. 2 a trade description was an indication of any matter in respect of goods, including their history. It was possible that the dealer's estimate fell within s. 2; in any event it amounted to a false trade description within s. 3 (3). Under s. 3 (3) anything was deemed to be a false trade description if it was likely to be taken as an indication of any of the matters specified in s. 2 and as such was false to a material degree. It was clear that the dealer's estimate was likely to be taken by the buyer as an indication of the history of the vehicle and as such was false to a material degree. Accordingly the appeal would be dismissed.

HOLLOWAY V CROSS (1980) Times, 20th November (Queen's Bench Division: DONALDSON LJ and HODGSON J).

2918   —— defence—exercise of due diligence

The defendant, manager of a firm of motor dealers, bought a van from auctioneers with an odometer recording 36,000 miles. He sold it to a customer who subsequently discovered that it had travelled more than 97,000 miles. The defendant therefore returned the deposit and took back the van which he then advertised for sale, making no reference to the mileage. The van was seen by a trading standards officer who established that it was being offered for sale and recorded the mileage which was still shown as 36,000. The defendant was charged with contravening the Trade Descriptions Act 1968, s. 1 (1) by supplying and offering to supply a van to which a false trade description was applied by means of a false odometer reading. The justices dismissed the information on the ground that the defendant had established the defence of due diligence under s. 24 (1) of the Act, and that there had been nothing to indicate that the van was for sale since it was merely parked outside his residence. On appeal by the prosecutor, *held*, there was no evidence to show that the defendant had discharged the burden of proof on him, by taking all reasonable precautions and by exercising all due diligence as required by s. 24 (1), to avoid the commission of an offence since he had not displayed a disclaimer or inquired into the van's history. Further, evidence of his conversation with the officer and the terms of a newspaper advertisement established that he was offering the same vehicle for sale within the meaning of s. 6 (1). The case would be remitted with a direction to convict.

STAINTHORPE v BAILEY [1980] RTR 7 (Queen's Bench Division: LORD WIDGERY CJ, DAVIES and ROBERT GOFF JJ). *Simmons v Potter* [1975] RTR 347, 1975 Halsbury's Abridgment para. 3342 applied.

2919   —— test to be applied

Motor traders sold a vehicle described on the sales invoice as a used 1975 vehicle. The vehicle had been manufactured in 1972 as a van, but was subsequently converted to a caravanette, and was first registered in 1975. The traders were acquitted on a charge of applying a false trade description to the vehicle contrary to the Trade Descriptions Act 1968, s. 1, the justices being of the opinion that the vehicle was a new vehicle when registered in 1975 and also a used vehicle as it was three and a half months old on the date of sale. On appeal, *held*, the question that the justices should direct themselves to consider was what was the impression given by the words used to the reasonable man; the purchaser in a given case. This question should not be concerned with "newness" or the fact that in the instant case the vehicle had not been used between 1972 and 1975, but with whether an average customer would be likely to believe on reading the description that 1975 was the year of manufacture. The justices did not consider that question and did not therefore come to a correct determination in law. The appeal would be allowed.

ROUTLEDGE v ANSA MOTORS (CHESTER LE STREET) LTD (1979) 123 Sol Jo 735 (Queen's Bench Division: LORD WIDGERY CJ, EVELEIGH LJ and KILNER BROWN J).

2920   Information in advertisements—sealskin goods

The Trade Descriptions (Sealskin Goods) (Information) Order 1980, S.I. 1980 No. 1150 (in force on 3rd September 1980), imposes requirements as to the information to be given regarding goods made of sealskin, including information in certain advertisements for the supply to retail customers of sealskin goods. It is an offence to supply or offer to supply such goods, or to publish such an advertisement with respect to which the requirements are not complied with.

TRADE MARKS, TRADE NAMES AND DESIGNS

Halsbury's Laws of England (3rd edn.), Vol. 38, paras. 811–1135

2921   Article

Comparative Advertising and Trade Mark Infringement, Philip J. Circus: 130 NLJ 5.

2922   Convention country—Korea

The Trade Marks (Republic of Korea) (Convention) Order 1980, S.I. 1980 No. 571 (in force on 12th May 1980), discharges any remaining obligations of the United Kingdom under the International Convention for the Protection of Industrial Property by declaring the Republic of Korea to be a Convention country for all the purposes of the Patents and Designs Act 1907 relating to trademarks.

2923   Designs rules

The Designs (Amendment) Rules 1980, S.I. 1980 No. 96 (in force on 27th February 1980, except r. 2 which came into force on 6th May 1980), further amend the Designs Rules 1949 so as to increase certain fees payable under them with effect from 6th May 1980. In the case of fees paid in advance for the extension of the copyright period in a design in respect of any period beginning on or after 6th May 1980, the fees are increased with effect from 27th February 1980. The Designs (Amendment No. 2) Rules 1978, 1978 Halsbury's Abridgment para. 2855 are revoked.

2924   Fees

The Trade Marks (Amendment) Rules 1980, S.I. 1980 No. 221 (rr. 1, 3 in force on 14th March 1980 and r. 2 in force on 6th May 1980), further amend the Trade Marks Rules 1938 by increasing certain fees payable under them. The new fees become payable on or after 6th May 1980, except in the case of renewal fees paid in advance in respect of the period beginning on or after that date, which are increased from 14th March 1980. The rules substitute a new schedule for the existing Schedule 1 and revoke the Trade Marks (Amendment) Rules 1978, 1978 Halsbury's Abridgment para. 2869.

2925   Gun Barrel Proof Act 1978—commencement

The Gun Barrel Proof Act 1978 (Commencement No. 2) Order 1980, S.I. 1980 No. 640 brought into force on 5th June 1980 the remaining provisions of the Act not already in force.

2926   Infringement—ghost mark used to protect unregistrable name— bona fide use

The plaintiffs, cigarette manufacturers, selected the name "Merit" for a new brand which was under consideration. However they were advised that the name was unregistrable as a trade mark and could only be considered for use as an unregistered brand name. Although the project was subsequently abandoned the ghost mark "Nerit" was registered allegedly with a view to continuing a similar project in the future. The following year the defendants launched a new brand of cigarettes using the name "Merit". Accordingly the plaintiffs made a limited introduction of cigarettes under the name "Nerit" so that the mark could not be taken off the register for non-use, and brought an action claiming an injunction to restrain the defendants from infringing their registered trade mark "Nerit". The defendants contended (i) that the mark "Nerit" was invalid within the meaning of the Trade Marks Act 1938, s. 68 (1); (ii) the mark was not capable of distinguishing the plaintiff's goods within s. 10 of the Act; and (iii) there had been no bona fide use of the mark within s. 26 (1) (a). *Held,* (i) since the words "proposed to be used" in s 68 (1) did not exclude a contingent intention to use a trade mark, the plantiffs had established that "Nerit" was a mark which at the time of its registration they proposed to use. (ii) "Nerit" was capable of distinguishing the goods to which it applied within s. 10. (iii) However, the plaintiffs did not intend and did not use "Nerit" as a genuine commercial trade mark, since their only purpose was to try to secure a monopoly right to an unregistered word. Accordingly such an intention and use were not bona fide within s. 26 and "Nerit" would therefore be removed from the register. IMPERIAL GROUP LTD v PHILIP MORRIS & CO LTD [1980] FSR 146 (Chancery Division: BALCOMBE J). *Electrolux Ltd Electrix Co Ltd* (1954) 71 RPC 23, CA considered; *Baume and Co Ltd v Moore Ltd* [1958] 2 All ER 113, CA distinguished.

2927   Passing off—business carried on abroad—foreign company in- tending to conclude franchise agreement in UK—business reputation

The plaintiffs were engaged in business largely in the United States. They supplied footwear for athletes, under the name of "The Athlete's Foot", and granted franchises to independent stores to carry on business under that name. During negotiations for a franchise agreement in relation to the United Kingdom the plaintiffs discovered that the defendants, shoe retailers, had registered two business names, namely "Athlete's Foot" and "Athlete's Foot (Mail Order)", but they were not being used. Although a prospective franchisee visited the defendants' shop with a view to establishing a chain of franchised shops, no agreement was concluded. Subsequently, the defendants opened a department which they called "Athlete's Foot Bargain Basement" and offered goods for sale by mail order under that name. The plaintiffs applied for an interlocutory injunction to restrain the defendants from passing off their trading operations as and for trading operations carried out under franchise from the plaintiffs. *Held*, (i) it was necessary to consider the strength of the plaintiffs' case in greater detail than usual since a decision on the motion either way would profoundly affect the rights of the parties if at the trial a different result was reached. (ii) The plaintiffs were not entitled to take the benefit of, or rely on the activities of their prospective franchisee, since although discussions had taken place, they only related to the preparations for accepting a franchise. (iii) The present case supported the view that no trader could complain of passing off as against him in any territory in which he had no customers, or anyone who was trading with him. The plaintiffs had no market in the United Kingdom and accordingly no goodwill which could be harmed. The motion would be dismissed.

ATHLETE'S FOOT MARKETING ASSOCIATES INC v COBRA SPORTS LTD [1980] RPC 343 (Chancery Division: WALTON J). *Alain Bernardin et Compagnie v Pavilion Properties Ltd* [1967] RPC 581, *Amway Corporation v Eurway International Ltd* [1974] RPC 82, 1974 Halsbury's Abridgment para. 509 applied, *American Cyanamid Co v Ethicon Ltd* [1975] 1 All ER 504, HL, 1975 Halsbury's Abridgment para. 1864 distinguished.

2928   Registration—application—five evenly spaced strips on length of toothpaste

The applicants sold toothpaste in tubes under the trade mark "SIGNAL". They applied for registration of a mark consisting of five evenly spaced red strips on the length of the toothpaste. Prior to extrusion, the toothpaste in the tube was white. The application was dismissed and on appeal, *held*, the strips appeared only upon use, after purchase. A trade mark had to have some sort of visual representation so that the mark could be used in the course of trade as a representation which could be seen by the purchaser at the time of purchase. The appeal would accordingly be dismissed. The application would however be remitted to the Registry for amendment so as to cover such a representation.

UNILEVER'S (STRIPED TOOTHPASTE) TRADE MARK APPLICATION [1980] FSR 280 (Chancery Division: WHITFORD J).

2929   —— —— surname—ordinary signification of word

The applicants applied to register the mark "CANNON" in Part A of the register in respect of various specified tobacco goods. The application was refused on the ground that one of the ordinary significations of the word was a surname and it was therefore excluded from registration under the Trade Marks Act 1938, s. 9 (1). On appeal, *held*, a word might have more than one ordinary signification, as in this case. The applicants' contention that objection could only be taken if the surname was the primary, dominant or paramount signification was incorrect. The word in question was, according to one of its ordinary significations, a surname and in the absence of evidence of distinctiveness registration should be refused. The appeal would be dismissed.

CANNON TRADE MARK [1980] RPC 519 (Court of Appeal: BUCKLEY, ACKNER and OLIVER LJJ). *Swallow Raincoats Ltd's Application* (1947) 64 RPC 92 applied.

2930   —— likelihood of confusion

A company's application to register "CHINA-THERM" as a trade mark in respect of various plastic, thermally-insulated cups and containers was refused on the ground that the mark was likely to deceive or cause confusion within the meaning of the

Trade Marks Act 1938, s. 11. The company appealed. *Held*, the public would be likely to think that cups and containers advertised as "CHINA-THERM" were made of china and the use of the words "CHINA-THERM" in that association would accordingly misdescribe the character or quality of the goods. The appeal would be dismissed.

CHINA-THERM TRADE MARK [1980] FSR 21 (Chancery Division: WHITFORD J). *Re Seligmann's Application* (1953) 91 RPC 52, *Treasury Trade Mark* [1973] RPC 551 and *Royal McBee Corpn's Applications* [1961] RPC 84 distinguished.

2931   Trade Marks Rules

The Trade Marks (Amendment No. 2) Rules 1980, S.I. 1980 No. 1931 (in force on 5th January 1981), further amend the 1938 Rules by providing that the Patent Office, Trade Marks Registry, is to be open until midnight for the receipt of documents only.

TRADE UNIONS

Halsbury's Laws of England (3rd edn.), Vol. 38, paras. 601–677

2932   Action in furtherance of trade dispute—existence of dispute—effect on recovery of money paid under duress

During a dispute between shipowners and a union a vessel was "blacked" and in order to secure her release the owners complied with union demands by paying a sum into the union's welfare fund. The owners sought to recover that sum on the basis that it had been obtained by duress and because it was paid over subject to a void trust. The union appealed from a decision upholding the owners' claims. *Held*, the judge found that the payment was subject to a trust which was void. However, the union rules concerning the fund fitted the concept of a contract just as well as they fitted that of a trust. Since that construction was equally permissible and would lead to the validity of the fund's purposes, that was the choice the law should make. Accordingly, the owners had no equitable interest in the money paid to the fund by virtue of any resulting trust, because the money had been paid under a valid contract.

The union's reply to the owners' contention that the payment was made under duress was that the demand for payment was part of a trade dispute within the Trade Union and Labour Relations Act 1974, s. 29 (1), and therefore was not actionable by virtue of s. 13 (1). That contention was correct since the dispute was connected with terms and conditions of employment. The appeal on these points would be allowed.

UNIVERSE TANKSHIPS INC OF MONROVIA v INTERNATIONAL TRANSPORT WORKERS' FEDERATION [1980] IRLR 363 (Court of Appeal: MEGAW, BRIGHTMAN and WATKINS LJJ). Decision of Parker J [1980] IRLR 239 reversed in part.

2933   —— interlocutory injunction to restrain action—call to private sector to take industrial action—coercive effect on government—whether action in contemplation or furtherance of dispute

Following a dispute over pay between the British Steel Corporation (BSC) and its employees, a strike was called by the steel workers' union, the Iron and Steel Trades Confederation (ISTC). Two weeks later, the union resolved to call upon workers in the private sector of the steel industry to join the strike. There had been no dispute between the union and the private employers. The union felt however that the dispute was becoming a political matter and that they were being singled out for direct government and BSC attack. Therefore, the involvement of the private sector would be a method of bringing pressure to bear on the government who had control over the BSC's finances. The BSC would thus in turn be able to increase the workers' wages. An application by the private sector employers for an injunction to restrain the union from involving their employees in the strike was refused on the ground that the Trade Union and Labour Relations Act 1974, s. 13 (1), as amended, provided protection for "actions that were taken in furtherance of a trade dispute". The judge based his decision on the House of Lords' decision in *Express Newspapers Ltd v MacShane*, where the test for such an action was held to be purely subjective. The Court of Appeal reversed this decision on the grounds, inter alia, that the original trade dispute between the ISTC and BSC about wages had generated a second dispute between the ISTC and the government which did not fall within the definition of a "trade dispute". The court further held it had a discretion to restrain a strike which would have disastrous economic consequences for the country. On appeal by the ISTC, *held*, it could not be said that the act of calling out the private steel workers was not an act done in furtherance of the existing dispute between the BSC and ISTC. The test of whether such an action was done in furtherance of a trade dispute was subjective, as seen from the *MacShane* case. Therefore, if the union honestly believed that their acts, aimed at putting pressure on the government, were the only way to bring the strike to a successful end, then they were acts done in furtherance of a trade dispute and consequently immune from an action in tort. The argument that Parliament could not have intended such an immunity to be extended to actions which had the object of coercing the government, could not be upheld. Where the meaning of the statutory words was plain, it was not for judges to go beyond their rôles as interpreters because they considered that the results of strict interpretation would be inexpedient, unjust or immoral. Particularly in the controversial field of industrial relations, Parliament's opinion was paramount. If the national interest required that limits should be put on the use of "industrial muscle", the law as it stood had to be changed by Parliament and not by the judges. The appeal would accordingly be allowed.

DUPORT STEELS LTD v SIRS [1980] 1 All ER 529 (House of Lords: LORD DIPLOCK, LORD EDMUND-DAVIES, LORD FRASER OF TULLYBELTON, LORD KEITH OF KINKEL and LORD SCARMAN). Decision of the Court of Appeal (1980) Times, 28th January, reversed. *Express Newspapers Ltd v MacShane* [1980] 1 All ER 65, HL, 1979 Halsbury's Abridgment para. 2828 applied.

2934   —— —— **circumstances governing grant of injunction**

The owners of a vessel, wishing to employ a crew cheaply, decided to fly a flag of convenience and to arrange for another company, Saguaro, to employ and pay the crew, rather than employing the crew themselves. The International Transport Workers Federation (ITF) became aware of the situation and arrangements were made for Saguaro to fly the flag on ITF terms, and the vessel accordingly received a "blue" certificate. However, the certificate lapsed and the Yugoslav crew, which was being employed at wages much lower than ITF terms, complained to the ITF. The ITF instructed another union to "black" the vessel, with the result that she was unable to leave port. The owners acceded to ITF's demand for a crew employed on ITF terms, but refused to concede back pay to the Yugoslav crew. The owners applied for an injunction restraining the "blacking", submitting that the dispute was not with the owners but with Saguaro; thus there was no reasonable prospect of the industrial action succeeding, as the owners could not influence Saguaro. Further it was submitted that the employers were Saguaro and not the owners. *Held*, a trade dispute existed and the action taken against the vessel was in furtherance of a trade dispute. An artificial separation had been created between the owners and the function of manning the vessel; in fact the relationship between the owners and Saguaro was so close that any dispute with Saguaro was also with the owners. Thus the industrial action would bring pressure to bear on whoever was responsible for payment of wages. Since there was likely to be statutory immunity for the industrial action the injunction would be refused.

THE MARABU PORR, PORR v SHAW, JOHNSON AND HOLDEN [1979] 2 Lloyd's Rep 331 (Court of Appeal: LORD DENNING MR, SHAW and TEMPLEMAN LJJ).

2935   A newspaper sought an injunction to restrain certain trade unions from inducing or procuring the newspaper's employees to break or not perform their contracts of employment on 14th May, the day of the TUC one-day national strike. The newspaper contended that the unions were unlawfully inducing their members to break their contracts by issuing instructions to them not to work. *Held*, it was not disputed that the strike was political and that the unions were not therefore entitled to the immunity afforded to an action in furtherance of a trade dispute. The court would grant the injunction requested. It was in the public interest and in that of union members that the latter be made aware that the union was not lawfully entitled to incite its members thus, and that members who did break their contracts would not be protected from action by their employers.

EXPRESS NEWSPAPERS LTD V KEYS [1980] IRLR 247 (Queen's Bench Division: GRIFFITHS J).

2936   —— —— meaning of "dispute"

A company's business involved the developing and marketing of computer services. The company planned to do business with certain health authorities who employed a large number of National Association of Local Government Officers (NALGO) members. The union objected to trade between the company and the health authorities, primarily because of its concern for the jobs of its members. It felt that the employment of independent contractors such as the company would eventually restrict the size of the computer staff within the health service and might deprive them of the opportunity to do research and developmental work. NALGO consequently sent out a circular instructing its members not to co-operate with the company. On the company's application for an interim injunction to restrain the union from implementing that action, *held*, the question was whether NALGO's action was protected by the Trade Union and Labour Relations Act 1974, s. 13 (1), as amended, as being an action in contemplation or furtherance of a trade dispute. Under s. 29 (1), a trade dispute was defined as a dispute between employers and workers. The test of the existence of such a dispute was subjective, as held in the case of *Express Newspapers Ltd v MacShane*. It was reasonable, in the circumstances, for NALGO to have foreseen that the enforcement of their action might have led to disputes with the health authorities. Therefore it could be said that the circular was distributed in contemplation of those disputes. Further, for the purposes of s. 29 (4), (6) of the Act, there was also a dispute between the company and NALGO, the former being employers, albeit not of NALGO members, and the latter being workers. As there were no other special circumstances to justify the granting of an interlocutory injunction, the application would be dismissed.

HEALTH COMPUTING LTD V MEEK [1980] IRLR 437 (Chancery Division: GOULDING J). *Express Newspapers Ltd v MacShane* [1980] 1 All ER 65, HL, 1979 Halsbury's Abridgment para. 2828 applied.

2937   —— picketing—code of practice

Pursuant to his power under the Employment Act 1980, s. 3 the Secretary of State has issued a Code of Practice on Picketing. The Code is expressed to provide practical guidance on picketing in trade disputes for those who may be contemplating, organising or taking part in a picket and for those who, as employers or workers or members of the general public, may be affected by it. The code is divided into several sections: A, the introduction; B, picketing and the civil law; C, picketing and the criminal law; D, role of the police; E, limiting numbers of pickets; F, organisation of picketing; G, essential supplies and services and an Annex, secondary action and picketing.

2938   —— —— —— commencement

The Employment Code of Practice (Picketing) Order 1980, S.I. 1980 No. 1757 (in force on 17th December 1980), brings into force on that date the Code of Practice on Picketing, para. 2937.

2939   Advisory, Conciliation and Arbitration Service—statutory duties—validity of decision to defer inquiries pending judicial proceedings

A trade union, the Engineers' and Managers' Association (EMA) sought recognition on behalf of professional staff at an engineering works. EMA started a recruitment campaign in the works but the Trade Union Congress (TUC) Disputes Committee made an award, in favour of a rival union, that EMA had infringed the disputes principles in the 1939 Bridlington agreement and instructed it to cease recruitment and not to seek recognition. In April 1977 EMA made an application to ACAS for recognition, and in October 1977 EMA issued a writ against the TUC claiming that its award was invalid. In deference to this trial ACAS, in November 1977, decided to postpone its inquiries as the outcome of the trial would be a material factor in the recognition issue. At this point there was a reasonable prospect of an early trial. EMA issued a writ against ACAS, asking for a declaration that ACAS in refusing or failing to proceed upon its reference was in breach of its statutory duties under the Employment Protection Act 1975. At first instance this was refused. Subsequently, despite hopes for an early trial, the "TUC" trial was fixed for March 1980. Thus in May 1979, thirteen months after the first instance decision to refuse the declaration ACAS sought, the Court of Appeal reversed this decision, taking the view that the lapse of time was such that it was now unreasonable for ACAS to persist any longer in deferring the inquiry. On appeal from the Court of Appeal decision, *held*, LORD DIPLOCK and LORD KEITH OF KINKEL dissenting, when a recognition issue was referred to ACAS under ss. 11–16 of the Act, ACAS had a discretion to suspend its inquiry or defer its report if it was of the opinion that this would promote the improvement of industrial relations, including the extension of collective bargaining, or if it was thought that, unless there was a suspension or deferment, industrial relations would be worsened. In the instant case the initial decision to suspend the inquiry had not been unreasonable; neither had it been unreasonable of ACAS to continue with the suspension, despite the lapse of time. When the issue came before the Court of Appeal all the factors which had made ACAS decide on suspension remained relevant and it still remained ACAS's duty, on industrial relations grounds, to take account of the TUC award, if lawful, before determining the reference.

LORD DIPLOCK considered that ACAS's decision to suspend the inquiry was not simply an exercise of its discretion on how the reference should be conducted but was an abdication of its statutory functions; for where the issue involved the possibility of workers remaining unrepresented for a long period of time, ACAS was under a duty to play an active part in ending the impasse and could not sit back and wait for the outcome to be fought out in another forum.

The appeal would be allowed.

ENGINEERS' AND MANAGERS' ASSOCIATION v ADVISORY, CONCILIATION AND ARBITRATION SERVICE (No. 2) [1980] 1 All ER 896 (House of Lords: LORD WILBERFORCE, LORD DIPLOCK, LORD EDMUND-DAVIES, LORD KEITH OF KINKEL and LORD SCARMAN). Decision of the Court of Appeal [1979] 3 All ER 227, 1979 Halsbury's Abridgment para. 2833, reversed.

2940   Certification officer—fees

The Certification Officer (Amendment of Fees) Regulations 1980, S.I. 1980 No. 1708 (in force on 8th December 1980), increase certain fees payable to the certification officer and revoke the Certification Officer (Amendment of Fees) Regulations 1979, 1979 Halsbury's Abridgment para. 2834.

2941   Closed shop agreements and arrangements—code of practice

Pursuant to his power under the Employment Act 1980, s. 3, the Secretary of State has issued a Code of Practice on Closed Shop Agreements and Arrangements. The Code is expressed to provide practical guidance on the formulation and operation of closed shop agreement, that is collective agreements that have the effect of requiring employees to be, or remain, members of one or more Unions. The code is divided into several sections: A, the introduction; B, legal rights of individuals; C, closed shop agreements and arrangements, including the scope and content of agreements, secret ballots and the operation of new or existing agreements; D, union treatment of members and applicants; E, the closed shop and the freedom of the press and an Annex containing the definition of a union membership agreement.

2942 —— —— **commencement**

The Employment Code of Practice (Closed Shop Agreements and Arrangements) Order 1980, S.I. 1980 No. 1758 (in force on 17th December 1980), brings into force on that date the Code of Practice on Closed Shop Agreements and Arrangements, para. 2941.

2943   Collective bargaining—disclosure of information

A trade union recognised by the company sought information from the company relating to, inter alia, gross profits made by the company in the United Kingdom and gross profits earned by the company on the contract for servicing aircraft at three airports. The company was not prepared to make such disclosures largely on the grounds that disclosure would cause substantial injury to it for reasons other than its effect on collective bargaining (Employment Protection Act 1975, s. 18 (1) (e)) and the matter was referred to the Central Arbitration Committee under s. 19. On the reference, the committee said that it was not convinced that the information sought was such that, without it, the union representatives would be impeded to a material extent in carrying on collective bargaining (s. 17 (1) (a)). However, the committee added that it was totally convinced that the information was protected under s. 18 (1) (e) as disclosure of profits in the United Kingdom could have an adverse effect on the company's overseas trading position and disclosure of particular profits (or losses) made at one airport could damage the company's bargaining position in relation to future tenders for similar contracts. See Central Arbitration Committee award no. 78/584 (*Airwork Services Ltd v Amalgamated Union of Engineering Workers (Engineering Section)*) available from HMSO.

2944   A transport executive operated, inter alia, a bus service. When the daily waybill of bus conductors and one-person bus operators was analysed any "cash shorts" and "cash overs" were disclosed. Cash shorts were deducted from wages and certain cash overs were recovered by individuals. The unions requested the offsetting of cash shorts against cash overs; the transport executive made a limited offer to offset sums up to £1 per week but this was not accepted by the unions. In connection with this offer the transport executive supplied the unions with the historical data connected with cash shorts and cash overs in four consecutive weeks in 1978. The transport executive said that it was prepared to make such information available again; but questioned the need to provide it under the disclosure provisions of the Employment Protection Act 1975 or the desirability of doing so on a continuing basis. A complaint was presented by one union on behalf of itself and another union to the Central Arbitration Committee under s. 19 (1) of the Act seeking an award that the transport executive should disclose information as to cash overs. The Committee said that it thought that each individual should be aware of any cash short or cash over in his waybill and that individuals were more clearly aware of cash shorts than cash overs. However, the committee added that it did not think that such information relating to individuals' claims should be the subject of a declaration under s. 19. See Central Arbitration Committee award no. 78/807 (*Tyne and Wear Passenger Transport Executive v General and Municipal Workers' Union and the Transport and General Workers' Union*) available from HMSO.

2945   A company employing more than 200 employees did not recognise any union for collective bargaining purposes. The Association of Scientific, Technical and Managerial Staffs ("the union") made a formal reference to the Advisory, Conciliation and Arbitration Service ("ACAS") on the question of recognition in respect of ten of the employees. ACAS reported that the company should recognise the union for collective bargaining purposes; but the company did not do so. The company also failed to provide information requested by the union as it regarded its duty to provide information under s. 17(1) of the Employment Protection Act 1975 as limited to the provision of information when collective bargaining had already taken place. On a reference to the Central Arbitration Committee, the committee ruled that the terms of s. 17(2)(b) were intended to deal with just such a situation and that, despite the absence of any collective bargaining, the company was under a duty to provide information. See Central Arbitration Committee award no. 78/626 (*Holo-Krome Ltd v Association of Scientific, Technical and Managerial Staffs*) available from HMSO.

2946   —— —— **job evaluation scheme**

A company operated a salaried staff job-evaluated pay structure. In relation to the employees in question the scheme was non-participative. There were eight grades and all jobs were the subject of agreed job description. Jobs were evaluated by reference to a points rating system and factor comparison techniques. Individual employees could appeal against their own assessments to departmental managers and then to a job evaluation officer. If a departmental manager rejected an appeal, the employee could take the matter up with the union. The company refused to disclose certain details of the job evaluation scheme to the union on the ground that in respect of the employees in question only individual rights of representation existed and that, in this respect the union was not recognised. The union complained to the Central Arbitration Committee. The committee considered that where an employer agreed to a union representing its members at an appeal stage of a job evaluation scheme, it was desirable and necessary for the union to have sufficient information about the scheme for the representation to have some meaning. The union was accordingly recognised for collective bargaining purposes and the committee made a declaration requiring the necessary information to be disclosed. See Central Arbitration Committee award no. 78/708 (*G K N Sankey Ltd v Association of Scientific, Technical and Managerial Staffs*) available from HMSO.

2947   —— —— **productivity scheme**

A union complained to the Central Arbitration Committee that the employer had failed to disclose information relating to a productivity scheme as requested by the union. In fact the employer had offered to disclose the information in confidence to a limited number of union officials. The union felt that it could not, however, accept this offer since their officials could not reasonably conceal information affecting remuneration from their members. Further, they had specific instructions from their members to obtain the information for them. The committee considered whether disclosure of information in confidence constituted disclosure for the purposes of the Employment Protection Act 1975 and came to the conclusion that it did not. See Central Arbitration Committee award no. 78/711 (*International Publishing Corpn v National Union of Journalists*) available from HMSO.

2948   **Employer—liability in conversion—refusal to release goods induced by fear of industrial action**

See *Howard E. Perry & Co Ltd v British Railways Board*, para. 2854.

2949   **Employment Act 1980**

The Employment Act 1980 provides for payment out of public funds towards trade unions' expenditure in respect of ballots, for the use of employers' premises in connection with ballots and for the issue by the Secretary of State of Codes of Practice for the improvement of industrial relations. It also makes provision in respect of exclusion or expulsion from trade unions and otherwise amends the law relating to workers, employers, trade unions and employers' associations and repeals the Trade Union and Labour Relations Act 1974, s. 1A. The Act received the royal assent on 1st August 1980 and ss. 1, 3, 20 (1), 21 came into force on that date. S.I. 1980 No. 1170 brought the following provisions into force on the following dates: ss. 7, 19 (b), (c) and parts of s. 20 (2) and (3) and Schs. 1, 2 on 15th August 1980;

ss. 4, 5, 10, 15–18 and parts of ss. 20 (2), (3), Schs. 1, 2 on 8th September 1980; ss. 2, 6, 8, 9, 11–14, the remainder of s. 20 (2) and Sch. 1 and part of s. 20 (3) and Sch. 2 on 1st October 1980. Section 19 (a) and that part of s. 20 (3) and Sch. 2 which relates to the repeal of those provisions of the Trade Union and Labour Relations Act 1974 which provide for the preparation of a charter relating to the freedom of the press, came into force on 22nd December 1980: S.I. 1980 No. 1926.

Section 1 empowers the Secretary of State to make regulations establishing a scheme providing for payments by the Certification Officer towards expenditure incurred by independent trade unions in respect of secret ballots for specified purposes. The Secretary of State may by order specify other purposes. Section 2 requires an employer, so far as is reasonably practicable, to comply with a request by an independent trade union for a secret ballot to be held on his premises. Section 3 empowers the Secretary of State, after consultation with the Advisory, Conciliation and Arbitration Service, to issue Codes of Practice containing practical guidance for promoting the improvement of industrial relations. Any Code is subject to approval by both Houses of Parliament.

Section 4 applies to employments to which a union membership agreement applies and confers on every person who is, or is seeking to be, in such employment the right not to have an application for membership of a specified trade union unreasonably refused and not to be unreasonably expelled from a specified trade union. Complaints of infringement of this right are to be made to an industrial tribunal and an appeal lies to the Employment Appeal Tribunal on any question of law or fact. Under s. 5, a person whose complaint has been declared to be well-founded may apply to an industrial tribunal if he has been admitted or re-admitted to membership of the union for compensation for any loss sustained. If he has not been admitted or re-admitted, he may apply to the Employment Appeal Tribunal for such compensation as is just and equitable in all the circumstances. In both cases the maximum amount of compensation is specified.

Section 6 provides that in determining the fairness of a dismissal, an industrial tribunal must take into account the size and adminstrative resources of the employer's undertaking. The requirement concerning the onus of proof is amended. Section 7 extends the grounds upon which dismissal for non-membership of a trade union is to be regarded as unfair where there is a union membership agreement. The grounds, as extended, are where the employee genuinely objects on grounds of conscience or other deeply-held personal conviction to being a member of any union or of a particular union, where he was not a member of a relevant union when the union membership agreement took effect, or, in the case of an agreement coming into effect after the commencement of this section, the agreement was not approved in a ballot in which at least eighty per cent of those to be covered supported it. Section 8 extends the qualifying period for bringing a complaint of unfair dismissal to two years in the case of any employee whose employer and any associated employer have together employed no more than twenty employees during his employment, unless the dismissal relates to trade union membership or activities or was on certain medical grounds. It also reduces from two years to one year the minimum length of a fixed term contract of employment in which the parties may agree to waive the employee's right to complain of unfair dismissal. Section 9 amends the entitlement to a basic award and provides that the amount may be reduced where the employee has unreasonably refused an offer of reinstatement or because of his conduct. The minimum entitlement to two weeks' pay is abolished. Under s. 10, an employer may join as a party in unfair dismissal proceedings a trade union or other person who he claims induced him to dismiss the employee by calling or threatening a strike or other industrial action because the employee was not a trade union member. The industrial tribunal may make an order requiring that party to pay to the employer a contribution in respect of compensation awarded. Provision is also made for indemnity in respect of union membership clauses.

Section 11 concerns the right to return to work after maternity absence and provides for written notification and confirmation of intention to return to work. Section 12 provides that where an employer with five or less employees finds it not reasonably practicable to reinstate an employee in her original job or to give a suitable one after maternity absence, he is relieved of the obligation to reinstate. An employer is also relieved of the obligation to reinstate where it is not reasonably practicable for a reason other than redundancy for him to reinstate an employee and he offers her suitable alternative employment. Section 13 confers a right not to be unreasonably refused time off during working hours to receive ante-natal care. An employee who is permitted such time off is entitled to be paid remuneration at the appropriate rate. If she is unreasonably refused time off or the employer fails to pay her the appropriate remuneration an employee may complain to an industrial tribunal, which may award her an amount equal to the remuneration she would have received if the time off had not been refused.

Section 14 provides that no more than five days' guarantee pay is payable in any period of three months, instead of fixed three-month periods, as formerly. Section 15 extends an employee's right not to have action short of dismissal taken against him to compel him to belong to a union to employees not covered by a union membership agreement and to those covered by such an agreement where they would be protected against unfair dismissal under s. 7. A right of joinder analogous to that contained in s. 10 is provided.

Section 16 modifies the Trade Union and Labour Relations Act 1974, s. 15, so that it applies to peaceful picketing in contemplation or furtherance of a trade dispute only when carried out by a person attending at or near his own place of work, or, if he has been dismissed, his former place of work, or by a trade union official accompanying a member of that union whom he represents and who is picketing at his own place of work. The immunities from actions in tort conferred by the 1974 Act, s. 13, do not apply to an act done in the course of picketing unless done during attendance within s. 16. Section 17 provides that the immunities conferred by the 1974 Act, s. 13, do not apply where a person induces a breach of contract, except a contract of employment, by means of secondary industrial action, unless the secondary action meets certain requirements. The main requirements are that the purpose or principal purpose of the action should be directly to prevent or disrupt the supply during a trade dispute of goods or services between an employer who is a party to the dispute and an employer whose employees are taking the action, and that it is likely to achieve that purpose. There will also continue to be immunity where secondary action involves employees of associated employers of the employer in dispute or employees of their customers if the purpose or principal purpose of the action is directly to prevent or disrupt the supply during the dispute of goods or services from the associated employer to the customer, which but for the dispute would have been supplied by the employer in dispute. Under s. 18, the immunities conferred by the 1974 Act, s. 13, do not apply where a person induces an employee of one employer to break his contract of employment in order to compel workers of another employer to join a particular trade union unless they are working at the same place.

Section 19 repeals the Trade Union and Labour Relations Act 1974, s. 1A, which provides for a charter on the freedom of the press; the Employment Protection Act 1975, ss. 11–16, which establish a procedure for dealing with issues relating to the recognition of trade unions; and the 1975 Act, s. 98, Sch. 11 and the Road Haulage Wages Act 1938, under which new terms and conditions of employment may be substituted for existing terms and conditions. Section 20 and Schs. 1 and 2 deal with interpretation, minor and consequential amendments and repeals. Section 21 deals with short title, commencement and extent.

2950   Funds—political funds

See *Parkin v Association of Scientific, Technical and Managerial Staffs*, para. 2959; *Reeves v Transport and General Workers Union*, para. 2960.

2951   —— trade union ballots

The Funds for Trade Union Ballots Regulations 1980, S.I. 1980 No. 1252 (in force on 1st October 1980), establish a scheme, as authorised by the Employment Act 1980 s. 1, para. 2949, under which the Certification Officer will make payments to independent trade unions in respect of postal, printing and stationery expenditure which they have incurred in holding secret postal ballots for certain prescribed purposes.

2952   —— **welfare fund**

See *Universe Tankships Inc of Monrovia v International Transport Workers' Federation*, para. 2932.

2953   **International Labour Conference—recommendations and conventions—implementation**

See para. 1340.

2954   **Recognition—duty of Post Office to consult with appropriate organisation—appropriateness of organisation—test to be applied**

See *R v Post Office, ex parte Association of Scientific, Technical and Managerial Staffs*, para. 2173.

2955   —— **recommendation by Advisory, Conciliation and Arbitration Service—effect of non-compliance with recommendation by company**

A union complained to the Central Arbitration Committee under the Employment Protection Act 1975, s. 16 that a company was not complying with a recommendation of the Advisory, Conciliation and Arbitration Service (ACAS) that the union should be recognised by the company for collective bargaining purposes in respect of certain of its employees. It was proposed that the committee should make an award in relation to the terms and conditions of employment of those employees. It was further proposed the the award be of such substantial proportions as to penalise the company for not complying with the recommendations of ACAS. The committee decided that the complaint was well founded and proceeded to deal with the claim as to terms and conditions. It rejected, however, the claim that it should make a penal or punitive award on the ground, inter alia, that there was no authority in the statute for making such an award. See Central Arbitration Committee award no. 78/808 (*John Wyeth & Brother Ltd v Association of Scientific, Technical and Managerial Staffs*) available from HMSO.

2956   —— —— **validity of recommendation**

The Advisory Conciliation and Arbitration Service were asked to decide a question of recognition involving a union that wished to represent the professionally qualified engineers working within a company. There were already a number of unions representing the company's employees, and these unions opposed the recognition of the union. ACAS recommended that the union should not be recognised. The Court of Appeal held that the ACAS report was a nullity as it did not contain the necessary findings on which to base a decision on whether or not to recommend recognition, and that ACAS had not given priority to the need to reform the collective bargaining machinery as against the need to improve industrial relations. Further ACAS was in breach of art. 11 of the European Convention on Human Rights in not recommending recognition. On appeal to the House of Lords, *held*, the Employment Protection Act 1975 entrusted the decision on whether to recommend recognition entirely upon ACAS and there was no provision for an appeal to the courts on the decision. The lawfulness of the acts of ACAS were still subject to judicial review, but the courts could not interfere with a decision of ACAS unless it could be shown that no reasonable body charged with the responsibilities of ACAS could have exercised its powers in such a way. Thus it could not be categorically stated that the duty to encourage the extension of collective bargaining took priority over the duty to promote the improvement of industrial relations, as the relative importance of each was a matter for ACAS to decide in each case; and although ACAS should not allow the threat of industrial action by other unions to fetter its impartiality in arriving at its decision, nevertheless this was a factor it could legitimately take into account. Section 12 (4) of the Act did not state upon what questions ACAS was to make its findings but only that it should set out its findings in its report, and unless no reasonable body could have reached the conclusion ACAS reached on those findings, its conclusion could not be overturned; the conclusions ACAS had reached in the instant case did follow logically from the findings set out in the report.

Although art. 11 of the European Convention sought to protect the right to join a trade union, it did not follow that every trade union which enjoyed support from employees within a company should be recognised for collective bargaining purposes. The appeal would be dismissed.

UNITED KINGDOM ASSOCIATION OF PROFESSIONAL ENGINEERS v ADVISORY CONCILIATION AND ARBITRATION SERVICE [1980] 1 All ER 612 (House of Lords: LORD WILBERFORCE, LORD DIPLOCK, LORD EDMUND-DAVIES, LORD KEITH OF KINKEL and LORD SCARMAN). Decision of Court of Appeal (1979) 123 Sol Jo 79, 1978 Halsbury's Abridgment para. 2880 reversed.

2957   **Rules—construction—"affecting a majority of the union"**

The National Executive Council (NEC) of the National Union of Journalists voted for a strike of its members employed by provincial newspapers, and disruptive measure to be applied by its other members. When the strike was settled disciplinary action was taken against those members who had failed to comply with the NEC's instructions. Rule 20 (b) of the union's rules provides that no withdrawal from employment affecting a majority of union members could be sanctioned without a ballot. A ballot had not been taken and the plaintiffs, members against whom action had been taken, successfully sought an interim injunction restraining the union from taking further disciplinary action and an order restoring them to membership pending trial of the action. The union appealed and the question arose as to the meaning of "affecting a majority of the union". *Held*, the balance of convenience required the continuance of the injunction. Serious issues of disputed fact were likely to arise for determination at a later trial which could not be decided on at an interlocutory stage and the status quo between the plaintiffs and the union, with the plaintiff members being treated as full union members, should, in such a situation, be maintained. Further it was self evident that any journalist suffering from a reduction in normal professional earnings by complying with the NEC order, or suffering as a result of others complying with that order, were "affected" within r. 20 (b) and that the NEC had acted unconstitutionally in calling a strike without holding a ballot. The appeal would accordingly be dismissed.

PORTER v NATIONAL UNION OF JOURNALISTS; PRITCHARD v NATIONAL UNION OF JOURNALISTS (1980) Times, 31st July (House of Lords: LORD DIPLOCK, VISCOUNT DILHORNE, LORD SALMON, LORD RUSSELL OF KILLOWEN, LORD KEITH OF KINKEL). Decision of the Court of Appeal [1979] IRLR 404, 1979 Halsbury's Abridgment para. 2842 affirmed.

2958   —— —— **welfare fund—validity of purposes**

See *Universe Tankships Inc of Monrovia v International Transport Workers' Federation*, para. 2932.

2959   —— **political fund—application of funds for political objects— affiliation to political party—whether bar to donations to other parties**

A branch of a trade union made a resolution requesting the national executive council (NEC) to refund to the branch one-third of its political levy, under r. 36 of the union rules, for it to be donated to the Conservative Party for promoting a better understanding of the policies of Conservative trade unionists within the union and for ensuring their co-operation. The NEC refused on the ground that the request was contrary to the rules as the union had affiliated to the Labour Party and that it was a condition of affiliation that money might not be donated to other political parties. The plaintiff, a member of the trade union, brought an action against the union contending that under the union rules the branch had a degree of autonomy sufficient to enable it to donate part of the fund to a political party whose objects were inconsistent with those of the Labour Party. *Held*, r. 36 contained no express limitation; any limitation had therefore to be found by implication from the rules as a whole, together with all the surrounding circumstances. The affiliation merely indicated the union's policy of support for the Labour Party; it did not limit the discretion of the branch to make a contribution to the Conservative Party if it so chose. However, the resolution stated the purposes for which the Conservative Party was to use the payment, and r. 36 (b) stated that any payment out of the fund had to be in furtherance of political objects defined in the Trade Union Act 1913, s. 3. The first purpose, regarding the understanding of Conservative trade unionists' policies, was a proper political object, but the second purpose, to ensure their co-operation and help, did not fall within the definitions in s. 3 and r. 36. The NEC were accordingly entitled to say that the request was for an improper purpose. The plaintiff, however, was entitled to a declaration dealing with the general point of principle, that the affiliation did not impose an additional limitation on the exercise of the branch's discretion.

PARKIN v ASSOCIATION OF SCIENTIFIC, TECHNICAL AND MANAGERIAL STAFFS [1980] ICR 662 (Queen's Bench Division: WOOLF J).

2960 —— —— **meaning of "relieved from payment"**

The Trade Union Act 1913, s. 5 provides that a union member can give notice that he objects to contributing to a union's political fund and thereby be exempted from making those payments.

The employee was a member of a union which had an agreement with his employer that if a member signed a form of authority, union subscriptions would be deducted from the employee's wages and remitted to the union. The rules of the union's political fund provided that a member who was exempt would be "relieved from the payment". The employee, who was exempt from the political levies, contended that the levy should not be deducted from his wages at source and that the system of refunding payments was not permissible under the rules. He also contended that if a member had to receive a refund he suffered a disadvantage in breach of the rules. He appealed under the 1913 Act, s. 5 as provided by the Employment Protection (Consolidation) Act 1978 s. 136 (2). The union cross-appealed contending that the Certification Officer had been wrong to hold that a union member was not "relieved" from payment within the meaning of the rules by a refund made soon after the contribution was due and that it was not bound to pay the refund in advance. *Held,* although the rules indicated that a member was to pay only the net amount of subscription, it was necessary to read them as a whole. There was no absolute rule that relief had to be given when payment was made. Since the wages were paid by computer and the system could not be adapted to enable the employee to pay a reduced contribution, there was no breach of the rules if the levy was refunded in advance. However, there was sufficient compliance with the rules if the refund was made as soon as possible after the payments were due, but it should be made automatically. The system did not place the employee at a substantial disadvantage as compared with other union members. The cross-appeal would be allowed and the order requiring the union to pay the refund in advance would be set aside and the appeal would be dismissed.

REEVES v TRANSPORT AND GENERAL WORKERS UNION (1980) Times, 24th April (Employment Appeal Tribunal: SLYNN J presiding).

TRANSPORT

Halsbury's Laws of England (3rd edn.), Vol. 31, paras. 639–1403

2961 **Common transport policy**

See EUROPEAN COMMUNITIES.

2962   Community buses—fitness, equipment and use

The Community Bus (Amendment) Regulations 1980, S.I. 1980 No. 144 (in force on 5th March 1980), amend the requirements of the Community Bus Regulations 1978, 1978 Halsbury's Abridgment para. 2887 regarding the fire extinguishing apparatus and first aid equipment carried by a community bus.

2963   —— road service licences

The Community Bus (Amendment) Regulations 1980, S.I. 1980 No. 1358 (in force on 6th October 1980), amend the Community Bus Regulations 1978, 1978 Halsbury's Abridgment para. 2887, in relation to road service licences, in consequence of the Transport Act 1980, para. 2986.

2964   Hackney carriage—fares

The Hackney Carriage Fares (Amendment of Byelaws) Order 1980, S.I. 1980 No. 496 (in force on 21st April 1980), empowers a local authority to increase taxi fares which are fixed by byelaw, with a view to offsetting higher operating costs attributable to the increases in the rates of excise duty on petrol and diesel oil (as from 26th March 1980) and in the rates of vehicle excise duty (as from 27th March 1980). The power is exercisable by resolution at any time before 30th June 1980 or at the first meeting of the local authority on or after that date. Any such resolution would authorise a surcharge of not more than three pence in respect of each hiring and would provide for a notice relating to the surcharge to be displayed in each hackney carriage. The order also requires the local authority to take certain steps to publish the resolution.

2965   International passenger services

The Road Transport (International Passenger Services) Regulations 1980, S.I. 1980 No. 1459 (in force on 3rd November 1980), supplement and enforce certain EEC Council and Commission Regulations relating to the international carriage of passengers by coach and bus. The Road Transport (International Passenger Services) Regulations 1973 as amended (see 1979 Halsbury's Abridgment para. 2845) are revoked.

2966   London Transport—bus services—agreements with independent undertakings—appeals

The London Bus Services (Appeals) Regulations 1980, S.I. 1980 No. 1355 (in force on 6th October 1980), prescribe the time and the manner in which certain appeals under the Transport (London) Act 1969 are to be made.

2967   Minibus—fitness, equipment and use

The Minibus (Conditions of Fitness, Equipment and Use) (Amendment) Regulations 1980, S.I. 1980 No. 142 (in force on 5th March 1980), amend the Minibus (Conditions of Fitness, Equipment and Use) Regulations 1977, 1977 Halsbury's Abridgment para. 2896 by introducing new requirements regarding the fire extinguishing apparatus and first aid equipment carried by a minibus.

2968   —— permit—grant by designated body

The Minibus (Designated Bodies) Order 1980, S.I. 1980 No. 1356 (in force on 6th October 1980), replaces the Minibus (Designated Bodies) Order 1977, 1977 Halsbury's Abridgment para. 2898, as amended. The new order designates the bodies which, in addition to traffic commissioners, may grant permits under the Minibus Act 1977 for the use of certain vehicles by educational and other bodies. The order also provides for returns to be made relating to the grant of permits.

2969   —— —— **prescribed form**

The Minibus (Permits) (Amendment) Regulations 1980, S.I. 1980 No. 1357 (in force on 6th October 1980), further amend the 1977 Regulations, 1977 Halsbury's Abridgment para. 2898, by revising the definition of the expression "minibus".

2970   **National Freight Corporation—pensions**

See PENSIONS AND SUPERANNUATION.

2971   **New bus grants**

The New Bus Grants (Extension of Period and Reduction of Rate) Order 1980, S.I. 1980 No. 1105 (in force on 30th July 1980), provides that new buses are eligible for grant under the Transport Act 1968, s. 32 if first available for use before 1st April 1984 and reduces the rate of grant payable.

2972   **Passenger vehicles—experimental areas**

The Passenger Vehicles (Experimental Areas) Designation Order 1980, S.I. 1980 No. 413 (in force on 18th April 1980), designates Swinton with Warthermarske in the district of Harrogate, North Yorkshire as an experimental area for the purposes of the Passenger Vehicles (Experimental Areas) Act 1977, 1977 Halsbury's Abridgment para. 2899.

2973   **Pensions**

See PENSIONS.

2974   **Public service vehicles—drawing of trailers**

See para. 2389.

2975   —— **driver—duty to take reasonable precautions to ensure safety of passengers**

The defendant was the driver of a school bus with a manually operated passenger door. A schoolgirl asked him to stop the bus; she opened the door herself with directions from the defendant who remained in his seat. When she closed the door, she trapped her coat and was dragged some distance along the road. The defendant was charged with failing to take all reasonable precautions to ensure the safety of passengers alighting from the bus in contravention of the Public Service Vehicles (Conduct of Drivers, Conductors and Passengers) Regulations 1936, reg. 4. *Held*, it would not have been reasonable for the defendant to open the door every time a child wanted to get off the bus since it was difficult for him to get to the door from his seat. Moreover, such action would have increased the risk of an accident by leaving the bus controls unattended. Accordingly, the defendant had taken all reasonable precautions to ensure his passengers' safety.

EDWARDS v RIGBY [1980] RTR 353 (Queen's Bench Division: WALLER LJ and PARK J).

2976   —— **fitness, equipment and use**

The Public Service Vehicles (Conditions of Fitness, Equipment and Use) (Amendment) Regulations 1980, S.I. 1980 No. 141 (in force on 5th March 1980), amend the Public Service Vehicles (Conditions of Fitness, Equipment and Use) Regulations 1972 by introducing new requirements relating to the fire extinguishing apparatus and first aid equipment carried by public service vehicles.

2977   The Public Service Vehicles (Conditions of Fitness, Equipment and Use) (Amendment) (No. 2) Regulations 1980, S.I. 1980 No. 1097 (in force on 27th August 1980), amend the Public Service Vehicles (Conditions of Fitness, Equipment and Use) Regulations 1972 by (i) prescribing the conditions of fitness to be complied with by certain vehicles; (ii) providing that requirements relating to brake connections do not apply to certain vehicles which have been type approved regarding their brakes; (iii) modifying the requirements regarding the width of gangways; (iv) revoking requirements relating to side overhang and hub projection and (v) providing more adequately for the height of certain exits and the availability of emergency exits in the event of a vehicle falling on its side.

2978   —— **licences—driver and conductor's licence**

The Public Service Vehicles (Drivers' and Conductors' Licences) (Amendment) Regulations 1980, S.I. 1980 No. 634 (in force on 9th June 1980), amend the Public Service Vehicles (Drivers' and Conductors' Licences) Regulations 1934 by increasing the fee for a driver's licence to £1·50 and abolishing the fee for a duplicate licence.

2979   The Public Service Vehicles (Drivers' and Conductors' Licences) (Amendment) (No. 2) Regulations 1980, S.I. 1980 No. 914 (in force on 31st July 1980), amend the Public Service Vehicles (Drivers' and Conductors Licences) Regulations 1934 by revoking the references to the licensing of conductors and disapplying certain provisions as regards badges issued to persons to whom licences to act as conductors were issued.

2980   The Public Service Vehicles (Conduct of Drivers, Conductors and Passengers) (Amendment) Regulations 1980, S.I. 1980 No. 915 (in force on 31st July 1980), amend the Public Service Vehicles (Conduct of Drivers, Conductors and Passengers) Regulations 1936 in relation to the abolition of the licensing of conductors of public service vehicles.

2981   —— —— **road service licences**

The Public Service Vehicles (Road Service Licences and Express Services) Regulations 1980, S.I. 1980 No. 1354 (in force on 6th October 1980), deal with the procedure relating to applications for road service licences under the Transport Act 1980, para. 1409 and fees for such licences. These regulations further prescribe various matters in relation to the classification of a service as an express carriage service.

Earlier regulations dealing with road service licences are revoked.

2982   —— **licences and certificates—fees**

The Public Service Vehicles (Licences and Certificates) (Amendment) Regulations 1980, S.I. 1980 No. 635 (in force on 9th June 1980), amend the Public Service Vehicles (Licences and Certificates) Regulations 1952 by increasing the following fees: (i) the fee for a public service vehicle licence to £65; (ii) the fee for a certificate of fitness to £35; (iii) the fees for approval of a vehicle as a type vehicle; (iv) the fee for a road service licence to £9 for each year or part of a year and (v) the maximum fee for a copy of the publication "Notices and Proceedings" to £1. The 1980 Regulations also abolish the fees for duplicate licences and certificates and for copies of permits under the Transport Act 1968, s. 30.

These regulations have been revoked in part; see para. 2981.

2983   —— **seating capacity**

The Public Service Vehicles and Trolley Vehicles (Carrying Capacity) (Amendment) Regulations 1980, S.I. 1980 No. 76 (in force on 21st February 1980), amend the Public Service Vehicles and Trolley Vehicles (Carrying Capacity) Regulations 1954 by altering the rule for determining the number of passengers who may be seated in a public service vehicle.

2984   **Taxicab—fares for hiring—London**

The London Cab Order 1980, S.I. 1980 No. 588 (in force on 18th May 1980), increases the existing fares and extra charges payable for the hiring of a motor cab in the Metropolitan Police District and the City of London in respect of all journeys beginning and ending there.   It also makes new provision in respect of the extra charges for the carriage of luggage and for hirings at night, at weekends and on public holidays.   If a cab is fitted with a taximeter which is not capable of recording the new fares automatically, a notice setting out the fares payable in relation to the fares shown on the meter must be prominently displayed in the cab.

2985 The London Cab (No. 2) Order 1980, S.I. 1980 No. 939 (in force on 4th August 1980), further amends the London Cab Order 1934 in relation to the fares prescribed for the hiring of a motor cab in the Metropolitan Police District and the City of London for journeys beginning and ending there.   The order makes provision for the fares payable where a cab is fixed with an electro-mechanical taximeter which is capable of recording only part of the fares introduced by the London Cab Order 1980, para. 2984.   The conversion from fares shown on the meter (from £2.90) to fares payable by the hirer is set out in the Schedule to the order.   The existing fares payable for the hiring of a cab are not increased.

2986   Transport Act 1980

The Transport Act 1980 makes various changes in the law relating to transport and road traffic.   It replaces (in part re-enacting with amendment) the principal existing provisions relating to public service vehicles, provides for the reconstitution of the National Freight Corporation and makes changes in the arrangements by which Government support is provided for the historic pensions obligations of the British Railways Board and the National Freight Corporation.   The Act received the royal assent on 30th June 1980 and Pt. II (except s. 51 (2) and Sch. 7), Pt. III, ss. 66–68, 70, Sch. 9, Pt. II (and s. 69 so far as it relates to that part) came into force on that date. Sections 1 (3) (part), (4) (part), 27, 36, 39, 43 (1) (part), 64, 69 (part) and Schs. 5, Part I (part) and 9, Part I (part) came into force on 31st July 1980: S.I. 1980 No. 913. Sections 1 (3) (part), (4) (part), 2–15, 28 (1)–(5) (part), (7)–(10) (part), 29, 32, 33, 35, 37, 38 (part), 40, 41 (part), 42 (part), 43 (1) (part), (2), 44 (part), 61, 62, 65, 69 (part), Schs. 1, Parts I, II, III, 4, 5 (part), 9 (part) came into force on 6th October 1980: S.I. 1980 No. 1353; and Sch. 1, Part IV and Sch. 2 were brought into force on the same date: S.I. 1980 No. 1424.   Section 51 (2), Sch. 7 and Sch. 9, Pt. III (and s. 69 so far as it relates to that Part) come into force on the appointed day within the meaning of Pt. II.   The remaining provisions come into force on a day or days to be appointed.

In Part I, which is concerned with public service vehicles, s. 1 sets out the main purposes for which Part I is put forward and lists the major repeals which result.   By s. 2 small vehicles in which passengers are carried otherwise than in the course of a business of carrying passengers are excluded from the licensing provisions and stage, express and contract carriages are reclassified by s. 3 and Sch. 1.   Section 4 requires road service licences to be obtained for the operation of stage carriage services but not express carriage services.   Sections 5–10 deal with the granting, revocation and suspension of road service licences and the criteria and conditions upon which they may be granted.   By s. 11 the normal duration of a road service licence is to be 5 years.   Sections 12–15 and Sch. 2 enable trial areas to be designated in which road service licences are not to be required for stage carriage services.   Sections 16–18 are concerned with the fitness of public service vehicles.   Sections 19–31 and Sch. 3 provide for a system of public service vehicle operator licensing which replaces the present system of public service licensing, with ss. 28 and 29 providing rights of appeal for applicants for licences or licence-holders, and for certain other persons having standing in the matter, against decisions of the traffic commissioners.   Other matters connected with public service vehicles are dealt with in ss. 32–44, Schs. 4 and 5.

In Part II, which deals with the transfer of the undertaking of the National Freight Corporation to a company limited by shares on a day to be appointed, s. 45 and Sch. 6 provide for the transfer and ss. 46–51 and Sch. 7 deal with matters concerning the dissolution of the Corporation, the securities, reserves and dividends of the successor company, the funding of certain obligations of the successor company and other supplementary provisions.

Part III alters the method by which Government financial assistance is being provided towards the fulfilment of certain obligations (the relevant pension obligations) owed by the British Railways Board and the National Freight Corporation to certain of their pension schemes. By s. 52 the Minister of Transport is under an obligation to make payments to the schemes and "relevant pension obligations" is defined in s. 53. Section 54 provides for the determination of the proportion of the relevant pension obligations which is unfunded and s. 55 for the determination of the total amount of pension payments made by each scheme and the proportion of that total which corresponds to the relevant pension obligations in relation to the scheme. Section 56 provides for the reduction of the Minister's payments in certain circumstances and s. 57 for the exclusion of payments in respect of certain transfer values. Sections 58–60 and Sch. 8 deal with repeals, definition of terms and other supplemental matters.

Part IV contains miscellaneous provisions. By s. 61 a motor insurance policy or security covering private use of a vehicle is automatically extended to cover use of the vehicle under a car-sharing arrangement, irrespective of any restriction on or exclusion of such use. Section 62 redefines the vehicles which qualify for new bus grant and the services which qualify for fuel duty rebate in consequence of the reclassification contained in s. 3 and excludes services not available to the general public from qualifying. By s. 63 certain articulated passenger vehicles are to be treated as single motor vehicles thus, making them eligible to be treated as public service vehicles. Section 64 prohibits the use of roof-signs on vehicles other than taxis. Sections 65–69 and Sch. 9 deal with repeals and certain other matters. Section 70 provides for citation and commencement and, in particular, provides that commencement orders may contain transitional provisions and savings.

TRESPASS

Halsbury's Laws of England (3rd edn.), Vol. 38, paras. 1194–1282

2987 Trespass to land—failure to take breath test—arrest—validity

See *Morris v Beardmore*, para. 2359.

2988 —— trespass on adjoining property—injunction

The plaintiff, a company, and the defendants, a bank, owned adjoining premises. The defendants' property was in a dangerous condition and they had a statutory duty to remedy the defective state of the building. It was impossible to repair the building without entering onto the plaintiff's land. The defendants entered into negotiations seeking permission to enter onto the plaintiff's land in order to carry out the remedial work but permission was consistently refused. The defendants commenced repair work to their building but in doing so entered onto the plaintiff's land, erecting scaffolding and dumping debris from the repair work. The plaintiff moved for interlocutory injunctions, both prohibitory and mandatory, until the trial of the action for trespass, earlier ex parte relief in the form of negative injunctions having been granted. *Held*, the defendants' intentional action of entering onto the plaintiff's land without permission in order to repair a building for their own commercial benefit was a flagrant invasion of another's rights of property. Although the actual damage likely to be caused was slight and would not command a large sum in compensation, it was a fit case for a prohibitory injunction and there were no grounds for the court to suspend it. Therefore the negative injunctions previously given would be continued. There was no dispute in the case as to any relevant fact or point of law and no conceivable reason in law for the defendants' acts was given. The case was therefore one of the rare class of cases where, even on an interlocutory

motion, a mandatory order, ordering the defendants to remove the scaffolding and
debris, would be made.

JOHN TRENBERTH LTD V NATIONAL WESTMINSTER BANK LTD (1979) 39 P & CR
104 (Chancery Division: WALTON J). *Woollerton & Wilson Ltd v Richard Costain
Ltd* [1970] 1 WLR 411 not followed.

2989 Trespass to the person—assault—defence—use of force reasonable in circumstances

Northern Ireland

A soldier in Northern Ireland, who had received information that a bomb attack on
a bank was likely to take place, instructed four soldiers to take up positions on a roof
overlooking the bank. Two men were seen approaching the night safe which they
attempted to open, when three others appeared, and a scuffle ensued. After one of
the soldiers shouted at them to halt, the three men began to run. Although he
threatened to fire at them they did not stop and were subsequently killed when all
four soldiers fired. They were found not to have been armed, and the widow of one
of the men brought an action against the Ministry of Defence. She claimed damages
on the ground that his death had been caused by the negligence of the ministry, its
servants and agents and by assaults and batteries committed by them. The judge
withdrew the question of negligence from the jury, on the basis that an answer to the
claim based on assault, would have constituted an answer to the claim based on
negligence. Judgment was given for the ministry and the widow appealed. The
appeal was allowed and a new trial ordered on the ground that in considering
whether the use of force by the soldiers was reasonable in the circumstances for the
prevention of crime, as provided for by the Criminal Law Act (Northern Ireland)
1967, s. 3 (1), the jury should also have been directed to take into account the
circumstances in which the preparatory steps were taken to prevent the supposed
bomb attack. The ministry appealed. *Held*, s. 3 (1) not only provided a defence for
a person accused of a crime, but also for a person sued. The question which had to
be determined was whether the force used was reasonable in the circumstances. The
only circumstances which were relevant for the purposes of s. 3 (1) were the
immediate circumstances in which the force was used. In the present case, only
the four soldiers had used force. Accordingly, they would not have been deprived
of their defence had any defects been established with respect to the planning of the
operation. Furthermore since there had been no allegations of negligence in the
statement of claim against anyone other than the four soldiers, it was not open to
the plaintiff subsequently to seek to establish facts which would amount to negligence
on the part of any other person. Accordingly the appeal would be allowed.

The court stressed the importance of pleadings in civil actions and pointed out that
despite wide powers to permit amendments such permission might cause injustice,
when an adjournment would be necessary particularly in trials by jury.

FARRELL V SECRETARY OF STATE FOR DEFENCE [1980] 1 All ER 166 (House of
Lords: VISCOUNT DILHORNE, LORD EDMUND-DAVIES, LORD FRASER OF TULLYBELTON,
LORD RUSSELL OF KILLOWEN and LORD LANE).

The Criminal Law Act (Northern Ireland) 1967, s. 3 (1) corresponds to the
Criminal Law Act 1967, s. 3 (1).

2990 —— battery—medical operation without consent

Canada

Prior to her operation a patient told the anaesthetist not to inject her left arm. The
anaesthetist ignored her warning and the patient suffered a severe and unexpected
reaction when the anaesthetic solution leaked into the tissue of her arm. She
brought an action for damages for personal injuries. *Held*, although the needle
slipping out and leaking the solution was not an infrequent occurrence, there was no
negligence on the part of the anaesthetist who had exercised reasonable skill in
placing the needle in and monitoring the anaesthetic during the operation.
However, the anaesthetist was liable in battery. All surgical operations constituted
a battery unless the patient consented. In this case the patient had expressly instructed
the anaesthetist not to inject her arm. Further, in battery all damage was recoverable

as the limitation devices of foresight and remoteness were not applicable to intentional torts as they were in negligence.

ALLAN v NEW MOUNT SINAI HOSPITAL (1980) 28 OR (2d) 356 (High Court of Ontario).

2991 —— medical practitioner

See *Chatterton v Gerson*, para. 1892; *McLean v Weir and Goff*, para. 2047; *Hopp v Lepp*, para. 2055.

TRUSTS

Halsbury's Laws of England (3rd edn.), Vol. 38, paras. 1346–1833

2992 Articles

Half a Loaf: Financial Provision on Death, Martin L. Parry: 124 Sol Jo 621.

Secret Trusts: The Fraud Theory Revisited, David Hodge: Conv (NS) 341.

Trustee Exemption Clauses and the Unfair Contract Terms Act 1977, W. Goodhart: Conv (NS) 333.

2993 Breach of trust—settlement of majority shareholding in private company—bank as trustee—duty to prevent speculative investment by company

The defendant bank was the trustee of a settlement consisting of ninety-nine per cent of the shares in a private company. Despite the bank's controlling interest in the company's shares no bank nominee or representative was on the Board. The bank was required to raise money for death duties on the cesser of certain life interests and asked the Board to examine the possibility of a public quotation of the company's shares. It was informed that this would be more successful if the company had investments in property development. The bank agreed to the policy of investment in development. At the annual general meeting and in subsequent monthly Board meetings the Chairman introduced several development projects for the Board's consideration, and, without consulting the bank, embarked on two projects at sites in London and Guildford. The Board did not provide the bank with, and the bank did not insist on, a regular flow of information and as the bank was content to receive only such information as was dispensed at annual meetings, it was unaware of the hazardous nature of the projects and did not interfere. The Guildford project provided a substantial capital profit but the London project sustained a heavy loss, reducing the market value of the shares and causing a substantial loss to the trust fund. The plaintiffs, as beneficiaries under the settlement, brought an action against the bank for breach of trust. *Held*, it was a trustee's duty to conduct trust business with the same care as a reasonably prudent businessman would have extended to his own affairs. A majority shareholder in a private company would not have been content to rely on such information as he was given at annual general meetings. Notwithstanding the high calibre of the Board, the bank was under a duty as a trustee to ensure that it received an adequate flow of information in time for it to protect the beneficiaries' interests and was in breach for neglecting to obtain such information. Further, a professional corporate trustee, such as a bank, owed a higher duty of care and was liable for loss caused to a trust by neglect to exercise the special skill and care it professed to have. The loss would not have occurred had the bank intervened to prevent the company's participation in the projects and it was liable for failure to intervene. The bank was entitled to plead the Limitation Act 1939 as a defence to a claim in respect of income lost on money spent prior to six years before the writ in action was commenced. The court would reject the plaintiff's contention that the right to action had been concealed by a fraud within s. 26 (b) of the Act. Fraud related to unconscionable conduct and, as the bank had been unaware that it was acting in breach of trust there was no concealment by it.

BARTLETT v BARCLAYS BANK TRUST CO LTD [1980] 1 All ER 139 (Chancery Division: BRIGHTMAN J). *Speight v Gaunt* (1883) 9 App Cas 1, *Re Lucking's Will Trusts, Renwick v Lucking* [1967] 3 All ER 726, *Kitchen v RAF Association* [1958] 2 All ER 241 and dictum of Lord Denning MR in *King v Victor Parsons & Co* [1973] 1 All ER at 209, applied.

2994   —— trustee's liability—compensation

The trustees of a settlement were held liable for breach of trust by failing to prevent the directors of a family company, in which the trustees held ninety-nine per cent of the shares, from embarking on a hazardous project which resulted in a loss to the company. On the question of compensation for the breach, *held*, the obligation of a defaulting trustee was essentially that of effecting restitution to the trust estate and was fundamentally different from the liability of a contractual or tortious wrongdoer for damages. Thus, tax was not to be taken into account in assessing the amount of compensation payable. The tax liability of the individual beneficiaries in relation to capital and income was irrelevant because it did not arise at the point of restitution to the trust estate, but at the point of distribution of capital or income. This was so notwithstanding that it produced an unjust bias against the fiduciary wrongdoer compared with the contractual or tortious wrongdoer where the breach had not enriched the defaulting trustee as in this case. Further the appropriate rate of interest payable by a defaulting trustee was that allowed from time to time on the courts' short-term investment account established under the Administration of Justice Act 1965, s. 6 (1).

BARTLETT v BARCLAYS BANK TRUST CO LTD (No. 2) [1980] 2 WLR 430 (Chancery Division: BRIGHTMAN LJ).

For proceedings on breach of trust see *Bartlett v Barclays Bank Trust Co Ltd* [1980] 1 All ER 139, para. 2993.

2995   Express trust—creation of trust—verbal agreement supported by evidence

Canada

For many years the plaintiff contributed substantial amounts of money to his mother for the benefit of the family in which there were thirteen children. Apart from his regular earnings, he accumulated larger sums which he also paid to his mother. On several occasions she had stated that she was keeping those sums invested for him and that he would receive them on her death. He also helped to run the family business which was subsequently sold and a residential property bought. In addition to acquiring property, the mother also spent large sums on jewellery. Ultimately she conveyed her entire estate, including her jewellery, by inter vivos gifts and by will to her seven youngest children. The plaintiff brought an action against the defendant executors and beneficiaries of the estate claiming that certain money which he had paid to his mother had been held on trust for him and that accordingly he was entitled to a proportionate share of the property and jewellery. *Held*, the existence of an express trust had been established in respect of certain amounts of the plaintiff's income, since his evidence had been supported in a number of material facts and no particular words were needed to create such a trust. However, his regular wages were not subject to the trust in that it was contemplated that they would primarily be used for the benefit of the family. In the absence of evidence to the contrary, it would be presumed that the mother had not expended trust money before using the available funds. Accordingly, the mixed assets would be treated as subject to the trust to the amount of the proven interest of the plaintiff and no allowances would be made in respect of accretions resulting from inflationary or other increases in the value of the trust fund. The plaintiff would be given judgment in personam against the estate and, to the extent that recovery would not be possible, against the children in the amount to which his income was subject to the trust.

KONG v KONG [1979] 6 WWR 673 (Supreme Court of British Columbia). *Re Diplock* [1950] 2 All ER 1137, HL applied.

2996   **Public Trustee—fees**

The Public Trustee (Fees) Order 1980, S.I. 1980 No. 370 (in force on 1st April 1980), re-enacts with amendments the provisions of the Public Trustee (Fees) Order 1977, 1977 Halsbury's Abridgment, para. 2919, and subsequent amending orders.

2997   **Trust for sale—unmarried couple—purchase of house in joint names—purpose of trust—discretion of court to order sale**

The parties, who were unmarried, lived together in the man's house. They subsequently had a child and the mother's children from her previous marriage joined them. They purchased a house on a joint mortgage which was conveyed into their joint names as trustees upon a trust for sale. When the parties separated, the mother continued to live in the house with the three children and the father applied to the court under the Law of Property Act 1925, s. 30 for the sale of the house. On appeal by the father against the court's order granting the application but postponing the sale until the parties' child attained the age of sixteen, *held*, s. 30 gave the court a discretion to intervene when trustees under a trust for sale were unable to agree that a property should be sold. The primary question was whether the court should come to the aid of the applicant at the particular moment and in the particular circumstances when the application was made to it. In the exercise of its discretion, the court had to consider the underlying purpose of the trust. In the present case, it would be wrong to order a sale since the underlying purpose was to provide a home for the parties and the children for the indefinite future, and the interests of the children both legitimate and illegitimate had to be considered. Further, the father had no immediate need to realise his investment. Accordingly, his application would be dismissed, and it would be left open to him to apply at a later date if the circumstances changed.

RE EVERS' TRUST, PAPPS V EVERS [1980] 3 All ER 399 (Court of Appeal: ORMROD, EVELEIGH and TEMPLEMAN LJJ).

2998   **Trust funds—purchase of land with funds—land conveyed to trustees—power of trustees to confirm conveyance and reject a tenancy—doctrine of election**

The defendant made a settlement on his wife and children. The trustees of the fund signed the settlement, but left the management of the trust to the defendant. Subsequently, the defendant purchased a farm with money from trust funds which he conveyed into the names of the trustees, and let it to a tenant who paid rent into the trust account. Fourteen years later the trustees learnt of the purchase and the tenancy agreement. They refused the rent and brought possession proceedings against the tenant. On appeal against an order that the tenant deliver up possession to the trustees, *held*, under the doctrine of election, the trustees could not confirm the conveyance of the land to them and reject a tenancy for which rent had been paid into the trust funds. There was a clear election by the trustees, when they learnt of the purchase, to affirm the defendant's actions in buying the farm and conveying it to them, and they could not ratify that advantage and repudiate the disadvantage of the tenancy. Accordingly the appeal would be allowed.

SMITH V HOBBS (1980) Times, 13th November (Court of Appeal: LORD DENNING MR, BRIGHTMAN LJ and SIR GEORGE BAKER).

2999   **Trust property—mixed assets—subject to trust to extent of proven interest of beneficiary**

See *Kong v Kong*, para. 2995.

3000   **Trustee—duty to convert residuary personalty settled in succession—whether also applicable to residuary realty**

See *Lottman v Stanford*, para. 1243.

UNFAIR DISMISSAL

Halsbury's Laws of England (4th edn.), Vol. 16, paras. 615–639:15

3001   Article

Unfair Dismissal and the Merits of an Industrial Dispute, John McMullen: 130 NLJ 670.

3002   Capability or qualifications—employment of unqualified teacher—dismissal on availability of qualified teacher—whether dismissal unfair

See *Birmingham City Council v Elson*, para. 998.

3003   —— ill health—lack of consultation prior to dismissal

A barman in a workmen's camp in the Shetlands was dismissed without prior consultation on the grounds of his ill health. He complained to an industrial tribunal, which held that he had been unfairly dismissed. On appeal, *held*, consultation prior to the dismissal of an employee on the grounds of ill health was not always necessary. The purpose of consultation was so that the situation could be evaluated, balancing the employer's need for the work to be done against the employee's need for time to recover his health. Consultation was only relevant where it affected the outcome of the proposed dismissal. It was self evident that in the present case a healthy employee was necessary and any consultation would not have affected the proposed dismissal. Further, the fact that contractual provisions for warnings and appeals had not been carried out did not render the dismissal unfair. These provisions applied specifically to disciplinary matters and it was impossible to apply such procedures to cases of genuine ill health. Nor was there a duty on the employers to offer any alternative employment as the employee was employed to work in the Shetlands where special physical and mental qualities were required. The employee's dismissal was therefore fair.

Taylorplan Catering (Scotland) Ltd v McInally [1980] IRLR 53 (Employment Appeal Tribunal: Lord McDonald MC presiding).

3004   Compensation—assessment—calculation of compensatory award—associated employers—local authorities

An employee who was unfairly dismissed from the last in the succession of four local authorities for whom he had worked, unsuccessfully claimed that the local authorities were "associated employers" within the Employment Protection (Consolidation) Act 1978, s. 153 (4), enabling him to recover compensation under Sch. 13, para. 18 in respect of the total period of employment. On appeal, *held*, s. 153 (4) provided that two employers were to be treated as associated only if one was a company of which the other had control or if they were both companies of which a third person had control. A local authority was not a company and the definition in the section was exhaustive. The employee's appeal would be dismissed.

Merton London Borough Council v Gardiner [1981] 2 WLR 232 (Court of Appeal: Watkins and Griffiths LJJ).

3005   —— basic award—calculation of basic award—minimum age limit

In a case where an employee aged seventeen was found to have been unfairly dismissed and was granted a compensatory award but no basic award because of his age, it was held that although a minimum basic award of two weeks' pay was provided for under the Employment Protection (Consolidation) Act 1978, s. 73, it was based on the employee's age and length of service. No provision for a minimum basic award was made for employees below the age of eighteen and had Parliament intended there to be an automatic entitlement to the minimum basic award, the provisions would have been formulated differently.

Kunz Engineering Ltd v Santi [1979] IRLR 459 (Employment Appeal Tribunal: Lord McDonald MC presiding).

3006   —— qualifying period—whether employee "absent from work"

See *Corton House Ltd v Skipper*, para. 1015.

3007   Complaint to industrial tribunal—agreement to preclude—validity of agreement—duty of conciliation officer

An employee who had been arrested on suspicion of theft from his employees was suspended. He reached an agreement with his employers whereby he would receive a sum of money and resign. A conciliation officer from the Advisory, Conciliation and Arbitration Service (ACAS), recorded the details of the settlement although he had taken no part in its negotiation. The employee was informed by the police that he would not be prosecuted, and therefore he brought a claim for unfair dismissal. The employer's contention, that the claim had been settled within the meaning of the Trade Union and Labour Relations Act 1974, Sch. 1, para. 32 (2) (d) and that the employee was therefore precluded from bringing the action, was upheld by the Employment Appeal Tribunal. On appeal, *held*, the Employment Appeal Tribunal had correctly concluded that the employee was precluded from making a complaint because he had agreed to a settlement, within the meaning of para. 32 (2) (d), in respect of which an ACAS officer had taken action in accordance with para. 26, which required only that the officer endeavour to promote a settlement. Thus, notwithstanding that the agreement was reached by the parties themselves, the officer recording the terms of the settlement was sufficient to amount to an action in an endeavour to promote a settlement without it being determined by an industrial tribunal within the meaning of para. 26 (2).

Moore v Duport Furniture Products Ltd; Moore v Advisory, Conciliation and Arbitration Service [1980] ICR 581 (Court of Appeal: Stephenson, Waller and Cumming-Bruce LJJ). Decision of Employment Appeal Tribunal [1979] ICR 165, 1978 Halsbury's Abridgment para. 2928 affirmed.

Trade Union and Labour Relations Act 1974, Sch. 1, paras. 26, 32 now Employment Protection (Consolidation) Act 1978, ss. 134 (3), 140.

3008   —— complaint made out of time—reasonable practicality of making complaint within time limit

The Court of Appeal has dismissed an appeal by an employee who had sought to bring a complaint of unfair dismissal to an industrial tribunal outside the prescribed three month time limit. The Employment Appeal Tribunal had held that, as the employee had relied on the skilled, albeit incorrect, advice of a Citizen's Advice Bureau, she could not claim that it was not reasonably practicable for her to have made the claim within the time limit. The Court of Appeal upheld the tribunal's decision on the ground that the question, as to whether the claim could have been made within the time limit, was one of fact for the industrial tribunal to decide.

Riley v Tesco Stores Ltd [1980] ICR 323 (Court of Appeal: Stephenson and Waller LJJ and Dame Elizabeth Lane).

3009   An employee was dismissed. The day before the expiry of the three-month period for presenting a complaint of unfair dismissal under the Employment Protection (Consolidation) Act 1978, s. 67 (2), the employee's complaint of unfair dismissal was sent by his solicitors by first class mail to the central office of the industrial tribunals. The letter only arrived four days later. On the hearing of a preliminary issue that the complaint was out of time, *held*, it was reasonable to expect that a letter sent by first class mail would, in the ordinary course of post, arrive the following day. In the light of the circumstances it was not reasonably practicable for the claim to have been presented within time.

Beanstalk Shelving Ltd v Horn [1980] ICR 273 (Employment Appeal

Tribunal: SLYNN J presiding). *Anglo Continental School of English (Bournemouth) Ltd v Gardiner* [1973] ICR 261 and *Dedman v British Building & Engineering Appliances Ltd* [1974] ICR 53 applied.

3010 —— **effective date of termination of employment—whether complaint time barred**

An employee received a letter from her employer terminating her employment. It stated that she had been given three months' notice of dismissal with effect from 5th November 1979 and was not expected to work out her notice period but would receive moneys in lieu of notice. On 22nd February 1980 she made a complaint of unfair dismissal. On the question of whether the claim was time barred under the Employment Protection (Consolidation) Act 1978 *held*, where notice of termination of employment was given the effective date of termination was the date when the notice expired and the fact that a person was not required to work during the period of notice did not mean that the employment was terminated earlier than the date specified. Accordingly, her employment was terminated three months from 5th November and her claim was not time barred.

ADAMS V GKN SANKEY LTD [1980] IRLR 416 (Employment Appeal Tribunal: SLYNN J presiding). *Brindle v H. W. Smith (Cabinets) Ltd* [1972] IRLR 125, CA applied.

3011 —— **right to bring complaint—whether sub-postmaster employed under contract of service**

See *Hitchcock v Post Office*, para. 1022.

3012 **Conduct—absenteeism—absenteeism due to minor ailments**

An employee was summarily dismissed for persistent absenteeism due to minor ailments and an industrial tribunal found the dismissal to be unfair. On appeal by the employer, *held*, the tribunal had erred in its decision. Where an employee had an unacceptable level of absenteeism what was required was (i) that there had been a fair review by the employer of the employee's attendance record and (ii) that the employee had been given the appropriate warnings as to the consequences of her conduct and further, given an opportunity to make representations to the employer. In the present case as this had been complied with and there was no adequate improvement in the employee's attendance record the employer was justified in treating the persistent absences as a sufficient reason for dismissal. The appeal would be allowed.

INTERNATIONAL SPORTS CO LTD V THOMSON [1980] IRLR 340 (Employment Appeal Tribunal: WATERHOUSE J presiding).

3013 —— —— **absence without leave**

An employee went on leave to Jamaica without his employers' permission. During his absence he was sent a letter of dismissal and subsequently successfully complained to an industrial tribunal of having been unfairly dismissed. The employers appealed on the ground, inter alia, that the employee had repudiated his contract and had not been dismissed. *Held*, the common law principle that a contract was not discharged by the repudiatory conduct of one party unless that conduct had been accepted by the innocent party applied to contracts of employment under the present employment legislation. Accordingly the employers, by their letter of dismissal, had accepted the employee's repudiatory conduct and had terminated his contract. They had, however, acted unreasonably in dismissing him by letter and the employee had been unfairly dismissed and should be re-engaged. The appeal would, accordingly, be dismissed.

LONDON TRANSPORT EXECUTIVE V CLARKE [1980] ICR 532 (Employment Appeal Tribunal: MAY J presiding).

This decision has been reversed by the Court of Appeal; see (1981) Times, 25th February.

3014   —— criminal offence—indecent assault—whether dismissal unfair

In a case concerning a teacher who was convicted of indecent assault on one of his pupils and sentenced to imprisonment but the conviction was later quashed, the local education authority stated that it regarded his contract of employment as being automatically terminated with his conviction. On his release he unsuccessfully sought re-engagement as a teacher with the local education authority and subsequently claimed that he had been unfairly dismissed. *Held*, the teacher's complaint of unfair dismissal would not succeed because he had not, in effect, been dismissed. The authority was entitled to treat the teacher's contract of employment as having come to an end through frustration when he was sentenced to imprisonment, even though it was aware that he was appealing.

HARRINGTON V KENT COUNTY COUNCIL [1980] IRLR 353 (Employment Appeal Tribunal: TALBOT J presiding).

3015   —— dishonesty—theft from employer—reasonable suspicion of dishonesty—validity as reason for dismissal

See *Monie v Coral Racing Ltd*, para. 3024.

3016   —— —— —— sufficiency of reason for dismissal—reasonableness in circumstances

The employee, a meat salesman, was seen selling to a customer meat that was not normally sold at his stall, and the employer's stock of meat was found to be down at the end of that day. He was interviewed by the police the next day, and his employer decided that there was a strong suspicion of dishonesty. The manager concerned subsequently told the employee that he was going to be dismissed for gross misconduct and asked him if he had anything to say. The employee merely replied that he had done nothing wrong. He was dismissed, and successfully claimed that the dismissal was unfair. On appeal, it was held that the tribunal had been entitled to conclude that the employer had not acted reasonably in failing to gather further evidence and to give the employee an opportunity to defend himself. On the employer's further appeal, *held*, there was material on which the tribunal could have concluded that the employee was not given a sufficient opportunity to explain what had happened. There was evidence of unfair procedure and the decision of the tribunal, therefore, could not be categorised as perverse. The appeal would be dismissed.

W. WEDDEL & CO LTD v TEPPER [1980] IRLR 96 (Court of Appeal: STEPHENSON, WALLER and CUMMING-BRUCE LJJ).

3017   —— refusal to obey lawful instructions—sufficiency of reason for dismissal

The employee was employed by a trade union as their publications officer, under the general direction of the union's General Secretary, with responsibility for the organisation and production of the union newspaper. On the General Secretary's instructions and without the employee's authorisation the newspaper published an article attacking the plaintiffs and which resulted in a libel writ being issued against the employees and the printers of the newspaper. Subsequently terms of a settlement were agreed, including that there was to be an undertaking by the employee and printers not to publish, either by themselves or their officers, servants or agents, further libels upon the plaintiffs. When asked to sign the undertaking the employee refused to do so on the grounds that he would then be liable for the acts of all union officers and agents over whom he had no control. He was subsequently summarily dismissed and brought an action claiming that the dismissal was unfair. *Held*, where the reason for dismissal was a refusal to obey a lawful order, in determining whether in the circumstances the employers were reasonable in treating that as a reason for dismissal, there had to be considered not only the nature of the order but also the circumstances surrounding the giving of that order, and furthermore the reasons stated by the employee for not carrying out the order. In the circumstances the employee's refusal was justified and his dismissal was unfair.

UNION OF CONSTRUCTION ALLIED TRADES AND TECHNICIANS v BRAIN [1980] IRLR 357 (Employment Appeal Tribunal: TALBOT J presiding).

3018 Constructive dismissal—circumstances entitling employee to terminate employment—change in job content

An employee, a sales manager, gave three months' notice of termination of his contract of employment following a disagreement with his employers. The employee intended to work with a rival company and as a result the employers removed his duties as sales manager and changed the basis of his remuneration. The employee regarded this as a demotion and left before the term of his notice had expired. He claimed that he had been constructively dismissed. Both an industrial tribunal and the Employment Appeal Tribunal found that the employee had been constructively dismissed and held that the dismissal was unfair. The employers appealed. *Held*, the Employment Appeal Tribunal had correctly concluded that there was no error of law in the industrial tribunal's decision that the employee had been unfairly dismissed. The industrial tribunal was entitled to find that the employers had repudiated the employee's contract of employment when they, in effect, demoted him. The Employment Appeal Tribunal was not wrong in finding that there was no error of law in the industrial tribunal's decision that the employers had failed to show that the dismissal was fair and that they had acted unreasonably. The appeal would be dismissed.

FORD v MILTHORN TOLEMAN LTD [1980] IRLR 30 (Court of Appeal: STEPHENSON, CUMMING-BRUCE and DONALDSON LJJ). Decision of the Employment Appeal Tribunal [1978] IRLR 306, 1978 Halsbury's Abridgment para. 2954 affirmed.

3019 —— —— contractual term for cost of living payments

An employee resigned and subsequently claimed that he had been constructively dismissed on the grounds that he was contractually entitled to receive cost of living increases awarded by his employers and that he had been refused such increases. An industrial tribunal found that the employee was entitled to be paid the cost of living increases and that by withholding such payments the employers were in breach of contract amounting to a repudiation of the employee's contract of employment. The employee was therefore entitled to resign and claim constructive dismissal. On appeal by the employers, *held*, although the industrial tribunal had not erred in law in reaching the conclusion that the employers were in breach of their contract with the employee to pay him cost of living expenses, in finding that the employee was entitled to resign and claim constructive dismissal, the tribunal had misdirected itself by failing to consider whether or not there was a genuine dispute about the construction of the contract of employment. It was a general principle in relation to repudiation of a contract that where there was a genuine dispute as to the construction of a contract, the courts were unwilling to hold that an expression of an intention by one party to carry out the contract only in accordance with its own, erroneous interpretation of it amounted to a repudiation, and the same was true of a genuine mistake of fact or law. The appeal would be allowed and the case remitted to the industrial tribunal for further consideration.

FRANK WRIGHT & CO (HOLDINGS) LTD v PUNCH [1980] IRLR 217 (Employment Appeal Tribunal: WATERHOUSE J presiding).

3020 Contract of employment

See EMPLOYMENT.

3021 Dismissal—employee attending unauthorised mass meeting—repudiation of contract by employee—whether employer entitled to treat contract as automatically terminated

An employer warned shop stewards that if employees attended an unauthorised mass meeting during working hours they would be risking "the sack". The employer also notified all employees that they would be regarded as in breach of their contracts of employment if they attended the meeting. Almost half the workforce went to the meeting, and the employer informed each of those employees that in so doing they had broken their contracts and had consequently automatically terminated their employment. On an employee's claim that he had been unfairly dismissed, a tribunal concluded that the employee had repudiated his contract of employment and that he had not been dismissed. The employee appealed on the preliminary point of whether he had been dismissed in law. *Held*, the employee had repudiated his contract of employment and the tribunal had not erred in considering the antecedent history of the troubles in so deciding. However, the tribunal had erred in concluding that the repudiation constituted a termination of the contract by the employee. If an employer elected to treat an employee's repudiation as discharging the employer from further performance of the contract, it was the employer and not the employee who terminated the contract within the meaning of the Trade Union and Labour Relations Act 1974, Sch. 1, para. 5 (2) (*a*). In the instant case, the employee's fundamental breach did not fall into the category of breaches where no effective option was left to the employer. The employer was able to and did make an election to treat the contract as discharged in consequence of the employer's breach. The appeal would be allowed to the extent that a finding that the employee was dismissed would be substituted for the finding of the tribunal.

RASOOL v HEPWORTH PIPE CO LTD (No. 1) [1980] IRLR 88 (Employment Appeal Tribunal: WATERHOUSE J presiding). *Western Excavating (ECC) Ltd v Sharp* [1978] 1 All ER 713, CA, 1977 Halsbury's Abridgment para. 2960 applied; *Pepper v Webb* [1969] 1 WLR 514 followed; *Gannon v J C Firth Ltd* [1976] IRLR 415, 1976 Halsbury's Abridgment para. 2693 not followed.

Trade Union and Labour Relations Act 1974, Sch. 1, para. 5 (2) (a) now Employment Protection (Consolidation) Act 1978, s. 55 (2).

3022 Dismissal procedure—code of practice—failure to comply—effect of failure

See *Rasool v Hepworth Pipe Co Ltd (No. 2)*, para. 3036.

3023 —— employee absent from disciplinary hearing—whether breach of natural justice

An employee was suspended for being drunk whilst at work. He was subsequently interviewed, in the presence of trade union officials, by the departmental manager. The employee's request for witnesses to testify as to his fitness for work was refused and he was dismissed in accordance with the terms of the disciplinary code. The employee appealed against the decision to the general manager. The employee was not present at the appeal but was represented by trade union officials. The dismissal was confirmed but an industrial tribunal found that, because the company had adopted a defective procedure in investigating the matter, the dismissal was unfair. The company appealed. *Held*, the concept of natural justice did not include the automatic right to be present throughout a disciplinary hearing, provided that the employee's interests were safeguarded by a representative, in the present case a trade union official. The dismissal was not rendered unfair by the refusal to hear witnesses testifying as to the employee's fitness to work. The test was whether, on the balance of probabilities, the employer would have taken the same course had the further evidence been heard. It was clear from the tribunal's decision that further evidence as to the employee's suitability to work would have made no difference to the outcome and the appeal would be allowed.

GRAY DUNN & CO LTD v EDWARDS [1980] IRLR 23 (Employment Appeal Tribunal: LORD MCDONALD MC presiding).

3024 —— internal appeal—dismissal confirmed on new ground— admissibility of new ground

An employee was the area manager of a number of betting shops. His employers discovered that money had been stolen from a safe in circumstances such that only the employee or an assistant manager could have taken it. The employers could not discover who was responsible and dismissed both men for dishonesty. The employee's internal appeal was dismissed on the ground that he had not exercised proper control over the money and was guilty of misconduct. The Employment Appeal Tribunal decided that although the employee could not be fairly dismissed on the basis of a mere suspicion of theft, his employers could rely on the subsequent finding of misconduct at the internal inquiry. On appeal by the employee, *held*, (i) under the Trade Union and Labour Relations Act 1974, Sch. 1, para. 6 (1), a dismissal was fair if an employer showed that the reason for dismissal was acceptable under the Act; no reference was made to any reason other than that given at the time of dismissal. Therefore, the employers could not rely on the reason given for affirming the dismissal at the internal inquiry. (ii) In deciding whether an employee could be fairly dismissed due to a reasonable suspicion of dishonesty rather than actual belief, the test to be applied was prescribed by 1974 Act, Sch. 1, para. 6 (8). Under Sch. 1, para. 6 (8), the employers had to show that they acted reasonably in treating their original reason as a sufficient reason for dismissing the employee. Looking at the matter from the view of an ordinary businessman, the employers had clearly discharged the onus of proof. The appeal would be dismissed.

MONIE v CORAL RACING LTD (1980) Times, 1st November (Court of Appeal: STEPHENSON and DUNN LJJ and SIR DAVID CAIRNS). Decision of Employment Appeal Tribunal [1979] ICR 254, 1979 Halsbury's Abridgment para. 2889 affirmed on different grounds. *Savage v J Sainsbury Ltd* [1980] IRLR 109, CA, applied.

1974 Act, Sch. 1, para. 6 (1), (8) now Employment Protection (Consolidation) Act 1978, s. 57 (1), (3).

3025   Employment Act 1980

See para. 2949.

3026   Excluded employment—age limit—normal retiring age

The provisions of a company pension scheme altered the normal retiring age for male employees from sixty-five to sixty. A letter, sent to employees after they had joined the scheme, stated that in certain circumstances employment would be continued after the normal retiring age. An employee, on reaching his sixtieth birthday, was dismissed. He complained of having been unfairly dismissed. *Held*, where there was a question as to whether the normal retiring age had been changed, it had to be seen whether the contractual position between the parties had been altered. This involved an inquiry as to whether the employee had understood the change and consented to it. In the present case the employee knew of the change of the retiring age before entering into the new pension scheme. This was not affected by the subsequent letter. He had therefore been fairly dismissed.

BP CHEMICALS LTD v JOSEPH [1980] IRLR 55 (Employment Appeal Tribunal: SLYNN J presiding).

3027

The minimum age of retirement in the Civil Service was sixty years, and although retention beyond that age was discretionary it was intended that employees should stay until they were sixty-five or had achieved twenty years' service. The plaintiff, who was sixty-one and had completed nineteen years of service at the time of his dismissal, appealed against a decision that he was precluded from bringing a claim for unfair dismissal by virtue of the Trade Union and Labour Relations Act 1974 Sch. 1, para. 10 (b), which provides that the right not to be unfairly dismissed does not apply to an employee who has attained the normal retiring age in his undertaking. *Held*, the normal retiring age was that fixed by the contract of employment, namely the age at which a person could be compulsorily retired, even though he could be retained after that age. The normal retiring age was therefore sixty, and the appeal would be dismissed.

HOWARD v DEPARTMENT OF NATIONAL SAVINGS [1981] 1 All ER 674 (Court of Appeal: LORD DENNING MR, ACKNER and GRIFFITHS LJJ). Decision of Employment Appeal Tribunal [1979] ICR 584, 1979 Halsbury's Abridgment para. 2911, affirmed. *Nothman v Barnet London Borough Council* [1979] 1 WLR 67, HL, 1978 Halsbury's Abridgment para. 2901 applied.

1974 Act, Sch. 1, para. 10 (b) now Employment Protection (Consolidation) Act 1978, s. 64 (1).

3023 —— **employment for less than qualifying period—date of termination of employment**

An employee began work with his employers on 8th February 1978. He was dismissed, without notice, by a letter dated 20th July 1978. He claimed that he had the necessary twenty-six weeks' continuous service required under the Trade Union and Labour Relations Act 1974, Sch. 1, para. 10 to make a complaint of unfair dismissal. He contended that (i) his dismissal amounted to a repudiation of contract and was not effective until he accepted the repudiation; (ii) the dismissal did not take effect until actual receipt of the letter when he returned from holiday on 30th July. On appeal *held* (i) by virtue of 1974 Act, Sch. 1 para. 5 (2) (a) an employee was dismissed if his contract of employment was terminated and it required no acceptance by the employee to effect the termination of employment. (ii) Summary dismissal of an employee by letter did not take effect until the employee had read or had reasonable opportunity of reading the letter. The termination therefore took effect on 30th July. Adding to this one week's statutory notice of termination that he should have been given, the employee had the requisite twenty-six weeks' continuous service and an industrial tribunal had the jurisdiction to hear his complaint of unfair dismissal.

The appeal would be allowed and the case remitted to a differently constituted industrial tribunal to be considered on its merits.

BROWN v SOUTHALL & KNIGHT [1980] ICR 617 (Employment Appeal Tribunal: SLYNN J presiding).

Trade Union and Labour Relations Act 1974, Sch. 1, paras. 5 (2) (a), 10 are now Employment Protection (Consolidation) Act 1978, ss 55, 64 (1).

The qualifying period of twenty-six weeks for unfair dismissal complaints is now fifty-two weeks: Unfair Dismal (Variation of Qualifying Period) Order 1979, 1979 Halsbury's Abridgment para 2917.

3029 —— —— **dismissal for taking part in trade union activities or for industrial action**

See *Drew v St. Edmundsbury Borough Council*, para. 3052.

3030 —— —— **employee accumulating previous qualifying period before period increased**

The Court of Appeal has affirmed a decision of the Employment Appeal Tribunal to the effect that the Unfair Dismissal (Increase of Qualifying Period) Order 1979, 1979 Halsbury's Abridgment para. 2874, was effective to increase the qualifying period of service for a complaint of unfair dismissal to fifty-two weeks. Accordingly, an industrial tribunal had no jurisdiction to entertain a claim by an employee who had not accumulated fifty-two weeks' service even though, prior to the change, he had worked the twenty-six weeks previously required for making the claim. This service did not give him a vested right to make a complaint as he was not dismissed before the date when the new Order came into force.

CAPON v REES MOTORS [1980] ICR 553 (Court of Appeal: ROSKILL and ACKNER LJJ). Decision of the Employment Appeal Tribunal (1980) Times, 20th February, affirmed.

3031 —— —— **summary dismissal—employee suspended pending domestic appeal—effective date of termination of contract**

An employee was summarily dismissed less than four months after his employment began. He appealed against the dismissal under the company's disciplinary procedure, which provided that pending the decision of an appeal against dismissal, the employee would be suspended without pay but, if reinstated, he would receive full back pay for the period of suspension. This appeal was unsuccessful and he was notified of the decision four months after the summary dismissal. The employee claimed that he had been unfairly dismissed, but the company argued that he did not have the requisite twenty-six weeks' continuous service. The employee successfully contended that his employment was not effectively terminated until he received notification that his appeal had failed, at which date he had the required service. The tribunal's decision was subsequently set aside. The employee appealed. *Held*, the effective date of termination of the employee's employment was the date when he was summarily dismissed and he did not therefore have the requisite twenty-six weeks' continuous service and was not qualified to make a complaint of unfair dismissal. On its proper interpretation, the company's disciplinary procedure provided that if an appeal did not succeed and the original decision to dismiss was affirmed, dismissal took effect on the original date. The appeal would be dismissed.

SAVAGE V J SAINSBURY LTD [1980] IRLR 109 (Court of Appeal: ROSKILL and BRIGHTMAN LJJ and SIR DAVID CAIRNS). Decision of Employment Appeal Tribunal [1978] IRLR 479, EAT, 1978 Halsbury's Abridgment para. 1024 affirmed.

The qualifying period for complaints of unfair dismissal has been increased to fifty-two weeks: Unfair Dismissal (Variation of Qualifying Period) Order 1979, 1979 Halsbury's Abridgment para. 2917.

3032   —— police service—whether police cadet an "employee"

See *Wiltshire Police Authority v Wynn*, para. 2160.

3033   Fixed term contract—effective date of termination

A part-time teacher was employed under a fresh contract each academic year; the contract required her to teach such courses as might be needed during the year. When her contract was not renewed, she complained that she had been unfairly dismissed. Her employer appealed against the decision of the Employment Appeal Tribunal that she had been dismissed under the Trade Union and Labour Relations Act 1974, Sch. 1, para. 5 (2) (b) contending that she had not been employed under a fixed term contract. *Held*, a contract for a fixed term meant one which specified the expiry date and therefore a contract to teach certain courses of indefinite length could not be for a fixed term. However, the contract in question required the teacher to be available for work from the beginning of the academic year until the end; it was clearly for a fixed term although the courses could be stopped at any time during the year. Accordingly the appeal would be dismissed.

WILTSHIRE COUNTY COUNCIL V NATIONAL ASSOCIATION OF TEACHERS IN FURTHER AND HIGHER EDUCATION [1980] IRLR 198 (Court of Appeal: LORD DENNING MR, LAWTON and ACKNER LJJ). Decision of the Employment Appeal Tribunal [1978] IRLR 301, 1978 Halsbury's Abridgment para. 2963, affirmed.

1974 Act, Sch. 1, para. 5 now Employment Protection (Consolidation) Act 1978, s. 55.

3034   Industrial action—dismissal of striking employees—whether "relevant employees"

The Employment Protection (Consolidation) Act 1978, s. 62 provides that if an employee claims he has been unfairly dismissed, and at the date of dismissal the employee was taking part in a strike or other industrial action, an industrial tribunal must not determine whether the dismissal was fair or unfair unless it is shown that one or more relevant employees of the same employer have not been dismissed.

An employee was one of a number of boilermakers and went on strike for more pay. B, another employee who was not involved in the dispute, refused to cross the boilermaker's picket line and stayed away from work for a month. He did not inform the employers that he was on strike. He returned to work and crossed the picket line every day until he was dismissed on the ground of redundancy. At the same time as B's dismissal the employee and other boilermakers, who were on strike, were dismissed. The employee complained to an industrial tribunal of having been unfairly dismissed on the ground that B was a "relevant employee" within the 1978 Act, s. 62 and that he had not been "dismissed", since for the purposes of the section the dismissal had to take place while B was on strike. On the question as to whether the tribunal had jurisdiction to hear the complaint, *held*, B's withdrawal of labour was considered to be support for the boilermakers' strike and in so doing he was taking part in the strike. He was therefore a "relevant employee" within the meaning of s. 62. The wording of s. 62 was clear and there was no justification for reading additional words into the statute that "dismissed" meant "dismissed during the strike". Although B had been dismissed on the ground of redundancy after he had returned to work, at the time of the hearing he was a relevant employee who had been dismissed and the tribunal was therefore precluded from hearing the complaint.

McCormick v Horsepower Ltd [1980] ICR 278 (Employment Appeal Tribunal: Talbot J presiding).

3035   —— **distinction between industrial action and taking part in trade union activities**

See *Drew v St. Edmundsbury Borough Council*, para. 3052.

3036   —— **participation in industrial action—employee attending unauthorised mass meeting—whether meeting "other industrial action"**

An employee's contract of employment was terminated as a result of his attending an unauthorised trade union meeting at the employers' factory during working hours. The employee complained to an industrial tribunal of having been unfairly dismissed. The tribunal found that the employee had been unfairly dismissed in that, (i) at the date of dismissal the employee was not taking part in "other industrial action" as opposed to a strike, within the meaning of Trade Union and Labour Relations 1974, Sch. 1, para. 7 (1) (b), as amended; (ii) the employer had acted unreasonably in treating the conduct of the employee as a sufficient reason for dismissing him, because the employer was in breach of the recommendations in the Industrial Relations Code of Practice, para. 15 (b) regarding disciplinary procedure. The employers cross-appealed contending that although the employee was dismissed at law, he had not, however, been unfairly dismissed. *Held*, (i) the reference to "strike" in para. 7 did not limit the interpretation of "other industrial action". The limitation that an employee must be taking part in industrial action at the date of the dismissal was itself an important restriction on the application of the provision so that an unduly restrictive interpretation of industrial action itself was inappropriate. It was incorrect to interpret the phrase narrowly in terms of specific intention. The nature and effect of the concerted action were probably of greater importance. Attendance at an unauthorised meeting fell short of "other industrial action" and it was more properly regarded as a trade union activity. The tribunal, therefore, had not erred in its finding. (ii) The tribunal, however, erred in deciding that the dismissal was unfair solely because the employers failed to comply with the Industrial Relations Code of Practice, para. 15 (b). Failure to comply with the recommendation was insufficient to make the dismissal unfair although under the Employment Protection Act 1975, s. 6 (ii) that had to be taken into account. When a tribunal did consider the failure to be the sole reason for deciding a question in a particular way, it was necessary to look at the reasoning with particular care. Paragraph 15 (b) was intended to avoid strikes rather than secure preferential treatment for certain union members and in the present case the relevance of the provision was doubtful. If there was a failure by the employers to comply with the provision, it was an insufficient reason to make the dismissal unfair. The cross-appeal would therefore be allowed with the result that the employee had failed to establish that he had been unfairly dismissed.

Rasool v Hepworth Pipe Co Ltd (No. 2) [1980] IRLR 137 (Employment Appeal Tribunal: Waterhouse J presiding).

For other proceedings see *Rasool v Hepworth Pipe Co Ltd (No. 1)* [1980] IRLR 88, para. 3021.

3037   —— —— **employee on sick leave—whether employee taking part in industrial action**

The employers, newspaper publishers, were involved in an industrial dispute with their journalists, all members of the appropriate trade union. The journalists refused to handle work done by non-union employees and went on a one-day strike. As a result of further industrial action after the strike all the journalists were dismissed. A journalist, who had taken part in the one-day strike, failed to return to work the following day due to illness. He complained to an industrial tribunal that his dismissal was unfair on the ground that since he had not been at work he had not taken part in any further industrial action within the meaning of the Trade Union and Labour Relations Act 1974, Sch. 1, para. 7. *Held*, taking part in industrial action within the meaning of the 1974 Act, Sch. 1, para. 7 was not limited to the particular moment an act was done. The journalist had joined in the industrial action before his absence and had not indicated to his employers that he no longer intended to take industrial action. On this basis it was assumed that he would have continued to take industrial action had he not been ill. He therefore had been dismissed and his dismissal was not unfair.

WILLIAMS v WESTERN MAIL AND ECHO LTD [1980] ICR 366 (Employment Appeal Tribunal: SLYNN J presiding).

Trade Union and Labour Relations Act 1974, Sch. 1, para. 7 now Employment Protection (Consolidation) Act 1978, s. 62.

3038   —— **participation in strike—dismissal of employees—offer of reengagement—whether change of capacity**

Following their dismissal during a strike, National Theatre stagehands were invited to apply for reengagement on condition that they would be treated as being on second warning in the internal grievance procedure. They rejected the offer and applied for compensation for unfair dismissal. The industrial tribunal held that it had no jurisdiction by virtue of the Employment Protection (Consolidation) Act 1978, s. 62, which provides that a claim of unfair dismissal at the time of a strike cannot be heard unless the employee concerned has not been offered reengagement while others have. The stagehands claimed that the condition, which affected their security of employment, constituted a change in "capacity" as used in the definition of "job" in s. 153 (1), and was an offer of a different job. *Held*, on the natural meaning of the words, the condition did not prevent the offer being an offer of reengagement within s. 62 (4) (c) and the stagehands were not entitled to bring a claim under s. 62 (2) (b).

WILLIAMS v NATIONAL THEATRE BOARD LTD (1980) Times, 7th November (Employment Appeal Tribunal: SLYNN J presiding).

3039   **Industrial tribunal—matters to be considered—relevance of common law and statutory duties of employer**

The applicant was one of a group of employees whose jobs required them to work in an area affected by hot rubber fumes. Acting on certain information, the employees refused to work in the area until the fumes were cleared. The employer suggested the use of masks as a temporary measure and a large majority of the employees agreed to accept the masks and resume normal working. The applicant, however, continued to refuse to work in the area until the fumes cleared. He was eventually dismissed. An industrial tribunal concluded that his dismissal was fair. The applicant appealed, contending that the tribunal had erred in failing to have regard to the common law duty owed by the employer to the applicant to provide a safe system of work, and to the statutory duty imposed by the Factories Act 1961, s. 63 (1), which provides for the removal of fumes. *Held*, the basic function of an industrial tribunal in an unfair dismissal case was to make findings as to whether the employer had acted reasonably in the circumstances. A tribunal might have regard to the employer's legal obligations, but it should not normally make findings as to whether or not those obligations had been breached. Further, the question as to whether an employer was in breach of his statutory duty under s. 63 (1) was a matter for the courts, not for industrial tribunals. It might be proper for a tribunal to have regard to such provisions, but only as a factor in determining whether or not an employer had acted reasonably. The appeal would be dismissed.

LINDSAY v DUNLOP LTD [1980] IRLR 93 (Employment Appeal Tribunal: LORD MACDONALD MC presiding).

3040 ———— **procedure—correct approach to unfair dismissal claims**

An employee brought a claim of unfair dismissal on the ground that his employers had not followed the agreed disciplinary procedure. His complant was upheld and an appeal, *held*, the proper approach to unfair dismissal claims were contained in the Trade Union and Labour Relations Act 1974, Sch. 1, para. 6 (8). A tribunal was required to look at every aspect of the case. The employer had to show that he had acted reasonably and fairly, and whether he did depended on what the employee had been proved or was known to have done, the circumstances in which the misconduct occurred and his behaviour when found out and asked for an explanation. Each case had to be decided on its own merits. Furthermore it was unwise for the Court of Appeal or the Employment Appeal Tribunal to set out guidelines and wrong to make rules and presumptions for industrial tribunals to follow when applying the provisions of the 1974 Act, Sch 1, para. 6 (8). The Employment Appeal Tribunal had misdirected itself in adjudging that because the disciplinary procedure had not been followed the dismissal was therefore automatically unfair.

BAILEY v BP OIL (KENT REFINERY) LTD [1980] ICR 642 (Court of Appeal: LAWTON and SHAW LJJ and SIR STANLEY REES).

Trade Union and Labour Relations Act 1974, Sch. 1, para. 6 (8) is now the Employment Protection (Consolidation) Act 1978, s. 57 (3).

3041 **Other substantial reason—breakdown in working relationship—reasonableness of dismissal**

An employee was employed as a secretary to the manager of a branch of a pharmaceutical wholesale dealer for two and a half years. During that time there were three branch managers and she got on well with the first two, her work being at all times satisfactory. A conflict of personalities developed between her and the third branch manager and she was dismissed within six months of his appointment. The employee unsuccessfully applied to an industrial tribunal for compensation for unfair dismissal and subsequently appealed on the ground that the industrial tribunal had erred in finding that the reason for dismissal was capable of constituting some "other substantial reason" within the Employment Protection (Consolidation) Act 1978, s. 57 (1). *Held*, where a dismissal was due to a breakdown in a working relationship it was necessary, before deciding whether or not the dismissal was fair, to ascertain whether the employers had taken reasonable steps to try to improve the relationship. In order to establish that the dismissal was fair, the employers had to show not only that there had been a breakdown but that the breakdown was irredeemable. Since the industrial tribunal had failed to look at that aspect of the matter, it had erred in law and its decision would be set aside and a finding that the dismissal was unfair substituted.

TURNER v VESTRIC LTD [1980] ICR 528 (Employment Appeal Tribunal: PHILLIPS J presiding).

3042 ———— **employer's genuine but erroneous belief that continued employment unlawful**

An employee, a Tunisian national, was dismissed when his employers were informed by the Department of Employment that it would be illegal to continue to employ him as he was no longer qualified for a work permit. This information was wrong as the employee did not need a work permit. He complained that the dismissal was unfair. *Held*, the employers had not established under the Employment Protection (Consolidation) Act 1978, s. 57 (2)(d), that the employee's continued employment would have involved a breach of the law. This provision could not be expanded to include the concept of a genuine but erroneous belief on the part of an employer.

However, such a genuine belief could constitute some other reason of a kind such as to justify the dismissal within s. 57 (1) (b). Hence the dismissal was not unfair.

BOUCHAALA V TRUSTHOUSE FORTE HOTELS LTD [1980] IRLR 382 (Employment Appeal Tribunal: WATERHOUSE J presiding).

3043　　　—— homosexual activities—reasonableness of dismissal

An employee was employed as a maintenance handyman at the employers' children's camp. He was dismissed on grounds of his homosexual activities although his job did not require him to be in contact with the children. He claimed that he had been unfairly dismissed but an industrial tribunal found that the dismissal was for a substantial reason within the provisions of the Employment Protection (Consolidation) Act 1978, s. 57 (1) (b) and was therefore fair. He appealed. *Held*, under s. 57 (1) an employer needed only show, on the balance of probabilities, that the reason for dismissal was one of those expressly specified in the section, or if not, was one which he considered to be substantial and of a kind such as to justify the dismissal. The present case was one where the area of decision regarding the reason for dismissal was indeterminate and provided the employer approached the matter fairly he could not be faulted for doing what, in his opinion, was just. The appeal would be dismissed.

SAUNDERS V SCOTTISH NATIONAL CAMPS ASSOCIATION LTD [1980] IRLR 174 (Employment Appeal Tribunal: LORD MCDONALD MC presiding).

3044　　　—— illness—employee's refusal to accept change in place of work

A sales engineer was employed as a export sales engineer. His contract of employment provided that his duties would be those "as required by the managing director". He became ill and was advised not to visit hot climates. He refused to transfer to a comparable post dealing with domestic sales offered to him by his employers and was consequently dismissed. An industrial tribunal found his dismissal fair but the Employment Appeal Tribunal allowed his appeal. On appeal, *held*, the employers had the right to transfer the engineer in accordance with his contract of employment. It was not therefore unfair to dismiss him for refusing to transfer to home duties. The appeal would accordingly be allowed.

DEELEY V BRITISH RAIL ENGINEERING [1980] IRLR 147 (Court of Appeal: STEPHENSON and WALLER LJJ and DAME ELIZABETH LANE). Decision of Employment Appeal Tribunal [1979] IRLR 5, 1979 Halsbury's Abridgment para. 2942 reversed.

3045　　　—— marriage to employee of rival agency—insufficiency of notice

The defendant, a female employee of a travel agency, was unmarried when she started work which involved access to confidential information about the business. She subsequently married an employee of a rival travel agency. Prior to the marriage, the two agencies, being worried about possible leakages, decided that the defendant would be dismissed in preference to her husband as he was to be the breadwinner. The defendant was dismissed two days after the marriage with two weeks' pay in lieu of notice. An industrial tribunal awarded her £1,666 compensation for unlawful discrimination under the Sex Descrimination Act 1975, ss. 1 (a), 3 (1) (a) and for unfair dismissal under the Employment Protection (Consolidation) Act 1978. The employers appealed. *Held*, the essential question under the 1975 Act was whether the employers who were alleged to have discriminated had treated a woman less favourably than they would have treated a man. While it was accepted that one of the couple had to go because of the risk of industrial espionage, there was no evidence as to what would have been done if the defendant was the breadwinner. It was likely in those circumstances that the husband would have been dismissed. The tribunal was therefore wrong to hold that there was discrimination under s. 1 (1) (a) as it had no material ground for concluding that the agency had treated the defendant less favourably than they would have treated a man. The tribunal had also erred in assuming that because the close association between the defendant and her husband arose from marriage, that it was discrimination on the ground of marital status within s. 3 (1) (a) of the 1975 Act.

A similar risk of information being passed could have arisen in the case of two members of the same family. However, while the tribunal was entitled to conclude that the defendants dismissal had been "for some other substantial reason" within the meaning of s. 57 (1) of the 1978 Act, that dismissal was unfair because the agency had not given her sufficient notice of their intention to dismiss her. The defendant was thus entitled to £300 as compensation for unfair dismissal and the appeal would be allowed in part.

SKYRAIL OCEANIC LTD v COLEMAN [1980] ICR 596 (Employment Appeal Tribunal: SLYNN J presiding).

3046   —— reorganisation of business

An area health authority appointed an employee as a general administrative assistant to head a particular department. Shortly after his appointment, the authority decided to reorganise the department and informed the employee that he would be transferred to another post. The employee responded by saying that the new post was a waste of his specialist knowledge and experience and that he had no alternative but to resign. On the questions whether the employee was entitled to claim that he had been constructively dismissed and that the dismissal was unfair, *held*, although the authority's attempt to change the employee's job and place of work amounted to a breach of the employee's contract of employment, justifying the employee in resigning and claiming constructive dismissal, in the circumstances the dismissal was for "some other substantial reason" under the Employment Protection (Consolidation) Act 1978, s. 57. Reorganisation or restructuring of a business fell within the meaning of "some other substantial reason" for dismissal and hence the dismissal was not unfair.

GENOWER v EALING, HAMMERSMITH AND HOUNSLOW AREA HEALTH AUTHORITY [1980] IRLR 297 (Employment Appeal Tribunal: SLYNN J presiding).

3047   Pregnancy—return after confinement—continuity of employment

In a case where an employee was dismissed shortly after having exercised her right to return to work after pregnancy, it was held that, if during a period when there was no contract of employment a woman was absent from work wholly or partly because of pregnancy, then those weeks counted in computing her period of employment and there was no break in continuity.

MITCHELL v BRITISH LEGION CLUB [1980] IRLR 425 (Employment Appeal Tribunal: TALBOT J presiding).

3048   Redundancy—selection of redundant employees—unlawful discrimination on ground of sex

See *Noble v David Gold & Sons (Holdings) Ltd*, para. 2588.

3049   Reinstatement—application—whether appropriate remedy

In a case where a teacher complained of unfair dismissal the Employment Appeal Tribunal decided in her favour but in the circumstances found it impossible to make an order for re-instatement. The Employment Appeal Tribunal refused leave to appeal against the decision. The teacher applied to the Court of Appeal for leave to appeal. *Held*, the Employment Appeal Tribunal had properly exercised its discretion in determining the appropriate remedy for unfair dismissal under the Employment Protection (Consolidation) Act 1978, s. 69. The unfair dismissal legislation was concerned with whether an employee was unfairly dismissed and if so how reasonably and sensibly to compensate the unfairly dismissed employee. The circumstances in the present case made re-instatement impossible and as no issue of law was raised in the appeal, leave to appeal would be refused.

NOTHMAN v LONDON BOROUGH OF BARNET (No. 2) [1980] IRLR 65 (Court of Appeal: ORMROD and CUMMING-BRUCE LJJ and SIR DAVID CAIRNS).

For previous proceedings see 1978 Halsbury's Abridgment para. 2961.

3050   Termination of employment—whether dismissal or by agreement

See *Midland Electric Manufacturing Co Ltd v Kanji*, para. 1081.

3051   Trade union membership or activities—dismissal in pursuance of closed shop agreement—refusal to join designated union

A milk roundsman was dismissed as the result of his refusal to join a designated union. An industrial tribunal dismissed his complaint of unfair dismissal and the employee appealed on the ground that the tribunal had erred in its construction of the Trade Union and Labour Relations Act 1974, Sch. 1, para. 6 (5), as amended by the Trade Union and Labour Relations (Amendment) Act 1976, contending that the employer should have proved that it was the practice for all employees to belong to the designated union. *Held*, in substituting "employees for the time being", in the 1976 Act, for "all the employees," in the 1974 Act, the requirements had been relaxed to increase the effectiveness of a union membership agreement. It was a question of fact for the tribunal as to whether it was usual for employees to belong to the union and there was no rule that almost all employees must belong. There was evidence on which it could be concluded that a practice had been established, and the appeal would be dismissed.

TAYLOR V CO-OPERATIVE RETAIL SERVICES LTD (1980) Times, 24th October (Employment Appeal Tribunal: SLYNN J presiding). *Home Counties Dairies Ltd v Woods* [1977] ICR 463, 1976 Halsbury's Abridgment para. 2722, disapproved.

3052   —— distinction between taking part in union activities and industrial action

An employee, a trade union member, was dismissed after less than twenty-six weeks' continuous employment for repeatedly complaining about health and safety matters. He complained that the dismissal was unfair and an industrial tribunal found that, although the employee claimed to be following a union "go slow" directive, the directive was not concerned with health and safety matters and he was not dismissed for taking part in union activities, an inadmissible reason within the Employment Protection (Consolidation) Act 1978, s. 58. He was held to have been dismissed for taking part in industrial action, which was not a union activity, and since he had not been continuously employed for twenty-six weeks the tribunal had no jurisdiction to hear his complaint. On appeal, *held*, there was a distinction in the 1978 Act for the purposes of unfair dismissal between a dismissal for taking part in union activities and a dismissal for industrial action. Since the employee was dismissed for taking part in industrial action, he was not dismissed for an inadmissible reason and the twenty-six week qualifying period applied. The tribunal had no jurisdiction to hear the complaint and the appeal would be dismissed.

DREW V ST. EDMUNDSBURY BOROUGH COUNCIL [1980] ICR 513 (Employment Appeal Tribunal: SLYNN J presiding).

The qualifying period for a complaint of unfair dismissal is now fifty-two weeks: Unfair Dismissal (Variation of Qualifying Period) Order 1979, 1979 Halsbury's Abridgment para. 2917.

VALUE ADDED TAX

Halsbury's Laws of England (4th edn.), Vol. 12, paras. 846–1053

3053   Appeal—appeal to tribunal—jurisdiction of tribunal

Value added tax tribunal decision:

B ROFFEY (trading as RIBBLESDALE LEASING ASSOCIATES) V CUSTOMS AND EXCISE COMRS (1980) MAN/80/130 (unreported) (applicant filed Notice of Appeal; no formal response from commissioners but two months later sent letter contending that there was no decision against which appeal could be brought; held commissioners in breach of mandatory direction to serve notice under Value Added Tax Tribunals Rules, r. 6 (2), as amended; however no jurisdiction to hear appeal because no decision which could form basis of appeal; appeal dismissed).

3054   —— —— —— **review of commissioners' discretion**

Certain items were disallowed by the commissioners under the Value Added Tax (Works of Art, Antiques and Scientific Collections) Order 1972, on the grounds that proper records had not been kept by a company of numismatists in respect of those items and thus they did not qualify for the margin scheme set out in the order. On appeal against assessment, the value added tax tribunal held that it had jurisdiction to review the commissioners' decision and to go into all matters relating to the appeal de novo, substituting their own decision for that of the commissioners. The Court of Appeal upheld the tribunal's decision and the commissioners appealed to the House of Lords. *Held*, LORD SALMON dissenting, the tribunal had no power to interfere with the commissioners' decision. It could only consider whether the conditions laid down in the Order had been complied with and could not review the commissioners' discretion under art. 3 (5) of the 1972 Order to recognise or not recognise records kept by the company as being sufficient. The appeal would therefore be allowed.

CUSTOMS AND EXCISE COMRS v J. H. CORBITT (NUMISMATISTS) LTD [1980] 2 All ER 72 (House of Lords: LORD DIPLOCK, LORD SIMON OF GLAISDALE, LORD SALMON, LORD SCARMAN and LORD LANE). Decision of Court of Appeal [1979] STC 504, 1979 Halsbury's Abridgment para. 3036 reversed.

3055   See also *J. M. Patel (trading as Magsons) v Customs and Excise Comrs*, para. 3059.

3056   —— **costs—disputed decision withdrawn—effect on award of costs**

Value added tax tribunal decision:
BRITISH INSTITUTE OF MANAGEMENT v CUSTOMS AND EXCISE COMRS [1980] VATTR 42 (decision by commissioners with respect to tax chargeable on supplies made by applicant; applicant appealed; decision withdrawn by Commissioners before hearing of appeal; tribunal held that all further proceedings should be stayed except in relation to costs; application for costs; costs would be excluded which were not costs of or incidental to or consequent upon the appeal or which were not necessary or proper for the attainment of justice; accordingly, costs incurred prior to commissioners' decision excluded; costs incurred after that date but before service of notice of appeal included; such costs incurred after withdrawal of decision by commissioners as were reasonable and proper to obtain direction staying proceedings and award of costs included).

3057   —— **time for service of notice—discretion of tribunal to extend time**

Value added tax tribunal decisions:
SHIELDFIELD PROCESSORS AND REFINERS v CUSTOMS AND EXCISE COMRS (1980) MAN/79/140 (unreported) (applicant applied for extension of time to bring appeal against assessment; commissioners had obtained judgment in High Court for sum assessed; tribunal had no jurisdiction to entertain appeal once final judgment obtained unless judgment set aside; application dismissed). *Digwa v Customs and Excise Comrs* [1978] VATTR 119, 1978 Halsbury's Abridgment para. 3014 applied.

3058   BRADLEY v CUSTOMS AND EXCISE COMRS (1979) MAN/79/143 (unreported) (applicant failed to serve notice of appeal against assessment within required time; commissioners issued writ of summons against the applicant for outstanding tax; applicant applied for extension of time within which to serve notice of appeal; power to extend time exercisable where trader had been bona fide confused about tax affairs, had since resolved problems and the matter was purely within jurisdiction of tribunal and not of High Court; extension granted on facts and applicant's circumstances). *Customs and Excise Comrs v Holvey* [1978] 1 All ER 1249, 1977 Halsbury's Abridgment para 3033, applied.

3059   Assessment—retailers' scheme—change of scheme by retailer—retrospective effect

Value added tax tribunal decision:

J. M. PATEL (TRADING AS MAGSONS) v CUSTOMS AND EXCISE COMRS (1980) LON/80/39 (unreported) (retail tobacconist and newsagent sought to change from one Retailers' Special Scheme to another; contended that change should be backdated to date when he began to operate first scheme; Value Added Tax (Supplies by Retailers) Regulations 1972, reg. 6, provides that, save as the commissioners may otherwise allow, retailers may change scheme after expiration of one year from its adoption; question whether words "save as the commissioners may otherwise allow" enabled commissioners to permit change of scheme with retrospective effect; words did have that effect; however, tribunal had no jurisdiction to decide whether application should be permitted to take effect retrospectively since decision was matter of discretion for commissioners). *Customs and Excise Comrs v J. H. Corbitt (Numismatists) Ltd* [1980] 2 All ER 72, HL, para. 3054 applied.

3060   Exempt supply—application of Community legislation—effect

See Case 126/78: *NV Nederlandse Spoorwegen v Secretary of State for Finance*, para. 1212.

3061   —— betting, gaming and lotteries—bingo—consideration for entry fee

Value added tax tribunal decision:

TYNEWYDD LABOUR WORKING MEN'S CLUB AND INSTITUTE LTD v CUSTOMS AND EXCISE COMRS (1980) LON/76/195, LON/80/287, LON/80/288 (unreported) (working men's club charged entry fee on bingo nights when live entertainment also provided; question whether entry fee was consideration for provision of bingo facilities and exempt, or consideration for provision of live entertainment; evidence that fees designed to meet cost of entertainment; part consideration for bingo and part for entertainment).

3062   —— education

The Value Added Tax (Education) Order 1980, S.I. 1980 No. 1604 (in force on 17th November 1980), extends the exemption in Finance Act 1972, Sch. 5, Group 6, items 1 and 2 (a) to cover research by a school or university, and research by other organisations if that research is of a kind provided by a school or university and is provided otherwise than for profit. It also extends the exemption in item 6 to cover facilities provided by an association of youth clubs to its members.

3063   ——health

The Value Added Tax (Health) Order 1980, S.I. 1980 No. 1602 (in force on 17th November 1980), qualifies the exemption for care or medical or surgical treatment under Finance Act 1972, Sch. 5, Group 7, item 4, by excluding institutions approved, licensed, registered or exempted from registration under local legislation or general legislation applied locally.

3064   —— —— manufacture of dental appliances

Value added tax tribunal decision:

BENNETT v CUSTOMS AND EXCISE COMRS (1979) LON/79/231 (unreported) (tribunal upheld the commissioners' contention that a manufacturer of crowns and bridges for dental surgeons and dentists was a dental technician within the meaning of Finance Act 1972, Sch. 5, Group 7, item 2: expert evidence showed that such a person was a dental technician both on the basis of the normal everyday use of the words and in medical and dental terminology; supplies he made were accordingly exempt).

3065   —— land—accommodation—holiday homes—life-time rights of occupation for portion of each year

Value added tax tribunal decision:
AMERICAN REAL ESTATES (SCOTLAND) LTD V CUSTOMS AND EXCISE COMRS (1980) EDN/80/5 (unreported) (applicants assessed to tax on sales of rights to occupy houses for a specified number of weeks in the year for holiday purposes; occupants joined club and houses conveyed to trustee on trust for club members; tribunal upheld assessment; right to occupy house at particular periods of year did not amount to granting of a major interest in building and not therefore zero-rated within Finance Act 1972, Sch. 4, Group 8, item 1; further, although there was a licence to occupy land attracting exemption from tax, the holiday homes fell within the exception to the exemption as holiday accommodation in a house with the 1972 Act, Sch. 5, Group 1, item 1, notwithstanding that there was a long term commitment to that accommodation).

3066   —— —— interest in or right over land—non-exclusive licence

Value added tax tribunal decision:
J. A. KING V CUSTOMS AND EXCISE COMRS (1980) LON/79/226 (unreported) (company allowed people to use fields for grazing horses in consideration of weekly payments; fields also used for grazing by company; contended supply was exempt under Finance Act 1972, Sch. 5, Group 1, item 1, as being grant of right over land or of licence to occupy land; contention rejected; grant was of non-exclusive licence; grant of non-exclusive licence for purpose of grazing did not constitute licence to occupy land within item 1; hence supply not exempt).

3067   —— postal services—cost of delivery of goods by post

Value added tax tribunal decision:
BSN (IMPORT AND EXPORT) LTD V CUSTOMS AND EXCISE COMRS (1980) LON/80/220 (unreported) (retailer invoiced mail order customers charging cost of postage separately; claimed service was exempt from value added tax as the conveyance of postal packets by post office; commissioners contended payment was consideration for service of procuring post office to deliver goods; hence service supplied by retailer not post office, and not exempt).

3068   —— sports competitions

The Value Added Tax (Competitions) Order 1980, S.I. 1980 No. 1909 (in force on 1st January 1981), exempts from value added tax the supply of a right to enter a competition in sport or physical recreation where the entry fees are wholly allocated towards the provision of prizes, or where the right to enter the competition is granted by a non-profit-making body established for purposes of sport or physical recreation.

3069   —— trade unions and professional bodies—association of taxi cab proprietors

Value added tax tribunal decision:
CITY CABS (EDINBURGH) LTD V CUSTOMS AND EXCISE COMRS (1980) EDN/79/30 (unreported) (association of taxi cab proprietors provided certain services for members including radio taxi service in return for subscriptions; contended facilities were exempt supplies under Finance Act 1972, Sch. 5, Group 9; association was not a trade union or other organisation of persons having as its main object the negotiation on behalf of its members of the terms and conditions of their employment, as members were all employers or self-employed; nor was it a

professional association since driving a taxi cab was a trade, not a profession; hence association not exempt).

3070   Finance Act 1980

See para. 2328.

3071   General regulations

The Value Added Tax (General) Regulations 1980, S.I. 1980 No. 1536 (in force on 17th November 1980), consolidate and amend the Value Added Tax (General) Regulations 1977, 1977 Halsbury's Abridgment para. 3052 and the amendments to those regulations.

3072   Imported goods—relief

The Value Added Tax (Imported Goods) Relief Order 1980, S.I. 1980 No. 1009 (in force on 15th August 1980), gives effect to Council Directive (EEC) 74/651 as amended by Council Directive (EEC) 78/1034, and Council Directive (EEC) 78/1035. It provides for the admission into the United Kingdom without payment of value added tax of certain small non-commercial consignments of goods sent from abroad by a private individual to another private individual in the United Kingdom for the personal or family use of the recipient.

3073   Imposition of VAT—Isle of Man

The Value Added Tax (Isle of Man) Order 1980, S.I. 1980 No. 183 (in force on 1st April 1980), provides for the modification of various enactments relating to value added tax, enabling the United Kingdom and the Isle of Man to be treated as a single area for the purposes of that tax. The Value Added Tax (United Kingdom and Isle of Man) (Consolidation) Order 1978, 1978 Halsbury's Abridgment para. 3033 and the Value Added Tax (United Kingdom and Isle of Man) Order 1978, 1978 Halsbury's Abridgment para. 3032 are revoked.

3074

The Value Added Tax (Isle of Man) (No. 2) Order 1980, S.I. 1980 No. 866 (in force on 24th June 1980), provides for the modification of various enactments relating to value added tax, enabling the United Kingdom and the Isle of Man to be treated as a single area for the purposes of that tax. The order, made as a consequence of the Value Added Tax (Gold) Order 1980, para. 3118, Value Added Tax (Transport) Order 1980, para. 3121, and the Value Added Tax (Cars) Order 1980, para. 3077, modifies those provisions.

3075

The Value Added Tax (Isle of Man) (No. 3) Order 1980, S.I. 1980 No. 1952 (arts. 1, 2 (1) in force on 17th December 1980 and art. 2 (2) on 1st January 1981), modifies the Value Added Tax (General) Regulations 1980, para. 3071, the Value Added Tax (Repayment to Community Traders) Regulations 1980, para. 3085 and the Value Added Tax (Special Provisions) Order 1977, 1977 Halsbury's Abridgment para. 3053 in furtherance of the Agreement between the United Kingdom and the Isle of Man that both countries are to be treated as a single area for the purposes of value added tax.

3076   Input tax—deduction—exceptions—business entertainment

A company carried on a business of direct selling through a pyramid of distributors. Training meetings for the distributors took place, at which meals and overnight accommodation were provided. The commissioners contended that the provision of such facilities amounted to business entertainment within the Value Added Tax (Special Provisions) Order 1977, and hence the company was not entitled to credit in respect of input tax under the Finance Act 1972, s. 3. *Held*, "business entertainment" was defined in the 1977 order as entertainment (including hospitality of any kind) provided by a taxable person in connection with a business carried on by him. The provision of food and accommodation was a provision of hospitality in connection with the company's business, notwithstanding that the company's motive in providing food and accommodation was exclusively for business purposes. Hence the provision of food and accommodation amounted to business entertainment and the company was not entitled to credit for input tax.

CUSTOMS AND EXCISE COMRS v SHAKLEE INTERNATIONAL [1980] STC 708 (Queen's Bench Division: WOOLF J). Decision of value added tax tribunal (1978) LON/78/210 (unreported), 1979 Halsbury's Abridgment para. 2986 reversed.

3077   —— —— **motor cars**

The Value Added Tax (Cars) Order 1980, S.I. 1980 No. 442 (in force on 30th April 1980), consolidates and revokes the Value Added Tax (Cars) Order 1977, 1977 Halsbury's Abridgment para. 3061, as amended. Article 3 of order revokes altogether the 1977 Order, art. 5 relating to the non-deductibility of input tax on certain goods installed in a motor car after car tax had been paid and supplied with it at the standard rate of tax, and amends art. 8. Articles 4, 5 and 6 contain provisions concerning the deduction of input tax on the supply or importation of new or used motor cars, the self-supply of certain motor cars and the charging of tax, subject to specified conditions, on the margin on sales of used motor cars. Article 7 removes from the scope of the tax disposals by finance houses and insurers of used motors which have been acquired by them in certain specified circumstances.

3078   —— —— **supply for purposes of business—supply of racehorse for promotional purposes**

Value added tax tribunal decisions:

BRIDGE BOOK CO LTD v CUSTOMS AND EXCISE COMRS (1980) LON/80/18 (unreported) (company carried on book trade business of buying and selling remainders in paperbacks; sought to deduct as input tax, tax on purchase and stabling costs of racehorses on basis that they were used for purpose of business within Finance Act 1972, s. 3; claimed that racing activities enabled company to do business with publishers of paperbacks; although company indirectly derived some benefit from racing activities, acquisition and use of horses was not primarily for use for purposes of company's business; hence tax not deductible).

3079   MSS (NORTH WEST) LTD v CUSTOMS AND EXCISE COMRS [1980] VATTR 29 (company supplying non-ferrous metals sought to deduct input tax on the purchase and training of a racehorse; company bought racehorse for promotional purposes; burden of proof on company to show that purchase of horse was for the purpose of business carried on by the company; test was subjective; however, it was not sufficient merely to state that the purchase was for promotional purposes; tribunal unable to see any connection between the name of the horse, "Metalco", company and nature of its business; too tenuous to suppose that such a business could be promoted by advertising through the medium of a racehorse; hence tax not deductible).

3080   SKELTOOLS LTD v CUSTOMS AND EXCISE COMRS (1980) LON/80/63 (unreported) (company carrying on business in high precision engineering; products difficult to promote by conventional advertising; director, who owned stud farm, leased race horses for a nominal sum to company to race under company's name; company deducted input tax claiming supplies made for purpose of company's business; test was subjective; company had bona fide intention of acquiring services for purpose of its business; director had no personal interest in horse racing and immediate benefit accrued to company and not to the stud; hence tax deductible).

3081   —— —— **whether amount improperly charged for tax recoverable**

Value added tax tribunal decision:

HEARNE v CUSTOMS AND EXCISE COMRS (1980) MAN/80/8 (unreported) (appellant purchased vehicle from vendor and was charged value added tax although vendor not a registered trader nor a taxable person for purposes of tax; appellant unable therefore to recover sum for input tax as transaction not susceptible to output tax).

3082   Liability to tax—duty to keep records—whether taxpayer entitled to be paid for his work

Value added tax tribunal decision:

WAJZNER v CUSTOMS AND EXCISE COMRS (1979) MAN/79/110 (unreported) (appellant deducted sum from amount due to commissioners as recompense for time and labour expended in keeping required records; Finance Act 1972, s. 34 (1) clearly stipulated that every taxpayer was required to keep such records as required by the commissioners and there was no provision or authority to pay the expenses of such persons; only Parliament could make such a provision; appellant not therefore entitled to deduct sum for expenses).

3083   —— group of companies—tax due from representative member of group—whether tax recoverable from other member

Company A and company B were members of the same group of companies, of which company A was treated as the representative member for the purposes of the Finance Act 1972, s. 21. Both companies went into liquidation on the same date, company A owing a substantial amount in VAT, in its capacity as representative member. The question arose whether the commissioners were entitled, by virtue of the 1972 Act, s. 41, to rank as preferential creditors in the winding up of company B in respect of the tax due to them from company A, for which under s. 21 company B was jointly and severally liable. *Held*, as soon as VAT became due under s. 21 from the representative member of a group of companies, it became due also from the other members of the group. Hence the commissioners were entitled to claim preferentially in the winding up of company B for any unpaid tax due from company A.

RE NADLER ENTERPRISES LTD [1980] STC 457 (Chancery Division: DILLON J).

3084   Refund—bad debt—insolvency of company

Value added tax tribunal decision:

SNOWDON v CUSTOMS AND EXCISE COMRS (1979) MAN/79/109 (unreported) (supplier liable to commissioners for payment of tax whether or not has received payment from recipient of supply; applicant applied for relief upon a bad debt incurred by him with a company; receiver appointed to debtor company but no winding up proceedings imminent or likely; under Finance Act 1978, s. 12 relief limited to where company insolvent and winding up order made; no refund therefore available to applicant).

3085   —— EEC scheme

The Value Added Tax (Repayment to Community Traders) Regulations 1980, S.I. 1980 No. 1537 (in force on 1st January 1981), implement in the United Kingdom a scheme which will operate throughout the Community for the refund of value added tax incurred by registered taxable persons in member states other than those in which they are registered.

3086   Registration—liability to be registered—partnership

Value added tax tribunal decision:

SAUNDERS v CUSTOMS AND EXCISE COMRS, SORRELL v CUSTOMS AND EXCISE COMRS [1980] VATTR 53 (commissioners claimed two firms only entitled to one registration pursuant to Finance Act 1972, s. 22 (1), as they comprised one partnership; firms run by two separate persons but both agreed to become limited partner in other one's firm, so that in event of one becoming ill, other could take over; under Limited Partnership Act 1907, s. 4 (2) limited partner not liable to pay debts of firm, therefore also not liable to pay firm's VAT; each firm thus entitled to separate registration).

3087 Relief—charitable organisation—hardship

Value added tax tribunal decision:

MARK HALL AND NETTESWELL COMMUNITY ASSOCIATION v CUSTOMS AND EXCISE COMRS (1980) LON/80/31 (unreported) (appellant association was registered charity which carried on catering service as part of operations; tax was incorrectly calculated over 3½ years and consequently underpaid; commissioners assessed correct tax; appellant pleaded both hardship and that under EEC Sixth Directive should be exempt from tax as charity; tribunal upheld assessment; had no power for mercy and exemption for charities under Sixth Directive not enacted into English law).

3088 —— special provisions

The Value Added Tax (Special Provisions) (Amendment) Order 1980, S.I. 1980 No. 1603 (in force on 17th November 1980), amends the Value Added Tax (Special Provisions) Order 1977, 1977 Halsbury's Abridgment para. 3053. It extends the relief from tax for certain transfers of a business as a going concern and also contains a new relieving provision which removes from the scope of the tax the assignment of hire-purchase or conditional sale agreements to banks or other financial institutions.

3089 Supply of goods and services—gifts—business incentive scheme

The High Court has dismissed an appeal by a company which contended that goods costing less than £10 each supplied to persons who were appointed as agents were gifts and that therefore their value should be taken as nil under the Finance Act 1972, Sch. 3, para. 6. The supplies therefore fell to be determined on their open market value in accordance with s. 10 (3). Nor did they qualify for calculation under the retailers' special schemes, whereby retailers were permitted to calculate value added tax on the value of their gross takings, as the scheme related only to retail sales to customers and not to transactions which were not sales.

GUS MERCHANDISE CORPN LTD v CUSTOMS AND EXCISE COMRS [1980] STC 480 (Queen's Bench Division: WOOLF J). Decision of value added tax tribunal [1978] VATTR 28, 1979 Halsbury's Abridgment para. 3015 affirmed.

3090 —— nature of supply—membership of golf club

Value added tax tribunal decision:

DOWNES CREDITON GOLF CLUB v CUSTOMS AND EXCISE COMRS (1979) CAR/79/203 (unreported) (certain local businessmen decided to create a golf club for the area; persons wishing to contribute to the club's capital requirements and who also later wished to pay a membership subscription in order to enjoy the club's facilities, paid their contribution in the form of an entrance fee which granted them temporary membership until such time as the amount of the first subscription was agreed; commissioners assessed club to tax on basis that entrance fees, as well as subscription fees, were taxable at standard rate; entrance fee was compulsory payment before election to membership and unless member paid that fee and subscription he was not entitled to benefit of membership; allocation of funds received as consideration irrelevant; club supplied membership in consideration of both fees and therefore tax chargeable at standard rate on both fees).

3091 —— services supplied for a consideration—assessment by reference to consideration for which goods supplied later sold by retail

Value added tax tribunal decision:

CLUB CENTRE OF LEEDS LTD v CUSTOMS AND EXCISE COMRS (1980) MAN/79/146 (unreported) (commissioners have power to direct, if necessary for protection of the revenue, that value for tax purposes of supplies made by taxable person to a number of individuals for later resale, should be determined not by reference to consideration received for such supplies but by reference to consideration for which goods so supplied are later sold by retail; appellant, wholesale supplier of greetings cards to charitable and other organisations, appealed against issue of such a direction against him; direction only necessary where trader carrying on business in manner designed to avoid accountability for tax and could not be made merely to obtain maximum tax revenue from supplies made by trader; appellant had carried on a business in same way before introduction of value added tax, therefore no evidence of evasion; appeal allowed).

3092 —— —— consideration not consisting of money

A golf club required its members to pay an annual subscription and make interest-free loans to the club, in order to raise money to improve the club's facilities. In return, membership and the right to use the club's facilities were conferred. The club was assessed to value added tax on the basis that the monetary consideration by way of subscription was not the whole consideration for the supply of facilities and that therefore the Finance Act 1972, s. 10 (3) applied and the value of the facilities supplied was, under s. 10 (5), their market value. The club successfully appealed against the assessment, and the commissioners appealed against the tribunal's decision. *Held*, the loans were a provision for the use of money only and constituted consideration not consisting of money within the meaning of s. 10 (3). Therefore, the value of the facilities supplied, their market value under s. 10 (5), was the total of the subscriptions together with the interest which the loans would have attracted had the money loaned been invested on the open market. The appeal would accordingly be allowed.

Customs and Excise Comrs v Exeter Golf and Country Club Ltd [1980] STC 162 (Queen's Bench Division: Griffiths J). Decision of value added tax tribunal [1979] VATTR 70, 1979 Halsbury's Abridgment para. 3012, reversed.

3093 —— —— meaning of consideration

Value added tax tribunal decision:

Landmark Cash and Carry Group Ltd v Customs and Excise Comrs [1980] VATTR 1 (association appealed against assessment in respect of supply of taxable services made by it in the course of business; association was national marketing umbrella for suppliers involved in cash and carry grocery trade; basic objective was to improve members' profitability by promotional campaigns; members paid basic subscription on entry; association entered into agreements with certain members whereby basic targets for growth were set and on the target being attained the association received payment; no new customers were introduced to the members but due to the association's promotional activities their turnover was consistently increased and most of the association's income was derived from such payments; entry into agreements and achievements of targets was something done by the association in consideration for the payments to it; therefore association, in relation to the payments, was making taxable supplies in the course of business; appeal would be dismissed).

3094 —— supply and delivery of goods—whether delivery separate supply

Value added tax tribunal decisions:

Lylybet Dishwashers (UK) Ltd v Customs and Excise Comrs (1980) LON/79/244 (unreported) (appellant company sold dishwashers which were chargeable to VAT at higher rate; company contended that delivery of goods was separate supply taxable at standard rate; another company, belonging to same group, which made separate charge for delivery of goods was chargeable to VAT on delivery charges at standard rate; however the same did not apply to applicant as it charged customers just one purchase price covering goods and delivery).

3095 Coleman v Customs and Excise Comrs (1980) LON/80/256 (unreported) (appellant in business as newsagent and tobacconist; for inclusive price supplied and delivered newspapers; used Scheme G under Notice 727 entitled "Special Schemes for Retailers" to calculate output tax on supplies of goods made by him; appellant contended he had to exclude from gross takings amount attributable to his charges for delivering newspapers as Scheme G could not be used to calculate output tax on any services; contended had to deal with said amount in normal VAT way outside Scheme G; commissioners contended that inclusive price was consideration for supply of goods rather than part consideration for supply of goods and part separate consideration for supply of services; it would follow that whole price must be included in gross takings and dealt with under Scheme G; commissioners' contention upheld).

3096   —— **supply in the course of business—food purchased for cooking at client's home**

Value added tax tribunal decision:

NORMAN v CUSTOMS AND EXCISE COMRS (1979) LON/79/174 (unreported) (appellant's business involved shopping for and cooking food for home entertaining by client; commissioners claimed cost of food taxable as it was supplied to client in course of business; appellant contended he supplied shopping and cooking services but not food, which he bought as client's agent; no evidence to show parties consented to agency relationship; food supplied in course of business and liable to tax).

3097   —— —— **shootings over private land**

Value added tax tribunal decision:

LORD FISHER v CUSTOMS AND EXCISE COMRS [1979] VATTR 227 (landowner arranged shootings over his land to which he invited friends and relatives who were asked to make contributions to cost; commissioners assessed him to tax on basis that contribution paid by each gun was consideration for right to take game and therefore taxable; right to shoot for consideration was supply of services; however supplies not made in course of business but in course of arranging shoot, for pleasure and social enjoyment; landowner's appeal therefore allowed).

3098   —— —— **supply by club, association or organisation**

Value added tax tribunal decision:

BELVEDERE AND CALDER VALE SPORTS CLUB v CUSTOMS AND EXCISE COMRS (1980) MAN/79/129 (unreported) (sports club assessed to tax on match fees paid by members under Finance Act 1972, s. 45, on basis that club ran a business whereby it granted to its members right to use facilities, in particular facilities relating to playing of individual matches in consideration of which each member paid a subscription and a match fee; therefore match fees represented part of consideration for grant of right to use club's facilities, grant of such right was taxable supply of services and total consideration for grant liable to tax; assessment upheld; services were supplied by club and were available to any member who had occasion to use them; hence were facilities within s. 45; both subscriptions and match fees together constituted consideration for provision by club of facilities available to members and match fees accordingly fell within s. 45).

3099   —— —— **training and racing of horses at stud farm**

Value added tax tribunal decision:

ISMAY v CUSTOMS AND EXCISE COMRS [1980] VATTR 19 (business of applicant running stud farm and breeding race horses for sale; applicant contended, for purposes of claiming input tax, that training and racing horses undertaken solely in course of business; tribunal found as fact that in order to develop successful brood mares, was essential that horses were trained as racehorses and raced; services supplied in training and racing therefore supplied in course of business).

3100   —— time of supply—no goods supplied when invoice issued

Value added tax tribunal's decision:

WELDONS (WEST ONE) LTD v CUSTOMS AND EXCISE COMRS (1980) LON/80/196 (unreported) (appellant sold pine beds; suppliers had cash flow problems and appellant advanced payment of £12,000; invoice included value added tax; appellant appealed against assessment made on account of input tax incorrectly claimed on non-supply; although supply treated as taking place when invoice issued, there was no description in invoice to identify goods supplied; total amount payable including tax, amount of tax chargeable at each rate and total amount of tax chargeable not shown; invoice not therefore tax invoice for value added tax purposes and no claim to deduct input tax could be allowed).

3101   —— —— supply before increase in rate

Value added tax tribunal decision:

J. D. FOX LTD v CUSTOMS AND EXCISE COMRS (1980) LON/80/237 (unreported) (furniture manufacturers appealed against assessment to tax in respect of goods ordered before, and delivered after, an increase in the rate of tax; company argued that relevant tax point was at payment of the deposit when an invoice was issued; invoice did not comply with the Value Added Tax (General) Regulations 1977, reg. 9 (1), therefore it was not a tax invoice but receipt of deposit was receipt of money in respect of the supply of goods within the Finance Act 1972, s. 7 (4); accordingly the relevant tax points were when the deposit was paid, to the extent of the deposit amount only; and on delivery, in respect of the balance of the price; the appeal would be dismissed).

3102   —— —— —— whether liable at new rate

Value added tax tribunal decision:

GLASGOW VENDING SERVICES v CUSTOMS AND EXCISE COMRS (1980) LON/79/334 (unreported) (14th June 1979 value added tax raised from eight to fifteen per cent operative from 18th June 1979; cigarette vending machine operator unable to make necessary alterations to machines until end of July; assessed to tax on fifteen per cent from 18th June; tribunal upheld assessment; under Finance Act 1972, s. 72 (a) supply deemed to take place at time of removal of goods; operator liable to account for tax at fifteen per cent for all takings removed from machines after 18th June).

3103   —— transport of goods—cash-on-delivery service—liability to tax

See Case 126/78: *NV Nederlandse Spoorwegen v Secretary of State for Finance*, para. 1212.

3104   Zero rating—books etc.—children's cut-out doll dressing book

Value added tax tribunal decision:

W F GRAHAM (NORTHAMPTON LTD) v CUSTOMS AND EXCISE COMRS (1980) LON/79/332 (unreported) (question whether supply of cut-out doll dressing books was zero rated as either books or children's picture or painting books or whether chargeable at standard rate as toys; book consisted of sixteen pages, four pages contained narrative of 1,500 words and other pages contained pictures of dolls and clothes to be cut out; word "book" to be construed in ordinary sense of word; not picture or painting book as painting not dominant factor; although there would be little left of book once pictures had been cut out, nevertheless at time when product taxable it was still a book in ordinary sense of word; supply zero-rated).

3105   —— building work—building materials

Value added tax tribunal decision:

PROPAFLOR LTD v CUSTOMS AND EXCISE COMRS (1980) LON/79/247 (unreported) (company manufactured and supplied platform flooring systems; company also supplied carpet to bond to top surface of flooring; carpet not building material within meaning of Finance Act 1972, Sch. 4, Group 8, item 3, therefore not zero rated). *Customs and Excise Comrs v Westbury Developments (Worthing) Ltd* [1979] STC 665, 1979 Halsbury's Abridgment para. 2985 applied.

3106 —— —— construction or alteration of building—installation of clock

Value added tax tribunal decision:

OTTERY ST. MARY CLOCK APPEAL COMMITTEE V CUSTOMS AND EXCISE COMRS (1980) LON(C)/80/6 (unreported) (new clock attached to exterior wall of building to replace old clock; installation involved bricking up window aperture; question whether supply of clock zero-rated as being supply in course of alteration of building; work was permanent and irreversible and was a structural alteration to building, but was not substantial in relation to building as a whole; hence did not qualify for zero-rating).

3107 —— —— —— installation of double-glazing windows

Value added tax tribunal decision:

GUARDIA SHUTTERS LTD V CUSTOMS AND EXCISE COMRS (1980) LON/80/149 (unreported) (supplies of double-glazing windows assessed to tax at zero-rate on basis that they constituted "alteration" of a building within Finance Act 1972, Sch. 4, Group 8; item 2; the supplier was also the manufacturer of a thermal shutter, which had the same effect as double-glazing but was a kind of blind, made of vertical panels, fitted to the inside of a window; supplies of thermal shutters assessed to tax at standard rate as installation did not amount to "alteration"; supplier appealed against assessment in respect of supplies of double-glazing at zero-rating, which he considered to benefit his competitors; "alteration" was to be limited to substantial alteration to the fabric or structure of a building so as to become an integral part of such fabric or structure; installation of double-glazing did not therefore amount to "alteration" and was taxable at standard rate).

3108 —— —— —— repair or maintenance

The foundations of some houses were damaged by subsidence and the taxpayers, who were builders, were employed to underpin them. As the original foundations were defective and could not be repaired the taxpayers constructed additional foundations leaving the original foundations unaltered. They were assessed to value added tax under Finance Act 1972, Sch. 4, group 8, item 2, on the basis that although there had been a supply of services in the course of alteration of the buildings, the work was maintenance and thus excluded from the zero-rating provisions of group 8. Questions arose as to the interpretation of "maintenance" within the provisions of the 1972 Act. *Held*, the interpretation of a word in a statute such as "maintenance" was a question of law and such a word should be given its ordinary, natural meaning as read by the "reasonable man". "Maintenance" generally involved work of minor significance. It did not involve making a building better than when it was first constructed. The work which was done in the present case was not done to any existing part of the building but involved an extension downwards to the existing building. Accordingly, it was not capable of falling within the ordinary meaning of "maintenance" and thus was a zero-rated supply.

ACT CONSTRUCTION LTD V CUSTOMS AND EXCISE COMRS [1980] STC 716 (Court of Appeal: LORD DENNING MR, BRANDON and ACKNER LJJ) Decision of Parker J [1979] STC 358, 1979 Halsbury's Abridgment para. 3041 affirmed. *Pearlman v Keepers and Governors of Harrow School* [1979] 1 All ER 365, 1978 Halsbury's Abridgment para. 1766, applied.

3109 Value added tax tribunal decision:

MIDGLEY V CUSTOMS AND EXCISE COMRS (1980) LON/80/134 (unreported) (appellant owned semi-detached house of architectural and historic interest; work carried out involving fixing cornice, corbels and block moulds to front of house in order to make it similar in appearance to other house of pair; whether work zero-rated as being supply in course of alteration of building; work was permanent and irreversible, was of a structural nature and was substantial in relation to the building as a whole; hence constituted an alteration; alteration was to correct imbalance between pair of semi-detached houses and could not therefore constitute repair or maintenance; supply accordingly zero-rated).

3110   —— —— **grant of major interest in building—holiday homes**

See *American Real Estate (Scotland) Ltd v Customs and Excise Comrs*, para. 3065.

3111   —— **exports—necessity for documentary proof of export**

The taxpayer was assessed to value added tax in respect of wholesale export sales made over the counter to overseas customers who had failed to complete forms proving export, as required by the Value Added Tax Notice 703, para. 10, which had to be satisfied before the goods could be zero-rated. He successfully appealed on the ground that the requirements were unreasonable and exceeded the powers given by the Finance Act 1972, s. 12 (7). On appeal by the Commissioners, *held*, the strict conditions were necessary for the purpose of preventing tax evasion. They were not void as being unreasonable, and they had been rightly applied by the commissioners. The appeal would be allowed.

HENRY MOSS OF LONDON LTD v CUSTOMS AND EXCISE COMRS (1980) Times, 11th December (Court of Appeal: LORD DENNING MR and SHAW LJ). Decision of Forbes J [1979] STC 657, 1979 Halsbury's Abridgment para. 3047 reversed.

3112   —— —— —— **misdescription of goods on shipping documents**

Value added tax tribunal decision:

MIDDLESEX TEXTILES LTD v CUSTOMS AND EXCISE COMRS [1979] VATTR 239 (applicant exported lengths of cotton material to Nigeria: Government of Nigeria had placed ban on importation of textiles therefore applicant misdescribed packages of cloth on bills as personal effects, printed books and spare parts; under Finance Act 1972, s. 12 (6) supply of goods is zero rated if commissioners are satisfied that person supplying them has exported them and under s. 12 (7) commissioners may make regulations providing for zero rating of supplies of goods if goods are exported and other specified conditions are satisfied; despite misdescriptions on proofs of export tribunal satisfied, on evidence presented, that goods sent out by applicant or his agent were exported under s. 12 (6); but goods sent out by customers did not fall under s. 12 (6) as they were not exported by applicant who was merely the supplier; these goods were however exported under s. 12 (7) as they were supplied to persons who were not taxable persons and were not resident in the United Kingdom and sufficient evidence had been adduced to show that they had in fact been exported; supplies therefore chargeable to tax at zero rate).

3113   —— **food—supply in course of catering**

Value added tax tribunal decisions:

COPE v CUSTOMS AND EXCISE COMRS (1980) LON/79/303 (unreported) (appellant operated at various racecourses mobile catering stall and tents from which he supplied seafood to be consumed on the racecourse; contended supplies zero-rated as not made in the course of catering because not supplied for consumption on the premises on which they were supplied; premises from which supplies made was stall or tent; seafood consumed on racecourse which was not premises on which food was supplied; hence supplies not in course of catering and were zero-rated).

3114   PARKER v CUSTOMS AND EXCISE COMRS (1980) MAN/80/58 (unreported) (appellant contended supply of food at football game was supply of food of a kind used for human consumption and zero-rated; commissioners contended supplies were made in course of catering and therefore tax chargeable at standard rate; test was whether food was consumed on the premises; irrelevant whether food and facilities provided by same person; food was purchased in one part of football stand and consumed in seats or en route to seats; commissioners' contention upheld).

3115   —— —— **supply of food used for human consumption**

Value added tax tribunal decisions:

DARLINGTON BOROUGH COUNCIL v CUSTOMS AND EXCISE COMRS (1980) MAN/80/20 (unreported) (council owned licensed abattoir; granted facilities to a contractor to slaughter animals therein; charges for service made to customers by both contractor and council; council assessed to tax at standard rate in respect of charges; council contended abattoir was business engaged in supply of food for human consumption and charges therefore zero-rated; services supplied by council did not include slaughter or processing of the carcases, which were carried out by contractor; nor was contractor an agent or servant of council; two separate charges made by two principals, one by contractor for killing and preparation of meat, other by council for various toll charges and levies; assessment therefore upheld).

3116   SONI v CUSTOMS AND EXCISE COMRS [1980] VATTR 9 (appeal against decision that traditional Indian delicacy "paan" not food and not eligible for zero-rating; paan made up of number of ingredients including betel nuts and wrapped in betel leaves; eaten after meals with main purpose of stimulating digestive juices, but as well as being stimulant also provided nourishment; paan was food for although main purpose was that of stimulant, did not preclude it being food if also provided nourishment).

3117   —— **fuel and power—restriction and withdrawal of zero rating**

The Value Added Tax (Fuel and Power) Order 1980, S.I. 1980 No. 440 (in force on 1st May 1980) restricts the zero-rate of value added tax on hydrocarbon oils to fuel oil, gas oil and kerosene which, on delivery from bond, have not borne the full rate of excise duty. All other hydrocarbon oils become liable to value added tax. The Order also withdraws the zero-rating from lubricating oils and all other lubricants. Solid fuel is eligible for zero-rating only when held out for sale solely as fuel.

3118   —— **gold**

The Value Added Tax (Gold) Order 1980, S.I. 1980 No. 303 (in force on 1st April 1980), amends the Finance Act 1972, Sch. 4, Group 12 by restricting the supply of gold (including gold coins) at the zero-rate to supplies made between central banks, or between a central bank and a member of the London Gold Market. The term "authorised dealer in gold" no longer has any legal status.

3119   —— —— **dealings on terminal market**

The Value Added Tax (Terminal Markets) (Amendment) Order 1980, S.I. 1980 No. 304, amends the Value Added Tax (Terminal Markets) Order 1973.

The 1973 Order zero rates certain supplies of goods and services in the course of dealings on specified terminal markets, which involve goods ordinarily dealt with on those markets. The 1980 Order extends the zero rating to supplies in the course of dealings on the London Gold Market, which is now added to the list of terminal markets.

3120   —— **overseas trader—agency**

See *Customs and Excise Comrs v Johnson*, para. 46.

3121   —— **transport—supply of services to overseas businessmen**

The Value Added Tax (Transport) Order 1980, S.I. 1980 No. 305 (in force on 1st April 1980), amends the Value Added Tax (Consolidation) Order 1978, 1978 Halsbury's Abridgment para. 3034. The 1978 Order amended the Finance Act 1972, Sch. 4, Group 10 by adding item 12 to Group 10, which provides zero rating relief for certain services supplied to foreign business customers at a port or customs and excise airport, in connection with the importation or exportation of goods. The 1980 Order extends the relief to those services when supplied at a place other than a port or customs and excise airport, including the Irish Land Boundary.

WAR AND EMERGENCY

Halsbury's Laws of England (3rd edn.), Vol. 39, paras. 18–240

3122 Pensions

See PENSIONS AND SUPERANNUATION.

WATER SUPPLY

Halsbury's Laws of England (3rd edn.), Vol. 39, paras. 241–652

3123 Abstraction of underground water—abstraction in excess of statutory limit—damage—nature of cause of action

Canada

Landowners sought to claim damages in respect of subsidence caused to their land by the abstraction of large quantities of underground water by a public authority in the course of the construction of a sewer. Under the Ontario Water Resources Act 1970 the abstraction of underground water in excess of the statutory limit, which had been exceeded by the public authority, was prohibited. Preliminary questions arose as to whether an owner of land which had been damaged by such unlawful abstraction of water had a right of action in nuisance or negligence or for breach of statutory duty. *Held*, the relevant statutory provisions, which imposed a restriction on the common law right to abstract underground water rather than creating a statutory duty, had been enacted for the purpose of protecting landowners from damage by excessive pumping. Accordingly, any abstraction of water above the permitted limit was unlawful and, insofar as it caused damage to other property, was actionable in nuisance. With respect to negligence, the effect of the statute was to define what was a reasonable amount of water which could be abstracted; the abstraction of any further amount was thus unreasonable and gave rise to a cause of action in negligence. Further, the imposition by the statute of a penalty for a breach of its provisions did not prejudice the right of any person for whose protection the statute had been enacted to sue for damages.

RE NATIONAL CAPITAL COMMISSION (1979) 97 DLR (3d) 631 (Supreme Court of Canada). *Langbrook Properties Ltd v Surrey County Council* [1969] 3 All ER 1424 referred to.

For the corresponding English legislation see the Water Resources Act 1963, ss. 23, 24.

3124 River authority area—water abstracted for agricultural use—easement at common law—effect on easement of statutory restrictions

See *Cargill v Gotts*, para. 963.

3125 Water authorities—limit of borrowing power

The Water Authorities and National Water Council (Limit for Borrowing) Order 1980, S.I. 1980 No. 170 (in force on 9th February 1980), specifies a new limit of £4,500 million on borrowing by regional water authorities, the National Water Council and local authorities under the Water Act 1973, Sch. 3, para 34 (5).

3126 Water mains—power to lay mains—duties of landowner

Scotland

A Scottish statute empowered a local water authority to lay a water main on giving notice to the owner and occupier of the land. It also conferred incidental powers such as powers of access and inspection. After the main was laid and compensation paid the landowner carried out tipping operations which resulted in an overburden several feet deep being heaped over the main. *Held*, the statute had created a servitude and the servient owner was not entitled to do anything which materially interfered with or rendered more expensive the authority's right of access.

CENTRAL REGIONAL COUNCIL V FERNS 1980 SLT 126 (Outer House).

The corresponding English provision is the Water Act 1945,Sch. 3, Pt V, s. 19.

WATERS AND WATERCOURSES

Halsbury's Laws of England (3rd edn.), Vol. 39, paras. 653–1128

3127   Article

Coastal Zone Management Law: A Case Study of the Severn Estuary and Bristol Channel; John Gibson (study of problems afflicting the coastal zone with implications of national relevance): [1980] JPL 153.

3128   Land drainage—water authority expenses

The Water Authority Expenses (Limitation of Precepts) Order 1980, S.I. 1980 No. 2017 (in force on 1st April 1981), is made under the Land Drainage Act 1976, s. 46, which empowers a water authority, in respect of each local land drainage district in its area, to issue precepts to a county council or London borough council requiring payment of the amount of the land drainage expenses of the water authority apportioned in respect of any part of the local land drainage district which is within the council's area. The aggregate amount for which such precepts may be issued for any one financial year, in the absence of special consent, is limited to the amount calculated by multiplying the estimated penny rate product for the area of the council comprised within the relevant local land drainage district by such a number as may be specified. This order specifies 2·5 as the number.

WEIGHTS AND MEASURES

Halsbury's Laws of England (3rd edn.), Vol. 39, paras. 1129–1272

3129   Article

Weights and Measures Act 1979: New Law, New Directions, R. G. Lawson: 129 NLJ 1251.

3130   Marking of goods and abbreviations of units

The Weights and Measures (Marking of Goods and Abbreviations of Units) (Amendment) Regulations 1980, S.I. 1980 No. 8 (in force on 1st February 1980), amend the 1975 Regulations regs. 11, 12, 1975 Halsbury's Abridgment para. 514 which relate to the use of metric and imperial units in the marking of containers.

The basic requirement remains that where a container is required to be marked with quantity by measurement, that marking is to be in metric units, but may also be in imperial units. Pre-packed goods required to be made up in specified quantities and which, after 1st February 1979, are required to be made in metric markings only, are required to be marked in both metric and imperial units for one year.

Other pre-packed goods which, after 1st February, were required to be made up in imperial quantities must also show both metric and imperial quantities.

Milk marked in imperial units is only to be marked in terms of the pint, quart or gallon.

3131   Measuring equipment—liquid fuel delivered from road tankers

The Measuring Equipment (Liquid Fuel delivered from Road Tankers) (Amendment) Regulations 1980, S.I. 1980 No. 1993 (in force on 1st February 1981), amend the 1979 Regulations, 1979 Halsbury's Abridgment para. 3073.

3132   Measuring instruments—EEC requirements

The Measuring Instruments (EEC Requirements) (Electrical Energy Meters) Regulations 1980, S.I. 1980 No. 886 (in force on 22nd July 1980), apply the Measuring Instruments (EEC Requirements) Regulations 1975, 1975 Halsbury's Abridgment para. 3515, with modifications to electrical energy meters to which Council Directive (EEC) 76/1891, 1976 Halsbury's Abridgment para. 1109 applies.

3133

The Measuring Instruments (EEC Requirements) Regulations 1980, S.I. 1980 No. 1058 (in force on 1st September 1980), replace the 1975 Regulations, 1975 Halsbury's Abridgment para. 3515, as amended. The regulations implement Council Directive (EEC) 71/316 (OJ No. L206, 6.4.71), as amended, relating to measuring instruments and methods of metrological control, and also the Council Directives relating to particular categories of instruments.

3134   —— —— fees

The Measuring Instruments (EEC Requirements) (Fees) (Amendment) Regulations 1980, S.I. 1980 No. 168 (in force on 10th March 1980), amend the Measuring Instruments (EEC Requirements) (Fees) Regulations 1979, 1979 Halsbury's Abridgment para. 3078 by increasing certain of the fees payable in connection with services provided by the Department of Trade in respect of EEC pattern approval of certain specified measuring instruments.

3135   —— liquid fuel and lubricants

The Measuring Instruments (Liquid Fuel and Lubricants) (Amendment) Regulations 1980, S.I. 1980 No. 1878 (in force on 31st December 1980), amend the Measuring Instruments (Liquid Fuel and Lubricants) Regulations 1979, 1979 Halsbury's Abridgment para. 3079, by (i) removing requirements that measuring instruments be marked with particulars of authorised modifications to approved patterns, (ii) prescribing the limits of error for quantities of 200 ml., (iii) confining to testing with a view to passing as fit for use for trade the application of the provision in reg. 29 relating to limits of error, where the errors are all errors in excess or all errors in deficiency, and (iv) clarifying the circumstances in which it is lawful to destroy, obliterate or deface a stamp on a measuring instrument and to use that instrument for trade unstamped.

3136   Milk and solid fuel vending machines

The Weights and Measures (Milk and Solid Fuel Vending Machines) Regulations 1980, S.I. 1980 No. 246 (in force on 18th April 1980), replace the Weights and Measures (Milk and Solid Fuel Vending Machines) Regulations 1965, as amended. The regulations specify the manner in which information is to be displayed on or in such vending machines, by means of which pre-packed milk and solid fuel are for sale, and the units of measurements to be used in marking the machines with any information about the quantity of each item for sale therein.

3137   Packaged goods

The Weights and Measures (Packaged Goods) (Amendment) Regulations 1980, S.I. 1980 No. 1064 (reg. 6 in force on 1st January 1981, the remainder on 1st September 1980), amend the Weights and Measures (Packaged Goods) Regulations 1979, 1979 Halsbury's Abridgment para. 3082.

3138 **Units of measurement**

The Units of Measurement Regulations 1980, S.I. 1980 No. 1070 (regs. 1 (3) (b), 3–7, Schs. 1, 2, in force on 1st October 1981, the remainder in force on 1st September 1980), implement Council Directive (EEC) 71/354 as amended, in so far as it has not yet been implemented. They also implement Council Directive (EEC) 80/181, (O.J. No. L39, 15.2.80) which amends the former Directive and replaces it as from 1st October 1981. These regulations also replace the Units of Measurement Regulations 1976, 1976 Halsbury's Abridgment para 2157, as from 1st October 1981.

The regulations define and authorise, as from 1st October 1981, in the circumstances specified in Council Directive (EEC) 80/81, the use of the units of measurement set out in the regulations, Sch. 1 and the prefixes and symbols set out in Sch. 2 for such use in conjunction with those units. They also provide that certain units of measurement listed in Sch. 3 are not authorised for use in those circumstances from the 1st September 1980 in relation to certain units and 1st January 1980 in relation to other units. Consequential amendments are made to the Weights and Measures Acts 1963 and 1967 and to certain statutory instruments which refer to the units no longer authorised to be used by these regulations.

3139 The Units of Measurement (No. 2) Regulations 1980, S.I. 1980 No. 1742 (in force on 12th December 1980), implement Council Directive (EEC) 71/354, as amended, in relation to byelaws made by local authorities under the Weights and Measures Act 1963, Schs. 6, 7, relating to solid fuel and wood fuel, in so far as the byelaws refer to tons, hundredweights, quarters and stones which are not authorised for use in the circumstances specified in Council Directive (EEC) 80/81.

The regulations also clarify, amend and revoke certain provisions in the Units of Measurement Regulations 1978 and 1980, 1978 Halsbury's Abridgment para. 1031 and para. 3138 respectively.

WILLS

Halsbury's Laws of England (3rd edn.), Vol. 39, paras. 1273–1720

3140 **Article**

Reforming the Law of Wills, R. D. Mackay 130 NLJ 1108.

3141 **Construction—residuary gift—residuary gift to "heirs and surviving issue"—meaning**

A will contained a gift of residue to trustees on trust to pay income to two persons for life, the survivor to receive the whole of the income. On the survivor's death, the capital was to be divided equally between three other persons "or their heirs and surviving issue". On the question of construction of the gift, *held*, (i) on the death of the persons entitled to the income for life, the residue was to be divided equally between the three other persons. If any of them had died, then because the gift over was substitutional in nature, their share was to be divided among their heirs and surviving issue. The gift over was a gift to two separate categories of beneficiary, namely the heirs and the surviving issue, and not to a composite class of both. (ii) As to the meaning of the word "heirs", the Law of Property Act 1925, s. 132 provided that a limitation of real or personal property in favour of the heir of a deceased which, before 1926 would in the case of freehold land have conferred on the heir an estate by purchase, operated to confer a corresponding equitable interest in the property on the person who would, under the rules in force before 1926, have been the heir of the deceased in respect of his freehold land. By virtue of this section the substitutional gift operated to confer an equitable interest in the property on the persons who were heirs in the strict pre-1926 sense. "Surviving issue" referred to surviving children but not surviving children of all degrees. The date for ascertaining the categories of heirs and surviving issue was the death of the relevant praepositus and since there was nothing in the will to indicate severance they took as joint tenants and not tenants in common.

RE BOURKE'S WILL TRUSTS; BARCLAYS BANK TRUST CO LTD v CANADA PERMANENT TRUST CO [1980] 1 All ER 219 (Chancery Division: SLADE J). *Re Noad (deceased)* [1951] 1 All ER 467 applied.

3142 **—— —— whether an original or substitutional gift**

Canada

A testator provided that the residue of his estate was to be shared equally amongst his children. If any of his children died leaving issue, the issue was to take the parent's share of the residuary estate. Two of the testator's children predeceased him and left surviving issue. On construction of the provision it was held that, where a testator used general terms which were applicable to a child who had predeceased the testator, as well as to a child then living, a gift to the issue of any children who had died took effect as an original gift and not as a substitutional gift to such issue.

RE DAVISON (1979) 99 DLR (3d) 80 (Supreme Court of Nova Scotia, Trial Division). *Loring v Thomas* [1861–73] All ER Rep 620 applied.

3143 **Making and revocation of wills—Law Reform Committee's recommendations**

The Law Reform Committee's 22nd report (on the making and revocation of wills) has been published as Cmnd. 7902. The recommendations which require changes in the law include a relaxation of the requirements as to the position of the testator's signature. The committee recommend that the will should be admitted to probate if it is apparent on its face that the testator intended his signature to validate it, regardless of the position of the signature. An acknowledgement of his signature by an attesting witness should have the same effect as his actual signature. The wording of the first exception to the rule that marriage revokes a will, contained in the Wills Act 1837, s. 18, should be brought into line with the Administration of Estates Act 1925, ss. 46 and 47. The "contemplation of marriage" test under s. 177 of the 1837 Act should be modified. The committee also recommend that where a will is revoked by marriage and the testator at the time of the marriage was incapable through mental disorder of managing his affairs, the beneficiaries (if they are persons for whom the testator, had he not been suffering from mental disorder, might have made provision) should be able to apply to the court for reasonable provision; likewise the Attorney-General should be able to make application to the court on behalf of any charity for which the testator had made provision in his revoked will.

INDEX

DAMAGES—*continued*
  personal injury—
    deduction of supplementary benefit, 781
    expiry of limitation period, 1802
    quantum of—
      ankle, 849, 867, 878
      arm, 847, 867
      asbestosis, 797
      back, 828 *et seq.*
      brain, 790, 791
      burns, 802–804
      chest, 847
      elbow, 851–853, 875
      examples, 801 *et seq.*
      eyes, 818, 819
      face, 809, 816, 817, 866
      finger, 809, 846, 855–857
      foot, 878–880
      general, 839, 863
      hand, 876
      head, 805 *et seq.*
      hernia, 798, 799
      hip, 834, 848–850
      housekeeping ability, loss of, 779
      knee, 813, 817, 835, 870 *et seq.*
      leg, 850, 859 *et seq.*, 873
      multiple injuries, 793–796
      neck, 810, 820 *et seq.*, 844
      negligent caesarean section, 800
      nervous shock, 2050
      paraplegia, 792
      rib, 811
      scar, 868
      shoulder, 824–827, 845
      skull, 814, 815
      spine, 836 *et seq.*
      thigh, 812, 868, 869
      thumb, 858
      wrist, 815
    supervening injury, effect of, 780
  prospective loss of employment, for, 865
  remoteness, 777
  solicitor's failure to secure good title in property,
    2812

DANGEROUS DRUGS
  conspiracy to produce, forfeiture order, 577
  cultivation, 583
  distribution, 587
  offence, appeal against sentence, 2552 *et seq.*
  possession, evidence, 688
  supply, 587

DANGEROUS GOODS
  carriage by sea, 2629, 2630

DANGEROUS SUBSTANCES
  restrictions on marketing and use, 2264
  safety requirements, 455

DEATH
  quantum of damages, 783 *et seq.*

DEEDS
  construction, ambiguity, 884
  escrow, when deed effective, 886

DEFENCE COUNSEL
  duty to cross-examine, 686

DEFENCE WORK
  grant for removal of, 984

DEER
  antlers in velvet, with—
    production of, 140
    prohibition of removal, 142
    removal without anaesthetic, 141

DENTAL APPLIANCES
  charges, 2017

DENTAL TREATMENT
  charges, 2017, 2018
  lists of dentists, 2023
  remuneration for dentists, 2023

DEPENDENCY BENEFIT
  amendment of regulations, 2725, 2726

DEPENDENT RELATIVE
  student's allowance for, 997

DEPORTATION
  European Communities, between member states,
    1175

DERELICT LAND
  clearance areas, 2866

DESIGNS RULES
  fees, 2923

DETENTION
  Air Force, 2427

DEVELOPING COUNTRIES
  iron and steel products, relief from customs duty,
    757

DEVELOPMENT
  permitted—
    appeals, 2869
    planning application, 2869

DEVELOPMENT COUNCIL
  Apple and Pear, 2895, 2896

DEVELOPMENT LAND TAX
  legislation, 2328
  liability, date of disposal, 888

DIPLOMATIC SERVICE
  disputes, 1327
  personal privilege, 1326

DISABLED PERSON
  employment by company, 370
  social security questions, 2727

DISCOVERY
  disclosure—
    contempt, whether, 889
    documents, public interest immunity, 900
    medical evidence, 2242
    source of documents, 896
  exercise of judicial restraint, 900
  inspection, patent, 892

HERRING
prohibition of fishing, 1273–1275

HIGHWAY
cycle racing on, 2345, 2346
duty to maintain, straying dogs, 1397
footpath—
    obstruction, 1404
    rights of public, 1403
    stopping up, 1402
hazard warning device, 2398
local authority, discretion, 1403
motorway, consent of minister, 1395
new street byelaws, 1400
obstruction, 1397, 1398
pitching a stall, 1398
recommendations of Law Commission, 1399
removal of vehicle from, 2400
road, meaning, 1405
straying dogs, on, 1397
traffic signs, 2421

HILL LIVESTOCK
compensatory allowances, 103

HIP
injury to, quantum of damages, 834, 848–850

HIRE PURCHASE
conditional sale agreement, accelerated payment
    clause, 1407
consumer credit business—
    advertisements, 1409, 1411
    extortionate credit bargain, 1419
    quotations, 1415

HISTORIC BUILDINGS
criteria for listing, 2077

HOME-GROWN CEREALS
levy to finance Authority, 105

HOME OFFICE
prison department, 2255

HONG KONG
application of Hague Rules, 2604, 2605

HORSE
breeding, 157

HORTICULTURE
capital grant scheme, 56
co-operation, grant for, 60, 61
grant for improvements, 94–101

HOSPITAL
charges, road accident victim, 2021
part payment for accommodation, 2024
premises, meaning, 1920
private—
    application for controlled works, 1918
    appointment and powers of inspectors, 1919
    notifiable change, 1921
    notifiable works, 1921
private patient, availability for, 2024

HOURS OF WORK
baking industry, 1012

HOUSE OF COMMONS
members' fund, 2079
Opposition, salaried members of, 449
Speaker, salary of, 449

HOUSE OF LORDS
petition for leave to appeal, 2223

HOUSEKEEPING DUTIES
loss of ability to perform, 779

HOUSING
accommodation, transfer by local authority, 1833
action area—
    approved expenditure, 1440
    compulsory acquisition in, 411
furnished, rent assessment committee, 1737
Greater London Council, homesteading scheme,
    1832
home insulation scheme, 1463
home purchase assistance, price limits, 1422
homeless person—
    intentionally homeless, 1430, 1433, 1434
    local authority, statutory duties, 1427 et seq.
improvement—
    area, 1439
    assistance for, 1424
    grant, increased amount of, 1443
    notice, 1446
    qualifying lender, 1425
    repair grants, and, 1441 et seq.
legislation, 1436
local authority—
    accommodation, transfer of, 1833
    acquisition of dwelling house in clearance area,
        409
    mortgage, 1423
    notice to quit, 1447, 1448
    right to buy, 1449 et seq.
        maximum discount, 1451
        mortgage costs, 1454
        mortgage limit, 1455
        statutory notices, 1452, 1456
    right to mortgage, 1457
    sale of, 1458
    Welsh form, 1457
purchase—
    assistance for, 1424
    qualifying lender, 1425
qualifying lenders for subsidies, 1424
rent—
    allowance subsidy, 1438
    rebates and allowances, 1459, 1460
secure tenancies, exceptions, 1748
sound insulation from airport noise, 199, 200
subsidies, qualifying lenders, 1424
thermal insulation scheme, 1464
transfers to local authorities, 1835

HOUSING ACTION AREA
approved expenditure, 1440
compulsory acquisition in, 411

HUMAN RIGHTS
contracting parties, obligations of, 1470
European Convention, application to national
    law, 1469

VALUE ADDED TAX—*continued*
registration, partnership, 3086
relief—
charity, 3087
hire-purchase or conditional sale agreement, 3088
imported goods, 3072
transfer of business, 3088
sports competition, 3068
supply—
business, in course of, 3097
goods and services—
consideration for, 3090, 3092
delivery services, 3094, 3095
gifts, 3089
in course of business, 3096
special consideration, 3091
stud farm, 3099
time of supply, 3101, 3102
in course of business, 3098
time of, 3100
transport of goods, 1212
zero rating—
abattoir, 3115
books, etc., 3104
building materials, 3105
building work, 3065, 3106, 3108
building work, double-glazing windows, 3107
construction or alteration of building, 3109
existence of agency relationship, 46
export, 3111, 3112
food, 3113, 3114, 3116
fuel and power, 3117
gold, 3118, 3119
transport, 3121

VANUATU
independence, 349

VEAL
frozen, levy-free import, 54

VEGETABLES
plant breeders' rights, 112
potatoes, fees in respect of, 117

VEHICLE LICENCE
duration and rate of duty, 2381

VENDING MACHINE
milk, 3136
solid fuel, 3136

VETERINARY DRUGS
sale or supply, 1904, 1905

VETERINARY INSPECTION
European Communities, 1170

VETERINARY SURGEON
Commonwealth practitioner, 1923
examination fees, 1923
foreign practitioner, 1923
qualifications of EEC national, 1924
registration fees, 1926
unqualified person, restriction on practice, 1925

VITAMINS
drops for child, 2803
tablets for expectant mother, 2803

WAGES COUNCIL
pin, hook and eye, and snap fastener, 1038

WALES
airport shops, 181
election forms, 1009
housing, local authority right to buy, 1450, 1453
Welsh language teaching, 978
Welsh television, 2830
wool marketing, 134

WAR
civilian's pension, 2137–2139
pensions committees, 2140

WAREHOUSING
excise, 765

WARRANT OF ARREST
execution of, 666

WASTE
special, control of, 1090
toxic and dangerous, 1090

WATER
agricultural use, abstracted for, 963

WATER AUTHORITIES
expense of land drainage, 3128
limit on borrowing power, 3125

WATER MAIN
power to lay main, duties of landowners, 3126

WATER SUPPLY
unlawful abstraction of water, right of action, 3123

WEIGHTS AND MEASURES
marking of goods, 3130
units of measurement, 3138, 3139

WELFARE FOOD
vitamins, 2803

WIDOW
social security benefit, 2706

WILL
construction—
heirs and surviving issue, 3141
original and substitutional gift, 3142
Law Reform Committee, report of, 3143

WINE
replanting, 91

WIRELESS TELEGRAPHY
exemption from requirement of licence, 2834
licence charges, 2832, 2833

WORDS AND PHRASES

act done by reference (Race Relations Act 1976, s. 2 (1) (c))..2278
actions in contemplation or furtherance of a trade dispute (Trade Union and Labour Relations
    Act 1974, s. 13 (1))..2933, 2936
actual occupation (Land Registration Act 1925, s. 70 (1) (g))..2012
agricultural building (Rating Act 1971, s. 4 (3))..2282
amount of any expenditure (Finance Act 1965, Sch. 6, para. 4 (1) (b))..286
ancillary services (Council Directive (EEC) 67/228, Annex B, item 5)..1212
any other judge (RSC Ord. 79, r. 9 (12))..655
any proceedings . . . are finally decided (Legal Aid Act 1974, s. 13 (1))..1773
appellate court..1774
applied to charitable purposes (Income and Corporation Taxes Act 1970, s. 360 (1) (c))..1567
appointment (Medical Act 1956, s. 28 (1))..1893
arrangements (Finance Act 1973, s. 29 (1) (b) (ii))..1560
article (Obscene Publications Act 1959, s. 1 (2))..616
at reasonable expense (Housing Act 1974, s. 89 (3) (c))..1446
bankers' books (Bankers' Books Evidence Act 1879, s. 7)..681
bankers' books (Bankers' Books Evidence Act 1879, s. 9)..210
bankruptcy (Bankruptcy Act 1914, s. 122)..240
British court (Bankruptcy Act 1914, s. 122)..240
business entertainment (Value Added Tax (Special Provisions) Order 1977)..3076
by reference to this Act (Race Relations Act 1976, s. 2 (1) (c))..2278
capacity (Prevention of Bribery Ordinance (Laws of Hong Kong, 1974 rev., c. 201), s. 4 (2)
    (a))..574
change of beneficial ownership (Bank of England Exchange Control Notice No. E.C. 7, para.
    88)..1094
charge on the land (General Rate Act 1967, s. 17B)..2307
charitable purposes (Finance Act 1965, s. 35 (1))..1567
circumstances, the continuance or possible recurrence of which (Coroners (Amendment) Act
    1926, s. 13 (2) (e))..520
circus (Dangerous Wild Animals Act 1976, s. 5)..139
claims (Arbitration Act 1950, s. 27)..162
collective work (Copyright Act 1911, ss. 5 (2), 35 (1))..501
competent authority of the host country (Council Directive (EEC) 64/221)..1507
competition (Lotteries and Amusements Act 1976, s. 14 (1) (b))..258
concerned in (Income and Corporation Taxes Act 1970, s. 488 (2) (ii))..1538
consistently (Children Act 1948, s. 2 (1) (b) (v) (as substituted))..1957
continues to be employed (Employment Protection (Consolidation) Act 1978, s. 33 (3)
    (a))..1062
continuously employed (Employment Protection (Consolidation) Act 1978, s. 81 (1))..1067
court (RSC Ord. 52, r. 1 (2) (a) (iii))..465
court below (RSC Ord. 59, r. 15)..1036
court of first instance..1774
credit token (Consumer Credit Act 1974, s. 14 (1))..1412
criminal cause or matter (Supreme Court of Judicature (Consolidation) Act 1925, s. 31 (1)
    (a))..718
custody (Bank of England Exchange Control Notice No. E.C. 7, para. 88)..1094
damage (Carriage by Air Act 1961, Sch. 1, art. 26 (2))..197
damage (Criminal Damage Act 1971, ss. 1, 3)..578
damage (Warsaw Convention, art. 26 (2))..197
danger (Domestic Proceedings and Magistrates' Courts Act 1978, s. 16 (3))..1486
debts (Finance Act 1965, s. 22 (1) (a))..287
decision (Lands Tribunal Act 1949, s. 3 (4))..2287
decision . . . on an appeal (Town and Country Planning Act 1971, s. 242 (3) (b))..2861
defective (Indictments Act 1915, s. 5)..710

851

directly interested (Industrial Tribunals (Labour Relations) Regulations 1974, Sch. r. 13 (1))..1052
directly interested (Social Security Act 1975, s. 19 (1))..2788
dismissed (Trade Union and Labour Relations Act 1974, Sch. 1, para. 5 (2))..3028, 3031
dismissed (Trade Union and Labour Relations Act 1974, Sch. 1, para. 7 (1) (as amended))..3021
domestic sewage (Public Health (Drainage of Trade Premises) Act 1937, s. 14)..2269
drives (Road Traffic Act 1972, s. 99 (b))..2364
drives ... recklessly (Road Traffic Act 1972, s. 8 (1) (as substituted))..2413
driving or attempting to drive ... (Road Traffic Act 1972, s. 8 (1))..2362
employed (Finance (No. 2) Act 1975, Sch. 12)..1556
employed (Schools Regulations 1959, reg. 18; Schools Regulations 1968, reg. 2)..998
employee (Trade Union and Labour Relations Act 1974, s. 30 (1))..2160
employment (Trade Union and Labour Relations Act 1974, s. 30 (1))..998
employment agency (Sex Discrimination Act 1975, ss. 15, 82)..2575
entry clearance (Immigration Act 1971, s. 33 (2))..1501
entry visa or equivalent document (Council Directive (EEC) 68/630, art. 3 (2))..1177
evidence in law (Forgery Act 1913, s. 3 (3) (g))..594
examine any witness (Coroners' Rules 1953, r. 16)..520
explosion..1640
facilities ... to the public (Sex Discrimination Act 1975, s. 29 (1))..2586
factory (Factories Act 1961, s. 175 (1))..1387
fails (Road Traffic Act 1972, s. 9 (3))..2357
firearm (Licensing Act 1872, s. 12)..1258
fixed deductions (Employment Protection (Consolidation) Act 1978, s. 8 (b))..1087
fixed term (Employment Protection (Consolidation) Act 1978, s. 83 (2) (b))..1067
fixed term (Trade Union and Labour Relations Act 1974, Sch. 1, para. 5 (2) (b))..3033
force reasonable in the circumstances (Criminal Law Act 1967, s. 3 (1))..2989
fraud (Bills of Exchange Act 1882, ss. 29 (2), 30 (2))..263
full-time course of study (Statement of Changes in Immigration Rules 1980, r. 22)..1497
furtherance of a trade dispute (Trade Union and Labour Relations Act 1974, s. 13 (1) (as amended))..2933, 2936
gross amount of wages (Employment Protection (Consolidation) Act 1978, s. 8)..1087
harbour (Immigration Act 1971, s. 25 (2))..1529
heirs (construction of will)..3141
homeless intentionally (Housing (Homeless Persons) Act 1977, s. 17 (1))..1434
in addition to being chargeable to income tax at the basic rate (Finance Act 1973, s. 16 (1))..1564
in connection with (General Rate Act 1967, s. 26)..2282
in connection with (Inland and Corporation Taxes Act 1970, s. 461, para. D)..1543
in the proceedings (Legal Aid Act 1974, s. 9 (6))..1790
income tax ... payable ... for that year (Income Tax (Sub-contractors in the Construction Industry) Regulations 1975, reg. 13 (1) (a))..1558
incurred (Employment Appeal Tribunal Rules 1976, r. 21 (1))..1035
industrial action (Trade Union and Labour Relations Act 1974, Sch. 1, para. 7 consolidated in Employment Protection (Consolidation) Act 1978, s. 62)..3037
insured (fire insurance policy)..1642
intention to deceive (Forgery Act 1913, s. 3 (3))..593
interest in possession (Finance Act 1975, Sch. 5, para. 6 (2))..1368
interest on a loan (Finance Act 1974, Sch. 1, para. 9)..1582
issued to the public (Copyright Act 1956, s. 49)..513
judgment or order (County Court Rules 1936 (as amended 1936–1978), Ord. 27, r. 1)..1241
justice of the case may require (Arbitration Act 1950, s. 27)..162
legal proceedings..2254
liberty to apply (applications in Family Division)..2213
like work (Equal Pay Act 1970, s. 1 (4))..2582, 2588
livestock (Rating Act 1971)..2284
living together as husband and wife (Domestic Violence and Matrimonial Proceedings Act 1976, s. 1 (2))..1489
lotteries (Lotteries and Amusements Act 1976, s. 1)..258
maintenance (Finance Act 1972, Sch. 4, group 8, note (1))..3108
maintenance (Inheritance (Provision for Family and Dependants) Act 1975, s. 1 (2) (b))..2194

maliciously (Offences against the Person Act 1861, s. 20)..642
matters of bankruptcy (Bankruptcy Act 1914, s. 122)..240
may recognise as sufficient (Value Added Tax (Works of Art, Antiques and Scientific Collections) Order 1972, art. 3 (5))..3054
member of . . . tenant's family (Rent Act 1977, Sch. 1, para. 3)..1752
notwithstanding that no asset is acquired (Finance Act 1965, s. 22 (3))..287
occupied (Finance Act 1965, s. 33)..298
office (Income and Corporation Taxes Act 1970, s. 181)..1602
only or main residence (Finance Act 1974, Sch. 1, para. 4 (1))..1583
opinion (Council Directive (EEC) 64/221, art 9)..1176
opportunity of realising a gain, provided directly or indirectly (Income and Corporation Taxes Act 1970, s. 488 (8))..1539
ordinarily resident (Local Education Authority Awards Regulations 1979, reg. 13)..976, 977
ordinarily resident (Warsaw Convention, art. 28 (1))..195
ordinary rules (Legal Aid Act 1974, Sch. 2 para. 4 (1))..1788
other industrial action (Trade Union and Labour Relations Act 1974, Sch. 1, para. 7 (1) (b))..3036
overriding interest (Land Registration Act 1925, s. 70 (1) (g))..2012
particulars (Income and Corporation Taxes Act 1970, s. 490)..1541
party to (Income and Corporation Taxes Act 1970, s. 488 (2) (ii))..1538
perils of the seas (Marine Insurance Act 1906, Sch. 1, r. 7)..1652
permission (Motor Vehicles (Construction and Use) Regulations 1973, reg. 115 (1))..2399
permit (Road Traffic Act 1972, s. 84 (2) (as amended))..2375
persistently ill-treated (Children Act 1975, s. 12 (2) (e))..1951
pitches (Highways Act 1959, s. 127 (c))..1398
place of work (Rent Act 1977, Sch. 15, para. 5 (1))..1728
plant (Finance Act 1971, s. 41 (1))..1548, 1549, 1592
political objects (Trade Union Act 1913, s. 3)..2959
power (RSC Ord. 24, r. 2 (1), 3 (1))..902
presented (Bills of Exchange Act 1882, s. 45)..262
preserving meat (Standard Industrial Classification)..2913
proceedings (Legal Aid Act 1974, s. 13 (1))..1772
proceedings commenced (Criminal Law Act 1977, Sch. 14, para. 1)..1857
process (Capital Allowances Act 1968, s. 7 (1) (e))..1547
property . . . recovered or preserved (Legal Aid Act 1974, s. 9 (6))..1790
publication (Copyright Act 1956, s. 3 (5) (b))..510
purpose of enlarging church (Disused Burial Grounds Act 1884, s. 3)..967
rating of the work (Equal Pay Act 1970, s. 1 (2) (b) (as amended))..2581
reasonable in the circumstances (Criminal Law Act (Northern Ireland) 1967, s. 3 (1))..2989
reasonably practicable (Trade Union and Labour Relations Act 1974, Sch. 1, para. 21 (4))..3008
reasonably suitable to the needs of the tenant as regards character (Rent Act 1977, Sch. 15, Part IV, para. 5 (1) (b))..1727
reckless driving (Criminal Law Act 1977, s. 50)..2412
recklessly (Road Traffic Act 1972, s. 1 (as amended))..2412
recklessly (Road Traffic Act 1972, s. 2 (as substituted))..2413
recommendation (Council Directive (EEC) 64/221, art. 9)..1176
refuses (Road Traffic Act 1972, s. 9 (5))..2357
relating to trial on indictment (Courts Act 1971, s. 10 (5))..718
relevant employees (Employment Protection (Consolidation) Act 1978, s. 62 (4) (b))..3034
remunerative full-time work (Supplementary Benefits Act 1976, s. 6)..2777
repairs (Income and Corporation Taxes Act 1970, s. 130 (d))..1592
repository (Town and Country Planning (Use Classes) Order 1950, Sch.)..2881
required (Offices, Shops and Railway Premises Act 1963, s. 23)..1390
requirements (Supplementary Benefit Act 1976, Sch. 1, para. 3)..2768
residence (Capital Gains Tax Act 1979, ss. 101 (1), 102 (1))..292
restrictions imposed by law (Income and Corporation Taxes Act 1970, s. 290 (4))..384
road (Road Traffic Act 1972, s. 196 (1))..1405
same household (Domestic Violence and Matrimonial Proceedings Act 1976, s. 1 (2))..1489
security (RSC Ord. 23)..2203
series (Criminal Law Act 1977, s. 23 (7))..729
shot gun (Firearms Act 1968, s. 57 (4))..1263